INTERNATIONAL BUSINESS TRANSACTIONS

INTERNATIONAL BUSINESS TRANSACTIONS

Second Edition

By

Ralph H. Folsom
University Professor of Law
University of San Diego Law School

Volume 1
Chapters 1–18

PRACTITIONER TREATISE SERIES

WEST
GROUP
A THOMSON COMPANY

ST. PAUL, MINN., 2002

Practitioner Treatise Series, and the West Group symbol
are registered trademarks used herein under license.

COPYRIGHT © 1995 By WEST PUBLISHING CO.
COPYRIGHT © 2002 By WEST GROUP
            610 Opperman Drive
            P.O. Box 64526
            St. Paul, MN 55164–0526
            1–800–328–9352

ISBN 0–314–26254–7

 *TEXT IS PRINTED ON 10% POST CONSUMER RECYCLED PAPER*

To
Sailors and Their Love of the Sea,
especially Captain Pixie Haughwout

*

Preface

International business transactions present a wonderfully vast and complex area of law and practice. The scope is truly global and the pace of change is breathtaking. Even after years in the field, international business transactions remain enthralling and intimidating. This professional treatise will hopefully make it a little easier for others to share in the excitement.

This treatise has been substantially revised, expanded and updated. Numerous sample international business agreements have been included throughout.

There are six new international sales and letters of credit chapters whose text was generously written by Professor John A. Spanogle of the George Washington University National Law Center. These chapters cover international sales law, commercial terms, bills of lading, documentary letters of credit, standby letters of credit and international electronic commerce.

Professor Michael Gordon kindly revised and updated the text of the chapters on sales agent and distributorship agreements, countertrade agreements, U.S. export controls, the Foreign Corrupt Practices Act and U.S. boycott and anti-boycott law. Likewise, he also revised the chapters on foreign direct investment, choice of business structure, choice of ownership, investing in NAFTA, investing in developing and nonmarket economies, currency controls, protecting against investment losses and expropriation. In addition, Professor Gordon prepared the new chapter on international business litigation.

I am responsible for the new chapters on international commmercial arbitration and the World Trade Organization. I also revised the chapters on U.S. tariff law, customs law, antidumping duties, subsidies and countervailing duties, U.S. import controls, escape clause and market disruption proceedings, Section 301 proceedings, antitrust laws, U.S. free trade agreements, franchising, patent and knowhow licensing, counterfeit and gray market imports, and investing in Europe.

Very happily, Attorney and USD Adjunct Professor of Law Geoffrey Leibl has revised his superb chapter on international business immigration.

The style of this treatise is largely textual combined with extensive footnoting to relevant legal sources and short bibliographies at the end of each chapter. In addition, when space permitted, selected documents and materials of unusual value were added. There is, of course, no substitute for careful, individually-tailored legal draftsmanship. The authors and contributors make no warranty of any kind, express or implied, including any warranty of merchantability or the fitness for a particular purpose of any sample agreements appearing in this treatise.

Please send along your comments and suggestions for the next edition and the annual supplements to this book.

RALPH H. FOLSOM
RFOLSOM@SANDIEGO.EDU

January 2002

Acknowledgements

Many persons have contributed to the development and publication of the first and second editions of this treatise. I acknowledge and thank all of them for their assistance. In addition to my longstanding colleagues, Professors Michael Gordon and John A. Spanogle, special thanks are due to the following:

Alex Daman, Esq. for assistance in preparing the chapters on foreign investment control laws and the regulation of foreign investment in the United States.

Prof. W. Davis Folsom of the University of South Carolina (Beaufort) School of Business Administration for his analysis of the economics of the Canada-United States Free Trade Agreement and NAFTA.

Ronald Halpern, Esq. and Ralph Lake, Esq., Vice Presidents and General Counsels to the Promus Companies in Memphis, for permission to reprint their international hotel franchise and management agreements.

Frank E. Kear, Esq., General Counsel to Solar Turbines, Inc. in San Diego, for permission to reprint their international manufacturers representative agreement.

Charles Saunders, Jr., Associate General Counsel, Ashland Chemical, Inc., for permission to reprint the Ashland Chemical Antiboycott Compliance Guide and Policy Statement.

Ozzie Schindler, Esq., for assistance in preparing the chapter on branches and subsidiaries.

H. Lawrence Serra, Esq. of San Diego for permission to reprint his international sales and joint venture licensing agreements.

Nancy Fuller-Jacobs, Esq. of San Diego for permission to reprint her manufacturer's agent agreement.

Professor James Nafziger of Willamette College of Law for the China international sales agreements.

The Dow Chemical Company Legal Department for permission to reprint selected chemicals industry agreements.

Aaron X. Fellmeth, Esq. of Bryan Cave LLP (Los Angeles) for permission to reprint his international technology license agreement.

Joseph Lo, Esq., for permission to reprint his China Joint venture agreement.

Peter W. Knapp, Esq. of Hamilton Sunstrand Corp. for permission to reprint selected aerospace industry agreements.

*

International Business Transactions Practitioner Treatise

———————

Useful Websites

Compiled by Prof. Ralph Folsom

Bank for International Settlements (BIS)
http://www.bis.org/

Bilateral investment treaties
http://www.sice.oas.org/bitse.asp

Bureau of Export Administration (BXA)
http://www.bxa.doc.gov

Chinalaw Web (University of Maryland)
http://www.qis.net/chinalaw/

Commerce Department
http://www.doc.gov

Convention on International Sale of Goods
http://cisgw3.law.pace.edu

Customs Service
http://www.customs.ustreas.gov

European Union
http://europa.eu.int

European Union Research
http://www.lib.berkeley.edu/GSSI/eugde.html
http://www.eurunion.org/infores/resguide.htm

Export Import Bank of the United States
http://www.exim.gov

Free Trade Area of the Americas (FTAA)
http://www.alca.ftaa.org/

International Economic Law
http://www.asil.org/resource/iell.htm

International Trade
http://www.11rx.com/features/trade2.htm

Import Administration–International Trade Administration (ITA), U.S. Department of Commerce
http://www.ita.doc.gov/import_admin/records/

International Standards Organization (ISO)
http://www.iso.ch/

International Trade Commission
http://www.usite.gov

International Labour Organization (ILO)
http://www.ilo.org

International Chamber of Commerce (ICC)
http://www.iccwbo.org

International Monetary Fund (IMF)
http://www.imf.org/

Internet Chinese Legal Research Center (Washington University in St. Louis)
http://law.wustl.edu/Chinalaw/ (links for Mainland China, Taiwan, and Hong Kong)

Latin American Trade and Information Network
http://www.latinet.com/

Lawsnet (Chinese Law Index)
http://www.lawsnet.com/china/chinaindex.htm

Lex Mercatoria
http://lexmercatoria.org

Multilateral Investment Guarantee Agency (MIGA)
http://www.miga.org/

NAFTA Resources
http://www.lanic.utexas.edu/la/Mexico/nafta/index.html

NAFTA Secretariat
http://nafta-sec-alena.org/english/index.htm

NAFTA–Organization of American States–Trade Unit
http://www.sice.oas.org/tradee.asp#NAFTA

NAFTA Information–U.S. Customs Service
http://www.customs.usteas.gov/nafta/inde.htm

NYU School of Law Library Research Guide—WTO/GATT Research by Jeanne Rehbert
http://www.law.nyu.edu/library/wto_gatt.html

Office of United States Trade Administration
http://www.ita.doc.gov

Private International Law
http://www.state.gov/www/global/legal_affairs/private_intl_law.html

Organization for Economic Co-operation and Development (OECD)
http://www.oecd.org/

The World Bank–International Trade Division
http://www.worldbank.org/html/iecit/iecit.html

Trade Information Center–International Trade Administration (ITA)
U.S. Department of Commerce
http://infoserv2.ita.doc/tic.nsf

United Nations Conference on Trade and Development (UNCTAD)
http://www.unctad.org/

United States Court of International Trade
http://www.uscit.gov/

United States International Trade Commission(ITC)
http://www.usitc.gov

World Customs Organization (WCO)
http://www.wcoomd.org/frmpublic.htm

World Trade Organization
http://www.wto.og

*

WESTLAW® Overview

Folsom's *International Business Transactions* offers a detailed and comprehensive treatment of legal principles and issues relating to the law of international business. To obtain supplemental information to the information contained in this book, you can access WESTLAW, a computer-assisted legal research service of West Group. WESTLAW contains a broad library of legal research resources, including case law, domestic and foreign statutes, current developments and many information databases.

Learning how to use these materials effectively will enhance your legal research. To help you coordinate your book and WESTLAW research, this volume contains an appendix listing WESTLAW databases, search techniques and sample problems.

THE PUBLISHER

*

Summary of Contents

*

Table of Contents

―――――――

Volume 2

INTERNATIONAL BUSINESS TRANSACTIONS

*

Chapter 1

INTERNATIONAL SALES LAW

Table of Sections

A. INTRODUCTION

B. SCOPE AND GENERAL PROVISIONS OF CISG

C. CONTRACT FORMATION

D. RIGHTS AND OBLIGATIONS OF THE PARTIES

E. REMEDIES

Sec.

A. INTRODUCTION

§ 1.1 Introduction to CISG

On April 10, 1980 a diplomatic conference meeting in Vienna adopted the United Nations Convention on Contracts for the International Sale of Goods (1980)(hereafter CISG).[1] CISG governs the sale of goods between parties in the United States and parties in over forty other countries, unless the parties to the sale contract have expressly "opted out" of the Convention. CISG entered into force on January 1, 1988, thirteen months after the United States had ratified the Convention and deposited its instruments of ratification with the United Nations. As a self-executing treaty, no separate implementing legislation is needed. As federal law, it supersedes Article 2 the UCC where it is applicable. CISG is available to be used by private parties in ordinary commercial litigation before both federal and state courts in the United States.

At the time of ratification, the United States declared one reservation, a reservation under Article 95 that the United States is not bound by Article 1(1)(b). The effect of this reservation is that the courts of the United States are bound under international law to use CISG only when the places of business of both parties to the sale contract are each in different States, and both of those different States are Contracting States to CISG. Thus, CISG governs all contracts for the international sale of goods (unless the parties "opt out" under Article 6) between parties whose principal places of business are in the United States and other Contracting States.

§ 1.1
1. United Nations Convention on Contracts for the International Sale of Goods, Apr. 11, 1980, U.N. Doc. A/CONF.97/18, Annex I (1980), 19 I.L.M. 671 (entered into force Jan. 1, 1988) [hereinafter CISG].

As of March 8, 2001, there were fifty-eight Contracting States to CISG. In addition to the United States, they included: Argentina, Australia, Austria, Belarus, Belgium, Bosnia and Herzegovina, Bulgaria, Burundi, Canada, Chile, China, Croatia, Cuba, Czech Republic, Denmark, Ecuador, Egypt, Estonia, Finland, France, Georgia, Germany, Ghana, Greece, Guinea, Hungary, Iraq, Italy, Kyrgystan, Latvia, Lesotho, Lithuania, Luxembourg, Mauritania, Mexico, Moldova, Mongolia, the Netherlands, New Zealand, Norway, Peru, Poland, Romania, the Russian Federation, Singapore, Slovakia, Slovenia, Spain, Sweden, Switzerland, Syria, Uganda, Ukraine, Uruguay, Uzbekistan, Yugoslavia and Zambia. The effect of the earlier ratification of Yugoslavia on its former constituent parts which are now independent states is not yet clear. It would be possible to argue that, as then constituent parts of States which adopted CISG, they are still bound by the Convention through the action of their previous governments, but the United Nations Treaty Section has taken the position that each state must make a positive indication of its intention to be so bound before it will consider them as a Contracting State. As of March 8, 2001, only Macedonia had not done so. This position of the U.N. office may be followed by the United States courts or not. However, counsel should be cautious about assuming that such former constituent parts of Contracting States are still Contracting States after gaining independence.

Other states are expected to ratify or adopt CISG in the near future. This will increase the impact and effectiveness of CISG in unifying international sales law. A current and complete list of Contracting States to this Convention can be obtained through the internet from the U.N. Treaty Section.[2]

§ 1.2   The United Nations Commission on International Trade Law

CISG was drafted by the United Nations Commission on International Trade Law (UNCITRAL), and adopted and opened for signature and ratification by a U.N.-sponsored diplomatic conference held at Vienna in 1980.[1] The mandate of UNCITRAL is the unification and harmonization of international trade law. The purpose of such unification is to reduce legal obstacles to international trade, and to promote the orderly development of new legal concepts to assist further growth in international trade. Although there are other international organizations engaged in similar work, the United Nations General Assembly created UNCITRAL in 1966 to establish a globally representative organization with representatives from all geographical regions and from all legal systems, including from both developed and less developed countries.

---

2. UNCITRAL Status of Conventions and Model Laws may be found at http://www.uncitral.org/en-index.htm.

tracts for International Sale of Goods, *Official Records*, A/CONF. 97–19.

§ 1.2

1. The signing took place on April 11, 1980. United Nations Conference on Con-

UNCITRAL consists of thirty-six member nations, but almost as many other nations usually attend meetings as observers, as do international organizations (e.g., ICC, IMF). Decisions are taken by consensus of both members and observers, not by vote. Thus, the process requires compromise and persuasion, rather than alignments; and the arguments are usually neither political nor dialectic, but are pragmatic, much as they should be in a well-taught law school seminar. The consensus requirement makes progress excruciatingly slow, but the difficulties in harmonizing systems from developed and less developed countries, from capitalist and socialist countries, and from common law and civil law legal systems are great. Further, the attainment of such consensus can help to promote wide acceptance of the results of UNCITRAL's product—as in the case of CISG.

In its first stage of work, UNCITRAL prepared four pieces of legislative work in its program on unification of international commercial law. One is CISG, discussed further below. A second is the Convention on the Limitation Period in the International Sale of Goods, adopted in New York in 1974.[2] This Convention establishes a limitation period of generally four years, and attempts to bridge the difference between common law "statutes of limitation" (a procedural law approach to termination of rights of action) and the civil law "prescription periods" (a substantive law approach to such problems). A 1980 protocol aligned the provision of this convention on limitation periods with the provisions of CISG.[3]

The third legislative work is the United Nations Convention on the Carriage of Goods by Sea of 1978, also called "the Hamburg Rules," which regulates international bills of lading.[4] The Hamburg Rules are a revision of the Hague Rules (the Brussels Convention of 1924),[5] and the Hague–Visby Rules.[6] The primary difference is that the Hamburg Rules were significantly affected by the participation of less developed countries (LDCs) in their drafting. LDCs did not participate in the drafting of the Hague Rules in Brussels in 1924. The Hamburg Rules entered into force in 1992, and has twenty six Contracting States as of September 1, 1999.[7]

2. United Nations Convention on the Limitation Period in the International Sale of Goods, *opened for signature* June 14, 1974, U.N. Doc. A/CONF.63/15 (1974).

3. The 1980 diplomatic conference that adopted the CISG also adopted a protocol to the 1974 text to conform the provisions of the two conventions. Protocol Amending the Convention on the Limitation Period in the International Sale of Goods, Apr. 11, 1980, U.N. Doc. A/CONF.97/18, Annex II (1980).

4. *United Nations Convention on the Carriage to Goods by Sea*, signed at Hamburg on March 31, 1978. They are in force.

5. *International Convention for the Unification of Certain Rules of Law Relating to Bills of Lading* signed at Brussels, August 25, 1924 and entered into force June 2, 1931, better known as the Hague Rules. They are in force.

6. *Protocol to Amend the 1924 Convention, ibid.* The Protocol was signed at Brussels, February 23, 1968 and entered into force June 23, 1977, and is often referred to as the *Visby Rules*. The Visby Rules do not stand alone but are amendments to the Hague Rules and the resulting rules are known as the Hague/Visby Rules. They are in force.

7. United Nations Convention on the Carriage of Goods by Sea, Hamburg, Mar. 31, 1978, U.N. Doc. A/Conf. 89/13, 17 I.L.M. 608 (1978), entered into force Nov. 1, 1992.

In August, 1987, UNCITRAL issued the Convention on International Bills of Exchange and International Promissory Notes (hereafter CIBN), which was adopted by the United Nations General Assembly and opened for signature and ratification in 1988.[8] This Convention establishes provisions for a new, optional, negotiable instrument which will be adaptable for use in the different domestic banking and legal systems—including under the Uniform Commercial Code (hereafter UCC), the British Bills of Exchange Act, and the civil law Uniform Law for Bills of Exchange (Geneva Conventions of 1930 and 1931). The United States signed this convention in 1988.

In its second stage of work, UNCITRAL has produced more model laws than conventions. As is discussed in Chapter 3, it has promulgated the U.N. Convention on Independent Guarantees and Stand-by Letters of Credit, which entered into force in January, 2000.[9] In the 1990s, UNCITRAL published the Model Law on International Credit Transfers (1992)[10] (an EU directive is based on this model law),[11] the Model Law on Procurement of Goods and Services (1994)[12] (four nations have enacted similar legislation),[13] (the Model Law on Electronic Commerce)[14] (Korea and Illinois have enacted similar legislation), and the Model Law on Cross–Border Insolvency.[15]

In addition, UNCITRAL has adopted the UNCITRAL Model Law on International Commercial Arbitration (1985),[16] which has been enacted in 28 nations and four states in the United States; and a Legal Guide on Drawing Up International Contracts for Construction of Industrial Works,[17] which has been widely used in LDC development projects, even before its final adoption by UNCITRAL, because of its perceived balance,

8. United Nations Convention on International Bills of Exchange and International Promissory Notes, *opened for signature* Dec. 9, 1988, 28 I.L.M. 176.

9. U.N. Convention on Independent Guarantees and Stand-by Letters of Credit, *in Report of the United Nations Commission on International Trade Law*, 28th Sess., U.N. Doc. A/50/17, Annex (1995).

10. Model Law on International Credit Transfers, *in Report of the Working Group on International Payments*, U.N. Commission on International Trade Law, 21st Sess., U.N. Doc. A/CN.0/341, Annex (1990).

11. Directive 97/5/EC of the Europe Parliament and of the Counsel of 27 January 1997 on cross-border credit transfers, *Official Journal No. L 043, 14/02/1997 P. 0025–0031.*

12. Model Law on Government Procurement, *in Procurement: Report of the Secretary–General*, [1989] 20 20 Y.B. Int'l Trade L. Comm'n 116, U.N. Doc. A/CN.9/WG.V/WP.22.

13. Status of Conventions and Model Laws (*Last updated on 20 February 2001*), U.N. Commission on International Trade Law, http://www.uncitral.org/english/status-e.htm.

14. Model Law on Electronic Commerce, *in Report of the United Nations Commission on International Trade Law*, 29th Sess., U.N. Doc. A/51/17, Annex (1996); Y.B. Int'l Trade L. Comm'n 237, *Vol. XXVII*, U.N. Doc. A/CN.9/SER.A/1996.

15. Model Law on Cross–Border Insolvency, *in Report of the United Nations Commission on International Trade Law*, 30th Sess., U.N. Doc. A/52/17, Annex (1997); Y.B. Int'l Trade L. Comm'n 305, U.N. Doc. A/CN.9/SER.A/1997.

16. Model Law on International Commercial Arbitration, *in Report of the United Nations Commission on International Trade Law*, 18th Sess., U.N. Doc. A/40/17, Annex (1985); Y.B. Int'l Trade L. Comm'n 393, U.N. Doc. A/CN.9/SER.A/1985.

17. Legal Guide on Drawing Up International Contracts for Construction of Industrial Works, U.N. Commission on International Trade Law, U.N. Doc. A/CN.9/SER.B/2.

fairness and attention to detail. UNCITRAL is continuing its tradition of promoting unification in the area of financial transactions by preparing a Model Law on International Receivables Financing.[18]

UNCITRAL is not the only international organization currently making proposals for the unification and harmonization of international law. The International Institute for the Unification of Private Law (UNIDROIT) held a diplomatic conference in Toronto in 1988 to adopt the Convention on International Lease Financing,[19] which has eight Contracting States and entered into force in 1995, and the Convention on International Factoring,[20] which has six Contracting States and entered into force in 1995. These two conventions, together with CISG and CIBN, may form an alternative source of law in international transactions for issues now analyzed under UCC Articles 2, 3 and 9. The OAS has also been active in this field on a hemisphere-wide basis.[21]

In addition, UNIDROIT has prepared and issued in 1994 the Principles of International Commercial Contracts.[22] The Principles are applicable to all contracts, not just sales of goods, and their provisions are set forth in more general terms. If CISG is the international analogue to UCC Article 2 in the United States law, then the Principles are the international analogue to the Restatement of Contracts in U.S. law. They are not intended to be adopted as a convention or enacted as a uniform model law. Instead, they are expected to be used by international commercial arbitrators, and even by judges where local law is ambiguous. Some of the specific concepts are discussed later in this chapter. The substantive rules of the Principles are often different from those of CISG, because the Principles were not drafted by official delegations of governments, and the individual drafters could adopt what they considered to be "best practices" in commerce.

§ 1.3 A Short History of the Drafting of CISG

CISG is the product of 50 years of effort by several organizations, all of which are still involved in the process of unification and harmonization of international commercial law. In 1930, the International Institute for the Unification of Private Law (UNIDROIT) began preparation of a uniform law on international sales, using a committee of experts originally from England, France, Germany and Scandinavia, but later ex-

---

18. Draft Convention on Assignment in Receivables Financing, in *Report of the Working Group on International Contract Practices*, U.N. Commission on International Trade Law, 31st Sess., U.N. Doc. A/CN.9/WG.II/WP.104 (1999).

19. UNIDROIT Convention on International Financial Leasing, May 28, 1988, 27 I.L.M. 931. The United States has signed this convention. *Id.*

20. UNIDROIT Convention on International Factoring, May 28, 1988, 27 I.L.M.

943. The United States has signed this convention. *Id.*

21. See, e.g., Inter–American Convention on Contracts for the International Carriage of Goods by Road, July 15, 1989, 29 I.L.M. 83; Inter–American Convention on International Commercial Arbitration, Jan. 30, 1975, 14 I.L.M. 336.

22. See Perillo, UNIDROIT Principles of International Commercial Contracts: The Black Letter Text and a Review, 63 Fordham L. Rev. 281 (1994).

panded.[1] Drafts were produced in 1935, 1936 and 1939, but World War II intervened and prevented further development of the project.[2] However, some basic principles were established by these early drafts, and continue in CISG: 1) the provisions should not be developed by selecting an existing system and amending it, or by putting together the existing rules of the different current legal systems, but by developing a new system which is internally consistent and includes modern provisions needed by businesses;[3] 2) the provisions should apply only to international sales, and therefore not disturb existing traditions applicable to domestic sales;[4] and 3) party autonomy should be fully protected.

In 1951, after World War II, UNIDROIT resumed preparation of a uniform law, and completed a final draft in 1963.[5] In 1964, the government of the Netherlands convened a diplomatic conference which adopted two conventions: the Uniform Law on the International Sale of Goods (ULIS) and the Uniform Law on the Formulation of Contracts for the International Sale of Goods (ULF).[6] The principal participants in the drafting of these two conventions were Western European nations, and they were criticized by many socialist and less developed countries as not adequately accommodating the interests of non-European parties. Only eight nations adopted ULIS, and seven adopted ULF. Although each convention came into force, they were not adopted widely enough to have much impact on world trade.

After the formation of UNCITRAL in 1966, that body carried out a survey of governments and concluded that ULIS and ULF would not be widely adopted. It therefore undertook to revise the texts of those two conventions to make them more acceptable to governments. Between 1970 and 1978, two new drafts for rules governing international sales, replacing ULIS and ULF, were prepared by a carefully balanced Working Group of UNCITRAL members, with many observers also participating.[7] In 1978, UNCITRAL further modified, then adopted the new drafts, but consolidated them into a single text, issued in all official United Nations languages—so that there are six authoritative texts of CISG in six different languages—English, French, Spanish, Arabic, Chinese and Rus-

§ 1.3

1. Gutteridge, *An International Code of the Law of Sale*, 14 Brit. Y.B. Int'l L. 75, 82 (1933).

2. The 1939 Text is reprinted in UNIDROIT, *Unification of Law: 1948* at 101–159 (1948). For a discussion of the 1935 draft, see Rabel, *A Draft of an International Law of Sales*, 5 U. Chi. L. Rev. 543 (1938).

3. See Keyes, *Toward a Single Law Governing the International Sale of Goods—A Comparative Study*, 42 Calif. L. Rev. 653, 661–662 (1954).

4. See Rabel, *A Draft of an International Law of Sales*, supra note 2; and Rabel, *The Hague Conference on the Unification of Sales Law*, 1 Am. J. Comp. L. 58, 60 (1952).

5. UNIDROIT, Projet de loi uniforme sur la formation des contrats de vente internationale des objets mobiliers corporels et rapport (1959), *reprinted in* II Hague Conference Records & DOcuments 421–432.

6. 834 U.N.T.S. 107 (1972). The texts are also available in 1 Hague Conference Records & Documents 333–354.

7. For a more comprehensive discussion of the history of the drafting of CISG, see Winship, the Scope of the Vienna Convention on International Sales Contracts in Galston and Smit, International Sales: The United Nation's Convention on Contracts for the International Sale of Goods, at 1–2 to 1–16 (1984).

sian.[8] However, one remnant of the prior ULIS—ULF division is incorporated into CISG. CISG Article 92 allows a Contracting State to declare, at the time of ratification or adoption, a reservation that it will not be bound by Part II of the Convention (Contract Formation) or by Part III of the Convention (Sale of Goods), which was the division between ULF and ULIS.

The United Nations General Assembly convened a diplomatic conference in Vienna in March—April of 1980, attended by delegates from 62 nations, which made a few further amendments of the text and then adopted the United Nations Convention on Contracts for the International Sale of Goods. The diplomatic conference did not authorize the preparation of any official commentary, although many legal scholars use the UNCITRAL Commentary, which was prepared for use at the diplomatic conference, but does not incorporate the changes made at the conference.[9] Thus, it must be used carefully and with great discretion, preferably by persons already familiar with the history and development of the text.

Under Article 99(1), CISG entered into force on January 1, 1988, thirteen months after the deposit with the United Nations of instruments of ratification from ten Contracting States. The United States, along with China and Italy deposited its instruments of ratification of CISG with the United Nations on December 11, 1986.

UNCITRAL has placed the substantive sales law rules into the text of the Convention itself, so that the "private law" rules are part of the Convention, and are directly adopted by ratification. Thus, CISG is a "self-executing" treaty, and in the United States ratification of CISG meant the automatic adoption of the substantive provisions on sales, without any need for separate implementing legislation. The main purpose of CISG is to avoid conflicts of law problems, not to aggravate them. Thus, it is important that the scope of application of CISG be clear, both as to the circumstances where it does apply, and those where it does not.

There is now a substantial body of caselaw under CISG. Unfortunately, it is reported in the language of each deciding jurisdiction. There are, however, abstracts of the decisions in English available from two sources: UNCITRAL itself (the CLOUT cases[10]) and the Rome Institute (the UNILEX cases).[11] The following survey of CISG will include the caselaw development, but will refer to the English-language abstracts for decisions written in foreign languages.

---

8. For the history of the drafting within UNCITRAL, see Honnold, *The Draft Convention on Contracts for the International Sale of Goods: An Overview*, 27 Am. J. Comp. L. 223 (1979).

9. See Secretariat, Commentary on the Draft Convention on Contracts for the International Sale of Goods, A/CONF.97/5 (14 March 1979), *reprinted in* Official Records 14–66. The proponents of an official commentary believed that its explanation would

prove helpful to practitioners and would facilitate ratification. Such a commentary would have paralleled the Official Comments is the UCC. A/CONF.97/8, page 26.

10. UNCITRAL CLOUT (Case Law on UNCITRAL Texts) Cases, A/CN.9/SER.C/ABSTRACTS/1, et seq.

11. UNILEX: International Case Law and Bibliography on CISG (M. Bonell, ed., 1995).

B.   SCOPE AND GENERAL PROVISIONS OF CISG

§ 1.4   The Sphere of Application of CISG

The first six articles of CISG define its sphere of application. Under CISG Article 1 the Convention is applicable only to contracts for the sale of goods which are international and which have a minimum amount of contact with a contracting State. Article 1 requires that a sale of goods contract be both "international" and also bear a stated relation to a Contracting State before the contract can be governed by the Convention. In determining whether "a contract is for the international sale of goods," the convention does not define "contract" on "sale" or "goods", but Article 1 does define in some detail the amount of "internationality" required, and the necessary amount of contact with a Contracting State or States.

Under Article 1, a contract is sufficiently international to be governed by the convention if the seller's and the buyer's "places of business are in different States."[1] There is no requirement that the goods be shipped between different states, nor that the offer and acceptance occur in different nations.[2] Neither the location of the goods themselves, nor the location of negotiations between the parties, is necessarily dispositive. Instead, the "place of business" of each party must be located, and must be in a different State. In a contract involving two Austrian citizens one of whom had his place of business in Italy, the court held that CISG applied, and not Austrian law.[3]

The application of the Convention depends upon both parties being aware that the transaction is international, and that the places of business are in different nations. Thus, if the foreign place of business of one of the parties is not disclosed to the other party by a local agent, the Convention cannot govern the transaction.[4]

What is "a place of business"? Although the term in the English language version may be ambiguous, the term in the French (tablissemant) and Spanish (establecimiento) language versions refer to a permanent place of business.[5] CISG does not define what a "place of business" is, although the drafting history of the Convention suggests that a permanent establishment is required and that neither a warehouse nor the office of a seller's agent qualifies as a "place of business." This interpretation has been adopted by the courts. A seller's "liaison office" in buyer's nation was held by the Paris Court of Appeal not to be a "place of business," because it was not an autonomous legal entity, so that orders through that office were subject to CISG.[6] Even the presence

---

§ 1.4

1. CISG art. 1(1).

2. Cf., ULF, supra § 1.3, note 6.

3. UNILEX Case D. 1998–17.2.

4. CISG, art. 1(2).

5. Official Records of the 1980 Conference 73, Analysis of Comments and Proposals: (Comment by ICC); Honnold, Documentary History of the Uniform Law for International Sales 394 (189).

6. UNILEX Case D–1995–1, CLOUT 155.

of a liaison office combined with a lengthy stay by one party's representatives in the nation of the other party to enter into and complete contract negotiations did not create a "place of business" in that country by the first party, as long as the first party's foreign place of business was disclosed.[7] There is an arbitral discussion to the contrary,[8] but the decision may be better analyzed as one involving multiple offices under CISG Art. 10, with the foreign office being more closely connected to the transaction.

This "place of business" criterion will cause difficulty whenever one or both parties have more than one place of business. However, CISG does provide some help in such situations by specifying which "place of business" is to be considered. If a party has multiple places of business, one of which is in the same State as the other party's place of business, the issue of "internationality" becomes more complicated. Which place of business is used to determine the applicability of the Convention? CISG Article 10(a) directs that use of the place of business having "the closest relation to the contract *and* its place of business."[9] Thus, the determinative "place of business" in the Convention analysis is different from those which use the place of incorporation,[10] or the "seat." Instead, it depends upon the relationship of the transaction to a particular office. It is further limited to the transaction-office relationship according to the facts which appear from (1) the contract form, (2) the dealings between the parties, or (3) information disclosed by the parties before the contract if formed.[11]

Where one office is more closely associated with the formation of the contract and a second office is more closely associated with a party's performance of its contractual obligations, there is an unresolved issue concerning which of those offices is the relevant "place of business." The only assistance furnished by Article 10(a) in such situations is to limit the usable facts in making a choice between multiple offices to those circumstances known to "the parties" before a binding contract is formed. However, this process limitation should permit well-advised parties to resolve possible ambiguities by stating in the contract which office of each party they believe to have "the closest relationship to the contract." Since the literal limitation in the Convention is to circumstances known to "the parties," each party should ensure that the other party is aware of its status.

What minimum amount of contact with Contracting States is required? There are two methods available to meet this requirement, but in the some States the second method is precluded by a permissible reservation under CISG Article 95. One method of meeting the requirement, which is universally available, is that each party has its relevant "place of business" in a different Contracting State.[12] This method does

---

7. UNILEX Case D. 1994–31.

8. ARB. ICC (Paris) 7531/1993 (1994).

9. CISG, art. 10 (a) (emphasis added).

10. Barcelona Traction [1970] I.C.J. Rep. 3.

11. CISG art. 1(2).

12. CISG art. (1) (a).

not depend upon the vagaries of conflicts of law doctrines, and provides certainty to the parties in designing the transaction and to courts in analyzing and deciding issues from such transactions.

The Convention does not govern all contracts for the international sale of goods, but only those contracts which have a substantial relation to one or more Contracting States—that is, States which ratified, accepted, approved or acceded to the Convention so as to become parties to the Convention. CISG Article 1 makes the Convention applicable to sales contracts where the places of business of the parties are in different States, and either (a) both states are Contracting States,[13] or (b) only one State is a Contracting State and private international law choice-of-law rules lead to the application of the law of a Contracting State.[14] Thus, CISG will govern a contract of sale between parties, where each party has its place of business in a different Contracting State. For a United States buyer or seller, that means that CISG will govern any transactions, in the absence of any contrary choice of law clause, where the other party to the transaction has its place of business in France, China, Italy or any of the other Contracting States.[15]

The other method of meeting the requirement of sufficient contact with a Contracting State, is to have one of the parties have its place of business in a Contracting State, and for that State's laws to govern the contract under the normative rules of "private international law" choice of law doctrines.[16] Thus, a contract between a seller in Germany (a Contracting State) and a buyer in the United Kingdom (not a Contracting State) would be governed by CISG if the applicable choice of law doctrines made the law of the seller's place of business the governing law.[17]

This second method of meeting the requirement of sufficient contact with a Contracting State is not normally available, however, to a buyer or a seller which has its principal place of business in the United States. When it ratified CISG, the United States declared a reservation that its courts would not be bound by Article 1(1)(b).[18] The United States' version of the Convention is that it is not applicable when a contract is between parties having places of business in different States and only one State is a Contracting State, even though choice-of-law rules lead to the application of the law of the Contracting State. Thus, a contract of sale between a United States party and another party in N, a non-Contracting State, will not be governed by CISG, even though United States law is applicable under usual choice-of-law rules. If United States law applies, but CISG does not, what law does govern the contract? Instead of CISG, United States law for domestic sales transactions would

---

13. *Id.*

14. CISG art. (1)(b).

15. See the list of Contract States in § 1.1, supra.

16. CISG art. 1 (1)(b).

17. See, the Convention the Law Applicable to Contractual Obligations (EC) (Rome, 1998), Art. 4.

18. This reservation is permitted under CISG art. 95.

govern, which means the Uniform Commercial Code (UCC) is applicable in forty-nine states (all but Louisiana).[19]

This reservation was included in the Convention by UNCITRAL to prevent the possibility that the formation of the contract by would be governed by the law of one state and the performance of the contract would be governed by the law of a different state.[20] However, the motivation for the United States declaration is probably a belief that the UCC is superior as a sales law to CISG. Therefore CISG was considered helpful to United States interests only where it provided a clear resolution of the choice-of-law issues.[21] It was believed that, if a court first had to resolve such choice-of-law issues and determined that United States law applied, it might as well apply the "best" United States law—the UCC. Thus, a sales contract between a United States party and another party in N, a non-Contracting State, will not be governed by CISG.

This analysis of the non-application of CISG to a contract between a party whose place of business is in the United States and a party whose place of business is in a non-contracting state should be consistent, whether the action is brought in the courts of the United States or in the courts of France, which has no reservation concerning CISG Article 1(1)(b). For the purposes of interpreting CISG Article 1(1)(a), the United States is a Contracting State in all jurisdictions. But, for the purposes of interpreting CISG Article 1(1)(b) the United States is not to be regarded as a Contracting State.

§ 1.5 Choice of Law Clauses

Under CISG the parties may expressly determine not to be governed by ("opt out of") the Convention.[1] Thus, even if CISG is applicable under its Article 1, the parties may choose a different law to govern the contract. If such a decision is made, care must be used in drafting the statement of exclusion. The parties can attempt to exclude the Convention either by expressly choosing a different law or by stating that CISG is not applicable. However, only if parties have done both will their intent be clear enough that they can be certain that it will be followed by courts.

For example, in the United States, a simple statement that a contract "shall be governed by New York law" is ambiguous, because a court could hold that the New York law concerning international sales is CISG, through federal pre-emption doctrines. Thus, if the parties decide to exclude the Convention, it should be expressly excluded by language

---

19. Although the reservation formally states that U.S. courts are "not bound" by CISG, they are not expressly prohibited from using CISG either. How should a court make that choice? The State Department explanation for the U.S. reservation under Article 95 is premised on the concept that use of the UCC is preferable to use of CISG. U.S. State Department, Legal Analysis of the United Nations Convention on

Contract for the Internal Sale of Goods (1980), Appendix B.

20. J. Honnold, Uniform Law for International Sales under the 1980 United Nations Convention (3d ed. 1999), at § 47.

21. See note 19, supra.

§ 1.5

1. CISG art. 6.

which states that it does not apply and also states what law shall govern the contract. ("This contract shall not be governed by the United Nations Convention on Contracts for the International Sale of Goods, 1980, but shall be governed by the New York Uniform Commercial Code for domestic sales of goods and other New York laws.") It is necessary to designate the law of a particular jurisdiction, in addition to CISG, in any choice of law clause because CISG, like any other single statute, will not furnish a complete legal regime.

Opting out of CISG in other legal regimes of Contracting States requires equal clarity. A simple statement that a contract "shall be governed by the law of France" is not so ambiguous, because CISG was incorporated into the laws of France when the Convention was adopted.[2] If the parties choose "the law of France," under French law the contract is one for an international sale, and the French law governing international sales is CISG.[3] In order to "opt out" of CISG would require at least: "This contract shall be governed by the laws of France applicable to domestic contracts of sale, and shall not be governed by the United Nations Convention on Contracts for the International Sale of Goods, 1980." Clauses with less clarity may fail. For example, references in a contract to the law of domestic contracts (the German Civil Code) were held to be not sufficient to indicate that the parties intended to derogate from CISG and apply the law for domestic contracts.[4]

Partial derogation from CISG provisions is also permitted.[5] Thus, specific clauses in contracts establishing different rules for transmission errors[6] and time for notification[7] have been held to derogate from CISG Articles 27 and 39, respectively.

If the parties can "opt out" of CISG, can they also "opt in"? Under CISG Article 1(1)(b), the parties may also use the rules of "private international law" including choice of law clauses, to "opt in" to the Convention.[8] The choice of law clause used to accomplish this result can be relatively simple ("this contract shall be governed by the laws of France") for the reasons explained above.[9] However, because at least one court has misperceived such language,[10] it is probably better to provide additional clarity here, also: "This contract shall be governed by the laws of France, including the United Nations Convention on Contracts for the International Sale of Goods, 1980."

This "opting in" process is accomplished by use of CISG Article 1(1)(b). However, the United States has declared a reservation to CISG that its courts are not "bound" by that paragraph of Article 1.[11] Can a

---

2. UNILEX Case D. 1994–32. At least one Italian court misperceived the issue and applied Italian domestic law in such circumstances. UNILEX Case D. 1993–3.

   3. See, e.g., Cases D. 1993–1, 1994–30.

   4. UNILEX Case D. 1995–12.

   5. CISG art. 6.

   6. UNILEX Case D. 1991–6.

   7. UNILEX Case D. 1994–18.

   8. See text at § 1.4, note 16, supra.

   9. See text and authorities at notes 2–4, supra.

   10. See UNLIEX Case D. 1993–3.

   11. See text at § 1.4, notes 18–21, supra.

United States party to an international sale contract "opt in" to CISG when Article 1(1)(a) is not applicable? For example, can a sales contract between a United States party and another party in N, a non-Contracting State, by made subject to CISG by including a clause stating: "This contract shall be governed by the United Nations Convention on Contracts for the International Sale of Goods, 1980."

First, it should be noted that, although CISG gives wide recognition to "party autonomy" (the ability of the parties to determine the terms of their deal), in Article 6 it only recognizes the ability of the parties to exclude the Convention. Only in Article 1(1)(b) does have provisions allowing adoption of the Convention through "party autonomy," and this is the provision excluded by the United States Article 95 reservation. Usually the United States court try to recognize "party autonomy," especially in international transactions, and they have permitted the parties to select their own dispute resolution forum in a wide range of circumstances.[12] However, difficulty arises under current United States law. The Convention does not apply through its own terms. The contract does not involve parties in two Contracting States, and the United States reservation makes private international law choice-of-law rules (including "party autonomy" rules) irrelevant as to whether CISG applies.

Under the *Erie*[13] doctrine, the relevant choice of law rules should be furnished by state law—the UCC, and, the UCC does limit "party autonomy." Under the UCC choice law provisions, parties may choose the law applicable to their contract from among those jurisdictions "having a reasonable relation to the transaction."[14] Yet, the whole purpose of the United States' reservation was to limit the influence of CISG to transactions with Contracting States only.[15]

The authorities are unanimous in believing that CISG will be applied in such a case, but provide no consistent rationale.[16] One argument is based on the reasoning in *M/S Bremen v. Zapata Off–Shore Co.*,[17] and the line of cases following it, in which the United States Supreme Court upheld the ability of parties to an international transaction to select their forum for dispute resolution. Those cases involved a forum selection clause rather than a choice of law clause, and neither the interpretation of a convention nor a sale of goods was involved, so the particular technicalities of CISG and the UCC were not analyzed. However, one federal appellate court has interpreted *Bremen* as controlling for choice of law clauses, but without any significant analysis of the differences.[18] Thus the perception of Bremen is that the United States Supreme Court will uphold any party choice clause in any contract for an

---

12. The foundation case is M/S Bremen v. Zapata Off–Shore Co., 407 U.S. 1, 92 S.Ct. 1907, 32 L.Ed.2d 513 (1972).

13. Erie R.R. Co. v. Tompkins, 304 U.S. 64, 58 S.Ct. 817, 82 L.Ed. 1188 (1938).

14. UCC § 1–105.

15. see text and authorities at § 1.4, notes 18–21, supra.

16. See, e.g., Honnold, supra § 1.4, note 20, at § 83; Winship, International Sales Contracts under the 1980 Vienna Convention, 17 U.C.C. L.J. 55 (1984).

17. Supra, note 12.

18. *Milanovich v. Costa Crociere, S.p.A.*, 954 F.2d 763 (D.C.Cir.1992).

"international" transaction, under a general policy encouraging private contractual choice for dispute resolution in the context of international trade. A "strict construction" of the United States reservation under Article 95 might be construed as a limitation on that general policy. However, it may seem more likely that the courts will attempt to fulfill the parties' directions, but analytical difficulties remain.

Another line of analysis relies upon interpretation of the state law (the UCC) itself. The language of Comment 1 of the Official Comments to UCC § 1–105 states: "[A]n agreement as to the choice of law may sometimes take effect as a shorthand expression of the intent of the parties as to matters governed by their agreement, even though the transaction has no significant contact with the jurisdiction chosen." By analogy, this argument supports application of some, if not all, of the provisions of CISG under the circumstances where the parties clearly manifest their interest in having the Convention govern their transaction.

There are many attorneys who will seek to "opt out" of CISG for all contracts under all conditions, simply because they do not understand it as well as they understand the UCC. However, such action may be a disservice to the clients' interests. There may be many circumstances when a seller of goods in an international transaction will be placed in a much more awkward position by the UCC and its "perfect tender" and "rejection" rules than it will be under the rules of CISG. In such transaction, automatic rejection of CISG should be resisted, unless the attorney is willing to write comparable seller-friendly rules into the contract as express terms of the contract. At least one author has stated that negotiating an international sales contract, or automatically opting out of CISG, without understanding how it affects the client's interests, constitutes malpractice.[19]

§ 1.6 Transactions Excluded from the Convention

CISG Articles 2 and 3 exclude a series of types of transactions from the Convention's application. Sales to consumers were excluded in order for CISG not to conflict with special national legislation (usually "mandatory law") to protect consumers.[1] The criteria for such consumer transactions is whether the goods are "bought for personal family or household use," which will be familiar to U.S. attorneys, since it is

19. Brand, Professional Responsibility in a Transnational Practice, 17 J. Law & Com. 301, 335–36 (1998).

See also Gordon, Some thoughts on the Receptiveness of Contract Rules in the CISG and the UNIDROIT Principles as Reflected in One State's (Florida) Experience of (1) Law School Faculty, (2) Members of the Bar with an International Practice and (3) Judges, 46 Am. J. Comp. L. 361 (1998). In it only 30% of practitioners who were members of the international law section

indicated a "reasonable" Knowledge of CISG, and only 2% claimed a "strong" knowledge of it. Although 40% of the judges handled international contracts cases, most were unfamiliar with CISG, and some believed that "CISG must be a federal law which is applicable in federal courts, not in state courts." Most faculty did not include CISG in their contracts or sales courses.

§ 1.6

1. CISG Art. 2(a).

derived from language used in the UCC[2] and the federal Truth in Lending Act (TILA).[3] The issues which arise under that language will also be familiar to U.S. attorneys. One ambiguity is whether the goods must be so used by the immediate buyer in the transaction. Or, can it be eventually used by that buyer's sub-buyer or other remote buyer? U.S. interpretation has uniformly held the former, that the buyer must intend to so use the goods. Other issues relate to whether buyer's intended use must be known to seller at the time of the conclusion of the contract, whether seller has a duty to inquire about intended use, and effect actual changes in use. An Austrian court, in a contract for the sale of Lamborghini automobile, stated that application of the exclusion language depended upon the proposed use of the car as understood by the parties, and not on the actual use, and ruled that CISG did not govern the sale.[4]

The exclusion of consumer goods contains an exception which allows CISG to apply if seller "neither knew or ought to have known" of buyer's use for personal purposes.[5] Thus, if buyer's purchase is in fact for "personal, family, or household use," seller would seem to have the burden of proving that it neither knew of that use, nor should have realized such intended use from the transaction facts. This may explain the results in some cases. In the Lamborghini sale, the Austrian court observed that seller had not presented evidence that it neither knew nor ought to have known of buyer's personal use.[6] However, a contract for the sale of a generator and spare parts for "a sailing yacht cruising the Carribean Sea" was held to be governed by CISG by a German court.[7]

Sales of ships, vessels, hovercraft and aircraft are also expressly excluded.[8] This exclusion seems to be derived from the prior conventions ULIS and ULF,[9] which excluded sales of such goods because they were often treated as "immovables" (real property) under civil law national legislation, because such goods were precisely identifiable by serial number and subject to registration. The ULIS and ULF exclusions were intended to apply only to those ships, etc., which were subject to such registration. This limitation does not appear in the text of CISG, however. Thus, there is an issue of whether either the registration or the size of the ship, etc., is relevant to this exclusion. Since most individual "rowboat" sales are sales to consumers, they would already be excluded under CISG art. 2 (a). However, it is unclear whether CISG covers commercial sales of large numbers of such "rowboats" by a manufacturer to a dealer. The one issue settled by the caselaw is that sales of parts of aircraft are covered by CISG, even though those parts themselves may be precisely identifiable by serial number and may be subject to registra-

---

2. UCC § 9–109.

3. 15 USC § 1663 (h), TILA § 103 (h).

4. UNILEX Case D. 1997–4.3; CLOUT Case 190

5. CISG Art. 2(a).

6. UNILEX Case D. 1997–4.3, CLOUT Case 190.

7. UNILEX Case D. 1995–27.1.

8. CISG Art. 2(e).

9. Supra § 1.3 note 6, ULIS Art. 5(1)(b), ULF Art. 1(6)(b).

tion.[10] Implicitly, this decision indicates that the necessity of registration may be irrelevant to an interpretation of the exclusion under CISG art. 2 (e).

Growing crops and timber have traditionally been considered part of the realty until severance (harvesting). If the crops or timber were sold in a present sale while growing, the harvest had not yet occurred and the sale was of realty. Even in a contract to sell crops or timber in the future, the sale was of realty if the severance was to be done by buyer. Only if seller contracted to sever as well as to sell could the contract be construed as the sale of "future" goods. At the turn of the century, sales statutes began to incorporate the doctrine of "constructive severance." If the growing corps were to be severed as part of the contract of sale, they were "constructively severed" from the realty by the conclusion of the contract, and were therefore converted into personalty. In this manner the sale of growing corps could become a sale of chattels. Other legal regimes constructed similar legal fictions to allow such sales to be considered sales of personalty. It is not clear whether these local doctrines are to be incorporated into CISG.

Sales of some intangible rights or claims—investment securities (stocks, shares), negotiable instruments, money and electricity—are expressly excluded from CISG, even though they may have a tangible "token."[11] Although CISG does not define the word "goods," these two provisions attempt to limit the concept to tangible items. A Swiss court has held that a contract for the purchase of corporate shares is not covered by CISG,[12] and an arbitral tribunal determined that a contract for the transfer of a quota relating to goods was not governed by CISG.[13]

Contracts for the transfer of information (an intangible) which is contained in a tangible (e.g., a computer disc) creates special difficulties in interpreting the term "goods" under CISG. While it is presumed that contracts concerning intellectual property rights (patent, copyright and trademark) are not for the sale of goods, but are licences, the intellectual property may be contained in a disc or a computer or a camera, each of which is a "good." In a non-electronic transaction, a German court held that a contract for market research was not a contract for the sale of "goods," even though the market research was to be contained in a written report to be furnished to the buyer.[14] The court emphasized that the concept of goods required that the tangible thing delivered be the principal object of the contract.

In contracts for the sale of things electronic, the sale of computer hardware, such as computer components, has been held to be governed by CISG.[15] Should that line of analysis be extended to cover the software

10. United Technologies Int'l Pratt & Whitney Com'l Engine Bus. v. Malev Hungarian Airlines, UNILEX Case D. 1992–40. The decision is translated and published in full text in 13J. Law and Com 31 (1993).

11. CISG Art. 2(d) and (f).

12. UNILEX Case D. 1998–17.1.

13. UNILEX Case D. 1993–27.

14. UNILEX Case D. 1994–21, CLOUT Case 122.

15. UNILEX Case D. 1993–23, CLOUT Case 281.

that is included in the sale of "loaded" computer, or the sale of a car or a camera with "embedded" software? The purchase of software downloaded over the internet would at least seem not to involve a sale of "goods." In the United States, the National Conference of Commissioners on Uniform State Laws (NCCUSL) has wrestled extensively with these questions, and seems to provide different answers depending upon the composition of the drafting committees.[16] The one CISG decision on the issue, by a German court, held a sale of software to be governed CISG.[17] The court identified the computer program as "standard software," this implying that it was not specially designed for the buyer, and perhaps that it was a mass-marketed, pre-packaged product. Both considerations could influence a court to consider the software product to be goods. More importantly, however, the court does not indicate that the sale was subject to any written contract of sale or license for use.

An analogy from the non-electronic world may be helpful in analyzing software sales. A contract calling for the submission of a manuscript for a book is not a contract for the sale of goods, even thought the manuscript will be on paper or a disc.[18] It is basically a contract for the author's services. However, a contract for the sale of a commercial lot of printed books (or only one book) is for the sale of tangible items—the books, and not the printer's services. There is no such clear bright line in software sales, since many software sales involve some adaptation to the user's precise situation. Nevertheless, a criterion which is based on the difference between "off the shelf" software and individually designed software may be helpful even when the software sold exhibits some characteristics of each, because one characteristic or the other may predominate.

§ 1.7 Types of Sales Transactions Excluded from the Convention

Although there are many issues concerning the definition of "goods,"[1] there are also many "transactions in goods" which may or may not be "sales." Neither the term "goods" nor the term "transactions" is defined in the Convention.

Auction sales are excluded from CISG. Like consumer contracts, this is another type of contract which is often subject to specialized national legislation. However, a court in the Netherlands has ruled that CISG did govern a sale in which Dutch seller directed a German "buyer," which was itself an auctioneer, to sell a painting "by auction."[2] The decision draws a distinction between a sale "by auction" and "an order to sell by auction." The analysis of this case turns upon the fact that the auction-

---

16. Compare the drafts of UCITA (Uniform Computer Information Act) with each of the two proposed drafts of UCC Article 2. For further discussion of this subject, see Chapter 8, infra.

17. UNILEX Case D. 1995–3.1; CLOUT Case 131.

18. See case cited at note 14, supra.

§ 1.7

1. CISG art. 2(b).

2. UNILEX Case D. 1997–12.1.

eer, the party plaintiff, was the "buyer" in the transaction in litigation, and the court characterized the auction as a second contract which was not the subject of the litigation. Thus, although the sale by the auctioneer to the subsidiary buyer was "by auction," that sale was not involved in the litigation. The transfer by the seller to the auctioneer was not "by auction", but the court found that it was subject to the rules governing "sales" of goods.

Execution sales and sales order by governmental authority are also excluded from CISG.[3] Such sales are often subject to special rules of court and legislature rules. The scope of this exclusion is not well-defined. It may include, for example, sales of goods which were warehoused, or collateral which is seized by the warehouse or a creditor "under authority of law," and which are then sold at public or private sale under the provision of that same law.[4]

"Services" contracts are also expressly excluded from CISG.[5] However, there are many contracts which involve both obligations to provide goods and also obligations to provide related services. In such transactions, when is CISG the governing law? The stated criterion is that CISG does not apply when the "preponderant part of the obligations of the party who furnishes the goods consists of . . . labor or other services."[6] The authorities seem to be in agreement that a "preponderant part" requires that more than 50% of the purchase price be attributed to labor or other services. Thus, the sale of a water tank did not become a "services contract" just because the contract required both provision and installation of the goods.[7] Further, if a CISG is applicable to a mixed service and sale contract it will govern both sales and services aspect of that contract, unless the contract is severable under national domestic law.[8]

Distribution agreements in their usual form are not covered by CISG,[9] although the Convention will govern the separate contracts under those distribution agreements which are actual orders for goods.[10] Thus, distribution agreements, like franchising and marketing contracts, are regarded as "service contracts and not contracts for sale of goods."[11] The same analysis applies to joint venture agreements.[12] As one U.S. court stated, a distribution contract would be within CISG only if it contained definite terms of the delivery of specific goods.[13] That case involved a contract for sale of identified goods, but no breach of the contract was

---

3. CISG art. 2(c).

4. See, e.g., UCC §§ 2–710, 9–504.

5. CISG art. 3(2).

6. Id.

7. UNILEX Case D. 1996–15.1, CLOUT Case 196.

8. P. Schlechtriem, Uniform Sales Law 32 (1986).

9. UNILEX Cases D. 1996–3.3, CLOUT Case 126.

10. UNILEX Case D. 1996–9, CLOUT Case 169; UNILEX Cases D. 1997–11, 12.

11. UNILEX Case D. 1997–2, CLOUT Case 192.

12. UNILEX Case D. 1998–24.

13. Helen Kaminski PTY Ltd. v. Marketing Australia Products Inc. (S.D.N.Y. 1997), UNILEX Case D. 1997–14.

claimed concerning those identified goods. The breach was claimed only for goods ordered later, and not identified in the distribution agreement.

Another excluded type of contract is the traditional "maquiladora" transaction, in which a United States party ships parts of a product to a party in Mexico (or other low-wage country) for the non-U.S. party to assemble the parts and ship the assembled product back to the United States. Is this transaction a pair of cross-border sales of goods, and thus governed by CISG, or a contract for the services of the non-U.S. party, which is not governed by CISG? CISG Article 3(b) excludes contracts where the preponderant part of the obligations of one party are labor or other services. However, there is a second CISG provision which is expressly applicable when the party who "orders the goods" also supplies some of the materials for producing those goods.

This provision first states that contracts for sales of future goods ("goods to be manufactured of produced" after the conclusion of the contract) are governed by CISG.[14] It then makes an exception, however, for those transactions in which the purported buyer ("the party who orders the goods") will provide "a substantial part of the materials necessary" for the completed goods. Note that the deliberate use of "a substantial part" in CISG Article 3(1) is in contrast with the use of "the preponderant part" in CISG Article 3(2), and indicates that the purported buyer need not provide as much as 50% of the necessary materials in order for this exclusion to become applicable. An Austrian court has ruled that a transaction was excluded from CISG in which an Austrian firm provided that raw materials to a Yugoslav company to process into brushes and brooms.[15] There was no discussion of any materials being furnished by the Yugoslav company.[16]

Barter transactions provide an issue of applicability which is outside CISG articles 2 and 3. Is a barter transaction, in which goods are exchanged for other goods, a "sale"? Professor Honnold argues that such transactions are "sales" because CISG Article 53 refers to buyer's obligation to "pay the price for the goods" without requiring that he "price" be a monetary obligation.[17] However, the word "pay" is usually related to tender of money and not to a tender of goods, so Article 53 may not settle this point.[18]

Where a countertrade transaction is structured to use three interrelated contracts—one for the sale of the primary goods, a second for the exchange sale of the countertrade goods, and a protocol to define the

---

14. UNILEX Case D. 1991–9, CLOUT Case 2.

15. UNILEX Case D. 1994–27, CLOUT Case 105.

16. An interpretation which seems more problematic, at least on the reported facts, is UNILEX Case D. 1993–7, in which a French Court excluded CISG from application because the purported buyer provided "specification and design" to the seller, but not materials.

17. J. Honnold, Uniform Law for International Sales § 56.1 (3d ed. 1999).

18. See also, P. Schlechtriem, Commentary on the U.N. Convention on Contracts for the International Sale of Goods, at 22 (1998).

relationship between other two[19]—there often is a price specified for each of the goods involved, the two sale contracts in such transactions would be governed by CISG. However, many such sales contracts, especially those for the sale of the exchange goods, are not sufficiently specific in identifying the quantities and types of goods to be purchased under the countertrade agreement. Thus, although the purported contract would be governed by CISG, the Convention might well determine that no valid contract was formed.[20]

§ 1.8   Issues Excluded from the Convention

The Convention expressly includes two sets of issues which arise under a sale contract, and expressly excludes three sets of issues from its coverage—thereby remanding those latter issues of the substantive law of the legal regime indicated by choice of law doctrines (private international law rules). The issues covered by the Convention are the formation of the contract and the rights and obligations of the parties to the contract.[1] The excluded issues are the "validity" of the contract,[2] property (or title) issues,[3] and liability for death or personal injury.[4]

The language in the preamble to CISG art. 4 concerning "formation" refers to Part II of the Convention[5] and the language concerning "rights and obligations" of the parties refers to Part III of the Convention.[6] Included within the concept of "obligations" is the concept of remedies for beach.[7]

In the language of the preamble to CISG Article 4, only the obligations of the buyer and the seller are expressly mentioned, which has lead to some debate over whether CISG would also govern the rights and obligations of persons who were not immediate parties to the sale contract.[8] Such persons would include manufacturers of the product or its parts which had sold their product to seller or to persons in the chain of distribution who were prior to the seller, and sub-buyers of the goods who purchased from the buyer.

The archetypical example is the manufacturer of a car or electric blanket who attaches a standard form "warranty in a box" to the goods, while the retailer (seller) sells the goods "as is."[9] If the courts read the "buyer-seller" language of CISG Article 4 literally, CISG provides no

---

19. McVey, Countertrade: Commercial Practices, Legal Issues and Policy Dilemmas, 16 Law & Pol'y Int'l Bus. 1 (1984).

20. For further discussion of this issue, see § 1.11, infra.

§ 1.8

1. CISG art. 4 (preamble).

2. CISG art. 4(a).

3. CISG art. 4(b).

4. CISG art. 5.

5. CISG art. 14–24.

6. CISG arts. 25–88.

7. Part III of the Convention, Chapter II covers obligations of the seller, and Section III of that chapter comprises the remedies for seller's breach of its obligations. Likewise, in Part III of the Convention, Chapter III covers obligations of the buyers, and Section III of that chapter comprises the remedies for buyer's breach of its obligations.

8. Honnold, § 1.7 note 17, supra, at 63.

9. See Reitz, "Manufacturers' Warranties of Consumer Goods," 75 Wash. U.L. Rev. 357 (1997).

basis for a claim against the manufacturer, as it is not a seller in this contract. Note, however, that since CISG does not cover this aspect of the contract, local domestic law should be consulted and may provide a cause of action. To the extent that the courts are willing to recognize that the manufacturer has been involved in the sale contract through its "warranty in a box," even though not a formal party, then CISG may be used to provide the cause of action.

To date, the cases have held that such lawsuits are not covered by CISG.[10] Although a French appellate court considered that a "warranty in a box" ("document of guarantee") was a sale contract and gave a right of action against the manufacturer, the Cour de Cassation reversed.[11] It held that the document of guarantee did not create a sale contract, and that CISG Article 4 limited the application of CISG to the buyer-seller relationship.

CISG Article 4 has also been used to exclude many non-sale issues, especially agency issues, from analysis under CISG. Such issues include the liability of a purported "agent" who represented a non-existing principal,[12] whether a person paid by a buyer was an agent of the seller or not,[13] and whether a right to payment could be assigned.[14] Non-agency issues excluded have included estoppel,[15] promissory estoppel,[16] unjust enrichment claims,[17] the validity of forum selection clauses[18] and the assignments of burdens of proof.[19]

CISG Article 4(a) excludes issues of "validity" from the coverage of the Convention but does not define "validity." There are concepts which are clearly within this concept (capacity illegality, fraud and duress), and other issues which present much closer cases. Thus, the domestic law rules which invalidate sale of contraband items would not be affected by CISG, and the local courts would continue to apply such local rules to international sales transactions. Would duress include only "gun at the head" type duress, or also economic duress? CISG provides no guidance other than to indicate that these issues are determined outside the Convention. Thus, a court should consult the local domestic law on the subject, or other law made applicable under the transaction.

The impact of other local, domestic regulatory statutes, such as unfair competition laws, would also be preserved under CISG art. 4(a). Thus, German domestic unfair competition laws were held to be outside CISG and applicable to an asserted franchising agreement. However, the German law involved did not invalidate the individual sales contracts

---

10. UNILEX Case D. 1994–16 (Manufacturer not a party to the sales contract).

11. UNILEX Case D. 1999–1.

12. UNILEX Case D. 1990–6, CLOUT Case 5.

13. UNILEX Case D. 1997–8.2.

14. UNILEX Case D. 1994–3, CLOUT Case 80.

15. UNILEX Case D. 1994–24.

16. UNILEX Case D. 1997–8.

17. UNILEX Case D. 1997–15.1.

18. UNILEX Case D. 1993–24.

19. UNILEX Case D. 1993–1, CLOUT Case 103.

under the flawed franchising agreement, as those individual sales contracts were considered to be valid.[20]

The impact of general doctrines concerning mistake, hardship and unfairness presents a more difficult analytical problem. The courts have reached different conclusions concerning whether "mistake" doctrines are outside CISG, so that domestic law my be consulted. In one Swiss case, a buyer sought excuse from an agreement under Swiss domestic mistake doctrines, because the buyer had not read the contract it signed.[21] The court held that claims of mistake created "validity" issues, so that Swiss domestic law could be consulted. However, a German court has held that it was precluded from considering the German domestic law of mistake, since CISG exhaustively covered the subject-matter area.[22]

There has been a fair amount of litigation concerning general terms of the contracting parties, statutes regulating the use of "general terms", and CISG, especially Article 4(a). Most of the court decisions on this issue have held that questions of the validity of general conditions must be determined by local law and not by CISG principles.[23] A clause disclaiming seller liability for conformity of the goods was subject to German domestic law on such clauses and ruled invalid.[24] Contractual "penalty" clauses have been both upheld[25] and invalidated,[26] but in all cases the court ruled that the analysis of such clauses involved concepts outside of CISG, so domestic law must be consulted. However, in one case, a Hungarian court struck down a liquidated damages clause using CISG Article 4(a), and allowed a greater recovery under the Convention provisions.[27]

One issue under United States law is whether the restrictions in the UCC on disclaimers of warranty create a "validity" issue or not. The UCC provision requires that a disclaimer of the warranty of merchantability use the term "merchantability" and be conspicuous.[28] Is this an issue of "validity" under United States law? A second issue concerns the UCC restrictions on seller's clauses which limit the buyer's remedies to repair or replacement, and thereby exclude the remedies of avoidance of the contract (rejection of the goods) or an action for damages, especially consequential damages.[29] A third issue concerns penalty clauses which provide for a significantly larger payment to the aggrieved party than any actual damages which reasonably could be expected. The relevant UCC provision makes such clauses "void as a penalty."[30]

To date, there are no judicial decisions on any of these issues in the United States arena. The academic analyses of the first two issues take

20. UNILEX Case D. 1997–13.

21. UNILEX Cases D. 1995–23. Accord, UNILEX Case D. 1997–6.

22. UNILEX Case D. 1993–16.

23. UNILEX Case D. 1994–12, D. 1995–1, D. 19972.1; CLOUT Case 232.

24. UNILEX Cases D. 1996–5.5.

25. UNILEX Case D. 1995–22.

26. UNILEX Case D. 1992–2, 1997–2.1.

27. UNILEX Case D. 1992–2.

28. UCC § 2–316(2).

29. UCC § 2–719 (2).

30. UCC § 2–718(1), last sentence.

widely different approaches. Professor Murray has argued that "validity" issues can only arise if the entire contract is voided by the domestic law, not just a single clause within the contract.[31] Thus, CISG would allow a court to go outside CISG and consult domestic law only for sales of heroin or sales of stolen goods—and then only if the actual thief was the seller.[32] Thus, neither the UCC rules on disclaimers of warranty or limitations on remedy could never be considered to be rules of validity.

Professor Hartnell argues that CISG Article 4(a) is designed to protect domestic law rules designed to protect the fairness of a particular clause or of the bargain as a whole.[33] Since the UCC provisions restricting clauses that disclaim warranties or limit remedies are designed to protect fairness, they would qualify as rules of "validity" under CISG and the United States domestic rules would apply to international sales contracts governed by CISG.

Professor Honnold argues that whether such rules are rules of validity depends in part, on the factual situation in which they are used.[34] He would turn first to the provisions of CISG Article 8 on the proper construction of the contract, and believes that proper construction could obviate the need to consult domestic rules on validity. However, he also suggests that where the same operative facts are covered by both a CISG provision and a domestic law rule, the CISG rule should prevail.

Despite all this sophisticated analysis, the CISG cases from other jurisdictions, especially those concerning general terms in contracts, suggest a far lower standard. Those decisions indicate that, if certain conduct or a certain clause is prohibited under the domestic law applicable to the contract, the courts will look outside the Convention and apply the prohibitive rules to the contract as rules of validity.[35] Thus, the standard adopted abroad resembles the standard proposed by Professor Hartnell.[36]

The long debate about the status of the UCC warranty disclaimer and remedy limitation provisions should be contrasted with the wide acceptance of the status of the limitation on penalty clauses.[37] There seems to be general agreement that common law courts will hold such clauses to be invalid, even in contracts otherwise subject to CISG. That wide acceptance may be due to the fact that the UCC makes such clauses "void," rather than merely prohibited or unconscionable. It may also be due to the fact that the rule arises out of the common law cases and pre-

31. J.E. Murray, Contracts, § 155B (1990).

32. Transfers of the thief could have "voidable title" UCC § 2–403.

33. Hartnell, Rousing the Sleeping Dog: The Validity Exception to the Convention on Contracts for the International Sale of Goods, 18 Yale Int'l L.1 (1993).

34. J. Honnold, § 1.4, note 20, supra, at §§ 65, 67. See also, Winship, Commentary on Professor Kastely's Rhetorical Analysis, 8 Nw. J. Int'l L. & Bus. 623 (1988).

35. See text and authorities at notes 23–27, supra.

36. Supra, note 33.

37. UCC § 2–718(1), last sentence.

dates the UCC.[38] Or, it may be due to the foundations of their rule on public policies against non-compensatory remedies and potential *in terrorem* use of contract language.[39]

Another set of issues excluded from CISG coverage concerns property rights to the goods, including title to the goods and the rights and obligations of third parties to the contract.[40] The primary issue raised in litigation over this provision has been the effect of "retention of title" clauses, in which seller attempts to retain title in the goods after they are delivered to the buyer until the buyer pays for the goods. The legal status of such clauses is a property issue and is therefore outside the scope of CISG.[41] Thus, any determination of the effect of such clauses depends upon applicable domestic law, even though CISG applies to the analysis of the remainder of the contract.[42]

§ 1.9   General Provisions of CISG

Articles 7–13 contain its "general principles." These provisions deal with interpretation of the Convention and filling gaps in its provisions,[1] interpretation of international sales contracts,[2] a few definitions,[3] and a replacement for the Statute of Frauds.[4] Article 7 is designed to assist in interpretation of the Convention itself, while Articles 8 and 9 are designed to assist in interpretation of the contract terms. Article 8 concentrates on statements and conduct by the parties themselves as indications of contract terms, while Article 9 concentrates on sources external to the parties, such as trade usage. The provisions of Article 10 concerning multiple business offices have already been discussed in relation to their impact on Article 1.[5]

At first glance, CISG Article 7(1) appears to be a set of "pious platitudes," without any particular analytical content. However, it is intended to provide several inhibitions to the local courts of a State which will decide disputes under the Convention from applying their local law, rather than the Convention, to these international disputes. Thus, in interpreting the concepts stated in the Convention, such as "reasonable time," regard for the "international character" of the Convention is imposed upon courts in an attempt to lead them to use international practice rather than domestic practice or precedent. This preference for international practice is stressed further by the directive "to promote uniformity of its application." The latter is intended to establish foreign decisions under CISG as more persuasive than local decisions on domestic sales law.[6] Even the doctrine of "good faith," well-

38. A. Farnsworth, Contracts 935–37 (3d ed. 1990).

39. See, Lloyd, Penalties and Forfeitures, 29 Harv. L. Rev. 117 (1915).

40. CISG art. 4 (b).

41. UNILEX Case D. 1992–4.

42. UNILEX Case D. 1995–15.1.1.

§ 1.9

1. CISG art. 7.

2. CISG arts. 8 and 9.

3. CISG arts. 10 and 13.

4. CISG arts. 11 and 12.

5. See text and authorities supra § 1.4, notes 10–13.

6. Compare the effect of UCC § 1–102 (2)(c) in persuading the courts of the different individual states of the United States to regard decisions under the UCC of courts in

known in most local law, is muted. Although the UCC imposes an obligation of good faith on each of the parties to a sale,[7] CISG Article 7(1) only refers to good faith in relation to interpretation of the Convention, not of the contract, by courts.

Article 7(2) continues this approach in regard to supplementary principles of law, or "gap-fillers." Unlike the corresponding provision in the UCC, these supplementary principles are not to be gathered from United States domestic law, but either from "general principles" found within the Convention or international law or, if none can be found, from principles found in the law applicable under normal choice-of-law rules. The danger to uniform application is that local courts will discover many "gaps," no usable "general principles" derivable from the Convention, choose their own law as applicable, and easily fall back on their own familiar supplementary principles of law.

Article 8 attempts to establish rules for interpreting the contract itself, and its terms. It establishes a three-tier hierarchy: (1) Where the parties have a common understanding or intent concerning the meaning of a provision, that common understanding is to be used in any interpretation. (2) Where the understandings or intent of the parties diverge, and one party "knew or could not have been unaware" of the other party's intent, the latter party's interpretation prevails.[8] And (3), where the parties were unaware of the divergence, their statements and conduct are each to be subjected to a "reasonable person" standard.[9] The Convention does not attempt to resolve the interpretation problems created if each party's understanding of the other's statements is possible under this "reasonable person" scrutiny.[10] In evaluating party conduct and statements, a court can look to the negotiating history of the contract and to the actual administration of terms of the contract by the parties.[11] (Termed "course of performance" under the UCC).[12]

Article 8(1) has been interpreted to require courts to consider subjective intent while interpreting both the statements and the conduct of the parties.[13] Article 8(3) also can direct a court to a very different approach to contract interpretation than is usual in other U.S. contract cases. Its requirement that a court give consideration to all relevant circumstances is a clear direction to consider parol evidence even when there is a subsequent written agreement. It has also been suggested that both provisions can be used to promote the actual intent of the parties in the battle of the forms transaction, to avoid the "last shot" doctrine.[14]

---

other states as persuasive (not binding) precedent. The hope is for the same effect under CISG art. 7(1).

7. UCC § 1–203.

8. CISG art. 8(1).

9. CISG art. 8(2).

10. See discussion of "mistake" doctrines in § 1.8. supra.

11. CISG art. 8(3).

12. UCC § 2–208.

13. *MCC-Marble Ceramic Center, Inc. v. Ceramica Nuova d'Agostino, S.p.A.*, 144 F.3d 1384 (11th Cir.1998), cert. denied 526 U.S. 1087, 119 S.Ct. 1496, 143 L.Ed.2d 650 (1999).

14. See discussion at § 1.13, notes 16–21 infra.

Article 9(1) allows the parties to include "any usage" to which they have agreed. The drafting history indicates that this paragraph refers only to express agreements to include usage, although the express agreement need not be written. Further, "any" usage may be so incorporated, including local ones, not just international usage. If so incorporated, usage is considered to be part of the express contract items, but is not the governing law of the contract. However, since Article 6 allows the express terms of the contract to vary the provisions of the Convention, agreed usages will prevail over CISG provisions where CISG is the governing law. The one exception to the last statement is Article 12, which is applicable only if one of the parties has its place of business in a Contracting State which has declared a reservation under Article 96. Under that reservation, which is considered to be "mandatory law" and may not be derogated by the contract terms, contracts must be evidenced by a writing if so required by the local law of the Contracting State.

Article 9(2) concerns the incorporation of usages by implication. Both less developed countries (LDCs) and nonmarket economies (NMEs) sought to limit the application of implied usages. Thus, if the parties do not expressly agree to incorporate a usage, it is available in interpreting the contract only if "the parties knew or ought to have known" of it, it must be a usage in international (not merely local) trade, it must be widely known to others in this international trade, and it must be "regularly observed" in that trade. This seems to set a very high standard for any party assuming the burden of proof, although the principle issue in litigation is likely to concern the delineation of the specific "trade" involved.

Article 11 provides that a contract for the international sale of goods is enforceable, even though it is not written, and may be proven by any means. Thus, there is no equivalent in the Convention of the common law Statute of Frauds. However, Articles 12 and 96 allow a Contracting State to declare a reservation that the local law of that Contracting State shall govern the form requirements of the sale contract "where any party has his place of business in that State." Such a reservation may be declared at any time, but it is applicable only to the extent that the domestic law of the State making the reservation "requires contracts of sale" to be in writing. The United States has not made this declaration, so its Statute of Frauds provisions in the UCC are not applicable to contracts under the Convention.[15] However, the local law of parties from other States may be applicable if they have the required local legislation. The former Soviet Union was the strongest proponent of the Article 96 reservation, and the Russian Federation, Belarus and the Ukraine made this declaration when they adopted the Convention.

If the Article 96 reservation has been declared, the parties may not under CISG Article 6 agree otherwise.[16] This gives the local law the effect of "mandatory law" under the Convention. However, it should be

---

15. UCC § 2–201.   **16.** CISG art. 12.

noted that a telex or a telegram can be used under Article 13 to satisfy the "writing" requirement.[17] Further, a telex or a telegram qualify as a "writing" regardless of the formal requirements of the local law. Articles 12 and 96 only make unenforceable those contracts which are "other than in writing" (a Convention term), and Article 13 then defines "writing," as used in CISG, to include a telex or telegram.

C. CONTRACT FORMATION

§ 1.10 Contract Formation in General

The contract formation provisions (Articles 14–24) form a separate "part" of CISG–Part II. A Contracting State may declare a reservation at the time of ratification that it will not be bound by Part II, even though it is bound by the rest of CISG.[1] This is an historical appendix to the Convention, arising out of the separation between ULF and ULIS.[2] The Article 92 reservation has been declared by the Scandinavian nations,[3] which have also made a declaration under Article 94 that CISG will not apply to contracts between parties which have their places of business in Scandinavian states.

Although every first-year American law student studies about "offer, acceptance and consideration," those three elements of contract formation are not present in other legal systems. Civil law emphasizes the agreement process, and does not include a "consideration" requirement.[4] An examination of most commercial transactions will show that there is no real issue concerning consideration in most of them. An examination of most "consideration" cases will show that few of them are commercial contracts—rather, they are aunts attempting to induce nephews not to smoke.[5] Thus, it should not be surprising to learn that CISG has no requirement of "consideration" in its contract formation provisions.

As was discussed in the previous section, the writing requirements of the Statute of Frauds are also not applicable, unless one of the parties has a place of business in a Contracting State which has declared a reservation under Article 96.[6] However, the parties to an informal contract may agree to require any formalities they desire, including requiring that a contract may be validly concluded only with a written, signed final agreement. Such a term, if agreed by both parties is an enforceable derogation from CISG Article 23.

Part II of CISG focuses on "offer"[7] and "acceptance."[8] In Convention terminology, a contract "is concluded" (becomes binding) "when an

---

17. CISG art. 13.

§ 1.10

1. CISG art. 92.

2. See discussion at § 1.3, above.

3. Denmark, Finland, Norway and Sweden.

4. See generally, Nicholas, "Introduction to the French Law of Contract," in

Contract Law Today: Anglo–French Comparisons (. Harris & D. Tallon, eds. 1989).

5. Hamer v. Sidway, 124 N.Y. 538, 27 N.E. 256.

6. See § 1.9, above.

7. CISG arts. 14–17.

acceptance of an offer becomes effective."[9] There is no need for consideration, and no formal requirements.

However, it is also clear that agreements can be reached without clearly identifiable elements of offer and acceptance, and that such offers fall within the scope of CISG rules.[10] Such agreements may be formed by the conduct of the parties, which recognize the existence of an agreement, and would establish that a contract had indeed been concluded without a formal offer or acceptance.[11]

§ 1.11   The Offer

Under CISG, the concept of an "offer" has three requirements.[1] First, it must be "a proposal for concluding a contract," which is a standard provision. Second, it must indicate "an intention to be bound in case of acceptance," which will distinguish an offer from a general sales catalogue or advertisement or a purchase inquiry.[2] Article 14 (2) elaborates on this concept by making proposals addressed to the general public to be presumptively not offers "unless the contrary is clearly indicated." Third, an offer must be "sufficiently definite." This provision is directed toward only three contract terms: the description of the goods, their quantity and their price. Other terms can be left open, but not those three. The criteria for judging definiteness are somewhat ambiguous. The offer is definite enough if the goods are "indicated," which does not seem to require that they be described with any particularity. Similarly, an offer is definite if it "expressly or impliedly fixes or makes provision for determining the quantity and the price," but it is not clear whether failure to meet that criterion requires a finding of indefiniteness.

However, the caselaw seems to be more restrictive. Where "during the course of negotiations" the parties agreed on the quantity of the test-tubes but did not agree on the quality of the test-tubes, the court concluded that the buyer and the seller had not created an agreement through the exchange of messages.[3] Therefore, there was no contract, and the seller had no right to recover the price of the test-tubes. The abstract does not state whether the parties agreed upon the price. If they had done so, the court could have found that the price was evidence that there had been agreement as to the quality of the test tubes.

This CISG provision seems more restrictive than the comparable UCC provision on open, or flexible, price contracts, and it was intended to be more restrictive, because many civil law states do not recognize such open-price contracts. Article 55 might seem to be helpful, but its

8. CISG arts. 18–22.

9. CISG art. 23.

10. P. Schlechtriem, Commentary on the U.N. Convention on Contracts for the International Sale of Goods 102 (2d., 1998)

11. CISG art. 9 (1); CLOUT Case 52 (Hungary, 1992).

§ 1.11

1. CISG art. 14.

2. CISG art. 14 (1).

3. CLOUT Case 135 (Germany, 1995)

provisions are available only where a contract has already been "validly concluded," which assumes either a valid offer or the creation of a contract without an identifiable offer and acceptance.[4] The Convention language is flexible enough, however, to authorize most forms of flexible pricing. Thus, the contract does "make provision for determining the price" where the price is to follow an index specified in the contract, has an escalator clause, or is to be set by a third party. Arguably, the latter would include "lowest price to others" clauses. The principal problem not resolved under the foregoing analysis may be only the order for a replacement part in which no price is stated. It is here that Article 55 is certainly useful. The offeror may have "implicitly" agreed to pay seller's current price for such goods, and Article 55 fixes the price as that generally charged at the time the contract is "concluded."

Open quantity contracts, such as those for requirements, output and exclusive dealings, may cause less difficulty. In each such contract, there arguably is a "provision for determining the quantity" through facts which will exists after the parties become bound, even if the precise number cannot be fixed in advance. Thus, an order for an approximate quantity of natural gas met the requirements of Article 14, because it complied with usage regularly applied in the natural gas trade.[5] Similarly, an order for "a certain quantity" of furs, followed by receipt and resale of specific furs, satisfied the definiteness requirements.[6] However, in view of the requirements of CISG Article 14, it is usually preferable to include either estimated quantity amounts or minimum quantity amounts, to assure that there is a fixed or determinable quantity provision.

Assortment is a final problem concerning "definiteness."[7] However, a clause which permits either the buyer or the seller to specify a changing assortment during the period of the contract would seem to make a provision for determining both quantity and type of goods. The major hurdle in such cases is the requirement that the offer "indicate the goods" and be "sufficiently definite." But Article 14 (1) does not require that the offer "specify" the goods, and so clauses which allow later selection of assortment are presumably authorized, if the parties take care in describing the type of goods from which the assortment will be selected. In a case involving aircraft engines, where seller's offer stipulated one set of engines if a Boeing aircraft were selected by the buyer, and a different set of engines if Airbus was selected, the court held that this was not an offer under CISG Article 14.[8] Thus, a contract was not concluded even though a Letter of Intention had been signed by the parties.

4. See notes 10 and 11 to § 1.15, *supra*.

5. UNILEX Case D. 1996–3.1.

6. UNILEX Case D. 1994–29.

7. Compare UCC § 2–311.

8. United Technologies Int'l Pratt & Whitney Com'l Engine Bus. v. Malev Hungarian Airlines, UNILEX Case D. 1992–40. The decision is translated and published in fall text in 13 J. Law and Com 31 (1993).

§ 1.12   Firm Offers

CISG Article 14 provides the prerequisites of an offer, but the three following articles concern the withdrawal, revocation and termination of an offer.[1] Many of these provisions resemble the civil law in substance, scope and style, more than comparable common law models. "Withdrawal" of an offer is permissible only before the offer is received by the offeree.[2] After such receipt, the only recourse of the offeror is to attempt to "revoke" the offer.

Under CISG, any attempt to revoke an offer must be received by the offeree before the offeree has dispatched an acceptance.[3] However, not all offers are revocable.

One of the consequences of the abandonment by CISG of the "consideration" requirement is that the traditional common law analysis of the revocability of an unaccepted offer has no foundation without the consideration doctrine. The traditional common law doctrine made an offer revocable at will until accepted, unless there was an agreement supported by consideration to keep it open (such as an option).[4] In German law, an offer is binding and irrevocable, unless the offeror states that it is revocable.[5] These two approaches are opposites, and the compromise adopted by CISG uses neither of these approaches.

Under the second paragraph of Article 16, an offer originating under the Convention is revocable unless "it indicates" that it is not revocable. In adopting this position, the Convention rejects both the common rule that an offer is always revocable and the German civil law rule that an offer is not revocable unless it is expressly stated to be revocable. This basic concept is similar to that used in creating a "firm offer" under the UCC,[6] but no "signed writing" is required. There are two ways in which an offer can become irrevocable under Article 16: (1) through the offeror's statements and (2) through reasonable reliance by the offeree. The first of these approaches incorporates civil law norms, while the second applies common law norms.

An offeror can indicate that an offer is irrevocable "by stating a fixed time for acceptance or otherwise." The first reference seems relatively clear, and would include a statement that an offer will be held open for a specified period and no longer. But, what is included in "or otherwise"? For example, does it include a statement that an offer will *lapse* after a specified period? That does not necessarily waive the offeror's right to withdraw the offer earlier, but the delegates at the Diplomatic Conference could not agree on how their language applied in

---

§ 1.12

1. CISG arts 15–17

2. CISG art 15 (2)

3. CISG art. 16(1).

4. Dickenson v. Dodds, L.R.2 Ch. Div. 463 (1876).

5. Eorsi, "Article 16," in Commentary on the International Sales Law: The 1980 Vienna Convention 155 (C. Bianca & M. Bonell, eds., 1987).

French law permits revocation, but requires indemnification of the offeree for revocation. However, this approach was not discussed at the Vienna Conference. Id.

6. UCC § 2–205.

that hypothetical case.[7] The criteria for irrevocability of an offer after reasonable reliance by an offeror under Article 16 (2) (b) seem to follow United States caselaw and the Second Restatement of Contracts, Section 87.

Despite the seeming ambiguity of these concepts and the Convention language, no cases been reported which arise under Article 16 (2). Courts which are presented with these issues may consult the principles of CISG Article 8 on the interpretation of the statement of parties. Under 8 (1), the issue would be whether the offeree knew or could not have been unaware that the offeror intended the offer to be revocable. If both offeror and offeree are from common law states, there may be such an intention, although it is not conclusive since both parties' understandings arise from a common law background in which offers are revocable in the absence of consideration, or a signed writing. If both parties are from civil law backgrounds the opposite construction of intention may be possible. It could be argued that Article 8 is irrelevant to this determination, since the language of CISG Article 16 (2) (a) asks what the offer indicates, not what the person making the offer intended to indicate. However, it is unlikely that the drafters of CISG intended to set aside the general interpretive rules of Art. 8 in interpreting any of the substantive provisions, including the provisions of Article 16.

§ 1.13 Acceptance

CISG defines "acceptance" as either a statement or "other conduct" by an offeree "indicating assent to an offer."[1] Silence is not necessarily acceptance, although the negotiations and other prior conduct of the parties may establish an implicit understanding that lengthy silence followed by affirmative conduct is acceptance. But in *Filanto*, the first CISG case decided by a United States court, the court used the prior relations of the parties, including exchanges of draft contracts, to find that a lengthy failure to object by one party to a proposed final draft of the other party, followed by the beginning of performance by the proposing party, was an acceptance which created an express "agreement in writing" for purposes of the Federal Arbitration Act.[2]

The Filantro decision has been criticized many times.[3] In part, the decision seems to state that there can be a contract to arbitrate which is

---

7. Eorsi supra note 4. "The common law delegations maintained that even if the offer states a fixed time for acceptance, this, in itself, does not necessarily mean that the offer is irrevocable. After all, revocability was stated in the offer. Thus, the common law delegations were inclined to read the civil law language in the common law way." Id.

§ 1.13

1. CISG Art. 18 (1).

2. Filanto S.p.A. v. Chilewich Int'l Corp., 789 F.Supp. 1229 (S.D.N.Y.1992).

Ironically, the opinion is principally an analysis of the "federal law of contracts" that has grown up around the 1958 New York Convention on the Recognition and Enforcement of Arbitral Awards and the federal legislation implementing that treaty. 9 U.S.C. §§ 201–209.

3. See, e.g., Winship, The U.N. Convention and the Emerging Caselaw, Emptio–Venditio Internationes 227–237 (1997); Van Alstine, Consensus, Dissensus and Contractual Obligation Through the Prism of Uniform International Sales Law, 37 Van. Int'l

separate from the sales contract and is separately formed. The concept that the dispute resolution clause can create valid obligations, when no sales contract was ever formed to support it, seems contrary to CISG Art. 8 (1). The antecedents of such an analysis are all in arbitration cases and not in sales cases. However, the federal law governing formation of an arbitration contract may be different from the state law governing formation of the underlying sales contracts. The decision's determination that the silence of one party is acceptance relies on past conduct, without indicating which actions were referenced. *Filanto* and a recent German decision both represent judicial hostility to the possible return under CISG to the "last shot" doctrine in the "battle of the forms" transaction, discussed below.

Article 18(2) determines when an "indication of acceptance" is effective for "concluding" the contract. Thus, along with Articles 16(1) and 22, it forms the Convention's analog to "the mailbox rule"—except that the CISG rules are different. At common law, "the mailbox rule" passed the risk of loss or delay in the transmission of an acceptance to the offeror, once the offeree has dispatched the acceptance.[4] It also chose that point in time to terminate the offeror's power to revoke an offer and to terminate the offeree's power to withdraw the acceptance. Under CISG however, an acceptance is not effective until it "reaches" (is delivered to) the offeror.[5] Thus, risk of loss or delay in transmission is on the offeree, who must now inquire if the acceptance is not acknowledged. On the other hand, the offeror's power to revoke under CISG is terminated upon dispatch of the acceptance[6]—which is the common law rule. However, the offeree's power to withdraw the acceptance terminates only when the acceptance reaches the offeror. Thus, an acceptance sent by a slow transmission method allows the offeree to speculate for a day or two while the offeror is bound. A telex will release the offeree from the acceptance.

Even though Article 18(1) states that acceptance by conduct alone is possible, the remaining paragraphs of Article 18 seem to imply that in the usual case the offeree must notify the offeror that acceptance by conduct is forthcoming. Article 18(3) indicates that acceptance by conduct without notice is possible only when that procedure is allowed by the offer, by usage or by the parties' prior course of performance. If so allowed by the offer, the acceptance by conduct, such as shipping the goods without notice, is effective upon dispatch of the goods, rather than upon their delivery to the offeror. However, notification of the acceptance may reach the offeror indirectly through third parties, such as banks or carrier.

The traditional analysis of the CISG approach to the "battle of the forms" is quite different than that of the UCC, and closer to the common

L. 1 (1996); Nakata, Filanto SPA v. Chilewich Int'l Corp., 7 Transnat.Law.141 (1994).

4. See Adams v. Lindsell, 1 B. & Ald. 631, 106 Eng. Rep. 250 (K.B.1818).

5. CISG art 18(2).

6. CISG art. 16 (1).

law "mirror-image" analysis.[7] Under CISG, if the buyer's purchase order form and seller's order acknowledgment form differ as to any material term, there is no offer and acceptance.[8] Instead, there is an offer, followed by a rejection of that offer and a counter offer (usually the seller's order acknowledgment form). The rejection of the original offer terminates the original offer under CISG.[9] Thus, (theoretically) the parties cannot "conclude" a contract by exchanging conflicting forms; and if one party reneges on its obligations, before performance, it probably is not bound to perform.

Under an express exception to the "mirror-image" rule, a non-mirror image response can be an acceptance if it contains additional or different terms which do not materially alter the terms of the offer.[10] However, "materially alter" is defined in the last paragraph of Article 19, and would include any term which relates to the quality of the goods or the extent of one party's liability to the other.[11] Most order acknowledgment forms contain an additional or different term which does materially alter the terms of most purchase orders. Thus, the express exception will not be applicable in the majority of "battle of the forms" cases.

However, the vast majority of transactions involving exchanges of such forms are performed by the parties, despite the lack of a contract formed by the exchange of forms. Once the goods have been shipped, accepted and paid for, there has been a transaction; and a contract underlying that transaction has been formed by the parties—what are its terms? To put the same question in a different way, is the seller's shipment of the goods "conduct" by the seller which accepts the terms in the buyer's purchase order? Or, is the buyer's acceptance and payment for the goods "conduct" which accepts the terms in the seller's acknowledgment form? The common law analysis would make the terms of the form last sent to another party controlling,[12] since that last form (usually seller's) would be a counter offer and a rejection and termination of all prior unaccepted offers. If the Convention is the governing law, and if no contract has been formed by the exchange of forms, when seller ships the goods, they are shipped under the terms of the only non-terminated offer, which often is the seller's order acknowledgment form.[13] When buyer accepts the goods, it may be argued that buyer also accept seller's terms as contained in the order acknowledgment form. Thus, buyer would be bound by the terms as set forth in seller's order acknowledgment form.[14]

If the buyer accepts the seller's terms by accepting the goods, no contract would be formed until the goods have been shipped by the seller and have been accepted by the buyer, so that the contract would be

7. Poel v. Brunswick—Balke—Collender, 216 N.Y. 310, 110 N.E. 619 (1915).

8. CISG art. 19(1).

9. CISG art. 17.

10. CISG art. 19(2).

11. CISG art. 19(3).

12. See Poel, supra note 7.

13. CISG art. 17.

14. CISG art. 18(1). So held in UNILEX Case D. 1996–10.1.

formed by the conduct of the parties. It may be worth noting that both the United States and civil law regimes have developed more sophisticated methods of dealing with the "battle of the forms" than the "mirror-image" rule followed by the "last shot" principle, but they each use different mechanisms, and the Convention drafters were unable to agree on any of them.[15] Despite the seeming clarity of CISG Articles 18 and 19, there is great resistance against going back to 19th century contract principles. A German decision held that a variation in an acceptance was nonmaterial which limited the buyer's ability to notify the seller of product defects to a 30–day period.[16] Professor Honnold would use the gap-filling provisions of CISG when the parties are not in actual agreement on the terms that lead to a dispute, adopting a "knock-out" doctrine in principal.[17] In *Filanto*, discussed above,[18] the court used prior conduct of the parties to find the existence of a contract where exchange of forms was followed by one party's silence. All of these authorities seem to agree that the mirror-image and last-shot doctrines should not be resurrected, and that there are more sophisticated analytical tools to resolve the battle of forms under CISG.

Professor Van Alstine argues that the problem with the traditional analysis relying on CISG art. 18 (1) is the assumption that the buyer's act of accepting the goods indicates assent to the counter-offer.[19] It is far more likely that the buyer acted without knowledge of the terms of the seller's form. He would argue that the buyer's act should be interpreted in accordance with CISG art. 8(1) or (2). In some cases this analysis will lead to the determination that there is a contract. In other cases, however, the result is indeterminate under the Convention because the buyer did not intend to accept the seller's terms. In these latter cases, the failure to provide an answer may be designated as a gap to be filled in accordance with CISG Article 7 (2). If so, it may be argued that the Convention has a general principle that the parties must act in good faith, which means in this context that contract terms are those that the parties agree upon, together with the gap-filling provisions of the Convention. Alternatively, if the general principle of good faith is deemed unsatisfactory, the answer may be filled by recourse to the national law designated by of conflict of laws rule.

---

15. Compare UCC § 2–207.

Under the UCC, one can argue for several different analytical approaches. However, the traditional analysis is that an agreement was formed by the writings of the parties under 2–207(1), and the terms in the offeree's response (often the seller's acknowledgment form) drop out under UCC § 2–207(2). This is a "first shot" rule which rewards the initiator of the transaction (the first offerror) by giving it the terms of that offer.

For the analysis under French law, see Vergne, the "Battle of the Forms" under the 1980 United Nations Convention Contract for the International Sale of Goods, 33 Am J. Comp. L. 233, 250–51 (1985).

For an analysis under German law, see H. Silberberg, The German Standard Contracts Act 18–19 (1979). The German statute results in the use of a "knock out" rule for the battle of the forms.

16. UNILEX Case D. 1991–7.

17. J. Honnold, supra § 1.4, note 20, at § 170.4.

18. Supra, note 2.

19. Van Alstine, supra note 3. Compare this reasoning to the analytical pattern used in MCC–Marble, supra § 1.9, note 13.

One recent German decision may have adopted Professor Honnold's approach to this issue, not only finding a contract in the "battle of the forms" situation, but using a "knock out" rule to determine the terms of the contract.[20] The parties exchanged standard forms, but the abstract does not state which form was the "last" sent. The court held that seller's choice of law clause had not become part of the contract. Instead, because their intention to be bound was shown by their performance of the contract, the court reasoned that the parties intended implicitly to derogate from CISG Article 19(1) and to permit a non-mirror image positive response to be an "acceptance." The court then ruled that the terms of the contract consisted of the agreed terms, plus "any standard terms which were common in substance," and the conflicting standard terms were excluded.[21]

It is always possible to attempt to "win" the battle of the forms, through derogation of Articles 7 and 8, by inserting a clause in the acknowledgment form that states: "Our obligations are conditional upon your assent to all our terms." However, if everyone uses such clauses in their forms, then no contract is ever formed by the writings, and we return to the "last shot" doctrine, with fax machines working overtime.

In summary and in comparison to the UCC, CISG reduces the flexibility of the parties by prohibiting some open price terms; CISG expands the "firm offer" concept and applies it to more offers; and in the battle of the forms, CISG may delay the formation of a contract through the "mirror image" rule, and may use the "last shot" principle to make to offeree's (usually seller's) terms control the transaction. However, on the last points, both the courts and the authors who have written on the subject have suggested ways of avoiding this traditional analysis.

D. RIGHTS AND OBLIGATIONS OF THE PARTIES

§ 1.14 Seller's Obligations—Delivery

The seller is obligated to deliver the goods and any related documents and to transfer "the property in the goods" to the buyer.[1] In addition, the seller is obligated to deliver goods which conform to the contract as to quantity, quality and title.

Some of these obligations are governed by domestic law, and not the Convention, because the Convention "is not concerned with" the effect of the contract on "the property in the goods sold."[2] Domestic law, therefore, determines whether "the property" passes from seller to buyer at the "conclusion" (formation) of the contract, upon delivery, or at some other time;[3] whether a certificate of title is required; and

---

20. UNILEX Case D. 1995–26.

21. Note that this result is comparable to the result under local domestic law, The German Standard Contracts Act. See authority cited at note 15, supra.

§ 1.14

1. CISG Art. 30.

2. CISG Art. 4(b).

3. For such domestic law in the United States, see UCC §§ 2–401 to 2–403.

whether seller may retain title as security for the purchase price or other debts.[4]

"Delivery" under CISG is a limited concept, relating to transfer of possession or control of the goods. The CISG draftsmen did not attempt to consolidate all the incidents of sale—physical delivery, passing of risk of loss, passing of title, liability for the price, and ability to obtain specific performance, etc.—into a single concept or make them turn on a single event, as has been done in many sales statutes.[5] Instead, they followed the format of the UCC in providing separate provisions for each of these concepts.[6]

As to the place of delivery, CISG recognizes four distinct types of delivery terms: (1) delivery contracts in which the seller must deliver to the place specified in the contract; (2) shipment contracts, in which the contract "involves carriage of the goods," but does not require delivery to any particular place; (3) sales of goods at a known location which are not expected to be transported; and (4) sales of goods whose location is not known or specified, and which are not expected to be transported.[7]

In "destination" or delivery contracts, the seller may be obligated to deliver the goods to the buyer's place, or to a sub-buyer's place, or to any location specified. However, it should be noted that CISG has no provisions directly describing seller's duties in such contracts, for they are expressly excluded from Article 31, and all interpretation is left to contract terms only. The goods must be conforming when delivered,[8] not merely when shipped, unless performance is excused by force majeure.[9]

In a shipment contract, the seller is not obligated to accomplish delivery of goods to their destination, or to any particular place, but it is clear that transportation of the goods by an independent third party carrier is involved. Since the goods are to be "handed over" to the carrier and not to the buyer, transactions involving carriage by the buyer seem to be excluded from this provision. It is not clear, however, whether the reference to a carrier must be express (such as through commercial terms like "FOB" or "CIF")[10] or whether they can also be implied from the facts (the goods and seller are located in State A and buyer plans to use or resell them in State B). The UNILEX case abstracts are all unclear on this particular issue.[11] Thus, it is preferable for the contract of sale to specify expressly whether carriage of the goods by a third party is intended or not.

The shipment contract may require seller to take more than one action to accomplish its obligation of "delivery." First, the seller must

---

4. In the United States, any retention of title of security under UCC Article 2 is subject to the secured transactions provisions of UCC Article 9.

5. See, e.g., the Sale of Goods Act 1893 (U.K.)

6. CISG arts. 31, 69, 57 and 46, respectively. The comparable UCC provisions are UCC §§ 2–509, 2–509, 2–511, and 2–716.

7. CISG art. 31.

8. CISG arts. 36, 69.

9. CISG art. 79.

10. See discussion of "commercial terms" in Chapter 2, infra.

11. See, e.g. UNILEX Cases D. 1995–27; D. 1997–14.1.

transfer ("hand over") the goods to a carrier—the first carrier.[12] There is no duty under CISG for seller to arrange for the carriage of the goods, such as the one imposed by the UCC.[13] Commercial terms may impose such a duty,[14] but the Convention does not. Second, depending upon the sale contract terms, seller must either "effect insurance" coverage of the goods during transit or, at buyer's request, provide the buyer all available information necessary to effect insurance.[15] Third, if the goods are not "clearly identified to the contract" by the shipping documents or by their own markings, seller must notify buyer of the consignment specifying the goods.[16] Finally, the contract may require seller to arrange for the transportation of the goods, in which case seller must contract for "appropriate" carriage under "usual terms."[17]

Where carriage of the goods is not "involved," the buyer may or may not be told where the goods are or will be. Absent a contrary provision in the contract, in such a transaction, if buyer is told the location of the goods she is expected to pick them up at that location; otherwise at the seller's place of business. The seller's obligation under CISG is to put the goods "at buyer's disposal" at the appropriate place.[18] The Convention is not clear as to whether this requires notification to buyer, but it would require notification to any third party bailees to allow the buyer to take possession.

Where the delivery of the goods is to be accomplished by tender or delivery of documents, CISG merely requires that the seller conform to the terms of the contract.[19] The second and third sentences of Article 34 establish the principle that a seller who delivers defective documents early may cure the defects until the date due under the contract, if possible, and buyer must take the cured documents, even though the original tender and cure has caused damage to buyer.

The time requirements for seller's performance, as stated in CISG, all relate to the contract terms: the goods or documents must be delivered on or before a stated or determinable date set in the contract, within a stated or determinable span of time specified in the contract, or, if no date or span of time is set, within a "reasonable time."[20] "Reasonable time" is not defined, and will depend on trade usage, but at least it precludes demands for immediate delivery.

The Convention has no provisions concerning seller's duties in regard of export and import licenses and taxes, but leaves the determination of these incidents of delivery to the contract terms, or usage. Where these issues are not covered by the contract terms or usage, the concepts are to be interpreted according to the general principles of CISG.

---

12. CISG art. 31 (a).

13. See UCC § 2–504 (a).

14. See generally, Chapter 2, infra.

15. CISG art. 32(3).

16. CISG art. 32(1).

17. CISG art. 32(2).

18. CISG art. 31(b), (c).

19. CISG art. 34.

20. CISG art. 33.

§ 1.15   Seller's Obligations—Quality of the Goods

Under CISG, the seller's obligation is to deliver goods of the quantity, quality, description and packaging required by the contract.[1] In determining whether the quality of the goods conforms to the contract, the Convention eschews such separate and independent doctrines as "warranty" and "strict product liability" from the common law analysis, as well as "fault" or "negligence" from civil law. Instead, CISG focuses on the simpler concept that the seller is obligated to deliver the goods as described in the contract, and then elaborates on the connotations of that contractual description. This approach, however, produces results which are comparable to the "warranty" structure of the UCC, but without the divisions between express and implied warranties.[2] This is a pattern of analysis which has long been urged by Professor John Honnold for the UCC itself.[3]

The basic requirements are that the goods conform to the contract description,[4] that the goods be fit for ordinary use and properly packaged,[5] that they be fit for any particular use made known to the seller,[6] and that they conform to any goods which seller has held out as a sample or model.[7] Each of these obligations, however, arises out of the contract, so that the parties may "agree otherwise" and limit seller's obligations concerning quality.[8]

In *Rotorex*, the court held that failure of the goods to comply with affirmative contractual performance standards (contractual specifications regarding cooling capacity and power consumption) constituted a breach.[9] Any trade usage recognized by CISG would also be applicable to the contractual description.[10]

There are no conditions on the imposition on seller of the obligation of fitness for ordinary use. All the contracts governed by CISG will be commercial contracts,[11] so that there is no need for the UCC limitation to a "merchant" seller.[12] One issue not expressly resolved is whether the "ordinary use" is defined by seller's location or by buyer's location, if "ordinary use" in each is different. One United States court has cited, with seeming approval, the analysis of a German court that the seller is

---

§ 1.15

1. CISG art. 35.

2. Compare CISG art. 35 to UCC §§ 2–314 and 2–315. The UCC creates a series of "warranties" from seller to buyer. Some warranties are "express" under UCC § 2–313, others are "implied" under UCC §§ 2–314 and 2–315. The primary reason for the differentiation under UCC concepts is that "implied" warranties can be "disclaimed" under UCC § 2–316(2), while "express warranties" cannot.

3. See, e.g., J. Honnold, Law of Sales and Sales Financing, 28–32 (4th ed. 1976).

4. CISG art. 35 (1). Compare UCC § 2–313.

5. CISG art. 35 (2)(a) and (d). Compare UCC § 2–314.

6. CISG art. 35(2)(b). Compare UCC § 2–315.

7. CISG art. 35(2)(c). Compare UCC § 2–313(1)(c).

8. CISG art. 6. Compare UCC § 2–316 (disclaimers of warranty).

9. Delchi Carrier SpA v. Rotorex Corp., 71 F.3d 1024 (2d Cir.1995).

10. CISG art. 9(2).

11. CISG art. 1(1).

12. See UCC § 2–314(1).

generally not obligated to supply goods that conform to public laws and regulations enforced at buyer's place of business, but with three recognized exceptions.[13] The exceptions enumerated were: (1) if the public laws and regulations of the buyer's state are identical to those enforced in the seller's state; (2) if the buyer informed the seller about those regulations; *or* (3) if, due to special circumstances, seller knew or should have known about the regulations in the buyer's state. The concept of "special circumstances" includes the seller having a branch office in the buyer's state.

The obligation of fitness for a particular purpose arises only if (1) the buyer makes the particular purpose known to the seller (expressly or impliedly) at or before the "conclusion of the contract," (2) the buyer also relies on seller's skill and judgment, and (3) such reliance is reasonable.[14] There is no express requirement that the buyer inform the seller of the buyer's reliance, but only that the buyer inform the seller of the particular purpose. More importantly, there is no requirement that the buyer inform the seller of any of the difficulties which the buyer may know are involved in designating or designing goods to accomplish this particular use. However, it is likely that courts can avoid any abuse of these gaps in the statute by the "reasonable reliance" criterion. In the text of the Convention, the assignment of burdens of proof on such issues is not clear. Most courts have usually placed this burden on the buyer,[15] although one court placed it on the seller,[16] or have allocated it according to the domestic law of the forum.[17]

Seller is relieved of any of the obligations under Article 35(2) against defects in quality whenever buyer is aware or "could not have been unaware" of a defect at the time the contract is "concluded." However, knowledge gained at the time of delivery or inspection of the goods will not affect seller's obligation.[18] The "could not have been unaware" language is the subject of much dispute among common law and civil law authorities. Most common law authorities consider it to be "subjective" and relate to buyer's actual state of mind, rather than to impose "constructive knowledge" on the buyer for items he should have learned. In practice, the usual dispute seems to arise out of the sale of used goods or "seconds," where the courts refuse to allow claims for defects which were not notified to the buyer, but which seem to be predictable for such goods.[19] A court will refuse to relieve the seller of its obligation of non-conformity, even though the buyer "could not have been unaware" of the non-conformity, when the seller was aware of non-conformity and

13. Medical Marketing Int'l, Inc. v. Internazionale Medico Scientifica, S.R.L., 1999 WL 311945 (E.D.La.1999). The court held that the decision of an arbitral tribunal was not in manifest disregard of the German Supreme Court decision. See UNILEX Case. D. 1995–9.

14. CISG art. 35(2)(b).

15. UNILEX Cases D. 1993–22; D 1994–20.1.

16. UNILEX Case D. 1996–10.5.

17. UNILEX Cases D. 1993–1; D. 1998–1.1.

18. CISG art. 35(3).

19. UNILEX Case D. 1997–20.

did not inform the buyer of it.[20]

Under CISG Article 35, a seller is generally not obligated to supply goods that conform to the public laws and regulations in the buyer's state. However, there are at least three exceptions to this general rule. First, if those laws and regulations are identical to those in the seller's state, the goods must conform to them. Second, if the buyer informs the seller about the laws and regulations in its state, the goods must conform to them. And, third, if the seller knew or should have known of the laws and regulations in the buyer's state due to special circumstances, such as having a branch office in buyer's state, then the goods must conform to them.[21]

Under CISG the conformity of the goods to all the contract, and to these standards, is to be tested "at the time when the risk [of loss] passes to the buyer."[22] The time at which the risk of loss passes will be explored in depth later.[23] How long do these obligations continue? Although the less developed countries sought a statutory provision requiring "a reasonable time" for the duration of such obligations, such a provision was not included. Instead, CISG defers to the contract, and speaks of long term obligations of quality which arise from a "guarantee ... for a period of time."[24] However, it is clear that any nonconformity concerning the quality of the goods which exists at the time the risk of loss passes is actionable, even if discovered later. Thus, the buyer is still able to recover for any nonconformity which becomes apparent long after delivery, but the buyer may have to prove that the defect was present at delivery and was not caused by buyer's use, maintenance or protection of the goods.[25]

If the goods are defective, seller may have a disclosure obligation. Under Article 40 there is an obligation to notify buyer of any nonconformity not only if known to seller, but also if "he could not have been unaware." If seller does know of a defect and does not notify, then seller may not be able to rely on buyer's failure to inspect the goods quickly or to notify seller of any discovered defects. Thus, even though the buyer may lose its right to rely on a nonconformity because the buyer did not inspect the goods "within as short a time as is practicable,"[26] or did not notify the seller of any defects, specifying the nature of the defects, within a reasonable time after it discovered or "ought to have discovered" them,[27] the buyer's right to rely on the nonconformity revives if the seller, in turn, knew of the nonconformity and did not notify the buyer of it.

20. UNILEX Case D. 1996–5.5. Compare CISG art. 40.

21. See *Medical Marketing Int'l, Inc. v. Internazionale Medico Scientifica, S.R.L.,* 1999 WL 311945 (E.D.La.1999).

22. CISG art. 36(1).

23. See § 1.25, infra.

24. CISG art. 36(2).

25. See UNILEX Case D. 1996–5.2.1, in which the goods, delivered under an FOB contract, were non-conforming when they reached their destination. The Commission held that the goods were not canned or packaged properly, so the non-conformity related back to a time before delivery.

26. CISG art. 38.

27. CISG art. 39.

Can seller exclude these obligations concerning the quality of the goods by terms in the contract—and, if so, how? CISG Article 6 states that the parties may, by agreement, derogate from any provision of the Convention, and Article 35(2) supports that ability to limit obligations concerning the quality of the goods. However, it is also clear that the standard United States formulation in domestic contracts—disclaiming implied warranties[28]—will be inapposite, since the CISG obligations are neither "warranties" nor "implied." New verbal formulations should be found, which deal directly with the description of the goods and their expected use.

If a contract is framed in the usual language, which is appropriate for contracts subject to the UCC,[29] but the contract is actually governed by CISG, a court would have two possible analytical approaches. One would arise from the concept that the term "warranties" has little meaning in the CISG context, and the drafters deliberately avoided using it, because the term has many different meanings in different legal regimes. Thus, use of such language by a seller should not be allowed to destroy the legislatively imposed duties of quality. The other approach would allow a court to inquire of the parties whether they understood the concepts of "warranty," "express" and "implied"—i.e., whether they were familiar with the United States domestic legal approach in this area. If so, CISG Article 8(1) would allow the court to interpret the language according to the parties intentions.[30]

The major unresolved issue is the extent to which local law regulating disclaimers will impact on the international contracts governed by CISG. Such local law covers a spectrum from prohibitions on disclaimers in printed standard terms[31] to the "how to do it manual" set out in UCC § 2–316. It is likely that the former raises a question of "validity," and therefore governs contracts arising under CISG; but there is a three-way argument as to whether the UCC provisions raise issues of "validity," and therefore whether they govern CISG contracts. The distinction drawn seems to depend upon whether the local public policy prohibits conduct completely, or allows it but only within certain conditions.[32] Whether the United States courts will accept such a distinction is conjectural at this point. However, they should, at the least, draw a distinction between those UCC provisions which require language to be

28. The so-called "standard manufacturers warranty," usually reads as follows:

Seller warrants this product to be free from defects in material and workmanship for [amount of time]. Seller makes No other EXPRESS WARRANTY and NO IMPLIED WARRANTIES. Seller's obligation is limited to repair or replacement of defective parts without charge to Buyer.

29. See UCC § 2–316 (2), (3).

30. The *MCC–Marble* case, supra § 1.9, note 13, would allow U.S. courts to examine the background of the transaction to determine the parties' intentions.

31. The German Standard Contracts Act, translated and published in H. Silberg. The German Standard Contracts Act, 27–29 (1979).

32. See Hartnell, "Rousing the Sleeping Dog: The Validity Exception to the CISG," 18 Yale Int'l L. 1 (1993); S. Honnold, supra § 1.4, note 20, at § 236; Longobardi, "Disclaimers of Implied Warranties: The 1980 United Nations Convention on Contracts for the International Sale of Goods", 53 Fordham L. Rev. 863 (1985).

"conspicuous" and those provisions which require a particular linguistic formula, such as use of the word "merchantability."

§ 1.16 Seller's Obligations—Property Issues

Even though CISG Art. 4(b) states that the Convention is not concerned with property or title to the goods sold, CISG does impose obligations on sellers that the goods be sold free of any claims concerning title to the goods or claims on infringement of intellectual property rights.[1] Seller's obligation concerning title to the goods under CISG is to deliver the goods not only free from any encumbrances on their title, but also free from any claim of a third party.[2] The issue concerning who actually has valid title to particular goods is outside the scope of the Convention under Article 4 (b), and would be left to local law. But the scope of seller's obligation to deliver what it has promised is within the scope of the Convention.

A second issue is whether seller is required to convey only a valid title to the goods, or is also required to convey title that will not be contested–a warranty of "quiet possession." The common law required that seller provide a warranty of "quiet possession."[3] The legal issue is whether the Convention language should be interpreted to require that seller convey title that is free from all claims, or only title that is free from valid claims. The language in the English version is not clear and, the debates and legislative history suggest conflicting interpretations, but the language in the French and Spanish versions suggest that the goods are to be free from all claims.[4] There are no CISG cases yet which analyze the issue.[5]

Although the obligation is very broad, it probably is not breached by claims which are frivolous on their face or by state restrictions on use of the goods. The parties may derogate from the terms of these provisions of CISG by agreement, but buyer's knowledge that the goods are subject to a bailee's lien does not necessarily imply such an agreement. Instead, buyer may expect seller to discharge the lien before tender of delivery.

In addition to good title and "quiet possession," seller is obligated to deliver the goods free from patent, trademark and copyright claims assertable under the law of the buyer's "place of business" or the place where both parties expect the goods to be used or resold.[6] This obligation is, however, subject to multiple qualifications. First, seller's obligations arise only with respect to claims of which "seller knew or could not have

§ 1.16

1. CISG arts. 41, 42.

2. CISG art. 41.

3. See UCC § 2–312, and especially Comment 1

4. See Honnold supra § 1.4, note 20, at § 266, and especially authorities cited in his note 4.

5. The one case to date citing CISG art. 41 dealt with seller's ability to place geographic limits on buyer's resale of the goods. See UNILEX Case D. 1996–3.1.

6. CISG art. 42.

been unaware."[7] Second, seller has no obligation with respect to intellectual property rights or claims of which buyer had knowledge when the contract was formed.[8] Third, seller is not liable for claims which arise out of its use of technical drawings, designs or other specifications furnished by buyer, if seller's action is in "compliance with" buyer's specifications.[9] It is clear that this provision applies when seller is following specifications required by the contract, but its application is not clear when seller is merely following "suggestions" of buyer as to how best to meet more general contract provisions. Fourth, seller is excused from these obligations if buyer does not give notice of breach[10]—unless seller knew of the claim, which knowledge may be required in order to create liability initially.[11]

With all these qualifications on the seller's obligation, does the mere assertion of an intellectual property infringement claim create a violation of seller's title obligations? In order to have a violation, the buyer must show that "seller knew or could not have been unaware" the third party claims. One survey of the legislative history concludes that it does not require the seller to research the trademark and copyright registries of the buyer's country, but only requires seller to use due care.[12] That interpretation would preclude a warranty of quiet enjoyment, because buyer has no absolute claim, but only a knowledge or negligence-based claim.

It can also be argued that mistake of law will excuse seller, or at least that the seller has performed its obligations concerning intellectual property rights if it has relied on trustworthy information from a lawyer that there are no such rights which might be infringed by use or resale of the goods, because seller could not then "know" of the possible claims of infringement.

The UCC approach to these problems is to allow buyer, when sued by a third party claimant, to "vouch in" the seller, so as to allow the seller to defend itself directly.[13] However, there is no "vouching in" provision in CISG. Thus, buyers who are confronted with third party claims are left to local procedural devices for protection, such as collateral estoppel.

§ 1.17 Buyer's Obligations

Buyer has two primary obligations in a sale contract under CISG: to pay the price, and to take delivery of the goods.[1] The former duty is the

---

7. CISG art. 42(1).

8. CISG art. 42(2)(a).

9. CISG art. 42 (2)(b).

10. CISG art. 43(1).

11. CISG art. 43 (2). Compare UCC § 2–312(3).

12. Shinn, "Liabilities Under Article 42 of the U.N. Convention on the International Sale of Goods," 2 Minn. J. Global Trade 115 (1993).

The only CISG decision to date, involves a situation in which the third party claimant had already obtained an infringement judgment against the buyer. See UNILEX Case D. 1996–6.0.1.

13. See UCC § 2–607(5)

§ 1.17

1. CISG art. 53.

more important of the two. In addition, there are several derivative preliminary duties which Professor Honnold refers to as "enabling steps."[2]

Unless the sale contract expressly grants credit to buyer, the sale is a cash sale, and payment and delivery are concurrent conditions. Further, payment is due when seller places the goods, or their documents of title, "at buyer's disposal according to the contract."[3] If the sales contract involves carriage of the goods, seller may ship the goods under negotiable documents of title and demand payment against those documents,[4] even though no particular method of payment was actually agreed upon by the parties. In such circumstances, buyer still has a right of inspection before payment. If, however, buyer has expressly agreed to "pay against documents" (such as through the use of CFR or CIF term), the buyer has agreed to pay upon tender of the documents, regardless of whether the goods have yet arrived, and without inspection of the goods.[5]

If the buyer is to pay against "handing over" of the documents, or handing over the goods, the place of "handing over" is the place of payment. Otherwise, the place of seller's business is the place of payment, unless the contract provides otherwise.[6] Such a provision requires the buyer to "export" the funds to seller, which is a critical issue when buyer is from a country with a "soft" currency, or with other restrictions on the international transfer of funds. In addition the buyer has an obligation to cooperate and take all necessary steps to enable payment to be made, including whatever formalities may be imposed by the buyer's country to obtain administrative authorization to make a payment abroad.[7] Failure to take such steps may create a breach by the buyer even before payment is due.

In addition to the payment provisions, Article 55 addresses the problem of open-price contracts, an issue discussed previously in this chapter.[8] Professor Honnold believes that Article 55 permits initial indefiniteness of the price, and allows a court to enforce such contracts at "the price generally charged at the conclusion of the contract."[9] Most other writers conclude that the Article 55 provisions are available only for supervening indefiniteness of a contract which initially had a method of determining the price.[10] Such a situation arises often when an index adopted by the contract is no longer calculated or published. However, the Article 55 solution would be to adopt the price charged when the contract was initially formed, which seems unduly harsh towards the

---

2. J. Honnold, supra § 1. 4, note 20, at § 323.

3. CISG art. 58.

4. CISG art. 58(2).

5. CISG art. 58 (3).

6. CISG art. 57.

7. CISG art. 54.

8. See text at § 1.16, supra.

9. J. Honnold, supra § 1. 4, note 20, at 150–56.

10. See, e.g., Eorsi, "Article 14," in Commentary International Sales Law: The 1980 Vienna Sales Convention, 136–44 (C.M. Bianca & M.J. Bonnell eds., 1987); P. Schelchtreim, Uniform Sales Law: The UN Convention on Contracts for the International Sale of Goods, 50–52 (1986).

seller. To avoid this possibility, sellers using flexible pricing contracts will wish to provide many fall-back indices, in case some should fail.

The cases, however, have not been so doctrinaire. Where the offer indicated a range of prices for goods with a range of quality, the court held that the offer was sufficiently definite, since it was possible to price each item according to its quality.[11] Where the parties agreed to a sale without stating a price, but essentially "agreed to agree" later on the price for each shipment, the purported offer neither contained a price term nor made a provision for determining the price.[12] However, in two cases where the seller and buyer agreed to a sale with no price term, then the goods were shipped and accepted by buyer, the courts found that a binding contract existed.[13] In each case, seller had included an invoice stating a price with the goods, and buyer had not contested that price at the time of receipt.

The buyer's second obligation, to take delivery, also poses duties of cooperation. The buyer must not only take over the goods, but also do everything that could reasonably be expected in order to enable the seller to make delivery.[14] This includes a duty to make the expected preparations to permit seller to make delivery and may include such acts as providing for containers, transportation, unloading and import licenses.[15]

§ 1.18 Buyer's Inspection and Notice of Defects

The buyer has a right to inspect the goods before taking delivery and the duty to notify the seller of any non-conformities.[1] Where the contract involves the carriage of goods, the buyer may defer the inspection until the goods have arrived at their destination.[2] Timeliness of inspection is important, and several decisions hold that the buyer is not permitted to pass the goods on to sub-purchasers and await their complaints, but has an affirmative duty to inspect the goods immediately when they arrive.[3]

The buyer may also have a natural incentive to inspect at the place of delivery (e.g., shipment) because the goods must be conforming at the time the risk passes, which will be at the place or port of shipment in the usual FCA, FOB or CIF contract.[4] There are numerous specialized

---

11. UNILEX Case D. 1994–29.

12. UNILEX Case D. 1995–7.2.

13. UNILEX Cases D. 1995–15 and D. 10.1.

14. CISG art. 60.

15. *Id.*

§ 1.18

1. CISG art. 38(1). Compare UCC § 2–513, which gives the buyer a right to inspect the goods before it must either accept or pay for them. Even when shipment of

the goods is involved, buyer may inspect after arrival at their destination before acceptance or payment, unless otherwise agreed. UCC § 2–513(1). However, buyer is not permitted to inspect before payment where the contract provides for payment against documents, UCC § 2–513(3).

2. CISG art 38(2).

3. See, e.g., UNILEX Case D. 1995–10.1. A delay of twenty days to inspect frozen bacon is unreasonably long. Buyer did not inspect but waited for its customs to do so.

4. See, generally, Chapter 2, infra.

inspection companies that will, for a fee, inspect goods for a distant buyer.

The buyer must notify the seller within a reasonable after the buyer discovers any nonconformity.[5] The notice must specify the nature of the lack of conformity. If it fails to duly notify the seller without a reasonable excuse, the buyer may not rely on the lack of conformity in any remedy proceeding. If there is a reasonable excuse, the buyer may still reduce the price of the goods in accordance with the special formula of Art. 50.[6] This latter provision was included in the CISG as a result of pressure from developing countries who complained that it was often difficult for them to inspect and notify promptly.

There has been more litigation over the effectiveness of such notices than over any other single issue, but the results are usually not surprising.[7] For example, where buyer notified seller that the goods (shoes) had "poor workmanship and improper fitting," the court held that the notice was defective in that it was not specific enough.[8]

The contract may include such terms as a provision on how many days the buyer will have to inspect, where the inspection will take place, how many days the buyer will have to notify the seller of the defects, how and where the notice is to be sent, and a statement as to when specification of a defect is sufficient.

§ 1.19   Cure

If the seller delivers non-forming goods, it will often wish to cure any defects in the goods delivered. It is for that reason that the Convention requires early notice by the buyer to the seller of any defects in the goods or their tender of delivery. The primary issues arise from defects in quantity or quality of the goods or the timeliness of the delivery. The Convention has different rules for cure which depend upon whether the defects were discovered before or after the contract date for delivery.

Where a non-conforming tender is made before the contract date for delivery, the seller has the right to remedy any lack of conformity, "provided that the exercise of this right does not cause the buyer unreasonable inconvenience or unreasonable expense."[1] The cure may be repair, replacement or making up a shortage in quantity. If seller cures

---

5. CISG art. 39. Compare UCC § 2–607, which requires the buyer which has accepted nonconforming goods to notify seller "of breach" within a reasonable time of discovery, or its "barred from any remedy" under the UCC—unless the contract terms provide otherwise, UCC § 2–607(3)(a).

6. CISG art. 44.

7. Consult the "Cases listed by Issue" section of UNILEX under Article 39.

8. CLOUT Case 3.

§ 1.19

1. CISG art. 37. Compare UCC § 2–508(1), which allows a seller who had tendered delivery before the contract delivery date to cure any non-conforming tender, if there is notice and cure be accomplished before the contract delivery date.

the non-conformity, it is still liable to the buyer for any damages caused by the defects.[2]

CISG Article 37 speaks of the seller having a "right" to cure the non-conformity of a tender before the date for delivery. Thus, the buyer is obligated to permit the seller to cure.[3] If the buyer prohibits the seller from attempting cure, that is a breach of buyer's obligations, so the buyer will be responsible for any damages which arise from not permitting the cure.[4] That article expressly contemplates repair or replacement as recognized forms of cure. Whether other forms of redress, such as offering of a money allowance,[5] can be used is not clear.[6] Given the objectives of Article 37, the list of specific forms of remedy should not be read as exclusive and the buyer should be obligated to accept a tendered cure as long as it does not cause the buyer unreasonable inconvenience or unreasonable expense.

Even after the date for delivery has passed, the seller may remedy the non-conformity but its right to do so is subject to more conditions. In addition to not causing the buyer unreasonable inconvenience or unreasonable expense, the seller must cure without unreasonable delay.[7] Unlike the specific references in CISG Article 37 to various ways a non-conformity tender might be remedied, CISG Article 48 says only that the seller may remedy any failure. Given that the basic objectives of Article 48 are the same as that of Article 37, the seller should not be limited in the form of cure as long as the conditions (e.g., no unreasonable delay, expense or inconvenience) are satisfied.

If asked whether it will accept cure, the buyer apparently has the option to say "No" under CISG.[8] If the buyer does so and the seller proceeds nevertheless to make a conforming tender, the buyer would not be obligated to accept the tender. One arbitral award has stated that the seller's right to cure after the delivery date is dependent on the consent of the buyer.[9] If the buyer does agree to the seller's offer of cure, it may not seek a remedy which as inconsistent with seller's offered performance, such as avoidance of the contract.

If the buyer wishes to avoid the contract after seller has made an offer to cure the non-conformities, that is still possible under the opening clause of CISG Article 48(1). However, to be authorized to avoid the contract, the buyer must comply with all of the requirements of CISG Article 49.[10] Suppose the seller had attempted to cure, but the performance remains non-conforming. Has the seller "performed" its obli-

---

2. *Id.*

3. CISG art. 61(1).

4. See CISG art. 74.

5. Compare CISG art. 50.

6. Compare UCC § 2–508(2).

7. CISG art. 48. Compare UCC § 2–508(2) which gives to the seller a more limited right to cure even after the contract delivery date. It is available only if the seller had "reasonable grounds to believe" that the non-conforming tender "would be acceptable" to buyer, even though defective. If so, seller must notify buyer of the intention to cure, and then may "substitute a conforming tender" within a reasonable time of the contract date.

8. CISG art 48 (2).

9. UNILEX Case D. 1994–31.

10. See further discussion with respect to the remedy of avoidance at § 1.

gations under CISG? Can the buyer seek further attempts to cure? To date these issues have not been analyzed in the reported decisions.

§ 1.20　Risk of Loss

Most international sales will involve transportation of the goods, even though no such transportation is necessary for CISG to apply.[1] The basic rule, under CISG and domestic law, is that the buyer bears the risk of loss to the goods during their transportation by a carrier, unless the contract provides otherwise.[2] The contract will often contain a term which expressly allocates the risk of loss, such as "FOB" or "CIF," and such terms supersede the CISG provision.[3] If there is no such delivery term, under CISG the risk in a shipment contract passes to the buyer when the seller completes its delivery obligations under CISG Article 31, which is when the goods are "handed over" by the seller to the first carrier.[4] They need not be on board the means of transportation, or even pass a ship's rail—any receipt by a carrier will do. Further, they need not be "handed over" to an ocean-going or international carrier—possession by the local trucker who will haul them to the port is sufficient. However, if the seller uses its own vehicle to transport the goods, seller bears the risk of loss until the goods are handed over to an independent carrier, or to the buyer.

Where the contract requires that the seller deliver the goods to buyer's location, or that seller provide part of the transportation and then "hand the goods over to a carrier at a particular place," seller bears the risk of loss to that location or particular place.[5] Thus, in a contract between a Buffalo, N.Y., seller and Beijing, China, buyer: (1) in a shipment contract (FCA Buffalo), the risk would pass to buyer when the goods were delivered to the first carrier in Buffalo;[6] (2) in a destination contract (DDU Beijing), the seller would bear the risk during transit, and risk would not pass to buyer until the goods were delivered in Beijing;[7] and (3) in a transshipment contract (FAS New York City), the seller would bear risk from Buffalo to "along side" a ship in New York harbor, and buyer would bear the risk thereafter.[8]

If the goods are not to be transported by a carrier (e.g., when the buyer or an agent are close to the seller and will pick up the goods), the risk passes to buyer when the buyer picks them up or, if the buyer is late in doing so, when the goods are "at his disposal" and the delay in

§ 1.20

1. See discussion of CISG art. 1 at § 1.4, supra.

2. CISG art. 67(1), UCC § 2–509(1).

3. See discussion of risk of loss, generally, throughout Chapter 2 on Incoterms. However, use of commercial terms is a derogation from CISG art. 67, even when there is no reference to Incoterms. See, e.g., UNILEX Case D. 1995–28.1.1.

4. The risk of loss passes to the buyer when the seller has completed its delivery obligations under CISG art 31(a).

5. CISG art. 67(1), second sentence.

6. See § 2.8, infra. Even if the contract had a C & F term, the risk of loss would pass upon delivery to the carrier at the port of shipment, Buffalo. See UNILEX Case D. 1995–28.1.1.

7. See § 2.19 infra.

8. See § 2.9, infra.

picking them up causes a breach of contract.[9] The goods cannot, however, be "at his disposal" until they have first been identified to the contract.

In most situations, title and risk are treated separately. Thus, manipulation of title through the use of title retention clauses or documents of title, such as negotiable bills of lading, is irrelevant and has no effect on the point of transfer of risk of loss. However, if the goods are already in transit when sold, the risk passes when the contract is "concluded."[10] This rule reflects a use of "title" concepts in risk allocation, even though it may be practically impossible to determine whether damage to goods in a ship's cargo hold occurred before or after a sale contract was signed.

Just as title and risk are treated separately, so also breach and risk are treated separately. If seller is in breach of contract when the goods are shipped, these basic risk of loss rules are not changed, which is contrary to the position of the UCC.[11] Thus, a breach by seller, whether it is a "fundamental beach" under CISG Article 25 or not, is irrelevant to determine risk allocation or the point when the risk of loss passes to the buyer. However, if the seller does commit a fundamental breach of contract in shipment contract, further damage to the goods during transit will not deprive buyer of its right to avoid the contract under CISG.[12] Likewise, a non-fundamental breach in a shipment contract, plus damage in transit, will not create a right for buyer to avoid the contract.

§ 1.21 Excused Performance

Under CISG, performance of an obligation of a party is excused when that party's failure to perform the obligation was due to an "impediment" which was beyond that party's control, and which the party "could not reasonably be expected to have taken [it] into account" when the contract was made.[1] In addition, the party seeking excuse must prove that it could neither avoid nor overcome the "impediment." The excuse is available only so long as the impediment continues,[2] and the party seeking excuse must notify the other party to the contract both of the "impediment" and of its effect on performance.[3]

Even if the party seeking excuse proves all these elements, it is protected only from damage claims.[4] It is not protected from other remedial actions by the other party, such as avoidance of the contract or restitution of benefits received from the other party or derived from goods received.

This brief summary of the provisions of Article 79 should demonstrate that great weight is placed on the concept of "impediment." In

---

9. CISG art. 69.

10. CISG art. 68.

11. UCC § 2–510.

12. CISG art. 49

§ 1.21

1. CISG art. 79(1).

2. CISG art. 79(3).

3. CISG art. 79(4).

4. CISG art. 79(5).

part, that word was chosen because it was believed to be not an operative word used to define excused performance in any current legal regime.[5] Thus, it is not connected to the operation of any domestic legal system; it creates a blank slate for development of CISG concepts,[6] although the of the word "impediment" does create nuances from which analytical conclusions may be drawn. The drafters of the CISG provisions deliberately rejected a proposal to use the word "circumstances," rather than "impediment."[7] "Impediment" was thought to reflect a requirement of an outside force which arose to prevent performances, rather than a change in the general economic climate. Thus, recessions or increases in inflation rates were not expected to qualify as impediments, although even Professor Honnold accepts that extreme cases of economic dislocation may qualify as an "impediment."[8] The language in Article 79 does not, however, resolve the issue of whether it can excuse only a complete failure to perform (deliver or pay for goods), or whether it can also be used to excuse defective performance (late delivery or delivery of non-conforming goods). Professor Honnold argues for the former interpretation, although that argument seems to ignore the literal language of the provision which allows excuse of "any" obligation. The debates in the Working Group indicate that it was intended to excuse only the obligation to deliver or pay, and not to include obligation to deliver conforming goods.[9]

While the CISG provisions may seem open-ended and subject to widely varying interpretation, the cases involving CISG Article 79 are clear. With one possible exception,[10] the decisions have all ruled against the party seeking excuse. Thus, a buyer is not excused from payment because the funds were stolen from "a foreign bank" through allegedly criminal conduct.[11] Transferring the funds to seller is part of buyer's obligations,[12] and at buyer's risk.

Most of the cases involve defaults by seller's suppliers. The CISG provisions establish a high standard for obtaining excuse because a third party, such as seller's supplier, has defaulted. The party to the sales contract (seller) is excused by a default of a third party (supplier) only if both the seller and the supplier can show that they failed due to an impediment which was beyond their control, not expected, and unavoid-

5. See J. Honnold, supra § 1.7, note 17 at §§ 425–432.

6. For example, CISG art. 79 is deliberately different from UCC § 2–615, which would be the analogous UCC provision. The CISG provision can be used by both buyer and seller, while the UCC provision is expressly limited to use by sellers only. Further, the CISG provision can be used to excuse "any" obligation, while the UCC provision is limited to late delivery. It was the limitations (or sometimes expansions) in domestic laws that the drafters sought to avoid by using a new word which started

with no precedential interpretation baggage.

7. Honnold, supra note 5, at § 427.

8. *Id.*, at § 432.2.

9. B. Nicholas, Chapter 5, in International Sales (Galston & Smit, eds. 1984).

10. See UNILEX Case D. 1995–15.2. However, that case seems to turn more on an interpretation of German agency law than on CISG art. 79.

11. UNILEX Case D. 1998–5.2.

12. CISG art. 57(1)(a).

able and not overcomable.[13] Thus, the seller must be able to prove that some "impediment" prevented the supplier from performing. Financial difficulties of the supplier do not meet that standard, and seller assumes the risk of supplier's ability to continue to perform.[14] If the supplier furnished non-conforming goods to the buyer, there is no excuse unless the problems causing the non-conformity were beyond the supplier's ability to control, as well as the seller's.[15] Where the goods are not delivered at all, seller faces a double difficulty. First, it must prove that the problems causing the non-delivery were beyond the supplier's ability to control.[16] In addition, the seller must prove that it was not possible for it (the seller) to obtain conforming substitute goods from another source.[17] To date no seller has overcome this double burden.

E. REMEDIES

§ 1.23 Remedies in General

The organization of CISG treats buyer's remedies for seller's breach in a separate chapter of the convention from the seller's remedies for buyer's breach.[1] Thus, the buyer has four potential types of remedies under CISG: "avoidance" of the contract,[2] price adjustment,[3] specific performance,[4] and an action for damages.[5] The first two of these remedies may be undertaken without judicial intervention, the latter two involve proceedings in court or before an arbitral tribunal.

If the buyer breaches, the seller has five potential types of remedies: suspension of performance,[6] "avoidance" of the contract,[7] reclamation of the goods (including protection of them if they have been delivered),[8] an action for the price,[9] and an action for damages.[10] The first of these remedies may be undertaken without judicial intervention, the third may or may not involve judicial assistance, and the last two involve proceedings in court or before an arbitral tribunal.

The informal remedies which do not require judicial intervention are preferred by merchants because of their low cost; and merchants who have traded with each other in the past, and hope to do so in the future, are much more likely to use these remedies than to go to court. Thus, to

13. CISG art. 79(2).

14. UNILEX Case D. 1996–3.4.

15. UNILEX Case D. 1999–3.

16. UNILEX Case D. 1995–34; UNILEX Case 1995–10.0.1, CLOUT Case 140.

17. UNILEX Case D. 1997–4.4.

§ 1.23

1. Buyer's remedies are in CISG Part III, Chapter II, arts. 45–52. Seller's remedies are in CISG Part III, Chapter III, arts. 61–65. The measurement of damages for both parties, however, is aggregated in still another chapter: CISG Part III, Chapter V, arts. 74–77.

2. CISG art. 49.

3. CISG art. 50.

4. CISG art. 46, which in the United States is also subject to art. 28.

5. CISG art. 45 (1)(b), referring to arts. 74–77.

6. CISG art. 71.

7. CISG art. 64.

8. CISG arts. 85–88.

9. CISG art. 62, which in the United States may or may not be subject to art. 28.

10. CISG art. 61(1), referring to arts. 74–77.

your authors, the more important differentiation is between informal (non-judicial) remedies and remedies which require formal proceedings in court or an arbitral tribunal; and we have organized the following discussion of CISG remedies around that principle.

§ 1.24   Suspending Performance

Under CISG, a party who has yet to perform may suspend its performance if "it becomes apparent" that the other party "will not" render the required counterperformance.[1] Thus, a seller who has not yet shipped the goods may suspend that performance if it learns that the buyer is insolvent or that there is a "serious deficiency ... in his creditworthiness."[2] The seller may also suspend its performance if the buyer fails to perform necessary, agreed upon preliminary steps, such as a failure to open a letter of credit[3] or to provide specifications for the goods.[4]

The provision is neutral between buyers and sellers. Thus, a buyer who has agreed to pay, or to prepay, for the goods may suspend that performance if it learns that there is a "serious deficiency" in seller's ability to perform,[5] or that necessary preparations for performance have not been made.[6] Seller's preparations for performance which are necessary include making shipping insurance arrangements[7] or obtaining the proper documents.[8]

Despite the facial neutrality of the provision between sellers and buyers, the cases all involve suspensions of performance by sellers, usually because they have not been paid for prior deliveries. There seems to be a split in the reasoning in the decisions to date. The Austrian Supreme Court has held that a seller may not suspend performance merely because the buyer has failed to pay for prior installments of goods shipped under a contract.[9] It stated that the seller was entitled to suspend its performance only if it could establish that the buyer was unable to pay (financial difficulty or insolvency), and that proof of the buyer's unwillingness to pay was insufficient.

The two other decisions on this issue seem to disagree. In one, a Belgian court held that a seven month delay in buyer's payment for an initial installment of goods allowed a seller to suspend performance in delivering the second installment.[10] The court reasoned that the seller could have a reasonable suspicion that the buyer would not pay for the second installment, but there is no indication that the buyer was in any

---

§ 1.24

1. CISG art. 71. Compare UCC § 2–702 which permits a seller to suspend performance, but relates this power to the buyer's insolvency.

2. CISG art. 71(1)(a).

3. CISG arts. 71(1)(b), 54. See UNILEX Case D. 1995–28.2 (failure to secure bank guarantee allows suspension of performance).

4. *Id.*, CISG art. 65.

5. CISG art. 71(1)(a).

6. CISG art. 71(1)(b).

7. CISG art 32(2), (3).

8. CISG art. 34.

9. UNILEX Case D. 1998–5.1, CLOUT Case 238.

10. UNILEX Case D. 1995–7.0.

financial difficulties or had any inability to pay. Thus, the unwillingness of the buyer to pay for prior deliveries was sufficient.

The second case involves a standard scenario. The seller delivers defective, but repairable goods. The buyer refuses to pay until the goods are repaired. The seller refuses to repair until paid. A sole arbitrator ruled that the seller was entitled to suspend its repair performance until it was paid.[11] Again, there was no discussion of the buyer's inability to pay.

This division of authority arises from the Austrian court's focus on CISG Article 71(1)(a), which requires inability to pay, and the other decisions focus on the preamble to Article 71(1) ("apparent that the other party *will not* perform"). Certainly the conditions stated in subparagraphs (a) and (b) to Article 71 (1) are an exclusive list. Thus, the analysis of the other two decisions would depend upon ruling that it was apparent that buyer would not pay in the future as a result of buyer's "conduct ... in performing the contract." (failure to pay for prior installments) under Article 71(1)(b).

A party who suspends performance must notify the other party of that suspension.[12] Failure to notify triggers the other party's rights to a remedy in accordance with the remedies provisions of CISG.[13] None of these remedies authorizes the other party to treat the suspension as ineffective because no notice has been given. However, the non-notified party may have an immediate cause of action for damages.[14]

The CISG permits a seller to suspend performance, if possible, after shipment of the goods but before delivery of them—stoppage in transit.[15] The CISG provision, however, only deals with rights and duties between the parties to the contract. There is a second question concerning whether a carrier will comply with the seller's direction to stop delivery. CISG does not require the carrier to do so, and the carrier's obligations are left to other law.[16] If the seller has possession of a negotiable bill of lading to its order, then the carrier is obligated under the contract of carriage to deliver the footwear to the seller. The CISG provision does not state any criteria for determining whether the stoppage is authorized, so the buyer has no ground under the sales contract to object to seller's stoppage or to challenge it.

However, if the buyer is the holder of the negotiable bill of lading, then the carrier is obligated to deliver the buyer.[17] If the carrier does so, then CISG provides no relief for the seller. If the carrier has not delivered the goods to the buyer, the seller may seek to obtain the bill of lading from the buyer and to enjoin the buyer from presenting the bill to the carrier. These remedies are not expressly provided for by the CISG, but the first sentence of CISG Article 71(2) expressly states that the

11. UNILEX Case D. 1995–29.
12. CISG art. 71 (3).
13. For the buyer, see CISG art. 45(1). For the seller, see CISG art. 61(1).
14. UNILEX Case D. 1991–1.
15. CISG art. 71(2).
16. CISG art. 71(2), last sentence.
17. See discussion in Chapter 3, infra.

seller is entitled to stop delivery even the buyer "holds a document which entitles [it] to obtain [the goods]." The remedies discussed merely give effect to this right.

The reasoning of the previous paragraph also applies to a transaction in which the buyer is the consignee of a non-negotiable bill of lading.

After the carrier has delivered the goods to the buyer, then it is no longer possible to stop delivery under CISG.[18] All that seller would have is an in personam claim against for the purchase price.[19] The CISG is silent on whether the seller might have an in rem right to recover the goods.[20]

§ 1.25   "Avoidance" of a Contract—Refusal to Accept Nonconforming Performance

Either a seller or a buyer can "avoid" a contract, under certain conditions, due to nonperformance or defective performance by the other party.[1] "Avoidance of the contract," in CISG terminology, is the equivalent of "cancellation of the contract" at common law and under the UCC.[2] Also note that "avoidance of the contract" under CISG is a different concept than "avoidance" under the UCC.[3]

For buyers, "avoidance of the contract" is a method of refusing to accept or keep defective goods or to pay for them. Thus, it is comparable to the rights of buyers under the UCC to "reject" the goods actually delivered before "acceptance,"[4] or to "revoke the acceptance" of goods previously accepted.[5] However, CISG does not adopt the distinctions between "rejecting of the goods" acceptance and "revocation of acceptance" contained in the UCC.[6] Further, CISG does not employ the concept of "acceptance" of the goods; so the buyer's taking delivery of the goods is not a crucial factual step in the analysis of buyer's position under the CISG.

Instead, the fundamental concept under CISG is to limit use of this remedy to situations which involve "fundamental breach" by seller, regardless of when the breach occurs.[7] What constitutes a "fundamental breach"? The Convention definition requires "such detriment to the other party as to substantially deprive him of what he is entitled to expect."[8] The drafting history of CISG indicates that "fundamental breach" seems to impose a stricter standard on buyer than the "substan-

---

18. CISG art. 71(2).

19. CISG arts. 61(1)(a), 62.

20. CISG art. 4(b).

§ 1.25

1. CISG arts. 49(1), 64(1).

2. UCC § 2–106(4). In both, the ending of the contract is for breach; and an action for damages survives the end of the contract.

3. See, UCC § 2–613.

4. UCC §§ 2–601, 2–612.

5. UCC §§ 2–606, 2–608.

6. UCC §§ 2–601, 2–602, 2–608, 2–612.

7. CISG art. 49(1)(a).

8. CISG art. 25.

tial impairment" test of the UCC.[9] However, there is no indication that the drafters contemplated the old English "fundamental breach" test, which required that the breach "go to the root" of the contract, but which was repudiated by the House of Lords in 1980.[10]

The seller must be substantially deprived of what it could reasonably expect. The reference to expectation is a reference to the quantity and quality of the goods, not to their market price. The focus is on the contract and what the seller is entitled to expect. This is an objective test, comparing the claimed defect in the goods to the reasonable expectation after buyer. The second clause of the CISG Article 25 requires a consideration of whether the substantial detriment was foreseeable. The motivation of the seller, such as an economic desire to get out of the contract is not legally relevant to the interpretation of CISG Article 25. However, it can also be argued that interpreting "fundamental breach" to promote the observance of good faith allows a court to consult the motivations for a breach. The current Common Law concept allowing parties to perform or pay damages is not accepted by civil law jurists. They seek to promote the performance of promises as an independent goal.

The two United States court decisions have not created an overwhelmingly high standard to meet the "fundamental breach" test. Nor have they required "perfect tender" or allowed non-functional defects to be considered as fundamental breaches. In one case, compressors for air conditioning units were delivered which did not have either the cooling capacity or the power consumption contained in the contract specifications. The court held that cooling capacity was an important factor in determining the value of air conditioner compressors, so that the buyer did not in fact receive the goods it was entitled to expect.[11] In the other case, mammography units were seized for non-compliance with U.S. administrative regulations. When the court decided that the seller in this case was obligated to furnish goods that conformed to the buyer's laws,[12] it also held that a breach of that obligation was a fundamental breach.[13]

Foreign cases have adopted the same approach. Where the buyer stated that "it was unable to work with" the substandard steel wire delivered by the buyer, the court held that since seller was unable to use the goods the defect was a fundamental breach.[14] However, where the buyer alleged only that the material used in the goods was different from the contract specifications, but did not allege that the goods could not be used or resold, the breach was not considered fundamental.[15] When a seller contracted to deliver in "July, August, September" and the buyer expected monthly installment deliveries, it was not a fundamental

9. UCC §§ 2–608, 2–612.

10. *Photo Production Ltd. v. Securicor Transport Ltd.*, [1980] 1 All Eng. Rep. 556.

11. Delchi Carrier SpA v. Rotorex Corp., 71 F.3d 1024 (2d Cir.1995)

12. See discussion in text at § 1.15, supra.

13. Medical Marketing Int'l, Inc. v. Internazionale Medico Scientifica, S.R.L. 1999 WL 311945 (E.D.La.1999).

14. CLOUT Case 235 (Ger. 1997).

15. UNILEX Case 1994–2.

breach to deliver the goods on September 26.[16] Such tender of delivery was within the agreed delivery period, so any delay was not a fundamental defect.

Where there was an exclusive dealership arrangement between seller and buyer, the fact that an agent of the seller sold to another retailer in the buyer's exclusive territory was held not to be a fundamental breach.[17] The court reasoned that because the seller had no knowledge of the agent's conduct, and that knowledge could not be imputed to the seller. On the other hand, where a seller stated that the resale location of the goods was critically important, and the buyer stated an intention to resell in South America, resale elsewhere was a fundamental breach.[18] At the conclusion of the contract, the buyer knew that it was important to the seller that the buyer not resell the goods in areas where other distributors sold those goods. The buyer breached the contract term with respect to the clothing delivered in the first installment. That breach could be treated as a fundamental breach, because the seller was substantially deprived of what it was entitled to expect under the contract,[19] and the buyer could foresee that the detriment would be substantial for the seller.[20]

Where as installment contract is involved, there are separate criteria for the avoidance with respect to an individual installment[21] and with respect to the whole contract.[22] For example, in the last case in the previous paragraph, although the resale of the first installment outside South America was a fundamental breach with respect to the first installment, it might not be a fundamental breach for the whole contract. To permit avoidance with respect to the whole contract, the seller would have to give "good grounds to conclude that a fundamental breach will reoccur with respect to future installments." In that case, the buyer had stated unequivocally that "its resale actions are of no concern to" the seller.[23] That statement gave the seller good grounds to conclude that the buyer would continue to breach the contract with regard to future installments as it had with respect to the first installment. If the buyer continued to breach the contract as it did, the seller would be deprived of what it is entitled to expect with respect to those installments and the buyer should have been able to foresee this.[24]

Given the uncertainties of the "fundamental breach" test, it will be very difficult for buyer, or buyer's attorney, to know how to react to any particular breach—and whether "avoidance" (cancellation) of the contract is permissible or not. Incorrect analysis could put buyer in the position of making a fundamental breach through its response. CISG Articles 47 and 49(1)(b) attempt to cure these uncertainties by offering

---

16. CLOUT Case 7 (Ger. 1990).

17. CLOUT Case 6 (Ger. 1991).

18. UNILEX Case 1995–7, CLOUT Case 154.

19. CISG art. 25, first clause.

20. CISG art. 25, second clause.

21. CISG art. 73(1).

22. CISG art. 73(2).

23. UNILEX Case D. 1995–7, CLOUT Case 154.

24. CISG arts. 72(2), 25.

buyer a method of formulating a supposedly strict standard for performance. If the seller fails to deliver the goods on the agreed delivery date, the buyer may notify the seller that performance is due by a stated new date (after the contract date for performance), and the seller's failure to perform by the new date permits the buyer to declare the contract avoided. However, the provision in CISG Article 49(1)(b) is available only for nondelivery by seller, not for delivery of nonconforming goods, and avoidance seems to be available only if seller does not deliver during the additional period allowed by the notice. Thus, it is not clear whether seller's delivery of nonconforming goods during the additional period permits avoidance or not. In other words, must the quality of a late delivery by seller meet a strict standard of "nonconformity," or only the standard of the "fundamental breach" test? There are other interesting issues of interpretation of this provision. How long an additional period must buyer give seller? Article 47 requires that it be "of reasonable length," but unless there is a custom on this issue, the buyer has no certainty that the period it gives in the Article 49(1)(b) notice is long enough, especially if long distances are involved.

The cases mostly involve buyers who quickly complain about the goods, hoping that the seller will cure the defect, and officially declare avoidance months later. They usually are not permitted to avoid the contract—the courts holding that their original complaints about the goods do not amount to a formal declaration of avoidance, and that their later declarations come too late.[25] However, in one case where the seller did unsuccessfully attempt to repair the defects, the period for sending a notice of avoidance seems to have been extended—for five weeks—even after the end of the unsuccessful repairs.[26]

As to the time period to be set by this notification to perform or else, the principle case involved "items related to printing machinery." The seller delivered only three out of nine promised items. The buyer then fixed an additional period of 11 days which was "too short to organize carriage by sea." But when seller still failed to deliver, the court held that the buyer could avoid the contract.[27] Thus, there is precedent for allowing the buyer's time desires to override the seller's time requirements for ordinary transport measures. The holding may be influenced by the fact that the buyer sent its declaration of avoidance seven weeks after delivery of the non-conforming goods. This delay was approved by the court because seller had offered only a partial delivery of the conforming goods in the interim.

The right to declare the contract avoided for the fundamental breach is lost if the buyer does not make the declaration within a

---

25. See, e.g., UNILEX Case D. 1994–7, UNILEX Case 1994–10.

26. UNILEX Case D. 1995–1.2. Compare that fact pattern to on in which the buyer declared the contract avoided four weeks after discovering the defect, and was

held to be too late UNILEX Case D. 1995–15.1.

27. UNILEX Case D. 1995–16, translated by P. Winship in J. Spanogle and P. Winship, International Sales Law at 257 (2000).

reasonable time after he knew or ought to have known of the breach.[28] The purpose of this notice is to give the seller an opportunity to cure the defects.[29]

Even if buyer seeks to "avoid the contract" after a "fundamental breach" by the seller, the seller has a right to "cure" any defect in its performance before avoidance is declared.[30] If seller's nonconforming tender is early, seller may cure by making a conforming tender up to the delivery date in the contract, whether the nonconformity would create a fundamental breach or not. However, seller's right to cure after the delivery date may be more problematic. Does the right to cure survive buyer's actual declaration of "avoidance of the contract"? Conceptually, it is difficult to sustain a finding of fundamental beach where seller has made a timely offer of cure. If seller's tender or offer of cure is made after the delivery date in the contract, seller still has a right to cure through late performance, but only if it can be done "without unreasonable delay," inconvenience or uncertainty of reimbursement expenses.[31] The cases have announced two different analytical approaches, one case held that the buyer could avoid the contract, despite the seller's offer to cure, because the seller's right to cure after the delivery date was dependent upon the buyer's consent.[32]

In the second case, the court found that the seller's breach was not fundamental, and that the seller had offered to furnish substitute conforming goods, but this offer was not accepted. The court ruled that determining the competing rights of the buyer to avoid the contract and the seller to cure defects in performance depended upon whether the defect was a fundamental breach of contract or not.[33] The buyer's right to avoid the contract could prevail over the seller's right to cure if there was a fundamental breach of contract. But, in this case, where the breach was not fundamental, the language of CISG Article 48 lead the court to decide that the seller's right to cure prevailed over the buyer's right to avoid the contract.

Must performance offered as cure meet a strict "nonconformity" test, or is it still subject to the "fundamental breach" test? CISG has no provisions on this issue. It is possible to argue that, if the seller delivers any attempt at cure, the buyer is not entitled to avoid under Art. 49 (1)(b), but may only recover any damages it has suffered. On the other hand, it seems strange to argue that the delivery a second round of defective goods constitutes "delivery of the goods" under Art. 49 (1)(b). Perhaps the seller, having breached once, should be considered to be on probation and must "get it right" during that probationary period.

The cases demonstrate that, for the buyer to be able to avoid the contract, it must inspect the goods in "as short a [time] as is practica-

28. CISG art. 49 (2)(b)(i). UNILEX Case D, 1992–10.

29. See discussion of "cure" at § 1.19, supra.

30. CISG art. 48(1).

31. Id.

32. UNILEX Case D.1994–31. The analysis seems to emphasize the conditions stated in CISG art. 48(2) and (3).

33. UNILEX Case D. 1997–4.

ble"[34]; notify seller of the nonconformity "within a reasonable time"[35]; and permit seller to attempt to cure any nonconformity, if the cure does not cause "unreasonable delay" or "inconvenience,"[36] To avoid the contract, the buyer must not only comply with the requirements of CISG Article 48 (1), but also those of CISG Article 49. Otherwise it is entitled only to seek the remedy of damages [37]or price reduction.[38] The thrust of the combination of all of these CISG provisions on avoidance is to require cooperation between the parties in resolving disputes over timeliness of delivery and quality of goods.

If the buyer properly avoids the contract and returns the goods, the buyer can still get its money back, even if it has already paid for the goods, under the restitutionary provisions of Article 81. However, the buyer must also return the goods "substantially in the condition which he receives them",[39] unless excused under CISG article 82(2). In the interim, the buyer must take reasonable steps to preserve them.[40] The seller must account for the goods if it is unable to return them "substantially in the condition in which it received them"[41] The buyer has right to deposit the goods in a public warehouse at the expense of the seller.[42] The buyer has a right to sell the goods under specified circumstances.[43]

Note that the seller of goods may be in a significantly better position under CISG than under the UCC, if the buyer claims a relatively minor fault in the goods. Although seller has a right to cure any defects under either statute, this right under the UCC has either time limitations or expectation requirements not stated in CISG.[44] Rejection merely because of a tender which is not "perfect" seems to be available under the UCC,[45] but is definitely not available under CISG.[46] Thus, the seller is less likely to find the goods rejected for an asserted minor non-conformity, and stranded an ocean or continent away, without any effective legal remedy.

§ 1.26 Non–Judicial Price Adjustment

In addition to refusing to accept goods which do not conform to the contract through "avoidance" (cancellation) of the contract,[1] the aggrieved buyer has another informal remedy which appears to give it the power of self-help. Under CISG, the buyer who receives nonconforming goods "may reduce the price" it pays to seller.[2] This remedy is available

34. CISG art. 38. See further discussion at § 1.18, supra.

35. CISG arts. 39, 48, see further discussion at § 1.18, supra.

36. CISG art. 48. See further discussion at § 1.19, supra.

37. CISG arts. 74–77. See further discussion at §§ 1.31–1.33, infra.

38. CISG art. 50. See further discussion at § 1.26, infra.

39. CISG arts, 81 (2), 82(1)

40. CISG art. 86(1).

41. CISG art. 84(2).

42. CISG art. 87.

43. CISG art. 88.

44. Compare UCC § 2–508 with CISG art. 37.

45. UCC § 2–601. Cf. UCC§§ 2–608, 2–612.

46. CISG art. 49 (1).

§ 1.26

1. See discussion at § 1.25, supra.

2. CISG art. 50.

whether the buyer has already paid or not. If the buyer has paid, the remedy is likely to require an action in court, rather than self help.

The Convention provision spells out a mathematical formula for calculating the permissible amount of the price reduction. The reduction requires a comparison of the value that the goods actually delivered at the time of that delivery to the value that conforming goods would have had at the time of that actual delivery. That ratio is to be applied to the contract price to determine the price to be paid under CISG Article 50. If the price of the goods has not changed between the time of contracting and, the delivery date, that formula gives the same result as would a damages calculation under the UCC. However, if the price of the goods has changed during the period, then the resulting calculations clash with normative results under common law doctrine, whether they are used to calculate expectation (benefit of the bargain), reliance or restitution interests.[3]

This type of self-help provision is familiar at civil law, as a method of compensating a aggrieved buyer when the seller is not "at fault," when there is no civil law cause of action for damages.[4] There is also a UCC provision which allows an aggrieved buyer to exercise self help in reducing the price of non-conforming goods, but it appears to be not widely used under the UCC.[5] Unlike the UCC provisions, there is no requirement of prior notice to the seller by the buyer before exercising this option. Proposals at the Diplomatic Conference to require a "declaration of price reduction" by the buyer were not accepted.[6]

There is little guidance in the provision on how to determine the value of the actual goods delivered at the time of delivery, or as to what evidence of value should be sent to the seller. The provision, therefore, seems better suited to deliveries which are defective as to quantity, rather than as to quality. One United States decision has indicated that, if the buyer resells the defective goods, the resale price is evidence of their value at the time of delivery; and that the seller is entitled to discover the resale prices.[7] Several foreign courts have dispensed with the formula stated in the provision and , where the buyer had the defective goods repaired, have given the buyer the costs of repair under CISG article 50.[8]

If the provision may be used for defects in quality, may it also be used in cases where the defect arises from claims under patent or other intellectual property regimes? A buyer attempting to use this self-help remedy must allow seller to attempt to cure, if seller so requests. On the

---

3. Flechter, More U.S. Decisions on the U.N. Sales Convention: Scope, Parol Evidence, "Validity," and Reduction of Price Under Article 50, 14 J. Law & Com. 153 (1995).

4. On the civil law foundation of Article 50, see Bergsten and Miller, The Remedy of Reduction of Price, 27 Am. J. Comp. L. 255 (1979).

5. UCC § 2–717.

6. See Bergsten and Miller, supra note 4. Cf. UNILEX Case D. 1994–7.

7. Interag Co., Ltd. v. Stafford Phase Corp., 1990 WL 71478 (S.D.N.Y.1990).

8. UNILEX Cases D. 1992–10, D. 1995–29.

other hand, a seller who is excused from performance by an Article 79"impediment"[9] will still be vulnerable to a price reduction under Article 50, even though the buyer could not bring an action for damages.[10]

§ 1.27 Reclamation of the Goods

If an unpaid seller is unable (for any reason) to obtain the price, it may seek to obtain the return of its goods from the defaulting buyer, after delivery, by "avoiding" the contract and seeking to reclaim them. Such reclamation is difficult at common law,[1] but the Convention may allow such reclamation. CISG Article 64 gives the seller the power to declare the contract "avoided" and does not distinguish between pre-and post-delivery situations. Article 81 requires "restitution . . . of whatever the first party has supplied" after avoidance. This analysis, however, is available only so long as third parties (buyer's creditors and trustees in bankruptcy) are not involved, for CISG does not affect title to the goods and third party rights,[2] and does not require a court to order "specific performance" which it would not order under its own law.[3]

A buyer who is in possession of goods after a contract has been avoided must take "reasonable" steps to preserve them.[4] Such steps may include depositing the goods in a warehouse at seller's expense.[5] If the seller has no agent in buyer's location, a buyer who avoids a contract or refuses to take delivery of goods which have been "placed at his disposal at their destination" must take possession of them "on behalf of the seller" if this can be done without payment of the price (i.e., without paying a negotiable bill of lading) and without "unreasonable inconvenience" or expense.[6] After such a taking of possession on behalf of the seller, the buyer must again take "reasonable" steps to preserve them.[7] If the goods are perishable, the buyer in possession may have to try to sell them and remit any proceeds to the seller, less the buyer's expenses of preserving and selling them.[8] CISG does not, however, contain any provisions which require a buyer in possession who has rejected the seller's tender to follow seller's instructions, such as to resell on seller's behalf, whether seemingly reasonable or not.

§ 1.28 Judicial Remedies

The more formal remedies available to an aggrieved party through court or arbitral tribunal proceedings are the buyer's action for specific

9. See discussion at § 1.21, supra.

10. This aspect conforms to the civil law derivation of the price reduction concept, to make the remedy available when the seller is not at "fault."

§ 1.27

1. See, e.g., UCC §§ 2–507 and 2–702, and their comments.

2. CISG art. 4.

3. CISG art. 28. See discussion at § 1.29, infra.

4. CISG art. 85.

5. CISG art. 87.

6. CISG art. 86 (2).

7. CISG art. 86(2), last sentence.

8. CISG art. 88.

performance, the seller's action for the price, and an action by either the buyer or the seller for damages.

This scheme is roughly comparable to the remedies available to an aggrieved buyer under the UCC. The difficulty facing the drafters of the Convention is illustrated by two facts: First, specific performance is the preferred remedy at civil law, while the action for damages is preferred at common law. Second, at civil law, a finding of "fault" is usually required for imposition of any recovery of damages, while the common law aggrieved party need show only "nonconformity." CISG had to bridge both gaps.

§ 1.29 Seller's Action for Specific Performance

CISG gives to the buyer who has not received the agreed performance from the seller a specifically enforceable right to "require performance" by the seller.[1] This reflects the basic civil law theory that legal compulsion of performance is the best relief to an aggrieved buyer, and that seller's actual performance is preferable to substitutional relief (such as a monetary award).[2] The reference to seller's "obligations" is not limited, and so can include court compulsion to provide goods of the agreed description quantity, quality and title (including intellectual property rights), as well as adhering to the agreed time, place & manner of delivery.

The provision permits the buyer to seek specific performance, but *does not require* it to do so. The buyer may still elect between seeking a performance remedy or a substitutional (i.e., damages) remedy. There are two limitations on the buyers' right to compel performance, One is that the buyer must not have previously sought an "inconsistent" remedy. For example, the buyer must not have previously "avoided", or sought to avoid, the contract. Since avoidance would terminate the contract, there would be no contract to enforce (specifically) after avoidance. The second limitation is that the court would order such performance under its own law in a similar case not governed by the Convention.[3] Thus, the buyer usually should not bring its action for specific performance in a common law court.

The CISG provision gives buyer the right to seek specific performance, rather than damages, but does not require it to do so. Thus, any preference for this remedy must arise from buyer's perspective, not from the court's. Even in civil law jurisdictions, buyers will often prefer to recover damages and purchase substitute goods, because of the expense and delays inherent in litigation.[4] Even if a court should prefer specific

§ 1.29

1. CISG art. 46(1).

2. See Beardsy, Compelling Contract Performance in France, 1 Hastings Int'l and Comp. L. Rev. 93 (1977). For the contrasting common law approach, see Farnsworth, Damages and Specific Relief, 27 Am. J.Comp.L. 247 (1979).

3. CISG art. 28.

4. There is significant evidence that substitutional relief is often sought in civil law commercial disputes. See, e.g., Ziegel, The Remedial Provisions of the Vienna Sales Convention: Common Law Perspectives, Ch. 9 in International Sales (N. Galston and H. Smit, eds. 1984).

performance, buyer can terminate this option by declaring the contract "avoided," which is an inconsistent remedy.

The CISG Article 28 limitation that the court "is not bound" to order specific performance unless it would do so in a case outside this Convention is applicable to all courts, both civil law and common law. However, it has a negligible effect on civil law courts because they are authorized to order seller's performance in many more cases.[5] Thus, if specific performance is sought in a civil law court, it will usually apply CISG Article 46 and order the seller to perform its obligations.

However, that would not be the analytical approach of a common law court. Under CISG Aricle 28, a United States court would not be required by CISG Article 46 to issue an order compelling the delivery if it would not do so in a similar domestic case. Although the UCC is designed to encourage courts to order specific performance, the case law does not demonstrate widespread interest in compelling performance.[6] If the goods are "unique" and they exist, then it is more likely the court will order specific performance. If, however, substitute goods are readily available in the market, it is less likely that the court would order specific performance. A United States court would be likely to issue a specific performance order if a requirements or a performance contact was involved.[7]

There are special provisions for specific performance orders which order seller to deliver substitute goods or to repair goods already delivered. Where the goods have been delivered, but are not conforming to the contract, the buyer may require specific performance in the form of delivery of conforming substitute goods only if the nonconformity amounts to a "fundamental breach,"[8] and the buyer has given the seller proper notice.[9] Likewise, buyer may require seller to repair the goods only if that is reasonable, "having regard to all the circumstances."[10] The principal difference between replacement and repair is that a buyer need not show that the non-conformities constitute a fundamental breach when requesting repair.

§ 1.30 Buyer's Action for the Contract Price

There is also a CISG provision which permits a court to issue a specific performance order against a buyer, requiring the buyer to perform its obligations.[1] The preferred remedy for an aggrieved seller, if buyer should breach, is a cause of action for the price, which is seller's functional equivalent of an action for specific performance. A cause of action for damages, but not the price, is distinctly secondary. In addition,

5. Tallon, Remedies, French Report in Contract Law Today: Anglo–French Comparison, 263–88 (D. Harris and D. Tallon, eds. 1989).

6. UCC § 2–716(1).

7. UCC § 2–716, comment 2.

8. See discussion at § 1.28, notes 7–24.

9. CISG art. 46(2).

10. CISG art. 46(3).

§ 1.30

1. CISG art. 62.

seller may wish to reclaim the goods if they are delivered or obtain some protection for them if they are refused.

As to the seller's recovery of the price, CISG Article 62 gives the seller a right to require buyer to pay the price unless the seller has resorted to an "inconsistent remedy."[2] Of course, there are implicit conditions on this right, first, that seller has itself performed to the extent required by the terms of the contract[3] and, second, that payment of the price is due.[4]

However, in common law jurisdictions, there is an issue of whether the seller's action for the price under CISG Article 62 an action for "specific performance," which is subject to the limitations of CISG Article 28. In other words, may a court order the buyer to pay the contract price of the goods, rather than mere damages, only if "the court would do so under its own law in respect of similar contracts of sale not governed by" CISG?[5] If it is an action for specific performance, then an aggrieved seller in the United States court would have to meet the requirements of the UCC[6] as well as the CISG,[7] before a United States court would order buyer to pay the price rather than damages. Under CISG Article 28, the issue is whether a judgment for the price requires the entry of a "judgment for specific performance." If not, then CISG Article 28 would seem to be inapplicable; and seller need meet only the requisites of CISG Article 62. The problem with this analysis is that the Convention and the UCC have different concepts of "specific performance."

From the UCC perspective the only provision which specifically mentions an action for "specific performance" is UCC § 2–716, which is expressly limited to a cause of action by seller. The buyer is given no comparable general cause of action to compel performance of buyer's obligations, except for a limited right to seek payment of the price—a monetary award.[8] Thus, from the UCC perspective the action for the price under UCC § 2–709 is merely another action for a monetary judgment, not one to compel conduct.

From the CISG perspective there is no separate action for the price as a monetary judgment, only CISG Article 62, which allows a court to compel three different types of conduct—payment of the price, taking delivery, or performance of other obligations. Payment of the price is within a list of specific performances which a court is authorized to compel.

2. "Avoidance" of the contract would be such an inconsistent remedy. See discussion at § 1.32, supra.

3. CISG art. 30.

4. CISG art. 58.

5. CISG art. 28.

6. UCC § 2–709.

7. CISG art. 62.

8. UCC § 2–709. There are other nonmonetary obligations of the buyer, such as duties of cooperation (UCC § 2–311), preparing to receive the goods, and opening a letter of credit. See text at not 12 infra.

The committee to revise UCC Article has considered revising UCC § 2–719 to permit buyer's to seek "specific performance."

On the issue of the applicability of Article 28, Professors Honnold and Farnsworth publicly disagree.[9] The question would seem to be open at this time, because no common law courts have ruled on the issues presented by CISG Article 28. The only ruling involving a U.S. party in an action for the price was by a Mexican arbitral tribunal which did not need to discuss the Article 28 issue.[10]

Some of the buyer's obligations are not monetary, such as preparing to take delivery of the goods or opening a letter of credit. CISG authorizes a court to compel such conduct by the buyer,[11] if the court would do so in a non-convention case.[12] However, each of these may require the discretionary actions of third parties who may not be subject to the jurisdiction of the court.

§ 1.31 Damages

CISG Articles 74–78 provide the aggrieved buyer with an action for damages for any breach of a party's obligations, and damages can be available when the contract has been "avoided" (cancelled) and also even when seller has successfully cured defects in its performance.[1] There is no requirement that buyer prove seller was at "fault" as a prerequisite to damage recovery. Both direct and consequential damages are recoverable; and expectancy, reliance and restitutionary interests are all protected.[2] Consequential damages are limited in the familiar manner that losses may not be recovered, which were neither actually foreseen nor should have been foreseen.[3] However, this may not be the same as the common law *Hadley v. Baxendale* test,[4] because recovery is available if the loss suffered is foreseeable as a "possible consequence of the breach of contract".[5] The aggrieved buyer must take "reasonable measures" to mitigate its damages.[6] Incidental damages relating to interest are covered separately.[7]

§ 1.32 Buyer's Damages

Where similar goods may be purchased in the market, the most usual measures of the aggrieved buyer's damages are either (1) the difference between the price of "cover" (substitute goods actually purchased) and the contract price, or (2) the difference between the market price for the goods and the contract price. The Convention provides for

9. Farnsworth, supra § 1.29, note 2; Honnold, supra § 1.4, note 20, at § 348.

10. UNILEX Case D. 1993–13.

11. CISG art. 62.

12. CISG art. 28. It is problematic whether a United States court could enter such an order. UCC § 2–716 is expressly limited to actions by sellers. The UCC approach instead is to make the buyer's conduct a condition precedent to seller's responsive conduct, and to award the seller damages if the buyer fails to perform.

§ 1.31

1. CISG arts. 45(2), 61(2), and 75. See also, CISG arts. 47(2), 48(1), 63(2).

2. Flechtner, Remedies under the New International Sales Convention: The Perspective from Article 2 of the U.C.C., 8 J. Law & Com. 53 (1988).

3. CISG art. 74.

4. 9 Ex. 341, 156 Eng. Rep. 145 (1854).

5. CISG art. 74, last sentence.

6. CISG art. 77.

7. CISG art. 78.

the recovery of each of these measures of damages,[1] but if buyer does purchase cover only the first measure is available.[2] The Convention gives no guidance on how to determine whether any particular purchase by buyer is a purchase of cover, or is ordinary inventory build-up. Where the market price differential is used, the market price is to be measured at the time of "avoidance" (cancellation),[3] unless buyer has "taken over" the goods, before cancelling, in which case, the market price is measured at the time of "taking over."[4]

The CISG measures of buyer's damages are remarkably similar to those in the UCC.[5] In the one CISG damage measurement case decided by United States courts, the court ruled that UCC caselaw could not be used to interpret CISG provisions unless the language of the UCC provision tracks that of the CISG provision.[6] The court also held that the broad, general language of CISG Article 74[7] was the primary criterion for damage measurement, and that all the subsequent provisions[8] were subsidiary to it. Finally, the court also ruled that, where there are gaps in the CISG provisions on measuring damages, that those gaps may be filled in by domestic law—the UCC.

The case involved a buyer which had lost sales due to seller's delivery of nonconforming goods, and which sought loss of profits for the sales lost until substitute, conforming goods had been found. The court found that the standard contract price—market price differential would not fully compensate the buyer for the "loss, including lost profits, suffered by" the buyer,[9] and chose Article 74 as its guide to damage measurement, not Articles 75 or 76. The lost profit damages were, however, recoverable only to the extent that they were reasonably foreseeable by the parties.[10] In measuring buyer's lost profits, the court found that CISG had no specific provision on the treatment of fixed and variable costs in determining buyer's lost profits. It therefore adopted the domestic law rule in which only the variable costs saved by the buyer are to be deducted from the lost sales revenues.

The courts also allowed the buyer to recover, as additional consequential and incidental damages:

(1) costs of buyer's attempts to cure, including reinspection and testing;

§ 1.32

1. The difference between "cover" and the contract price is provided in CISG Article 75. Compare UCC § 2–712.

The difference between market price and the contract price is provided in CISG Article 76(1). Compare UCC § 2–713.

2. CISG art. 76(1): "if he has not made a purchase or resale under Article 75."

3. CISG art. 76(1), first sentence.

4. CISG art. 76(1), second sentence.

5. Flechtner, supra § 1.31, note 2.

6. Delchi Carrier SpA v. Rotorex Corp., 71 F.3d 1024 (2d Cir. 1995).

7. "Damages ... consist of a sum equal to the loss ... suffered by the other party as a consequence of the breach." CISG art. 74.

8. CISG arts. 75–77.

9. CISG art. 74.

10. Delchi Carrier, S.p.A. v. Rotorex Corp., 1994 WL 495787 (N.D.N.Y.1994), aff'd 71 F.3d 1024 (2d Cir.1995).

(2) costs of expedited delivery of substitute conforming goods from another seller;

(3) costs of storing the non-conforming goods.[11]

(4) shipping and customs costs for the non-conforming goods;

(5) cost of materials and tools usable only with the non-conforming goods; and

(6) labor costs related to the production line shutdown.[12]

§ 1.33 Seller's Damages

CISG Articles 74–78 provide the unpaid seller (as well as an aggrieved buyer) with an action for damages and the general principles are the same as the discussion of buyer's remedies for seller's breach.[1] The most usual measures of an unpaid seller's damages are either (1) the difference between the contract price and the resale price if the goods were actually resold or (2) the difference between the contract price and market price for the goods at the time of avoidance of the contract. The Convention provides for recovery of each of these measures of damages,[2] but if seller resells the goods only the first measure is available.[3] The major practical problem concerning unpaid sellers is that the "lost volume" seller is not adequately protected by the above two measures of damages.[4] However, the CISG provisions which establish these measures state that they are not exclusive, and the basic principles of Article 74 specifically include recovery of lost profits.[5] Since the *Rotorex* case has established the primacy of Article 74 over the subsequent provisions, a court should be able to protect the lost volume seller. The *Rotorex* court awarded "lost profits" damages to a buyer, which should be persuasive precedent for making a comparable award to a "lost volume" seller.

The CISG measures of seller's damages are remarkably similar to those in the UCC.[6] The principal difference is that the CISG provisions on the difference between the contract price and the resale price contain no provisions covering notice of the resale of the goods, nor do they regulate the resale.[7]

---

11. *Id.*

12. Rotorex, supra note 6.

§ 1.33

1. See § 1.32, supra.

2. The difference between the contract price and the resale piece is provided in CISG Article 75. Compare UCC § 2–706.

The difference between the contract price and the market price is provided for in CISG Article 76(1) Compare UCC § 2–708(1).

3. CISG art. 76(1): "if he has not made a purchase or resale under Article 75."

4. Compare UCC § 2–708(2).

5. *Rotorex*, supra § 1.32, note 6.

6. Flechtner, supra § 1.31, note 2.

7. Compare UCC § 2–706 (2)–(6).

F.　SELECTED DOCUMENTS

§ 1.34　Sample International Product Sales Agreement (PRC) With Accompanying Irrevocable Bank Guarantee*

A–SAI PIPELINE PROJECT
CONTRACT NO. 91 ABC–123(4)567 DE
DATE: JUNE 19, 1991

China National Machinery Import & Export Corporation, Beijing China (hereinafter referred to as the "Buyer") as one party and BIG PUMP COMPANY (BPC) (hereinafter referred to as the "Seller") as the other party, have authorized the respective representatives from both parties to sign as a result of friendly negotiations, the present Contract under the following terms and conditions:

Chapter 1

Object of the Contract

1.1　The Sellers agrees to sell and the Buyer agrees to buy the crude oil engine driven pump sets for a-sai Pipeline Project

1.2　The contract equipments are detailed in the following appendixes of the Contract:

(1) the scope of supply as per appendix I,

(2) the technical requirements for crude oil engine driven pump set as per appendix II.

Chapter 2

Price

2.1　The total price of the Contract of the equipment, materials, spare parts, technical documents, training and technical services, etc. to be supplied by the Seller as stipulated in Chapter 1 of the Contract amounts to USD 1,839,856.00 (say: ONE MILLION-EIGHT HUNDRED THIRTY-NINE THOUSAND EIGHT HUNDRED AND FIFTY-SIX only).

2.2　The price under 2.1 is a firm and fixed price.

2.3　The price under 2.1 is for delivery of equipment, materials and spare parts, C&F Xingang, China. The technical documents shall be delivered by the Seller to the CIF Beijing Airport.

Chapter 3

Payment and Terms of Payment

3.1　All the payments between the Buyer and the Seller under the Contract shall be made by telegraphic transfer. Payments from the Buyer to the Seller shall be made through Bank of China, Beijing to . . . Payments from the Seller to the Buyer shall be made through . . . to Bank of China, Beijing. The Banking charges and other

---

* Courtesy of Prof. James Nafziger, University of Willamette College of Law. Prof.　Nafziger directs Willamette's longstanding summer legal studies program in Shanghai.

expenses for the remittance incurred in China shall be borne by the Buyer and those incurred outside China shall be borne by the Seller.

3.2   The price for the equipment, materials (including spare parts, technical documents, etc.) as stipulated in Clause 2.1 of Chapter 2, i.e. USD 1,834,856. (Say: ONE MILLION EIGHT HUNDRED THIRTY-NINE THOUSAND EIGHT HUNDRED FIFTY SIX only) shall be paid by the Buyer to the Seller according to the following schedule, terms and proportions:

    3.2.1   10% (ten percent) of the contract price as stipulated in Clause 2.1, i.e. USD 183,986 (Say ONE HUNDRED EIGHT-THREE THOUSAND NINE HUNDRED EIGHTY-SIX only) shall be paid by the Buyer to the Seller after the Contract has come into force and within 30 (thirty) days after the Buyer has received the following documents sent by the Seller and found them to be in order.

       A.   One photostatic copy of the export license issued by the relevant authorities of the Seller's country to the Seller or a statement that no export license is required.

       B.   One original and one copy of an irrevocable letter of credit issued by ... in favor of the Buyer. The letter of credit would be returned to the Seller when the documents listed in Clause 3.2.2 are received by the Buyer.

       C.   Performs invoice in quadruplicate.

       D.   Sight draft in duplicate.

     When making this payment, the Buyer shall at the same time submit to the Seller one original and one copy of an irrevocable letter of credit issued by the Bank of China, Beijing in favor of the Seller for 90% (ninety percent) of the contract price as stipulate in Clause 2.1.

    3.2.2   80% (eighty percent) of the contract price as stipulated in Clause 2.1, i.e. USD 1,471,885 (say ONE MILLION FOUR HUNDRED SEVENTY-ONE THOUSAND EIGHT HUN-DRED EIGHTY-FIVE only) shall be paid by the Buyer to the Seller after pump sets have been loaded on board the vessel as stipulated in Clause 4.1 of the Chapter 4 and within 30 days after the Buyer has received the following documents sent by the Seller and found them to be in order.

       A.   Three originals and one copy of the full set of clean On-Board Bills of Lading made out to order, blank endorsed and marked: notifying China Foreign Trade Transportation Corporation at the port of destination and "freight pre-paid".

       B.   Commercial invoice in quadruplicate.

       C.   Packing list in quadruplicate.

       D.   Quality certificate in quadruplicate.

E.   sight draft in duplicate.

3.2.3   10% (ten percent) of the contract price as stipulated in Clause 2.1, i.e. USD 183,985. (Say: ONE HUNDRED EIGHTY-THREE THOUSAND NINE HUNDRED EIGHTY-FIVE only) shall be paid by the Buyer to the Seller after the Contract Equipment has been accepted according to the stipulations of the Contract and within 30 days after the Buyer has received the following document sent by the Seller and found them to be in order.

A.   Commercial invoice in quadruplicate.

B.   One photostatic copy of the Certificate of Acceptance of the Contract Equipment signed by the Buyer and the Seller.

C.   Sight draft in duplicate.

D.   One original and one copy of an irrevocable letter of credit in the amount of 10% of the contract price made out by the Seller's Bank. The letter of guarantee shall be valid until the expiration of the warranty period.

E.   This payment shall be effected, latest 12 months after shipment.

Chapter 4

Delivery

4.1   The Seller shall complete the shipment on C&F basis of the equipment, materials and spare parts under the Contract No. 91 ABC–123(4)567 DE within 12 months from the date of the Contract. The delivery of equipment, materials and spare parts shall be effected C&F Xingang Port, Tianjin, the People's Republic of China.

4.2   The date of the bill of lading shall be the actual delivery date.

4.3   The Contract equipment to be supplied by the Seller shall be delivered C&F Xingang Port with a vessel designated by the Seller. Transshipment and partial shipment shall not be accepted. The contract good shall not be carried by a vessel flying the flag of the country which the Buyer cannot accept. The age of vessel should not exceed 15 years.

4.4   The Seller shall, twenty (20) days before the date of delivery as stipulated in 4.1, advise the Buyer by cable or telex of the Contract number, commodity name, approximate name, approximate measurement, the date of goods readiness, shipping port total gross weight, and total measurement of each piece twenty (20) metric tons in weight or $15 \times 3 \times 3$ metres in measurement. At the same time, the seller shall airmail to the Buyer the following documents, each in six (6) copies:

A.   The detailed list of the shipment covering Contract number, item number, name of the equipment and materials, specifications, type, quantity, unit/total price, unit weight, unit/total volume, the overall dimensions of each package (length × width × height), total number of packages, and name of loading port.

B. Overall packing sketch for each large piece exceeding thirty (30) metric tons in weight or 15 × 3 × 3 metres in measurement.

C. Description covering names, properties, special protective measures and way of handling an accident for any inflammable and dangerous goods shipped.

D. Description of special precautions to be taken for those goods with a special requirement for temperature, shock, etc., during the transportation.

4.5 Latest 7 days before loading the Seller shall inform the Buyer by telex on the name and nationality of the vessel, the expected date of loading and the expected arrival date at the destination port.

4.6 Within forty-eight (48) hours after shipment is effected, the Seller shall inform the Buyer by cable or telex of the Contract number, the date and number of bill of lading, name of the carrying vessel, as well as name of goods loaded, quantity, date of loading, total price, total number of packages, total weight and total volume.

4.7 The Seller shall, within five (5) days after shipment, send by the registered airmail two complete sets of the shipping documents (ie, bill of lading, commercial invoice, packing list and quality and quantity certificate each in one copy) with one set directly to the Buyer and one set directly to China National Foreign Trade Transportation Corp. at the port of destination. The Sellers shall send a complete set of shipping documents along with the carrying vessel to the port of destination. Should the Seller fail to do so, the Seller shall bear the penalty the Buyer pays to the Customs for the delay of the Custom's declaration because the aforesaid documents are not available at the time the goods arrive at the port of destination.

Chapter 5

Packing and marking

5.1 Goods shall be packed in strong wooden cases suitable for long distance ocean and inland transportation to withstand numerous handlings in loading and unloading and well protected against moisture, rain, shock, rust and rough handling. The Seller shall be liable for any rust, damage and loss attributable to inadequate or improper protective measures taken by the Seller in regard to the packing. For bare and exposed machines, tools, etc., subject to rust and corrosion, the surfaces must be coated with corrosion-resistant preservatives.

5.2 The Seller shall mark the following on the two adjacent sides of each case with indelible paint in conspicuous English printed words in size no less than five (5) cm.

A. Contract number: 91 ABC–123(4)567 DE

B. Shipping Mark: 91 ABC–123(4)567 DE

   Xingang, China

C. Case/Package number:

D. Port of destination:

E. Gross/Net weight: (kg)

F. Measurement: Length × Width × Height (mm)

G. Center of gravity or sliding point (for goods above five (5) metric tons only).

5.3 For bundles and goods without packing, labels indicating shipping mark and other information shall be tied with steel wire. Each case of the goods shall be marked with "Right side up", "Handle with care", "Keep dry", etc., and with other appropriate international trade practice marks according to the characteristics and features of the goods.

5.4 The technical documents delivered by the Seller shall be properly packed to withstand numerous handlings, long distance transportation and for protection against moisture and rain. The surface and adjacent sides of each package shall be marked with the following in English:

A. Contact number: 91 ABC–123(4)567 DE

B. Shipping mark: 91 ABC–123(4)567 DE

   Beijing Airport, China

C. Destination: Beijing Airport, China

D. Weight:

After delivery, the Seller shall send a list of the delivered technical documents to the Buyer.

Chapter 6

Inspection

6.1 .... months after signing the Contract, the Buyer shall send, ... technical personnel to the Seller's workshop to have a quality inspection of the equipment.

6.2 The Seller shall assist the Buyer's personnel in obtaining visas and provide them, free of charge, with necessary inspection tools, instruments, detailed information on inspection and performance tests, etc. In case discrepancies are found during the said inspection, the Buyer's inspectors shall have the right to make remarks, and the Seller shall take such remarks into consideration and take necessary measures to make the machines in question meet the contractual requirements. The Buyer's inspection personnel shall not sign any document related to the inspection of equipment, neither shall they take any responsibility thereof.

6.3 Upon the arrival of the goods at the job site, the China Commodity Inspection Bureau will carry out the open-package inspection at the Buyer's request, together with the Seller's inspector at Seller's option sent at the Seller's own expense. In case of any damage, defect or shortage due to the Seller's fault, the China Commodity Inspection Bureau shall issue an inspection certificate as an effective proof for the Buyer to lodge claim with the Seller for repair, replacement or supplemental deliveries which shall be made by the Seller, free job site. All expenses incurred therefrom shall be for the Seller's account.

Chapter 7

Site Installation, Check-up, Adjustment, Commission and S.A.T.

7.1 The BUYER shall perform the site installation. But the installation shall be executed according to the installation instruction manual to be submitted by the SELLER to the BUYER.

7.2 Upon completion of the site installation, representatives of the SELLER shall arrive at the installation site to provide site services, including check-up, adjustment, commission, S.A.T., and etc. of the pumpset and auxiliaries. The site representative of both sides shall arrange through consultation and coordination the above-mentioned work which should be executed with the supervision of the SELLER. The SELLER shall submit all major technical instructions to the BUYER in written form. Joint efforts shall be made by both sides for the check-up, adjustment, commission, S.A.T. and etc., which shall be completed within months after the Contract comes into effect. The check-up, adjustment, S.A.T. and etc. shall be performed and completed exactly according to the content specified in Appendix to the Contract.

7.3 Upon completion of S.A.T., representatives of both sides shall sign the certificate of S.A.T. and thereafter the pumpsets and auxiliaries shall be considered as accepted by the BUYER. The Certificate of S.A.T. shall be a prerequisite for the SELLER to be paid by the BUYER the amount of the Contract value specified in Clause 3.2.3 of the Contract.

7.4 If, due to any reason from the SELLER, the check-up, adjustment, commission and S.A.T. cannot be completed within the time duration specified in the Contract, then the SELLER shall continue the work until the completion of the above-mentioned work at its own cost and completed within a time limit agreed on by both parties.

7.5 If, during check-up and adjustment, commission, it is found that any equipment supplied by or through the SELLER is not operational due to defect or lack of supply, or if the performance of the system cannot meet the criteria specified in the Contract after the adjustment, then the SELLER shall solve whatever problem may occur at its own cost.

7.6 If, after the SELLER has made efforts within a reasonable extended period of time, any equipment or the pumpsets auxiliaries supplied is still not operational or cannot meet the performance criteria specified in the contract, then the SELLER shall compensate the BUYER for all of the direct loss, but not to exceed the total value of the Contract.

Chapter 8

Guarantee

8.1 The Seller shall guarantee that the equipment and materials are brand new and unused and of the best quality, with the specifications and performance conforming to the Contract stipulations and meet the requirements of long-term operation. The guarantee period of the equipment and materials in twenty-four (24) months from the date of shipment or twelve (12) months from the date of operation (whichever expires earlier).

8.2 Within the guarantee period, in order to ensure a timely and normal operation of the equipment, the Seller shall take effective measure in time, e.g. sending personnel to the job site, air freighting the urgently needed parts to the job site to remove the defects arising due to the Seller's reason.

8.3 In case any equipment supplied by the Seller fails to meet the guarantees specified in Appendix to the Contract due to the Seller's reason during performance commission, the Seller should revise the design, remove the defects or replace the equipment until the equipment is able to meet the guarantees. All expenses incurred therefrom shall be for the Seller's account.

Chapter 9

Penalties

9.1 In case the equipment and materials are not delivered according to the time schedule due to the Seller's fault, the Seller shall pay a penalty at the following rate:

0–1 week delay	No penalty.
2–3 week delay	1% of the total price of the delayed equipment and materials for each week delay.
4–8 week delay	2% of the total price of the delayed equipment and materials for each week delay.
9 or more week delay	3% of the total price of the delayed equipment and materials for each week delay.

Odd days less than one (1) week shall be counted as one (1) week. The total amount of the penalties shall not exceed 50 percent (50%) of the total price of the Contract amount, the payment of the penalties shall not release the Seller from this obligation of continuing delivery of the aforementioned equipment and/or materials. If the Seller is in penalty, the Buyer may deduct the amount of the penalty from the payment due the Seller.

Chapter 10

Force Majeure

The Sellers shall not be held responsible for the delay in shipment or non-delivery of the goods due to *Force Majeure*, which might occur during the process of manufacturing or in the course of loading or transit. The Sellers shall advise the Buyers immediately of the occurrence mentioned above and within fourteen days thereafter, the Sellers shall send by airmail to the Buyers for their acceptance a certificate of the accident issued by the Competent Government Authorities where the accident occurs as evidence thereof. Under such circumstances the Sellers, however, are still under the obligation to take all necessary measures to hasten the delivery of the goods. In case the accident lasts for more than 10 weeks, the Buyers shall have the right to cancel the Contract.

Chapter 11

Taxes

1. All taxes in connection with the execution of this Contract levied by the Chinese government on the Buyer (or Licensee) in accordance with the tax laws in effect shall be borne by the Buyer (or Licensee).

2. All taxes levied by the Chinese government on the Seller in connection with and in the performance of the present contract in accordance with the tax laws in effect shall be borne by the Seller.

3. All taxes arising outside of China in connection with the execution of this Contract shall be borne by the Seller (or Licensor).

Chapter 12

Arbitration

12.1 All disputes arising from the execution of or in connection with the Contract shall be settled through friendly consultation between both parties. In case no agreement can be reached, the disputes shall be submitted to arbitration. The arbitration shall take place in Stockholm, Sweden and be carried out according to the arbitration procedures and rules of the Arbitration Institute of the Stockholm Chamber of Commerce in Sweden. The arbitration award shall be final and binding on both parties, and both parties shall act accordingly.

12.2 In the course of arbitration both parties shall continue to execute their respective obligations under the Contract, except those under arbitration.

12.3 The arbitration fee shall be borne by the losing party.

Chapter 13

Effectiveness of the Contract and Miscellaneous

13.1 The Contract is effective on June 19, 1991.

13.2   Appendices. Technical Requirements of the Contract are an integral part of the Contract.

13.3   No assignment of any obligations arising under the Contract shall be made by either of the parties to a third party without the previous written consent of the other party.

Chapter 14

Legal Address

The Buyer:	China National Machinery Import & Export Corporation
Address:	Erligou, Xijiao, Beijing, China
Cable Address:	MACHIMPEX BEIJING
Telex:	22872 CMIEC CN
Fax:	8021323
The Seller:	Big Pump Company
Address:	250 Winter St SE, Salem, OR 97301, USA
Telex:	12345678BPC
Fax:	(503) 555–5286

BUYER: _____   SELLER: _____

Attachment For Contract No. 91 ABC–123(4)567 DE

IRREVOCABLE LETTER OF GUARANTEE
ISSUED BY (PRIME U.S. BANK)

(Specimen Form)

Date: _____

BENEFICIARY:

China National Machinery Import & Export Corp.
Beijing, China

With reference to Contract No. 91 ABC–123(4)567 DE signed on _____ between your Corporation (hereinafter referred to as Party A) and BIG PUMP COMPANY (hereinafter referred to as Party B) concerning the Package Supply by Party B to Party A of Supply under the Contract amounting USD _____ (Say US dollars _____), we, at the request of Party B, hereby open an irrevocable Letter of Guarantee No. _____ in favor of Party A amounting to ten percent (10%) of the total Contract price *i.e.*, USD 183,985 (Say US dollars _____). We are obliged to refund unconditionally said amount together with the interest at the annual rate of ten percent (10%) counting from the date of payment to the date of refund to you within 30 days after receipt of Party A's written Notice stating that Party B did not fulfill its obligations stipulated in the Contract.

The Letter of Guarantee shall become valid from the issuing date of this Letter and shall become null and void after Party B has completed the delivery of the Package Supply under the Contract.

§ 1.35 Sample International Commodity Sales Agreement (PRC)*

CONTRACT

No. _____

Beijing Date: _____

The Buyers: CHINA NATIONAL MACHINERY IMPORT & EXPORT CORPORATION, BEIJING BRANCH,
190 Chao Yang Men Nei Street; Beijing, People's Republic of China.

Cable Address: "MACHBRANCH" BEIJING TELEX:

The Sellers: _____

Cable Address:_____ TELEX:

1. This contract is made by and between the Buyers and the Sellers; whereby the Buyers agree to buy and the Sellers agree to sell the undermentioned commodity according to the terms and conditions stipulated below:

Item No. Commodity Specifications	Unit Quan.	Unit Price	Total Amount
Total Value:			

2. COUNTRY OF ORIGIN AND MANUFACTURERS:

3. PACKING: To be packed in strong wooden case(s) or in carton(s), suitable for long distance ocean/parcel post/air freight transportation and to change of climate, well protected against moisture and shocks.

   The Sellers shall be liable for any damage of the commodity and expenses incurred on account of improper packing and for any rust attributable to inadequate or improper protective measures taken by the Sellers in regard to the packing.

4. SHIPPING MARK: The Sellers shall mark on each package with fadeless paint the package number, gross weight, net weight, measurement and the wordings: "KEEP AWAY FROM MOISTURE" "HANDLE WITH CARE", "THIS SIDE UP" etc. and the shipping mark:

5. TIME OF SHIPMENT:

6. PORT OF SHIPMENT:

* Courtesy of Prof. James Nafziger, University of Willamette College of Law. Prof. Nafziger directs Willamette's longstanding summer legal studies program in Shanghai.

7. PORT OF DESTINATION: CHINA

8. INSURANCE: To be covered by the Buyers after shipment.

9. PAYMENT: Under (A) (B) (C) below:

    (A) Under Letter of Credit: The Buyers, upon receipt from the Sellers of the delivery advice specified in Clause 11 (1)a hereof, shall 15–20 days prior to the date of delivery, open an irrevocable letter of credit with Bank of China, Beijing, in favour of the Sellers, for the total value of shipment. The credit shall be available against Sellers' draft(s) drawn at sight on the opening bank for 100% invoice value accompanied by the shipping documents specified in Clause 10 hereof. Payment shall be effected (by the opening bank, for telegraphic transfer/airmail transfer) against presentation to them of the aforesaid draft(s) and documents. The Letter of Credit shall be valid until the 15th day after the shipment is effected.

    (B) On Collection: After shipment, the Sellers may draw on the Buyers at sight and send the draft(s) together with the shipping documents specified in Clause 10 hereof, to the Buyers through the Sellers' bankers and Bank of China, Beijing for collection.

    (C) By direct Remittance: Payment shall be effected by the Buyers, by telegraphic transfer/airmail transfer, within seven days after receipt from the Sellers of shipping documents specified in Clause 10 hereof.

10. DOCUMENTS:

    (1) In case of seafreight:

    Full set of clean on board ocean bills of lading marked "Freight to Collect"/"Freight Prepaid" made out to order blank endorsed notifying China National Foreign Trade Transportation Corporation at the port of destination.

    In case of airfreight:

    One copy of airway bill marked "Freight to Collect"/"Freight Prepaid" and consigned to the Buyers.

    In case of air parcel post:

    One copy of air parcel post receipt addressed to the Buyers.

    (2) Invoice in 5 copies indicating contract number and shipping mark (in case of more than one shipping mark, the invoice shall be issued separately, made out in details as per the relative contract).

    (3) Packing list in 2 copies issued by the Manufacturers.

    (4) Certificate of Quality and Quantity issued by the Manufacturers.

    (5) Copy of cable/letter to the Buyers advising particulars of shipment immediately after shipment is made.

In addition, the Sellers shall, within 10 days after shipment, send by airmail two extra sets of the aforesaid documents (except item 5) one set directly to the Buyers and one set directly to the China National Foreign Trade Transportation Corporation at the port of destination.

11. SHIPMENT:

(1) In case of FOB Terms:

a. The Sellers shall, 40 days before the date of shipment stipulated in the Contract, advise the Buyers by cable/letter of the Contract No, commodity, quantity, value, number of package, gross weight, measurement and date of readiness at the port of shipment for the buyers to book shipping space.

b. Booking of shipping space shall be attended to by the Buyers' Shipping Agents Messrs. China National Chartering Corporation, Beijing, China. (Cable address: Zhongzu Beijing).

c. China National Chartering Corporation, Beijing, China, or its Port Agents, (or Lines' Agents) shall send to the Sellers 10 days before the estimate date of arrival of the vessel at the port of shipment, a preliminary notice indicating the name of vessel, estimated date of loading, Contract No. for the Sellers to arrange shipment. The Sellers are requested to get in close contact with the shipping agents. When it becomes necessary to change the carrying vessel or in the event of her arrival having to be advanced or delayed the Buyers or the Shipping Agent shall advise the Sellers in time.

Should the vessel fail to arrive at the port of loading within 30 days after the arrival date advised by the Buyers, the Buyers shall bear the storage and insurance expenses incurred from the 31st day.

d. The Sellers shall be liable for any dead freight or demurrage, should it happen that they have failed to have the commodity ready for loading after the carrying vessel has arrived at the port of shipment on time.

e. The Sellers shall bear all expenses, risks of the commodity before it passes over the vessel's rail and is released from the tackle. After it has passed over the vessel's rail and been released from the tackle, all expenses of the commodity shall be for the Buyer's account.

(2) In case of C & F Terms:

a. The Sellers shall ship the goods within the shipment time from the port of shipment to the port of destination. Transhipment is not allowed. The contracted goods shall not be carried by a vessel flying the flag of the country which the Buyers can not accept.

b. In case the goods are to be despatched by parcel post/air-freight, the Sellers shall, 30 days before the time of delivery as stipulated in Clause 5, inform the Buyers by cable/letter of the estimated date of delivery, Contract No., commodity, invoiced value, etc. The Sellers shall, immediately after despatch of the goods, advise the Buyers by cable/letter of the Contract No., commodity, invoiced value and date of despatch for the Buyers to arrange insurance in time.

12. SHIPPING ADVICE:

The Sellers shall, immediately upon the completion of the loading of the goods, advise by cable/letter the Buyers of the Contract No., commodity, quantity, invoiced value, gross weight, name of vessel and date of sailing etc. In case the Buyers fail to arrange insurance in time due to the Sellers not having cabled in time, all losses shall be borne by the Sellers.

13. TECHNICAL DOCUMENTS:

(1) One complete set of the following technical documents written in English, shall be packed and despatched together with each consignment.

   a) Wiring instructions, diagrams of electrical connections and/or pneumatic hydraulic connections.

   b) Manufacturing drawings of easily worn parts and instructions.

   c) Spare parts catalogues.

   d) Erection, operation, service and repair instruction books.

(2) The Sellers shall in addition send to the Buyers by airmail the respective technical documents as stipulated in paragraphs a), b), c) and d) of Item (1) of this Clause within 00 months, after the signing of this Contract.

14. GUARANTEE OF QUALITY:

The Sellers guarantee that the commodity hereof is made of the best materials with first class workmanship, brand new and unused, and complies in all respects with the quality and specification stipulated in this Contract. The guarantee period shall be 12 months counting from the date on which the commodity arrives at the port of destination.

15. CLAIMS:

Within 90 days after the arrival of the goods at destination, should the quality, specification, or quantity be found not in conformity with the stipulations of the Contract except those claims for which the insurance company of the owners of the vessel are liable, the Buyers shall, on the strength of the Inspection Certificate issued by the China Commodity Inspection Bureau, have the right to claim for replacement with new goods, or for compensation, and all the expenses (such as inspection charges, freight for returning the goods and for sending the replacement, insurance premium, storage and loading and unloading charges etc.) shall be borne by the Sellers. As regards quality, the Sellers shall guarantee that if, within 12 months from the date of arrival of the goods at destination, damages occur in the course of operation by reason of inferior quality, bad workmanship or the use of inferior materials, the Buyers shall immediately notify the Sellers in writing and put forward a claim supported by Inspection Certificate issued by the China Commodity Inspection Bureau. The Certificate so issued shall be accepted as the base of a claim. The Sellers, in accordance with the Buyers' claim shall be responsible for the immediate elimination of the defect(s), complete or partial replacement of the commodity or shall devaluate the commodity according the state of defect(s). Where necessary, the Buyers shall be at liberty to eliminate the defect(s) themselves at the Sellers' expenses. If the Sellers fail to answer the Buyers within one month after receipt of the aforesaid claim, the claim shall be reckoned as having been accepted by the Sellers.

16. FORCE MAJEURE:

The Sellers shall not be held responsible for the delay in shipment or non-delivery of the goods due to Force Majeure, which might occur during the process of manufacturing or in the course of loading or transit. The Sellers shall advise the Buyers immediately of the occurrence mentioned above and within fourteen days thereafter, the Sellers shall send by airmail to the Buyers for their acceptance a certificate of the accident issued by the Competent Government Authorities where the accident occurs as evidence thereof.

Under such circumstances the Sellers, however, are still under the obligation to take all necessary measures to hasten the delivery of the goods. In case the accident lasts for more than 10 weeks, the Buyers shall have the right to cancel the Contract.

17. LATE DELIVERY AND PENALTY:

Should the Sellers fail to make delivery on time as stipulated in the Contract, with exception of Force Majeure causes specified in Clause 16 of this Contract, the Buyers shall agree to postpone the delivery on condition that the Sellers agree to pay a penalty which shall be deducted by the paying bank from the payment under negotiation. The penalty, however, shall not exceed 5% of the total value of the goods involved in the late delivery. The rate of penalty is charged at 0.5% for every seven days, odd days less than seven days should be counted as seven days. In case the Sellers fail to make delivery ten weeks later than the time of shipment stipulated in the Contract, the Buyers shall have the right to cancel the contract and the

Sellers, in spite of the cancellation, shall still pay the aforesaid penalty to the Buyers without delay.

18. ARBITRATION:

All disputes in connection with this Contract or the execution thereof shall be settled friendly through negotiations. In case no settlement can be reached, the case may then be submitted for arbitration to the Arbitration Committee of the China Council for the Promotion of International Trade in accordance with the Provisional Rules of Procedures promulgated by the said Arbitration Committee. The Arbitration shall take place in Beijing and the decision of the Arbitration Committee shall be final and binding upon both parties; neither party shall seek recourse to a law court of other authorities to appeal for revision of the decision. Arbitration fee shall be borne by the losing party. Or the Arbitration may be settled in the third country mutually agreed upon by both parties.

IN WITNESS THEREOF, this Contract is signed by both parties in two original copies; each party holds one copy

THE BUYERS: THE SELLERS:
CHINA NATIONAL MACHINERY IMPORT
AND EXPORT CORPORATION BEIJING
BRANCH

§ 1.36   Volume Purchase Agreement (Electronics)*

AMERITEK
7446 Industrial Drive
San Diego, California

> hereinafter referred to as
> AMERITEK

and

SIEMENS Aktiengesellschaft
Berlin and München
Federal Republic of Germany

> hereinafter referred to as
> SIEMENS

AMERITEK wishes to purchase and to sell Siemens MCS Product(s) in North America (USA, Mexico). Now, therefore, a volume purchase is agreed between the parties as follows:

1   Definitions

1.1   "Product(s)" means the Microelectronic hardware and software as listed in the current and future transfer price lists which Siemens shall update regularly. The current transfer price list is annexed as Annex A1 to this Agreement, which annexes may be amended from case to case.

---

* © By H. Lawrence Serra, Esq. San Die-   go. Reprinted with permission.

1.2   Designation NPR respecting products in Annex A1 denotes software products for which Siemens has no proprietary rights or hardware products from third party vendors for which it would be more convenient for AMERITEK to purchase directly from vendors.

1.3   "Documentation" means all guides, user-manuals, publications and other materials which facilitate the use of Product(s).

1.4   "Effective Date" of agreement means the date of the signature of each Annex An by both parties with regard to the Product(s) concerned.

2   Purchase

2.1   Siemens agrees to sell and AMERITEK agrees to purchase Product(s) in order to sell to customers in North America (USA, Canada and Mexico) and from time to time, when agreed to by Siemens, elsewhere in the world market. Siemens grants AMERITEK the non-exclusive right to make copies of users manuals in English. Terms and conditions have to be agreed upon separately.

2.2   Siemens entitles and is prepared to assist AMERITEK to buy any parts and components from Siemens and Siemens' vendors.

2.3   Annex A2 lists products specially made for Siemens by vendors. As AMERITEK cannot obtain these products on the open market, Siemens shall sell these products to AMERITEK.

3   Forecast and Orders

3.1   Orders are to be placed with:

Siemens AG, Abteilung WIS AZ 5, Balanstr. 73
8000 München 80, FRG.

3.2   AMERITEK is recommended to place an initial order for Product(s) as defined in Annex A3 at Effective Date.

3.3   All orders committed by Siemens shall remain fixed in price, mix and quantity and Product(s).

3.4   AMERITEK will provide Siemens with a rolling 12 month forecast, which will be reviewed by AMERITEK and provided to Siemens on a quarterly basis three weeks before the beginning of next quarter.

3.5   AMERITEK shall place orders in accordance with paragraph 3.3 which shall not exceed the following maximum variations in quantity from the originally forecasted quantities
quarter 1—plus/minus 0% (zero)
    " 2—plus minus 10% (ten)
    " 3—plus minus 25% (twenty five)
    " 4—plus minus 75% (seventy five)

3.6   Siemens will acknowledge quantities ordered in accordance to paragraphs 3.2 and 3.4.

3.7   Procedures according to paragraphs 3.3, 3.4, 3.5 shall not prevent AMERITEK from placing additional orders, which shall not be unreasonably rejected by Siemens.

3.8   Modifications on ordering and forecasting are subject to mutual agreement.

4   Prices

4.1   AMERITEK shall place orders for Product(s) on base of Siemens actual transfer price list in US–Dollars.

4.2   All prices are to be understood FOB Munich Airport according to INCOTERMS 1990 including export packaging.

4.3   Prices for initial order are based on actual transfer price list issued 25.12.90.

4.4   A discount of 40% (forty) of transfer list price for all hardware products shall be applied to all orders. Discounts for unbundled software products have to be negotiated separately.

4.5   If the reject rate for hardware products delivered to AMERITEK increases more than 3% per year (FOB Munich), Siemens shall compensate the value difference of such hardware products; provided, however, AMERITEK has proved reject rate.

4.6   The repair prices for these products are calculated in US–Dollars as percentage of the sales price being published in the actual transfer price list in accordance with the repair procedure for boards as described in Annex A4.

5   Terms of Payment

5.1   AMERITEK shall make payment for Product(s) purchased hereunder not later than 45 (forty five) days from date of invoice.

5.2   The line of credit is 50,000 US–Dollars (fifty thousand). AMERITEK shall supply with the order a letter of credit issued by First Interstate Bank for order amounts in excess of line of credit.

6   Deliveries

6.1   Deliveries shall be made to the address:

AMERITEK
7446 Industrial Drive
San Diego, California

or an address agreed upon separately, FOB Munich Airport according to INCOTERMS 1990.

6.2   Product(s) ordered by AMERITEK will be labeled and packed under AMERITEK's Logo.

6.3   No technical description for each Product is included.

6.4   Upon mutual agreement Siemens will supply AMERITEK with prototypes.

7   Updates and Modifications

7.1   Technical modifications and updates may be performed by Siemens to eliminate defects, to improve Product(s) and/or to bypass patent infringements. A modification requirement may be initiated by Siemens or AMERITEK in written form. Siemens shall inform AMERITEK sufficiently in advance of such modification and shall provide it with the necessary technical documentation.

7.2   Error Debugging for SW as far as listed in transfer price list.

An error will be reported by AMERITEK either by telex or by filling in an error form, both with allocated priority. Further, AMERITEK prepares additional documentation for diagnosis, if necessary. Siemens checks this error on a reference system. Warranty for software product(s) will be handled according to the corresponding software product sheet under terms and conditions to be agreed upon case by case.

8   Technical Assistance

8.1 Siemens is prepared to train AMERITEK's personnel (2 men, one week) on its premises free of charge to operate. All additional costs which are incurred by this training such as travel, accommodations, and living expenses shall be covered by AMERITEK.

8.2 Siemens agrees to provide AMERITEK additional technical assistance and training subject to mutual agreement.

9   Copyright and Trademarks

9.1 On request of AMERITEK, Siemens shall grant AMERITEK the non-exclusive right to copy documentation, under conditions to be agreed upon case by case.

9.2 AMERITEK agrees to use the international symbol "TM" for a trademark or "R" for registered trademark at the end of Siemens' product name, whenever this product name is mentioned in any AMERITEK brochures, documentation, or advertising. One reference to such a trademark claim in each publication is sufficient to give notice, but it should be with the first reference to Siemens' product name.

9.3 Manuals being supplied with Product(s) in accordance to 6.3 shall be identified by remark: "This manual is distributed under copyright of Siemens."

10   Patent Indemnity

10.1 If a third party rightfully raises claims due to patent infringement because of the delivery of the Product, Siemens will—subject to 10.2—as far as such claims are directed to Product(s) per se and not to its application, at its option and its costs and excluding further liability, obtain the right of use from the third party

or

modify the infringing parts

or

substitute for the parts infringing the patents noninfringing parts

or

take back the Product(s) concerned against reimbursement of the respective purchase price.

Claims shall be deemed justified only, if they are acknowledged by Siemens or finally adjudicated by a court of competent jurisdiction.

10.2 AMERITEK shall inform Siemens promptly, in case a third party raises a claim, whether directly or indirectly, against Siemens based on infringement of a patent relating to the Product. AMERITEK shall not on its own accept such third party claim. In accordance with any reasonable request from Siemens and to the extent so requested AMERITEK shall support Siemens' defense or any such third party claim, and Siemens shall reimburse AMERITEK for expenses thus arising.

11   Force Majeure—Excuse of Performance

Force Majeure and Excuse of Performance shall be determined under the applicable law.

12   Secrecy

Neither party shall make available to any third party any confidential information which may be acquired during the course of this Agreement, including without limitation the generality of the foregoing trade secrets, customer lists, and information concerning design or methods of manufacture. The aforesaid applies also after expiration of this Agreement.

However, this secrecy obligation does not apply to information which is in the public domain or which is proved to have been produced independently or to have been obtained legitimately from third parties.

13   Term and Termination

13.1 This Agreement shall become effective on Effective Date and shall continue thereafter, unless earlier terminated—according to 13.3— for 7 (seven) years.

13.2 It is automatically extended for further 12 (twelve)-months-periods unless written notice is given 3 (three) months prior to the end of a 12 (twelve)-months-period.

13.3 Either party may terminate this Agreement: (a) on thirty (30) days written notice, for material breach—to be sufficiently detailed in said written notice—unless the said breach is corrected within the said thirty (30) days or (b) immediately if the other party shall cease conducting business in the normal course, become insolvent, make a general assignment for the benefit of creditors, suffer or permit the appointment of a receiver for its business or assets, or shall avail itself of or become subject to any proceeding under the federal bankruptcy act or any other statute of any state relating to insolvency or the protection of rights of creditors.

14   Non–Assignability

Neither the benefits nor the obligation of this Agreement may be assigned or transferred in any manner.

15   Written Form and Modification of Agreement

This Agreement may not be modified, varied or extended, except by agreement in writing signed by both parties. This requirement of written form may be waived only in writing signed by both parties.

16   Arbitration

16.1 Any differences or disputes arising from this Agreement or from agreements regarding its performance shall be settled by an amicable effort on the part of both parties to the Agreement. An attempt to arrive at a settlement shall be deemed to have failed as soon as one of the parties to the Agreement so notifies the other party in writing. The arbitration proceedings shall be in English language.

16.2 If an attempt at settlement has failed, the disputes shall be finally settled under the Rules of Conciliation and Arbitration of the International Chamber of Commerce in Paris (Rules) by three arbitrators, fluent in the English language, appointed in accordance with the Rules.

16.3 The place of arbitration shall be Bern/Switzerland. The procedural law of this place shall apply where the Rules are silent.

16.4 The arbitral award shall be substantiated in writing. The arbitral tribunal shall decide on the matter of costs of the arbitration and on reasonable attorney fees.

17   Choice of Law

All disputes shall be settled in accordance with the provisions of this Agreement and all other agreements regarding its performance, otherwise in accordance with the applicable law in force in California without reference to other laws.

18   Supplementary to this Agreement the General Conditions of Supply and Delivery for Products and Services of the Electrical and Electronic Industry (Annex A5) shall apply in this actual version, as far as not otherwise agreed herein.

19   Supplementary to this Agreement the "General Terms for the Use of Software Products of the Components Group" (Annex A6) shall apply in its actual version, as far as not otherwise agreed herein.

In Witness Whereof, the parties hereto have caused this Agreement to be signed by their respective duly authorized officers.

AMERITEK   SIEMENS AKTIENGESELLSCHAFT

Signature: Signature:

§ 1.37 License to Manufacture Agreement (Electronics) (linked to previous Volume Purchase Agreement)

LICENSE TO MANUFACTURE AGREEMENT *

THIS AGREEMENT, effective as of _____, between AMERITEK, a corporation organized and existing under the laws of California, with offices at San Diego/California (hereinafter referred to as "Ameritek"), and Siemens Aktiengesellschaft, a German corporation, having principal offices in Berlin and Munich, Federal Republic of Germany, (hereinafter referred to as "Siemens");

WITNESSETH:

WHEREAS the parties concluded additionally a Volume Purchase Agreement (VPA) dated Jan. 7, 1991 and a letter of intent dated Dec. 21, 1990 which are referred to and incorporated by reference, for entering the North American Market with Siemens Micro Computer Systems (MCS) products.

WHEREAS, Siemens owns valuable proprietary information including knowhow and patent rights relating to development, manufacture and operation of such MCS products;

* © By H. Lawrence Serra, Esq. San Die-   go. Reprinted with permission.

WHEREAS, Ameritek desires to extend the cooperation with Siemens for the purpose of obtaining access to Siemens' proprietary information and knowhow as well as acquiring relevant rights for use of such knowhow for the manufacture and operation of Siemens MCS products and special equipment thereof.

NOW, THEREFORE, in consideration of the premises, the rights granted herein by Siemens to Ameritek and the covenants and conditions herein contained, the parties agree as follows:

ARTICLE 1

Definitions

1.1   The term "Contract Products" shall mean Siemens Micro Computer Systems (MCS) as defined in Annex 1 hereto.

1.2   The term "Contract Products" shall not include and therefore no rights and no information shall be granted with regard to the manufacture of basic or raw materials or parts used in Contract Products (for example the bare printed circuit board per se, wires, connectors, electric/electronic components of any kind) and of products not manufactured by Siemens Components Group.

Annex 1 may be amended by new/other types of Contract Products under terms and conditions to be agreed upon separately case by case with regard to Considerations (Article 5).

1.2   The term "Information" means written or otherwise recorded (Manufacturing Packages) or oral information available at Siemens which Siemens may dispose of concerning Contract Products including information on Improvements and relating to the design, manufacture and testing of Contract Products to the extent such information has been incorporated in and forms part of the manufacturing technique of Siemens.

1.3   The term "Improvement" means innovations and/or modification of less than 20% change in control flow made by one party on the particular Contract Product and introduced by it into its own manufacture of Contract Products.

1.4   The term "Patent" means any patent, patent application or other statutory protected right which may be granted to one party in USA, Canada or Mexico under and during the term of this Agreement.

ARTICLE 2

Rights Granted/Manufacturing Assistance/Supplies

2.1   Subject to the terms and conditions herein set forth, Siemens hereby grants and agrees to grant to Ameritek under the Information delivered under this Agreement and under Patents owned or controlled by Siemens the nonexclusive, nontransferable and nonassignable right to manufacture and to sell such manufactured Contract Products in USA, Canada and Mexico.

Ameritek shall be entitled to make any innovations and/or modifications including, but not limited to, Improvements of Contract

Products provided Siemens has given its written approval before, which shall not be unreasonably withheld. Such approval shall be withheld for example, if such innovations and/or modifications are Siemens-products already existing and/or under development by Siemens.

2.2   Until notice of termination is given by one party Siemens shall deliver to Ameritek recorded Information in form of Manufacturing Package appropriate for the manufacture, test and operation of Contract Products in accordance with Annex 2 hereto (details and time schedule).

2.3   Upon request of Ameritek Siemens is prepared—as far as reasonably acceptable, however, not more than one week for each type of Contract Products—to assist Ameritek's experts in the manufacture of Contract Products according to terms and conditions to be agreed upon separately by training in Siemens' facilities or delegating Siemens' experts to Ameritek.

2.4   Siemens is prepared to supply Ameritek with Contract Products under terms and conditions contained in the Volume Purchase Agreement, dated Jan. 7, 1991 between the parties.

2.5   Upon request of Siemens, Ameritek shall grant to Siemens required rights and licenses to make, have made, use, sell, lease or otherwise dispose of Ameritek's products including resident software and software-development-tools worldwide according to fair and reasonable terms and conditions to be agreed upon case by case.

ARTICLE 3

Consideration

3.1   In consideration of the rights granted to Ameritek and the transfer of Manufacturing Packages by Siemens Ameritek shall make the following payments after signature of this Agreement by both parties:

3.1.1   a lump sum of US Dollars 25,000,—(In Words: Twenty five thousand US Dollars) after signature of this Agreement by both parties and request of the Manufacturing Package by Ameritek for each type of Contract Products (Annex 1) according to Art. 2.2.

For all Manufacturing Packages in excess of 10 types of Contract Products requested within the first three years, commencing on request of the first Manufacturing Package by Ameritek, beforementioned lump sum shall be reduced to US Dollars 20,000,— (Twenty thousand US Dollars) for each type of Contract Product requested in excess of the first ten types of Contract Products. If Integritek has not requested Manufacturing Packages for a total of 15 types of Contract Products within such three year period, Ameritek shall pay the difference between lump sums already paid and US Dollars 350,000,—(Three hundred and fifty thousand US Dollars) at the end of said three year period. For Manufacturing Packages requested by Ameritek after said three year period Ameritek shall pay a lump sum of US Dollars 30,000,—(Thirty thousand US Dollars) for each type of Contract Product.

3.1.2 a royalty rate of 6.5% (six point five percent) of the Net Sales Price of Contract Products sold by Ameritek for a minimum period of seven (7) years after commencement of series production for each type of Contract Products.

"Net Sales Price" means the actual price invoiced by Ameritek to its customer for Contract Products reduced by costs for freight, packing, insurance, taxes, prepaid duties provided, however, such costs are explicitly invoiced to Ameritek's customer, as well as a reduction for supplies purchased from Siemens according to the Volume Purchase Agreement (2.4).

3.2   Contract Products shall be also considered sold when incorporated as part of Ameritek's System Products or when used by Ameritek itself or delivered by Ameritek for replacement purposes. In such cases "Net Sales Price" shall be the average-price charged by Ameritek to its customers for delivery of Contract Products. Royalty payments on Contract Products not accepted or returned to Ameritek for credit by its customer shall be credited on future royalty payments.

ARTICLE 4

General Provisions Relating to Royalties

4.1   Ameritek shall keep full and accurate records of all Contract Products manufactured and sold by Ameritek. Within thirty (30) days after the end of each calendar half year, Ameritek shall render a written royalty statement to Siemens, setting forth the total monetary amount of sales of Contract Products sold by Ameritek during the preceding semi-annual period, the amount of royalties payable hereunder on account thereof and the deductions made, if any; and Ameritek shall therewith pay the royalty due.

4.2   Siemens is entitled to request from Ameritek to pay interest to Siemens on any and all amounts of royalties that are at any time overdue and payable to Siemens, at a rate of 2% (two percent) above the discount rate of the Deutsche Bundesbank, Frankfurt am Main, as of the last day of the period for which payment is due.

4.3   At any time within 2 (two) years of the date a royalty statement is due under 4.1 Ameritek agrees to permit the aforesaid records and supporting information related to said settlement to be examined at all reasonable times on no less than 30 days notice by a representative reasonably acceptable to Ameritek which Siemens may designate in writing, in order to determine the accuracy of Ameritek's statements, and of the payments required to be made hereunder. Prompt adjustment shall be made to correct any errors or omissions in Ameritek's reports or figures disclosed by such audit. Neither such right to audit nor the right to receive adjustment shall be affected by any statement to the contrary appearing on checks or otherwise.

4.4   Any payment given under this Agreement shall be made in US Dollar to Siemens' account no. 203 848 at the Bayerische Vereinsbank (BLZ 700 202 70), Kardinal–Faulhaber–Str., D–8000 München 2, with the remark "VPA VLV".

ARTICLE 5

Improvements made by Integritek/Joint inventions

5.1 If during the duration of this Agreement and subject to Art. 2.1 Ameritek makes any Improvements with regard to Contract Products Ameritek shall communicate such Improvements to Siemens and hereby grants to Siemens, under such Improvements (including any Patent which may be issued thereon), a non-exclusive, non-transferable perpetual right to utilize and to grant sublicenses to its Subsidiaries.

Subsidiaries shall mean any and all business concerns which Siemens controls either directly or indirectly by means of stock, ownership, or voting rights of 50 percent or more.

Upon request of Siemens, Ameritek shall assist Siemens according to Art. 2 with regard to such Improvements.

5.2 If any joint invention will result from the cooperation under this Agreement, (i.e. inventions jointly made by employees of both parties) and the features of such joint invention cannot be separately applied for industrial property rights, the parties shall jointly apply for patent protection.

The details for applying for and maintaining of such patent shall be worked out by the parties on a case-by-case basis. So long as such patent is in force, Siemens and Ameritek shall each be entitled to practice and to license such patent without any financial compensation or the consent of the other.

ARTICLE 6

Term and Termination

6.1 This Agreement shall become effective on the date of signature by both parties and shall continue until December 31, 2007, unless terminated under the provisions of this Art. 6.

Subject to Art. 7.1 and other provisions which by express terms are intended to survive a termination of this Agreement, it may be terminated on two years notice on December 31 of any odd numbered calendar year (each second calendar year) by registered letter, however, not before December 31, 1997.

6.2 After termination of this Agreement according to 6.1, Ameritek may subject to Art. 3.1.2 continue to make use of the Manufacturing Packages delivered under this Agreement free of charge. If at this date Patents may exist Ameritek will be entitled to use such Patents to the extent Ameritek will have used such Patents according to Article 2 hereof during the term and until termination of this Agreement but will pay to Siemens a fair and reasonable royalty the amount of which will be mutually agreed upon at due time.

6.3   If Ameritek shall at any time default in making any payment provided under this Agreement or in making any report hereunder, or commit any material breach of any covenant or agreement herein contained, and shall fail to remedy any such default or breach or to correct any such report within 60 (sixty) days after written notice by Siemens, Siemens may, by notice in writing to this effect, and at its option, terminate this Agreement and the licenses hereunder, but such termination shall not prejudice Siemens' rights with its rights to recover any royalty or any sum due at the time of such termination nor shall it prejudice any cause of action or claims of Siemens accrued or to accrue on account of any breach or default by Ameritek.

6.4   Each party shall have the right to terminate this Agreement at any time upon or after the filing by the other party of a petition in bankruptcy or insolvency, or upon or after any adjudication that the other party is bankrupt or insolvent, or upon or after the filing by the other party of any petition or answer seeking reorganization, readjustment or arrangement of the other party under any federal or state law relating to bankruptcy or insolvency, or upon or after the appointment of a receiver for all or substantially all of the property of the other party or upon or after the making by such other party of any assignment or attempted assignment for the benefit of creditors, or upon or after the institution by the other party of any proceedings for the liquidation or winding up of its business, and upon the exercise of such right, this Agreement shall terminate within 30 (thirty) days after notice in writing to that effect has been given by one party to such other party.

The same shall also apply if Ameritek shall become controlled directly or indirectly by any third party, which is manufacturing products in the scope of Siemens-products, provided however, the interests of Siemens are jeopardized materially. "Control" means either direct or indirect ownership of more than 50% (fifty percent) of the shares or stock or the voting rights.

6.5   Termination of this Agreement, by regular termination or otherwise, shall not release the other party from any of its obligations hereunder with regard to Contract Products manufactured, or in the process of manufacture prior to termination, and shall not rescind or give rise to any right to rescind anything done or to claim return of, or cancellation of any payment made, obligation accruing, or other consideration given to Siemens hereunder, prior to the time of such termination.

6.6   No failure or delay on the part of one party to exercise its right of termination hereunder or any one or more defaults shall be construed to prejudice its right of termination for such or for any other subsequent default.

ARTICLE 7

General Provisions

7.1   Unless otherwise agreed to in writing each party shall maintain in confidence during the duration of this Agreement and thereafter any Information received from the other party pursuant to the terms of this Agreement and not divulge the Manufacturing Packages delivered or disclose any Information incorporated therein or orally provided to any third party or to personnel of one party not having a need to know, with the same degree of care as is used with respect to its own proprietary information except such Information is at the given time part of the public knowledge without the fault of the receiving party or was or is subsequently independently developed by the receiving party as proven by written records.

Each party agrees to and shall utilize the Information received hereunder solely for the purposes of and in accordance with the stipulations set forth under this Agreement.

7.2 As long as a party, in fulfilling its obligations under this Agreement, employs the same degree of care in that it otherwise employs in carrying out its business affairs, that party shall not be liable for any claim, whether of the other party or of a third party, that in any way relates to the sufficiency or utility of any Information furnished hereunder or to the use of any such Information including third party rights or that in any way relates to any product (including, but not limited to, a claim based on the quality, utility, merchantability or any other characteristic of such a product) made using any such Information.

7.3 Neither party shall be liable for delays in delivery or performance or non-delivery or for non-performance under this Agreement due to Force Majeure, e.g.; war, fire, strike, lockouts, flood, typhoons, earthquakes, etc., provided that the party seeking to be excused shall have notified the other party of the beginning and the end of any such circumstances and shall use every reasonable endeavour to minimize the prevention and, upon the ending of such circumstance, without undue delay resume the performance of its obligations. Where any such Force Majeure results, or is likely to result, in a disproportion between the relative undertakings of the parties under this Agreement, the parties shall reach a fair and equitable adjustment between them or the party not affected shall have the right to withhold its performance during the period of Force Majeure.

If no agreement is reached on such adjustment and the events of Force Majeure render the performance of the obligations impossible for a period exceeding 180 days, then the party aggrieved may terminate this Agreement by giving 90 day's notice to the party hindered by such Force Majeure. Such termination shall be avoided if the events of the Force Majeure cease during the period of notice.

7.4 All disputes arising in connection with this Agreement shall be finally settled by a Court of Arbitration consisting of three members, fluent in the English language, the chairman being of juridical education, to be convened in Bern, Switzerland, if not otherwise agreed upon under the auspices of and in accordance with the Rules and of Conciliation and Arbitration of the International Chamber of Commerce, Paris. The arbitration proceedings shall be in the English language.

The Court of Arbitration has to decide in accordance with Swiss law without reference to other laws. Judgment upon the award rendered may be entered in any court having jurisdiction or application may be made to such order of enforcement, as the case may be.

7.5 If any term, provision, covenant or restriction of this Agreement is held by a court of competent jurisdiction to be invalid, void, or unenforceable, the remainder of the terms, provisions, covenants and restrictions hereof shall remain in full force and effect and shall in no way be affected, impaired or invalidated, and the invalid or unenforceable term or provision shall be replaced by a term or provision that comes closest to expressing the intention of the invalid or unenforceable term or provision.

7.6 All changes and amendments including any Annexes to this Agreement must be in writing to be valid and marked so explicitly. This requirement of written form may be waived only in writing signed by both parties.

7.7 All notices herein shall be in writing. Written notices shall be delivered to the following addresses:

AMERITEK: Hubert Godfrey, Chief Executive Officer
                 7446 Industrial Drive
                 San Diego, California
                 U.S.A.

SIEMENS: Siemens Aktiengesellschaft
                 Unternehmensbereich Bauelemente
                 WISCO
                 Balanstraße 73
                 D–8000 München 80

7.8 Supplementary to this Agreement the regulations of the Volume Purchase Agreement including its Annexes shall apply.

IN WITNESS WHEREOF, the parties hereto have caused two (2) copies of this Agreement to be executed by their duly authorized officers as of the date first specified above.

Ameritek   Siemens Aktiengesellschaft

§ 1.38   International Contract for Sale of Secondary Galvanized Metal (Selective CISG Application)*

This contract number 062895 is dated this _____ day of July, 1995, between HAIFA TRADING, INC. ("BUYER") located at, _____ and ("Seller") located at 8363 Sultana Avenue, Fontana, California 92335.

TERMS AND CONDITIONS

1.   NAME OF COMMODITY; SPECIFICATIONS; COUNTRY OF ORIGIN; MANUFACTURER'S PACKING TERMS

A. **Commodity:** The material being sold is secondary galvanized steel rolled coils and sheets. The material should be secondary or better

---

* © By H. Lawrence Serra, Esq. of San   Diego. Reprinted with permission.

quality steel for commercial use, with United States as the Country of Origin of the product. SELLER and BUYER are merchants skilled and informed on the subject matter of secondary steel and acknowledge that each understands what the term "secondary steel for commercial use" means in custom and usage of their trade.

1. **Size and weight**: Ten to twenty percent (10%–20%) under 0.5MM one hundred percent (100%) under 1.2MM in thickness. No less than 800MM in width, and no less than 2,000 lbs. per coil in weight. The first shipment shall have at least 20% 0.5MM and under. The remaining shipments shall have at least 10–20% 0.5MM.

2. **Quantity**: 2,000 metric tons, plus or minus five percent (5%) in quantity allowed, in four (4) roughly equal shipments, containerized in containers arranged for, delivered, and pre-paid for by BUYER.

3. **Price**: U.S. $22.50 (U.S. Dollars) cwt EX WORKS ** SELLER's place of business, Fontana, California, to be loaded into container(s), arranged for, ordered by, and pre-paid for by BUYER.

4. **Total Amount**: Total contract value of the material is nine hundred ninety-two thousand, seventy U.S. dollars ($992,070.00) plus or minus five percent (5%).

5. **Time of Shipment:** The first of four containerized shipments of roughly five hundred (500) metric tons each should be within forty-five (45) days after receipt by SELLER of contract signed by BUYER, in form acceptable to SELLER, and no sooner than forty-eight (48) hours after confirmation to SELLER's satisfaction of BUYER's irrevocable deposit to SELLER's account by wire transfer to SELLER'a account (¶ 6 below) in the amount of U.S. $247,950.00. Total quantity of two thousand (2,000) metric tons will be shipped in four (4) roughly equal five hundred (500) metric ton shipments (containerized) within six (6) months of first shipment.

6. **Payment**: By four wire transfers in equal amounts of U.S. $ Two hundred forty-seven thousand nine hundred fifty U.S. dollars (U.S. $247,950.00) paid to SELLER's account referenced below. Each transfer shall be completed and irrevocable deposit confirmed to SELLER's satisfaction to SELLER's account at least forty-eight (48) hours before completion of EX WORKS obligations by SELLER of each of four shipments (containerized) of roughly five hundred (500) metric tons each. Upon confirmation to SELLER's satisfaction of irrevocable deposit to SELLER's account of each wire transfer in the amount of U.S. $ Two hundred forty-seven thousand nine hundred fifty U.S. dollars (U.S. $247,950.00), but no sooner than forty-eight (48) hours thereafter, SELLER shall forthwith undertake its EX WORKS obligations. Shipments may be slightly more or slightly less than five hundred (500) metric tons, so long as all four shipments constitute two thousand

_____

** As defined in INCOTERMS, except   paragraph 7e below.
that BUYER bears cost of inspection per

(2,000) metric tons plus or minus five percent (5%), without affecting the amount of any of the four wire transfers in the amount of Two hundred forty-seven thousand nine hundred fifty dollars ($247,950.00).

SELLER's wire transfer information is as follows:

Account No.:	
Bank:	Wells Fargo
	10535 Foothill Blvd. Suite 100
	Rancho Cucamonga, CA 91730
Telephone:	(909) 596–1507
Routing No.:	121000248
Manager:	Patty La Rue

7. **Documents**: To facilitate the BUYER to check shipped material, all documents shall be prepared as follows:

a. Commercial Invoice: Two (2) fully executed original copies of commercial invoices. Contract number shall be indicated on each invoice.

b. Packing List: Two (2) original copies.

c. Certificate of Origin: One (1) original for each of four shipments.

d. Certificate of Quality/Quantity/Weight of Goods: One (1) original and two (2) copies for each of the four shipments of five hundred (500) metric tons.

e. Inspection of Quality/Quantity/Weight: By independent inspector designated and paid for by BUYER, to be issued at the time of SELLER's loading of containers provided by BUYER at SELLER's place of business for each of the four shipments (containerized) of roughly five hundred (500) metric tons each.

All appropriate above-referenced forms shall be provided to SELLER.

8. Delayed Shipment/Postponement: SELLER may, with BUYER's consent, postpone shipment of above-referenced commodity not to exceed fifteen (15) days after each proposed shipment date for each of the four shipments (containerized) of roughly five hundred (500) metric tons each.

9. Force Majeure: SELLER shall use its best efforts to meet all obligations under this contract with reasonable promptness, and SELLER shall not be liable for failure or delay to perform any part of the contract because of Act of God, fire, labor disputes of any nature, inevitable accident, insurrection, civil disturbance or instability, or other causes beyond the control of SELLER, including without limitation, changes in governments' policies with respect to international trade, import or export, administration of import or export license procedures or requirements, or duties, quotas, fees, charges, taxes or any other requirements of any supra-national organization, national or subordinate government entity; nor shall SELLER be liable for its failure to perform

or its delay in performance, if caused or contributed to by the failure or delay to perform, or any of the reasons set forth in this paragraph, of any third party on which SELLER relies. Further, any such failure to perform, or delay to perform on the part of SELLER, shall be evaluated, and any remedies constructed in accordance with Article 79 of the United Nations Convention for Contracts on the International Sale of Goods (CISG), a copy of which Article is attached hereto.

10. Governing Law: BUYER and SELLER expressly agree that this contract shall NOT be governed by the U.N. Convention for Contracts on the International Sale of Goods (CISG) even if it is applicable as a matter of law by its terms, except that BUYER and SELLER specifically agree to the utilization of CISG Article 79 regarding failed or delayed performance as specified in ¶ 9 above. BUYER and SELLER agree that the law governing this contract and any disputes arising out of it shall be the commercial law of the State of California, United States of America, excluding the U.N. Convention for Contracts on the International Sale of Goods (CISG) except to the extent Article 79 is referenced for use in ¶ 9 above.

11. No Warranty (SALE "AS IS"): Sale of SELLER's products hereunder is a sale "AS IS", with no warranties of any sort, express, implied or statutory. BUYER specifically relies solely on the Certificates of Inspection for each shipment prepared by the independent inspector retained by BUYER (designated in ¶ 7e above) as to quality, quantity and weight of product.

12. BUYER Holds SELLER Harmless: BUYER holds SELLER harmless and indemnifies SELLER from any and all claims, causes of action, lawsuits and administrative proceedings, and the like that may arise in relation to this contract and its obligations. BUYER further agrees to defend SELLER from any claims, lawsuits, causes of action or administrative proceedings, or the like which may arise from this contract or its obligations.

13. Arbitration: All disputes in connection with this contract or the execution thereof shall be settled through friendly negotiations between the BUYER and SELLER. If no settlement can be reached, the dispute shall then be submitted to one (1) to three (3) arbitrator(s) mutually agreed upon by BUYER and SELLER, or failing such agreement, submitted to arbitrator(s) designated by the court under California Code of Civil Procedure § 1297.11, et seq. (International Mediation and Arbitration). Such arbitrator(s) must each have at least five (5) years experience in the secondary galvanized metal business. Specifically, SELLER and BUYER agree that any dispute regarding any aspect of this contract shall be directed as quickly as possible to conciliation as provided in California Code of Civil Procedure §§ 1297.341, et seq., and the procedures described in the provisions of California Code of Civil Procedure § 1297.11, et seq. shall be utilized by the parties and arbitrator(s) to direct the dispute directly and immediately to a friendly conciliation with such arbitrator(s), without the necessity of filing formal

pleadings by either party, but rather by submitting a clear and concise statement of the dispute (5 pages or less) by each party to the arbitrator(s) or conciliator(s). The award rendered by such arbitrator(s) or conciliator(s) shall be final and binding on both parties. The expense of such arbitration or conciliation, including reasonable attorneys' fees, shall be borne by losing party, unless that expense is otherwise allocated by the arbitrator(s) or conciliator(s).

Dated _____   Dated _____

BUYER   SELLER
HAIFA TRADING, INC.

By_____   By_____

§ 1.39 Purchase and Sale Agreement (Chemicals Industry)*

(Toll Agreement—Favors Buyer or Party tolling the product)

This Purchase and Sale Agreement ("Agreement") is between _____, a _____ corporation, located at _____ _____, ("Seller"), and **COMPANY**, a _____ corporation, located at _____. ("COMPANY").

In consideration of the mutual covenants set forth herein, Seller and COMPANY agree as follows:

1. TERM OF AGREEMENT.

This Agreement will be for an initial term of _____ beginning on , and ending on _____. This agreement may be renewed for additional one (1) year periods upon mutual written agreement.

2. PURCHASES AND SALES.

a. COMPANY agrees to buy from Seller and Seller agrees to sell to COMPANY the following product meeting the specifications set forth in Addendum A ("Product"):

Product Name	Estimated Quantity	Minimal Annual Quantity	Maximum Annual Quantity	Price (U.S. Currency)

b. In addition to the purchase price for Product, COMPANY will sell and deliver to Seller, at [no charge], _____ pounds of _____, meeting the specifications set forth in Addendum B ("Materials") for each pound of Product supplied under this Agreement.

3. PRODUCT ORDERS.

COMPANY will issue orders for Product at least _____ days before the delivery date which specify the quantity, time, and place for delivery of Product. Seller will timely manufacture and deliver Product as directed

* Courtesy of Dow Chemical Company Legal Department.

in COMPANY's orders for Product. Product will be shipped in mutually acceptable types and sizes of drums, bins, cartons or other shipping containers.

4.   PRODUCT SPECIFICATION, CERTIFICATIONS AND CHANGES.

a.   Seller will certify conformance of Product to the specifications with each delivery. COMPANY is not required to inspect Product for conformance to specifications.

b.   From time to time, COMPANY may request changes to the Product specifications which will not be effective unless agreed to in writing by Seller. If more than sixty (60) days pass following the receipt of COMPANY's request and Seller and COMPANY have not agreed upon mutually acceptable terms and conditions for delivering Product meeting the revised specifications, then COMPANY may, at any time thereafter, terminate this Agreement or wholly or partially cancel its remaining purchase obligations by sending 15 days' prior written notice and may purchase such quantity of Product from other sources.

5.   DELIVERY; TITLE; RISK OF LOSS.

a.   All Product will be shipped, FOB destination point, to the location specified in COMPANY'S order for the Product. Title to Product and all legal responsibilities associated therewith will remain with Seller until the Product is delivered to the FOB point. COMPANY may select the carriers and the routes.

b.   Materials will be shipped, FOB shipping point, to Seller's facility at _____. Title to Materials and all legal responsibilities associated therewith will transfer to Seller when the Materials are delivered to the FOB point. COMPANY will pay freight for Materials to Seller's facility. Seller will use the Materials exclusively to manufacture Product for COMPANY. Upon delivery of Materials to the FOB point, Seller will be solely responsible for the receiving, handling, storing, safekeeping, and disposal of Materials and will be liable for any loss or damage thereof. COMPANY may select the carriers and the routes. The parties shall mutually agree on the delivery dates for delivery of Material to Seller.

c.   Upon the expiration or termination of this Agreement, if COMPANY so requests, Seller will, according to such request, deliver and convey title to COMPANY remaining Product at the prices set forth in this Agreement and Materials which Seller has not earned. The parties will then settle the any remaining imbalances according to the terms contained in paragraph 8. Title and any responsibility for handling such Product or Materials shall not be deemed to have been conveyed or transferred to COMPANY until such Product or Materials have been delivered to COMPANY pursuant to the terms in paragraph 5(a) above, except COMPANY will pay freight for Materials.

6.   PAYMENT AND PAYMENT TERMS.

Seller will invoice COMPANY each month for Product delivered the preceding month. Payment terms are net 30 days from the date of receipt by COMPANY of Seller's invoice. The price listed in paragraph

2(a) is the entire amount that Seller shall charge COMPANY. Seller shall not charge COMPANY for any taxes, government charges, or other expenses beyond what is already included in the listed price. It shall be the responsibility of the Seller, and not of COMPANY, to file with the appropriate government authority any tax returns and to pay any tax (e.g., federal Superfund tax) that may be required as a result of Seller's or COMPANY's use of Materials or as a result of Seller's sale of Product to COMPANY. Upon request by COMPANY, Seller shall provide COMPANY with (a) proof of payment of any taxes, costs, and expenses that Seller may be charging COMPANY as part of the price listed in paragraph 2(a) and (b) information in enabling COMPANY to verify the accuracy of such charges. Seller shall hold harmless and indemnify COMPANY for any government charges or taxes (plus penalties and interest thereon), excluding COMPANY's income taxes or taxes measured on the income of COMPANY, which COMPANY may incur as a result of Seller's or COMPANY's use of Materials or as a result of Seller's sale of Product to COMPANY.

7. COMPETITIVE OFFERS.

If COMPANY can obtain comparable Product at a lower delivered cost from another party, then COMPANY may request Seller to meet such cost within 15 days of Seller's receipt of written notice from COMPANY. If Seller is unwilling to meet such cost within such notice period, then, at the expiration of such notice period, COMPANY may obtain the Product from such party and the quantity of such Product will be deducted from COMPANY's and Seller's obligations hereunder.

8. IMBALANCES.

Each party will, as soon as practical, following the end of each month, provide the other with a report stating the quantities delivered and received during the month and the calendar year pursuant to this Agreement, as well as exchange balance for such periods. The reports will be sent to COMPANY to the attention of _____, at _____ and to Seller to the attention of _____ at _____ _____. If quantities of Materials delivered by COMPANY are not in proportionate balance with the amount of Product delivered by Seller at the end of any calendar quarter, then within thirty (30) days Seller will itemize and document the difference to COMPANY. COMPANY will then, at COMPANY's option, (1) deliver Materials to Seller as necessary to correct the imbalance, or (2) take delivery of Product from Seller as necessary to correct the imbalance, or (3) either invoice or pay Seller, as applicable, for the price of Materials (i.e., the price of Materials as reported in the then most current [Chemical Marketing Reporter or other index or trade journal]) to correct the imbalance.

9. FACILITIES AND OPERATIONS.

a. Seller warrants that the facilities it will utilize in the performance of this Agreement will comply with all laws, regulations and ordinances governing construction and operation of such manufacturing facilities, including, without limitation, all environmental, health and safety laws. Seller has the responsibility to properly engineer, construct, maintain and operate such facilities. Seller will maintain all facilities and equipment used to perform its obligations pursuant to this Agreement in a good and serviceable condition.

b. Seller warrants to perform the following activities safely, properly and in conformance with all applicable laws, regulations and ordinances: manufacturing, receiving of Materials and raw materials, storing, blending, packaging, cleaning, performing analytical work, lot control marking, shipping, completing paperwork, and all other operations related to Seller's performance of this Agreement. Seller shall be deemed the generator and owner of any "Wastes" [which term, as used in this Agreement, includes the meaning of "hazardous substance" and/or "hazardous materials" which is "disposed or released" as provided in the Federal Comprehensive Environmental Response, Compensation and Liability Act ("CERCLA"), 42 U.S.C. 9601 *et seq.*, the meaning of "waste" as provided in the Federal Resource Conservation and Recovery Act ("RCRA"), 42 U.S.C. 6901 *et seq.* and includes waste of any kind including, without limitation, routine process waste and by-products which are disposed] generated in connection with Seller's performance under this Agreement, and as such shall be solely and independently responsible for any liabilities caused by such Wastes and shall safely, properly and in compliance with applicable laws, regulations and ordinances dispose of or arrange for the disposal of the same. On an annual basis, Seller will certify to COMPANY that all Wastes have been properly disposed of in compliance with applicable laws, regulations and ordinances. Seller's failure to fulfill the obligations of this paragraph 9 will be construed as a material breach of this Agreement.

10. SAFETY, SECURITY AND HYGIENE.

Seller will become familiar with all raw materials and Materials, Products and Wastes, used, produced or generated, respectively, while manufacturing Product. Seller will comply with the Federal OSHA "Hazard Communication Standard," codified as 29 C.F.R. 1910.1200, et seq., and any similar state "right-to-know" laws which are currently in force or may be enacted in the future. Seller is solely responsible for informing its employees of the chemical hazards associated with any products or chemicals handled pursuant to this Agreement and is also responsible for training its employees in the proper methods of handling such products and chemicals. Seller has an affirmative obligation, when in doubt about a product or chemical, to seek further information from COMPANY. Seller's failure to fulfill the obligations of this paragraph 10 will be construed as a material breach of this Agreement.

11. PRODUCT WARRANTY.

Seller warrants that Product delivered to COMPANY will (1) conform to the descriptions and specifications as set forth in this Agreement, (2) be of good quality and workmanship and free from defects, latent or patent, and (3) be merchantable and fit and sufficient for COMPANY's intended purpose. Payment, inspection, acceptance or use of Product will not affect Seller's obligation under this warranty.

12. INDEMNIFICATION.

Seller will indemnify, defend and hold COMPANY (including COMPANY's officers, directors, employees, servants, affiliates, agents, successors, and assigns) harmless from any and all liability, expense (including actual attorneys' fees and internal costs associated with internal attorney work), cost, loss or damage COMPANY may suffer as a result of claims, demands, costs, suits or actions (whether based on facts now known or later discovered) against COMPANY arising out of the following:

(A) The failure of Seller or those acting under or for Seller to comply with all federal, state and local laws, regulations and ordinances (including, without limitation, those related to the environment, health and safety) in connection with Seller's performance of this Agreement (including, without limitation, Seller's ownership or operation of its business and facilities);

(B) Any contamination of the environment or damage to natural resources at a facility owned or operated by Seller or a facility/location chosen by Seller for its disposal of Wastes or any other facility at which Seller's Wastes may be released or threatened to be released, including any liability imposed by federal, state and local laws, regulations and ordinances, including, but not limited to, the Federal Comprehensive Environmental Response Compensation and Liability Act (CERCLA), 42 USC 9601 et seq., the Federal Resource Conservation and Recovery Act (RCRA), 42 USC 6901 et seq., or comparable and applicable state legal requirements or any extension or revision thereof; or

(C) Any damage to any property, including damage to any environmental medium (air, water, groundwater, soil), or damage to natural resources, or death or injury of persons (including Seller's employees) arising out of (1) Seller's performance or nonperformance of this Agreement, (2) The Materials delivered or the Products ordered pursuant to this Agreement unless caused by the sole negligence of COMPANY, or (3) any design or manufacturing defect in the Product, whether latent or patent.

This paragraph 12 will apply regardless of the type of assertion being made including, without limitation, any legal, equitable, or admiralty causes of action or rights (including, without limitation, negligence, strict liability in tort, other tort, express or implied warranty, indemnity, contract, contribution or subrogation), whether the assertion is made by a party to this Agreement or any third party, and will apply to all types of damages (including, without limitation, direct, compensatory, incidental, consequential, exemplary, punitive, or special). In the event of a claim, COMPANY shall select the legal counsel and co-ordinate the defense. This paragraph 12 will survive the expiration or termination of this Agreement, and will be binding upon Seller's successors, assigns and trustees.

13. INSURANCE COVERAGE.

Seller will procure and maintain insurance in the following amounts, at its own expense, at all times while the Agreement is in effect:

(A) Workmen's Compensation insurance at statutory limits and Employers' Liability Insurance at not less than $1,000,000 aggregate; and

(B) Comprehensive General Liability Insurance (including contractual liability, products, and completed operations) with a bodily injury, death, and property damage combined single limit of $5,000,000 per occurrence; and

(C) Pollution and Environmental Impairment Insurance with a limit of $1,000,000 per occurrence and $2,000,000 aggregate.

Seller will furnish COMPANY a certificate(s) from an insurance carrier showing all insurance set forth above. The certificate(s) will include the following statement: "The insurance certified hereunder is applicable to all contracts between COMPANY and the Insured. This insurance may be canceled or altered only after ten (10) days' written notice to COMPANY." The insurance, and the certificate(s), will (1) name COMPANY (including COMPANY's officers, directors, employees, servants, affiliates, agents, successors, and assigns) as additional insureds with respect to Seller's performance under this Agreement, (2) provide that such insurance is primary to any liability insurance carried by COMPANY, and (3) provide that underwriters and insurance companies of Seller may not have any right of subrogation against COMPANY (including COMPANY's officers, directors, employees, servants, affiliates, agents, successors, and assigns). The insurance will contain an ordinary deductible. Failure of any of the terms and conditions of this paragraph 13 will be considered a material breach under this Agreement.

14. TERMINATION.

Either party may terminate this Agreement at any time, without further liability, by providing the other party with five (5) days' written notice upon the occurrence of any of the following events:

(A) The filing of bankruptcy for or on the part of the other party (or its parent organization or affiliate organizations);

(B) The appointment of a receiver, trustee or liquidator for all or substantially all of the assets of the other party (or its parent organization or affiliate organizations);

(C) An assignment by the other party (or its parent organization or affiliate organizations) for the benefit of its creditors;

(D) The filing of any petition by or against the other party (or its parent organization or any affiliate organizations) asking for a reorganization under any state insolvency law or under the Federal Bankruptcy Act;

(E) The failure of the other party to cure a material breach within thirty (30) days after having received written notice specifying the breach.

15.   LIENS, SETOFF & UCC FILINGS.

a.   Seller will keep Materials and Product free and clear of all liens, encumbrances, security interests and charges of any kind and character. Seller will indemnify, defend, and hold harmless COMPANY for all liens, encumbrances, security interests and charges that COMPANY may be compelled to pay in discharging such, including all costs and reasonable attorneys' fees.

b.   The parties shall have the right to setoff of any amounts due hereunder. The Parties acknowledge that the obligations to setoff are mutual under this Agreement.

c.   Upon passage of title in Materials to Seller, COMPANY shall have, and Seller hereby grants to COMPANY a purchase money security interest ("PMSI") in the Materials and its proceeds and products. Seller shall, at the request of COMPANY, execute such documents in connection with the Materials supplied pursuant to this Agreement as COMPANY may reasonably deem necessary, including but not limited to, the execution of any UCC statements. Seller further agrees, at the request of COMPANY, to disclose the names and addresses of its existing secured creditors. COMPANY may, at its expense, send a notice of its PMSI in the Materials to all such creditors.

16.   INDEPENDENT CONTRACTOR.

Seller is an independent contractor, with all the attendant rights and liabilities, and not an agent or employee of COMPANY. Any provision in this Agreement, or any action by COMPANY, which may appear to give COMPANY the right to direct or control Seller in providing Product means Seller will follow the desires of COMPANY in results only.

17.   FORCE MAJEURE.

a.   In the event of war, fire, flood, strike, labor trouble, breakage of equipment, accident, riot, action of governmental authority and laws, rules, ordinances and regulations (including, but not limited to, those dealing with pollution, health, ecology, or environmental matters), act of God, or contingencies beyond the reasonable control of Seller or COMPANY, interfering with the production, supply, transportation, or consumption practice of the party at the time respecting the Product or Materials covered by this Agreement, or in the event of inability to obtain on reasonable terms (other than price) any raw material (including energy source or power) used in connection therewith, delivery of quantities so affected may be delayed without liability during the duration of such occurrence only, but the Agreement will otherwise remain unaffected. The affected party will promptly notify the other party in writing after the commencement of such force majeure occurrence, setting forth the full particulars of such force majeure occurrence. The affected party will remedy such force majeure occurrence with all reasonable dispatch consistent with this paragraph and will promptly give written notice to the other party at the cessation of such force majeure occurrence.

b.   Notwithstanding the above, if the estimated duration of a force majeure occurrence which will interrupt, delay or decrease Seller's supply of Product to COMPANY is for more than 30 days, then COMPANY may, at its option, elect either to terminate the quantities of Product so affected from the Agreement altogether or terminate this Agreement by giving 10 days written notice thereof to Seller.

18.   RIGHT TO INSPECT.

COMPANY will have the right, but not the obligation, to inspect and test all Materials and Product during the period of manufacture and at all other times, at any place where the Materials, Products or Wastes may be located. The fact that COMPANY may have inspected, tested or failed to inspect or test Materials or Products will not affect any rights of COMPANY at law or at equity under this Agreement. This right will arise only upon the giving of reasonable notice to Seller and may occur only during the normal business hours of Seller.

19.   RIGHT TO AUDIT.

COMPANY will have the right but not the obligation to have the records of the Seller, insofar as such records relate to this Agreement, examined by an independent third party for the purpose of determining compliance with this Agreement. Such third party will be mutually acceptable to the parties. This right will arise only upon the giving of reasonable notice to the Seller and the records may be examined only during the normal business hours. If the examination reveals a breach, Seller will bear the cost of the examination; otherwise, COMPANY will bear such cost.

20.   ASSIGNMENT.

None of the rights, duties, or obligations under this Agreement may be assigned, delegated or transferred by either party without the other's written consent. All the processes associated with the manufacture of Product under this Agreement will take place only at Seller's facility located at ____; the work performed under this Agreement will not take place at any other facility without COMPANY's written consent. Seller will not subcontract any portion of this Agreement without COMPANY's written consent.

21.   WAIVER.

Waiver by either party of any breach, or failure to enforce any of the terms and conditions of the Agreement at any time, will not in any way affect, limit or waive the right of that party thereafter to enforce the Agreement and compel strict compliance with every term and condition of it.

22.   SEVERABILITY.

If any provision of this Agreement or the application thereof to any person or circumstance will, for any reason, and to any extent, be held to be invalid or unenforceable under applicable law, such provision will be deemed limited or modified to the extent necessary to make the same valid and enforceable under applicable law. If such invalidity becomes known or apparent to COMPANY and to Seller, COMPANY and Seller agree to negotiate promptly in good faith in an attempt to make appropriate changes and adjustments to achieve as closely as possible, consistent with applicable law, the intent and spirit of such invalid provision.

23. NOTICES.

All notices, request, demands and other communication under this Agreement will be in writing and will be deemed to have been duly given on the date of the service if served personally on the party to whom notice is to be given, or on the date of receipt if mailed to the party to whom notice is to be given by first class mail, registered or certified, postage prepaid or by overnight courier service (i.e., Federal Express or equivalent) and unless either party should notify the other of a change of address properly addressed as follows, or on the date of receipt where the intended recipient has acknowledged receipt:

To Seller: To COMPANY:

Seller Company   COMPANY
Attn: _____   Attn: _____
_____   _____
_____   _____

24. APPLICABLE LAW.

The validity, interpretation and performance of these terms and conditions will be governed by _____ law, including _____'s adaptation of the UCC, regardless of _____'s conflict-of-law rules.

25. TRADEMARKS.

Seller shall not obtain any rights in or to the use of the trademark _____, the COMPANY _____ trademark, the trade name COMPANY, or any other trademarks or service marks of COMPANY as a result of performing pursuant to this Agreement.

26. NONDISCLOSURE.

The Confidentiality Agreement executed by COMPANY and Seller, effective _____, as set forth in Addendum C to this Agreement is incorporated herein by reference; however, such Confidentiality Agreement shall be governed by its own terms and conditions.

27. ENTIRE AGREEMENT.

This Agreement (with its addenda) constitutes the full understanding of the parties, and is a final, complete and exclusive statement of the terms and conditions of their agreement. All representations, offers, and undertakings of the parties made prior to the effective date of this Agreement are merged herein. All modifications to this Agreement must be in writing and signed by an authorized representative of each party.

The parties have caused this Agreement to be executed by their duly authorized representatives as of the date corresponding to their respective signatures, but effective as of the date first written above.

SELLER   COMPANY

By: _____   By: _____
Name: _____   Name: _____
Title: _____   Title: _____
Date: _____   Date: _____

ADDENDUM A

to the
Purchase and Sale Agreement
between
COMPANY and Seller
Dated _____

PRODUCT SPECIFICATIONS

ADDENDUM B

to the
Purchase and Sale Agreement
between
COMPANY and Seller
Dated _____

MATERIALS SPECIFICATIONS

ADDENDUM C

to the
Purchase and Sale Agreement
between
COMPANY and Seller
Dated _____

CONFIDENTIALITY AGREEMENT

Selected Bibliography

C. Bianca and M. Bonell, eds., Commentary on the International Sales Law: The 1980 Vienna Sales Convention (1987).

M. Bonell, ed., UNILEX: International Case Law & Bibliography on CISG. (1995).

Brand, Professional Responsibility in a Transnational Transactions Practice, 17 J. Law & Com. 301 (1998).

E. Enderlein & D. Maskow, International Sales Law (1992).

Flechtner, Remedies under the New International Sales Convention: The Perspective from Article 2 of the UCC, 8 J. Law & Com. 53 (1988).

N. Galston and H. Smit, eds., International Sales (1984).

Hartnell, Rousing the Sleeping Dog: The Validity Exception to the Convention on Contracts for the International Sale of Goods, 18 Yale J. Int'l L. 1 (1993).

J. Honnold, Documentary History of the Uniform Law for International Sales (1989).

J. Honnold, Uniform Law for International Sales Under the 1980 United Nations Convention (3d ed. 1999).

Kiser, Minding the Gap: Determining Interest Rates under the U.N. Convention for the International Sales of Goods, 65 U. Chi. L. Rev. 1279 (1998).

P. Schlechtriem, Commentary on the UN Convention on the International Sale of Goods (CISG) (1998).

Shinn, Liabilities under Article 42 of the U.N. Convention on the International Sale of Goods, 2 Minn. J. Global Trade 115 (1993).

UNICITRAL, CLOUT (Case law on UNITRAL Texts) Cases, A/CN.9/SER.C/ABSTRACTS/1, et seq.

Winship, The U.N. Sales Convention and the Emerging Caselaw, Emptio–Vendito Inter Nationes 227 (1997).

Winship International Sales Contracts under the 1980 Vienna Convention, 17 U.C.C. L.J. 55 (1984).

Chapter 2

COMMERCIAL TERMS

Table of Sections

A. INTRODUCTION

B. INCOTERMS

C. THE INDIVIDUAL TERMS OF INCOTERMS

D. CISG, THE UCC AND INCOTERMS

A. INTRODUCTION

§ 2.1 Introduction

Chapter 1 illustrated how different rules are applicable to domestic and international sales of goods—respectively the Uniform Commercial Code (UCC) and the Convention on Contracts for the International Sales of Goods (CISG).[1] There are also differences between domestic and international commercial terms that provide rules for the delivery term in a contract for the sale of goods.

The UCC has its own definitions of such terms as "F.O.B." and "C.I.F."[2] The CISG does not have such definitions, and the CISG rules on delivery terms are very sparse.[3] Instead of incorporating detailed rules on the meaning of individual commercial delivery terms for the international sale, the drafters of the CISG could rely upon a written formulation of industry understanding of the meaning of such terms.[4] That written formulation is contained in Incoterms, published by the International Chamber of Commerce.[5] At least one author has concluded that Incoterms would qualify as an international "usage" under the CISG, and therefore would be available to fill in gaps in CISG provisions.[6]

Incoterms is an acronym for "International Commercial Terms" and was first published in 1936. It has been updated periodically since that time. Incoterms underwent major revisions in 1953 and 1990, and it was republished with new terms in 1967, 1976, and 1980.[7] The current version of Incoterms was published in 2000, and is known as Incoterms 2000.[8] It is substantially similar to the 1990 revision of Incoterms. These revisions of Incoterms have made the Incoterms definitions of commercial terms substantially different from the UCC definitions of similar terms.

§ 2.2 The Purpose of Commercial Terms

Where the goods are to be carried from one location to another as part of the sale transaction, the parties will often adopt a commercial

---

§ 2.1

1. *United Nations Convention on Contracts for the International Sale of Goods,* I.N. GAOR, U.N. DOC A/CONF.97/18 (1980), *reprinted in* 19 I.L.M. 671 (1980) [hereinafter CISG].

2. U.C.C. §§ 2–319 to–324.

3. CISG, *supra* note 1, art. 31. See discussion at § 1.14, supra.

4. *See* John Honnold, Uniform Law for Internation Sales Under the 1980 United Nations Convention ¶¶ 208, 211 (3d ed. 1999).

5. International Chamber of Commerce Incoterms 2000 (I.C.C. Publ. No. 560, 2000 Ed.) [Hereinafter Incoterms 2000].

6. Jan Ramberg, *Incoterms 1980, in* The Transnational Law of International Commercial Transactions 137 151 (Norbert Horn & Clive M. Schmitthoff eds., 1982); *see also* Texful Textile, Ltd. v. Cotton Express Textile, Inc., 891 F.Supp. 1381 (C.D.Cal.1995).

7. *See* Peter Winship, *Introduction* in Basic Instruments in International Economic Law, at 707 (Stephen Zamora & Ronald Brand eds., 1990).

8. Incoterms 2000, *supra* note 5.

term to state the delivery obligation of the seller. Such terms include F.O.B. (Free on Board), F.A.S. (Free Alongside) and C.I.F. (Cost, Insurance and Freight). These terms are defined in the UCC,[1] but the UCC definitions are seldom used intentionally in international trade. In fact, the UCC definitions are becoming obsolescent in domestic trade also, because the abbreviations used are now associated primarily with waterborne traffic, and the statutory terms do not include the new terminology associated with air freight, containerization, or multi-modal transportation practices.

In International commerce the dominant source of definitions for commercial delivery terms is "Incoterms," published by the International Chamber of Commerce (I.C.C.) and last revised by them in 2000.[2] Incoterms provides rules for determining the obligations of both seller and buyer when different commercial terms (like F.O.B. or C.I.F.) are used. They state what acts seller must do to deliver, what acts buyer must do to accommodate delivery, what costs each party must bear, and at what point in the delivery process the risk of loss passes from the seller to buyer. Each of these obligations may be different for different commercial terms. Thus, the obligations, costs, and risks of seller and buyer are different under F.O.B. than they are under C.I.F.

There are other sources of such definitions, in addition to the UCC and Incoterms, such as the American Revised Foreign Trade Definitions (1941).[3] It has been widely used in Pacific Ocean trade, but may be replaced by the more recently revised Incoterms.

B. INCOTERMS

§ 2.3 Incoterms as a Trade Usage

Since the I.C.C. is a non-governmental entity, Incoterms is neither a national legislation nor an international treaty. Thus, it cannot be "the governing law" of any contract. Instead, it is a written form of custom and usage in the trade, which can be, and often is, expressly incorporated by a party of the parties to an international contract for the sale of goods. Alternatively, if it is not expressly incorporated in the contract, Incoterms could be made an implicit term of the contract as part of international custom. Courts in France and Germany have done so, and both treatises and the UNCITRAL Secretariat describe Incoterms as a widely-observed usage for commercial terms.[1] This description should allow Incoterms to qualify under CISG Article 9(2) as a "usage . . . which in international trade is widely known to, and regularly observed by, parties to" international sales contracts, even if the usage is not

---

§ 2.2

1. *See,* e.g., U.C.C. §§ 2–319, 2–320.

2. *See* Incoterms 2000, § 2.1, note 5, *infra.*

3. Revised American Foreign Trade Definitions, *excerpted in* Andreas F. Lowenfeld,

International Private Trade ds–151–158 (1977).

§ 2.3

1. *See* Winship, *§ 2.1,*note 7, *supra* at 707–10.

global.[2]

Although the UCC has definitions for some commercial terms (e.g., F.O.B., F.A.S., C.I.F.), these definitions are expressly subject to "agreement otherwise."[3] Thus, an express reference to Incoterms will supercede the UCC provisions, and United States courts have so held.[4] Such incorporation by express reference is often made in American international sales contracts, especially in Atlantic Ocean trade. If there is no express term, and the UCC is the governing law rather than CISG, Incoterms can still be applicable as a "usage of trade" under the UCC.[5] The UCC criteria for such a usage is "a practice.... having such regularity of observance ... as to justify an expectation that it will be observed with respect to the transaction in question."[6] A usage need not be "universal" nor "ancient," just "currently observed by the great majority of decent dealers."[7]

§ 2.4 Categories of Commercial Terms

Incoterms gives the parties a menu of thirteen different commercial terms to describe the delivery obligations of the seller and the reciprocal obligations of the buyer to accommodate delivery. They include:

1) EXW (Ex Works)

2) FCA (Free Carrier)

3) FAS (Free Alongside Ship)

4) FOB (Free On Board)

5) CFR (Cost and Freight)

6) CIF (Cost, Insurance and Freight)

7) CPT (Carriage Paid To)

8) CIP (Carriage and Insurance Paid To)

9) DAF (Delivered at Frontier)

10) DES (Delivered Ex Ship)

11) DEQ (Delivered Ex Quay)

12) DDU (Delivered Duty Unpaid)

13) DDP (Delivered Duty Paid)

There are several types of divisions which one may make of these thirteen different terms. One is a division between the one term which does not assume that a carrier will be involved (EXW), and all the twelve other terms. A second division is between those six terms which require the involvement of water-borne transportation (FAS, FOB, CFR, CIF, DES and DEQ) and those six other terms which are applicable to any

2. CISG, art. 9(2), at 674.

3. U.C.C. §§ 2–319(1)(2), 2–320(2).

4. Phillips Puerto Rico Core, Inc. v. Tradax Petroleum Ltd., 782 F.2d 314 (2d Cir. 1985).

5. U.C.C. § 1–205(2).

6. U.C.C. § 1–205, cmt. 5; *see* Ramberg, *§ 2.1*, note 6, *supra.*

7. U.C.C. § 1–205, cmt. 5.

mode of transportation, including multi-modal transportation (FCA, CPT, CIP, DAF, DDU, and DDP). The UCC has none of the latter six terms, although the types of transactions they are designed for arise routinely, and can be handled under the UCC designations "F.O.B. place of shipment,"[1] "C. & F.", "C.I.F.,"[2] and "F.O.B. named place of destination."[3]

The twelve terms requiring transportation can also be divided into "shipment contract" terms (FCA, FAS, FOB, CFR, CIF, CPT, and CIP) and "destination contract" terms (DAF, DES, DEQ, DDU, and DDP.). The UCC and CISG both use this terminology.[4] The underlying concept is that, in shipment contracts seller puts the goods in the hands of a carrier and arranges for their transportation, but transportation is at buyer's risk and expense.[5] On the other hand, in destination contracts seller is responsible to put the goods in the hands of the carrier, arrange their transportation, and bear the cost and risk of transportation.[6] Unfortunately, many aspects of transportation usages have changed since 1952, and the UCC concepts do not always fit the practices now described in Incoterms.

The I.C.C. suggests that these thirteen commercial terms be divided into four principal categories, one for each of the different first letters of the constituent terms, E,F,C and D. The "E" term (EXW) is where the goods are made available to buyer, but use of a carrier is not expressly required. All other terms require the use of a carrier. The "F" terms (FCA, FAS, FOB) require seller only to assume the risks and costs to deliver the goods to a carrier, and to a carrier nominated by the buyer. The "C" terms require seller to assume the risks and costs to deliver the goods to a carrier, arrange and pay for the "main transportation" (and sometimes insurance), but without assuming additional risks due to post-shipment events. Thus, under "C" terms, seller bears risks until one point in the transportation (delivery to a carrier), but pays costs to a different point in the transportation (the agreed destination). The "D" terms (DAF, DES, DEQ, DDU and DDP) require the seller to deliver the goods to a carrier, arrange for their transportation, and assume the risks and costs until the arrival of the goods at an agreed country of destination.

§ 2.5   Revisions of Incoterms

Incoterms are periodically revised, lately about once every ten years. The last revision was in 2000 and is set forth in I.C.C. Publication 560. It has few changes from its immediately previous edition. The primary changes concern loading and unloading obligations under FCA, customs

§ 2.4

1. U.C.C. § 2–319(1)(a).

2. U.C.C. § 2–320(1)(2).

3. U.C.C. § 2–319(1)(b)

4. CISG, art. 31; U.C.C. §§ 2–504, 2–509.

5. U.C.C. § 2–504.

6. *See,* e.g., U.C.C. § 2–319(1)(b) ("F.O.B. place of destination" contracts).

clearance and duty obligations under FAS DEQ, and numerous wording changes to clarify various obligations.

The last significant revisions were in 1990 and are set forth in I.C.C. Publication No. 460.[1] In that 1990 revision, the I.C.C. included references to electronic messages and to new types of transport documents, such as air waybills, railway and road consignment notes, and "multimodal transport documents." The I.C.C. explained that these changes were needed because of "the increasing use of electronic data interchange (EDI)" and "changed transportation techniques," including "containers, multimodal transport and roll on-roll off traffic."[2]

However, other changes were made in the 1990 Revisions that were not explained. Many commercial delivery terms have incorporated payment and inspection obligations as part of their definitional scheme, particularly the concept of "payment against documents"[3] which precluded post-shipment inspection of the goods before payment. Under prior versions of Incoterms, these obligations and disabilities had been expressly stated in the definition of such terms as CIF and C & F.[4] In the 1990 and Revision of Incoterms, all references to payment terms and post-shipment inspection terms were deleted, leaving only a standard provision that buyer must pay for any *pre*-shipment inspection. These deletions were not explained in the 1990 Revisions, and are still omitted from the Incoterms 2000, without explanation.[5]

§ 2.6   The Format of Incoterms

The Incoterms 2000 obligations are arranged in a mirror-image format that sets forth the obligations of sellers and buyers in adjacent columns. Each column has numbered paragraphs, and each numbered paragraph refers to the comparable obligation of each party. The obligations covered include licenses and other formalities, contracts of carriage and insurance, physical delivery, risk of loss, division of costs, notices, transportation documents or equivalent electronic messages, and inspections.

Thus, the first set of paragraphs in the statement of rules for the interpretation of any Incoterm is a statement of the basic obligations of seller and buyer—to deliver the goods and a commercial invoice (or its electronic equivalent), and to pay the contract price. The second set of paragraphs allocates the responsibilities of the parties to procure export

---

§ 2.5

1. International Chamber of Commerce, Incoterms 1990 (I.C.C. Publ. No. 460, 1990 Ed.) [Hereinafter Incoterms 1990].

2. Incoterms 1990, *supra note*, at 6. *See also* Jan Ramberg, Guide to Incoterms 1990 (I.C.C. Publ. No. 461/90, 1991 & No. 505, 1996) for further explanation and elaboration on the use and meaning of the 1990 revision of Incoterms.

3. *See* Chapter 3.

4. *See* e.g., Incoterms 1980, CIF ¶ A1. "The buyer must: 1. Accept the documents when tendered * * * and pay the price as provided in the contract." The current version of this paragraph omits all reference to accepting documents and merely requires buyer to "pay the price."

5. Compare U.C.C. § 2–320(4). As to F.O.B. vessel and F.A.S. terms, see UCC § 2–319(4).

and import licenses and to carryout customs formalities. The third set of paragraphs allocates the responsibilities of the parties to arrange and pay for carriage and insurance during transportation of the goods. The fourth set of paragraphs specifies both the extent of seller's delivery obligation and buyer's obligation to take delivery. The fifth set of paragraphs specifies when the risk loss is transferred from the seller to the buyer.

The sixth set of paragraphs allocates the costs of transportation between the parties, including not only the freight and insurance costs already allocated in the third paragraph, but also loading costs and the administrative costs of customs clearance, even when no import duties are charged. The seventh set of paragraphs determines what notice each party must give to the others, when to give notice, and what each notice should say. The eight set of paragraphs specifies the type of transport document or other proof of delivery which seller must provide to buyer. The ninth set of paragraphs allocates who must pay the costs of packaging the goods, marking the packages, "checking operations" (measuring, weighing, counting), and any pre-shipment inspection. It does not, however, state when and whether buyer has a right to post-shipment inspection before paying for the goods. Finally, the tenth set of paragraphs sets forth miscellaneous obligations, such as duties of assistance and cooperation.

C. THE INDIVIDUAL TERMS OF INCOTERMS

§ 2.7 The Ex Works (EXW) Term

Under the Incoterms Ex Works (EXW) commercial term[1] (including Ex Factory and Ex Warehouse), the seller needs only to "tender" the goods to the buyer by placing them at buyer's disposal at a named place of delivery. Thus, seller has no obligation to deliver the goods to a carrier or to load the goods on any vehicle. Seller must also notify buyer when and where the goods will be tendered, but has no obligation to arrange for transportation or insurance. The risk of loss transfers to the buyer at the time the goods are placed at its disposal. Seller will normally provide a commercial invoice or its equivalent electronic message, but has no obligation to obtain a document of title or an export license. The Incoterms definition has no effect upon either payment or inspection obligations under the contract, except to require buyer to pay for any pre-shipment inspection. The Incoterms risk of loss provision is contrary to the default rules of both the UCC[2] and CISG,[3] which delay passing the risk until buyer's receipt of the goods, both because seller is more likely to have insurance and because seller has a greater ability to protect the goods.

§ 2.7

1. Incoterms 2000, § 2.1 note 5, *supra,* at 27–31.

2. UCC § 2–509(3).

3. CISG, art. 69(1).

§ 2.8   The Free Carrier (FCA) Term

Under the Incoterms Free Carrier (FCA) commercial term,[1] the seller is obligated to deliver the goods into the custody of a carrier, usually the first carrier in a multi-modal transportation scheme. The Incoterms definition of "carrier" includes freight forwarders. Seller has no obligation to pay for transportation costs or insurance. Usually the carrier will be named by, and arranged by, the buyer. However, seller "may" arrange transportation at buyer's expense if requested by the buyer, or if it is "commercial practice" for a seller to do so. But, even under such circumstances, seller may refuse to make such arrangements as long as it so notifies buyer. Even of seller does arrange transportation, it has no obligation to arrange for insurance coverage during transportation, and need only notify buyer "that the goods *have been* delivered into the custody of the carrier."[2] The risk of loss transfers to buyer upon delivery to the carrier, but buyer may not receive notice until after that time. The seller must provide a commercial invoice or its equivalent electronic message, any necessary export license, and usually a transport document that will allow buyer to take delivery—or an equivalent electronic data interchange message. The Incoterms definition has no provisions on either payment or post-shipment inspection terms under the contract.

§ 2.9   The Free Alongside Ship (FAS) Term

Under the Incoterms Free Alongside Ship (FAS) commercial term,[1] the seller is obligated to deliver the goods alongside a ship arranged for and named by the buyer at a named port of shipment. Thus, it is appropriate only for water-borne transportation, and seller must bear the costs and risks of inland transportation to the named port of shipment. Seller has no obligation to arrange transportation or insurance for the "main" (or water-borne) part of the carriage, but does have a duty to notify buyer "that the goods *have been delivered* alongside the named vessel."[2] The risk of loss will transfer to the buyer also at the time the goods are delivered alongside ship. Seller must provide a commercial invoice and usually a transport document that will allow buyer to take delivery, or the electronic equivalent of either. In a major change form prior versions of Incoterms, Incoterms 2000 requires seller to provide an export license, and to clear the goods for export from the place of delivery.[3] Seller must also pay any costs of export customs formalities and export taxes.

In addition, seller must provide packaging, to the extent it is customary to package the goods, marking, and checking operations. The latter include measuring, weighing, counting, and checking the quality of

§ 2.8

1. Incoterms 2000, § 2.1, note 5, *supra*, at 33–39.

2. *Id.*, at 36 (emphasis added).

§ 2.9

1. *Id.*, at 41–47.

2. *Id.*, at 44 (emphasis added).

3. Id. at ¶ A2.

the goods that are considered necessary for accomplishing delivery, but buyer must pay the cost of any pre-shipment inspection not required by the country of export.

The Incoterms 2000 Revision definition of FAS term has no provisions on either payment or post-shipment inspection terms under contract. However, in the prior 1980 version of Incoterms, the definition of FAS[4] did not provide that payment against documents was required in an FAS contract, while the 1980 Incoterms in its definitions of other commercial terms did contain such payment provisions.[5] Thus, it is more likely that the current version of Incoterms FAS is not intended to require payment against documents, to restrict inspection before payment, or to be used with negotiable bills of lading.

§ 2.10   The Free on Board (FOB) Term

Under the Incoterms Free on Board (FOB) commercial term,[1] the seller is obligated to deliver the goods on board a ship arranged for and named by the buyer at a named port of shipment. Thus, this term is also appropriate only for water-borne transportation, and seller must bear the costs and risks of inland transportation to the named port of shipment, and also of loading the goods on the ship (until "they have passed the ship's rail").[2] Seller has no obligation to arrange transportation or insurance, but does have a duty to notify buyer "that the goods *have been delivered* on board" the ship.[3] The risks of loss will transfer to the buyer also at the time the goods have "passed the ship's rail."[4] The seller must provide a commercial invoice, or its equivalent electronic message, any necessary export license, and usually a transport document that will allow buyer to take delivery—or an equivalent electronic data interchange message.[5] The seller must also provide an export license, and clear the goods for export from the place of delivery.[6] The seller must therefor pay any costs of customs formalities and export taxes.

In addition, the seller must provide all customary packaging and working, and pay for checking operations. The latter include measuring, weighing, counting, and checking of the goods considered necessary to accomplish delivery. However, buyer must pay the cost of any pre-shipment inspection not required by the country of export. The Incoterms definition has no provisions on either payment or post-shipment inspection terms under the contract.

---

4. International Chamber of Commerce, Incoterms: International Rules for the Interpretation of Trade Terms (I.C.C. Publ. No. 350, "FAS," 1980 Ed.) [Hereinafter Incoterms 1980].

    5. *Id.*, "CIF" ¶ A1, "C & F" ¶ A1.

§ 2.10

1. Incoterms 2000, § 2.1, note 5, *supra,* at 49–55

    2. *Id.*, at 50, ¶ A5

3. *Id.*, at 51 (emphasis added).

4. *Id.*, at 51.

5. For a more detailed analysis of the F.O.B. and FOB terms, see A. Frecom, *Practical Considerations in Drafting F.O.B. Terms in International Sales,* 3 Int'l Tax & Bus. Law 346 (1986).

6. Incoterms 2000, § 2.1, note 5, *supra,* at 51.

§ 2.11   The Cost, Insurance and Freight (CIF) Term

Under the Incoterms Cost, Insurance and Freight (CIF) commercial term,[1] the seller is obligated to arrange for both transportation and insurance to a named destination port and then to deliver the goods on board the ship arranged for by the seller. Thus, the term is appropriate only for water-borne transportation. Seller must arrange the transportation, and pay the freight costs to the *destination port*, but has completed its delivery obligations when the goods are "on board the vessel at the port of shipment." The seller must pay the freight and unloading costs of the carrier at the destination port under the CIF term, but the buyer must pay all other costs, including unloading costs not collected by the carrier. However, demurrage charges for the cost of docking the ship longer than agreed are to be borne by the party causing the delay.[2]

Significant litigation has arisen when the CIF contract specifies the arrival date at the port of destination. The U.S. courts have held that, since the 1980 Incoterms C & F was a shipment contract, the seller's obligations were fulfilled when the carrier took delivery of the goods. Thus, the buyer could not specify an arrival or delivery date after the sale contract has been formed.[3] If a CIF contract specifies an arrival or delivery date rather than a shipment date, the British decisions are split. One case held that, under an Incoterms CIF contract which specified a delivery date, the buyer could calculate an "appropriate latest delivery date," and that the seller is then entitled to calculate a "late date for loading" the goods on board the carrier. As long as the seller met that loading date, it was not liable for the carrier's subsequent late delivery to the port of destination, since seller's duties were completed upon a timely loading of the goods and notification to the buyer.[4] However, another court has held that a delivery date term is not inconsistent with Incoterms CIF. The court rejected an interpretation of CIF that requires the seller only to deliver to carrier and thereafter the risk of delay is on the buyer.[5]

The seller must arrange and pay for insurance during transportation to the *port of destination*, but the risk of loss transfers to the buyer at the time the goods "pass the ship's rail" at the *port of shipment*. The buyer bears the risk of damages that occur to the goods during transit, even though the seller has a duty to procure insurance against such risks.[6] Seller must notify buyer "that the goods have been delivered on

§ 2.11

1. Incoterms 2000, § 2.1, note 5, *supra*, at 66–71.

2. *In re* Commonwealth Oil Refining Co., 734 F.2d 1079 (5th Cir.1984).

3. Phillips Puerto Rico Core, Inc. v. Tradax Petroleum Ltd., 782 F.2d 314 (2d Cir. 1985).

4. P & O Oil Trading Ltd. v. Scanoil AB, [1985] 1 Lloyd's Rep. 389 (Q.B. 1984).

5. CEP Interagra SA v. Select Energy Trading, GmbH (Q.B. 1990), LEXIS, UK Library, Engcas File.

6. Establissements El Hadj Ousmanou Chetima risk of loss issues under Incoterms, see Daniel E. Murray, *Risk of Loss of Goods in Transit: A Comparison of the 1990 Incoterms with Terms from Other Voices,* 23 U. Miami Inter–Am. L. Rev. 93 (1991).

board" the ship to enable buyer to receive the goods.[7] Seller must provide a commercial invoice, or its equivalent electronic message, any necessary export license, and "the usual transport documents" for the destination port. Under the 1980 Incoterms, the transportation document was required to be a "clean negotiable bill of lading" and "a full set of 'on board' or 'shipped' bills of lading."[8] There is no such specification in the current revision of Incoterms, however. The stated purpose of the deletion was to allow for the development of electronic substitutes for such documents.

The Incoterms definition has no provisions on either payment or post-shipment inspection terms under the contract. However, it does require that the transportation document "must ... enable the buyer to sell the goods in transit by the transfer of the document to a subsequent buyer ... or by notification to the carrier," unless otherwise agreed.[9] As is explained below,[10] the traditional manner of enabling buyer to do this, in either the "payment against documents" transaction or the letter of credit transaction, is for seller to obtain a negotiable bill of lading from the carrier and to tender that negotiable document to buyer through a series of banks. The banks allow buyer to obtain possession of the document (and control of the goods) only after buyer pays for goods. Thus, buyer "pays against documents," while the goods are at sea, and pays for them before any post-shipment inspection of the goods is possible. This transaction should still be regarded as the norm under Incoterms CIF, and the definition of the term in the 2000 version does refer to the use of a negotiable bill of lading.

The 1980 version of Incoterms was more precise on these obligations, requiring buyer to "accept the documents when tendered by the seller ... and pay the price as provided in the contract."[11] The implication from this provision, as explained above, was that buyer had no right to inspect the goods before this payment against documents. However, ambiguity is introduced in the Incoterms 2000 CIF definition, because it also refers to the use of nonnegotiable documents as well.[12] On the other hand, the ICC's Introduction to the 1990 Incoterms recognized that the use of nonnegotiable documents is inappropriate in a "payment against documents" situation and thus would not "enable the buyer to sell the goods in transit by surrendering the paper document" to the sub-buyer.[13] The introduction then explains that sometimes the parties "may specifi-

7. Incoterms 2000, § 2.1 note 5, *supra*, at 68.

8. Incoterms 1980, § 2.9, note 4, *supra*, "CIF" ¶ A7. Under the 1953 Incoterms, a "clean negotiable bill of lading for the port of destination" was required. *In re* Commonwealth Oil Refining Co., 734 F.2d 1079 (5th Cir.1984); *cf.* Concord Petroleum Corp. v. Gosford Marine Panama S.A. ("The Albazero"), [1974] 2 Lloyd's Rep. 38 (Q.B.) (title to goods covered by a bill of lading issued to seller's order passes when the bill of lading is endorsed and mailed to buyer).

9. Incoterms 2000, § 2.1, note 5, *supra*, at 70.

10. *See* Chapter 3 on bills of lading and Chapter 6 on documentary letters of credit.

11. Incoterms 1980, § 2.9, note 4, *supra*, "CIF" ¶ B1. So held in Phillips Puerto Rico Core, Inc. v. Tradax Petroleum Ltd., 782 F.2d 314 (2d Cir.1985) (C & F contract).

12. Incoterms 1990, § 2.5, note 5, *supra*, at 54, 15.

13. *Id.*, at 15.

cally agree to relieve the seller from" providing a negotiable document when they "know that the buyer does not contemplate selling the goods in transit."[14] The 2000 Incoterms does not have any provisions on when title to the goods passes from the seller to the buyer.[15] Thus, when title issues arise the courts must turn to the applicable law of sales or of personal property for governing provisions.[16]

§ 2.12   The Cost and Freight (CFR) Term

The Incoterms Cost and Freight (CFR) commercial term[1] is similar to the CIF term, except that seller has no obligations with respect to either arranging or paying for insurance coverage of the goods during transportation. Under the CFR term, the seller is obligated to arrange for transportation to a named destination point and then to deliver the goods on board the ship arranged for by the seller. Thus, the term is appropriate only for water-borne transportation. Seller must arrange the transportation and pay the freight costs to the *destination port*, but has completed its delivery obligations when the goods are "on board the vessel" at the *port of shipment*.[2] The seller has no express obligation to arrange or pay for insurance on the goods during transportation, and the risk of loss transfers to the buyer at the time the goods "pass the ship's rail" at the *port shipment*. Seller must notify buyer "that the goods *have been delivered* on board" the ship to enable buyer to receive the goods.[3] The seller must also provide an export license, and clear the goods for export from the place of delivery. The seller must therefore pay any costs of customs formalities and export taxes.

The seller must provide a commercial invoice, or its equivalent electronic message, any necessary export license, and "the usual transport document" for the destination port.[4] In addition the seller must provide all customary packaging and marking, and pay for checking operations. The latter include measuring, counting, weighing and checking of the quality of the goods considered necessary to accomplish delivery. However, the buyer must pay the cost of any pre-shipment inspection not required by the country of export. As with CIF, the Incoterms CFR definition has no provisions on either payment or post-shipment inspection terms under the contract. However, it does require that the transport document "must ... enable the buyer to sell the goods in transit by the transfer of the document to a subsequent buyer,"[5] which had traditionally meant use of a negotiable bill of lading

---

14. *Id.*

15. Texful Textile Ltd. v. Cotton Express Textile, Inc., 891 F.Supp. 1381 (C.D.Cal.1995).

16. *Id.* The court used U.C.C. §§ 2–511 and 4–401 to resolve the issues. *See also* L. Galler, *An Historical and Policy Analysis of the Title Passage Rule inn International Sales of Personal Property*, 52 U. Pitt. L. Rev. 521 (1991).

§ 2.12

1. Incoterms 2000, § 2.1, note 5, *supra*, at 58–63.

2. *Id* at 58 (emphasis added).

3. *Id.* at 60 (emphasis added).

4. *Id.*

5. *Id.* at 60.

and payment against documents. Prior versions of Incoterms regarded this term as requiring payment against documents while the goods were still at sea, thus restricting port-shipment inspection of the goods before payment.[6] These provisions should still be regarded as the norm under Incoterms CFR.

§ 2.13 The Carriage and Insurance Paid to (CIP) Term

The Incoterms Carriage and Insurance Paid To (CIP)[1] commercial term is similar to the CIF term, except that it may be used for any type of transportation, including multimodal transportation, and not just for waterborne transportation. Under the CIP term, seller is obligated to arrange and pay for both transportation and insurance to a named *destination* place. However, seller completes its delivery obligations, and the risk of loss passes to the buyer, upon delivery to the first carrier at the place of shipment. The term is appropriate for multimodal transportation. Where more than one carrier is used, delivery is accomplished and the risk of loss passes, when the goods are delivered to the first "carrier." That "carrier" may be a freight forwarder under the I.C.C. definition of "carrier."

The insurance need be only on the minimum cover of the Cargo Clauses of the Institute of London Underwriters unless the parties expressly agree greater cover.[2] However, since CIP is often used for manufactured goods, and minimum cover is not appropriate for such goods, the CIP term should be used only when the buyer and the seller have communicated about the provision of additional cover (at buyer's expense), or buyer should procure additional cover, but not both.

Under the term, seller must notify buyer "that the goods have been delivered" to the first carrier, and also give any other notice required to enable buyer "to take the goods."[3] Seller must also provide a commercial invoice, or its equivalent electronic message, and "the usual transport document."[4] A list of acceptable transport documents is given, including a negotiable bill of lading and non-negotiable waybills and documents, but there is no requirement that the document enable buyer to sell the goods in transit.[5] The seller must also provide an export license, and clear the goods for export from the place of delivery. The seller must therefore pay any costs of export customs formalities and export taxes.

In addition, the seller must provide all customary packaging and marking, and pay for checking operations. The latter include measuring, counting, weighing, and any checking of the quality of the goods considered necessary to accomplish delivery. However, the buyer must pay the cost of any pre-shipment inspection not required by the country of export. There are no payment or post-shipment inspection provisions in

---

6. Incoterms 1980, § 2.9, note 4, *supra,* "C & F" ¶ B1.

§ 2.13

1. Incoterms 2000, § 2.1, note 5, *supra,* at 81–87

2. *Id.,* at 82.

3. *Id.,* at 84

4. *Id.,* at 86.

5. *Id.*

the Incoterms definitions. Further, the Introduction to the prior 1990 revision of Incoterms contrasted CIP with CIF, indicating that there is no requirement to provide a negotiable bill of lading under a CIP term.[6] Thus, unless the parties expressly agree to a "payment against documents" terms, it is more likely that the CIP commercial term is not, by itself, intended to require payment against documents or to restrict inspection before payment.

§ 2.14   The Carriage Paid to (CPT) Term

The Incoterms Carriage Paid to (CPT)[1] commercial term is similar to the CFR term, except that it may be used for any type of transportation, including multimodal transportation, and not just for waterborne transportation. Under the CPT term, the seller is obligated to arrange and pay for transportation to a named *destination* place. However, the seller completes its delivery obligations, and the risk of loss passes to the buyer, upon delivery to the carrier at the place of *shipment*. The term is appropriate for multimodal transportation. Where more than one carrier is used, delivery is accomplished, and the risk of loss passes, when the goods are delivered to the first "carriers." That "carrier" may be a freight forwarder under the I.C.C. definition. The CPT commercial term is similar to the CIP term, except that the seller had no duty to arrange or pay for insurance coverage of the goods during transportation.

Under CPT term, the seller must notify the buyer "that the goods have been delivered" to the first carrier and also give any other notice required to enable the buyer "to take the goods."[2] The seller must also provide a commercial invoice, or its equivalent electronic message, any necessary export license, and "the usual transport document."[3] A list of acceptable transport documents if given, and there is no requirement that the document enable the buyer to sell the goods in transit.[4] There are no payment or post-shipment inspection provisions in the Incoterms definitions. Further, the Introduction to the prior 1990 revision of Incoterms contrasts CPT with CFR, indicating that there is no requirement to provide a negotiable bill of lading under a CPT term.[5] Thus, unless the parties expressly agree to a "payment against documents" term, it is more likely that the CPT commercial term is not intended to require payment against documents or to restrict inspection before payment.

§ 2.15   Destination Terms

Incoterms provides five different commercial terms for "destination" or "arrival" contracts. Two of them, Delivered Ex Ship (DES)[1] and

---

6. Incoterms 1990, § 2.5, note 1, *supra,* at 15.

§ 2.14

1. Incoterms 2000, § 2.1, note 5, *supra,* at 73–79.

2. *Id.,* at 76

3. *Id.*

4. *Id.*

5. 1990 Incoterms, § 2.5, note 1, *supra,* at 15.

§ 2.15

1. Incoterms 2000, § 2.1, note 5, *supra,* at 97–103.

Delivered Ex Quay (DEQ)[2] should only be used for waterborne transportation. The other three, Delivered At Frontier (DAF)[3] Delivered Duty Unpaid (DDU)[4] and Delivered Duty Paid (DDP),[5] can all be used with any type of transportation, including multimodal transport. In all of them, seller is required to arrange transportation, pay the freight costs and bear the risk of loss to a named destination point. Although these definitions have no provisions on insurance during transportation, since seller bears the risk of loss during that event, seller must either arrange and pay for insurance or act as a self-insuror during transportation. There are also no provisions on payment or post-shipment inspection, but there is no requirement for use of negotiable bill of lading, and delivery occurs only after arrival of the goods. Thus, there is no reason to imply a "payment against documents" requirement if none is expressly stated. On the other hand, the parties are free to agree expressly on both a destination commercial term and a payment against documents term, if they so desire.

§ 2.16 The Delivery Ex Ship (DES) Term

The DES commercial term is appropriate only for water-borne transportation. Under the Incoterms DES commercial term, delivery occurs and the risk of loss passes when the goods are placed at buyer's disposal on board ship at the named destination port.[1] Thus, seller both arranges and pays for both transportation costs and any necessary insurance to the port of destination. To be "at buyer's disposal," the goods must be placed (at seller's risk and expense) so that they can be removed by "appropriate" unloading equipment. However, the goods need not be cleared for importation by customs officials; that is buyer's obligation. In DES shipments, seller must notify buyer of the estimated time of arrival of a named vessel at a named destination port. Also, in such shipments, seller must provide buyer with a commercial invoice or the equivalent electronic message and, "a delivery order and/or the usual transport document."[2] The documents listed include the negotiable bill of lading and non-negotiable waybills and documents. The seller must also provide an export license from the place of delivery. The seller must therefore pay any costs of export customs formalities and export taxes. However, the goods need not be cleared for importation by customs officials; that is buyer's obligation. In DES Shipments, the seller has no duty to provide an import license, unless otherwise agreed.

In addition, the seller must provide all customary packaging and marking, and pay for checking operations. The latter include measuring, counting, weighing and any checking of the quality of the goods considered necessary to accomplish delivery. However, the buyer must pay the

2. *Id.*, at 105–111.

3. *Id.*, 89–95.

4. *Id.*, 113–119.

5. *Id.*, 121–125.

§ 2.16

1. *Id.*, at 98.

2. *Id.*, at 98.

cost of any pre-shipment inspection not required by the country of export.[3]

§ 2.17   The Delivery Ex Quay (DEQ) Term

The Incoterms DEQ commercial term is appropriate only for water-borne transportation. Under the DEQ commercial term, delivery occurs when the goods are placed at buyer's disposal on the quay or wharf at the named destination port.[1] Thus, seller both arranges and pays for both transportation and any necessary insurance to the port destination. To accomplish delivery, seller must place the goods "at the disposal of the buyer on the quay (wharf)."[2] The designation of the particular quay may be agreed by the parties, determined by practice, or selected by the seller. The risk of loss passes from the seller to the buyer when the goods are at buyer's disposal on the quay.

In DEQ shipments, the seller must notify the buyer of the estimated time of arrival of a named vessel at a named destination port. Also, in DEQ shipments, the seller must provide the buyer with a commercial invoice or the equivalent electronic message, a "delivery order and/or the usual transport document."[3] The latter can be negotiable bill of lading or a non-negotiable waybill or document. The seller must also provide an export license, and clear the goods for export from the place of delivery. The seller must therefore pay any costs of export customs formalities and export taxes. However, the seller is not responsible for clearing the goods for import at the destination port or for paying import duties or taxes.[4] Clearing the goods for importation and paying import duties are now the buyer's responsibilities under DEQ. This is revision of prior interpretations of the DEQ term under prior versions of Incoterms[5]. Under those prior versions of Incoterms, the parties who used a DEQ term were supposed to specify either "Duty Paid" or "Duty Unpaid," because both DEQ (Duty Paid) and DEQ (Duty Unpaid) terms were in use. If "Duty Paid" was specified, or there was no specification, seller must "pay the costs of customs formalities ... duties, taxes ... payable upon ... importation of goods, unless otherwise agreed."[6] However, this election is no longer relevant under Incoterms 2000.

In addition, the seller must provide all customary packaging and marking, and pay for checking operations. The latter include measuring, counting, weighing and any checking of teh quality of the goods considered necessary to accomplish delivery. However, the buyer must pay the cost of any pre-shipment inspection not required by the country of export.

3. *Id.*, at 100.

§ 2.17

1. *Id.*, 108.
2. *Id.* at 106.
3. *Id.*, at 108.

4. *Id.*, at 108.

5. Incoterms 1990, § 2.5, note 1, *supra*, at 82

6. See e.g., Incoterms 1990, § 2.5, note 1, *supra*, at 82.

§ 2.18 The Delivery at Frontier (DAF) Term

The Incoterms DAF commercial term is most appropriately used with rail or road transportation. Under the DAF term delivery occurs when the goods are placed at the buyer's disposal at a named place at the frontier, but they need not be unloaded from the carrier.[1] A further designation of the particular frontier, and the particular place on a specified frontier, is crucial to the use of this term. The "frontier" can be that of the country of export, the country of destination, or some intermediate frontier.[2] It may also refer to a geographical frontier or the customs frontier of a country. However, once a particular point or place is designated, the term has great flexibility, because it *can* be used for any mode of transportation, including air and water-borne. Further, the parties can agree and specify in the contract, as a variant of the DAF term, that seller is responsible for unloading the goods, with its associated risks and costs.

In the absence of agreement, the risk of loss is upon the seller until the goods reach the designated point on the designated "frontier," but the risk of loss then passes to buyer upon arrival, without unloading. If the parties do not designate a destination point, it may be determined by custom; otherwise, seller may select the destination point unilaterally. The seller must arrange and pay for transportation to the frontier, and provide any necessary insurance. At the buyer's request, the seller may also contract for on-going transportation from the frontier to the final destination.[3] The seller must notify the buyer "of the dispatch of the goods." If such a notice would come to the buyer too late for buyer to arrange for delivery and on-going transport, then the seller must also send a notice of proposed dispatch to the buyer with sufficient time to make such arrangements.[4]

The seller must provide the buyer with a commercial invoice or the electronic equivalent and "the usual document or other evidence of the delivery" such as a delivery order.[5] The seller must also provide an export license, and clear the goods for export from both the place of delivery and any other country transited before the designated frontier. The seller must therefore pay any costs of customs formalities and export taxes in all such countries, but the seller has no duty with respect to import formalities or costs.

In addition, the seller must provide all customary packaging and marking, and pay for checking operations. The latter include measuring, counting, weighing and any checking of the quality of the goods considered necessary to accomplish delivery. However, the buyer must pay the cost of any pre-shipment inspection not required by the country of export.[6]

§ 2.18

1. Incoterms 2000, § 2.1, note 5, *supra*, at 90–92.

2. *Id.*, at 89.

3. *Id.*, at 90.

4. *Id.*, at 92.

5. *Id.*, at 94.

6. *Id.*, at 94–95.

§ 2.19   The Delivery Duty Unpaid (DDU) Term

The Incoterms DDU commercial term may be used with any mode of transportation, including multimodal. Under the DDU commercial term, delivery occurs when the goods are placed at buyer's disposal "on any arriving means of transport, not unloaded, at the named point of destination" in the country of importation.[1] The risk of loss is upon the seller until the goods arrive at the designated destination point, but it then passes to the buyer upon arrival, without unloading. If the parties do not designate a destination point, it may be determined by custom; otherwise, the seller may select the destination point unilaterally. The seller must arrange and pay for transportation to the destination point, and any necessary insurance. The seller must notify the buyer "of the dispatch of the goods."[2] If such a notice would come to the buyer too late for the buyer to arrange to take delivery, the seller must also send a notice of proposed dispatch to the buyer with sufficient time to make such arrangements.

The seller must also provide a commercial invoice or its electronic equivalent and the "delivery order and/or the usual transport document."[3] The latter can be a negotiable bill of lading or a non-negotiable waybill or document. The seller must also provide an export license, and clear the goods for export from the place of delivery. The seller must therefore pay any costs of export customs formalities and export taxes.[4] However, seller has no obligation to pay import duties or charges, unless the contract of sale expressly requires the seller to carry out some of the customs formalities.[5]

In addition, the seller must provide all customary packaging an marking, and pay for checking operations. The latter include measuring, counting, weighing, and any checking of the quality of the goods considered necessary to accomplish delivery. However, the buyer must pay the cost of any pre-shipment inspection not required by the country of export.[6]

§ 2.20   The Delivery Duty Paid (DDP) Term

The Incoterms DDP commercial term may be used with any mode of transportation including multimodal. Under the Incoterms DDP commercial term, delivery occurs when the goods are placed at buyer's disposal on any arriving means of transport not unloaded a the named place in the country of destination, cleared for importation into that country. Seller must pay all import duties and charges and complete all customs formalities at its risk and expense.[1] The risk of loss is upon the seller until the goods arrive at the designated destination point, but it

§ 2.19

1. *Id.*, at 114.
2. *Id.*, at 116.
3. *Id.*
4. *Id.*, at 116–117.

5. *Id.*, at 113.
6. *Id.*, at 122.

§ 2.20

1. *Id.*, at 122

passes to the buyer upon arrival, without unloading. If the parties do not designate a destination point, it may be determined by custom, otherwise, the seller may select the destination point unilaterally. The seller must arrange and pay for transportation to the destination point, and any necessary insurance. The seller must notify "of the dispatch of the goods."[2] If such a notice would come to the buyer too late for the buyer to arrange to take delivery of the goods, the seller must also send a notice of proposed dispatch to the buyer with sufficient time to make such arrangements.

The seller must also provide a commercial invoice or its equivalent electronic message and delivery order "and/or" the usual transport document.[3] The latter can be a negotiable bill of lading or a non-negotiable waybill or document. The seller must also provide an export license and clear the goods both for export from the place of shipment and for import into the country if destination.[4] The seller must therefore pay any costs of customs formalities and taxes in both the countries of export and import. However, a known variant is for the seller, which is bearing the costs of tariff duties and customs formalities, to be relieved of other taxes, such as value added tax, which are to be borne by the buyer. Such a division of costs, if applicable, must be expressly stated in the sale contract.[5]

In addition, the seller must provide all customary packaging an marking, and pay for checking operations. The latter include measuring, counting, weighing, and any checking of the quality of the goods considered necessary to accomplish delivery. However, the buyer must pay the cost of any pre-shipment inspection not required by the country of export.[6]

§ 2.21 Interpretation of Gaps in Incoterms

The deletions of the payment terms in the 1990 and 2000 Revisions of Incoterms leave a gap that must be filled from some other source of information. There are at least three sources of such information. One such source of payment and inspection terms is the prior versions of Incoterms, such as the 1980 Revisions, that included definitions which did include terms on payment and inspection.[1] The definitions in the 1990 Revision of Incoterms refer to "the usual transport document,"[2] and it can be argued that this reference incorporated the standards established in definitions from prior versions. Further, the deletions are not explained, except to indicate a desire not to impede the introduction of the use of EDI messages to handle transportation arrangements. On the other hand, the 1990 and 2000 Revisions establish several new terms, for which this approach will be ambiguous; and this approach,

2. *Id.*, at 124.
3. *Id.*, at 122.
4. *Id.*, at 124.
5. *Id.*, at 121.
6. *Id.*, at 124–25.

§ 2.21

1. Incoterms 1980, § 2.9, note 4, *supra* .

2. Incoterms 2000, § 2.1, note 5, *supra*, ¶ A8, at 46, 5.

over time, could be used to impede the use of EDI technology. However, some carryover use of such payment and inspection terms should be expected.

A second source of payment and inspection terms is national law, such as the UCC. In Sections 2–319 to 2–323, the UCC provides "default rules" for a number of commercial terms.[3] Under prior versions of Incoterms, these default rules were not applicable if the parties selected Incoterms, because the parties had "agreed otherwise." Now, however, that analysis may no longer stand. The parties have agreed that Incoterms will pre-empt UCC terms, where applicable; but Incoterms no longer has payment and inspection provisions, so the payment and inspection provisions of the UCC definitions may no longer be pre-empted. There are difficulties with this analytical approach. One is that many of the Incoterms commercial terms no longer correspond to their UCC namesakes.[4] A second is that the parties, by nominating Incoterms, may have intended to bypass all aspects of the statutory definitions and instead substitute definitions provided by custom and usage. Nevertheless, some use of the UCC and other definitions from national law should be expected, as a source of information to resolve the legal issues created by the deletion of the payment and inspection provisions in the Incoterms definitions.

If neither prior versions of Incoterms nor specific definitions in national law are deemed to be acceptable sources of information, then the general provisions of national law, whether contained in the UCC or CISG, give virtually no provisions for interpretation of the commercial terms, except to allow a court to consult customs and usage of trade. Custom and usage therefore can be a third source of such terms.[5] However, custom and usage must be proven as matters of fact, usually by expert testimony; and the proof must surmount several legal hurdles to be accepted by a court. And the use of experts and surmounting of legal hurdles was exactly what the parties thought they were avoiding by incorporating Incoterms into their contract. It is possible that those expectations may now be violated, at least as to payment and inspection terms. Thus, use of Incoterms definitions may subject the users to problems of proof of custom and usage that may not arise for the UCC definitions.

D.   CISG, THE UCC AND INCOTERMS

§ 2.22   Comparison of Incoterms with UCC and CISG

The CISG has no commercial terms which would compete with the terms of Incoterms. It does however create minimum default obligations for delivery for seller[1] and the passing of risk of loss.[2] These obligations

---

3. UCC §§ 2–319 to 2–323.

4. *See* §§ 1.23, 1.25 and 1.27, below.

5. *See,* e.g., UCC §§ 1–205, 2–208; (ISG), *supra* note 1, art. 9.

§ 2.22

1. CISG art. 31.

are comparable to, but different from, the Incoterms EXW Term. The UCC also provides minimum default obligations concerning delivery[3] and the passing of the risk of loss,[4] which also are comparable to, but different from, the Incoterms EXW term.

The UCC also has competing definitions of some commercial terms, F.O.B., F.A.S., C. & F., and C.I.F.[5] These definitions date from 1952, and are now in many ways different from the more modern definitions in Incoterms 2000. Perhaps more importantly, there are many new commercial terms in Incoterms 2000 which are not found in the UCC—FCA, CPT, CIP, DAF, DES, DEQ, DDU, DDP. The absence of these provisions from the UCC does not necessarily mean that the UCC does not cover the concepts embodied in them. Instead, it means that many of these concepts are covered by current UCC terms, but they are covered by a term using a different name than that used by Incoterms. Further, a current UCC term may not be applicable to a transaction covered by an Incoterm commercial term with a corresponding name. This difference of definitions creates many conflicts and confusions.[6]

§ 2.23   The EXW Term and Default Rules under CISG and UCC

Under the Incoterms Ex Works (EXW) commercial term (including Ex Factory and Ex Warehouse), the seller needs only to "tender" the goods to the buyer by placing them at the buyer's disposal at a named place of delivery and notifying the buyer of the time and place where the goods will be at its disposal. Thus, the seller has no obligation to deliver the goods to a carrier or to load the goods on any vehicle.[1] The risk of loss transfers to the buyer at the time the goods are placed at its disposal. Further, the seller has no obligation to arrange transportation of the goods; and if the seller does arrange transportation of the goods, it has no obligation to arrange for insuring the goods during transportation. The seller must provide a commercial invoice, but has no obligation to provide any transportation document.

The CISG default term on seller's delivery obligation is bifurcated, depending upon whether the contract involves carriage of the goods by a third party or not. EXW can cover both situations, although its preferred use seems to be for transactions in which third party carriers are not involved.[2] If the contract of sale does not involve the carriage of the goods, the CISG default rule is that seller's delivery obligation is completed when the goods are placed at the buyer's disposal at seller's place

---

2. CISG art. 67, 69.

3. UCC §§ 2–503, 2–504.

4. UCC § 2–509

5. UCC §§ 2–319, 2–320.

6. For further discussion of this point, and recommendations to the committee revising UCC Article 2, *see* Spanogle, Inco-

terms and UCC Article 2—Conflicts and Confusions, 31 Int'l Lawyer III (1997).

§ 2.23

1. See § 2.6, *supra*.

2. Incoterms 2000, § 2.1, *supra* note 5, at 27.

of business.[3] However, that the risk of loss does not pass to buyer until the buyer "takes over the goods," or until the buyer is in breach of the contract for failing to take delivery.[4] CISG is silent concerning notice, arrangements for transportation or insurance during transportation, commercial invoices, and transportation documents.

If the contract of sale does involve the carriage of goods, but no commercial term is used ("ship them by air"), the CISG default rule requires the seller to hand the goods "over to the first carrier."[5] In such cases CISG requires the seller to notify the buyer only if "the goods are not clearly identified to the contract by markings on the goods, by shipping documents or otherwise."[6] The risk of loss passes when "the goods are handed over to the first carrier,"[7] and they are also "clearly identified to the contract" by markings, documents, or notice to the buyer.[8] CISG is otherwise silent concerning arrangements for transportation, commercial invoices and transportation documents. However, if the seller is required to arrange transportation (for example, by industry practice), it must make a contract which has the "usual terms for such transportation."[9] That concept will often require the seller to also arrange for insurance during transportation of the goods. If the seller does not arrange for insurance during transportation, at the buyer's request, the seller must provide "all available information necessary" for the buyer to obtain such insurance.[10]

The UCC default term on seller's delivery obligation is also bifurcated, and depends upon whether delivery by carrier is "required or authorized by the agreement."[11] If delivery by carrier is not part of agreement, the UCC default rule is that the seller's delivery obligation is completed when the seller "puts and holds conforming goods at the buyer's disposition,"[12] usually at the seller's place of business,[13] and notifies the buyer that the goods are at its disposition.[14] The goods must be tendered "at a reasonable hour" and kept available for a reasonable period of time.[15] However, the risk of loss does not pass until the buyer "receives" the goods,[16] not upon mere tender of delivery. In such situations, the UCC is silent concerning arrangements for transportation, commercial invoices and transportation documents.

Thus, where a third party carrier is not involved, both CISG and the UCC also delay the time when the risks of loss passes from buyer to seller. Such risk passes to the buyer only when buyer "receives" or "takes over" the goods, not upon mere tender of delivery. The reasons

3. CISG art. 31 (c).
4. CISG art. 69.
5. CISG art. 31 (a)
6. CISG art. 32 (a)
7. CISG art. 67 (1)
8. CISG art. 67 (2)
9. CISG art. 32 (2).
10. CISG art. 32 (3).
11. UCC § 2–308, cmt. 1.
12. UCC § 2–503 (1).

13. UCC § 2–308 (a). But see, the special rules for "identified goods" known to be held at a different location under UCC § 2–308 (b).
14. UCC § 2–503 (1).
15. UCC § 2–503 (1)(a).
16. UCC § 2–509 (3). The UCC rule is limited to merchant sellers, but CISG is limited to commercial sales, CISG art. 2 (a).

given for this delay is that a merchant seller is more likely to have insurance covering the goods still in its possession than a buyer is to have insurance covering incoming, undelivered goods.[17] Also, the seller is still in control of such goods, and therefore has a greater ability to arrange adequate protection of them. The Incoterms EXW terms turns this philosophy upside-down without explanation.

If a third party carrier is involved, the UCC requires the seller to arrange for transportation[18] and usually for insurance,[19] as is explained more fully below.[20]

§ 2.24   The UCC "F.O.B. Place of Shipment" Term

The UCC does define "F.O.B.,"[1] but it is not a term requiring water-borne transportation. Further, the use of "F.O.B." in the UCC context is determinative of very little, because the UCC permits use of both "F.O.B. place of shipment"[2] and "F.O.B. place of destination."[3] The latter is more comparable to the Incoterms DDU term, and will be discussed below.[4]

The FCA term is the Incoterms commercial term which is most comparable to the UCC's "F.O.B. place of shipment" term under UCC § 2–319(1)(a). However, there are two levels of confusion. One is that Incoterms has an "FOB" term which is different,[5] and the UCC "F.O.B." term is more likely to be compared with the Incoterms "FOB" term. The other is that the obligations under FCA and the UCC "F.O.B. place of shipment" term are, in fact, different. The norm under the UCC's "F.O.B." is for seller to arrange transportation, while seller need do so under FCA only in special circumstances.[6] Further, if seller does ship, under the UCC seller usually must also arrange insurance coverage, unless instructed otherwise by buyer.[7] Under Incoterms FCA, seller does not seem ever to have any obligation to arrange for insurance coverage. Under the UCC "F.O.B. place of shipment" term, there is no implied special payment or inspection terms, no implied requirement of payment against documents or payment before inspection. This would also seem to be a preferable interpretation of the current Incoterms FCA term.

§ 2.25   The UCC "F.A.S. Vessel" Term

Under the UCC, the term "F.A.S. vessel"[1] requires the buyer to pay against a tender of documents, such as a negotiable bill of lading, before

---

17. UCC § 2–509, cmt. 3.

18. UCC § 2–504 (a).

19. UCC § 2–504, cmt. 3.

20. *See* discussion of UCC "F.O.B." term infra, § 2.24.

§ 2.24

1. UCC § 2–319 (1)

2. UCC § 2–319 (1) (a).

3. UCC § 2–319 (1) (b).

4. *See* text below, at § 2.28.

5. *See* text above, at § 2.8.

6. UCC §§ 2–319, 2–504

7. UCC § 2–504 requires the seller to make a "reasonable" contract for transportation; which in turn, requires that the goods be insured if it is "commercially reasonable" to do so.

§ 2.25

1. UCC § 2–319 (2).

the goods arrive at their destination and before buyer has any post-shipment opportunity to inspect the goods.[2] Otherwise, the UCC "F.A.S." term is similar to the Incoterms "FAS" term, including obligating the seller only to deliver the goods alongside a named vessel and not obligating the seller to arrange transportation to a final destination. However, in the prior 1980 version of Incoterms, the definition of FAS[3] did not provide that payment against documents was required under an FAS contract, and the 1980 Incoterms did contain such payment provisions in its definitions of other commercial terms.[4] Thus, it is more likely that the current version of Incoterms FAS is not intended to require payment against documents, to restrict inspection before payment, or to require use of negotiable bills of lading.

§ 2.26 The UCC "F.O.B. Vessel" Term

As has been discussed above, the UCC does define "F.O.B.,"[1] but it is not a term requiring waterborne transportation. The UCC also has a term "F.O.B. vessel,"[2] which does relate only to water-borne transportation, and therefore is most closely linked to the Incoterms FOB term. Under the UCC, the term "F.O.B. vessel" requires the buyer to pay against a tender of documents, such as a negotiable bill of lading, before the goods arrive at their destination and before buyer has any post-shipment opportunity to inspect the goods.[3] Otherwise, the UCC "F.O.B. vessel" term is similar to the Incoterms "FOB" term, including obligating the seller only to deliver the goods to a named ship's rail and not obligating the seller to arrange transportation to a final destination.

The current definition of Incoterms FOB is silent on buyer's payment obligations, but the definition of FOB in the 1980 version of Incoterms provided that payment against documents was not required for an FOB contract, while the 1980 Incoterms did contain such payment provisions in its definitions of other commercial terms. Thus, it is more likely that the current version of Incoterms FOB is not intended to require payment against documents or to restrict inspection before payment, unless such a term is expressly added or there is a known custom in a particular trade. In addition, it is more likely that negotiable bills of lading are not intended to be used with Incoterms FOB shipments, unless the parties specify "payment against documents" in the sale contract.

§ 2.27 The UCC "C.I.F." Term

The UCC also has a definition of "C.I.F." which requires the buyer to "make payment against tender of the required documents."[1] The UCC "C.I.F." term is otherwise similar to Incoterms CIF, in that it requires

2. UCC § 2–319 (4).
3. Incoterms 1980, § 2.9, note 4, *supra*.
4. *Id*. "CIF" ¶ A1, "C & F" ¶ A1.

§ 2.26
1. U.C.C. § 2–319 (1).

2. U.C.C. § 2–319 (1) (c).
3. U.C.C. § 2–319 (4).

§ 2.27
1. U.C.C. § 2–320(4).

seller to deliver to carrier at the port of shipment and bear the risk of loss only to that port, but to pay freight costs and insurance to the port of destination.[2]

§ 2.28 The UCC "F.O.B. Place of Destination" Term

The only UCC destination term is "F.O.B. destination,"[1] which seems similar to Incoterms the "DDU" term, but without much of the detail and precision. Where the seller is required to deliver the goods "at a particular destination," the seller's delivery obligation is satisfied when the goods are placed at the buyer's disposition at the designated destination point, and give the buyer any notification necessary to enable the buyer to take possession.[2] Rather than provisions concerning whether the goods are to be loaded or unloaded on the carrier, the seller's obligation to deliver is satisfied only when the goods "pass the ship's rail" at the destination point.

There are no provisions concerning whether the goods must be cleared for import into the destination country. The buyer must furnish facilities "reasonably suited to the receipt of the goods,"[3] a duty not established by any of the Incoterms delivery commercial terms.[4] Unless the contract of sale specifically requires the seller to deliver documents, the UCC has no provisions concerning the tender of a commercial invoice or transportation documents.[5] However, the comments to the UCC provisions acknowledge that such documents may be "plainly implicit in the particular circumstances of the case or in a usage of trade."[6]

Under the UCC, the risk of loss in an "F.O.B. destination" contract passes from the seller to the buyer when the goods are tendered[7] to the buyer, while still in the possession of the carrier, at the destination point.[8] This would seem to be similar to the point at which the risk passes under the Incoterms DDU commercial term, in which the risk passes when the goods are delivered, unloaded, at the destination point.[9] However, the UCC rule for the passing of the risk of loss is different if the seller tenders non-conforming goods. For non-conforming goods, the risk of loss does not pass to the buyer upon seller's tender of delivery, but only upon buyer's acceptance[10] or seller's cure of the non-conformity.[11] Thus, if the buyer's rightfully rejects the goods, and the defect is not or cannot be cured, then the risk of loss never passes to the buyer. Even if the buyer accepts non-conforming goods and later revokes that acceptance,[12] the risk of loss is still on the seller to the extent of any deficiency

2. U.C.C § 2–320(2).

§ 2.28
1. UCC §§ 2–503 (3), 2–319(1)(b).
2. U.C.C. § 2–302 (1), (3).
3. UUC § 503 (1)(b).
4. Compare Incoterms 2000, § 2.1, note 5, *supra*, at 115.
5. UCC § 2–503, cmt. 7.
6. *Id.*

7. For a definition of "tendered," see UCC § 2–503.
8. UCC § 2–509 (1)(b).
9. See § 2.19, *supra*.
10. UCC § 2–510(1).
11. *Id.*
12. UCC § 2–608.

of buyer's effective insurance coverage over the goods.[13]

Selected Bibliography

A. Frecon, Practical Considerations in Drafting F.O.B. Terms in International Sales, 3 Int'l Tax & Bus. Law. 346 (1986).

A. Garro, The U.N. Sales Convention in the Americas: Recent Developments, 17 J. Law & Com. 219 (1998).

International Chamber of Commerce, Incoterms 2000 (I.C.C. Publ. No. 560, 2000).

International Chamber of Commerce, Incoterms in Practice (C. Dibattista, ed. 1995).

B. Kozolchyk, Evolution and Present State of the Ocean Bill of Lading from a Banking Law Perspective, 23 Maritime L. & Com. 161 (1992).

D. Murray, Risk of Loss of Goods in Transit: A Comparison of the 1990 Incoterms with Terms from Other Voices, 23 U. Miami Inter–Am. L. Rev. 93 (1991).

J. Spanogle, Incoterms and UCC Article 2—Conflicts and Confusions, 31 The Int'l Lawyer 111 (1997).

W. Tetley, Marine Cargo Claims (3d ed. 1988).

J. White and R. Summers, Uniform Commercial Code (4th ed. 1995).

P. Winship, Introduction, in Basic Instruments in International Economic Law, 707 (S. Zamaro and R. Brand, eds. 1990).

13. UCC § 2–510(2).

Chapter 3

BILLS OF LADING

Table of Sections

A. INTRODUCTION

§ 3.1 Bills of Lading in International Business Transactions

When a buyer and seller in different countries decide to transact business with each other and they negotiate payment in cash instead of payment against credit, they incur many more risks than if they transact business domestically. The buyer would want to inspect the goods prior to payment to minimize its risks relating to the nonconforming quantity and quality of the goods, and the seller would want payment prior to shipping the goods to the buyer to minimize its risks of nonpayment.

A bill of lading is a document that is issued by a carrier to a shipper upon receipt of goods from the shipper. The use of a bill of lading alleviates some of the risks of the buyer and seller. In addition, bills of lading make it possible to have a cash international sales transaction without requiring a letter of credit by using a negotiable bill of lading and a series of collecting banks to require the buyer's payment of the price in full prior to obtaining physical possession of the negotiable bill of lading, and therefore prior to access to the goods.

§ 3.2 Descriptive Terms for Bills of Lading

At common law and under the U.S. Federal Bills of Lading Act,[1] there are two different types of bills of lading: a "straight," or non-negotiable, bill of lading, and an "order," or negotiable, bill of lading. These are also known in the trade as "white" and "yellow" for the different colors of paper on which they are often printed. They are specifically described below in §§ 3.3 and 3.4. Each type usually represents the shipper's contract with the carrier, and sets forth the terms of that contract expressly or incorporates a carrier's terms and tariffs by reference. Specifically, each type contains a statement of the contract of carriage between the shipper and the carrier and is the best evidence of the terms of that contract, and at the same time it is effectively a contract of bailment as a receipt from the carrier to the shipper.

Shippers and carriers often refer to an "on board" bill of lading. An "on board" or "loaded" bill of lading is either a non-negotiable or a negotiable bill of lading that has been issued once the goods have been loaded on board the vessel, providing that same assurance to the buyer.

A "clean" bill of lading is one that has no clause or notation on the face of the bill indicating visible or possible defects in the packaging or condition of the goods. Therefore, simple comments regarding amount, weight or other descriptions as provided by the shipper will not "foul" the bill of lading, provided that they do not incorporate other documents indicating defects in the cargo.

§ 3.2
1. 49 U.S.C. §§ 80101–80116.

In addition, the parties can negotiate either a "through" bill of lading, or a "multimodal" or "combined transport" bill of lading, when the carrier agrees to transport and deliver the goods to their final destination using connecting carriers such as railroads, trucks, and air carriers so that the bill of lading governs all of the links of transportation. The terms and conditions contained in such bills of lading may be found to apply to non-international or non-commercial carriers that may not otherwise benefit from such terms.

Furthermore, there are foreign bills of lading that create different combinations of rights and duties of the parties than those established under the common law "order" and "straight" categories.

Finally, this area of law, like many others, is entering into the electronic age. Electronic substitutes for non-negotiable bills of lading have been in use for about two decades and have proved to be successful. However, electronic substitutes for negotiable bills of lading have been less successful and are still in the developmental stage. (See F. Electronic Bills of Lading.)

B. TYPES OF BILLS OF LADING

§ 3.3 Non-negotiable or Straight Bills of Lading

A non-negotiable, or "straight," bill of lading is a receipt for the goods, and serves as a contract with the carrier stating the terms and conditions of carriage. A straight bill of lading is issued to a named person, the consignee.[1] Under the U.S. Federal Bills of Lading Act, a straight bill of lading must have the language "non-negotiable" or "not negotiable" on the bill of lading itself.[2]

Possession of the actual straight bill of lading does not confer rights over the goods or against the carrier to a person in possession of the paper who is not the consignee. In fact, the consignee does not need to be in possession of the bill of lading or produce the document in order to obtain the goods from the carrier.[3] The carrier fulfills its duty under the straight bill of lading by delivering and transferring title to the goods to the consignee.[4] The shipper can even change its mind at any time prior to the delivery of the goods and stop delivery or reroute delivery to another party by instructing the carrier in writing. Straight bills of

---

§ 3.3

1. A straight bill of lading under the Pomerene Act, the predecessor to the Federal Bills of Lading Act, was defined as "a bill in which it is stated that the goods are consigned or destined to a specified person."

2. 49 U.S.C. § 80103(b)(2).

3. For a discussion of the cases stating that the physical document need not be presented, see Chan, A Plea for Certainty: Legal and Practical Problems in the Presen-

tation of Non-negotiable Bills of Lading, 29 Hong Kong L.J. 44, 52 (1999).

4. 49 U.S.C. § 80110(b)(2). See Polygram Group Distrib., Inc. v. Transus, Inc., 990 F.Supp. 1454, 1459 (N.D.Ga.1997) (holding that delivery to a street address specified as consignee's place of business on a straight bill of lading and obtaining signature of general contractor working at that address satisfied delivery requirements imposed by the bill of lading).

lading are commonly used between related parties or merchants with ongoing business as it is the simplest method of conducting business. Straight bills of lading are often used in container transport and on short sea routes.[5]

Straight bills of lading are not negotiable documents and are not documents of title. Further, indorsements on straight bills of lading are irrelevant in making the bill negotiable or to giving rights to the indorsee.[6]

Straight bills of lading are also called "air waybills," "sea waybills" and "freight receipts," depending upon the intended method of main transportation for the goods. In fact, the sea waybill is the European equivalent to the U.S. straight bill of lading, and is referred to by Incoterms (in addition to the air waybill).[7]

§ 3.4 Negotiable or Order Bills of Lading

An "order," or negotiable, bill of lading serves as (1) a contract with the carrier, (2) a receipt for the goods, and (3) a document of title for the goods. A negotiable bill of lading is issued to a named person "or order." This allows the named person (the consignee) to indorse the bill of lading to "order" delivery of the goods to others.

If possession of the bill of lading is transferred to a third party, and the bill of lading is indorsed to that third party (either specially or in blank), then the third party becomes a "holder" of the bill of lading. Therefore, possession of the actual negotiable bill of lading, properly indorsed, confers rights over the goods and against the carrier to the person in possession of the document, the "holder." The original consignee may indorse the negotiable bill of lading either "in blank" by a bare signature (e.g., "Ralph Folsom") or by a "special indorsement," which specifies the name of the intended holder

(e.g., "Deliver the goods to Michael Gordon, or order, Ralph Folsom").[1]

Under a blank indorsement, any person in possession becomes a holder, and is entitled to demand delivery from the carrier. Under a special indorsement, only the named indorsee can become a holder, and only that person can demand delivery from the carrier or indorse the bill of lading to another party so as to make it a holder. Thus, the special indorsement better protects the interest of the parties from thieves and forgers than a blank indorsement.

---

5. See Chan, supra note 3, at 45.

6. See Kasden et al. v. New York, New Haven & Hartford R.R. Co., 104 Conn. 479, 133 A. 573, 574 (Conn. 1926) (stating that a straight bill issued by the carrier to the shipper and indorsed as "nonnegotiable" was not made negotiable by the shipper's subsequent indorsement on the bill of lad-

ing to deliver the goods to a third party or order). See also, 49 U.S.C. § 80108.

7. International Chamber of Commerce, Incoterms 2000, Pub. N. 560a.

§ 3.4

1. 49 U.S.C. § 80104(a).

A carrier under a negotiable bill of lading is required to obtain the original bill of lading prior to releasing the goods. If the carrier does not obtain the original bill of lading, it will be held liable to the shipper for misdelivery and conversion.[2] The negotiable bill of lading is used in the "payment against documents" transaction described below, and is required for CIF and CFR (C & F) contracts,[3] as well as the letter of credit transaction.[4] Under UCC commercial terms, the negotiable bill of lading should also be used with "F.O.B. vessel" and "F.A.S." commercial terms.[5]

Some commercial nations only recognize straight bills of lading and not negotiable bills of lading, but most commentators believe the United States' system of recognizing both types of bills of lading is preferable.

C. GOVERNING LAW

§ 3.5 International Conventions

Regulation of the terms of a bill of lading, or the relationship between a carrier and its customers, is the subject of three international conventions and three United States federal statutes. The three international conventions (the Hague Rules,[1] the Hague–Visby Rules,[2] and the Hamburg Rules[3]) B all encompass contracts of carriage and bills of lading, but have differing approaches and are progressively more customer-oriented.[4]

---

2. See Velco Enters. Ltd. v. S.S. Zim Kingston, Zim Israel Navigation Co., et al., 858 F.Supp. 36, 38 (S.D.N.Y.1994) (holding that when a carrier releases goods without requiring the person receiving the goods to produce the original bill of lading, the carrier is liable for conversion of the goods and misdelivery under the Federal Bills of Lading Act because a carrier has delivered the goods to one who is not lawfully entitled to possession of them.)

3. 3 J. White & R.S. Summers, Uniform Commercial Code § 29–4(a) (4th ed. 1995).

4. Id. at § 29–1(a).

5. See UCC § 2–319(1)(c), (2) and (4).

§ 3.5

1. Convention for the Unification of Certain Rules of Law Relating to Bills of Lading, Aug. 25, 1924, 51 Stat. 233, T.S. No. 931, 120 L.N.T.S. 155, reprinted in 3 T.J. Schoenbaum, Admiralty and Maritime Law 747 (2d ed. 1994) (hereinafter the Hague Rules) (enacted as 46 U.S.C. App. §§ 1300–1315 (1988)).

2. See Protocol to Amend the International Convention for the Unification of Certain Rules of Law Relating to Bills of Lading, Brussels, Feb. 23, 1968, 2 U.N.

Register of Texts ch. 2, at 180 (entered into force June 23, 1977), reprinted in 3 Schoenbaum, supra note 1, .5, at 753 (hereinafter the Visby Amendments) (together with the Hague Rules, the Hague–Visby Rules). The Hague–Visby Rules have been ratified by many countries, including Belgium, Denmark, Ecuador, Egypt, Finland, France, Germany, Italy, the Netherlands, Norway, Poland, Singapore, South Africa, Spain, the United Kingdom, and other signatory countries that represent a large percentage of the U.S. trade. 6 Benediction Admiralty 1–30 (7th ed. 1996).

3. United Nations Convention on the Carriage of Goods by Sea, Hamburg, Mar. 31, 1978, U.N. Doc A/Conf.89/13, 17 I.L.M. 608 (1978) (hereinafter the Hamburg Rules). Entered into force on Nov. 1, 1992, U.N. Doc. A/RES/48/34. As of March 8, 2001, there are twenty-seven Contracting States to the Hamburg Rules. See UNCITRAL Status of Conventions and Model Laws at http://www.uncitral.org/en-index.htm.

4. For discussions on the development and changes of these international conventions, see Samuel Robert Mandelbaum, Creating Uniform Worldwide Liability Standards for Sea Carriage of Goods Under the

The Hague Rules were adopted in 1924, and set forth rules governing shipowner liability to shippers for cargo loss and damage. The Hague Rules provide 17 defenses against carrier and shipowner liability, preclude contractual exculpatory clauses in bills of lading, and limit liability to a minimum of $500 per package or customary freight unit.[5] The Visby Amendment was adopted in 1968 and amended the Hague Rules; thus, they are referred to as the Hague–Visby Rules. The Visby Amendment addressed certain issues that had arisen under the Hague Rules, such as the broadness of the carrier defenses and the inadequacy of the $500 per package provision in light of multimodal transportation and containerized packaging. The Hague–Visby Rules define the term "package" to include containerized cargo, increase the per package liability to $663 (or $2 per kilogram, whichever is higher), and restrict a carrier's limitations of liability for damage caused by its own intentional or reckless actions.[6] The Hamburg Rules of 1978 is a major departure from the Hague and Hague–Visby Rules by substantially decreasing carrier and shipowner defenses and increasing potential liability. It eliminates many defenses leaving three from the 17 defenses provided in the previous conventions, increases liability per package to approximately $1,169 per package or customary shipping unit and provides the shipper an opportunity to recover based on the weight of the cargo instead, and includes liability for on deck cargo and shipments without a bill of lading for the first time (these items are specifically excluded by the prior conventions).[7] The Hamburg Rules have not been widely adopted, and a number of the adopting states are developing and/or landlocked states.

Some nations have chosen one set of rules to apply as mandatory law;[8] others such as Hague–Visby signatories apply different rules depending on the country of origin or whether the shipment is inbound or outbound, since the rules are not applicable of their own force for inbound shipments to a signatory country.[9]

The United States has enacted the Hague Rules into its domestic law as the Carriage of Goods by Sea Act (COGSA), but also has nonconforming pre-COGSA legislation (the Harter Act) in force. English law is based on the Hague/Visby Rules.

§ 3.6   Overview of United States Law

U.C.C. Article 7 would appear to regulate the relationship governing the transfer of the bill of lading, but in fact, except for intrastate

Hague, COGSA, Visby and Hamburg Conventions, 23 Transp. L.J. 471, 477 (1996); see also Yancey, Admiralty Law Institute: Symposium on American and International Maritime Law: Comparative Aspects of Current Importance: The Carriage of Goods: Hague, COGSA, Visby and Hamburg, 57 Tul. L. Rev. 1238 (1983).

5. See Mandelbaum, supra note 4, at 477.

6. See Edelman, Proposed Changes for Cargo Liability, 208 N.Y.L.J. 3 (1992).

7. See Mandelbaum, supra note 4, at 482–484. For an in-depth review of the Hamburg Rules, see Robert Force, A Comparison of the Hague, Hague–Visby, and Hamburg Rules: Much Ado About (?), 70 Tul. L. Rev. 2051 (1996).

8. For country-by-country information regarding the adoption of the Hague, Hague–Visby or Hamburg conventions and the effective date, see www.admiralty-law.com/cargo_regimes.htm.

9. Visby Amendment, supra note 2, Article 5.

transactions, the U.C.C. is preempted by federal law.[1] The Federal Bills of Lading Act[2] (formerly called the Pomerene Act), governs the transfer and transferability of all bills of lading originating in the United States and generated to cover both international and interstate shipments.[3] The form and content of bills of lading are also governed by the Harter Act,[4] and the Carriage of Goods by Sea Act.[5] With this multiplicity of statutes governing the terms of the bill of lading and its use, conflicting concepts from overlapping statutes can be expected.

§ 3.7   The Harter Act

The Harter Act, codified under the shipping title of the United States Code (46 U.S.C. §§ 190–96), governs liability for cargo between the vessel owner or carrier and the shipper in the domestic trade. The Harter Act was described as a restatement of the common law that applied to the duties and liabilities of a vessel to its cargo.[1] It was enacted by Congress in 1893 in order to remedy the abuses of shipowners who unreasonably limited their obligations as carriers through exculpatory provisions in bills of lading.[2] The Harter Act was a compromise between shippers who wanted carriers to be responsible for all forms of negligence and carriers who wanted full exemption from negligence claims.[3]

The Harter Act prohibits and nullifies language in a bill of lading that limits a carrier's liability for "negligence, fault, or failure in proper loading, stowage, custody, care, or proper delivery of any and all lawful merchandise or property committed to its or their charge."[4] Therefore, a choice of law provision choosing, for example, the Carriage of Goods by Sea Act to apply, may be nullified in certain circumstances where the parties seek to enforce a contractual term that broadens a carrier's immunities and defenses.[5] Furthermore, a carrier may not use language "whereby the obligations of the owner or owners of said vessel to exercise due diligence [to] properly equip, man, provision, and outfit said vessel, and to make said vessel seaworthy and capable of performing her intended voyage, or whereby the obligations . . . to carefully handle and stow her cargo and to care for and properly deliver same, shall in any

§ 3.6

1. See National Union Fire Ins. Co. v. Allite, Inc., 430 Mass. 828, 724 N.E.2d 677, 679 (Mass. 2000) (holding that the Federal Bills of Lading Act preempts Article 7 of the UCC, which applies only in cases of intrastate transportation of goods).

2. 49 U.S.C. §§ 80101–80116.

3. See 49 U.S.C. § 80102.

4. 46 U.S.C. §§ 190–196.

5. 46 U.S.C. App. §§ 1300–1315.

§ 3.7

1. See The Delaware, 161 U.S. 459, 471–72, 16 S.Ct. 516, 40 L.Ed. 771 (1896).

2. See Koppers Conn. Coke Co. v. James McWilliams Blue Line, Inc., 89 F.2d 865, 866 (2d Cir.1937), cert. denied, 302 U.S. 706, 58 S.Ct. 25, 82 L.Ed. 545.

3. See Hanover Ins. Co. v. Shulman Transp. Enter., Inc., 581 F.2d 268, 271 (1st Cir.1978).

4. 46 U.S.C. § 190.

5. See United States v. Ultramar Shipping Co., 685 F.Supp. 887, 896 (S.D.N.Y. 1987) (stating that "where the Harter Act would ordinarily apply to an event, it forbids and nullifies all contractual terms which broaden a carrier's immunities and defenses beyond those granted by the act itself.")

wise be lessened, weakened or avoided."[6] Finally, the Harter Act provides that a vessel owner exercising due diligence to make the vessel "seaworthy and properly manned, equipped, and supplied" will not be held liable in certain cases, including but not limited to errors in navigation or management of the vessel, dangers of the sea, acts of God, inherent defects in the goods, or acts or omissions of the shipper or owner of the goods.[7]

Basically, the Harter Act limits the carrier's ability to contract away its liability for exercising due diligence in preparing the vessel (and all aspects related thereto) for the carriage of the goods, and in exercising due care in its handling of the goods while in the carrier's possession. The exercise of due diligence is a condition precedent to any of the defenses, regardless of whether the lack of due diligence caused the damage.[8] Furthermore, the lack of due diligence on the part of an owner is not required to have a causal effect with the damages.[9] A carrier is held liable unless it can prove that it exercised due diligence at and before the voyage to make the vessel seaworthy, and can claim that the loss was caused by an act of God, an act of the shipper, an act of public enemies, an inherent vice of the goods, or one of the other defenses enumerated in the statute.[10]

The Harter Act also governs the type of information that a shipper must include in a bill of lading, such as quantity or number of packages and weight.[11]

§ 3.8   Carriage of Goods by Sea Act (COGSA)

COGSA, codified under the shipping title of the United States Code (46 U.S.C. App. §§ 1300–15), is derived from the Hague Rules.[1] At the time it was enacted in 1936, there was no international uniformity regarding cargo liability derived from bills of lading. For example, in the U.S., carriers could not limit their liability and were treated as insurers of the cargo, while in the U.K., carriers were permitted under the principle of freedom of contract to exonerate themselves from liability.[2] COGSA was enacted to establish uniform ocean bills of lading to govern the liability for cargo between the vessel owner or carrier and the shipper in international trade.[3]

6. 46 U.S.C. § 191.

7. 46 U.S.C. § 192.

8. See Ultramar Shipping, supra note 5, at 897; see also Hooper, Carriage of Goods and Charter Parties, 73 Tul. L. Rev. 1697, 1700 (1999).

9. See May v. Hamburg–Amerikanische P. Aktiengesellschaft (The Isis), 290 U.S. 333, 353–54, 54 S.Ct. 162, 78 L.Ed. 348 (1933). Furthermore, unseaworthiness as the subject of a covenant, as opposed to a condition of exemption under the Harter Act, would require a causal relationship with the damage. Id. at 354.

10. The carrier is essentially "an insurer, absolutely liable to the shipper for dam-

ages unless occasioned by an excepted cause under the Harter Act." PPG Indus., Inc. v. Canal Barge Co., Inc., et al., 438 F.Supp. 1238, 1241 (W.D.Pa.1977).

11. 46 U.S.C. § 93.

§ 3.8

1. For a description of the Hague Rules, see supra § 3.5.

2. See Hooper, supra § 3.7, note 8, at 1698.

3. See Robert C. Herd & Co., Inc. v. Krawill Mach. Corp., 359 U.S. 297, 301, 79 S.Ct. 766, 3 L.Ed.2d 820 (1959). International counterparts include the British Car-

COGSA applies to every bill of lading or document of title that evidences a contract for the carriage of goods by sea to or from a U.S. port, but does not automatically apply to solely domestic bills of lading.[4] It specifically excludes live animals and cargo on deck that is carried by contract,[5] and does not cover charter parties and other contracts of affreightment where there is no bill of lading or document of title.[6]

COGSA sets forth the responsibilities and liabilities of the carrier and the ship, including seaworthiness of the vessel (which includes the proper manning, maintenance, equipment, supplies, and preparation of the vessel so that it is fit for the cargo),[7] and proper care and loading of cargo.[8] COGSA does not require due diligence as a condition precedent to the use of a statutory defense, except for liability under the seaworthiness requirement.[9] Even then, a claimant has the burden of showing that the carrier's lack of due diligence in providing a seaworthy vessel and to properly load, stow, carry, discharge and deliver the cargo was a proximate cause of the loss, damage or delay.[10] In addition, COGSA states that a carrier will be held liable for damaged cargo resulting from an unreasonable deviation from the terms of the contract of carriage, for example, discharging the cargo and reloading it on another vessel, stowage in contravention to specific terms of contract of carriage, or a change in route to take on cargo resulting in delay of delivery.[11] Furthermore, COGSA provides a carrier with 17 defenses for "uncontrollable causes of loss," including defective navigation or management of the ship, fire, dangers of the sea, acts of God, seizure, acts or omissions of the shipper or owner of the goods, certain labor problems, inherent defects in the goods, insufficiency of packing or marks.[12]

One of the most well-known provisions of COGSA is the $500 per package limitation of liability for loss or damage to cargo,[13] which may be increased if the shipper declares a higher valuation or maximum amount of liability in the bill of lading.[14] Regardless of the valuation or maximum amount of liability, a carrier or ship will not be held liable for more than

---

riage of Goods by Sea Act of 1924 and the Barbados Carriage of Goods by Sea Act of 1926.

4. 46 U.S.C. App. §§ 1300 and 1312.

5. 46 U.S.C. App. § 1301(c).

6. 46 U.S.C. App. § 1305.

7. 46 U.S.C. App. § 1303(1).

8. 46 U.S.C. App. § 1303(2).

9. 46 U.S.C. App. § 1304(1).

10. Wood, Multimodal Transportation: An American Perspective on Carrier Liability and Bill of Lading Issues, 46 Am. J. Comp. L. 403, 407–08 (1998).

11. See 46 U.S.C. App. § 1304(4). Note that deviations are often not covered by a ship's P & I insurance.

12. 46 U.S.C. App. § 1304(2).

13. 46 U.S.C. App. § 1304(5) ("Neither the carrier nor the ship shall in any event be or become liable for any loss or damage to or in connection with the transportation of goods in an amount exceeding $500 per package . . .")

14. See Atlantic Mut. Ins. Co. v. Poseidon Schiffahrt, 206 F.Supp. 15, 19 (N.D.Ill. 1962), aff'd, 313 F.2d 872 (7th Cir.1963), cert. denied, 375 U.S. 819, 84 S.Ct. 56, 11 L.Ed.2d 53. This concept is embodied in the doctrine of "fair opportunity" to declare a higher value. See generally Hooper, supra note 8, .7. Note that neither the carrier nor the ship will be liable for an increased liability if the shipper has knowingly and fraudulently misstated the value of the goods on the bill of lading. Furthermore, the carrier may be subject to higher liability if damage is due to "unreasonable deviation" as described in this § 3.8.

the damage actually sustained.[15] An additional protection or limitation of liability under COGSA is that claims must be filed within a year following delivery of the subject goods.[16]

COGSA also governs the contents of a bill of lading, and provides that the carrier shall, on demand of the shipper, include identification marks on the cargo, the number of packages or pieces, or quantity or weight, as provided by the shipper, and the apparent order and condition of the goods unless the carrier reasonably believes that it is not accurate or has no reasonable means for checking.[17] If a carrier does provide any particulars on the bill of lading regarding the goods shipped, then the bill of lading will be treated as evidence that the goods, as detailed, were actually received by the carrier.[18] In addition, if a shipper provides any particulars (such as marks, number, quantity or weight) to the carrier, such particulars are to be guaranteed by the shipper who will be held liable to the carrier for any damages or expenses arising out of the inaccuracies.[19] There is an exception regarding weight information contained on a bill of lading: if bulk cargo is weighed by a third party and that information is contained in the bill of lading, then the carrier will not be deemed to have checked the weight, and the shipper will not be deemed to have guaranteed the weight.[20]

COGSA contains provisions that overlap with the Harter Act. COGSA will prevail for any loss or damage arising from an act, negligence or default in navigation or management of a vessel used for carriage of goods by sea.[21] When damage to goods occurs on land, the Harter Act will prevail and prohibit any disclaimers against liability.[22] The Harter Act by its terms still governs prior to loading and after discharge of cargo until delivery under the bill of lading is made.[23]

15. 46 U.S.C. App. § 1304(5).

16. 46 U.S.C. App. § 1303(6).

17. 46 U.S.C. App. § 1303(3). See Westway Coffee Corp. v. M. V. Netuno, 675 F.2d 30, 33 (2d Cir.1982) (finding that bill of lading containing weight description represents that the carrier has no reasonable grounds for suspecting that the weight of the goods actually received differs from the listed weight and that the carrier has reasonable means of checking the weight, therefore, the record constitutes a prima facie showing for recovery).

18. 6 U.S.C. App. § 1303(4). See Hecht, Levis & Kahn, Inc. v. The Javanese Prince, 210 F.Supp. 236, 238 (S.D.N.Y.1962) (stating that a carrier is bound by representations in the bill of lading stating that cargo was received in apparent good order).

19. 46 U.S.C. App. § 1303(5). This provision has not been uniformly enforced B courts have held that despite language indicating "shipper's weight, load and count," the purchaser of the bill of lading would still rely on that information and therefore

carriers in such circumstances should refuse to specify such information in a bill of lading pursuant to 46 U.S.C. App. § 1303(3)(c) or else face liability for misdescription. See e.g., Portland Fish Co. v. States S.S. Co., 510 F.2d 628, 633 (9th Cir.1974); Westway Coffee Corp. v. M/V Netuno, 528 F.Supp. 113, 116–17 (S.D.N.Y. 1981), aff'd, 675 F.2d 30 (2d. Cir.1982).

20. 46 U.S.C. App. § 1310.

21. 46 U.S.C. App. § 1301(e) defining carriage of goods by sea.

22. Compare 46 U.S.C. App. § 1304(2)(a) with 46 U.S.C. § 190. See Baker Oil Tools, Inc. v. Delta S.S. Lines, Inc., 562 F.2d 938, 940–41 (5th Cir.1977) (refusing to apply COGSA to liability caused by land transportation), reh'g denied, 571 F.2d 978 (5th Cir.), reh'g denied, 577 F.2d 1134 (5th Cir.).

23. 46 U.S.C. App. § 1311 (stating that COGSA does not supercede the Harter Act or other federal statutes insofar as they relate to duties, responsibilities and liabilities of the ship or carrier prior to the time

Many defenses available to a carrier under COGSA are not available under the Harter Act or other U.S. laws. For the reasons mentioned above, COGSA is commonly preferred as the choice of law to govern bills of lading, especially if carriage is interstate (not international so that COGSA may apply automatically) or the parties want COGSA to apply before and after the carriage of goods by sea.[24] It should be noted that any inconsistency between the Harter Act and COGSA will yield to the Harter Act.[25] Therefore, provisions in the bill of lading that resemble exoneration clauses or that insulate the carrier from liability that are permissible under COGSA may not be upheld under the Harter Act.[26]

Many scholars note that COGSA, having been enacted in 1936, does not adequately protect and serve modern maritime interests and is outdated compared to the domestic laws in many other nations. The Maritime Law Association of the United States (hereinafter the MLA) has been attempting to greatly reform COGSA and introduced a draft bill titled the Carriage of Goods by Sea Act of 1995.[27] This proposed law combined aspects of the Hague–Visby Rules and the Hamburg Rules and would significantly change the current allocation of risks and liabilities.[28] The proposal was presented to a U.S. Senate sub-committee in 1998, and the Senate sub-committee, in consultation with the MLA, has been drafting new texts (the most recent version in 1999).[29]

§ 3.9 Federal Bills of Lading Act

The Federal Bills of Lading Act (hereinafter the FBLA) (formerly called the Pomerene Act), codified under the transportation title of the United States Code (49 U.S.C.A. §§ 80101–80116), governs the transfer and transferability of all bills of lading generated to cover both international and interstate shipments. Congress enacted the FBLA in 1916, and recodified the FBLA in 1994. It did not intend to change the

when the goods are loaded or after the time the goods are discharged from the ship.) See Allied Chem. Int'l Corp. v. Companhia de Navegacao Lloyd Brasileiro, 775 F.2d 476, 482 (2d Cir.1985), cert. denied, 475 U.S. 1099, 106 S.Ct. 1502, 89 L.Ed.2d 903 (1986).

24. Parties in a domestic bill of lading may adopt COGSA as their choice of law. See Puerto Rico v. Sea–Land Serv., Inc., 349 F.Supp. 964, 968–69 (D.P.R.1970).

25. 46 U.S.C. App. § 1311. See Uncle Ben's Int'l Div. of Uncle Ben's Inc., et al. v. Hapag–Lloyd Aktiengesellschaft, 855 F.2d 215, 217 (5th Cir.1988). Note that in this case, COGSA's statute of limitations restriction was not considered to be inconsistent with the Harter Act.

26. See David Crystal, Inc. v. Cunard S.S. Co., 339 F.2d 295, 297 (2d Cir.1964) (clause excluding carrier liability for aban-

doning goods on wharf if they were not immediately received was not upheld), cert. denied, 380 U.S. 976, 85 S.Ct. 1339, 14 L.Ed.2d 271 (1965).

27. See Carriage of Goods by Sea Act, 1 to 16, Proposed Official Draft, Mar. Law. Assoc. (1995).

28. For an article discussing the need for reform and international uniformity, see Sturley, Uniformity in the Law Governing the Carriage of Goods by Sea, 26 J. Mar. L. & Com. 553 (1995).

29. Sixth Staff Working Draft of the Bill to Amend the Carriage of Goods by Sea Act, prepared by the drafters of the U.S. Senate, dated April 16, 1999. For more information regarding this Senate draft from the perspective of an author who is against this proposed litigation, see William Tetley, The Demise of the Demise Clause?, 44 McGill L.J. 807 (Dec. 1999).

substance of the Act, but it did reword and consolidate the prior provisions and change all the section numbers.

The FBLA governs all interstate and international shipments that use a bill of lading issued by a common carrier. By its terms, the statute governs the bill of lading if the goods are shipped from the United States to another country. The FBLA defines the different types of bills of lading (negotiable and non-negotiable),[1] and sets forth the rules that apply to a negotiable bill of lading [2] and non-negotiable bill of lading,[3] outlining the rights and duties attached to each type.

There are several notable provisions in the FBLA regarding potential liability for bills of lading: (1) a carrier's liability for misdelivery and conversion, (2) a carrier's liability for nonreceipt, misdescription and improper loading, and (3) the warranty liability of a person negotiating or transferring a bill of lading for value. The FBLA sets forth the requirements for a carrier to fulfill its duty to deliver goods, thus describing what is required to prove liability for a claim for conversion or misdelivery by the carrier, and some of the carrier's defenses to such a claim.[4] For example, the carrier must deliver the goods to a person entitled to possession (consignee in of a non-negotiable bill of lading or holder of a negotiable bill of lading),[5] and must obtain and cancel a negotiable bill of lading at the time of delivery.[6]

A carrier is liable for nonreceipt and misdescription if it either indicates its receipt of cargo on a bill of lading where no cargo was received, or if the goods do not correspond with the carrier's description of them on the bill of lading.[7] The FBLA does provide certain exceptions for a carrier's nonreceipt, misdescription and improper loading liability, such as when the goods are loaded by the shipper, the bill of lading indicates that the goods were "shippers weight, load and count" or the "contents are unknown," and in the case of nonreceipt or misdescription, the carrier does not have information contrary to that included on the bill.[8] This defense is not available for an indication of the weight of bulk freight on a bill of lading if a shipper provides facilities for the carrier to determine the weight and requests that the carrier provide such information in the bill of lading, or for the kind and quantity of bulk freight when the goods are loaded by a carrier.[9]

As further described below, the FBLA provides for automatic representations and warranties by a person negotiating or transferring a bill of lading for value, including that the bill is genuine, the transferor has title to the goods and the right to transfer the bill, and the transferor is

§ 3.9

1. 49 U.S.C. § 80103.

2. 49 U.S.C. §§ 80104 and 80105 (regarding indorsement, delivery and possession of the bill of lading, and title to the goods).

3. 49 U.S.C. § 80106.

4. 49 U.S.C. §§ 80110 and 80111.

5. 49 U.S.C. § 80111(a).

6. 49 U.S.C. § 80111(c).

7. 49 U.S.C. § 80113.

8. 49 U.S.C. § 80113(b) and (c).

9. 49 U.S.C. § 80113(d).

not aware of any fact affecting the validity of the bill.[10] These representations and warranties often arise in the context of a forged signature or a forged bill of lading.

The final provision worth noting assesses criminal liability for anyone fraudulently making or using a domestic or export bill of lading.[11]

The word "carrier" is not defined in the FBLA, so it is not clear whether documents issued by freight forwarders are covered by the FBLA. Further, the term "bill of lading" is not defined, so it is not clear whether air waybills or inland waterway documents are included.

§ 3.10 Choice of Law

As mentioned above, a choice of law clause choosing COGSA may not be applied if the circumstance requires application of a limitation of liability provision that is contrary to the Harter Act. Despite this possibility, U.S. bills of lading often indicate COGSA or the Hague Rules as the choice of law: not only because it maximizes a carrier's ability to defend against liability, but also because it is required by most protection and indemnity insurance carriers.[1]

In fact, other parties may take advantage of the COGSA defenses and the $500 limitation of liability through the use of several common provisions. The parties may choose COGSA to apply the entire time the goods are within the carrier's custody rather than from loading aboard the vessel to discharge of cargo from the vessel, or "tackle to tackle,"[2] and such a clause in the bill of lading is commonly referred to as a "Period of Responsibility Clause." In addition, the parties may make use of a Himalaya Clause, which is a clause contained in a "through" bill of lading that extends the COGSA immunities, defenses, limitations and protections of the carrier to third parties, such as stevedores and inland carriers. A "Clause Paramount" included in a bill of lading is similar to a traditional choice of law provision and designates the controlling law to govern the rights and liabilities of all of the parties to a bill of lading.

COGSA is automatically applicable to all shipments of goods between the U.S. and a foreign port. The Hague–Visby Rules, similar to COGSA, apply automatically to any bill of lading issued in a contracting state. What happens when a Clause Paramount designates one of these rules of law to apply? In the case of a bill of lading for cargo shipped from a Hague–Visby signatory country and destined for the U.S. there is a conflict in the choice of law provision, because both COGSA and the Hague–Visby Rules are considered mandatory. This situation is particularly interesting in light of the fact that the Hague–Visby Rules provide for a higher limitation of liability than the $500 limitation provided in

10. 49 U.S.C. § 80107(a).

11. 49 U.S.C. 80116.

§ 3.10

1. The Standard P & I Class rules state that liability for damage to cargo is conditioned upon the bill of lading or contract of

carriage indicating that such contract is subject to the Hague Rules or Hague–Visby Rules or to other rules containing similarly wide exemptions of carrier liability.

2. See 46 U.S.C. App. § 1307.

COGSA;[3] therefore, there is an incentive for the carrier to advocate that COGSA should apply.

U.S. courts have generally held that COGSA applies as a matter of law to the shipment of goods from a foreign port to the U.S., and therefore general foreign choice of law clauses are invalid to the extent they contradict COGSA.[4] The resolution of the limitation of liability issue depends on the language used in the bill of lading—whether the Paramount Clause specifically declares that a certain law should apply, the scope of the Paramount Clause, whether there is language regarding the parties intent to increase liability above the $500 COGSA limitation, and any other language of intent between the parties.[5] If the relevant provisions in a bill of lading are considered ambiguous, the language will be construed against the drafter, or the carrier.[6] Therefore, carriers should be very cautious regarding the language used in a bill of lading.

D. THE "PAYMENT AGAINST DOCUMENTS" TRANSACTION

§ 3.11 Overview

How does the "payment against documents" transaction work? When the buyer and the seller are forming their contract for the sale of the goods, the seller will insist that the buyer "pay against the documents," rather than after delivery and inspection of the goods themselves. Such a payment term must be bargained for and expressed in the sales contract since it will normally not be implied.

The seller will then pack the goods and prepare a commercial invoice. If the commercial term requires it (e.g., under a "CIF" or a "Cost, Insurance and Freight" term) seller will also procure an insurance certificate (another form of contract) covering the goods during transit. The seller then delivers the goods to the carrier, which issues a bill of lading and designates to whom the goods should be delivered. In the case of a negotiable bill of lading, it will require the carrier to deliver the goods only "to seller or order" B i.e., only to the seller or a person the seller may designate by an appropriate endorsement.

As stated above, a bill of lading serves as both a carrier contract and as a receipt for the cargo being sent. Under the terms of the bill of lading contract, in return for payment of the freight charge, the carrier promises to deliver the goods to either (1) the named "consignee" in a straight or non-negotiable bill of lading, or (2) the person in possession or the "holder" of a properly endorsed order or negotiable bill of lading. The issuance by the carrier of a bill of lading serves to assure the parties

3. See supra § 3.5.

4. See generally, Nakazawa and Moghaddam, COGSA and Choice of Foreign Law Clauses in Bills of Lading, 17 Mar. Law. 1 (1992).

5. See Jeffries, COGSA or Hague–Visby: Cargo Damages in International Shipments, 18 Hous. J. Int'l L. 767, 793–801 (1996).

6. See e.g., Francosteel Corp. v. M/V Kapetan Andreas G, 1993 A.M.C. 1924, 1928 (S.D.N.Y.1993).

that (1) the goods have been delivered to the carrier, and (2) that they are destined for the buyer either as consignee under a straight bill of lading or as the holder of a negotiable bill of lading.

§ 3.12 The Necessity of a Negotiable Bill of Lading

The negotiable bill of lading should be used in the payment against documents sale. Because the negotiable bill of lading acts as a document of title, the buyer is able to obtain delivery of goods *only if* the buyer has physical possession of a properly endorsed bill of lading. The buyer can only have physical possession of a properly endorsed bill of lading by paying in full the balance owed on the goods for the shipment.

Since a negotiable bill of lading controls the right to obtain the goods from the carrier, the collecting banks can control the carrier's delivery of the goods to the buyer by simply retaining possession of the order bill of lading. In other words, when a bank undertakes to collect funds from the buyer for the seller, it receives the bill of lading from the seller that has been issued by the carrier. The bank's control over the negotiable bill of lading as a document of title confers control over the goods. The buyer cannot obtain possession of the goods from a carrier without physical possession of the negotiable bill of lading, so after the banks have received that piece of paper from the seller, they can obtain payment (or assurances that the buyer will pay them) before the buyer receives the physical possession of the negotiable bill of lading and therefore the ability to obtain the goods from the carrier.

If a straight bill of lading is used in the payment against documents transaction, the buyer would be able to obtain delivery of the goods as the consignee even if no payment was made, and thus the seller would lose a valuable protection.

§ 3.13 Payment

Once the seller has obtained a negotiable bill of lading to his own order, how does he obtain payment? First, he attaches a "draft" to it, together with an invoice and any other documents required by the sales contract. Then the seller uses the banking system as a collection agent. The "draft" (sometimes also called a "bill of exchange") will usually be a "sight draft," which is payable "on demand" when presented to buyer. The draft is drawn for the amount due under the sales contract, and it is payable to the seller's order.

At the bank, the seller endorses both the draft and the negotiable bill of lading to the seller's bank, and will also transfer the other documents required by the sales contract. If no letter of credit is involved in the transaction, the bank will usually take these documents only "for collection," although it is also possible for the bank to "discount" or buy the documents outright and become the owner.

To understand the collection transaction by the banking system, consult the flow chart on the next page. The seller's bank is required to send the draft and its accompanying documents for presentment to the buyer by the buyer's bank. The seller's bank deals with "for collection" items individually, without assuming that they will be honored, and therefore without giving the seller a provisional credit in the seller's account until the buyer pays the draft.

See flow chart below showing payment against document transaction.

DIAGRAM OF AN INTERNATIONAL DOCUMENTARY SALE

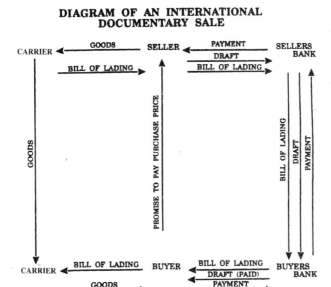

The draft, with its attached documents, will pass through "customary banking channels" to the buyer's bank (the "presenting bank"), which will notify the buyer of the arrival of the documents. The buyer's bank will demand that the buyer "honor" the draft, at which time the buyer can pay the amount of a demand draft, or "accept" or promise to pay a time draft later. The buyer may require the bank to "exhibit" the draft and documents to it to allow the buyer to determine whether they conform to the contract. If the buyer receives mere notice that the documents have arrived, the buyer has three banking days after the notice is sent to decide whether to "honor" the draft. However, if the draft and documents are exhibited directly to the buyer, the buyer must decide whether or not to honor the draft by the close of business on that same day, unless there are extenuating circumstances.

The buyer must "pay against the documents" and not the goods themselves, which is why it is preferable to specify the terms of the documents in the original contract for the sale of goods. Once the buyer has paid or made arrangements to pay the buyer's bank, it will obtain possession of the negotiable bill of lading and only then will it be entitled to obtain the goods from the carrier. The buyer never sees the goods, only the documents B so it inspects the documents rigorously to determine that they comply exactly with the requirements of the sale contract. Substantial performance by the seller in the tender of documents is not acceptable.

An international sale of goods involving payment against documents is diagrammed on this page.

§ 3.14 Risks of the Parties

Both parties face certain risks in this type of transaction that will affect both sides regardless of whether the buyer or seller is ultimately responsible for bearing the risks. For example, the goods could be lost or stolen. In such a situation, the value of the goods, the amount of time required to secure additional or replacement goods, and the demand for the goods on the buyer are factors that may be taken into account.

Some of these problems are recognized and dealt with in the standard handling of the "payment against documents" transaction. For example, insuring the goods against loss or theft is standard practice in the CIF transaction. Other problems, such as payment before inspection, make buyers feel unprotected, and they have searched for devices within the transaction that can afford them more protection. Such a device, in common use in modern transactions, is the Inspection Certificate.

Other risks relate directly to potential liabilities regarding bills of lading and are discussed under E. Inherent Risks and Liabilities Regarding Bills of Lading.

§ 3.15 Seller's Risks

What can go wrong from the seller's point of view? The seller will be paid before the documents or the goods are released to the buyer. If the buyer pays the buyer's bank, the proceeds are remitted immediately and automatically to the seller's bank account in the seller's nation. Therefore, the seller will not lose control of the goods without being paid for them.

However, the seller has shipped the goods to a foreign buyer prior to receiving any payment, and with no guarantee of payment from anyone other than the buyer. The buyer may refuse to pay the sight draft with documents attached when it arrives. This would give the seller a cause of action, but often the seller would have to go to a court in the buyer's jurisdiction for relief, which means bringing a suit abroad with its extra expense, delay and uncertainty. In addition, the seller could feel that it will be the target of discrimination in the courts of the buyer's nation.

The seller would still have control of the goods because after dishonor of the draft, the bill of lading will be returned to the seller. However, the goods would either be in transit or would have reached their foreign destination B one at which the seller is likely to have no agents and no particular prospects for resale. If the seller wanted to bring the goods back to its base of operations (and normal sales territory), it would have to pay a second transportation charge, and this may be substantial in relation to the value of the goods. Thus, the dishonor of the draft by the buyer can create economic circumstances where the seller's only rational option is a distress sale in the buyer's nation. This risk to the seller is inherent in the payment against documents transaction, unless the seller requires that the buyer also procure the issuance of a letter of credit. (See Chapter 6 for a complete description and discussion of the letter of credit transaction.)

§ 3.16   Buyer's Risks

What can go wrong from the buyer's point of view? In exchange for its payment of the purchase price of the goods, the buyer has a document from the carrier entitling it to delivery of the goods, an insurance certificate protecting the buyer against casualty loss, and perhaps an inspection certificate warranting that the goods conform to the sale contract. Therefore, the buyer should receive what it bargained for B delivery of conforming goods or insurance proceeds sufficient to cover any loss.

However, without the ability to inspect the actual goods before payment, the buyer cannot be absolutely assured that they conform to the contract. The buyer is forced to rely on information provided in the bill of lading, such as a description of the goods, quantity of boxes or weight of the cargo prior to payment for the goods. There could be misstatements or errors on the bill of lading so that the description conforms to the sales contract, but upon delivery, the buyer could find that the goods shipped are non-conforming. This non-conformity could range from the seller shipping scrap paper, to the seller shipping the correct goods in the wrong size or color. Similarly, the buyer could find that the labeling on the packaging is incorrect (which can cause problems with customs agents in both countries).

The buyer faces other risks—that the goods could have been stored or handled inappropriately by the carrier such that they are damaged in transit, or the bill of lading has been obtained by fraud or forgery. Some of these risks are inherent to any transaction using a bill of lading, and will be considered in the materials below.

E.   INHERENT RISKS AND LIABILITIES REGARDING BILLS OF LADING

There are certain problems that are uniquely related to any transaction using a bill of lading, and will be considered in the materials below:

(1) The loss of the bill of lading, followed by the forgery of a necessary indorsement and the carrier's misdelivery (delivery of the goods to the wrong person under a bill of lading).

(2) The misdescription of the goods by the shipper in the bill of lading followed by the carrier's delivery of goods which do not conform to the description in the bill of lading.

(3) The forgery of a complete bill of lading by the shipper without the carrier's knowledge.

§ 3.17 Misdelivery

Under a non-negotiable bill of lading, the carrier obligates itself to deliver the goods at the destination point to the consignee named in the bill of lading.[1] In short, the carrier is liable to the consignee of a straight bill of lading for misdelivery if it delivers the goods to anyone but the consignee or a person to whom the consignee delegates to receive them.[2] Thus, straight bills of lading are not appropriate for a "payment against documents" transaction, and the case reports are full of litigation where an attorney tried a short-cut using a straight bill of lading as the "easy" way to do this transaction, and sacrificed the client's interests.

Under a negotiable bill of lading, the carrier obligates itself to deliver the goods to the "holder" of the bill of lading at the destination point.[3] Thus, possession of the negotiable bill of lading becomes crucial and confers title over the goods. The carrier must see the actual bill of lading both to determine who has possession and to determine to whom the indorsements run.

In certain situations where the actual bill of lading is not available, the carrier will not be liable for delivery to a person entitled to possession of the goods pursuant to the FBLA.[4] For example, the New York Supreme Court held that a carrier was not liable for delivery without requiring the surrender of the bill of lading where the buyer was the true owner of the goods under the buyer's f.o.b. contract (in which the shipper passes title to the goods to the buyer upon delivery to the carrier).[5] More recently, a New Jersey District Court held that Honduran customs authorities were "persons entitled to possession" of jute bags since the bill of lading was not available for presentment to the customs authorities; therefore, the carrier was not liable for the bags being stolen while in the possession of the customs authorities.[6]

Notwithstanding the above situation, the carrier is liable to the holder of a negotiable bill of lading for misdelivery if it delivers the goods to anyone but the holder.[7] As stated above, the negotiable bill of lading is

---

§ 3.17

1. 49 U.S.C. § 80110.

2. See Richardson v. Railway Express Agency, Inc., 258 Or. 170, 482 P.2d 176, 178–79 (Or. 1971) (holding carrier liable under a straight bill of lading where shipper instructed carrier to hold the goods for pickup and instead the carrier delivered the goods to an address listed as shipper's street address on the bill of lading and did not obtain evidence that the person signing for the goods was entitled to possession).

3. 46 U.S.C. § 80110.

4. 46 U.S.C. § 80110(b)(1).

5. Miller v. New York Cent. R.R. Co., 205 A.D. 663, 200 N.Y.S. 287 (1923).

6. Ace Bag & Burlap Co., Inc. v. Sea-Land Serv., Inc., 40 F. Supp. 2d 233, 239–40 (D.N.J.1999).

7. 46 U.S.C. § 80111; see also 46 U.S.C. § 80114(b) (stating that delivery of goods pursuant to a court order "does not relieve a common carrier from liability to a person

a document of title because possession of it, properly indorsed, controls title to the document, title to the goods, and the direct obligation of the carrier to hold the goods and deliver them to the holder of the document. For this reason, the negotiable bill of lading is appropriate for a "payment against documents" transaction. The collecting banks can use their possession of such bills of lading to control title to both the goods and the document until they have collected the purchase price from the buyer.

The carrier has an obligation to take possession of the bill of lading and cancel it. Under § 80111(c) of the FBLA, "if a common carrier delivers goods for which a negotiable bill of lading has been issued without taking and canceling the bill, the carrier is liable for damages for failure to deliver the goods to a person purchasing the bill for value in good faith whether the purchase was before or after delivery and even when delivery was made to the person entitled to the goods."[8] The statute does provide certain exceptions to this provision.[9]

The holder of the bill of lading has absolute title to the goods in almost all cases. If the seller is not the owner of the goods, for example if the goods have been stolen at gunpoint from the "true owner," then no holder of the bill of lading will have title because the seller's claim of title is void. However, if the original owner voluntarily parted with the goods but was defrauded by the seller (for example, a cash sale in which the check bounces later), then the seller obtains voidable title[10] and can pass good title to a holder of the document who purchases it in good faith for value without notice.[11] The rights of such a good faith holder for value are also superior to any seller's lien or right to stop delivery of the goods in transit.

Under the FBLA, as under the UCC, any forgery of a necessary indorsement is not effective to create or transfer rights, regardless of whether the forgery is perfect. Further, any unauthorized signature by an agent is treated as a forgery, as long as it was made without actual, implied or apparent authority. The protection is illustrated in the situation where a thief steals a negotiable bill of lading from the holder who was in possession of the document under a special indorsement. As such, the holder's indorsement is necessary to transfer rights to the document or goods to any other party. Without that indorsement, the thief is not a holder and still has no rights. If the thief transfers the document to another party, that party also is not a holder and cannot obtain rights under the document without the holder's signature. The carrier is still obligated to deliver the goods only to the holder, the victim of the theft.

---

to whom the negotiable bill has been or is negotiated for value without notice of the court proceeding or of the delivery of the goods"). Note that under 46 U.S.C. § 80114(a) the court order requiring delivery of goods may require the posting of a surety bond prior to delivery.

8. 49 U.S.C. § 80111(c).

9. 49 U.S.C. § 80111(d).

10. U.C.C. § 2–403.

11. 49 U.S.C. § 80105.

Thus, if a collecting bank or another party takes the document under a special indorsement, it is protected from loss from theft of the paper and forgery, and even from unauthorized transfer by an agent.

If the carrier does deliver to the forger, or to someone who received the document from the forger without the holder's indorsement, the carrier is liable for misdelivery.[12] The forger is also liable, if he can be found. The person who received the goods and other transferees have all made warranties hat they had "a right to transfer the bill and title to the goods," when they had no such rights or title.[13]

In the case of a person who purchases or otherwise gives value for a valid bill of lading without notice that the bill of lading was obtained by breach of duty, fraud, accident, mistake, duress, loss, theft or conversion, the validity of the bill of lading will be upheld to the detriment of the original or rightful owner.[14] The rightful owner will have the same remedies for misdelivery as described herein.

The concept is that each person who takes the bill of lading should "know his indorser." If the goods are misdelivered, the party most easily found is the one who received the goods, and that party is liable. That party then has a warranty action against its transferor B and it is the person involved that is most likely to be able to find that transferor. The transferor, in turn, has a warranty action against its transferor B and so on back up the chain of transfers. This is not very efficient, however the purpose is to push liability back up the chain of transfers to the person who took from the forger, or even to the forger himself. In the meantime, the holder collects from the misdelivering carrier, which collects from its insuror.

Even collecting banks that transfer the document for value can be subject to this warranty liability. If the buyer pays, and those funds are transmitted to the forger, then the collecting banks have received value. However, such banks have at least three potential escape valves. One is to disclaim such warranty liability when indorsing the negotiable bill of lading. The statutory warranties do not arise if "a contrary intention appears."[15] Thus, a specific indorsement "XYZ Bank. Prior indorsements not guaranteed," or a general indorsement that the bank will not be responsible for quantity, quality, condition or delivery of the goods described in the bill would clearly disclaim liability for such a warranty.[16] A second avenue is to claim that the bank is only holding the document "as security for a debt," for the statute exempts such holders from warranty liability.[17] The difficulty with this avenue is that a collecting

---

12. 49 U.S.C. § 80111.

13. 49 U.S.C. § 80107.

14. 49 U.S.C. 80104(b).

15. 49 U.S.C. 80107(a). The statute reads "unless a contrary intention appears," and then describes the general warranties and liabilities assigned to a person negotiating or transferring a bill of lading.

16. See e.g, American State Bank v. Mueller Grain Co., 15 F.2d 899, 904 (7th Cir.1926), rev'd on other grounds, 275 U.S. 493, 48 S.Ct. 34, 72 L.Ed. 390 (1927); Johnston v. Western Md. R.R. Co., 151 Md. 422, 135 A. 185 (Md. 1926).

17. 49 U.S.C. 80107(b) ("A person holding a bill of lading as security for a debt and in good faith demanding or receiving payment of the debt from another person does

bank does not pay the seller until after it receives payment, so it never becomes a creditor, secured or otherwise. The third avenue is the International Chamber of Commerce "Uniform Rules for Collection" (hereinafter the I.C.C. Collection Rules) which provide that banks have no obligation to examine documents, other than to verify that they "appear to be as listed in the collection order."[18] That may indicate a blanket "contrary intention" under the statute. Any bank found to have warranty liability can pass this liability back to the transferor, as long as it can identify that transferor.

§ 3.18 Misdescription

The carrier in a shipment transaction has no privity with the contract between the buyer and the seller for the sale of goods, and therefore has no obligation to deliver goods that conform to the sale contract. However, the goods are described in the bill of lading, which constitutes part of the carriage contract. Thus, the carrier does have an obligation to deliver goods that conform to the description in the bill of lading. Under the FBLA, a carrier is liable for any failure to deliver goods that correspond to the description in the bill of lading, either as to quantity or as to quality.[1] This obligation is owed to the owner of the goods under a non-negotiable bill of lading and to the holder of a negotiable bill of lading. Therefore, if a bill of lading describes goods, and the described goods differ from the delivered goods, the carrier may be held liable to the shipper.[2]

The problem with this obligation is that the carrier usually does not know what it is carrying, since the goods are often in containers. Thus, the carrier knows that it received a container that was labeled "100 IBM word-processing computers." It will not, and is not expected to, open the container to check whether it contains computers, or to count how many items are in the container. Even if the carrier opened the container, it would not be expected to check whether each computer is in working order. Even if it did so check, it is not likely to have the expertise to determine whether each computer can perform the necessary routines to be a word processor. Thus, the carrier is not expected to warrant the description and capability of packaged goods given to it to transport.

To solve this problem, carriers are allowed, under the FBLA and COGSA, to effectively disclaim their obligations to deliver goods that conform to the description.[3] Appropriate disclaimer language is set forth in the statute and includes: "contents or condition of contents of

not warrant by the demand or receipt (1) the genuineness of the bill; or (2) the quantity or quality of the goods described in the bill.")

18. Uniform Rules for Collection, Article 2 (1978).

§ 3.18

1. 49 U.S.C.A. § 80113.

2. See Industria Nacional Del Papel, CA. v. M/V "Albert F", 730 F.2d 622, 624 (11th Cir.1984) (holding the vessel liable for non-delivery when goods received did not conform to the goods described in the bill of lading), cert. denied, 469 U.S. 1037, 105 S.Ct. 515, 83 L.Ed.2d 404 (1984).

3. 49 U.S.C.A. § 80113(b); 46 U.S.C. App. § 1303(3)(c).

packages unknown," "said to contain," and "shipper's weight, load and count." Other language conveying the same meaning can be used; the statutory linguistic formulas are not required.

According to these statutory provision, all of these disclaimers are effective only if the seller loads the goods.[4] This restriction seems appropriate for disclaimers of the "shipper's weight, load and count" variety, but seems inappropriate for disclaimers of the "said to contain" or "contents or condition of contents of packages unknown" variety. There are cases in which the carrier is held liable for misdescription despite stating "shipper's weight, load and count" in a bill of lading if the carrier issues a bill of lading and the shipper has in fact never loaded anything on board the carrier's cars.[5]

The disclaimers are not effective if the carrier knows that the goods do not conform.[6] The protection is available only to the uninformed carrier. However, when goods are loaded by a carrier, the carrier is obligated to count the number of packages and is expected to note the condition of the packages.[7] The carrier is also obligated to "determine the kind and quantity" (but not the quality) of any bulk freight that it loads.[8] For bulk freight, even where it is loaded by the seller, the carrier must still determine the kind and quantity of the freight if the seller so requests and provides adequate facilities for the carrier to weigh the freight.[9] In situations where the carrier must count packages or weigh the goods, disclaimers (such as "shipper's weight, load and count" or others indicating that the shipper described or loaded the goods) will not be effective.[10]

The disclaimers are also not effective if the carrier has reasonable grounds for suspecting that the goods do not conform, or has no reasonable means of checking for marks, number, quantity or weight.[11] In such situations, the carrier is expected to omit such information from the bill of lading. A carrier that instead uses disclaimer language such as "shipper's load and count" and "said to contain," will face potential

4. 49 U.S.C.A. 80113(b)(1).

5. See, e.g., Chicago and N. W. R. Co v. Stephens Nat. Bank, 75 F.2d 398, 400 (8th Cir.1935). See also, Portland Fish Co. v. States S.S. Co., 510 F.2d 628, 630–31 (9th Cir.1974) (stating that since the cargo was loaded by the carrier, the carrier should not have issued a bill of lading with a weight description if it had no reasonable means to check the weight of the cargo and therefore held that the carrier was estopped from denying that they had received anything other than what was listed on the bill of lading, despite a "shipper's load and count" clause).

6. 49 U.S.C. § 80113(b)(3).

7. 49 U.S.C. § 80113(d)(2); see Elgie & Co. v. S.S. "S. A. Nederburg", 599 F.2d 1177, 1180–81 (2d Cir.1979) (stating that carrier loading packaged goods is obligated to count packages and indicate that number in the bill of lading), cert. denied, 444 U.S. 1072, 100 S.Ct. 1016, 62 L.Ed.2d 753 (1980).

8. 49 U.S.C. § 80113(d)(2).

9. 49 U.S.C. § 80113(d)(1).

10. 49 U.S.C. § 80113(d)(2).

11. 46 U.S.C. ann. § 1303(3)(c), stating that "no carrier, master or agent of the carrier, shall be bound to state or show in the bill of lading any marks, number, quantity or weight which he has reasonable ground for suspecting not accurately to represent the goods actually received, or which he has had no reasonable means of checking."

liability.[12]

Thus, what is established is a system in which the carrier is responsible for checking some quantity terms, the number of cartons and the weight of a shipment. These are items that the carrier is likely to check in any event, to be certain that some cartons are not inadvertently left behind, and to determine the appropriate freight charge. However, the carrier is not required to check most quality terms, such as what goods are in a container and whether they are in operating condition.[13] The carrier can truthfully say that it has received 100 cartons "said to contain" IBM word processing computers, without opening the cartons; but it does need to count the number of cartons.

The intersection of these rules arise when the carrier accepts a sealed container supposed to contain 2000 tin ingots weighing 35 tons, and issues a bill of lading for a container "said to contain 2000 tin ingots." If the container is empty or weighs less than a ton and the carrier does not weigh it, the carrier's disclaimer is not likely to protect it.[14] The disclaimer will, however, protect the carrier if the shipper actually loaded the sealed container itself.[15]

Note that regardless of the description of quantity or other terms on the bill of lading, a carrier cannot avoid liability when the goods are damaged by the carrier's negligence.[16]

§ 3.19 Forged Bills of Lading

If the carrier issues a bill of lading for which there are no goods, the carrier will likely be held liable to the holder of a negotiable bill of lading. However, suppose the carrier never issued any bill of lading. Instead, a person unrelated to the carrier created a false bill of lading or forged a bill of lading, without authority from the carrier. The buyer who purchases such a forged bill of lading has paid funds to a forger, probably through a series of banks, and finds that the carrier has no goods to deliver. There is no misdelivery or misdescription claim against the carrier, for there never were any goods delivered to the carrier for it to redeliver or to describe. If the carrier did not issue the bill of lading and its "signature" is a forgery or is unauthorized, that signature is not "effective," and carrier will not be liable on the bill, absent some sort of actionable negligence.

12. See supra note 5, § 3.18.

13. See e.g., Mannell v. Luckenbach S.S. Co., 26 F.2d 908 (D.Wash.1928) (stating that the purchaser was not entitled to recover from a carrier for misdescription of the damaged goods where the bill of lading correctly described the kind and quantity of articles, without any description of the condition of the goods).

14. Berisford Metals Corp. v. S/S Salvador, 779 F.2d 841, 847–48 (2d Cir.1985), cert. denied, 476 U.S. 1188, 106 S.Ct. 2928, 91 L.Ed.2d 556 (1986).

15. See Dei Dogi Calzature S.P.A. v. Summa Trading Corp., 733 F.Supp. 773, 775–76 (S.D.N.Y.1990) (stating that carrier is not liable to shipper for losses resulting from receipt of container filled with water instead of leather items where bill of lading description of contents was prefaced by "said to contain" and the bulk freight was loaded by the shipper).

16. See Atlantic Coast Line R.R. Co. v. Hogrefe, 43 Ga.App. 520, 159 S.E. 760, 766–67 (Ga.Ct.App.1931).

The forger is liable for the fraud, if he can be found. Unlike the forged indorsement situation, there is no one who has received any goods, for there never were any goods to deliver. However, like the forged indorsement situation, each party that transferred the bill of lading for value makes warranties to later parties, and the first warranty is that "the bill is genuine."[1] If the bill of lading itself is forged that warranty is breached. Thus, all parties who transferred the bill and received payment funds can be liable to breach of warranty actions against them by later parties. The concept is that the last person to purchase the bill will "know its indorser," and be able to recover against its transferor. That transferor can, in turn, recover against its transferor, and so on up the chain of transfers, until the loss falls either on the forger or upon the person who dealt with and took the bill from the forger.

Collecting banks that have transferred the document for value can be subject to this warranty liability, but have the same three potential escape options discussed under forged indorsements: (1) a disclaimer of warranty through making "a contrary intention appear," (2) a claim that the bank is holding the document only "as security for a debt," and (3) the limitation in the I.C.C. Collection Rules that banks need examine only the appearance of the documents. Each of these approaches has analytical difficulties, as discussed above, but they may indicate a blanket intention to disclaim the statutory warranties implicitly. Any bank that is found to have warranty liability can pass this liability back to its transferor, as long as it can identify and find that transferor.

In addition, the FBLA provides for criminal liability and punishment of the fraudulent making or use of bills of lading, whether they are domestic, export or originate from foreign countries.[2]

F. ELECTRONIC BILLS OF LADING

§ 3.20 Introduction

The FBLA does not define "bills of lading" and does not require that a bill of lading be written on a piece of paper or signed by anyone. Thus, use of electronic bills of lading would seem to be a technical possibility. However, all of the primary rules of the federal law are filled with an implicit assumption that the bill of lading is a paper document. In fact, international maritime business law has been called a "law of document."[1] The references to indorsements in blank or to a specified person, transfer by delivery, and "person in possession" (holder) make sense only in a paper document transaction.

§ 3.19

1. 49 U.S.C. § 80107(a)(1).

2. See United States v. Castro, 837 F.2d 441, 444–46 (11th Cir.1988).

§ 3.20

1. See Dube, Canadian Perspectives on the Impact of the CMI Rules for Electronic Bills of Lading on the Liability of the Carrier Towards the Endorsee, 26 Transp. L. J. 107, 110 (Fall 1998).

The United Nations Commission on International Trade Law (hereinafter UNCITRAL) conducted a preliminary investigation into the legal ramifications of electronic data interchange in 1985, and prepared a preliminary study in 1990.[2] The study examined the issues and problems relating to the legal acceptance of non-written documents, and made recommendations in order to reduce the barriers to electronic data interchange. The study recommended, among other things, that states permit computer records to be admitted into evidence, computer-readable forms to be substituted for written documents, and electronic authentication of signatures.[3]

In the arena of electronic bills of lading, the largest challenge has been in making an electronic bill of lading negotiable so that it remains authentic and confidential.[4] Telecommunications technology can provide electronic messages that perform the main functions of the bill of lading as a receipt, transport contract and document of title. Thus, several types of bills of lading equivalents are currently in use, but most of them are used only as receipts for the goods and are generated by the carrier. Their utility is enhanced where a straight bill of lading (or waybill) does not need to be presented to the carrier to obtain possession of the goods. Unfortunately, the FBLA requires the carrier to deliver the goods only to a person who "has possession of the bill," even under a straight bill of lading,[5] and makes the carrier liable for damages if it does not take and cancel the bill when delivering the goods.[6] These requirements are often ignored by carriers in practice, and the parties merely exchange printed forms, but the statutory requirements do inhibit the acceptance of electronic bills of lading in the United States.

Despite the requirements regarding delivery by the carrier to only a party in possession of a bill of lading, the International Chamber of Commerce now authorizes the use of uniform electronic bills of lading, both negotiable and non-negotiable, for both motor carrier and rail carrier use. These have been authorized since 1982 and 1988 respectively. There is an assumption that such electronic bills of lading merely communicate information about the goods, the shipper, and the consignee. There are no provisions defining the rights and obligations of the parties to the electronic bill. Thus, the bills do not allow for further sale or rerouting of the goods in transit, or for using the bills of lading to finance the transaction. Under the regulations, negotiable uniform electronic bills of lading must "provide for endorsement on the back portion," but there is no explanation of how an electronic message has a "back portion," or how "endorsement" is to be effected.

---

2. UNCITRAL Electronic Data Interchange B Preliminary Study of Legal Issues Related to the Formation of Contracts by Electronic Means B Report of the Secretary General, 23rd Sess., P8, U.N. Doc. A/CN.9/333 (1990) (hereinafter UNCITRAL Study).

3. UNCITRAL Study, id. at P2(a).

4. See Dube, supra note 1, at 110.

5. 49 U.S.C. § 80110(a)(2).

6. 49 U.S.C. § 80110(c).

§ 3.21 Establishing a System and Format for Electronic Bills of Lading

There have been several programs to create electronic carrier-issued international receipts for goods. Atlantic Container Lines used dedicated lines between terminals at its offices in different ports to send messages between those offices. It generated a Data Freight Receipt that was given to the consignee or notify party. Such a receipt was not negotiable and gave buyers and banks little protection from further sale or rerouting of the goods by shipper in transit. The Cargo Key Receipt was similar, but also an advance over the prior approach, because it included a "no disposal" term in the shipper-carrier contract. Thus, this electronic message protected buyer from further sale or rerouting by seller in transit. It still could not be used to finance the transfer, however, because the electronic receipt, even if it named a bank as consignee, was not formally a negotiable document of title. The receipt was believed to give the bank only the right to prevent delivery to the buyer, not a positive right to take control of the goods for itself.

The Chase Manhattan Bank and the International Association of Independent Tanker Owners (Intertanko), created the SEADOCS Registry, which was intended to create a negotiable electronic bill of lading for oil shipments. The Registry acted as custodian for an actual paper negotiable bill of lading issued by a carrier, and maintained a registry of transfers of that bill from the original shipper to the ultimate "holder." The transfers were made by a series of electronic messages, each of which could be authenticated by "test keys," or identification numbers, generated by SEADOCS. SEADOCS would then, as agent, endorse the paper bill of lading in its custody. At the end, SEADOCS would electronically deliver a paper copy of the negotiable bill of lading to the last endorsee to enable it to obtain the goods from the carrier. While SEADOCS was a legal success, showing that such a program was technically feasible, it was not a commercial success and lasted less than a year when Chase discontinued its efforts.[1]

The Comite Maritime International has adopted Rules for Electronic Bills of Lading (hereinafter the CMI Rules).[2] Under the CMI Rules, any carrier can issue an electronic bill of lading as long as it will act as a clearinghouse for subsequent transfers. Each carrier has its own registry (usually per ship) and is not dependant upon the technology or software of any other party or a central registry.[3] Upon receiving goods, the carrier sends an electronic message to the shipper describing the goods, the contract terms, the location and date that the goods were received, and a "private key" which can be used to transfer shipper's rights to a third party. Under the CMI Rules, the shipper now has the "right of

---

§ 3.21

1. See Chandler, Maritime Electronic Commerce for the Twenty–First Century, 22 Mar. Law. 463, 469 (1998).

2. Comite Maritime International Rules for Electronic Bills of Lading (1990), re-

printed in Kelly, Comment: The CMI Charts a Course on the Sea of Electronic Data Interchange: Rules for Electronic Bills of Lading, 16 Mar. Law. 349 (1992).

3. See Dube, supra § 3.20, note 1, at 109.

control and transfer" over the goods, and is called a "holder." Under Rules 4 and 7, an electronic message from a shipper, which includes the private key, can be used to transfer the shipper's rights to a third party. The third party becomes a new holder when it sends a confirmation to the carrier that it intends to accept the transfer of ownership rights from the shipper. The carrier then cancels the shipper's private key and issues a different private key to the new holder. Upon arrival, the carrier will deliver the goods to the then-current holder or consignee designated by the holder.

Electronic bills of lading under the CMI Rules require the carrier to participate in the transaction. The use of the private key permits each transmission to be authenticated and makes the electronic bill of lading negotiable. The private key is not transferable, as it changes every time there is a new holder, and therefore the carrier is involved in the negotiation process every time the bill of lading is negotiated.[4]

To take advantage of the CMI Rules, the original parties to the transaction must agree that the CMI Rules will govern the "communications" aspects of the transaction B the rules are voluntary and do not automatically have the force of law.[5] The CMI Rules are not intended to govern the substantive laws of bills of lading provisions, only the electronic transfers of the electronic bill of lading. All parties also agree that electronic messages satisfy any national law requirements that a bill of lading be in writing. This is an attempt to create an "electronic" writing that is a negotiable document of title by contract and estoppel. Some commentators have observed that this is an attempt by private parties to create a negotiable document, a power usually reserved to legislatures. In addition, there is some concern that the CMI Rules do not address certain issues, such as what constitutes receipt of an offer or acceptance, or what happens when there is a system failure.[6]

The Commission of the European Committees has sponsored the BOLERO electronic bill of lading initiative, which is based on the CMI Rules, and supported by a consortium of carriers, shippers, banks, insurers and telecommunication companies. However, under the BOLERO system, neither a bank nor a carrier is the repository of the sensitive information of who has bought and sold the cargo covered by the electronic bills of lading. Instead BOLERO establishes a third party who is independent of the shipper, the carrier, the ultimate buyer and all intermediate parties as the operator of the central registry. The central registry and user-carriers, shippers, freight forwarders, and banks communicate through computer workstations that also permit communications between the parties themselves. The central registry maintains the shipping details in "consignment records," and access to such records is limited to those possessing authority through strong security controls and digital signatures. The digital signatures authenticate the message

---

4. See Dube, supra § 3.20, note 1, at 113.

5. See Chandler, supra note 1, at 475.

6. See Livermore and Euarjai, Electronic Bills of Lading: A Progress Report, 28 J. Mar. L. & Com. 55, 57 (1997).

sender and prevent modification of transactions. Trials began in 1995 on the BOLERO project with participants in Hong Kong, the Netherlands, Sweden, the United Kingdom and the United States. The BOLERO project has not been broadly accepted in the industry and has faced much difficulty B it has changed management and continues to struggle to maintain funding.[7]

American bankers have been skeptical of the device created by the CMI Rules. The registries maintained by each carrier do not have the same level of security associated with SWIFT procedures (Society for Worldwide Interbank Financial Telecommunication). [See "Electronic Letters of Credit" in Chapter 6.] In addition to fraudulent transactions, there is a risk of misdirected messages. Thus, a bank could find itself relying on "non-existent rights based upon fraudulent information in a receipt message transmitted to it by someone pretending to be the carrier." The banks are concerned as to whether carriers will accept liability in their new role as electronic registrars for losses due to such fraudulent practices.[8] The banks are also concerned that the full terms and conditions of the contract of carriage are not available to the subsequent "holders." Thus, use of the CMI Rules does not yet seem to be widely adopted, and bills of lading are still primarily paper-based in both the "payment against documents" and letter of credit transactions.

UNCITRAL adopted the Model Law on Legal Aspects of Electronic Data Interchange and Related Means of Communication (the "Model Law") in 1996.[9] The Model Law, using a "functional equivalence" approach, eliminates many barriers that had previously existed, such as testimonial value, recognition as a writing, and authentication.[10] The Model Law includes provisions that a data message satisfies any requirement that a document be in writing (Article 5), provides for electronic signatures (Article 6), and confirms that electronic data can be used as a document and as evidence (Articles 4 and 8).[11]

The experiments discussed above all attempted to substitute an electronic message for the paper-based bill of lading, but otherwise did not change the bill of lading system.

7. Bills of Lading for Europe (BOLERO). See Laryea, Paperless Shipping Documents: An Australian Perspective, 25 Mar. Law 255 (2000); Chandler, supra note 1, at 486–87; Livermore and Euarjai, Electronic Bills of Lading and Functional Equivalence, at http://eljiwarwick.ac.uk./jilt/ecomm/982liv/livermore.htm.

8. See Winship, in Current Developments Concerning the Forms of Lading (A.N. Yiannaopolis ed. 1995).

9. UNCITRAL Model Law on Electronic Commerce, G.A. Res. 162, U.N. GAOR, 51st Sess., U.N. Doc. A/RES/51/162 (1996).

10. See Livermore and Euarjai, supra note 6, at 56.

11. Id.

G.   SELECTED DOCUMENTS

§ 3.22   Sample Bill of Lading

INTERNATIONAL BILL OF LADING
NOT NEGOTIABLE UNLESS CONSIGNED "TO ORDER"

(2) SHIPPER/EXPORTER (COMPLETE NAME AND ADDRESS)	(5) BOOKING NO	(5A) BILL OF LADING NO
SANTA CLAUS COMPANY EAST AURORA, NEW YORK 14052	(6) EXPORT REFERENCES	A-10

(3) CONSIGNEE (COMPLETE NAME AND ADDRESS)	(7) FORWARDING AGENT F M C NO
TO ORDER OF SHIPPER	F.W. MYERS (ATLANTIC) & CO., INC. One World Trade Center New York, New York 10048 (212) 432-0670

(8) POINT AND COUNTRY OF ORIGIN
EAST AURORA, NEW YORK   FMC 1397

(4) NOTIFY PARTY (COMPLETE NAME AND ADDRESS)	(9) ALSO NOTIFY - ROUTING & INSTRUCTIONS
ALPHA COMPANY ATHENS GREECE	notify on arrival in NYC Mr. J. Emma Phone 432-0670 for pier delivery instructions EXPORT MOTOR FREIGHT TO DELIVER TO PIER DOCK RECEIPTS LODGE AT PIER

(12) PRE CARRIAGE BY ★	(13) PLACE OF RECEIPT BY PRE CARRIER ★
EXPORT MOTOR FREIGHT	EAST AURORA, NY

(14) VESSEL VCY FLAG	(15) PORT OF LOADING	(10) LOADING PIER/TERMINAL	(10A) ORIGINAL(S) TO BE RELEASED AT
SS LIVORNO	NEW YORK	Pier 29, Black Ball Terminal	

(16) PORT OF DISCHARGE	(17) PLACE OF DELIVERY BY ON-CARRIER ★	(11) TYPE OF MOVE (IF MIXED, USE BLOCK 20 AS APPROPRIATE)
ATHENS		

PARTICULARS FURNISHED BY SHIPPER

MKS & NOS / CONTAINER NOS (18)	NO OF PKGS (19)	HM	DESCRIPTION OF PACKAGES AND GOODS (20)	GROSS WEIGHT (21)	MEASUREMENT (22)
K ALPHA CO. ATHENS, GREECE ORDER NO. 1234 Made in U.S.A. NOS. 1-513			CONTAINER XTRU STC: 513 Cartons Childrens Toys IMPORT LICENSE #143210 Letter of Credit #34576 CLEAN ON BOARD G-DEST	9633 lbs.	2102.4 C.F.

These Commodities Licensed by the U.S. for Ultimate Destination GREECE
Diversion Contrary to U.S. Law Prohibited.

23) Declared Value $ _____ If shipper enters a value, carriers package limitation of liability does not apply and the ad valorem rate will be charged					(23A) RATE OF EXCHANGE	(24) **FREIGHT PAYABLE AT/BY**
TP	RATED AS	PER	RATE	PREPAID	COLLECT	LOCAL CURRENCY
TOTAL CHARGES						

☐ If this box is checked, goods have been loaded, stowed and counted by Shipper. Carrier has NOT done so and is not responsible for accuracy of count, condition or nature of goods described in PARTICULARS FURNISHED BY SHIPPER

THE RECEIPT, CUSTODY, CARRIAGE AND DELIVERY OF THE GOODS ARE SUBJECT TO THE TERMS APPEARING ON THE FACE AND BACK HEREOF AND TO CARRIER'S APPLICABLE TARIFF

In witness whereof three (3) original bills of lading all of the same tenor and date one of which being accomplished the others to stand void have been issued by the originating carrier for and on behalf of itself other participating carriers, the vessel and her master and owners or charterers

Dated ....

At ....

.... (Originating Carrier)

By ....

BILL OF LADING NO _____   DATE _____   ★ APPLICABLE ONLY WHEN USED FOR MULTIMODAL TRANSPORTATION

COMBINED TRANSPORT BILL OF LADING.

1. DEFINITIONS

"Carrier"	means the Owners or Charterer of the ocean vessel on whose behalf this Bill of Lading has been issued.
"Goods"	means the cargo accepted from the Shipper and includes any Container not supplied by or on behalf of the Carrier.
"Container"	includes any Container (including an open top Container) flat rack, platform, trailer, transportable tank, pallet or any other device used for the transportation of Goods.
"Merchant"	includes the Consignor, Shipper, Holder, Consignee, the receiver of the Goods, any person including any Corporation, Company or other legal entity owning or entitled to the possession of the Goods or this Bill of Lading and anyone acting on behalf of any such persons.
"Holder"	means any person for the time being in possession of this Bill of Lading to whom the property in the Goods has passed on or by reason of the consignment of the Goods or the endorsement of this Bill of Lading or otherwise.

"The Internal Law of a State" shall be deemed to exclude all principles of private international law applied by such State.

2. CARRIER'S TARIFF

The terms of the Carrier's applicable Tariff are incorporated herein. Copies of the relevant provisions of the applicable Tariff are obtainable from the Carrier upon request. In the case of inconsistency between this Bill of Lading and the applicable Tariff, this Bill of Lading shall prevail.

3. SUB-CONTRACTING

(1) The Carrier shall be entitled to sub-contract on any terms the whole or any part of the carriage, loading, unloading, storing, warehousing, handling and any and all duties whatsoever undertaken by the Carrier in relation to the Goods.

(2) The Merchant undertakes that no claim or allegation shall be made against any servant, agent, stevedore or sub-contractor of the Carrier which imposes or attempts to impose upon any of them or any vessel owned or chartered by any of them any liability whatsoever in connection with the Goods, and, if any such claim or allegation should nevertheless be made to indemnify the Carrier against all consequences thereof. Without prejudice to the foregoing, every such servant, agent, stevedore and sub-contractor shall have the benefit of all provisions herein benefiting the Carrier as if such provisions were expressly for their benefit, and all limitations of and exonerations from liability provided to the Carrier by law and by the terms hereof shall be available to them, and, in entering into this contract the Carrier, to the extent of those provisions, does so not only on its own behalf, but also as agent and trustee for such servants, agents, stevedores and sub-contractors.

(3) The expression "sub-contractor" in this clause shall include direct and indirect sub-contractors and their respective servants and agents.

4. DELIVERY OF CARGO BEYOND PORT OF DISCHARGE OR PLACE OF DELIVERY

In the event that Consignees/Receivers of cargo require the Carrier to deliver cargo at a port or place beyond the place of delivery originally designated in this Bill of Lading and the Carrier in its absolute discretion agrees to such further carriage, such further carriage will be undertaken on the basis that the Bill of Lading terms and conditions are to apply to such carriage as if the ultimate destination agreed with Consignees/Receivers had been included in the description of the transport on the reverse side of this Bill of Lading.

5. CARRIER'S RESPONSIBILITY

The Carrier undertakes responsibility from the place of receipt if named herein or from the port of loading to the port of discharge or the place of delivery if named herein as follows:

(1) If it can be proved that the loss or damage occurred while the Goods were in the custody of an inland carrier the liability of the Carrier and the limitation thereof shall be determined in accordance with the inland carrier's contracts of carriage and tariffs, or in the absence of such contracts or tariffs, in accordance with the internal law of the state where the loss or damage occurred.

(2) Where loss or damage has occurred between the time of receipt of the Goods by the Carrier at the port of loading and the time of delivery by the Carrier at the port of discharge, or during any prior or subsequent period of carriage by water, the liability of the Carrier shall be determined as follows:

- (a) If the carriage is to or from the United States of America, the "Carriage of Goods by Sea Act 1936" (COGSA) of the United States of America, shall apply.
- (b) For carriage in all other trades, the "International Convention for Unification of certain Rules relating to Bills of Lading", dated Brussels, August 25, 1924 (The Hague Rules, excluding Article IX), shall apply except when the "Hague Visby Rules" (dated Brussels, February 23, 1968) are compulsorily applicable at the port of loading in which case the "Hague Visby Rules" shall apply.

(3) Where it cannot be established where the loss or damage occurred the liability of the Carrier shall be determined in accordance with sub-paragraph 2 above.

In no event shall the liability of the Carrier exceed the amount of compensation payable under Clause. 6.

The Carrier shall be entitled to the full benefit of and right to all limitations of or exemptions from liability authorized by any provision of Section 4281 to 4289 of the Revised Statutes of the United States of America and amendments thereto and of any other provisions of the laws of the United States or of any other country whose laws shall apply.

Nothing in this Bill of Lading, expressed or implied, shall be deemed to waive or operate to deprive the Carrier of or lessen the benefits of any such rights, immunities, limitations or exemptions.

6. THE AMOUNT OF COMPENSATION

(1) For shipment to or from ports in the United States of America neither the Carrier nor the Ship shall in any event be or become liable for any loss or damage to or in connection with the transportation of Goods in an amount exceeding $500.00 per package lawful money of the United States of America, or in case of Goods not shipped in packages, per customary freight unit, or the equivalent of that sum in other currency, unless the nature and value of such Goods have been declared by the shipper before shipment and inserted on the face of this Bill of Lading and extra freight paid.

13. LIEN

The Carrier shall have a lien on the Goods and any documents relating thereto for all sums payable to the Carrier under this contract and/or any other contract and for general average contributions to whomsoever due and for the cost of recovering the same, and for that purpose shall have the right to sell the Goods by Public Auction or private treaty without notice to the Merchant. If on sale of the Goods the proceeds fail to cover the amount due and the cost incurred, the Carrier shall be entitled to recover the deficit from the Merchant.

14. OPTIONAL STOWAGE, DECK CARGO AND LIVESTOCK

(1) The Goods may be stowed by the Carrier in Containers or similar articles of transport used to consolidate Goods.

(2) Goods whether stowed in Containers or not, may be carried on deck or under deck without notice to the Merchant unless on the face hereof it is specifically stipulated that the Containers or Goods will be carried under deck, and if carried on deck, the Carrier shall not be required to note, mark or stamp on the Bill of Lading any statement of such on deck carriage. Such Goods (other than livestock) whether carried on deck or under deck and whether or not stated to be carried on deck shall participate in general average and shall be deemed to be within the definition of Goods for the purpose of the "Carriage of Goods by Sea Act 1936" (COGSA) of the United States of America or similar provisions of any other Act which may be applicable.

(3) Goods (not being Goods stowed in Containers other than flats or pallets) which are stated herein to be carried on deck and livestock, whether or not carried on deck, are carried without responsibility on the part of the Carrier for loss or damage of whatsoever nature arising during carriage by sea whether caused by unseaworthiness or negligence or any other cause whatsoever.

15. METHODS AND ROUTES OF TRANSPORTATION

(1) The Carrier may at any time and without notice to the Merchant:

- (a) use any means of transport or storage whatsoever;
- (b) transfer the Goods from one conveyance to another including trans-shipping or carrying the same on another vessel than the vessel named overleaf or on any other means of transport whatsoever and even though transhipment or forwarding of the Goods may not have been contemplated or provided for herein;
- (c) sail without pilots, proceed via any route, proceed to, return to and stay at any port or place whatsoever (including the port of loading herein provided) in any order in or out of the route or in a contrary direction to or beyond the port of discharge once or more often for bunkering or loading or discharging cargo or embarking or disembarking any person(s) whether in connection with the present a prior or subsequent voyage or any other purpose whatsoever, and before giving delivery of the Goods at the port of discharge or the place of delivery herein provided and with liberties as aforesaid leave and then return to and discharge the Goods at such port, tow or be towed make trial trips, adjust compasses, or repair or dry-dock, with or without cargo onboard;
- (d) load and unload the Goods at any port or place (whether or not any such port is named overleaf as the Port of Loading or Port of Discharge) and store the Goods at any such port or place;
- (e) comply with any orders or recommendations given by any government or authority or any person or body or purporting to act as or on behalf of such government or authority or having under the terms of the insurance on the conveyance employed by the Carrier the right to give orders or directions.

(2) Anything done or not done in accordance with sub-clause (1) or any delay arising therefrom shall be deemed to be within the contractual carriage and shall not be a deviation.

16. MATTERS AFFECTING PERFORMANCE

(1) If at any time the performance of the contract evidenced by this Bill of Lading is or is likely to be affected by any hindrance, risk, delay, difficulty or disadvantage of whatsoever kind which cannot be avoided by the exercise of reasonable endeavours, the Carrier (whether or not the transport has commenced) may without notice to the Merchant treat the performance of this contract as terminated and place the Goods or any part of them at the Merchant's disposal at any port or place whatsoever which the Carrier or Master may consider safe and advisable in the circumstances, whereupon the responsibility of the Carrier in respect of such Goods shall cease. The Carrier shall nevertheless be entitled to full freight and charges on Goods received for transportation, and the Merchant shall pay any additional costs of carriage to and delivery and storage at such port or place.

(2) The circumstances referred to in sub-clause (1) above shall include, but shall not be limited to, those caused by the existence or apprehension of war declared or undeclared, hostilities, warlike or belligerent acts or operations, riots, civil commotions or other disturbances, closure of, obstacles in or danger to any canal; blockade of port or place or interdict or prohibition of or restriction on commerce or trading; quarantine, sanitary or other similar regulations or restrictions; strikes, lockouts or other labour troubles whether partial or general and whether or not involving employees of the Carrier or his sub-contractors; congestion of port, wharf, sea terminal or any other place; shortage, absence or obstacles of labour or facilities for loading, discharge, delivery or other handling of the Goods; epidemics or diseases; bad weather, shallow water, ice, landslide or other obstacle in navigation or haulage.

17. PERISHABLE CARGO

Goods of a perishable nature shall be carried in ordinary Containers without special protection, services or other measures unless there is noted on the reverse side of this Bill of Lading that the Goods will be carried in a refrigerated, heated, electrically ventilated or otherwise specially equipped Container or are to receive special attention in any way.

The Merchant undertakes not to tender for transportation any Goods which require refrigeration without giving written notice of their nature and the required temperature setting of the thermostatic controls before receipt of the Goods by the Carrier. In case of refrigerated Container(s) packed by or on behalf of the Merchant, the Merchant undertakes that the Goods have been properly stowed in the Container and that the thermostatic controls have been adequately set by him before receipt of the Goods by the Carrier.

The Merchant's attention is drawn to the fact that refrigerated Containers are not designed to freeze down cargo which has not been presented for stuffing at or below its designated carrying temperature and the Carrier shall not be responsible for the consequences of cargo presented at a higher temperature than that required for the transportation.

If the above requirements are not complied with, the Carrier shall not be liable for any loss of or damage to the Goods howsoever arising.

(2) In all other trades where the Hague Rules apply the Carrier's maximum liability shall in no event exceed £100.00 lawful money of the United Kingdom per package or unit, unless the nature and value of such Goods have been declared by the shipper before shipment and inserted on the face of this Bill of Lading and extra freight paid.

7. GENERAL

(1) The Carrier does not undertake that the Goods shall arrive at the port of discharge or the place of delivery at any particular time or to meet any particular market or use and save as is provided in clause 4 the Carrier shall in no circumstances be liable for any direct, indirect or consequential loss or damage caused by delay. If the Carrier should nevertheless be held legally liable for any such direct or indirect or consequential loss or damage caused by delay, such liability shall in no event exceed the freight paid for the transport covered by this Bill of Lading.

(2) Save as is otherwise provided herein, the Carrier shall in no circumstances be liable for direct or indirect or consequential loss or damage arising from any other cause.

(3) The terms of this bill of Lading shall govern the responsibility of the Carrier in connection with or arising out of the supplying of a Container to the Merchant whether before or after the Goods are received by the Carrier for transportation or delivered to the Merchant.

8. NOTICE OF LOSS, TIME BAR

Unless notice of loss or damage and the general nature of such loss or damage be given in writing to the Carrier or his agents at the port of discharge or the place of delivery as the case may be before or at the time of removal of the Goods into the custody of the Merchant such removal shall be prima facie evidence of the delivery by the Carrier of the Goods as described in this Bill of Lading. If the loss or damage is not apparent, then notice must be given within three days of the delivery. In any event, the Carrier shall be discharged from any liability unless suit is brought within one year after delivery of the Goods or the date when the Goods should have been delivered.

9. SHIPPER-PACKED CONTAINERS

(1) If a Container has not been stuffed by the Carrier, this Bill of Lading shall be a receipt only for the Container(s) and the Carrier shall not be liable for loss of or damage to the contents and the Merchant shall indemnify the Carrier against any injury, loss, damage, liability or expense incurred by the Carrier if such injury, loss, damage, liability or expense has been caused by:

(a) The manner in which the Container has been filled, packed, stuffed or loaded: or

(b) the unsuitability of the contents for carriage in Containers; or

(c) the unsuitability or defective condition of the Container which would have been apparent upon reasonable inspection by the Merchant at or prior to the time the Container was filled, packed, stuffed or loaded.

(2) The Shipper shall inspect Containers before stuffing them and the use of the Containers shall be prima facie evidence of their being sound and suitable for use.

10. INSPECTION OF GOODS

The Carrier shall be entitled, but under no obligation, to open any Package or Container at any time and to inspect the contents. If it thereupon appears that the contents or any part thereof cannot safely or properly be carried or carried further, either at all or without incurring any additional expense or taking any measures in relation to such Package or Container or its contents or any part thereof, the Carrier may abandon the transportation thereof and/or take any measures and/or incur any reasonable additional expense to carry or to continue the carriage or to store the same ashore or afloat under cover or in the open, at any place, which storage shall be deemed to constitute due delivery under this Bill of Lading. The Merchant shall indemnify the Carrier against any reasonable additional expense so incurred.

The Carrier in exercising the liberties contained in this clause shall not be under any obligation to take any particular measures and the Carrier shall not be liable for any loss, damage or delay howsoever arising from any action or lack of action under this clause.

11. SHIPPER'S RESPONSIBLITY

(1) The Shipper warrants to the Carrier that the particulars relating to the Goods as set out overleaf have been checked by the Shipper on receipt of this Bill of Lading and that such particulars and any other particulars furnished by or on behalf of the Shipper are correct,

(2) The Shipper shall indemnify the Carrier against all loss, damage or expenses arising or resulting from inaccuracies or inadequacy of such particulars.

12. FREIGHT AND CHARGES

(1) Full freight hereunder shall be due and payable by the Shipper in cash without deduction on receipt of the Goods or part thereof by the Carrier for shipment and shall be deemed to have been fully earned upon such receipt of Goods. All charges due hereunder together with freight shall be due from and payable by the Shipper, Consignee, Owner of the Goods or Holder of this Bill of Lading (who shall be jointly and severally liable to the Carrier therefore) on demand at such port or place as the Carrier may require, vessel or other means of transportation of cargo lost or not lost from any cause whatsoever.

(2) The freight stated herein to be paid or payable has been calculated and based on the particulars of the Goods furnished by the Shipper to the Carrier. The Carrier shall be entitled at any time to open and re-classify or re-weigh or re-measure or re-value any Goods, and freight shall be paid on the proper classification or the excess weight or measurement or value.

(3) The Merchant's attention is drawn to the stipulations concerning currency in which the freight and charges are to be paid, rate of exchange, devaluation and other contingencies relative to freight and charges in the applicable Tariff.

(4) The freight has been calculated on the basis of particulars furnished by or on behalf of the Shipper. The Carrier may at any time open any Container or other Package or Unit in order to re-weigh, re-measure, re-classify or re-value the contents, and if the particulars furnished by or on behalf of the Shipper are incorrect, it is agreed that a sum equal to the difference between the correct freight and the freight charged shall be payable by the Merchant to the Carrier.

18. DANGEROUS GOODS

(1) The Merchant undertakes not to tender for transportation any Goods which are of a dangerous, inflammable, radioactive or damaging nature without previously giving written notice of their nature to the Carrier and marking the Goods and the Container or other covering on the outside as required by any laws or regulations which may be applicable during the carriage. The Carrier or the Master may however, in their absolute discretion reject any such cargo.

(2) If the requirements of sub-clause (1) are not complied with or if the Goods which were tendered in compliance with sub-clause (1) shall become a danger to the vessel, cargo or any other property or person, such Goods may be unloaded, destroyed or rendered harmless without compensation and the Merchant shall indemnify the Carrier against all loss, damage or expense which the Carrier could not avoid by the exercise of reasonable diligence by incurred as a result of the carriage of such Goods.

19. REGULATIONS RELATING TO GOODS

The Merchant shall comply with all regulations or requirements of Customs, port and other authorities, and shall bear and pay all duties, taxes, fines, imposts, expenses or losses incurred or suffered by reason thereof or by reason of any illegal, incorrect or insufficient marking, numbering or addressing of the Goods, and indemnify the Carrier in respect thereof.

20. NOTIFICATION AND DELIVERY

(1) Any mention in this Bill of Lading of parties to be notified of the arrival of the Goods is solely for information of the Carrier, and failure to give such notification shall not involve the Carrier in any liability nor relieve the Merchant of any obligation hereunder.

(2) The Merchant shall take delivery of the Goods within the time provided for in the Carrier's applicable Tariff.

(3) If the Merchant fails to take delivery of the Goods or part of them in accordance with this Bill of Lading, the Carrier may without notice unstow the Goods or that part thereof and/or store the Goods or that part thereof ashore, afloat, in the open or under cover. Such storage shall constitute due delivery hereunder, and thereupon all liability whatsoever of the Carrier in respect of the Goods or that part thereof shall cease.

(4) The Merchant's attention is drawn to the stipulations concerning free storage time and demurrage contained in the Carrier's applicable Tariff, which is incorporated in this Bill of Lading.

(5) The Carrier may in his absolute discretion receive the Goods as Full Container Load and deliver them as less than Full Container Load and/or as break bulk cargo and/or delivery of the Goods to more than one receiver. In such event the Carrier shall not be liable for any shortage, loss, damage or discrepancies of the Goods, which are found upon unpacking of the Container.

(6) If the Goods are unclaimed during a reasonable time, or whenever in the Carrier's opinion the Goods will become deteriorated, decayed or worthless, the Carrier may, at his discretion and subject to his lien and without any responsibility attaching to him, sell, abandon or otherwise dispose of the Goods at the sole risk and expense of the Merchant.

21. BOTH-TO-BLAME COLLISION CLAUSE

If the carrying ship comes into collision with another ship as a result of negligence of the other ship and any act, neglect or default in the navigation or the management of the carrying ship, the Merchant undertakes to pay the Carrier, or, where the Carrier is not the owner and in possesison of the carrying ship, to pay to the Carrier as trustee for the owner and/or demise charterer of the carrying ship, a sum sufficient to indemnify the Carrier and/or the owner and/or demise charterer of the carrying ship against all loss or liability to the other or non-carrying ship or her owners insofar as such loss or liability represents loss of or damage to, or any claim whatsoever of the Merchant, paid or payable by the other or non-carrying ship or her owners to the Merchant and set off, recouped or recovered by the other or non-carrying ship or her owners as part of their claim agaany shipsinst the carrying ship or her owner or demise charterer or the Carrier. The foregoing provisions shall also apply where the owners, operators, or those in charge or any ship or ships or objects, other than, or in addition to, the colliding ships or objects, are at fault in respect to a collision, contact, stranding or other accident.

22. GENERAL AVERAGE

(1) General average shall be adjusted at any port or place in the option of the Carrier in accordance with the York-Antwerp Rules 1974.

(2) If the Carrier delivers the Goods without obtaining security for general average contributions, the Merchant, by taking delivery of the Goods, undertakes personal responsibility to pay such contributions and to provide a cash deposit or other security for the estimated amount of such contribution as the Carrier shall reasonably require.

23. NEW JASON CLAUSE

(1) In the event of accident, danger, damage or disaster before or after the commencement of the voyage, resulting from any cause whatsoever, whether due to negligence or not, for which or for the consequence of which the Carrier is not responsible, by statute, contract or otherwise, the Goods and the Merchant shall jointly and severally contribute with the Carrier in general average to the payment of any sacrifices, losses or expenses of a general average nature that may be made or incurred and shall pay salvage and special charges incurred in respect of the Goods.

(2) If a salving ship is owned or operated by the Carrier, salvage shall be paid for as fully as if the said salvage ship belonged to strangers.

24. VARIATION OF THE CONTRACT ETC.

No servant or agent of the Carrier shall have power to waive or vary any terms of this Bill of Lading unless such waiver or variation is in writing and is specifically authorized or ratified in writing by the Carrier.

25. LAW AND JURISDICTION

Whenever the "Carriage of Goods by Sea Act of 1936" (COGSA) of the United States of America applies by virtue of clause 5.2(a) above this contract is to be governed by United States law and the United States Federal Court Southern District of New York is to have exclusive jurisdiction to hear all disputes hereunder.

In all other cases this Bill of Lading is subject to English law and jurisdiction.

[G4115]

Selected Bibliography

Andrewartha and Swangard, English Maritime Law Update: 1999, 31 J. Mar. L. & Com. 471 (July 2000).

Chan, A Plea for Uncertainty: Legal and Practical Problems in the Presentation of Non-negotiable Bills of Lading, 29 Hong Kong L.J. 44 (1999).

Chandler, Maritime Electronic Commerce for the Twenty–First Century, 22 Mar. Law. 463 (Summer 1998).

Donovan and Haley, Who Done it and Who's Gonna Pay?, 7 D.C.L.J. Int'l L. & Prac. 415 (Fall 1998).

Dube, Canadian Perspective on the impact of the CMI Rules for Electronic Bills of Lading on the Liability of the Carrier Towards the Endorsee, 26 Transp. L.J. 107 (Fall 1998).

Force, A Comparison of the Hague, Hague–Visby, and Hamburg Rules: Much Ado About (?), 70 Tul. L. Rev. 2051 (June 1996).

Hooper, Carriage of Goods and Charter Parties, 73 Tul. L. Rev. 1697 (May/June 1999).

Jefferies, COGSA or Hague–Visby: Cargo Damages in International Shipments, 18 Hous. J. Int'l L. 767 (Spring 1996).

Kelly, Comment, The CMI Charts a Course on the Sea of Electronic Data Interchange: Rules for Electronic Bills of Lading, 16 Mar. Law. 349 (Spring 1992).

Mandelbaum, Creating Uniform Worldwide Liability Standards for Sea Carriage of Goods Under the Hague, COGSA, Visby and Hamburg Conventions, 23 Transp. L.J. 471 (Spring 1996).

Livermore and Euarjai, Electronic Bills of Lading: A Progress Report, 28 J. Mar. L. & Com. 55 (Jan. 1997).

Nakazawa and Moghaddam, COGSA and Choice of Foreign Law Clauses in Bills of Lading, 17 Mar. Law. 1 (Fall 1992).

Southcott, Canadian Maritime Law Update: 1999, 31 J. Mar. L. & Com. 447 (July 2000).

Sturley, Uniformity in the Law Governing the Carriage of Goods by Sea, 26 J. Mar. L. & Com. 553 (1995).

Tetley, The Demise of the Demise Clause?, 44 McGill L.J. 807 (Dec. 1999).

Tetley, The Proposed New United States Senate COGSA: The Disintegration of Uniform International Carriage of Goods by Sea Law, 30 J. Mar. L. & Com. 595 (Oct. 1999).

Tiberg, Legal Qualities of Transport Documents, Tul. Mar. L.J. 1 (Winter 1998).

Wood, Multimodal Transportation: An American Perspective on Carrier Liability and Bill of Lading Issues, 46 Am. J. Comp. L. 403 (1998).

Yancey, Symposium on American and International Maritime Law: Comparative Aspects of Current Importance: The Carriage of Goods: Hague, COGSA, Visby and Hamburg, 57 Tul. L. Rev. 1238 (June 1983).

Chapter 4

SALES AGENT AND DISTRIBUTORSHIP AGREEMENTS

Table of Sections

A. INTRODUCTION

171

A. INTRODUCTION

§ 4.1 Need for a Written Agreement

Most products sold to purchasers in foreign lands involve the use of some person or entity in the foreign nation as the sales representative or distributor.[1] A small company may retain a representative in the foreign nation who handles many different, but usually compatible, products. A large company will have its own foreign agent or distributor.[2] It should be obvious that the commercial relationship between a U.S. producer and its foreign agent or distributor *must* be reduced to a written agreement. Because two different nations' laws may be involved, and probably two different cultures, the agreement should be sufficiently detailed to deal with the legal consequences reflecting such differences.

---

§ 4.1

1. Certainly a company in one nation may accept orders placed from abroad. Such sales require no foreign, local representation. The retention of a foreign agent or distributor often follows periodic but increasing sales placed directly to the home office from abroad.

2. While the direct sale from an order placed from abroad may be the prelude to the use of an agent or distributor, the successful use of an agent or distributor may in turn lead subsequently to manufacturing the products in the foreign nation. Subsequent chapters deal with licensing such production (Chapters 22–23), and direct foreign investment (Chapters 25–30).

§ 4.2 Problems Most Prevalent Upon Termination

A U.S. producer/seller may have its own complete distribution network in each foreign country in which it does business. That is frequently not the case, however. Much more likely is that the U.S. company will use some local person or entity for the distribution of its goods. Local distributors are used by U.S. companies just beginning to sell goods abroad, as well as by large multinationals with long experience abroad, but which do not have their own distribution networks. As in the case of any commercial contract, there are many possible areas for disagreement. But in the sphere of distribution agreements, the most difficult issues arise upon termination, especially when the foreign agent or distributor is terminated against its will. Termination issues are often difficult when both parties are in the United States. But they are exacerbated when the seller is in one nation, such as the United States, and the distributor is in another nation, particularly a developing nation.[1] The foreign distributor, often an individual or comparatively small corporation, may believe that it has been treated unfairly by the quite likely much larger foreign seller. This is especially true when the local distributor has worked to develop clients and goodwill for the foreign company. The consequence of complaints by local agents and distributors that they have been mistreated, especially terminated unfairly, by large foreign corporations, has been the enactment of host-nation regulation of many forms of distribution agreements.[2] These laws may be very favorable to the local agent or distributor, but one may look in vain for provisions in these foreign laws which offer the foreign producer or supplier compensation when the local distributor has performed unsatisfactorily.

§ 4.3 Effect of Changing Export Laws in the United States

A company dealing abroad through a foreign agent or distributor must be aware not only of any laws in the foreign nation that protect the

§ 4.2

1. It is not only developing nations which attempt to regulate the distribution of goods. Agency law in general affects such distribution and may be quite different and quite complex in other countries. See for example the law of Mexico, as discussed by Ignacio Gomez Palacio in Symposium, Establishing an Agency or Distributorship in Mexico, 4 U.S.-Mexico L. J. 72 (1996); or the law of Italy, as discussed in G. LaVilla & M. Caetella, The Italian Law of Agency and Distributorship Agreements (1977); or the law of Germany, as discussed in F. Staubach, The German Law of Agency and Distributorship (1977); or the law of France, as discussed in J. Guyenot, The French Law of Agency and Distributorship Agreements (1976).

2. For example, the "Statement of Motives" of the Puerto Rican law applicable to distribution agreements states:

> The Commonwealth of Puerto Rico cannot remain indifferent to the growing number of cases in which domestic and foreign enterprises, without just cause, eliminate their dealers, concessionaries [sic], or agents, as soon as these have created a favorable market and without taking into account their legitimate interests.

Quoted in Fornaris v. Ridge Tool Co., 423 F.2d 563, 565 (1st Cir.1970), *reversed* 400 U.S. 41, 91 S.Ct. 156, 27 L.Ed.2d 174 (1970).

rights of nationals who become agents and distributors, but also of U.S. laws that may affect the distribution of goods abroad. The United States has exerted with some frequency extraterritorial authority by way of laws that affect U.S. businesses doing business abroad. These rules have usually been motivated by political goals (e.g., the removal of a dictator from office), and have no direct relation to either the U.S. seller or the foreign buyer. The political goals may be strongly rejected by the foreign agent's or distributor's government. These rules may have significant impact. The U.S. party may be prohibited from exporting to the foreign nation, which leaves the foreign agent or distributor without products to sell, and therefor in jeopardy of serious financial losses. The U.S. exporter may be in breach of a distribution agreement if it is unable to fulfill orders. The agreement should have an excuse for nonperformance clause which covers such an event. Which U.S. laws may have such an effect are not easily identified. Foreign policy has caused various U.S. presidents to use export controls as a response to foreign political actions, such as when in 1982 the United States limited the transfer of goods to Europe that were destined for use in the construction of a gas pipeline from the then-USSR.

When the United States acts extraterritorially, the foreign government may attempt to "block" the long-arm extension of U.S. laws into the foreign territory. The foreign government may actually be the U.S. exporter's "best friend" in attempting to convince the U.S. government that the action is unreasonable and possibly unlawful under international law or trade agreements such as the NAFTA or the WTO/GATT.

B.   FORMS OF DISTRIBUTION

§ 4.4   Choice of Form

The two forms most frequently used to distribute products abroad are (1) an independent foreign agent, or (2) an independent foreign distributor. Usually the choice is made by the U.S. exporter. But in doing business abroad, especially in developing nations, the choice of the form of distribution may not be the prerogative of the U.S. company. The choice may be mandated by local law. Furthermore, there may be quite different choices.

§ 4.5   Independent Foreign Agent

An independent foreign agent, who may be called a "sales representative" or "commission agent", is a person in the foreign nation who does not take title to the goods and who usually is paid in some combination of salary and commissions. This person does not bear the risk that the buyer might not pay. That risk remains with the U.S. supplier. The foreign agent usually does not have the power to bind the U.S. supplier,[1] but may be considered to have implied power to do so, and

---

§ 4.5

1. The word "agent" in foreign sales use may mean more than or less than the

legal meaning of the word in U.S. law. United States agency law usually involves a consensual relationship where the agent

certainly may be given express authority to do so.[2] The independent agent obtains orders for sales abroad and sends those orders to the U.S. seller. Thus, there usually is no need for the agent to store goods in its nation.

The use of an independent foreign agent tends to create more legal problems for the company selling abroad than would the use of an independent foreign distributor. The agent, who may be called a distributor without regard to the legal distinction between the two, thus receives the greater focus of this chapter. Agency law may differ substantially in a foreign nation, especially nations with civil law tradition systems.[3] Furthermore, the laws of some nations blur the distinction between the two forms of distribution, and thus use of one form may not achieve the protection sought.

One important factor to understand is that the law of the agent's nation may regulate the nature of the agency relationship substantially more than is the practice in the United States. Civil law commercial codes may provide extensive detail regarding the agency relationship. Additionally, these rules may be mandatory and not subject to alteration by contract. Foreign law may outline different forms of agency with quite carefully delineated powers. The powers may or may not be in conflict with what the U.S. party might wish to arrange by contract. It is essential to understand the forms of agency which exist, and their respective roles, in any nation where the use of an agent is contemplated.

§ 4.6 Independent Foreign Distributor

An independent foreign distributor, in contrast to the usual kind of agent, buys the company's products and resells them through the foreign distributor's network.[1] The foreign distributor, in taking title to the goods, consequently assumes such risk as not being able to resell them. The distributor is the one whom the purchaser must pay, and therefore the distributor is at risk for nonpayment. Because the distributor is essentially buying the goods for resale, it must find storage for the goods prior to final sale and distribution.

Unlike the uncertainty existing in the case of the independent agent, the independent distributor does not have power to bind the supplier.

has certain power to bind the principal. But that power may be limited or removed altogether. It is important to realize that the general meaning of "agent" may differ from country-to-country, which emphasizes the need for contractual clarity in defining the relationship.

2. Agents are frequently used for sales to foreign governments, where contracts are often for very substantial amounts.

3. The civil law tends not to recognize the responsibility of a principal for acts of an undisclosed agent.

§ 4.6

1. The distributor, in contrast to an agent, thus has to make a financial commitment, and consequently is usually a larger and more formal entity than a foreign direct agent.

That is because the distributor buys the goods for resale, rather than entering into contracts on behalf of the principal as in the case of an agent. Of course the distributor might additionally have power to act as an agent for goods it does not obtain as a distributor. In such case, the issue of the power to bind the principal is present.

If an independent foreign distributor is chosen, the language in the distribution agreement should be as clear as possible in noting the principal-principal vice principal-agent relationship. Language used when establishing an independent contractor relationship may be useful in establishing an independent distributor relationship.

§ 4.7   Laws Protecting Agents and Distributors

Countries often have special laws which govern the distribution agreement between their nationals *as agents* and foreign businesses.[1] This is in addition to the domestic agency laws that apply to any agency relationship.[2] There are far fewer countries that have laws governing agreements between foreign business and local independent *distributors*.[3] However, the distinction between the two is sometimes blurred, but nevertheless remains an important distinction. For example, antitrust laws in some nations are enforced against distributorships but not against agencies. This may affect assigning a distributor exclusive selling rights.[4] Of course, when the agency form is that of an *employee* agent rather than an *independent* agent, the agency may clearly be exclusive. Some developing nations do not even recognize the distinction between their nationals as agents and their nationals as distributors, and govern both in one law.[5] But to be fair, what the U.S. supplier calls its foreign distributor is less important than being able to determine and formalize the characteristics of the relationship. If the characteristics suggest an agency, the host nation is likely to consider the person as an agent. The same is true for distributors.[6]

---

§ 4.7

1. Some nations mandate the use of local agents for the distribution of foreign goods. This tends to be the rule in developing nations, and includes much of the middle-East.

2. Appointment of an agent, particularly with power to bind the principal, may constitute doing business and subject the foreign business to jurisdiction and taxation.

3. An example is Belgium, one of the very few nations in the European Union to have legislation regulating distributorship agreements.

4. Chile allows an exclusive agency but not an exclusive distributorship.

5. This is true of many Latin American nations, but not of Brazil. Developing nations in other areas of the world, i.e., Africa and Asia, are more inclined to follow the general rule of regulating agents but not distributors.

6. There is considerable literature on the subject of foreign laws affecting agents/distributors. See, e.g., Georg Vorbrugg & Dirk H. Mahler, Agency and Distributorship Agreements Under German Law, 19 Int'l Lawyer 607 (1985); Jacques Sales, Termination of Sales Agents and Distributors in France, 17 Int'l Lawyer 741 (1983); Thad W. Simons, Termination of Sales Agents and Distributors in Belgium, 17 Int'l Lawyer 752 (1983); A.H. Puelinck & H.A. Tielemans, The Termination of Agency and Distributorship Agreements: A Comparative Survey, 3 Nw.J.Int'l L. & Bus. 452 (1981); Robert B. Cartwright & Samir Hamza, The Saudi Arabian Service Agents Regulation, 34 Bus.Lawyer 475 (1979); Salvador Juncadella, Agency, Distribution and Representation Contracts in Central Amer-

Where foreign laws applicable to distribution agreements have been enacted, they are likely to be designed to (1) benefit local agents/distributors, especially in the area of termination; (2) restrict (or prohibit) the use of agents/distributors, essentially to protect the public from unfair agents/distributors; or (3) apply domestic *labor* law to the distribution agreement, in addition to any special laws applicable to the distribution agreement. How these laws influence the distribution agreement is discussed below in the separate sections covering various distribution agreement provisions.

Civil law tradition nations tend to be more likely to restrict freedom to contract than common law tradition nations. Laws regulating agency and distributorship agreements in civil law countries may be separate and specific, or may be found in the civil or commercial codes.[7] Developing nations are most likely to have special laws affecting the agency/distributorship relationships.

Even where host nation law mandates use of local agents or distributors, it may be possible to use a local business entity as the agent even though the agency is majority owned by the U.S. company. But many host nations which mandate the use of local distributors additionally require at least majority host-nation ownership of artificial entities (i.e., local corporations).[8]

C. ABILITY TO CONTROL AGENT OR DISTRIBUTOR

§ 4.8 Aspects of Control

The sale of goods abroad to an independent distributor usually means the seller relinquishes control over such aspects as where the product may be resold and the price.[1] Loss of control over establishing the price may be enough to cause the seller to adopt an independent *agency* form of distribution, which may but does not assure ability to set the resale price.[2] Because title remains in the U.S. seller until the goods are sold in the foreign country by the agent, the seller should be able to

ica and Panama, 6 Lawyer of the Americas 35 (1974).

7. Distribution of products within the European Union involves national laws and EU law. Common or civil law tradition-based national laws, depending on the EU member state involved, are likely to govern the nature of the relationship, such as the powers of persons designated as agents. European Union law is likely to govern such aspects of distribution as territorial restrictions and price maintenance. See infra § 4.31.

8. Many nonmarket economies mandated local sales through a government state trading organization (STO) or foreign trade organization (FTO), a requirement which

has substantially been abandoned along with many other trade restrictions. But remnants of state involvement persist in some nations in transition from nonmarket to market economies, and there remain a number of nations still firmly committed to nonmarket policies.

§ 4.8

1. The U.S. export-control laws govern reexport and may place a burden on the U.S. exporter to assure that the goods are not reexported to certain destinations. See infra Chapter 16.

2. In many developing nations the government establishes price controls.

set the price.[3] The agent only has authority to find a buyer, but not set the terms of the sale. That remains the function of the seller.

A further element of control is the ability to appoint sub-agents or sub-distributors without the approval of the principal. An agent normally has no such authority, but an independent distributor will be able to hire and fire at will, unless there is some agreement regarding whom the distributor uses to deal with the foreign company's products.

If the agent is actually *employed* by the U.S. company, there is no question about the issue of control.[4] But when an agent is an employee, the employer becomes subject to labor laws of the host nation. That may create such problem as being unable to terminate the employee at will, at least without making a substantial severance payment.[5] It is not only developing nations' laws which grant greater rights to employees. The industrialized nations of Europe treat labor in a very different way than does the United States.[6] The U.S. company therefore may prefer to use an independent agent who is carefully kept independent of the company, and linked to the company as an agent by contract rather than by employment. Control will be contractually designated, but host-nation laws are likely to affect the contract. Some foreign nations do not distinguish carefully between an agent who is an employee and an agent who is not.[7] Where the distinction is made, and statutory protection is not given to the independent agent, the choice of an agent who is not an employee will usually be the preference of the U.S. company.

The fact that some laws may not acknowledge the distinction between an employee-agent and an independent agent does not mean that all laws will overlook that distinction. For example, the tax laws will generally accept the distinction, and thus income from sales by an employee-agent is income to the corporation, but not necessarily so in the case of an independent agent. Furthermore, a foreign nation may exert extraterritorial jurisdiction over the U.S. company which *employs* an agent in the foreign nation, but decline to do so when the U.S. company uses an *independent* agent in the foreign nation.

Choice of an independent distributor rather than an employee-agent may create antitrust problems. The distributorship agreement becomes an agreement between two different and independent entities, and

---

3. That may be a wholesale price and the U.S. seller may not be able to further control the retail price.

4. An employee-agent may be on commissions alone or a salary plus commissions. The independent agent is more likely to be solely on commissions.

5. Many developing nations have special agency/distributor laws because their labor laws do not apply to these relationships. Agents and distributors are thought to be able to bargain better than employees, but when that has proven not to be the case, it has been "remedied" by either enacting a special agent/distributor law, or by applying the labor laws to the agency/distributorship relationships.

6. See Clyde W. Summers, Worker Participation in the U.S. and West Germany: A Comparative Study from an American Perspective, 28 Am.J.Comp.L. 367 (1980).

7. Italy grants to self-employed agents nearly all the rights granted to employee agents. See A.H. Puelinck & H.A. Tielemans, The Termination of Agency and Distributorship Agreements: A Comparative Survey, 3 Nw.J.Int'l L. & Bus. 452, 456 (1981).

provisions such as an exclusive distributorship arrangement may conflict with local laws. The European Union imposes rules on exclusive distributorships which differ from those in the United States. Prohibitions on selling outside an exclusive territory, such as one of the EU nations, will not be recognized, although one may be able to mandate that the distributor *solicit* business exclusively in the applicable territory. European Union rules also address and prohibit resale price maintenance and minimum prices.[8]

Antitrust concerns similar to those involving exclusive distributorship arrangements may exist where the foreign independent distributor is prohibited from selling competing goods. This may create a problem with U.S. law in that it may foreclose other U.S. companies from entering the foreign market. It may conflict with host nation antitrust principles as well.

Use of an employee-agent may avoid these issues, because there is only a single entity involved and the control over the employee is obviously greater than over an independent agent. When there is any question regarding restraints on competition, the antitrust laws of both the United States and the foreign host nation must be consulted. The most developed antitrust law outside the United States is in the European Union. While many of the EU antitrust concepts parallel those in the United States, there are many significant differences, mandating an understanding of both.[9]

The ability to control the agent by means of the distribution agreement may depend upon whether the agent is in a country with a common law tradition or a country with a civil law tradition. Common law tradition nations tend to allow greater freedom to contractually create the full terms of the agreement, including termination provisions. Civil law tradition nations, contrastingly, more often include statutory restraints on freedom to contract, especially with regard to the right to terminate and rights created upon termination. Whether the nation has a common law or civil law tradition system, laws are dynamic and the attitude toward distribution agreements may change. Laws governing the transfer of technology and intellectual property have very substantially changed in the past two decades in developing nations, several of which realized that restrictive laws diminished the amount and quality of technology offered. Knowing foreign law usually means associating with local counsel. No one distributing products in many countries can be an expert in all the host-nation laws—the use of local counsel is critical. *

There is no single contract form which may be used throughout the world. But there are provisions which should be in every contract. Many of the areas to consider in drafting a contract are discussed below.

8. See infra § 4.31.   **9.** See infra Chapter 20.

§ 4.9 Areas to Consider

There are many areas of control which should be considered, not only those mentioned above dealing with setting prices and hiring sub-agents. Where control exists, the agent/distributor may be limited in many actions. That may include the ability to incur expenses on behalf of the principal, or to carry competing lines of products. Such actions as making corrupt payments to foreign officials may be closely monitored where control exists. There is an obvious benefit to having control. But with control may come responsibility for actions of the agent appearing to a third party to be within the agent's authority. Such responsibility may be avoided by using a distributor who is fully independent of the company. But where the host foreign nation does not recognize this independence, the worst of both worlds may exist. The company may have no control over the agent/distributor, but may be held responsible for much of the conduct of the agent/distributor.

D. CHOOSING THE AGENT OR DISTRIBUTOR

§ 4.10 Individual or Business Entity

A U.S. company should consider whether it is appropriate to hire an individual rather than a formal business entity as the foreign agent.[1] Whatever the choice, the foreign person or persons involved should have the same business expectations as the U.S. entity, including perhaps similar experience in advertising, marketing and credit policies. The U.S. party should know how the foreign party will operate, such as the extension of credit, use of sub-agents or distributors, use of retail stores, history of sales efforts for other U.S. or third-nation principals, compatibility of the product with other lines carried by the agent/distributor, and reputation for service.

The usual rule is to retain a business entity rather than an individual. The contract should clarify the identity of the parties to the distribution agreement. If the agent is an individual, local labor laws may apply even if the U.S. company attempts to define the local agent as an independent contractor. Labor laws in some developing nations are very protective. They often prohibit termination at will and require significant termination pay when termination is allowed.[2] Using independent contractor language is useful, such as specifying that the compensation is to be in the form of commissions or discounts rather than a salary. The agreement should not state required working hours, nor provide capital to commence the distributorship, nor offer the goods to the distributor on consignment, nor allow the use of the U.S. company's name.

§ 4.10

1. The agreement should clearly state the character of the agent/distributor.

2. The labor laws may have consequences even at the time of hiring, such as contributions to national social security, health, workers compensation and retirement funds.

§ 4.11   Nationality of the Agent/Distributor

A second and important consideration is the nationality of the agent/distributor. Some countries reserve to their own nationals distribution rights in the country. In most cases the agent/distributor will be a host-nation national. Such person should better understand the business culture and legal requirements of the nation. In some instances, U.S. persons move abroad and become agents or distributors of U.S. businesses. Their advantage is that they understand the business culture of the U.S. seller, including sales expectations, work ethic principles, and U.S. legal rules such as those governing foreign corrupt payments.

Obviously the first inquiry is whether the U.S. seller has a choice. The host-nation laws may mandate that agents/distributors be nationals, and thus the issue is moot. But if allowed, the distributorship could be a business entity controlled and perhaps owned by U.S. parties, but employing host-nation sales personnel.

§ 4.12   Special Problems

There have been special problems in obtaining distributors in the former Eastern European nations as they undergo restructuring of their economies. Old state-owned distributors often prove inadequate, particularly in developing new markets.[1] Some companies have used young and inexperienced distributors in each country, who in turn hire students and others part-time to take displays to various stores. Establishing a new distribution program takes considerable time in contrast to market economy nations. Many companies have first concentrated on the principal city, and later moved to regional cities, and finally developed national distribution. Some companies in Eastern Europe have opened brand-name stores under parent company management. This form of distribution requires a quite different form of agreement than that used for a traditional local distributorship. One reason to use this form is the desire to retain close control over retail operations, and to be able to watch for the sale of counterfeit items. The problems of operating distributorships in these nations indicate the fragility of such agreements and the need to tailor them to the circumstances in each nation.

The selected agent or distributor may expect, or by local law be required, to be the *exclusive* distributor of the goods. It should not be surprising that a successful local agent or distributor intending to expend considerable efforts on behalf of the company will expect to be the exclusive agent or distributor. With regard to distributorships, exclusivity may create problems, including antitrust issues.[2] Exclusivity

§ 4.12

1. Old state-owned distributors were often most concerned with how to dismantle the old business and gave little effort to developing new business.

2. The antitrust issues may be raised under both U.S. law and foreign law, especially in the European Union where anti-trust law is in a rapid stage of development (or perhaps catch-up). See U.S. Department of Justice, Antitrust Guide for International Operations (1988), allowing exclusive territories abroad depending on certain conditions, such as the effect on competitors of the U.S. supplier and absence of other anti-competitive conduct.

may be useful in providing protection to agents and distributors, but enforcement of exclusive territory provisions may raise legal issues.

E. THE AGREEMENT—PROVISIONS TO CUSTOMERS

§ 4.13 Language

The agreement must be in at least one language, and should be in *only* one language. If the parties insist on two or more languages, one should be designated as the official language, preferably English, the language of the U.S. entity. The party with whom the U.S. entity is dealing should understand English well enough to fully comprehend the agreement. Contrastingly, if the agreement is to be in the foreign language, the U.S. party should either understand the foreign language or have faith in the local foreign counsel retained to assist. Local law may require the agreement to be in the host-nation language rather than English.

§ 4.14 Agreement is the Full Agreement

The agreement should contain a provision that the parties concur that the written agreement represents the full agreement between the parties. If not included, the question of the admission of oral evidence may be more complex, and require consideration of rules of admissibility of evidence outside the written agreement, in different legal systems. Furthermore, by attempting to regulate the full range of expected conduct, the parties are likely to discover, during the negotiation process areas where there are differences that need to be resolved. Different countries mean different cultures, and different cultures mean different laws, policies and attitudes.

§ 4.15 Definitions

Although the agreement may attempt to define various terms, the parties may wish to include a provision that internationally recognized definitions, such as the International Chamber of Commerce's INCO-TERMS or the U.S. Chamber of Commerce's Revised American Foreign Trade Definitions, shall apply in the absence of a specific definition in the agreement. Important terms not defined in any adopted standard definitions should be clearly spelled out in the agreement.

§ 4.16 Services to be Performed by Agent/Distributor

A foreign distribution agreement should be very detailed with regard to the expected duties of the agent/distributor. Reasonable expectations of persons in one culture may be very different from those in another. For example, the agreement should specify how much stock the agent/distributor must carry. This is especially important when an independent distributor is used who purchases and assumes title to the goods and who may prefer to stock a very small part of the principal's line. Other areas to consider include the agent/distributor's role in sales campaigns and provision of periodic reports.

One alternative is to include a provision calling for the agent/distributor to use best efforts to promote and solicit sales. But perhaps the better method is to specify exactly how the agent/distributor is to carry out such activities. For example, the agreement may be more specific regarding any advertising the agent/distributor is required to undertake, including both the amount and locations. If the goods require installation and service, the agreement should state whether that is the duty of the agent/distributor, and how costs of installation and service are to be allocated.

If the arrangement is a distributorship where the distributor purchases and assumes title to the goods, the terms should be included in the agreement. This may include the form of payment, whether credit is extended, currency of payment, and terms of shipment of goods (i.e., FAS, FOB, CIF, etc.).[1] These terms not only are necessary for an independent distributorship agreement, but help affirm that the nature of the distributorship is not an agency agreement. If it is an agency agreement, it should state that the terms and conditions of sale are those which are presented to the agent from time-to-time.

The U.S. party should protect its intellectual property—trademarks and trade names, copyrights and patents. The contract should include statements affirming the U.S. party's ownership of the intellectual property involved, and stipulate that the agent/distributor is allowed to use that property only to promote and solicit sales. The agent/distributor should agree not to use deceptively similar names or marks, not to destroy or alter names or marks, and to allow only the U.S. party to sue for infringement. Intellectual property should be protected by local registration, and where available multi-state registration. Access of the agent/distributor to company knowhow should be limited to a need to know basis.

Compensation of the agent/distributor should be carefully defined in the agreement. If the arrangement is an independent distributorship, compensation in the form of commissions is obviously more appropriate than a salary. A salary is indicative of an agency relationship, not an independent distributorship. The compensation provisions should address how figures are calculated, for example what constitutes the total volume of sales if commissions are a percentage of total sales. The provisions should consider any applicable discounts, costs of shipping and insurance and taxes. Total sales should be stated to be total sales paid for, to allow for nonpayment by customers. Finally, the manner of payment should be included, usually by check but certainly in accordance with any local laws governing currency transfers.

§ 4.16

1. Use of INCOTERMS is recommended since some shipping terms (e.g., FOB) have different meanings in different nations.

§ 4.17 Compensation and Payment

Some nations limit the amount of commissions which agents may receive in their country, particularly when the sales are to the government. The local agent might wish to avoid such limits by other arrangements, such as amounts above the limit paid to a third-nation bank account.[1] Agreeing to such an arrangement may make the U.S. supplier a party to the breach of local laws, and jeopardize not only the particular agency agreement, but the right to do future business in the country. *Any* request for payment made to an account in a third nation should be of concern to a U.S. supplier, since it may also violate currency control laws and may be part of a scheme of tax evasion. The local agent may be compelled by local law to deposit all income received for services in an account in the host nation. Deposits in a third nation may also suggest that some of the agent's commissions are being used to pay government officials, which may implicate the U.S. principal or supplier not only in the violation of local law, but of the U.S. Foreign Corrupt Practices Act.[2] Any agreement should provide for the manner of compensation, and that procedure should clearly avoid allowing the foreign distributor to violate host-nation law. It should clearly avoid drawing the U.S. party into a breach of U.S. or host nation law, with possible criminal as well as civil sanctions.

Where there is a distributorship, the payment issues are usually less frequently subject to local limits, and less likely to raise FCPA issues. Distributors buy the U.S. party's goods, and issues of payment are likely to involve credit arrangements, payment in dollars, and use of traditional documents such as letters of credit.

§ 4.18 Choice of Law and Venue

Where there are no statutes to the contrary present, most courts will apply basic contract law to distributorship agreements. While there is some thought that distributorship agreements are *sui generis* and should have special conflicts of law rules, conflicts rules applicable to commercial contracts are generally used. But freedom to contract, more prevalent in common law than civil law tradition nations, is often restricted, especially in the area of the right to terminate.

Each party is likely to prefer its own law and courts as the applicable law and forum in the event of a dispute.[1] But since the agreement is to be carried out in a foreign nation, the law of that nation may be mandatory, and it may require the proceeding to be brought in local courts. That is more likely to be the case in a nation which has in place a statutory scheme governing distribution agreements, and even in

§ 4.17

1. Or to a bank account in the United States.

2. The FCPA is the subject of Chapter 17, infra.

§ 4.18

1. See generally Jay Greenfield, How to Avoid, Prepare for, and (Should All Else Fail) Win Supplier–Distributor Disputes, 33 Practical Lawyer 59 (1987).

a nation without such a law but where the laws are extensively codified. Where local law is mandatory, choice of law and venue provisions will not be honored by the courts.

The judiciary of the host nation may be viewed to be excessively protective of nationals, possibly mirroring the local statutory law. This protectionism may be endemic to the system, and may arise because of uncertainty of dealing with international commercial contracts. Where such bias is thought to exist, the best advice may be to choose arbitration, if available. Some nations prohibit arbitration altogether, others allow arbitration only if the arbitral forum and rules are domestic. Unfortunately, the biases of the judicial system may be reflected as biases of the local arbitration system. But the U.S. company should attempt to provide for third-nation arbitration, especially for compensation determination, and to specify in the agreement at least the situs of the arbitration and the rules of arbitration which are to be used. The U.S. party may prefer arbitration in the United States or perhaps at the International Chamber of Commerce in Paris, and the use of AAA or ICC rules of arbitration, respectively.

§ 4.19   Termination

It is very important to know what the termination laws are in any nation where a distributorship agreement is proposed. One may confront a rule that effectively means that the distributorship agreement may not be terminated or may not be renewed, without the payment of what may be a substantial amount of compensation to the local agent/distributor. The potential costs of a termination, which at first may seem quite reasonable and justified under the laws of the principal's nation, may be very extensive under the laws of the host nation. Because termination often follows a realization that the agent/distributor relationship did not function as expected, it is essential to choose the agent/distributor with great care. Since termination problems are the most significant and potentially most costly matter regarding distribution agreements, contracting with the kind of agent/distributor one really needs will minimize the occurrence of unhappy times.

In addition to being aware of local termination laws, the issue of termination should be discussed thoroughly with the agent/distributor. An agent/distributor who is terminated and who believes that the termination was fair and reasonable, may not attempt to seek additional protection under domestic laws.

Termination laws are more likely to be present in civil law tradition nations than common law tradition nations, and the causes for termination are likely to be limited by statute. Many European nations have detailed termination rules, which provide different rights depending upon the classification of the relationship.

§ 4.20   Termination—Right to Terminate

If restrictions on the termination of a distributorship agreement are imposed, they nevertheless usually allow termination where there is just cause. But what is just cause? It may be defined in the host-nation's statutes, but if it is not the contract should include a definition. For example, is the failure to meet contractually stipulated sales quotas just cause? It may not be in some countries.

The statutes may include other reasons allowing termination beyond just cause. The principal should know these reasons, and may wish to incorporate them into the agreement. An agreement may often be terminated on the date established in the agreement as the end of the relationship. Some nations, however, to protect their nationals, do not allow termination at will and thus may not even approve a fixed-term agreement. When a very successful distributorship comes to the end of a fixed time, the government may wish to protect its national from termination by the foreign party, which may plan to continue the distribution scheme as a company-managed enterprise. This has often been the case with franchises.[1] When the franchisor realizes how lucrative the arrangement has been for the franchisee (however magnified the profits were for the franchisor), the franchisor may attempt to "take over" the franchise by refusing to renew the agreement.[2]

If a distributorship agreement is silent as to expiration, host-nation law may either treat any termination as subject to the just cause/no just cause rules, or may allow termination after a period of time has elapsed, and usually with adequate pre-termination notice. Inappropriate notice may cause the termination to be treated the same as a termination not for just cause, with statutory indemnification provisions applicable.

The U.S. company should consider what should be just cause, and include as full a list as possible in the agreement. They may not all be acknowledged by local law as just cause reasons, and there is some concern that they will be considered the exclusive list of reasons, meaning that the agent/distributor may not otherwise be terminated. The agreement should consider actions which *immediately* terminate the agreement, such as bankruptcy or insolvency of the agent/distributor, nationalization of the property of the agent/distributor, transfer of ownership of the agency/distributorship, and inability to function for a period of time due to *force majeure* causes. The agreement might also include a provision which allows for termination if the agent's/distributor's government enacts new legislation governing the distributorship which allows compensation to the agent/distributor upon nonrenewal or termination.

A more difficult reason for termination is unsatisfactory performance, the most common reason cited for terminating an agreement. The agreement may attempt to state expected sales goals or minimum performance. But if the expectations prove unworkable, the agreement should be modified. Termination for unsatisfactory performance will usually require some notice, and may require an opportunity to have a

§ 4.20

1. See Chapter 22, infra.

2. Many nations have special laws applying exclusively to franchises, and addressing this issue.

second chance after renegotiating the minimum expectations. If the contract calls for minimum standards which are not met, and if the company neither terminates nor renegotiates, a later termination may be considered unreasonable since the company may have waived the standards by its inaction.

In any area where the company believes the agent/distributor might act to harm the relationship and provide cause for termination, the company should consider allowing for some period of time to cure the problem, after fair notification. The company must act with unquestioned fairness, particularly where restrictive host-nation laws exist.

§ 4.21   Termination—Notice of Termination

The host-nation statute may cover notice of termination, and may require that notice be given not only to the agent/distributor, but also to a government office. The provision may also state the amount of time that must be given between the notification and termination. Ineffective notice may not only be invalid as notice, but could lead to sanctions. The agreement should provide for the details of notice, including how it is to be sent, and that the notice period begins on the date of receipt. It should of course be sent by registered mail, with some form of return receipt.

Providing notice may act as a substitute for just cause in some nations. In other words, just cause may require little or no notice, while termination without just cause may be allowed if fair notice, possibly several months, is given. This is not likely to be the case, however, in many developing nations which have restrictive laws protecting agents/distributors. In such case reasonable notice may be required in addition to compensation.

§ 4.22   Termination—Rights Upon Termination

Terminated agents/distributors have various rights under the laws of different nations. If the agent/distributor is terminated with just cause, unless the agent/distributor is an employee or otherwise treated as such, there are likely to be limited rights, if any. But where the termination is without just cause, the rights may be extensive.

Usually rights upon termination involve some form of a monetary settlement. The amount may be a percentage of the principal's gross profits during the time the agreement was in effect, or it may be a multiple of what the agent/distributor earned during the life of the agreement or during a certain number of years. The calculation may also consider any unexpired term of the contract. The agent/distributor may have to be paid for any goods in his possession, for any goodwill established by the agent/distributor, for any promotional expenses assumed, and for any other expenses or investments made during the time of the agreement. The calculation of compensation, particularly where there is a dispute which may have to be decided in the courts, may prove expensive for the U.S. principal if a court in the host nation enjoins the

U.S. party from terminating the agent/distributor during the judicial proceeding, or where a new distributor appointment is delayed by the government pending the outcome of the proceeding.

If the agent was an employee or treated as such under host nation law, there also may be labor law consequences of the termination. These may be fixed amounts or amounts which must be calculated, and could amount to very considerable sums.

Knowledge of both the nature of statutory indemnification upon termination and how the judiciary treats termination may be useful. In some nations conservative judges are inclined to award low amounts to terminated agents/distributors. Furthermore, where inflation is not compensated by indexing, a lengthy judicial process may lead to an award that is much reduced by inflation.[1]

Upon termination, the agent/distributor may possess inventory. The agreement should specify what is to be done with that inventory, such as a promise by the principal to buy back inventory where the form of the distributorship is such that title has passed to the agent/distributor.

§ 4.23   Termination—Waiver of Termination Rights

Where termination rights exist, it may be possible to have the agent/distributor waive these rights. But that is not likely to be allowed, since the protective laws exist for the benefit of host-nation citizens. The laws or public policy of the country may reject any waiver of rights, because the agent/distributor is assumed to have little bargaining leverage. Many distribution agreements are fairly labeled "adhesion" contracts. The host-nation laws attempt to offset this aspect of distribution agreements, and do not allow waivers to nullify this protection granted to the local agent/distributor.

§ 4.24   Termination—Denial of Import Privileges

Where the process to determine the compensation of a terminated agent/distributor is continuing, the principal may be denied any further rights to import into the country. The principal thus may not shift the distributorship to another party and continue business while the indemnification process remains unfinished. However, the principal may not wish to send additional products to the country, that might be subject to attachment if the terminated agent/distributor receives a judgment (or pretrial attachment order) against the principal.[1]

---

§ 4.22

1. Where inflation is extremely high, an award not indexed may be insignificant.

§ 4.24

1. One of the hazards of establishing a distributorship in a nation which is part of an economically integrated area, such as the European Union, is that a judgment of one member nation may easily be enforce-

able in another. The foreign agent/distributor judgment creditor could attempt to enforce the judgment in the United States, where state law, which may vary considerably from state-to-state, will apply. This will be affected by the adoption of a widely accepted international convention on the enforcement of foreign judgments, currently being negotiated at the Hague. The convention is expected to be ready for adoption

§ 4.25   Termination—Denial of Export Privileges

The U.S. party should include a provision that allows suspension, or possibly even termination, of any obligations to provide products to fulfill orders, when the U.S. government imposes restrictions on exports for any reason. This is a kind of *force majeure* clause that may be especially important for agency agreements when orders are placed to the home entity in the United States, rather than with sales from stocks of a foreign distributor. But the distributor may also place orders for goods it does not stock, or the agent may have goods in stock. Thus, whichever agreement is used, some excuse for nonperformance clause may be appropriate.

§ 4.26   Duration of Agreement

The duration of the agreement creates two issues. The first is what term is allowed? The second is whether the agreement truly terminates at the end of the stipulated term. A U.S. company may prefer a short term so that it has an opportunity for an early review of the performance of the agent/distributor. The agent/distributor may prefer a longer term for fear that it will not be renewed if the performance is either very bad, or very good. If very bad there should be termination for just cause allowed. If very good, the agent/distributor is justified in thinking that the relationship should not be terminated, that might lead to the U.S. company replacing the distributor with someone at a lower salary or commission, or establishing a company-owned distribution network. The fixed term thus becomes interrelated with the issue of the right to terminate.

It is probably best to use a short and definite duration term, allowing the U.S. company to consider nonrenewal for legitimate reasons. The danger of not stipulating a term is that the agreement will be viewed as indefinite. Viewed as indefinite, it may not be terminated except for just cause and the payment of compensation.

If an agreement is renewed several times at the end of definite terms, the agreement may be come to be viewed as an agreement of indefinite duration, and thus require compensation at any subsequent termination. At the expiration of the first fixed term, it may be wise to draft an entirely new agreement. The agreement may say much the same as the first contract, but it will appear as a second, separate contract rather than a renewal of the first. If renewals are to be automatic, the contract should state that they are for clearly defined renewal periods, at which time the contract may again be renewed, or considered at an end.

§ 4.27   Rights Retained by the U.S. Company

The U.S. company may wish to state that it retains certain rights. These might include the right to enter into additional distribution

in 2002, but it may be later. See "Hague Conference—Jurisdiction/Judgments," at <http://www.net/e/workprog/jdgm.html> (visited Oct. 5, 2000).

agreements in the host nation, or to make direct sales in the agent's/distributor's territory.[1] The agent/distributor may not wish to lose exclusive territorial rights, and such provisions might state that such company actions would only occur if the agent/distributor failed to reach stated minimum goals, and perhaps after new negotiations regarding those minimum goals.

F. REGISTRATION OF THE AGREEMENT

§ 4.28 Notification or Approval

Some nations designate a government office for the registration of all distributorship agreements.[1] This may be merely a notification formality, or it may bring the government in as a third party, to *review* and *approve or reject* distributorship agreements that are filed with a government agency.[2] Registration may further involve public disclosure, and create problems regarding information that the foreign company would prefer to keep confidential.

G. JURISDICTION OVER UNITED STATES PRINCIPAL

§ 4.29 Who Asserts Jurisdiction?

Where a U.S. corporation uses a foreign agent as its distributor, the U.S. company may not be doing business in the foreign nation. But the notion of doing business as it is known in the United States may differ from doing business notions in the foreign country. Furthermore, some nations' laws governing distributorship agreements require that the foreign principal acknowledge jurisdiction of the host-nation's courts when hiring an agent. Other laws so define the business relationship that the foreign principal is considered to be a business establishment in the nation.[1]

§ 4.27

1. This could be an adjacent nation. For example, a distributorship for Costa Rica may or may not include as the territory other Central American nations, and Panama. The agreement should state the territory the agent/distributor is expected to cover, and that other territories are clearly left to the U.S. company. Such provisions, however, may conflict with antitrust rules that prohibit territorial allocations.

§ 4.28

1. The government may be the importer, and there may be special provisions regulating agents or distributors who sell to the government.

2. This is especially true of the Middle East nations.

§ 4.29

1. For tax purposes, the taxing jurisdiction may be defined in a tax treaty. The OECD model tax treaty includes a definition of a permanent establishment. Organization for Economic Cooperation and Development, Model Double Taxation Convention on Income and Capital (1977). Bilateral tax treaties may also define doing business. U.S. companies usually try to contractually define agents as independent contractors and make it clear that they have no power to bind the company. Such provisions help to create a wall between the agent and principal and lessen the risk of subjection of the principal to local taxation.

H. INTERNATIONAL UNIFICATION OF THE RULES OF AGENCY

§ 4.30   1983 Geneva Convention on Agency in the International Sale of Goods

The 1983 Geneva Convention on Agency in the International Sale of Goods[1] followed soon after the 1980 Vienna Convention on the International Sale of Goods (CISG),[2] which has been extremely successful and is law in the United States.[3] But the Agency Convention,[4] which had the participation of 49 nations (plus nine as observers), has been signed by only a few nations and has not been ratified by even one.[5] The Convention drafters accomplished a remarkable job in bringing together the different attitudes toward agents in common law tradition and civil law tradition nations. The Convention covers both the scope of authority of an agent and the termination of the authority of an agent. But the termination of authority only covers external relations, that is the relations between the agent or principal and third parties. It does not cover the more difficult internal relations between the agent and the principal. There are other areas not sufficiently covered in the Convention, including leasing and warehousing.

The Convention, and the few writings on its development, are useful in understanding some of the problems of attempting to unify an area where very different fundamental views exist regarding the institution of agency. The original goal of unification of all aspects of the law of agency was quite reduced in the Convention. The delegates agreed upon parting that further efforts needed to be made to develop international rules of agency.

§ 4.31   European Union Unification of the Rules Affecting Agents and Distributors

The Europeans issued a Directive Regarding Commercial Agents in December 1986. It is Council Directive 86/653, and coordinates member-state laws regarding self-employed commercial agents. This directive was inspired by existing French and German law. From a United States perspective, the directive is remarkably protective of the agent. It is particularly significant because many North American firms do business

---

§ 4.30

1. See *www.unidroit.org/english/conventions/c-ag.htm*. The United States is not a party to the agency convention.

2. The text of the CISG is at http:/www.uncitral.org/english/texts/sales/salescon.htm.

3. The United States is a party to the CISG. See U.S. Dep't of State, Treaties in Force (Jan. 1, 1999) at 467.

4. The background of the unification of the law of agency is discussed in Petar Sarcevic, The Geneva Convention on Agency in the International Sale of Goods, in Paul Volken & Petar Sarcevic (eds. & contribs.) International Sale of Goods: Dubrovnik Lectures 443 (1986).

5. Chile, France, Italy, Morocco, the Vatican and Switzerland signed the Convention when it was first opened for signature.

in Europe through commercial agents. The directive defines a commercial agent as a "self-employed intermediary who has continuing authority to negotiate the purchase or sale of goods on behalf of another person (the principal), or to negotiate and conclude such transactions on behalf of and in the name of that principal."

Directive 86/653 establishes various rights and obligations for commercial agents and principals, e.g., the agent's duty to comply with reasonable instructions and the principal's duty to act in good faith. In the absence of an agreed-upon method of compensation, customary local practices prevail (and if none, reasonable remuneration). Compensation may apparently be by commission or salary. Compensation rights before and after the effective period of the agency contract are specified. Directive 86/653 also establishes when the agent's commission becomes due and payable, as well as the conditions under which it is extinguishable. For example, the agent is entitled to compensation on all transactions where the agent has participated. Moreover, transactions that have been concluded during the term of the agreement with third parties the agent previously procured as customers for the principal fall within this rule. The agent is also entitled to compensation on transactions with customers located in the agent's area of responsibility or for whom the agent is an exclusive representative.

An important element concerns the notice and termination rights of the agent. Agency agreements for fixed periods of time that continue to be performed by both parties, upon expiration become contracts for an indefinite period. Minimum termination notice requirements are established of one month per year of service up to three years, and optional notice requirements up to six months for six years. The member states must provide for either a right of indemnification or for damages compensation, which must be claimed within one year of termination. The agency agreement cannot waive or otherwise "derogate" these rights. The indemnity cannot exceed one year's remuneration but does not foreclose damages. The indemnity is payable if the agent has brought in new customers or increased volumes with existing customers to the substantial continuing benefit of the principal, and if it is equitable in light of all circumstances.

The right to damages as a result of termination occurs when the agent is deprived of commissions which would have been earned upon proper performance to the substantial benefit of the principal. The agent may also seek damages when termination blocks amortization of the costs and expenses incurred on advice of the principal while performing under the agency contract. The death of the agent triggers these indemnity or compensation rights. They are also payable if the agent must terminate the contract because of age, infirmity or illness, causing an inability to reasonably continue service. No indemnity or damages may be had under specified circumstances, including when the agent is in default, justifying immediate termination under national law. "Restraint of trade" clauses (covenants not to compete) are permissible upon termination to the extent that they are limited to two years' duration and to the geographic area or customers of the agent. Restraint of trade clauses may be made a precondition to the payment of an indemnity.

A 1962 Commission Notice announced that agreements with "commercial agents" were outside Article 81(1), formerly 85(1) of the Rome Treaty, and therefore are not subject to notification.[1] The theory regarding exempting commercial agents from European antitrust law was their "auxiliary function" on behalf of principals who were subject to the law. In *Flemish Travel Agents*,[2] however, the European Court of Justice ruled that the relationship between suppliers and independent commercial agents could present competitive implications under the Treaty of Rome. The 1962 Notice defines "commercial agents" as those who undertake for a specified territory to negotiate or conclude transactions on behalf of an enterprise either in their own name or in the name of that enterprise. The key to distinguishing commercial agents from independent traders, who are subject to Article 81, is whether the intermediary assumes any risk in the transaction, including nonpayment, title to a considerable inventory of products, liability for substantial services to customers, or control over prices or terms of sale. This definition of "commercial agents" has been somewhat narrowed by case law.[3]

Regulation 1983/83 (exclusive distribution) and Regulation 1984/83 (exclusive purchasing),[4] were adopted in 1983 and replaced late in 2000. Exclusive dealing agreements ordinarily involve restrictions on manufacturers or suppliers and independent distributors of goods. These restraints concern persons whom the manufacturer may supply, to whom the manufacturer or distributor may sell, and from whom the distributor may acquire the goods or similar goods. Exclusive dealing agreements should be distinguished from agency or consignment agreements where title and most risk remain with the manufacturer until the goods are sold by their retail agents to consumers. The announced policy position is that competition law will not require a manufacturer to compete with its agents. Exclusivity in genuine retail agency agreements is therefore legal.[5]

Regulation 1983/83 acknowledged that many exclusive dealing agreements fell within the scope of the prohibitions of Article 81(1). Under Article 81(2) they would be automatically void. Regulation 1983/83 also recognizes that exclusive dealing activities can lead to an improvement in the distribution and competition of products sold in the European Union. While a manufacturer may be reluctant to sell and compete in new territories through nonexclusive distributors, it may be willing to do so through exclusive outlets. These retailers must often

§ 4.31

1. 1962 Official Journal 2921.

2. 1987 Eur.Comm.Rep. 3801.

3. See Cooperative Vereniging "Suiker Unie" V.A. v. Commission (1975) Eur. Comm.Rep. 1663.

4. See Delimitis v. Henninger Brau (1991) Eur.Comm.Rep. 935 (Case C–234/89)

(Regulation 1984/83 applied extensively to beer-supply agreements).

5. But see Re Pittsburgh Corning Europe (1973) Common Mkt.L.Rep. D2; Commission Announcement on Exclusive Agency Contracts Made with Commercial Agents, Official Journal 2921 (1962).

provide services, advertising or other goodwill to back-up the products. By removing the ability of distributors to sell competing brands, exclusive dealing creates a singular incentive to market the manufacturer's goods. In the context of the evolution of the European market, exclusive dealing may encourage greater penetration by producers who have traditionally sold only in their national markets.

Following the Article 81(3) formula, Regulation 1983/83 stated that consumers would receive a fair share of the resultant benefits from exclusive dealing agreements by virtue of their improved ability to obtain a wider range of goods. However, Article 81(3) requires that the restrictions used in exclusive dealing agreements be indispensable to their objectives, and that they do not substantially eliminate competition in the goods concerned. Regulation 1983/83 therefore exempted only agreements or concerted practices not in any way inhibiting parallel imports of the same goods from other exclusive dealers. The concern has been that exclusive dealing agreements are often accompanied by efforts at absolute territorial market protection, a practice considerably more restrictive of competition than mere exclusive dealing. Thus the manufacturer could not prevent the distributor from filling an order from outside the territory, provided that it did not actually solicit the order. Similarly, provisions that allowed the distributor to sell to only one market segment and not to other customers disqualified the agreement from the group exemption. The agreement could require the distributor to purchase a range of goods or minimum quantities, to sell the goods under trademarks of the manufacturer, and to promote sales of the goods through advertising, a sales network, adequate inventory and warranty services. It could also forbid the active seeking of orders (e.g., by advertisements) or the establishment of warehouses or depots outside the distributor's territory. Furthermore, in many cases the distributor could be limited by location clauses, designated areas of primary sales responsibility, etc.

Regulation 1983/83 provided an excellent example of Commission efforts to employ and develop law under Article 81 to serve the goal of economic integration. The formation of absolute territorial trade barriers, similar in impact to national tariffs and quotas that existed prior to the creation of the European Common Market, would negate some of the economic benefits of increased trade and economic integration. Yet to prohibit exclusive dealing entirely would deter cross-border sales by national manufacturers. Hence, under Regulation 1983/83, distributive competition among goods for sale was encouraged by permitting exclusive dealing agreements between manufacturers and independent distributors and by insuring that competition as between exclusive dealers in the same goods was also preserved. It was only absolute territorial exclusive dealing that precluded benefit from the group exemption. It was precluded whether achieved by the exercise of national patent, copyright or trademark rights, or simply by contractual restraints between manufacturers and their exclusive dealers. For example, when territorial protection for distributors was obtained by making slight changes to a product's content, this constitutes an Article 81 violation. Manufacturers and distributors may not seek product approvals which effectively divide up the common market in this manner.[6] This outcome protected *intrabrand* competition in ways that had largely been abandoned under U.S. antitrust law.[7]

Export bans applied by manufacturers to their European distributors attracted sizeable fines and penalties under Article 81.[8] For selective distribution systems where the supplier limits the number of "approved" distributors of its products who in turn may only sell to end-users and other "approved" distributors, the Commission has established regulatory guidelines.[9] These exempt selective distribution systems when there are objective, qualitative requirements for the dealer (such as technical qualifications) that are applied on a nondiscriminatory basis. However, when quantitative limitations (quotas for the number of resellers) are present, selective distribution systems are less likely to be allowed. Article 81 is generally applied to selective distribution systems under a rule of reason approach. For example, in *Metro–Saba*,[10] the European Court of Justice focused on high quality and technically advanced goods. Some intrabrand price competition could be sacrificed to adapt to the resale needs of such goods (e.g., warranties, after-sales servicing).[11]

Effective June 1, 2000, Commission Regulation No. 2790/1999 replaced Regulations 1983/83 and 1984/83. This regulation is more economic and less formalistic than Regulation 4087/88. Supply and distribution agreements of firms with less that 30 percent market shares are generally exempt; this is known as a "safe harbor." Companies whose market shares exceed 30 percent may or may not be exempt, depending upon the results of individual competition law reviews by the Commission under Article 81(3). In either case, no vertical agreements containing so-called "hard-core restraints" are exempt. These restraints concern primarily resale price maintenance, territorial and customer protection leading to market allocation, and in most instances non-compete covenants that last more than five years.

§ 4.32   International Chamber of Commerce

The International Chamber of Commerce has adopted a model

6. See Zera Montedison/Hinkins Staehler, Commission Decision of June 22, 1993.

7. Compare Continental TV, Inc. v. GTE Sylvania Inc., 433 U.S. 36, 97 S.Ct. 2549, 53 L.Ed.2d 568 (1977), *on remand* 461 F.Supp. 1046, (N.D.Cal.1978), *affirmed* 694 F.2d 1132 (9th Cir.1982).

8. See, e.g., John Deere & Co., 28 O.J.Eur.Comm. (No. L 35) 58 (1985) (fining respondent two million ECUs for violation of Article 81(1) for imposing, accepting or practicing bans on the export of its products by dealers or distributors to other EU countries); Sperry New Holland, a Division of

Sperry Corp., 28 O.J.Eur.Comm. (No. L 376) 21 (1985) (fining respondent 750,000 ECUs for violation of Article 81(1) for imposing, accepting or practicing a ban on export of SNH products by dealers or distributors to other EU countries).

9. See generally Regulation 1475/95 on selective distribution auto franchise agreements. This regulation is scheduled to expire in 2002.

10. 1977 Eur.Comm.Rep. 1875.

11. O.J.Eur.Comm. (No. L17) 1 (1976).

commercial agency contract and a model distributorship contract.[1] They are intended to reflect the specific needs of international trade, which, as the above commentary has indicated, differ significantly from one country to another. The model contracts consider prevailing international trade law practice and general principles recognized by domestic laws of various nations.

I. FINAL CONSIDERATIONS

§ 4.33 Laws Affecting Exports and Imports

Use of a distributorship agreement means the export of products from one nation, the United States, and the import into another. That involves export laws of the United States that may require licenses.[1] It also involves import controls of the foreign nation, which may mean quotas and tariffs, and many possible barriers such as packaging and safety-testing rules. Furthermore, other U.S. laws may be involved, such as antitrust and securities laws, the Foreign Corrupt Practices Act and antiboycott rules.[2]

The U.S. party is likely to be the one drafting the agreement. It must of course be consistent with the laws of the host nation. But where that law is doubtful or absent, the U.S. party should control the agreement, and be able to determine the characteristics of termination, and choice of law and forum.

§ 4.34 Strategic Alliances between Different Nation Manufacturers

Selling in every market throughout the world is an objective realizable by only a very few large multinational corporations. In order to sell in more markets than resources might otherwise allow, the formation of a strategic alliance may help reduce fixed costs. Such an alliance may also reduce the impact of protectionist policies that may close certain markets, whether due to cultural barriers, as in Japan, or to legal barriers, as in many developing nations. A strategic alliance may be especially useful to a new company with high technology and a quality product, but without a very well developed marketing system. Associating with a company in the host nation which has an established trading network should benefit both companies. How the alliance is structured depends on the bargaining position of the two companies, their common interests, and willingness to form certain types of associations. For example, they may form a new joint venture, or have the host-nation

---

§ 4.32

1. See   <www.iccwbo.org/home/state-ments_rules/menu_rules.asp>.

§ 4.33

1. The U.S. export control laws are discussed in Chapter 16, infra.

2. Antitrust laws are discussed in Chapter 20, infra, the Foreign Corrupt Practices Act in Chapter 17, infra, and the antiboycott rules in Chapter 18, infra.

marketing company acquire a minority interest in the manufacturing company and in return provide the needed marketing.

Another form of strategic alliance is for two companies, with established marketing networks in their own nations, to exchange products.[1] This form does not involve any equity exchange or purchase by one party of part of the other's shares.[2] A product exchange or swap is essentially a contractual alliance, with the contract providing for some method of valuation of the respective products, not unlike provisions of some countertrade agreements. The contract also would likely address issues of the level of promotion of the other's products. Of considerable concern is the possibility that such an agreement would be viewed as anticompetitive by one or both of the parties' nations, especially where final selling prices are fixed or territories are allocated.[3] The arrangement ought to be structured so as to avoid any application of a per se approach, and to fit within what is allowed under a rule of reason approach.

J.   SELECTED DOCUMENTS

§ 4.35   Sample Manufacturer's International Representative Agreement

REPRESENTATIVE AGREEMENT
BETWEEN
SOLAR TURBINES INTERNATIONAL COMPANY *
and

———————————

Effective Date: _____, 199__

Contents

§ 4.34

1. This has a very significant impact by eliminating research and development costs of the product acquired.

2. Thus reducing the costs of selling abroad.

3. See, e.g., United States v. Topco Associates, 405 U.S. 596, 92 S.Ct. 1126, 31 L.Ed.2d 515 (1972).

* Reproduced with permission of Mr. Frank E. Kear, Esq., General Counsel, Solar Turbines, Inc.

REPRESENTATIVE AGREEMENT

THIS AGREEMENT is entered into effect as of the _____ day of _____, 1990 between Solar Turbines International Company 2200 Pacific Highway, P.O. Box 85376, San Diego, California, 92138–5376, hereinafter referred to as "COMPANY", and _____, _____ [Address] _____, hereinafter referred to as "REPRESENTATIVE", who, in consideration of the mutual promises made herein and intending to be legally bound thereby, AGREE AS FOLLOWS:

ARTICLE 1

PARTIES AND PURPOSE

1.1 *Status of Company.*

COMPANY is a corporation duly organized and validly existing under the laws of the State of Delaware, United States of America, with its principal office located at San Diego, California. COMPANY is engaged in the business of selling for export products and services manufactured or supplied by Solar Turbines Incorporated, hereinafter referred to as "STI", and subsidiaries and affiliates thereof.

1.2 *Status of Representative.*

REPRESENTATIVE is a corporation duly organized, validly existing, and in good standing under the laws of _____, with power to own property and carry on its business as contemplated by this Agreement. REPRESENTATIVE has its primary office, place of business and business registration at ____[Address]____, Tel: _____, Telex: _____, Cable: _____, Fax: _____.

REPRESENTATIVE further represents that it has complied with registration and other requirements of _____ needed to carry on and fulfill the duties as contemplated by this Agreement.

1.3 *Purpose.*

COMPANY desires to appoint a REPRESENTATIVE for the Territory, as hereinafter defined, and REPRESENTATIVE declares it possesses the independent means, requisite skills, facilities and financial and physical resources to perform as such REPRESENTATIVE for the said Territory and Sales Responsibility and is willing to do so.

ARTICLE 2
REPRESENTATION

2.1 *Appointment.*

COMPANY hereby appoints REPRESENTATIVE as its [non]exclusive representative of COMPANY for the Territory for the sale of Goods (as further described in Article 2.2) in the Territory. REPRESENTATIVE hereby accepts the appointment as a[n non] exclusive representative.

2.2 *Goods.*

The Products and Services, collectively referred to herein as "Goods", covered by this Agreement are as described in Exhibit A, attached hereto and made a part hereof, and are limited to that as described. They may be subsequently enlarged upon, reduced or otherwise changed by written mutual consent of the parties.

2.3 *Territory.*

The Territory is as described in Exhibit B, attached hereto and made a part hereof, and is limited to that as described. The Territory may be subsequently enlarged, reduced or otherwise changed by the written mutual consent of the parties. Except as the COMPANY may authorize in writing hereafter, in accordance with Articles 5.7 and 5.8, REPRESENTATIVE shall not be entitled to compensation for any sale outside the Territory.

2.4 *Effective Date, Term, and Renewal.*

This Agreement shall be effective as of _____. Unless this Agreement is canceled or terminated as authorized herein, this Agreement shall expire on _____. Renewal of this Agreement may be accomplished by the written mutual consent of both parties within ninety (90) days prior to the expiration of this Agreement.

2.5 *Compensation.*

COMPANY shall pay to REPRESENTATIVE as the sole compensation for its services the compensation described in Exhibit C, attached hereto and made a part hereof. REPRESENTATIVE SHALL NOT BE PAID ANY COMPENSATION ON THE SALE OF GOODS IN THE TERRITORY INVOLVING:

2.5.1 Any sale in which COMPANY is formally notified in writing by a customer in the Territory that such customer precludes participation by REPRESENTATIVE in said sale, unless REPRESENTATIVE has already been involved in the sale. In such cases COMPANY and REPRESENTATIVE will mutually agree on a compensation level, providing compensation is not precluded by law.

2.5.2 Products or Services supplied by the REPRESENTATIVE when acting as a subcontractor to COMPANY or any affiliate of COMPANY; and

2.5.3 Business activity which violates the provisions of Article 3.5.

All compensation payable by COMPANY to REPRESENTATIVE under this Agreement shall be in the name of REPRESENTATIVE and shall be remitted to a bank account of REPRESENTATIVE in the country of residence or place of business of REPRESENTATIVE or where the services are to be rendered. Compensation will be remitted by COMPANY in accordance with the written instructions of REPRESENTATIVE, which shall be communicated to COMPANY in accordance with Article 5.1 within ninety (90) days of the effective date of this Agreement, provided such payment complies with all applicable laws, including laws relating to taxation and exchange controls.

Commissions shall be earned on each sale after the sale occurs and COMPANY receives payment therefore. Commissions shall be earned and paid in U.S. dollars on a pro rata basis within sixty (60) days after receipt of payment by COMPANY.

ARTICLE 3
OPERATIONS

3.1 *Prices and Acceptance of Orders.*

All prices for Goods are within the exclusive control of COMPANY. All orders are to be addressed to COMPANY at its principal office in San Diego for acceptance. COMPANY reserves the right in its sole judgment to accept or reject any orders. REPRESENTATIVE may *not* accept orders on behalf of COMPANY.

3.2 *Controlling Language.*

The English language shall be the controlling language for the purpose of interpreting this Agreement, and all correspondence between COMPANY and REPRESENTATIVE shall be in the English language.

3.3 *Duties of Representative.*

REPRESENTATIVE represents, covenants and warrants that during the term of this Agreement REPRESENTATIVE shall perform the duties set forth in this Agreement and Exhibit D.

3.4 *Independent Contractor Relationship.*

REPRESENTATIVE is not an agent or employee of COMPANY for any purpose whatsoever, but is an independent contractor, who shall have sole control of the manner and means of performing under this Agreement. All expenses and disbursements including, but not limited to, those for travel and subsistence, reasonable entertainment, office, clerical and general selling expenses, that may be incurred by REPRESENTATIVE in connection with this Agreement shall be borne wholly and completely by REPRESENTATIVE, and COMPANY shall not in any way be responsible or liable therefor. REPRESENTATIVE does not have, and REPRESENTATIVE represents, warrants, and covenants that REPRESENTATIVE shall not hold himself out as having, any right, power, or authority to create any contract or obligation, either expressed or implied, on behalf of, in the name of, or binding upon COMPANY, or to pledge COMPANY'S credit, or to extend credit in COMPANY'S name.

REPRESENTATIVE shall have the right to appoint or otherwise designate suitable and desirable salesmen, employees, agents, and representatives (herein collectively referred to as "REPRESENTATIVE's Agents"). REPRESENTATIVE shall be solely responsible for REPRESENTATIVE's Agents and their acts. REPRESENTATIVE's Agents shall be appointed at REPRESENTATIVE'S own risk, expense, and supervision; and REPRESENTATIVE's Agents shall not have any claim against the COMPANY for salaries, commissions, items or cost, or other form of compensation or reimbursement; and REPRESENTATIVE represents, warrants and covenants that REPRESENTATIVE's Agents shall be subordinate to REPRESENTATIVE and subject to each and all of the terms, provisions, and conditions applying to REPRESENTATIVE hereunder.

3.5 *Business Conduct.*

For purpose of this section the term "SOLAR" means COMPANY, Solar Turbines Incorporated, Solar Turbines, S.A., Solar Turbines Overseas Ltd., Solar Turbines International Company, and any parent, subsidiary or affiliate of the above existing during the term of this Agreement.

REPRESENTATIVE represents, warrants and covenants that during the term of this Agreement:

    3.5.1 REPRESENTATIVE has not and will not return at any time, in any form, directly or indirectly, any portion of the payments made to REPRESENTATIVE by SOLAR to any director, officer or employee of SOLAR;

    3.5.2 REPRESENTATIVE has not made or given and will not make or give at any time, directly or indirectly, any payment or thing of value, from the funds paid to it by SOLAR (or from any other funds if such payment is connected in any way to the transaction on which a Commission of Fee is paid or a Discount is allowed) (i) to any government official, (ii) to any representative or employee of a government entity, (iii) to any political party or officer thereof, (iv) to any candidate for public office, (v) to any employee or representative of any purchaser, or (vi) to any other person or entity, which is illegal under any applicable law;

3.5.3   Neither REPRESENTATIVE, nor any director, officer, manager or key employee of, nor any member of its, his or their immediate family is or will be (i) a government official or employee of a governmental entity or (ii) an official or employee of, or holder of a beneficial interest in, any purchaser;

3.5.4   No government official or representative or governmental entity or ultimate purchaser has or will have an ownership or beneficial interest in or management control of REPRESENTATIVE;

3.5.5   No government official or representative is or will be an officer, director, employee or agent of REPRESENTATIVE;

3.5.6   REPRESENTATIVE is and will remain registered as a representative of COMPANY under any applicable law and will conduct its activities as a representative in compliance with all applicable laws; and

3.5.7   REPRESENTATIVE will furnish to SOLAR annually a certificate from its independent auditors that the current examination of the books and records of REPRESENTATIVE does not disclose any violation of the above representations and covenants.   If REPRESENTATIVE does not have independent auditors, REPRESENTATIVE will furnish to SOLAR annually a certificate from its chief executive officer and its chief financial officer that REPRESENTATIVE has not and is not in violation of any of the above representations and covenants.

3.6   *Performance Review.*

In order that a satisfactory level of REPRESENTATIVE performance may be maintained, COMPANY and REPRESENTATIVE shall meet annually or as deemed necessary by COMPANY to review the performance of REPRESENTATIVE and the degree to which it has satisfied the performance expectations and business purpose established in this Agreement.   COMPANY's Managing Director responsible for the Territory shall communicate to REPRESENTATIVE the location, agenda, attendees and criteria for the annual performance review at least thirty (30) days prior to the date of the review.

REPRESENTATIVE shall cooperate with COMPANY by making available at the time of such review, those sales, service, and financial records which are necessary to adequately analyze the operation of REPRESENTATIVE's performance.   REPRESENTATIVE shall also make available at the time of such review those REPRESENTATIVE personnel whose attendance the COMPANY believes would contribute to the overall value of the review.   The conclusions and recommendations developed from the review shall be incorporated into a written report and supplied to REPRESENTATIVE.

3.7 *Use of Tradenames or Trademarks.*

REPRESENTATIVE shall not use the name Solar Turbines International Company, Solar Turbines S.A., Solar Turbines Overseas Ltd., Solar Turbines Incorporated, STI, Solar, Jupiter, Mars, Centaur, Saturn or any other tradename or trademark owned by or licensed for use by COMPANY or any parent or subsidiary or other corporation with whom COMPANY is affiliated as part of REPRESENTATIVE's name or in REPRESENTATIVE's advertising except with the prior written permission from a corporate officer of COMPANY. REPRESENTATIVE agrees upon cancellation or termination of this Agreement to immediately discontinue the use of any tradenames or trademarks which may have been approved, authorized or licensed in connection with this Agreement.

ARTICLE 4
CANCELLATION AND TERMINATION

4.1 *Cancellation.*

Either party shall have the right to cancel this Agreement immediately, prior to the expiration of the term (or any renewal term) hereof, upon the occurrence of any of the following events, by written notice in accordance with Article 5.1:

  4.1.2 The other party's insolvency;

  4.1.3 The other party's failure to maintain the current purpose and scope of its operations in and for the Territory; or

  4.1.4 The other party's breach or default of any of the terms, obligations, representations, covenants, or warranties under this Agreement, unless such breach or default is waived in writing by the nondefaulting party.

4.2 *Convenience Termination.*

Either party may at any time for convenience terminate this Agreement by giving written notice in accordance with Article 5.1, to the other party. Such notice of termination shall specify the date upon which the termination is to become effective and shall be given at least ninety (90) days before the effective date of termination.

4.3 *Procedures after Cancellation or Termination.*

Upon receipt of written notice of cancellation or convenience termination of this Agreement, REPRESENTATIVE shall immediately surrender all rights vested in it by this Agreement, shall immediately cease performance and shall thereafter refrain from holding itself out as an authorized representative of COMPANY.

Upon receipt of written notice of convenience termination REPRESENTATIVE shall not contact any customer during the period between the giving of notice of termination and the effective date of termination without specific advance written approval from COMPANY. However,

REPRESENTATIVE shall be entitled to receive commissions on all sales for which a written work authorization is received by COMPANY for a period of 180 days after notification. Compensation for such sales shall be payable in accordance with this Agreement.

Cancellation or convenience termination of this Agreement shall not relieve either party from keeping in confidence any and all trade secrets, proprietary data and information imparted by one party to the other hereunder, and each party agrees it will not knowingly use or permit the use of information obtained by it to the disadvantage of the other or for itself or any third party.

Upon cancellation or convenience termination, REPRESENTATIVE shall return to COMPANY any and all catalogs, price lists, service manuals, bulletins, owner's manuals, current advertising material and any and all other items and documents which have been furnished to REPRESENTATIVE by COMPANY.

ARTICLE 5

INTERPRETATION AND ENFORCEMENT

5.1   *Notice.*

Any notice, request, demand or other communication, herein referred to as "Notice", required or permitted hereunder shall be properly given when delivered; or in the event Notice is by telex then such Notice shall be properly given when sent by telex and the sender receives a telex "answer back" (followed by a signed copy by registered air mail), addressed:

  5.1.2   In the case of COMPANY to:

  Director of Sales

  Solar Turbines International Company

  P.O. Box 85376

  2200 Pacific Highway

  San Diego, California 92138–5376

  United States of America;

  Telex number 695045 (Solar); or Fax (619) 544–5263;

or such other person or address as COMPANY may from time to time furnish to REPRESENTATIVE by notice.

  5.1.3   In the case of REPRESENTATIVE to:

  _____

  Attn: _____

  _____

  _____

  Tel: _____

  Tlx: _____

  FAX: _____

or such other person or address as REPRESENTATIVE may from time to time furnish to COMPANY by Notice.

5.2 *Controlling Law.*

This Agreement has been accepted by Company and shall in all respects be governed by and construed in accordance with the laws of the State of California, United States of America, applicable to agreements made and to be performed entirely within such State, including all matters of construction, validity, and performance; such location having a reasonable relationship to the execution of and performance under this Agreement.

5.3 *Assignments/Personal Nature of Agreement.*

This Agreement may not be assigned by either party without the prior written consent of the other party, except that COMPANY may assign this Agreement to any parent, subsidiary or affiliated corporation without the consent of REPRESENTATIVE. Any assignment not consistent with this Article shall be a material breach of this Agreement. This Agreement is personal as to REPRESENTATIVE and _____, active participant(s) in the day-to-day management and operation of REPRESENTATIVE. Any assignment, sale or change in management or control of REPRESENTATIVE shall constitute grounds for cancellation of this Agreement pursuant to Article 4.1.

5.4 *Hold Harmless.*

REPRESENTATIVE shall hold COMPANY harmless from and against, and shall indemnify COMPANY for, any liability, loss, cost, expenses, or damages howsoever caused by reason of any injury (whether to body, property, or personal or business character or reputation) sustained by any person or property by reason of any act, neglect, default or omission of REPRESENTATIVE or REPRESENTATIVE's Agents, and REPRESENTATIVE shall pay all sums to be paid or discharged in case of any action or any such damages or injuries. If COMPANY is sued in any court for damages or is a party to any arbitration proceedings by reason of the acts of REPRESENTATIVE, then REPRESENTATIVE shall defend said action (or cause same to be defended) at its own expense and shall pay and discharge any judgment or arbitration award that may be rendered against COMPANY in any such action. If REPRESENTATIVE fails or neglects to so defend said action, the COMPANY may defend the same and any expenses including reasonable attorneys' fees, which it may pay or incur in defending said action and the amount of any judgment or arbitration award which it may be required to pay, shall be promptly reimbursed by REPRESENTATIVE on demand. Nothing herein is intended to nor shall relieve COMPANY from liability for its own acts, omission, default or negligence.

5.5 *Arbitration.*

5.5.1 *Rules.* Any controversy, claim or dispute between the parties hereto arising out of or related to this agreement or any breach thereof, which cannot be settled amicably by the parties, shall be submitted for arbitration in accordance with the provisions contained herein and the Rules of the American Arbitration Association ("Rules"); provided, however, that notwithstanding any provisions of such Rules, the parties shall have the right to take depositions and obtain discovery regarding the subject matter of the arbitration, as provided in Title III of Part 4 (commencing with Section 1985) of the California Code of Civil Procedure. The parties further agree to facilitate the arbitration by making available to one another and to the arbitrators for inspection and extraction all documents, books, records and personnel under their control, if determined by any arbitrator to be relevant to the dispute by conducting arbitration hearings to the greatest extent possible on successive, continuous days; and by observing strictly the time periods established by the rules of the arbitrators for the submission of evidence and of briefs. Judgment upon the award rendered by the arbitrators may be entered in any court having jurisdiction over the parties or their assets. The arbitrator shall award the prevailing party its costs including reasonable attorney fees. The arbitrators shall determine all questions of fact and law relating to any controversy, claim or dispute hereunder, including but not limited to whether any such controversy, claim or dispute is subject to the arbitration provisions contained herein. All proceedings shall be held in the English language.

5.5.2 *Notice.* Any party desiring arbitration shall serve on the other party and the San Diego Regional Office of the American Arbitration Association, in accordance with the aforesaid Rules, its Notice of Intent to Arbitrate ("Notice of Intent"), accompanied by the name of the arbitrator selected by the party serving the Notice of Intent. A second arbitrator shall be chosen by the other party, and a third arbitrator shall be chosen by the two (2) arbitrators so selected. If the party upon whom the Notice of Intent is served fails to select an arbitrator and advise the other party of its selection within thirty (30) days after receipt of the Notice of Intent, the second arbitrator shall be selected by the first arbitrator. If the two (2) arbitrators so chosen cannot agree upon a third arbitrator within ten (10) days after the appointment of the second arbitrator, the third arbitrator shall be selected in accordance with the Rules. The arbitration proceedings provided hereunder are hereby declared to be self-executing, and it shall not be necessary to petition a court to compel arbitration. Notwithstanding the foregoing, if the two parties can agree to a mutual arbitrator within thirty (30) days of the commencement of arbitration, then arbitration shall proceed by the one arbitrator so agreed upon.

5.5.3 *Consolidation.* If a controversy, claim or dispute arises between REPRESENTATIVE and COMPANY which is subject to the arbitration provisions hereunder, and there exists or later arises a controversy, claim or dispute between REPRESENTATIVE and COM-

PANY and any third party arising out of or related to the same transaction or series of transactions, said third party controversy, claim or dispute shall be consolidated with the arbitration proceedings hereunder; provided, however, that any such third party must be a party to an agreement with COMPANY or REPRESENTATIVE which provides for arbitration of disputes thereunder in accordance with rules and procedures substantially the same in all material respects as provided for herein or, if not, must consent to arbitration as provided hereunder.

5.5.4 *Venue.* All arbitration proceedings shall be held where best suited for the resolution of the dispute in light of the convenience of the parties and their documents and witnesses. If the parties are unable to promptly agree on such location, arbitration shall be conducted in San Diego, California.

5.5.5 *Time.* Notice of the demand for arbitration shall be filed in writing with the other party to this agreement and with the American Arbitration Association. The demand for arbitration shall be made within a reasonable time after the claim, dispute or other matter in question has arisen, and in no event shall it be made after the date when institution of legal or equitable proceedings based on such claim, dispute or other matter in question would be barred by the applicable statute of limitations.

5.5.6 *Cooperation.* Unless otherwise agreed in writing, each party shall carry on its responsibilities under this or any other Agreement between the parties during the arbitration proceedings.

5.6 *Documents Constituting Agreement.*

This Agreement consists of this Agreement form and the following exhibits which are attached hereto and incorporated herein by reference:

Exhibit A—GOODS;

Exhibit B—TERRITORY;

Exhibit C—COMPENSATION;

Exhibit D—DUTIES; and

Exhibit E—ADDITIONAL TERMS AND CONDITIONS

Nothing contained in any exhibit shall supersede or annul the terms and provisions hereof, unless the matter set forth in the exhibit shall specifically and explicitly so provide to the contrary; and in the event of any ambiguity in meaning or understanding between the Agreement proper and any Exhibit hereto, the Agreement shall control. No exhibit shall be of any force and effect unless it is initialed or signed by the parties to this Agreement.

5.7 *Integration, Entire Agreement.*

The term "Agreement" as used in this document includes the Agreement proper and all exhibits attached hereto, and constitutes the entire agreement and understanding between COMPANY and REPRESENTA-

TIVE concerning the subject matter hereof. This Agreement supersedes any and all other agreements, either oral or in writing, between the parties hereto with respect to the subject matter hereof and contains all the covenants and agreements between the parties with respect to said matter, and each party to this agreement acknowledges that no representations, inducements, promises or agreements, orally or otherwise, have been made by any party, or anyone writing on behalf of any party, which are not embodied herein, and that no other agreement, statement or promise not contained in this agreement shall be valid or binding. This Agreement may be amended only by an instrument in writing which expressly refers to this Agreement and specifically states that it is intended to amend it. No party is relying upon any covenants, warranties, representations, or inducements not set forth herein. No employee of COMPANY other than one of its corporate officers is authorized on its behalf to modify, change or waive any of the provisions of this Agreement or to change, add to or erase any of the printed portions of the form on which this Agreement or any Exhibit to this Agreement appears. No waiver by a party of any default by the other party in the performance of this Agreement shall apply to or be deemed a waiver of any prior or subsequent default hereunder.

If any term, covenant, condition or provision of this Agreement, or the application of such provision, shall be held invalid, illegal, or unenforceable for any reason, the remainder of this Agreement shall not be affected and every other term, covenant, condition and provision of this Agreement shall be valid and enforceable to the fullest extent provided by law.

5.8 *Survival.*

The provisions contained in this Agreement that by their sense and context are intended to survive the stated term of this Agreement, shall so survive the completion of performance or termination of this Agreement.

5.9 *Approval of Agreement.*

This Agreement shall not be binding upon COMPANY until approved on behalf of COMPANY by a corporate officer of COMPANY at its General Office.

The COMPANY retains the right at any time this Agreement is in effect to submit this Agreement for approval to reputable counsel, retained by COMPANY, in the country in which the REPRESENTATIVE is a resident or will be performing services, to the effect that this Agreement is legal, that the services to be rendered by the REPRESENTATIVE are legal and that the form of payment is legal under the laws of such country, or any other applicable law. The parties agree to modify this Agreement as may be required by opinion of such counsel. Failure of the parties to so modify this Agreement within ninety (90) days after Notice of such opinion is given to REPRESENTATIVE, in accordance with Article 5.1, shall result in automatic termination and cancellation of this Agreement and the provisions of Article 4.3 shall apply.

Executed by REPRESENTATIVE at _____, this _____ day of _____, 19__.

By: _____

Approved and executed by COMPANY at San Diego, California, this _____ day of _____, 19__.

SOLAR TURBINES
INTERNATIONAL COMPANY

By: _____

EXHIBIT A

GOODS

The "Goods" covered by this Agreement are limited to the "Products" and "Services" (also referred to herein as "Customer Services") described below.

A. *Products*

    1. The Products covered by this Agreement shall be limited to:

        a. New or reconditioned Saturn, Centaur and Mars series gas turbine mechanical drive, gas compressor and generator set packages (including their accessories and ancillary equipment);

        b. Package content supplied by COMPANY'S Construction Services Group;

        c. Customer Services included in the original order for Products in 1(a) and 1(b) above (as defined in Paragraph B hereof).

        d. Spare engines (including gas producers and power turbines);

        e. Parts and tools for Products;

        all as manufactured or offered for sale by COMPANY within the Territory.

    2. Without limitation and for clarification the following are specifically excluded from the term "Products" defined in Paragraph A.1. above unless specifically agreed to in writing by the parties prior to submittal of the proposal to the customer or end user:

        a. Jupiter GT 35 gas turbine packages,

    b. Driven equipment not manufactured by COMPANY and furnished as part of a mechanical drive package,

    c. Gas turbines or other drivers not manufactured by COMPANY,

    d. Combined cycle systems, packaged cogeneration systems, waste heat recovery systems or other development products of Company not regularly offered for sale,

    e. Electric motor driven compressors packaged by COMPANY,

    f. Products sold by or through COMPANY'S packagers and distributors, and

    g. Products purchased or leased by or through the United States Government or any agency thereof for its own use or the use of a Foreign Military Sale end user and installed in the Territory.

B. *Customer Services*

    1. The Customer Services covered by this Agreement shall be limited to the following, subject to the further exclusions and limitations in Paragraph B.2. below:

        a. Spare engines (including gas producers and power turbines);

        b. Parts and tools for Products;

        c. Overhauled and uprated components and assemblies;

        d. New and reconditioned major components and sub-assemblies;

        e. Package refurbishment (including ancillary equipment);

        f. Tooling, training, parts and documentation for customer owned overhaul facilities (overhaul technology transfer);

        g. Contracts for maintenance of Products;

        h. Call out and troubleshooting service;

        i. Product condition surveys;

        j. Product commissioning and installation;

        k. Compressor restaging;

        l. Maintenance planning programs;

        m. Projects involving mechanical, electrical and process technical modifications;

        n. Product training;

        o. Manuals, documentation, flow schematics, certifications and the like;

all as supplied or performed directly by COMPANY.

    2. Specifically excluded from the term "Customer Services" as defined in Paragraph B.1. above, are:

        a. Customer Services supplied or performed by Energy Services International Limited, an affiliate of COMPANY;

        b. Customer Services performed on Jupiter (GT 35) Gas Turbine Package and on equipment not manufactured or supplied by COMPANY, except as may be agreed to in writing by the parties prior to submittal of the proposal to the end user or customer;

c. Customer Services supplied for or performed on products purchased or leased by or through the United States Government or any agency thereof for its own use or the use of a Foreign Military Sale end user and installed in the Territory; and

d. Customer Services sold by or through COMPANY's packagers and distributors except as may be agreed to in writing by the parties prior to submittal of the proposal to the end user or customer.

_____
(Company)

_____
(Representative)

EXHIBIT B

TERRITORY

The Territory shall be limited to the following country or countries:

_____
(Company)

_____
(Representative)

EXHIBIT C

COMPENSATION

All compensation to REPRESENTATIVE shall be governed by the terms of Article 2.5 of the Agreement and this Exhibit C.

Commissions hereunder shall be earned on each sale after the sale occurs and when COMPANY receives payment. The commission shall be earned and paid in U.S. Dollars on a pro rata basis within sixty (60) days after receipt of payment by COMPANY. The commission amount shall be calculated as a percentage of the COMPANY's final purchase order or contract value of the Products in U.S. Dollars on an Ex Works point of shipment basis less any freight, packing, insurance, tariffs, taxes, and transportation. (herein "Sale Value").

A. *Products.*

REPRESENTATIVE shall be paid a commission of between three (3%) percent and five (5%) percent of the Sale Value of the Products as defined in Exhibit A based on the following cumulative annual sales volume:

Cumulative Annual Sales from zero to $_____ = 5%

Cumulative Annual Sales from $_____ to _____ = 4%

Cumulative Annual Sales above $_____ = 3%

On those sales where a substantial proportion of the total sales effort is performed by others or where substantial commercial concessions are required to meet competitive circumstances, the commission shall be reduced proportionally. COMPANY shall be the sole judge of when a substantial proportion of the sales effort is performed by others and of the proportion by which the commission is reduced, and shall promptly inform the REPRESENTATIVE in writing of such action.

COMPANY shall give written notification to REPRESENTATIVE of the commission level payable prior to submittal of quotation by COMPANY to the customer or end user if it is deemed that a "substantial portion" of the total Effort as performed by others and a lower commission is to be paid.

B. *Customer Services.*

1. REPRESENTATIVE shall be paid a commission of two percent (2%) on Customer Services as listed in Paragraph B.1. of Exhibit A when ordered separately from Products.

_____

(Company)

_____

(Representative)

C. *Retainer Fee.*

In addition to the above, Company shall pay REPRESENTATIVE a retainer fee of $_____ quarterly in advance only for so long as

REPRESENTATIVE employs the dedicated sales engineer required by Exhibit D.A.6.

_____

(Company)

_____

(Representative)

EXHIBIT D

DUTIES

REPRESENTATIVE represents, covenants and warrants that during the term of this Agreement, REPRESENTATIVE shall perform the following duties in addition to those set forth in the main body of the Agreement.

A. *Operating Duties.*

   1. Use its best efforts to develop a demand for and promote the sale of Products and Services offered for sale by COMPANY in accordance with its sales responsibility and maintain a sales and technical services office and specialized personnel as necessary to perform under this Agreement.

   2. Assume and pay all of the costs of conducting REPRESENTA-TIVE'S business hereunder, including commissions or other form of compensation to those in REPRESENTATIVE'S employ including, but not limited to REPRESENTATIVE's Agents.

   3. Provide and maintain physical facilities and staff commensurate with the sales potential in the Territory, and to provide office systems to maintain complete records of business transactions covered by this Agreement.

   4. Provide written notice to COMPANY before any closing, opening or relocating of its current principal, branch or subsidiary estab-lishments involved in REPRESENTATIVE's performance.

   5. Provide at all times sufficient working capital and net worth to enable REPRESENTATIVE to fully perform under this Agree-ment.

   6. Engage, train and maintain one or more fully-qualified sales engineers to obtain the maximum sales potential in the Territo-ry for the Products and Services covered by this Agreement. In no case shall REPRESENTATIVE dedicate less than the equiva-lent of _____ man-year per year on behalf of the company.

   7. Provide Sales and Service forecasts and reports at reasonable time periods as requested by COMPANY and cooperate with

COMPANY in the conducting of REPRESENTATIVE's performance review provided for in this Agreement.

_____

(Company)

_____

(Representative)

B. *Support Duties.*

REPRESENTATIVE will use reasonable efforts to:

1. Have key employees and managers attend COMPANY conducted training programs and appropriate sales and service meetings.

2. Make available temporary office space, communications facilities, clerical services and other reasonable support services to COMPANY personnel where available.

3. Assist COMPANY in collecting customer payments.

4. Provide transportation, translation and accommodations assistance if available and required.

5. Provide emergency assistance in the event of hostilities that are life-threatening to COMPANY employees.

6. Provide assistance to COMPANY in obtaining necessary permits or visas as may be requested from time to time, provided COMPANY reimburses REPRESENTATIVE its actual out of pocket costs and fees incurred in rendering such help.

_____

(Company)

_____

(Representative)

EXHIBIT E

ADDITIONAL TERMS AND CONDITIONS

None.

_____

(Company)

_____

(Representative)

§ 4.36 General Manufacturer's Agent Agreement*

This Manufacturer's Agent Agreement ("Agreement") is made this _____ day of _____, 1992, by and between Plant Equipment, Inc., a

* Courtesy of Nancy Fuller-Jacobs, Esq.

California corporation ("Principal"), having a principal office at 28075 Diaz Road, Temecula, California, USA, and _____, a(n) _____ ("Agent"), having a principal office at _____. Principal and Agent may be hereinafter collectively referred to as the Parties.

Recitals

A. Principal is in the business of manufacturing or supplying various telecommunications equipment.

B. The Agent declares that it possesses the financial and physical resources to promote the sale and use of the products of the Principal and is desirous of developing demand for and selling such products as authorized herein.

C. The Principal is desirous of having the Agent develop demand for and sell its products on the terms and conditions set forth herein.

ARTICLE 1. AGENCY

Exclusive Appointment

Section 1.01. (a) The Principal appoints the Agent as exclusive sales representative for the sale of its products within the country of Canada. The territory so described, and as may be subsequently enlarged, reduced, or otherwise changed in area with the mutual consent of the parties hereto, is hereinafter referred to as the "territory."

(b) During the continuance of this Agreement, the Principal shall not appoint any other or different person, firm, or corporation to sell the same products in the territory.

(c) Except as the Principal may authorize in writing hereafter, the Agent shall not sell any of the Principal's products outside of the territory.

Compensation

Section 2.02. The Principal shall pay to the Agent as compensation for his services a commission of _____ percent of the net invoice value of all shipments of its products to any part of his territory for which the Principal shall have received payment. The Principal shall pay the commissions on the _____ day of each month for all shipments paid for during the preceding calendar month.

Term

Section 2.03. This Agreement shall continue in full force for a period of two (2) years commencing from the date of this Agreement.

ARTICLE 3. OPERATIONS

Samples ad Advertising Matter

Section 3.01. The Principal at its own expense shall furnish the Agent a reasonable supply of samples and advertising matter to be used by him in connection with his agency hereunder. Samples are the exclusive property of the Principal and, on termination of this Agreement, the Agent shall return them to the Principal at the Principal's expense.

Quoting Prices

Section 3.02. In obtaining sales of the products of the Principal, the Agent shall quote only the prices and terms set forth in Schedule A attached hereto and made a part hereof, and as may be revised from time to time.

Forwarding Orders

Section 3.03. The Agent shall forward all orders promptly to the Principal and each order shall be subject to the Principal's acceptance. In the case of each order accepted, the Principal shall forward to the Agent two copies of invoices covering shipment of the ordered products.

Authority to Employ Salesmen

Section 3.04. The Agent shall have full authority to employ such salesmen at such compensation and on such other conditions as he deems proper to sell the products of the Principal in the territory. The contract which the Agent makes with such salesmen shall contain a provision that the salesmen are the employees of the Agent and are to be paid by him alone and, that in employing the salesmen, he is acting individually and not as an agent or attorney for the Principal.

Payment of Expenses

Section 3.05. The Agent shall assume and pay all the costs of conducting the sales agency hereunder, including commissions or other compensation to salesmen in his employ.

ARTICLE 4. TERMINATION

Grounds

Section 4.01. Either party, at its election, may treat this Agreement breached and, without prejudice to any other of its rights, may forthwith terminate this Agreement by written notice to the other party on occurrence of any of the following events:

(a) There shall be a substantial failure by the other party to perform one or more of its obligations hereunder which shall not have been cured within thirty (30) days after written notice specifying the nature of such failure.

(b) The other party shall make a general assignment for the benefit of creditors.

(c) A receiver of all or substantially all of the property of the other party shall be appointed and not removed within thirty (30) days.

(d) The other party shall file a petition for reorganization under the provisions of federal bankruptcy laws.

(e) The other party shall file a petition for an arrangement under federal bankruptcy laws.

(f) The other party shall become or be declared insolvent.

(g) The other party shall file a petition in bankruptcy or shall be adjudged a bankrupt.

Applicability of Terms After Termination

Section 4.02. In the event of termination, this Agreement shall remain applicable to any orders for products which the Agent has previously placed and to any other orders which may be executed within sixty (60) days subsequent to the effective date of termination.

ARTICLE 5. INTERPRETATION AND ENFORCEMENT

Notices

Section 5.01. Any notice, request, demand, or other communication required or permitted hereunder shall be deemed to be properly given when deposited in the United States mail, postage prepaid, or when deposited with a public telegraph company for transmittal, charges prepaid, addressed:

(a) In the case of the Principal, to _____ "corporate name, name of officer concerned, street address, city, and state", or to such other person or address as the Principal may from time to time furnish to the Agent.

(b) In the case of the Agent, to _____ "specify relevant data as in subsection (a) and as appropriate to the form of organization", or to such other person or address as the Agent may from time to time furnish to the Principal.

Controlling Law

Section 5.02. The validity, interpretation, and performance of this Agreement shall be controlled by and construed under the laws of the State of _____, the state in which this Agreement is being executed.

Assignment

Section 5.03. The Agent shall not assign this Agreement without the prior consent of the Principal in writing.

Completeness of Instrument

Section 5.04. This instrument contains all of the agreements, understandings, representations, conditions, warranties, and covenants made between the parties hereto. Unless set forth herein, neither party shall be liable for any representations made, and all modifications and amendments hereto must be made in writing.

Executed on _____, 19__, at _____ [city and state].

PRINCIPAL

_____

[typed name of principal]

By _____
[signature]

AGENT

_____

[typed name of agent]

By _____
[signature]

§ 4.37 Authorized Repair Facility Agreement (Aerospace)*

* Courtesy of Peter W. Knapp, Esq. of the   Hamilton Sunstrand Corp.

TABLE OF CONTENTS

AUTHORIZED REPAIR FACILITY AGREEMENT

This Authorized Repair Facility Agreement is entered into this day of _____, 2001 ("Effective Date"), by and between XYZ CORPORATION, a corporation organized and existing under the laws of _____, United States of America having an office at _____ and ABC CORPORATION, having an office at _____(hereinafter referred to as "ARF"). XYZ and ARF may be referred to individually as the "PARTY" or collectively as the "PARTIES".

RECITALS

A.　　XYZ is engaged in the business of designing, manufacturing, marketing and repairing power units, including spare parts and components thereof, utilized for power on various aircraft; and

B.　　ARF is in the business of providing overhaul, repair and other support services to operators of aerospace engines and power units; and

C.　　ARF desires to perform certain services for XYZ as an authorized commercial repair facility for power units and associated components manufactured or supplied by XYZ; and

D.　　XYZ and ARF desire to set forth the terms and conditions under which ARF shall provide repair and overhaul services for the aircraft power units; and

E.　　XYZ owns or controls know-how, trade secrets and other proprietary technical information necessary or useful in the repair of those power units and components and is willing to authorize the repair of same to ARF on a non-exclusive basis; and

F.　　ARF has established or wishes to establish facilities with tools, test equipment, spare parts inventory, staff, training and/or experience appropriate for an authorized repair facility, and desires to provide those services, for owners and operators of XYZ power units in accordance with XYZ's standards and requirements, subject to the applicable regulatory authorities' approvals and XYZ policies and procedures.

NOW THEREFORE

In consideration of these premises and the mutual promises and covenants contained herein, the PARTIES hereby agree as follows:

DEFINITIONS

Action Item System - The system established by XYZ to provide Customers and ARF with a documented means of asking for technical assistance regarding the Repairs of XYZ Products and interpretation of appropriate Manuals.

Agreement - This ARF Agreement including all appendices, amendments, and orders issued hereunder.

Airworthiness Authority - means the United States Federal Aviation Administration (FAA), and/or Civil Aviation Authority of China (CAAC), and/or European Joint Aviation Authority (JAA), or any other applicable airworthiness authority for Customers defined in **Appendix B**.

Anniversary Date - the yearly recurring date of the Effective Date.

AOG (Aircraft-On-Ground) - An Aircraft is unable to continue or be returned to revenue service until an appropriate corrective action is taken.

Approved or Authorized Repairs – those specific Repairs included in **Appendix A** hereto and/or those Repairs for which XYZ has issued a written amendment to this Agreement.

ARF (Authorized Repair Facility) - An Overhaul and/or Repair facility owned and/or operated by ABC or any other Authorized Repair Facility which is authorized by XYZ to perform Repairs of XYZ Power Units, LRUs and/or component parts.

Assembly - Receiving, disassembly, cleaning, inspection, non-destructive testing (NDT), reassembly, test, and final inspection of a Product.

Component Repair/Non-Routine Work - The work performed on parts to return such parts to Serviceable condition through the accomplishment of approved Repair processes.

Customer - Any owner or operator of an XYZ Power Unit.

Cycle – One Power Unit cycle, which begins at the initiation of start, continues through ready-to-load condition, and ends at Power Unit shutdown. Component service life is expressed in total hours operated or number of cycles. Maintenance limits and scheduled removal increments are expressed in cycles or Power Unit operating hours.

Exchange Unit - An unserviceable Power Unit exchanged for a Serviceable unit, with title transfer.

Field-of-Use - The commercial aircraft operated within the countries listed in **Appendix G** to this Agreement.

FOD (Foreign Object Damage) - Damage caused to the Power Unit by ingestion of a foreign object or objects, including but not limited to de-icing fluid or other "soft FOD".

Gross Invoice Price – Total billing amount to customers of ARF including freight, taxes, duties and other incidental charges.

Industrial Property Rights – Any and all proprietary information including, but not limited to, drawings, specifications, know-how and any inventions, including any patents, utility models or patent applications, results of technical investigations owned or controlled by XYZ and directed to the Repair of XYZ components.

Life Limited Component – A component having a specific service life which is expressed in total hours operated or total number of cycles.

Line Replaceable Unit (LRU) - Any component replaceable in the aircraft as identified in XYZ's documentation.

Low Cycle Fatigue – Materials fatigue resulting from stress-induced starting and stopping of the Power Unit and which is related to total number of Power Unit cycles.

Manual(s) - Engine Repair Manual, Component Maintenance Manual, Workscope Planning Guide, Service Information Letters, and Service Bulletins.

Net Invoice Price – Invoice Price billed to customers of ARF excluding: 1) freight and shipping expenses (including insurance) paid by ARF; 2) all sales, use and excise taxes; 3) customs duties; 4) consular fees and agent's comissions; 5) discounts, returns and allowances given by ARF, to the extent that such charges are included in the gross invoice price; 6) the invoice price of all Repair work subcontracted to a XYZ facility or another XYZ Authorized Repair Facility; and, 7) the actual price paid for any parts purchased from XYZ and used for the Repair billed to ARF's customer.

MSA - An XYZ Maintenance Support Agreement, which includes an XYZ Maintenance Service Plan.

On Condition Inspection – An unscheduled maintenance action (inspection or test) to determine the condition and serviceability of the Power Unit or its components.

Overhaul - A major maintenance or Repair action taken to restore the service life of the Power Unit or a major module of the Power Unit. An Overhaul requires evaluation and or inspection, as well as Repair(s), based on criteria included in the applicable Manual(s). An Overhaul may also include incorporation of Product improvements based on Service Bulletins in effect at that time.

Product - The commercial PSXXX Power Unit installed in commercial aircraft, including any parts or components utilizing XYZ know-how, trade secrets and other proprietary technical information owned or controlled by XYZ.

Power Unit – A power unit which is a gas turbine engine including accessories and controls, specifically identified as the PSXXXX.

PSXXX - XYZ's Power Unit System shipset including the Power Unit, and the Electronic Sequence Unit (ESU).

Repair - A maintenance or Overhaul action taken to restore the unserviceable Power Unit, its module(s), and/or component parts to acceptable limits of operation or serviceability as defined in Manual(s) or Action Item System documentation.

While the primary intent of a given Repair is to resolve the apparent problem and return the Power Unit, module(s), or components to service, all parts exposed during a Repair must conform to parts inspection limits noted in the applicable Manual(s) or Action Item System documentation in order for the Repair to result in a Serviceable condition. Repairs are performed at the request of the Customer and with the understanding that, unless otherwise directed by the Customer or XYZ for MSA/warranty Repairs, parts are Repaired rather than replaced with new hardware. Customers should be advised that Repairs, while typically cost less than replacing new hardware, may affect Turn-Around-Time. Customers must also be advised that Power Unit life expectancy, other than that directly related to the Repaired item(s), will not be affected.

Repairable - A Power Unit, module, or component which can be returned to Serviceable condition consistent with criteria set forth in the applicable Manual(s) or Action Item System documentation. All maintenance and Repair work performed must be in accordance with procedures, tolerances and limits documented in the applicable Manual(s) and/or Action Item System documentation.

Scrap Parts – Parts determined to be unserviceable and not Repairable based on criteria included in the applicable Manual(s) and/or Action Item System documentation.

Service Territory – Those areas of the world where ARF is authorized to perform services under this Agreement.

Serviceable - The condition of an item, based on criteria included in the applicable Manual(s)and/or Action Item System documentation, such that it may be placed in aircraft service.

Services – Performance of periodic inspections or Repairs which return product to serviceable condition in the manner and in accordance with Manual(s) and/or Action Item System documentation, and in accordance with the terms and conditions set forth in this Agreement.

Spare Part - Any new or Serviceable Product used as a replacement for any similar Product, or which may be required for the maintenance, modification, or Repair of a Product.

TAT (Turn-Around-Time) - The time needed to Repair, service or check out a Product for recommitment to operational service or the total number of calendar days required to complete a specified task(s) from receipt of a Product by ARF to availability for return shipment.

Wear Limits – Dimensional limits for acceptable wear of a component or part based on criteria included in the applicable Manual(s) and/or Action Item System documentation.

XYZ - XYZ Customer Corporation.

Article 1 - ARF's Obligations

XYZ appoints ARF as an XYZ Authorized Repair Facility (ARF), subject to the terms and conditions set forth in this Agreement. In consideration of its appointment for the term hereof, ARF shall pay to XYZ the sum of $XXX USD for each Product Line authorized, due and payable by wire transfer on the date of execution of this Agreement. In the event the PARTIES mutually agree, in their absolute discretion, to renew this Agreement at the expiration hereof, for one (1) or more additional five (5) year periods, and conditional upon the ARF's compliance with the terms and conditions hereof, the then applicable ARF fee for the Power Unit model(s) covered by this Agreement for any such five (5) year renewal periods shall be waived.

1.1　Adequate Technical Service Organization: ARF will maintain an adequate technical service organization to accomplish Overhaul and Repair to service Power Units in support of the Customer base. ARF agrees to provide XYZ Power Unit Customers with trouble-shooting assistance and field support as defined herein.

1.2　Services Provided to Customers of XYZ Power Units: ARF will provide maintenance and Repairs, and perform inspections and tests in accordance with applicable Manuals, Action Item System documentation, XYZ issued technical documents, and procedures as recommended by XYZ's representative(s). ARF shall perform any required work based on a thirty (30) day Turn-Around-Time, or within a specified time period as otherwise mutually agreed between ARF and XYZ or Customer. ARF will provide a no-charge loaner Product to Customer(s) at ARF's expense in the event that ARF is responsible for not meeting the Turn-Around-Time. The no-charge loaner Product shall be made available to the Customer provided the Customer is experiencing an AOG or impending AOG situation and the Customer has provisioned to at least a 95% protection level based on XYZ's recommendation.

　　1.2.1　ARF will charge Customers direct for all Repair services except for Customers covered under a valid XYZ warranty or MSA. ARF will be responsible for all receivables collection and credit control with respect to such Repair services. XYZ will be responsible for MSA administration and MSA fee collection. ARF Repair prices shall be furnished to Customers and XYZ upon request.

　　1.2.2　ARF is authorized to perform warranty Repairs and Repairs covered under a valid MSA. In the event of a warranty or MSA Repair, ARF must comply with the warranty/MSA procedures, guidelines, and General Terms and Conditions set forth in **Appendix A**. Any inquiries of such guidelines shall be directed to XYZ's Warranty Administration organization. MSA and/or warranty repairs shall be directed to ARF at the sole discretion of XYZ.

　　1.2.3　In performing Product Repairs, ARF will only use new or Serviceable Spare Parts approved by XYZ, as described in XYZ Manuals, publications or instructions, except for standard aircraft parts, which meet all Airworthiness Authority requirements. Any non-XYZ standard parts such as MS/AN parts, must be completely interchangeable with the XYZ-specified parts and must meet applicable quality requirements for aircraft service.

    1.2.4 ARF agrees that Repair services provided by ARF in accordance with this Agreement shall comply with applicable government and Airworthiness Authority requirements relating to such sales and services, and that ARF shall be fully responsible for performing any required inspection(s) and/or obtaining any required approval(s). ARF will promptly notify XYZ of any change in its authority from the Airworthiness Authorities or its capacity or capability to perform the XYZ Repair work.

1.3   ARF will accept Repair service orders for XYZ Power Units only from Time and Material Customers within the Field of Use unless otherwise authorized by the prior written consent of XYZ.

1.4   ARF will ensure that XYZ Repair operations and XYZ hardware will be separate and inaccessible to other Power Unit manufacturers.

1.5   <u>Hardware Disposition</u>: ARF will disposition failed or unserviceable Power Units, modules and/or components as directed by XYZ. Such direction may include, but is not limited to, return of such items to XYZ.

1.6   <u>Proprietary Information</u>: Manuals and other XYZ Proprietary Information are the property of XYZ and shall not be, in whole or in part, copied, transferred, or disclosed for any purpose outside the terms of this Agreement without the prior written consent of XYZ. ARF will protect XYZ's proprietary rights by treating all information relating to the design, manufacture, performance or maintenance and Repair of XYZ Power Units as information proprietary to XYZ. ARF may advise Customer of the existence and nature of this Agreement, and to the extent necessary for sales and service activities, to disclose XYZ's non-proprietary data relating to the nature, performance and support of Power Units. The provisions of this paragraph will survive any termination or expiration of this Agreement and will prevail for a period of not less than ten (10) years from the termination or expiration date of this Agreement or as required by law or subpoena. Data will not be considered confidential if:

At the time of disclosure, the data is provided to the Customer by ARF to comply with Airworthiness Authority certification requirements; or the data is already publicly available as evidenced by written publications or otherwise; or if after disclosure to the other PARTY, the data becomes publicly available by written publication or otherwise through no fault of the other PARTY; or if the other PARTY has the information in their possession at the time of disclosure without restriction as to its use; or if the data is requested by law or in response to subpoena.

This document contains information which is confidential and proprietary to XYZ. As a condition of, and as consideration for receiving this document, the recipient agrees that this document and the information contained herein shall not be disclosed outside the recipient or duplicated or used for any purpose other than proposal/quotation or product performance/conformance evaluation without XYZ's prior written consent. This restriction does not limit the recipient's right to disclose or use information contained in this document if it is publicly available or properly obtained from another source without restriction. The information subject to this restriction is contained on all pages referring to this notice.

1.6.1   Upon termination or expiration of this Agreement, ARF agrees that it will return XYZ proprietary data and all copies, in whatever form, and will not, either directly or through any affiliated companies, use or employ any of the proprietary data for further service and Repair of the Power Unit or for any other purpose. Upon termination or expiration of this Agreement ARF will return such proprietary data to XYZ within thirty (30) days.

1.6.2   No patent licenses are granted by XYZ under this Agreement, and no rights of use in data are granted or are to be inferred hereunder, except as expressly provided for herein.

1.6.3   In providing information, XYZ makes no representation or warranty, express or implied, as to its adequacy, sufficiency or freedom from any defect of any kind, including, without limitation, freedom from patent infringement that may result from its use.

1.7   Repair Procedures: Prior to the development of any Repair procedures, tooling drawings, specifications, improvements in XYZ's Power Units (including parts thereof), or XYZ Repairs introduced by ARF during the life of this Agreement, ARF will contact XYZ to determine the extent, if any, of XYZ's cooperation. No unauthorized Repair procedures shall be implemented in the Repair of any Product before ARF obtains XYZ's express written consent. The proportion of XYZ's participation in any Repair procedure development will determine what items developed will be considered the intellectual property to one or both of the PARTIES. ARF hereby grants to XYZ a royalty-free nonexclusive right to use such improvements during the term of this Agreement and thereafter. In the event ARF develops a Repair procedure solely at ARF's cost, XYZ shall be entitled to a royalty payment in the amount of twenty-five percent (25%) of the Net Invoice price for each Repair performed by ARF using such Repair procedure.

1.7.1   When mutually agreed upon between ARF and XYZ, certain test and trouble-shooting procedures, tool drawings, or specifications developed solely by ARF may be designated as proprietary to ARF and will not be published in XYZ Manuals.

1.8   Changes to Repair Documentation: From time to time XYZ may issue special Repair instructions to ARF which may modify the method(s) for Repair of Product(s), limit Repair options previously permitted by published documentation, change acceptable Repair limits, require replacement of parts previously considered Repairable for which history indicates may have a limited life, require minimum Product configurations, specify Repair sources for specific Repair methods, or impose other conditions upon ARF which in XYZ's judgment will increase the reliability of the Repaired part. ARF shall incorporate such special Repair instructions in all future Services performed as soon as reasonably practical following notification of such changes.

1.9   Quality Control Requirements: ARF shall have in place adequate and appropriate formal quality control processes which address the control and disposition of parts, Spare Parts, processes, personnel and equipment. Such processes shall conform to the requirements of the local Airworthiness Authority and shall be subject to an audit by XYZ. ARF shall have available complete, up-to-date XYZ Repair Manuals for Power Units and other related publications and specifications in sufficient quantities relative to the facility shop organization and volume of Power Units processed. All XYZ Repairs performed by ARF shall be inspected and accepted subject to XYZ authorized and approved inspection and quality assurance procedures. ARF shall not subcontract aspects of its operation which are subject to quality control without the prior written approval of XYZ. However, it is agreed that XYZ shall supply ARF with a list of the Repair suppliers/subcontractors designated by XYZ to perform specialized Repairs, where applicable. In addition, ARF may subcontract minor Repairs or minor sub-processes that meet both ARF's quality control processes and XYZ's quality system requirements as set forth in this Agreement (as shall be flowed down by ARF to its subcontractor). However, the scope of such minor Repairs and/or sub-processes shall be confirmed by ARF in regular coordination with XYZ's Repair support department. In no event is ARF authorized by XYZ to sub-contract any elements of Repair work which XYZ considers an integral core part of this ARF appointment, including, but not limited to, such tasks as inspection, Power Unit test, Assembly, repair of rotating hardware or other major Repairs, disassembly, Power Unit Repair, etc. ARF agrees that it shall remain at all times, responsible for any work contracted out of its facility.

    1.9.1   ARF shall establish an effective means of self-audit to ensure constant internal surveillance regarding proper implementation of the ARF quality system, and establish an information feedback system to XYZ regarding field-encountered Power Unit problems or suggestions for service Manual improvements.

1.10   Personnel Training Requirements: ARF will ensure an adequate level of training for its technically-qualified specialists and will send these individuals to XYZ for the training required for the proper operation, maintenance, and Repair of any XYZ Power Unit for which ARF performs maintenance or Repair actions. ARF acknowledges that the minimum qualifications for trained personnel should be those set forth by the local Airworthiness Authority who is granting ARF operating approval. Scheduled training classes conducted by XYZ at XYZ's facilities will be provided free of charge; however, ARF will be responsible for the transportation and expenses of ARF's employees while they are participating in the training program at XYZ's facilities. Upon request, XYZ will also provide training programs and related customer support on-site at ARF's facility. The charges for such services are set forth in **Appendix E.** ARF is authorized to provide Customer training courses on the proper operation and troubleshooting of all XYZ Power Units covered by this Agreement.

1.11   Customer Availability: To ensure an adequate level of customer support, ARF will provide a twenty-four (24) hour telephone number service informing Customers of Repair and/or Spare Parts availability status for any Aircraft-on-Ground (A.O.G.) situations for XYZ Power Units covered by this Agreement.

1.12   Joint Meetings: ARF will periodically participate in joint XYZ - ARF meetings for purposes of program coordination and information exchange. ARF will be responsible for costs and expenses incurred by ARF's employees or agents in connection with such joint meetings.

1.13   Records maintenance: ARF will keep complete, separate, and accurate records of all XYZ Power Units, modules and/or components maintained and Repaired by ARF for a period of six (6) years after such services are performed. Such records will be kept in sufficient detail to enable XYZ to ascertain the extent of Power Unit maintenance or Repairs performed. These records will be submitted to XYZ quarterly in a format to be mutually agreed upon, and will include, but not be limited to:

- Customer name and address
- Aircraft model, serial number, registration number and total hours
- Type of installation (name of installer)
- Power Unit operating hours and starts including both total hours/starts and the number of hours/starts since last maintenance action, if available. If not available, total aircraft operating hour and start data should be provided and the records so noted.
- A list of parts Repaired and/or replaced during the shop visit, including the serial numbers (S/Ns), where applicable.
- A detailed description of any discrepancies found during maintenance and Repair.

1.14   Audits: ARF shall provide to XYZ or its designee, on reasonable prior notice, suitable access and facilities to conduct periodic audits of ARF's personnel, procedures, books and records, facility and quality issues, during normal business hours.

1.14.1   XYZ shall have the right to conduct an initial facility audit on all aspects of the facility affecting the quality of ARF's services.

1.14.2   XYZ reserves the right to request audited financial statements as required during the life of the Agreement and ARF shall comply within ninety (90) days of the request thereof.

1.14.3   The foregoing audits will be subject to a charge as set forth in **Appendix E.**

1.14.4   Any proprietary or competitive information disclosed in the course of these audits shall be subject to the confidentiality provisions set forth in Article 1.6.

1.14.5   ARF shall promptly comply with any corrective actions identified by XYZ. XYZ reserves the right to terminate this Agreement if ARF is deemed to be adversely affecting the quality of its services and has failed to rectify any identified defects in the manner and/or time frame acceptable to XYZ.

Article 2 - ARF's Facility

2.1   <u>Test Cell:</u> ARF shall have a test cell, which shall be an immovable structure, successfully correlated with an XYZ reference test cell. The test cell correlation exercise will require three (3) phases.

Phase 1: Test Cell Shakedown
Phase 2: Power Unit Calibration
Phase 3: Test Cell Correlation

The test cell correlation exercises shall comply with the requirements outlined in the XYZ Test Cell Acceptance Process Manual, as may be amended from time to time, a copy of which has been provided to ARF under separate cover.

2.1.1   Phase 1: Test Cell Shakedown

2.1.1.1   ARF shall execute a functional check of all systems following construction of and modifications to a test cell.

2.1.1.2   The shakedown shall be performed with a suitable Power Unit capable of covering the complete test cell rated-power range. It is ARF's responsibility to provide a shakedown Power Unit. XYZ does not recognize the validity of a calibrated correlation Power Unit following use as a shakedown Power Unit.

2.1.1.3   XYZ will not be present during the shakedown phase, but may be consulted.

2.1.1.4   ARF shall forward the results of the shakedown test to XYZ for review and acceptance before the test cell correlation. The results shall cover the complete scope of the applicable XYZ Power Unit Repair Manual test section, and shall contain, as a minimum, copies of the shakedown test log, performance calculation curve and copies of any computer or calculator programs and printouts. ARF shall also include information relating to the size and type of test cell, Power Unit models to be tested, description of major items of equipment and instrumentation, and test cell drawings showing general installation.

2.1.1.5   The shakedown data shall be approved by XYZ before proceeding with the correlation exercise.

2.1.2   Phase 2: Power Unit Calibration

2.1.2.1   The correlation Power Unit is calibrated by being installed in a XYZ baseline test cell. Two (2) sets of multi-point tests are then run. The objective is to prove the performance, repeatability and stability of the Power Unit and to correct any flaws that it may contain. The data obtained is processed using an XYZ-developed program, which is identical to that which will be used at ARF's facility. The XYZ representative conducting the calibration is present at all times and is usually the same as that assigned to conduct the correlation at ARF's facility. Following a satisfactory calibration, the Power Unit and slave equipment is shipped back to ARF's facility.

2.1.2.2 ARF shall identify and provide a Power Unit(s) for the test cell correlation. The Power Unit must be capable of covering the highest power range of the XYZ Power Unit tested in the test cell.

2.1.2.3 The calibrated Power Unit shall not be run without the presence of an XYZ representative.

2.1.2.4 The charges for XYZ Power Unit calibration services are set forth in **Appendix E.**

2.1.3 Phase 3: Test Cell Correlation

2.1.3.1 An XYZ representative shall conduct the correlation exercise at ARF's facility, using a suitable Power Unit(s) previously calibrated at XYZ. ARF shall have test cell calibrating and troubleshooting equipment available on site and be prepared to adequately support the test cell correlation exercise.

2.1.3.2 The acceptability of the correlation exercise, and subsequent approval of the test cell, shall be determined by the XYZ representative conducting the exercise. The approval will be based upon the ability of the facility to perform all Repair Manual test section requirements, the degree of repeatability and deviation observed between the calibration and correlation runs.

2.1.3.3 Upon a successful test cell correlation exercise, XYZ shall issue a test cell acceptance letter and, if required, test cell recommendations. The test cell recommendations shall be implemented to the mutual satisfaction of ARF and XYZ.

2.1.3.4 The validity of the test cell acceptance will be limited to a maximum of five (5) years. Subsequent test cell correlation will not require a test cell shakedown, unless the test cell has been modified or moved to a different location.

2.1.3.5 The charges for XYZ test cell correlation services are set forth in **Appendix E.**

2.2   Service Tooling and Service Tooling Designs (Drawings)

2.2.1 ARF shall retain, for Power Unit Repairs, a complete set of applicable XYZ service tooling, to the latest XYZ designs.

2.2.2   XYZ shall provide ARF all necessary Service Tooling Design and technical data to manufacture or procure a complete set of service tooling and test equipment required for the Repair of Power Units.

XYZ assumes no responsibility for tooling manufactured or purchased by ARF.

2.2.3   ARF shall not disclose XYZ Service Tooling Designs to any third party, without the express prior written authorization of XYZ and shall comply with all the terms and conditions set forth in Article 1.6.

2.2.4   ARF shall use the Service Tooling Designs solely for the purpose of manufacturing Power Unit tools to be used in its facility.

2.2.5   ARF shall not rent, sell or otherwise transfer to any third parties, tools manufactured from XYZ Service Tooling Designs.

2.2.6   ARF is responsible for the cost and proper maintenance of any tooling and test equipment necessary to accomplish the Power Unit Repair.

2.3   Spare Parts: ARF shall maintain an adequate inventory of Spare Parts to replace unserviceable parts removed from the Customer's Power Unit. ARF's failure to comply with this requirement shall be considered default and may lead to termination of this Agreement in accordance with Article 8. ARF understands and agrees that it will obtain only Power Unit Spare Parts from XYZ as an Authorized Repair Facility for use in Repair work. Unless otherwise specifically provided for herein, ARF agrees that Power Unit Spare Parts will not be sold, shipped, transferred or in any other manner redistributed to any person or organization without XYZ's express consent. ARF shall act as a Spare Parts distributor to only those Customers experiencing an AOG or pending AOG. ARF understands and agrees that its affiliated companies, other divisions and facilities (generally, "ARF's affiliates") have not been designated by XYZ as an Authorized Repair Facility. ARF represents to XYZ that it will not resell or transfer Spare Parts to its affiliates.

2.3.1   Parts Provisioning

ARF shall conduct material requirements planning so as to ensure timely Spare Parts ordering and scheduling in accordance with **Appendix C** and XYZ's published lead-times and terms and conditions of sale contained in XYZ's Commercial Airline Price Catalog(s). If deemed necessary by XYZ, Spare Parts provisioning conferences will be required. XYZ may review ARF's Spare Parts inventory records and orders from time to time and will provide provisioning assistance and recommendations as requested by the ARF during such reviews.

2.3.2   Published Lead-time

The delivery of Spare Parts at published lead-time is conditional upon ARF fulfilling all of the terms and conditions of this Agreement, including, without limitation, those terms and conditions relating to order performance and expedite control.

2.3.3   Provisioning Performance Fee

As appropriate, ARF shall pay to XYZ on each Anniversary Date of this Agreement, the fee as described and calculated in accordance with **Appendix C.**

2.3.4   Parts Order Administration

By the first (1st) Anniversary Date, ARF shall establish and maintain with XYZ, electronic communications capabilities for Spare Parts order administration in accordance with XYZ's recommendations. XYZ will assist ARF in defining and establishing appropriate electronic interface. ARF may establish electronic capabilities through a mutually agreed third party.

2.3.5   Serviceable Parts

ARF shall maintain a pool of Serviceable Spare Parts in quantities required to support XYZ Customers in accordance with XYZ policies.

2.4   Safety and Forecasting Support Record Access: ARF shall maintain the following data for each Power Unit shop visit and provide XYZ with such data within ninety (90) days of completion of the Power Unit. All data will be communicated electronically to XYZ. Data shall be used exclusively by XYZ for the purpose of facilitating XYZ's ability to compile Power Unit reliability data, forecast Spare Parts consumption and ensure superior quality operator support.

Category A - Power Unit and Module History
Example: Power Unit time/cycle/removal history and ownership records;

Category B - Major Event Notification and Shop Investigation
Example: data establishing symptom and cause for event such as catastrophical failures;

Category C - Power Unit Repair Summary (Shop Finding Report)
Example: data on Power Unit refurbishment such as Spare Parts consumed and replaced, parts Repaired, Power Unit overall condition, etc;

Category D - Quarterly Shop Repair Forecast
Example: data for planning such as anticipated shop Repairs, actual Spare Parts inventory records and actual spare Power Unit inventory;

Category E - Annual Summary of Shop Events
Example: data for planning; historical shop activity (prior year's actual events), actual Spare Parts inventory records and actual spare Power Unit inventory.

The detailed specifications of the data required are set forth in **Appendix F**.

2.4.1   ARF shall establish with XYZ customer support and Spare Part sales, electronic communications capabilities, procedures and formats for supplying the information described above, details of which are contained in **Appendix**

F. XYZ will assist ARF in defining and establishing appropriate electronic interface. It is ARF's responsibility to establish and maintain the necessary electronic communications capabilities with XYZ.

2.4.2   Based on the information supplied by ARF and other third parties, XYZ will supply the following information to ARF:

i) Number of Power Units delivered;
ii) Total forecast Repairs for the market as a whole, with ARF's share.

The information supplied will be the most accurate information available to XYZ at the time.

Article 3 - XYZ's Obligations

XYZ agrees that during the term of this Agreement, XYZ will provide on a non-exclusive basis the following services to ARF for the Repair of Power Units.

3.1   Visits to ARF: XYZ will periodically send an XYZ representative to visit ARF for purposes of familiarization and problem review.

3.2   Technical Support and Other Communication: XYZ will provide ARF in a timely manner, technical data and service information for the Power Units, in the same form as released and used by XYZ to service the Power Units. XYZ will promptly advise ARF of any significant service related problems, which are either Power Unit or service-oriented.

3.2.1   All standard XYZ service information and assistance will be provided in English. Any requirements to translate technical information, interpretations or clarifications into any other language, or to convert XYZ measurements into different units will be at a charge to be mutually agreed upon by the PARTIES. If any part of the technical information furnished hereunder does not conform with the technical information released and used, XYZ will, upon reasonable notice, correct the discrepancy in question by furnishing amended technical information.

3.2.2   XYZ Customer Support will act as the single point of contact between ARF and XYZ for ARF technical issues. XYZ Product Support Engineering (PSE) will provide technical assistance through XYZ's Action Item System in response to ARF's requests for information involving Repair documentation, practices and procedures.

3.2.3   XYZ Customer Support will also act as the single point of contact between ARF and XYZ for Repair facility financial and business issues.

3.3   Warranty and MSA Provisions: Within ninety (90) days of ARF's warranty or MSA Repair activity, XYZ will indemnify ARF for labor performed and material used in fulfilling XYZ's applicable printed warranty or MSA requirements. Such indemnification will be made subject to ARF's submission of required documentation in the manner and form prescribed by XYZ. The detailed procedures, guidelines, and general terms and conditions imposed on ARF by XYZ in fulfilling XYZ's Power Unit warranty and MSA Repairs are set forth in **Appendix A**.

The only warranties made by XYZ are those expressly provided for in this Agreement. Any other statements expressed in this Agreement, including but not limited to, specifications, drawings, or Manuals shall not be deemed to constitute a warranty of the Products. THE WARRANTIES SET FORTH IN THIS AGREEMENT ARE EXCLUSIVE AND NO OTHER WARRANTIES OF ANY KIND, WHETHER EXPRESS OR IMPLIED, INCLUDING ALL WARRANTIES OF MERCHANTABILITY AND FITNESS FOR A PARTICULAR Power UnitRPOSE, AND ALL WARRANTIES ARISING FROM COURSE OF DEALING OR USAGE OF ARTICLE ARE THE SOLE AND EXCLUSIVE REMEDIES OF ARF FOR ANY CLAIMS, EXPENSES, OR DAMAGE ARSING OUT OF OR RELATED TO PRODUCTS DELIVERED UNDER THIS AGREEMENT. IN NO EVENT WILL XYZ BE LIABLE IN TORT OR IN CONTRACT FOR ANY INCIDENTAL, SPECIAL, INDIRECT, OR CONSEQUENTIAL DAMAGES.

3.4   <u>XYZ Inventory</u>:   XYZ will maintain a stock of the commonly used Repair or replacement parts in quantity and types reasonably related to the Power Units. XYZ agrees to furnish these parts to ARF at the published catalog price and lead times current at the time the order is placed. Expedited Spare Parts orders (not ordered to established lead times) shall be subject to an expedite fee of twenty-five percent (25%) of XYZ's Commercial Airline Catalog price at the time of order.

3.5   <u>Spare Part Warranty</u>:   New parts supplied by XYZ are warranted to be, at the time of delivery, free from defects in material and workmanship. Each new Spare Part purchased by ARF will carry an XYZ standard warranty of six (6) months from date of sale to Customer or twelve (12) months after shipment to ARF whichever occurs first. The general terms and conditions for XYZ's Spare Parts shall be in accordance with XYZ's Commercial Airline Price Catalog.

3.6   <u>Publication of New Spare Part Pricing</u>:   XYZ will publish new Spare Part prices to primary commercial Customers on an annual basis. ARF will be advised of new prices sixty (60) days prior to the effective date of the new XYZ Commercial Airline Price Catalog(s). While best efforts will be made to ensure accuracy, occasional errors may occur when preparing this catalog. XYZ reserves the right to correct any such errors without prior notice.

3.7   <u>Notice of Configuration Changes</u>:   To the extent practical, XYZ will provide ARF with information on hardware modifications and service changes prior to the release of the information to aircraft Customers. XYZ will utilize good faith to notify ARF at least thirty (30) days prior to the release of significant configuration changes. Such notification will be provided in a document, which will be held confidential in accordance with Article 1.6. This document will outline the changes(s) to be implemented and will provide warranty coverage information as well as any other pertinent information relative to economic considerations.

Article 4 - Loan and Exchange Units

4.1   ARF shall maintain sufficient quantities of spare Power Units, accessories (LRUs) and components in quantities required to support all its Customers with loan, rental or Exchange Units.

    4.1.1   ARF, at its discretion, may utilize Power Units as rental units to Customers or provide Exchange Units to Customers during the time the Customer Power Unit is being Repaired. If XYZ requests ARF to provide a Power Unit owned by ARF to a Customer on a rental basis when an XYZ rental unit is not otherwise available, then XYZ will restore ARF's Power Unit to Exchange Unit status or will compensate ARF in the form of a Spare Parts credit, for the reduced value of the unit.

    4.1.2   Each Exchange Unit and Serviceable Spare Part purchased from XYZ by ARF will carry XYZ standard warranty coverage of six (6) months from date of sale to Customer or twelve (12) months after shipment to ARF whichever occurs first. Any warranty extension programs developed by XYZ for Exchange Units and/or Serviceable Spare Parts will be implemented and available to ARF for those Products designated by XYZ.

Article 5 - Loss, Damage and Delay

The PARTIES will not be liable for loss, damage, detention, or delay resulting from causes beyond reasonable control, or from fire, weather, or other concerted action of workers, act or omission of any Government authority, insurrection or riot, embargo, fuel shortage, inability to obtain transportation, or inability to obtain necessary labor materials or manufacturing facilities from usual sources. In the event of a delay due to such causes, XYZ shall be entitled to an equitable adjustment in delivery schedule for any Power Units or Spare Parts scheduled for delivery to ARF.

Article 6 - Risk of Loss

Risk of loss of supplies or any part of same shall pass to ARF upon delivery "Ex Works" XYZ's facility (I.C.C. Incoterms, 2000). All deliveries shall be made "Ex Works" freight forwarder selected by ARF. ARF will take the necessary steps to assure that XYZ retains a security interest in deliverable items until payment is received by XYZ.

Article 7 - Term of Agreement

Except as otherwise expressly provided, the term of this Agreement and of any and all rights granted and obligations assumed hereunder will begin on the Effective Date of this Agreement and will continue for a period of five (5) years unless terminated as provided in Article 8 of this Agreement.

Article 8 - Termination

8.1   In the event that either PARTY breaches any material provision of this Agreement, the other PARTY may terminate this Agreement effective thirty (30) days after the breaching PARTY has been given written notice of the default and has failed within that time period to correct such default.

8.2   Termination of this Agreement shall not prejudice or otherwise affect the rights or liabilities of either PARTY with respect to breach of this Agreement, nor shall it relieve either PARTY of its rights or obligations with respect to parts sold to or ordered by ARF, or any indebtedness owing by either PARTY to the other, or the obligation of ARF to keep books and records, or the obligation of the PARTIES to treat information as confidential in accordance with this Agreement. Upon termination for any reason, neither PARTY shall be liable for consequential or indirect damages such as, without limitation, lost profits on sales or anticipated sales, or commitments made in connection with the development of ARF's business.

8.3   Should either PARTY become insolvent, or perform or permit any act of bankruptcy, liquidation or re-organization (with the exception of a voluntary re-organization within a PARTY's own group of companies not further to its bankruptcy, insolvency, liquidation or other similar proceedings) or if a receiver, trustee or custodian is appointed to a PARTY's property or a substantial part thereof, the other PARTY may, at its option, terminate this Agreement immediately by written notice.

8.4   This Agreement may be terminated for convenience at any time by XYZ, without cause, by giving written notice to ARF no less than ninety (90) days prior to the proposed termination date.

8.5   If any governmental approvals or authorization shall be rescinded, or not renewed when required, or shall otherwise cease to be effective, XYZ may at its sole option, give notice of the suspension of this Agreement pending reinstatement by the applicable governmental authorities. If such approvals or authorizations are not reinstated within ninety (90) days, XYZ may forthwith give notice of termination of this Agreement (or part thereof), in which event this Agreement (or part thereof) shall terminate when such notice is given. ARF shall immediately give notice to XYZ of any change in the status of such governmental approvals or authorization upon its first knowledge thereof.

8.6   ARF agrees to notify XYZ immediately of any change or anticipated change in the nature of its ownership or business, including, without limitation, a deterioration in its financial situation, or any other circumstances which may in any way affect ARF's performance under this Agreement. XYZ reserves the right to terminate this Agreement for any reason including, without limitation, if (i) XYZ determines, in its absolute discretion, that any such change may result in a conflict of interest or otherwise prejudice the ability of ARF to perform its obligations hereunder or (ii) such change results in ARF being effectively owned or operated, directly or indirectly, by a competitor or supplier of XYZ. In the event of any ownership changes involving ARF or business change as defined above, should XYZ agree to continue doing business with ARF or the new owner(s), XYZ reserves the right to charge the then applicable ARF fee at such time.

8.7   Upon termination for any reason, ARF shall provide XYZ with the opportunity to bid on the repurchase of any surplus Power Units and related parts, service tooling and equipment (herein collectively referred to as "Surplus Power Units"). ARF shall accept any reasonable offer made by XYZ pursuant to this provision. In addition and without prejudice to the foregoing, if ARF desires to sell any Surplus Power Units to a third party, ARF shall first give to XYZ an irrevocable option to purchase the Surplus Power Units at the price and on those terms and conditions offered to ARF by the third party. ARF shall give to XYZ a copy of the offer received (hereinafter referred to as the "Offer"), which shall have been made in good faith.

To exercise this option, XYZ shall notify ARF within thirty (30) days of receipt of a copy of the Offer, failing which XYZ shall be deemed to have consented to the sale of the Surplus Power Units to the third party.

If XYZ has or is deemed to have consented to the sale of the Surplus Power Units to a third party, then ARF shall sell to the same third party, but strictly in compliance with the Offer.

8.8   Upon termination, ARF shall advise all Customers that it is no longer an XYZ appointed authorized repair facility.

8.9   In the event this Agreement is not renewed, ARF agrees that it will not directly or indirectly market or sell the repair of Product for a period of not less than fifteen (15) years from the termination or expiration date of this Agreement, without the prior written consent of XYZ.

Article 9 - Assignment

This Agreement is personal to XYZ and ARF. Any assignment of the rights or obligations hereunder by either PARTY, whether in whole or in part, will only be made with the prior written consent of the other PARTY, which consent will not be unreasonably withheld. Notwithstanding anything to the contrary, XYZ reserves the right to assign this Agreement, in full or any part thereof, to any affiliate, subsidiary or division of XYZ.

Article 10 - Advertising

Any ARF advertising or display which includes a reference to XYZ, XYZ Products, or the aircraft in which XYZ Products are installed or which reproduces any trademark owned by or licensed to XYZ, shall be submitted to XYZ Product Support Business Management for approval before publishing. ARF shall comply with any requirement made by XYZ in connection with such advertising or display. For the purpose of this Article 10, advertising includes, but is not limited to, news releases, sales literature, website, promotional brochures (including photographs and films) and public announcements whether printed or electronically transmitted.

Article 11 - XYZ Trademark

11.1 ARF shall not, in its trade or corporate names or otherwise, use the words "ABC Customer", "Customer", or any other trade name or trademark used by or licensed to XYZ or any subsidiary or affiliate of XYZ.

11.2 Nothing in this Agreement shall be construed as granting a license or any other right under any trademark, service mark, or copyright of XYZ.

Article 12 - Limitation of Rights and Liability

12.1 <u>Limitation of Rights</u>: This Agreement does not confer or grant, in any manner whatsoever, express or implied, any authorization to manufacture or sell, or any right to sub-authorize to any third party the manufacture or Repair of any Power Units or components of Power Units which incorporate patents, copyrights or any other rights held by XYZ.

12.2 <u>Limitation of XYZ's Liability</u>: The total liability of XYZ on any claim, whether in contract, tort, (including negligence) or otherwise, arising out of, connected with, or resulting from the manufacture, sale, delivery, resale, Repair, replacement or use of any Power Unit or the furnishing of any service in connection with this Agreement shall not exceed the price allocable to the Power Unit or service or part thereof which gives rise to the claim.

12.3 <u>Incidental or Consequential Damages</u>: IN NO EVENT, SHALL XYZ BE LIABLE FOR ANY SPECIAL, INCIDENTAL OR CONSEQUENTIAL DAMAGES INCLUDING, BUT NOT LIMITED TO, DAMAGES FOR LOSS OF REVENUE, COST OF CAPITAL, CLAIMS OF CUSTOMERS FOR SERVICE INTERRUPTIONS, AND COSTS INCURRED IN CONNECTION WITH SUBSTITUTES, FACILITIES OR SUPPLY SOURCES.

Article 13 - Indemnification

13.1 <u>ARF's Indemnification of XYZ</u>: ARF shall indemnify and hold XYZ, its agents, employees, distributors, and dealers harmless from and against any and all liabilities, claims, demands, losses, and causes of action whatsoever (including without limitation, costs and expenses in connection therewith) resulting from the injury to or death of any employee, representative, agent, or student/trainee or for the loss of or damage to the property of either PARTY, suffered or sustained in the course of or in connection with the performance of this Agreement except to the extent such injury, death, loss or damage shall have been caused by negligent acts of XYZ or XYZ's employees or representatives.

13.2 <u>Attorney's Fees</u>: Such indemnities will include reasonable attorney's fees associated with the defense of any indemnified claim, loss, damage, cost or expense, but limited by comparative fault or negligence on the part of the indemnified PARTY.

13.3 <u>Defense of Claims Brought Against ARF</u>: XYZ will handle all claims and defend any suit or proceeding brought against ARF so far as based on a claim that Products or service (or any part thereof) furnished by XYZ under this Agreement constitute an infringement of any patent of the United States, provided XYZ is notified promptly in writing and given authority, information and assistance by ARF for the defense of same.

Article 14 - Insurance

ARF shall carry aircraft products liability insurance in respect of ARF's activities and those of its employees in an amount of not less than XXXX U.S. dollars and shall submit to XYZ a certificate of insurance evidencing such coverage prior to the start of work. XYZ shall receive at least thirty (30) days prior written notice in the event of cancellation or reduction of coverage amount of the above insurance. ARF shall maintain this aircraft products liability coverage for as long as Power Units remain in service. ARF, its agents and subcontractors shall provide certificates of such insurance to XYZ when requested.

Article 15 - Taxes

ARF shall be responsible for all taxes, duties, interest, penalties and other charges of any nature whatsoever directly resulting from the transactions under this Agreement and will reimburse XYZ for any such charges XYZ may be required to pay. ARF and XYZ agree to cooperate to secure, where applicable, any certificates of tax exemption or any tax recoveries.

Article 16 - Export Restrictions

Each PARTY hereby acknowledges that the Products which are the subject of this Agreement, and any data relating thereto, are subject to the provisions of United States export control laws as enacted and amended from time to time, and the regulations issued thereunder. ARF will not directly or indirectly transfer any proprietary information or technical data, or any Products utilizing any such information or data obtained from XYZ to any country for which the U.S. Government, or any agency thereof, at the time of export, requires an export authorization or other Governmental approval, without first obtaining the written consent and/or applicable authorization of the U.S. Department of Commerce or other agency, as appropriate, of the U.S. Government when required by an applicable statute or regulation.

Article 17 - Governing Laws

This Agreement shall be governed by and interpreted in accordance with the laws of the State of California, U.S.A. In the event, however, that ARF and XYZ fail to resolve any disputes through negotiations, ARF and XYZ hereby irrevocably consent and agree that any legal action, suit or proceeding arising out of or in any way connected with this Agreement, shall be instituted in the courts of the city of XXXX, State of California, U.S.A. The PARTIES to this Agreement shall not be bound by the United Nations Convention on Contracts for the International Sale of Goods. The Parties expressly disclaim the applicability of said Convention.

Article 18 - Independent Contractor

ARF shall act as an independent contractor and nothing contained herein, express or implied, should at any time be construed to create the relationship of employer and employee, partnership, principal and agent, joint venture, pooling or similar relationship between ARF and XYZ.

Article 19 - Illegal, Invalid or Unenforceable Provisions

In the event any material or essential provision contained in this Agreement is held by a competent authority to be illegal, invalid, or unenforceable under any law applicable in any jurisdiction, the PARTIES agree, as to such jurisdiction, to reasonably negotiate an appropriate and equitable amendment to this Agreement. If the PARTIES are unable to agree on an appropriate and equitable amendment, this Agreement shall, at the option of either PARTY, be terminated by giving written notice to the other PARTY. In the event any provision of this Agreement is held by a competent authority to be illegal, invalid, or unenforceable under any law applicable in any jurisdiction, and such provision is not material or essential to this Agreement, this Agreement shall be continued as to such jurisdiction as if such invalid or unenforceable provision was not included.

Article 20 - Notices

All notices issued by either PARTY, must be in writing and addressed as follows:

For XYZ Corporation:　　　　　　　　XYZ Corporation

　　　　　　　　　　　　　　　　　　_____

　　　　　　　　　　　　　　　　　　Attention:
　　　　　　　　　　　　　　　　　　Manager, Customer Support
　　　　　　　　　　　　　　　　　　Facsimile Number: XXXXX

For ABC Corporation:　　　　　　　　_____

　　　　　　　　　　　　　　　　　　_____

Attention: _____
Facsimile Number: _____

Article 21 - Waiver of Rights

The failure of either PARTY to enforce at any time any of the provisions of this Agreement or exercise any of the rights hereunder shall not be construed as a waiver of such provisions or rights.

Article 22 - Compliance with Laws

ARF agrees that it will comply with all international, federal, state, and local laws applicable to the performance of this Agreement and specifically including those relating to the export of Power Units and technical data and the requirements of Airworthiness Authorities.

Article 23 - Amendment

No amendment or modification of this Agreement shall be binding upon either PARTY unless agreed to in writing by the duly authorized officers or representatives of both PARTIES.

Article 24 - Entire Agreement

This Agreement, together with any document referred to in this Agreement, comprises the entire Agreement between the PARTIES with respect to the subject matter hereof and supersedes all prior agreements, communications, understandings, exchange of correspondence, representations, and negotiations between the PARTIES with respect to the subject matter hereof and shall enure to the benefit of any successors and assigns.

Article 25 - Order of Precedence

Should any inconsistencies or contradictions appear between this Agreement and its appendices or attachments or any document incorporated by reference or any order issued hereunder, the following order of precedence shall govern:

1. This Agreement   2. The Appendices or Attachments   3. Other written documents

Article 26 - Signatures

IN CONSIDERATION OF THE ABOVE, the PARTIES hereto have caused this Agreement to be executed by their duly authorized representatives.

ABC CORPORATION   **XYZ CORPORATION**

By:_____   By: _____

Name:_____   Name: _____

Title:_____   Title: _____

Date: _____   Date: _____

APPENDIX A - WARRANTY/MSA

TERMS AND CONDITIONS

1. ARF warrants to XYZ and Customers that all ARF Repairs performed pursuant to this Agreement shall conform to the applicable Power Unit Repair Manual and be free from defects in workmanship. ARF agrees to extend to the Customer, on behalf of XYZ, the warranty that Repairs pursuant to this Agreement shall be free from defects in material and such material warranty shall extend for a period of six (6) months after Customer receives the Product after Repair by ARF.

    1.1 ARF will promptly provide to the Customer or XYZ, such labor and material as necessary to correct any defects in workmanship. In such circumstances, XYZ will not grant ARF a labor allowance or authorize credit for material used or parts replaced.

    1.2 ARF will be solely responsible for adjudication of Product failures occurring during the ARF warranty period, which are caused by or attributable to defects in ARF's workmanship.

2. In the event XYZ is responsible for all or part of a Product failure covered under a valid XYZ warranty or MSA agreement, XYZ agrees to pay ARF the labor rate set forth in **Appendix E,** for labor and other services performed by ARF in fulfilling the applicable printed XYZ warranty, MSA Repairs and XYZ directed configuration campaign changes, provided however, reports and invoices covering the work or services performed, are in accordance with the requirements set forth herein. XYZ's standard Power Unit warranty and MSA terms do not include removal and replacement of the Power Unit from an installation. The Product removal and replacement expense shall be the responsibility of ARF, or Customer. Reimbursement to ARF for warranty and MSA Repair efforts will only include the shop labor Repair man-hours associated with the affected XYZ hardware and will not include maintenance task time attributed to installation, such as access to components. XYZ's reimbursement to ARF for labor hours for specific work actions shall be based on ARF's actual labor hours incurred, but in no event shall be greater than XYZ's established labor allowance for specific work actions as set forth in **Appendix B.**

3. XYZ will replace at no charge, or at its option reimburse ARF in the form of a Spare Parts credit, for each XYZ Repair or replacement Spare Part installed or furnished by ARF in fulfilling the applicable printed XYZ warranty and/or MSA Repair. The reimbursement credit to ARF will be equal to XYZ's Commercial Airline Catalog price at the time of Product failure or the invoice price paid by AFR for the Spare Part, whichever is less. ARF shall submit a formal, written warranty claim notice (Attn: Warranty Administration) requesting a credit for the material and labor cost expended to Repair the Power Unit. The request for reimbursement shall itemize each part replaced with its cost, and provide a detailed breakdown of the labor hours expended. To qualify for reimbursement, the formal claim notice must be submitted within ninety (90) days of the Power Unit removal date. After final approval by XYZ, any such credit

owed to ARF by XYZ for warranty or MSA Repairs, will be credited against ARF's existing, or forthcoming purchase of Spare Parts from XYZ.

4.   XYZ's MSA Repair coverage shall be in accordance with the applicable contractual agreement executed by XYZ and Customer. In the event the required MSA Repair exceeds $XXX, ARF shall obtain written approval from XYZ prior to commencing the MSA Repair or replacement action. ARF shall not charge XYZ for consumable (expendable) hardware or nonrepairable LRUs used or replaced during MSA Repairs.

5.   XYZ's Product Warranty Coverage is subject to the following terms:

5.1   The Product shall be returned to ARF for full investigation within sixty (60) days after discovery of the defect.

5.2   The Customer provides ARF with a report of the defect together with details of any Repair work performed on the Product from the date the Customer first received the Product.

5.3   The Product shall have been stored, operated and maintained in accordance with XYZ Manuals and instructions.

5.4   The Product has not been subject to misuse, neglect, corrosion, accident or other adverse operating condition that may have caused undue deterioration or distress or suffered distress due to Foreign Object Damage.

5.5   The Product has not been Repaired or subject to any other work by a non XYZ authorized repair facility, and/or incorporated replacement parts other than those purchased from XYZ or from an XYZ-approved source.

5.6   The failure of the Product to operate satisfactorily has not been caused by an installation or system interface problem in an installation or application not approved by XYZ for the Power Unit in question.

5.7   The Customer shall be liable for pro-rata Repair charges relating to the rectification of reasonable wear and tear unrelated to the warranty claim.

5.8   The correction of any failure, deficiency, or malfunction shall not extend the original warranty period. After Repair of each Product by ARF, the remainder of the original warranty will apply, except for ensuing failures resulting from ARF workmanship, or failure of parts procured from a vendor other than XYZ or XYZ-approved source.

5.9   Warranty labor covers the cost of Power Unit and component testing and includes only the work required to Repair the primary failure and resultant damage to the equipment.

5.10   Warranty parts include only those parts required to Repair the primary failure, resultant damage, and expendable items, including miscellaneous supplies and parts required to accomplish the warrantable Repair and test.

5.11   Scheduled and routine maintenance and inspection, including but not limited to disassembly, Assembly, cleaning, inspection, and all field Repair effort required as a result of normal wear and tear, as delineated in the applicable Manual(s) and other like documentation are specifically excluded from warranty coverage.

6.   Procedures for Administration are as follows:

6.1   ARF shall administer all applicable XYZ Power Unit warranty programs in accordance with the XYZ Warranty Instructions Manual (WIM), as may be amended from time to time, a copy of which has been provided to ARF under separate cover.

6.2   For warranty Repair or replacement actions that are less than $XXX, ARF shall have sole discretion to adjudicate the warranty claim. In the event the required warranty Repair or replacement exceeds $XXX, ARF shall obtain written approval from XYZ prior to commencing a warranty Repair or replacement action. The XYZ Field Service Representative reserves the right to be present at ARF's shop during the removal and inspection of the failed Power Unit and its parts. XYZ also reserves the right to review each claim in detail, including requests for additional pertinent data, prior to final acceptance. In no event will XYZ be financially liable for Repair costs incurred by ARF, if ARF failed to obtain prior written approval from XYZ Warranty Repair Administration when Repair or replacement action values exceed $XXX.

6.3   ARF shall advise XYZ in writing, via warranty claim, of any failure subject to the conditions of the warranty within a maximum of ninety (90) days of the discovery of such failure and shall return the part to XYZ, as required, within thirty (30) days following the date of notification. Parts that have a commercial catalog value equal to or greater than $XXX must be returned. Any other part determined by XYZ to require evaluation for any reason whatsoever, may be required to be returned.

6.4   Copies of maintenance logbook pages for the Product that failed and any other additional information requested by the XYZ Field Service Representative must be submitted with the warranty claim if available. Claims submitted without this information may result in delay and rejection of the claim.

6.5   Power Units, subassemblies, or piece parts, which are damaged but are potentially Repairable, as determined by XYZ's Service Representative, but where such Repair is beyond the capability of ARF, shall be returned to XYZ with a warranty claim for Repair.

6.6   ARF shall notify XYZ of Power Units removed prematurely as a result of failure, the determination of removal causes and shall submit all reports to XYZ in accordance with the XYZ Warranty Instructions Manual (WIM).

6.7   ARF shall maintain written communication with XYZ with regard to Customer disputes and timely disposition of warranty claims.

6.8   ARF shall participate in automated warranty processing procedures and the supply of all requested data concerning parts removed from Power Units.

6.9   ARF shall isolate all Customer material subject to a claim in warranty in order to ensure traceability of the parts and parts condition until ninety (90) days following the final disposition of a claim by XYZ.

6.10   ARF shall submit to XYZ supporting documents confirming that the warranted unserviceable material has been dispositioned (i.e. returned to XYZ, scrapped or held in an isolated area in accordance with the XYZ WIM).

6.11   In all matters pertaining to the administration of XYZ warranty programs, ARF shall invoice the Customer net of any and all applicable commercial support and warranty credits and indicate on the Customer's invoice all applicable details of commercial and warranty credits, the whole in accordance with the XYZ WIM. All warranty claims submit to XYZ by ARF shall be in U.S. dollars.

6.12   XYZ shall be entitled to require an accident investigation to be performed either at XYZ or XYZ's designated facility. In the event of an investigation on a Power Unit previously Repaired at a XYZ designated facility, a representative of such facility may be present during such investigation.

6.13   If an XYZ published Repair scheme exists, warranty indemnification on replacement components at any time after ninety (90) days from the publication of such Repair in the applicable XYZ Technical Publication shall be limited to the average Repair cost of such Repair as established by XYZ.

6.14   If deemed necessary by XYZ, ARF shall maintain in its facility, suitable digital cameras and appropriate electronic communications equipment to be used to transmit parts condition information to XYZ.

6.15   In the event of a premature Power Unit removal, XYZ reserves the right to recall the Power Unit and/or parts for investigation, or Repair at a facility designated by XYZ Warranty Administration.

6.16   XYZ Warranty Administration shall monitor ARF's performance based on, but not limited to the following criteria:

    i)   Power Unit removal cause and removed parts condition;
    ii)   claims accuracy and timeliness;
    iii) complete supporting documentation;
    iv)   invoicing practices;
    v)   Customer satisfaction; and
    vi)   Repair warranty administration process including compliance with XYZ Warranty Administration Instructions and the implementation of XYZ's recommendations and other applicable instructions.

6.17   XYZ reserves the right, upon reasonable notice, to audit ARF warranty administration process on any or all of the elements indicated above and ARF agrees to promptly comply with any recommendations made by XYZ's Warranty Administration. These audits will be subject to the audit provisions set forth in Article 1.11.

APPENDIX B - IN-HOUSE WARRANTY/MSA SERVICE LABOR ALLOWANCE

SERVICE LABOR ALLOWANCE SHOP REPAIR TIMES

The following provides the shop labor hours standard Repair times:

TBD

REPAIRS NOT COVERED BY SERVICE LABOR ALLOWANCE LIST

If a maintenance or Repair action is required which is not set forth on the Service Labor Allowances list, the XYZ Field Service Representative will determine the labor allowances commensurate with the necessary Repair work.

APPENDIX C - PROVISIONING PERFORMANCE

1.   <u>Provisioning Performance Fee:</u> The Provisioning Performance Fee is structured as an incentive for ARF to conduct material requirements planning to ensure timely parts ordering and scheduling consistent with XYZ's published lead-time requirements with a minimum of expedite requests. Notwithstanding assessment of the fee payable to XYZ, ARF's failure to comply with this requirement shall be considered default and may lead to termination of this Agreement in accordance with Article 8.

XYZ recognizes that Spare Part shortages and expedite activities are a function of Spare Parts support and Customer's demand and as a consequence XYZ anticipates an acceptable allowance for these circumstances. XYZ will provide to ARF, on a monthly basis, ARF's performance measurements for review and corrective action if necessary.

1.1   <u>Order Performance:</u> ARF is contracted to provide published lead-time or greater for a minimum of 75% of both items and dollar value ordered on a consistent basis over the contract anniversary period. (It will be the lesser of the items or dollar value which will be used to calculate order performance.) Order performance also includes delivery schedules that do not have abnormal quantity requirements. Order quantity deliveries must be mutually agreed to between both PARTIES.

1.2   <u>Expedites:</u> ARF is contracted to ensure that expedite activity as defined herein is maintained below a maximum of 10% for both items and dollar value ordered on a consistent basis over the contract anniversary period. (It will be the greater of the items or dollar value which will be used to calculate the expedites performance.) This includes existing orders rescheduled and requiring expedite activity.

   A. Expedite = Aircraft on ground (AOG) only, requiring XYZ to make every attempt to ship Parts within 24 hours.

   B. Expedite = Line stoppage or shortage requiring XYZ to make every attempt to ship Parts within 72 hours.

   C Expedite = Potential line stoppage or shortage requiring XYZ to make every attempt to ship Parts within 7 calendar days.

1.3   <u>Exceptions:</u>   XYZ will not penalize ARF for expedite activity related to HS performance or XYZ directed field support.

1.4   <u>Provisioning Performance Fee Calculation:</u> The Provisioning Performance Fee, if applicable, will be invoiced by XYZ on each Anniversary Date and shall be calculated in relation to ARF's performance against established criteria as outlined in paragraphs 1.1 and 1.2. of this Appendix II. The fee will be calculated by taking the 12 month average of both order performance and expedite criteria and comparing them to the Provisioning Performance Fee Structure chart and table attached. The fee may range from a minimum of 0% to a maximum of 4% of total sales during the measurement period.1.1

| | APPENDIX C TABLE | | | | |
	Provisioning Performance Fee Structure				
	Applicable Charges (%) for each category based on Performance/Expedites	0%	1% each of sales	2% each of sales	4% each * of sales
End year 1	Order Performance (%) Expedites (%)	70-100 0-10	65-69 11-15	60-64 16-20	59 or < 20 or >
End year 2	Order Performance (%) Expedites (%)	75-100 0-10	70-74 11-15	65-69 16-20	64 or < 20 or >
Year 3/5	Order Performance (%) Expedites (%)	SAME	SAME	SAME	SAME

Charges calculation = Sum of Order Performance + Expedites

Example End Year 1:

Order Performance at 67% Charges = 1%
Expedites at 17% Charges = 2%
Total Applicable Charges = 3%

* Note: The total combined charges to any Customer will not exceed a maximum of 4%.

| | APPENDIX C TABLE | | | | |
	Provisioning Performance Fee Structure				
	Applicable Charges (%) for each category based on Performance/Expedites	0%	1% each of sales	2% each of sales	4% each * of sales
Anniversary Date of Agreement	Order Performance (%) Expedites (%)	75-100 0-10	70-74 11-15	65-69 16-20	64 or < 20 or >

Charges calculation = Sum of Order Performance + Expedites

Example:

Order Performance at 72% Charges = 1%
Expedites at 17% Charges = 2%
Total Applicable Charges = 3%

* Note: The total combined charges to any Customer will not exceed a maximum of 4%.

APPENDIX D - LABOR PRICE ESCALATION

Unless otherwise provided for herein, the base prices set forth in this Agreement are subject to an annual (January 1) adjustment for inflation/deflation, beginning on January 1, 2002, in accordance with the following:

One hundred Percent (100%) of the base price shall constitute the labor portion subject to adjustment utilizing United States Department of Labor, Bureau of Labor Statistics publication "Employment and Earnings", Table C-2, SIC-Code 372, Average Hourly Earnings.

In accordance with the formula:

$$P = P_o\left(\frac{L}{L_o}\right)$$

Whereby:

P   =   New escalated price
P_o =   Base price in 2001 dollars
L   =   Table C-2, SIC-372 average for the months of June, July, and August of the year preceding the year of delivery and/or services rendered
L_o =   Table C-2, SIC-372 average for the months of June, July, and August of the year 2000

XYZ will increase or decrease the base year prices by a percentage increase/decrease in the aforesaid index for the year of delivery of the product and/or time of services rendered. Final Agreement prices will be determined by January 1, of the year of delivery or service based on the Economic Price Adjustment above utilizing the most current index published. In the event the index specified above is discontinued or significantly altered, both PARTIES shall agree upon the use of a new index or the adjustment to the new index.

APPENDIX E - CHARGES

All fees and rates are expressed in 2001 economics and are valid until December 31, 2001. These fees and rates shall be subject to adjustment in accordance with **Appendix D**.

Power Unit CALIBRATION & TEST CELL CORRELATION CHARGES

Large Power Units $XXX USD (PS XXXX)

Small Power Units $XXX USD (PS XXXX)

Plus actual transportation and living expenses.

Flat rate test cell correlation charges include a maximum of forty (40) hours on site. If ARF is deemed responsible for any delay, a daily charge of $ XXX USD plus living expenses will be applicable for the additional time spent on ARF's premises.

XYZOMER SUPPORT SERVICES

Available in addition to test cell correlation, training, etc., XYZ will provide consulting services charged at:

$XXX USD Per Diem
plus airfare and expenses.

INITIAL FACILITY AUDIT CHARGES

Audit $ XXX USD
Plus airfare and expenses for a maximum of four (4) representatives.
Flat rate shop review charges include a maximum of five (5) days per representative on site.

SUBSEQUENT FACILITY AUDIT CHARGES

Charges to be determined at time of audit dependent on the nature of the audit.
Plus Airfare and expenses.

SERVICE TOOLING DESIGNS

Update service (2 years) $XXX USD (per Power Unit family)

ON-SITE REPAIR LEVEL TRAINING

Per Diem Charge $XXX USD
Plus Airfare, accommodations, and living expenses.

WARRANTY AND MSA LABOR RATE

The warranty and MSA labor rate shall be (USD $ XXX. /hr.) or ARF's posted rate, whichever is lower shall apply.

APPENDIX F - SAFETY & FORECASTING SUPPORT RECORD ACCESS

The following describes the data exchange requirements.

A standard form is not available for category "A", "B", and "C" data. ARF shall provide such data as described herein using its own report formats. A standard form is provided for category "D" and "E" data and should be used.

ARF must ensure that the data elements for category "A", "B" and "C" as described herein are included in the required reports. Example: "Power Unit Condition Summary Sheets", "Investigation Reports", etc.

All data in this Appendix should be submitted by ARF to XYZ as follows:

Category "A", B", and "C" data to:

> Attn: XYZ Field Representative

Category "D" and "E" data to:

> Attn: Repair Administration
> Customer Support
> Fax: XXXXXXXX

CATEGORY 'A' DATA

Power Unit, Module and Accessory History

FREQUENCY: Monthly

SUBMITTED BY: ARF   **SUPPLIED TO:** XYZ Field Representative

The following data elements, encompassing 'Power Unit, Module and Accessory History' should be included with all detailed reports describing the scheduled or unscheduled maintenance, Repair and investigation of XYZ Power Units, modules and accessories.

Data Element

1.   Operator Name and Address (Owner's name if different).
2.   Power Unit Model.
3.   Power Unit /Module Serial Number(s).
4.   Aircraft Model and Serial Number/Tail Number if available.
4a. Application.
4b. Work order number.
5.   Power Unit/Module/Accessory Removal Date.
5a. Reason for removal (Planned or Unplanned).
5b. Accessory part name(s), part number(s) and serial number(s).
6.   Total Time and Cycles since new. (Power Unit/Module/Accessory) (TSN - CSN).

7.   Time and Cycles Since Last Unscheduled Repair, if applicable (TSR,CSR).

If available, provide name of shops last visited for Repair as applicable including dates performed (month and year).

If available, provide reason(s) for last shop visit and brief summary.

CATEGORY 'B' DATA

Major Power Unit Event Notification and Shop Investigation

FREQUENCY: Monthly

SUBMITTED BY: Facility   **SUPPLIED TO:** XYZ Field Representative

The following data elements, resulting from major events such as unscheduled removals (*) or accidents of XYZ Power Units, should be included in your investigative reports.

Please note that data in Categories 'A' and 'C' (Power Unit Module and Accessory History and Power Unit Repair/Repair Summary) should be included with or follow the investigation report.

In some cases, participation of XYZ Service Investigation either through a visit to the Repair facility, or through examination of selected material forwarded to XYZ, may be requested by ARF or XYZ.

The need for on-site participation is dependent on the nature of the event and determined by review by both ARF and XYZ Customer Support.

(*) Does not include removals for scheduled maintenance and removals in response to an Airworthiness Authority Directive, or XYZ's or OEM's documents and/or instructions.

Data Elements or Information

1.   Report a major event to your XYZ Field Representative immediately upon receipt of Power Unit/module or contact by operator including:

   Power Unit serial/model numbers, aircraft serial/model numbers, operator name, circumstances of event, event date, (accessory name, part number and serial number if implicated in event).

2.   Preliminary information Report must be submitted to XYZ within twenty-four (24) hours of immediate notification to your XYZ Field Representative.

3.   Reason for removal including brief description of problem/symptoms reported, relevant troubleshooting or prior maintenance.

4.   Description of significant teardown observations, identification of major parts affected (including part numbers and serial numbers) contributory to the problem including photographs.

5.   Results of testing and analysis (examples: accessories and metallurgical).

6.   Discussion of conclusions including probable/possible causes, recommended corrective action such as incorporation of existing Service Bulletins, stipulation of maintenance practices.

CATEGORY 'C' DATA

Power Unit and Accessory Repair and Repair Summary

FREQUENCY: Monthly

SUBMITTED BY: Facility   **SUPPLIED TO:** XYZ Field Representative

The following data elements, which characterize the general condition of Power Unit parts and accessories and describe reassembly, should be included in 'Power Unit and Accessory Repair and Repair Summary' report. This type of report should also include the data specified under Category 'A', Power Unit, Module and Accessory History.

While the Category 'B' report, Major Power Unit Event Notification and Shop Investigation, focuses on unplanned Power Unit removals and establishing their cause, the following data elements are more generic and focus on describing the condition of parts replaced or Repaired due to unacceptable 'wear and tear'.

Data Elements or Information

1.   Reason for removal including brief description of problems/symptoms reported (if any).

2.   Description of teardown observations including identification and condition of major Power Unit and accessory parts to be replaced or Repaired (include photographs). Example: Hot section parts, fuel pumps, etc.

3.   Results of any testing and analysis including appropriate comments on ease of qualification testing.

4.   Summary of conclusions including recommended corrective action to improve part condition (example: washing to alleviate sulphidation) or incorporate existing Product improvements (Service Bulletins). Also include identification of Parts suffering significant damage that might be classified as 'in pending failure'.

5.   Classification of work performed and reference work order number, examples:
     - Time expired Repair
     - Power Unit planned removal as dictated by Power Unit condition trend monitoring
     - Test only

6.   Listing of 'Repaired' and 'new' replacement parts. Also include listing of major parts (example: blades & vanes) that were inspected and installed ' as is ' (i.e.: no Repair required) including:
     - Part name, part number, serial number of original and replacement parts

- Time and cycles of original parts
- Indicate whether replaced 'new' or 'Repaired' and quantities
- Description of each part condition

7. Listing of 'Repaired' and 'new' replacement accessories including:
   - Accessory name, part number, serial number
   - Accessory time
   - Indicate whether replaced 'new' or 'Repaired'

8. Listing of life limited parts including:
   - Part name, part number, and serial number
   - Time and cycles expired and remaining
   - Indicate whether replaced 'new' or 'Repaired'

9. Listing of Service Bulletin records including:
   - Listing of bulletins incorporated this and previous shop visits
   - Indicate 'new' or 'Repaired'
   - Highlight Airworthiness Directives complied with

10. Power Unit Test Cell Certificate including:
    - Include comments on ease of meeting test requirements
    - Performance data (speed and temperature margin, trim, etc.) including a list of actual performance parameters and limits that apply
    - Oil and fuel type

CATEGORY 'D' DATA

Quarterly Shop Visit Forecast

FREQUENCY: Quarterly

SUBMITTED BY: Facility   **SUPPLIED TO:** XYZ Customer Account Representative
Customer Support

In order to ensure efficient worldwide provisioning of Spare Parts and services, the Quarterly Shop Visit Forecasts are needed to support this aspect of business planning. The following data elements characterize shop planning and activity, are detailed and should be provided in a form identical or similar to the following table.

Data Element

1. Power Unit Parts Inventory Record.
2. Forecast Shop Visits - Power Units.
2. Spare Power Units.

REPAIR FACILITY
QUARTERLY SHOP VISIT FORECAST

Customer: *Quarter::*   *to:*

Customer code: *to:*

ENGINE MODEL	H.S.I		REPAIR		OVERHAUL	
	1ST Qtr.	2nd Qtr.	1ST Qtr	2nd Qtr	1ST Qtr	2nd Qtr
PSXXXX						

OTHER INFORMATION

INVENTORY as of :			SPARE ENGINES as of:		
ENGINE MODEL	VALUE ($)		ENGINE MODEL	Available	In Use
	New	Serviceable			
PSXXXX			PSXXXX		

CATEGORY 'E' DATA

Annual Summary of Shop Events

FREQUENCY: Annually (To be submitted 31 January)

SUBMITTED BY: Facility   **SUPPLIED TO:** Customer Account Representative
                                                     Customer Support

Will be used by XYZ to correlate and verify detailed information provided during the year.

Data Element

1.   Shop Activity.

APPENDIX G - FIELD OF USE

The Territory for which ARF is authorized to perform Repairs will include the countries listed above and, where applicable, their recognized successors in the same geographical area. If and so long as transactions with any country in the Territory are or become prohibited by the laws or public policy of the United States of America, such country will be excluded from the Territory and ARF will not perform work for or make shipments to any organization in such country.

APPENDIX H – Product Lines/Engine Models Authorized under this Agreement

(TBD)

§ 4.38 Maintenance Support Agreement (Aerospace)

THIS AGREEMENT, made and entered into as of _____("Effective Date"), by and between **XYZ CORPORATION,** a corporation organized and existing under the laws of _____, United States of America, having offices at _____ (hereinafter referred to as **SELLER**), and _____ having offices at _____ (hereinafter referred to as **BUYER**). SELLER and BUYER may be referred to individually as a "Party" or collectively as the "Parties":

<u>Recitals</u>

WHEREAS, BUYER operates, or intends to operate, a fleet _____ Aircraft in BUYER's commercial revenue service; and

WHEREAS, SELLER manufactures, markets, sells, and supports its Model PSXXX Power Unit Systems for installation and operation on board such Aircraft; and

WHEREAS, SELLER, an approved FAA Repair station maintains and operates certain facilities for the Repair, maintenance, modification and functional testing of PSXXX Power Unit System and other of SELLER's aerospace products; and

WHEREAS, BUYER has selected the PSXXX Power Unit System and shall install or have installed such system into BUYER's new _____ Aircraft; and

WHEREAS, BUYER and SELLER desire to set forth the terms and conditions under which SELLER shall provide maintenance support of such product.

NOW, THEREFORE, in consideration of the mutually agreed to conditions, covenants and promises set forth herein, the parties hereby agree to the following terms and conditions:

*Courtesy of Peter W. Knapp, Esq. of the Hamilton Sunstrand Corp.

TABLE OF CONTENTS

PART I - DEFINITIONS

1.0   DEFINITIONS

The following definitions shall apply to terms employed in this Agreement, unless other meaning or definition is expressly indicated:

"**Agreement**" means this Maintenance Support Agreement (MSA) including all appendices, amendments, and Orders issued hereunder or otherwise in connection herewith.

"**Aircraft**" means the _____ regional aircraft, and/or derivatives thereof, owned or leased and operated by BUYER, with Power Unit System installed.

"**Airworthiness Authority**" means the United States Federal Aviation Administration (FAA), and/or European Joint Aviation Authority (JAA).

"**AOG**" (Aircraft-On-Ground) means that an Aircraft is unable to continue or be returned to revenue service until an appropriate corrective action is taken.

"**PSXXX Power Unit or Power Unit**" means SELLER's Power Unit (Power Unit), P/N XXXX series less the Electronic Controller.

"**PSXXX System or Power Unit System**" means SELLER's Model PSXXX Power Unit System shipset, P/N XXXX series including the Power Unit, the Electronic Controller, P/N XXXX.

"**PSXXX EC or EC**" means solely the Electronic Controller of the PSXXX System.

"**Power Unit Cycle**" means one (1) start/stop event recorded by the EC.

"**Power Unit Operating Hour**" means each hour or part thereof elapsing from the moment operation of the Power Unit is commenced until that operation of the Power Unit is next shutdown recorded by the EC. For purposes of all calculations under this Agreement measured in Power Unit Operating Hours, such Power Unit Operating Hours (or part thereof) shall be rounded off to the nearest minute.

"**BUYER**" or "**Operator**" means _____ Airlines and its successors and permitted assigns.

"**Chargeable Repair**" means the Repair, replacement or reconditioning of a component by SELLER which will be separately charged to BUYER (i.e., not covered by the Maintenance Service Plan set forth in Article 1.0 of the Special Terms of this Agreement) where such Repair, replacement or reconditioning was necessitated or caused by any of the following:

- a Repair for maintenance convenience, unless such Repair was directed by SELLER and/or the OEM or otherwise authorized by SELLER and/or the OEM; or
- parts required for compliance with issued Airworthiness Authority directives, which are not the sole responsibility of SELLER; or

- missing parts or covers; or
- any operation, service, maintenance, or repair which is not in accordance with SELLER's Service Bulletin, Service Information Letter, Manuals or other technical / operational documentation; or
- damage, where prior to the failure of the removed Power Unit, LRU, module or component, SELLER offered a written remedy in the form of a Maintenance Manual instruction, Service Bulletin or information letter for such failure and BUYER did not accomplish such remedy within a period specified by the Maintenance Manual instruction, Service Bulletin or Service Information Letter; or
- removal/installation of hardware not supplied by SELLER; or
- shipping, handling or other outside influenced damage; or
- Test OK/No Fault Found Removals, or
- Foreign Object Damage (FOD).

"Component" means a genuine SELLER part, necessary for the operation of the Power Unit, and normally supplied by the SELLER as part of the Power Unit build specification unless otherwise specified within this Agreement.

"Exchange Unit" means a serviceable Product transferred to BUYER in return for a non-serviceable Product.

"Entry into Service" means the date of delivery of new Aircraft by the OEM to BUYER.

"FOD" (Foreign Object Damage) means damage to any portion of the Power Unit caused by, or initiated by, an outside source, foreign object, or debris.

"Line Replaceable Unit" or **"LRU"** means any component replaceable in the Aircraft as identified in SELLER's documentation.

"Low Cycle Fatigue Limited" means parts, the service life of which is expressed in total hours operated or number of Power Unit Cycles, which total hours operated or number of Power Unit Cycles form the baseline for scheduled removals and must not be exceeded.

"Maintenance Support Plan" or **"MSP"** means the services, and fees therefor, that SELLER provides to BUYER under this Agreement.

"Major Repair" means a Repair, or reconditioning requiring a complete disassembly, inspection and rebuild of the core Power Unit in SELLER's facility to bring the Power Unit to the current build standard as set forth in the Workscope Planning Guide.

"MTBUR" means "Mean Time Between Unscheduled Removals", a performance figure, calculated by dividing the total Power Unit Operating Hours accrued in a given period by the number of Unscheduled Removals that occurred during the same period with respect to the same Power Unit Systems.

"No Fault Found Removals" means Product passes operational as-received acceptance test in accordance with Repair criteria, with no anomalies found. Product is considered flight-worthy and may be returned to service as is.

"OEM" means: XXXX, manufacturer of the _____ Aircraft.

"On Condition Maintenance" means a primary maintenance process having repetitive inspections or tests to determine the condition of units, systems, or portions of structures with regard to continued serviceability (i.e. corrective action is taken when required by item condition).

"Order" means any purchase order and amendments thereto issued pursuant to this Agreement including the Terms and Conditions herein. BUYER's preprinted terms are agreed to not be applicable, unless agreed otherwise in writing.

"Product" means any new, serviceable or repairable PSXXX System or part thereof provided by SELLER to BUYER for installation in or use in conjunction with an Aircraft.

"Repair" means the return to serviceable condition of a Product.

"Rotable Pool" means a stock of SELLER owned Exchange Units.

"Scheduled Removal" means removal of a Product from an Aircraft in response to an Airworthiness Authority Directive, or SELLER's or OEM's documents and/or instructions.

"SELLER" means XYZ CORPORATION.

"Service Bulletins" means documents issued periodically to airlines by SELLER and/or the OEM detailing recommendations and incorporation instructions for any special inspections, modification improvements, and unit upgrades on SELLER Product.

"Service Bulletin Modification Record" means the configuration, which reflects incorporation of Service Bulletins into the PSXXX System, which designates responsibility for incorporation costs.

"Spare Part" means any new or serviceable Product used as a replacement for any similar Product, which is installed on an Aircraft or which, may be required for the maintenance, modification, or Repair of a Product.

"Turn-Around-Time" means that time needed to Repair, service or checkout a Product for recommitment to operational service or the total number of calendar days required to complete a specified task(s) from receipt of a Product by SELLER to availability for return shipment.

"Unapproved Parts" means a part, component, or material used therein that has not been manufactured in accordance with SELLER approved procedures and/or Repaired by a SELLER approved Repair/overhaul facility.

"Unscheduled Removal" means any removal of a Power Unit from an Aircraft except, Scheduled Removals, and Chargeable Repairs.

PART II - SPECIAL TERMS

1.0   MAINTENANCE SERVICE PLAN (MSP)

This MSP is provided in substitution of SELLER's Power Unit warranty, and will provide Aircraft maintenance support to BUYER's Aircraft based on a Power Unit Operating Hour rate. Unless specifically provided for herein, this plan does not cover normal on-wing or line maintenance activities, or the consumable hardware required for such activities. Line Replaceable Units that are not classified as repairable are excluded. The Power Unit Operating Hour rate per Power Unit Operating Hour as set forth below is in 2001 economics, subject to escalation in accordance with **Appendix C**. The Power Unit Operating Hour rate is specifically conditioned upon Power Unit utilization and operation consistent with BUYER's declarations as set forth in **Appendix B**.

PERIOD	POWER UNIT OPERATING HOUR RATE
0 to 60 months from the Effective Date of this Agreement	$ _____ USD

This plan will be administered in accordance with the following:

A.   SELLER shall provide shop level Repair services for BUYER-owned or operated Power Unit Systems and repairable LRUs set forth in **Appendix A**, to return equipment to a serviceable condition. This MSP includes the consumable and expendable hardware utilized in conjunction with the shop Repair of Power Units and repairable LRUs. SELLER shall use serviceable parts, as appropriate, to Repair Product. SELLER may maintain a Rotable Pool of Products for the purpose of providing prompt service to BUYER. Products returned to BUYER may be assembled with parts other than parts contained in the Products initially delivered to SELLER. This could include the shipment of an Exchange Unit. Any part(s) replaced by an Exchange Unit shall become SELLER's property. The Exchange Unit shall become BUYER's property.

B.   New Power Unit Systems will be covered by this Maintenance Service Plan commencing from the date of Entry into Service. Existing Power Unit Systems currently in revenue service may be incorporated into this Maintenance Service Plan upon BUYER's payment to SELLER of an entry fee equal to the then current Power Unit Operating Hour rate multiplied by the number of Power Unit Operating Hours accumulated since new, or in the event a Power Unit has completed a non-warranty Major Repair, the then current Power Unit Operating Hour rate multiplied by the Power Unit Operating Hours accumulated from the date of the non-warranty Major Repair. Additionally, BUYER is responsible for all cost to upgrade the Power Unit System to the current build standard as set forth in the Workscope Planning Guide, prior to entry into this Maintenance Service Plan.

C.   BUYER agrees to make monthly payments to SELLER based on an estimated fixed billing rate for each Aircraft in BUYER's fleet. The monthly estimated billing rate shall be determined by calculating the actual average monthly Power Unit Operating Hours per Aircraft for the preceding six (6) month period multiplied by the then current Power Unit Operating Hour Rate. In the event BUYER is unable to provide SELLER with actual Power Unit Operating Hour data to establish the initial Power Unit Operating Hour billing rate, an estimated Power Unit Operating Hour billing rate for the first six (6) month billing period shall be mutually agreed upon by the Parties. The estimated monthly billing rate shall apply to each Aircraft in BUYER's fleet and shall remain fixed for a period of six (6) months. Within ten (10) days after completion of each six (6) month billing period, BUYER shall provide to SELLER actual Power Unit Operating Hour data for the respective period as follows: Aircraft tail number; Power Unit serial number; date of reading; total hours from the hour meter; and total Power Unit Cycles from the Power Unit Data Memory Module. SELLER shall reconcile the estimated billings against actual Power Unit Operating Hours for the applicable six (6) month period and provide BUYER an invoice adjustment with the following monthly billing. During such reconciliation, the monthly estimated billing rate shall be adjusted for the following six (6) month billing period based on actual average Power Unit Operating Hour utilization for the preceding six (6) month period.

D.   In the event BUYER desires to introduce a Power Unit System into the existing Maintenance Service Plan, BUYER shall provide SELLER a written request containing the appropriate Power Unit serial number, Power Unit Operating Hours, total Power Unit Cycles from the Power Unit Data Memory Module, and any other information SELLER may require to evaluate BUYER's request. SELLER shall maintain an invoice history serial number file recording Power Unit Operating Hours and Power Unit Cycle history for each Power Unit. In the event of a Product removal, BUYER shall provide to SELLER, in addition to the Power Unit data identified above, the date of the removal and installation of the substitute Product.

E.   BUYER shall maintain records and other documents to sufficiently demonstrate Power Unit Operating Hours. BUYER shall provide SELLER reasonable access to such records as is required to support BUYER's payments. SELLER shall have the right at any time to audit BUYER records in this regard but such audit shall be performed on a non-interference basis.

F.   When a Power Unit is returned to SELLER's facility, or SELLER's authorized facility for Repair, the number of Power Unit Operating Hours in the Power Unit log book shall be compared to the Power Unit Operating Hours maintained in SELLER's invoice history serial number file. If there is a discrepancy, the Power Unit Operating Hours in the Power Unit log book shall be used to adjust the billing during the following billing rate reconciliation.

G.   Except as provided for herein, during the term of this Agreement, BUYER agrees to return all Products to SELLER's facility, or SELLER's authorized facility for Repair. SELLER agrees to Repair or provide an Exchange Unit for each Product and return the Product to BUYER in a serviceable condition within the Turn-Around-Time specified in Article 7.1 of the General Terms.

H.   BUYER shall return all unserviceable repairable Product within seven (7) calendar days of removal. Failure to do so may subject BUYER to SELLER's then current lease and/or late return charges as applicable.

I.   BUYER shall be responsible to perform all line maintenance or "on-wing" maintenance of Product on an On-Condition basis in accordance with line maintenance procedures detailed in Aircraft manufacturer's and SELLER's approved Maintenance Manuals, Service Bulletins (SBs), Service Information Letters (SILs), and specific Power Unit Maintenance Tasks.

J.   Chargeable Repairs are excluded from this plan.

K.   Transportation costs to and from SELLER's facility, or SELLER's authorized facility shall be the responsibility of BUYER.

L.   Power Units operated by military, paramilitary or other government agency without the prior knowledge and approval of SELLER are not eligible under this plan.

M.   Power Units that have become part of any pool of Power Units, an arrangement by which the Operator is entitled to an exchange, withdraw and/or use Power Units held by another participant are not eligible under this plan.

2.0   SERVICE BULLETIN IMPLEMENTATION

Upon execution of this Agreement, SELLER shall provide BUYER with a Workscope Planning Guide for review and approval. Once approved by BUYER, the Workscope Planning Guide will be used as the authority to upgrade units returned for Repair with the appropriate Service Bulletins. SELLER will accomplish review of the Workscope Planning Guide on a semi-annual or "as required" basis and will provide recommended updates to the Workscope Planning Guide to BUYER as necessary. BUYER shall not unreasonably withhold timely approval of such updates.

SELLER will incorporate applicable Service Bulletins, as specified in the Workscope Planning Guide, at the first available shop visit at SELLER's facility, or SELLER's authorized repair facility. However, should BUYER desire earlier incorporation of selected Service Bulletins, SELLER will work with BUYER to establish a schedule to perform such modifications at BUYER's expense. While it is SELLER's intent to incorporate Service Bulletins in accordance with the Workscope Planning Guide, a Product may be repaired without incorporation of all Service Bulletins when it is necessary to maintain adequate inventory for BUYER's needs. SELLER will endeavor to incorporate those Service Bulletins not incorporated at the next shop visit. Further, Exchange Units will be functionally interchangeable but may not be fully modified to the standard. After Power Unit Repair and Service Bulletin incorporation, SELLER will properly identify all upgraded LRUs per the Service Bulletin and revise the appropriate Engine Log Book accordingly.

3.0 POWER UNIT CYCLE LIMITATION

The Power Unit Operating Hour rate identified above is contingent upon actual Power Unit utilization not exceeding _____ (__) Power Unit Cycles per Power Unit Operating Hour. Should BUYER's annual average Power Unit Cycles per Power Unit Operating Hour exceed (__) Power Unit Cycles per Power Unit Operating Hour, the Power Unit Operating Hour rate shall be adjusted upwards in accordance with the following formula:

$$\frac{\text{Fleet average Power Unit Cycles per Power Unit Operating Hour}}{(\textit{Power Unit Cycles per Power Unit Operating Hour})} \quad \text{x} \quad (\text{Power Unit Operating Hour rate}) \quad = \quad \begin{array}{c}\text{Adjusted Power Unit}\\ \text{Operating Hour rate}\end{array}$$

4.0 POWER UNIT REMOVAL

In the event that any or all Aircraft are removed from this Maintenance Service Plan during the term of this Agreement through loan, lease, or sale of the Aircraft by BUYER, absent SELLER's express written consent, BUYER shall compensate SELLER for the remaining Power Unit System life. The remaining Power Unit System life shall be calculated in accordance with the following formula:

From the MTBUR fleet average for the twelve (12) month period preceding the date of the Power Unit removal, taken from SELLER's invoice history serial number file of Power Unit Operating Hours and Power Unit Cycle history ("MTBUR Hours"), shall be subtracted Power Unit Operating Hours accumulated since last shop visit, or Power Unit Operating Hours accumulated since Power Unit installation, whichever occurred last, through the date the Power Unit was removed from the Maintenance Service Plan ("Accumulated Hours"). This figure shall be multiplied by the then current Power Unit Operating Hour rate, and BUYER shall remit this total to SELLER.

The formula for each removed Power Unit is as follows:

(MTBUR Hours - Accumulated Hours) x Power Unit Operating Hour rate = Payment

NOTHING IN THIS ARTICLE SHALL BE CONSTRUED AS A LIMITATION OR NEGATION OF SELLER'S RIGHTS OR LEGAL REMEDIES IN THE EVENT OF BUYER'S DEFAULT OR TERMINATION OF THIS AGREEMENT.

PART III - GENERAL TERMS

1.0   AIRCRAFT

BUYER agrees to specify and install the PSXXX System for all Aircraft and to maintain and operate Aircraft with the PSXXX System installed for the term of this Agreement.

2.0   WARRANTY DISCLAIMER

This Agreement is in substitution of SELLER's warranty for new PSXXX Power Unit(s).

2.1   Exclusivity

UNLESS OTHERWISE SPECIFICALLY PROVIDED FOR HEREIN, THE PRODUCT AND/OR SERVICE TO BE FURNISHED IS PROVIDED WITHOUT WARRANTY. NO WARRANTIES OF ANY KIND, WHETHER EXPRESS OR IMPLIED, INCLUDING ALL WARRANTIES OF MERCHANTABILITY AND FITNESS FOR A PARTICULAR PURPOSE, SHALL APPLY; AND ALL WARRANTIES ARISING FROM COURSE OF DEALING OR USAGE OF TRADE ARE SPECIFICALLY EXCLUDED.

IN NO EVENT SHALL SELLER BE LIABLE IN TORT (INCLUDING NEGLIGENCE OR STRICT LIABILITY) OR IN CONTRACT OR UNDER ANY OTHER LEGAL OR EQUITABLE THEORY FOR ANY INCIDENTAL, SPECIAL, INDIRECT, OR CONSEQUENTIAL LOSS OR DAMAGE, OR OTHER ECONOMIC LOSS.

3.0   ESCALATION / ECONOMIC ADJUSTMENT

Unless otherwise noted, all dollar amounts set forth herein are deemed to be in January 2001 economics, and shall be adjusted to the date of performance per **Appendix C.**

4.0   DELIVERIES

Unless otherwise noted, all dollar amounts for services or Product set forth herein are quoted "Ex Works" (I.C.C. Incoterms, 2000) SELLER's facility. All deliveries shall be made "Ex Works" freight forwarder selected by BUYER. Spare Parts or hardware sold under this Agreement or related Order shall become the property of BUYER upon delivery of the parts by SELLER to the carrier designated by BUYER at SELLER's "Ex Works" distribution point or, in the absence of such designation, to the carrier selected by SELLER for shipment to BUYER.

5.0   SPARE PARTS

BUYER agrees to purchase from SELLER the Spare Parts required for BUYER's operational and maintenance needs subject to the terms and conditions of SELLER's current Spare Parts Catalog for a 95% protection level based on airline industry standards. Spare Parts purchased by BUYER directly from SELLER are warranted according to the terms of the Spare Parts Catalog.

Repairs, maintenance and modification of Product using parts purchased from SELLER must be performed by technically competent personnel, utilizing tooling and test equipment as specified in SELLER's approved Maintenance Manuals, Service Bulletins, and Service Information Letters, in a repair facility approved by SELLER and appropriate Airworthiness Authority. Use of unapproved parts may be considered a material breach of this agreement and may be a reason to invalidate provisions of this agreement.

IN EVENT THAT BUYER USES UNAPPROVED PARTS, SUCH PARTS ARE NOT COVERED BY SELLER'S WARRANTY AND SELLER IS NOT RESPONSIBLE OR LIABLE FOR ANY DIRECT, INDIRECT, SPECIAL, INCIDENTAL OR CONSEQUENTIAL DAMAGES OR COSTS ARISING FROM OR RELATED TO THE USE OF SUCH PRODUCTS OR SERVICES. BUYER AGREES TO DEFEND, INDEMNIFY AND HOLD SELLER HARMLESS FROM ANY AND ALL CLAIMS, LOSS OR EXPENSE RESULTING DIRECTLY OR INDIRECTLY FROM SUCH USE.

6.0   PAYMENT

Payment in U.S. Dollars (USD) shall be due upon services rendered or material shipped according to the terms of net thirty (30) days from the date of invoice, facsimile or other electronic means. Invoice copies shall be sent to BUYER by electronic means, with the original invoice forwarded to BUYER by mail. SELLER shall have the right to impose a finance charge of one and one-half percent (1-1/2%) per month, on all past due amounts. Payments should be mailed to the "Remit To" address shown on the invoice. SELLER reserves the right to modify or withdraw credit terms at any time without notice and to require guarantees, security, or payment in advance for the amount of the Order involved. SELLER shall be entitled to set off any amount owing from BUYER to SELLER against any amount payable under this Agreement.

7.0   PRODUCT SUPPORT SERVICES

7.1   Turn-Around-Time

SELLER shall maintain a not-to-exceed thirty (30) calendar day average Repair/exchange Turn-Around Time (TAT) for the Power Unit, and a not-to-exceed forty five (45) calendar day average Repair/exchange (TAT) for repairable LRUs excluding transportation and customs clearance time. This TAT is expressly conditioned upon BUYER's acceptance of Exchange Units.

7.2   Rotable Pool

Throughout the term of this Agreement, SELLER shall have available a Rotable Pool of Power Units and LRUs on an exchange basis for BUYER's use, contingent upon SELLER's non-performance to the terms of this Agreement, and BUYER experiencing an AOG or impending AOG situation. This Rotable Pool of spares shall be made available at no charge to BUYER upon request, on the condition that BUYER has provisioned to at least a 95% protection level based on airline industry standards. Title to the Exchange Unit shall pass from SELLER to BUYER on the date of shipment of the replacement unit, and from BUYER to SELLER upon receipt of the returned Exchange Unit at SELLER's facility.

7.3   Data Retrieval

BUYER shall provide Product operating performance data to SELLER on a monthly basis.

7.4   Field Service

During the term of this Agreement, SELLER shall furnish without additional charge, periodic technical representative visits to BUYER.

7.5   Lease Unit

If BUYER has provisioned to a less than 95% protection level based on airline industry standards, Power Units shall be provided by SELLER on a lease basis ("Lease Power Unit"), if requested, to BUYER during emergency situations.

8.0   TRAINING AND MANUALS

The appropriate classroom and hands-on training, as well as all training materials for the Power Unit, shall be provided to BUYER free of charge at SELLER's training center in XXXX, California, U.S.A. Further refresher training or training for additional staff in the future, shall also be provided free of charge at the regularly scheduled training periods.

At SELLER's discretion, on-site training may be available, if requested by BUYER. Travel expenses and SELLER labor costs for the on-site training shall be the responsibility of BUYER. SELLER shall deliver all required print manuals to BUYER free of charge prior to entry of Aircraft into service. This will include a free of charge revision service for the term of this Agreement.

9.0   ADMINISTRATIVE ARTICLES

9.1   Assignment

No Order subject to these standard terms and conditions of sale or any service interest hereunder shall be assignable by BUYER, unless such assignment is agreed to in writing by the SELLER. SELLER may without advance notice to the BUYER assign any such purchase order or any interest therein.

9.2   Amendments

Oral statements and understandings are not valid or binding. No amendment of this Agreement shall be effective unless the parties hereto duly execute a written agreement, signed by their duly authorized officers.

9.3   Interpretation of Law

This Agreement shall be governed by and interpreted in accordance with the laws of the State of California, U.S.A. In the event, however, that BUYER and SELLER fail to resolve any disputes through negotiations, BUYER and SELLER hereby irrevocably consent and agree that any legal action, suit or proceeding arising out of or in any way connected with this Agreement, shall be instituted in the courts of the city XXXX, State of California, U.S.A.

9.4   Diversion

SELLER's obligations under this Agreement are subject to any required export authorization from the United States Government. Moreover, no export and/or re-export of the hardware supplied under this Agreement may be made to some countries without prior United States Government authorization. It is the responsibility of BUYER to secure the proper authorization and/or license for the exportation from the State Department through the local United States Embassy, and to comply with all applicable governmental laws and regulations.

9.5   Non-Waiver

SELLER's or BUYER's failure at any time to enforce any provision of this Agreement does not constitute a waiver of such provision or prejudice either party's right to enforce such provision at any subsequent time.

9.6   Headings

Article and paragraph headings used in this Agreement are for convenient reference only and do not affect the interpretation of the Agreement.

9.7   Partial Invalidity

If any provision of this Agreement or any order based thereon is or becomes void or unenforceable by force or operation of law, the other provisions shall remain valid and enforceable, and the Parties shall substitute for the stricken provision another provision of as similar effect as is permitted by law so as to accomplish the legally permissible purposes of the Parties which were intended by the stricken provision.

9.8   Entire Agreement; Order of Precedence

This Agreement sets forth the entire agreement, and supersedes any and all prior understandings, representations and communications between BUYER and SELLER, whether written or oral, related to the subject matter of this Agreement. In the event of a conflict or inconsistency between the terms of the following documents, the following order of precedence shall control: 1) The Special Terms of this Maintenance Support Agreement, 2) The General Terms of this Maintenance Support Agreement, 3) Appendices and Attachments to this Agreement, 4) SELLER's Spare Parts Catalog.

9.9   Notices

Notices required or authorized hereunder shall be given in writing via first class mail, postage prepaid, by hand, TWX, Facsimile or other electronic means and the date upon which such notice is received by the addressee shall be deemed to be the date appearing therein. In the event of a facsimile transmission, the facsimile shall be deemed received only if the sending machine produces a receipt evidencing error free transmission to the intended recipient.

All notices to BUYER shall be as follows:

_____

_____

_____

Attention: _____

Telephone: (   ) _____

Fax: (   ) _____

All notices to SELLER shall be as follows:

XYZ CORPORATION

_____

_____

Attention:	Manager, Contracts
Telephone:	XXXXX
Fax:	XXXXX

9.10   Inspection and Acceptance

Upon receipt of Product by BUYER at BUYER's facility, BUYER may inspect the Product to ensure compliance with the terms of the Order under which the Product was ordered, and with the terms of this Agreement. BUYER shall accomplish such inspection and acceptance within thirty (30) days after receipt of the Product. BUYER shall promptly notify SELLER of any discrepancies discovered as a result of such inspection. After such thirty (30) day inspection and acceptance period, the Product shall be conclusively deemed as accepted by BUYER.

9.11   Compliance with Law

BUYER shall comply with all laws and regulations relating to the possession, leasing, operation, control, use, maintenance, delivery and/or return of the Product and shall defend, indemnify, and hold SELLER harmless from any and all costs and expenses in connection with any actual or asserted violations.

9.12   Confidentiality

BUYER agrees to retain in confidence all information received from SELLER with respect to any Product in this Agreement and not to use such information for any purpose not contemplated by this Agreement or disclose such information to any other party unless the information: is in the public domain through no act of BUYER; is previously known to BUYER on a nonconfidential basis; is received by BUYER from a third party having no obligation of confidentiality to SELLER; or is required to be disclosed by law or legal process. Any expiration or termination of this Agreement shall not alter the rights or obligations of strict confidentiality, including but not limited to the obligations of BUYER arising during the term hereof with respect to information disclosed by SELLER to BUYER prior to such expiration or termination.

9.13   Termination

9.13.1 Default

Should either Party fail to perform any of their duties or material obligations under this Agreement, and such failure continues for thirty (30) days after written notice of such default from the other Party, then the non-defaulting Party may terminate this Agreement within a reasonable period of time thereafter, effective immediately upon written notice of termination to the defaulting Party, without prejudice to any other rights or remedies the non-defaulting Party may have.

9.13.2 Bankruptcy

In the event either Party (i) makes a general assignment for the benefit of creditors or becomes insolvent, (ii) files a voluntary petition in bankruptcy, (iii) petitions for or acquiesces in the appointment of any receiver, trustee, or similar officer to liquidate or conserve its business or any substantial parts of its assets, (iv) commences under the laws of any competent jurisdiction any proceeding involving its insolvency, bankruptcy, reorganization, readjustment of debt, dissolution, liquidation or any other similar proceeding for the relief of financially distressed debtors, (v) becomes the object of any proceeding or action of the type defined in (iii) or (iv) above and such proceeding or action remains undismissed or unstayed for at least thirty (30) days, or (vi) is divested of a substantial part of its assets for at least thirty (30) days, it shall constitute an anticipatory breach of contract by that Party for the purpose of any determination of the other Party's rights and remedies at law, including the right to terminate this Agreement by providing written notice of termination to the other Party

9.14 Excusable Delay

SELLER shall not be responsible nor be deemed to be in fault on account of delay in the delivery of Products due to causes beyond SELLER's fault or negligence, including but not limited to, acts of God, fires, floods, explosions, earthquakes, epidemics or quarantine restrictions, acts of Government, wars, insurrections, riots, failures of transportation, strikes or labor troubles causing cessation, slowdown or interruption of work. In the event delivery of any Product is delayed by one or more of the above causes, SELLER shall promptly notify BUYER of any such delay and the expected extent thereof. For delays not classified as excusable, BUYER shall have access to SELLER's Rotable Pool should such delayed delivery result in BUYER's line spares reaching a critical level.

9.15 International Sale of Goods

The Parties to this contract or order shall not be bound by the United Nations Convention on Contracts for the International Sale of Goods. The Parties expressly disclaim the applicability of said Convention.

9.16　LIMITATION OF LIABILITY

UNDER NO CIRCUMSTANCES SHALL SELLER BE LIABLE FOR ANY INCIDENTAL, SPECIAL OR CONSEQUENTIAL DAMAGES OF ANY NATURE WHATSOEVER INCLUDING WITHOUT LIMITATION, LOST PROFIT, REVENUE, CONTRACTS OR DESIGN, WHETHER OR NOT SUCH CLAIMS ARE BASED IN CONTRACT OR TORT, INCLUDING NEGLIGENCE (ACTUAL OR IMPUTED) STRICT LIABILITY OR UPON ANY OTHER LEGAL THEORY.

10.0　TERM OF THE AGREEMENT

This Agreement shall remain in effect from the date first written above for a period of five (5) years or until terminated pursuant to the terms and conditions herein, or by mutual agreement.

IN CONSIDERATION OF THE ABOVE, the parties hereto have caused this Agreement to be executed by their duly authorized representatives.

_____　　　　**XYZ CORPORATION**

By:_____　　　By: _____

Name:_____　　　Name: _____

Title:_____　　　Title:_____

Date:_____　　　Date: _____

APPENDIX A - REPAIRABLE LRUs

LINE REPLACEABLE UNITS (LRU) COVERED UNDER THE MSP

1. The following LRUs are subject to coverage under this Agreement. The identified LRUs are those supplied by SELLER to the airframe manufacturer, as specified in the Power Unit build specification, and do not include items such as the support frame, engine mounts, blankets, fire loop, or any other airframe manufacturer installed or supplied items.

2. In the event a covered Component is designated as Low Cycle Fatigue Limited (LCF), SELLER will replace the Component at the time of shop visit, provided however, the cycles remaining on the subject Component are insufficient to reach the next forecasted shop visit. SELLER may, at its option, elect to install repaired LCF Components.

PSXXX Series

PART NUMBER	NAME/NOMENCLATURE

APPENDIX B – OPERATOR PROFILE

1.0   OPERATOR PROFILE

1.1   The *__Hourly Rate__* is based on the operator profile declared by BUYER. Any modifications to operator profile or changes in geographical or operating environment must be reported promptly to SELLER and may result in an adjustment to the **Hourly Rate** referenced in this Agreement.

1.2   The Operator profile under this Agreement is for Power Units used in the Transport Flight profile submitted by BUYER as indicated below and which are operated within the limitations specified in the applicable section of the aircraft flight manual.

The Power Unit fleet under this Agreement shall consist of __ installed Power Units and __ Power Unit spares as referenced below.

1.2.1   annual utilization of each installed Power Unit of no less than _____ Power Unit Operating Hours;

1.2.2   average Power Unit Cycles per Power Unit Operating hour not to exceed ___ Power Unit Cycles;

1.2.3   Spares protection level **95**%;

1.2.4   Provisioning Period **180** days;

1.2.5   Maintenance bases: One (1);

1.2.6   Regular scheduled airline passenger revenue service commencing _____ *date* _____;

1.2.7   Aircraft delivery schedule.

A/C NUMBER	A/C MSN	Delivery Date
1		
2		
3		
4		
5		
6		
7		
8		
9		
10		
11		
12		
13		
14		

APPENDIX C - PRICE ESCALATION

Unless otherwise provided for herein, the base prices set forth in this Agreement are subject to an annual (January 1) adjustment for inflation/deflation, beginning on January 1, 2002, in accordance with the following:

Fifteen Percent (15%) of the base price shall constitute the material portion subject to adjustment utilizing United States Department of Labor, Bureau of Labor Statistics, "Wholesale prices - Metal and Metal Products (Code 10)".

Fifteen Percent (15%) of the base price shall constitute the material portion subject to adjustment utilizing United States Department of Labor, Bureau of Labor Statistics, "Industrial Commodities".

Seventy Percent (70%) of the base price shall constitute the labor portion subject to adjustment utilizing United States Department of Labor, Bureau of Labor Statistics publication "Employment and Earnings", Table C-2, SIC-Code 372, Average Hourly Earnings.

In accordance with the formula:

$$P = P_0\left(.15\frac{M}{M_0} + .15\frac{IC}{IC_0} + .70\frac{L}{L_0}\right)$$

Whereby:

P	=	New escalated price
P_0	=	Base price in 2001 dollars
M	=	Code 10 index average for the months of August, September and October of the year preceding the year of delivery and/or services rendered.
M_0	=	Code 10 average for the months of August, September and October of the year 2000
IC	=	Industrial Commodities index average for the months of August, September and October of the year preceding the year of delivery and/or services rendered.
IC_0	=	Industrial Commodities average for the months of August, September and October of the year 2000
L	=	Table C-2, SIC-372 average for the months of August, September and October of the year preceding the year of delivery and/or services rendered
L_0	=	Table C-2, SIC-372 average for the months of August, September and October of the year 2000

Seller will increase or decrease the base year prices by a percentage increase/decrease in the aforesaid indices for the year of delivery of the product and/or time of services rendered. The adjustments for the three (3) indices will be combined and the base price subject to adjustment in accordance with the above outlined provisions.

Final Agreement prices will be determined by January 1, of the year of delivery based on the Economic Price Adjustment above utilizing the most current indices published. In the event the indices specified above are discontinued or significantly altered, both parties shall agree upon the use of a new index or the adjustment to the new index.

§ 4.39 International Distributorship Agreement (Electronics)*

Table of Contents

Section

T TECHNOLOGIES, INC.
INTERNATIONAL DISTRIBUTORSHIP AGREEMENT

This Agreement is made and entered into by and between T, Inc., a Massachusetts corporation, with its principal office at _____ U.S.A. ("T") and ABC GmbH, with its principal office at _____, Germany ("Distributor") on the date of signature hereof set forth below, _____.

Preliminary Statement

T desires to grant to Distributor the right to sell, license and distribute certain T products subject to the terms and conditions of this Agreement, and Distributor desires to receive such grant. Accordingly, in consideration of the covenants contained herein the parties hereto mutually agree as follows:

1. Definitions: In this Agreement the following terms shall have the following meanings:

1.1 "Products" means the software, disks, documentation media, supplies, and products, singularly and collectively, described on Exhibit A attached hereto and made a part hereof.

* Courtesy of Professor Edward Eberle of Roger Williams University School of Law.

1.2 "Territory" means the area described on <u>Exhibit B</u> attached hereto and made a part hereof.

1.3 All terms of this Agreement (such as, not by way of limitation, "cost", "payments", "amounts", "value", "discounts", "price", "credits", "set-off", "dollars", or "$") shall be calculated and construed in terms of currency of the United States of America.

2. <u>Grant of Distributorship.</u>

2.1 <u>Appointment.</u> Subject to the terms and conditions of this Agreement, T appoints Distributor as a distributor to import, promote, distribute by means of sublicenses, deliver and service the Products in the Territory for the term specified in <u>Section 17.1.</u>

2.2 <u>Acceptance.</u> Distributor accepts the foregoing appointment, represents that it has adequate facilities and personnel to perform the services hereinafter set forth and agrees, upon the terms and conditions set forth in this Agreement, to use its best efforts to promote the distribution of the Products to customers within the Territory and at all times to carry out a merchandising policy designed to promote and maintain the goodwill which is now associated with the name and reputation of T and its Products. In addition by accepting this appointment, Distributor understands that it is subject to all of the terms and conditions of T's merchandising and credit policies as they now exist or may hereafter exist and that sublicenses granted by Distributor to customers shall be in accordance with the applicable T software license terms and conditions then in effect.

2.3 <u>No Solicitation Outside Territory.</u> Distributor will not establish a branch office or warehouse, and will not actively solicit sales or licenses of the Products, outside the Territory.

2.4 <u>Distribution Outside the Territory.</u> Although Distributor is not prohibited from distributing the Products outside the Territory, it is mutually understood and agreed that T's policy may be to require that some or all of the price of or license fees for Products distributed by Distributor outside the Territory be paid to the person whose area of primary responsibility is such area outside the Territory. It is further understood and agreed that in such event T's policy shall also be to require that Distributor be paid some or all of the price of or license fees for Products distributed by other persons in the Territory. In such cases, T will determine in an equitable manner the price of or license fees for Products to be paid to Distributor and any other persons, which determination shall be final and binding on Distributor and any such other persons.

2.5 <u>Reservation of Rights.</u> T reserves the right to itself to sell, license and/or service, but shall not appoint other distributors to sell, license and/or service, the Products to customers in the Territory. Notwithstanding the foregoing, should this Agreement terminate in any manner, T shall have the right, upon termination of this Agreement or delivery to Distributor of written notice of termination thereof, to appoint other distributors to sell, license and/or service the Products to customers in the Territory.

2.6 <u>Subdistributors</u>. Distributor may not, without the prior written approval of T, appoint subdistributors or agents for the dale or license of the Products in the Territory; and such appointments shall be subject to terms prescribed by T.

3. <u>Prices, Terms and Payment</u>.

3.1 <u>T's Prices and Terms</u>. Distributor will place orders for the Products from T for its own account at prices and upon the general terms and conditions fixed by T from time to time. All prices are F.O.B. list price T's warehouse in _____ ("Warehouse"), plus delivery costs to Distributor (including, not by way of limitation, inland and marine freight, export charges, import duties, insurance and brokerage) less any trade discounts established by T. T's current F.O.B. list prices with applicable trade discounts are set forth on <u>Exhibit A</u>. T's current general terms and conditions are set forth on <u>Exhibit C</u>, attached hereto and made a part hereof, which terms and conditions shall control to the extent they are not inconsistent with any terms or condition of this Agreement.

3.2 <u>Distributor's Prices; House Accounts; Billing</u>. Distributor shall be entitled to establish its resale or relicense prices for Products with respect to customers in the Territory except with respect to any house accounts of T set forth on <u>Exhibit B</u>, which prices T shall establish. T's current prices for such house accounts are set forth on <u>Exhibit B</u>. T will notify Distributor in writing of any change in house accounts, or prices at which Products are to be sold or licensed to house accounts, at least 30 days prior to the effective date of the change. Distributor will be responsible for quoting, billing, and all sales and license activities with respect to customers in the Territory.

3.3 <u>Payments</u>. All payments shall be made in U.S. dollars in accordance with T's general terms and conditions then in effect. The ability of Distributor to complete payments in the currency of the United States is of the essence of this Agreement. If by virtue of any law, regulation or order of any government authority in the Territory, Distributor is unable to make payments in accordance with this Agreement and T's general terms and conditions, T may elect to terminate this Agreement immediately.

3.4 <u>No Deductions</u>. The Distributor agrees that in making payments to T no deductions for warranty or other claims against T shall be made unless Distributor receives prior written notice of the approval of the claim by T.

3.5 <u>Right to Set-off</u>. T shall have the right to set-off at any time (before, during, or after termination of this Agreement) amounts owed by Distributor to T and its subsidiaries and affiliates against amounts owed by T to Distributor.

3.6 <u>Security Interest</u>. For the purpose of securing payment to T, the title to the Products shall be and remain in T until receipt by T in cash or property acceptable to T of the full purchase price therefor. T shall have the right to repossess and resell or relicense such Products until title passes to Distributor, notwithstanding that the risk of loss or damage shall have passed to Distributor.

4. <u>Minimum Orders and Inventories</u>.

4.1 <u>Minimum Orders</u>. Distributor will order minimum quantities of the Products as shown on <u>Exhibit D</u>, attached hereto and made a part hereof, for the periods therein specified and thereafter in the amounts agreed upon by the parties from time to time, but in no event less than the amount specified in the latest period set forth on <u>Exhibit D</u>.

4.2 <u>Inventory</u>. Distributor will maintain an inventory of the Products sufficient to meet not less than 45 days' order requirements for the Territory, based upon the minimum order requirements set forth on <u>Exhibit D</u>.

5. <u>Acceptance of Orders and Shipment</u>.

5.1 <u>Acceptance by T</u>. No order placed by Distributor shall be binding on T until the same has been accepted by T. Upon acceptance by T, each such order shall constitute a binding agreement of T to ship, and of Distributor to pay for, the Products ordered under the terms of this Agreement.

5.2 <u>Inconsistent Terms</u>. Any terms or conditions stated in Distributor's order or T's acceptance inconsistent with this Agreement shall be null and void.

5.3 <u>Shipment</u>. T shall ship the Products to Distributor within a reasonable time after acceptance of any order. All Products shall be shipped to Distributor in T's standard packages. Shipment by packages in any size other than standard will be billed to Distributor at a rate 10% higher than the standard packaging rate. Shipping dates shall be approximate and shall be computed from the date of acceptance of the order by T. Weights given shall be estimated weights. All typographical and clerical errors shall be subject to correction. T shall in no event be obliged to make any such shipment if such shipment would, at the time thereof, constitute a violation of any laws, regulations, or policies of the Territory or the United States of America.

5.4 <u>Export Licenses and Fees</u>. Distributor shall provide all documentation and written assurances required by the United States Department of Commerce to obtain export licenses and shall comply with the regulations of the United States Office of Export Administration. Customers of the Distributor shall also provide all required import licenses and permits, satisfy all import formalities and comply with the regulations of the United States Office of Export Administration. Distributor shall be responsible for all duty and license fees, taxes, and any other fee or charge related to import or export of the Products into the Territory.

5.5 Risk of Loss. T's obligations to effect shipment of the Products shall be fully discharged, and all risk of loss or damage shall pass to Distributor when the Products are delivered to a common carrier in the U.S.A., even though legal title is retained by T for security purposes.

5.6 Acceptance by Distributor. Distributor shall be entitled to conduct a reasonable investigation of the Products at the port of entry in the Territory. All claims for defects in the Products or shortages shall be made in writing by Distributor within 10 days of the receipt of the Products. Acceptance of the Products by Distributor shall constitute a waiver of all claims by Distributor for loss or damage due to defects or shortages in the Products, or to delay in delivery of the Products.

5.7 Return Authorization. The Products shall not be returned by Distributor without authorization and instructions from T, nor shall T accept returned Products except in accordance with such authorization and instructions.

5.8 Cancellation. No order for Products from Distributor may be cancelled, suspended or modified without T's written consent and then only upon terms which will indemnify T against loss arising from such cancellation, suspension or modification.

6. Rights Reserved by T.

6.1 Change in Products, Prices or Terms. T retains and shall have the right, exercisable in its sole discretion, any time and from time to time to alter, modify or discontinue any Products or change the price of any Products or general terms and conditions without liability to Distributor. T will notify Distributor in writing of any change in its Products, prices, or its general terms and conditions at least 30 days prior to the effective date of the change.

6.2 Change of Grant. T shall have the right amend, modify, delete, add to or otherwise revise the rights granted in Section 2 and on Exhibits A and B upon 90 days prior written notice to Distributor. Such actions shall be accomplished by amending Exhibits A and B to this Agreement, which shall set forth the effective date of any change in the above terms and be sequentially numbered, signed and dated by T. Any dispute concerning the scope or definition of the Products or Territory shall be decided by T whose determination thereon shall be final and binding.

7. Independent Contractor. Distributor shall act solely as an independent contractor and shall have no legal power or authority whatsoever, expressed or implied, oral or written, to act for, bind or commit T in any manner or to any thing whatsoever. The parties

agree that nothing in this Agreement is intended to effect the appointment of Distributor as an agent of T or to create or evidence a joint venture between the parties. Distributor shall not take any action which has the effect of creating the appearance of its having authority to assume or create obligations on T's behalf.

8. <u>Products</u>.

8.1 <u>No Competing Products</u>. During the term of this Agreement, Distributor shall not manufacture, sell or distribute any goods or products which are functionally similar to the Products or which T determines to be competing with the Products or any other products the promotion and sale of which will interfere with or adversely affect the promotion and sale of T's Products, without T's prior written consent.

8.2 <u>No Changes</u>. Distributor shall not change, alter, or modify any of the Products in any manner without the prior written consent of T.

8.3 <u>Packages; Labels</u>. Distributor shall distribute the Products only in packages and under labels and packaging designs which have received the prior written approval of T.

9. <u>Advertising and Promotion</u>.

9.1 <u>T Assistance</u>. T shall from time to time furnish Distributor with reasonable quantities of sales literature, samples, displays, promotional materials and press releases relating to the Products and other Product data which T considers helpful in advancing the sale or license and service of the Products. Distributor may reproduce at its own expense such materials, provided that such reproduction contains all applicable copyright and proprietary rights legends sufficient to protect and preserve T's rights therein and provided a licensing agreement has been signed by T and samples of such reproductions are approved by T.

9.2 <u>Best Efforts</u>. Distributor will use its best efforts to promote and enhance the goodwill of the Products and of the trademarks specified in <u>Section 12</u> and will give the Products prominence in its promotional and advertising activities.

9.3 <u>Cost</u>. Distributor will assume the full cost of all its advertising, promotional, and selling expenses, including, but not limited to, correspondence with customers, travel and entertainment expenses, and salaries and commissions of salesmen and/or agents and other personnel in the Territory.

9.4 <u>Trade Shows</u>. Distributor shall, at its own expense, attend such trade and industry meetings, shows and conventions in the Territory as in its judgment will promote the distribution of Products.

9.5 <u>Training</u>. Distributor shall attend training courses in marketing, operations and maintenance of the Products to be held at locations specified by T not less often than once each year. All travel and subsistence expenses incurred by Distributor in attending training courses shall be borne by Distributor.

9.6   Additional Investment. Except as otherwise specified herein, Distributor shall undertake and continue the performance of this Agreement solely with the employees and facilities presently owned, leased, employed or contracted by it, and shall not make any investments in fixed assets or otherwise, or contract additional employees or agents, without the prior written consent of T, which shall not be unreasonably withheld.

10.   Information Furnished by Distributor.

10.1   Product Failures. Distributor will immediately notify T in writing of any Products failures or customer complaints concerning the Products.

10.2   Price List. Distributor will furnish T copies of its price list for the Products and advise T promptly of any change therein.

10.3   Advertising. Distributor will submit to T in advance details of all proposed advertising of the Products and shall not use any advertising or promotional materials prior to obtaining T's written approval of such materials.

10.4   Competition. Distributor will keep T fully informed concerning competition in the Territory.

10.5   Sublicense and Inventory Reports. Distributor will furnish T quarterly sublicense and inventory reports with respect to the Products.

10.6   Additional Market Information. Distributor shall forward to T such additional information as may aid T in the development of more efficient marketing aids, advertising, product literature, product comparisons and the like.

11.   Warranty, Service and Returns.

11.1   Customer Warranty. T warrants its Products to the ultimate customer subject to the provisions of a written warranty set forth in the applicable documentation for the Product, which may be modified from time to time.

11.2   No Warranties to Distributors. T extends to Distributor no warranties with respect to the Products, expressed or implied, oral or written. T DISCLAIMS ANY IMPLIED WARRANTIES OF MERCHANTABILITY OR FITNESS FOR A PARTICULAR PURPOSE WITH RESPECT TO THE PRODUCTS.

11.3   No Inconsistent Warranty. Distributor will not give to any ultimate customer, purchaser, licensee or user of the Products any guarantee or warranty with respect to Products, or any instruction for use or care of Products, which is different from the warranty set forth in the applicable documentation for the Product, without the prior written consent of T.

11.4 Customer Service. Distributor shall be responsible for handling all warranty problems, returns and customer service within the Territory and shall undertake or arrange all necessary service on delivered Products in the Territory.

11.5 Customer Inquiries. T shall forward to Distributor for its handling a copy of all inquiries received from the Territory along with a coy of any acknowledgements T may have made and T shall make available to Distributor such sales, product and technical information as T may consider advantageous and helpful to Distributor in handling such inquiries. Distributor will supply T with information as to the disposition of all referred inquiries.

11.6 Returns and Replacements. T shall permit Distributor to return Products for repair or replacement in accordance with T's stated warranties for such Product and its Marketing Policy then in effect. All transportation and related charges in connection with the return and replacement of such Products shall be borne by Distributor. No Products shall be returned by Distributor without authorization and instructions from T, nor shall T accept returned Products except in accordance with such authorization and instructions.

11.7 Responsibility on Termination. Upon termination of this Agreement by either party Distributor shall remain liable for replacement or service according to and for the period of any warranty given to its customers in connection with the purchase or license of the Products.

12. Trademarks, Trade Names, Logotypes.

12.1 Right to Use. T hereby authorizes Distributor to use the trademarks, trade names, logotypes or other proprietary information of T including, without limitation, those set forth on Exhibit F, attached hereto and made a part hereof (the "Trademarks"), in connection with the sublicense of the Products in the Territory during the term of this Agreement, but for no other purpose. Nevertheless, Distributor shall acquire no rights to the Trademarks by its permitted use thereof.

12.2 Acknowledgment. Distributor acknowledges the validity of the Trademarks, and T's ownership thereof, and will respect, protect and safeguard T's rights therein. In connection with any reference to the Trademarks, Distributor shall clearly indicate T's ownership of the Trademarks and shall not in any manner represent that it has any ownership interest in the Trademarks or registrations thereof, and the Distributor acknowledges that no action by it or on its behalf shall create in Distributor's favor any right, title or interest in or to the Trademarks.

12.3 No Alterations. Distributor will not alter, deface, remove, cover up, or mutilate in any manner whatsoever any Trademarks or serial or model number, brand or name which T may attach or affix to the Products.

12.4 <u>Legal Compliance</u>. Distributor undertakes that when referring to the Trademarks, it will diligently comply with any law pertaining to Trademarks at any time in force in the Territory, including compliance with marking requirements.

12.5 <u>No Registration</u>. Distributor will not use or register at any time during the term of this Agreement, or after its termination, any word, symbol or combination thereof which is confusingly similar to any of the Trademarks.

12.6 <u>Notification</u>. Distributor will promptly notify T of the use by any person of trademarks or trade names which are similar to the Trademarks or of any instances of possible infringement or violation of the Trademarks or other commercial rights of T which may come to Distributor's attention. Distributor furthermore agrees that it shall not at any time take any action in the courts, administrative agencies, or otherwise to prevent the infringement, imitation, illegal use, or misuse of the Trademarks, it being clearly understood by Distributor that such action falls wholly with T as sole owner of the Trademarks.

12.7 <u>Assistance</u>. Distributor will assist T in taking all steps to protect or defend its rights in the event of any possible violation or infringement of the Trademarks or other commercial rights of T, whether in the courts, administrative agencies, or otherwise, and to make promptly available to T, its representatives and attorneys all of the Distributor's files, records and other information pertaining to the advertising, promotion, distribution, sale and licensing of the Products.

13. <u>Copyrights</u>. Distributor recognizes the validity of T's copyright in any Products, documentation, written material or packaging to which T shall have made a claim to copyright protection and Distributor specifically recognizes T's exclusive right to copyright protection and/or registration of any translation of the Products, documentation, advertising, promotional or descriptive material furnished Distributor by T.

14. <u>Confidentiality</u>. In addition to and not in lieu of any term or condition set forth on <u>Exhibit C</u>, this Agreement, the Products and any drawings, specifications, documents, prints, catalogs, price books, price lists, promotional lists, customer lists, sales and company policy manuals, marketing information or technical or other data or information provided by T to Distributor or acquired by Distributor in connection with this Agreement is strictly confidential and shall not be used to the detriment of T or the benefit of any other person or for any purpose other than in connection with this Agreement. Except as permitted by this Agreement, Distributor shall not disclose to third-parties or copy or use or employ, either during the term of this Agreement or after its termination, any confidential or proprietary information of T of whatever nature ("Confidential Information"), including, but not limited to, the

information and documentation set forth above, but not including any information which is (i) public information or (ii) was known to Distributor prior to entering into a distributorship relationship with T, or (iii) becomes public information other than as a result of any breach of any obligation or duty of any person to T. Confidential Information is and will remain the exclusive property of T and will be held in trust by Distributor for the exclusive benefit of T.

15.   Government Regulation.

15.1   Import Licenses. Distributor agrees to obtain at its own expense any import license, foreign exchange or currency exchange permit, or other permit or approval it may need for the performance of its obligations under this Agreement, and in essence, to comply at its own expense, with all applicable laws, regulations and orders of the government of the Territory or any instrumentality thereof, including, not by way of limitation, any requirements for the registration or recording of this Agreement with governmental entities in the Territory.

15.2   Export Regulations. T is subject to U.S. laws and regulations governing the export of U.S. products and technology. Distributor agrees that it will not directly or indirectly engage in any acts which would constitute a violation of such laws or regulations.

16.   Indemnification. Distributor will indemnify and hold T harmless from and against any and all losses, damages, claims, liabilities, cost or expenses based upon or relating to activities of Distributor in violation of the terms and conditions of this Agreement or any applicable law, decree or regulation or the maintenance of the Products purchased or licensed in the Territory through the Distributor.

17.   Terms and Termination.

17.1   Term. The term of this Agreement shall be one year, commencing on the date hereof, subject to automatic renewal for additional six-month periods in the absence of notice by either party of a contrary intention at least 90 days prior to the end of any extended term.

17.2   Immediate Termination by Either Party. Either party may terminate this Agreement immediately upon written notice to the other party should (a) a trustee or receiver be appointed to administer or conduct the business and affairs of the other party, (b) an application for bankruptcy or rehabilitation proceedings be filed by or against the other party, (c) a court of competent jurisdiction attach or take custody of all or a significant portion of the assets of the other party, or (d) should the other party make an assignment of all or a significant portion of its assets or properties for the benefit of creditors.

17.3   Immediate Termination by T. T may terminate this Agreement immediately by written notice to Distributor (a) in the event of a material change in the ownership or control of Distributor, (b) if any of the sovereign entities or political subdivisions in the Territory whether by legislation or decree, prevents payments being made under Section 3 of this Agreement, or (c) default by Distributor of its obligations under Sections 12, 13, 14 or 15 or the inability or prospective failure of Distributor to perform is obligations thereunder.

17.4 Default. In addition to and not in limitation of the rights granted under Sections 17.2 and 17.3 hereof, in the event that either party defaults in the performance of any of the provisions of this Agreement, the other party may, at its sole discretion, render written notice at least 30 days in advance to the other party specifying the cause of such default. If such default is not cured by the defaulting party within 30 days, this Agreement shall be deemed to terminate as of the date 30 days from the date of the notice. Failure by either party to provide notice with respect to any default shall not prejudice the right of such party to provide notice and effect termination for subsequent defaults.

17.5 Automatic Termination. If any of the sovereign entities or political subdivisions in the Territory enacts legislation, whether in the form of a law, decree or regulation, relating to the relationship created by this Agreement which grants rights to Distributor which are not granted by this Agreement, this Agreement shall terminate automatically one day prior to the date such legislation becomes effective.

18. Effect of Termination.

Upon Termination of this Agreement:

18.1 No Damages. T will not be liable for compensation or damages of any kind, whether on account of the loss by Distributor for current or prospective profits, anticipated sales, expenditures, investments or commitments made in connection with this Agreement; or on account of any other thing or cause whatsoever, and the parties hereby waive any rights which may be granted to them by sovereign entities or political subdivisions in the Territory which are not granted to them by this Agreement.

18.2 Return of Information. Distributor will return all drawings, specifications, documents, prints, catalogs, price books, price lists, promotional lists, customer lists, sales and company policy manuals, marketing information, and any other data or information, whether or not Confidential Information, provided by T to Distributor in connection with this Agreement, together with all copies thereof, or otherwise dispose of the same as instructed by T.

18.3 Purchase of Inventory. T may, but has no obligation to, repurchase or resell at the price Distributor acquired from T or the fair market value thereof, whichever is less, such of Distributor's inventory of the Products as shall be in good and saleable condition.

19. Arbitration.

19.1 Disputes. Any controversy or claim arising out of or relating to this Agreement, or the breach thereof, shall, unless otherwise expressly provided herein, be settled by arbitration in accordance with the Rules of the American Arbitration Association, and judgment upon the award rendered by the Arbitrator(s) may be entered in any court having jurisdiction thereof.

19.2 Venue and Jurisdiction. All proceedings hereunder shall take place in the Commonwealth of Massachusetts. The parties hereto expressly consent to and accept the exclusive jurisdiction of the courts of Massachusetts with respect to the enforcement of their rights under this arbitration clause, or with respect to the determination of any claim, dispute, or disagreement which may arise concerning the interpretation, performance, or breach of this Agreement.

20. Miscellaneous.

20.1 Successors and Assigns; Assignment. This Agreement shall be binding upon and inure so the benefit of the parties and their respective assigns, executors, heirs or successors. This Agreement, and any rights hereunder, may not be assigned by Distributor without the prior written consent of T.

20.2 Notices. All notices and requests provided for herein shall be in writing and in English and may be delivered personally or may be sent by cable or air mail, return receipt requested, and shall be deemed effective from the date of delivery, transmission or mailing, as the case may be. Unless the parties agree otherwise, all notices shall be addressed to the parties at the addresses set forth above.

20.3 Modification. This Agreement may not be modified except as specified in Section 6 without the prior written consent of both parties. Approvals or consents hereunder of a party shall also be in writing.

20.4 Waiver. The waiver by either party of a breach or default in any of the provisions of this Agreement by the other party shall not be construed as a waiver of any succeeding breach of the same or other provisions; nor shall any delay or omission on the part of either party to exercise or avail itself of any right, power, or privilege that it has or may have hereunder operate as a waiver of any breach or default by the other party.

20.5 Survival. Upon termination of this Agreement in any manner, the provisions of this Agreement which are expressed to survive this Agreement or to apply notwithstanding termination hereof shall be observed by Distributor.

20.6 Force Majeure. Neither party shall be liable to the other party for any loss, damage, delay or failure of performance resulting directly or indirectly from any cause beyond its reasonable control, including force majeure, strikes, or the laws, regulations, acts or failure to act of any governmental authority.

20.7 <u>Captions</u>. The captions in this Agreement are for convenience of reference only and shall not define or limit the provisions hereof.

20.8 <u>Entire Agreement</u>. This Agreement, including the general terms and conditions set forth on <u>Exhibit C</u> as they may be modified from time to time in accordance with this Agreement, constitutes the entire Agreement between the parties and supersedes all prior and contemporaneous agreements between the parties with respect to the subject matter of this Agreement, whether expressed or implied, oral or written.

20.9 <u>Severability</u>. The invalidity, in whole or in part, of any provision, term or condition of this Agreement shall not affect the validity of any other such provision, term or condition.

20.10 <u>Counterparts</u>. This Agreement may be executed in one or more counterparts, each of which shall be deemed to be an original, but all of which will constitute one and the same instrument.

20.11 <u>Governing Law</u>. This Agreement shall be exclusively governed by, and construed and interpreted in accordance with, the laws of the Commonwealth of Massachusetts, U.S.A. The English text of this Agreement shall control over any translation hereof.

IN WITNESS WHEREOF, this Agreement has been executed by the parties as of the date first set forth above.

Accepted by Distributor,
ABC GmbH:

Accepted by T, INC.:

BY: _____   BY: _____

NAME: _____   NAME: _____

TITLE: _____   TITLE: _____

DATE: _____   DATE: _____

Selected Bibliography

Michael Joachim Bonell, The 1983 Geneva Convention on Agency in the International Sale of Goods, 32 Am. J. Comp. L. 717 (1984).

Dennis Campbell & Louis Lafili (editors), Distributorships, Agency and Franchising in an International Arena: Europe, The United States, Japan and Latin America (1990).

Thomas F. Clasen, International Agency and Distribution Agreements (1991).

Thomas F. Clasen & Christian G. Cabou, EC Regulation of Agency and Distribution Arrangements, in European Community Law After 1992 (Ralph H. Folsom et al., eds. 1992).

Ovido M. Giberga, The Legal Pitfalls of Negotiating With Foreign Agents, 5 Preventive L. Rep. 3 (1986).

Hamza & Stovall, Registering Agreements (Agency and Distributorship: Egyptian Law & Practice) 12 Middle East Executive Rep. (Mar. 1989).

Karl G. Herold & David D. Knoll, Negotiating and Drafting International Distributing Agency and Representative Agreements: The United States Exporter's Perspective, in Negotiating and Drafting International Commercial Contracts (1986), reprinted in 21 Int'l Lawyer 939 (1987).

International Chamber of Commerce, Model Commercial Agency Contract.

Henry T. King, Jr., Legal Aspects of Appointment and Termination of Foreign Distributors and Representatives, 17 Case W.Res.J.Int'l L. 91 (1985).

Carolita L. Oliveros, International Distribution Contract Materials, ALI–ABA Course of Study, March 23, 1995 (C998 ALI–ABA 811).

A.H. Puelinck & H.A. Tielemans, The Termination of Agency and Distributorship Agreements: A Comparative Survey, 3 Nw.J.Int'l L. & Bus. 452 (1981).

Jacques Sales, Termination of Sales Agents and Distributors in France, 17 Int'l Lawyer 741 (1983).

Andre M. Saltoun, International Distribution and Sales Agency Agreements, 7 Hastings Int'l & Comp. L. Rev. 303 (1983).

Andre M. Saltoun & Barbara C. Spudis, International Distribution and Sales Agency Agreements: Practical Guidelines for U.S. Exporters, 38 Bus.Law. 883 (1983).

Petar Sarcevic, The Geneva Convention on Agency in the Law of International Trade, in Paul Volken et al. (eds.), International Sale of Goods: Dubrovnik Lectures, ch. 14 (1986).

Thad W. Simons, Jr., Termination of Sales Agents and Distributors in Belgium, 17 Int'l Lawyer 752 (1983).

Thompson (ed.), Commercial Agency and Distribution Agreements in Europe (Brit.Inst.Int'l & Comp.L.1964).

Utz Toepke, EEC Law of Competition: Distribution Agreements and their Notifications, 19 Int'l Lawyer 117 (1985).

Georg Vorbrugg & Dirk H. Mahler, Agency and Distributorship Agreements Under German Law, 19 Int'l Lawyer 607 (1985).

C. C. A. Voskuil & J. A. Wade (eds. & contribs.), Hague–Zagreb Essays on the Law of International Trade, 157–294 (1983).

Guy-Martial Weijer (ed.), Commercial Agency and Distribution Agreements: Law & Practice in the Member States of the European Community (1989).

Kojo Yelpaala, Strategy and Planning in Global Product Distribution—Beyond the Distribution Contract, 25 Law & Pol'y Int'l Bus. 839 (1994).

Symposium, Establishing an Agency or Distributorship in Mexico, 4 U.S.–Mexico L.J. 72 (1996).

Note, EEC—Article 85—Selective Distributorship Agreements May Not Include Prohibition on Exports, 10 Ga.J.Int'l & Comp.L. 673 (1980).

Chapter 5

COUNTERTRADE AGREEMENTS

Table of Sections

A. INTRODUCTION

A. INTRODUCTION

§ 5.1 Countertrade in the Post World War II Years

Countertrade is barter in modern clothes. It developed rapidly as a form of doing business with the USSR and Eastern European nations in the 1970s and 1980s, before major economic and political reforms tended to diminish its emphasis as a means of doing business.[1] Although some nations announced that as part of their reforms from nonmarket to market economies they would discontinue the use of countertrade, some of the same reasons that previously existed which encouraged the use of countertrade, i.e., shortage of hard currency, have persisted and have caused these nations to continue its use. Increased countertrade has been part of the dynamic growth in world trade since World War II, and part of the changing conditions in trading patterns.[2]

The use of countertrade has not depended on the size of the transaction. It has been used for some very large natural resource

§ 5.1

1. The Council for Mutual Economic Aid (CMEA or COMECON), the socialist bloc's modest attempt at economic integration, had requirements that member-nation sellers had to obtain contracts to sell their goods before they could import Western goods.

2. It has been estimated as accounting for 8–10 percent of world trade. Group of Thirty (G30) Report (Mar. 1986). A United States International Trade Commission report in 1985 suggested that 5.6 percent of U.S. exports involved countertrade.

ventures in the former Soviet Union, and for many relatively small transactions in Eastern European nations. The success that countertrade achieved in nonmarket economy nations caused it to spread; it has been used increasingly in transactions with developing nations.[3] Countertrade is not limited to nonmarket or developing nation trade, however. One form of countertrade, offsets (discussed below), is being used for many military equipment and large civilian aircraft sales to developed nations. It is thus no longer considered the "dark" side of international trade, but a legitimate form of doing business.

The above comments illustrate the use of countertrade by geographical sectors, by nonmarket economy nations, by developing nations and by the industrialized nations. It might also be identified with reference to either a product or service basis. It has often been the only form available where the goods or services were not of sufficiently high priority to gain import permission and consequent access to scarce hard currency. The exporter of sophisticated computer hardware usually has had little trouble in demanding traditional forms of documentary sales, cash in the form of some hard currency in return for the needed goods. But where the goods or services are of less priority for a nation's perceived development needs,[4] or where the goods or services are available from many sources, countertrade may be the only way to successfully market them.

§ 5.2 Why Engage in Countertrade?

Before one characterizes countertrade as any form of rightful heir to free trade, it must be acknowledged as a form of trade which is often an involuntary transaction. It consumes more time than a cash transaction. It gives the U.S. exporter products it may not want and cannot easily sell, sometimes because of poor quality. In view of such unattractive characteristics of countertrade, why do U.S. and other industrialized nations' companies engage in countertrade? In a great many cases not because they want to, but because it is the only way to trade or invest in the particular product or service. Additionally, it may be the way to gain a foothold in a market, to be positioned favorably for the time when countertrade is not mandatory and exchangeable currency is available.

The U.S. company would almost always prefer to be paid in its own or another nation's hard currency. That currency is freely convertible. The reason for countertrade is often that the foreign party (or that party's nation) is short of convertible currency. It is easier to understand the complexities of countertrade when it is accepted that it is usually not the preferred method of trade, but does have some justifications which lead parties to agree to one form of countertrade or another.

3. It was largely the product of the debt crisis in the early 1980s, certainly as much so as the product of witnessing the success of countertrade by nonmarket economies.

4. This is especially true where there is a development plan which outlines what the nation's needs are for the next 5–10 years. If the products planned for export to such a country are not on the "list", they will be unlikely to be approved as a transaction involving scarce hard currency.

One might use countertrade to avoid or evade taxation, but that is not usual for a professional, commercial transaction. It is rather more common between individuals who know each other, such as a person who has a hobby making concrete garden statuary and trades a fountain to a local restaurant for a dozen "free" dinners. Or the plumber who does some work on a lawyer's house in exchange for a will.[1] Tax avoidance was probably not an issue, but a consequence of not even thinking it was necessary to include the value of each item received as income. These simple transactions constitute countertrade, but in its most simple form—barter.

Countertrade as a form of international trade may be used to penetrate new markets which have been closed due to traditional trading relationships or patterns. Some persons have viewed countertrade as a necessary way of prying open formerly closed markets.[2] Purchasers often build good relations with suppliers and tend to avoid even listening about other available substitutes. It is commonplace in Japan especially, and often misunderstood in the United States as creating intentional trade barriers. Coerced or voluntary countertrade may be an effective way to create new markets for new products.[3]

Countertrade is not only intended to keep scarce hard currency within the foreign nation that demands countertrade, but to create jobs as well. It thus is not only practiced by third world and nonmarket economies, but by many industrialized nations.[4] Selling military equipment, or large aircraft, is very likely to involve some countertrade as part of the sales agreement. This is a voluntary form of countertrade, part of the negotiating process to obtain a sale, and viewed as a legitimate part of fair trade, or trading on an "even playing field." Selling commercial aircraft from the United States to Japan is likely to involve manufacturing some of the aircraft parts in Japan. If the U.S. company does not agree to such countertrade, Airbus in Europe is likely to win the contract by agreeing to this form of countertrade.

The motivation and even mandate to engage in countertrade will vary from country-to-country. Some Eastern European nations have made countertrade mandatory, but the trend is away from such restrictive use. Some nations use countertrade to attempt to keep a general

§ 5.2

1. This is obviously more likely in a small town where people frequently "exchange" their work products, than in a large city. One may reasonably doubt that a huge New York City law firm engages in such barter of its services.

2. Stanislaw J. Soltysinski, "Statement: In Defense of Countertrade," 5 J. Com. Bus. & Capital Market L. 341 (1983).

3. It is estimated that countertrade grew from about two percent of world trade in 1976 to something between five percent and 25 percent by the mid-1980s. Philip Rowberg, Jr., Countertrade as a

Quid Pro Quo for Host Government Approval of a Joint Venture, in David N. Goldsweig (ed.), Joint Venturing Abroad: A Case Study (ABA 1985). The movement towards market economies in Eastern Europe and former USSR countries has reduced countertrade because some of those nations consider countertrade a characteristic identified with the socialist, nonmarket form of economy they are rejecting.

4. Australia, Belgium and Canada, for example. See Cedric Guyot, Countertrade Contracts in International Business, 20 Int'l Lawyer 921, 943 (1986).

balance of trade in all industries, and others try to maintain a balance in each industrial sector (e.g., vehicles) or even each separate industry (e.g., trucks). Because countertrade tends to increase when a nation has a serious shortage of hard currency, the rules of the countertrade game are constantly changing. Participants enter and exit usually not according to any philosophical commitment to or rejection of countertrade, but because sales are best or only achieved by playing the game.

Because various forms of countertrade are often given different names, some definitions should be useful. They are not always carefully separated in use, but they help to illustrate how many variations of centuries-old "barter" modern commerce has been able to create.

B. FORMS OF COUNTERTRADE

§ 5.3 Barter

"Countertrade" has many faces. It is often nothing more than simple "barter," two parties exchanging goods, usually of similar value. Any difference in the values is normally paid in cash, but barter is often thought of as a transaction without cash, partly because the parties lack any currencies. It is actually the one form of countertrade that is usually accomplished without any cash involvement. As young people we have probably all at one time engaged in barter, trading "things" with friends, perhaps stamps, or baseball cards, or dolls, or marbles or Pokemon cards. We never thought of involving any money in the exchange. The reason for the exchange may well have been that we did not have any money, and thus added to our collections by disposing of other things less desired. That sounds remarkably like a modern countertrade transaction by a nation short of hard currency or lacking credit.

Barter may be on a much larger scale than exchanging marbles or one rifle for fifteen buffalo hides. Many commercial transactions, particularly with Eastern European countries, have been basically barter transactions. For example, New Zealand has exchanged lamb for Iranian oil. A U.S. liquor company has sent its products abroad in exchange for bananas. The list of such examples is very long.

Barter agreements are not always simple, cash-less, single-document arrangements. They sometimes involve two separate documentary sales, often with letters of credit, and a linking or protocol agreement which includes provisions which make the transaction an exchange or barter transaction. But this tends to be more descriptive of a more complex form of barter, really *counterpurchase*.

§ 5.4 Counterpurchase

Counterpurchase occurs usually after one party, for example a company in the United States, finds a market for its goods in another, for example Poland. The U.S. company agrees to purchase Polish products of the same value as the U.S. company's goods. The Polish goods are usually unrelated to the U.S. goods. It sounds like barter described above. But barter usually has two parties interested in each other's goods. In much counterpurchase, where it may be fairly called an involuntary transaction, one party would prefer to sell its goods for cash, but is forced into a countertrade agreement because of the currency shortage of the other nation. A company, whether Boeing or Airbus, selling commercial aircraft to Poland, would prefer to be paid in dollars or francs or pounds or deutschmarks. The company really does not want glassware, or canned hams, or coal. But if it wishes to sell the aircraft, it may have to accept the Polish products and arrange for their sale in the United States or some third nation.[1]

The counterpurchase agreement will provide for the date by which the seller must purchase the agreed amount of countertrade goods. Some nations require all agreements to be 100 percent counterpurchase, that is the seller must purchase as much as it sells. Such an arrangement means there will effectively be no net exchange of currency. But the nation demanding countertrade may even attempt to negotiate 150 percent countertrade, requiring that the foreign party essentially sell, on behalf of the nation demanding countertrade, some of its products and return hard currency for the 50 percent excess. For example, a U.S. company sells a lathe valued at $10,000 to a Hungarian company, and must take $15,000 in value in Hungarian goods. But the U.S. company does not keep the $15,000 received for selling those goods, it must turn over to the Hungarian company $5,000. The U.S. company has become little more than a sales agent for Hungarian goods, at least with respect to the $5,000 worth of goods.

There is always concern that if the U.S. exporter purchases the foreign countertrade goods *before* selling its own goods, the foreign nation will use the hard currency obtained from such sale for some purpose other than to obtain the U.S. exporter's products. In such case it is useful to establish an escrow account in a third nation and have all the hard currency resulting from the U.S. purchase deposited in that account, to be used by the nation only to buy specified products from the U.S. exporter.

Counterpurchase accounts for a considerable percentage of countertrade, perhaps as much as 50–60 percent. There are many potential problems, both with regard to locating products for countertrade in the foreign nation, establishing their value, drafting the agreement, and selling the products in the United States or a third nation. The countertrade or protocol agreement must be carefully drafted, although it is likely that some control of its terms will be maintained by the foreign nation, which may have laws or regulations governing such issues as the required percentage of counterpurchase, time limits for meeting such purchase commitment, and penalties for failure to meet the time limit. All are discussed below.

§ 5.4

1. Because it involves imports of the Polish products into the United States or a third nation, tariffs and non-tariff barriers may have to be confronted.

One issue frequently involved in either common barter or the more sophisticated counterpurchase is setting a value for the goods. Returning to trading items as a child, if you were trying to trade an 1898 postage stamp, you might have said it was "worth" three 1904 stamps. But your friend may have disagreed, saying the 1904 stamps were rarer and at best the trade should be one for one. The same problem may occur in modern countertrade. In establishing the price you wish to receive for your lathe sold to the Hungarian party, you may inflate the price above what would be the cash price so as to cover the "extra" costs attributable to countertrade. One of these costs is the uncertainty of the value of the products received from Hungary. You may be asked to and accept Hungarian wine as the countertrade products. But at what price will the wine sell in the United States—$6 or $12 a bottle? The Hungarian company may argue the latter, but unless there is an established market for such wine in the United States, the price agreed per bottle is somewhat of a "rolling of the dice". One can understand why companies forced into countertrade may increase substantially the price of their goods in order to cover some very unknown costs of countertrade.

§ 5.5 Compensation or Buyback

This form of countertrade involves a relationship linking the seller's product and the countertrade goods.[1] The seller's "product" is sometimes equipment, or technology, or even an entire manufacturing plant. In return the seller receives products produced by the foreign purchaser with the equipment or technology, or in the plant. Obviously, it may take a long period of time to pay for the value of a plant by way of accepting products produced in that plant, and the agreement will be for a considerable duration. One of the most notable examples of buyback involved the Occidental Petroleum sale to the USSR of an ammonia plant, paid for by taking part of the ammonia production once the plant was operating.

There is usually less concern about the disposition of *compensation* goods in contrast to *counterpurchase* goods. As noted above, counterpurchase may involve very different goods than what the U.S. company sold, i.e., airplanes for canned hams, or liquor for bananas. In compensation agreements, the goods are often products which the seller is at the least familiar with, and possibly even sells, in the regular course of its business. Thus, a U.S. automobile manufacturer might establish a plant in China, and take in exchange a percentage or fixed number of the production, which it in turn markets along with the production of its own U.S. plants.[2] An obvious concern in such case is to assure that the Chinese products meet quality standards of other plants. Returning countertrade products is costly and has proven all too frequent in many

---

§ 5.5

1. See Leo G.B. Welt, Unconventional Forms of Financing: Buyback/Compensation/ Barter, 22 N.Y.U. J. Int'l L. & Pol. 461 (1990); Jerzy Rajski, Some Legal Aspects of International Compensation Trade, 35 Int'l & Comp.L.Q. 128 (1986).

2. The experience of producing the "Jeep" in the People's Republic of China is related in Jim Mann, Beijing Jeep (1989).

countertrade arrangements with nonmarket and developing nations. At least in a compensation agreement, the seller may have some say over quality in the production of the goods, while in a counterpurchase agreement it will be necessary to carefully examine any prospective products to assure that they will be marketable in the United States or a third nation.

Compensation agreements are often for very large dollar amounts. A chemical plant may be constructed in return for many years of a percent of the production. An automobile manufacturing plant may also require many automobiles over many years to pay for the cost of the plant. Counterpurchase agreements may be for large amounts, such as the sale of airplanes, but they are usually much smaller-value contracts than compensation agreements.

§ 5.6　Offsets

Sometimes used interchangeably to describe either counterpurchase or compensation forms of countertrade, an *offset* arrangement is technically quite different. It is very much used in aerospace, especially in the defense industry, but also quite often for civilian aircraft sales. Offsets constitute an agreement by the foreign seller to include as part of the sale in the foreign nation the use of parts or services from local suppliers. It is really a local content requirement and is becoming increasingly more common.[1] The local supplier could be owned by the U.S. party (a foreign subsidiary), and might be established for that very purpose. Often a joint venture is established to provide the local production. The net result is that some of the production takes place in the foreign nation which is purchasing the item, expectantly at less cost to the nation's possibly limited supply of hard currency, and with an increase in local jobs.

The U.S. government has been sufficiently concerned that offset agreements have a damaging impact on the U.S. economy that Congress in 1984 amended the Defense Production Act to require annual reporting by the President on the impact of offsets on "defense preparedness, industrial competitiveness, employment, and trade."[2] The general view of the U.S. government is not favorable toward countertrade, yet it realizes that countertrade is often required for U.S. firms to be competitive. Curiously, it (actually the Department of Defense) has promoted the use of offsets for many defense-related items.

Offsets have been used and encouraged by such nations as Belgium and Canada for 20 years. Most firms in Western Europe, as well as Canada, Australia and New Zealand, use offsets for large military

---

§ 5.6

1. It might also involve regular counterpurchase, buying unrelated products and selling them in the home nation or a third nation.

2. 50 U.S.C.A. app. § 2099 (1986). Subsequent amendments have extended the re-

porting requirements. The reporting process and results of the report prepared in 1985 are discussed in Judith K. Cole, Evaluating Offset Agreements: Achieving a Balance of Advantages, 19 Law & Pol'y Int'l Bus. 765, 781 (1987).

contracts. Boeing in the United States has agreed with the United Kingdom to use a 130 percent offset in sales of military aircraft.[3]

The Feingold Amendment to the Foreign Relations Authorization Act in 1995 amended the Arms Export Control Act to require the President to certify to Congress whether an offset agreement involving certain high-value weapon sales abroad constitutes a government-to-government or a direct commercial sale.[4] U.S. contractors may not give incentive payments to U.S. persons to persuade them to buy goods or services from a foreign country which has an offset agreement with the contractor. The amendment arose from concern that Northrop offered more than $1 million to a customer of Harnischfeger Industries to encourage the customer to buy machinery from a Finnish company to help meet Northrup's offset obligations in a $3 billion sale of jet fighters to Finland. A Memorandum of Understanding (MOU) between Finland and the United States only discouraged offsets, it did not prohibit them.

Offsets are prohibited in the NAFTA agreement, but there is a major exception for defense procurement.[5]

§ 5.7 Switch Trading

Switch trading is less a form of countertrade than a manner of clearing accounts among a number of transactions, or even among a number of nations. If our seller of airplanes to Poland is unable to find sufficient Polish products to meet the counterpurchase percentage requirement in the contract, it may learn that Poland is selling certain goods to Canada and has a surplus of Canadian dollars which the Polish government is willing to apply to the agreement. These Canadian dollars are called "clearing dollars." But Poland may wish to retain all the Canadian-transaction hard currency for other uses, because it lacks scarce hard currencies of any denomination.

If the clearing transaction is with a nation with soft currency, it may be easier to work the switch. For example, if the Polish goods are sold in Argentina rather than Canada, Poland may welcome the U.S. seller taking Argentine currency, since it is not acceptable in many international transactions (and may be available to the seller at a discounted price). The U.S. seller may be willing to take the Argentine currency if it is buying products from Argentina, or commencing an investment there and needs some local currency.[1]

---

3. Economist 89 (Dec. 20, 1986).

4. Current reporting requirements are in the Defense Production Act Amendments of 1992. Contractor reporting where involved in offset agreements exceeding $5 million for the sale of weapons systems or defense related items to foreign purchasers. 15 C.F.R. Part 701—"Reporting of Offsets Agreements in Sales of Weapons Systems or Defense Related Items to Foreign Countries or Foreign Firms." See 59 FR 61796 (2 Dec. 1994).

5. See Richard J. Russin, Offsets in International Military Procurement, 24 Pub. Cont. L.J. 65 (1994).

§ 5.7

1. The Argentine adoption of the dollar as a dual currency will increase the acceptability of the Argentine peso in international transactions, including switch trading.

Companies usually turn to professional help for switch trading. There are a number of multinational companies which act as countertrade facilitators using computer technology. Usually based in developed nations, e.g., London or Vienna, these facilitators bear the risk, buying the product from the seller, paying for it with vouchers (which are exchangeable for products or services from the firm's clients), or sometimes cash plus vouchers. The services obtained might even be travel (accommodations) and advertising.[2] The persons who arrange these clearing transactions are called "switch traders". They obviously add an additional cost to the transaction. Indeed, countertrade has several "hidden" costs which may arise to take away or diminish an expected profit. One of those costs is the higher cost of negotiating a countertrade agreement than a simple single documentary sale. Such costs will be added to the selling price.

§ 5.8 Bilateral Clearing Accounts

Occasionally two nations will agree to purchase goods from each other in a determined amount. They are "clearing units" or an artificial use of a set currency, usually the dollar. The trade is designed to remain in balance. If it becomes out of balance the clearing units may be sold, often at a discount and often using a switch trader.

§ 5.9 Investment Commitment

In this form the seller agrees to invest a certain amount of money in the foreign country. The amount to be invested may be a percentage of the sales of the seller's products, or a fixed amount to be taken out of the proceeds of such sales in a fixed amount/percentage over a period of time. In some cases, companies invest the proceeds of their sales not because of any investment commitment, but because there is a shortage of hard currency in the foreign nation and the seller is essentially locked into leaving the proceeds of the sale of the goods in the country. An investment is often the most appropriate use of such funds.

C. THE COUNTERTRADE AGREEMENT

§ 5.10 Single versus Three Agreements

It is possible to have a single agreement provide for (1) the sale of goods from the United States to a foreign nation, (2) the purchase of countertrade goods from that foreign nation by the U.S. company selling the first goods above, and (3) the elements unique to the countertrade relationship, such as consequences of failing to fulfill the countertrade goods purchase.[1] But it is more common and less complex to view the

---

2. See G. Cassidy, Financing Strategies—Barter's Rebirth, East–West Commersant, Dec. 1, 1995.

§ 5.10

1. A single agreement may be preferred if the foreign party is thought to be unreliable and likely to default. The single contract may allow the U.S. party to withhold deliv-

relationship as three agreements.[2] Because counterpurchase is the most common form of countertrade, the following outlines a typical counterpurchase transaction.[3]

§ 5.11 The First Agreement

The first agreement is for the sale of goods by the U.S. seller to the foreign buyer, for example a Polish enterprise. This is a standard sales contract, a documentary sale as discussed in earlier chapters. There will also be a letter of credit obtained by the Polish purchaser in favor of the U.S. seller, probably confirmed by a U.S. bank. While obtaining a letter of credit from a purchaser in a nation with uncertain hard currency reserves may be difficult, because there is to be a second agreement which generates sufficient hard-currency to pay for the first, the letter of credit should be available. Many nonmarket economy and developing nation buyers do not have easy access to lines of credit, and thus the letter of credit could become a very major obstacle to the transaction. The U.S. party will not wish to extend credit and effectively finance the transaction—a practice often asked of Western sellers.

§ 5.12 The Second Agreement

The second agreement is another standard documentary sale, this time the sale of Polish products to the U.S. party, with the latter obtaining a letter of credit in favor of the Polish seller. This second agreement may not be as clear as the first, because the U.S. seller may need time to locate appropriate countertrade products. But it is dangerous to sell the U.S. products to the foreign purchaser under a countertrade commitment, and later discover that there are no acceptable foreign nation goods to purchase to fulfill the countertrade commitment. The U.S. party may wish to have a provision in the first agreement which invalidates its obligations under the second agreement if the first agreement is canceled by the Polish buyer or the government.[1] The three agreements should all be negotiated at the same time. The U.S. party may not be able to determine an export price for its products until it knows of the costs associated with marketing the selected countertrade goods. It will certainly wish to add on such costs, or it will have to absorb them against its expected profit.

§ 5.13 The Third Agreement—The Protocol

The third agreement is the "protocol". It is usually not very long, but it is absolutely critical to the countertrade arrangement. The proto-

---

ery of its exports if the other party defaults. But the fear of a single contract is that the U.S. party will deliver first, and if the U.S. party does not subsequently find appropriate countertrade goods, the foreign party will not pay for the U.S. goods.

2. If letters of credit are used, they add additional agreements.

3. This transaction is adapted from a hypothetical problem contained in the au-

thors' casebook, Ralph H. Folsom, Michael Wallace Gordon & John A. Spanogle, Jr., International Business Transactions (West Pub. Co., 4th ed. 1999).

§ 5.12

1. This might appear in the protocol agreement.

col agreement serves to link the first two agreements. The three agreements thus form a three-contract aggregate that constitutes the full countertrade arrangement. The protocol actually may be the first agreement signed, requiring the parties to enter into the other two agreements. *Both* of the separate purchase agreements must be signed for either to be valid. The protocol provides for penalties if the Polish buyer accepts and pays for the goods, but the U.S. seller fails to fulfill the countertrade agreement. It allows the U.S. party to refuse to perform the second purchase agreement if the Polish buyer does not fulfill the requirements of the first purchase agreement. The U.S. seller does not want to be in the difficult position of having delivered the goods to the Polish buyer, yet not be entitled to payment until it has acquired and paid for the countertrade Polish goods. That would allow the Polish buyer to receive the equipment, place pressure on the government to block the U.S. seller from finding and purchasing Polish goods, and avoid having to pay for the U.S. goods it has received. This is why the use of letters of credit is advisable. The U.S. seller will be entitled to receive payment from a U.S. confirming bank as soon as it has shipped the goods and presented the documents to the bank. The documents will include no reference to the protocol agreement, that could cause rejection of the documents and nonpayment by the bank.

The Polish buyer may not wish to sign only the first purchase agreement and hold off execution of the second until the U.S. seller has located acceptable countertrade goods. Consequently, all the contracts may be signed at the same time, with the U.S. party agreeing to purchase the required dollar amount of Polish goods within a fixed period of time, often six months, but sometimes even two to three years.

There may be other provisions in the protocol agreement allowing the U.S. party to transfer the countertrade purchase obligation to a third party; providing that if the U.S. seller were to be required to pay a penalty under the countertrade agreement, it would remain entitled to be paid under the first purchase agreement (although it is contemplated that such payment will occur well before the second purchase agreement might be considered breached); and stating that there are no territorial or price restrictions on the disposal of the countertrade goods.

Although the Polish buyers (or Polish government regulations or policies) may have wanted the U.S. seller to take specified goods, the U.S. buyer may insist on having the agreement provide only that a fixed value of goods must be purchased within six months, or some other agreed upon period. The U.S. seller will want the agreement to state that if the goods it locates for purchase are not those delivered, or if the quality is not as specified, then the obligation to purchase any countertrade goods is extinguished. But the Polish party may not agree to this, and the U.S. seller may have to accept the possibility of returning the wrong or poor-quality goods and taking another shipment. Experience with countertrade in Eastern European countries suggests that poor quality is a very serious problem, and that countertrade goods are very often of unacceptable quality. The U.S. party may prefer to find goods *before* contracting and specify them in the contract, or at least list a variety of goods that are acceptable.

The six month period to locate goods may also be considered too brief. Delay is a routine incident of dealing with many developing and nonmarket economy nations. A longer period, two or three years, is preferable. But the foreign officials may be rigid in their insistence on a short term. It is obviously a matter of bargaining power and skill. If a longer term is allowed, thought should be given to the currency in which the purchase requirement is stated. If in the foreign currency, the obligation may actually be reduced in dollar terms if that foreign currency is falling against the dollar. As in the case of all international transactions, currency fluctuations may provide a party with a windfall or a loss. The longer the time granted to fulfill the commitment, the more likely is the impact of changing currency values.

The Polish buyers may also insist on including a penalty provision in the contract that requires the U.S. seller to pay some amount, perhaps ten percent of the value of the contract, if the countertrade goods are not purchased within the specified period. The Polish party may even wish to have such promise supported by what seems quite clearly a standby (or "suicide") letter of credit. But the U.S. party should only agree to the penalty and guarantee if the Polish party agrees that such payment would release the U.S. party from any further obligation to purchase Polish goods.

The U.S. party may want a provision allowing inspection of the countertrade goods by an agent to assure adequate quality, as well as a right to return any of the goods upon the U.S. party's receipt and inspection of the goods, and discovery that they are not the stipulated quality.

It should be apparent from the above discussion of several aspects of a countertrade arrangement that careful specification of times to fulfill the contracts is essential, and that the U.S. party should have a right to reject the goods for inadequate quality. Countertrade may involve an involuntary purchase by the U.S. party. The reason that the agreement is involuntary is often that the foreign goods are not able to be sold without the coercion of countertrade because they are not up to the standards required by most buyers.

Any profit on the sale of the U.S. party's goods may be quickly eroded by the time spent in returning countertrade goods and finding acceptable substitute goods, if that is required. If the U.S. party is willing to accept the payment of a penalty for failing to find acceptable products, perhaps the foreign party must accept a penalty in the form of releasing the U.S. party from any further obligation, if the initial purchase of countertrade goods requires the return of those goods because of unacceptable quality. The contract for the purchase of Polish products should clearly specify what is acceptable quality. Because this is a separate contract, it should be viewed as enforceable (and be financed) as any regular commercial documentary sale. The third contract or protocol may link obligations, however, and excuse performance of one of the initial two agreements if the other is breached.

While the above discussion suggests that the second contract may be concluded after the first (after countertrade goods are found), the two should be negotiated at the same time. The urge to sell goods should not lead the U.S. seller to make some "loose" arrangement to purchase countertrade goods, only to discover later that this arrangement places difficult or impossible burdens upon the U.S. seller, which quickly erodes the profit on the initial sale.

D.   NEGOTIATING A COUNTERTRADE AGREEMENT

§ 5.14   Understanding Countertrade

Before negotiating a countertrade agreement with a foreign purchaser, it is useful to know some of the countertrade experiences and practices of different nations. Such publications as Business Eastern Europe often describe both the changing legal rules of countertrade in different nations, and business issues confronted by specific countertrade agreements.[1]

Companies sometimes create countertrade units within the company to negotiate agreements, while other companies prefer to assign a single executive to the task. If the countertrade products are to be used in-house by the U.S. company (often not possible due to poor quality), the purchasing officers may be involved. In such case, the countertrade coordinator may be part of the purchasing department. But in the majority of cases, where the products are not to be used in-house, the task of the countertrade executive is to satisfy the countertrade obligation at the least cost to the company.

It is helpful to understand the reason a government wants countertrade. It may be that there is a shortage of hard currency, or an emphasis on job creation, or the nation may be attempting to pry open foreign markets perceived as closed (a kind of "try it you will like it" theory). If the reason for countertrade is understood, the requirements of a successful agreement are more easily identified. A willingness to learn about and to adapt to local countertrade interests may be the key to obtaining contracts for the U.S. exporter's products or investor's direct foreign investment.

§ 5.15   Length of Time to Negotiate

The negotiating process in concluding a countertrade agreement may seem inordinately long. It is fair to assume that it will take longer to negotiate than a regular documentary export sale. Additional time

§ 5.14
1. Business Eastern Europe is published   weekly by Business International.

means additional expense, which must be factored into the total costs equation. It is often difficult to find appropriate goods, and once they are found and become part of a countertrade agreement, they may not be available again as countertrade goods in response to a future sale of more goods to that foreign nation. Once the foreign nation learns that the goods have a market abroad, the government may take over that market and the next time around the U.S. exporter will discover that the goods no longer are listed as available for countertrade. The U.S. party's efforts have created a market abroad which the foreign party will subsequently exploit to earn hard currency. The U.S. party is left to find new goods to fulfill the countertrade requirements.

§ 5.16   Definition of the Goods

Defining the countertrade goods is important. The U.S. party may wish the definition to be very broad, but the nation demanding countertrade may try to narrow the definition to include only goods it has had trouble selling in the West. The U.S. party may wish to have no definition at all, but to be allowed to find any products of the foreign nation.

§ 5.17   Quality

Demanding that the countertrade goods meet quality specifications is no less important than any other aspect of a countertrade agreement. In some cases it may be the *most* important. The experience of many U.S. companies which have engaged in countertrade is that a high percentage of countertrade goods, as much as 60 percent, have to be returned. This adds an expense that must be considered at the time of negotiating the initial sale and the acceptance of countertrade. The agreement should cover both the quality of the countertrade goods and the procedures and cost allocations for returned goods. The U.S. company will want to be excused from any obligation to take further goods in countertrade, but it may be necessary to keep receiving similar goods until they are satisfactory in quality.

Poor quality has been a consistent complaint in dealing with Eastern European countries.[1] The foreign goods should be inspected *before* shipment, to avoid costly and time consuming repackaging and reshipping after they have been received in the United States, and rejected for poor quality. Inspection in the foreign nation may help to quickly identify problems in production and assist in improving the quality of future goods. Eastern European officials have often admitted that quality is a serious problem, but with a sense of frustration and few suggestions for solutions other than careful inspection. Poor quality is usually not intentional, but rather attributable to an inability to produce goods of a quality demanded in international markets, after functioning so long

§ 5.17   Eastern Europe.
1. Examples often appear in Business

solely in the domestic market where there were no competitive goods of any better quality.

§ 5.18 Quantity

The U.S. company may be dealing over a long term and wish to state quantities of countertrade goods it is required to purchase on a yearly basis. The foreign nation may wish to have the quantity based on a shorter period, for its own domestic planning requirements. But that may be difficult for the U.S. company. The compromise may be to use *value* per time period rather than *number* per time period.

§ 5.19 Prices

One method of setting the price of goods is to use a per-unit price. But that may be hard to define, other than in compensation or buy-back agreements. Where an agreement is for several years, determining prices may be impossible. But it may be considered very desirable, if not mandatory, by the foreign nation for planning purposes. Base prices may be used, with some form of annual adjustment, essentially an escalation provision. It may not be easy to draft such a provision and may result in an unrealistic price which is not welcome to one party. It may be necessary to provide for a negotiation between the parties each year, to determine a price which allows the goods to be sold competitively in the intended markets.

§ 5.20 Other Trade Rules Applicability

Engaging in countertrade does not mean that the foreign nation will waive other trade requirements. For example, the foreign countertrade goods may require an export permit. The countertrade agreement should provide that the foreign party must obtain any such export permit, just as the U.S. party is responsible for any export permission needed in the United States. If the contract is with an independent entity, the agreement may state that it is subject to obtaining permits from the appropriate government agencies. The agreement should clearly indicate which party is responsible for obtaining the necessary permits.

In addition to export permits, there may be export tariffs. They may be greater for countertrade sales than for cash sales. The agreement should clarify who is to pay these tariffs. If title passes in the foreign nation prior to export, the U.S. party could be left with goods subject to export tariffs and an export permit. Both would add unexpected costs to the transaction.

§ 5.21 Percentage of Countertrade Demanded

The company may be asked to accept as countertrade $120 worth of goods for every $100 it exports.[1] Such a commitment is to be avoided,

---

§ 5.21

1. Boeing accepted 130 percent countertrade to sell its airborne warning and con-

especially if the countertrade goods the U.S. party accepts are difficult to market. An equivalency formula ($100 of value for $100 of value) is better, but if the goods are *very* difficult to market, it may be appropriate to agree to accept only $80 worth of the foreign goods for each $100 exported. Called the "compensation ratio", in actual practice it is often reduced to as low as 20–30 percent, not 80–120 percent.[2] If the U.S. goods are high on the priority list of imports for the foreign nation, the negotiated percentage may be quite low.[3] The demand is sometimes not based on percentage, but on the purchase of a certain dollar value within a given period.

§ 5.22 Discount for Costs of Disposing Countertrade Goods

Another important consideration is the percentage of the value of the sales by the U.S. company which constitutes the costs of counter-trade, often called a discount or "disagio". This percentage, sometimes only a few points, may be as high as 30 percent of the total value of the sales. It compensates the U.S. seller for the additional costs of counter-trade, and is the amount by which the value of the goods will be reduced in selling them to third parties, or to a trading entity which will sell them to a third party. It is to some degree a measure of the economic inefficiency of countertrade as compared to free trade.

§ 5.23 Nonperformance Penalties

If the U.S. company fails to purchase the goods in the amount and within the time as agreed, it may be required to pay a penalty. The amount is usually a percentage of the total value of the goods. Some-times it is quite nominal, but sometimes it is very high. The penalty level, if any, will depend on the priority of need of the goods by the foreign nation, and the total value of the countertrade. An important element of the agreement is whether the U.S. party is relieved of any further obligation to purchase when it pays a penalty. It would certainly prefer such an arrangement. But if the penalty is really to be a penalty, it may be considered compatible with a demand for specific performance even after the payment of the penalty.

Penalties are almost always only to be paid by the Western party, not by the foreign party which has demanded countertrade. A U.S. party is quite obviously going to use whatever bargaining power it has to eliminate any penalty provision proposed for a countertrade agreement. If it is only able to make the sale with a countertrade agreement which

trol system (AWACS) to the British over a British competitor. See Brown, Boeing Team Offers British 130% Offsets for AWACS Buy, Aviation Wk. & Space Tech., Nov. 17, 1986, at 24.

2. The determining factor may be the foreign nation's supply of hard currency.

3. If the foreign nation has an annual, or longer (five year), plan, it may have set aside sufficient reserves to obtain the goods. If the Western party knows this, it has a better bargaining position.

contains a penalty provision, it should negotiate both the lowest possible penalty, plus a similar penalty for nonperformance by the foreign party.

§ 5.24   Selection of Goods

How to evaluate the foreign products that are proposed to be taken in countertrade may be difficult. How acceptable will Hungarian wine be? Where will it fit in the U.S. market? Could it be sold in third nations, particularly close to the source, such as Western Europe? The Hungarian government may try to value each bottle at $10 while the consumer market in the United States would pay no more than $6. It is essential to know the likely price of disposition of the goods in the United States or other market before concluding the contract. There are international trading companies which may assist in identifying acceptable quality goods from particular nations, and in avoiding other poor quality goods from those nations.[1]

§ 5.25   Release of United States Party

When the U.S. party has fulfilled the countertrade agreement, it should obtain a letter or statement from the foreign party indicating satisfaction of the agreement.

§ 5.26   Renegotiation

An additional area to consider is being able to renegotiate the contract if problems arise in locating acceptable products, if they prove to be of poor quality, or if they are not delivered within the time specified.

§ 5.27   Dispute Resolution

Countertrade agreements should have provisions for dispute resolution. The protocol agreement may be particularly unique and difficult for a court to understand. If judicial resolution is preferred, there should be some provision for selecting the forum and the applicable law. Arbitration may be preferred, but if selected there should be some identification of what is subject to arbitration, how the arbitrators are to be selected, where and under what rules arbitration is to be conducted, and a statement as to the intention that the arbitration decision shall be binding.

When the countertrade agreement is more in the nature of counterpurchase, meaning that the U.S. exporter receives goods that may be entirely unrelated to what it has exported, as opposed to a compensation agreement, there are additional problems, some of which are outlined in the above section dealing with the third or protocol agreement. Dealing with different products may be difficult for the U.S. company's adminis-

§ 5.24

1. The International Trade Administration of the Department of Commerce lists international trading houses in the United States which assist in countertrade.

trative staff, which may have little experience with the countertrade products and how to market them. If the U.S. company has received canned hams as part payment for an aircraft, the hams will either have to find their way into the food distribution market, or the company's employees will have to eat a lot of ham in the company cafeteria. The employees may not be pleased to receive even more as a Christmas bonus.[1]

A countertrade agreement for counterpurchase is best drafted with a "best efforts" clause, rather than a commitment with a penalty for nonfulfillment. But the ability to negotiate that kind of flexible deal will depend on a mixture of the company's desire to penetrate the market and competition. But if the "best efforts" of the U.S. company prove not to be successful in obtaining and marketing countertrade goods, there may be no next time in selling products to that nation. Future contracts are likely to depend a great deal on the success of earlier ones. Perhaps the best advice is to allow the U.S. party to find and accept *any* local goods, rather than specifying certain goods. But even if that flexibility is possible, it is best to have a fairly good idea of what goods are available and the company's capacity to dispose of them in its own nation or a third nation.

E. COUNTERTRADE IN THE CONTEXT OF A JOINT VENTURE

§ 5.28 Compensation Countertrade and a Joint Venture

Approval of a joint venture by a foreign government may be conditioned upon the joint venture exporting products of a set amount, possibly related to the value of equipment, machinery and technology imported by the joint venture. The products exported are most likely those to be produced by the joint venture, and in such case would constitute compensation or buy-back countertrade. Such arrangement has been most often associated with nonmarket economy nations, but may take place with developing nations. The joint venture agreement might mandate countertrade, or it may be the natural result of a shortage of hard currency, requiring the company to take out its profit in the form of part of the production of the joint venture.

Compensation assures the joint venture of a market for part of its production. This may mean the foreign company will work hard to achieve the lower costs necessary to export goods long before otherwise expected. If the wage rates are low and production efficient, the compensation-agreement goods may actually be obtained for less than the U.S. company could itself produce them. Costs attributable to countertrade may be very difficult to measure, especially in a nonmarket economy

§ 5.27

1. McDonnell–Douglas agreed to accept, in partial exchange for its aircraft, numerous items including hams. See Grant T. Hammond, Offset, Arms and Innovation, 10 Wash.Q. 172, 176 (Winter 1987).

enterprise, but the increasing costs of a countertrade agreement must be calculated and added to the agreement.

If the company takes back part of its production, it will have to be able to market that production. It may not wish to "compete" with its home plant production and may have to look for new foreign markets. For example, if a U.S./Polish joint venture is producing furniture in Poland and the U.S. company does not wish to sell its compensation products in the United States, it will have to find new markets, perhaps in Europe. That may involve problems in the chosen market area with subsidies, dumping, tariffs, and the myriad of other problems facing imports. German furniture makers may no more wish to have the furniture sold in Germany than the parent company wishes to have the furniture compete with its own products in the United States.

F. POLICY POSITIONS CONCERNING COUNTERTRADE

§ 5.29 Governments and International Organizations

Governments and international organizations may have very different views regarding countertrade. These views may be expressed in laws or departmental statements. They obviously should be considered by a company planning or subjected to countertrade.[1]

§ 5.30 United States Government Policy

The U.S. government has made no statement regarding countertrade,[1] although it is generally opposed to government *mandated* countertrade.[2] A policy was established in 1983 but never made official. That policy stated that the United States believed countertrade to be contrary to the free trading system, but it would not attempt to restrict U.S. companies from engaging in countertrade. U.S. agencies were prohibited from promoting countertrade, and they are to advise companies that countertrade products remain subject to U.S. trade laws, including tariffs and quotas. Despite these restrictions, the Department of Agriculture is clearly allowed by law to barter agricultural commodities held by the government, and the Department of Defense is allowed by law to barter U.S. National Defense Stockpile commodities. For example, a 1982 agreement between Jamaica and the United States traded Jamaican bauxite to be added to the National Defense Stockpile in exchange

§ 5.29

1. See Department of Commerce, Individual Country Practices in International Countertrade (1992).

§ 5.30

1. See Marie J. Oh, The Need for a United States Countertrade Policy, 7 Nw. J.Int'l L. & Bus. 113 (1985).

2. See Pompiliu Verzariu, Trends and Developments in International Countertrade, 2 Bus. Am. (Nov. 2, 1992).

for U.S. dairy products held by the Commodity Credit Corporation.[3] In reality, each department within the U.S. government is likely to view countertrade uniquely. Most acknowledge it to be one of the many forms of international business which is going to be used with or without the blessing of the government. The Internal Revenue Service has expressed concern about countertrade transactions which avoid taxation. Simple barter is usually undeclared as a taxable transaction. The U.S. seller receives products in lieu of taxable dollars, and will use the products in its own operations rather than sell them in another ordinarily taxable transaction. But the way counterpurchase is often structured, with separate documentary sales and a third protocol agreement, should not result in a transaction which escapes taxation.

Government expressions tend to object to countertrade because it allegedly distorts free trade and is not economically efficient. It is contrary to the free trade system promoted by the WTO nations. The receipt or "purchase" of the foreign goods in countertrade is viewed as involuntary, and harmful to other sellers whose products would be preferred in a fully arm's length transaction. But no U.S. trade law expressly deals with countertrade.[4] Goods involved in countertrade are essentially indistinguishable from other goods. Statistics maintained by the United States do not help in identifying a transaction as part of countertrade.

Offset countertrade was the subject of a U.S. government study required under 1984 amendments to the Defense Production Act.[5] The study found that nearly all transactions where offset was used involved NATO countries or others with which the United States has special agreements regarding national defense. But the report suggested that the figures illustrate that the magnitude of such sales is quite small in proportion to the total exports by the subject companies for their military production sales. Countertrade allowed U.S. companies to remain competitive in foreign sales although their principal sales were to the U.S. government, allowed foreign governments to strengthen certain industries and gain needed foreign exchange, and increased foreign competition.[6] The report never responded to Congressional desire to learn more about the frequency of use of offsets, the dollar amounts involved in offset agreements, which nations most used offsets, and what products were principally involved. Congress requested the General Accounting Office to study the report.

---

3. See Note, Bauxite for Butter: The U.S.–Jamaican Agreement and the Future of Barter in U.S. Trade Policy, 16 Law & Pol'y Int'l Bus. 239 (1984).

4. It might be possible to bring a Tariff Act of 1930 § 337 action against a countertrade arrangement on the grounds that it is an unfair import practice. 19 U.S.C. § 1337. But § 337 received a GATT death penalty ruling and may be eliminated from U.S. law.

5. Defense Production Act Amendments of 1984, codified as amended at 50 U.S.C.A. app. § 2099.

6. Office of Management & Budget, Impact of Offsets in Defense–Related Exports x-xi 1985.

The International Trade Commission undertook a separate study of countertrade in general and offsets in particular. These two provided the Congress with some of the information missing in the report noted above. The Omnibus Trade and Competitiveness Act of 1988 established a Barter Office in the Department of Commerce.[7] The Office is responsible for organizing and disseminating countertrade information, and for providing assistance to enterprises seeking barter and countertrade opportunities. It also notifies government agencies of countertrade opportunities to assist in the disposition of U.S. government owned surplus commodities.

The 1989 National Defense Authorization Act caused the president to adopt a policy on offsets in military exports.[8] The policy, announced in 1990, reemphasizes the commitment of the United States to free and fair trade, and the belief that offsets for military exports are "economically inefficient and market distorting."[9] But acknowledging that United States firms must be able to compete for military export sales, the policy forbids U.S. agencies from encouraging, entering into or committing U.S. firms to any offset arrangement regarding the sale of defense goods or services. Government funds may not be used to finance offsets in security assistance transactions beyond then current policies. This policy essentially left the policy of offsets with private companies. The policy can only be altered by the president through the National Security Council. The policy lastly requires the Secretary of Defense, in coordination with the Secretary of State, to consult with foreign nations to attempt to gain agreements to limit the adverse effects of offsets in defense procurement.

The U.S. Export–Import Bank, and other insuring or export credit institutions (Coface, ECGD), have generally disliked countertrade and for the most part refused to insure countertrade risks. The private market provides some insurance, but at higher cost. Insurance is thought necessary in much export trade because of the chronic debt of many nations, repeated recessions and uncertain government participation and changing policies toward imports. The Export–Import Bank will not finance the countertrade portion of a transaction, but it will finance the U.S. export portion. Repayment to the bank may not be dependant upon the success of the full countertrade agreement. The bank will consider the impact of the full transaction on U.S. industry, and tends not to finance projects where U.S. produced-goods are adversely affected by the countertrade goods.

The Overseas Private Investment Corporation (OPIC) is not allowed to participate in any project which involves performance requirements that adversely affect U.S. trade, but OPIC has substantial discretion in evaluating projects.

7. 102 Stat. 1107, § 2205(b).

8. 10 U.S.C.A. § 2505.

9. Id. The U.S. government offsets policy is included in Department of Commerce, International Countertrade, A Guide for Managers and Executives 4 (1992).

§ 5.31 United States Trade Law

Any countertrade arrangement is subject to U.S. trade law. Countertrade goods might be challenged under countervailing duty law if the foreign goods were subsidized,[1] or under antidumping law if the foreign goods are being sold at less than fair value in the United States.[2] The fact that the goods are part of a countertrade transaction does not insulate them from countervailing or antidumping duties. Nor will it insulate them from charges under any one of numerous other U.S. laws governing various aspects of international trade. Such challenges could create problems under the protocol agreement, and even give rise to the application of contract penalty provisions.

In addition to the countervailing duty and antidumping duty laws mentioned above, a Department of Commerce guide identifies the following additional provisions of the principal laws governing U.S. international trade which might be violated by a countertrade transaction:[3]

(1) Escape Clause or safeguard provisions, often referred to as Section 201 actions;[4]

(2) Responses to unfair methods of competition and unfair acts in the importation of goods, often referred to as Section 337 actions;[5]

(3) Imports which threaten national security, sometimes referred to as Section 232 actions;[6]

(4) Imports from communist countries which materially injure domestic injuries, often called "market disruption" or Section 406 actions;[7] and

(5) Acts which violate trade agreements, or deny U.S. rights under such agreements, or are unjustifiable, unreasonable or discriminatory restrictions, often called Section 301 actions.[8]

The Department of Commerce guide also notes the following additional acts and applicable sections as affecting countertrade:

(1) Commodity Credit Corporation Charter Act of 1949;[9]

(2) The Agricultural Act of 1949;[10]

(3) Federal Property and Administrative Services Act of 1949;[11]

---

§ 5.31

1. 19 U.S.C.A. § 1671 et seq.; 19 U.S.C.A. § 1303; infra, chapter 13.

2. 19 U.S.C.A. § 1673 et seq.; infra, chapter 12.

3. See Department of Commerce, International Countertrade: A Guide for Managers and Executives 5 (1992).

4. 19 U.S.C.A. § 2251; infra, chapter15.

5. 19 U.S.C.A. § 1337, infra, chapter 24.

6. 19 U.S.C.A. § 1862.

7. 19 U.S.C.A. § 2436, infra, chapter 15.

8. 19 U.S.C.A. § 2411, infra, chapter 19.

9. 15 U.S.C.A. § 714b(h), authorizing the Commodity Credit Corporation to exchange agricultural commodities for foreign strategic and critical material.

10. 7 U.S.C.A. § 1421 et seq., amended by Food Security Act of 1985, 7 U.S.C.A. § 1431(d)(requiring a pilot program for exchanging agricultural commodities for foreign produced strategic and other materials, which expired in 1987).

11. 40 U.S.C.A. § 485(f)(allowing an agency to receive property in lieu of cash for surplus property where received property has strategic or critical value).

(4) The Agricultural Trade Development and Assistance Act of 1954;[12]

(5) Foreign Assistance Act of 1961;[13]

(6) Agricultural Trade Act of 1978;[14]

(7) Agricultural Adjustment Act;[15]

(8) The Strategic and Critical Materials Stock Piling Act;[16] and

(9) Conventional Forces in Europe Treaty Implementation Act of 1991.[17]

§ 5.32 United States Antitrust Law

U.S. antitrust law may apply to countertrade. Section 1 of the Sherman Act and other provisions that address trade restraints may apply. The countertrade portion of the transaction is not free trade, and the barter arrangement may be a kind of mutual patronage that may be suspect under antitrust theory. There have been no cases that involve allegations that countertrade violated the antitrust laws.

§ 5.33 Western European Nations

Western European nations have been uncertain about the benefits of countertrade. That may be attributed to Western European nations viewing Eastern Europe as "their" territory, and consequently disliking U.S. exporters agreeing to countertrade in order to gain access to countries which have more traditional trade linkages with Western Europe. An example is Airbus Industrie, spokespersons for which have condemned countertrade as "potentially distortive and disruptive to the growth of trade, in as much as it replaces the pressures of competition and market forces with reciprocity, protection and price-setting."[1] Western European nations do engage in considerable countertrade and much of the tone of the discussion above regarding the United States applies equally to Western Europe.

12. 7 U.S.C.A. § 1727(g)(allowing exchange of agricultural commodities owned by Commodity Credit Corporation for (1) strategic or other material not produced in the U.S., (2) items in connection with foreign economic or military aid programs, and (3) materials or equipment needed for offshore construction programs).

13. 22 U.S.C.A. § 2751 et seq. (Allowing president to provide assistance under Act in exchange for strategic raw materials).

14. 7 U.S.C.A. § 5624 (allowing agricultural commodities to be exchanged for foreign products).

15. 7 U.S.C.A. § 624 (authorizing fees or quotas on imported agricultural commodities, including those imported under countertrade, where they harm a price support program in the United States).

16. 50 U.S.C.A. § 98 et seq. (governing the management of the National Defense Stockpile and allowing barter for acquiring and disposing of strategic and critical materials).

17. It allows payment in natural resources or other materials in exchange for assistance in dismantling nuclear weapons of former USSR.

§ 5.33

1. Pierre Chanut commenting at a Vienna conference on countertrade in 1984. See Int'l Trade Rptr. 489 (October 17, 1984).

§ 5.34 Nonmarket Economy Nations

The nonmarket economies engaged extensively in countertrade until the commencement of reforms in the mid-late 1980s.[1] Countertrade was indeed most associated with Eastern European nations in the 1980s. In their efforts to assume more market economy structures, several of these nations have since rejected countertrade as a mark of what they no longer wish to be: nations with unwanted currencies which force poor quality goods on others through countertrade transactions. But with shortages of hard currency, and some difficulty in penetrating Western nation markets, they have retained countertrade as one of the forms of doing business. Russia has used countertrade rather extensively, especially in trading its oil to Cuba for sugar rather than worthless Cuban pesos. Russia has also traded natural gas to the Ukraine for such goods as uniforms and steel tubing. Russian tax inspectors have complained about the use of countertrade, because it easily avoids taxes and is often used by companies that have no bank accounts to seize for taxes.

§ 5.35 Developing Nations

Countertrade developed rather rapidly in the 1980s in some developing nations, especially in Indonesia and in several nations in Latin America.[1] Many of the Latin American nations have adopted laws which clearly allow countertrade.[2] These laws often provide for the creation of public or private trading companies with various incentives to increase the nation's exports. Exemptions may be granted from income taxes on profits from the sale of exported goods, and from laws requiring the surrender of foreign exchange obtained from countertrade export sales. Most countertrade laws have applied to private-sector imports, but there has been considerable debate regarding extending countertrade mandates to public-sector imports, i.e., government procurement.[3]

§ 5.36 Middle–East Nations

Countertrade in local manufactured products has not been a major factor in sales to the Middle–East, mainly because of the lack of exporta-

§ 5.34

1. See, e.g., Silverman, New Thinking: Current Aspects of East–West Countertrade, 3 Annual Conf. on Intellectual Property 4 (1990); Franz M. Horehager, Countertrade with the Soviet Union, 11 Whittier L.R. 347 (1989); Marcy Marino, Note, Bartering with the Bolsheviks: A Guide to Countertrading with the Soviet Union, 8 Dick.J.Int'l L. 269 (1990).

§ 5.35

1. See, e.g., Singapore Supports Countertrade While Letting Barter Die Out, 15 East Asian Executive Repts. 20 (1993); Alberto del Campo Wilson, Advantage and Disadvantage of Countertrade: The Argentine View as an Importing Country, 17 Int'l Bus.Lawyer 369 (1989); M. M. Kostecki, Countertrade: Guidelines for Developing Countries (1988); Sarah C. Carey & Sheila Avrin McLean, The United States, Countertrade and Third World Trade, 20 J.World Trade L. 441 (1986).

2. See generally Department of Commerce, Individual Country Practices in International Countertrade, (1992).

3. It is this form of countertrade requirement that creates concern in the industrialized nations, which have generally been opening government procurement under changes negotiated in the GATT and WTO agreements.

ble finished products from that area. Where there are such products, however, cash-short governments have pushed countertrade.[1] Oil barter is very prevalent, however, and often crude oil is priced under a "net-back" system, using market-related *product* prices. As oil prices drop, countries have swapped oil to finance major purchases, especially military products. Dealing with Iraq, a country in near bankruptcy in the early 1990s, generally meant using switch trading (using other credit lines).

§ 5.37 United Nations

The view of the UN is quite different than that of the United States, Western Europe or the OECD, each of which have expressed opposition to countertrade as hindering free trade. The UN, often dominated by nonmarket economy and developing nations which have viewed countertrade more positively, is assisting individuals in drafting countertrade agreements.

Several countertrade studies have been conducted by the U.N. Nations Commission on International Trade Law (UNCITRAL) and the ECE Committee on the Development of Trade. UNCITRAL completed a Legal Guide on International Countertrade Transactions.[1] The Guide considers various legal issues associated with countertrade, and constitutes one of the most important sources of information on this often illusive and secretive subject.

The ECE Committee on the Development of Trade considered several documents regarding countertrade transactions in its 1988 meeting, including sample counterpurchase and buy-back agreements.

§ 5.38 GATT/WTO

Countertrade is not the form of free trade on which the GATT was based. Since the GATT addressed many areas which constitute abuses of free trade, it might well have considered countertrade an appropriate topic.[1] But the WTO Agreement does not address countertrade as a specific form of trade.

§ 5.36

1. See Countertrade Offset Program (Kuwait), 16 Middle East Executive Rep. 27 (1993); Abla Abdel–Latif, The Egyptian Experience with Countertrade: Case Studies, 24 J.World Trade 17 (No. 5, 1990); Somay, Countertrade and Turkey, 12 Middle East Executive Rep. 8 (1989); Bruno, Countertrade in the Middle East, 7 Middle East Executive Rep. 18 (1984).

§ 5.37

1. U.N. Comm'n on Int'l Trade Law (UNCITRAL): Legal Guide on Int'l Countertrade, ch. II,¶ 25, U.N. Doc. A/CN.9/SER.B/3, U.N. Sales No. E.93.V.7 (1993). The Legal Guide is described in

James C. Nobles and Johannes Lang, The UNCITRAL Legal Guide on International Countertrade Transactions: The Foundations for a New Era in Countertrade? 30 Int'l Law. 739 (1996).

§ 5.38

1. See, e.g., William D. Zeller, Countertrade, the GATT, and the Theory of the Second Best, 11 Hastings Int'l & Comp.L.R. 247 (1988);Frieder Roessler, Countertrade and the GATT Legal System, 19 J.World Trade L. 604 (1985); Vincene Verdun, Are Governmentally Imposed Countertrade Requirements Violations of the GATT?, 11 Yale J.Int'l L. 191 (1985); Edward Michael Rieu, Note, The Application of the General

Countertrade may involve subsidies, where it increases exports of U.S. products that otherwise might be obtained by the foreign nation from other, traditional markets. But when the United States takes products from a developing nation in return for goods the developing nation could not otherwise afford due to a lack of hard currency, it is helping the developing nation create new markets, which is consistent with the WTO Agreement on Subsidies and Countervailing Measures. If the developing nation is viewed to be allocating its hard currency for other purchases, as opposed to having inadequate hard currency for any purchases, it is less clear that countertrade would be WTO consistent.

If a WTO benefit is being nullified or impaired by a countertrade agreement, a nation might attempt to use GATT Article XXIII to initiate a complaint. But if countertrade results in trade being initiated, is anything being impaired other than "potential" trade? One might also consider Article I MFN treatment under the GATT and conclude that the special arrangements made to admit nonmarket nations to the WTO in Article XVII do not allow countertrade.

§ 5.39   OECD

The Organization for Economic Cooperation and Development has undertaken studies of countertrade.[1] Its study of East–West trade in 1981 warned against a policy of "no policy", because countertrade was developing at a rapid rate and decisions of firms might be contrary to the interests of the member nations of the OECD and their relations with the nations engaged in East–West trade.

G.   CONCLUSIONS

§ 5.40   Future of Countertrade

Countertrade began to intensify in use after World War II, mainly as the hard currency-short Eastern European nations increased trade with Western nations which were reluctant to buy the former nations' products. But countertrade quite rapidly spread to many other parts of the world, especially developing nations. Latin American countertrade has increased substantially since the early 1980s. Although some of the Eastern European nations have stated that they will reduce countertrade as part of their market economy oriented reforms, much seems to depend on their ability to successfully market their products abroad. Countertrade is here to stay. To be successful in countertrade arrangements, a company must learn how to accomplish some very complex negotiating, which cannot but help it in other trading as new, esoteric

Agreement on Tariffs and Trade to the Countertrade Practices of the Less-developed and Developing Countries: Proposed Amendments to the GATT, 16 Calif.West.Int'l L.J. 312 (1986).

§ 5.39

1. OECD, East–West Trade, Recent Developments in Countertrade (1981); OECD, Countertrade: Developing Country Practices (1985).

forms arise. Additionally, a company that has been willing to accept countertrade to gain entry to a market may be in a very advantageous position when the nation becomes better off in accumulating hard currency for direct cash purchases.

Some countertrade may distort free or nearly free markets, partly because it is bilateral rather than multilateral trade. Imports under a countertrade agreement may disadvantageously affect the market, and may cause unemployment and depressed prices. Because it is often difficult to identify a true price for the countertrade goods, it is hard to identify and measure dumping. Whatever distortions in free trade are attributed to countertrade, it is a method of international trading which sophisticated trading enterprises must learn and add to more common forms. The expertise in countertrade transactions has lagged behind the number of transactions. Experience and a long-term approach to countertrade are necessary ingredients to success. Some companies have suggested that it takes at least three years to show results from an in-house countertrade entity, and a General Electric spokesperson noted that GE had "nurtured" its trading capability over a 20 year period.[1] Countertrade is thus usually considered to be a service center in the same way as market research or finance, rather than a separate profit center.[2] However it is considered, company willingness to use countertrade may result in rewards for the additional effort.

H. SELECTED DOCUMENTS*

§ 5.41 Counterpurchase Contract With India

No. MMTC/91–92   Dated:

This Agreement hereinafter referred to as "Countertrade Agreement" is made this _____ day of _____ 1991 between the Minerals & Metals Trading Corporation of India Ltd., New Delhi, represented by their Export Division (hereinafter referred to as "MMTC"), which expression shall unless excluded by or repugnant to the context include its successors and assignors, of the first part and M/s _____, a company established under the laws of and having its Regd. office at _____ and represented by their duly constituted attorneys (hereinafter referred to as "Overseas Supplier") of the second part.

AND WHEREAS THE Overseas Supplier has signed a contract with MMTC No. _____ dated _____ (hereinafter referred to as "Import Contract") for supply of _____ valued at US $_____

---

§ 5.40

1. Int'l Trade Rptr. 489 (Oct. 17, 1984). But in 1986 GE Trading announced that it was halting its countertrade program. Losses on large transactions caused several major countertraders to make similar announcements. But others, including Mitsui and Mitsubishi, were making announcements to increase countertrade.

2. The company may bill product divisions for the countertrade services when a sale is made.

* Documents 2.41 through 2.47 are reprinted from the Department of Commerce "International Countertrade: A Guide for Managers and Executives."

AND WHEREAS it was provided in Clause No. _____ of the Import Contract that the Overseas Supplier shall purchase or cause to be purchased Indian Goods, Commodities, Services (hereinafter referred to as "Goods") from Indian Companies and export the Goods from India for an amount and within a time period in accordance with the provisions of this Agreement.

NOW THEREFORE IT IS MUTUALLY AGREED TO BETWEEN THE PARTIES HERETO AS FOLLOWS:

DEFINITION OF TERMS

Clause 1

1.1   In this Agreement, unless the context otherwise provides

1.2   Indian Goods, Commodities and Services, means, any goods, commodities, services manufactured/produced within India with the exclusion of Free Trade Zones or Export Promotion Zones, so designated by Appropriate authorities. It shall also include services by Indian companies outside India, the earnings from which is fully repatriated to India. Indian companies means any corporate body established under the law of India, including sole proprietorship.

1.3   Countertrade means purchase and export of goods, commodities and services from India by an Overseas Supplier of a value equivalent to a specified percentage of the value of the import contract, payments for either link of the transaction to be on mutually acceptable terms.

1.4   For the purpose of countertrade under this Agreement, the list of goods can include items listed in Annexure–1 and excludes all items listed in Annexure–2 enclosed.

PURCHASE AND EXPORT

Clause 2

2.1   The Overseas Supplier shall purchase Indian goods, directly or through MMTC, from Indian companies and export them from India in accordance with this Agreement.

2.2   The sum of such purchase of goods and their subsequent export from India under this Agreement shall be in the value of _____ based on the FOB prices of goods so purchased and exported out of India (hereinafter referred to as "Export Obligation").

2.3   Subject to Sub-clause 2.4, the Overseas Supplier shall commence export of goods from India subsequent to the date of the Countertrade Agreement and shall complete such exports up to a total sum as per Sub-clause 2.2, and do so no later than 12 months from the date of the import contract.

2.4   Notwithstanding the provisions in Sub-clause 2.3, if the Overseas Supplier is not able to complete the obligations for exports of Indian goods as per Sub-clause 2.2, within the time period stipulated in Subclause 2.3, they may at the discretion of MMTC for reasons other than force majeure under Clause 8, be granted an extension of the period stipulated in Sub-clause 2.3 based on MMTC's evaluation of the need for granting such an extension which shall not exceed _____ months in total.

2.5   The date of export performance by the Overseas Supplier, as per this Agreement, shall be linked to the dates of the bill of lading of the export.

2.6   The Overseas Supplier may send an enquiry to MMTC for the goods they intend to purchase and export as per this Agreement. Wherever MMTC is able to make an offer directly as principal on competitive terms, MMTC and the Overseas Supplier will enter into separate contracts for each transaction on mutually agreed terms and conditions. Alternatively, the Overseas Supplier may at its option make arrangements for purchases from alternate sources of supply within India. However, such deals must be referred to MMTC immediately upon finalization indicating the export deal finalization date, the goods proposed to be bought, the name of the buyer, the name of the Indian seller, the goods' prices/quantity, the total value, the payment terms, etc., along with the agreement duly signed by the Indian seller in terms of Sub-clause 2.7 for our specific approval before proceeding with the exports. In all such cases, the Overseas Supplier shall indemnify MMTC from all losses, obligations, risks and responsibilities arising out of such arrangement.

2.7   In case of payment on CAD basis, the Indian seller will be required to enter into an agreement with MMTC as per Annexure 6 appended to this Agreement.

2.8   Payments for exports of goods by the Overseas Supplier in terms of this Agreement shall be governed by the "documentation procedure" relating to export documentary credits, as per Annexure 3 appended to this Agreement.

PERFORMANCE BANK GUARANTEE

Clause 3

3.1   The Overseas Supplier shall furnish to MMTC within 15 days of the signing of this Agreement a security deposit in the form of an export performance bank guarantee (hereinafter referred to as "EPBG") as per Annexure 4 attached herewith. The EPBG shall be confirmed by an Indian nationalized bank, having its duly authenticated branch office in Delhi. This security deposit in the form of EPBG shall be for a sum of US $_____ being _____ percent of the value of the export obligation of the Overseas Supplier as per Sub-clause 2.2 of this Agreement. The amount secured herein shall be payable to MMTC on demand, notwithstanding any arbitration proceedings under Clause 11, for any breach of any provisions of this Agreement, on the part of the Overseas Supplier. The validity of this EPBG shall be from the date of the issue up to two months after the stipulated period for completion of the export obligations.

3.2   The validity of the EPBG shall be extended by the Overseas Supplier for a further period up to _____ months in case any extension is granted as per Sub-clause 2.4 of this Agreement.

3.3   MMTC shall release the EPBG after deducting the amount of liquidated damages, if any, due to MMTC under Clause 8 of this Agreement after the export obligations of the Overseas Supplier as per various clauses of this Agreement have been duly fulfilled.

Clause 4

4.1   The Overseas Supplier would have to submit "non negotiable" copies of the various export shipping documents to MMTC as proofs of exports required to be made by him as per Sub-clause 2.2 of this Agreement. These documents must be presented to MMTC within 30 days from the date of B/L in accordance with the documentation procedure as per Annexure 3, otherwise countertrade credit will not be allowed by MMTC.

4.2   Within 15 days from the submission of documents as per Clause 4.1, in case the documents are in order and evidence satisfactory fulfillment of the countertrade obligation, MMTC will issue a certificate confirming the acceptable value of exports as per Annexure 5 attached herein, towards the value accountable towards the fulfillment of the export obligation of the Overseas Supplier.

ASSIGNMENT

Clause 5

5.1   The Overseas Supplier can purchase from India directly or through nominees. Nominees/assignees may be changed on a selective basis, as and when necessary, with mutual written consent of both MMTC and the countertrade obligant. The nominee/assignee cannot sub-assign in full or part the benefits and the obligations so assigned to them by the Overseas Supplier to any fourth party nor can they nominate a fourth party to fulfill the obligations so assigned to them as above. The consent for assignment of benefits and obligations of the Overseas Supplier as per this Agreement to a third party(ies) shall be given entirely at the discretion of MMTC and the same shall not relieve the Overseas Supplier from any liabilities or obligations under this Agreement.

Clause 6

6.1   If the import contract is cancelled for any reason whatsoever, the Overseas Supplier's obligation under this contract shall not, to the extent of the value of goods purchased by MMTC under the import contracts, be relieved; PROVIDED ALWAYS that such cancellation shall not prejudice or affect any right of action or remedy which shall have accrued or shall accrue thereafter to MMTC.

Clause 7

7.1   This Agreement shall be deemed to have been completed upon the occurrence of any of the following events:

7.1.1   MMTC releases the EPBG upon fulfillment of export obligations as per Clause 2.2.

7.1.2   The Overseas Supplier has paid the liquidated damages to MMTC as per Clause 8.

7.1.3   The import contract is cancelled for any reason as provided under relevant clauses of the import contract.

Clause 8

8.1   Subject to any extension of time that may be allowed by MMTC under Sub-clause 2.4 of this Agreement, the failure of the Overseas Supplier to fulfill the countertrade obligations as per this Agreement shall be subject to liquidated damages in the following manner:

8.1.1   If only less than 50 percent of the export obligations has been fulfilled within the time period specified under Clause 2 of this Agreement, than 100 percent of the EPBG would be forfeited.

8.1.2   If only 50 percent or more of the export obligations as per Sub-clause 2.2 of this Agreement has been fulfilled within the stipulated time as per Clause 2 of this Agreement, then the encashment of the EPBG would be on a pro-rata basis of the unfulfilled part of the export obligations.

Clause 9

9.1   The Overseas Supplier shall not be liable for any delay due to labor strike, fire, floods, war, riot and any other circumstances beyond its control by reason of Force Majeure and which materially affects the due performance of its export obligations under this Agreement. The Overseas Supplier shall notify the MMTC with documentary proof as soon as any such Force Majeure occurs.

9.2   The Overseas Supplier shall provide MMTC with all the necessary proof of the occurrence of any of the aforementioned events and of their effect on the Overseas Supplier's export obligations, should it wish to apply for an extension of the date of completion of the export obligations under Sub-clause 2.4. Failure to provide MMTC with the necessary proof shall not entitle the Overseas Supplier to make a claim under this Clause. MMTC shall be entitled to conduct an investigation into the delay immediately, and if the Overseas Supplier is unable to fulfill its export obligations under this Agreement within the period stipulated in Sub-clause 2.4 by reason of Force Majeure as above, MMTC shall, if it has reasonable grounds for believing the reason given in the notice, extend the period of completion of the export obligations as MMTC thinks fit.

Clause 10

10.1   All export purchases and subsequent exports of goods as per this Agreement shall be subject to the policy, guidelines and procedures laid down by the Government of India from time to time during the time this Agreement is in force.

ARBITRATION

Clause 11

11.1   Any dispute/difference arising out of this Agreement shall be settled in a friendly and amicable manner between the two parties. Should this not be possible, then the procedures under the Indian Arbitration Act will apply. The place of arbitration shall be New Delhi. The arbitrator shall give reasoned award.

Clause 12

12.1   Normally, all export invoicing and Letters of Credit would be in freely convertible U.S. dollars. Should any export be invoiced in any other freely convertible currency, then, for the purpose of assessment of fulfillment under the Agreement, the invoice value would be converted into U.S. dollars at the rate of exchange prevailing between these currencies on the date of the presentation of documents to the bank for payment. The rate of exchange would be as determined by the Reserve Bank of India.

COMMUNICATION

Clause 13

13.1   All communications shall be made to the party at the address first set forth above or communicated in writing by either party to another.

Clause 14

14.1   This Agreement shall be governed and construed in accordance with the laws of India.

14.2   The Overseas Supplier hereby irrevocably submits to the exclusive jurisdiction of the Courts of India.

ADDITIONALITY

Clause 15

The purpose of the Counterpurchase Agreement is to generate additional exports and not to divert existing exports from India.

Additionality is to be seen with reference to the base level of export of the individual Indian exporter. In this regard, exports of the Indian exporter for a particular commodity and to a particular destination in the base year would be relevant.

An Additionality Certificate is to be furnished by the Indian exporter accordingly.

IN WITNESS WHEREOF, the parties hereto have caused this Agreement to be executed in their respective names and by their only authorized representatives, the day and year first above written.

Signed for and on behalf of	Signed for and on behalf of
The Minerals & Metals Trading	Overseas Supplier/Countertrade
Corporation of India Ltd.,	Obligant
New Delhi	

In the presence of
Witness
1.
2.

§ 5.42   Counterpurchase Contract With Russia

Concerning the cooperation in the erection of a complex for the production of polyester fibers, polyester threads and their raw materials in Russia, and the delivery of chemicals and cotton entered into by the Ministry for Foreign Trade of Russia, Moscow, as the party of the first part and the firms [NAMES] as the parties of the second part.

WITNESSETH

Article 1

1.1   The parties to this agreement shall cooperate in erecting a complex for the production of polyester fibers, polyester threads, and their raw materials in Russia, comprising:

	Capacity in Tons/Year
Polyester Fibers	35,000
Polyethylene Terephthalate (Granulate)	57,000
Polyester Threads	24,000
Polyester Threads	28,000
Polyester Fibers	50,000
Polyester Fibers	50,000

1.2   The firms listed below shall submit technical and commercial offers for the licensing, transfer of technical documentation for the delivery of the complete equipment (hereinafter called "equipment") and the granting of services on the facilities listed under numeral 1.1, not later than by the deadline listed below, to V/O "Techmashimport" Moscow:

(a) [GENERAL CONTRACTOR FIRM'S NAME] for the facilities

(b) [ENGINEERING FIRM'S NAME] according to the know-how of [TECHNOLOGY LICENSOR'S NAME] for the facilities:

Polyester Fibers	35,000	tons/year	April 15, 197–
Polyethylene Terephthalate (Granulate)	57,000	"	June 15, 197–
Polyester Threads	24,000	"	June 15, 197–
Polyester Threads	28,000	"	July 15, 197–
Polyester Fibers	50,000	"	July 1, 197–
Polyester Fibers	50,000	"	Sept. 1, 197–

Article 2

2.1 V/O "Techmashimport" and the firms mentioned under numeral 1.2 shall, if they agree on reciprocally acceptable technical and commercial terms, conclude agreements about the licensing and transfer of the technical documentation (including the projection documentation), delivery of the equipment and the performance of services, including supervision of the erection, start of the operation of the facilities and training of Soviet technical personnel for which the corresponding firms shall present offers as per numeral 1.2.

V/O "Techmashimport" and the firms mentioned above shall agree on the method of the conclusion of the agreements, including their sequence.

The technical documentation and equipment to be furnished by the suppliers for the facilities listed in numeral 1.1 shall be on the level of world engineering standards in the area involved, which will assure the production of products with a high value.

The warranty conditions and the liability of said suppliers for meeting the responsibilities assumed by them shall be determined in agreements to be concluded between V/O "Techmashimport" and the said firms.

2.2 V/O "Techmashimport" has the right to request offers on licensing, transfer of technical documentation, delivery of equipment and performance of services for the facilities listed in numeral 1 at all times from any third party firms. If *comparable* offers from any third party firms prove to be more favorable for V/O "Techmashimport", the aforementioned suppliers shall improve the conditions of their offers. If during the negotiations no agreement is reached about reciprocally acceptable technical and commercial terms, V/O "Techmashimport" may conclude agreements with third party firms.

Article 3

3.1 The parties to the agreement rely on the premises that the purchase of the licenses, technical documentations, equipment and services listed under article 1 of this agreement will be effected on the condition of the granting of long-term, project-bound *bank loans* for *85%* of the contractual amounts, 15% of the contractual values being paid in cash. It is further assumed that the detailed terms of these loans shall be set forth in the agreement(s) between the Foreign Trade Bank of Russia and the banks of the [WEST EUROPEAN COUNTRY]. If it should turn out that it is impossible to obtain bank loans, both sides shall search for other forms of credit.

3.2 The parties to the agreement further assume that under the licensing, delivery of technical documentation and equipment, and under the performance of services from countries with which the USSR maintains loan agreements on a government level, the financing of such operations shall take place under the terms of the credit agreements concluded on government levels.

3.3 The parties to the agreement are obligated to promote the credit negotiations. The supplier firms of the [WEST EUROPEAN COUNTRY] shall use their influence so that the loans will be made available by the banks at the best possible terms.

Credit negotiations shall be conducted as rapidly as possible. Such discussions shall be attended on the one hand by representatives of the Ministry for Foreign Trade of Russia and the Bank for Foreign Trade of Russia and on the other hand, the [WEST EUROPEAN COUNTRY] banks and the supplier firms, in order to reach an agreement about the essential terms of the loan contracts to be entered into.

Article 4

4.1 The buyers, [NAMES OF THREE WEST EUROPEAN BUYERS], shall conclude at the same time long-term agreements with the vendors V/O "Sojuzchimexport" and/or V/O "Exportljon", Moscow, concerning the supply of chemicals and cotton from Russia, if they agree on reciprocally acceptable terms.

The total value of these agreements shall correspond with the entire value payable by V/O "Techmashimport" in foreign exchange to the supplier firms according to the agreements covering licenses, technical documentation, equipment and services, including interest on loans.

4.2 The vendors and buyers listed under numeral 4.1 shall sell and/or purchase the following products and quantities:

BUYER	PRODUCT	QUANTITIES IN 1000 TONS/YEAR	START OF DELIVERIES
[BUYER A]	DMT	20	198–
	Para–Xylol	20	Will be agreed on by the end of 198–
	Methanol	30	198–
[BUYER B]	Methanol	40	198–
	Ortho Xylol	20	Will be agreed on by the end of 198–
	Acetic Acid	10	198–
[BUYER C]	Cotton	30	198– (198–; 19,000 tons)

4.3 The parties to the agreement assume thereby that in view of the expected price trends, the full value will have to be reached not later than 12 years effective with the beginning of the deliveries as set forth under numeral 4.1.

If the *full value* cited in numeral 4.1 is reached earlier than at the aforementioned deadline, the obligations of the parties to the agreement concerning the sale and/or purchase of the products are considered as having been met.

If it becomes obvious that the total value cited in numeral 4.1 for all contracts cannot be reached within the time limit quoted in said numeral, the buyer(s) unable to attain the total value cited in its (their) *individual contract* shall try to reach an agreement in time with V/O "Sojuzchimexport" and/or V/O "Exportljon" about increasing the scope of the delivery of the goods according to numeral 4.2 and/or about an extension of the above time limit by reciprocal accord. If Russian foreign trade associations can offer other products, this question may be decided on by mutual agreement between the contracting parties.

Article 5

5.1 The prices for the chemicals mentioned in article 4 of this agreement shall be determined by the parties to the contract per metric ton net, CIF West European basic ports.

The prices shall be determined for a period of 6 months, in each case 2 months prior to the start of such a period (or for other periods to be agreed on between the parties to the contract), on the basis of the world market prices which are determined on the basis of the following documents:

— Agreements in effect on export and import transactions, except transactions of the vendor with RGW countries and transactions of the buyer with his branches and under barter transactions;

— Inquiries and quotation of the firms;

— Customs statistics of the countries into which said chemicals will be exported;

— Publications (newspapers, magazines, etc.) reproducing the trends of market development for these products;

— Other representative and objective data on the market situation of these products.

5.2 The prices for cotton shall be determined by V/O "Exportljon" and [BUYER C] per metric ton net CIF West European basic ports for periods to be agreed on on the basis of world market quotations. V/O "Exportljon" and [BUYER C] shall premise themselves in their agreements on prices for cotton on the principle of cooperation, reciprocal benefit and competitive conditions according to the international commercial practice for cotton.

Article 6

6.1 The agreements about the delivery of equipment according to article 2 and the long-term agreements about the delivery of chemicals and cotton according to article 4 shall become effective simultaneously, with the premise that the agreements about the delivery of chemicals and cotton according to article 4 shall be concluded prior to or simultaneously with the contracts on the delivery of equipment according to article 2.

A tie-in of the sale of Russian products with the purchase of licenses, technical documentation, equipment and services by V/O "Techmashimport" can be established only in the agreements between V/O "Sojuzchimexport" and V/O "Exportljon" and the buyer firms involved. The parties to the agreement shall take every possible measure for the agreements to be concluded as soon as possible following the execution of the present contract.

These agreements will become effective only following the resolution of financing problems in connection with the loans to be granted for the licenses, technical documentation, equipment and services to be performed.

6.2 Each contracting partner is liable only for the accomplishment of the obligations it assumes in each individual agreement on the basis of this contract.

Article 7

7.1 In consideration of the high significance of the cooperation of the partners to this contract, under the present agreement, and of the large scope of the reciprocal deliveries of equipment and merchandise on a long-term basis, the parties to the agreement shall engage in joint efforts to take all measures necessary to secure the obligations assumed according to this agreement.

7.2 Any disputes and differences of opinion which could arise out of this agreement shall be solved by way of negotiations between the contracting partners under this agreement. The invocation of any courts (including arbitration courts) by the contracting parties under this agreement is ruled out.

Article 8

Agreements concluded in harmony with the present agreement shall provide for licensing conditions, terms of delivery, including among other matters, scope, prices, delivery dates, terms of payment, warranties, shipping conditions, liability of the contractual partners according to the contracts for compliance with their terms, type of settlement of possible disputes, etc.

Article 9

The present agreement becomes effective as of the date of signing and remains in force until all obligations under the contracts concluded on its basis have been complied with.

This present agreement has been signed on February 20, 197–, in two originals, each original being drawn up in the Russian and [WEST EUROPEAN] languages, in [WEST EUROPEAN CITY], whereby both texts are equally binding.

    For the Russian side   For the [WEST EUROPEAN] side

[Author's Note: This contract form was adapted from a form applicable to the former USSR.]

§ 5.43   Offset Agreement With Israel

Standard document provided to contractors/suppliers bidding on public tenders by Israel's Industrial Cooperation Authority (ICA), the public agency charged with negotiating and ensuring compliance with offset commitments.

AGREEMENT

between

_____ with its registered office a _____

_____

(hereinafter called _____),

and

Industrial Cooperation Authority with its principal office at 35, Shaul Hamelech Blvd, Tel Aviv (hereinafter called ICA). An agreement to promote an Industrial Cooperation based on reciprocity.

DEFINITIONS

The "Supply Contract" means a contract to be made between _____ with _____ (hereinafter called _____) relating to the provisions of _____ .

"Industrial Goods" means goods, the substantial manufacturing of which has been performed in Israel, mainly by the Electrical, Electronic, Plastic and Metal Industries, or by other industries approved by ICA. Those goods may be either purchases, subcontracting or others as agreed by the parties.

"Substantial Manufacturing" means at least 35% value added.

OPERATIVE PROVISIONS

1. This agreement shall come into force on the date the "Supply Contract" comes into force (hereinafter called Effective Date).

2. Subject to hereinafter, _____ undertakes within _____ years of the "Effective Date", to reciprocate in the areas as detailed in paragraph 11 below.

3. The value of the total reciprocity according to paragraph 2 above, will be 35% of the invoiced price in the "Supply Contract" (Invoiced price means escalated price updated).

4. Notwithstanding the foregoing, any obligations of _____ to purchase goods and/or services hereunder is based upon the condition that the goods and services being offered to _____ from Israeli suppliers are competitive.

5. The undertaking shall be carried out:

    ___% i.e. $_____ within the first period year of the agreement,

    ___% i.e. $_____ within each of the _____ following years.

6. If the agreement specifies that the fulfillment should be carried out during a period which exceeds three (3) years, the residual amount of the undertaking after the third year, should be linked to the official inflation rate in the country of the seller in supply contracts which have no escalation clause.

7. Concerning purchases:

    a. Engineering Services and/or manufactured goods may be valued as at the point of delivery to the purchasing entity or as C.I.F. port entry at the option of _____.

    b. The _____ will prove to satisfaction of ICA the performance of its obligation by presenting documentation asked by ICA.

    c. ICA will be informed, twice a year (December and June) of the current status of purchases made or carried to be made from Israel under this Agreement. Meetings between ICA and _____ will be held regularly to discuss the progress of this Agreement. Such meetings being held at mutually convenient times and venues.

    d. Within 90 days of the "Effective Date" of this Agreement, _____ will:

        1) Submit to ICA lists of subjects/items in which _____ is interested, i.e.: to invest, co-produce, cooperate with Israeli industry or purchase.

        2) Make a survey of Israeli industry by sending a survey team.

        3) Name or appoint its representative in Israel for the purpose of fulfiling its obligations under this Agreement and inform ICA of the above.

8. _____ will do its utmost that its orders will have the potential of being repeated or extended. Where appropriate, in requests for quotations to Israeli suppliers, special emphasis should be placed on the fact that the order may be repeated; with mention being made of the exact period of supply.

9. In order to enable _____ to fulfill its commitments outlined in this Agreement, ICA will endeavour to assist _____'s request in obtaining bids from suitable Israeli sources, whenever asked to do so.

10. All correspondence relating to purchases from the Israeli source will be directed by _____ to the relevant Israeli suppliers.

11. The following transactions, according to ICA's priority, shall be credited to _____'s purchase obligations:

    a. Direct investment in Israeli Industry. Any investment shall be credited against _____'s obligation to an amount of 200% of the fully paid-up capital in an Israeli company, invested in foreign currency.

    b. Transfer of industrial property rights of any kind, confirmed in advance by ICA, but only to the extent of the added value of export orders received by the Israeli licensee or recipient of the industrial property rights for the specific goods utilizing such property rights as confirmed by ICA.

    c. Co-development, and/or co-production, and/or co-marketing by the Seller and Israeli Industry, after approval by ICA. The approval will specify the terms and the conditions.

d. Sub-contracting by the Seller to Israeli Industry.

e. Purchases from Israeli Industry with priority to: metal, electrical, electronics, plastics and optics.

f. Transportation services purchased from an Israeli company, excluding for the delivery of goods to Israel, but limited to 10% of the offset purchasing under paragraph 2.

g. All the above transactions if carried out by a third party who designated _____ to be the beneficiary of such transactions for the purpose of fulfilling _____'s offset purchase obligation, provided that ICA has given its preliminary consent to such transaction, but limited to 50% of the value of the overall commitments. Above includes purchases by affiliated companies within the corporation (if applicable).

12. _____ shall be excused from any obligation under this Agreement or may terminate this Agreement to the extent that performance of any obligation of this Agreement is prevented or impeded due to an act of the Israeli Government, not related to an act of any third country. For the avoidance of doubt, it is agreed that such exemption is only to the extent of the effect of such prevention and limited to the item of such prevention.

13. _____ declares that it will give priority and make the effort, time and manpower, to achieve the goals of this Agreement within the timetable stated.

14. This Agreement will be governed by the law of the State of Israel and the appropriate courts shall be the courts in Israel.

15. All correspondence with ICA will be held through:
   a. for European companies—
   The European representative
   Industrial Cooperation Authority
   Embassy of Israel
   120 Bd. Malesherbes, 75017 Paris
   Tel.: 47 66 45 86

   b. for U.S. and Canadian companies—
   The U.S. Director
   Industrial Cooperation Authority
   Government of Israel Trade Center
   350 5th Ave., New York, NY 10118
   Tel.: (212) 560–0667

Date: Date:

Signed by: _____   Signed by: _____
       for and on behalf of ICA   for and on behalf of

Name and Title: _____   Name and Title: _____

§ 5.44 General Guide for the Offset Program of the Korean Telecommunication Authority

1. PURPOSE
The purpose of this "Guide" is to outline definitions, objectives, basic guidelines and procedures in support of the Offset program directed by the Korea Telecommunication Authority (KTA).

2. SCOPE OF APPLICATION
This "Guide" applies to all agencies under the KTA and Korean industries as well as all foreign contractors participating in offset programs of the KTA.

3. DEFINITIONS

    A. Offset Program:
The Offset program is work, or the provision of work, or other compensatory opportunities, directed to the Republic of Korea by foreign contractors as a result of receiving, or in anticipation of receiving, an order for equipment, material (including spare parts) or services in which the Government of the Republic of Korea is involved.

    B. Direct Offset:
Activities in the Direct Offset category are those which are directly related to the original purchase, by the Republic of Korea, of foreign equipment, material or services. Direct Offset includes the following:

        (1) Provision of opportunities to manufacture and export parts and components.

        (2) Transfer of technology to achieve the capability to manufacture, and/or manage the production of, parts and components to meet the follow-on logistic support.

        (3) Transfer of technology to obtain the maintenance capability.

        (4) Assistance in establishing industrial facilities and/or provision of equipment and tooling.

        (5) Assistance in obtaining maintenance opportunities in overseas markets for which the Republic of Korea has the technological ability.

    C. Indirect Offset:
Activities in the Indirect Offset category are those activities which are not directly related to the production of equipment originally purchased. Indirect Offset activities include the following:

        (1) Korean Industry Participation (KIP).

            (a) Activities in paragraphs 3.B.(1) through (5) which are not directly related to the original purchase.

            (b) Opportunities to participate in major research and development projects.

            (c) Assistance in establishing industrial facilities and/or provision of equipment or tooling.

            (d) Assistance in creating new employment opportunities.

            (e) Any approved activity that will enhance further Korean national, economic or industrial interests.

        (2) Counterpurchase:
Counterpurchase activities include those which are related to the purchase of telecommunication articles and general commodities. It should be noted that credit for the purchases of telecommunication articles and general commodity items will be allowed only if such purchases have been given prior approval from KTA. Counterpurchase activities include the following:

    (a) Direct purchase of, and/or assistance in selling, tele-communication articles from original Korean sources.

    (b) Direct purchase of, and/or assistance in selling, general commodities from original Korean sources.

D. Memorandum of Agreement (MOA) for Offset programs:

An addition to the basic contract setting forth the obligations and understandings of foreign contractors and the Government of the Republic of Korea with respect to the Offset program.

4. BASIC OBJECTIVES AND GUIDELINES

A. OBJECTIVES

The primary objective of the Offset program is to assist the Republic of Korea in developing and expanding its manufacturing and industrial capability. The program is intended to increase technological and industrial capabilities with an emphasis on the area of telecommunication industry.

B. GUIDELINES

(1) The Offset program will apply, on a case-by-case basis, to all major equipment, material and services purchased directly by the government of the Republic of Korea for more than one million U.S. dollars.

(2) The national goal for an individual Offset program will be at least 50% of the basic contract value. At least 20% of the basic contract value will be in the Direct Offset Category.

(3) Offset programs will be considered on a competitive basis and foreign contractors will submit Offset proposals to KTA within a required period of time. The content of the proposals will be an important factor in awarding final contracts.

(4) A Memorandum of Agreement for the Offset program will be part of, and attached to, the basic contract.

5. EVALUATION CRITERIA

A. GENERAL STANDARD

(1) The technological sophistication, the total dollar value and the length of time to complete the Offset program will be major factors in the evaluation process.

(2) It is expected that Korean equipment, material and services will be used to the maximum extent possible. Priority will be given to those Offset proposals containing a greater amount of Korean material and services.

(3) KTA will not approve those activities that do not meet selection criteria.

(4) On a case-by-case basis, a multiple factor from 3 to 10 will be given as an incentive to a foreign contractor who provides facilities, equipment and tooling.

(5) If foreign contractors, acting as intermediaries, assist in any of the following activities after receiving prior approval from KTA, such assistance will be calculated by using a factor of from 0.5 to 1.0 on a case-by-case basis:

(a) Provision of opportunities for KIP.

(b) Assistance in selling telecommunication.

      (c) Assistance in selling specific products which have never been previously exported to a third party.

      (d) Assistance in selling general commodities which have never been previously exported to a specific country.

(6) In calculating Offset credit for projects where Korean companies are utilized, only the value of the equipment, material or services provided by the Republic of Korea will be considered for Offset credit.

(7) The value of technology/know-how transfer, technical assistance and training will be calculated using the following criteria:

      (a) Technology Transfer

—Direct Offset Technology: (telecommunication field)	10% to 15% of work value provided by the contractor.
—Indirect Offset Technology: (telecommunication field)	8% to 12% of work value provided by the contractor.
—Indirect Offset Technology: (commercial)	4% to 7% of work value provided by the contractor.

      (b) Technical Assistance

Actual value of costs of transportation, lodging, food, and other costs associated with providing assistance.

      (c) Training

Credit for training will be calculated using a rate of $5,000 per class plus other costs associated with providing assistance.

(8) Financial assistance (loans) and other intangible assistance approved by KTA will be considered on a case-by-case basis.

B. CATEGORY CLASSIFICATION

The following categories are listed in order of importance:

(1) Category "A"

High national priority activities which greatly affect economic and industrial development objectives related to direct offset.

      (a) Creation, or improvement, of self-reliance by providing for:

—Ability to independently produce equipment (components).

—Ability to jointly produce equipment (components).

—Ability to produce spare parts independently.

—Ability to maintain equipment independently.

      (b) Provision of opportunities to manufacture and export parts and components.

      (c) Assistance in obtaining maintenance opportunities in overseas markets for which the Republic of Korea has the technological capability.

      (d) Assistance in establishing industrial facilities and/or provision of equipment or tooling.

      (e) Other activities which greatly contribute to national interests.

(2) Category "B"

Priority activities which contribute to economic and industrial development and diversification.

(a) Direct Offset which does not extensively contribute to national interests.

(b) Indirect Offset (KIP) which extensively contributes to national interests.

(3) Category "C"

Desirable activities which support economic/industrial growth and favorably affect the international balance of payments.

(a) Indirect Offset (KIP) which does not extensively contribute to national interests.

(b) Direct purchase of, and/or assistance in selling communication articles from original Korean sources.

(4) Category "D"

(a) Acceptable activities which contribute to economic growth in areas that do not require extensive assistance.

(b) Direct purchase of, and/or assistance in selling general commodities approved by KTA from original Korean sources.

(5) Category "E"

Incidental activities which satisfy unique requirements of KTA. These activities will be considered on a case-by-case basis (e.g., studies, management development assistance and other assistance).

(6) Category "F"

Unacceptable activities which do not satisfy KTA requirements and/or activities which do not require external assistance such as exhausted export quotas or production capacity which has been exceeded.

C. WEIGHTED VALUES OF CATEGORIES

In general, but not as an absolute rule, the following weighted values will be given to the categories listed:

CONTENT OF PROPOSALS	CATEGORIES	WEIGHTED VALUES
HIGH NATIONAL PRIORITY ACTIVITY	A	5
PRIORITY ACTIVITY	B	4
DESIRABLE ACTIVITY	C	3
ACCEPTABLE ACTIVITY	D	2
INCIDENTAL ACTIVITY	E	1
UNACCEPTABLE ACTIVITY	F	0

D. OFFSET EVALUATION METHODS

The degree of fulfillment of KTA's basic offset objective is evaluated and calculated as follows:

(1) KTA's basic offset objective

—Offset percentage: 50% of basic contract value (of which at least 20% is in the direct offset category of the basic contract value).

—Offset category: Category "C" or better.

—Offset execution period: Completed within basic contract period.

(2) Evaluation formula

$$\frac{(\text{Offset percentage} \times \text{Weighted value})/\text{Weighted offset execution period} \times 100}{\text{KTA's objective offset percentage} \times 3}$$

The weighted offset execution period is calculated as follows:

$$\frac{1 + \text{Time exceeded basic contract period}}{\text{Basic contract period}}$$

6. TERMS AND CONDITIONS

A. All calculations will be made in U.S. dollars.

B. Offset programs will be conducted, wherever possible, in annual increments which will parallel the payment schedule of the basic contract.

C. Offset programs shall be fulfilled within an agreed period of time, usually within the time period of execution of the basic contract.

D. Costs for technology related to the execution of the basic contract will be provided as an offset credit.

E. Royalties and license fees for products currently being purchased in Korea will be granted offset credit.

F. Any expenses incurred by the contractor in the execution of the offset program will not be included as part of the offset program.

G. Offset credit for cost of material used on items manufactured or assembled under the offset program will not be allowed for imported material when the end product is retained within the Republic of Korea. However, imported material costs will be counted when the end product is exported for sale.

H. Cost of shipping related to the offset program will not be included in calculating offset credit. However, if companies use Korean shipping to transport material not related to the offset program, the value of the shipping will receive credit on a case-by-case basis.

I. The terms and conditions of the basic contract shall apply to the offset commitment to the extent applicable except as specified in the offset agreement.

J. If the basic contract comes to termination, in whole or in part, or if the scope of the contract is reduced through negotiated changes, the offset commitment will be proportionately reduced.

K. When submitting requests for offset credit, a copy of the Irrevocable Letter of Credit must be attached. However, shipping documents or export permits with purchase orders may also be used to verify contracts.

L. In executing the offset program, all values of KIP (Direct and Indirect), determined by prior KTA approval, that exceed program goals will be credited to the foreign contractor for follow-on contracts.

M. If the offset execution period is required to be extended beyond the basic contract period, when submitting an offset proposal, the contractor should request KTA approval. Such an approved offset program will require a 10% performance bond for the amount of the remaining offset commitment as a security when the basic contract is completed.

N. If the committed offset is not achieved within the execution period, KTA will be entitled to receive from the performance guarantee fund an amount equal to 10% of the unfulfilled portion of the offset commitment.

7. CONTENT OF OFFSET PROPOSALS

   A. Offset proposals can take many forms. Prospective foreign contractors are required to determine the structure and content of their proposals as specified in this "Guide".

   B. Offset proposals submitted in response to requests for contracts will be clearly defined, demonstrably viable and normally competitive with overseas prices and deliveries.

   C. The following content will be included in offset proposals:
     (1) Contract value or estimated contract value
     (2) Offset value and percentage
       (a) Direct offset value and percentage
       (b) Indirect offset value and percentage
         a. KIP value and percentage
         b. Counterpurchase value and percentage
     (3) Fulfillment time period (month/years)
     (4) Commitment to, or assurance of, fulfillment
     NOTE: Details will be stated in attachments.

8. PROCEDURES FOR SUBMISSION AND REVIEW OF THE OFFSET PROGRAM PROPOSALS

   A. Offset proposals should be submitted to the offset program office (KTA) in writing together with a draft MOA within the period specified in the request for proposal (RFP), indicating in detail a contractor's commitment to the offset program and outlining the offset program execution plan.

   B. Within four weeks after the receipt of the offset proposal and draft MOA by the offset program office, each foreign contractor will meet with the assigned offset project manager and discuss the details of the proposal. If the submitted proposal is not feasible or does not satisfy KTA's basic offset objectives, continued revisions and supplemental actions will be taken. If a satisfactory proposal is not submitted within the closing period, it will be disadvantageous to the contractor.

   C. All discussions between the contractor and the offset project manager will be completed before signing the MOA. The MOA will be signed by a designated representative of KTA and a representative of the contractor.

9. REPORTING
Foreign contractors will be required to report quarterly to the offset program office on the progress of implementation of offset commitments. Reports will include details of opportunities offered Korean industries and contracts concluded. Upon conclusion of offset commitments, both parties will sign a statement certifying the conclusion of the offset program.

10. PENALTIES
A monetary penalty clause is included in the terms and conditions of this "Guide". In all cases, however, failure to comply with the intent of this "Guide" or other regulations governing offset pro-

grams or failure to meet offset program obligations could result in action being taken to preclude that particular contractor from business activities in KTA for more than two years.

11.   OTHER ADMINISTRATIVE ACTIVITIES
     A.   PROCEDURES FOR OFFSET PROGRAMS

Foreign Contractor	*	Requests survey of Korean industrial capabilities and marketing related to offset programs
	*	If required, requests recommendations for Korean industrial sources
KTA	*	Arranges for foreign contractor's requests after consulting proper concerned agencies of KTA
	*	Informs foreign contractor of arrangements
Foreign Contractor	*	Surveys Korean industries recommended by KTA
	*	Submits acceptable offset proposal and a draft MOA within a specified period of time
KTA	*	Refines foreign contractor's proposal and prepares alternatives for negotiations
	*	Concludes negotiations upon the completion of discussions and signs an appropriate agreement (MOA)
	*	Evaluates offset proposals and submits results to the Review Council

     B.   ASSISTANCE TO FOREIGN CONTRACTORS
KTA offers information and advice, and maintains a record of the capabilities of Korean industries interested in working with foreign contractors.

§ 5.45   International Buy–Back Contracts (UN ECE) *

CHAPTER ONE: SOME PRELIMINARY ISSUES

1. SCOPE OF THIS GUIDE

Parties to a buy-back deal may want to regulate their rights and obligations in a simple manner, and include the relevant provisions in the same contractual document that regulates the primary transaction. However, they often prefer to use several contracts. This Guide deals with that manner of proceeding.

In principle, the rights and obligations of the parties under the primary transaction are similar to those usually agreed upon in international contracts for the sale of Equipment/Technology. The same can be said about the terms and conditions of the subsequent contracts implementing the sale and purchase of the specific buy-back products.

* This section on International Buy–Back Contracts was prepared by the Committee on the Development of Trade of the Economic Commission for Europe, of the United Nations.

Yet, in buy-back there is a special relationship between these contracts. The equipment/technology that is involved in the setting up of the production facilities emanates from the party who commits himself to the subsequent purchase of products produced thereby.

For that reason this Guide will discuss not only problems relating to the buy-back contract itself, but will also briefly address some of the main issues of the primary contract.

2. DEFINITIONS

In this Guide, the terms below will have the following meanings:

Equipment/Technology means the machinery and/or equipment and/or patents and/or know-how and/or technical assistance that will enable the manufacturing of the Products.

Primary Contract means the contract that regulates the rights and obligations of the respective parties with regard to the supply of the Equipment/Technology.

Original Seller means the party to the Primary Contract who supplies the Equipment/Technology agreed upon therein.

Original Buyer means the party to the Primary Contract who purchases the Equipment/Technology agreed upon therein.

Products means the products that are manufactured by using the Equipment/Technology and are sold and purchased by way of buy-back.

Plant means the industrial or other works where the Products are manufactured.

Buy-back Contract means the contract which the Original Seller and the Original Buyer conclude simultaneously with the Primary Contract, and which regulates their rights and obligations, as parties to the Buy-back Contract, with regard to the sale and purchase of the Products.

Buy-back Seller means the Original Buyer in his capacity as party to the Buy-back Contract.

Buy-back Purchaser means the Original Seller in his capacity as party to the Buy-back Contract.

Implementing Contract means the contract that regulates the rights and obligations of the parties to that contract with regard to the sale and purchase of the specific buy-back Products arising out of the Buy-back contract.

Implementing Seller means that party to the Implementing Contract who supplies the Products agreed on therein. He usually is the party who is the Original Buyer and the Buy-back Seller, but he may also be a third party.

Implementing Buyer means the party to the Implementing Contract who purchases the Products agreed on therein. He may, in fact, be the party who is the Original Seller and the Buy-back Purchaser, but he may also be a third party.

Assignor means the Buy-back Purchaser, or, as the case may be, the Buy-back Seller, who has assigned his rights and obligations under the Buy-back Contract to a third party.

Assignee means the third party to whom the Assignor has assigned his rights and obligations under the Buy-back Contract.

CHAPTER TWO: THE PRIMARY CONTRACT

The conformity of the Products with the requirements agreed upon in the Buy-back Contract (see Chapter Three, Section 3) depends, among other things, on the Equipment/Technology that is sold under the Primary Contract, on the manner in which the Equipment/Technology is transferred and used in the Plant, and on the quality control policies and procedures that are instituted at the Plant. The parties to the Primary Contract should therefore draft particularly carefully those parts of the contract that regulate these questions. A brief account of the issues involved is given below. For further details, parties should consult existing guides and model contracts dealing with these matters.

1. MACHINERY AND EQUIPMENT

(a) Description

If the Original Seller is to supply machinery and/or equipment, the Primary Contract should contain a clear description thereof, and of the respective performance requirements.

As a rule, supply of machinery and equipment includes delivery of the technical documentation necessary for their proper use. If this is the case, the Primary Contract should specify the documents and stipulate how they will be handed over to the Original Buyer.

(b) Installation

If installation of the machinery and equipment is included in the Primary Contract, it should specify the respective obligations of the parties in this regard.

(c) Commissioning, test runs, and acceptance

When appropriate, the Primary Contract should specify the conditions for, and duration of, the commissioning of the machinery and equipment. Similarly, details on the test runs where the performance of the machinery and equipment are proven, should be agreed upon. Finally, the Primary Contract should set forth the terms and conditions under which the supply of the machinery and equipment will be accepted.

(d) Guarantees

The Primary Contract should set out the quality guarantee (material and workmanship guarantee) and performance guarantee (technological guarantee) of the machinery and equipment.

2. PATENTS, KNOW–HOW, AND TECHNICAL ASSISTANCE

Often a buy-back transaction includes not only the sale by the Original Seller of production machinery and equipment, but also a grant of license to use the Original Seller's patent rights and/or know-how relating to the manufacture of the Products. As part of the transaction, the Original Seller may also render to the Original Buyer technical assistance relating to the manufacture of the Products.

(a) Scope of license

The Primary Contract should define the patents, technical information and other know-how that the Original Seller will license to the Original Buyer.

(b) Disclosure

The parties should agree on the manner (e.g., handing over of specifications, drawings, computer diskettes, etc.) in which the technical information will be disclosed by the Original Seller to the Original Buyer.

(c) Technical assistance

The parties may wish to agree that the Original Seller will arrange for his own technical personnel to visit the Plant to assist the Original Buyer in undertaking the manufacture and sale of the Products and/or train the Original Buyer's personnel in this respect. If this is the case, the Primary Contract should specify the number of the Original Seller's personnel that will be involved, and the time periods that will be used for this purpose.

Sometimes it will be necessary for the representatives of the Original Buyer to visit the plant of the Original Seller in order to become familiar with and/or be trained in the manufacturing of the Products. In that case, the Primary Contract should contain provisions defining the scope and duration of such visit(s) or training, and the number of Original Buyer's personnel that will be involved therein.

3. QUALITY CONTROL AND GUARANTEES

(a) Quality control

To ensure that the Products are of the agreed specification, performance and quality, the parties may wish to institute appropriate quality control policies and procedures. Quality control provisions might further stipulate procedures to be followed in the event that the Products do not meet the agreed specifications, performance or quality.

(b) Guarantees

Matters related to the guarantee of the Products can, of course, be agreed upon in the Buy-back Contract and, if necessary, even in the individual Implementing Contracts. However, the parties may wish to include appropriate provisions already in the Primary Contract. This might be the case, for example, when Products will be sold to third parties under the trade mark of the Original Seller. He has then a direct interest in ensuring that appropriate guarantee standards are applied also with regard to such third parties.

CHAPTER THREE: BUY–BACK CONTRACT

1. THE BUY–BACK COMMITMENT

(a) *The requirement of buy-back*

If the sale of Equipment/Technology involves a buy-back commitment, the Buy-back Purchaser will often have to take specific measures to fulfil that undertaking. It is therefore very important that the Original Buyer informs the Original Seller of the buy-back requirement before negotiations on the substance of the Primary Contract begin. An early notice of the buy-back requirement will be of benefit to both parties since it allows the Original Seller to study, before the parties use time and expenses in negotiating the Primary Contract, whether or not he is willing, or able, to commit himself to the buy-back undertaking proposed by the Original Buyer.

Consequently, already at this stage the Original Buyer should, whenever possible, propose concrete details for the transaction, including the proposed total value, and the time period for fulfillment, of the buy-back obligation.

(b) *Mutual commitments*

If buy-back is accepted and agreed on by the parties, the Buy-back Contract should contain in one of its first paragraphs a clear commitment by the Buy-back Purchaser to purchase, on agreed terms, Products, and an equally clear commitment by the Buy-back Seller to sell said Products.

2. THE BUY–BACK PRODUCTS

(a) *Definition*

Definition of the Products is usually not a problem in buy-back. However, if the Equipment/Technology permits the production of a wide range of Products, the parties may wish to agree on a mechanism according to which the assortment of the Products to be sold and purchased under the Buy-back Contract will be agreed upon.

(b) *Availability of Products*

Once the parties have agreed that the Buy-back Purchaser will purchase Products, it may be very important for him to be sure that he will in fact receive the Products. The parties may therefore wish to include in the Buy-back Contract a commitment by the Buy-back Seller whereby he warrants that agreed amounts of Products will be available at the time of performance. The Buy-back Contract should also stipulate the legal consequences if Products are subsequently not available (see section 15 below).

3. CONFORMITY OF THE PRODUCTS
(a) Specification and quality

With regard to the conformity of the Products the parties may simply refer to those provisions of the Primary Contract where the specifications and quality of the Products are defined, and stipulate that the Products to be delivered must correspond to such specifications and quality.

(b) Quantity and assortment

Regarding the quantity and, when applicable, assortment of the Products, the parties may refer to the requirements set forth in the individual Implementing Contracts to be concluded within the framework of the Buy-back Contract.

4. TOTAL VALUE OF BUY–BACK COMMITMENT
(a) Value should be defined

The Buy-back Contract should contain a provision defining the value of the buy-back commitment—i.e., the value for which the Buy-back Purchaser will purchase products within the framework of the Buy-back Contract. This amount may be equal to, or lower or higher than, the price of the Equipment/Technology sold under the Primary Contract.

(b) Alternative ways of defining

The value of the buy-back commitment can be agreed in absolute money terms or as a percentage of the total price of the Equipment/Technology sold under the Primary Contract.

(c) Basis of calculation, etc. should be specified

The value of the buy-back commitment may be defined in terms of a percentage of the price of the Equipment/Technology, if such price (or the basis on which it will be calculated) is stated in unambiguous terms. That may not always be the case. Thus, for instance, the price of technical assistance might not be included in the price of the Primary Contract, but be invoiced separately on a time-basis. In such cases, the value of the buy-back commitment should be defined in a way which permits taking into account the final price of the technical assistance.

The Buy-back Contract must define clearly the value for which the individual Implementing Contracts will be applied against the Buy-back Purchaser's total undertaking (for instance, whether it is the FOB- or the CIF-value of the respective Implementing Contracts). Further, if the Implementing Contracts are to be invoiced in a currency other than the currency in which the aggregate value of the buy-back undertaking is set forth in the Buy-back Contract, the parties should agree in the said contract on the exchange rate at which the Implementing Contracts shall be applied against the aggregate buy-back undertaking; in doing so, they should take into account the applicable foreign exchange regulations (see also subsection 5(d) below).

5. PRICE OF THE PRODUCTS

(a) Reasons for deferring the setting of prices

In buy-back the parties to the Buy-back Contract could in principle agree on the prices of the Products, since the parties to that contract will also be parties to the subsequent Implementing Contracts.

Substantial time may pass after the signing of the Primary Contract and the Buy-back Contract before commercial manufacture of Products is started at the Plant. During that period prices of raw materials and components may change, and the same may happen to the costs of labour. The market situation for the Products may also be different when commercial production begins.

For these and similar reasons the parties to the Buy-back Contract may wish to leave the final agreement on the prices to be made only at the time when the individual Implementing Contracts are concluded.

(b) Guidelines and standards

Nevertheless, the parties to the Buy-back Contract may wish to set, in that contract, certain guidelines or standards to be applied when prices are subsequently determined. There are various ways in which that can be done.

Thus, reference can be made, for example, to the prices charged generally for the types of products that are similar to the Products. Or the parties could refer to the price of the said types of products in the territory in which the Products will be consumed or re-sold. If it can be expected that no products of the same type will be offered for sale in that territory, reference may have to be made to the fair market value of the Products themselves in the said territory.

(c) Most-favoured purchaser terms

In order to ensure that the Buy-back Purchaser or his Assignees will not be undersold in the agreed territory due to the fact that the Buy-back Seller grants more advantageous conditions to other purchasers, the parties may wish to agree in the Buy-back Contract that the Buy-back Purchaser and his Assignees shall be granted most-favoured purchaser conditions with regard to the buy-back products. The parties should bear in mind any relevant anti-dumping, cartel or other similar legislation.

(d) Currency

The parties should agree in the Buy-back Contract on the currency in which the buy-back products shall be quoted and paid for. If the currency of payment is other than that of quotation, the parties should also agree on the method to be used when the currency of quotation is converted into the currency of payment (see also subsection 4(c) above).

6. ASSIGNMENT

(a) *Reasons for Assignment*

In buy-back, both the Buy-back Purchaser and the Buy-back Seller may find it necessary to assign their rights and obligations, either entirely or partly, to a third party in particular. If the Products cannot be used in-house by the Buy-back Purchaser, there are various alternative ways in which he can dispose of them.

For example, he can purchase the Products himself and then resell them, or he can assign the buy-back obligation directly to an Assignee who will then conclude Implementing Contracts with the Buy-back Seller, take delivery of the Products and either use them himself or resell them. There may, of course, be occasions when the Buy-back Purchaser can use a part of the Products himself, and perhaps resell another part, but will still need to assign the rest of the commitment to a third party.

(b) *Assignment by agreement, approvals and duty to inform*

If it is the common intention of the parties that assignment in some form should be possible, they should provide for this possibility in the Buy-back Contract. When appropriate, an approval from relevant authorities and/or financial institutions should be obtained for the assignment.

The parties may also wish to agree in the Buy-back Contract that if a party assigns his rights and obligations under the contract to an Assignee, he must give the other party notice thereof. If they so agree, they should also include in the contract provisions on the legal consequences of a failure to give such notice.

(c) *Legal effect of assignment*

The legal effect of assignment is that usually all rights and obligations of the Assignor with regard to the assigned portion will terminate and be vested in the Assignee. Therefore, if it is the intention of the parties that the Assignor will remain responsible, together with the Assignee, for the fulfillment of the assigned obligations, they should include a provision to that effect in the Buy-back Contract.

(d) *The Assignee and the other party to be bound to each other*

In cases where it is agreed that a party to a Buy-back Contract will have the right to assign some part, or the whole, of his rights and obligations to a third party, the parties should provide in the Buy-back Contract that the Assignor shall include in his agreement with any Assignee a clause whereby the Assignee commits himself to be bound by the provisions of the Buy-back Contract with regard to the assigned portion.

To counter balance this provision, the parties may wish to agree that, again with regard to the assigned portion, the other party shall in turn become bound vis-à-vis the respective Assignee.

7. RE–SALE OF THE PRODUCTS

(a) Re-sale territory to be defined

In the event that the buy-back products are to be re-sold, either by the Buy-back Purchaser or by an Assignee, the parties to the Buy-back Contract may wish to consider whether they should define the territory where re-sale can take place.

(b) Rules of competition to be observed

It should be observed, however, that territorial restrictions may in certain circumstances violate national or international rules of competition, or otherwise be un-enforceable in practice. The situation should therefore be studied carefully in each individual case.

8. REFERENCE

In the event that the Buy-back Purchaser's commitment will be discharged through Implementing Contracts, entered into within the framework of the Buy-back Contract, it is important that each Implementing Contract that falls into this category is indeed recognized and recorded as such. For this purpose, the Buy-back Contract should contain a provision stipulating that each Implementing Contract must explicitly refer to the Buy-back Contract and state that it is made in fulfillment of the Buy-back Contract. Such a reference will facilitate the monitoring and recording of the individual Implementing Contracts.

9. TERMS OF DELIVERY

Usually the parties of the Buy-back Contract will also be the parties to the individual Implementing Contracts. If this is the case, they may wish to agree already in the Buy-back Contract on the terms of delivery to be used in the Implementing Contracts.

10. TIME SCHEDULES FOR PERFORMANCE

(a) Commencement of delivery

Since the Products will be manufactured at the Buy-back Seller's Plant, deliveries can begin only after some time has passed from the completion of the performance test and acceptance of the Equipment/Technology under the Primary Contract. The parties should therefore define in the Buy-back Contract the time period that will be required for the first delivery to take place.

(b) Estimated time schedule

If the fulfillment of the buy-back commitment will be extended over a period of several years, as is often the case, the parties may not wish to agree in advance on binding yearly quotas for deliveries, but rather to create, in a form of an estimated time schedule, only a broad framework within which to operate.

(c) Actual quantities and assortments

With regard to the actual quantities and, when applicable, actual assortments, of the Products, the parties may wish to agree upon a mechanism according to which these will be defined. For example, the Buy-back Contract could stipulate that actual quantities and assortments will be negotiated and agreed upon in individual Implementing Contracts. These would be concluded between the parties an agreed number of days or months before the beginning of the next delivery period (year, quarter or month).

Even if agreement on binding quantities and assortments is left for subsequent Implementing Contracts, the parties may wish to set out in the Buy-back Contract some guidelines in that respect. They might stipulate, for instance, that when actual quantities and assortments are negotiated, the Buy-back Purchaser's own needs for Products and/or prevailing market conditions in the agreed re-sale territory will be taken into account. On the other hand, the Buy-back Contract might also provide for certain minimum quantities that must always be purchased and/or maximum quantities that cannot be exceeded unless both parties agree thereto.

(d) Final date

While certain flexibility in the fulfillment of the buy-back commitment may suit both parties, they may wish to include in the Buy-back Contract a final date by which all Implementing Contracts must have been concluded.

11. LACK OF CONFORMITY

Since the parties to the Buy-back Contract will, as a rule, also be parties to the Implementing Contracts, and since the buy-back Products are well known to them, they may wish to agree already in the Buy-back Contract on their respective rights and obligations in the event that the Products are not in conformity with the agreed requirements. If the Buy-back Purchaser uses the Equipment/Technology to manufacture identical or similar products himself, the provisions he uses in contracts with his own customers might be used as a model when drafting the respective clauses of the Buy-back Contract.

12. PAYMENT

(a) Terms of payment

The Buy-back Contract should state how and against what documents payment of deliveries under Implementing Contracts will be effected, whether any securities of payment will have to be arranged by the Buy-back Purchaser or, as the case may be, by his Assignee. The Buy-back Contract should also define what requirements such securities of payment, if agreed upon, should fulfill as well as which of the parties will be responsible for the costs involved in the agreed payment arrangements.

(b) Escrow arrangements

In appropriate circumstances the parties might also agree on an escrow arrangement. Thereby, the value of the Products delivered under the Primary Contract—or the proceeds received from their re-sale—is placed by the Original Buyer on an escrow account with a bank or another third party, and is subsequently used to pay for some or all of the buy-back Products.

13. MONITORING THE PERFORMANCE

(a) Evidence accounts

The parties should agree in the Buy-back Contract on how the performance of the various obligations of the parties is monitored. A rather simple mechanism is that each party records those steps that are taken on his side in fulfillment of the respective obligations within the framework of the Buy-back Contract. Thus, in such a record (sometimes called an "evidence account") an entry could be made of each Implementing Contract concluded, each delivery completed, and each payment made within the framework of the Buy-back Contract.

(b) Assignee(s) to inform Assignor

In the event of assignment, the Assignor normally has no particular interest in monitoring the fulfillment of the assigned portion; his rights and obligations with regard to that portion will have terminated (see subsection 6(d) above). However, if it is agreed that the Assignor will remain, together with the Assignee, responsible for the fulfillment of the buy-back obligation, the Assignor should require that the Assignee inform him about all Implementing Contracts that he concludes within the framework of the Buy-back Contract. If this is done, the Assignor will be able to follow the development of the situation and, when called for, take appropriate measures to secure the timely fulfillment of the buy-back obligations.

(c) Evidence accounts to be compared and agreed

Since both parties to the Buy-back Contract should be informed of how the contract is being performed, the parties should agree in the contract that their evidence accounts will be compared and agreed upon on a regular basis. In the contract the parties could also agree that evidence accounts thus compared and agreed shall constitute final and conclusive evidence as to the performance of their obligations under the Buy-back Contract.

14. LIABILITY

(a) Liquidated damages

Failure by either party to fulfill his obligations under the Buy-back Contract may imply liability to damages. If this question is not regulated in the Buy-back Contract or in the Implementing Contract(s), disputes will be settled in accordance with the rules of the applicable law.

It may be agreed in the Buy-back Contract that the non-compliance by a party or his Assignee with the obligations thereunder gives birth to an obligation to pay liquidated damages—i.e., damages which are determined in advance by the parties themselves in the Buy-back Contract. The amount of the liquidated damages can be agreed as an absolute sum of money or, as is more usual, as a given percentage of the value of that part of the buy-back commitment which has remained unfulfilled.

(b) Bank guarantee

In appropriate circumstances the parties may wish to agree that the commitment by a party, and—as the case may be—his Assignee, to pay liquidated damages should be backed by a bank guarantee obtained by the party (or his Assignee). If this is the case, the parties should include in the Buy-back Contract provisions defining the amount of the bank guarantee, the bank in which it should be obtained, and the form and content it should have.

(c) Non-fulfillment caused by the other party

It is a general principle of contract law that a party may not claim damages for non-fulfillment of the agreed obligations by the other party if such non-fulfillment is a result of a failure by the first-mentioned party to meet his own commitments under the contract.

The parties may therefore wish to underline this principle in the Buy-back Contract by stating that no liquidated damages will be payable by a party insofar as the lack of performance of his obligations is due to an event which the other party has caused.

15. RELIEF FROM LIABILITY

(a) Circumstances to be defined

The parties to the Buy-back Contract may wish to provide in their contract for those circumstances which might bring relief from liability for consequences of failure to perform contractual obligations. Where the parties fail to make such provision, the circumstances prompting relief from liability for consequences of failure to perform contractual obligations result from the law applicable to their contract.

The parties might stipulate that a party is not liable for failure to perform any of his obligations if he can prove that the failure was due to an impediment occurring after the signing of the Buy-back Contract, and which was beyond his control, and that he could not reasonably have been expected to have taken the impediment into account at the time of the conclusion of the contract, or to have avoided or overcome it or its consequences. Examples of such situations are: war, civil strife, interference by public authorities, fire, natural disasters, etc.

(b) Procedure

In addition to the circumstances prompting relief from liability for failure to perform contractual obligations, the contract should also specify the procedure in the event of a party invoking relief. The following items constitute the most important provisions in this respect: the party which fails to perform and which is claiming relief should, without undue delay, give notice to the other party of the commencement of the impediment and of its inability to perform its obligations; the parties should specify the consequences for failure to give such notice (for example, payment of damages); and the right to terminate the contract in the event of a protracted impediment.

16. TERMINATION OF PRIMARY CONTRACT OR IMPLEMENTING CONTRACT

(a) Primary Contract

Since the manufacture of Products is possible only in the event that the Equipment/Technology is successfully transferred and accepted, it is clear that if this does not happen, and the Primary Contract is therefore terminated, there is no basis for the implementation of the Buy-back Contract either. The Buy-back Contract should therefore stipulate that if the Primary Contract is subsequently terminated without the Equipment/Technology having been transferred and accepted, the Buy-back Contract shall automatically become null and void.

(b) Implementing Contracts

With respect to Implementing Contracts, the parties should agree whether, and under what conditions, the Buy-back Purchaser will be deemed to have fulfilled, in spite of the termination of an Implementing Contract, that part of his buy-back obligation which corresponds to the value of the Implementing Contract so terminated, and include corresponding provisions in the Buy-back Contract.

17. PRIOR COMMITMENTS, EFFECTIVE DATE, AMENDMENTS, AND GOVERNING LANGUAGE

(a) Prior commitments

The parties to the Buy-back Contract may wish to include therein a provision, often found in commercial contracts, stating that the contract supersedes and invalidates all other commitments or representations which the parties may have made either orally or in writing prior to the date of signature of the contract.

(b) Effective date

The parties should agree on the date on which the Buy-back Contract enters into force. This date may be, for example, the date of the signing of the contract. On the other hand, if the effectiveness of the Buy-back Contract is subject to approval by competent authorities and/or financial institutions having an interest in the matter, the parties may wish to agree that each party must notify the other of approvals obtained in their respective countries, and that the date (of the latest) of such notification(s) will be the date when the Buy-back Contract enters into force. Finally, the parties should provide that if such approvals are not obtained within an agreed period, each party has the right to rescind the Buy-back Contract.

(c) Amendments

The Buy-back Contract should stipulate that any amendments to it will be effective only if made in writing and signed by legally authorized representatives of the parties, and if approved, when applicable, by the competent authorities and/or financial institutions.

(d) Language

It is to be recommended that the contracts used in the buy-back transaction be drawn up in one language only. As a consequence, disagreements based merely on differences in terminology or expression are avoided. If several languages are used, it is desirable that the parties designate one of the languages used as the governing language which shall be decisive in cases of dispute. In any event, if the contract is drawn up in more than one language, the parties should endeavour to ensure that the texts are identical.

18. APPLICABLE LAW

The parties should agree on the law which governs the contracts used in the buy-back transaction, and in accordance with which the contracts are to be construed.

19. SETTLEMENT OF DISPUTES

(a) Rules or institutions to be designated

With regard to any dispute or difference arising from or in connection with the interpretation or execution of the contracts used in the buy-back transaction, the parties should try to negotiate amicably before having recourse to arbitration. Should, however, the parties be unable to settle such dispute or difference, international business practice presents adequate conciliation and arbitration procedures to enable the parties to select the one appropriate to a particular case. The parties should state in the contract which arbitration rules will be applied, and/or which arbitration institution shall be competent, for the settlement of eventual disputes between them. If the parties wish to resort to *ad hoc* arbitration, they should specify how the arbitration court will be set up and function.

(b) Number of arbitrators to be agreed

Under many arbitration rules, the parties may agree on the number of arbitrators.

(c) Language of arbitration procedure

The parties may wish to agree on the language to be used in the arbitration procedure.

(d) Place of arbitration

The parties may wish to agree on the place where the arbitration will be held.

ANNEX

This Annex contains alternative clauses for a Buy-back Contract. Because of this, the document should be adapted to the specific circumstances of the transaction in question.

BUY–BACK CONTRACT

Between

Alpha _____ [1]
of 1, Alpha Street, 00100 Alphatown, Alphaland
(hereinafter "Alpha")

and

Beta _____ [1]
of 1, Beta Street, 00100 Betatown, Betaland
(hereinafter "Beta")

WHEREAS

Under a Primary Contract dated _____ 19__ (hereinafter the "Primary Contract")/ [2] and the Technical Assistance Contract dated _____ 19__ (hereinafter the "Technical Assistance Contract")/ Alpha has sold to Beta, and Beta has purchased from Alpha, under the terms and conditions set forth in the Primary Contract/and the Technical Assistance Contract/, the machinery/and/equipment/and/patents/and/know-how/and/technical assistance/specified therein (hereinafter "the Equipment/Technology"), to manufacture _____ (hereinafter "the Products") in Betaland.

By way of buy-back, and under the terms and conditions set forth in this Contract, Beta agrees to sell to Alpha, and Alpha agrees to purchase from Beta, Products as specified herein.

NOW, THEREFORE, the parties to this Contract agree as follows:

ARTICLE 1—THE BUY–BACK COMMITMENT

1.1   Alpha hereby agrees to buy (or cause the purchase) from Beta, under the terms and conditions set forth in this Contract, Prod-

---

§ 2.48

1. Indicate legal form of party.

2. The words, or groups of words, separated by strokes are alternative formulations. Delete the one(s) not applicable.

ucts manufactured by Beta using the Equipment/Technology sold by Alpha, and take delivery of the said Products.

1.2   Beta hereby agrees to sell to Alpha (or to his assignee (as defined below in Article 6)), under the terms and conditions set forth in this Contract, such Products, and to accept the purchase by Alpha of such Products as buy-back within the framework of this Contract.

ARTICLE 2—THE PRODUCTS

2.1   The assortment of Products to be sold and purchased under this Contract is agreed upon by the parties in accordance with the provision of Article 10 below.

2.2   Beta hereby warrants that sufficient Products of the agreed assortment will be available at the times specified in ARTICLE 10 of this Contract.

ARTICLE 3—CONFORMITY OF THE PRODUCTS

3.1   The Products to be delivered shall correspond to the specifications and quality agreed upon in the Primary Contract, and must be of the quantity and assortment required by the individual purchase contracts (hereinafter "Implementing Contract(s)") to be concluded within the framework of this Contract between Beta/or his Assignee (as defined below in Article 6)/ in his capacity of seller of the Products (hereinafter "the Implementing Seller"), and Alpha/or his Assignee (as defined below in Article 6)/ in his capacity of buyer of the Products (hereinafter "the Implementing Buyer").

3.2   The Products must be contained or packaged in the manner required by the respective Implementing Contract.

ARTICLE 4—TOTAL VALUE OF THE BUY-BACK COMMITMENT

4.1   During the term of this Contract Alpha shall purchase from Beta Products for the value of/

(A) [3] _____ [4]   (B) not less than _____ per cent (__%) of the total _____ [5] price of the Primary Contract as specified in Article X of the Contract/plus not less than _____ per cent (__%) of the total price of the technical assistance invoiced in accordance with Article X of the Technical Assistance Contract.

4.2   The value of each of the Implementing Contracts to be applied against Alpha's buy-back commitment under this Contract shall be _____ [5] value of the respective Implementing Contract.

---

3. When alternative formulations comprise entire clauses, sentences, or half-sentences, the various alternatives are indicated with capital letters (A), (B), etc.

4. Indicate amount and currency.

5. Insert here the relevant term of delivery, e.g. FOB, CIF, etc.

4.3   The value of each of the Implementing Contracts, if invoiced in a currency other than the currency in which Alpha's buy-back commitment is set forth hereabove, shall be applied against Alpha's commitment at the exchange rate quoted by the Central Bank of _____ [6] at the date of the invoice issued in respect of such Implementing Contract.

ARTICLE 5—THE PRICE OF THE PRODUCTS

5.1(A) The prices of the Products offered under this Contract shall correspond to/

5.1(B) The prices of the Products shall be agreed upon from case-to-case by the respective Implementing Seller and Implementing Buyer of the Products.

(A–1) [7] the price generally charged at the time of the conclusion of the respective Implementing Contract for such products under comparable circumstances in the trade concerned.[8]

(A–2) [7] the fair/average/market value of the Products in the Territory (as defined below in para. 7.1) under competitive terms of delivery and payment.

(A–3) [7] the prices of competing products, of essentially similar specifications and quality standards than those of the Products, in the Territory (as defined below in para. 7.1) under competitive terms of delivery and payment.

(A–4) [7] the quotation of the Product at the _____ exchange [9] on the date when the respective Implementing Contract is concluded.

6. Indicate the name of the country.

7. A–1 to A–4 are alternative formulations of 5.1(A).

8. This alternative is based on Article 55 of the United Nations Convention on Contracts for the International Sale of Goods (1980).

9. Indicate the name of agreed commodity exchange.

5.1(C) Alpha/and the Assignee(s)/shall be granted most-favoured-customer conditions in the Territory with regard to the Products.

5.2   The prices of the Products shall be quoted and paid for in _____.[10]

ARTICLE 6—ASSIGNMENT

6.1(A) Alpha shall not be entitled to assign its buy-back undertaking under this Contract, either as a whole, or any part of it, to any other entity/without the express written consent of Beta/.[11] Such consent shall not be unreasonably withheld.

6.1(B) Alpha may assign the whole, or a part, of its buy-back undertaking under this Contract, to any third party.

6.2   In the event that Alpha (hereinafter "the Assignor") shall assign any part of its buy-back commitment under this Contract to a third party (hereinafter "the Assignee")/

(A)   all rights and obligations of the Assignor under this Contract with regard to the assigned part shall terminate at the time when the assignment contract between the Assignor and the Assignee becomes effective, and the respective rights and obligations shall be vested in the said Assignee; provided that in the said agreement the Assignee assumes all the obligations of the Assignor agreed upon in this Contract with regard to the part so assigned.

(B)   the Assignor shall remain responsible,/jointly/jointly and severally/ with the Assignee, for the fulfillment of all of its obligations agreed upon in this Contract.

6.3   Alpha agrees to include in its agreement with any Assignee appropriate provisions whereby the Assignee commits itself to be bound by this Contract with regard to the assigned part of the buy-back commitment, as if this Contract had originally been executed by the Assignee. In consideration for the said commitment, Beta agrees to be bound by this Contract against the respective Assignee, with regard to the assigned part of the buy-back commitment, as if this Contract had originally been executed with the Assignee.

6.4   In the event that a party shall assign any part of its buy-back obligations under this Contract to an Assignee, it must give

10. Indicate currency.

11. Replace "Beta" with the name of the appropriate Government body in Beta-land, when applicable.

notice to the other party of the assignment. If the notice is not received by the other party within a reasonable time after the assignment, the party will be liable for the damages resulting from such non-receipt.

ARTICLE 7—RE–SALE OF THE PRODUCTS

7.1　　Alpha/or its Assignee(s)/shall have the right to re-sell the Products in the territory agreed upon below in paragraph 7.2 (hereinafter "the Territory").

7.2(A)　The Territory shall include all countries in the world.

7.2(B)　The territory shall include the countries set forth in Appendix ( ) with respect to each of the Products or Product groups mentioned therein.

　　(C)　　Alphaland.

7.3　　The Products shall not be re-sold outside the Territory without the written consent of Beta.[12]

7.4　　It is agreed by the parties hereto that the restrictions set forth in paragraphs 7.2 and 7.3 above shall be construed as undertakings from the part of Alpha/or the Assignee/to refrain from actively putting the Products in the market outside the Territory.[12][13]

ARTICLE 8—REFERENCE

Each Implementing Contract as may be entered into by a /party or its Assignee/in accordance with the terms of this Contract, must explicitly refer to this Contract and state that the said Implementing Contract is made in fulfillment hereof. The parties agree to include in their agreements with any Assignee appropriate provisions to that effect.

ARTICLE 9—TERMS OF DELIVERY

Unless otherwise agreed in the individual Implementing Contracts, the terms of delivery of the Products will be _____.[5]

ARTICLE 10—TIME SCHEDULES FOR PERFORMANCE

10.1　Deliveries of the products by Beta will commence _____ /days/ months/ after the completion of the performance test and acceptance of the Equipment/Technology under the Primary Contract/and the Technical Assistance Contract.

10.2　It is presently estimated that the buy-back commitment agreed upon in Article 4 above will be fulfilled according to the following schedule:

Years	Value
19__	_____
19__	_____
19__	_____
etc.	Total _____

12. Not applicable if alternative A is chosen.

13. Should be included if Alphaland or any of the countries listed in *Appendix* ( ) are member countries of the European Economic Community (EEC).

10.3   Actual quantities and assortments of Products to be delivered will be negotiated and agreed upon in the individual Implementing Contracts to be concluded not later than _____ days/months/ before the beginning of each year/quarter/month with regard to the said /year/quarter/month.

10.4   When actual quantities and assortments are agreed upon, Alpha's remaining buy-back commitment /and/Alpha's own needs for Products/and/prevailing market conditions in the Territory for the various assortments of the Products/ will be taken into consideration. It is agreed, however, that, until the total buy-back commitment has been fulfilled, the value of Products to be sold by Beta and bought by Alpha each calendar year will be at least _____/ and not more than _____./.

10.5   Sufficient Implementing Contracts to cover the whole of Alpha's buy-back obligation as agreed under paragraph 4.1 above, must be concluded by _____ 19___.

ARTICLE 11—LACK OF CONFORMITY

11.1   Alpha must examine the Products delivered to him within as short a period as is practicable in the circumstances.

11.2   Alpha loses the right to rely on a lack of conformity of the Products if it does not give notice to Beta specifying the nature of the lack of conformity within _____ [14] after it has discovered or ought to have discovered it.

11.3   Further rights and obligations of the parties with regard to the lack of conformity of the Products will be governed.

(A)   by the provision of the law applicable to this Contract.

(B)   by the provision of the Guarantee Conditions attached to this Contract as *Appendix* ( ), and by the provisions of the law applicable to this Contract.

ARTICLE 12—PAYMENT OF THE PRODUCTS

12.1   The Products shall be paid for in the currency agreed upon in paragraph 5.2 above, and in the manner set forth in paragraph 12.2 below.

12.2   Each delivery of the Products shall be paid against the original documents set forth in paragraph 12.3 below/

(A)   through direct bank transfer to the bank account in Betaland of the Implementing Seller of the respective Products.

(B)   through an irrevocable and transferable Letter of Credit, allowing partial and trans-shipments, to be opened in the amount of the respective Implementing Contract at the latest _____ days after the signing of the said Contract, in the respective Implementing Seller's favour, and to be confirmed by the Bank in Betaland designated by the said Implementing Seller, such Letter of Credit to be valid for a

14. Indicate time period.

period of _____ days/weeks/months after the agreed date of delivery of the respective Products.

12.3 The/Products/Letter of Credit/shall be payable against the following documents:

— _____

— _____

— _____

12.4 The Implementing Buyer shall bear all exchange and bank charges as well as any other costs,/including the confirmation charges of Letters of Credit /but excluding the charges of the Bank of Betaland/ for transferring the funds to the Implementing Seller's account.

ARTICLE 13—MONITORING THE PERFORMANCE

13.1 Both Alpha and Beta shall keep records on all Implementing Contracts concluded within the framework of this Contract. Each such record (hereinafter "the Evidence Account") shall be in the form set forth in *Appendix* ( ) to this Contract.

13.2 The Evidence Accounts maintained by Alpha and Beta shall be compared and agreed by the parties through exchanges of letters on a quarterly basis during the term of this Contract, the first occasion being no later than __/__/19__

13.3 Alpha and Beta hereby agree that the Evidence Accounts, compared and agreed in accordance with paragraph 13.2 above, shall constitute final and conclusive evidence as to the performance of their obligations under this Contract.

ARTICLE 14—LIABILITY

14.1 In the event that Alpha's buy-back commitment, agreed upon in this Contract, has not been fully performed by the date mentioned in paragraph 10.5 above, Alpha shall, upon written demand by Beta, remit to Beta as agreed and liquidated damages _____ per cent (__%) of the value of the Products yet to be purchased under paragraph 4.1 hereof.

14.2 Notwithstanding the provisions of paragraph 14.1 above, Alpha shall not be obligated to make any payment mentioned therein insofar as the lack of performance of Alpha's buy-back commitment is due to the failure of the Implementing Seller to deliver Products of the quality, price or cumulative value, specified in ARTICLES 3, 5 and 10, respectively, of this Contract.

14.3 If the lack of performance of Alpha's buy-back commitment is due to the reasons set forth in paragraph 14.2, Beta shall, upon written demand by Alpha, remit to Alpha as agreed and liquidated damages _____ per cent (__%) of the value of the Products yet to be purchased under paragraph 4.1.

14.4 As guarantee for the due performance of its obligations under this ARTICLE 14 Alpha shall issue to Beta a bank guarantee, acceptable to Beta, for the sum of _____.[4] The bank guarantee shall be essentially of the form and contents as set forth in *Appendix* ( ) attached to this Contract.

14.5 As a guarantee for the due performance of its obligation under this ARTICLE 14 Beta shall issue to Alpha a bank guarantee, acceptable to Alpha, for the sum of _____.[4] The bank guarantee shall be essentially of the form and contents as set forth in *Appendix* ( ) attached to this Contract.

14.6 The payment by the respective party of the agreed and liquidated damages, set forth in paragraphs 14.1 and 14.3 above, shall be in full and final settlement of all claims that the other party may have against the first party arising out of or in connection with the breach by the first party of his obligations under this Contract.

ARTICLE 15—RELIEF [15]

15.1 A party is not liable for a failure to perform any of his obligations if he proves that the failure was due to an impediment beyond his control and that it could not reasonably be expected to take the impediment into account at the time of the conclusion of the contract or to have avoided or overcome the impediment or its consequences.

15.2 Exemption under this ARTICLE 15 shall be available to the affected party for the period during which the impediment prevents it from fulfilling his obligations under this Contract. If the effect of the impediment lasts for more than _____[14] months, each party shall be entitled to terminate this Contract upon written notice to the other, and neither party shall be liable to the other for any expenses or losses thereby incurred.

15.3 The party who fails to perform must give notice to the other party of the impediment and its effects on his ability to perform. If the notice is not received by the other party within a reasonable time after the party who fails to perform knew or ought to have known of the impediment, he is liable for damages resulting from such non-receipt.

15.4 A party may not rely on a failure of the other party to perform, to the extent that such failure was caused by the first party's act or omission.

ARTICLE 16—THE EFFECT OF THE TERMINATION OF THE PRIMARY CONTRACT OF THE IMPLEMENTING CONTRACTS

16.1 In the event that the Primary Contract should subsequently be terminated without the Equipment/Technology having been transferred and accepted, this Contract shall become automatically null and void and with no effect.

16.2 For the purposes of this Contract, Alpha's buy-back commitment, agreed upon herein, or a respective part thereof, as the case may be,/

(A) shall be deemed fulfilled even if any Implementing Contract should later be terminated/through no

(B) shall not be deemed fulfilled insofar as any Implementing Contract should later be terminated,

15. This Article 15 is based on Articles 79 and 80 of the United Nations Convention on Contracts for the International Sale of Goods (1980).

fault on the part of Alpha/for whatever reason/.

irrespective of the grounds for which the Implementing Contract was terminated. In this case Alpha shall be obligated to conclude (a) fresh Implementing Contract(s) corresponding to the value of the terminated Implementing Contract(s) such fresh Implementing Contracts to be then carried out in accordance with the provisions of this Contract.

ARTICLE 17—PRIOR COMMITMENTS, EFFECTIVE DATE, AMENDMENTS, AND GOVERNING LANGUAGE

17.1   Except as otherwise expressly provided in this Contract, this Contract supersedes and invalidates all other commitments or representations which may have been made by Alpha and Beta either orally or in writing prior to the date of signature of this Contract.

17.2   This Contract shall come into effect only /upon the entering into force of the Primary Contract/and/upon the signing of this contract by both parties/and/upon the approval of this Contract by the competent authorities and/or /financial institutions/in/Betaland/ and/or /Alphaland. Beta shall immediately notify Alpha/and/Alpha shall immediately notify Beta/by cable or telex of such approval, and the date of/such notification/the latest of such notifications/shall be the date on which this Contract comes into effect. Unless the approvals are obtained within _____/days/ months/from the signing of this Contract, it shall be considered null and void and with no effect.

17.3   Amendments to this Contract will be effective only if they are made in writing and signed by legally authorized representatives of the parties/, and if approved by the competent authorities /and/or/ financial institutions in/Betaland/and/Alphaland.

17.4   The _____ [16] text of this Contract is the governing text.

ARTICLE 18—APPLICABLE LAW

This Contract shall for all purposes be governed by, and construed in accordance with, the law of _____.[17]

ARTICLE 19—SETTLEMENT OF DISPUTES

19.1   All disputes or differences which may arise between the parties out of or in connection with this Contract, and which cannot be

16. Indicate language.   17. Indicate country.

settled amicably shall be subject to arbitration by _____ [18] arbitrator(s) under the rules of _____.[19]

19.2 The award of the arbitrator(s) shall be final and binding on the parties.

19.3 The arbitration proceedings shall be conducted in the _____ [16] language.

19.4 The place of arbitration shall be _____.[20]

_____   _____ 19__

Alpha   Beta

By _____   By_____

Selected Bibliography

Judith K. Cole, Evaluating Offset Agreements: Achieving a Balance of Advantages, 19 Law & Pol'y Int'l Bus. 765 (1987).

Robert F. Dodds, Jr., Offsets in Chinese Government Procurement: The Partially Open Door, 26 Law & Pol'y Int'l Bus. 1119 (1995).

Andrew Gordon, Countertrade: Developed and Developing Countries Are Getting into Offset—For Civil and Military Purchases, Euromoney Trade Fin. and Banker Int'l, Feb. 18, 1986, Lexis, News Library, TXPRIM File.

Cedric Guyot, Countertrade Contracts in International Business, 20 Int'l Lawyer 921 (1986).

John C. Grabow, Negotiating and Drafting Contracts in International Barter and Countertrade Transactions, 9 N.C.J. Int'l L. & Comm. Reg. 255 (1984).

Department of Commerce, Individual Country Practices in International Countertrade (1992).

Department of Commerce, International Countertrade: A Guide for Managers and Executives (1992).

Scott J. Lochner, Guide to Countertrade and International Barter, 19 Int'l Lawyer 725 (1985).

Thomas B. McVey, Countertrade: Commercial Practices, Legal Issues and Policy Dilemmas, 16 Law & Pol'y Int'l Bus. 1 (1984).

Paul Mishkin, Countertrade, 17 Int'l Bus.Lawyer 402 (1989).

Adrian A. Montague, An Introduction to Countertrade, 17 Int'l Bus.Lawyer 360 (1989).

OECD, East–West Trade, Recent Developments in Countertrade (1981).

18. Indicate number of arbitrators.   **20.** Indicate place and country.
19. Indicate applicable rules.

OECD, Countertrade: Developing Country Practices (1985).

Rowberg, Jr., Countertrade as a Quid Pro Quo for Host Government Approval of a Joint Venture, in D. Goldsweig (ed.) Joint Venturing Abroad: A Case Study 211 (ABA 1985).

Symposium, Countertrade, 5 J. Com.Bus. & Capital Market L. 341 (1983).

Controller General, U.S. Gen. Accounting Office, Trade Offsets in Foreign Military Sales, Appendix I, 3 Doc. No. GAO/NSIAD–84–102 (1984).

Pompiliu Verzariu, Countertrade, Barter and Offsets: New Strategies for Profit in International Trade (1985).

Leo B. Welt, Trade Without Money: Barter and Countertrade (1984).

Linda A. Whisman, Countertrade: A Reading List, 19 Int'l Lawyer 1013 (1985).

Chapter 6

DOCUMENTARY LETTERS
OF CREDIT

Table of Sections

A. INTRODUCTION

§ 6.1 Introduction—The Transactional Problem

Unlike most domestic sales transactions, in a sale of goods across national borders the exporter-seller and importer-buyer may not have previously dealt with one another; or each may know nothing about the other, or the other's national legal system. The seller does not know: (1) whether the buyer is creditworthy or trustworthy; (2) whether information received on these subjects from the buyer's associates and bankers

368

is reliable; (3) whether exchange controls will hinder movement of the payment funds (especially if payment is in "hard currency" from a "soft currency" country); (4) how great the exchange risk is if payment in buyer's currency is permitted, and (5) what delays may be involved in receiving unencumbered funds from buyer.

On the other hand, the buyer does not know: (1) whether the seller can be trusted to ship the goods if buyer prepays; (2) whether the goods shipped will be of the quantity and quality contracted for; (3) whether the goods will be shipped by an appropriate carrier and properly insured; (4) whether the goods may be damaged in transit; (5) whether the seller will furnish to the buyer sufficient ownership documentation covering the goods to allow the buyer to claim them from the customs officials; (6) whether the seller will provide the documentation necessary to satisfy export control regulations and import customs and valuation regulations (e.g., country of origin certificates, health and other inspection certificates); and (7) what delays may be involved in receiving unencumbered possession and use of the goods in the buyer-importer's location.

Where the parties are strangers, these risks are significant, possibly overwhelming. Since they operate at a distance from each other, seller and buyer cannot concurrently exchange the goods for the payment funds *without the help of third parties*. The documentary sale, involving the use of a letter of credit, illustrates how these potentially large risks can be distributed to third parties who have special knowledge, can properly evaluate each risk assumed, and thereby can reduce the transaction risks to insignificance.

§ 6.2 The Documentary Sale Transaction

The third party intermediaries enlisted are banks (at least one in buyer's nation and usually a second one in seller's nation) and at least one carrier. Thus, the parties involved are: (1) a buyer, who is also presumably a "customer" of (2) a Buyer's Bank, (3) a seller, (4) a bank with an office in seller's nation (hereafter "Seller's Bank"), and (5) at least one carrier. Among them, these parties are able to take a large risk which is not subject to any firm evaluation, and divide it into several small, calculable risks, each of which is easily borne by one party. Thus, the documentary sale is an example that not all risk allocation is a "zero sum game," but may in fact create a "win-win" situation.

These parties will be related by a series of contracts—but not all of the parties to the transaction will be parties to each contract. The contracts include (A) the sale of goods contract between the buyer and the seller; (B) the bill of lading, a receipt and contract issued by the carrier; and (C) the letter of credit, a promise by Buyer's Bank (and, if confirmed, also by Seller's Bank) to pay seller under certain conditions concerning proof that seller has shipped the goods.

(A) The contract underlying the entire series of transactions is the contract for the sale of goods from buyer to seller. The buyer and the seller are parties to this contract, but the banks and the carrier are not parties. The seller is responsible to deliver the contracted quantity and quality of goods, and buyer is responsible for taking the goods and paying the stated price. (For conditions and further elaborations on this point, see the discussion of the Convention on Contracts for the International Sale of Goods in Chapter 1.)

(B) In documentary sales, buyers and sellers are usually distant from each other, and the goods must be moved. Thus, an international carrier of the goods is usually employed, and either the seller or the buyer will make a contract with the carrier to transport the goods. (For our illustration, seller will make that contract). The seller (or, in the language of a contract of carriage, "shipper") makes a contract with carrier that the goods will be transported to the buyer's ("consignee's") location.

This second contract in our transaction will be expressed in the "bill of lading" issued by the carrier. Under the terms of the bill of lading contract, in return for payment of the freight charge, carrier promises to deliver the goods to either (1) the named "consignee" in a "straight" (or non-negotiable) bill of lading, or (2) the person in possession ("holder") of an "order" (or negotiable) bill of lading.[1] The order (negotiable) bill of lading should be used in the documentary sale (letter of credit transaction), so that the buyer is able to obtain delivery of goods *only if* buyer has physical possession of the bill of lading.[2] Such a bill of lading controls access to and delivery of the goods, so that the bill of lading is also a "document of title."

(C) Before the seller ("shipper") delivers the goods to the carrier, the seller wants assurance that payment will be forthcoming. A promise from the buyer may not be sufficient. Even a promise from a bank in the buyer's nation may not be sufficient, because the seller does not know them or know about them. Instead, the seller wants a promise from a bank known to it, and preferably in the seller's location.

What the seller wants is the third contract in our transaction—a confirmed, irrevocable letter of credit. A letter of credit is a contract—an undertaking (promise) by a bank (usually the Buyer's Bank) that it will pay to seller (or, "will honor drafts drawn on this bank by seller for") the amount of the contract price. The bank's promise is conditioned upon seller's presenting evidence that the goods have been shipped via carrier to arrive in buyer's port, along with any other documents required by the contract for the sale of goods. What would furnish such evidence? The bill of lading between the seller and the carrier, the second contract in our transaction, furnishes the evidence that the seller has shipped the goods.

Further, if it is a negotiable bill of lading, it also controls the right to obtain the goods from carrier. Thus, a negotiable bill of lading delivered by the seller to the Seller's Bank will assure the Bank that: (1) the goods

§ 6.2

1. See § 3.4, supra.

2. See § 3.4, notes 2–4, supra.

have been delivered to carrier, (2) they are destined for the buyer and not some third party, and (3) Bank can control the carrier's delivery of the goods to the buyer by simply retaining possession of the order bill of lading. In other words, when a bank pays seller, it receives from seller a "document of title" issued by carrier which gives the bank control of the carrier's delivery of the goods. The buyer cannot obtain possession of the goods from a carrier without physical possession of the bill of lading, so after the banks have paid the seller for that piece of paper, they can obtain payment (or assurances that the buyer will pay them) before the buyer receives the ability to obtain the goods from the carrier.

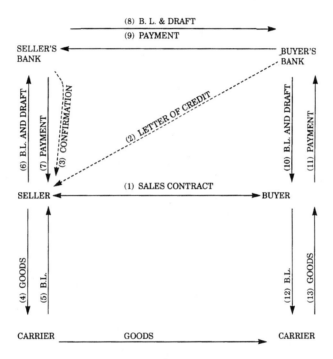

How does the international documentary sales transaction work? An international documentary sale is diagramed above. When the buyer and the seller are forming their contract for the sale of the goods, the seller will insist that the contract have both a "Price" term and a "Payment" term. For maximum protection, the seller will seek payment to be by "Confirmed, Irrevocable Letter of Credit," and should specify what documents are required with great detail. The reason for putting this payment term in the sales contract is that, since the buyer is expected to establish a letter of credit and "to pay against the documents," rather than after delivery and inspection of the goods themselves, that payment term must be bargained for and expressed in the sales contract. It will not normally be implied.[3]

---

3. See § 1.17, supra.

What documents will be required? Usually, they include:

(1) a transport document, usually a negotiable bill of lading (showing transportation company's receipt of the goods to be shipped and the obligation to deliver them only to the holder of the document).[4]

(2) a commercial invoice (which sets out the terms of purchase such as grade and number of goods, price, etc.)

(3) an insurance document, such has a policy of marine insurance (if goods are to go by sea)[5]

(4) a certificate of inspection (issued by a commercial inspecting firm and confirming that the required number and type of goods are being shipped)[6]

(5) certificate of origin (relevant to the rules of origin used by customs personnel in importer's country for determining tariff assessments).[7]

Other documents may be required by the contract between the parties,[8] but it may not require the beneficiary to perform non-documentary conditions.[9]

If buyer agrees to a letter of credit payment term, buyer (or, in the language of the letter of credit), the "applicant"[10] or the "customer"[11] or an "account party" will contract with Buyer's Bank ("issuer" or "issuing bank") to issue a letter of credit ("credit") to seller ("beneficiary"). The letter of credit is a direct promise by the issuing bank that it will pay the contract price to the seller ("beneficiary"), on the condition that the seller presents to it the documents specified in the letter of credit (and also specified previously in the sales contract). The Buyer's Bank will be aware of the buyer's creditworthiness, and there will be a contract between the buyer and the Buyer's Bank (the "credit application agreement") which makes appropriate arrangements to obtain the funds from the buyer (through either immediate payment or future repayment of a loan). These arrangements will be made before the letter

---

4. *See* ICC, Uniform Customs and Practices for Documentary Credits, art. 23 (ICC Publ. 500, 1993) (hereafter, the UCP).

In addition to the negotiable bill of lading, the UCP also permits the use of non-negotiable sea waybills (UCP art. 24), charts party bills of lading (UCP art. 25), multi modal transport documents (UCP art. 26), air transport documents (UCP art. 27), road, rail or inland waterway transport documents (UCP art. 28), courier and post receipts (UCP art. 29), and transport documents issued by freight forwarder.

5. *See* UCP arts. 34, 35.

6. *See* UCP arts. 20, 21. Inspection certificates may be issued either by an inde-

pendent inspection company contracted for by either the buyer or the seller, or by a governmental entity.

7. *See* UCP arts. 20,21.

8. *E.g.,* an export license or a health inspection certificate may be required to show that the goods are cleared for export.

9. UCP art. 13(c). The provision in Revised UCC § 5–108(g) is significantly more limited.

10. Uniform Customs Practices art. 2; Revised UCC § 5–102 (a)(2).

11. UCC (1962) § 5–103 (1)(g).

The UCP uses both terms in UCP art. 2, and uses "the Applicant" thereafter.

of credit is issued, for the Buyer's Bank is bound to the letter of credit terms after issuance if it is irrevocable.

If the seller requires an obligation of a bank in the seller's jurisdiction, the letter of credit must be confirmed by a Seller's Bank ("confirming bank").[12] The Buyer's Bank will forward its letter of credit to the seller through another bank, the Seller's Bank, which is usually a correspondent bank to the Buyer's Bank. By merely indicating "We confirm this credit," the Seller's Bank makes a direct promise to the seller that it will pay the contract price to the seller, if the seller presents the required documents to it. Confirmation of a letter of credit must be bargained for and specified in the sales contract.

If no confirmation of the credit is required by the sales contract, Buyer's Bank can forward the letter of credit through a "notifying bank" or an "advising bank"[13] which is near the seller. These banks act as the agents of the issuing bank and have only a duty to communicate the terms of the credit accurately. They are not obligated to the seller, but will take the documents and forward them to the Buyer's Bank for collection purposes only.

There are many other categories of banks which may be involved in the letters of credit transaction. Any bank which is authorized to pay against the documents is a "nominated bank",[14] whether it also undertakes an obligation to pay or not. "Nominated banks" are usually located in the same jurisdiction but may be located elsewhere. Thus, a "confirming bank" is a nominated bank which also undertakes to pay the credit. A bank which is a nominated bank and has given value for the documents is a "negotiating bank."[15] A "collecting bank" is one which acts as an agent of the beneficiary to take the documents for collection only, and to forward them to the issuer or confirmer.

Once the letter of credit is issued and confirmed, the seller will pack the goods and prepare a commercial invoice, and procure an insurance certificate (another form of contract) covering the goods during transit. If an inspection certificate is required, the goods will be made available to the inspector designated in the sales contract, and the inspecting firm will issue a certificate (another contract) stating that the goods conform to the description in the sales contract. The seller will also prepare the necessary documents for the customs officials in its nation (e.g., export license) and in the buyer's nation (certificate of origin). The seller then sends the goods to the carrier, which issues a negotiable bill of lading as a combination receipt and contract. This bill of lading will commonly be a negotiable document and require carrier to deliver the goods only "to seller or order"—i.e., only to seller, to such other persons as seller may designate by an appropriate endorsement.[16]

12. UCP art. 9; Revised UCC § 5–10 2(a)(4).

13. UCP art. 7; Revised UCC § 5–102 (a)(1).

14. UCP art. 10 (b)(i), (c)i Revised UCC § 5–102 (a)(11).

15. UCP art. 10 (b)(ii).

16. *See* discussion in Chapter 3, supra.

The Seller now has the complete set of documents needed, and takes these documents to the Seller's Bank, which (as a confirming bank) is obligated to pay the seller the contract price upon presentation of the documents. To obtain payment, the seller attaches a "draft"[17] to the documents; and in the letter of credit the banks have promised to honor such a draft. The draft (sometimes also called a "bill of exchange)" resembles a check written by the seller and drawn on the Seller's Bank or on the Buyer's Bank for the amount of the contract price.[18] A draft can be payable on demand ("at sight") in a cash sale, or payable at a later time (e.g. "30 days after sight") in a credit sale. If a "demand draft" is used, the bank will pay the amount immediately, usually by crediting the seller's account either in the Seller's Bank or in some other bank designated by the seller.

If the sales contract has been a sale on credit, the draft will be a "time draft" (e.g. "pay 30 days after sight") and is different from a check in that respect.[19] In that case, the issuer or confirming bank need not pay upon presentment of the draft and documents, but it must "accept"[20] the time draft when it is presented. This "acceptance" creates a promise, an obligation on the part of the issuer or confirming bank, a promise or undertaking that it will pay at the later time stated in the draft.[21] This promise through "acceptance of the draft" is directly enforceable against the party accepting by the "holder"[22] of the draft, and against a "holder in due course,"[23] deprives the acceptor of most of its potential defenses against payment.[24] Thus, if the confirming bank accepts a time draft and the buyer later becomes insolvent, the confirming bank which has accepted the draft must still pay the time draft when it matures. With the bank obligated on the time draft, the seller can immediately raise funds by selling the paper on the strength of the bank's credit.

In return for the bank's payment, the seller will endorse both the draft and the negotiable bill of lading to the Seller's Bank and transfer the other documents to it. The Seller's Bank, in turn, will endorse and will forward the draft, with the required documents attached to the Buyer's Bank. It thus, presents the draft (with the accompanying documents) to the Buyer's Bank for payment.[25] The Buyer's Bank is obligated under the letter of credit to "honor" (accept) the draft and to reimburse the Seller's Bank if the documents attached to the draft are conforming. Since there is already a correspondent relationship between the two banks, the Buyer's Bank will credit the Seller's Bank's account with the amount of the draft. The Buyer's Bank then advises the buyer that the documents have arrived and that payment is due. Since the buyer and the Buyer's Bank usually have an established relationship, the usual

17. Revised UCC § 3–104(e).

18. Revised UCC § 3–104 (f).

19. Revised UCC § 3–104 (f).

20. Revised UCC § 3–401 (a).

21. *Id.*

22. UCC § 1–201 (20); Revised UCC § 3–301.

23. Revised UCC § 3–302.

24. Revised UCC §§ 3–305(b), 3–306.

25. Revised UCC § 3–501.

course of events will be for the bank to be authorized to charge the amount of the draft to the buyer's bank account, and to forward the documents to the buyer. If the buyer has arranged for credit from the Buyer's Bank, the credit will be advanced when the draft and documents arrive. If there was not an established relationship between the buyer and its bank, the buyer would be required to pay (or to arrange sufficient credit for) the draft before the documents were released to it. As the draft and documents are forwarded from the seller to the Seller's Bank to the Buyer's Bank to the buyer, each of these parties will endorse the bill of lading to the next party.

The buyer, like the banks, must pay "against the documents" and not the goods themselves, which is why it is necessary to specify the terms of the documents in the original contract for the sale of goods, and then repeat those specifications precisely in the letter of credit. Once the buyer had paid, or arranged to pay, the Buyer's Bank, it will obtain possession of the bill of lading and only then will it be entitled to obtain the goods from carrier.

After it has obtained possession and endorsement of the bill of lading, the buyer uses the negotiable bill of lading to obtain the goods from the Carrier. Note that the buyer has effectively paid for the goods while they were at sea, long before their arrival. In fact, the buyer was bound to pay for the goods as soon as the draft and required documents were presented to the Seller's Bank. If the goods failed to arrive the buyer must look to its Insurance Certificate for protection and reimbursement.[26] When the goods arrive, carrier may not release them to the buyer unless it is in possession of the negotiable bill of lading, properly endorsed *to* the buyer.[27] Further, the terms of the bill of lading will prohibit the buyer from even inspecting the goods unless it has obtained physical possession of the bill of lading. Thus, until the banks are satisfied that they will be paid by the buyer, they can control the goods by controlling the bill of lading.

§ 6.3   Risk Allocation in the Letter of Credit Transaction—In General

Note the limited risks to each party. If the seller ships conforming goods, it has independent promises of payment from both the buyer and two banks. The banks' promises are enforceable despite assertions of non-conformity of the goods, so long as the documents conform. Seller's Bank never sees the goods, only the documents—so the bank inspects the documents rigorously to determine that they comply exactly with the requirements of the letter of credit, for the documents are its only protection. Substantial performance by seller is not acceptable.[1]

---

26. See discussion of CIF in Chapter 2, supra.

27. See discussion in Chapter 3, supra.

§ 6.3

1. UCP art. 13(a). For further discussion of this issue, see text at § 6.6, notes 7–17, infra.

Thus, as a practical matter, the seller is at risk only if the Seller's Bank fails (and also the Buyer's Bank and the buyer), a risk it can probably evaluate. If the Seller's Bank unjustifiably refuses to perform its obligation, the seller has a cause of action in a local court against a "deep pockets defendant."

Even though the Seller's Bank is obligated to pay the seller on the documents, it is entitled to reimbursement from the Buyer's Bank and from the buyer, and practically is at risk only if the Buyer's Bank (and the buyer) fails or refuses to perform its obligations. Thus, a Seller's Bank has the credit risk concerning solvency of the Buyer's Bank, which it can evaluate better than either the buyer or the seller, and concerning breach of contract, which, since it has multiple level relationships with Buyer's Bank, it is in a better position to induce compliance than the other parties. Thus, when the seller ships and procures conforming documents, there is a risk of nonpayment only if both Buyer's Bank and Seller's Bank fail.

The Buyer's Bank is at risk only if the buyer fails or refuses to perform. If the buyer cannot pay (becomes insolvent) or will not (wrongfully rejects the goods), the Buyer's Bank must still pay the seller against conforming documents. The Buyer's Bank has protection from the bill of lading, including possible resale of the goods, but it is also in a particularly good position to investigate and to evaluate the risk of the buyer's insolvency, and to either obtain funds from the buyer when issuing the letter of credit or sue the buyer for breach of contract if there is a wrongful refusal to pay. Further, the Buyer's Bank had an opportunity to evaluate all of these risks before issuing the letter of credit, and it could adjust its price (fee or interest rate) to compensate for any increased risk.

On the other hand, for its payment of the price, the buyer has a document from the carrier entitling it to delivery of the goods, an insurance certificate protecting the buyer against casualty loss and perhaps an inspection certificate warranting that the goods conform to the sale contract. In other words, the buyer should receive what it bargained for—delivery of conforming goods or insurance proceeds sufficient to cover any loss.

One large risk has been reduced to several smaller ones, and each smaller risk placed on a party which can fairly evaluate it. The lack of substantial risk in the vast bulk of these transactions can be seen by looking at the usual bank charges for this service.

B. BASIC CONCEPTS AND SOURCES OF RULES

§ 6.4 The Governing Rules

The law relating to letters of credit developed before World War I principally in England, and thereafter by courts in the United States.[1] In

---

§ 6.4   1. See J. Dolan, The Law of Letters of the United States, the governing law is usually the applicable state's version of Article 5 of the Uniform Commercial Code. However, most of UCC Article 5 is not mandatory law, and therefore most Article 5 provisions defer to the contract terms of the parties as expressed in the contract.[2]

UCC Article 5 had recently been revised. The Revised Article 5 was adopted by the Uniform Commissioners and the American Law Institute in 1995, and has been enacted by 47 state legislatures, including, after a long delay, the state of New York.[3] In this chapter there will be references to both versions of the UCC, which will distinguish between the original UCC Article 5[4] (hereafter the 1962 version) and the Revised UCC Article 5.[5]

The International Chamber of Commerce (I.C.C.) has developed and published the Uniform Customs and Practices for Documentary Credits (the UCP), which is incorporated by reference in most international letters of credit. The UCP constitutes a rather detailed manual of operations for banks, but they are a restatement of "custom" in the industry, and they do not purport to be law. They are incorporated as an express statement of contract terms and banking trade usage, and the UCP contract terms furnish the rules which usually determine the actions of the parties.

The I.C.C. published the original version of the UCP in 1933, and has published a revision of the UCP about every ten years. The most recent version of the UCP is the 1993 Revision (I.C.C. Publ. No. 500).[6] The rules set forth in the 1993 version are relatively similar to those of prior versions, but there are some differences.

According to the UCP, it is binding if "incorporated into the text of the Credit."[7] Thus, the UCP is applicable to any letter of credit which expressly incorporates the UCP into its terms. However, the UCP is silent as to implicit incorporation of its terms, such as by custom and usage. The language in the 1993 version of the UCP was amended supposedly to require express incorporation,[8] but it used neither the word "expressly," nor the word "only."

There is no need for a "choice of law" conflict between the UCC and the UCP. One is legislation, the other represents the agreed terms of the parties. Since the UCC Article 5 is not mandatory law, and most of its provisions are not mandatory law,[9] it would seem that the UCP provi-

---

Credit (rev. ed. 1999) at §§ 3.01–3.04.

2. For a list of the few provisions in Revised UCC Article 5 which are not open to variant by agreement of the parties, see Rev. UCC § 5–103(c).

3. See http://www.nccusl.org/unifor-mact_factsheets/uniformacts-fs-ucca5.htm.

4. E.g., UCC § 5–102 (1962).

5. E.g., Rev. UCC § 5–102.

6. I.C.C. Uniform Customs and Practices for Documentary Credits (hereafter the UCP) (I.C.C. Publ. No. 500, 1993).

7. UCP art. 1.

8. Dolan, supra note 1, Unofficial Comment to UCP art. 1. However, UCC § 1–205(2) allows inclusion of a proven trade usage. As to whether UCC Article 5 allows consultation of custom, see Dolan, supra note 1, at § 4.07.

9. See note 2, supra.

sions would prevail over the "gap-filler" provisions of UCC Article 5. However, in New York, Alabama, Arizona and Missouri, a non-uniform amendment to the 1962 UCC § 5–102(4)[10] states that the UCP alone governs if it is incorporated into the credit. That provision should make such credits subject to 1940s caselaw,[11] but some of the relevant courts have wisely ignored the provision or used UCC Article 5 by analogy, when necessary.[12] However, the New York Court of Appeals has stated that the New York non-uniform amendment does not displace UCC provisions which codify pre-UCC New York caselaw.[13] The Revised UCC Article 5 provides that the UCP, if expressly chosen by the parties, prevails over all the non-mandatory UCC provisions.[14]

The primary difference between the UCC provisions and the UCP is that the UCC has provisions on fraud and on enjoining payment against documents where fraud or forgery exist,[15] and the UCP has none. Otherwise, their scope, coverage and substance are quite similar.[16] The absence of provisions on fraud and enjoining payment should be expected, however, in the drafting of a set of contract terms to be consented to by the parties. Thus, the UCP provisions will have more impact on the analysis of non-fraud issues, and the UCC Article 5 provisions will be used to resolve issues related to allegations of fraud. Therefore, this chapter will describe the UCP rules for all non-fraud issues, and the UCC provisions on fraud will be described in the next chapter, on standby letters of credit, because that is the transaction which underlies most of the fraud cases[17].

§ 6.5 Applicable Law

One provision which is noticeably absent from the UCP is a term which selects the law applicable to the transaction in the absence of an express choice of law by the parties. The UCC both allows the parties to select the law of any jurisdiction as the law applicable to the letter of credit,[1] and also provides "gap-filler" provisions if the parties do not make such a choice.[2] If no choice is made, "the liability" of each party is

10. NY UCC § 5–102(4) (McKinney Supp. 1995); Ala. Code § 7–5–102(4) (1993); Ariz. Rev. Stat. § 47–5702(4)(1988); Mo. Rev. Stat. § 400.5–102(4) (Vernon Supp. 1994).

11. So held in Newport Indus., N. Am., Inc. v. Berliner Handels Und Frankfurter Bank, 923 F.Supp. 31 (S.D.N.Y.1996); Oei v. Citibank, NA, 957 F.Supp. 492 (S.D.N.Y. 1997).

12. Brenntag Int'l Chemicals, Inc. v. Nordeutsche Landesbank GZ, 70 F.Supp.2d 399 (S.D.N.Y.1999).

13. United Bank, Ltd. v. Cambridge Sporting Goods Corp., 41 N.Y.2d 254, 360 N.E.2d 943, 392 N.Y.S.2d 265 (1976).

14. Revised UCC § 5–116(c).

15. Revised UCC § 5–109; UCC § 5–114(1962).

16. See, e.g., Gustavus, Letter of Credit Compliance under Revised UCC Article 5 and UCP 500, 114 Banking L.J. 55 (1997); Comment, Letters of Credit: A Comparison of Article 5 of the UCP, 41 Loy. L. Rev. 735 (1996).

17. See § 7.13, supra.

§ 6.5

1. Revised UCC § 5–116(a). The general choice of law provisions in UCC Article 1 allow choice of the law of any state or nation if the "transaction bears a reasonable relation to" that state or nation. UCC § 1–105(1).

2. Revised UCC§ 5–116(b). The general choice of law provisions in UCC Article 1 provide that the court in a state which has enacted the UCC shall use its own law (its

governed by the law of the jurisdiction where it is "located."[3] Presumably, the rights of each party are not governed by the law where it is located, but are co-extensive with the liabilities of each of the other parties. However, the Revised UCC provisions concern only the liabilities of each of the issuer, the nominated person and the advisor, and does not include the applicant. Apparently, the choice of law for the applicant is left to the contract between the applicant and the issuer, or to general conflict doctrines.

The UCP establishes four categories of banks in the letter of credit transaction: an issuing bank an advising bank, a confirming bank, and a nominated bank, and they are located in different jurisdictions. An issuing bank is usually located in the buyer's jurisdiction and promises to honor drafts on itself, if the documents stated in the letter of credit (conforming documents) are presented to it.[4] An advising bank is usually located in the seller's jurisdiction and advises the beneficiary (usually the seller) of the documentary credit, but makes no promise to pay against documents.[5] It is obligated to take "reasonable care" to check the authenticity of the credit before advising, but is not otherwise obligated. A confirming bank is also usually located in seller's jurisdiction and receives the credit from the issuing bank and adds its own promise to honor drafts presented to it if accompanied by conforming documents.[6] A nominated bank is often located in Seller's jurisdiction, but may be in a third jurisdiction, and is designated by the issuing bank to pay or negotiate the drafts which accompany the required documents.[7] It may, or may not, be a confirming bank, but a confirming bank is a nominated bank. Outside the United States, the courts will not use the UCC provisions, but will use their own choice of law doctrines. They will uphold a choice of law clause stated in the letter of credit contract,[8] but a choice of law clause stated in the underlying sale contract is not necessarily applicable to the letter of credit contract. If there is no choice of law clause, the traditional doctrine is that the applicable law is the law of the place of performance of the contract, or, in the letter of credit context, the place of payment of the credit against presentation of the documents. Thus, where a straight credit is issued (only the issuer may pay), the law of the issuer's location is applicable.[9] Where there is a

own state's version of the UCC) if the transaction bears an "appropriate relation" to the forum state. UCC § 1–105(1), last sentence.

3. Revised UCC § 5–116(b). A person is "located" at the address stated on the person's undertaking, from which the undertaking was issued.

4. UCP art. 9(a). The UCC equivalent is the "issuer," Rev. UCC § 5–102(a)(9).

5. UCP art. 7. The UCC equivalent is the "advisor," Rev. UCC§ 5–102(a)(1).

6. UCP art. 9(b). The UCC equivalent is the "confirmer," Rev. UCC § 5–102(a)(4).

7. UCP art. 10(b)(i), (c). The UCC equivalent is the "nominated person," Rev. UCC § 5–102(a)(ii).

Under the UCP, if the letter of credit does not state expressly that honor is available only with the issuing band, either the credit must designate a specific bank that is authorized to honor it or it becomes "freely negotiable credit" and any bank is authorized to honor it.

8. Bonny v. Society of Lloyd's, 3 F.3d 156 (7th Cir.1993), cert denied 510 U.S. 1113, 114 S.Ct. 1057, 127 L.Ed.2d 378 (1994).

9. Sinotani Pacific Pte Ltd. v. Agricultural Bank of China, 1999–4 Singapore L. R. 34 (C.A. 1999).

confirmed letter of credit, the law of the confirming bank is applicable, because that is the jurisdiction where payment of the beneficiary is made against presentation of the documents.[10]

The traditional doctrine applies the same law to all segments of the credit transaction. The Revised Article 5 doctrine will change this approach, however, and apply different rules to the obligations of the issuer and of the confirmer. This, in turn, could lead to the use of different standards for determining strict compliance, or different rules for transmission errors or effectiveness of communication. The law which governed the liability of the nominated bank in a "freely negotiated credit"[11] could not be determined until after the seller had presented the credit to that bank for honor.

§ 6.6   Basic Legal Principles

There are two basic principles of the letter of credit rules promulgated by the UCP (and also of UCC Article 5). One is that the banks' obligations under the letter of credit are independent of the buyer's and seller's obligations under the contract for the sale of goods–the Independent Principle.[1] The promises of an issuing bank or a confirming bank are not subject to claims or defense by the applicant (Buyer) that the beneficiary (Seller) has not performed its obligations under the sales contract.[2] The issuing and conforming banks have made their own undertakings to the beneficiary that the banks will perform if the beneficiary (Seller) performs its obligations under the letter of credit contract, regardless of whether those obligations fulfill the sales contract obligations or not. Although the bank's obligations may not be subject to contract claims and defenses, they may still be subject to claims by the applicant (Buyer) relating to fraud by the beneficiary (Seller),[3] as will be discussed below.[4] As has been discussed previously,[5] the UCP has no provisions concerning fraud, and therefore such issues must be analyzed under UCC Article 5, where U.S. law is applicable.

The second principle is that banks deal only with documents, and not with the goods or any issues concerning performance of the sale contract.[6] However, since the banks pay the beneficiary (Seller) against the documents, and never see the goods, banks insist on "perfect tender" and "strict compliance" with all documentary conditions.[7] The

---

10. Power Curber Int'l Ltd. v. National Bank of Kuwait, [1981] 3 All Eng. Rep. 607 (CA), noted (1981) J. Bus. Law 384; Offshore Int'l SA v. Banco Cent. SA, [1976] 2 Lloyd's Rep. 402 (QB).

11. See note 7.

§ 6.6

1. UCP art. 3; Newport Indus. NA v. Berliner Handels Und Frankfurter Bank, 923 F.Supp. 31 (S.D.N.Y.1996).

2. UCP art. 3(a); Banca Del Sempione v. Provident Bank, 160 F.3d 992 (4th Cir. 1998).

3. Rev. UCC § 5–109, UCC (1962) § 5–114.

4. See § 7.13, infra.

5. See supra § 6.4, at note 15.

6. UCP art. 4.

7. UCP art. 13(a). Buckley, The 1993 Revision of the UCP, 28 Geo. Wash. J. Int'l and Econ. 256 (1994), raises the issue of whether the language added in the 1993 revisions referring to "international standard banking practice" loosens the "strict compliance" doctrine, and concludes that it

primary document for describing the goods in a documentary sale transaction is the commercial invoice. The description in the commercial invoice must be specific and must "correspond with the description in the credit;" descriptions in all other documents can be general and need only be "consistent" with the description in the credit.[8] Thus, where a credit called for "100% acrylic yarn" and the invoice merely stated "imported acrylic yarn," the credit was not satisfied, even though the packing list stated "100% acrylic yarn."[9] The archetypical case of the strict compliance doctrine was an English court's determination that "machine shelled groundnut kernels" was not the same description as "Coromandel groundnuts," even though it was agreed that the same goods were described by either label. Bankers could not be expected to know that, or to find it out.[10]

Many of the cases which litigate issues concerning the strict conformity of documents seem to revolve around discrepancies in transportation terms. Express conditions in the credit that loading, presentment or other acts must be performed by a certain time will be strictly enforced.[11] So also, a discrepancy in the location of shipment or delivery will fail to comply with the terms of a credit.[12] A credit calling for "Full Set Clean on board ocean bills of lading" is not satisfied by a tender of "truckers bills of lading," even though evidence was presented that the bills of lading were in customary Mexican form and that Mexican truckers did not specify on the bill of lading that the goods were "on board."[13] Nor is the "Full Set Clean on Board Bills of Lading" requirement satisfied by air waybills, even though air delivery may be preferable.[14] Discrepancies which seem not to warrant rejection include technically invalid clauses in bills of lading which limit the carrier's liability.[15]

does not, because of the reference to "as reflected in these Articles."

A "substantial performance standard under several First Circuit cases appears to be no longer viable." Flagship Cruises Ltd. v. New England Merchants Nat. Bank, 569 F.2d 699 (1st Cir.1978); Banco Espanol de Credito v. State Street Bank and Trust, 385 F.2d 230 (1st Cir.1967), cert. denied, 390 U.S. 1013, 88 S.Ct. 1263, 20 L.Ed.2d 163 (1968). See Rev. UCC § 5–108 and Comment.

8. UCP art. 37(c).

9. Courtaulds North America, Inc. v. North Carolina Nat. Bank, 528 F.2d 802 (4th Cir.1975).

10. J.H. Rayner & Co. Ltd. v. Hambros Bank Ltd. [1943] 1 K.B. 37 (Court of Appeal).

11. Voest–Alpine Int'l Corp. v. Chase Manhattan Bank, NA, 545 F.Supp. 301 (S.D.N.Y.1982).

12. Bank of Nova Scotia v. Angelica–Whitewear Ltd., 36 Dom. L.R. 4th 161 (Can. 1987); Bucci Imports, Ltd. v. Chase

Bank Int'l, 518 N.Y.S.2d 15, 132 A.D.2d 641 (1987).

In a pre-UCC case, the seller-shipper did not prepay the freight charges on a CIF contract, but instead credited the freight charges against the amount of the invoice price, and then submitted the resulting documents to the issuing bank. The issuing bank rejected the documents, and refused to pay the draft accompanying the documents, as non-conforming. It argued that the documents did not strictly comply with CIF terms. However, in Dixon, Irmaos & Cia, Ltda v. Chase Nat. Bank, 144 F.2d 759 (2d Cir.1944), the court held that the documents were conforming because of "ancient usage" which permitted shippers to take such action.

13. Marine Midland Grace Trust Co. of N.Y. v. Banco Del Pais, S.A., 261 F.Supp. 884 (S.D.N.Y.1966).

14. Board of Trade v. Swiss Credit Bank, 597 F.2d 146 (9th Cir.1979).

15. British IMEX Indus., Ltd. v. Midland Bank, Ltd., [1958] 1 All Eng. Rep. 264.

There is authority that questions concerning strict compliance are issues of law, and not issues of fact for a jury.[16]

Recent UCP cases have involved substitutes for original documents. In *Western Int'l Forest Products v. Shinhan Bank*,[17] the letter of credit required the presentation of an original of an inspection certificate along with other documents. The designated inspector executed an inspection certificate and faxed it to the seller. The seller stamped the faxed copy "original" and sent it to the freight forwarder. When the documents were presented to the issuer, it refused payment, and the court upheld its action. Only the inspector could authenticate a copy. In another case, the letter of credit required the presentation of the original letter of credit and a promissory note. The beneficiary presented copies of both, an indemnity, and an affidavit that the originals were lost. The bank refused payment, and the court upheld that action.[18]

Not all discrepancies are permit the banks to refuse payment, however. In *Automation Source Corp. v. Korea Exchange Bank*,[19] the issuing bank detected two discrepancies. First, the shipping documents listed two "notifying parties," while the letter of credit required that the shipping documents instruct the consignee to notify the applicant. Second, two of the packages in the shipping documents listed identical contents, but had different weights. The court noted that the second notify party had been added at the request of the applicant and rejected any claim that listing an extra notify party created an ambiguity; but the court remanded the case for a factual determination as to whether any banking custom existed on duties to deliver documents to such parties. The court held that, since the letter of credit did not refer to the weight of the shipment, any discrepancy in weights would relate to the sales contract; and, under the "independence principle" be irrelevant to the issuer's obligation under its letter of credit contract.

C. HONOR AND DISHONOR

§ 6.7 Wrongful Dishonor of a Credit

If the issuing bank or the confirming bank dishonors the credit, and refuse to pay when the documents are presented, the dishonor may be rightful or wrongful. If there truly are discrepancies between the specifications in the credit and the documents actually presented (and they are not waived),[1] the banks are entitled to dishonor, although they must follow the notice procedures specified in the UCP to protect themselves.[2]

16. Siderius, Inc. v. Wallace Co., 583 S.W.2d 852 (Tex.Civ.App.1979).

17. 860 F.Supp. 151 (S.D.N.Y.1994).

18. Brul v. MidAmerican Bank and Trust Co., 820 F.Supp. 1311, 22 U.C.C. Rep.Serv. 2d 1125 (D.Kan.1993). UCC (1962) § 5–113 permitted issuers to take indemnities, but did not require them to do so. Rev. UCC Article 5 has no such provisions.

19. 249 A.D.2d 1, 670 N.Y.S.2d 847, 37 U.C.C. Rep.Serv.2d 372 (App.Div.1998).

§ 6.7

1. UCP art. 14 (c). See further discussion at § 6.10, notes 8–11, infra.

2. See generally UCP art. 14. For further discussion see § 6.10, infra.

If the procedures are correctly followed, there is no liability of anyone on the credit, and no successful litigation on the credit[3] should ensue. For example, in *Western International Forest Products*, supra,[4] the issuer properly dishonored under the "strict compliance" principle, the beneficiary (seller) sued the issuing bank—-and lost. Most of the cases involving rightful dishonor involve litigation over the timeliness and effectiveness of the notice of dishonor to prior parties.

If the issuer dishonors a presentation of documents which do comply strictly to the letter of credit, that is a wrongful dishonor. It is also a breach of one or more contracts. First, it is a breach of the letter of credit contract, for which the beneficiary will have a cause of action. Second, it may be a breach of the credit application agreement between the applicant and the issuer for which the applicant may have a cause of action. The former is governed by statute the letter is not. The UCP has no provisions on the subject.

The Revised Article 5 gives the beneficiary of a letter of credit whose presentation was wrongfully dishonored a cause of action against the issuer.[5] In addition it establishes the amount of damages which the aggrieved beneficiary may claim as "the amount of money that is the subject of the dishonor."[6] This amount does not necessarily equate to the actual damages suffered by the beneficiary. The beneficiary has no obligation to mitigate damages, but if it does actually avoid part of the loss, the recovery is reduced by the amount of the loss avoided. In addition, the aggrieved beneficiary can recover incidental damages and interest, but not consequential damages.

If the issuer wrongfully dishonors a presentation, the applicant may also be damaged. The most common harm is damage to the applicant's reputation in the trade, and an unwillingness of suppliers to accept subsequent letters of credit from the applicant. Prior to the revisions of UCC Article 5, it was usually held that the applicant was not actually a party to the letter of credit, so that it could not bring an action on the letter of credit itself for wrongful dishonor of the credit.[7] Instead, the applicant's right to sue the issuer for wrongful dishonor would arise out of the credit application agreement, and would be analyzed under ordinary contract law. It would also depend upon the terms of the credit application agreement, which might or might not include a clause disclaiming liability of the issues for wrongful dishonor.[8]

That analytical approach may be pre-empted under the revisions to UCC Article 5. Under Revised UCC Article 5, the applicant is given a

3. There may well, however, be successful litigation between the buyer and the seller for breach of the sale of goods contract. See UCC article 2.

4. Supra, § 6.6, note 17.

5. Rev. UCC § 5–111 (a). The provision in the original version was UCC § 5–115(1)(1962).

6. *Id.* Under the 1962 version, however, the damages measurement provision produced a recovery closer to actual damages.

7. Interchemicals Co. v. Bank of Credit, 222 A.D.2d 273, 635 N.Y.S.2d 194 (App.Div. 1995).

8. *Id.* In *Interchemicals*, the application agreement did include such a waiver.

statutory cause of action against the issuer for wrongful dishonor of the credit.[9] This cause of action would arise out of the statute, not the agreement, and would be analyzed according to the statutory terms, not the terms of the agreement. The most important statutory term regulating this cause of action is that the applicant can never recover consequential damages, even if foreseeable.[10] Thus, applicant's recovery for the most common form of harm—-damage to reputation—-would seem to be foreclosed in the statutory action. However, the contract cause of action under the credit application agreement may survive the enactment of the statutory cause of action, because the Official Comments state that "this section does not bar recovery ... for breach ... of common law duties outside of this article."[11]

The Comments do pose one circumstance in which the statutory action by the applicant is expected to be successful. Where the applicant has back-to-back credits,[12] the wrongful dishonor of the documents under the first credit prevents the applicant from properly performing its obligations as beneficiary under the second credit. The Official Comments indicate that recovery of damages to the applicant from the issuer of the first credit should be expected in such a situation.[13]

§ 6.8 Wrongful Honor of the Credit

The issuing or confirming bank may honor the credit, paying the beneficiary or accepting a time draft when the documents are presented and this honor may be rightful or wrongful. If there are no discrepancies between the specifications in the credit (or they are waived)[1] and the documents actually presented, the banks are obligated to honor the presentation, and are entitled to reimbursement from the applicant. After the letter of credit is honored, the beneficiary has received payment or the acceptance of its time draft,[2] so its claims should be satisfied and no litigation on the credit should ensue.

After a letter of credit has been honored, the issuer will seek reimbursement from the applicant under the credit application agreement. Alternatively, if that is not available, the issuer can seek reimbursement under banking custom or applicable law.[3] If the documents are conforming, so that the banks rightfully honored the beneficiary's presentation, the applicant has no defense to the issuer's reimbursement claim. The issuer has performed its contractual obligation to the applicant and is entitled to counterperformance. If the issuer granted credit to the applicant, the issuer has consciously taken the risk that the applicant would be unable to pay, and should have made provision for that possibility through taking collateral, obtaining a third party's guarantee, or seeking pre-payment.

---

9. Rev. UCC § 5–111 (b).

10. *Id.*

11. Rev. UCC § 5–111, Comment 4.

12. *See* discussion at § 6.13, infra.

13. Rev. UCC § 5–111, Comment 2.

§ 6.8

1. See discussion in § 6.9, infra.

2. See discussion in § 6.2, supra.

3. See, e.g., Rev. UCC § 5–108(i).

On the other hand, if the documents have discrepancies and the issuer honors the beneficiary's presentation, that is a wrongful honor. The issuer may still seek reimbursement from the applicant, arguing that it has a right to such reimbursement even if it paid against documents that did not strictly comply with the letter of credit. The issuing bank may even debit the applicant's account with the bank, and compel the applicant to litigate to seek an order to re-credit that account.[4] There is a split of opinion as to whether the issuer is entitled to be reimbursed for a wrongful honor.[5]

The division of opinion arises from the difference between the letter of credit contract and the credit application agreement. The former is governed by statute, the latter is not. the standards for breach of each type of contract may be different.[6] Before either the UCC or the UCP, the law was relatively clear. A wrongful honor was a bar to recovery from the applicant by the issuer.[7]

The UCP has no provisions directly addressing the subject, although two UCP Articles can be used to formulate the various conflicting arguments. One argument is that, although the beneficiary is held to a "strict compliance" standard under the letter of credit,[8] the issuing bank is held to a lesser standard, because its liability arises under the credit application agreement, not the letter of credit. This argument finds some support in UCP Article 13(a), which fixes a standard of examination for banks that only requires them to use "reasonable care, to ascertain whether or not [the documents] appear, on their face, to be in compliance ..."[9] They argue that "reasonable care" and "appearance" language, when applied to ordinary contracts, connotes only a substantial performance standard.

The contrary position draws support from the construction of UCP Article 14, which equates the examinations of nominated banks, confirming banks and issuers, and then applies the same standards to each.[10] There seems to be agreement that nominated banks and confirming banks must meet a strict compliance standard, and that, for those banks, the "reasonable care" and "appearance" language applies to the examination process, not to the standard of compliance.[11]

The Revised UCC Article 5 also has no provisions directly addressing the issue. The applicant is not given (or denied) a cause of action for

---

4. Oei v. Citibank NA, 957 F.Supp. 492 (S.D.N.Y.1997).

5. See Dolan, supra § 6.4, note 1 at § 9.03.

6. Id.

7. Anglo–S. Am., Trust Co. v. Uhe, 261 N.Y. 150, 184 N.E. 741 (1933); Equitable Trust Co. v. Dawson Partners, Ltd., 27 Lloyd's Rep. 49 (H.L. 1927), H. Harfield, Bank Credits and Acceptances, 105–108 (5th ed. 1974). Cf., Bank of New York and Trust Co. v. Atterbury Bros., 226 App.Div. 117, 234 N.Y.S. 442 (1929) (proper person

paid under variant of specified name); Bank of Montreal v. Recknagel, 109 N.Y. 482, 17 N.E. 217 (1888) (non-material variation excused).

8. See discussion supra, § 6.6 at notes 7–19.

9. UCP art. 13(a).

10. UCP art. 14(a).

11. Bank of Cochin Ltd. v. Manufacturers Hanover Trust Co., 612 F.Supp. 1533 (S.D.N.Y.1985); aff'd 808 F.2d 209 (2d Cir. 1986).

wrongful honor.[12] The obligation of the issuer, that it "shall dishonor a presentation that does not appear [on its face strictly] to comply"[13] is made clear, but the UCC standard is ambiguous. The UCC ambiguity has many of the same dimensions as the similar ambiguity in the UCP, but the "appearance" must be one of strict compliance. These statutory duties can probably be modified by "agreement otherwise," so interpretation of the credit application agreement may be more important than interpretation of either the UCC or the UCP. Such agreements may include issuer disclaimers of liability for wrongful honor as well as wrongful dishonor.[14]

The cases are split, with a majority favoring no reimbursement from the applicant to the issuer after the issuer has wrongfully honored the presentation,[15] but in many of these cases the pronouncement is dictum.[16] The latter group of cases more often turns on the effectiveness, or lack thereof, of notices and other process requirements between the parties. The cases which apply a standard of less than strict compliance for the issuer to obtain reimbursement after wrongful honor involve a failure of the issuer to certify documents before forwarding them to the applicant[17] and a change of status by an employee designated to sign for a corporation—but the correct party did sign.[18]

If the issuer debits the applicant's account, the applicant may sue the issuer to have the account recredited.[19] If the applicant cannot, or does not wish to, sue the issuer, it probably does not have a cause of action against the confirming bank. The applicant is not a party to the letter of credit, has no contractual relationship with the confirming bank, and therefore lacks the necessary privity of contract to sue.[20]

If the issuer has wrongfully honored the beneficiary's presentation, and cannot obtain reimbursement from the applicant, it may seek to recover from the beneficiary. It may seek to recover directly from the beneficiary on a breach of warranty, or indirectly as an assignee or subrogee of the applicant's rights. The UCC provides that the beneficiary gives a warranty to the issuer that there is no fraud or forgery of the

---

12. Note that Rev. UCC § 5–111(b) applies only to cases of wrongful dishonor.

13. Rev. UCC § 5–108(a), (e).

14. See Interchemicals, § 6.7, note 7, supra.

15. Oei v. Citibank NA, 957 F.Supp. 492 (S.D.N.Y.1997); Pioneer Bank and Trust Co. v. Seiko Sporting Goods USA Co., 184 Ill.App.3d 783, 132 Ill.Dec. 886, 540 N.E.2d 808 (1989); Gulf So. Bank and Trust Co. v. Holden, 562 So.2d 1132 (La.App.1990). Contra: Transamerica Delaval, Inc. v. Citibank, 545 F.Supp. 200 (S.D.N.Y.1982); and case cited in notes 17, 18, infra.

16. Bank of Nova Scotia v. Agelica–Whitewear Ltd., 36 Dom. Rep. 4th 161 (Can. 1987); Computer Place Services Pte Ltd. v. Malayan Bank Bhd, 1996–3 Singapore L.R. 287 (High Ct. 1996); Philadelphia Gear

Corp. v. Central Bank, 717 F.2d 230 (5th Cir.1983); International Leather Distributors, Inc. v. Chase Manhattan Bank, N.A., 464 F.Supp. 1197 (S.D.N.Y.1979), aff'd 607 F.2d 996 (2d Cir.1979).

17. Morgan Guaranty Trust Co. v. Vend Technologies, Inc., 100 A.D.2d 782, 474 N.Y.S.2d 67 (1984).

18. First National Bank v. Carmouche, 504 So.2d 1153 (La.Ct.App.), rev'd on other gnds. 515 So.2d 785 (La.1987).

19. Oei, supra note 16.

20. Dulien Steel Products, Inc. v. Bankers Trust Co., 298 F.2d 836 (2d Cir.1962); United States v. Foster Wheeler Corp., 639 F.Supp. 1266 (S.D.N.Y.1986).

documents, but that warranty is not so broad as to cover all discrepancies in the documents, or even simple breach of contract.[21] The beneficiary also gives a warranty to the applicant but it is different in substance. The beneficiary warrants to the applicant that the documents do not violate the sales agreement.[22] The difference between these warranties is to promote finality to the letter of credit transaction, so that litigation between parties to the letter of credit transaction does not continue over obligations on the sales transaction, after the letter of credit is paid.[23] Except in New York, and other states with the same non-uniform amendment, incorporation of the UCP by the parties should not limit the availability of the UCC warranties.[24]

§ 6.9   Examination of the Documents for Discrepancies

Discrepancies in tendered documents are an everyday occurrence. The Preface to the 1993 version of the UCP states that some surveys find that fifty percent of documents presented are rejected for discrepancies.[1] There is also expert testimony in one case stating that discrepancies are discovered in nearly one half of all documentary transactions.[2] Other commentary and cases indicate between one half and two thirds of all such presentations contain at least one discrepancy.[3] That rate of error should not be surprising if one understands that the presentation may consist of 967 pages of documents.[4] However, it is clear that the "strict compliance" standard itself causes problems.

Under the UCP, "banks must examine all documents ... with reasonable care, to ascertain whether or not they appear, on their face, to be in compliance ..." "and" Compliance ... shall be determined by international standard banking practice as reflected in these Articles.[5] According to the draftsmen, the reference to "international banking practice" was added ti the 1993 version of the UCP in order to prevent "sharp, dishonest or negligent" use of strict compliance standards, and therefore to add some flexibility to the previous standards. But, since the "international ... practice" must be "as reflected in these Article," it is difficult to be certain whether any change is intended at all, since no other UCP provision deals with the issue.[6] Further, there may be no "international standard banking practices," since practices in London are different from those in developing countries. Thus, the prior "strict

---

21. Rev. UCC § 5–110(a)(1). See Mennen v. J.P. Morgan and Co., 91 N.Y.2d 13, 666 N.Y.S.2d 975, 689 N.E.2d 869 (N.Y. 1997).

22. Rev. UCC § 5–110(a)(2).

23. Rev. UCC § 5–110; Comment 2.

24. Chase Manhattan Bank v. Am–Tak Furniture Importers, Inc., 269 A.D.2d 882, 706 N.Y.S.2d 297 (App.Div.2000).

§ 6.9

1. UCP, Preface

2. Banker's Trust Co. v. State Bank of India, [1991] 1 Lloyd's Rep. 587, affirmed [1991] 2 Lloyd's Rep. 443 (C.A.).

3. Buckley, The 1993 Revision of the UCP, 28 Geo. Wash. J. Int'l Law and Econ. 256 (1994).

4. Banker's Trust Co., supra note 2.

5. UCP art. 13(a).

6. Buckley, supra note 3.

compliance" standard, with all its rejections of documents, is likely to continue.

When documents are tendered to an issuing or a confirming bank (or a nominated bank acting for them), it has two duties. One is to examine the documents to determine whether they conform to the terms of the letter of credit.[7] The second is to act upon any discrepancies found.[8]

The examination must be, not only thorough, but also quick. If the bank does discover discrepancies, it may reject the documents without consulting its customer, the applicant (Buyer). However, in many situations, the discrepancies may be trivial or typographical, and the applicant-buyer may want the payment made, and the goods delivered, despite the discrepancy. Thus, the UCP allows, but does not require, the bank to consult the applicant, its customer, for a waiver of the discrepancies it has discovered.[9] That provision does not permit the bank to seek help from the applicant to find further discrepancies.[10] About 90% of the time that they are consulted by the issuing bank, applicants will in fact waive the discrepancies discovered by the bank.[11] Thus, the system continues to work despite possible rejection of the documents in half the cases, because the non-bank parties (Buyer and Seller) want the transaction to be completed despite the technical difficulties imposed by the banking system.

The UCP gives the bank a "reasonable time, not to exceed seven banking days ... to determine whether to take up or refuse the documents."[12] This does not mean that all banks have seven days to examine the documents. Instead, banks have a "reasonable time" with an outside fixed time limit. As will be discussed in the next section,[13] the length of a reasonable time will vary with the amount and complexity of the documents, whether the defects are curable within the life of the credit, whether consultation with the applicant is required to seek a waivers of discrepancies, and whether any discrepancies are found.

However, if the bank discovers no discrepancies, so that there is no need for consultation with the applicant, the reasonable time for examination may be very short. For example, in one reported case, the employees of the issuing bank were able to examine 967 pages of documents twice in the period of two and a half days.[14] If the bank decides to accept the documents, it must honor the accompanying draft, and remit any proceeds to the beneficiary.[15]

---

7. UCP art. 13(a).

8. See § 6.10, infra.

9. UCP art. 14(a).

10. So held in Banker's Trust Co., supra note 2, and E & H Partners v. Broadway Nat. Bank, 39 F.Supp.2d 275 (S.D.N.Y. 1998).

11. Buckley, supra not 3.

12. UCP art. 13(b).

13. See discussion § 6.10, notes 11–12 infra.

14. Banker's Trust Co., supra note 2.

15. UCP art. 14(a).

§ 6.10   Notification of Discrepancies

On the other hand, if the bank discovers discrepancies, it must act to notify the person presenting the documents. It is under these circumstances that the "reasonable time" and the "seven banking days" limits may generate time pressures. This is due to the number of different actions which usually must be squeezed into the relevant time period. First, the bank must examine the document for discrepancies, as was discussed in the preceding section. Second, if discrepancies are found, the bank is authorized by the UCP to "approach the Applicant for a waiver of the discrepancy."[1] Third, if discrepancies are found, the bank must prepare a notification of dishonor which specifies all, not merely some, of the discrepancies relied upon to dishonor the presentation.[2]

The seven-day deadline should not become a "reasonable time" in all transactions, especially in simple transactions where all the documents can be examined in an hour or two. If seven banking days did become the norm, a beneficiary would not know for three weeks whether the funds were firm or not in transactions involving a non-confirmed letter of credit with a local nominated bank. Current practice is much quicker than that.

The cases make it clear that "seven banking days" is not a safe harbor provision. The bank has only a "reasonable time," and that may be significantly less than seven days.[3] Delays of over seven banking days are almost always too long,[4] although there are cases in which longer delays have been permitted under special circumstances.[5] Several cases have held that the reasonableness of any delay is an issue of fact for the jury or other trier of fact,[6] but this has been criticized.[7]

If the bank discovers discrepancies, as it will in half of the presentations,[8] it is authorized to contact the applicant, describe the discrepancies, and ask the applicant whether it chooses to waive the discrepancies or not.[9] Although the UCP does not require banks to do this, it may be expected by the applicant, the bank's customer, and therefore be commercially necessary, even if it is not legally necessary. It has been

§ 6.10

1. UCP art 14(d)(i).

2. UCP art. 14(e).

3. Datapoint Corp. v. M and I Bank, 665 F.Supp. 722 (W.D.Wis.1987) But see Bombay Industries, Inc. v. Bank of New York, 27 U.C.C. Rep.Serv.2d 987 (Sup.Ct. 1995), rev'd 233 A.D.2d 146, 649 N.Y.S.2d 784 (App. Div. 1996).

4. Bank of Cochin Ltd. v. Manufacturers Hanover Trust Co., 808 F.2d 209 (2d Cir.1986); Kuntal, S.A. v. Bank of New York, 703 F.Supp. 312 (S.D.N.Y.1989); Hamilton Bank, N.A. v. Kookmin Bank, 44 F. Supp. 2d 653, 38 UCC Rep.Serv.2d 930 (S.D.N.Y.1999), aff'd in part, vac'd in part 245 F.3d 82 (2d Cir.2001).

5. Alaska Textile Co. Inc. v. Chase Manhattan Bank, N.A. 982 F.2d 813 (2d Cir. 1992).

6. Hellenic Republic v. Standard Chartered Bank, 244 A.D.2d 240, 664 N.Y.S.2d 434, 36 U.C.C. Rep.Serv.2d 502 (App.Div. 1997); Rhode Island Hospital Trust Nat. Bank v. Eastern General Contractors, Inc., 674 A.2d 1227 (R.I.1996) (Standby letters of credit).

7. Barnes and Byrne, Survey: Letters of Credit: 1998 Cases, 54 Bus. Law. 1885 (1999).

8. See authorities cited at § 6.9, notes 1–3, supra.

9. UCP art. 14(c).

estimated that such waivers are granted in 90% of the transactions in which they are sought.[10] However, the bank must seek a waiver from the applicant based on the bank's examination of the documents, not assistance from the applicant in discovering discrepancies.[11]

Thus, the "seven banking days" deadline includes not only time to examine the documents presented, but also time to consult the bank's customer (Buyer) about waiving the discrepancies *and* notifying the party from whom the documents were received. It is the latter two requirements which can create difficulties. It is easier to deduce a "reasonable time" for clerks to examine documents than it is to determine such a time period for consulting with the customer, the applicant, and obtaining a response. The issuing bank may also wish to delay notification of prior parties about any discrepancies, because it must be very careful in making that notification.

If the bank discovers discrepancies, and the applicant does not waive the discrepancies, then the issuer should dishonor the presentation of the draft and documents.[12] If it does determine to dishonor the presentation, then it must act to notify the person who presented the documents both of the fact of dishonor and the reasons for dishonor. In its notice of dishonor, simply stating that the documents are defective ("discrepant docs") is not sufficient, the notice must also specify what the discrepancies are.[13] If it fails to notify, on a timely basis,[14] specifying the defects, it "shall be *precluded* from claiming that the documents are not in compliance with the terms and conditions of the Credit."[15] Most of the reported cases involve some dispute over whether the dishonoring bank has properly fulfilled its notification obligations or whether it is "precluded" to defend its dishonor on this basis.

In addition to specifying what the discrepancies are, the UCP also requires any bank which rejects a presentation of documents to "state all discrepancies" that it will rely upon in its notice to the person who presented the documents.[16] Failure to state all the discrepancies "precludes" the bank from claiming non-compliance due to any unstated discrepancies,[17] without the necessity of proving waiver or estoppel. Thus, banks which reject documents have only one chance to identify all the discrepancies on which they can ever rely. The rationale for this rule is to inform the beneficiary (Seller) of all the discrepancies at once, so that it can determine whether they all can be cured and whether such cure is cost-effective. But the rule can also lead the issuing bank to delay

10. See Buckley, § 6.9, note 3, supra.

11. See Banker's Trust Co., § 6.9, note 2, supra.

12. UCP art. 14(b) states that the bank "may" refuse to take-up the documents. However, if it does take them up, it may not be entitled to reimbursement. See § 6.8, supra, on Wrongful Honor.

13. See., e.g., Creaciones Con Idea, S.A. v. MashreqBank PSC, 51 F. Supp. 2d 423,

38 UCC Rep.Serv.2d 946 (S.D.N.Y.1999); Hamilton Bank, supra note 4.

14. See discussion at notes 11–12, supra.

15. UCP art. 14(e). (emphasis added).

16. UCP art. 14(d). See authorities cited at note 14, supra.

17. UCP art. 14(e).

notification for additional re-examinations to ensure that all defects are discovered.

In addition to provisions specifying time limits and specification of discrepancies of the notification of dishonor, the UCP also has provisions specifying the manner in which the notice must be communicated. The notice must be sent "by telecommunication" if possible;[18] use of a courier will not be proper.[19] However, a telephone call is subject to misinterpretation, or at least different interpretations, and is likely to produce litigation.[20]

The bank may not be required to follow this procedure if the credit has expired.[21] However, the simple fact that the beneficiary sent documents which were clearly discrepant, or that the beneficiary knew that they were discrepant, will not excuse the issuing bank from strict compliance with the notice requirements.[22] The price of not strictly following the UCP is "preclusion" from being able to raise the discrepancies at all in defense of the dishonor.

§ 6.11　The Documents in the Letter of Credit Transaction

Under the UCP, banks deal only in documents.[1] The parties may provide conditions upon the credit, as long as compliance with those conditions can be satisfied through documentary evidence. Thus, letters of credit must state precisely the documents, and the terms of the documents, against which payment is to be made.[2] It is the responsibility of the issuing bank and its customer, the applicant (Buyer), to ensure that satisfaction of each condition can be evidenced by documents. Otherwise, the condition need not be satisfied. The UCP provides that if a letter of credit contains any condition which is not satisfied by a document to be presented to evidence compliance with it, the bank can ignore that condition as though it were not written.[3]

The most important of the documents required by a letter of credit is the transportation document. Under prior versions of the UCP, this had referred to ocean bills of lading, evidencing an assumption that the goods would be carried by sea. However, there are new developments in the transport industry and new technological applications. Thus, the 1993 revision of the UCP provides separate articles for negotiable ocean bills of lading,[4] non-negotiable sea waybills,[5] charter party bills of lading,[6]

---

18. UCP art. 14(d)(1).

19. Hamilton Bank, supra note 4.

20. Bombay Industries, Inc. v. Bank of New York, 32 U.C.C. Rep. Serv. 2d 1155 (N.Y.Sup.Ct.1997).

21. Todi Exports v. Amrav Sportswear, 1997 WL 61063 (S.D.N.Y.1997).

22. Hamilton Bank, supra note 4, Bombay Indus., supra note 21.

§ 6.11

1. UCP art. 4.

2. UCP art. 5(b).

3. UCP art. 13(c).

4. UCP art. 23.

5. UCP art. 24.

6. UCP art. 25.

multi-modal transport documents,[7] air transport documents,[8] road, rail or inland waterway transport documents,[9] and courier and post receipts.[10]

Under the UCP, an ocean bill of lading must name the port of loading, the port of discharge, the carrier and specify the parties which will be acceptable signatories.[11] Banks have no duty, however, to check the signature or initials accompanying an "on board" notation, absent a special arrangement with the bank.[12] The bill of lading may indicate an "intended vessel." In such cases, any "on board" notation must specify the vessel on which the goods have been loaded.[13] The medieval custom of issuing "a set" of bills of lading, and hoping one of them would arrive and be honored, is now disapproved; and the UCP seeks to have only a single original bill of lading issued as the norm.[14]

A charter party bill of lading does not identify the carrier, and is now a permissible transport document for use with a letter of credit. The UCP relieves the banks from any duty to examine the terms of the charter party, under the assumption that only sophisticated parties with considerable knowledge of the trade will use them.[15]

In multimodal transportation arrangements, the bill of lading is likely to be issued by a freight forwarder and not by a carrier. Thus, it does not name a carrier and it does not contain a receipt by the bailee (who is the carrier), which is the norm for documents of title.[16] However, if the letter of credit authorizes its use, such a transportation document may be used, if the freight forwarder issues it as either a multi-modal transport operator or an agent for a carrier.[17] Otherwise, such "house bills" of freight forwarders are not acceptable transport documents for letters of credit under the UCP.

If the original documents are lost or destroyed, a bank may accept copies of the documents as originals, if the copies have been signed.[18] Allowable signatures includes handwriting, facsimiles, perforated signatures, stamps, symbols, and other mechanical and electronic methods.[19] In the past, many civil law countries (e.g., Germany) have not accepted facsimile signatures and have ruled that *any* non-handwritten signature is invalid, but these rules are changing with the advent of e-commerce.[20]

---

7. UCP art. 26.

8. UCP art. 27.

9. UCP art. 28.

10. UCP art. 29.

11. UCP art. 23. Compare the discussion in Chapter 3, supra.

12. UCP art. 23(a)(i).

13. UCP art. 23 (a)(ii).

14. UCP art. 23(a)(iv).

15. UCP art. 25(a)(iii).

16. UCP art. 25(b).

17. UCP art. 26(a).

18. UCP art. 30.

19. UCP art. 20(b).

20. The provisions of the German Civil Code are now supplemented by the German Digital Signature Law. That law will be further amended to comply with the EU Electronic Signature Directive. For further discussion, see § 8.12, infra.

D. OTHER TRANSACTIONS

§ 6.12 Electronic Letters of Credit

Electronic communication has taken over some aspects of letters of credit practice, but not others. They dominate the issuance process in bank-to-bank communications, and are sometimes used by applicants to stimulate the issuance process. However, at this time they have not been able to create an entirely paperless transaction pattern for many reasons. First, the beneficiary still wants a piece of paper committing the banks to pay upon specified conditions. Second, electronic bills of lading still are not accepted in most trades as transferable documents of title for the reasons discussed in Chapter 3, supra. Thus, in the collection of the letter of credit, physical documents will be forwarded, while funds settlement may be electronic.

About three quarters of letter of credit communication between banks, for other banks' issuance, advice, confirmation or negotiation of letters of credit is paperless; and the communication is electronic. While bank-to-bank communication is electronic, bank-to-beneficiary (Seller) communication is still paper-based. Letter of credit issuers can now communicate directly with beneficiaries' computers, however, and use of this practice should be expected to increase. The UCP rules are now written in terms of "teletransmissions," rather than paper-based terminology, which facilitates the use of electronic practices.

Most bank-to-bank communication concerning letters of credit are routed through the dedicated lines of SWIFT (the Society for Worldwide Interstate Financial Telecommunications). SWIFT is a Belgian not-for-profit organization owned by banks as a cooperative venture for the transmission of financial transaction messages. It requires all such messages to be structured in a uniform format, and uses standardized elements for allocating message space and for message text. Thus, messages can be communicated on a computer-to-computer basis without being re-keyed.

A bank issuing a letter of credit communicates that message to the nearest SWIFT access point. The message is then routed on a dedicated data transmission line to a regional processor, where it is validated (see below). From the regional processor, it is routed over a dedicated line to one of two main switches located in either the United States or Europe. From there it is routed through a regional processor to a SWIFT access point to the receiving bank. The message switching and sometimes necessary storage can be performed by computers, if the standardization of the format of the financial messages is sufficiently developed and comprehensive. SWIFT seems to have achieved this level of uniformity.

The bank which receives a SWIFT electronic letter of credit message does not have to send a reply stating that it accepts the request to advise or the authorization to negotiate or pay the letter of credit. It needs only to perform by advising, negotiating or paying, and it is entitled to reimbursement by the issuing bank. However, the SWIFT messages only transmit the letter of credit and their authorizations and requests.

SWIFT messages do not effect the settlements of letters of credit or other transfers of funds between issuing banks and other banks. SWIFT is not a clearing house for bank settlements like, for example, CHIPS (Clearing House for Interbank Payment Systems). Under the SWIFT letter of credit system, participating banks must use other arrangements (such as CHIPS) to settle their accounts and accomplish a transfer of funds.

SWIFT relies upon both incryption of messages and authentication to provide security to its users. The authentication of SWIFT messages is accomplished by the use of algorithms, which are mathematical formulas that calculate the contents of a message from header to trailer. If a SWIFT message requires authentication, and all letter of credit messages do, the issuing bank computes the contents and compiles a result based on the number of characters and data fields. At the regional processor, SWIFT checks the authentication trailer for the number of characters in the authentication. However, a more rigorous authentication will be performed by the receiving bank, using an algorithm contained in an authentication key provided by the issuing bank. The computations involving these authentication procedures will indicate a mismatch if the message is fraudulent or has been altered. There are also "log in" procedures, application-selection procedures, message numbering and error checking capabilities, and control of access to the system hardware. SWIFT also retains records of each transaction. In all, the security devices are numerous and complex.

Most SWIFT messages are delivered within minutes of their issuance by a bank, although delays of up to two hours are possible. Thus, delays in the system are slight, but present. When is the issuer of an electronic letter of credit bound? The UCP provides no set rules on the issue, but Revised UCC Article 5 establishes that such messages are effective and enforceable upon transmission by the issuer, not delivery to the receiving bank.[1] Revised UCC and SWIFT rules require no reply.[2] This UCC rule conforms to the understanding of bankers involved in the trade.

Under SWIFT rules, Belgian law governs all relations between SWIFT and its users. SWIFT is liable for negligence or fraud of its own employees and agents and for those parts of the communication system that it controls, such as regional processors, main switches and the dedicated lines that connect them. But SWIFT disclaims liability for those parts of the communication system that it does not control, such as the bank computers that issue and receive messages and the dedicated lines from bank to a regional processor. Even where SWIFT is liable, its liability is limited to "direct" damages (loss of interest), and liability for indirect (consequential) damages is not available. Whether Belgian law also governs relations between SWIFT and the non-bank parties to the

§ **6.12**
1. Rev. UCC § 5–106(a).

2. Rev. UCC § 5–106(a).

transaction (applicants and beneficiaries), or between banks and their customers, does not seem yet to have been tested in court.

It is now possible for an applicant (Buyer, in the documentary credit transaction) to draft a proposed electronic letter of credit. The electronic proposed credit can then be transmitted to the issuing bank for it to issue over the SWIFT system. This procedure is usually used where the applicant seeks multiple credits and there is a master agreement between the issuing bank and the applicant. The issuing bank will first check to see whether the proposed credit is authorized and contains the required security codes. Then it will determine whether it is within the previously authorized credit limits and is stated in the standardized elements and uniform format for electronic messages. Both SWIFT and UCP requirements must be analyzed, and changes in the proposed message may be necessary. Thus, the procedures are not yet fully automatic.

On the other end of the electronic communications, the beneficiary (Seller, in the documentary sale), who must be induced to part with value on the basis of the bank's promises, wants a "hard copy", a written letter of credit in the traditional form. The receiving bank therefore will convert the SWIFT electronic message into such a written, paper credit. However, the SWIFT message has been designed for bank-to-bank use, and not necessarily for use by beneficiaries, which creates some problems. First, it does not bear a signature in the traditional sense, even though it has been thoroughly authenticated within the computer-based transmission mechanisms. Thus, the beneficiary is entitled to doubt whether the sending bank is bound to the beneficiary to perform by the written credit derived from the SWIFT electronic message.

The issue if usually framed as: "Is the SWIFT message to be considered to be *the* operative credit instrument as far as the beneficiary is concerned?" The issue is of importance to beneficiaries not only in the original issuance of the credit, but also in the myriad of amendments to the credit which may follow. Under SWIFT rules, SWIFT users treat the electronic message as a binding obligation, and treat the authentication as the functional equivalent of a signature. However, the beneficiary is not a SWIFT user, and banking practice has been that a beneficiary can rely on an electronic message only after it has been issued in a paper-based format, properly signed or otherwise authenticated. The Revised UCC states that a letter of credit "may be issued in any form," including an electronic format,[3] but that provision does not necessarily answer the question as to whether the unsigned, paper-based transcription of a SWIFT message, generated by the recipient of that message, is the operative credit instrument and binds the issuing bank.

Under the UCP, whether an electronic message is the operative credit instrument or not depends upon the terminology in the message itself. The UCP provides that, if the electronic message states "full

---

3. Rev. UCC § 5–104.

details to follow," or states that a mail confirmation will be the operative credit instrument, then the electronic message is not that instrument, and the subsequent message is.[4] However, another provision of the UCP states that other authenticated electronic messages to advise or amend credits *are* the operative credit instrument.[5] In the latter transactions, mail confirmations should not be sent, and are to have no effect if sent.

However, there is some doubt as to whether SWIFT-generated transcriptions are subject to the UCP. SWIFT internal rules provide that credits issued through its system are subject to the UCP, but the transcription into a hard copy may bear no reference to the UCP. The UCP states that the UCP provisions govern "where they are incorporated into the text of the credit."[6] That language is deemed, in some parts of the world, to require an express reference to the UCP in the message to the beneficiary.

The attempts to create an electronic bill of lading have been discussed earlier in Chapter 3. If successful, an electronic bill of lading could help facilitate the electronic letter of credit transaction. However, to date, while electronic bills of lading have been used successfully to replace the straight (non-negotiable) bill of lading, its use to replace the negotiable bill of lading has been met with skepticism. Although SE-DOCS showed that an electronic approach was technically feasible, it was not a commercial success. American bankers have been skeptical of their rights to any actual goods under electronic bills of lading issued under CMI (Comite Maritime International) Rules. However, the Commission of the European Communities has just initiated the BOLERO program under the CMI Rules, and it may prove to be more successful. It is discussed in more detail in Chapter 3.

The experiments discussed above all attempted to substitute an electronic message for the paper-based bill of lading, but otherwise did not change traditional letter of credit system, based on the bill of lading. A very different approach is proposed in an experiment called Trade Card. This approach attempts to provide an electronic system, rather than just an electronic message in a paper-based system. It is loosely based on a credit card or debit card system used by banks. However, for this system to be feasible, all the parties must be members of the Trade Card system. This includes not only the shipper, the carrier and all of the banks involved, but also all of the potential buyers of the goods while they are in transit. Whether Trade Card will be a success remains to be seen, because only a pilot program has been initiated to date. Even if Trade Card should not be successful, one should expect that there will be other attempts to create an electronic letter of credit transaction which follows an electronic model, not the traditional model but with an electronic bill of lading.

4. UCP art. 11(a)(ii).   **6.** UCP art. 1.
5. UCP art. 11(a)(i).

§ 6.13   Back-to-Back and Revolving Credits

Brokers of goods have a problem because they often have two transactions in the same goods. They will sell the goods to a buyer in one transaction and then buy them from a supplier in a separate transaction. If both sales transactions involve payment by letters of credit, the broker will be the beneficiary (seller) of the letter of credit in the first transaction and the applicant (buyer) in the second. If the documents required by each letter of credit are *identical*, the broker can assign its rights in the first credit to the issuing bank of the second credit. Such arrangements are facilitated if the credits specify the use of time drafts (e.g., "pay 30 days after sight"). This arrangement is a "back to back credit" and allows broker to finance its purchase of the goods from supplier with the credit of its buyer. Such arrangements work more easily using general letters of credit, although special credits can be used by giving an issuing bank a security interest in its proceeds.[1]

However, back to back credits can also become unworkable if one of the credits is amended, and no similar amendment is made to the other credit.[2] Thus, most banks prefer not to use the back to back letter of credit transaction. Instead, they recommend that sellers and brokers obtain financing through a "transferable letter of credit"[3] or an "assignment of proceeds" from a letter of credit.[4]

A transferable letter of credit is one that expressly states that it can be transferred by the original beneficiary to third parties, who become new and substitute beneficiaries. Thus, a broker who is the beneficiary of a transferable letter of credit can use its rights under that credit to finance the purchase of the goods from suppliers by transferring part of the broker's rights under the credit to the suppliers.[5] Partial transfers are allowed, so the broker can use this device to finance purchases from several suppliers.[6] However, although substitute commercial invoices and drafts may be used, all other necessary documents must be presented to the original applicant, which will reveal the identity of the substitute beneficiary. That may compromise commercially sensitive information, and so brokers tend to avoid use of such credits.

The beneficiary of a letter of credit may irrevocably assign a portion of the credit's proceeds to a third party.[7] If the proceeds are assigned, the advising bank notifies the assignee of the assignment. Thus, a broker who is the beneficiary of a letter of credit that permits assignment of proceeds can use its rights under that credit to finance the purchase of the goods from a supplier by assigning a part of the broker's rights under the credit to the supplier. The assignment of proceeds does not change the parties to the letter of credit. The original applicant is

§ 6.13

1. A "general" letter of credit does not restrict the beneficiary's right to transfer its rights thereunder, while a "special" letter of credit limits permissible transferees, usually to one or more banks.

2. See generally, UCP art. 5.

3. UCP art. 48(a).

4. UCP art. 49.

5. UCP art. 48(b).

6. UCP art. 48(g).

7. UCP art. 49.

obligated to pay only if it receives documents which conform to the credit, so the assignee will not be paid unless it ships the goods using conforming documents. The assignee is not a party to the original credit, it may not know what the terms of the credit are, and must trust the broker (the original beneficiary) to fulfill those terms. The assignment is not governed by the UCP, but by the applicable law of contract.[8]

Rapid expansion of turn-key construction contracts (e.g. for building a complete steel mill or cement plant needing someone only to "turn a key" to begin plant operation) has expanded use of "revolving" letters of credit as a vehicle for ensuring that contractors are given progress payments promptly as initial construction pleases are completed and to permit further construction phases to occur. Revolving letters of credit are usually clean,[9] sight letters of credit.

In the transaction the applicant is an importer, often a third world government. The beneficiary is a foreign construction company, and the documents it presents to the issuing bank are, at most, invoices for provision of services and raw materials. As the credit is drawn down to make partial payments to the beneficiaries, the applicant is obligated to provide further funds to the issuer to restore the fund supporting the letter of credit to an argued level.

Such revolving letters of credit do not become "exhausted" in the normal sense of that word,[10] since the fund is periodically replenished. However, they are subject to rules similar to those for fixed credits. There are differences from the "fixed" letter of credit, however, and they may be important. First, the applicant (importer) pays, by way of a letter of credit, to import services and raw materials rather than finished goods. Second the applicant-importer restores the amount of the letter of credit (by payment to the issuer) to an agreed level of further payment to the beneficiary following each draw that the beneficiary makes upon the letter of credit for payment. Revolving letters of credit may be documentary (requiring presentation of a certificate of construction phase completion), but "red tape" in obtaining such interim certifications prompts many contractors to seek less formal arrangements, requiring the account party to trust the contractor not to draw upon the letter before such action is appropriate. As a result, the payment ceiling (amount) of the revolving letter of credit will usually be a modest fraction of the total value of the construction contract.

---

8. *Id.*

9. A "clean" letter of credit is one for which documents are not required for payment.

10. A "fixed" letter of credit becomes "exhausted" when either the full amount has been paid out or the time period for drawing upon the letter has expired.

E.   SELECTED DOCUMENTS

§ 6.14   Letter of Credit—Confirmed, Irrevocable

Marine Midland Bank—Western
   Buffalo, New York
To: Santa Claus Company
   East Aurora, New York

Letter of Credit # 34576
Issued on May 1, 2000
From: Alpha Company
     Athens, Greece

Gentlemen:

We are instructed by Commercial Bank of Greece, Athens, Greece, to inform you that they have opened their irrevocable credit in favor for account of Alpha Company, Athens, Greece, for the sum in U.S. dollars not exceeding a total of about $21,000.00 (Twenty One Thousand and $^{00}/_{100}$ Dollars), available by your drafts on the Commercial Bank of Greece, to be accompanied by:

1. Full Set On Board Negotiable Ocean Bills of Lading, stating: "Freight Prepaid," and made out to the order of Commercial Bank of Greece.
2. Insurance Policy or Certificate, covering Marine and War Risk.
3. Packing List.
4. Commercial Invoice in triplicate:

Covering   252 Pcs. 930 Play Family Garage

                 252 Pcs. 942 Play Family Lift & Load

                 360 Pcs. 300 Scoop Loader

                 360 Pcs. 313 Roller Grader

                 360 Pcs. 307 Adventure People & Their Wilderness Patrol

                 360 Pcs. 839 Medical Kit

                 225 Pcs. 993 Play Family Castle

Total Value $20,072.55 C.I.F. Athens, Greece

Import Lic. No. 143210, Expires July 13, 2000

5. Shipper's Export Declaration

    Partial Shipment Permitted.   Transshipment Not Permitted.

    Merchandise must be shipped on SS Livorno.

All documents must indicate Letter of Credit No. 34576, Import License No. 143210, expires July 13, 2000.

All drafts must be marked "Drawn under Letter of Credit No. 34576, confirmed by Marine Midland Bank-Western". Drafts must be presented to this company not later than July 1, 2000.

This credit is subject to the Uniform Customs and Practices for Documentary Credits (1993 Revision) International Chamber of Commerce Publication No. 500.

We confirm the credit and thereby undertake to purchase all drafts drawn as above specified and accompanied by the required documents.

By:

International Credit Department

Selected Bibliography

Barski, Letters of Credit: A Comparison of Article 5 of the UCC and the UCP, 41 Loy L. Rev. 735 (1996).

Buckley, The 1993 Revision of the UCP, 28 Geo. Wash. J. Int'l Law & Econ. 256 (1994).

Chung, Developing a Documentary Credit Dispute Resolution System: An ICC Perspective, 19 Fordham Int'l L.J. 1349 (1996).

J. Dolan, The Law of Letters of Credit (Rev. ed. 1999).

Goode, Abstract Payment Undertakings in International Transactions, 22 Brook. J. Int'l L. 1 (1996).

Kozolchyk, The "Best Practices" Approach to the Uniformity of Commercial Law: The UCP 500 and the NAFTA Implementation Experience, Ariz. J. Int'l & Comp. L. 443 (1996).

C. Schmitthof, Export Trade (9th ed., 1990).

Whitaker, Letters of Credit and Electronic Commerce, 31 Idaho L.Rev. 699 (1995).

White, The Influence of International Practice on the Revision of Article 5, Nw. J.Int'l L. & Bus. 189 (1995).

Chapter 7

STANDBY LETTERS OF CREDIT

Table of Sections

A. INTRODUCTION

A. INTRODUCTION

§ 7.1 Introduction

Just like traditional letters of credit, standby letters of credit, are mechanisms for allocating risks among parties in commercial transactions. By placing in the hands of a neutral third party the responsibility for making payment when certain conditions are met, one party to a transaction is able to avoid the risk of nonpayment or nonperformance.

Third world governments often require a financial assurance (by way of a financial guarantee) that foreign firms which undertake to supply goods or to perform a construction project will do so competently

401

and in accordance with the terms of the contract covering the sale or project. Performance bonds can serve as an adequate assurance, but the United States banks are barred from issuing insurance contracts, including performance bonds. They have, however, developed an alternative– the *"standby" letter of credit*, which is a second type of letter of credit transaction. It involves a letter of credit which is issued by the seller's bank and runs in favor of the buyer–truly a backwards arrangement-and payable against a writing which certifies that the seller has not performed its promises. Such a standby letter of credit is not for the purpose of ensuring payment to the seller for the goods shipped. Instead, this standby letter of credit is used as a guarantee, or a performance bond, or as insurance of the seller's performance. Under current federal law, banks are not allowed to issue guarantees or performance bonds or insurance policies.[1] However, the use of standby letters of credit can accomplish the same results, and is not prohibited by bank regulatory agencies. The result has been the creation of a new commercial device, which is now commercially accepted for its own value, and which has supplanted the performance bond in many fields of endeavor.

The standby letter of credit has become an indispensable tool for financing international commercial transactions, with a two fold increase in use since 1970. Standby Letters of credit now exceed Commercial Letters of Credit by a five to one ratio.[2]

§ 7.1

1. 12 U.S.C.A § 24 (Seventh).

2. Based on the Call Reports for the Second Quarter of 1999, the top 300 U.S. banks reported outstanding standby obligations of U.S.$29 billion in commercial LCs. The more recently available figures place the amount of standbys outstanding by non-U.S. banks to U.S. beneficiaries at $450 billion. Assuming conservatively that the amount of standbys by non-U.S. beneficiaries is $100 billion, that would place the amount of standbys outstanding at $765 billion. See Byrne, *Overview of Letter of Credit Law and Practice in 1999,* Documentary Credit World.

§ 7.2   Transaction Pattern of the Standby Letter of Credit

Below is an example of a standby letter of credit issued by seller's bank from *Dynamics Corp. of America v. Citizens & Southern Nat. Bank,* 356 F.Supp. 991 (N.D.Ga.1973).

TO: THE PRESIDENT OF INDIA

INDIA

BY ORDER OF: ELECTRONICS SYSTEMS

DIVISION OF DYNAMICS CORPORATION OF AMERICA

For account

of same

GENTLEMEN:

WE HEREBY ESTABLISH OUR IRREVOCABLE CREDIT IN YOUR FAVOR, FOR THE ACCOUNT INDICATED ABOVE, FOR A SUM OR SUMS NOT EXCEEDING IN ALL FOUR HUNDRED TEN THOUSAND FOUR HUNDRED SEVENTY TWO AND 60/100 US DOLLARS (US$410,472.60)—AVAILABLE BY YOUR DRAFT(S) AT sight,

DRAWN ON: us

Which must be accompanied by:

1. Your signed certification as follows: "The President of India being one of the parties to the Agreement dated March 14, 1971 signed and exchanged between the President of India and the Dynamics Corporation of America for the license to manufacture, purchase and supply of radio equipment as per Schedule I thereof for the total contract value of $1,368,242.00, does hereby certify in the exercise of reasonable discretion and in good faith that the Dynamics Corporation of America has failed to carry out certain obligations of theirs under the said Order/Agreement. . . ."

In it, the seller (account party) has contracted to have the seller's bank (issuing bank) issue an irrevocable letter of credit in favor of the third world government (beneficiary) that payment will be made upon presentation of a document which is only a simple statement by the beneficiary that the account party has failed to carry out its obligations under a contract (called a "suicide credit"). Some require no document, but provide for payment to be made upon the beneficiary's demand.

This transaction is almost a mirror image of the letter of credit in the documentary sale. In the standby credit, the account party is the seller or contractor (more analogous to the seller than to the buyer), the beneficiary is the purchaser (not the seller), and the documents do not control goods and have no independent value of their own. Often the required documentation is a mere certification by the beneficiary that the contractor has failed to perform under the contract, or perhaps, has failed to return an advance payment.

§ 7.3 Differences with Commercial Letter of Credit

The function of a standby letter of credit differs substantially from that of the traditional letter of credit, even though both are governed by the same substantive rules of law and practice. The fundamental difference between a standby and a commercial letter of credit is that the obligation for the commercial letter of credit arises out of documents showing that the beneficiary has performed. In contrast, the obligation of a standby letter of credit arises from documents showing that the principal has failed to perform.

The standby letter of credit is primarily a risk-shifting device, with the advantage of providing the beneficiary with swift and easy access to funds in case of a default by the customer, much as if the customer had left a cash deposit with the beneficiary. The standby letter of credit is often preferable to a cash deposit, however, because it does not require the customer to part with any funds until after payment is demanded on the standby letter of credit.

Under the standby letter of credit the beneficiary may draw only after the customer defaults on the underlying contract. The traditional letter of credit usually requires a third party to generate some of the documents that the beneficiary must present to the issuer (usually a bill of lading); under the standby letter of credit, the beneficiary usually generates all of the necessary documents himself (usually a simple statement that the customer is in default).

Due to their contingent nature, standby letters of credit are riskier to a bank than ordinary letters of credit. The bank does not and cannot "look behind" the allegation of its customer's non-performance or delay payment in order to investigate the validity of the allegation. The bank cannot assert any defenses (except fraud) which the customer may have against the beneficiary. Standby letters of credit typically are unfounded (that is, they are not supported by funds on deposit with the bank), because banks do not anticipate having to pay out on them; the customer simply guarantees that the bank will be reimbursed if it is forced to pay out on the letter.

Under suicide credits payable upon unilateral demands, the account party's exposure may be enormous and the legal protections against arbitrary demands are limited to the fraud exception. Thus, standby credits tend, by their nature, to rely more heavily on the good faith of the parties than the commercial credit. This reliance on good faith exist because under a commercial credit it is more difficult for the beneficiary to make a fraudulent call on the credit as it has to present documents generally prepared by third parties, such as shipping companies and freight forwarders, in support of a call under the credit.

B. TRADITIONAL SOURCES OF RULES

§ 7.4 Sources of Law and Rules/Governing Rules

Standby letters of credit are governed by the Uniform Customs and Practices for Documentary Credits (UCP)[1], and are governed by the same rules as those applicable to documentary credits "to the extent they may be applicable."[2]

Standby letters of credit share two basic principles of commercial letters of credit. One is that the banks' obligations under the letter of credit are *independent* of the buyer's and seller's obligations under the contract for the sale of goods.[3] The "independence principle" posits that the contract for sale of goods between buyer and seller is conceptually and actually independent from the letter of credit contract. Historically, the independence principle has been recognized for the predictability and certainty that it offered to sellers, who were often reluctant to send goods abroad without payment.

The second is that banks deal only with documents, and not with performance of the underlying sales contract.[4] If the documents presented conform precisely to the terms of the letter of credit, the Confirming Bank and the Issuing Bank are obligated to pay the beneficiary or to honor its draft. The beneficiary is not subject to defenses arising out of the underlying sales transaction, so the conformity of the goods is, with exceptions noted below, irrelevant to the bank's decision. The decision is to be based upon the documents alone. Further, the documents need not conform to the underlying sales contract either, so long as they comply with the letter of credit.[5] However, the bank's promises may still be subject to claims by the applicant (Buyer) of fraud by the beneficiary (Seller). The UCP has no provisions concerning fraud, and therefore such issues must be analyzed under U.C.C. Article 5[6], where U.S. law is applicable.

Some legal commentators question whether the traditional "independence principle" of letter of credit rules is being or should be applied to standby credits, in light of the facts that such letters do not assure an exporter about payment for goods to be shipped, but serve principally a non-payment function to assure an importer (beneficiary) about payment if an exporter (the account party) does not deliver on its contract (to supply goods, services or raw materials). However, the text of both the UCP and Revised Article 5 make it clear that the drafters intended to

---

§ 7.4

1. Uniform Customs and Practices for Documentary Credits (UCP500) (International Chamber of Commerce, Pub. No.500 (1993)).

2. UCP Art. 1.

3. UCP Article 3.

4. UCP Article 4.

5. UCP Article 3(a).

6. Article 5 of the Uniform Commercial Code (U.C.C. §§ 5–101–117 (1999)).

cover standby letters of credit, and to apply the "independence principle" to such bank obligations.

Both U.C.C. Article 5 and the UCP have recently been revised. The Revised Article 5 was adopted by the Uniform Commissioners and the American Law Institute in 1995, and by the end of 2000, 47 U.S. and the District of Columbia had adopted the revision.[7] The most recent version of the UCP is the 1993 Revision.[8] The rules set forth in each are relatively similar, but there are some differences. The UCP provisions will have more impact on the analysis of non-fraud issues, and the U.C.C. Article 5 provisions will be used to resolve issues related to allegations of fraud.

§ 7.5 Revised UCC Article 5

U.C.C. Article 5 has considerable significance in the field of letters of credit. Until the formulation of the United Nations Convention on Independent Guarantees and Standby Letters of Credit[1], it was the only modern attempt at a statute regulating letters of credit. Although a model code, it was adopted by every U.S. state. Moreover, it has provided a context for the development of U.S. letter of credit law which, because of the economic and political position of the U.S., has been influential beyond its borders. While the original version of U.C.C. Article 5, released in 1952, was largely declaratory of general principles of letter of credit law, it captured the fraud exception in a manner that has been highly influential. During the last decade the model code was completely revised. The process occurred simultaneously with the formulation of the U.N. Convention and the revision of the UCP and was influenced considerably by these efforts.

Revised Article 5 "clearly and forcefully states the independence of the letter of credit obligations from the underlying transaction that was unexpressed in, but was a fundamental predicate for, the original Article 5."[2] Certainty of payment, independent of other claims, setoffs or other causes of action, is a core element of the commercial utility of letters of credit.

The revision authorizes the use of electronic technology[3]; expressly permits deferred payment letters of credit.[4]

UCC Section 116–5(c) expressly recognizes that if the UCP is incorporated by reference into the letter of credit, the agreement varies the provisions of Article 5 with which it may conflict except for the non-variable provisions of Article 5.

---

7. See table of adoptions available in: *http://www.nccusl.org/uniformact_factsheets/uniformacts-fs-ucca5.htm*.

8. I.C.C. Publ. No. 500.

§ 7.5

1. UN Convention on Independent Guarantees and Standby Letters of Credit, available in *www.uncitral.org*.

2. Prefatory Note, Art. 5 (UCC §§ 5–103(d) and 5–108(f)).

3. UCC § 102(a)(14) and 5–104.

4. (UCC § 102 (a)8).

§ 7.6   Uniform Customs and Practices for Documentary Credits (UCP)

The UCP is a set of industry rules that banks and trade finance institutions submit to voluntarily through express provision in the terms of a commercial letter of credit.

The International Chamber of Commerce (I.C.C.) has developed and published the Uniform Customs and Practices for Documentary Credits (UCP), which is incorporated by reference in most international letters of credit. The UCP constitutes a rather detailed manual of operations for banks, but they are a restatement of "custom" in the industry, and they do not purport to be law.

The UCP apply only if the operating banks, particularly the issuing bank, make the credit subject to the UCP. The general provisions of the UCP stipulate that the Customs govern all credits that do not expressly provide for the contrary. If the parties expressly incorporate the UCP, they become terms of the engagement and will apply. If the parties expressly reject the Uniform Customs, under the terms of Article 1 they do not apply. If the credit is silent, to the extent that a party proves that the UCP "fill in points that the parties have not considered and in fact agreed upon."

The UCP have, since 1983, included standby letters of credit within their scope. Article 1 of the UCP brings out more sharply than its predecessor the need for textual incorporation: "The Uniform Customs and Practice for Documentary Credits... shall apply to all Documentary Credits (including to the extent to which they may be applicable, Standby letter(s) of credit) where they are incorporated into the text of the credit. They are binding on all the parties thereto, unless otherwise expressly stipulated in the credit." However, UCP 500 is essentially a set of rules for commercial letters of credit.

The beneficiary of the standby credit is not a performing party of the underlying transaction, but the party entitled to receive performance, and his entitlement to make a demand for payment arises not because of his own performance, but because of the other party's failure to perform. The result of this fundamental distinction is that most of the provisions of the UCP are simply not applicable to standby credits.

Despite persistent talk of the impending revision of UCP500, the I.C.C. Banking Commission agreed that any revision be postponed several years in order to permit necessary studies as to the need and extent of any revisions and to assess the impact of ISP98.[1]

§ 7.6

1. Statement of the Revision of UCP (ICC Commission on Banking Technique & Practice, Nov. 1999 DCW 8).

C. NEW SOURCES OF RULES

§ 7.7 New International Rules for Standby Letters of Credit

Even though both the UCP and Revised U.C.C. Article 5 expressly include standby letters of credit within their coverage, it is clear that they were designed to cover the documentary letter of credit transaction and not the standby transaction. Thus, they impose many unnecessary document-related conditions on the use of standbys. In response to these difficulties, the United Nations Commission on International Trade Law (UNCITRAL) has developed the United Nations Convention on Independent Guarantees and Stand-by Letters of Credit (1995) which entered into force on January 1, 2000. For the same reason, the International Chamber of Commerce (I.C.C.) has developed the Rules on International Standby Practices (ISP 98)[1], which became effective on January 1, 1999. The Convention currently has five Contracting States (Ecuador, El Salvador, Kuwait, Panama and Tunisia). The ISP 98 was designed to replace the UCP and be its equivalent to international practice regarding standby letters of credit.

§ 7.8 United Nations Convention on Independent Guarantees and Stand-by Letters of Credit (1995)

The United Nations Commission on International Trade Law (UNCITRAL) prepared the United Nations Convention on Independent Guarantees and Stand-by Letters of Credit (CIGSLC). The UN Convention was adopted and opened for signature by the General Assembly by its resolution 50/48 of December 11, 1995,[1] and entered into force on January 1, 2000.[2]

The Convention is designed to facilitate the use of independent guarantees and standby letters of credit. The CIGSLC uses the term "undertaking" to refer to both type of instruments.

The Convention gives legislative support to the autonomy of the parties to apply agreed rules of practice such as the UCP and the Uniform Rules for Demand Guarantees (URDG).[3] It supplements their operation by dealing with issues beyond the scope of such rules. It does so in particular regarding the question of fraudulent or abusive demands for payment and judicial remedies in such instances.

The focus of the Convention is on the relationship between the issuer and the beneficiary. The relationship between the issuer and the account party largely falls outside its scope.

§ 7.7

1. International Standby Practices 1998 (ISP 98) (I.C.C. Pub. No 590).

§ 7.8

1. Explanatory Note by UNCITRAL secretariat of the United Nations Convention on Independent Guarantees and Standby Letters of Credit, available in (*www.uncitral.org*).

2. The Convention has been signed by four states (including the US) and ratified by five (but not the US), Ecuador, El Salvador, Kuwait, Panama and Tunisia. See UNCITRAL Status of Conventions and Model Laws, at http://www.uncitral.org/en-index.htm.

3. Uniform Rules for Demand Guarantees (URDG) (I.C.C.), Pub. No 458, (1992).

Full freedom is given to the parties to exclude completely the coverage of the Convention,[4] with the result that another law becomes applicable. Since the Convention, if it is applicable, is to a large extent suppletive rather than mandatory, wide breath is given to exclude or alter the rules of the Convention in any given case.

Letters of credit other than standby letters of credit are not covered by the Convention. However, the Convention does recognize a right of parties to international letters of credit to "opt into" the Convention.[5]

The Convention applies to an "international" undertaking if the place of business of the issuer is in a state that has adopted the Convention or if the rules of private international law lead to the application of the laws of such a state, unless the undertaking excludes the application of the CIGSLC.[6] The Convention also applies if it expressly states that it applies to an international letter of credit.[7] An undertaking is international if any of two of the issuer, the applicant, the confirmer or the beneficiary are located in different states.[8]

The Convention defines as "independence,"[9] an undertaking which is not dependent upon the existence or validity of the underlying transaction, or upon any other undertaking. An independent undertaking must not be subject to any terms or conditions not appearing in the undertaking. To be independent from the underlying transactions, the undertakings covered by the Convention must possess a "documentary" character. The effect of this rule is that an undertaking which is subject to "non-documentary" conditions is outside the scope of the Convention.

The Convention contains a general rule that interpretation of the Convention should be with a view to its international character and the need to promote uniformity in its application.[10] In addition, interpretation is to have regard for the observance of good faith in international practice.

The Convention provides rules on several aspects of the form and content of undertakings. The rights and obligations of the issuer and the beneficiary are determined by the terms and conditions of the undertaking.[11] Express reference is made in the Convention to rules of practice, general conditions or usages (e.g. UCP,URDG) to which the undertaking may be expressly made subject.

The United Nations Convention complements the UCP and reinforces its use. The United Nations Convention differs from the UCP in that it is public law, not private law. Unlike the UCP, it also provides for injunctive relief to thwart fraudulent demands.

Now that the Convention has entered into force, letters of credit can be issued subject to its provisions. Indeed, even in countries where the

---

4. CIGSCL Article 1.

5. CIGSCL Article 1(2).

6. CIGSLC Art. 1(1).

7. CIGSLC Art. 1(2).

8. CIGSLC Art. 4 (1).

9. CIGSLC Article 3.

10. CIGSLC Article 5. Compare to CISG art. 7(1), discussed in § 1.8, supra.

11. CIGSLC Article 13(1).

Convention has not been adopted, standby letters of credit may be issued subject to it if so permitted by the choice of law rules of the issuer's state. Since many such rules emphasize party autonomy, such a result may be possible in a number of different countries.

§ 7.9 Rules on International Standby Practices (ISP 98). Drafting History

The International Standby Practices (ISP 98) were issued in draft form in the fall of 1997. The International Institute of Banking Law and Practice, Inc., the main sponsor of ISP 98, and the ICC Publishing ultimately agreed to the publication of the Rules, which are available for banks to incorporate into their standby credits as of January 1, 1999.[1]

The UCP have, since 1983, included standby letters of credit within their scope. However, there is an understanding that UCP is essentially a set of rules for commercial letters of credit and are inapplicable to most standby credits.

Some legal scholars argued that independent bank guarantees, while different in form, are functionally the equivalent of standby, and that the same law should apply to them. Moreover, that the Uniform Rules for Demand Guarantees (URDG), a product of the ICC Banking Commission, governing independent bank guarantees, may constitute an adequate regime for standby letters of credit.[2] Looking at the drafting history, it may be only "an accident of banking politics that the URDG did not cover standby credits in the first place."[3]

Since independent bank guarantees have traditionally been the product of European Banks, it appears that U.S. bankers were largely left out of the drafting process. The Chair and the major participants, understandably, were not U.S. bankers.[4] US bankers were, however, very much involved in the drafting of the UCP 500, promulgated in 1993. It may be then, that the US bankers, who had achieved a measure of hegemony in the UCP drafting process were unhappy at the prospect of having a European Law Professor and European bankers draft rules for the quintessential US product, the standby credit. Whatever the reason, UCP 500, promulgated the year after the URDG, continued to cover the

---

§ 7.9

1. In April 1998, after some revision, the ISP received endorsement when the ICC, approved them and recommended adoption. Report from an ICC affiliate announced that the vote of the Commission was 32 in favor and 9 opposed, with 46 Commission members abstaining or failing to participate. News Briefs, Documentary Credits Insight, (ICC Paris), Spring 1998 at , 24., cited in Dolan, *Analyzing Bank Drafted Standby Letter of Credit Rules, The International Standby Practice (ISP98),* 45 Wayne L. Rev. 1865 (2000).

2. See for example Goode, *Abstract Payment Undertakings and the Rules of the International chamber of Commerce,* 39 St. Louis L.J. 725 (1995)

3. Dolan, *Analyzing Bank Drafted Standby Letter of Credit Rules, The International Standby Practice (ISP98),* 45 Wayne L. Rev. 1865 (2000), 1874.

4. The Chair for the URDG Drafting Group was Professor Roy Goode from St. John's College Oxford.

standby, even though the URDG regime is far more congenial to the standby than the UCP.[5]

Ultimately U.S. bankers decided that UCP 500 was indeed sufficiently inhospitable to the standby such that there was a need for a separate regime. By the time the acknowledged that need, the URDG, with no mention of the standby and no incorporation of standby locution, was in place.[6]

§ 7.10 The Rules of ISP 98

ISP 98 endeavors to set forth uniform rules and regulations governing standby letters of credit that would be widely accepted, as well as to streamline and standardize customs and practices. It also addresses issues unique to standby letters of credit, and clarifies the application of rules to standby letters of credit.

There are basic similarities with the UCP because standby and commercial practices are fundamentally the same. However, ISP 98 differs from the UCP in style and approach. The ISP 98 contains 89 rules in contrast to the UCP's 49 and cover many areas with regard to which the UCP is silent. The most significant differences between the UCP and the ISP 98 exist in the issuer's and the beneficiary's respective rights and obligations.

Like the UCP and the URDG, the ISP will apply to any independent undertaking issued subject to it. The choice of which set of rules to select is, therefore, left to the parties. The ISP is designed to be compatible with the UN Convention and also with local law, whether statutory or judicial, and to embody standby letter of credit practice under that law.

ISP 98 clarifies terminology used in letters of credit, and restates basic principles of letter of credit law in order to obviate the need for placing these principles in each standby letter of credit.[1]

ISP 98 applies to both domestic and international standby credits expressly stated to be subject to it (notwithstanding that ''international'' is used in the title of ISP 98).[2] Is intended to apply to any standby Letter of Credit that is issued subject to ISP 98. Parties need to incorporate ISP 98 by reference before it becomes applicable as the ''governing law'' of the standby letter of credit.

ISP 98, like the UCC and the UCP, contains only a few provisions concerning the contract between the issuer and the account party. These

---

5. Dolan, *Analyzing Bank Drafted Standby Letter of Credit Rules, The International Standby Practice (ISP98),* 45 Wayne L. Rev. 1865 (2000), 1874.

6. According to Professor Dolan, the drafting history takes on some significance by virtue of the fact that the provisions of ISP 98 that maybe ''inefficient and unfair'' are completely absent from the URDG. That absence may reflect the inadequacy of the URDG or it may reflect the reason that

U.S. bankers have been dissatisfied with the URDG. Dolan, *Analyzing Bank Drafted Standby Letter of Credit Rules, The International Standby Practice (ISP 98),* 45 Wayne L. Rev. 1865 (2000), 1875.

§ 7.10

1. ISP 98, Rules 1.06, 1.07, 1.10.

2. ISP 98, Rule 1.01(b).

concern the issuer's right to be paid certain charges for issuing the credit, to reimbursement and limitations on its liability to the applicant.

Neither the UCP nor ISP 98 prescribe rules concerning when the issuer may or should refuse an otherwise complying presentation because the beneficiary's draw is fraudulent. The UCP does not mention the exception. The ISP 98 states expressly that it does not provide "defenses to honor based on fraud, abuse or similar matters."[3] Some have raised a question as to whether this difference between the UCP and ISP 98 leaves open the possibility of banks becoming defendants in securities fraud litigation by having aggressive plaintiffs' counsel alleging the bank permitted a drawing because of a reckless state of mind.

ISP 98 rule 3.06 is the first existing rule actually permitting electronic presentation of documents under a standby LC. It enables members of S.W.I.F.T. to make electronic presentation in situations where the only required document is a demand whether or not the credit expressly permits it. In addition, ISP 98 proposes basic definitions should the standby permit or require presentation of documents by electronic means. While electronic presentation is relatively easy for standbys, it is much more difficult for commercial letters of credit that require presentation of documents of title.

ISP 98 applies to the obligation of the applicant to reimburse the issuer of a standby letter of credit, and even create indemnification obligations on the part of the applicant against certain cost of the issuer.[4] The UCP does not specifically address these obligations.

Under ISP 98, certain provisions of a standby letter of credit may be waived unilaterally by the issuer, without effect on the applicant's reimbursement obligations to the issuer.[5]

The ISP establishes a three-day safe harbor for examination of documents, within which notice of dishonor is deemed to be reasonable.[6] It continues the seven-day rule of the UCP, beyond which notice of dishonor is deemed to be unreasonable. The statement of discrepancies need not be detailed.[7]

The ISP also sets out standards for documentary compliance.[8] Regarding the extent to which the documents presented under a standby must match the wording of the letter of credit, Rule 4.01 states the general principle that demands must comply on their face with the terms and conditions of the standby. Rule 4.09 contains specific rules for applying this principle. The UCP does not provide such detail in determining when a presentation is in compliance.

§ 7.11   Use of ISP 98

To date, there are no cases from courts or arbitrators construing ISP 98. As to its use, the reports vary. One of the most important issuers

---

3. ISP 98, Rule 1.01(b).
4. ISP 98, Rule 8.03.
5. ISP 98, Rule 3.11.
6. ISP 98, Rule 5.01.

7. ISP 98, Official Comments to Rule 5.02.
8. ISP 98, Rule 4.09.

of standbys reports that 60% of new standbys issued are subject to ISP 98.[1] Other banks report less use, and a few banks have refused to issue standbys subject to the new rules during 1999. U.S. acceptance outside New York has been slower as banks and the parties to standbys acquaint themselves with the new rules. ISP standbys have been issued to and accepted by agencies of the U.S. federal government, agencies of U.S. local governments, Fortune 500 corporations, some major insurance companies, and some of the major financial beneficiaries.

§ 7.12 The Debate over ISP 98

Considering its significance for standby letters of credit and detailed text and rules, it is not surprising to find out considerable amount of literature produced on the International Standby Practices. As is the case with any new set of international standards, there are different views and perspectives on different legal issues arising from ISP 98. Nonetheless, one conclusion common to experts and scholars is that ISP 98 fills a need in the standby regulation.

Among the opinions published on the ISP 98, some attorneys consider them too academic.[1] Others regard ISP 98 as filled with detail and estimate that the broad scope of the ISP creates traps for those not intimately familiar with it and its Official Comments.[2] This is because "virtually every aspect of a standby letter of credit governed by the ISP will require reference to the rules for appropriate direction."[3]

Even though Professor John Dolan recognizes the extensive consultations undertaken during the drafting process, he highlights that "there were non-bankers and non-bank lawyers involved in the fashioning of the ISP 98" and, that "virtually all sponsors of the Rules are connected to banking." He concludes that "ISP 98 in many respects has struck a balance that renders it inefficient by imposing educational and other transactions costs on the commercial parties, who are less able to bear them, rather than on the banks that issue standby credits."[4] Moreover that "the presences of unfair provisions in ISP 98 will encourage some commercial parties to eschew them entirely."[5]

§ 7.11

1. Byrne, *Overview of Letter of Credit Law and Practice in 1999*, Documentary Credit World.

§ 7.12

1. See, for example, Sullivan, *The ISP: Too Academic?*, Trade & Forfeiting Rev., Oct. 1999 18.

2. Byrne, The Official Commentary on the international Standby Practices (Institute of International Banking Law & Practice, Inc.), 1998.

3. Kenney, A Road Map To the International Standby Practices (1999).

4. Professor Dolan applies Professor Rubin's theses to ISP 98. Rubin argues that the absence of consumer representatives at the drafting table skewed the statutory result away from consumer interests and in favor of the well represented banking interests Rubin also contended that allocation of costs in a statutory product will yield waste if that allocation puts costs on parties who, often by virtue of information asymmetry, are less well able to shoulder them than another party. See Dolan, *Analyzing Bank Drafted Standby Letter of Credit Rules, The International Standby Practice (ISP 98)*, 45 Wayne L. Rev. 1865 (2000), 1868.

5. *Id.*

According to Professor James Byrne, chair of the ISP Working Group that served as the drafting committee for the Rules, "much of the effort was directed at removing unintentional traps that are present in the UCP and in providing clear rules for problems that the UCP does not address." In responding critics, he considers that the criticisms, have hardly been serious and that "rules were not drafted in favor of any party. The goal was to make them neutral payment devices."[6] He deems the process by which ISP 98 was developed as "the most collaborative and open of any rule making exercise in the field of international banking operations."[7]

D. THE ISSUE OF FRAUD

§ 7.13 The "Fraud Defense"

Where the documents are forged or fraudulent, or there is a fraud in the transaction, however, a different analysis is applied. The "independence principle" promotes the utility of the letter of credit transaction, by offering certainty of payment to the beneficiary who complies with a credit's requirements. But where there is fraud or forgery, rather than a "mere" breach of the underlying sales contract, a counter principle comes into play. "There is as much public interest in discouraging fraud as in encouraging the use of letters of credit."[1] Where the seller's fraud has been called to the bank's attention before the drafts and documents have been presented for payment, the principle of the "independence of the bank's obligation under the letter of credit" should not be extended to protect the unscrupulous seller.[2]

Thus, there are two competing principles, and the courts have created compromise which limit the impact of the independence principle when there are forged or fraudulent documents, or fraud in the transaction. Vexing problems are raised by claims of fraud and, more particularly, of "fraud in the transaction", but the doctrine that there is a "fraud exception" to the "independence principle" seems to be generally recognized. However, there is still a significant debate about how broad and extensive the fraud exception should be.

This "fraud exception" is available where the credit is expressly subject to the UCP, even though the UCP has no specific provisions on the subject. Since the UCP is silent, the courts have generally held that

---

6. He identifies, among other criticism that "there is no case law interpreting the rules. It has also been suggested that the ISP does not represent customary standby practice in the same sense as does the UCP." Moreover, he says that "critics tend to include attorneys who litigate, people who have no notion of standby practice, or regional pockets with some particular bias or concern." See Byrne, *Overview of Letter of Credit Law and Practice in 1999*, Documentary Credit World.

7. Byrne, *Overview of Letter of Credit Law and Practice in 1999*, Documentary Credit World.

§ 7.13

1. *Dynamics Corp. of America v. Citizens & Southern Nat. Bank*, 356 F.Supp. 991 (N.D.Ga.1973).

2. *Sztejn v. J. Henry Schroder Banking Corp.*, 177 Misc. 719, 31 N.Y.S.2d 631 (1941).

the UCC provisions govern as a "gap filling provision." The principle underlying this approach is that the courts will not allow their process to be used by a dishonest person to carry out a fraud. Most of the cases have arisen in New York courts, where there is a non-uniform amendment to the UCC, discussed above, making it inapplicable to credits expressly subject to the UCP. New York's highest court has permitted the account party to seek to maintain an injunction against payment of a credit subject to the UCP. In doing so, the court used pre-UCC case law as its precedent, but used all the concepts expressed in the UCC. This approach has been followed in both the state and federal courts in cases arising out of New York.

While the concept of enjoining payment due to fraud has not been widely used in the documentary letter of credit transaction, it has been widely sought in the standby letter of credit transaction. Some limiting concepts in the documentary letter of credit transaction, such as "strict compliance" of the documents, become somewhat meaningless when the "document" becomes a mere allegation by one party that the other party failed to perform properly under the contract. When the limitations which give structure to the transaction become meaningless, the transaction can become a breeding ground for fraud.

Under Revised UCC 5–109, there is a series of limitations on the availability of the fraud exception for use by the beneficiary. The first limitation is that "the issuer shall honor presentation, if honor is demanded by a nominated person who has given value in good faith without notice of material injury or fraud." Thus, confirming banks who have paid against the documents in good faith and without notice of any defense to, or defect in, the documents are entitled to reimbursement, despite fraud on the beneficiary. So also is an advising bank which has been authorized to pay against the documents, rather than merely to accept the documents for collection. Under the UCC, if the documents are presented by such a confirming bank, or authorized advising bank, and the documents appear on their face to comply with the credit, the issuing bank *must* pay the confirming bank, even though the documents are forged or fraudulent or there is fraud in the transaction.

A second limitation is that, if the documents are presented by anyone else (beneficiary, advising bank authorized to take for collection only, confirming bank which took with notice of defects or defenses, etc), the issuing bank *may* still pay, even though it has been notified that the documents are forged or fraudulent, or that there is fraud in the transaction, as long as it acts in good faith. In the latter case, the issuing bank may also refuse to pay, but that is not very likely. Reasons for the issuing bank not refusing to pay range from its reluctance to be known as an unreliable source of funds in letter of credit transactions to its inability to evaluate the available evidence of fraud, especially on an *ex parte* basis. Banks are paid to handle documents, not to become judge and jury.

The account party is, however, given the power to obtain a court order against payment, so long as it can prove forgery, fraud or fraud in the transaction. Thus under the UCC, if the account party obtains a court injunction against payment form a court having proper jurisdiction, the issuing bank is permitted to dishonor the presentment. But the Revised UCC Article 5 leaves only a very narrow avenue for the account party to seek and obtain judicial intervention through injunctive relief in the letter of credit transaction. To beneficiaries, the concept creates great uncertainty about prompt payment, because they know nothing about the judicial system and fear the worst. To account parties, the concept has created a theoretical argument, but there have been very few reported cases in which they were successful.

The Revised Article 5 limits itself in several ways:

First, the fraud must be "material," but material is not defined. The Comments to Revised 5–109 cite some prior decisions favorably, but its meaning will be decided on a case by case basis.

Second, the account party must present sufficient evidence of fraud or forgery, not merely allegations of it.

Third, all the procedural requirements for injunctive or other relief must be met.

Fourth, the relief can be denied if third parties are not "adequately protected," and no relief will be granted if a confirming or advising bank has paid funds to the beneficiary. However, this concept has been expanded in the Comments to include protection against incidental damages, such as legal fees, by *bonds* or otherwise. All of these are limitations which have been found in the prior cases and which would be expected in an action for injunctive relief.

The principal new limitation is one stated in Revised 5–109. A forgery or a fraud in the document may permit an injunction of payment if perpetrated by anyone, but a fraud in the underlying transaction is cognizable only if it is "committed by the beneficiary," and not by some third party, such a carrier. The difference between the two concepts is illustrated by the approach of English and Canadian courts to the fraud exception.

The English and Canadian courts have each recognized the "fraud exception," based upon the persuasive precedent of the American cases. However, each of them, in addition to the requirements of the pre-Revision UCC, place great stress on the *scienter* requirements of common law fraud and require the account party to establish that the beneficiary itself made, or was responsible for, the misrepresentation that was the foundation for the fraud claim. A misrepresentation made by any other party to the transaction would not permit an injunction against payment of the beneficiary. Thus, the House of Lords, while recognizing, the basic fraud concept, refused to extend it to protect the buyer when the fraud was committed by a third party (a loading broker) without seller's knowledge.[3] Under the English–Canadian formulation: (1) Where the credit requires loading by May 15 and the bill of lading shows loading on the 16th, the bank must dishonor. (2) Where the credit requires loading on May 15, and bank knows that the beneficiary has altered a document in a non-apparent manner, the bank must dishonor. (3) But, where the credit requires loading by May 15, and bank knows that a freight forwarder has altered a document in a non-apparent manner, the bank must *honor* the credit.

Under Revised 5–109, American courts would reach such a result if the misrepresentation was considered a fraud in the underlying transaction. However, such a misrepresentation is more likely to be considered arising out of the document itself. If so, the identity of the perpetrator would be irrelevant. Revised 5–109 does not attempt to define fraud, which is a product of case law and varies widely from state to state.

The traditional difference between fraud doctrines and breach of contract concepts was that the former consider the state of mind of the seller, while breach of contract concerns only whether the goods lived up to a particular objective standard set by their description. Fraud concepts have expanded enormously since 1952, and conduct which not have been actionable during the first half of the 20th Century is now routinely within current case law concepts. The modern fraud doctrines often do not require any evil intent, but only that seller know that a particular fact is not true—or, that he does not know whether a particular fact is true or not when he states it—or, that he believes that a fact is true when is not, and a court decides that he should have made a more thorough investigation before speaking.

As an outgrowth of the 1979 change of government in Iran, increased attention was given to the potential that a standby letter's beneficiary could require payment for what was characterized as "bad faith" or "arbitrary" reasons, or at least for reasons not related to the contractor's intentional failure to perform on the contract (e.g., perhaps because of conditions surrounding a civil insurrection).

Many courts have declined to enjoin payment because of insufficient evidence of fraud. Other courts have been willing to issue a "notice of injunction" requiring issuers to give some prior notice (usually three to ten days) to the account party before transferring money to the beneficiary of a standby credit after demand for payment, while a few courts have granted preliminary injunctions of indefinite duration.

Although the customer may sometimes have payment enjoined when fraud is present, he is obligated to reimburse the bank if the bank has made a payment in good faith, even upon a fraudulent demand.

The fraud in the transaction exception created in *Stejn* has been codified in section 5–114 of the UCC, and has been accepted by courts in

---

3. *United City Merchants (Investments) Ltd. v. Royal Bank of Canada (The Ameri-* *can Accord),* 1983 A.C. 168 (H.L. 1982)

England. In cases involving traditional letters of credit, the courts have given the fraud in the transaction exception a narrow reading, confining its application to cases of egregious fraud on the part of the beneficiary. This narrow reading apparently is justified on the ground that a broader rule would defeat the certainty of letter of credit transactions and undermine of the basic purposes of the letter of credit—assuring prompt payment to the beneficiary.

§ 7.14 Fraudulent or Abusive Demands for Payment Under the United Nations Convention on Independent Guarantees and Stand-by Letters of Credit

A main purpose of the UN Convention on Independent Guarantees and Stand-by Letters of Credit is to establish greater uniformity internationally in the manner in which issuers and courts respond to allegations of fraud or abuse in demands for payment under standby letters of credit.

Article 19 of the Convention indicates the situations in which a court may interfere with a complying drawing under an independent undertaking. As is apparent from the drafting history of the provision, it is intended to provide a rigorous standard by which the availability of relief is to be determined.

The Convention provides a general definition of the types of situations in which an exception to the obligation to pay against a facially compliant demand would be justified.[1] The definition encompasses fact patters covered in different legal systems by notions such as "fraud" or "abuse of right." The definition refers to situations in which is manifest and clear that any document is not genuine or has been falsified, that no payment is due on the basis asserted in the demand or that the demand has no conceivable basis. Additionally, the Convention provides examples of cases in which a demand would be deemed to have no conceivable basis.[2]

The Convention seeks to strike a balance between different interests and considerations at play. By allowing discretion to the issuer acting in good faith, the Convention takes into account the concern of issuers over preserving the commercial reliability of undertakings as promises that are independent from underlying transactions.

At the same time, the Convention affirms that the applicant, in the situations referred to, is entitled to provisional court measures to block payment.[3] This recognizes that it is proper role of courts, and not of issuers, to investigate the facts of underlying transactions.

Apart from entitling an applicant or an instructing party to provisional court measures blocking payment or freezing proceeds of an

---

§ 7.14

1. Article 19(1), CIGSLC.

2. Article 19(2), CIGSLC.

3. Article 19(2), CIGSLC.

undertaking in the types of cases referred to above, the Convention establishes a standard of proof to be met in order to obtain such provisional measures on the basis of immediately available strong evidence of a high probability that the fraudulent or abusive circumstances are present. Reference is also made to consideration of whether the applicant would be likely to suffer serious harm in the absence of the provisional measures and to the possibility of the court requiring security to be posted.

While authorizing provisional court measures in the cases concerned, the Convention is aimed at minimizing the use of judicial procedures to interfere in undertakings by limiting the granting of provisional court measures to those types of cases, with one additional type of case. Provisional court orders blocking payment or freezing proceeds are also authorized in the case of use of an undertaking for a criminal purpose.[4]

Selected Bibliography

Stern, The Independence Rule in Standby Letters of Credit, 52 U. Chi. L. Rev. 218 (1985).

Blodgett & Mayer, International Letters of Credit: Arbitral Alternatives to Litigating Fraud, 35 Am. Bus. L. J. 443 (1998).

Hinchey, Guarantees of Performances, June 19, 1998, Center for International Legal Studies, Salzburg Conference, International Construction, Law and Dispute Resolution.

Goode, Abstract Payment Undertakings and the Rules of the International Chamber of Commerce, 39 St. Louis L.J. 725 (1995).

Gabriel, Standby Letter of Credit Does the Risks Outweigh the Benefits?, 1988 Columb. Bus. L. Rev. 705 (1988).

Dolan, Analyzing Bank Drafted Standby Letter of Credit Rules, The International Standby Practice (ISP 98), 45 Wayne L. Rev. 1865 (2000).

Dole, The Essence of a Letter of Credit under Revised U.C.C. Article 5: Permissible and Impermissible Non–Documentary Conditions Affecting Honor, 35 Hous. L. Rev. 1079 (1998).

Kenney, A Road Map to the International Standby Practices, Feb. 1999, McKenna & Cuneo, L.L.P., Los Angeles,

Pitney, Hardin, Kipp & Szuch LLP, A Brief Look at the New Letter of Credit Rules: International Standby Practices 1998, January 1999.

Available in: **www.phks.com/html_refs/alerts/finan_alert_99jan.shtml** (Feb. 9, 2001)

Noah & Taylor, Introduction to Standby Practices (ISP 98), Jan. 27 1999.

---

4. Article 20(3), CIGSLC.

Available in: **www.wtci.org/program-reports/isp98pro.htm** (Feb. 9, 2001)

Rendell, Stand By for New Set of Rules of Letters of Credit, The National Law J., Nov. 2, 1998.

Available in: **www.pattonboggs.com/news/views/1999/11/letters.html** (Feb. 9, 2001)

Spjut, Documentary and Standby Letters of Credit, The Turin Group–Financial Services.

Available in **www.toerien.com/advice_column/doc_standby_letters_credit_.htm** (Feb. 9, 2001)

Lipton, Documentary Credit Law and Practice in the Global Information Age, 22 Fordham Int'l L.J. 1972 (1999).

Byrne, Overview of Letter of Credit Law and Practice in 1999, Documentary Credit World.

Byrne, The Official Commentary on the international Standby Practices (Institute of International Banking Law & Practice, Inc., 1998).

Chapter 8

INTERNATIONAL ELECTRONIC COMMERCE

Table of Sections

A. INTRODUCTION TO E–COMMERCE TRANSACTIONS

§ 8.1 Introduction

In their simplest form, traditional commercial transactions might be considered as revolving around the exchange of goods or services for money. But actually a great deal more is involved, the creation of the goods or services themselves, their distribution directly or through a variety of third parties, matching (or creating) customer needs with

421

those goods and services, providing ongoing support, and establishing the terms, conditions, and pricing for the transaction, all involve complicated tasks with potential legal import. Many of the legal and business issues associated with these tasks are managed through various contractual arrangements with the appropriate parties.

Today's confluence of computerization, the Internet, and a variety of other communications technologies, is altering the historic business models and traditional contracting practices. With E-Commerce one is dealing with an intangible, digital, world where tangible "things" are arguably less important; and access to the digital elements at the core of a transaction (often along with the associated documents) is both easier and more widely spread than with real world "chains" of physical interactions. Thus, the traditional relationships among the parties to a transaction are affected, and concerns regarding the management, communication, and security of the digital information involved rise to a new level.[1]

The recent phenomenal growth of E–Commerce caught the legal regimes of the world unprepared. None was ready for the legal problems caused by the new forms of contract-making, payment, performance, and information exchange brought about by the application of new technologies. The law also adapts to changing technologies, however it commonly takes some time for legal rules and principles to adjust to new circumstances, and consequently there is often a lag between the time new business practices are created and changes in the legal rules. They have done their best to adapt traditional rules to new business patterns, but each legal regime has adapted in a different manner. Thus, there is little consistency in the rules applicable to E–Commerce transactions which cross national borders.

Such a lack of consistency is not new, but the problems are magnified by two practical aspects of E–Commerce. One is that the parties often do not know when an E–Commerce transaction involves dealings across national boundaries. A website with a ".com" address may literally be located anywhere in the world. Thus, the website address of each party, which may be the only information each has of the other, may not reveal the transborder nature of the transaction. The second aspect is that the amount of writing on a screen—and the attention span of parties acting at "Internet speed"—is limited. Accordingly, long sophisticated contracts with lots of form-pad clauses are "out" in E–Commerce. In particular, most E–Merchants believe that too many other terms have priority over choice of law and choice of forum clauses, for example, so they do not appear in the terms of many E–Commerce

---

§ 8.1

1. The phenomenon is not new. Consider the following statement:

"The businessman of the present day must be continually on the jump, the slow express train will not answer his purpose,

and the poor merchant has no other way in which to work to secure a living for his family. He *must* use the telegraph." (Emphasis in the original.) Statement in 1868 by W.E. Dodge *quoted in* Tom Standage, THE VICTORIAN INTERNET (1999) at 166.

contracts. Thus, a second potential device for revealing the transborder nature of the transaction is usually missing.

There are a variety of new contract issues created by E–Commerce, including how to satisfy requirements for agreements in writing and signatures, authentication and attribution of communications without personal contact, security and integrity of electronic messages, and express and implied terms and conditions for both commercial and consumer contracts. E–Commerce also raises jurisdictional issues, ranging from choice of law to presence in a jurisdiction for purposes of being sued in a civil action to presence in a jurisdiction for purposes of regulation by public authorities. The public authorities not only wish to prevent fraud and deception by E–Merchants, but also to regulate privacy, intellectual property and taxation issues, among others. In all these areas, there are very few statutory rules or decided cases; and, where there are, the existing rules and approaches to E–Commerce differ from one legal regime to another.

Thus, there is a perceived need, not only for statutory rules to facilitate E–Commerce, but for such rules to be similar across national borders, since it is not usually clear where the parties are located. In the absence of clear rules, parties have attempted to address many of these issues through their private contractual dealings, with varying degrees of success. Additionally, attempts to legislatively create similar rules in different jurisdictions, through international treaties, regional directives, or model legislation, continue to be proposed from time to time. The concerns over *whether* a contract can be formed electronically in recent years led to a burst of legislative activity at the state, federal and international levels. At the international level, UNCITRAL has issued two Model Laws: The UNCITRAL Model Law on Electronic Commerce,[2] and the UNCITRAL Model Law on Electronic Signatures[3]. The European Union has similarly been active in addressing these issues on a regional level. At the U.S. federal level, Congress has enacted the E–Sign law. At the state level, there have been many enactment of state laws, and the National Conference of Commissioners is also proposing uniform acts in the field. In addressing the various issues raised by E–Commerce, the parties' private contractual solutions and those enabled or facilitated by these new statutory measures are interrelated and interdependent, and must be considered together.

§ 8.2   Private Contractual Measures Enabling E–Commerce—Trading Partner Agreements

Trading Partner or EDI Agreements were among the first tools used to address the issues raised by E–Commerce, and continue to serve that role to day in a number of different types of business relationships. EDI Agreements are used to facilitate electronic information exchange and to

2. UNCITRAL Model Law on Electronic Commerce, U.N. Doc. A/RES/51/162, 16 December, 1996.

3. UNCITRAL Model Law on Electronic Signatures, U.N. Doc. A/CN.9/WG.IV/WP.88, January 30, 2001.

regulate many aspects of the relationship between the parties who do business with each other through electronic communication. The agreement may be just between two parties, or it may encompass a whole network of interrelated businesses either with a master agreement covering all parties or a series of standardized individual contracts.

EDI Agreements date back to the 1960s when they were first used by the large companies in the transportation industry and later by manufacturers to manage B2B transactions with established partners, purchasers, or suppliers conducted over private networks. Prior to the spread of the Internet, many of these networks used technical standards and formats which were not common across the marketplace or even within a given industry. An important part of the function of the EDI Agreement is to establish precisely what is technically required for the parties' computers to "talk" to one another. Thus, unlike relatively free form messaging, found in the text of email for example, the EDI Agreement established the *specific* format and content to which communications between the parties must conform so that their computers could appropriately execute the directions contained in the message. Once these technical standards are set, the parties benefit by the ability of their respective computer systems and software applications being able to directly read and process orders, shipping instructions, inventory management information, billing, etc.—the types of routine and repetitive tasks which are well suited to automation and would be less error prone if processed by computer. When EDI transaction processing is combined with electronic funds transfers, which financial institutions began developing at roughly the same time, the foundation is created for entirely computerized supply transactions which require little or no human intervention.

Transactions conducted with EDI pose a number of technical issues, some of which have been greatly eased as the technology continues to evolve. EDI first developed in the mainframe computer era, when there were *no* graphical interfaces or fill-in-the-blank electronic forms, and *every* element of the messages exchanged between the parties had to be precisely specified in order to be recognized operate properly on the parties' computers. Thus, to facilitate EDI transactions, technical standards for EDI messaging developed to help simplify the demands on competing computer systems. This is seen both with regard to particular industries, such as with the Society for Worldwide Interbank Financial Telecommunication (SWIFT) standards which are widely used for international financial transactions, and in more generalized standards such as those promulgated by the ANSI ("American National Standards Institute") program or in the United Nation's EDIFACT ("Electronic Data Interchange for Administration, Commerce, and Transport") standards. Accordingly, Trading Partner or EDI Agreements traditionally included lengthy technical specifications, or referenced an appropriate set of technical standards, which incidentally had the effect of locking the parties into specific technologies and making it difficult to migrate to newer technologies without losing the investment in their "legacy" systems. Moreover, the amount of technical work and investment in common systems needed to make this type of automated transaction processing work meant that EDI was not well suited to casual business relationships, but rather to established, stable, supply chains. However, while perhaps cumbersome, in the right circumstances, such as with a buyer's desire to improve its "just in time" parts supply system, EDI systems can be quite useful.

More recently, with the open and flexible technology such as that embodied in graphical web-based Internet communications, EDI is no longer confined primarily to large companies or parties involved in long term business relationships utilizing "closed" value-added-networks or "VANS." There is now a movement towards "Open EDI," forms of interaction which are less dependent upon a single, common set of computer protocols mandated by a contract put in place by the parties. There are even new forms of businesses being created, which bundle order processing, catalog or other "back office" EDI services among their capabilities, and which contract these services out to other companies thereby helping to enable the creation of so-called "virtual" enterprises.

Transactions conducted with EDI similarly pose a number of legal issues. Particularly when these agreements were first being developed and used, there were concerns over the ability to form legally enforceable contracts through electronic communications. Questions were frequently raised as to whether electronic communications could meet the traditional "writing" and "signature" requirements present in various jurisdictions. Additionally, the nature of electronic communications also prompted renewed focus on the "authentication" and "attribution" of communications from remote parties, and the related issues of the parties' ability to repudiate the content of any given communication. These were not entirely new issues. As noted earlier, businesses began substituting electronic communications for written documents since at least the time of the telegraph. However, to avoid the legal debates surrounding these issues in an electronic contracting environment, EDI agreements were typically executed by the parties in "hard copy" *before* engaging in the electronic communications they contemplated, much as they would with any master purchasing/supply agreement. In this manner, and against a background where the law governing electronic transactions was at best arguable, the parties created their own "enabling rules" for E–Commerce in their private contracts—and created for themselves the degree of legal certainty needed to conduct business electronically. The contract formation issues were minimized by employing a traditional contract vehicle up front, which then spelled out both the technical and legal consequences of the parties' subsequent electronic interactions. However, this approach is also inherently limited, as it depends upon establishing a continuing relationship with one's contractual partners and is therefore not well suited to one time transactions, which can be particularly limiting when dealing with mass market or consumer transactions. Accordingly, other private contractual approaches to enabling E–Commerce developed, such as "shrinkwrap" or "clickwrap" contracting.

§ 8.3 Private Contractual Measures Enabling E–Commerce—Shrinkwrap and Clickwrap Agreements

As more and more transactions moved online, new contractual approaches were needed to enable electronic transactions with consumers or end-users. Many of these would involve parties without any preexisting contractual relationship, so the example of the EDI Agreement developed primarily to serve a network of established B2B business relationships would not work. Close at hand, however, was another contractual model which could easily be adapted to online electronic contracting, that model was the "shrinkwrap" contract or license agreement developed by the software industry for mass market B2C transactions.

As the personal computer proliferated over the last twenty years, computer software became more of a commodity to be sold and employed by end-users remote from the developer both physically and legally. Given the ease with which software can be reproduced and duplicated, developers who were concerned over their intellectual property rights sought ways to continue to control the software which was being distributed on disks in mass-market transactions, and also to limit the liabilities and warranties which might otherwise accompany a sale of goods. Their solution was to rely upon a standardized software license which was provided with the disk or diskette-and to treat the transaction as a "license" of the software on the disk for a one-time license fee rather than a "sale" of the media on which the software resided. In order to bolster the argument, early license agreements were physically displayed on the outside of the packaging with the notation that breaking the shrinkwrap was a manifestation of the end-user's consent to be bound by the license. In this manner, developers hoped to both highlight the nature of the transaction as a license rather than as a commodity sale, and to minimize the possibility that the end-user could later challenge the terms of the license as a "surprise" not discovered until the packaging was opened.

The software industry quickly adopted the shrinkwrap concept and the use of these types of licenses has become such a common and well-known practice that the actual agreements are no longer typically displayed on the exterior of the packaging. The courts, however, were less eager to accept the shrinkwrap approach to contracting. As late as 1991 in *Step-Saver Data Systems, Inc. v. Wyse Technology* the Third Circuit U.S. Court of Appeals treated the terms of a software license agreement shipped with the product following a telephone order as "additional terms" to which the end-user had not consented under UCC § 2–207(2), and therefore not part of the parties' contractual agreement.[1] The trend since the mid 1990s, however, with cases such as

§ 8.3

1.   939 F.2d 91 (3d Cir. 1991).

ProCD, Inc. v. Zeidenberg;[2] *Hill v. Gateway 2000, Inc.;*[3] and *M.A. Mortenson Company Inc. v. Timberline Software Corporation,*[4] has been to uphold the validity of shrinkwrap software license agreements, although individual terms of these standard contracts might still be struck down as "unconscionable" in appropriate cases.[5] Courts in other jurisdictions are generally following a similar trend in their caselaw when considering whether shrinkwrap agreements are valid and enforceable.

As the Internet exploded with the advent of the World Wide Web, software distribution and other transactions increasingly moved "online" and the shrinkwrap model was naturally modified to suit the online environment. While it might be argued that posting standard terms and conditions on a website, without more, binds those who look at or use the website—the physical act of "clicking" on a link, typing "I agree," or some other actual manifestation of assent, bolsters the argument that an agreement between the parties was reached much as opening the box was initially viewed as manifesting assent to be bound by the terms of a shrinkwrap license. Various terms my be applied to this type of contracting, such as "clickwrap," "click-through," "point-and-click," or "webwrap" agreements, for example.

One of the first cases to address this form of contracting, the Sixth Circuit U.S. Court Of Appeals 1996 decision in *CompuServe v. Patterson,*[6] upheld an online Software Registration Agreement and an accompanying Service Agreement and Rules of Operation based upon the plaintiff's "manifesting assent" by typing the word "agree" at the appropriate places indicated on the online screens. Courts have subsequently upheld agreements to be bound by standard form online contract terms based upon clicking on an online button or link, as for example in *Hotmail Corp. v. Van$ Money Pie, Inc.,*[7] *Groff v. America Online,*[8] and *Caspi v. Microsoft Network.*[9] In each of these cases, the design of the online offering was such that the user could not proceed to the next step and utilize the service without manifesting their agreement with some sort of physical act. Additionally, unlike *Patterson*, the agreements related purely to the use of online services, and not the provision of goods or software arguable covered by the U.C.C .. The agreements were upheld, even though formulated entirely online, by parties with no prior rela-

2. 86 F.3d 1447 (7th Cir. 1996).

3. 105 F.3d 1147 (7th Cir. 1997).

4. 140 Wash.2d 568, 998 P.2d 305 (Wash.2000).

5. *See e.g.* Brower v. Gateway 2000, Inc., 246 A.D.2d 246, 676 N.Y.S.2d 569, 37 U.C.C. Rep. Serv.2d 54 (N.Y. App. Div. 1998), which held that Gateways's arbitration clause, which required the use of International Chamber of Commerce procedures, imposed excessive costs on individual consumers. Under the ICC rules and advance deposit of $4,000 was required, of which $2,000 was not refundable even if the consumer prevails in the dispute.

6. 89 F.3d 1257 (6th Cir. 1996).

7. 47 U.S.P.Q.2d 1020 (BNA), 1998 WL 388389 (N.D. Cal. 1998). The Hotmail decision is also interesting as it involved the provision of a *free* service. In effect, the decision confirms that Hotmail users were bound to abide by Hotmail's terms of use in exchange for receiving free web-based email.

8. 1998 WL 307001 (R.I. Super. 1998).

9. 323 N.J. Super. 118, 732 A.2d 528 (1999), cert. den., 162 N.J. 199, 743 A.2d 851 (1999).

tionship, and with no pre-existing hardcopy agreement to be bound by contracts formed electronically.

§ 8.4 Legislative Measures Enabling E–Commerce

Given the speed with which technology is changing business practices related to E–Commerce, the gradual adaptation of existing legal rules to the new modes of doing business through caselaw is viewed by many as simply being too slow. Just as E–Merchants clamor for more legal certainty in the rules surrounding their enterprises; legislatures and academicians on the national, regional, and international levels also want to demonstrate their receptiveness to these new ways of doing business. This has led to an explosion of new statutes, codes, and model laws on E–Commerce around the world.

These new statutory schemes have multiple purposes. Several of them are pure "enabling" measures, aimed simply at clarifying and confirming the ability to form contractual agreements electronically, for example. This is the most basic function for any statutory e-commerce measure, and one which deals with many of the same issues which underlie the private contractual approaches to E–Commerce. However, as legal systems generally get more comfortable with the notion of entering into binding agreements electronically, many of these e-commerce statutory measure are pushing ahead to deal with substantive issues beyond merely contract formation in cyberspace. Many of the statutory schemes deal with the terms found in "standard" electronic contracts, and raise the types of issues which might cause concern in any form contract. Are any of the standard terms unconscionable? Are they sufficiently clear and conspicuous so as to fully bind the user? Do the existing approaches to warranties and consumer protection measures need to be altered when dealing with E–Commerce? Are there particular public policy issues, such as privacy issues, associated with E–Commerce transactions? Do existing contractual and legal remedies work with E–Commerce transactions? And even at the most fundamental level, are there particular problems with choice of law and choice of forum in the global marketplaces found in cyberspace?

Whatever the scope of their coverage, the national regional, and international statutory schemes and the private contractual solutions devised for these issues are inextricably intertwined. Private contractual approaches and statutory measure borrow freely from one another in all jurisdictions, and their interplay helps inform the debate over what approaches will be most successful in the global marketplace for E–Commerce transactions.

B.   INTERNATIONAL MODEL LAWS

§ 8.5 UNCITRAL Model Law on Electronic Commerce— In General

UNCITRAL (the organization which developed CISG) developed a

Model Law on Electronic Commerce, which it adopted in 1996.[1] The Model Law is a minimalist approach to legislation, seeking to facilitate E–Commerce transactions and not to regulate them. This Model Law is now available to all legal regimes for enactment to provide guidance for E–Merchants and their customers. The UNCITRAL Model Law is intended to provide a legal guide in order to facilitate modern business transactions in the electronic environment. The fundamental principle of this Model Law is that data messages should not be discriminated against, in other words, that there should be no disparity of treatment between data messages and paper documents. Under this basic principle, Articles 5 to 10 address the issues of legal recognition of data messages,[2] admissibility and evidential weight of data message,[3] the concepts of "writing," "signature" and "original" in the aspect of electronic commerce,[4] and retention of data messages.[5] Articles 11 to 15 furnish a set of provisions dealing with formation of electronic contracts and the communication of data messages.

Finally, Articles 16 and 17 create provisions for two specific transactions: the carriage of goods and transportation documents. As of March 8, 2001, legislation based on the UNCITRAL Model Law on Electronic Commerce has been enacted by Australia, Bermuda, Columbia, France, Hong Kong, Ireland, the Philippines, the Republic of Korea, Singapore and the state of Illinois. Further enactments are expected.[6]

§ 8.6 UNCITRAL Model Law on Electronic Commerce— Non Discrimination

In its non-discrimination provisions, the UNCITRAL Model Law provides for equality of treatment between paper documents and electronic messages.[1] It provides that "date messages" are not to be denied legal effect because they are electronic,[2] and that any "writing" requirement is satisfied by a data message which is acceptable for subsequent reference.[3] Legal requirements for a "signature" are met by a data message if there is a method which is "reasonable for the circumstances" to identify both the identity of the person sending the message and that person's approval of the message.[4] An electronic data message is allowed to satisfy evidentiary requirements, and an evidentiary requirement for "an original document" is satisfied by an electronic data message whose information integrity can be assured, and whose information can be displayed.[5] Finally, record retention requirements may be

§ 8.5

1. General Assembly Resolution 51/162 of 16 December 1996; Y.B. Int'l Trade L. Comm'n 237, Vol. XXVII.

2. Electronic Commerce Model Law, supra § 8.1, note 2, Article 5.

3. *Id.*, at Article 9.

4. *Id.*, at Article 6, 7, 8.

5. *Id.*, at Article 10.

6. See http:www.uncitral.org/en-index.html.

§ 8.6

1. Electronic Commerce Model Law, arts. 5–10.

2. *Id.*, at art. 5.

3. *Id.*, at art. 6(1).

4. *Id.*, at art. 7(1)(b).

5. *Id.*, at art. 8(1).

satisfied for data messages by appropriate electronic retention.[6]

Article 5 is the direct presentation of the non-discrimination principle discussed above. It states that "information shall not be denied legal effect, validity or enforceability solely on the grounds that it is in the form of a data message."[7] The basic concept of this language is that a party of the transaction cannot solely rely on the ground that the information is in the form of a data message to deny its legal effect. At the same time, however, information contained in a data message is not necessarily valid on the sole ground that it is in the form of part of a data message.[8]

The Model Law on Electronic Commerce also addresses the issue of legal recognition of data message, in terms of the admissibility and evidential weight of data message in legal proceedings.[9] According to Article 9, the fact that an information is in the form of data message cannot be used as the sole ground to deny the admissibility as evidence of that data message. In case the data message is the best evidence one part could obtain, the fact that it is not in its original form should not be used as the ground to deny the admissibility of the data message. Since the term "best interest" is not used in many non-common law jurisdictions, however, the paragraph of Article 9 containing this term can be ignored when enacting the Model Law. On how the evidential value of data message should be assessed, Paragraph (2) of Article 9 sets up the guidelines. The evidential value depends on whether the data message was generated, stored or communicated in a reliable manner.

May contract terms and conditions be "incorporated by reference" in electronic commerce? For example, may a seller fail to state, in a legal document, certain provisions and conditions in the text but are referred to and detailed elsewhere. Because electronic commerce relies heavily on the mechanism of incorporation by reference, a standard of the legal validity of those incorporated provisions becomes critical to the growth of electronic commerce. By stating that the legal effect of information shall not be denied solely on the ground that it is not contained in the data message, but only referred to in that data message, the Model Law in fact recognizes that the incorporated terms and provisions should be treated as if they had been fully stated in the text of that data message.[10] Since the principle in conventional paper transactions is that provisions incorporated by reference should be regard as if they are fully stated in the text, the Model Law, in this respect, expands the applicability of this paper transaction principle to the electronic scenario.

In traditional paper-based transactions, "writing," "original" and "signature" are the fundamental concepts which support the validity of

---

6. *Id.*, at art. 9.

7. *Id.*, at art. 5.

8. UNICTRAL Model Law on Electronic Commerce, Guide to Enactment (hereafter Guide) ¶ 46.

9. Electronic Commerce Model Law, art. 9.

10. *Id.*, at art. 5 bis.

the transaction. Adopting the new "functional-equivalent" approach, the Model Law defines these three concepts in the electronic context.[11]

Information meets the requirement of writing in the applicable State law, if the information is accessible so one can use it at some later time as reference.[12] The word "accessible" implies that the information in the form of data message should be retrievable, reproducible, readable and interpretable. Computer processing is also covered under the term "usable" in the Article.

Any legal requirement of signature is met if a reliable method is used to identify the person and, at the same time, to identify that person's approval of the information contained in the data message.[13] There are three statutory requirements for an effective electronic signature: the method used must be able to identify the person himself; the method used must also identify the person's approval the data massage, and the method must be reliable. Only after these criteria are met, will the data message be regarded as authenticated with sufficient credibility and therefore be enforceable in legal proceedings under the statute.

There are two requirements for a data message to be deemed to be the equivalent of an original.[14] First, there must be a reliable assurance as to the integrity of the information at the time when it was first generated in its final form.[15] Second, the information must be capable of being displayed to the person to whom it is to be presented.[16] Necessary additions to the data message, for example, endorsement, would not affect its originality as long as the content of the data message remain complete and unaltered.

Retention of data message is also crucial to the validity of electronic transaction. There are three requirements for the retention of electronic documents to be deemed the equivalent of paper documents.[17] First, the information must be accessible so as to be usable for subsequent reference. Second, the data message must be retained in the format which accurately reflects the original content. And, third, the data message retained must reflect the origin, destination, date and time when it was sent or received. In short, all important transmittal information has to be stored and other transmittal information can be exempted without damaging the integrity of the data message.

§ 8.7   UNCITRAL Model Law on Electronic Commerce—Contract Formation

Articles 11 to 15 of the UNCITRAL Model Law on Electronic Commerce address issues relating the contract formation and communication of data messages. These more specialized rules may be varied by

---

11.   *Id.*, at arts. 6, 7 and 8.
12.   *Id.*, at art. 6.
13.   *Id.*, at art. 7.
14.   *Id.*, at art. 8.

15.   *Id.*, at art. 8(1)(a).
16.   *Id.*, at art. 8(1)(b).
17.   *Id.*, at art. 10.

agreement between the parties.[1] These rules concern formation, attribution of messages, and acknowledgment and time of receipt of data messages. As to attribution, a message is deemed to be sent by a designated originator if it is sent either by an authorized person or by a machine that is programmed by the originator to operate automatically. The addressee of the data message is authorized to rely on it as being from the originator if either an agreed-upon security procedure has been used or the originator enabled the actual sender to gain access to a message identification method.

Article 11 concerns the issue of the validity of contract formed by exchange of data messages. It establishes the legal effectiveness of data messages by stating that a contract shall not be denied validity on the sole ground that it was formed by exchange of data messages.[2] This article covers not only the case in which both the offer and the acceptance are communicated by electronic means but also the case in which only the offer or only the acceptance is communicated electronically.

Article 12 functions as supplement to article 11 by stating that in addition to the data messages related to the conclusion of the contract, data messages that relate to the performance of contractual obligation shall also not be denied legal effectiveness solely on the ground that they are in the form of a data message.[3]

The Model Law also establishes a set of rules on attribution of data messages.[4] The underlying issues are under what circumstances should a data message be considered as a message of the originator, and under what circumstances should the originator be bound by the addressee's response or action.

First, a party is bound as an originator by a data message if it has actually sent that message.[5]

Second, a party is deemed to be bound by a message if the sender had the authority to act on behalf of the originator in respect of that data message,[6] or if the data message was sent automatically by an information system programmed by or on behalf of the originator.[7] In such circumstances, the data message is deemed to be sent by the originator.

Third, the addressee "is entitled" to rely on a data message as being that of the originator: if the addressee properly applied an authentication procedure previously agreed to by the originator for that purpose.[8] The addressee is also "entitled" to rely on a data message which results from the action of an unauthorized person who nevertheless had access

---

§ 8.7

1. Electronic Commerce Model Law, art. 11. This provision also allows the parties to agree that they will be bound only by paper-based communications, such as a formally-signed written document, prepared by attorneys and signed by corporate executives, to conclude the contracts.

2. *Id.*

3. *Id.*, at art. 12.

4. *Id.*, at art. 13.

5. *Id.*, at art. 13(1).

6. *Id.*, at art. 13(2)(a).

7. *Id.*, at art. 13(2)(b).

8. *Id.*, at art. 13(3)(a).

to the originator's authentication procedure.[9] Under both circumstances, the originator would be stopped if the addressee relies and acts on the data message.

But the originator would not be entitled to rely on the message in two types of situation. First, if the addressee received notice from the originator that the data message is not from the originator while the addressee had reasonable time to act on the notice, the message would no longer bind the originator.[10] Second, where the data message is sent by an unauthorized person who had access to the originator's authentication process, the originator is not bound if the addressee knew or should have known that the data message was not from the originator.[11]

If the data message is deemed to be binding or the addressee is entitled to rely upon the message, and the addressee is entitled to action it.[12] However, the addressee is never entitled to act on a message if it knew or should have known that the data message was not from the originator.[13] If the addressee knew or should have known that the data message was a duplicate, he is not entitled to regard the data message as a separate data message and to act on that assumption.[14] A major problem with electronic data messages is that they get lost much more often than messages sent through the U.S. Post Office. Thus, acknowledgment of receipt of electronic message is much more important to the parties than is acknowledgment of paper-based messages, and the parties often stipulate in their agreements that data messages must be acknowledged. If they so agree, under the UNCITRAL Model Law, acknowledgment can be accomplished either by the method agreed upon or, where no specific acknowledgment method has been agreed, any communication or conduct can be sufficient.[15] Even where the parties have not agreed to require acknowledgment, the originator of a data message may unilaterally require it by stating in the body of the message that it is conditional on acknowledgment.[16] Such a message is deemed "never been sent" until acknowledgment is received. Receipt of a message generally requires that the message enter an information system outside the control of the originator or its agents.[17]

The Model Law on Electronic Commerce also addresses the legal issues arising from the usage of acknowledgment procedures. Where the originator has requested or has agreed with the addressee that receipt of a data message is to be acknowledged. Any communication or any conduct of the addressee which is sufficient to indicate to the originator that the message has been received is a valid acknowledgment, if no particular form or particular method is agreed upon by both parties.[18]

---

9. *Id.*, at art. 13(3)(b).

10. *Id.*, at art. 13(4)(a).

11. *Id.*, at art. 13(4)(b). This exception applies only to the provision in Article 13(3)(b).

12. *Id.*, at art. 13(5).

13. *Id.*, last sentence.

14. *Id.*, at art. 13(5).

15. *Id.*, at art. 14(2).

16. *Id.*, at art. 14(3).

17. Id., at art. 15(1).

18. *Id.*, at art. 14(2).

Further, where the parties have agreed that receipt of a data message is to be acknowledged, and the originator has stated that the data message is conditional on receipt of the acknowledgment, the originator's data message is not effective until the acknowledgment is received;[19] finally, if the parties have agreed to acknowledge receipt, and the originator has not stated that the data message is conditional on receipt of the acknowledgment, until an acknowledgment is received by the originator, the originator may by notice request that the addressee send an acknowledgment within a specified time. If the addressee does not send acknowledgment within the time specified, the data message loses its effect.[20]

It may be essential to determine the time and place of offer and acceptance to business transactions. The Model Law defines these concepts in the electronic context.[21] The core concept in this provision depends upon the time that a data message enters a certain information system. For example, the dispatch of a data message is defined as the moment when a data message enters an information system outside the control of the originator.[22] Similarly if the originator has designated an information system, the receipt of a data message occurs at the time when the data message enters that information system designated by the originator.[23] On the other hand, if the originator does not designate an information system, receipt occurs when the data message enters the information system of the addressee.[24]

§ 8.8 UNCITRAL Model Law on Electronic Commerce— Specialized Provisions

There are other provisions in the UNCITRAL Model Law which are specific to the contracts for the carriage of goods and to transportation documents. These provisions generally permit electronic data messages to replace bills of lading and waybills, even where local statutes require a writing on a paper document.[1] They also provide that legal rules which compel the use of paper documents in carriage contracts are satisfied by such data messages.[2]

§ 8.9 UNCITRAL Model Law on Electronic Signatures

In addition to the Model Law on Electronic Commerce, UNCITRAL has also prepared a Model Law on Electronic Signatures.[1] The UNCITRAL Model Law on Electronic Signature can be regarded as a supplementary document to the UNCITRAL Model Law on Electronic Commerce.[2] The Electronic Signature Model Law deals specifically with the

---

19. *Id.*, at art. 14(3).

20. *Id.*, at art. 14(4).

21. *Id.*, at art. 15.

22. *Id.*, at art. 15(1).

23. *Id.*, at art. 15(2)(a).

24. *Id.*, at art. 15(2)(b).

§ 8.8

1. *Id.*, at art. 16.

2. *Id.*, at art. 17.

§ 8.9

1. UN document, A/CN.9/483.

2. See discussion at §§ 8.5–8.8, *supra*.

legal issues arising from the wide usage of electronic signatures in the modern electronic business transactions. Its principle provisions relate to party autonomy, validity, reliability, and certification authorities.

The Model Law applies party autonomy principles to electronic signatures, so that the provisions of the Draft are not mandatory. Instead, parties are permitted to vary the conditions and provisions by agreement, so as long as their electronic signatures are valid under the applicable State law.[3]

After defining itself as non-mandatory law, the Model Law on Electronic Signatures builds a foundation by establishing criteria for "valid" signatures and "reliable" signatures. If the applicable State law requires a "signature," whether by mandatory provisions or not, Model Law enables a reliable electronic signature to meet this requirement.[4] An electronic signature deemed to be reliable if three requirements are met. First, the signature creation data[5] must be linked to, and only to, the signatory. Second, at the time when the signatory signs, the signature creation data must be under the sole control of the signatory. And third, any alteration to the electronic signature must be detectable after signing. There is a fourth requirement where the signature is required also to assure the integrity of the signed information—any alteration made to that information after signing must be detectable.[6]

Any person, organization or authority may be competent to determine which electronic signature satisfy the tests enumerated above, if it is specified by the enacting State. The determination should be consistent with recognized international standards.[7]

After defining "valid" and "reliable" with respect to signatures, the Model Law imposes duties on persons who claim the ability to provide such signatures—signatories. A signatory's basic obligation is to exercise reasonable care to secure the authenticity of the electronic signature. If a signatory breaches the duty of reasonable care, it will be liable for the legal consequences.

In particular, where the signature creation data can be used to create a signature that has legal effect, the signatory shall exercise reasonable care to avoid unauthorized use of these data. If the signatory knows that the signature creation data have been compromised or may have been compromised, it must provide notice of this fact to those who may reasonably rely on the electronic signature. Where a certificate is used to authenticate the electronic signature, the signatory should exercise reasonable care to ensure the accuracy and completeness of all relevant materials.[8]

The certification service provider's basic responsibilities are to: act in accordance with its presentation with respect to its policies and

---

3. *Id.*, at art. 5.
4. *Id.*, at art. 6(1)(2).
5. *Id.*, Signature creation data is defined as the data that can create the signature.
6. *Id.*, at art. 6(3).
7. *Id.*, at art. 7.
8. *Id.*, at art. 8(1).

practices; exercise reasonable care to ensure the accuracy and completeness of all relevant materials; and provide technical measures to facilitate a relying party to ascertain a series of important information in determining the authenticity of the electronic signature.[9]

Similarly, a relying party shall exercise reasonable care in verifying the reliability of an electronic signature or validity of the information provided by the certification service provider.[10]

The Model Law provides a list of factors to be taken into account in order to determine the "trustworthiness" of systems, procedures and human resources utilized by the certification service provider.[11]

Although all of the foregoing provisions develop a national system for creating valid and reliable electronic signatures, the most important issue in international E–Commerce concerns the recognition of electronic signatures from other legal regimes. The Model Law states the non-discrimination rule on the reliability of certificates and electronic signatures. According to this provision, a certificate or an electronic signature issued outside the enacting State should have the same legal effect in the enacting State as if it is issued in the enacting State. The test here is that it must offer a substantially equivalent level of reliability. Geographic factors are excluded in determining the legal effect of a certificate and an electronic signature. If the parties want to set their own standard of recognition, however, they can realize it by an agreement valid under the applicable State law.[12]

C. REGIONAL LAWS

§ 8.10 European Union—Background to the eEurope Initiative

The European Union began considering the advent of the "Information Society," and the need to establish a Pan–European information technology infrastructure with the 1994 white paper on "Growth, Competitiveness and Employment: the Challenges and Courses for Entering into the XXIst Century" prepared by former European Commission Vice–President Martin Bangemann. The Bangemann Report led to the establishment of an Information Society Project (now Promotion) Office within the EU,[1] and a series of actions plans to promote the Information Society in Europe. These plans were intended to formulate strategies to change the existing regulatory and legal framework, technical infrastructure, and the cultural attitudes necessary to promote the Information Society. This led most recently to the eEurope Initiative to further accelerate the development of an European Information Society.[2]

---

9. *Id.*, at art. 9.

10. *Id.*, at art. 11.

11. *Id.*, at arts. 10 and 9(1).

12. *Id.*, at art. 12.

§ 8.10

1. See "Europe's Europe's Way to the Information Society—An Action Plan," COM(94) 347 final, 19.07.1994.

2. "eEurope—An Information Society for All," COM(99) 687 final, 8.12.1999.

The EU efforts to coherently address the impact of technology on European society as a whole results in a very different approach to many of the issues raised by E–Commerce than that seen in the United States for example. It is an approach which is inherently multinational, and characterized by a conscious effort to harmonize or approximate legal rules throughout the different member countries in the EU. At the same time it is an approach which also consciously seeks to identify and remove barriers to the development of E–Commerce and other Information Society services. Although only one aspect of the broader European Information Society initiatives, measures related to E–Commerce have been central to the various EU action plans. These measures include the 1997 European Initiative on Electronic Commerce,[3] which focused on primarily on developing infrastructure and protecting consumers' economic and legal interests; the related 1997 Distance Selling Directive;[4] the 1999 Electronic Signature Directive;[5] and most recently the Electronic Commerce Directive in 2000.[6] There are also several other important measures aimed at particular issues, such as the Privacy Directive,[7] which have a significant impact upon online transactions but which would not themselves be considered as "enabling" legislation for E–Commerce transactions. Unlike the UNICTRAL Model Law, however, all these measures have immediate legal impact within the European Union.

§ 8.11 European Union—Distance Selling Directive

The Distance Selling Directive is intended to promote European consumer confidence in E–Commerce, by guaranteeing that the local consumer protection laws will apply to contracts concluded at a distance.[1] By relying upon the protections of local laws, presumably concerns over the nature and amount of information provided by sellers, the privacy accorded to information provided by consumers, aggressive marketing techniques, and payment fraud resulting from online transactions would be ameliorated. The Directive, however, applies to all types of contracts concluded by any means where the supplier and consumer are not in each others physical presence including those created by mail, telephone, videophone, radio, fax, and email, for example, and is not

3. "A European Initiative on Electronic Commerce," COM(97) 157 final, 16.6.1997.

4. Directive 1997/7/EC of the European Parliament and of the Council of 20 May 1997 on the Protection of Consumers in respect of Distance Contracts, *Official Journal L 144, 04/06/1997.*

5. Directive 1999/93/EC of the European Parliament and of the Council of 13 December 1999 on a Community framework for Electronic Signatures, *Official Journal L 013, 19/01/2000.*

6. Directive 2000/31/EC of the European Parliament and of the Council of 8 June 2000 on certain legal aspects of information society services, in particular electronic commerce, in the Internal Market, *Official Journal L 178, 17/07/2000.*

7. Directive 95/46/EC of 24 October 1995 on the protection of individuals with regard to the processing of personal data and on the free movement of such data., *Official Journal L 281, 23.11.1995.*

§ 8.11

1. Directive 1997/7/EC of the European Parliament and of the Council of 20 May 1997 on the Protection of Consumers in respect of Distance Contracts, *Official Journal L 144, 04/06/1997.*

confined just to online transactions.[2] Each member state in the EU was required to implement the Directive's requirements in their national law, in this manner the various national laws on distance contracts through the EU "approximate" one another and achieve the same objectives.[3]

The Directive imposes a number of requirements. Certain types of technologies, such as automated calling machines or faxes, may not be used for unsolicited marketing without prior consent, and others may not be employed over the consumer's objection.[4] Prior to concluding the contract, consumers are to be provided with certain information in "clear and comprehensible form" covering a variety of basic details about the supplier; the cost, terms, and conditions of the transaction; and, significantly, the consumer's right to withdraw or cancel the transaction.[5] This information must be provided either in writing or in some other "durable" media accessible to the consumer prior to delivery or completion of performance of the contract.[6] Orders placed through distance selling must ordinarily be filled within 30 days.[7] Consumers are typically given 7 business days to withdraw from a distance contract for any reason, with no penalty, and the consumer's reimbursement following withdrawal must be processed within 30 days.[8] If the supplier failed to provide the requisite information in advance of the transaction, the time period for the consumer to exercise this right of withdrawal expands to three months.[9]

Not all distance selling transactions are covered however. There are exemptions for financial services contracts, auctions, immovable property, sales of everyday consumable goods by door-to-door salesagents; accommodation, transport, catering or leisure services for specific dates, and vending machines.[10] Additionally, absent agreement, the consumers right of withdrawal does not apply to services begun before the expiration of the withdrawal period; commodities whose price fluctuates in financial markets beyond the control of the supplier; certain custom produced/personalized goods; audio/video/software products unsealed by the consumer; periodicals; gaming or lottery services.[11]

Thus, while not exclusively aimed at E–Commerce, the Distance Selling Directive imposes a number of specific requirements on E–Merchants who will be selling to consumers within the EU. These requirements will affect the nature of the transactions conducted with consumers in Europe, the manner in which they are conducted, and even the design of the online systems by which they are accomplished.

2. *Id.*, Art. 2 & Annex1.

3. *Id.*, Art. 15. EU member nations were given until the end of 2000 to implement the Directive.

4. *Id.*, Art. 10.

5. *Id.*, Art. 4.

6. *Id.*, Art. 5.

7. *Id.*, Art. 7.

8. *Id.*, Art. 6.

9. *Id.*

10. *Id.*, Art. 3.

11. *Id.*, Art. 6(3).

§ 8.12   European Union—Electronic Signature Directive

The Electronic Signature Directive,[1] like the Distance Selling Directive, is aimed at harmonizing the national law among the various member states. The Directive was intended to create a single common legal framework for electronic signatures within the EU.[2] An electronic signature is defined as any "data in electronic form which are attached to or logically associated with other electronic data and which serve as a method of authentication."[3] This definition is intended to be technologically neutral, and to apply to any and all forms of electronic signatures. However, the Directive expressly states that it is *not* intended to address national or European legal requirements as to the form or use of documents, nor the conclusion or validity of contracts.[4] It was issued in an effort simply to forestall the proliferation of different standards for electronic signatures and services related to providing such signatures at a time when several nations were considering different approaches and technologies.

The Directive establishes that a signature may not be denied legal effect of validity solely on the grounds that it is in electronic form.[5] Additionally, member states within the EU are prohibited from imposing obligations which would restrict the free flow of electronic signature services across national borders.[6] In accord with the emphasis on consumer protection in many European measures, the Directive imposes a number of obligations upon general providers of electronic signature services, but not upon those who use electronic signature technologies within their own closed or proprietary systems.[7] In particular, Certification Service Providers (CSPs), those who provide an "electronic attestation which links signature-verification data to a person and confirms the identity of that person," are to be supervised and regulated in the country where they are established[8] and are liable for the certifications they issue.[9] The establishment of national voluntary accreditation schemes to bolster public confidence in electronic signatures is encouraged,[10] and intended to promote the cross border acceptability of electronic signatures and their accompanying certifications.[11]

§ 8.13   European Union—Electronic Commerce Directive

Based upon the aims and objectives stated in the 1997 Initiative,[1]

§ 8.12

1. Directive 1999/93/EC of the European Parliament and of the Council of 13 December 1999 on a Community framework for Electronic Signatures, *Official Journal L 013, 19/01/2000.*

2. *Id.,* Art. 1.

3. *Id.,* Art. 2.

4. *Id.,* Art. 1.

5. *Id.,* Art. 5.

6. *Id.,* Art. 4.

7. *Id.,* Preamble (16).

8. *Id.,* Art. 3.

9. *Id.,* Art. 6.

10. *Id.,* Art. 3.

11. *Id.,* Art. 7.

§ 8.13

1. "A European Initiative on Electronic Commerce," COM(97) 157 final, 16.6.1997.

the Electronic Commerce Directive[2] endeavors to establish a more certain and comprehensive legal framework to generally enable E–Commerce transactions within the member states of the EU. As such, the Directive covers a number of issue areas beyond merely electronic contracting,[3] such as rules regarding the establishment of service providers,[4] information to be provided by service providers,[5] information to be provided in connection with commercial communications such as advertising or direct marketing,[6] liabilities of Internet intermediaries,[7] online dispute resolution processes,[8] and the general role of national authorities.[9]

There is a general "right of establishment" guaranteed by the treaties establishing the European Union. The Directive clarifies that electronic service providers are "established" where they effectively pursue an "economic activity using a fixed establishment for an indefinite period. The presence and use of the technical means and technologies required to provide the service do not, in themselves, constitute an establishment of the provider."[10] It then continues to generally prohibit member states from requiring prior-authorization to establish electronic service provider operations, or from imposing other requirements which do not generally apply to the same services or operations conducted by other means.[11] However, the use of "codes of conduct" or other voluntary measures established at the Community level with input from appropriate trade, professional, and consumer associations is encouraged.[12] Deviations from the "country or origin" and "mutual recognition" principles which underlie the Directive are permitted for public policy purposes such as crime prevention, combating hate crimes, the protection of minors, and the protection of public health. However, any such measures which are imposed must be necessary, proportionate to their objective, and the European Commission has been notified.[13]

Additionally, the Electronic Commerce Directive compliments the notice/disclosure provisions of the Distance Selling Directive by requiring that electronic service providers make "easily, directly, and permanently available" certain information such as its name, physical address, email address, an VAT or similar registrations, and any supervisory or professional regulatory bodies to which it might be subject—and that any pricing information which is provided must be clear and unambiguous.[14]

"Commercial communications"[15] are recognized as an integral part of any Information Society service, and also subject to special require-

---

2. Directive 2000/31/EC of the European Parliament and of the Council of 8 June 2000 on certain legal aspects of information society services, in particular electronic commerce, in the Internal Market, *Official Journal L 178, 17/07/2000.*

3. *Id.,* § 3.

4. *Id.,* § 1.

5. *Id.*

6. *Id.,* § 2.

7. *Id.,* § 4.

8. *Id.,* Ch.IV.

9. *Id.*

10. *Id.,* Art. 2.

11. *Id.,* Art. 4.

12. *Id.,* Art. 16.

13. *Id.,* Art.3.

14. *Id.,* Art. 5.

15. The Directive generally defines "commercial communications" as "any form of communication designed to pro-

ments. Advertising, direct marketing and similar communications must be clearly identified as "commercial communications" and identified as to their origin, and any conditions attached to promotional offers must be clearly identifiable and easily accessible.[16] Moreover, unsolicited email solicitations must be "identifiable clearly and unambiguously as such as soon as it is received" and service providers using unsolicited email are required to comply with opt-out registers.[17] Regulated professions, such as lawyers or accountants, are specifically authorized to use electronic commercial communications but remain subject to the rules applicable to their professions.[18]

Service providers who are merely passive conduits for Information Society services supplied by others are generally insulated from any liability, so long as they did not initiate or modify the transmission or the content of the communication, nor select the recipient of the transmission.[19] This immunity specifically extends to caching operations, or the "automatic, intermediate, and temporary storage" of information;[20] hosting operations;[21] or any obligation to engage in general monitoring of the service user's activities.[22] However, nothing in the Directive precludes member states within the EU from requiring that service providers inform the authorities of illegal activities which do come to their attention, or from acting to terminate or prevent an infringement in accordance with local judicial or administrative processes.[23]

Means for resolving disputes arising out of the provision of Information Society services are also addressed. In addition to encouraging the formulation of EU-wide voluntary codes of conduct,[24] the member states are directed to ensure that appropriate means for alternative dispute resolution processes exist—both offline and online—particularly for consumer disputes.[25] The member states are also directed to facilitate cross-border cooperation and promote the effective investigation and legal redress of infringements or violations throughout the EU.[26]

At the heart of this framework, however, are the provisions enabling the formation of electronic contracts. Although brief, these provisions are significant in providing a firm basis for E–Commerce, and expanding upon the foundation established in the Electronic Signature Directive. In Article 9, the Electronic Commerce Directive states that the "Member States shall ensure that their legal system allows contracts to be formed by electronic means."[27] It then continues to specify that national laws should neither create obstacles to the contractual process, nor impede

mote, directly or indirectly, the goods, services, or image of a company, organization, or person or pursuing a commercial, industrial or craft activity or exercising a regulated profession." *Id.,* Art. 2.

16. *Id.,* Art. 6.

17. *Id.,* Art. 7.

18. *Id.,* Art. 8.

19. *Id.,* Art. 12.

20. *Id.,* Art. 13.

21. *Id.,* Art. 14.

22. *Id.,* Art. 15.

23. *Id.,* Art. 12(3); 13(2); 14(3); 15(2).

24. *Id.,* Art. 16.

25. *Id.,* Art. 17.

26. *Id.,* Arts. 18–20.

27. *Id.,* Art. 9.

the effectiveness or validity of contracts formed by electronic means.[28] Only four categories are exempted from this mandate: contracts which must be registered with a public authority (e.g. real estate transfers), contracts requiring the use of a notary or similar public authority, contracts governed by family law, or contracts governed by the law of succession.[29] Even within these categories, member states wishing to derogate from the general obligations of Article 9 must notify the Commission, and justify their continued exemption every five years.[30]

Additionally, when contracts are to be concluded electronically, the E–Merchant must clearly and unambiguously explain—in advance—the languages in which the contract will be available, the steps involved to form the contract, precisely who will fulfill the contract, and the means for correcting any order entry errors. This information must be made available in a manner in which it may be stored and reproduced. The Directive imposes these requirements on all electronic contracts, except those concluded "exclusively" by means of individual communications such as email.[31] Moreover, the Directive also requires that the receipt of orders placed electronically must be acknowledged "without undue delay and by electronic means," and specifically rejects the "mailbox rule" by stating that both orders and acknowledgments are "received" when they are accessible to the recipient.[32] These requirements ordinarily apply equally to consumers and those pursuing a trade, business, or profession—although those who are not consumers may agree to dispense with receiving the required information or order acknowledgments.[33]

Thus, reflecting the more comprehensive approach which come from having a regional authority such as the European Union, the enabling legislation in the EU strives to facilitate the formation of electronic contracts—but does so in the broader context of its efforts to accelerate the formation of an Information Society. Accordingly, it attempts to integrate the issues associated with E–Commerce within its plans for an eEurope.

§ 8.14 European Union—Personal Data Protection Directive

The European Union has adopted a personal data protection directive that applies to international electronic commerce. Council Directive 95/46 (effective October 1998) requires each member EU state to protect the processing of personal data. The deadline for implementation is January 1, 2002. Under this directive, any information relating to natural persons must be secure, current, relevant and not excessive in content. In most cases, personal data may be processed only with the consent of the individual involved. Processing data revealing racial or ethnic origin, political opinions, religious beliefs, philosophical or ethical

28. *Id.*
29. *Id.*, Art. 9(2).
30. *Id.*, Art. 9(3).
31. *Id.*, Art. 10.

32. *Id.*, Art.11.
33. *Id.*, Arts. 10(1), 11(1).

persuasion, and health or sexual life is rarely permitted without written consent.

Directive 95/46 guarantees individual access to processed information and notice of its use. Individuals may object at any time to the legitimacy of personal data processing. They may also demand erasure without cost of personal data before it is disclosed to or used by third parties for direct mail marketing.

Data processors are required to make extensive disclosures to individuals and to governments. Such disclosure duties, for example, apply to virtually all web sites that invite registration. National authorities are empowered where appropriate to access, erase or block information held by data processors. Private civil liability and public penalty remedies are administered under member state laws, which allow electronic commerce consumers to sue in their countries of residence.

Article 25 of Directive 95/46 mandates a prohibition against the transfer of personal data to non-member states (like those of North America) that fail to ensure an "adequate level of protection." Hence the adequacy of United States laws offering personal data protection is generally at issue. Exemptions from this scrutiny exist for "unambiguous" consents, when the data is necessary for contract performance between individuals and data processors (e.g., billing), the transfer is legally required or serves "important public interests," the transfer is necessary to protect the individual's "vital interests," or the transfer comes from an open, public register.

Practically speaking, Directive 95/46 governs most global businesses since it is very difficult to segregate European Union data from that collected elsewhere. Both online and offline data processors fall within its scope. The directive's impact has been felt, for example, in restrictive orders denying U.S. direct mail companies access to European mailing lists. More broadly, the European Commission and the U.S. Department of Commerce have sought to defuse the potentially explosive issue of the "adequacy" of U.S. law on personal data privacy. Early in 2000, agreement was reached to create a "safe harbor" for U.S. firms from EU data privacy litigation or prosecution. To obtain such immunity, U.S. data processors can: (1) formally agree to be subject to regulatory oversight in a member EU state; (2) sign up with a U.S. self-regulating privacy group that is supervised by the U.S. Federal Trade Commission or the Department of Transportation; (3) demonstrate to European satisfaction that relevant U.S. laws are comparable to Directive 95/46; or (4) agree to refer privacy disputes to a European panel of data protection authorities.

Financial services (including insurance) are not covered by these safe harbor provisions. In 2001, the European Union proposed standardized financial services contracts that would subject U.S. data processors to European jurisdiction.

To date, only a handful of U.S. companies have signed up with self-regulatory privacy groups (such as BBBOnline) to obtain shelter from Directive 95/46. Some U.S. companies (e.g., Amazon.com) assert that they are in compliance. Others (e.g., DoubleClick.com) have selectively curtailed their use of "cookies" to track online users. Many seem blissfully unaware of the scope and intensity of Directive 95/46.

D. UNITED STATES LAWS

§ 8.15 United States—Federal Laws

The Electronic Signatures In Global and National Commerce Act (E–SIGN Act), became effective in the United States on October 1, 2000.[1] The E–SIGN Act implements a national uniform standard for all electronic transactions. Its provisions cover electronic signatures, electronic contracts and electronic records. The E–SIGN Act includes several key provisions that address its: (1) scope; (2) application; (3) consumer consent requirements; (4) validity requirements for electronic signatures, electronic contracts and electronic records; (5) retention requirements for electronic contracts and records; (6) notarization rules; and (7) national uniform standards for the banking, insurance and stock industries.

The E–SIGN Act regulates any transactions in interstate and foreign commerce. In this regard, the E–SIGN Act applies to any transaction "relating to the conduct of business, consumer or commercial affairs between two or more persons." The provisions of the E–SIGN Act may be superceded by a state statute, so long as that state statute is the Uniform Electronic Transaction Act as reported by the National Conference of Commissioners on Uniform State Laws.[2] Otherwise, the E–SIGN Act does not alter the obligations of persons under any requirements imposed by statute, regulation or other rule of law. In this regard, the E–SIGN Act does not restrict the scope or availability of any other federal or state statute, regulation and other rule of law that requires, authorizes or otherwise allows for the use of electronic signatures or electronic records if it is consistent with the provisions of this Act.

"Electronic signatures" are defined very broadly under the E–Sign Act. The statutory definition is "an electronic sound, symbol or process attached to or logically associated with a contract or other record and executed or adopted by a person with the intent to sign the record."[3] It thus as intended to include telephone keypad agreements (e.g., "press 9 to agree to 7 to hear this menu again") and click wrap agreements. Moreover, a contract or other record may not be denied legal effect because its is in an electronic format and a contract may not be denied legal effect solely because an electronic signature was used in its formation. Consistent with the UNCITRAL Model Law on Electronic Commerce,[4] the E–SIGN Act does not require the use of electronic signa-

---

§ 8.15

1. Electronic Signatures in Global and National Commerce Act of 2000 (hereafter E–SIGN Act) Pub.L. No. 106–229, 114 Stat. 464, 15 U.S.C. § 7000–7006, 7021, 7031 (West. Supp. 2000).

2. See discussion at § 8.16, infra.

3. E–SIGN Act, § 106(5).

4. See discussion at § 8.7, supra, at note 1.

tures, electronic contracts or electronic record. Instead, it seeks to facilitate the use of these electronic communications by upholding their legal effect. The E–SIGN Act is also technology-neutral and does not require a specific type or method that businesses and consumers must use or accept in order to conduct their electronic transaction.

There are special provisions for consumer contracts. The E–SIGN Act assumes that many consumers will want a paper (hardcopy) record of the transaction, while others prefer not to be bothered with paper. The Act provides that a consumer may elect to receive an electronic record in substitution of a required written record if: "(1) the consumer affirmatively consents to receive an electronic record" and (2) before consent "is provided with a clear and conspicuous statement informing the consumer of rights or options to have the record provided or made available on paper." However, the pre-consent notice may state that the seller will refuse to deal if the consumer wants paper. The consumer must also have some ability to access the electronic records to which the consent applies. However, this requirement may be met if the consumer confirms electronically that he or she can access the electronic records in the specified formats, or the consumer acknowledges or responds affirmatively to an electronic query that asks whether the consumer can access the electronic record. Any consent of a consumer applies only to the particular transaction that gave rise to the obligation to provide the record.

The E–SIGN Act does not alter the existing contract law as to the validity and enforceability of an electronic contract. Instead, it provides substitute methods of satisfying the requirements of contract law. Where a Statute of Frauds provision requires a contract to be in writing, then an electronic contract must be in a form that is capable of being retained and accurately reproduced at the time of entering into the contract. If an electronic contract meets the validity requirement of a writing under existing substantive contract law, it is then legally enforceable. "If a customer chooses to use a device, such as a Palm Pilot or cellular phone, that does not have a printer or a disk drive allowing the customer to make a copy of the contract at the time of contracting, the contract will only be valid and legally enforceable if it was capable of being retained and reproduced" at the time of entering into the contract. In addition, an electronic signature is only valid under the E–SIGN Act if the signatory intends to sign the contract. Thus, the person or entity accepting an electronic signature has a duty of care to determine whether the electronic signature was really created by the person to whom it is attributed.

The E–SIGN Act forbids states from prohibiting parties from using electronic signatures and electronic records in lieu of paper records and hand-written signatures. If parties to a transaction agree, either electronically or otherwise, on the terms and conditions on which they will accept and use electronic signatures and electronic records in their dealings with one another, a state cannot refuse to give legal effect to the parties agreement.

Any state of federal requirements for the retention of paper-based records is satisfied if an electronic record "accurately reflects" the necessary information and the electronic record is accessible to all the necessary parties. The retention requirement only requires that the electronic record be in a form that is capable of accurately reproducing the contained information. The accessibility requirement "does not require businesses to provide direct access to its facilities nor does it require businesses to update electronic formats as technology changes."

§ 8.16   United States—State Laws

In the United States, the National Conference of Commissioners on Uniform State Laws has adopted two different proposed uniform acts to facilitate electronic commerce. One is the Uniform Electronic Transactions Act (UETA), which is similar in scope and substance to the UNCITRAL Model Law on Electronic Commerce[1] and the federal E–SIGN Act.[2] It applies to all types of electronic messages and contracts, and seeks to validate and facilitate their use at a very basic level. As of June 2000 UETA was enacted in 14 states.[3]

The second is the Uniform Computer Information Transactions Act (UCITA) which applies only to software licensing transactions, and incorporates very detailed provisions concerning every aspect of the transaction. Its format is similar to UCC Article 2 on sales of goods, and at one time was intended to be UCC Article 2B, until it was rejected by the American Law Institute as not sufficiently balanced. As of June, 2000 UCITA was enacted in three states.[4]

UCITA also rejects many of the concepts in both the UNCITRAL Model Law and UETA. Thus, the Uniform Commissioners have proposed two different uniform acts whose provisions conflict on such basic terms as authentication and attribution. The introduction and adoption of differing state, national and international legislation with conflicting provisions to govern E–Commerce is likely to create difficulties for all the participants in a transaction where the location of the parties is unknown. These difficulties are likely to grow as more non-U.S. parties participate in E–Commerce, and a greater proportion of such transactions are across national boundaries.

Selected Bibliography

American Bar Association, Model Trading Partner Agreement, 45 Bus. Law. 1721.

§ 8.16

1. See discussion at §§ 8.5–8.8, supra.

2. See discussion at § 8.15, supra.

3. California, Hawaii, Indiana Kansas, Kentucky, Maryland, Minnesota, Nebraska, Ohio, Oklahoma, Pennsylvania, South Dakota, Utah, and Virginia. See http://www.mbc.com/ecommerce/legis.ucvue.htm for a current list of States where UETA has been adopted.

4. Maryland, Oklahoma and Virginia. See http://www.mbc.com/ecommerce/legis.ucvue.htm for a current list of States where UCITA has been adopted.

Boss, Electronic Commerce and the Symbiotic Relationship Between International and Domestic Law Reform, 72 Tul. L. Rev. 1931 (1998).

Costa, Minimum Contracts in Cyberspace: A Taxonomy of the Case Law, 35 Hous. L. Rev. 453 (1998).

Effross, The Legal Architecture of Virtual Stores, 34 San Diego L. Rev. 1263 (1999).

Overby, UNCITRAL Model Law on Electronic Commerce: Will Cyberlaw Be Uniform? 7 Tul. J. Int'l and Comp. L. 219 (1999).

Patience, Global Internet Project Warns EC Jurisdiction Model, 1999 WL 17640524 (1999).

Scoville, Clear Signatures, Obscure Signs, 17 Cardozo Arts and Ent. L.J. 345 (1999).

T. Smedinghoff, Online Law (1996).

Symposium, Intellectual Property and Contract Law in the Information Age, 13 Berkeley Tech. L.J. 809 (1998).

Wimmer, Enforcing Click–Wrap Licenses, E–Litigation, Clicks and Contracts, 14 Corporate Counsellor 1 (Sept. 1999).

J. K. Winn and B. Wright, The Law of Electronic Commerce (4th ed., 2000).

Winn and Wrathall, Who Owns the Customer? The Emerging Law of Commercial Transactions in Electronic Customer Data, 56 Bus. Law. 213 (2000).

Chapter 9

AN INTRODUCTION TO IN-TERNATIONAL TRADE LAW—THE WTO

Table of Sections

A. THE WORLD TRADE ORGANIZATION (WTO)

B. CLEARING U.S. CUSTOMS

C. REGULATING U.S. TRADE

United States regulation of international trade is a complex affair. This chapter introduces and briefly summarizes the actors and institutions most commonly involved in customs and regulatory determinations affecting imports into the U.S. This summary is intended for persons unfamiliar with U.S. import law and should be read before reviewing the much more detailed chapters that follow. Many of the actors and institutions discussed in this introductory chapter are also involved in the regulation of United States exports.

A. THE WORLD TRADE ORGANIZATION (WTO)

The need to balance the protection of local industries from harm by foreign competitors and the encouragement of trade across national borders is a recurrent theme in the law of international business transactions. There has been a shift in recent years toward freer international trade because of diminished restrictions on imported goods. However, trade problems associated with the movement of goods across national borders still arise because of restrictive trade devices which impede or distort trade. Common devices include tariff barriers (e.g., import duties and export duties) as well as certain nontariff trade barriers (NTBs) such as import quotas, import licensing procedures, safety, environmental and other minimum manufacturing standards, import testing requirements, complex customs procedures (including valuation), government procurement policies, and government subsidies or countervailing measures. For example, during a part of 1982, France required that all video recorders entering France had to do so through a small customs post at Poitiers and carry documentation written in French. Product distribution practices have been an effective NTB in Japan. The Japanese have also banned from importation a food preservative which is essential to preserve the edibility of certain agricultural products from abroad.

Efforts by countries to limit disruptive trade practices are commonly found in bilateral treaties of friendship, commerce and navigation (FCN), which open the territory of each signatory nation to imports arriving from the other signatory nation. Such bilateral FCN treaty clauses are usually linked to other preferential trade agreements. In a bilateral arrangement, such linkage will most often be through a reciprocal "most favored nation" (MFN) clause. In a MFN clause, both parties agree not to extend to any other nation trade arrangements which are more favorable than available under the bilateral treaty, unless the more favorable trade arrangements are immediately *also* available to the signatory of the bilateral treaty.

In various parts of the world, two or more countries have joined in customs unions or free trade areas in order to facilitate trade between those countries and to acquire increased bargaining power in trade discussions with countries which already enjoy a strong trade position.

The General Agreement on Tariffs and Trade (GATT), now replaced by the new World Trade Organization (WTO), was an international arrangement with over one hundred countries as Contracting States which regularly held multilateral trade negotiations (MTN) seeking ways of making international trade more open. These periodic negotiations cumulatively reduced tariff barriers by an average of up to eighty percent below those existing three decades before. After the most recent multilateral negotiations, the Uruguay Round, average tariff rates of developed countries on dutiable manufactured imports were cut from 6.3 percent to 3.9 percent. Tariff reductions are one of the success stories of GATT. But not all nations participated in the GATT or are members of its replacement, the WTO. For example, both Russia and China are seeking membership in the WTO, but are not yet Members. Nontariff trade barriers (NTBs) are also addressed in the WTO Covered Agreements, which include agreements designed to lessen or to eliminate NTBs such as complex customs valuation procedures, import licensing systems, product standards, subsidies and countervailing duties, and dumping practices.

§ 9.1   The General Agreement on Tariffs and Trade: History and Provisions

Participants in the Bretton Woods meetings in 1944 recognized a post-War need to reduce trade obstacles in order to foster freer trade. They envisioned the creation of an International Trade Organization (ITO) to achieve the desired result. Fifty-three countries met in Havana in 1948 to complete drafting the Charter of an ITO that would be the international organizational umbrella underneath which negotiations could occur periodically to deal with tariff reductions. A framework for such negotiations had already been staked out in Geneva in 1947, in a document entitled the General Agreement on Tariffs and Trade (GATT). Twenty-three nations participated in that first GATT session, India, Chile, Cuba and Brazil representing the developing world. China participated; Japan and West Germany did not. Stringent trading rules were adopted only where there were no special interests of major participants to alter them. The developing nations objected to many of the strict rules, arguing for special treatment justified on development needs, but they achieved few successes in drafting GATT.

The ITO Charter was never ratified. The United States Congress in the late 1940s was unwilling to join more new international organizations, thus U.S. ratification of the ITO Charter could not be secured. Nonetheless, and moving by way of the President's power to make executive agreements, the United States did join twenty-one other countries, as Contracting Parties, in signing a Protocol of Provisional Application of the General Agreement on Tariffs and Trade (61 Stat.Pts. 5, 6) (popularly called the "GATT Agreement").

From 1947 to 1986, GATT was concerned primarily with international trade of goods. The central features of GATT, as reflected by the Articles of the Agreement, include Article I, which makes a general commitment to the long standing practice of most favored nation treatment (MFN) by requiring each Contracting Party to accord unconditional MFN status to all other Contracting Parties. Thus, any privilege granted by any Contracting Party to any product imported from any other country must also be "immediately and unconditionally" granted to any "like product" imported from any Contracting Parties.

Although addressed to national treatment regarding internal taxation and regulation, GATT Article III incorporates the practice of according national treatment to imported goods by providing, with enumerated exceptions, that the products of one Contracting State, when imported into any other Contracting State, shall receive most favored nation (MFN) treatment. In this context, MFN treatment requires that the products of the exporting GATT Contracting State be treated no less favorably than domestic products of the importing Contracting State under its laws and regulations concerning sale, internal resale, purchase, transportation and use.

In addition to requiring MFN treatment, GATT prohibits any use of certain kinds of quantitative restrictions. Although GATT does permit "duties, taxes or other charges", Article XI prohibits the use of other "prohibitions or restrictions" on imports from Contracting Parties. It specifically prohibits the use of "quotas, import or export licenses or other measures" to restrict imports from a Contracting Party. Article XIII requires non-discrimination in quantitative trade restrictions, by barring an importing Contracting State from applying any prohibition or restriction to the products of another Contracting State, "unless the importation of the like product of *all* third countries . . . is similarly prohibited or restricted." (emphasis added).

While GATT does permit nondiscriminatory "duties, taxes and other charges," the powers of a Contracting Party are limited even as to these devices. First, GATT Article X requires that notice be given of any new or changed national regulations which affect international trade, by requiring the prompt publication by any Contracting Party of those "laws, regulations, judicial decisions and administrative rulings of general application"

> which pertain to the classification or the valuation of products for customs purposes, or to rates of duty, taxes or other charges, or to requirements, restrictions or prohibitions on imports or exports or on the transfer of payments therefor, or affecting their sale, distribution, transportation, insurance, warehousing, inspection, exhibitions, processing, mixing or other use. . . .

Second, the Contracting Parties commit themselves, under GATT Article XXVIII to a continuing series of MTN ("from time to time") to seek further reductions in tariff levels and other barriers to international trade. Such negotiations are to be "on a reciprocal and mutually advantageous basis." GATT negotiated tariff rates (called "concessions" or "bindings"), which are listed in the "tariff Schedules", are deposited with GATT by each participating country. These concessions must be granted to imports from any Contracting Party, both because of the GATT required MFN treatment, and also because Article II specifically requires use of the negotiated rates.

Framers of GATT were well aware that a commitment to freer trade could cause serious, adverse economic consequences from time to time within part or all of a country's domestic economy, particularly its labor sector. The GATT contains at least seven safety valves (in nine clauses of the Agreement) to permit a country, in appropriate circumstances, to respond to domestic pressures while remaining a participant in GATT. Two safety valves deal with antidumping duties and countervailing subsidies.

"Dumping" occurs when the products of one country are introduced into the commerce of another country at less than the fair value of the products, at least as measured by the normal sale price in the domestic market of the exporting company. Article VI recognizes that dumping must be prevented, if it causes or threatens material injury to an established industry in the importing Contracting State or materially retards the establishment of a domestic industry in it. Article VI permits a country to impose an antidumping duty under appropriate circumstances when dumping has caused such harm.

A "subsidy" or "bounty" may be bestowed by the exporting Contracting State on goods produced within its territory. Article VI also recognizes that such subsidies must be prevented, if they cause or threaten material injury to an established industry of the importing Contracting State or materially retard the establishment of a domestic industry in it. The Article authorizes a country to impose a countervailing duty as a special duty levied for the purpose of offsetting any bounty or subsidy bestowed, directly or indirectly, by a Contracting State on merchandise produced and exported from it. However, the countervailing duty must not be levied in an amount greater than the estimated bounty or subsidy granted.

§ 9.2 The GATT Multinational Trade Negotiations (Rounds)

Under the auspices of GATT Article XXVIII, the Contracting Parties committed themselves to hold periodic multinational trade negotiations (MTN or "Rounds"). They have held eight such Rounds to date.

While the first five Rounds concentrated on item by item tariff reductions, the "Kennedy Round" (1964–1967) was noted for its achievement of across-the-board tariff reductions. In 1961, GATT began to consider how to approach the increasing trade disparity with the developing world. In 1964, GATT adopted Part IV, which introduced a principle of "diminished expectations of reciprocity". Reciprocity remained a goal, but developed nations would not expect concessions from developing nations which were inconsistent with developmental needs. For the developing nations, nonreciprocity meant freedom to protect domestic markets from import competition. Import substitution was a major focus of developmental theory in the 1960s, and developing nations saw keeping their markets closed as a way to save these domestic industries. Although they also sought preferential treatment of their exports, that was a demand which would remain unsatisfied for another decade.

The "Tokyo Round" (1973–1979) engendered agreements about several areas of nontariff barrier (NTB) trade restraints. Nearly a dozen major agreements on nontariff barrier issues were produced in the Tokyo Round. In the early 1970s, national and regional generalized preference schemes developed to favor the exports of developing nations. The foreign debt payment problems of the developing nations suggest that they need to generate revenue to pay these debts, and that developmental theory must shift from import substitution to export promotion.

In 1986, the "Uruguay Round" of multilateral trade negotiations began at a Special Session of the GATT Contracting States. This Uruguay Round included separate negotiations on trade in goods and on trade in services, with separate groups of negotiators dealing with each topic. Subtopics for negotiation by subgroups included nontariff barriers, agriculture, subsidies and countervailing duties, intellectual property rights and counterfeit goods, safeguards, tropical products, textiles, investment policies, and dispute resolution. The negotiating sessions were extraordinarily complex, but were able to achieve a successful conclusion at the end of 1993. In 2001, the "Qatar Round" of WTO negotiations was launched.

Because protectionist barriers to international trade in services were stifling, the United States and several other countries insisted that there should be a General Agreement on Trade in Services (GATS). In the United States, trade in services accounts for two-thirds of the Nation's GNP; services provide work for nearly two-thirds of the work force. Services account for almost one-third of U.S. trade abroad.

The 1947 GATT Agreement and its subsequent multinational negotiating rounds were quite successful in reducing tariff duty levels on trade in goods. This was its original purpose, and the mechanism was well-adapted to accomplishing that purpose. However, its effectiveness was also limited to trade in goods, and primarily to reduction of tariffs in such trade. It was not designed to affect trade in services, trade-related intellectual property rights or trade-related investment measures. As tariff duty rates declined, the trade-distorting effects of these other issues became relatively more important.

Even within "trade in goods," the 1947 GATT had limitations. It included a Protocol of Provisional Application which allowed numerous grandfathered exceptions to Members' obligations under the GATT Agreement. The Protocol exempted from GATT disciplines the national laws of Member States which were already enacted and in force at the time of adoption of the Protocol. Further, the 1947 GATT did not have an institutional charter, and was not intended to become an international organization on trade. It did later develop institutional structures and acquired quasi-organizational status, but there was always a lack of a recognized organizational structure. This lack was most often perceived in the inability of GATT to resolve disputes which were brought to it.

Dispute settlement procedures were dependent upon the acquiescence of the individual Member States.

§ 9.3 The World Trade Organization (WTO) and GATT 1994

The WTO is the product of the Uruguay Round of GATT negotiations, which was successfully completed in 1994. The Uruguay Round produced a package of agreements, the Agreement Establishing the World Trade Organization and its Annexes, which include the General Agreement on Tariffs and Trade 1994 (GATT 1994) and a series of Multilateral Trade Agreements (the Covered Agreements), and a series of Plurilateral Trade Agreements.[1]

GATT 1947 and GATT 1994 are two distinct agreements. GATT 1994 incorporates the provisions of GATT 1947, except for the Protocol of Provisional Application, which is expressly excluded. Thus, the problems created by exempting the existing national laws at the time of the adoption of the Protocol will now be avoided by this exclusion in the Covered Agreements. Otherwise, in cases involving a conflict between GATT 1947 and GATT 1994, GATT 1947 controls. The WTO will be guided by the decisions, procedures and customary practices under GATT.

Annexed to the WTO Agreement are several Multilateral Trade Agreements. As to trade in goods, they include Agreements on Agriculture, Textiles, Antidumping, Subsidies and Countervailing Measures, Safeguards, Technical Barriers to Trade, Sanitary and Phytosanitary Measures, Pre-shipment Inspection, Rules of Origin, and Import License Procedures. In addition to trade in goods, they include a General Agreement on Trade in Services and Agreements on Trade–Related Aspects of Intellectual Property Rights and Trade–Related Investment Measures. Affecting all of these agreements is the Understanding on Rules and Procedures Governing the Settlement of Disputes. All of the Multilateral Trade Agreements are binding on all Members of the World Trade Organization.

In addition to the Multilateral Trade Agreements, there are also Plurilateral Trade Agreements which are also annexed to the WTO Agreement. These agreements, however, are not binding on all WTO Members, and Members can choose to adhere to them or not. They include Agreements on Government Procurement, Trade in Civil Aircraft, International Dairy and an Arrangement Regarding Bovine Meat. States which do not join the plurilateral trade agreements do not receive reciprocal benefits under them.

The duties of the World Trade Organization are to facilitate the implementation, administer the operations and further the objectives of all these agreements. Its duties also include the resolution of disputes under the agreements, reviews of trade policy and cooperation with the

§ 9.3

1. *See* 33 Int. Legal Mat. 1130 (1994).

International Monetary Fund (IMF) and the World Bank. To achieve these goals, the WTO Agreement does provide a charter for the new organization, but provides for only a minimalist institution, with institutional and procedural capabilities, but with no substantive competence being given to the organization itself. Thus, there is a unified administration of pre-existing and new obligations under all agreements concerning trade in goods, including the Uruguay Round Agreements. In addition, the administration of the new obligations on trade in services and intellectual property are brought under the same roof.

On the other hand, both the International Monetary Fund (IMF) and the World Bank have executive powers for their institutions, which the WTO does not have. The WTO as an institution has no power to bring actions on its own initiative. Under the provisions of the WTO Agreement, only the Members of WTO can initiate actions under the Dispute Settlement Understanding. Enforcement of WTO obligations is primarily through permitting Members to retaliate or cross retaliate against other members, rather than by execution of WTO institutional orders. However, the WTO has an internationally recognized organizational structure, which is a step forward from the status of GATT as an organization.

§ 9.4 WTO Decision–Making

The World Trade Organization is structured in three tiers. One tier is the Ministerial Conference, which meets biennially and is composed of representatives of all WTO Members. Each Member has an equal voting weight, which is unlike the representation in the IMF and World Bank where there is weighted voting, and financially powerful states have more power over the decision-making process. The Ministerial Conference is responsible for all WTO functions, and is able to make any decisions necessary. It has the power to authorize new multilateral negotiations and to adopt the results of such negotiations. The Ministerial Conference, by a three-fourths vote, is authorized to grant waivers of obligations to Members in exceptional circumstances. It also has the power to adopt interpretations of Covered Agreements. When the Ministerial Conference is in recess, its functions are performed by the General Council.

The second tier is the General Council which has executive authority over the day to day operations and functions of the WTO. It is composed of representatives of all WTO Members, and each member has an equal voting weight. It meets whenever it is appropriate. The General Council also has the power to adopt interpretations of Covered Agreements.

The third tier comprises the councils, bodies and committees which are accountable to the Ministerial Conference or General Council. Ministerial Conference committees include Committees on Trade and Development, Balance of Payment Restrictions, Budget, Finance and Administration. General Council bodies include the Dispute Settlement Body, the

Trade Policy Review Body, and Councils for Trade in Goods, Trade in Services and Trade–Related Intellectual Property Rights. The Councils are all created by the WTO Agreement and are open to representatives of all Member States. The Councils also have the authority to create subordinate organizations. Other committees, such as the Committee on Subsidies and Countervailing Measures are created by specific individual agreements.

Of the General Council bodies, the two which are likely to be most important are the Dispute Settlement Body (DSB) and the Trade Policy Review Body (TPRB). The DSB is a special meeting of the General Council, and therefore includes all WTO Members. It has responsibility for resolution of disputes under all the Covered Agreements, and will be discussed in more detail below, under Dispute Resolution.

The purpose of the Trade Policy Review–Mechanism (TPRM) is to improve adherence to the WTO agreements and obligations, and to obtain greater transparency. Individual Members of WTO each prepare a "Country Report" on their trade policies and perceived adherence to the WTO Covered Agreements. The WTO Secretariat also prepares a report on each Member, but from the perspective of the Secretariat. The Trade Policy Review Body (TPRB) then reviews the trade policies of each Member based on these two reports. At the end of the review, the TPRB issues its own report concerning the adherence of the Member's trade policy to the WTO Covered Agreements. The TPRB has no enforcement capability, but the report is sent to the next meeting of the WTO Ministerial Conference. It is then up to the Ministerial Conference to evaluate the trade practices and policies of the Member.

The process of decision-making in the WTO Ministerial Conference and General Council relies upon "consensus" as the norm, just as it did for decision-making under GATT 1947. "Consensus", in this context means that no Member formally objects to a proposed decision. Thus, consensus is not obtained if any one Member formally objects, and has often been very difficult to obtain, which proved to be a weakness in the operation of GATT. However, there are many exceptions to the consensus formula under WTO, and some new concepts (such as "inverted consensus", discussed below) which are designed to ease the process of decision-making under WTO.

Article IX(1) of the WTO Agreement first provides that "the practice of decision-making by consensus" followed under GATT shall be continued. The next sentence of that provision, however, states that "where a decision cannot be arrived at by consensus, the matter at issue shall be decided by voting", except where otherwise provided. The ultimate resolution of the conflict between these two sentences is not completely clear.

There are a number of exceptions to the requirement for consensus that are expressly created under the WTO Agreement. One such exception is decisions by the Dispute Settlement Body, which has its own rules (see below). Another set of exceptions concerns decisions on waivers, interpretations and amendments of the Covered Agreements. Waivers of obligations may be granted and amendments adopted to Covered Agreements only by the Ministerial Conference. Amendments of Multilateral Trade Agreements usually require a consensus, but where a decision on a proposed amendment cannot obtain consensus, the decision on that amendment is to be made in certain circumstances by a two-thirds majority vote. In "exceptional circumstances", the Ministerial Conference is authorized to grant waivers of obligations under a Covered Agreement by a three-fourths vote. Another exception to the consensus requirement allows procedural rules in both the Ministerial Conference and the General Council to be decided by a majority vote of the Members, unless otherwise provided.

However, in addition to these express exceptions, Article IX (1) seems to indicate that where a decision would normally be made by consensus, but consensus cannot be obtained, the matter will then be decided "by voting." Whether this provision destroys the basic consensus requirement whenever there is an impasse is not yet clear. It is possible that any issue which fails to obtain a consensus, but has majority support, can be determined "by voting", as long as there is no other express provision. It is also not completely clear what procedure is to be used to satisfy the "by voting" standard. It is also possible, however, that this provision is only to be applied to decisions which the Ministerial Conference must make to assure the continuance of a workable WTO system. An illustration of such a decision could be the continuation, modification or termination of the dispute settlement procedure.

§ 9.5 WTO Agreements and U.S. Law

The WTO Covered Agreements concern not only trade in goods, but also trade in services (GATS), and trade-related aspects of intellectual property (TRIPS). The basic concepts that GATT applied to trade in goods (described above) are now applied to these areas through GATS and TRIPS. In the WTO Covered Agreements, the basic concepts of GATT 1947 and its associated agreements are elaborated and clarified. In addition, there is an attempt to transform all protectionist measures relating to agriculture (such as import bans and quotas, etc.) into only tariff barriers, which can then be lowered in subsequent MTN Rounds (a process known as "tariffication"). WTO also contains some superficial provisions on trade-related investment measures (TRIMS). Some of the WTO provisions, particularly those concerning trade in goods, will be discussed in more detail below in relation to United States trade law.

As of 2001, there were 141 Member States of the World Trade Organization. This does not include Russia or the People's Republic of China, although Russia is seeking membership and China is expected to join in 2001. The United States enacted legislation to implement WTO and the Covered Agreements on December 3, 1994. The implementing legislation was submitted to Congress under the "fast track" procedures of 19 U.S.C.A. § 2112, which required that the agreement and its implementing legislation be considered as a whole by Congress, and which also prohibits Congressional amendments to the implementing legislation. The Congressional authority for "fast track" procedures also required that the President give ninety days notice of his intention to enter into such an agreement. This "fast track" legislation expired on October 3, 1994, and has not yet been renewed.

Neither GATT 1947 nor the WTO Agreement, GATT 1994 and the other Covered Agreements have been ratified as treaties, and therefore comprise international obligations of the United States only to the extent that they are incorporated in United States' implementing legislation. GATT 1947 was not considered controlling by the courts of the United States, and these courts have always held themselves bound to the U.S. legislation actually enacted.[1] The WTO Covered Agreements will be considered to have a non-self-executed status, and therefore are likely to be regarded in the same manner as GATT 1947.

§ 9.6 WTO Dispute Settlement/U.S. Disputes

WTO provides a unified system for settling international trade disputes through the Dispute Settlement Understanding (DSU) and using the Dispute Settlement Body (DSB). The DSB is a special assembly of the WTO General Council, and includes all WTO Members. There are five stages in the resolution of disputes under WTO: 1) Consultation; 2) Panel establishment, investigation and report; 3) Appellate review of the panel report; 4) Adoption of the panel and appellate decision; and 5) Implementation of the decision adopted. There is also a parallel process for binding arbitration, if both parties agree to submit this dispute to arbitration, rather than to a DSB panel. In addition, during the implementation phase (5), the party subject to an adverse decision may seek arbitration as a matter of right on issues of compliance and authorized retaliation.

Although the DSU offers a unified dispute resolution system that is applicable across all sectors and all WTO Covered Agreements, there are many specialized rules for disputes which arise under them. Such specialized rules appear in the Agreements on Textiles, Antidumping, Subsidies and Countervailing Measures, Technical Barriers to Trade, Sanitary and Phytosanitary Measures, Customs Valuation, General Agreement on Trade in Services, Financial Services and Air Transport Services. The special provisions in these individual Covered Agreements govern, where applicable, and prevail in any conflict with the general provisions of the DSU.

Under WTO, unlike under GATT 1947, the DSU practically assures that panels will be established upon request by a Member. Further, under WTO, unlike under GATT 1947, the DSU virtually ensures the adoption of unmodified panel and appellate body decisions. It accom-

---

§ 9.5

1. *See, e.g.,* Suramerica de Aleaciones Laminadas, CA v. United States, 966 F.2d

660 (Fed.Cir.1992).

plishes this by requiring the DSB to adopt panel reports and appellate body decisions automatically and without amendment unless they are rejected by a consensus of all Members. This "inverted consensus" requires that all Members of the DSB, including the Member who prevailed in the dispute, decide to reject the dispute resolution decision; and that no Member formally favor that decision. Such an outcome seems unlikely. This inverted consensus requirement is imposed on both the adoption of panel reports or appellate body decisions and also on the decision to establish a panel.

The potential resolutions of a dispute under DSU range from a "mutually satisfactory solution" agreed to by the parties under the first, or consultation phase, to authorized retaliation under the last, or implementation, phase. The preferred solution is always any resolution that is mutually satisfactory to the parties. After a panel decision, there are three types of remedies available to the prevailing party, if a mutually satisfactory solution cannot be obtained. One is for the respondent to bring the measure found to violate a Covered Agreement into conformity with the Agreement. A second is for the prevailing Member to receive compensation from the respondent which both parties agree is sufficient to compensate for any injury caused by the measure found to violate a Covered Agreement. Finally, if no such agreement can be reached, a prevailing party can be authorized to suspend some of its concessions under the Covered Agreements to the respondent. These suspended concessions, called "retaliation," can be authorized within the same trade sector and agreement; or, if that will not create sufficient compensation, can be authorized across trade sectors and agreements.

Phase 1: Consultation. Any WTO Member who believes that the Measures of another Member are not in conformity with the Covered Agreements may call for consultations on those measures. The respondent has ten days to reply to the call for consultations and must agree to enter into consultation within 30 days. If the respondent does not enter into consultations within the 30 day period, the party seeking consultations can immediately request the establishment of a panel under DSU, which puts the dispute into Phase 2.

Once consultations begin, the parties have 60 days to achieve a settlement. The goal is to seek a positive solution to the dispute, and the preferred resolution is to reach whatever solution is mutually satisfactory to the parties. If such a settlement cannot be obtained after 60 days of consultations, the party seeking consultations may request the establishment of a panel under DSU, which moves the dispute into Phase 2.

Third parties with an interest in the subject-matter of the consultations may seek to be included in them. If such inclusion is rejected, they may seek their own consultations with the other Member. Alternatives to consultations may be provided through the use of conciliation, mediation or good offices, where all parties agree to use the alternative process. Any party can terminate the use of conciliation, mediation or good offices and then seek the establishment of a panel under DSU, which will move the dispute into Phase 2.

Phase 2: Panel establishment, investigation and report. If consultations between the parties fail, the party seeking the consultations (the complainant) may request the DSB to establish a panel to investigate, report and resolve the dispute. The DSB must establish such a panel upon request, unless the DSB expressly decides by consensus not to establish the panel. Since an "inverted consensus" is required to reject the establishment of the panel and the complainant Member must be part of that consensus, it is very likely that a panel will be established. Roughly 100 panels were established in the first five years of operation of the DSU.

The WTO Secretariat is to maintain a list of well-qualified persons who are available to serve as panelists. The panels are usually composed of three individuals from that list who are not citizens of either party. If the parties agree, a panel can be composed of five such individuals. The parties can also agree to appoint citizens of a party to a panel. Panelists may be either nongovernmental individuals or governmental officials, but they are to be selected so as to ensure their independence. Thus, there is a bias towards independent individuals who are not citizens of any party. If a citizen of a party is appointed, his government may not instruct that citizen how to vote, for the panelist must be independent. By the same reasoning, a governmental official of a non-party Member who is subject to instructions from his government would not seem to fit the profile of an independent panelist.

The WTO Secretariat proposes nominations of the panelists. Parties may not normally oppose the nominations, except for "compelling reasons." The parties are given twenty days to agree on the panelists and the composition of the panel. If such agreement is not forthcoming, the WTO Director–General is authorized to appoint the panelists, in consultation with other persons in the Secretariat.

Complaints brought to DSB panels can involve either violations of Covered Agreements or nonviolation nullification and impairment of benefits under the Covered Agreements. A prima facie case of nullification impairment arises when one Member infringes upon the "obligations assumed under a Covered Agreement." Such infringement creates a presumption against the infringing Member, but the presumption can be rebutted by a showing that the complaining Member has suffered no adverse effect from the infringement.

The panels receive pleadings and rebuttals and hear oral arguments. Panels can also engage in fact development from sources outside those presented by the parties. Thus, the procedure has aspects familiar to civil law courts. A panel can, on its own initiative, request information from any body, including experts selected by the panel. It can also obtain confidential information in some circumstances from an administrative body which is part of the government of a Member, without any prior consent from that Member. A panel can establish its own group of experts to provide reports to it on factual or scientific issues. In a series of rulings commencing with the *Shrimp-Turtles* decision in 1998, the WTO Appellate Body has affirmed the right of panels and itself to elect to receive unsolicited informational and argumentative briefs or letters from non-governmental organizations (NGOs), business groups and law firms.

A panel is obligated to produce two written reports—an interim and a final report. A panel is supposed to submit a final written report to the DSB within six months of its establishment. The report will contain its findings of fact, findings of law, decision and the rationale for its decision. Before the final report is issued, the panel is supposed to provide an interim report to the parties. The purpose of this interim report is to apprize the parties of the panel's current analysis of the issues and to permit the parties to comment on that analysis. The final report of the panel need not change any of the findings or conclusions in its interim report unless it is persuaded to do so by a party's comments. However, if it is not so persuaded, it is obligated to explain in its final report why it is not so persuaded.

The decisions in panel reports are final as to issues of fact. The decisions in panel reports are not necessarily final as to issues of law. Panel decisions on issues of law are subject to review by the Appellate Body, which is Phase 3, and explained below. Any party can appeal a panel report, and as is explained below it is expected that appeals will usually be taken.

Phase 3: Appellate review of the panel report. Appellate review of panel reports is available at the request of any party, unless the DSB rejects that request by an "inverted consensus." There is no threshold requirement for an appellant to present a substantial substantive legal issue. Thus, most panel decisions are appealed as a matter of course. However, the Appellate Body can only review the panel reports on questions of law or legal interpretation.

The Appellate Body is a new institution in the international trade organization and its process. GATT 1947 had nothing comparable to it. The Appellate Body is composed of seven members (or judges) who are appointed by the DSB to four year terms. Each judge may be reappointed, but only once, to a second four year term. Each judge is to be a recognized authority on international trade law and the Covered Agreements. To date, Appellate Body members have been drawn mostly from the academe and retired justices. They have come from Germany, Japan, Egypt, India, New Zealand, the Philippines, Argentina and the United States. The review of any panel decision is performed by three judges out of the seven. The parties do not, however, have any influence on which judges are selected to review a particular panel report. There is a schedule, created by the Appellate Body itself, for the rotation for sitting of each of the judges. Thus, a party might try to appear before a favored judge by timing the start of the dispute settlement process to arrive at the Appellate Body at the right moment on the rotation schedule, but even this limited approach has difficulties.

The Appellate Body receives written submissions from the parties and has 60, or in some cases 90, days in which to render its decision. The Appellate Body review is limited to issues of law and legal interpretation. The panel decision may be upheld, modified, or reversed by the Appellate Body decision. Appellate Body decisions will be anonymous, and ex parte communications are not permitted, which will make judge-shopping by parties more than usually difficult.

Phase 4: Adoption of the panel or Appellate Body decision. Appellate Body determinations are submitted to the DSB. Panel decisions which are not appealed are also submitted to the DSB. Once either type of decision is submitted to the DSB, the DSB must automatically adopt them without modification or amendment at its next meeting unless the decision is rejected by all Members of the DSB through the form of "inverted consensus" discussed previously.

An alternative to Phases 2 through 4 is arbitration, if both parties agree. The arbitration must be binding on the parties, and there is no appeal from the arbitral tribunal's decision to the DSB Appellate Body.

Phase 5: Implementation of the decision adopted; Compensation; Retaliation. Once a panel or Appellate Body decision is adopted by the DSB, implementation is a three-step process. In the first step, the Member found to have a measure which violates its WTO obligations has "a reasonable time" (usually 15 months) to bring those measures into conformity with the WTO obligations. That remedy is the preferred one, and this form of implementation is the principal goal of the WTO implementation system. To date, most disputes have resulted in compliance in this manner. If the adequacy of compliance is disputed, such disputes typically return to the WTO panel that rendered decision on the merits which also determines, acting as an arbitrator, the amount (if any) of authorized retaliation. The retaliation process is discussed below.

If the violating measures are not brought into conformity within a reasonable time, the parties proceed to the second step. In that second step, the parties negotiate to reach an agreement upon a form of compensation which will be granted by the party in violation to the injured party. Such compensation will usually comprise trade concessions by the violating party to the injured party, which are over and above those already available under the WTO and Covered Agreements. The nature, scope, amount and duration of these additional concessions is at the negotiating parties' discretion, but each side must agree that the final compensation package is fair and is properly related to the injury caused by the violating measures. Presumably, any such concessions need not be extended under MFN principles to all WTO members.

If the parties cannot agree on an appropriate amount of compensation within twenty days, the complainant may proceed to the third step. In the third step, the party injured by the violating measures seeks authority from the DSB to retaliate against the party whose measures violated its WTO obligations. Thus complainant seeks authority to suspend some of its WTO obligations in regard to the respondent. The retaliation must ordinarily be within the same sector and agreement as the violating measure. "Sector" is sometimes broadly defined, as all trade in goods, and sometimes narrowly defined, as in individual services in the Services Sectoral Classification List. "Agreement" is also broadly defined. All the agreements listed in Annex IA to the WTO Agreement are considered a single agreement. If retaliation within the sector and agreement of the violating measure is considered insufficient compensation, the complainant may seek suspension of its obligations across sectors and agreements.

The DSB must grant the complainant's request to retaliate within 30 days unless all WTO members reject it through an "inverted consensus." (Article 22.6, D.S.U.) However, the respondent may object to the level or scope of the retaliation. The issues raised by the objection will be examined by either the Appellate Body or by an arbitrator. The respondent has a right, even if arbitration was not used in Phases 2 through 4, to have an arbitrator review in Phase 5 the appropriateness of the complainant's proposed level and scope of retaliation. The arbitrator will also examine whether the proper procedures and criteria to establish retaliation have been followed. The Phase 5 arbitration is final and binding and the arbitrator's decision is not subject to DSB review.

In addition to objecting to the level of authorized retaliation, the responding WTO member may simultaneously challenge the assertion of noncompliance (Article 21.5, D.S.U.). This challenge will ordinarily be heard by the original panel and must be resolved within 90 days. Thus the request for authorized retaliation and objections thereto could conceivably be accomplished before noncompliance is formally determined. In practice, WTO dispute settlement has melded these conflicting procedures such that compliance and retaliation issues are decided together, typically by the original panel.

The amount of a U.S. retaliation permitted against the EU after the WTO *Bananas* and *Beef Hormones* decisions were not implemented by the EU was contested. The arbitration tribunals for this issue were the original WTO panels, which did not allow the entire amount of the almost $700 million in retaliatory tariffs proposed by the United States. The U.S. was authorized and has levied retaliatory tariffs amounting to about $300 million against European goods because of the EU failure to implement those WTO decisions. Since 2000, Congress has authorized rotating these tariffs in "carousel" fashion upon different European goods. The threat of carousel retaliation contributed to an April 2001 settlement of the *Bananas* dispute.

In a landmark ruling, a WTO panel acting as an arbitrator has authorized Ecuador to remove protection of intellectual property rights regarding geographical indicators, copyrights and industrial designs on European Union goods for sale in Ecuador. This authorization is part of Ecuador's $200 million compensation in the *Bananas* dispute. The WTO panel acknowledged that Ecuador imports mostly capital goods and raw materials from the European Union and that imposing retaliatory tariffs on them would adversely harm its manufacturing industries. This risk supported "cross-retaliation" under Article 22.3 of the DSU outside the sector of the EU trade violation.

Both "compensation" in the second step and "retaliation" in the third step of implementation provide only for indirect enforcement of DSB decisions. There is no mechanism for direct enforcement by the WTO of its decisions through WTO orders to suspend trade obligations. Some commentators believe that retaliation will be an effective implementation device; others believe that it will prove ineffective. The division represented by these conflicting views represents two different approaches to the nature of both international law and international trade law. One approach seeks a rule-oriented use of the "rule of law"; the other seeks a power-oriented use of diplomacy. The United States and less developed countries have traditionally sought to develop a rule-oriented approach to international trade disputes. The European Union and Japan have traditionally sought to use the GATT/WTO primarily as a forum for diplomatic negotiations, although the EU has begun to file more formal complaints.

U.S. Involvement in WTO Dispute Resolution. The WTO dispute resolution process has been invoked more frequently than many expected. The United States has been a complainant or a respondent in dozens of disputes. It lost a dispute initiated by Venezuela and Brazil (WT/DS 2 and 4) concerning U.S. standards for reformulated and conventional gasoline. The offending U.S. law was amended to conform to the WTO ruling. It won on a complaint initiated jointly with Canada and the European Union (WT/DS 8, 10 and 11) regarding Japanese taxes on alcoholic beverages. Japan subsequently changed its law. When Costa Rica complained about U.S. restraints on imports of underwear (WT/DS 24), the U.S. let the restraints expire prior to any formal DSB ruling at the WTO. Similar results were reached when India complained of U.S. restraints on wool shirts and blouses (WT/DS 23). The United States won a major dispute with Canada concerning trade and subsidies for periodicals (WT/DS 31). This celebrated *Sports Illustrated* dispute proved that WTO remedies can be used to avoid Canada's cultural industries exclusion under NAFTA.

In the longstanding *Bananas* dispute (WT/DS 27) noted above, the United States joined Ecuador, Guatemala, Honduras and Mexico in successfully challenging EU import restraints against so-called "dollar bananas." The EU failed to comply with the Appellate Body's ruling, and retaliatory measures were authorized and imposed. In April 2001, the *Bananas* dispute was settled on terms that convert EU quotas to tariffs by 2006. A patent law complaint by the U.S. against India (WT/DS 50) prevailed in the DSB and ultimately brought changes in Indian law regarding pharmaceuticals and agricultural chemicals. In *Beef Hormones* (WT/DS 26 and 48), also noted above, the European Union once again lost before the Appellate Body. It refused to alter its import restraints and presently faces retaliatory tariffs on selected exports to Canada and the United States.

The United States prevailed against Argentina regarding tariffs and taxes on footwear, textiles and apparel (WT/DS 56). It lost a challenge (strongly supported by Kodak) to Japan's distribution rules regarding photo film and paper (WT/DS 44). In this dispute the U.S. elected *not* to appeal the adverse WTO panel ruling to the Appellate Body. In contrast, the European Union took an appeal which reversed an adverse panel ruling on its customs classification of computer equipment (WT/DS 62, 67 and 68). The U.S. had commenced this proceeding. Opponents in many disputes, Japan, the United States and the European Union united to complain in WT/DS 54, 55, 59 and 64 that Indonesia's National Car Programme was discriminatory and in breach of several WTO agreements. They prevailed and Indonesia altered its program.

India, Malaysia, Pakistan and Thailand teamed up to challenge U.S. shrimp import restraints enacted to protect endangered sea turtles (WT/DS 58). The WTO Appellate Body generally upheld their complaint and the U.S. has moved to comply. The adequacy of U.S. compliance is being challenged by Malaysia. The European Union and the United States jointly opposed Korea's discriminatory taxes on alcoholic beverages (WT/DS 75 and 84). This challenge was successful and Korea now imposes flat non-discriminatory taxes. The United States also complained of Japan's quarantine, testing and other agricultural import rules (WT/DS 76/1). The U.S. won at the WTO and Japan has changed its procedures.

In a semiconductor dumping dispute, Korea successfully argued that the U.S. was not in compliance with the WTO Antidumping Agreement (WT/DS 99/1). The United States amended its law, but Korea has instituted further proceedings alleging that these amendments are inadequate. The United States did likewise after Australia lost a subsidies dispute relating to auto leather exports (WT/DS 126/1). The reconvened WTO panel ruled that Australia had indeed failed to conform to the original adverse DSB decision. A U.S. challenge concerning India's quotas on imports of agricultural, textile and industrial products was upheld (WT/DS 90/1). India and the United States subsequently reached agreement on a timeline for removal of these restraints.

Closer to home, New Zealand and the United States complained of Canada's import/export rules regarding milk (WT/DS 103/1). Losing at the WTO, Canada agreed to a phased removal of the offending measures. The United States also won against Mexico in an antidumping dispute involving corn syrup (WT/DS 132/1), but lost a "big one" when the DSB determined that export tax preferences granted to "Foreign Sales Corporations" of U.S. companies were illegal (WT/DS 108/1). It has been estimated that unless the U.S. complies with this ruling the European Union will be authorized to retaliate up to $4 billion annually. The United States has expanded the FSC regime by removing the requirement that eligible goods be manufactured in the U.S. It claims that this change makes the FSC program not contingent upon exports, and thus WTO-legal. The European Union is challenging this assertion of compliance before the WTO.

Another "big one" went in favor of the United States. The European Union challenged the validity under the DSU of unilateral retaliation under Section 301 of the Trade Act of 1974 (WT/DS 152/1). Section 301 has been something of a bete noire in U.S. trade law, but the WTO panel affirmed its legality in light of Presidential undertakings to administer it in accordance with U.S. obligations to adhere to multilateral WTO dispute settlement.

U.S. involvement in WTO dispute settlement continues to be extensive. The Appellate Body ruled that U.S. countervailing duties against British steel based upon pre-privitization subsidies were unlawful (WT/DS 138/1). The European Union prevailed before a WTO panel in its challenge of the U.S. Antidumping Act of 1916 (WT/DS 136). U.S. complaints against Korean beef import restraints and procurement practices were upheld (WT/DS 161/1, 163/1). Canada's patent protection term was also invalidated by the WTO under a U.S. complaint (WT/DS 170/1). European Union complaints concerning U.S. wheat gluten quotas (WT/DS 166/1) and the royalty free small business provisions of the Fairness in Music Licensing Act of 1998 (WT/DS 160/1) have been sustained. The *Wheat Gluten* dispute questions the legality of U.S. "causation" rules in escape clause proceedings under Section 201 of the Trade Act of 1974.

The United States has also settled a number of disputes prior to WTO panel decisions, and remains in consultation on other disputes that may be decided by a WTO panel. For the latest summary of all WTO disputes, including many not involving the United States, see www.wto.org.

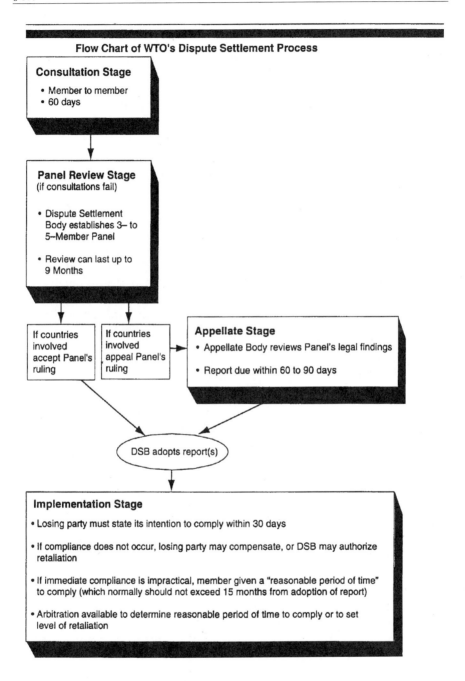

Flow Chart of WTO's Dispute Settlement Process

Consultation Stage

• Member to member
• 60 days

Panel Review Stage
(if consultations fail)

• Dispute Settlement
  Body establishes 3– to
  5–Member Panel

• Review can last up to
  9 Months

If countries involved accept Panel's ruling

If countries involved appeal Panel's ruling

Appellate Stage

• Appellate Body reviews Panel's legal findings

• Report due within 60 to 90 days

DSB adopts report(s)

Implementation Stage

• Losing party must state its intention to comply within 30 days

• If compliance does not occur, losing party may compensate, or DSB may authorize retaliation

• If immediate compliance is impractical, member given a "reasonable period of time" to comply (which normally should not exceed 15 months from adoption of report)

• Arbitration available to determine reasonable period of time to comply or to set level of retaliation

§ 9.7   Import Quotas and Licenses Under the WTO

Quantity restrictions, such as numerical quotas on the importation of an item or upon a type of item, continue to exist, despite GATT Article XI which calls for their elimination. Import quotas may be "global" limitations (applying to items originating from anywhere in the world), "bilateral" limitations (applying to items originating from a particular country) and "discretionary" limitations. Quantitative limitations may have arisen from a Treaty of Friendship, Commerce and Navigation or from a narrow international agreement, such as agreements on trade in textiles and textile products. Discretionary limitations, when coupled with a requirement that importation of items must be licensed in advance by local authorities, provide an effective vehicle for gathering statistical data and for raising local revenues. "Tariff-rate quotas" admit a specified quantity of goods at a preferential rate of duty. Once imports reach that quantity, tariffs are normally increased.

The WTO has significantly reduced the number of trade quotas. The Agreement on Textiles will ultimately eliminate the quotas long maintained under the Multi–Fibre Arrangement. Voluntary export restraints (quotas) are severely limited by the Safeguards Agreement. In addition, the WTO removes trade quotas by pressuring for "tariffication," or replacing them with tariffs—sometimes even at extraordinarily high tariff rates. Tariffication is the approach adopted in the Agriculture Agreement. It is expected that such high tariff rates will be reduced in subsequent negotiating Rounds. Import licensing schemes are also being phased out under WTO agreements.

§ 9.8 GATT/WTO Nontariff Trade Barrier Codes

There are numerous nontariff trade barriers applicable to imports. Many of these barriers arise out of safety and health regulations. Others concern the environment, consumer protection, product standards and government procurement. Many of the relevant rules were created for legitimate consumer and public protection reasons. They were often created without extensive consideration of their international impact as potential nontariff trade barriers. Nevertheless, the practical impact of legislation of this type is to ban the importation of nonconforming products. Thus, unlike tariffs which can always be paid, and unlike quotas which permit a certain amount of goods to enter the market, nontariff trade barriers have the potential to totally exclude foreign exports.

Multilateral GATT negotiations since the end of World War II have led to a significant decline in world tariff levels, particularly on trade with developed nations. As steadily as tariff barriers have disappeared, nontariff trade barriers (NTBs) have emerged. Health and safety regulations, environmental laws, rules regulating products standards, procurement legislation and customs procedures are often said to present NTB problems. Negotiations over nontariff trade barriers dominated the Tokyo Round of the GATT negotiations during the late 1970s. A number of NTB "codes" (sometimes called "side agreements") emerged from the Tokyo Round. These concerned subsidies, dumping, government procurement, technical barriers (products standards), customs valuation and import licensing. In addition, specific agreements regarding trade in bovine meats, dairy products and civil aircraft were also reached. The

United States accepted all of these NTB codes and agreements except the one on dairy products. Most of the necessary implementation of these agreements was accomplished in the Trade Agreements Act of 1979.

Additional GATT codes were agreed upon under the Uruguay Round ending in late 1993. They revisit all of the NTB areas covered by the Tokyo Round Codes and create new codes for sanitary and phyto-sanitary measures (SPS), trade-related investment measures (TRIMs), preshipment inspection, rules of origin, escape clause safeguards and trade-related intellectual property rights (TRIPs). The United States Congress approved and implemented these Codes in December of 1994 under the Uruguay Round Agreements Act.

One problem with nontariff trade barriers is that they are so numerous. Intergovernmental negotiation intended to reduce their trade restricting impact is both tedious and difficult. There are continuing attempts through the World Trade Organization to come to grips with additional specific NTB problems. Furthermore, various trade agreements of the United States have been undertaken in this field. For example, the Canadian–United States Free Trade Area Agreement and the NAFTA built upon the existing GATT agreements to further reduce NTB problems between the United States, Canada and Mexico.

In the *EU Beef Hormones* case, the EU banned imports of growth-enhancing hormone-treated beef from the U.S. and Canada as a health hazard. The Appellate Body ruled that, since the ban was more strict than international standards, the EU needed scientific evidence to back it up. However, the EU had failed to undertake a scientific risk assessment, and the EU's scientific reports did not provide any rational basis to uphold the ban. In fact, the primary EU study had found no evidence of harm to humans from the growth-enhancing-hormones. The Appellate Body ruled that the ban violated the EU's SPS obligations and required the EU to produce scientific evidence to justify the ban within a reasonable time, or to revoke the ban. Arbitrators later determined that 15 months was a reasonable time, but the EU has failed to produce such evidence and the U.S. has retaliated.

§ 9.9   The WTO Agreement on Agriculture

Agricultural issues played a central role in the Uruguay Round GATT negotiations. More than any other issue, they delayed completion of the Round from 1990 to 1993. The agreement reached in December of 1993 is a trade liberalizing, market-oriented effort. Each country has made a number of commitments on market access, reduced domestic agricultural support levels and export subsidies. The United States Congress approved of these commitments in December of 1994 by adopting the Uruguay Round Agreements Act.

Broadly speaking nontariff barriers (NTBs) to international agricultural trade are replaced by tariffs that provide substantially the same level of protection. This is known as "tariffication." It applies to virtually all NTBs, including variable levies, import bans, voluntary export restraints and import quotas. Tariffication applies specifically to U.S. agricultural quotas adopted under Section 22 of the Agricultural Adjustment Act. All agricultural tariffs, including those converted from NTBs, are to be reduced by 36 and 24 percent by developed and developing countries, respectively, over 6 and 10 year periods. Certain minimum access tariff quotas apply when imports amount to less than 3 to 5 percent of domestic consumption. An escape clause exists for tariffed imports at low prices or upon a surge of importation depending upon the existing degree of import penetration.

Regarding domestic support for agriculture, some programs with minimal impact on trade are exempt from change. These programs are known as "green box policies." They include governmental support for agricultural research, disease control, infrastructure and food security. Green box policies are also exempt from GATT/WTO challenge or countervailing duties for 9 years. Direct payments to producers that are not linked to production are also generally exempt. This will include income support, adjustment assistance, and environmental and regional assistance payments. Furthermore, direct payments to support crop reductions and *de minimis* payments are exempted in most cases.

After removing all of the exempted domestic agricultural support programs, the agreement on agriculture arrives at a calculation known as the Total Aggregate Measurement of Support (Total AMS). This measure is the basis for agricultural support reductions under the agreement. Developed nations must reduce their Total AMS by 20 percent over 6 years, developing nations by 13.3 percent over 10 years. United States reductions undertaken in 1985 and 1990 suggest that little or no U.S. action will be required to meet this obligation.

Agricultural export subsidies of developed nations must be reduced by 36 percent below 1986–1990 levels over 6 years and the quantity of subsidized agricultural exports by 21 percent. Developing nations must meet corresponding 24 and 14 percent reductions over 10 years.

All conforming tariffications, reductions in domestic support for agriculture and export subsidy alterations are essentially exempt from challenge for 9 years within the GATT/WTO on grounds such as serious prejudice in export markets or nullification and impairment of agreement benefits. However, countervailing duties may be levied against all unlawfully subsidized exports of agricultural goods except for subsidies derived from so-called national "green box policies" (discussed above).

§ 9.10 WTO Public Procurement Code

Where public procurement is involved, and the taxpayer's money is at issue, virtually every nation has some form of legislation or tradition that favors buying from domestic suppliers. The Tokyo Round GATT Procurement Code was not particularly successful at opening up government purchasing. Only Austria, Canada, the twelve European Union states, Finland, Hong Kong, Israel, Japan, Norway, Singapore, Sweden,

Switzerland and the United States adhered to that Procurement Code. This was also partly the result of the 1979 Code's many exceptions. For example, the Code did not apply to contracts below its threshold amount of $150,000 SDR (about $171,000 since 1988), service contracts, and procurement by entities on each country's reserve list (including most national defense items). Because procurement in the European Union and Japan is often decentralized, many contracts fell below the SDR threshold and were therefore GATT exempt. By dividing up procurement into smaller contracts national preferences were retained. United States government procurement tends to be more centralized and thus more likely to be covered by the GATT Code. This pattern may help explain why Congress restrictively amended the Buy American Act in 1988.

Chapter 13 of the North American Free Trade Area Agreement opened government procurement to U.S., Canadian and Mexican suppliers on contracts as small as $25,000. However, the goods supplied must have at least 50 percent North American content. These special procurement rules effectively created an exception to the GATT Procurement Code which otherwise applied. The thresholds are $50,000 for goods and services provided to federal agencies and $250,000 for government-owned enterprises (notably PEMEX and CFE). These regulations are particularly important because Mexico, unlike Canada, has not traditionally joined in GATT procurement codes.

The Uruguay Round Procurement Code took effect in 1996 and replaced the 1979 Tokyo Round GATT Procurement Code. The Uruguay Round Code expanded the coverage of the prior GATT Code to include procurement of services, construction, government-owned utilities, and some state and local (subcentral) contracts. The U.S. and the European Union applied the new Code's provisions on government-owned utilities and subcentral contracts as early as April 15, 1994.

Various improvements to the procedural rules surrounding procurement practices and dispute settlement under the Uruguay Round Code attempt to reduce tensions in this difficult area. For example, an elaborate system for bid protests is established. Bidders who believe the 1979 Code's procedural rules have been abused will be able to lodge, litigate and appeal their protests. The Uruguay Round Procurement Code became part of U.S. law in December of 1994 under the Uruguay Round Agreements Act. The United States has made, with few exceptions, all procurement by executive agencies subject to the Federal Acquisition Regulations under the Code's coverage (i.e., to suspend application of the normal Buy American preferences to such procurement).

B.   CLEARING U.S. CUSTOMS

§ 9.11   Introduction

Suppose you wish to export goods to the United States. U.S. customs must be cleared. The following material summarizes the issues and actors most likely to be encountered. A more detailed review of customs classification, origin and valuation law is presented in Chapter 5 and Chapter 4 analyzes U.S. tariff and duty free entry law.

Many disputes in the customs area arise over the classification of imported goods under the Column 1 customs schedule. The rate of duty depends upon such classification, and substantial amounts may depend upon the outcome. The classifications are enunciated in abstract terms, so that overlap is possible; and, where such overlap exists, the importer wants to choose the classification with the least duty. Other disputes concern the place of origin of the goods. The country of origin may determine whether the goods enter under Column 1 or Column 2 tariffs, or perhaps duty free.

§ 9.12   Entry Formalities

The formalities of entry of imported goods are usually handled by a customs broker, but as an attorney you need to understand them for the same reasons that you need to understand other parts of the transaction. Customs brokers are licensed and regulated by federal law as administered by the U.S. Customs Service. The consignee, or an agent such as a customs broker, will file an "entry" form with the United States Customs Service and also documents sufficient to enable the customs officer to determine whether to release goods or not. At the same time, or within ten days, the consignee or agent must file an "entry summary" form. This form will be used by the customs officers to determine duties, collect aggregate statistics, and determine conformity of merchandise with United States domestic health and safety legal requirements. Alternatively, the consignee or agent may file only the "entry summary" form and its required documents as a substitute for both "entry" and "entry summary" forms. Estimated customs duties are also to be deposited at the time of filing either entry documentation or entry summary documentation.

The customs entry procedure was significantly streamlined in 1978 to allow immediate release of the imported goods after filing of entry documentation only, without posting of a bond to cover customs duties, and with no requirement of deposit of estimated duties until the entry summary is filed subsequently (within ten days). The customs service sends importers consolidated periodic statements for all entries made during a billing period, rather than requiring settlement on an entry-by-entry basis. Further streamlining, including a national electronic customs automation program, was implemented by the Customs Modernization Act of 1993.[1]

§ 9.13   Customs Documentation and Liability

The documentation required by the customs service is an entry form (Customs Form 3641), a commercial invoice, a packing list, and other

§ 9.12   1.   Public Law 103–182 (Title VI).

evidence of the right to make entry—such as a bill of lading. In most transactions, the bill of lading requirement is satisfied by a "carrier's certificate," a certified statement by the importing carrier that a designated person or firm is the owner or consignee for customs purposes. Other documents may be needed for a particular type of shipment—e.g., export country documents for importation of certain textiles under bilateral textile agreements, meat products, steel shipments over $10,000, etc. Careful attention must be paid to preparation and presentation of the necessary customs documents. Harsh civil penalties apply to false and material statements, acts and omissions.[1] Such penalties may be assessed for misdescriptions of goods, undervaluations and false claims of tariff exemption whether intentionally or negligently caused.[2] Only clerical errors will be excused. Pre-penalty notice to the importer must be given by the Customs Service. After a reply period, the penalty may be assessed. The importer may appeal all such customs penalties to the Court of International Trade (CIT) for *de novo* review.

The Customs Service has stepped up its compliance audits which can now be undertaken with the assistance of the Internal Revenue Service. The importer's duty to show reasonable care is sanctionable by substantial civil penalties, as are record keeping and false statement requirements. These changes follow the Customs Modernization Act of 1993, Public Law No. 103–182.

The Customs Service normally examines at least one package per invoice and at least ten percent of the packages of merchandise. However, the Customs Service may examine either more or less than this. It has the authority to examine every package, if that is believed necessary. On the other hand, it may open only one package where the goods are uniform; and, at designated ports, the district director has discretion to release designated merchandise without any examination. The purpose of customs examinations is to determine, first, whether the goods are accurately invoiced as to description and quantity; then second, the dutiable status of the goods and the proper amount of customs duty owed. In addition, the examination is to determine whether the required "country of origin" markings appear, and whether the packages contain any prohibited articles.

The importer is liable for all import duties. It is liable even if the Customs Service releases the goods in error without payment, or if the importer pays its agent the customs broker, but the customs broker fails to pay the United States Customs Service. The liability for customs duty constitutes a "lien" on the goods, and the government's claim for unpaid

§ 9.13

1. See 19 U.S.C.A. § 1592. But foreign companies cannot be held negligently liable for aiding and abetting customs negligence of another party. See United States v. Hitachi America, Ltd., 172 F.3d 1319 (Fed.Cir. 1999). They can be held liable for knowingly doing so. Id.

2. See, e.g., United States v. Ven–Fuel, Inc., 758 F.2d 741 (1st Cir.1985) (importer liability for negligently filed false statement); United States v. Frowein, 727 F.2d 227 (2d Cir.1984) (omissions' liability).

duties takes priority over other creditors in bankruptcy. If goods are reimported, they are dutiable on each successive importation unless they are personal or household effects, tools of the trade or professional books, automobiles taken abroad for non-commercial use, goods sent abroad for repair (although dutiable for the value of the repair) and domestic animals sent abroad for pasturage for eight months.

A nonresident may enter imported goods, but it must post a bond provided by a resident corporate surety. A foreign corporation entering imported goods must have a resident agent. That agent may be a corporate officer, regular employee, or customs broker, as long as they have a proper power of attorney, are a resident of the United States, and are authorized to accept service of process on behalf of the importer.

Since the consignee did not ship or load the goods, the consignee cannot declare of his or her own knowledge that the goods conform to the bill of lading. Thus, the "consignee's declaration" merely requires a declaration that, to the best of its knowledge, the goods are what the invoice says they are. Where the named consignee is not the actual owner of the imported goods and wishes to be relieved of liability for increased and additional customs duties, an actual owner's declaration may be filed, stating that the consignee is not the actual owner and furnishing the name and address of the actual owner. If the entry is made by a customs broker or other agent, a customs power of attorney must be executed by the consignee or owner. An agent must file this power of attorney with the customs district office, but a customs broker need only keep it in its own files, available for inspection.

The requirements for "informal entries" and "mail entries" are somewhat less elaborate. The informal entry is available for shipments having a value of less than $250, including installments of less than $250 (if the other installments arrive at different times), and for shipments of personal and household effects and books for libraries. The informal entry requires no customs invoice, but a commercial invoice is needed for goods purchased for import or intended for resale in the United States. Mail entry is also available where the imported goods are sent by sealed letters or parcel post. In such entries, the duties on parcels with a value under $250 can be collected by the postal carrier, and there is no need to clear these mailed shipments personally. It should be noted, however, that mailed imports are still subject to customs inspection. Parcel post packages must have attached to them a customs declaration form provided by a foreign post office giving an accurate description and the value of the contents. Customs officers may open for examination mail which appears to contain matter other than correspondence, if they have "reasonable cause to suspect" the presence of either merchandise or contraband.[3]

There are, however, classes of transactions in which the importer need not pay any duty—or at least not pay duty at that time. These transactions involve goods which are entered into a bonded warehouse or

3. United States v. Ramsey, 431 U.S. 606, 97 S.Ct. 1972, 52 L.Ed.2d 617 (1977).

a foreign trade zone.[4] In these transactions, the duty is not due on the imported goods until they are withdrawn from the warehouse or foreign trade zone, and they may be so withdrawn only by the importer or actual owner. In warehouses and foreign trade zones, the goods may be cleaned, sorted, repacked, or even undergo manufacturing operations (car parts to finished automobile), including smelting or refining—or they may simply be stored, awaiting better market conditions or awaiting their turn to be admitted under an import quota program.

§ 9.14   Customs Classification

Prospective rulings on customs classification issues may be obtained.[1] An importer may request a ruling from the Commissioner of Customs on the proper classification of goods whose importation is merely contemplated, and which have not arrived in the United States. Such a request, if properly presented, will be answered by a "ruling letter," which is binding on all Customs Service personnel; but only if the actual import transaction corresponds with the transaction described in the letter requesting the ruling.

The initial product and origin classification of the imported goods is made by the importer, consignee, or broker.[2] But this classification is subject to disapproval by the District Director. If an improper classification is found, the District Director notifies the importer of the proposed change of rate and amount of tariff duty.[3] The importer then normally has 20 days to pay the increase in the duty or seek further administrative review before the imported goods will be "liquidated" (sold) to cover the unmet charges.

If the importer seeks a review of the Customs classification, the importer bears the burden of proof that Customs is wrong.[4] The importer's protest will be reviewed first by the District Director, and then may be reviewed by the Regional Commissioner or the Commissioner of Customs, especially in cases of first impression.[5] If Customs denies the protest, the importer may seek judicial review in the Court of International Trade.[6] Ordinary Customs Service classification decisions are not entitled to judicial deference.[7]

The classification problem may be illustrated as follows: Are parts of a wooden picture frame, imported piece by piece in separate packages for later assembly within a country, to be assessed duties prescribed for wood picture frames or for strips of wood molding? Is "wood picture frame" even an appropriate nomenclature, or should what is commonly

4. See Chapter 11.

§ 9.14

1. 19 C.F.R. § 177.

2. 19 C.F.R. § 141.90.

3. 19 C.F.R. § 152.2.

4. Corning Glass Works v. United States, 448 F.Supp. 262 (Cust.Ct.1977), re-versed on other grounds 586 F.2d 822 (Cust. & Pat.App.1978).

5. 19 C.F.R. §§ 173, 174.

6. 19 C.F.R. § 175.

7. United States v. Mead Corp., 533 U.S. 218, 121 S.Ct. 2164, 150 L.Ed.2d 292 (2001).

known to be a wood picture frame have a tariff nomenclature of "art object" or "forest product" or simply "personal belonging?"

For decades, most of the countries in the world, except the United States and Canada, classified imports according to the Brussels Tariff Nomenclature (BTN), which identifies items along a progression from raw materials to finished products. The United States had its own system of classification set out in the Tariff Schedule of the United States (TSUS). However, beginning in 1982, the United States initiated steps to convert the TSUS into a Harmonized Commodity, Description and Coding System (HS) of classification, in common with the classification system used by most other countries and developed by the Customs Cooperation Council in Brussels. The United States adopted the Harmonized System as the Harmonized Tariff Schedule (HTS) for classification of all imports by enactment of the Omnibus Trade and Competitiveness Act of 1988, with an effective date of Jan. 1, 1989. Many nations have adopted HS and use it for U.S. exports.

§ 9.15 Customs Valuation

Even though an imported item may be classified and have a known rate of duty, expressed as a percentage of the item's value, difficulty may still arise in getting the importer and customs authorities to agree upon the item's value. For decades, United States Customs valuation of an imported item was gauged by the American Selling Price (ASP) of the item—i.e. the usual wholesale price at which the same item manufactured in the United States was offered for sale.

However, Article VII of GATT requires that "value for customs purposes ... should not be based on the value of merchandise of national origin or on arbitrary or fictitious values." The 1979 Tokyo Round produced the Customs Valuation Code, which established the details of an approach which was quite different from ASP. The GATT approach was incorporated into the U.S. Trade Agreements Act of 1979.[1] United States Customs valuation is now calculated by the "transaction value" of the imported item and, if that cannot be determined, by certain fall-back methods which are, in descending order of eligibility for use, the transaction value of identical merchandise, the transaction value of similar merchandise, the resale price of the merchandise with allowances for certain factors (deducted value) or the cost of producing the imported item (computed value). "Transaction value" is "the price actually paid or payable for the merchandise when sold for exportation to the United States" plus certain amounts reflecting packing costs, commissions paid by buyer, any assist, royalty or license fee paid by buyer, and any resale, disposal or use proceeds that accrue to seller.

§ 9.16 Rules of Origin

When a country's tariff schedules provide that duties on an imported item may vary depending upon the country from which the item

§ 9.15   1. See Chapter 11.

comes, certain "rules of origin" may come into play. Two common situations raising questions of origin are when a product is shipped to the United States from Country "X" but has been manufactured in fact in Country "Y", and when a product is shipped to the United States from Country "X", in which the product was made, but certain component parts of the product have originated in Country "Y".

A statutory "rule of origin" is provided in the Trade Agreements Act of 1979.[1] This general "substantial transformation" rule of origin reflects longstanding Customs Service regulations[2] and is relevant in determining the rate at which customs duty is charged (MFN or not). It also has deep roots in the jurisprudence of the Supreme Court,[3] and principally asks whether the product has changed in name, character or use. In most cases, this approach applies for purposes of United States country of origin marking requirements and determination of the origin of goods subject to U.S. import quotas.[4] Variations on the substantial transformation theme occur for goods subject to voluntary trade restraints (VERs),[5] economic sanctions,[6] country of origin marking requirements,[7] antidumping and countervailing duty circumvention law,[8] customs duty drawback (refunds or waivers),[9] and government procurement preferences.[10]

Different more quantitative (value-added) rules of origin usually apply for goods from developing nations seeking duty free entry into the United States.[11] The Canada–United States Free Trade Agreement and the NAFTA generally replace the substantial transformation test with origin criteria emphasizing changes in HTS tariff classifications along with regional value content which are treated as the equivalent of a substantial transformation.[12] Product specific rules of origin have been created for textiles,[13] motor vehicles,[14] electronics and other goods.[15]

§ 9.16

1. 19 U.S.C.A. § 2518(4)(B): "An article is a product of a country . . . only if . . . it is wholly the growth, product, or manufacture of that country . . . , or . . . in the case of an article which consists in whole or in part of materials from another country . . . it has been substantially transformed into a new and different article of commerce with a name, character, or use distinct from that of the article or articles from which it was so transformed."

2. See 19 C.F.R. § 134.1(b).

3. See Anheuser–Busch Brewing Ass'n v. United States, 207 U.S. 556, 28 S.Ct. 204, 52 L.Ed. 336 (1908).

4. See Chapter 14.

5. See Superior Wire v. United States, 669 F.Supp. 472 (C.I.T.1987), affirmed 867 F.2d 1409 (Fed.Cir.1989).

6. Re Marking of Felt Manufactured from South African Wool, 24 Customs Serv. Dec. 30 (Jan. 17, 1990).

7. See Uniroyal v. United States, 542 F.Supp. 1026 (C.I.T.1982), affirmed 702 F.2d 1022 (Fed.Cir.1983).

8. See 19 U.S.C. § 1677j.

9. See Anheuser–Busch Brewing Ass'n v. United States, 207 U.S. 556, 28 S.Ct. 204, 52 L.Ed. 336 (1908).

10. See 19 U.S.C.A. § 2518(4)(b); 19 C.F.R. Part 177.

11. See Chapter 10.

12. See Chapter 21.

13. See 19 C.F.R. § 12.130; Mast Industries, Inc. v. United States, 652 F.Supp. 1531 (C.I.T.1987), affirmed 822 F.2d 1069 (Fed.Cir.1987).

14. See 19 C.F.R. § 10.84.

15. See also Chapter 11 for product-specific NAFTA origin rules.

One thoughtful commentator has concluded that the substantial transformation test of origin is inherently ambiguous, complex and difficult to apply consistently. He notes that in determining whether merchandise has emerged from a manufacturing process with a new name, character or use, the courts consider the following factors:

> (1) the value added to the merchandise at each stage of manufacture;
>
> (2) the degree and type of processing that occurred in each country;
>
> (3) the effect of processing on the article;
>
> (4) the markets in which the article was sold at each stage of production;
>
> (5) the capital costs of the processing;
>
> (6) the manner in which the article was used before and after processing;
>
> (7) the durability of the article before and after processing;
>
> (8) the lines of distribution in which the article was sold;
>
> (9) the article's name or identity in commerce before and after processing; and
>
> (10) the tariff classification of the merchandise before and after processing.[16]

§ 9.17 The WTO and Rules of Origin

The Uruguay Round accord on rules of origin is, in reality, an agreement to agree. A negotiations schedule was established along with a WTO Committee to work with the Customs Cooperation Council on harmonized rules of origin. Certain broad guiding principles for the negotiations are given and considered binding until agreement is reached. These principles are:

- rules of origin applied to foreign trade must not be more stringent than applied to domestic goods.

- rules of origin must be administered consistently, uniformly, impartially and reasonably.

- origin assessments must be issued within 150 days of a request and remain valid for three years.

- new or modified rules or origin may not be applied retroactively.

- strict confidentiality rules apply to information submitted confidentially for rule of origin determinations.

16. Maxwell, Formulating Rules of Origin for Imported Merchandise: Transforming the Substantial Transformation Test, 23 Geo.Wash.J.Int'l L. & Econ. 669, 673 (1990).

C. REGULATING U.S. TRADE

The international trade of the United States is regulated by a number of different governmental bodies. The International Trade Administration is part of the Commerce Department, which in turn is part of the Executive Branch of the federal government. The Commerce Department also contains the Office of Export Licensing and the Office of Anti-boycott Compliance. The International Trade Commission is an independent federal government agency, and the Court of International Trade is part of the Judicial Branch of the United States government. Lastly, the Office of the United States Trade Representative works directly under the President.

§ 9.18 International Trade Administration (ITA)

The International Trade Administration (ITA) is an administrative agency. In broadest terms, the ITA is to foster, promote and develop world trade, and to bring U.S. companies into the business of selling overseas. At a practical level, the ITA is designed to be helpful to the individual business by providing it with information concerning the "what, where, how and when" of imports and exports, such as information sources, requirements for a particular trade license, forms for an international license agreement or procedures to start a business in a foreign country. The ITA provides business data and educational programs to United States businesses. In addition to these duties, the ITA also decides whether there are subsidies in countervailing duty (CVD)[1] cases or sales at less than fair value in antidumping duty (AD) cases.[2] Prior to 1980, such decisions were made by the Treasury Department. The ITA is not, however, involved in decision-making in escape clause (Section 201), market disruption (Section 406) and unfair import practices (Section 337) proceedings.

§ 9.19 International Trade Commission (ITC)

The United States International Trade Commission (ITC) is an independent bipartisan agency created in 1916 by an act of Congress. The ITC is the successor to the United States Tariff Commission. In 1974, the name was changed and the ITC was given additional authority, powers and responsibilities. The Commission's present powers and duties include preparing reports pertaining to international economics and foreign trade for the Executive Branch, the Congress, other government agencies and the public. To carry out this responsibility, the ITC conducts investigations which entail extensive research, specialized studies and a high degree of expertise in all matters relating to the commercial and international trade policies of the United States. Statutory investigations conducted by the ITC include unfair import trade practice determinations (Section 337 proceedings),[1] domestic industry injury de-

§ 9.18
1. See Chapter 13.
2. See Chapter 12.

§ 9.19
1. See Chapter 24.

terminations in antidumping and countervailing duty cases,[2] and escape clause and market disruption import relief recommendations.[3] The ITC also advises the President about probable economic effects on domestic industries and consumers of modifications on duties and other trade barriers incident to proposed trade agreements with foreign countries.

The ITC is intended to be a quasi-judicial, bipartisan, independent agency providing trade expertise to both Congress and the Executive. Congress went to great lengths to create a bipartisan body to conduct international trade studies and provide reliable expert information. The six Commissioners of the ITC are appointed by the President and confirmed by the United States Senate for nine year terms, unless appointed to fill an unexpired term. The presence of entrenched points of view is inhibited because a Commissioner who has served for more than five years is not eligible for reappointment. Not more than three Commissioners may be members of the same political party. The Chairman and Vice–Chairman are designated by the President for two year terms. No Chairman may be of the same political party as the preceding Chairman, nor may the President designate two Commissioners of the same political party as Chairman and Vice–Chairman. Congress further guaranteed the independence of the ITC from the Executive Branch by having its budget submitted directly to the Congress. This means that its budget is not subject to review by the Office of Management and Budget.

§ 9.20   Court of International Trade (CIT)

The United States Court of International Trade (CIT) is an Article III court under the United States Constitution for judicial review of civil actions arising out of import transactions and certain federal statutes affecting international trade. It grew out of the Board of General Appraisers (a quasi-judicial administrative unit within the Treasury Department which reviewed decisions by United States Customs officials concerning the amount of duties to be paid on imports in actions arising under the tariff acts) and the United States Customs Court which had essentially the same jurisdiction and powers. The President, with the advice and consent of the Senate, appoints the nine judges who constitute the Court of International Trade. Not more than five of the nine judges may belong to any one political party.

The geographical jurisdiction of the Court of International Trade extends throughout the United States, and it is also authorized to hold hearings in foreign countries. The court has exclusive subject-matter jurisdiction to decide any civil action commenced against the United States, its agencies or its officers arising from any law pertaining to revenue from imports, tariffs, duties or embargoes or enforcement of these and other customs regulations. This includes disputes regarding trade embargoes, quotas, customs classification and valuation, country of origin determinations and denials of protests by the U.S. Customs

---

2. See Chapters 12 and 13.   **3.** See Chapter 15.

Service. The court's exclusive jurisdiction also includes any civil action commenced by the United States that arises out of an import transaction, and authority to review final agency decisions concerning antidumping and countervailing duty matters, the eligibility of workers, firms and communities who are economically harmed by foreign imports for trade adjustment assistance, disputes concerning the release of confidential business information, and decisions to deny, revoke or suspend the licenses of customs brokers. However, the CIT does *not* have jurisdiction over disputes involving restrictions on imported merchandise where public safety or health issues are raised. This limitation on CIT jurisdiction arises because such issues involving domestic goods would be determined by other regulatory bodies, and only referral to United States District Courts can ensure uniform treatment of both imports and domestically produced goods.

The standard for the judicial review exercised by the CIT varies from case to case. In some instances, such as confidentiality orders, a *de novo* trial is undertaken. In others, notably antidumping and countervailing duty cases, the standard is one of substantial evidence or arbitrary, capricious or unlawful action or an abuse of discretion. In trade adjustment assistance litigation, the administrative determinations are considered conclusive absent substantial evidentiary support in the record with the CIT empowered to order the taking of further evidence. Unless otherwise specified by statute, the Administrative Procedure Act governs the judicial review by the CIT of U.S. international trade law. The CIT possesses all the remedial powers, legal and equitable, of a United States District Court, including authority to enter money judgments for or against the United States, but with three limitations. First, in an action challenging a trade adjustment ruling, the court may not issue an injunction or writ of mandamus. Second, the CIT may order disclosure of confidential information only as specified in Section 777(c)(2) of the Tariff Act of 1930. Third, the CIT may order only declaratory relief for suits brought under the provision allowing the court accelerated review because of a showing of irreparable harm.

The CIT must give due deference to Customs Service regulations under *Chevron* rules[1] even when undertaking *de novo* review.[2] CIT decisions are first appealed to the Court of Appeals for the Federal Circuit (formerly to the Court of Customs and Patent Appeals), and ultimately to the United States Supreme Court.

§ 9.21   United States Trade Representative (USTR)

Removing trade barriers is usually done on a reciprocal basis, and requires lengthy bargaining and negotiations between the sovereigns. Congress is not adapted to carry on such negotiations, so it routinely

§ 9.20

1. Chevron, U.S.A., Inc. v. Natural Resources Defense Council, Inc., 467 U.S. 837, 104 S.Ct. 2778, 81 L.Ed.2d 694 (1984).

2. United States v. Haggar Apparel Co., 526 U.S. 380, 119 S.Ct. 1392, 143 L.Ed.2d 480 (1999).

delegates limited authority to the President to negotiate agreements reducing trade restrictions. Recent efforts to reduce trade restrictions have been multilateral, bilateral and trilateral. In all cases, Congress has given quite broad authority to the President, or his representative, to reduce or eliminate United States tariffs on a reciprocal basis.

The power to negotiate for international trade advantage within the framework of GATT or elsewhere was summarized in a 1975 letter by the (then) Acting Assistant Secretary of State for Congressional Relations, Mr. Kempton Jenkins, to a Congressional committee:[1]

> The Trade Act of 1974, [19 U.S.C. § 2101 et seq.] which became law on January 3, 1975, provides the President with substantial new authority in the area of trade negotiations. He may, under certain circumstances, enter into trade agreements, and, as a result thereof, decrease existing tariffs or harmonize, reduce or eliminate nontariff barriers to and other distortions of trade. This authority may be exercised through both multilateral and bilateral trade agreements. Agreements regarding nontariff barriers are subject to congressional approval.... Finally, Title IV of the Trade Act contains a number of limitations on the President's authority to make commercial agreements with nonmarket economy countries, including provisions relating to congressional approval or disapproval of such agreements.[2]

In response to Section 1104 of the Trade Agreements Act of 1979,[3] the President reviewed the structure of the international trade functions of the Executive Branch. Although this did not lead to the establishment of a new Department of International Trade and Investment, it did lead to enhancement of the Office of the Special Representative for Trade Negotiations,[4] which has since been renamed the United States Trade Representative (USTR). The powers of the USTR were expanded and its authority given a legislative foundation.

The USTR is appointed by the President, with the advice and consent of the Senate.[5] The Office of the USTR has been the principal vehicle through which trade negotiations have been conducted over the past several years on behalf of the United States. Among other things, the USTR has had continuing responsibility in connection with implementation and development of the Codes produced by the 1979 Tokyo Round of the GATT. This role is authorized by section 2 of the Trade Agreements Act of 1979 (to an extent not in conflict with existing United States statutes). The USTR is the contact point for persons who desire an investigation of instances of noncompliance with any trade agreement. The USTR also negotiates "orderly marketing agreements" and

§ 9.21

1. See 69 Am.J.Int'l Law 651–52 (1975).

2. Section 1102 of the Omnibus Trade and Competitiveness Act of 1988 (P.L. 100–418) extended until June 1, 1993 the President's authority under the Trade Act of 1974.

3. P.L. 96–39.

4. The office had been established by an Executive Order in 1963.

5. 19 U.S.C.A. § 2171.

"voluntary restraint agreements" with foreign governments that are willing to restrict the flow of goods into the United States.

In 1988, the duties of the USTR were significantly expanded in conjunction with an overhaul of Section 301 of the Trade Act of 1974.[6] Section 301 creates a controversial unilateral trade remedy which principally has been used to obtain foreign market access for U.S. exports. Prior to 1988, the President directly administered Section 301. Thereafter, as amended by the Omnibus Trade and Competitiveness Act, the USTR assumed this role along with new duties governing the Super 301 and Special 301 procedures created in 1988. Moreover, since the 1988 Act expanded the coverage of Section 301 and introduced mandatory (not discretionary) remedies, the USTR has been in the spotlight of many domestic industry complaints about foreign governments. Such complaints can reach breaches of international agreements as well as unjustifiable, unreasonable or discriminatory foreign country practices.

§ 9.22   U.S. Import Regulation (Chart)

Proceeding	ITA Determinations	ITC Determinations	Presidential Determinations	Remedies	Judicial Appeals
Subsidies	Bounty or Grant	Domestic Injury	N/A*	Countervailing Tariff Duty	CIT****
Dumping	Sales at Less Than Fair Value	Domestic Injury	N/A*	Antidumping Tariff Duty	CIT****
Escape Clause "201 action"	N/A	Import Surge, Domestic Injury	Remedies (if any)*	Tariffs, Quotas OMAs*, Adjustment Action or Assistance	Limited***
Market Disruption "406 action"	N/A	Import Surge, Domestic Injury	Remedies (if any)*	Tariffs, Quotas OMAs*	Limited***
Unfair Import Practices "337 action"	N/A	Unfair Import Practices, Domestic Injury**	Nullification of ITC Remedies	General Exclusion and Cease & Desist Orders, Customs Seizures	Federal Circuit Court of Appeals

*   President may negotiate settlement with foreign governments (OMAs) or exporters (VRAs).
**   Not needed in intellectual property cases.
***   See Sneaker Circus Inc. v. Carter, 566 F.2d 396 (2d Cir.1977) and Maple Leaf Fish Co. v. United States, 762 F.2d 86 (Fed.Cir.1985) (judicial review of ITC and President limited to procedural irregularities and clear misconstructions of statute). The use and remedies of escape clause proceedings are also limited by the Canadian–American and North American free trade agreements.
****   Binational or trinational panels replace CIT judicial review under the Canadian–American and North American free trade agreements.

§ 9.23   U.S. Export Regulation (Chart)

Offense/ Proceeding	Commerce Dept. Determinations	USTR Determinations	SEC/Justice Dept. Determinations	Remedies/Sanctions
Export Licensing	Licenses	—	—	Criminal and civil penalties; denial of export privileges
Assisting in Boycott of Israel	Unlawful refusals to act or unlawful furnishing of information	—	—	Tax penalties; civil and criminal penalties; denial of export privileges
Payments to Foreign Officials, Political Candidates or Agents	—	—	Record keeping and accounting violations by issuers (non-issuer determinations by Justice Dept.); illegal payment violations (Justice)	Civil and criminal penalties

6.   See Chapter 19.

| Foreign Country Practices "301 action" | — | Breach of int'l agreement; * unjustifiable,* unreasonable,** discriminatory ** practices | — | Negotiated settlements; mandatory/discretionary U.S. trade sanctions |

* Mandatory U.S. trade sanctions.
** Discretionary U.S. trade sanctions.

Selected Bibliography

American Bar Ass'n, Rules of Origin (standing Committee on Customs Law) (1991).

Bhala, Enter the Dragon: An Essay on China's WTO Accession Saga, 15 Amer. Univ. Int'l L.Rev. 1469 (2000).

Bhala, The Bananas War, 31 McGeorge L. Rev. 843 (2000).

Bhala, The Precedent Setters: De Facto *Stare Decisis* in WTO Adjudication, 9 J. Transnat'l Law & Policy 1 (1999).

Demeret, The Metamorphoses of the GATT: From the Havana Charter to the World Trade Organization, 34 Columbia J. Transnat'l L. 123 (1995).

Maxwell, Formulating Rules of Origin for Imported Merchandise: Transforming the Substantial Transformation Test, 23 Geo.Wash.J.Int'l L. & Econ. 669 (1990).

Kennedy, The GATT–WTO System at Fifty, 16 Wisc. Int'l L.J. 421 (1994).

Re, Litigation Before the U.S. Court of International Trade, 19 U.S.C.A. XI–XLVII (Pocket Part).

U.S. International Trade Commission, Annual Reports.

Chapter 10

UNITED STATES TARIFFS AND DUTY FREE IMPORTS

Table of Sections

A. THE U.S. HARMONIZED TARIFF SCHEDULE

§ 10.1 Introduction

This chapter focuses on United States tariffs under the Harmonized Tariff Schedule (HTS). Column 1 tariffs, known as most-favored-nation (MFN) tariffs, are the lower and most likely to be applicable. Column 2 tariffs, originating in the Smoot–Hawley Tariff Act of 1930, are the higher and least likely to be applicable. In addition, there are a variety of duty free entry programs to which the U.S. subscribes. This chapter selectively reviews duty free entry under the Generalized System of Tariff Preferences of the United States (GSP), the Caribbean Basin Initiative, the Andean Trade Preference Act and Section 9802.00.80 of the HTS. Duty free entry is, of course, the ultimate goal of all exporters and importers involved in United States trade. The Israeli and Canadian–American Free Trade Area Agreements, as well as the North American Free Trade Agreement (NAFTA), are treated separately in Chapter 15.

United States tariffs generally take one of three forms. The most common is an ad valorem rate. Such tariffs are assessed in proportion to the value of the article. Tariffs may also be assessed at specific rates or compound rates. Specific rates may be measured by the pound or other weight. A compound rate is a mixture of an ad valorem and specific rate tariff. Tariff rate quotas involve limitations on imports at a specific tariff up to a certain amount. Imports in excess of that amount are not prohibited, but are subject to a higher rate of tariff. Thus tariff rate quotas tend to restrict imports that are in excess of the specified quota for the lower tariff level.

§ 10.2 The Origins of United States Tariffs

Article I, Section 8, of the United States Constitution authorizes Congress to levy uniform tariffs on imports. Tariff legislation must originate in the House of Representatives. Although tariffs were primarily viewed as revenue-raising measures at the founding of the nation, it was not long before tariffs became used for openly protectionist purposes. The Tariff Act of 1816 initiated this change in outlook. During much of the Nineteenth Century, the United States legislated heavy protective tariffs. These were justified as necessary to protect the country's infant industries and to force the South to engage in more trade with the North (not with Europe). Exceptions were made to the high level of tariffs for selected United States imports. These typically flowed from conditional most-favored-nation reciprocity treaties. The first of these treaties involved Canada (1854) and Hawaii (1875).

As the United States moved into the 20th Century, additional tariffs in excess of the already high level of protection were authorized. "Countervailing duty" tariffs were created in 1890 to combat export subsidies of European nations, particularly Germany. After 1916, additional duties could also be assessed if "dumping practices" were involved. Early American dumping legislation was largely a reaction to marketplace competition from foreign cartels. Throughout all of these years the constitutionality of protective tariffs was never clearly resolved. In 1928, however, the United States Supreme Court firmly ruled that the enactment of protective tariffs was constitutional.[1] This decision, followed by the crash of the stock market in 1929, led to the enactment of the Smoot–Hawley Tariff Act of 1930. This Act set some of the highest rates of tariff duties in the history of the United States. It represents the last piece of tariff legislation that Congress passed without international negotiations. These tariffs remain part of United States law and are generally referred to as "Column 2 tariffs" under the Harmonized Tariff Schedule (HTS).

Since 1930, changes in the levels of tariffs applicable to goods entering the United States have chiefly been achieved through international trade agreements negotiated by the President and affirmed by Congress. During the 1930s and 40s, the Smoot–Hawley tariffs generally applied unless altered through bilateral trade agreements. The Reciprocal Trade Agreements Act of 1934[2] gives the President the authority to enter into such agreements, and under various extensions this authority remains in effect today. An early agreement of this type was the Canadian Reciprocal Trade Agreement of 1935.

§ 10.3   Column 1 Tariffs and the GATT/WTO

The Trade Agreements Extension Act of 1945 authorized the President to conduct multilateral negotiations in the trade field. It was out of this authority that the General Agreement on Tariffs and Trade (GATT) was negotiated. The GATT became effective on January 1, 1948 and was implemented in the United States by executive order. Indeed, despite its wide-ranging impact on United States tariff levels since 1948, the GATT has never been ratified by the United States Congress. Nevertheless, it is the source of the principal tariffs assessed today on imports into the United States. These duties, known as most-favored-nation (MFN) tariffs or "Column 1 tariffs," have been dramatically reduced over the years through successive rounds of trade negotiations. They are unconditional MFN tariffs, meaning that reciprocity is not required in order for them to apply. Multilateral tariff agreements have predominated over bilateral negotiations since 1948.

The term "most-favored-nation" is misleading in its suggestion of special tariff arrangements. It is more appropriate and since 1998 officially correct to think of MFN tariffs as the normal level of U.S. tariffs, to which there are exceptions resulting in the application of

§ 10.2   2. 48 Stat. 943 (1934).
1. J.W. Hampton v. United States, 276
U.S. 394, 48 S.Ct. 348, 72 L.Ed. 624 (1928).

higher or lower tariffs. After the Tokyo Round of GATT negotiations in 1978, the average MFN tariff applied to manufactured imports into the United States was approximately 5.6 percent. Reductions in this level to approximately 3.5 percent have been accomplished under the Uruguay Round of 1994.

Tariff cuts on a wide range of information technology products were agreed to late in 1996. The United States, the European Union and most of East Asia agreed to abolish tariffs on computers, electrical capacitors, calculators, ATM's, fax and answering machines, digital copiers and video cameras, computer diskettes, CD–ROM drives, computer software, fiber optical cables and hundreds of other items by the year 2000. This agreement covers more than 90 percent of all information technology trade.

In early 1997, agreement on liberalizing trade and reducing tariffs on basic telecommunications equipment was reached by 69 nations. This agreement took effect Feb. 5, 1998. Later that year, a WTO declaration imposed standstill obligations on all members to continue to refrain from applying customs duties to electronic commerce while negotiations are underway for more permanent rules in this area.

§ 10.4 Column 2 Tariffs

Between 1948 and 1951 the United States granted Column 1 most-favored-nation tariff treatment to goods originating from virtually every part of the world. Commencing in 1951, goods originating in nations controlled by communists were withdrawn from such tariff treatment. This had, and to some degree continues to have, the effect of treating the importation of goods from communist nations under Column 2 United States tariff headings. As a practical matter, very few such imports can overcome the high Smoot–Hawley tariffs embodied in Column 2.

The designation of which nations are "communist" for these purposes has varied over time. Yugoslavia was generally not treated as a communist country and its goods therefore entered under Column 1 MFN tariffs. Goods from Slovenia, Croatia, Macedonia and Bosnia–Hercegovina presently do so as well. Central and Eastern European nations were sometimes treated as communist countries, particularly during the 1950s and 1960s. This is no longer the case, and at this point nearly every European and Baltic nation has been granted MFN status under United States tariff law. Belarus, Kazakhstan, Turkmenistan, Georgia, Azerbaijan, Tajikstan, Moldava, Kyrgyszstan, Armenia, Uzbekistan, the Russian Federation and Ukraine are also MFN beneficiaries. It is perhaps more useful, therefore, to indicate those nations that do not presently benefit from most-favored-nation tariff treatment. These include Cuba, Serbia, Afghanistan, Laos, and North Korea. Negotiations regarding MFN tariff status for goods from many of these nations are ongoing. Goods from some of these nations are totally embargoed as a matter of national security; the law in this area is covered in Chapter 8. The most current listing of those nations whose products are subject to Column 2 tariffs can be found in General Headnote 3(b) to the HTS.

§ 10.5　The Jackson–Vanik Amendment

Section 402 of the 1974 Trade Act presently governs American grants of most-favored-nation tariff status.[1]　This is commonly known as the "Jackson–Vanik Amendment."　Under its terms, no products from a nonmarket economy nation may receive MFN treatment, nor may that country participate in U.S. financial credit or guaranty programs, whenever the President determines that it denies its citizens the right or opportunity to emigrate, imposes more than nominal taxes on visas or other emigration documents, or imposes more than nominal charges on its citizens as a result of their desire to leave.　These statutory conditions are widely thought to have been the product of United States desires to have the Soviet Union permit greater exodus of its Jewish population during the early 1970s.　However, the passage of the Jackson–Vanik Amendment was an important factor in the Soviet decision to withdraw from a broad trade agreement with the United States at that time, and led to sharply curtailed Jewish emigration from the Soviet Union.

The application of Jackson–Vanik by the President is subject to a waiver by executive order whenever the President determines that such a waiver will substantially promote the objectives of freedom of emigration and the President has received assurances that the emigration practices of a particular nonmarket economy nation will lead substantially to the achievement of those objectives.　If the President decides to exercise this waiver authority, the waiver must be renewed annually and reported to Congress.　These reports and the exercise of presidential waivers have over the years been contentious.　At one point Congress had the power to veto presidential waivers under the Jackson–Vanik Amendment.　However, a 1983 decision of the United States Supreme Court strongly suggested that these veto powers were unconstitutional.[2]　The Customs and Trade Act of 1990 amended the Trade Act of 1974 so as to permit Congress to jointly resolve against presidential Jackson–Vanik waivers.　These resolutions can be vetoed by the President, and the President's veto can in turn by overridden by Congress.　It is thought that these amendments resolved the constitutional problems associated with Congressional vetoes of presidential action.

Congress and the President have disagreed significantly over the renewal of most-favored-nation treatment for Chinese goods.　Questions surrounding China's emigration policies, and its general human rights record, were downplayed by U.S. authorities for many years prior to Tiananmen Square.　As internal discord within China increased, especially in Tibet and more generally in connection with the Democracy

§ 10.5
1. 19 U.S.C.A. § 2432.

2. See Immigration and Naturalization Service v. Chadha, 462 U.S. 919, 103 S.Ct. 2764, 77 L.Ed.2d 317 (1983).

Movement, the Jackson–Vanik amendment came to the forefront of Sino–American trade relations. President Bush's renewal of China's most favored nation status in June of 1990, 1991 and 1992 was heavily criticized.

Jackson–Vanik has become the political fulcrum of Sino–American trade relations. Congress has threatened but not yet achieved a veto of the President's renewal of MFN tariffs for Chinese goods. Early in 1992, Congress adopted the United States-China Act of 1991. This law would have prohibited the President from recommending further extensions of MFN status to China unless he reports that the PRC has accounted for citizens detained or accused in connection with Tiananmen Square and has made significant progress in achieving specified objectives on human rights, trade and weapons proliferation. President Bush vetoed the Act and the Congress was unable to override that veto.

In 1993, President Clinton renewed China's MFN status subject to some general human-rights conditions, including "significant progress" in releasing political prisoners, allowing international groups access to prisons and respect for human rights in Tibet. This seemed to pacify Congress for the moment. But it engendered hostility and resistance in China. Less publicly, the United States business community opposed the linkage of human rights to MFN tariffs as its PRC trade and investment commitments and opportunities were endangered. China, meanwhile, had developed the world's fastest growing economy and it decided to force the issue. If anything, abuse of human rights in the PRC actually increased early in 1994, notably prior to a well-publicized visit of the U.S. Secretary of State. With Congress increasingly split on the issue, President Clinton made what will probably prove to be an historic reversal in policy. In June of 1994, he renewed China's MFN tariff status without human rights conditions, limiting its coverage only as regards Chinese-made ammunition and guns.

President Clinton renewed China's MFN tariff status each year after 1994. Congress did not seek to override these decisions. In 1998, for the first time, President Clinton waived the Jackson–Vanik requirements for Vietnam. This waiver survived Congressional scrutiny. It opens the door to EXIMBANK and OPIC programs, as well as Column 1 MFN tariffs on Vietnamese goods entering the United States.

Should China or Vietnam join the World Trade Organization, the Jackson-Vanik amendment will no longer apply. WTO members receive MFN tariff status automatically and unconditionally.

§ 10.6 Duty Free Entry

At the other end of the spectrum, some goods may enter the United States at less than most-favored-nation tariff levels or duty free. This occurs because of special tariff preferences incorporated into United States law. It is important to realize that these preferences create valuable trading opportunities for U.S. importers and exporters located in qualified nations. These people are the clients for whom lawyers work to secure duty free entry into the United States market.

Perhaps the widest of the duty free programs is known as the Generalized System of Preferences (GSP) adopted through the GATT. The GSP is a complex system of duty free tariff preferences benefiting selected goods originating in developing nations and intended to foster their economic improvement. Another way in which goods may enter the United States duty free is under the North American, Israeli or Canadian–U.S. Free Trade Agreements.[1] Duty free importation of goods from Israel will be complete by 1995 and from Canada by 1998. Most trade within North America will be duty free by 2003.

A third program is the Caribbean Basin Economic Recovery Act of 1983 (also known as the Caribbean Basin Initiative), which permits certain goods to enter the United States market duty free. To a significant degree, the CBI duty free program was duplicated in the Andean Trade Preference Act of 1991 benefiting Colombian, Ecuadorian, Bolivian and Peruvian goods. Another important "duty free" category allows fabricated U.S.-made components shipped abroad for assembly to return to the U.S. without tariffs on the value of the components. Authorization for this importation is found in Section 9802.00.80 of the Harmonized Tariff Schedule. Goods of this type are subject to a United States Customs duty limited in amount to the value added by foreign assembly operations. This provision is perhaps best known in connection with Mexican maquiladoras.

The least restrictive rules of origin for duty free entry of goods into the United States apply to its insular possessions. These include American Samoa, Guam, Johnson Island, Kingman Reef, Midway Islands, Puerto Rico, the U.S. Virgin Islands and Wake Island. Generally speaking, goods from such possessions may contain up to 70 percent foreign value and still be admitted duty free.[2]

Some of these duty free programs overlap and effectively compete with each other. It might be helpful to think of them in terms of concentric geographic circles. The widest circle is Section 9802.00.80 which applies to the entire globe. The next circle represents the GSP system and most developing nations. Inside that circle is the Caribbean Basin Initiative, the Andean Initiative, and U.S. insular possessions followed by the North American, Israeli and Canadian–U.S. Free Trade Area Agreements. A manufacturer based in the Caribbean may seek duty free entry into the United States market under Section 9802.00.80, the GSP program or the CBI, but not the North American, Israeli or Canadian agreements. To developing nations outside Israel, Mexico and the Caribbean, NAFTA, the CBI and the Israeli agreement are selectively discriminatory duty free programs that undermine their GSP benefits. Canada, of course, is not a developing nation so its goods would not otherwise qualify for duty free treatment in the absence of the free trade agreement.

Unusual trade opportunities can arise by linking U.S. duty free entry programs with those of the European Union (EU). For example, the Union has its own complicated and different GSP program, its equivalent of Section 9802.00.80, and two selective duty free programs for developing nations. The latter are known as its Mediterranean Policy and Lomé Conventions.[3] A producer in Israel can quite possibly gain duty free access to the EU (under its Mediterranean Policy) and to the United States (under the Israeli–U.S. FTA). A producer in Jamaica might achieve similar results under the Lomé Conventions, the CBI and/or the GSP programs of the EU and the United States.

§ 10.7 HTS Sample

A sample taken from the Harmonized Tariff Schedule of the United States is presented below. This sample facilitates an understanding of applicable United States tariffs. The customs duties payable in the United States will either be "most-favored-nation" tariffs (shown in the tariff schedule below under Rates of Duty, Column 1, General) or the much higher Smoot–Hawley Tariff Act of 1930 (Column 2). However, some goods may enter the U.S. at reduced tariff levels or duty free under the Caribbean Basin Initiative (symbol "E" in schedule below), the ANDEAN Trade Preference Act (symbol "J"), the Generalized System of Tariff Preferences ("GSP") (symbol "A"), the Canada (symbol "CA"), Israeli (symbol "IL") or North American (symbol "CA" for Canada, symbol "MX" for Mexico) Free Trade Agreements and other special laws. This preferred tariff treatment is indicated in the "Special" Column 1 Rates of Duty. Other goods benefiting from special treatment include automotive products (symbol "B") and civil aircraft (symbol "C").

HARMONIZED TARIFF SCHEDULE of the United States

Heading/ Subheading	Stat. Suf- fix	Article Description	Units of Quantity	Rates of Duty 1 General	Special	2
8507		Electric storage batteries, including separators therefor, whether or not rectangular (including square); parts thereof:				
8507.10.00		Lead-acid storage batteries, of a kind used for starting piston engines....................	....	5.3%	Free (A,B,C,E,IL,JMX) 2.1% (CA)	40%
	20	Used batteries, for recovery of metal	No. v kg			
		Other: 12 V batteries:				
	30	Not exceeding 6 kg in weight	No.			
	60	Exceeding 6 kg in weight.........	No.			
	90	Other	No.			
8507.20.00		Other lead-acid storage batteries............	....	5.3%	Free (A,B,C,E,IL,JMX) 2.1% (CA)	40%
	20	Used batteries, for recovery of metal	No. v kg			
		Other:				
	40	12 V batteries......................	No.			
	80	Other	No.			
8507.30.00		Nickel-cadmium storage batteries..........	....	5.1%	Free (A*,B,C,E,IL,JMX) 2% (CA)	40%

3. See generally, R. Folsom, European Union Law (West Group), Chapter 6.

	10	Sealed............................	No.			
	90	Other............................	No.			
8507.40.00	00	Nickel-iron storage batteries...............	No.	5.1%	Free (A,B,C,CA,E,IL,JMX)	40%
8507.80.00	00	Other storage batteries...................	No.	5.1%	Free (A,B,C,CA,E,IL,JMX)	40%
8507.90		Parts:				
8507.90.40	00	Of lead-acid storage batteries...........	X	5.3%	Free (A,B,C,E,IL,JMX) 2.1% (CA)	40%
8507.90.80	00	Other...............................	X	5.1%	Free (A,B,C,E,IL,JMX) 2% (CA)	40%

Exporters, importers and other interested parties may get advisory advance rulings on the dutiable status of merchandise by writing the Director of the port or customs district where the goods will be entered. The procedures applicable to such rulings are given in 19 C.F.R. Part 177. Binding decisions on dutiable status can be had from the Regional Commissioner, New York Region or the U.S. Customs Service in Washington, D.C. These decisions will not be changed at a later date so as to result in higher tariffs without advance notice and an opportunity to show reliance by the importer on the advance ruling.

B. FOREIGN TRADE ZONES AND BONDED WAREHOUSES

§ 10.8   Foreign Trade Zones

The United States has authorized the creation of numerous foreign trade zones.[1] These zones are typically established in enclosed areas near ports of entry into the United States. However, foreign trade zones are treated as being outside the customs territory of the United States.[2] They are subject to state and local public health, labor and other laws. But state regulations regarding food, drugs or cosmetics do not apply to goods transshipped through foreign trade zones.[3] Goods that are imported into a United States foreign trade zone receive different treatment depending on their status. Goods treated as "privileged foreign merchandise" are assessed tariffs according to their condition and quantity upon entry into the zone. This means that the tariff in effect at that time will apply.[4] However, although the goods are considered liquidated upon entry into the zone, the actual tariffs are not payable until the merchandise is later removed into the United States customs territory. This status thus has the advantage of securing an advance determination of the U.S. tariffs due. This determination will continue to be binding even if the goods are thereafter manufactured, processed or manipulated in the zone prior to entry into the United States customs

§ 10.8

1. 19 U.S.C.A. §§ 81a–81u. See 15 C.F.R. Part 400 (General regulations and rules of procedure); 19 C.F.R. Part 146 (General provisions); 19 C.F.R. Part 196 (Exportation and removals).

2. See Hawaiian Independent Refinery v. United States, 460 F.Supp. 1249 (Cust. Ct.1978).

3. 3M Health Care, Ltd. v. Grant, 908 F.2d 918 (11th Cir.1990).

4. But see Inter–Maritime Forwarding Co. v. United States, 192 F.Supp. 631 (Cust. Ct.1961) (tariff-rate quota merchandise may be subject to higher rates).

territory. This will be true even if the effect of such alterations is to change the ordinary tariff classification of a product.

Another status of goods entering U.S. foreign trade zones is that of "nonprivileged foreign merchandise." Goods of this kind are not tariffed until they leave the zone and enter the United States customs territory. Thus their value, condition and classification, as well as the applicable tariff, will be determined only at that later date. However, the value subject to U.S. tariffs as applied to nonprivileged merchandise does not include the cost of processing in the foreign trade zone, general expenses and profits attributable to zone operations, incidental expenses incurred in the zone such as packing, and freight, insurance and related costs.[5] Thus, to a very large degree, the value added in the foreign trade zone is exempt from United States tariffs. The privileged foreign merchandise and nonprivileged foreign merchandise statuses are the most prevalent in U.S. foreign trade zones. Other possible statuses include privileged domestic merchandise, nonprivileged domestic merchandise and zone-restricted merchandise.

Once goods have entered a United States foreign trade zone, they may be held in storage, exhibited, broken up, repackaged, distributed, sorted, graded, cleaned, mixed with foreign or domestic merchandise, assembled, manufactured or otherwise processed. Certain kinds of operations are prohibited in U.S. foreign trade zones. These include those relating to tobacco and liquor as would incur an excise tax in the United States, and retail sales (except with respect to domestic or duty paid or duty free goods).

There has been a substantial growth in the use of United States foreign trade zones. One reason for this is the ability to take advantage of differences in the United States tariff structure. For example, when a finished product is tariffed at a notably lower rate than the raw materials or components from which it is made, it can be quite desirable to bring those materials or components into a foreign trade zone and thereafter manufacture them into finished goods. In one case, for example, Japanese steel plates were brought into a foreign trade zone on a nonprivileged basis and manufactured into barges. Had the plates come into the U.S. Customs territory directly they would have been subject to a 7.5 percent tariff. Barges, on the other hand, are not subject to United States tariffs and therefore when they left the foreign trade zone they entered the United States on a duty free basis.[6] However, machinery imported into a foreign trade zone in order to process materials into finished goods is subject to U.S. tariff duties,[7] whereas foreign merchandise (namely oil) that is "consumed" inside an FTZ is not dutiable.[8]

5. See 19 C.F.R. § 146.48(e).

6. Armco Steel Corp. v. Stans, 431 F.2d 779 (2d Cir.1970).

7. Nissan Motor Mfg. Corp., U.S.A. v. United States, 693 F.Supp. 1183 (C.I.T.

1988), affirmed 884 F.2d 1375 (Fed.Cir. 1989).

8. Hawaiian Independent Refinery v. United States, 460 F.Supp. 1249 (Cust.Ct. 1978).

Another advantage of foreign trade zones is that United States import quotas do not apply. Thus, if an import quota is about to be reached, goods can be put into a foreign trade zone for storage until the next quota period and thereafter entered into the United States Customs territory. Goods from nonmarket economies ordinarily subject to Column 2 United States tariffs can be brought into a foreign trade zone and if they undergo substantial transformation may emerge in the form of a product that will be tariffed at the lower Column 1 rate.[9]

A very large percentage of the goods processed in United States foreign trade zones are automotive products. This is the case despite the historical intent that foreign trade zones were to benefit exporters rather than importers. Foreign trade zones are established by approval of the Foreign Trade Zones Board, an interagency committee composed of the Secretaries of Commerce, Treasury and the Army or their designees.[10] The Board may prohibit or restrict any FTZ proposal if it is deemed detrimental to the public interest, health or safety.[11] It has done so reasonably often when proposed zones conflict with powerful domestic lobbies (steel, textiles, sugar). In addition to general purpose FTZ, subzones designed specifically for use by a single firm are possible.[12]

§ 10.9 Bonded Warehouses

Temporary duty free importation of goods into the U.S. can also be achieved through bonded warehouses for a maximum of five years. The goods may be stored, cleaned, packed, manipulated or manufactured in such warehouses. Customs Service regulations authorize eight varieties of bonded warehouses.[1] Tariffs are paid when the goods are withdrawn for consumption in the United States at the rate then applicable. Manipulation of the goods in a warehouse to achieve a different tariff classification is allowed. No duties need be paid if the goods are exported, supplied to international vessels or aircraft or destroyed under Customs Service supervision. Goods held in customs-bonded warehouses are exempt from state and local personal property taxes.[2] Applications to establish bonded warehouses are processed through district Customs Service directors. Extensive record-keeping requirements apply.[3]

C. THE U.S. GENERALIZED SYSTEM
OF PREFERENCES (GSP)

§ 10.10 Statutory Authorization

The Generalized System of Preferences (GSP) originated in United Nations dialogues between the developed and the developing world.

---

9. See Chinese Chemicals, Customs Service Decision 79–41.

10. See 15 C.F.R. Part 400.

11. 19 U.S.C.A. § 81o.

12. See Armco Steel Corp. v. Stans, 303 F.Supp. 262 (S.D.N.Y.1969), affirmed 431 F.2d 779 (2d Cir.1970).

§ 10.9

1. See 19 C.F.R. § 19.1.

2. Xerox Corp. v. County of Harris, 459 U.S. 145, 103 S.Ct. 523, 74 L.Ed.2d 323 (1982).

3. See 19 C.F.R. § 19.12.

The third world successfully argued that it needed special access to industrial markets in order to improve and advance their economies. One problem with this approach is that it is contrary to the unconditional most-favored-nation principle contained in the GATT. Nevertheless, in 1971 the GATT authorized its parties to establish generalized systems of tariff preferences for developing nations. The European Union, Japan and nearly all other developed nations adopted GSP systems before the United States. Although similar in purpose, each of these systems is governed by a unique body of law of the "donor" country.

It was not until the Trade Act of 1974 that a GSP system was incorporated into United States tariff law. The Trade Act authorized GSP tariff preferences for ten years. The program was renewed in the Trade Act of 1984 for an additional nine years ending in July 1993. Incremental extensions have since been made pending a program review. At this point, tens of billions of dollars worth of goods enter the U.S. market duty free under the GSP program, but it is estimated that more imports could achieve this status if traders better understood the GSP.

Title V of the Trade Act of 1974 contains the provisions authorizing the United States GSP program.[1] The United States GSP system, as presently operated, designates certain nations as "beneficiary developing countries." Unless a country is so designated, none of its imports can enter duty free under the GSP program. In addition, only selected goods are designated "eligible articles" for purposes of the GSP program. Thus, for duty free entry under the GSP program to occur, the goods must originate from a beneficiary nation and qualify as eligible articles.

§ 10.11 USTR Petition Procedures

Any United States producer of an article that competes with GSP imports can file a petition with the United States Trade Representative (USTR) to have a country or particular products withdrawn from the program. This petitioning procedure can also be used in the reverse by importers and exporters to obtain product or beneficiary country status under the United States GSP program. The President is given broad authority to withdraw, suspend or limit the application of duty free entry under the GSP system.[1] Specific products from specific countries may be excluded from GSP benefits. In one case, for example, the President's decision to withdraw GSP benefits for "buffalo leather and goat and kid leather (not fancy)" from India was affirmed.[2] In another decision, the President's discretionary authority to deny GSP benefits to cut flowers from Colombia was similarly upheld.[3]

§ 10.10
1. 19 U.S.C.A. §§ 501–506.

§ 10.11
1. See 19 U.S.C.A. § 2464(a).

2. Florsheim Shoe Co. v. United States, 744 F.2d 787 (Fed.Cir.1984).

3. Sunburst Farms, Inc. v. United States, 797 F.2d 973 (Fed.Cir.1986).

The President is required to take into consideration the impact of duty free entry on U.S. producers of like or directly competitive products. There is a set of regulations, codified at 15 C.F.R. Part 2007 and reproduced in part in Section 10.26 of this chapter, which details the petitioning procedures used in connection with the certification of GSP eligible products or countries. These regulations require the domestic competitor to cite injury caused by duty free GSP imports. Within 6 months after the petition is filed, and a review by the United States Trade Representative (USTR) acting with the advice of the International Trade Commission (ITC) has been undertaken, a decision on the petition will be rendered by the USTR.

§ 10.12   Competitive Need Limitations

There are two statutory limitations on the applicability of duty free GSP entry. These are known as the "competitive need" limitations. They are found in Section 504 of the Trade Act of 1974, codified at 19 U.S.C.A. § 2464(c). The first statutory limitation focuses upon dollar volumes. Duty free entry is not permitted to any eligible product from a beneficiary country if during the preceding year that country exported to the United States more than a designated dollar volume of the article in question. There is a statutory formula for establishing this dollar volume limitation. In recent years, the maximum dollar volume limitation has ranged between 75 and 80 million dollars. The second statutory limitation on duty free GSP entry is framed in terms of percentages. Duty free entry is denied to products if during the preceding year the beneficiary country exported to the United States 50 percent or more of the total U.S. imports of that particular product.[1]

A complex system of waivers applies to the competitive need formulae. These are administered by the USTR and the President acting on advice of the International Trade Commission.[2] Basically, there are five possibilities for waivers of the competitive need limitations. The first can occur if the President decides that there is no like or directly competitive article produced in the United States and the imported product is exempt from the percentage but not the dollar value competitive need limitation. The second can occur under circumstances where the President determines that the imports in question are de minimis. The third possibility involves imports from the least developed developing nations, after notice to Congress. A list of these countries can be found in HTS General Note 3(c)(ii)(B) reproduced in Section 10.25. A fourth opportunity for a competitive need waiver exists when there has been an historical preferential trade relationship between the United States and the source country, and there is a trade agreement between that country and the United States, and the source country does not

§ **10.12**

1. See West Bend Co. v. United States, 10 Court of International Trade 146 (1986) (competitive impact still must be proven).

2. See 19 U.S.C.A. § 2464(c).

discriminate against or otherwise impose unjustifiable or unreasonable barriers to United States commerce.

Lastly, the President is authorized to waive the competitive need requirements of the GSP program if the International Trade Commission decides that the imports in question are not likely to have an adverse effect on the United States industry with which they compete, and the President determines that such a waiver is in the national economic interest.[3] In making waiver determinations, the President must consider generally the extent to which the beneficiary country has assured the United States that it will provide equitable and reasonable access to its markets and basic commodity resources. The President must also consider the extent to which the country provides adequate and effective means for foreigners to secure and exercise intellectual property rights. Once a waiver of the competitive need limitations is granted, it remains in effect until circumstances change and the President decides that it is no longer justified. Attorneys can play a useful role in monitoring Department of Commerce trade statistics to determine how close imports are coming under the competitive need formulae to restriction. By shifting to purchases of similar goods from another country, importers can preserve duty free entry and avoid the affects of these statutory restraints.

§ 10.13 Country Eligibility

At present, thousands of products from over one hundred countries benefit from duty free GSP entry into the United States.[1] A list of GSP qualified nations and territories is presented in HTS General Note 3(c)(ii) reproduced in Section 10.25. Goods from insular possessions of the United States (e.g., American Samoa and the U.S. Virgin Islands) ordinarily receive duty free GSP entry "no less favorable" than allowed GSP beneficiary nations.[2] The President's power over the list of eligible countries and eligible products is wide and politically sensitive. For example, the President is required to evaluate, in determining whether a country is eligible under the U.S. GSP program, if it is upholding "internationally recognized workers' rights." Such rights include the right of association, the right to organize and bargain collectively, a prohibition against forced or compulsory labor, a minimum age for employment of children, and acceptable working conditions (minimum wages, hours of work, and occupational safety and health.)[3] The President must report annually to the Congress on the status of internationally recognized workers' rights in every GSP beneficiary country, but the issue is not open to private challenge.[4]

3. See 19 U.S.C.A. § 2464(c)(3)(A).

§ 10.13

1. See Executive Order 11888 (Nov. 24, 1975, 40 F.R. 55276, extensively amended, for a detailed listing of eligible products and countries).

2. 19 U.S.C.A. § 2462(d).

3. 19 U.S.C.A. 2462(a).

4. See International Labor Rights Education & Research Fund v. Bush, 752 F.Supp. 495 (D.D.C.1990), affirmed 954 F.2d 745 (D.C.Cir.1992).

The President must also consider whether the foreign country is adequately protecting United States owners of intellectual property, (compliance with TRIPs is not necessarily sufficient), and whether its investment laws adversely affect U.S. exports. In addition, when designating GSP beneficiary nations, the Trade Act requires the President to take into account various factors which amount to a U.S. agenda on international economic relations during the 1990s:

(1) the desires of the country;

(2) its level of economic development;

(3) whether the EU, Japan or others extend GSP treatment to it;

(4) the extent to which the country provides equitable and reasonable access to its markets and its basic commodity resources, and the extent to which it will refrain from unreasonable export practices;

(5) the extent to which it provides adequate and effective intellectual property rights; and

(6) the extent to which it has taken action to reduce trade distorting investment practices (including export performance requirements) and reduced barriers to trade in services.[5]

No communist nations and no oil restraining OPEC nations (Indonesia, Ecuador and Venezuela are excepted) may benefit from the GSP program. Furthermore, the President must not designate countries that grant trade preferences to other *developed* nations. The President must also consider, in making GSP decisions, whether beneficiary countries are cooperative on drug enforcement, whether they are expropriators of U.S. property interests, whether they offer assistance to terrorists, and whether they are willing to recognize international arbitration awards. The President may waive the expropriation requirement if it is determined that the country in question has paid prompt, adequate and effective compensation or entered into good faith negotiations or arbitration with the intent to do so.

The statutory bar against communist, oil restricting OPEC and preferentially trading countries as GSP beneficiaries is absolute. The bar against expropriating, drug dealing, arbitration award unenforcement, terrorist aiding and workers rights nonrecognition beneficiaries is discretionary with the President. The goods of such nations may still qualify if the President determines that GSP duty free entry would be in the national economic interest of the United States.[6] In applying these country eligibility criteria, past Presidents have disqualified a variety of nations from the U.S. GSP program. For example, Romania, Nicaragua, Paraguay, Chile, Burma, the Central African Republic and Liberia have all been disqualified in the past for failure to meet the workers' rights standards. Argentina and Honduras have lost GSP benefits for perceived failures to adequately protect U.S. pharmaceutical patents. Pana-

5. 19 U.S.C.A. § 2462(c).   6. 19 U.S.C.A. § 2462(b).

ma under General Noriega was rendered ineligible in 1988 because of the failure to cooperate on narcotics. The President's review of a country's eligibility under the GSP program is ongoing. This has led to the reinstatement of GSP beneficiary nations. Russia was made a GSP beneficiary by President Clinton in the Fall of 1993. Any country designated as a beneficiary nation under the GSP program that is subsequently disqualified by exercise of Presidential discretion, or graduated, must receive 60 days notice from the President with an explanation of this decision.[7] This, in effect, presents the opportunity to reply and negotiate.

Since the GSP program originated within the GATT/WTO nearly all the beneficiary countries are members of that organization. It is not, however, mandatory for a developing nation to be a member of the WTO in order to receive GSP trade benefits from the United States. Because China is not yet a WTO member, and for other reasons, its goods do not qualify for GSP duty free entry. Other nations whose goods are not eligible are specifically listed in the Trade Act: Australia, Austria, Canada, European Union States, Finland, Iceland, Japan, Monaco, New Zealand, Norway, Republic of South Africa, Sweden, and Switzerland.[8]

§ 10.14 Product Eligibility

For each designated GSP beneficiary country, the President also issues a list of products from that country that qualify for duty free entry into the United States. The statutory authorization for the United States GSP program generally excludes leather products, textiles and apparel,[1] watches,[2] selected electronics and, certain steel, footwear and categories of glass from being designated as eligible articles.[3] All these goods are thought to involve particular "import sensitivity."

The UNCTAD Certificate of Origin Form A is ordinarily required of the foreign exporter when GSP eligible merchandise is involved. A complex body of "rules of origin" determine where goods are from for purposes of the United States GSP program. Basically, for goods to originate in a beneficiary country, at least 35 percent of the appraised value of those goods must be added in that nation.[4] The statutory rules of origin for GSP eligible goods are found in 19 U.S.C.A. § 2463(b).[5] A federal Circuit Court of Appeals has ruled that a "two-stage" substantial transformation process must also occur in order to qualify goods for GSP

---

7. 19 U.S.C.A. § 2462(a).

8. 19 U.S.C.A. § 2462(b).

§ 10.14

1. See Luggage and Leather Goods Mfrs. of America, Inc. v. United States, 588 F.Supp. 1413 (C.I.T.1984) (man-made fiber flat goods are textile and apparel articles).

2. See North American Foreign Trading Corp. v. United States, 600 F.Supp. 226 (C.I.T.1984), affirmed 783 F.2d 1031 (Fed. Cir.1986) (exemption for watches includes solid-state digital watches).

3. 19 U.S.C.A. § 2463(c).

4. See Madison Galleries, Ltd. v. United States, 870 F.2d 627 (Fed.Cir.1989).

5. 19 U.S.C.A. § 2463(b). Eligible articles qualifying for duty-free treatment:

(b)(1) The duty-free treatment provided under section 501 shall apply to any eligible article which is the growth, product, or manufacture of a beneficiary developing country if—

(A) that article is imported directly from a beneficiary developing country

purposes.[6] Thus, the value of U.S.-grown corn did not count towards meeting the 35 percent requirement because the intermediate products into which it was turned did not qualify as Mexican in origin for lack of substantial transformation into a new and different article of commerce.[7] But the assembly of integrated circuits in Taiwan from slices containing many integrated circuit chips, gold wire, lead frame strips, molding compound and epoxy (all of which were U.S. in origin) did constitute a substantial transformation of such items into a new article of commerce. Thus the circuits could be deemed from Taiwan for purposes of the 35 percent value added GSP rule.[8]

One unusual feature of the rules of origin for the United States GSP program is that which favors selected regional economic groups. Goods made in the ANDEAN pact, ASEAN or CARICOM may be designated as "one country" for purposes of origin. So too may goods produced in the East African Community, the West African Economic and Monetary Union and the Southern African Development Community. This means that the value added requirement as applied in these regions is met if 35 percent of the value added has been created inside each group as opposed to inside any one nation of the group. It is notable that many other third world regional economic groups are not similarly treated, e.g. the Central American Common Market, MERCOSUR, and the Gulf Council of the Middle East.

§ 10.15   Graduation

As nations develop, U.S. law either bars their participation in the GSP program absolutely or vests discretion in the President to remove

into the customs territory of the United States; and

(B) the sum of (i) the cost or value of the materials produced in the beneficiary developing country or any 2 or more countries which are members of the same association of countries which is treated as one country under section 502(a)(3), plus (ii) the direct costs of processing operations performed in such beneficiary developing country or such member countries is not less than 35 percent of the appraised value of such article at the time of its entry into the customs territory of the United States.

(2) The Secretary of the Treasury, after consulting with the United States Trade Representative, shall prescribe such regulations as may be necessary to carry out this subsection, including, but not limited to, regulations providing that, in order to be eligible for duty-free treatment under this title, an article must be wholly the growth, product, or manufacture of a beneficiary developing country, or must be a new or different article of commerce which has been grown, produced, or manufactured in

the beneficiary developing country; but no article or material of a beneficiary developing country shall be eligible for such treatment by virtue of having merely undergone—

(A) simple combining or packaging operations, or

(B) mere dilution with water or mere dilution with another substance that does not materially alter the characteristics of the article.

6. See Torrington Company v. United States, 764 F.2d 1563 (Fed.Cir.1985). See generally Cutler, United States Generalized System of Preferences: the Problem of Substantial Transformation, 5 North Carolina Journal of International Law & Commercial Regulation, 393 (1980).

7. Azteca Mill. Co. v. United States, 890 F.2d 1150 (Fed.Cir.1989).

8. Texas Instruments Inc. v. United States, 681 F.2d 778 (C.C.P.A.1982). See Madison Galleries, Ltd. v. United States, 688 F.Supp. 1544 (C.I.T.1988) (blank porcelain from Taiwan substantially transformed when painted and fired in Hong Kong).

nations or products from its scope. Since 1984, developing nations with a per capita gross national product in excess of $8,500 are totally ineligible for GSP duty free entry. The Bahamas, Bahrain, Brunei, Israel, Nauru and Bermuda have been disqualified under this rule. In addition, the President has a broad authority to "graduate" countries from the United States GSP program. The basic concept here is that certain nations are sufficiently developed so as to not need the benefits of duty free entry into the United States market. Discretionary graduation is based on an assessment of the economic development level of the beneficiary country, the competitive position of the imports and the overall national economic interests of the United States.[1]

In recent years, Presidents have been graduating more and more products from countries like India and Brazil. In January of 1989, President Reagan graduated all products from Hong Kong, Singapore, South Korea and Taiwan. At that time, these countries were the source of about 60 percent of all goods benefiting from the United States GSP program. Mexico then emerged as the chief beneficiary country under the program until late in 1993 when all of its products were removed from the GSP treatment in anticipation of the North American Free Trade Agreement. In 1997, President Clinton graduated Malaysia entirely from the GSP program.

§ 10.16 Judicial and Administrative Remedies

Legal challenges to presidential revocations of duty free GSP treatment were originally filed with the U.S. Customs Court. This was the case despite contentions of inadequate legal remedies in that court and the fact that plaintiff could not pursue class action relief except in federal district court.[1] Litigation involving the GSP program is now commenced in the U.S. Court of International Trade.

The goods entering the United States duty free through the GSP program remain subject to the possibility of escape clause relief under Section 201 of the Trade Act of 1974.[2] Moreover, such goods may also be restrained pursuant to Section 232 of the Trade Expansion Act of 1962 in the name of the national security of the United States.[3] These protective trade remedies are discussed in other chapters.[4]

D. CARIBBEAN BASIN INITIATIVE, ANDEAN AND AFRICAN TRADE PREFERENCES

§ 10.17 Introduction

The European Union has had for many years a policy which grants substantial duty free entry into its market for goods originating in

§ 10.15

1. See 47 Fed.Reg. 31,099, 31,000 (July 16, 1982).

§ 10.16

1. Barclay Industries, Inc. v. Carter, 494 F.Supp. 912 (D.D.C.1980).

2. See 19 U.S.C.A. § 2251.

3. See 19 U.S.C.A. § 2463(c)(2).

4. See Chapters 8 and 9.

Mediterranean Basin countries. The United States has duplicated this approach for the Caribbean Basin. This is accomplished through the Caribbean Basin Economic Recovery Act of 1983.[1] For these purposes, the Caribbean Basin is broadly defined to include nearly all of the islands in that Sea, and a significant number of Central and South American nations bordering the Caribbean. So defined, there are 28 nations which could qualify for purposes of the United States Caribbean Basin Initiative. As with the GSP program, the Caribbean Basin Initiative (CBI) involves presidential determinations to confer beneficiary status upon any of these eligible countries. However, unlike the GSP, there are no presidential determinations as to which specific products of these countries shall be allowed into the United States on a duty free basis. All Caribbean products except those excluded by statute are eligible. Moreover, there are no "competitive need" or annual per capita income limits under the CBI. Lastly, unlike the GSP program which must be renewed periodically, the Caribbean Basin Initiative is a permanent part of the U.S. tariff system.

The United States has maintained a steady trade surplus with Caribbean Basin countries. Leading export items under the CBI are typically beef, raw cane sugar, medical instruments, cigars, fruits and rum. The leading source countries have often been the Dominican Republic, Costa Rica and Guatemala. The value of all CBI duty free imports now exceeds $1 billion annually, but the CBI countries fear a diversion of trade and investment to Mexico as the North American Free Trade Agreement (NAFTA) matures.

§ 10.18 CBI Country Eligibility

The President is forbidden from designating Caribbean Basin Initiative beneficiaries if they are communist, have engaged in expropriation activities, nullified contracts or intellectual property rights of the U.S. citizens, failed to recognize and enforce arbitral awards, given preferential treatment to products of another developed nation, broadcast through a government-owned entity United States copyrighted material without consent, failed to sign a treaty or other agreement regarding extradition of United States citizens, failed to cooperate on narcotics enforcement, or failed to afford internationally recognized workers rights. For these purposes, the definition of workers rights enacted in connection with the GSP program applies.[1] Since 2000, CBI countries must also show a commitment to implementing WTO pledges.

These prohibitions notwithstanding, the President can still designate a Caribbean Basin country as a beneficiary if he or she determines that this will be in the national economic or security interest of the

§ 10.17

1. Public Law 98–67, 97 Stat. 384 codified at 19 U.S.C.A. § 2701 et seq.

§ 10.18

1. See text at Note 3, § 4.13, supra.

United States. However, this can be done only in connection with countries that are disqualified as being communist, expropriators, contract or intellectual property nullifiers, nonenforcers of arbitral awards, unauthorized broadcasters, or those who fail to provide for internationally recognized workers rights. Thus, if a Caribbean nation is disqualified because it grants preferential trade treatment to products of another developed nation or refuses to sign an extradition treaty with the United States, there is no possibility of its designation as a beneficiary nation under the Caribbean Basin Initiative. As with the GSP statutory requirements, if the basis for the disqualification is expropriation or nullification of benefits, the President may override this disqualification if that nation is engaged in payment of prompt, adequate and effective compensation or good faith negotiations intended to lead to such compensation.

In addition, the President is required to take various factors into account in designating beneficiary countries under the Caribbean Basin Initiative. These include:

(1) the desire of that country to participate;

(2) the economic conditions and living standards of that nation;

(3) the extent to which the country has promised to provide equitable and reasonable access to its markets and basic commodity resources;

(4) the degree to which it follows accepted GATT rules on international trade;

(5) the degree to which it uses export subsidies or imposes export performance requirements or local content requirements which distort international trade;

(6) the degree to which its trade policies help revitalize the region;

(7) the degree to which it is undertaking self-help measures to promote its own economic development;

(8) whether it has taken steps to provide internationally recognized workers rights;

(9) the extent to which it provides adequate and effective means for foreigners to secure and enforce exclusive intellectual property rights;

(10) the extent to which the country prohibits unauthorized broadcasts of copyrighted material belonging to U.S. owners; and

(11) the extent to which it is prepared to cooperate with the United States in connection with the Caribbean Basin Initiative, particularly by signing a tax information exchange agreement.

Under these criteria, the President has designated a large number of the 28 eligible nations as beneficiary countries under the Caribbean Basin Initiative. These include Antigua and Barbuda, Aruba, the Bahamas, Barbados, Belize, the British Virgin Islands, Costa Rica, Dominica, the Dominican Republic, El Salvador, Grenada, Guatemala, Guinea, Haiti, Honduras, Jamaica, Monserrat, the Netherlands Antilles, Nicaragua, Panama, St. Christopher–Nevis, St. Lucia, St. Vincent and the Grenadines, and Trinidad and Tobago. The nations not designated as beneficiary countries under the Caribbean Basin Initiative to date include Anguilla, Suriname, the Cayman Islands and the Turks and Caicos Islands. Cuba is not even listed among the nations eligible for consideration in connection with the Caribbean Basin Initiative.

U.S. Presidents have typically required of each potential beneficiary a concise written presentation of its policies and practices directly related to the issues raised by the country designation criteria listed in the Caribbean Basin Economic Recovery Act. Wherever measures were in effect which were inconsistent with the objectives of these criteria, U.S. presidents have sought assurances that such measures would be progressively eliminated or modified. For example, the Dominican Republic promised to take steps to reduce the degree of book piracy and the Jamaican and Bahamian governments promised to stop the unauthorized broadcast of U.S. films and television programs.[2]

§ 10.19　CBI Product Eligibility

Unless specifically excluded, all products of Caribbean Basin nations are eligible for duty free entry into the United States market. Certain goods are absolutely excluded from such treatment.[1] These include footwear, canned tuna, petroleum and petroleum derivatives, watches, and certain leather products. It should be noted that this listing of "import sensitive" products is different from but overlaps with that used in connection with the United States GSP program. Since 2000, products ineligible for CBI benefits enter at reduced tariff levels corresponding to Mexican goods under NAFTA . . . so-called "NAFTA parity".

One of the most critical of the products that may enter the United States on a duty free basis is sugar. But the President is given the authority to suspend duty free treatment for both sugar and beef products originating in the Caribbean Basin or to impose quotas in order to protect United States domestic price support programs for these products.[2] Sugar exports have traditionally been critical to many Caribbean Basin economies. Nevertheless, sugar import quotas into the United States from the Caribbean have been steadily reduced in recent years. For example, by 1988 the sugar quota allocations for some CBI countries reached a low of 25 percent of their 1983 pre-Caribbean Basin Initiative allocations.[3] Many consider the few duty free import benefits obtained under the Initiative to be more than counterbalanced by the loss in sugar exports to the United States market.

2. 19 U.S.C.A. § 2702.

§ 10.19

1. See 19 U.S.C.A. § 2703(b).

2. 19 U.S.C.A. § 2073(c) and (d).

3. See Fox, Interaction of the Caribbean Basin Initiative and U.S. Domestic Sugar Price Support: A Political Contradiction, 8 Mississippi College Law Review 197 (1988).

The rules of origin for determining product eligibility in connection with the Caribbean Basin Initiative are virtually the same as discussed previously under the GSP.[4] As a general rule, a substantial transformation must occur and a 35 percent value added requirement is imposed (but 15 percent may come from the United States). This percentage is calculated by adding the sum of the cost or value of the materials produced in the beneficiary country or two or more beneficiary countries plus the direct cost of processing operations performed in those countries.[5] It should be noted that this approach effectively treats all of the CBI-eligible nations as a regional beneficiary since the 35 percent required value can be cumulated among them.

As under the GSP program, the President is given broad powers to suspend duty free treatment with reference to any eligible product or any designated beneficiary country.[6] Import injury relief under Section 201 of the Trade Act of 1974 can be invoked in connection with Caribbean Basin imports. And the equivalent of that relief is authorized specifically for agricultural imports upon similar determinations by the Secretary of Agriculture.[7] The effects of these protective proceedings may be diminished in the context of Caribbean Basin imports. Whenever the International Trade Commission is studying whether increased imports are a substantial cause of serious injury to a domestic industry under Section 201 or its agricultural equivalent, the ITC is required to break out the Caribbean Basin beneficiary countries. The President is given the discretion if he or she decides to impose escape clause relief to suspend that relief relative to Caribbean Basin imports. A similar discretion is granted to the President in connection with national security import restraints under Section 232 of the Trade Expansion Act of 1962. However, these discretionary provisions relate only to those goods that are eligible for duty free entry under the Caribbean Basin Initiative.[8]

In 1986, President Reagan initiated a special program for textiles produced in the Caribbean. Essentially, this program increases the opportunity to sell Caribbean textile products when the fabric involved has been previously formed and cut in the United States. If this is the case, there are minimum guaranteed access levels that are different from those quotas which traditionally apply under the Multi–Fiber Arrangement. This program is run in conjunction with Section 9802.00.80 of the Harmonized Tariff Schedule of the United States.[9]

The U.S.–Caribbean Basin Trade Partnership Act of 2000 grants duty-free and quota-free access to the U.S. market for apparel made from U.S. fabric and yarn. Apparel made from CBI fabric is capped for duty free into the United States. CBI textiles and apparel are subject to market surge safeguards comparable to those under NAFTA.

4. See HTS General Note 3(c)(v).

5. 19 U.S.C.A. § 2703(a).

6. 19 U.S.C.A. § 2702(e).

7. 19 U.S.C.A. § 2703(f).

8. See 29 U.S.C.A. § 2703(e).

9. See 51 Fed.Reg. 21,208 (June 11, 1986).

§ 10.20   Andean Trade Preferences

The Andean Trade Preference Act (ATPA) of 1991 [1] authorizes the President to grant duty free treatment to imports of eligible articles from Colombia, Peru, Bolivia and Ecuador. Venezuela is not included as a beneficiary country under this Act. The Andean Trade Preference Act is patterned after the Caribbean Basin Economic Recovery Act of 1983. Goods that ordinarily enter duty free into the United States from Caribbean Basin nations will also enter duty free from these four Andean countries. The same exceptions and exclusions discussed above in connection with the Caribbean Basin Initiative generally apply. However, while the CBI is a permanent part of United States Customs law, the ATPA is only authorized initially for a period of ten years. Furthermore, the guaranteed access levels for Caribbean Basin textile products, separate cumulation for antidumping and countervailing duty investigations, and the waiver of the Buy American Act for procurement purposes are not authorized by the ATPA. Broadly speaking, the passage of the ATPA represents fulfillment of the elder President Bush's commitment to assist these nations economically in return for their help in containing narcotics.

§ 10.21   African Trade Preferences

The Africa Growth and Opportunity Act of 2000 (Public Law No. 106-200, 114 Stat. 252) granted duty-free and quota-free access to the U.S. market for apparel made from U.S. fabric and yarn. Apparel made from African fabric is capped for duty free entry. The least developed sub-Saharan countries enjoy duty-free and quota-free apparel access regardless of the origin of the fabric.

The Act also altered U.S. GSP rules to admit certain previously excluded African products on a duty-free basis, including petroleum, watches and flat goods. Sub–Saharan countries can export almost all products duty-free to the United States. These countries are encouraged to create a free trade area with U.S. support.

African exports are subject to import surge (escape clause) protection and stringent rules against transshipments between countries for purposes of taking advantage of U.S. trade benefits.

E.   GOODS INCORPORATING UNITED STATES COMPONENTS

§ 10.22   Section 9802.00.80 of the HTS

Section 9802.00.80 of the Harmonized Tariff Schedule of the United States (formerly Section 807.00 of the Tariff Schedule of the United States) is an unusual "duty free" provision. This section allows for the

§ 10.20   § 3201 et seq.
1. Public Law 102–82, 19 U.S.C.A.

duty free importation of United States fabricated components that were exported ready for assembly abroad. If qualified, goods assembled abroad containing U.S. components are subject only to a duty upon the value added through foreign assembly operations. In order for this to be the case, Section 9802.00.80 requires that the components be fabricated and a product of the United States, that they be exported in a condition ready for assembly without further fabrication, that they not lose their physical identity by change in form, shape or otherwise, and that they not be advanced in value or improved in condition abroad except by being assembled and except by operations incidental to the assembly process such as cleaning, lubricating and painting.

The regulations issued in connection with Section 9802.00.80 indicate that there are other incidental operations which will not disqualify components from duty free re-entry into the United States. These include removing rust, grease, paint or other preservative coatings, the application of similar preservative coatings, the trimming or other removal of small amounts of excess material, adjustments in the shape or form of a component required by the assembly that is being undertaken, the cutting to length of wire, thread, tape, foil or similar products, the separation by cutting of finished components (such as integrated circuits exported in strips), and the calibration, testing, marking, sorting, pressing and folding and assembly of the final product.[1] In contrast, the regulations also provide examples of operations that are not considered incidental to assembly for these purposes. These examples include the melting of ingots to produce cast metal parts, the cutting of garments according to patterns, painting which is intended to enhance the appearance or impart distinctive features to the product, chemical treatment so as to realize new characteristics (such as moisture-proofing), and the machining, polishing or other treatment of metals which create significant new characteristics or qualities.[2]

If all of the Section 9802.00.80 criteria are met, the tariff that will be assessed upon the imported assembled product will be limited to a duty upon the full value of that product less the cost or value of U.S. made components that have been incorporated into it.[3] Those who seek to take advantage of Section 9802.00.80 must provide the United States Customs Service with a Foreign Assembler's Declaration and Certification. This is known as Form 3317. The assembly plant operator certifies that the requirements of Section 9802.00.80 are met, and the importer declares that this certification is correct. Billions of dollars of ordinarily tariffed value have been excluded as a result of this Customs law provision. Motor vehicles, semiconductors, office machines, textiles and apparel, and furniture are good examples of the kinds of products assembled abroad with fabricated U.S. components so as to meet the requirements of Section 9802.00.80. Historically, many of these prod-

---

§ 10.22

1. 19 C.F.R. § 10.16(b).

2. 19 C.F.R. § 10.16(c).

3. See generally 19 C.F.R. § 10.14 et seq.

ucts have been assembled in Japan, Germany or Canada. In more recent times, the assembly operations to which Section 9802.00.80 frequently applies have more commonly been found in the developing world.

§ 10.23 Mexican Maquiladoras

Section 9802.00.80 is applicable to goods imported into the United States from anywhere in the world. However, it is most frequently associated and used in connection with Mexican maquiladoras. Maquiladoras are "in-bond" assembly plants located in Mexico that often take advantage of the duty free potential of Section 9802.00.80. Maquiladoras have enjoyed a phenomenal popularity since 1982 when the Mexican peso was dramatically devalued. This had the practical effect of rendering Mexican labor costs lower than those of Taiwan, Hong Kong, Singapore and South Korea. These Asian nations were traditionally low-cost assembly plant centers. Since 1982, thousands of maquiladoras have been established in Tijuana, Ciudad Juarez, Neuvo Laredo and other border cities. They provide Mexico with hundreds of thousands of jobs and are a major source of foreign currency earnings. Electronics, apparel, toys, medical supplies, transport equipment, furniture and sporting goods are examples of the types of industries that have been attracted south of the border. United States components, when assembled in maquiladoras and qualifying under Section 9802.00.80, are exported and then reimported on a duty free basis.

The maquiladora industry has enjoyed explosive growth. Mexican law, like Section 9802.00.80, supports this growth. Various decrees permit goods to enter Mexico on a duty free basis *under bond* for purposes of assembly in maquiladoras. Mexican law permits duty free importation of equipment, technology and components for six months. At the end of that period the goods must be exported from Mexico, typically back to the United States. Except with special permission, which has been increasingly granted by the authorities, maquiladora-assembled goods may not enter the Mexican market. Investors may own maquiladoras, typically using 30–year land trusts (fideicomiso) and Mexican subsidiaries. Alternatively, they may lease assembly plant space from a Mexican company and operate a maquiladora from that space. The simplest way to enter into maquiladora assembly operations is to contract with a Mexican company to assemble the goods in question.

In 1998, Mexico's Ministry of Commerce and Industry Development (SECOFI) published an amended Maquiladora Decree. The revised Decree streamlines regulation of maquiladoras in Mexico, notably reducing SECOFI's discretion to deny, suspend or cancel maquila programs. A translation of the new Decree can be found at www.natlaw.com.

The net result of the United States and Mexican law in this area is to create an interdependent legal framework mutually supportive of maquiladora operations. Many have characterized this legal framework as a "co-production" or "production sharing" arrangement between the two countries. However, utilization of maquiladoras is not limited to U.S. firms nor United States' components. Japanese and Korean companies have become major investors in maquiladora industries. To the extent that they utilize U.S. components, they may benefit from the duty free entry provisions of Section 9802.00.80.

Until late in 1993, there was also a link between the United States System of Generalized Preferences (GSP) and Mexican maquiladoras. Under the rules of origin that govern the GSP program, if at least 35 percent of the value of a maquiladora product was of Mexican origin, it could qualify entirely for duty free entry into the United States. The possibility of this result caused many users of maquiladoras to seek out Mexican suppliers in order to try to meet the 35 percent rule of origin. This incentive was enhanced by the fact that South Korea, Singapore, Taiwan and Hong Kong were all graduated from the United States GSP program in 1989. Mexico was the largest source of GSP qualified goods entering the United States market prior to December, 1993 when all of its products were removed from the GSP program.

The North American Free Trade Area incorporating Mexico, Canada and the United States furthers the investment trend in Mexico. Nearly all Mexican-made goods will eventually be able to enter the United States market on a duty free basis.[1] NAFTA phases out over seven years the duty free entry Section 9802.00.80 benefits currently applied to Mexican maquiladoras, but not as regards goods assembled with United States components outside North America.

§ 10.24 Section 9802.00.80 Case Law

There is a surprisingly large body of case law interpreting Section 9802.00.80. Much of it was developed when this provision was formally known as Section 807 of the Tariff Schedule of the United States. One issue is whether the United States components have been advanced in value or improved in condition abroad. If this is the case, duty free re-entry into the United States is prohibited. An early decision of the Court of Customs and Patent Appeals held that the export of U.S. fish hooks, which were assembled abroad into individually packaged assortments so as to meet the requirements of retail purchasers in the United States, were not advanced in value or improved in condition so as to be disqualified.[1] In another decision, U.S. revolvers were rechambered in Canada such that they no longer fired with accuracy .38 caliber bullets as originally designed. This change in condition caused the revolvers to be disqualified under Section 9802.00.80.[2] United States tomatoes shipped to Canada in bulk and sorted, graded as to color and size, and

§ 10.23

1. See Chapter 21.

§ 10.24

1. United States v. John V. Carr & Son, Inc., 496 F.2d 1225 (C.C.P.A.1974).

2. A.N. Deringer, Inc. v. United States, 386 F.Supp. 518, 73 Cust.Ct. 144 (1974).

repackaged in smaller cartons were not changed, advanced in value or improved in condition so as to be disqualified from duty free re-entry.[3]

The buttonholing in Mexico of U.S. shirt components (cuffs and collar-bands) did not advance them in value nor improve their condition as a result of this incidental operation.[4] But polyester fabric exported from the United States to Canada where it was dyed and processed, and then exported back to the United States as finished fabric did involve an advancement in value and changing of the condition of the U.S. component so as to disqualify it from duty free entry.[5] Similarly, glass pieces produced in annealled form in the United States which were sent to Canada for heat treatment and returned for use as pieces of tempered glass were not capable of benefiting from duty free entry.[6] Terminal pins of U.S. origin were shipped to Mexico and incorporated into header assemblies and relays. This operation constituted an assembly which did not advance the value of the terminals nor improve their condition.[7]

Another requirement of Section 9802.00.80 is that the United States component be fabricated and ready for assembly without further fabrication. Circuit boards for computers made in the United States from foreign and U.S. parts qualify as fabricated components for these purposes.[8] In this case, the programmable read only memory (PROM) was programmed in the United States causing it to undergo a substantial transformation and become a United States product. Aluminum foil, tabs, tape, paper and mylar made in the United States and shipped to Taiwan in role form where they were used together with other articles of U.S. origin to produce aluminum electrolytic capacitors were not eligible for duty free entry because they were not "fabricated components" upon departure from the United States to Taiwan.[9] The fact that gold wire made in the United States was not cut until used for transistors assembled in Taiwan did not make it a U.S. component that was not ready for assembly abroad without further fabrication. The cutting of the gold wire was an incident of the assembly process.[10] But the assembly in Ecuador of flattened cylinders and ends into tunafish cans which were then packed with tuna and shipped back to the United States did not qualify under Section 9802.00.80.[11]

3. Border Brokerage Co., Inc. v. United States, 314 F.Supp. 788, 65 Cust.Ct. 50 (1970).

4. United States v. Oxford Industries, Inc., 668 F.2d 507 (C.C.P.A.1981). See United States v. Mast Industries, Inc., 668 F.2d 501 (C.C.P.A.1981) (buttonholing and pocket slitting operations incidental to assembly process do not lead to duty free entry disqualification.)

5. Dolliff & Co., Inc. v. United States, 455 F.Supp. 618 (Cust.Ct.1978), affirmed 599 F.2d 1015 (C.C.P.A.1979).

6. Guardian Industries Corp. v. United States, 3 C.I.T. 9 (1982).

7. Sigma Instruments, Inc. v. United States, 565 F.Supp. 1036 (C.I.T.), affirmed 724 F.2d 930 (Fed.Cir.1983).

8. Data General Corp. v. United States, 4 C.I.T. 182 (1982).

9. General Instrument Corp. v. United States, 67 Cust.Ct. 127 (1971).

10. General Instrument Corp. v. United States, 462 F.2d 1156 (C.C.P.A.1972).

11. Van Camp Sea Food Co. v. United States, 73 Cust.Ct. 35 (1974).

The failure to lock knitting loops to keep the knitting from unravelling in the United States meant that knitted glove shelves were not exported in a condition ready for assembly without further fabrication. The importer of those gloves was not entitled to duty free entry for the value of the shelves.[12] On the other hand, pantyhose tubes made in the United States were fully constructed and secured from unravelling by stitches. A closing operation did not create a new toe portion and the goods were permitted the benefits of Section 9802.00.80.[13] Likewise the joinder of molten plastic to the upper portion of a shoe abroad did not prevent the shoe vamp from duty free entry upon return to the United States. This operation did not constitute further fabrication of the vamp.[14]

The scoring and breaking of silicon slices along designated "streets" was an incidental operation to the assembly of transistors and therefore the slices were entitled to duty free entry into the United States.[15] Magnet and lead wire made in the U.S. and exported to Taiwan where it was wound into coils and cable harness put into television deflection yolks were entitled to duty free entry.[16] The two-step assembly process in this case did not defeat the application of Section 9802.00.80. The burning of slots and holes in steel Z-beams in order to incorporate them into railroad cars was an operation incidental to the assembly process and therefore the beams were not dutiable.[17]

For Section 9802.00.80 to apply the components must be assembled abroad. It has been held that a needling operation causing fibers to be entwined with exported fabric in order to create papermaker's felts constituted an assembly abroad for these purposes.[18] Likewise the adhesion of Canadian chemicals to sheets of the United States polyester involved an assembly.[19] Another requirement of Section 9802.00.80 is that the components not lose their physical identity by change in form, shape or otherwise. Fabric components used to make papermaker's felts which were needled abroad and thus perforated with holes and changed in width did not lose their physical identity and therefore continued to qualify for duty free re-entry.[20] The absence of a loss of physical identity was apparently included as a requirement of Section 9802.00.80 in order to exclude U.S. components that are chemical products, food ingredients, liquids, gases, powders and the like. These products would presumably lose their physical identity when "assembled" abroad.[21]

12. Zwicker Knitting Mills v. United States, 613 F.2d 295 (C.C.P.A.1980).

13. L'Eggs Products, Inc. v. United States, 704 F.Supp. 1127 (C.I.T.1989).

14. Carter Footwear, Inc. v. United States, 669 F.Supp. 439 (C.I.T.1987).

15. United States v. Texas Instruments, Inc., 545 F.2d 739 (C.C.P.A.1976).

16. General Instrument Corp. v. United States, 499 F.2d 1318 (C.C.P.A.1974).

17. Miles v. United States, 567 F.2d 979 (C.C.P.A.1978).

18. E. Dillingham, Inc. v. United States, 470 F.2d 629 (C.C.P.A.1972).

19. C.J. Tower & Sons of Buffalo, Inc. v. United States, 304 F.Supp. 1187 (Cust.Ct. 1969).

20. E. Dillingham, Inc. v. United States, 470 F.2d 629 (C.C.P.A.1972).

21. See United States v. Baylis Bros., Co., 451 F.2d 643 (C.C.P.A.1971).

§ 10.25   Metals Processed Abroad

Section 9802.00.60 of the Harmonized Tariff System of the United States allows for duty free re-entry of U.S. metal objects that have been sent abroad for processing. Goods that qualify under this provision are subject to a duty only on the value of the foreign processing. In order to qualify, the metal must be further processed once it returns to the United States. The processing that is done abroad, like the assembly of products from U.S. components under Section 9802.00.80, is typically undertaken in low cost labor environments. This processing may involve the melting, machining, grinding, drilling, tapping, threading, cutting, punching, rolling, forming, plating and galvanizing of the United States metal.[1] Thus, for example, when aluminum sheets are made abroad from aluminum ingots originating in the United States, and then returned to the country to be cut into appropriate sizes and shapes, this is presumably the type of activity that would benefit from the tariff preferences found in Section 9802.00.60. The exporter of the metals must certify their condition at the time of exportation using Customs Form 4455. This same person must also certify the nature of the further processing that will ultimately be performed in the United States. Utilization of this provision, although not insignificant, is substantially less than the volume of goods assembled abroad from fabricated United States components under Section 9802.00.80.

Selected Bibliography

Cutler, United States Generalized System of Preferences: the Problem of Substantial Transformation, 5 North Carolina Journal of Int'l Law & Commercial Reg., 393 (1980).

DeVault, Political Pressure and the U.S. Generalized System of Preferences, 22 Eastern Econ. J. 35 (1996).

Fox, Interaction of the Caribbean Basin Initiative and U.S. Domestic Sugar Price Support: A Political Contradiction, 8 Mississippi College Law Review 197 (1988).

Glick, The Generalized System of Preferences, 30 Federal Bar News & J. 284 (1983).

Glick, The Generalized System of Preferences Revisited, 32 Federal Bar News & J. 139 (1985).

Lansing and Rose, Granting and Suspension of Most–Favored–Nation Status for Nonmarket Economy States, 25 Harvard Int'l L.J. 329 (1984).

Note, An Investors' Introduction to Mexico's Maquiladora Program, 22 Texas Int'l L.J. 109 (1986).

§ 10.25

1. See U.S. International Trade Commission Publication 1688 (April 1985).

Note, International Trade: Elimination of Tariffs on Caribbean Products—Caribbean Basin Economic Recovery Act, 25 Harvard Int'l L.J. 245 (1984).

Note, Texas–Mexico Twin Plants System: Industry and Item 807.00 of the U.S. Tariff Schedule, 16 Texas Tech L.Rev. 963 (1985).

Peterson, *The Maquiladora Revolution in Guatemala* (1992).

Stras, Foreign Trade Zones: A Community's Competitive Edge, 37 Fed.B.News & J. 155 (1990).

U.S. International Trade Commission, Report on the Impact of the Caribbean Basin Economic Recovery Act on U.S. Industries and Consumers (issued annually).

Chapter 11

CUSTOMS CLASSIFICATION VALUATION AND ORIGIN

Table of Sections

A. THE ROLE OF CLASSIFICATION AND VALUATION

§ 11.1 Purpose of Classification and Valuation

What customs officials do is to classify and value imported merchandise. The importer (and the exporter) may disagree with the conclusions reached as to the classification of the merchandise, its country of origin, and its valuation. Where they disagree, there are avenues of appeal. This chapter concentrates on who plays a role in classification and valuation, and how they undertake their roles.

Foreign goods entering the United States must be identified and assigned a value. The identification process is called classification. There are actually two forms of classification. The first is classification to determine the nature of the product, such as whether an imported doll wig made from human hair should be classified as a wig of human hair, a part of a doll, or a toy.[1] The second is classification by country to determine in what country or countries the product was made. If the doll wig was made in Argentina from human hair from Cuba, is the doll wig a product of Argentina or Cuba? This form of classification by country is more commonly referred to as the determination of the country of origin, and may involve quite formal rules of origin.

Knowing the nature of the product will allow Customs to determine the proper tariff. But tariffs differ for each foreign nation. Consequently, knowing the country of origin informs Customs which tariff column to use, such as one for countries granted most favored nation (MFN) status, countries denied such status, or countries with special tariff levels such as Canada and Mexico under the North American Free Trade Agreement (NAFTA), Caribbean Basin beneficiaries under the Caribbean Basin Economic Recovery Act, or other such agreements. Furthermore, identification of the country of origin may mean the product cannot be imported because it is from a country whose products are embargoed by the United States for reasons of foreign policy, such as Cuba. But even if the product and its source has been identified, Customs must know the value of the product before the tariff may be determined.[2]

---

§ 11.1

1. A hypothetical problem involving imported doll wigs and the process of classification and valuation was included in R. Folsom, M. Gordon & J. Spanogle, International Business Transactions: A Problem Oriented Coursebook 276 (2d ed. 1991). The hypothetical in the 1999 edition of this book involves classifying peanut butter-jelly swirl.

2. Assigning a value to an import is called valuation. Customs officials must be able to determine a value in order to calculate the appropriate import tariff. The task is easier if the product is entitled to duty free entry. In such case the valuation is not needed for purposes of collecting a tariff. But valuation remains useful for gathering information regarding the value of various classes of imports for statistical purposes.

§ 11.2   The Actors Who Classify and Value—The Customs Service

The United States Customs Service is part of the Department of the Treasury. It is assigned the role of administering the entry of goods into the United States.[1] Extensive regulations governing such entry are outlined in Title 19 of the Code of Federal Regulations.[2]

A Customs Service official at the port of entry makes a determination regarding the correctness of the documentation presented by the importer. If the Customs official rejects the documentation, that official's decision may be appealed to the District Director (Regional Commissioner if for the port of New York), and to the Commissioner of Customs.[3]

Judicial review of the decisions of Customs regarding classification or valuation go to the United States Court of International Trade (CIT),[4] which has exclusive jurisdiction.[5] Appeals from the CIT may be made to the Court of Appeals for the Federal Circuit (CAFC).[6] From these specialized courts, appeals are ultimately made to the United States Supreme Court.

On the international level there are other actors involved in classification and valuation. The most important follows:

Secretariat of the Customs Cooperation Council (CCC). This Brussels based organization is the administrative entity formed under the Convention on the Commodity Description and Coding System (the Convention). The CCC has sought since 1970 to develop an internationally accepted "Harmonized Commodity Coding and Description System" which nations would adopt as domestic law for classifying goods for all purposes, including the application of tariffs and gathering statistics. Its system, the Customs Cooperation Council Nomenclature (CCCN), was formerly known as the Brussels Tariff Nomenclature (BTN). The CCCN has evolved into the Harmonized Tariff Schedule (HTS), and is the system in use in the United States.

The Customs Cooperation Council (CCC) has been composed of four committees which have dealt with the HTS, one of which remains active. It is the Harmonized System Committee, which administers the Convention.

§ 11.2

1. 19 U.S.C.A. § 1500, granting Customs authority to appraise, classify and liquidate merchandise entering the United States.

2. Title 19 of the C.F.R. is divided into three chapters. Chapter I includes parts 1–199 entitles United States Customs Service, Department of the Treasury. Chapter II and Chapter III include parts 200 to the end and are entitled United States International Trade Commission, and International Trade Administration, Department of Commerce, respectively.

3. 19 C.F.R. §§ 173–174. There is a process for omitting the review by the district director in certain instances, by application for "further review." See 19 C.F.R. § 174.23–174.27.

4. 19 C.F.R. § 176.

5. The CIT is the successor to the Customs Court.

6. The CAFC is the successor to the Court of Customs and Patent Appeals.

§ 11.3 The Sources of Law for Classification and Valuation

The process of classification (of the item and the country of origin) and valuation requires us to turn to separate rules. Classification of products or materials requires use of the Harmonized Tariff Schedule adopted by the enactment of the Omnibus Trade and Competitiveness Act of 1988, the HTS comprising extensive schedules of products. Classification of the country of origin tends to focus on theory developed in cases. Valuation requires use of provisions in the Tariff Act of 1930 which generally following the GATT Customs Valuation Code. The statutory development of classification of products and valuation follows.

Classification. Although most nations for many decades used the internationally accepted Brussels Tariff Nomenclature (BTN), the United States refused to participate. The United States long used its own system of classification, included in the Tariff Schedule of the United States (TSUS). This quite obviously created a very different set of classifications for United States exports destined to a nation using the BTN, in comparison to the classifications of products entering the United States from other nations. What might be very narrowly defined in one system might be very broadly defined in another. It made it quite difficult to achieve fairness in seeking to lower tariffs for certain products. What was called a widget in the foreign nation, might be a gadget in the United States. The United States was increasingly isolated in using its own system, and it became apparent that it was the United States TSUS which would have to give way to the BTN. In 1982, after much urging from other major trading partners, the United States began to convert to the HTS, the effective successor to the BTN. That conversion was completed by adoption of the HTS for all imports in the Omnibus Trade and Competitiveness Act of 1988, effective January 1, 1989.[1] Most United States exports enter other nations under the HTS, and now the same is true for products of those other nations which enter the United States.

The HTS has twenty sections, the majority of which group articles from similar branches of industry or commerce. Examples of sections are Section I which includes live animals and animal products, Section II which includes vegetable products, Section III which includes animal or vegetable fats, Section IV prepared foodstuffs, Section V mineral products, etc. These twenty sections are divided into 96 chapters. Finally, the 96 chapters in total list approximately 5,000 article descriptions in the heading and sub-heading format, as discussed below. These provisions apply to all goods entering the customs territory of the United States, which includes the 50 states, the District of Columbia and the Commonwealth of Puerto Rico.

§ 11.3

1. P.L. 100–418, title I, §§ 1202–1217, Aug. 23, 1988, 102 Stat. 1107. The HTS is not published in the U.S.Code. The United States International Trade Commission maintains the current version, which is available from the Superintendent of Documents, U.S. Government Printing Office, Washington, D.C., 20402.

Valuation. For many years the United States used the American Selling Price (ASP) system to determine the value of an imported good. That system valued an imported good at the level of the usual wholesale price at which the same product was offered for sale if manufactured and sold in the United States. The valuation thus had no relation to the costs of production in the foreign nation. The ASP system was much criticised abroad.[2] Many other nations, especially in Europe, used a system based on the 1950 convention which established the Brussels Definition of Value. The Brussels Definition was thought to be too general by many, and it was not adopted by either the United States or Canada. Harmonization of customs valuation became one of the most important topics at the 1979 GATT Tokyo Round, which produced the GATT Customs Valuation Code.[3] The GATT Code adopted a very different approach to valuation than the ASP. Valuation is basically calculated by the "transaction" value, or if that cannot be determined, by several fall-back methods in a descending order of allowable application. The United States abandoned the ASP by adopting the GATT Customs Valuation Code in the Trade Agreements Act of 1979.[4]

Because of the replacement of the TSUS with the HTS for classification of imports, and the replacement of the ASP with the GATT Customs Valuation Code for valuation of imports, the United States uses classification and valuation systems harmonized with those of its major trading partners.

The next step in the development of customs valuation comes with the implementation of the Uruguay Round. The World Trade Organization replaces the GATT, and incorporates customs valuation provisions rather than having them exist as a separate external code. There were three principal amendments to the Customs Valuation Code, all discussed below. Of considerable importance to customs procedures was the addition of provisions allowing preshipment inspection.[5] These provisions attempt to balance the interests of some nations in contracting with outside companies to determine whether imports were fairly valued in the invoice, with the interest of exporting nations to reduce or remove impediments to trade, not to increase them.

B. CLASSIFICATION—THE FRAMEWORK OF THE HARMONIZED TARIFF SCHEDULE OF THE UNITED STATES

§ 11.4 Sample Provisions of the Harmonized Tariff System

Immediately below is a very small part of the very large classification schedules of the United States.[1] These provisions help to illustrate

2. Such criticism was quite expected since United States domestic producers could indirectly control the valuation applied to foreign competitors' imports.

3. Its importance is reflected by its adoption by the European Union, Canada and the United States, plus such major trading nations as Australia, Japan, Spain (prior to joining the EU) and Sweden, and even important developing nations such as Argentina, Brazil, and India.

4. 19 U.S.C.A. § 1401a.

5. See Creskoff, Pre–Shipment Inspection Programs: The Myth of Inconsistency with GATT Customs Valuation Provisions, 35 Fed.Bar News & J. 83 (1988).

two features of the HTS. First are the Notes which precede the chart and provide some comments on such areas as what the chapter does or does not not cover. Second is the schedule of tariffs with the various columns.

CHAPTER 67

PREPARED FEATHERS AND DOWN AND ARTICLES MADE OF FEATHERS OR OF DOWN; ARTIFICIAL FLOWERS; ARTICLES OF HUMAN HAIR

Notes

1. This chapter does not cover:

(a) Straining cloth of human hair (heading 5911);

(b) Floral motifs of lace, of embroidery or other textile fabric (section XI);

(c) Footwear (chapter 64);

(d) Headgear or hair-nets (chapter 65);

(e) Toys, sports equipment, or carnival articles (chapter 95); or

(f) Feather dusters, powder-puffs or hair sieves (chapter 96).

Heading Subheading	Stat. Suf. & cd	Article Description	Units of Quantity	Rates of Duty 1 General	Rates of Duty 1 Special	Rates of Duty 2
6703.00		Human hair, dressed, thinned, bleached or otherwise worked; wool or other animal hair or other textile materials, prepared for use in making wigs or the like:				
6703.00.30	00 1	Human hair	kg	3.1%	Free (A, E, I)	20%
6703.00.60	00 4	Other	kg	4.7%	Free (A, E*, I)	35%
6704		Wigs, false beards, eyebrows and eyelashes, switches and the like, of human or animal hair or of textile materials; articles of human hair not elsewhere specified or included: Of synthetic textile materials:				
6704.11.00	00 3	Complete wigs	No.	2.8%	Free (A*, E, I)	35%
6704.19.00	00 5	Other	X	2.8%	Free (A*, E, I)	35%
6704.20.00	00 2	Of human hair	X	2.8%	Free (A*, E, I)	35%
6704.90.00	00 7	Of other materials	X	2.8%	Free (A*, E, I)	35%

§ 11.5 The Meaning of the Headings in the HTS

The heading in the above excerpt is used under the General Rules of Interpretation to assist in determining the classification.[1] Thus, were the goods false eyelashes made of human hair for human adult use, it would appear that Chapter 67 is the correct chapter to apply. But more than one heading may seem appropriate for a commodity, as will be discussed below.

§ 11.4

1. See Harmonized Tariff Schedule of the U.S., Annotated for Statistical Reporting Purposes (ITC Publ. 2030).

§ 11.5

1. General Rules of Interpretation are reproduced in the Selected Documents section.

§ 11.6 The Meaning of the Notes in the HTS

The notes at the beginning of chapters in the HTS are often useful in classification. They are to be used along with the terms of the headings, under the General Rules of Interpretation.[1] For example, according to Note 1, Chapter 67 is not to be used for footwear, which is the subject of Chapter 64. These "chapter notes" should not be confused with the Explanatory Notes to the Harmonized System.[2] Nor should they be confused with the General Notes to the HTS.[3]

§ 11.7 The Meaning of the Columns in the HTS

Assuming one is not driven from the seemingly applicable chapter by the notes, the next step is to look at the columns. The United States HTS combines the international use of six digits by adding additional digits for even further subdivisions and for statistical use. Using the above excerpt the first column, titled "Heading/Subheading", has eight digits. The first six are the heart of the HTS, and must be adopted by all contracting nations. The first two (67 in the excerpt) repeat the chapter. The second two designate the heading (03 for Human hair, etc., 04 for Wigs, etc., in the excerpt). The next two are subheadings. This completes the international system, but the United States in some cases adds two more further sub-subheadings (.30 for Human hair and .60 for Other in the excerpt).[1] Finally, in the columns titled "Stat. Suf. & cd", additional numbers help to maintain records for statistical purposes.

The three column section titled "Rates of Duty" is what finally discloses the rate of duty for the article which has been classified. Column 1 rates are those applied to nations which receive most favored nation (MFN) status. The "General" column applies to most MFN nations. The "Special" column applies to nations which have tariff preferences which make these nations even more favored than the most favored. They may be commodities which enter duty free or with tariffs less than the general MFN rate. The capital letters denote different special preferential tariff programs. For example, A means nations qualifying under the Generalized System of Preferences (GSP),[2] B means commodities under the Automotive Products Trade Act, C means products under the Agreement on Trade in Civil Aircraft, CA means com-

§ 11.6

1. Id.

2. The Explanatory Notes to the Harmonized System are part of the documents of the Customs Cooperation Council in Brussels which may have some influence on the classification. They are discussed in § 5.8, infra.

3. These General Notes identify the customs territory of the United States, list nations to which Column 2 rates of duty apply, define symbols for special treatment such as the Caribbean Basin nations, give definitions, abbreviations, items exempted from coverage and rules on commingled goods. See ITC Pub. 2333 (1991).

§ 11.7

1. The use of an additional four digits is permitted by the Convention and other nations have adopted their own form of using these additional digits. Such use will lead to some lessening of the uniformity of the system.

2. An A* appears if a country is specifically ineligible.

modities under the Canada–United States Free Trade Agreement, E means commodities under the Caribbean Basin Economic Recovery Act,[3] IL means commodities under the United States–Israel Free Trade Area, and NA means commodities under the North American Free Trade Agreement.

Column 2 applies to all nations which are not entitled to Column 1 rates of duty. These countries are listed in General Note 3(b). They include principally nations under communist or socialist rule. They are essentially "least" favored nations, although that term perhaps ought to be saved for those nations which are excluded from trading with the United States altogether.

While it might seem that the HTS offers a fairly easy resolution to classification, that is true only when a commodity clearly fits into only one chapter, one heading, and if present one sub-heading. Fortunately, that is often the case. But many commodities are not so clearly allocated within the system, and there may be multiple possibilities for their classification. That will be the subject of much of the remainder of this chapter.

C. CLASSIFICATION—DETERMINING THE PROPER RATE OF DUTY

§ 11.8 Applying the General Rules of Interpretation

Classifying goods is the job of the Customs Service. But the importer (also the foreign exporter) is obviously interested in the classification because if the goods are classified with a high rate of duty applicable, the transaction may not go forward. Thus, the United States importer will wish to consider the classification. If the importer's conclusion is not the same as the Customs Service (meaning undoubtedly that the later will be a classification at a higher rate of duty), the importer may (1) decide not to import the goods, (2) pay the higher duty, or (3) challenge the Customs determination.

The process of determination, whether conducted by Customs or the importer, must use the rules of interpretation of the United States. They are the General Rules of Interpretation and the Additional U.S. Rules of Interpretation.[1] A walk through those rules ought to illustrate how difficult classification may be.

Headings and relevant section or chapter notes (Rule 1). The legal classification of a good is determined according to (1) the terms of the *headings,* and (2) any relative *section* and *chapter notes.*[2] This means the section, chapter and sub-headings are subordinated to the headings

3. The symbol E* appears if a country is ineligible.

2. General Rules of Interpretation 1.

§ 11.8

1. Both are included in the Selected Documents section of this chapter.

in importance. If the headings and notes do not otherwise require, one turns to the additional provisions of the General Rules,[3] and also to the Additional U.S. Rules of Interpretation.[4] The General Rules specifically note that the "table of contents, alphabetical index, and titles of sections, chapters and sub-chapters" are only for reference, not legal classification.[5]

Heading references to articles (Rule 2(a)). When any reference in a heading is to an *article,* as opposed to a material or substance, the reference is to be understood to mean that article incomplete or unfinished if the article in an incomplete or unfinished state "has the essential character" of the complete or finished article.[6] The reference to an article is also to mean that article unassembled or disassembled.[7] This emphasis on the *material* as well as on the *function* of the good replaces emphasis on how the goods are used under the TSUS.

Heading references to a material or substance. (Rule 2(b)). When the reference in a heading is to a *material* or *substance,* as opposed to an article, the reference is to be understood to mean mixtures or combinations of that material or substance with other materials or substances.[8] Furthermore, any reference to goods of a given material or substance should include a reference to goods consisting wholly or partly of such material or substance. The obvious problem with this is that when the goods are only partly of the material or substance, the other party may have its own classification. That is also true when there are mixtures or combinations. The Rules acknowledge this and require one to move on to Rule 3.

Classification under two or more headings—most specific description (Rule 3(a)). When goods may be classified under two or more headings,[9] the most specific description is preferred over the *more general description.*[10] But if each possibly applicable heading refers only to a *part* of the material or substances in mixed or composite goods, or of the items in a set for retail sale, the headings must be considered equally specific. That is so even if one heading provides a more complete or precise description of the goods.[11] In such case one must move on to Rule 3(b). This Rule 3(a) is somewhat parallel to the long used "rule of relative specificity" and decisions under that rule may continue to be of some use.[12]

3. Id.

4. The Additional U.S. Rules of Interpretation are found immediately following the General Rules in the HTS, as adopted in the United States. These additional rules often include methods of interpretation used under the prior classification system in the United States.

5. General Rules of Interpretation 1.

6. General Rules 2(a).

7. Id. Rule 2 generally follows the previous position under the TSUS.

8. General Rules 2(b).

9. This applies to Rule 2(b) discussed above and to any other situation where two or more headings seem possibly applicable.

10. General Rules 3(a).

11. Id.

12. That includes the doctrine that an *eo nomine* description prevails over headings having only general or functional descriptions.

Classification under two or more headings—essential character (Rule 3(b)). Inability to classify under the most specific description test in Rule 3(a) requires classification with regard to that material or component which gives the items their *essential character.*[13] There was no similar provision in the TSUS,[14] and "essential character" is not defined in the HTS. It has some parallel under the TSUS definition of the term "almost wholly of." One must turn to the cases as they develop, although some past United States cases defining "almost wholly of" may be useful when defining "essential character."

Classification under two or more headings—last in numerical order (Rule 3(c)). If classification is not possible using either the most specific description or essential character tests, the rules move from a substantive classification method to one based simply on location. The proper classification is to be the heading which occurs last in numerical order among those which might be applicable.[15]

Goods unclassifiable under Rules 1–3—most akin (Rule 4). When there are no headings which seem directly applicable, and which might lead to the use of Rules 1–3 above, the goods are to be classified under the heading to which the goods are *most akin.* It is not expected that this test will have to be used very frequently. This is essentially a "do the best the headings allow" test, and may result in two or more headings being equally "most akin." In such case one would seem to try to find which is "more" akin. If there is still uncertainty, move on to Rule 5.

Specially shaped or fitted cases for goods—classed with their contents (Rule 5(a)). Containers, such as camera cases, musical instrument cases, gun cases, drawing instrument cases, and necklace cases, which are "specially shaped or fitted" are to be classified with the goods they serve, if they enter with those goods and are suitable for long term.[16] But the rule does not apply if the containers give the whole its essential character.[17]

Packing materials and containers—classed with their contents (Rule 5(b)). Subject to the provisions of Rule 5(a) above, packing materials and containers which enter with the goods and classified with the goods if they are the normal kind used as packing or containers.[18] But this is not true when the materials or containers are suitable for repetitive use.

These above rules 5(a) & (b) are quite specific and apply only in a very limited situation. In most cases when one is going through the list and has not yet found a clear classification after using Rule 4, it will be necessary to go on to the final General Rule 6 for additional guidance.

---

13. General Rules 3(b).

14. A "chief value" determination applied, no less capable of exact determination.

15. General Rules 3(c).

16. General Rules 5(a).

17. For example, expensive carved tea caddies containing tea would not be classified as tea, because the container is not shaped to fit the tea (as is a musical instrument case) and the container gives the whole (tea plus caddy) the essential character.

18. General Rules 5(b).

Subheadings and subheading notes (Rule 6). Subheadings, which are found in the first "Heading/Subheading" column of each chapter in the tariff schedules, may more specifically define goods than the heading. When subheadings or subheading notes are used, and there are two or more subheadings on the same level which seem possibly applicable, the process follows the outline in the rules discussed above.[19]

§ 11.9   The Additional U.S. Rules of Interpretation

The above six General Rules of Interpretation are the contribution to classification provided by the HTS system. But when the United States adopted that system, it added to the General Rules its own "Additional U.S. Rules of Interpretation."[1] One thus must check these rules to determine whether in a given situation their use is (1) consistent with the General Rules, (2) helpful where the General Rules do not lead to a satisfactory conclusion, or (3) conflict with the conclusion reached under the General Rules. The additional U.S. Rules of Interpretation consist of a four part provision.

Classification controlled by use other than actual use (U.S. Rule 1(a)). If classification is controlled by use other than actual use, and there is no special language or context which mandates otherwise, the use must be the use in the United States. It is to be the use in the United States at or immediately prior to the time of importation. Furthermore, the controlling use must be the *principal* use (which exceeds any other single use).[2] This is a change from the past reference to chief use (which exceeds all other uses).

Classification controlled by actual use (U.S. Rule 1(b)). The rule is similar to the above, being the actual use in the United States and the use to which the goods are actually put with proof so provided within three years of the date of entry.[3]

Parts and accessories—general v. specific (U.S. Rule 1(c)). Where there is a provision specifically describing a part or accessory, that must be used over a general "parts and accessories" provision.[4] Thus, the import of bicycle chains would be classified as bicycle chains if such is described specifically, not under a "catch-all" "other parts and accessories" category. Such rule certainly is consistent with the preference for a specific description over a general description contained in the General Rules. The General Rules do not contain a rule for parts. Individual chapter and section notes, however, sometimes include parts rules.

Textile materials (U.S. Rule 1(d)). Principles of section XI, which govern mixtures of two or more *textile* materials, apply to goods in any provision which names a textile material.[5] Textiles have their own mystique, and

19. General Rules 6.

§ 11.9

1. The Additional Rules are included in the Selected Documents section to this chapter.

2. U.S. Rules 1(a).

3. U.S. Rules 1(b).

4. U.S. Rules 1(c).

5. U.S. Rules 1(d).

are subject to many special trading rules throughout the world. This provision assures that special rules of classification for textile materials are applied throughout the tariff schedules wherever a textile material is mentioned.

What if a conflict arises between the application of the General Rules and the Additional U.S. Rules? There is no guidance in the rules, but it seems likely that the Additional U.S. Rules would be deemed to supplant as well as supplement. But the likelihood for such conflict is slim, the Additional U.S. Rules were not intended to set forth views where the United States differs with the HTS, but where it believes there are necessary supplementary rules to express.

Application of the above rules is not easy, and certainly does not mean that all reasonable minds (including those found in the Customs Service) will reach the same conclusion when applying the General and Additional U.S. Rules. But we have not exhausted the assistance provided. There is one important source to consider, the "United States Customs Service, Guidance for Interpretation of Harmonized System." [6]

§ 11.10 United States Customs Service, Guidance for Interpretation of Harmonized System

When the HTS was adopted in 1989, there was some question as to how Customs would use some of the materials developed over the years as the HTS developed. Of specific concern was the use of the Explanatory Notes to the Harmonized System, and reports of the Nomenclature Committee which administered the Customs Cooperation Council (CCC) Nomenclature. Additionally unclear was how letters from the Secretariat of the CCC would be used, and also rulings and regulations from the customs administrations of other nations. The United States Customs Service soon issued the *Guidance for Interpretation of Harmonized System.*[1] The guide makes several points quite clear.

United States Customs Service does not seek uniformity of interpretation with other nations. Uniformity is considered to be the function of the Harmonized System Committee (HSC) under Article 7 of the Convention, not the function of the United States Customs Service. The United States is not to alter "sections, chapters, headings or subheadings" of the HTS, and will consider background documents to avoid such alterations. But the Customs Service will not attempt to make its interpretations of the HTS consistent with interpretations in other HTS member nations. If serious inconsistency in interpretation results, it is likely that the HTS will be modified to minimize the inconsistency, such as by further refining the classifications.

Use of Explanatory Notes to the Harmonized System. These notes are the official interpretation of the Harmonized System by the Customs

6. This guidance is included in the Selected Documents section to this chapter.

§ 11.10
1. 54 Fed.Reg. 35127 (1989). See Selected Documents in this chapter.

Cooperation Council. They are considered useful for guidance by Customs, but are not treated as dispositive. That is the Custom Service's interpretation of the intention of Congress in adopting the HTS.[2] The Explanatory Notes are amended from time to time and reflect changes in interpretation. They thus must be consulted periodically as changes are adopted. Status similar to the Explanatory Notes is to be given only, as Congress stated, to "similar publications of the Council." The only similar publication is the Compendium of Classification Opinions.

Use of the Compendium of Classification Opinions. These opinions are decisions of the Harmonized System Committee on the classification of different products. They result from requests presented to the HSC. They are considered to have the same weight as Explanatory Notes and are the official interpretation of the HSC on the particular issue decided.

Harmonized System Committee Reports. The HSC has periodically issued reports on various subjects. They do not have the weight of the Explanatory Notes or Compendium of Classification Opinions, but may be helpful in determining the intention of the HSC. Reports of committees of the HSC, such as the Nomenclature Committee, carry virtually no weight, but may nevertheless be of some assistance in interpretation. Of even less use are the "working documents" of the Nomenclature and Classification Directorate of the CCC. They are the basis of discussions in HSC sessions, but they may not reflect the intent of the HSC.

Rulings of Other Countries. Because other nations which have adopted the HTS use the same General Rules of Interpretation, Section and Chapter Notes, and first six digits in the classification tables, decisions of their customs administrations are sometimes presented to the United States Customs Service. Customs does not follow other nations' rulings because it believes that they "may have been subject to political realities or domestic regulations which are different from our own." What this means is not further defined, but may serve to illustrate that there may be political pressure to classify goods so as to more readily admit them to, or more readily exclude them from, the United States. In any event, these foreign rulings are considered "merely instructive of how others" classify imports.

Position papers. Before a session of the HSC, United States Customs, the International Trade Commission and the Bureau of Census prepare position papers for the session. These papers do not reflect the Customs position in the interpretation of the HTS and are considered to have no value, although they are occasionally circulated and obtained by importers or their counsel.

These notes, opinions, reports, rulings and papers all add to the process of interpretation a layer which did not exist before the adopted of the HTS by the United States. Awareness of their use by the Customs Service may prove helpful to United States counsel, but they

2. See Conf.Rep. No. 100–576, 100th Cong., 2d Sess. 549 (1988).

should not expect to be given weight beyond that announced by the Customs Service and described above.

§ 11.11 Decisions of United States Courts

While it may seem strange to suggest that decisions of United States courts may not be applicable in interpreting the HTS, that may be correct for decisions interpreting the prior TSUS.[1] Interpretations of the United States HTS are to follow the procedure outlined above. Certainly decisions rendered subsequent to the adoption of the HTS in 1988, which interpret the HTS, will be useful. But in so many cases decisions have very little usefulness since they apply to very narrow issues affecting specific goods where there are two or more classification possibilities. Some earlier decisions may be useful to understand the analytical process used by the courts.[2] Although the HTS has a different process, the approach used in the past may find use in the future.

One example is the application of General Rule of Interpretation 3(a), which uses a kind of "rule of relative specificity" under the wording "most specific description." United States decisions applying the rule of relative specificity may be used in interpreting Rule 3(a).[3]

D. COUNTRY OF ORIGIN

§ 11.12 Introduction—Substantial Transformation

A second form of classification is to determine the country of origin of the items to be imported. Determination of the proper classification discussed above does not disclose whether Column 1 or Column 2 rates of duty apply. Furthermore, if Column 1 rates of duty are applicable, the goods may qualify for special treatment if they are from a country of origin included by the code letters in the Special part of Column 1. Finally, knowing the country of origin may invoke more general prohibitions of trade with that country, since the United States nearly always has several nations with which it does not trade by legislative or presidential declaration.[1]

There are other reasons to wish to know the country of origin. The United States may limit the products which enter from a specific foreign nation. That limitation might be the result of a formal quota,[2] or an informal voluntary restraint agreement (VRA). VRAs have covered a great many products (i.e., steel, vehicles, electronics), and have been a

§ 11.11

1. See JVC Company of America v. United States, 234 F.3d 1348 (Fed.Cir. 2000).

2. For example, the Mattel, Inc. v. United States decision, 287 F.Supp. 999 (Cust. Ct.1968), might be used when the issue involves priority of one classification over another.

3. See, e.g., Great Western Sugar Co. v. United States, 452 F.2d 1394 (C.C.P.A. 1972).

§ 11.12

1. These prohibitions may extend to both exports and imports, but may have certain exceptions, such as medical supplies.

2. Quotas are regulated by the Customs Service. See 19 C.F.R. Part 132.

major device adopted by the United States (and other areas such as the European Union) as executive policy in order to discourage legislative action to establish mandatory and involuntary quotas to reduce trade imbalances.[3] The WTO Safeguards Agreement has reduced the frequency of their utilization.

Counsel representing an importer must know the framework for determining the country of origin of articles.[4] Eligibility of entry often depends on country of origin determination.[5] Country of origin law is not found in as consolidated a framework as for classification of the goods discussed above. Such classification takes one exclusively to the HTS, although working within that system is not a simple matter. Determination of the country of origin requires the use of rules which may be applicable in quite different areas. The most fundamental rule for determining the country of origin is *substantial transformation.* While there are several references to various aspects of the rule of origin in different sources of law, the substantial transformation test, in its various costumes, is *the* test.

§ 11.13   Sources of Law

Tariff Act of 1930. Section 304 of the Tariff Act requires that every article of foreign origin or its container which is imported into the United States be marked in a conspicuous place with the English name of the country of origin.[1]

Trade Agreements Act of 1979. Section 308,[2] provides various definitions, including a rule of origin for eligible products. The definition focuses on the substantial transformation concept,[3] leaving to the courts the meaning of substantial transformation.

The basic rule is that of substantial transformation, and it has origins both in this statute and much earlier case law. It is discussed below.

3. See, e.g., Note, Voluntary Restraint Agreements: Effects and Implications of the Steel and Auto Cases, 11 N.C.J. Int'l L. & Com.Reg. 101 (1986).

4. Counsel may wish to obtain a ruling from Customs in advance of importation. See 19 C.F.R. §§ 177.1–177.11.

5. The United States must know whether the country of origin is one entitled to most favored nation treatment.

§ 11.13

1. 19 U.S.C.A. § 1304. For example the product would have to say "Made in Spain" rather than "Made in Espana". The HTS governs treatment of containers and holders for imported merchandise. See 19 C.F.R. § 1202. The purpose of the rule is essentially to inform the public. The Trademark Act of 1946, 15 U.S.C.A. §§ 1051–1127, does not allow admission of goods of foreign origin if they have a mark or name intended to lead the United States public to believe the product was made in the United States, or any country other than its true country of origin.

2. 19 U.S.C.A. § 2518.

3. "An article is a product of a country or instrumentality only if (i) it is wholly the growth, product, or manufacture of that country or instrumentality, or (ii) in the case of an article which consists in whole or in part of materials from another country or instrumentality, it has been substantially transformed into a new and different article of commerce with a name, character, or use distinct from that of the article or articles from which it was so transformed." 19 U.S.C.A. § 2518(4)(B).

Code of Federal Regulations, Country of Origin Marking. Part 134 of 19 C.F.R. provides rules governing country of origin *marking.* These regulations implement or reflect the provisions noted above in both the Tariff Act of 1930 and the HTS. The regulations define articles that are subject to marking, with special rules for articles repacked or manipulated, and ones usually combined with another article.[4] Rules also specify how containers or holders must be marked,[5] exceptions to the marking requirements,[6] method and location of marking,[7] and the consequences of finding articles not legally marked.[8] The consequences are essentially (1) to properly mark the goods, or (2) to return the goods to the foreign nation, or (3) to destroy the goods.[9]

Generally, a single country of origin must be determined for labeling purposes, even though the product may have been made in several countries. The country of origin as determined by Customs may not disclose other nations which participated in the process. That may be important to the United States consumer, who may not wish to purchase products from a country substantially benefiting from the sale, but not the official country of origin. And it may be important to the United States government, which may not trade with the country which has substantially benefited, but which is not the official country of origin.

Special Rules—The North American Free Trade Agreement (NAFTA). In drafting the NAFTA, as in drafting the earlier Canada–United States Free Trade Agreement, there was considerable concern that products would enter into the United States as products of Canada or Mexico which actually had little fabrication or processing in those countries. The result was the adoption of special NAFTA rules of origin (discussed in Chapter 21), which include articles governing customs procedures for the certification of origin. The procedures create a North American "Certificate of Origin" and extensive verification provisions. The Certificate of Origin is provided by the exporter when the importer wishes to claim the duty free tariff treatment offered by the NAFTA.[10] Certificates are not required for goods of a value of $1,000 or less or where the member state has waived their use.[11] A member state may conduct a verification by questionnaires or visits to the exporter, or by other procedures the member states establish.[12] Verification is of considerable concern to the United States, which does not wish Mexico to be used as a base for transshipping products from outside the NAFTA area, especially from Asia.

Decisions of United States Courts. There are several areas where Customs is required to determine the country of origin. Products from countries with which the United States does not trade may be transshipped through a country with which the United States does trade.

4. 19 C.F.R. §§ 134.13–134.14.

5. 19 C.F.R. §§ 134.21–134.26.

6. 19 C.F.R. §§ 134.31–134.36.

7. 19 C.F.R. §§ 134.41–134.47.

8. 19 C.F.R. §§ 134.51–134.55.

9. 19 C.F.C. § 134.51(a).

10. NAFTA Art. 501.

11. NAFTA Art. 503.

12. NAFTA Art. 506.

Products from countries subject to high rates of duty in Column 2 may be transshipped through countries subject to lower rates of duty in Column 1. Products with most favored nation Column 1 rates of duty may be transshipped through a country with special access, such as a Caribbean nation. Exporters from a nation which has agreed to a voluntary restraint agreement may try to exceed the agreed upon numbers by having the products transshipped through a nation without any such quota. As the United States enters into free trade agreements such as NAFTA, other nations may attempt to take advantage of that relationship by having goods transshipped through Canada or Mexico into the United States.

Fortunately, some case law has evolved addressing the country of origin issue. Cases involving one specific area may be helpful in addressing another. For example a case which has attempted to identify the country of origin to determine whether the agreed amount under a voluntary restraint agreement has been exceeded,[13] may be helpful where products are alleged to be violating the rules of the generalized system of preferences. Thus, in attempting to deal with a country of origin issue, cases outside the scope of the form of entry (i.e., GSP, VRA, NAFTA, etc.) must be consulted. The sense of the cases is that the same test of substantial transformation is applied, whether the matter involves quota restrictions or trade preferences.[14]

§ 11.14 Applicable Legal Theories

There is some consistency in the approach to identifying the country of origin. More is obviously needed than to read the label which states the country of origin. A nation may do little more to an item than sew on a label which states that the item is a product of the country. The label may well be a product of the country, but that may be the only part of the item which is. It is the product itself which must be measured. The tests tend to be product specific. Since there are so many product variations, there are also many variations in application.

Substantial transformation test. The principal focus in a country of origin determination is whether the product was substantially transformed in the country stated to be the country of origin.[1] One of the principal cases defining substantial transformation in the United States, an early United States Supreme Court decision, involved drawbacks.[2] Substantial transformation would occur if the product was transformed into a new and different article "having a distinctive *name, character or*

13. See, e.g., Superior Wire, A Div. of Superior Products Co. v. United States, 669 F.Supp. 472 (C.I.T.1987), affirmed 867 F.2d 1409 (Fed.Cir.1989).

14. See Ferrostaal Metals Corp. v. United States, 664 F.Supp. 535, 538 (C.I.T.1987) (case law does not suggest that the court should depart from "policy-neutral rules governing substantial transformation in or-der to achieve wider import restrictions in particular cases.").

§ 11.14

1. This test is in the Trade Agreements Act of 1979. See 19 U.S.C.A. § 2518(4)(B).

2. Anheuser–Busch Brewing Ass'n v. United States, 207 U.S. 556, 28 S.Ct. 204, 52 L.Ed. 336 (1908).

use.'' [3] But while this case may be a standard, it has been applied in many different ways.[4] A name change alone would not always be sufficient, such as from "wire" to "wire rod".[5] But changing heat treated steel to galvanizing steel was sufficient, because it involved a substantial manufacturing leading to the substantial transformation that had to occur.[6] The character of the steel was changed. The annealing process strengthened the steel, and the galvanizing process made it resistant to corrosion.

Courts have tended to concentrate more on changes in *character* or *use* than in name. They often develop subtests appropriate for a particular kind of article. For example, is *significant value* added, or how much *additional costs* are incurred? But each test creates some subjective evaluation, leading to a sort of sense of whether the product is really from the state country. While the substantial transformation test has been criticized,[7] it remains the applicable law.

Value added test. This test allows a more exacting process. How much value has been added as a percent of the value of the original product? There may be situations where there has been no substantial transformation, but there has been significant value added.[8] What if a completed shirt with K–Mart logo buttons has those buttons removed and buttons are added with the logo of the most prestigious (currently) designer? If the result is the retail price may be trebled would that satisfy the value added test? There has certainly been minimal processing. Was the added value any more than the cost of the new buttons and their application? Isn't the high price really added in the United States by the consumers' willingness to pay more for apparent prestige? It seems that there must be some real value, such as labor or capital equipment, added in the country claiming to be the country of origin.

Considerations. However a court reaches a decision in a country of origin question, it is likely to have considered most of the following changes:

1. Change in name (and change in tariff classification);

2. Change in physical appearance;

3. Change in material substance (at each stage of manufacture);

4. Change in apparent use;

3. Id. at 562, 28 S.Ct. at 206.

4. But it is applied by the courts. See, e.g., Texas Instruments Inc. v. United States, 681 F.2d 778, 782 (C.C.P.A.1982).

5. See Superior Wire, A Div. of Superior Products Co. v. United States, 669 F.Supp. 472 (C.I.T.1987) (the court noted that in recent years the focus was on a change in use or character).

6. Ferrostaal Metals Corp. v. United States, 664 F.Supp. 535 (C.I.T.1987) (there

was a "significant altering" of the "mechanical properties and chemical composition of the steel").

7. Maxwell, Formulating Rules of Origin for Imported Merchandise: Transforming the Substantial Transformation Test, 23 J. Int'l L. & Econ. 669 (1990).

8. One may nevertheless claim this to be a substantial transformation of value, if not of substance.

5.   Change in value of item in the mind of the consumer;

6.   Additional capital vested in article;

7.   Additional labor vested in article;

8.   Type of processing;

9.   Affect of processing; and

10.   Change in method of distribution.

There is no secret formula for determining which factor, if any, will play the most significant role. The end result may seem much like a test parallel to pornography—"I'll know it when I see it."

E.   VALUATION—THE FRAMEWORK OF VALUATION LAW IN THE UNITED STATES

§ 11.15   United States Law

The law applicable to classification of products is quite clearly limited to the United States adoption of the HTS. The law applicable to classification of the country of origin tends to evolve in case law applying variations on the theme of substantial transformation. The law applicable to valuation is included in the United States Tariff Act of 1930, as amended, but within the confines of the United States commitment to the GATT Customs Valuation Code, and the successor World Trade Organization provisions regulating customs valuation evolving from the Uruguay Round.

The United States Tariff Act of 1930 for the most part incorporates the GATT Customs Valuation Code of 1979.[1] But because the United States adopted that GATT Code in 1979 amendments to the Tariff Act of 1930, some of the prior methods of interpretation of valuation may continue to be considered by courts.[2]

§ 11.16   The Law of the GATT/WTO

Of the several codes adopted by the GATT in the Tokyo Round and renewed in the Uruguay WTO Round, the Agreement on the Implementation of Article VII of the General Agreement on Tariffs and Trade (GATT Customs Valuation Code) is of considerable importance to the United States.[1] Article VII of the GATT, titled "Valuation for Customs Purposes", had much earlier established a form of transaction value, but it was not until the Customs Valuation Code was adopted that the form

§ 11.15

1. 19 U.S.C.A. § 1401a. See Sherman, Reflections on the New Customs Valuation Code, 12 Law & Pol'y Int'l Bus. 119 (1980).

2. The same is true of other areas with pre-Code established procedures. See Snyder, Customs Valuation in the European Economic Community, 11 Georgia J. Int'l & Comp.L. 79 (1981).

§ 11.16

1. Geneve, 1979, GATT, 26th Supp. BISD 116 (1980). See Davey, Customs Valuation: Commentary on the GATT Customs Valuation Code (1989).

of valuation by a descending order of tests was introduced. That form of valuation was incorporated into the United States law in 1979 and is the source of law to which one must turn for valuation of imports.

F. VALUATION—DETERMINING THE PROPER VALUE

§ 11.17 Appraisal of Imported Merchandise

Imports of merchandise are valued according to a series of alternative methods.[1] But they are not alternative methods in the sense that Customs may use any method it chooses. Nor may Customs reject information provided if based on the use of generally accepted accounting procedures.[2] The methods of valuation are set forth in the order of use which must be followed. Most valuations never go beyond the first, the transaction value.

§ 11.18 Transaction Value

Customs first considers the transaction value.[1] The transaction value is often referred to as the *invoice* value, since, in the absence of over or under invoicing, that would be the value of the transaction. The statute refers to the transaction value as the *price actually paid or payable.*[2] It is the price when sold for exportation to the United States and thus is usually a wholesale price.[3] It may be confusing where there are several contracts in addition to the actual contract between the buyer-seller, such as between a party to the sale and the party's parent entity,[4] or between a foreign seller and United States company acquiring items purchased by the foreign seller from a foreign manufacturer.[5] The transaction value may or may not include some elements about which there may be doubt as to application of duty. Rebates to the price actually paid or payable made after the merchandise has entered the United States are disregarded in determining the transaction value.[6] For example, quota charges clearly separated on the invoice are never-

§ 11.17

1. Merchandise is defined as of the same class or kind as other merchandise if within a group or range which is produced by a particular industry or industrial sector. 19 U.S.C.A. § 1401a(e)(2).

2. 19 U.S.C.A. § 1401a(g)(3).

§ 11.18

1. 19 U.S.C.A. § 1401a(a)(1)(A).

2. 19 U.S.C.A. § 1401a(b)(1). Price actually paid or payable is defined in 19 U.S.C.A. § 1401a(b)(4). Disbursements by the buyer for the benefit of the seller are included, as when the buyer disburses some funds to the agent's seller who assists in bringing about the sale. Moss Mfg. Co.,

Inc. v. United States, 714 F.Supp. 1223 (C.I.T.1989), affirmed 896 F.2d 535 (Fed. Cir.1990).

3. That would not be the case for direct purchases of large items, such as a United States customer directly purchasing a yacht from a German builder.

4. Nissho Iwai American Corp. v. United States, 786 F.Supp. 1002 (C.I.T.1992).

5. See Brosterhous, Coleman & Co. v. United States, 737 F.Supp. 1197 (C.I.T. 1990).

6. 19 U.S.C.A. § 1401a(b)(4)(B). See Allied Int'l v. United States, 795 F.Supp. 449 (C.I.T.1992) (importer has the burden of showing that the rebate occurred on or before date of entry).

theless includable.[7] Dividing the assembly (service) price from the consumer (sale of goods) price for made-to measure clothing does not relieve the importer from duty on the former portion, the full cost is subject to duty.[8]

Added to the transaction value are five other categories of associated costs. Some are costs which may be part of the price paid or payable and thus subject to valuation. But some are costs which, if not subject to tariffs, could be split off from the price of the goods and paid separately, thus avoiding or evading proper duty.[9] These additional costs subject to duty are:

1. Packing costs incurred by the buyer.[10] If incurred by the seller they would be part of the price paid for the merchandise, probably buried in the price of the goods.

2. Selling commission incurred by the buyer.[11]

3. Any assist, apportioned as appropriate.[12] An assist includes a very broad range of benefits, and is the subject of an extensive definitional provision.[13]

4. Any royalty or license fee related to the goods which the buyer pays directly or indirectly as a condition of the sale.[14] This can be a difficult provision to interpret. If a buyer pays a flat fee per year directly to the designer of the goods, no matter how many are sold, the buyer may escape duty. But any payment which is related to the number sold seems subject to duty.

5. Any direct or indirect accrual to the seller from the subsequent resale, disposal, or use of the goods.[15] This prevents the sale at a low base price, with the buyer required to pass on a percentage to the seller after the goods are resold.

In order to include any of the above five additions it must be shown that they have not been included already in the price paid or payable by "sufficient" information.[16] The statute defines sufficient information as used in this section and others in the valuation provisions.[17] Where sufficient information is not available but there is a belief that one or

7. Generra Sportswear Co. v. United States, 905 F.2d 377 (Fed.Cir.1990).

8. E.C. McAfee Co. v. United States, 842 F.2d 314 (Fed.Cir.1988).

9. See All Channel Products v. United States, 787 F.Supp. 1457 (C.I.T.1992), judgment affirmed 982 F.2d 513 (Fed.Cir.1992) (inland freight charges separately invoiced properly included in transaction value); United States v. Arnold Pickle & Olive Co., 659 F.2d 1049, 68 C.C.P.A. 85 (1981) (inspection costs).

10. 19 U.S.C.A. § 1401a(b)(1)(A).

11. 19 U.S.C.A. § 1401a(b)(1)(B). See Jay–Arr Slimwear Inc. v. United States, 681 F.Supp. 875 (C.I.T.1988).

12. 19 U.S.C.A. § 1401a(b)(1)(C).

13. 19 U.S.C.A. § 1401a(h)(1). See, e.g., Texas Apparel Co. v. United States, 883 F.2d 66 (Fed.Cir.1989), cert. denied 493 U.S. 1024, 110 S.Ct. 728, 107 L.Ed.2d 747 (1990) (sewing machine costs constitute an assist in manufacturing jeans). See Collins, The Concept of Assist as Applied to Customs Valuation of Imported Merchandise, 1991 Detroit Col.L.R. 239.

14. 19 U.S.C.A. § 1401a(b)(1)(D).

15. 19 U.S.C.A. § 1401a(b)(1)(E).

16. 19 U.S.C.A. § 1401a(b)(1).

17. 19 U.S.C.A. § 1401a(b)(5).

more of the five additional amounts exist, the transaction value is considered not to be determinable.[18] One would have to move to the next section in the chronology of applicable provisions.

Where the transaction value is determinable under the above discussed provisions, it is to be considered the *appraised* value only if certain further conditions exist. If they do not exist, one must also move to the next applicable method of valuation.[19]

First, the buyer must be able to dispose of or use the goods without restriction, except restrictions that (1) are required by law, (2) limit resale to a geographical area, or (3) do not substantially affect the value.[20]

Second, there may not be any condition or consideration affecting the sale of or the price paid or payable where the value of the condition or consideration cannot be determined.[21]

Third, no part of the proceeds from the use or resale may accrue directly or indirectly to the seller, unless that amount is calculable under the provisions noted above.[22]

Fourth, the buyer and seller are either unrelated, or if related the transaction is acceptable under the discussion below regarding related buyers and sellers.[23] The statutes define related persons under special rules.[24]

Often the buyers and sellers are related. The most common relationship is that of a parent and subsidiary. Intraorganization transfers are often conducted with prices that are not truly reflective of arm's length prices, sometimes to avoid taxes, sometimes to avoid tariff duties, sometimes for other purposes.[25] Because of the unique nature of related buyers and sellers, separate provisions apply. The transaction value in a sale from a related seller to buyer is the appraised value, as long as (1) the circumstances of the sale do not suggest the relationship influenced the price, and (2) the transaction value approximates either the transaction value in an unrelated parties transaction, or the deductive value or computed value for identical or similar merchandise.[26] This exception introduces the concept of *deductive* value and *computed* value, both alternative valuations methods discussed below. The exception also requires defining both *identical* merchandise and *similar* merchandise. Definitions of both are in the statutes.[27] The comparison values referred

18. Id.

19. In rejecting use of transaction value, there must be more than mere suspicion that the value is not fairly reflective of sales in the market. See Texas Instruments Inc. v. United States, 500 F.Supp. 922 (Cust.Ct. 1980), judgment vacated 8 C.I.T. 1, 5 ITRD 2543 (C.I.T.1984).

20. 19 U.S.C.A. § 1401a(b)(2)(A)(i).

21. 19 U.S.C.A. § 1401a(b)(2)(A)(ii).

22. 19 U.S.C.A. § 1401a(b)(2)(A)(iii). The above provision is 19 U.S.C.A. § 1401a(b)(1)(E).

23. 19 U.S.C.A. § 1401a(b)(2)(A)(iv).

24. 19 U.S.C.A. § 1401a(g)(1).

25. Transfer pricing is discussed in chapter 24.

26. 19 U.S.C.A. § 1401a(b)(2)(B).

27. 19 U.S.C.A. § 1401a(h)(2) & (4).

to above must be values for merchandise entering the United States at
or about the same time as the merchandise in question.

Values used for comparison purposes may consist of identical or
similar goods,[28] but differences in the method of sales may distort the
comparison. Consequently, the values used must consider differences, if
based on sufficient information, in commercial levels, quantity levels and
any costs, commissions, values, fees and proceeds in § 1401a(b)(1),
discussed above.[29]

While the above identifies provisions which designate the composition of the transaction value, there are also specific items which are not
to be included in that value. They include two specific areas.

First, transaction value should not include any reasonable cost or
charge for either (1) construction, erection, assembly, or maintenance of,
or technical assistance to the merchandise after importation, or (2)
transportation after importation.[30]

Second, transaction value should not include the customs duties or
other federal taxes imposed upon importation, nor federal excise tax.[31]

Transaction value of identical and similar merchandise. This separate
section largely draws from the above section those provisions applicable
to determining transaction value where it is necessary to refer to
identical or similar merchandise. The identical merchandise value
method is used when the above transaction value cannot be determined
or used, and if the identical merchandise value cannot be used the
similar merchandise value is used.[32] Where the transaction value has
been determined above for identical merchandise or for similar merchandise, as defined in the statute,[33] it is to be adjusted. That adjustment
requires consideration of any different commercial level or quantity level
of sales for the comparison identical or similar merchandise.[34] The
adjustment must be based on sufficient information. Where there are
two or more comparison transactions, the appraisal of the imported
merchandise will be based on the lower or lowest of the comparison
values, thus resulting in a favorable conclusion for the importer.[35]

§ 11.19 Deductive Value

The most important question is when is the deductive method of
valuation to be used? It is used when the above transaction value does
not lead to a determination acceptable to Customs.[1] But the importer

---

28. See Walter Holm & Co. v. United States, 3 C.I.T. 119 (1982) (use of value of exports of cantaloupes through Laredo, Texas, to determine value of same items through Nogales, Arizona).

29. 19 U.S.C.A. § 1401a(b)(2)(C).

30. 19 U.S.C.A. § 1401a(b)(3)(A). International transportation is separately excluded in 19 U.S.C.A. § 1401a(b)(4)(A).

31. 19 U.S.C.A. § 1401a(b)(3)(B).

32. 19 U.S.C.A. §§ 1401a(a)(1)(B) & (C).

33. 19 U.S.C.A. § 1401a(h)(2) & (4).

34. 19 U.S.C.A. § 1401a(c)(2).

35. Id.

§ 11.19

1. 19 U.S.C.A. § 1401a(a)(1)(D).

may request that the computed value discussed below be used in place of the deductive value.[2] If use of the computed value does not prove possible, the deductive value is next used.[3]

In using deductive value, it may be applied to the merchandise being appraised, or to either identical or similar merchandise.[4] The deductive value focuses on unit value,[5] and constitutes the most appropriate value as determined in one of three ways.

The first method of determining deductive value applies where the merchandise imported is sold (1) in the condition as imported and (2) at or about the date of importation. The deductive value is the unit price at which the merchandise is sold in the greatest quantity.[6]

The second method applies where the merchandise imported is sold in the condition as imported but not at or about the date of importation. The deductive value is the unit price at which the merchandise is sold in the greatest quantity, but within 90 days after importation.[7]

The third method is where the merchandise is neither sold in the condition imported nor within 90 days after importation. The deductive value is the unit price at which the merchandise, after further processing, is sold in the greatest quantity within 180 days of importation.[8] But this third method applies only at the election of the importer, upon notification to the customs officer.[9]

If none of these deductive methods apply, which also means the transaction value was first ruled inapplicable, the next test to apply will be the computed value method.

If the deductive method proves applicable, there may be some applicable reductions from the unit price. They include commissions, additions for profit and expenses, costs of domestic and international transportation, customs duties and other federal taxes on the merchandise, and where the third method of deductive value is used, the costs of additional processing.[10] Deductions for profits and expenses must be consistent with profits and expenses in the United States for similar merchandise, and any state or local taxes on the importer relating to the sale of the merchandise is considered an expense.[11]

There may also be an increase to the unit price, if such costs have not already been included, amounting to the packing costs incurred by the importer or buyer.[12]

2. 19 U.S.C.A. § 1401a(a)(2).

3. Id.

4. 19 U.S.C.A. § 1401a(d)(1).

5. Unit value is the price the merchandise is sold (1) in the greatest aggregate quantity, (2) to unrelated persons, (3) at the first commercial level after importation (at level i and ii discussed below), or after further processing (at level iii discussed below), (4) in a total volume which is both greater than the total volume sold at any other unit price, and sufficient to establish the unit price. 19 U.S.C.A. § 1401a(d)(2)(B).

6. 19 U.S.C.A. § 1401a(d)(2)(A)(i).

7. 19 U.S.C.A. § 1401a(d)(2)(A)(ii).

8. 19 U.S.C.A. § 1401a(d)(2)(A)(iii).

9. Id.

10. 19 U.S.C.A. § 1401a(d)(3)(A).

11. 19 U.S.C.A. § 1401a(d)(3)(B).

12. 19 U.S.C.A. § 1401a(d)(3)(C).

A final provision requires that in calculating deductive value one disregards any sale to a person who supplies an assist for use in connection with the merchandise.[13]

Where deductive value is inapplicable, or where the importer has chosen to pass over deductive value, the next method is computed value.

§ 11.20 Computed Value

Computed value is used when transaction and deductive value methods have not provided an appropriate result. But the importer may skip over using deductive value and use the computed value.[1] The computed value constitutes the sum of four parts.[2]

First, the cost or value of materials and fabrication or processing.[3] It does not include any internal tax by the exporting country if the tax is remitted upon exportation.[4]

Second, profit and expenses of the amount usually associated with the same kind of merchandise.[5] They are based on producer's profits and expenses, unless inconsistent with those for sales of the same class or kind of merchandise by producers in the country exporting to the United States, in which case there is a calculation of such profits and expenses using the "sufficient information" procedure.[6] The foreign assembler's profit for integrated circuits and transistors assembled in Curacao were properly included, but Customs also should have applied same rationale in determining general expenses.[7] The costs of a warranty for aircraft should also be included as profit, less expenditures the manufacturer-seller may establish have been incurred by the warranty obligations in curing defects.[8]

Third, any assist if not included in the amount above.[9] Computing the value of jeans would allow the addition of the cost or value of the sewing machines used to produce the jeans.[10]

13. 19 U.S.C.A. § 1401a(d)(3)(D).

§ 11.20

1. 19 U.S.C.A. § 1401a(a).

2. 19 U.S.C.A. § 1401a(e)(1). For cases which have used the constructed value approach, see Texas Instruments, Inc. v. United States, 3 C.I.T. 114 (1982) (values of integrated circuits and transistors); New York Credit Men's Adjustment Bureau, Inc. v. United States, 314 F.Supp. 1246 (Cust. Ct.1970), affirmed 342 F.Supp. 745 (Cust. Ct.1972).

3. 19 U.S.C.A. § 1401a(e)(1)(A). See Texas Apparel Co. v. United States, 698 F.Supp. 932 (C.I.T.1988), affirmed 883 F.2d 66 (Fed.Cir.1989), cert. denied 493 U.S. 1024, 110 S.Ct. 728, 107 L.Ed.2d 747 (1990).

4. 19 U.S.C.A. § 1401a(e)(2)(A).

5. 19 U.S.C.A. § 1401a(e)(1)(B). See Texas Instruments Inc. v. United States, 500 F.Supp. 922 (Cust.Ct.1980), judgment vacated 8 C.I.T. 1, 5 ITRD 2543 (C.I.T. 1984); Braniff Airways, Inc. v. United States, 2 C.I.T. 26 (1981).

6. 19 U.S.C.A. § 1401a(e)(2)(B).

7. Texas Instruments Inc. v. United States, 500 F.Supp. 922 (Cust.Ct.1980), judgment vacated 8 C.I.T. 1, 5 ITRD 2543 (C.I.T.1984).

8. Braniff Airways, Inc. v. United States, 2 C.I.T. 26 (1981).

9. 19 U.S.C.A. § 1401a(e)(1)(C).

10. Texas Apparel Co. v. United States, 698 F.Supp. 932 (C.I.T.1988), affirmed 883 F.2d 66 (Fed.Cir.1989), cert. denied 493 U.S. 1024, 110 S.Ct. 728, 107 L.Ed.2d 747 (1990).

Fourth, packing costs.[11]

§ 11.21   Value When Other Methods Are Not Effective

If the value cannot be determined under the above discussed methods, there is a final method of calculation of value. It is to derive a value using the methods set forth above, adjusting them to the extent necessary to achieve a reasonable result.[1] But in making such appraisal, the statute prohibits using any of seven items.[2] They are:

(1) United States selling price of United States produced merchandise,

(2) any system using the higher of two alternatives,

(3) domestic market price in country of exportation,

(4) cost of production for identical or similar merchandise which differs from such cost of production determined under the computed value method,

(5) price for export to a country other than the United States,

(6) minimum values, or

(7) arbitrary or fictitious values.

As first noted, transaction value expressed in the invoice is used in the vast majority of cases. When there is some challenge to transaction value, the procedure may become very complex. Any of the determinations of Customs may be challenged, but the cost of such challenge for all but the largest importers will often result in paying the Customs determined value, or not importing the goods. Counsel will calculate the possible rates of duty under all the possible alternatives and will only import the products if the rate of duty is acceptable and does not cause the price for resale to be either excessive, or more than would result from using United States products which may cost more to produce, but do not have added duty.

Selected Bibliography

American Bar Association, Rules of Origin (Standing Committee on Customs Law 1991).

Chaplin, An Introduction to the Harmonized System, 12 N.C.J.Int'l L. & Com.Reg. 417 (1987).

Davis, A Substantial Transformation of the Country of Origin Substantial Transformation Test?, 19 Inter–Am.L.R. 493 (1988).

Galligan, It's a Bird, It's a Plane—What is It?: Understanding Customs Classification, 5 Software L.J. 673 (1992).

11.   19 U.S.C.A. § 1401a(e)(1)(D).   **2.**   19 U.S.C.A. § 1401a(f)(2).

§ 11.21

1.   19 U.S.C.A. § 1401a(f)(1).

Hall, Values Greatest Hits (And Misses): A Complete History of Judicial Decisions Concerning Value, 25 J. Law & Policy Int'l Bus. 51 (1993)

Hayward and Long, Comparative Views of U.S. Customs Valuation Issues in Light of the U.S. Customs Modernization Act, 5 Minn. J. Global Trade 311 (1996).

LaNasa, Rules of Origin and The Uruguay Round's Effectiveness in Harmonizing and Regulating Them, 90 Amer. J. Int'l L. 625 (1996).

Maxwell, Formulating Rules of Origin for Imported Merchandise: Transforming the Substantial Transformation Test, 23 J.Int'l L. & Econ. 669 (1990).

McCall, What is Asia Afraid Of? The Diversionary Effect of NAFTA's Rules of Origin on Trade Between the United States and Asia, 25 Cal. West. Int'l L.J. 389 (1995).

Orr, Evaluation of Country of Origin Standards as Applied in the Textile Industry, 7 Houston J.Int'l L. 305 (1985).

Schueren, Customs Classification: One of the Cornerstones of the Single European Market, But One Which Cannot be Exhaustively Regulated, 28 Common Mkt.L.R. 855 (1991).

Sherman, Reflections on the New Customs Valuation Code, 12 L. & Pol'y Int'l Bus. 119 (1980).

Silverstein, Country of Origin Marking Requirements Under Section 304 of the Tariff Act: An Importer's Map Through the Maze, 25 Am. Bus.L.J. 285 (1987).

Snyder, Customs Valuation in the European Economic Community, 11 Georgia J.Int'l & Com.L. 79 (1981).

Stepp, The 1984 "Country of Origin" Regulations for Textile Imports: Illegal Administrative Action Under Domestic and International Law?, 14 Georgia J.Int'l & Comp.L. 573 (1984).

Usher, Customs Valuation: The Reliability (Or Otherwise) of Invoice Prices, 5 Europ.L.R. 304 (1980).

Chapter 12

ANTIDUMPING DUTIES

Table of Sections

A. INTRODUCTION

A. INTRODUCTION

§ 12.1 Dumping—What Is It and Why Is It Done?

Dumping involves selling abroad at a price that is less than the price used to sell the same goods at home (the "normal" or *"fair"* value). To be unlawful, dumping must threaten or cause material injury to an industry in the export market, the market where prices are lower. Dumping is recognized by most of the trading world as an unfair practice (akin to price discrimination as an antitrust offense). Dumping is the subject of a special GATT code which establishes the basic parameters for determining when dumping exists, what constitutes material injury and the remedy of antidumping tariffs. Such tariffs can amount to the margin of the dump, i.e. the difference in the price charged at home and (say) the European Union or the United States.

The economics of dumping as an unfair trade practice arise from a producer's opportunity to compartmentalize the global marketplace for its goods. Such opportunities permit it to offer the product for sale at different prices in different sectors and thereby maximize its revenues. Only if trade barriers or other factors insulate each market sector is there an opportunity to vary substantially the price in different sectors of the global market. For example, a producer can safely "dump" in an overseas market at cheap prices and a high volume only if it can be sure that the market in its home country is immune from penetration (arbitrage) by the products sold abroad. The objective of dumping may be to increase long term marginal revenues or to ruin a competitor's market position (predatory pricing). On the other hand, the dumping may not represent an unfair trade practice, but only short term interests related to distress sales, introductory offers or loss leaders. Dumping to develop a new foreign market or brand awareness in an existing market may make sense as a marketing technique. There is great difficulty in determining which type of dumping is being practiced in any particular case.

B. GATT/WTO ANTIDUMPING LAW

§ 12.2 GATT and The Tokyo Round Antidumping Code (1979)

The General Agreement on Tariffs and Trade (1947) has always been concerned with dumping practices.[1] GATT Article VI allows GATT Contracting Parties to impose antidumping duties to offset the margin of dumping, but only if it can be shown that such dumping causes or threatens to cause "material injury" to competing domestic industries. The material injury requirement is intended to prevent trading countries from overly enforcing their antidumping laws, and using them as weap-

---

§ 12.2

1. General Agreement on Tariffs and Trade (hereafter GATT), 55 U.N.T.S. 194 (1947, as amended). The GATT provisions on antidumping duties are set forth in GATT Article VI.

ons to protect domestic industries. It also provides a degree of uniformity in national antidumping measures. Under the GATT, antidumping duties may be imposed only if both material injury and a causal link between the dumped goods and the injury can be shown. These requirements derive from the concern that member countries might otherwise impose antidumping duties even though the allegedly dumped imports cause only marginal injuries. However, the causal link element was not intended to require that the imports be the principal cause of the injuries.

The GATT Antidumping Code of 1979,[2] adopted during the Tokyo Round of negotiations, is an attempt to ensure uniformity of its member countries' antidumping laws and provides a detailed framework of antidumping regulation. It builds upon the earlier 1967 Kennedy Round GATT Antidumping Code that the U.S. failed to implement. One of the characteristics of the injury determination proceeding the 1979 Code requires is its complex factual nature. It is essentially a fact-finding investigation; the allegations, evidence, and nature of the dispute are extremely complex. The types of injury may be very different from one industry to another and thus seemingly similar circumstances may lead to opposite or at least differing conclusions. Because of this unique fact-specificity of the injury determination, it is unavoidable that antidumping laws would be different from one country to another without some unifying guidance.

Concerns that each country's having a different regime of antidumping law would impede the unrestrained flow of international trade led the GATT member countries to agree on the GATT Antidumping Code (1979).[3] A list of its present signatories is footnoted.[4] The Code directs that material injury determinations should involve (1) an objective examination of the volume of the concerned dumped imports, (2) the effect of those imports on prices in the domestic market for like products, and (3) the consequent impact of those imports on domestic producers of like products.[5] It cautions that no one or several of these factors can necessarily give decisive guidance.[6] The Antidumping Code also provides that the investigating authorities shall consider: whether there has been a significant increase in the volume of dumped imports, either in absolute terms or relative to production or consumption in the importing country; whether there has been a significant price undercutting by the dumped imports as compared with the price of a like product

2. Agreement on Implementation of Article VI of the General Agreement on Tariffs and Trade (Tokyo Round GATT Anti-Dumping Code) (Geneva, 1979) GATT, 26th Supp. B1SD 171 (1980). Reprinted at 18 Int'l Legal Mat. 621.

3. Vermulst, Injury Determinations in Antidumping Investigations in the United States and the European Community, 7 N.Y.L.Sch.J.Int'l & Comp.L. 301, 313 (1986).

4. As of June 1993, the following countries had accepted the Tokyo Round GATT Antidumping Code: Australia, Argentina, Brazil, Canada, the Czech Republic, Egypt, the twelve European Union states, Finland, Hong Kong, Hungary, India, Japan, Korea, Mexico, New Zealand, Norway, Pakistan, Poland, Romania, Singapore, Slovakia, Sweden and Switzerland.

5. Tokyo Round GATT Antidumping Code, Art. 3(1).

6. Id., Art. 3(2).

of the importing country; or whether the effect of such imports is otherwise to depress prices to a significant degree or to prevent price increases which otherwise would have occurred to a significant degree.

The Tokyo Round GATT Antidumping Code envisions that in examining the impact of dumped imports on the domestic industry, the investigating authorities will evaluate all relevant economic factors and indices having a bearing on the state of the industry. It then gives a nonexhaustive list including: actual and potential decline in output, sales, market share, profits, productivity, return on investments, or utilization of capacity; factors affecting domestic prices; and actual and potential negative effects on cash flow, inventories, employment, wages, growth, the ability to raise capital or investments.[7]

As part of an effort to bring its antidumping law more in line with the GATT standard, the United States amended the Tariff Act of 1930, the principal antidumping statute, through enactment of the Trade Agreements Act of 1979.[8] Among other things, these amendments first introduced the concept of material injury into the United States antidumping law. The GATT allows its member countries to take antidumping measures if dumping causes or threatens material injury to an established industry or materially retards the establishment of a domestic industry.[9]

§ 12.3   The WTO Antidumping Code (1994)

Late in 1993, the Uruguay Round of GATT negotiations were concluded and President Clinton notified Congress of his intent to sign the many agreements involved. One of these agreements is yet another attempt at clarification of antidumping law. The Uruguay Round GATT Antidumping Code focuses upon dumping determinations (particularly criteria for allocating costs) and material injury determinations (particularly causation). *De minimis* dumping, defined as less than 2 percent of the product's export price, is not subject to antidumping duties and signatories must terminate such investigations immediately. Cumulation of imports in injury determinations is permitted, as is the filing of petitions by unions and workers. When another signatory challenges the implementation of the Code, World Trade Organization dispute settlement panels will have binding authority to resolve the dispute without hearing new evidence and allowing for "competing, reasonable interpretations" of the Code under national laws.

§ 12.4   U.S. Implementation of the WTO Antidumping Code

Congress ratified and implemented the Uruguay Round accords in

---

7. Id., Art. 3(3).

8. Pub.L. No. 96–39, § 101, 93 Stat. 162 (1979) (current version at 19 U.S.C.A. § 1673).

9. GATT Art. 6(1).

December of 1994 under the Uruguay Round Agreements Act.[1]

Section 733(b) of the Tariff Act (1930)[2] has been amended by the addition of a subparagraph providing for a de minimis dumping margin. The administrating authority, in making its preliminary determination, must disregard any weighted average dumping margin that is de minimis, i.e., any average dumping margin that is less than two percent ad valorem or the equivalent specific rate for the subject merchandise. Any weighted average dumping margin that is de minimis must also be disregarded by the administrating authority when making its final determinations.[3]

A significant effect of the Uruguay Round Agreements Act (URAA) is that it has reduced the discretion previously available to the administrating authorities by imposing strict statutory time limits. In the case of an antidumping petition, the administrative authority must make an initial determination within twenty days after the date on which a petition is filed. This time limit may be extended to forty days in any case where the administrative authority is required to poll or otherwise determine support for the petition by the industry and exceptional circumstances exist.[4] Time limits are also imposed on the Commission in their determination of whether there is a reasonable indication of injury.[5]

The Uruguay Round Agreements Act authorizes an adjustment to sales-below-cost calculations for start-up costs,[6] thought to be particularly beneficial to high-tech products. It adds a new "captive production" section[7] intended to remove such internal sales from ITC injury determinations. The URAA, however, fails to fully implement the average-to-average or transaction-to-transaction dumping calculations mandated by the Antidumping Code. Rather, weighted average approaches will only be used in the investigatory phase, not in subsequent administrative reviews where the traditional U.S. calculation of dumping margins by comparing individual U.S. sales to average home or third country sales will continue.[8] Adjustments for profits from further manufacturing, selling and distribution of products in the U.S. are authorized.[9] And the URAA strengthens existing U.S. anticircumvention provisions despite their absence from the Uruguay Round Antidumping Code.[10] It also reinforces U.S. law on exclusion of sales below cost from normal value calculations in the home market.[11]

The URAA requires that the International Trade Commission provide all parties to the proceeding with an opportunity to comment, prior to the Commission's vote, on *all* information collected in the investiga-

§ 12.4

1. Public Law No. 103–465, 108 Stat. 4809.

2. 19 U.S.C.A. 1673b(b).

3. 19 U.S.C.A. 1673d(a).

4. 19 U.S.C.A. 1673a(c).

5. 19 U.S.C.A. 1673b(a).

6. 19 U.S.C. § 1671.

7. 19 U.S.C. § 1677b(f)(1)(c)(iii).

8. 9 U.S.C. § 1677a(d)(3).

9. 9 U.S.C. § 1677a(d)(3).

10. 19 U.S.C. § 1677j.

11. 19 U.S.C. § 1677b(d)(3).

tion. The URAA also generally requires imports from a country subject to investigation to be deemed negligible if the imports amount to less than 3 percent of the volume of all such merchandise imported into the United States in the most recent 12–month period preceding the filing of the petition for which data are available. If imports from a country are deemed negligible, then the investigation regarding those imports must be terminated.

Under the URAA, the Commission is ordinarily required to consider cumulation of imports from two or more countries when the imports are subject to investigations as a result of petitions filed on the same day. The Commission must make any cumulative analysis on the basis of the same record, even if the simultaneously filed investigations end up with differing final deadlines.

The URAA requires the International Trade Commission to consider the magnitude of the dumping margin (although not the magnitude of the margin of subsidization) in making material injury determinations. Lastly, the Commission must conduct a review no later than five years after an antidumping or countervailing duty order is issued to determine whether revoking the order would likely lead to continuation or recurrence of dumping or subsidies and material injury. Known as the "sunset provision," this new requirement will result in review of all existing antidumping and countervailing duty orders.

A WTO panel has ruled that the Commerce Department's refusal to revoke an antidumping order against South Korean DRAMS was inconsistent with Article 11.2 of the Antidumping Code. Hence, U.S. regulations regarding the likelihood of continued dumping after a 3–year hiatus are suspect under the Code.[12] The Court of International Trade, on the other hand, found the U.S. regulations in question consistent with the WTO Antidumping Code.[13] The Court took the position that the WTO panel ruling was not binding precedent, merely informative.

C.   U.S. ANTIDUMPING LAW

§ 12.5   The Evolution of U.S. Antidumping Law

The United States was an early advocate of the perspective that dumping constitutes an unfair international trade practice. Indeed, United States objections to dumping were recorded as the subject of a protest by Secretary of the Treasury Alexander Hamilton in 1791. In general, United States antidumping statutes compare the price at which articles are imported or sold within the United States with their price in the country of their production at the time of their export to the United States. This approach was first established by the Antidumping Act of 1916, a rarely invoked criminal statute, which is functionally similar to price discrimination antitrust statutes applicable to domestic business.[1]

12. See BNA–ATRR (12–16–98) at 2097.

13. Hyundai Electronics Co. v. United States, 53 F.Supp.2d 1334 (C.I.T.1999).

§ 12.5

1. 39 Stat. 798, 15 U.S.C.A. §§ 71–77.

This statute, which also created a private remedy for treble damages, requires proof of an intent to seriously injure or destroy a U.S. industry. This burden of proof has made it almost impossible to prevail as a treble damages dumping plaintiff.[2]

The United States law on antidumping is now set forth in Title I of the Trade Agreements Act of 1979, codified at 19 U.S.C.A. §§ 1671–1677g (as amended). Prior noncriminal antidumping provisions, dating from the Antidumping Act of 1921,[3] were repealed. The new provisions are comparable to, but not always identical with, the GATT and the Tokyo Round GATT Antidumping Code. The principal U.S. antidumping regulations are found in 19 C.F.R. Part 353.

Modern United States law on antidumping provides an increasingly used and effective private international trade remedy. Prior to 1974, the Treasury Department exercised great discretion over whether to impose antidumping duties. Domestic producers might complain, but the Treasury did not have to act at all or within any time limits and its negative decisions were not subject to judicial review. The Trade Act of 1974, by imposing time limits and clarifying judicial review, marked the arrival of U.S. antidumping law as private remedy.

Unlike early U.S. countervailing duty law, the Antidumping Act of 1921 required proof of injury or the threat thereof to a U.S. industry before duties could be levied. As a matter of practice, the Treasury had always interpreted the Act as requiring proof of *material* injury, an interpretation that eventually caused Congress to shift the determination of injury (but not the determination of dumping) to the U.S. Tariff Commission.[4] This bifurcation of the administration of U.S. antidumping law is now carried over in the roles played by the International Trade Administration (ITA) and International Trade Commission (ITC). On the issue of requiring proof of material injury, Congress remained adamantly opposed even to the point of rejecting this standard as part of the Kennedy Round GATT Antidumping Code.[5] It was not until the same standard was also incorporated in the Tokyo Round Antidumping Code that Congress finally relented and made proof of material injury necessary under the Trade Agreements Act of 1979.[6] This Act also transferred the dumping determination from the Treasury to the Commerce Department and continued the trend towards structured procedural rights in U.S. antidumping proceedings.

U.S. law places authority for administering antidumping (AD) law in two different governmental agencies. The "Administering Authority",[7] responsible for all administration except injury determinations, is the

---

2. See In re Japanese Electronic Products Antitrust Litigation, 807 F.2d 44 (3d Cir.1986), cert. denied 481 U.S. 1029, 107 S.Ct. 1955, 95 L.Ed.2d 527 (1987).

3. 42 Stat. 9.

4. Customs Simplification Act of 1954, 68 Stat. 1136, 1138.

5. See Renegotiations Amendments Act of 1968, 82 Stat. 1345.

6. 93 Stat. 148.

7. 19 U.S.C.A. § 1673(1).

Secretary of Commerce,[8] who has designated the International Trade Administration (ITA) as the administering agency. Injury determinations are the responsibility of the International Trade Commission (ITC).[9]

Under current United States law, dumping occurs when foreign merchandise is sold in the United States at "less than its fair value" (LTFV).[10] "Fair value", in turn, is usually determined by the amount charged for the goods in the exporter's domestic market (the "home market").[11] If such sales are both at LTFV and cause or threaten "material injury" to a domestic industry, or retard its development, then an antidumping duty "shall" be imposed. Thus antidumping duties are a statutory remedy, one which the President cannot veto or affect except by negotiation of an international trade agreement. When this occurs, agreement is typically reached with foreign governments to restrain the flow of the offending goods into the U.S. market. These agreements are known as VERs ("voluntary" export restraints). If the complaining U.S. industry is not satisfied with such an agreement, it may generally pursue an antidumping proceeding to its conclusion in spite of the President by refusing to withdraw its complaint.[12] This gives the domestic industry substantial leverage and influence over VER negotiations.

The antidumping duty is in addition to the usual customs duties charged on such products, and is in the amount of the "dumping margin," the difference between the price at which the goods are sold for export to the United States ("United States price")[13] and the "home market" price.[14] The dumping margin may be different for similar merchandise from different foreign states, and may also be different for different manufacturers from the same foreign state.

§ 12.6   The Dumping Determination

The ITA determines whether foreign merchandise is or is likely to be sold in the United States at less than fair value (LTFV) by comparing the "foreign market value" (FMV) to the "United States price" (USP) for such merchandise. If the former exceeds the latter, dumping can be found, which places great stress on the definitions of these two terms. Since the FMV is normally calculated as an average price, and the USP is a transaction-specific price, dumping can be found despite the fact that the average USP exceeds the average FMV.

8. Prior to 1980, the Treasury Department was the "administering authority", but the Secretary of Commerce was so designated in 1980. See President's Reorganization Plan No. 3 of 1979, 44 Fed.Reg. 69,273 (1979); and Executive Order 12188, 45 Fed.Reg. 989 (1980).

9. 19 U.S.C.A. §§ 1673(2) and 1677(2).

10. 19 U.S.C.A. § 1673(1). Thus, in place of the GATT formulation of "less than its normal value" (Tokyo Round

GATT Antidumping Code, Art. 2(1)), the United States AD statute substitutes "fair" value. As is discussed below, no substantive difference is created however.

11. 19 U.S.C.A. §§ 1673, 1673b(b)(1)(A).

12. See 19 U.S.C.A. § 1673c(a).

13. 19 U.S.C.A. § 1677a.

14. 19 U.S.C.A. § 1677b.

§ 12.7 Foreign Market Value

"Foreign market value" is the weighted average wholesale F.O.B. shipment price of the merchandise in the exporter's home (foreign) market—after many adjustments to assure comparability.[1] If sales in the home market are nonexistent or too small to form an adequate basis for comparison, usually less than 5 percent, then export sales to other countries may be used.[2] Export sales to other countries may be used even when they comprise less than 5 percent of export sales to the United States.[3] Sales intended to establish fictitious markets in the source country cannot be considered.[4]

If comparable merchandise is not offered for sale either in the home market or for export to other countries, the ITA is authorized to calculate a "constructed" foreign market value.[5] Such constructed values are most often used when the ITA determines that the merchandise is being sold at less than the cost of production,[6] and also for imports from nonmarket economies.[7]

The time and place to be used in establishing the home market value is often crucial. The time is when the merchandise is first sold within the United States by the importer to a person who is not related to the importer.[8] That is also the date for determining the exchange rate to be used in converting prices in foreign currency into United States dollars.[9] When the goods are manufactured in one country and then shipped to another, from which they are exported to the United States, there is a question as to whether the foreign market value is to be determined according to prices in the country of manufacture or the country of transshipment. The statute does provide a partial answer. The prices in country of transshipment are to be used when:

(1) the manufacturer sells to "a reseller" and the manufacturer does not know to what country the reseller intends to export the merchandise;

(2) the merchandise is exported to a country other than the United States, enters into the commerce of that other country, but is not substantially transformed in that country; AND

(3) the goods are later exported to the United States.[10]

In determining foreign market value, averaging and generally recognized sampling techniques may be used whenever there is a significant volume of sales or number of adjustments. The samples are selected by

§ 12.7

1. 19 U.S.C.A. § 1677b(a)(1)(A); 19 C.F.R. § 353.46.

2. 19 U.S.C.A. § 1677b(a)(1)(B); 19 C.F.R. § 353.48.

3. Certain Dried Salted Codfish from Canada, 50 Fed.Reg. 20,819 (1985), 7 ITRD 2121.

4. 19 U.S.C.A. § 1677b(a)(1), (5).

5. 19 U.S.C.A. § 1677b(a)(2); 19 C.F.R. § 353.50.

6. 19 C.F.R. § 353.51.

7. 19 U.S.C.A. § 1677b(c).

8. 19 U.S.C.A. § 1677b(a)(1). Prior to 1984, the time used was the time of export of the merchandise to the United States.

9. 19 C.F.R. § 353.60(a).

10. 19 U.S.C.A. § 1677b(g).

the Secretary, but must be "appropriate" and "representative." [11] Insignificant adjustments "may" be disregarded, and will ordinarily be disregarded when their individual *ad valorem* effect is less than 0.33 percent, or when a group of adjustments has an *ad valorem* effect of less than 1.0 percent of the foreign market value.[12]

Other issues relating to the determination of foreign market value are discussed below. These problems include issues arising out of sales at less than costs of production, constructed values, imports from non-market economy countries, special rules for multinational corporations, and adjustments necessary to get comparable prices.

§ 12.8 United States Price

To determine whether dumping exists, it is necessary to compare the "foreign market value" to the "United States price," which is either the "purchase price" or the "exporter's sales price." [1] The "purchase price" is the price at which the goods were purchased in a foreign market prior to importation into the United States, if the purchase was from a producer or reseller of the merchandise to a non-related buyer for export to the United States.[2] The purchase price may, however, not be the price of the last sale before importation. Where the producer sells to a reseller knowing that the reseller will, prior to importation into the United States, resell the goods for export to the United States, the ITA has used the price between the producer and reseller as the purchase price.[3]

The "exporter's sales price" is the price at which the goods are sold or are likely to be sold in the United States, either before or after importation, by an "exporter." [4] "Exporter" is a defined term, and includes not only the actual exporter from or producer in a foreign market, but also any agent or related entity in the United States which, directly or indirectly, is controlled by or controls that actual exporter or producer.[5] It also includes entities which are controlled (20 percent or more of voting power) by a third party which controls (20 percent or more of voting power) the actual exporter or producer. Thus, use of the "exporter's sale price" is an attempt to avoid transfer sale problems, and to prohibit use of prices arising out of sales between related parties.[6]

The determination of whether to compare the "purchase price" or the "exporter's sales price" to the "foreign market value" does not depend upon whether the sale occurred before or after the importation. Instead, the purchase price will be used for comparison only if the sale transaction resulted in the goods being shipped directly to a United States purchaser through customary commercial channels for the parties

11. 19 C.F.R. § 353.59(b).

12. 19 C.F.R. § 353.59(a).

§ 12.8

1. 19 U.S.C.A. § 1677a(a).

2. 19 U.S.C.A. § 1677a(b).

3. Sandvik AB v. United States, 721 F.Supp. 1322 (C.I.T.1989).

4. 19 U.S.C.A. § 1677a(c).

5. 19 U.S.C.A. § 1677(13).

6. PQ Corp. v. United States, 652 F.Supp. 724 (C.I.T.1987).

involved, and the exporter's related United States sales agents act only as communications links and documentation processors.[7]

§ 12.9 Sales Below Cost

Sales at less than cost of production are to be disregarded in determining "foreign market value;" but only if the below-cost sales have been over an extended time, in substantial quantities, and will not permit recovery of all costs within a reasonable time in the normal course of trade.[1] Thus, recovery of start up costs can properly be prorated over commercially normative periods. Omission of sales below cost from FMV calculations naturally raises the average FMV and increases the potential to find dumping. Inclusion has the opposite effect.

The central question in most antidumping proceedings is whether and to what degree the foreign producer or exporter is making a portion of its sales in its own market at below cost of production.[2] The ITA interprets "extended time" to mean the investigation period, usually the most recent six months.[3] More than ten percent of total sales, measured by volume, will meet the "substantial quantities" requirement, although fifty percent is sometimes required for fresh agricultural products. Sales are below cost is they do not recover total costs, both fixed and variable, over a commercially normative period.[4] Thus, a significant volume of sales by a foreign producer at prices which cover only its variable costs can be disregarded by the ITA in its calculation of foreign market value.

§ 12.10 The DOC's Policy Concerning Application of the "10–90–10" Test

Trade law practitioner Irwin P. Altschuler of the Washington, D.C. firm of Manatt, Phelps & Phillips has summarized below the approaches taken by the ITA in determining whether to exclude or include sales below cost in calculating foreign market value under what is known as the "10–90–10" test. Petitioners for U.S. antidumping relief will be pleased that a model-by-model analysis under this test is now the official policy of the ITA. This policy was announced in an unpublished, unnotified bulletin dated Dec. 15, 1992 (reproduced in the Selected Documents section of this chapter).

Under the statute, the Department of Commerce (DOC) is authorized to disregard below cost sales in the calculation of foreign market value (that is, not use them as the basis for price-to-price

7. Internal–Combustion Industrial Forklift Trucks from Japan, 52 Fed.Reg. 45,003 (1987).

§ 12.9

1. 19 U.S.C.A. § 1677b(b). See generally Timken Co. v. United States, 673 F.Supp. 495 (C.I.T.1987) (review of ITA practice on sales below cost).

2. Palmeter, Antidumping Law: A Legal and Administrative Nontariff Barrier, in Down in the Dumps, at 73 (R. Boltuck and R.E. Litan, eds.) (Brookings, 1991).

3. 19 C.F.R. § 353.42(b).

4. Palmeter, supra Note 2.

comparisons) if they were made in substantial quantities, over an extended period of time, and at prices that would prohibit the recovery of all costs over a reasonable period of time.[1] To determine whether below cost sales were made in substantial quantities, the DOC has always utilized the "10–90–10" test. Under this test, if less than 10 percent of sales are below cost, then the DOC will use all reported home market sales in the calculation of FMV. If more than 10 percent but less than 90 percent of home market sales were made at below cost, the DOC will disregard all sales made below cost and only include above cost sales in the calculation of FMV. If 90 percent or more of reported sales are below cost, then the DOC would disregard all reported sales and use constructed value to calculate FMV.

The question then arises as to how the DOC applies the 10–90–10 test. Respondents have always favored a "universal" or "macro" application of the test—that is, applying the 10–90–10 test to *total* home market sales of the merchandise subject to review. Under the *universal* test, below cost sales may still be used for fair value comparisons if such sales constitute less than 10 percent of *total* home market sales. Petitioners have always favored a "model-by-model" analysis which would maximize the number of sales eliminated from fair value comparisons.

It has been the ITA's policy to apply a combination of the two tests. The DOC would first apply the universal test, and if between 10 percent and 90 percent of total home market sales were below cost, the DOC would determine that there was a substantial quantity of below cost sales. The DOC would then conduct further analysis and compare home market prices to cost a second time, by applying the 10–90–10 test on a *model-by-model* basis to determine whether and the extent to which to exclude sales for purposes of fair value comparisons.[2] If under the universal test, less than 10 percent of sales were below cost, or more than 90 percent of sales were below cost, application of the model-by-model test would be unnecessary since either all sales would be considered (less than 10 percent of all sales below cost) or none of the sales would be considered (more than 90 percent of all sales below cost).

The DOC's Policy Bulletin No. 92/3 announces that from December 12, 1992 forward, the DOC will apply the 10–90–10 test on a *model-by-model basis only*. The DOC will no longer use the universal test or the combination test in applying the 10–90–10 test. The DOC policy bulletin further states that the policy will be applied in active anti-dumping cases where there has not been a preliminary determination and in cases where the final results are pending if the issue was raised by the parties.

§ 12.10

1. 19 U.S.C.A. § 1677b(b).

2. See e.g., Certain Carbon Steel Butt–Weld Pipe Fittings from Thailand, 57 Fed. Reg. 21,065, 21,070 (1992).

The ITA may investigate the cost of production on its own motion, and must begin such an investigation if it has reasonable grounds to believe or suspect that sales are being made in the exporter's home market at less than cost of production.[3] Petitioners need produce only enough evidence to create such reasonable grounds for belief, and meet no higher burden of proof, although company-specific sales data is usually necessary.[4] If the ITA disregards some sales because those sales are at below cost prices, it is to determine foreign market value from the remaining sales, unless the remaining sales are an inadequate basis for determining that value. In the latter case, the ITA uses a constructed value to determine foreign market value.[5]

§ 12.11 Nonmarket Economies Included

A constructed value is always used to determine the "foreign market value" of imports from nonmarket economy countries.[1] The actual prices used in the exporter's (home) foreign market are deemed irrelevant because they are assumed to be determined bureaucratically and not by market forces. They are not sufficiently subject to the forces of competition to form an accurate standard for comparison.[2]

The statute defines "nonmarket economy country" in terms of a determination by the ITA,[3] and insulates that administrative determination from judicial review.[4] Within that procedure, the statute gives the ITA a criterion—whether the country's economy operates on "market principles" so that (home market) sales reflect "fair value"—and five factors to consider.[5] The factors include the convertability of the foreign country's currency, the extent to which wages and prices are determined by government control or free bargaining, the extent of governmental ownership of the means of production and the receptivity to private foreign investment. Although the statute speaks in terms of a country by country decision, the ITA has more often analyzed the particular industrial segment involved.[6] In 1992, the ITA indicated that determinations regarding nonmarket economy status will follow its traditional practice and focus upon government involvement in fixing prices and production, private versus collective ownership and the degree of market pricing for industrial inputs. Under these criteria, many believe that the People's Republic of China or at least the Southern Coastal region

3. 19 U.S.C.A. § 1677b(b).

4. Huffy Corp. v. United States, 632 F.Supp. 50 (C.I.T.1986).

5. 19 C.F.R. § 353.51(b).

§ 12.11

1. 19 U.S.C.A. § 1677b(c).

2. The courts came to the same conclusion before the enactment of the 1988 Omnibus Trade and Competitiveness Act. See

Georgetown Steel Corp. v. United States, 801 F.2d 1308 (Fed.Cir.1986).

3. 19 U.S.C.A. § 1677(18)(A), (C).

4. 19 U.S.C.A. § 1677(18)(D).

5. 19 U.S.C.A. § 1677(18)(B).

6. See, e.g., Certain Headwear from China, 54 Fed.Reg. 11,983, 54 Fed.Reg. 18,561 (1989); Natural Menthol from the People's Republic of China, 46 Fed.Reg. 3,258 (1981).

thereof may be treated as a market economy source under U.S. anti-dumping law.[7]

§ 12.12 Nonmarket Economy Constructed Values

If the imports are from a nonmarket economy (NME) country, the statute directs the ITA to "construct" a foreign market value by determining the factors of production (labor, materials, energy, capital, etc.) actually used by the NME to produce the imported goods.[1] A value for each of those factors of production must then be determined according to the prices or costs in a market economy, but the ITA is directed to use countries "considered to be appropriate." Surrogate countries are appropriate if they are at the same level of economic development and are significant producers of comparable merchandise.[2]

To the cost of production, as constructed by this use of factors of production, the ITA is directed to add amounts for general expenses, profits, containers and packing for shipment to the United States. The amounts for general expenses and profits are to be derived from sales of the same class or kind of merchandise in the "country of exportation,"[3] but that really means the surrogate "appropriate" market economy country. The general expenses must be at least 10 percent of the cost of production, and profit must be at least 8 percent of the cost of production plus general expenses.

Several problems arise in the application of this scheme. First, "appropriate" market economy countries may be limited or not available. Second, the surrogate market economy countries selected may be obviously inappropriate, when compared to the level of economic development of the NME.[4] Third, producers in such countries may not furnish the necessary information, even though the ITA is authorized to use the "best available information."[5] Fourth, there is no necessary relationship between the price so constructed by the ITA and any price which the NME producer may decide to charge. This leaves the NME producer or exporter always open to dumping charges, and there is no pre-transaction analytical path for avoiding the dumping charges.

In recognition of some of these difficulties, the statute provides an exception to the construction method outlined above, allowing the use of a different method of constructing a foreign market value for imports from a NME. This second method may be used if the ITA finds that the best available information on factors of production is not adequate. The second, less preferred method of constructing foreign market value of

---

7. See Chrome–Plated Lug Nuts from China, 57 Fed.Reg. 15,052 (1992).

§ 12.12

1. 19 U.S.C.A. § 1677b(c)(1).

2. 19 U.S.C.A. § 1677b(c)(4).

3. 19 U.S.C.A. § 1677b(e)(1)(B).

4. The statutory language has, in the past, allowed Canadian prices to be applied to goods produced in Poland, and Paraguayan prices to commodities from China. See Natural Menthol from the People's Republic of China, 46 Fed.Reg. 3,258 (1981); Electric Golf Cars from Poland, 40 Fed.Reg. 25,497 (1975).

5. 19 U.S.C.A. § 1677b(c)(1).

exports from NMEs, is to find a "surrogate" market economy country that produces the same or goods similar to the merchandise imported from the NME, and base the foreign market value on the price of the goods imported from the surrogate country.[6] Such a construction methodology does not require the ITA to break the pricing of the goods into factors of production.

§ 12.13 Market Economy Constructed Values

The ITA may use constructed values not only for imports from NME countries, but in other circumstances as well. It is directed to construct a foreign market value whenever merchandise comparable to the imported merchandise is not offered for sale either in the home market of the foreign producer or exporter or for export from that home market to other countries.[1] A constructed foreign market value is also to be used when so many sales in the home market are below cost of production, and therefore are disregarded, that the remaining sales provide an inadequate basis for determining foreign market value.[2]

In the circumstances above (not involving NME merchandise), foreign market value is constructed by calculating the actual producer variable costs of production (materials, labor, energy, etc.), then adding industry-normative amounts for general overhead, profit, containers and packing.[3] The "general expenses" usually include a portion of all fixed costs fully allocated to the portion of merchandise exported to the United States, and must be at least ten percent of variable costs, and may be higher if that is done by other producers in the exporting country in the ordinary course of trade. A minimum profit of eight percent is also added, but again may be higher if other producers in the exporting country generally seek higher percentage profits in the ordinary course of their trade.

Actual costs of inputs purchased by the producer from third parties "may be disregarded" if the producer and the third party are related in any way, including the common ownership of five percent of voting stock by any third party.[4] If the actual cost of the input is disregarded, the ITA is directed to look first at other transactions in the market, and if none to use the best evidence available. Where a "major input" is provided by a related person, and there are reasonable grounds to believe it was furnished at below the cost of production, the ITA is authorized to consult the best evidence available.[5]

There is a special rule for determining the foreign market value of merchandise produced by a corporation having production facilities in

---

6. 19 U.S.C.A. § 1677b(c)(2). Until 1988, this method of construction was the normal method for constructing a foreign market value for imports from a NME.

§ 12.13

1. 19 U.S.C.A. § 1677b(a)(2); 19 C.F.R. § 353.50.

2. 19 U.S.C.A. § 1677b(b); 19 C.F.R. § 353.51(b).

3. 19 U.S.C.A. § 1677b(e)(1).

4. 19 U.S.C.A. § 1677b(e)(2), (4).

5. 19 U.S.C.A. § 1677b(e)(3).

two or more countries, where there are insufficient sales by that producer in its home market on which to base a comparison of its export sales to the United States.[6] If the foreign market value of the goods produced in the country of exportation is less than the price of the goods produced in the corporation's facilities in another country, the ITA "shall" construct a foreign market value which reflects the price of the goods produced in the nonexporting country.

§ 12.14   Similar Merchandise and Price Adjustments

All of the analysis above depends upon a comparison of the prices of "such or similar merchandise."[1] Since merchandise sold in foreign markets is often different, due to cultural, technical or legal constraints, the determination of comparability of merchandise sold in the foreign market to the imported merchandise is often a crucial one. The statute provides a definition, with a hierarchy of criteria.[2] Thus, merchandise which is identical in physical characteristics, and produced in the same country by the same person as the imported merchandise is to be categorized as such or similar merchandise.[3]

If such identical merchandise is not available, the ITA next looks for merchandise which is produced in the same country by the same person which has component materials and is approximately equal in value to the imported merchandise.[4] If neither of the above is available, the ITA is to look at merchandise produced in the same country by the same person, used for the same purpose and "may reasonably be compared with" the imported merchandise.[5] In practice, the ITA considers similarities in the physical characteristics, use and expectations of ultimate purchasers, including advertising of the product, and distribution channels.[6]

A considerable number of adjustments are necessary to obtain comparable prices for goods sold in home markets and for export to the United States. To obtain the United States price, packing costs and container costs are added to the purchase price or exporter's sales price, if they are not already included in that price.[7] Other amounts added to obtain the United States price include any import duties or other taxes which are rebated or not collected by the country of exportation, and which are imposed on similar merchandise sold in the country of exportation.

Adjustments deducted from the purchase price or exporter's sales price include any expenses, such as freight or insurance, included in that price and attributable to the costs of bringing the goods from the country

---

6. 19 U.S.C.A. § 1677b(d).

§ 12.14

1. 19 U.S.C.A. § 1677b(a)(1)(A).

2. 19 U.S.C.A. § 1677(16).

3. 19 U.S.C.A. § 1677(16)(A).

4. 19 U.S.C.A. § 1677(16)(B).

5. 19 U.S.C.A. § 1677(16)(C).

6. 3.5 inch Microdisks and Coated Media from Japan, 54 Fed.Reg. 6433, 11 ITRD 1767 (1989); Antifriction Bearings from West Germany, 54 Fed.Reg. 18,992, 11 ITRD 2204 (1989).

7. 19 U.S.C.A. § 1677a(d)(1).

of export to the United States and most export taxes of the exporting country.[8] There are also deductions for any commissions and other expenses for selling in the United States and the costs of additional processing or assembly in the United States after importation and before sale.[9] But the additional cost of U.S. product liability insurance is not an allowable adjustment.[10]

Adjustments and exchange rate conversions are also made to determine the foreign market value of the goods. Exchange rate conversions are required whenever the USP or FMV sales are not in U.S. dollars. The rates for the relevant sales period as determined quarterly by the Federal Reserve Bank of New York are ordinarily used except when those rates are fluctuating rapidly.[11] In such cases, the ITA will test whether the dumping margin remains if the rates from the prior quarter are used. If the margin disappears, the dumping is attributed to exchange rate fluctuations and the ITA may determine that no dumping occurred.

To obtain an equivalent of the conditions of the United States price, an amount equal to the packing costs and container costs for shipment to the United States is added to the foreign market value.[12] Allowances may be made for sales at different trade levels (wholesale versus retail), quantity or production cost justified discounts, differences in the circumstances of sale and for physical differences in the merchandise.[13] Differences in the circumstances of the sale include credit terms, warranties, servicing, technical assistance, and advertising allowances. Adjustments for cost differences in the circumstances of sale are allowable even if they do not give rise to comparable price increases in the foreign market.[14] And even if they involve rebates or discounts not made available to all purchasers.[15] These decisions reflect the substantial deference given by the Court of International Trade and appellate courts to the ITA on the important issue of adjustments to its FMV and United States Price calculations.

§ 12.15 The Injury Determination

Antidumping proceedings in the United States are conducted in two stages. In the second stage, the International Trade Commission (ITC) must determine whether the dumping has caused material injury to

8. 19 U.S.C.A. § 1677a(d)(2). See Zenith Electronics Corp. v. United States, 755 F.Supp. 397 (C.I.T.1990) affirmed 988 F.2d 1573 (Fed.Cir.1993).

9. 19 U.S.C.A. § 1677a(e).

10. See Carlisle Tire & Rubber Co. v. United States, 622 F.Supp. 1071 (C.I.T. 1985).

11. 19 C.F.R. § 353.60(b); see Washington Red Raspberry Commission v. United States, 859 F.2d 898 (Fed.Cir.1988).

12. 19 U.S.C.A. § 1677b(a)(1).

13. 19 U.S.C. § 1677b(a)(4). See Smith–Corona Group v. United States, 713 F.2d 1568 (Fed.Cir.1983), cert. denied 465 U.S. 1022, 104 S.Ct. 1274, 79 L.Ed.2d 679 (1984) (advertising and rebate sale adjustments upheld) (physically different accessory adjustments upheld).

14. See Atlantic Steel Co. v. United States, 636 F.Supp. 917 (C.I.T.1986) (credit and warehousing costs).

15. Zenith Radio Corp. v. United States, 783 F.2d 184 (Fed.Cir.1986).

concerned domestic industries.[1] This section reviews the material injury determination under United States law, including market definition, injury factors and causation.

The Tariff Act provides that an affirmative injury determination should be made when an industry in the United States is "materially" injured or is threatened with material injury by reason of dumped imports, or the establishment of an industry in the United States is materially retarded.[2] The "material injury" standard is applied to established industries, and is defined in the statute.[3] The "threat of material injury" standard is separately stated, but has a substantial overlap with the material injury criteria.[4] The standard for "material retardation" of the establishment of an industry is applied to new industries which have made a substantial commitment to begin production, or have recently begun production.[5]

§ 12.16   Like Domestic Products

Both the ITA and the ITC must determine what constitute "like products" in performing their duties under U.S. antidumping law. The ITA necessarily focuses upon which foreign products are like those alleged to be dumped in the United States. And the ITC must define the relevant domestic industry producing like products in making its injury assessment. The term "like products" is defined by statute as one which is "like, or in the absence of like, most similar in characteristics and uses" to the foreign product under investigation. Although this definition applies to both the ITA and the ITC, they do not always agree on the outcome.[1]

The determination of like products can be influential to ITA dumping and particularly ITC injury decision-making. In one case, for example, the ITC excluded large screen TVs from the U.S. domestic industry definition. This had the effect of giving Japanese TV exports a much larger market share in the U.S., thus supporting an affirmative injury determination.[2] In another decision, the ITC defined the U.S. industry as canned mushrooms, noting that fresh mushrooms were not always interchangeable. This narrow market definition again supported a preliminary injury determination.[3] Variations on the theme of defining "like products" can occur if the ITC decides it is appropriate to exclude domestic companies that also import the allegedly dumped goods

---

§ 12.15

1. See 19 U.S.C.A. § 1673(2).

2. 19 U.S.C.A. § 1673(2).

3. 19 U.S.C.A. § 1677(7).

4. 19 U.S.C.A. § 1677(7)(F).

5. BMT Commodity Corp. v. United States, 667 F.Supp. 880 (C.I.T.1987), affirmed 852 F.2d 1285 (Fed.Cir.1988), cert. denied, 489 U.S. 1012, 109 S.Ct. 1120, 103 L.Ed.2d 183 (1989).

§ 12.16

1. See Tantalum Electrolytic Fixed Capacitors from Japan, U.S.I.T.C. Publ. No. 789 (Oct. 1976).

2. Television Sets from Japan, U.S.I.T.C. Publ. No. 367 (March 1971).

3. Canned Mushrooms from the People's Republic of China, U.S.I.T.C. Publ. No. 1324 (Dec. 1982).

or are related to the importer or foreign producer.[4] The ITC may also define the domestic industry regionally in situations where that reflects market realities.[5] Thus, which U.S. firms (and their relative state of economic health) are included or excluded in the ITC's like products definition of the domestic industry is an important threshold issue in material injury analysis.

§ 12.17 Material Injury

There are two potential positions on the meaning of "material." The first is that the term material means any economic harm that is more than trivial, inconsequential or *de minimis*. The second is that material injury means a higher threshold, something not quite as hurtful as the "serious injury" required for escape clause relief,[1] but yet still serious in the ordinary sense of that word. The consensus was that the spirit of Article VI of the GATT was intended to procure the higher standard.[2]

The Tariff Act incorporated the concept of materiality when the Act was amended by the Trade Agreements Act of 1979 in an effort to bring United States law into conformity with the Tokyo Round GATT Antidumping Code. Before the amendment, the ITC used a standard of injury known as the *"de minimis"* standard [3] with congressional approval.[4] Under that standard, antidumping duties could be imposed if the injury was more than *de minimis*.[5]

The Tariff Act defines material injury as "harm which is not inconsequential, immaterial, or unimportant." [6] This is the same standard that applies in CVD proceedings "under the Agreement" [7] and much of the law in the area may therefore be treated as interchangeable. Although the material injury definition seems to require a higher standard than a mere injury requirement, the Senate Finance Committee report did not consider them inconsistent. It stated that the material injury standard was nothing more than a codification of the *de minimis* standard as it had been construed by the ITC.[8] The ITC's subsequent interpretations suggest that it understood the material injury requirement to codify the *de minimis* rule.[9]

---

4. 19 U.S.C.A. § 1677(4)(B).

5. 19 U.S.C.A. § 1677(4)(C). See National Pork Producers Council v. United States, 661 F.Supp. 633 (C.I.T.1987).

§ 12.17

1. See Chapter 8.

2. Hudec, United States Compliance with the 1967 GATT Antidumping Code, in 1 Antidumping Law; Policy and Implementation 217 (Michigan Yearbook of International Legal Studies 1979).

3. See Titanium Sponge from the U.S.S.R., 33 Fed.Reg. 10,769, 10,772 (1968).

4. See S.Rep. No. 1298, 93d Cong., 1st Sess. 180 (1974).

5. See, e.g., Cast Iron Soil Pipe from Poland, USTC 214 (AA 1921–50) (1967).

6. 19 U.S.C.A. § 1677(7)(A).

7. See Chapter 7.

8. Senate Comm. on Finance, Trade Agreements Act of 1979, S.Rep. No. 249, 96th Cong., 1st Sess. 87.

9. Vermulst, supra Note 2, § 6.3, at 364–76.

After the development of the Tokyo Round GATT Antidumping Code, however, the United States amended its statutes to incorporate the Code's principles. The Tariff Act requires the ITC to consider three basic economic aspects in applying the injury standard:

> (1) The volume of imports of the merchandise subject to investigation;

> (2) The effect of these imports on prices in the United States for like products; and

> (3) The impact of these imports on domestic producers of like products, but only in the context of domestic United States production operations.[10]

The Commission is required to explain its analysis of each factor considered and explain its relevance to the agency's determination. The Tariff Act, however, also provides that the "presence or absence" of any of these three factors should "not necessarily give decisive guidance" to the ITC in its material injury determination, and the Commission is not required to give any particular weight to any one factor.[11] The factors are examined through extensive statistical analyses. The analysis is performed for the domestic industry as a whole, and not on a company-by-company basis.[12] The ITC may select whatever time period best represents the business cycle and competitive conditions in the industry, and most reasonably allows it to determine whether an injury exists.[13]

Volume of Imports

In compliance with Tokyo Round GATT Antidumping Code Article 3(2), the Tariff Act requires the ITC to consider the absolute volume of imports or any increase in volume of imports in evaluating the volume of imports subject to investigation. This assessment may be made in relation to production or consumption in the United States. The standard in this evaluation is whether the volume of imports, viewed in any of the above ways, is significant.[14]

Data relating to the volume of imports are an important factor in the ITC's injury determinations.[15] In particular, the ITC is more concerned with the dynamics of the market share, such as a significant rise

---

10. 19 U.S.C.A. § 1677(7)(B). See Angus Chemical Co. v. United States, 140 F.3d 1478 (Fed.Cir.1998) (three factors are mandatory for ITC to consider).

11. 19 U.S.C.A. § 1677(7)(E)(ii). See e.g., Iwatsu Elec. Co. v. United States, 758 F.Supp. 1506, 13 ITRD 1120 (C.I.T.1991) (ITC may weigh each factor in light of circumstances and need not find all economic factors negative before it makes a finding of injury). Compare Tokyo Round GATT Antidumping Code Art. 3(2).

12. Copperweld Corp. v. United States, 682 F.Supp. 552 (C.I.T.1988).

13. 19 U.S.C.A. § 1677(7)(C)(iii); Kenda Rubber Industrial Co., Ltd. v. United States, 630 F.Supp. 354 (C.I.T.1986).

14. 19 U.S.C.A. § 1677(7)(C)(i).

15. See, e.g., Certain Seamless Steel Pipes and Tubes from Japan, 47 Fed.Reg. 11,331 (1982) (affirmative preliminary injury determination) (Japanese import tonnage in the heat-resisting category almost tripled during the period of investigation and import penetration nearly doubled).

in market penetration, than it is with the size of market share.[16] It is also primarily concerned with the effects that market share changes might have on profits and lost sales.[17] Injury can be found when an importer has a small market share, but imports from a single country are increasing rapidly and the domestic industry reduces its prices during the period of investigation.[18] On the other hand, a large market share for the importer, coupled with increases in production, domestic shipments, exports, employment and profits of the domestic industry, may indicate no injury.

Price Effects

While price issues are obviously crucial to any determination of dumping margins, they have no strict correlation to injury determinations. However, under the Tariff Act, the ITC when making an injury determination may consider the effect of the dumped imports upon prices for like products in the domestic market. This is done to the extent that such a consideration assists in evaluating whether (1) there is significant price underselling by the imported merchandise as compared with the price of like products of the United States,[19] and (2) whether the effect of the imported merchandise is otherwise to depress domestic prices to a significant degree or prevent price increases, which otherwise would have occurred to a significant degree.[20] If there is no price underselling, but instead the exporters cut their U.S. prices to effectively meet price competition from U.S. producers, this is traditionally considered only "technical dumping" and precludes a finding of material injury.[21] The rationale for this approach focuses upon the purposes behind AD law; to prevent unfair not procompetitive trade practices. Thus, technical dumping constitutes a defense to U.S. material injury determinations.

Price underselling is not a *per se* basis for a finding of injury. For example, if the demand for the product is not price sensitive, price underselling will not be a central consideration in any injury finding. There may be no injury from price underselling, even though the domestic producers lost sales in the United States, if the domestic producers' inability to sell goods was not caused by dumped imports. For example, the industry's decline may have been caused by its failure

16. *J. Pattison,* Antidumping and Countervailing Duty Laws 4–2 (1992).

17. See, e.g., Tubeless Tire Valves from Federal Republic of Germany, 46 Fed.Reg. 29,794 (1981) (dumped imports of tubeless tire valves from West Germany caused United States producers to lose sales).

18. Barbed Wire and Barbless Wire Strand from Argentina, 7 ITRD 2610, I.T.C. Pub. No. 1770 (October 1985) (increase from 0.5 to 4.0 percent of market). However, import penetration of only 0.2 percent has been found incapable of causing materi-

al injury. Alberta Pork Producers' Marketing Board v. United States, 669 F.Supp. 445 (C.I.T.1987), appeal after remand 683 F.Supp. 1398 (C.I.T.1988).

19. 19 U.S.C.A. § 1677(7)(C)(ii)(I).

20. 19 U.S.C.A. § 1677(7)(C)(ii)(II).

21. Asphalt Roofing Shingles from Canada, 2 ITRD 5171 (Oct. 1980); Rayon Staple Fibers from France and Belgium, U.S.I.T.C. Inv. No. AA1921–17 and 18 (1961).

to develop, produce and market a competitive product. A more extensive analysis of causation issues appears in the next subsection.

Substantial underselling, on the other hand, will lead to an affirmative injury finding, where the market is price sensitive.[22] The ITC looks for a pervasive pattern of underselling, which can occur even where there are instances of overselling as well.[23] When the ITC finds that demand for a specific product is price sensitive and importers are engaging in price underselling, it further examines whether domestic producers are being forced into price suppression[24] or actual price cutting[25] due to this price underselling. Since price suppression can be as severe a burden to domestic producers as can an actual price cutting, the ITC will find an injury if it determines that because of the less-than-fair-value price of the dumped imports, domestic producers have lowered or have been unable to raise their prices to accommodate rising costs.[26]

Domestic Industry Impact

The impact on a domestic industry of an allegedly dumped product is probably the most important factor in any injury analysis. The Tariff Act employs the same criteria as are set out in the Tokyo Round GATT Antidumping Code.[27] It then provides supplemental factors for ITC consideration, adding the actual and potential negative effects on the existing development and production efforts of the domestic industry, including efforts to develop a derivative or more advanced version of the like product.[28] The ITC relies primarily on two of these factors in

22. The ITC views a product as price sensitive when its price is the most important factor in purchasing the product. In Tubeless Tire Valves from the Federal Republic of Germany, 46 Fed.Reg. 29,794 (1981), the ITC relied upon the testimony of buyers who had switched their sourcing from domestic producers to the imports that price was the most important factor in purchasing decisions, with availability a secondary but often critical factor. Id. at 29,795.

23. Metallverken Nederland B.V. v. United States, 728 F.Supp. 730 (C.I.T. 1989), on remand 12 ITRD 1784 (1990), action dismissed 744 F.Supp. 281 (C.I.T. 1990).

24. Price suppression arises when the domestic industry can affect smaller price increases on those articles directly competitive with dumped imports than it can on those articles that directly compete with non-dumped imports. Tapered Roller bearings from Japan, 40 Fed.Reg. 26,312, 26,-314–26,315 (1975).

25. Price cutting arises when the domestic industry is compelled to lower its prices to meet the prices of dumped imports in an attempt to protect its market share.

26. See, e.g., Unrefined Montan Wax from East Germany, 46 Fed.Reg. 45,223, 45,224 (1981).

27. 19 U.S.C.A. § 1677(C)(iii) provides:

In examining the impact required to be considered under subparagraph (B)(iii), the Commission shall evaluate all relevant economic factors which have a bearing on the state of the industry in the United States, including, but not limited to—

(I) actual and potential decline in output, sales, market share, profits, productivity, return on investments, and utilization of capacity,

(II) factors affecting domestic prices,

(III) actual and potential negative effects on cash flow, inventories, employment, wages, growth, ability to raise capital, and investment, and

(IV) actual and potential negative effects on the existing development and production efforts of the of the domestic industry, including efforts to develop a derivative or more advanced version of the like product.

28. 19 U.S.C.A. § 1677(7)(C)(iii)(IV).

making this determination. First, the industry must be in a distressed or a stagnant condition. Second, the ITC analyzes whether low domestic price levels are a factor in the industry's difficulties (e.g., high unemployment or low capacity utilization rate), and whether the low prices are causing low profits.[29]

The ITC will often base an affirmative determination of material injury on severe downward trends in profitability among domestic producers. For example, a drop in the ratio of net profit to sales from 5.55 percent to 1.05 percent over a three year period, coupled with a 75 percent decline in the aggregate profit in the relevant industry in the same period, has resulted in an affirmative determination of material injury.[30] Thus, it is not necessary that an industry suffer an actual loss as a prerequisite to a finding of material injury.

When a negative injury determination has been made despite the industry's declining profitability, the ITC may find alternative injury factors such as general economic conditions and industry overexpansion, which are unrelated to dumping or subsidization of foreign goods.[31] On the other hand, absent other severe injury factors, a general upward trend and strong profitability of domestic firms is likely to result in a negative determination.[32]

The effect of dumped imports on employment in the relevant domestic industry is also considered. Employment data are not dispositive due to the broad spectrum of economic factors related to such data, and many of those factors may not be attributable to dumping. However, changes in domestic employment during the period of dumping are one factor to be considered. For example, the ITC has found a 35 percent drop in employment during the period of dumping to be a reasonable indication of material injury.[33] On the other hand, where employment and man-hours worked have increased in the domestic industry, this data will be cited by the ITC as a factor in its determination that there has been no material injury.[34] But such negative determinations are usually made only when other factors also indicate no material injury is present.

The utilization of plant capacity has been considered a factor in many determinations, but such capacity utilization data is treated ambiguously because it is dependent upon diverse factors. For example, a reasonable indication of material injury has been found when capacity utilization fell from 88 percent to 77 percent in two years.[35] However,

29. Vermulst, supra Note 2, § 6.3, at 369.

30. Sugars and Syrups from Canada, 46 Fed.Reg. 51,086 (1981).

31. See, e.g., Silicon Metal from Canada, 44 Fed.Reg. 13,590 (1981).

32. Motorcycle Batteries from Taiwan, 46 Fed.Reg. 53,235 (1981) (negative final injury determination) (data regarding profitability data showed the industry as a whole to be prosperous during times of greatest import penetration).

33. Montan Wax from the German Democratic Republic, 45 Fed.Reg. 73,821 (1980).

34. Portable Electric Nibblers from Switzerland, 45 Fed.Reg. 80,209 (1980).

35. Carbon Steel Wire Rod from Brazil, Belgium, France, and Venezuela, 47 Fed. Reg. 13,927 (1982).

no material injury has been found when capacity utilization went from 85 to 77 percent and the decline was found to be caused by frequent equipment breakdowns and quality control disruptions.[36]

§ 12.18   Threat of Material Injury

A good example of the analysis of the *threat* of material injury standard before the Court of International Trade (CIT) is found in Rhone Poulenc, S.A. v. United States.[1] This case involved the shipment of package anhydrous sodium metasilicate (ASM) from France to the United States. The U.S. industry was comprised of four companies, only one of which was demonstrably injured. *Rhone Poulenc* was an appeal to the CIT from an ITC decision concerning the "threat of material injury" standard. The court first determines the relevant market, then rejects the importers argument that present market penetration by imports is the crucial fact in determining whether such a threat exists. Instead, the court states that it is proper for the ITC to consider, in determining the likelihood of future injury, the developing trends in all the indicators used to determine whether actual injury has occurred. These indicators of actual injury include the volume of imports, the effect of imports on prices, and the impact of the imports on the domestic industry. The ITC is permitted, however, to look at likely future conduct of producers.

In *Rhone Poulenc,* the court finds that the volume of imports, although now only 4.4 percent, had increased rapidly, and that fact was significant. The importer argued that this rapid increase had leveled off but the court determined that the leveling off was primarily due to the cash bond requirement imposed after the ITA Preliminary Decision on sales at LTFV. The facts also showed that the foreign source operated at less than its maximum capacity, and that its efficiency would improve if it operated at maximum capacity. Thus, the importers could expand their foreign supply quickly to increase market penetration.

The ITC and CIT also found that there was price undercutting by the importers, which caused lost sales. These lost sales, in turn, had a negative effect on domestic industry prices. Because ASM is a fungible good, there is decreasing demand for it, and ASM buyers are price sensitive. A direct causal relation between the lost sales and present injury to the domestic injury does not need to be proven, so long as the ITC finds that the lost sales "indicate" a threat to future sales, production and profit.

The importers raised the question of whether the ITC can look at the injury to each producer separately, or can look only at the domestic injury as a whole. The court responded that enough producers must be threatened such that their collective output is a major proportion of domestic production. Further, different domestic producers can be subject to different kinds of threats, as long as the single source of all

36. Crystal from Austria and Italy, 45 Fed.Reg. 31,830 (1980).

§ 12.18

1. 592 F.Supp. 1318 (C.I.T.1984).

such threats is imports. The CIT holds that this burden was met, and threat of material injury proved.

§ 12.19 Causation

Causation of material injury by dumping is a required element which must be found independently of the finding of material injury, threat of material injury or the material retardation of the establishment of a domestic industry. However, there is a tendency to enter an affirmative injury determination when dumping and material injury to a concerned industry are found, without a lengthy analysis of the causal link between them. In a negative injury determination, on the other hand, the ITC may engage in a rather detailed analysis of causation.

The Tariff Act requires a simple causation element, stating that material injury must be caused "by reason of" the dumped imports.[1] The same standard applies in CVD proceedings "under the Agreement" and once again the law in this area is largely interchangeable. The causation requirement is not a high one. Imports need only be *a* cause material injury, and need not be the most substantial or primary cause of injury being suffered by domestic industry. This causation element of an affirmative injury determination can be satisfied if the subsidized imports contribute even minimally to the conditions of the domestic injury.[2] Under this "contributing cause" standard, causation of injuries may be found despite the absence of correlation between dumped imports and the alleged injuries if there is substantial evidence that the volume of dumped imports was a contributing factor to the price depression experienced by the domestic injury.[3]

In examining the causal link between the dumped imports and the material injury, the ITC is willing to recognize that there can be causal factors other than dumping which can be responsible for the alleged injury in a particular proceeding.[4] For example, the ITC has found no causal link between dumped imports and the condition of the industry when the industry prospered during times of greatest import penetration and did less well during times of decreased imports.[5] The existence of

§ 12.19

1. 128. 19 U.S.C.A. § 1673(2): If . . . (2) the Commission determines that—

(A) an industry in the United States—

(i) is materially injured, or

(ii) is threatened with material injury, or

(B) the establishment of an industry in the United States is materially retarded,

by reason of imports of that merchandise . . . , then there shall be imposed upon such merchandise an antidumping duty. . . .

2. British Steel Corp. v. United States, 593 F.Supp. 405, 413 (C.I.T.1984).

3. Id.

4. Such extraneous factors include:

(1) Volume and prices of imports not sold at less than fair value;

(2) Contraction in demand or changes in patterns of consumption;

(3) Trade restrictive practices of and competition between foreign and domestic producers;

(4) Developments in technology; and

(5) The export performance and productivity of the domestic industry.

S.Rep. No. 249, 96th Cong., 1st Sess. 57 (1979).

5. Motorcycle Batteries from Taiwan, 47 Fed.Reg. 13,619 (1982).

extraneous injury factors will not, however, necessarily preclude an affirmative finding of material injury for purposes of the Tariff Act [6] as long as the dumping is a contributing cause to the material injury of the domestic industry. The ITC is not required to weigh the effects from the dumped imports against the effects associated with other factors. For example, in evaluating causation, the ITC may uncover other major causes for the problems of the domestic industry. These may include huge unnecessary expenses, chronic excess capacity, inefficiency, poor quality, price sensitivity or increased domestic competition. Nevertheless, the presence of such major alternative causes of injury does not foreclose the possibility that imports have been *a* contributing cause of the industry's problems.[7]

The ITC may, but is not required to, consider the margin of dumping when evaluating causation. In practice the margin of dumping is an important factor in the ITC's causation analysis.[8] The ITC may also include or exclude sales at fair value in calculating the dumping margin for this purpose.[9] If the dumping margin is slight or substantially lower than the margin of underselling,[10] this may indicate that the injury was not caused by the dumped imports. The imports will still be able to undersell domestic producers, even if the prices of the imports are raised to their fair values. If, on the other hand, the dumping margin is higher than the margin of underselling, thereby enabling the foreign exporters to undersell domestic producers, material injury may be said to have been caused by the dumping because the foreign exporters were able to undersell only because of the higher dumping margin. Though it may be useful as one factor in determining causation, the size of the dumping margin is usually not determinative in injury determinations. For example, the ITC has found no causation of injury despite dumping margins of 50 percent and 36 percent.[11]

6. At least one Commissioner has argued that although this traditional analysis may be useful in determining material injury, it is not a proper tool to resolve the issue of causation because it does not do well in separating the effects of dumped imports from the effects of other factors operating in the marketplace. Instead she advocates what is termed the elasticity analysis. This new approach analyses the elasticity of domestic demand for the product under investigation to determine the effect on the domestic injury of unfair imports, as separated from many other factors that affect the concerned industry. See H. Blinn, The Injury–Test under United States Antidumping and Countervailing Duty Laws as Interpreted by the International Trade Commission and the Department of Commerce: A Comparison Study of the Conventional "Trend–Analysis" and the "Elasticity-test" 23–30 (1991).

7. Iwatsu Electric Co. Ltd. v. United States, 758 F.Supp. 1506 (C.I.T.1991) (small telephone systems); United Engineering & Forging v. United States, 779 F.Supp. 1375 (C.I.T.1991), opinion after remand 14 ITRD 1748 (C.I.T.1992) (crankshafts).

8. Hyundai Pipe Co., Ltd. v. United States, 670 F.Supp. 357, 8 ITRD 2044 (C.I.T.1987).

9. Algoma Steel Corp. v. United States, 865 F.2d 240 (Fed.Cir.1989), cert. denied 492 U.S. 919, 109 S.Ct. 3244, 106 L.Ed.2d 590 (1989); Floral Trade Council of Davis, Cal. v. United States, 704 F.Supp. 233 (C.I.T.1988).

10. Certain Spirits from Ireland, 46 Fed.Reg. 38,780 (1981) (negative injury determination) (subsidy was so small as to have a "minuscule possible price effect").

11. Fall Potatoes from Canada, 48 Fed. Reg. 43,412 (1983).

§ 12.20   Cumulative Causation

Can "material injury" be caused by imports from several exporters in more than one country through the cumulative effect of many small injuries? There are arguments against cumulating each source of dumping to determine whether it is a cause of injury. Such cumulation could penalize small suppliers who would not have caused injury if their dumping had been examined in isolation.[1] Nevertheless, the injury to a domestic industry is measured by the cumulated results of dumping on the ground that injury caused by "many nibbles" is just as harmful as that caused through "one large bite." Cumulation provides administrative ease, since the antidumping agency is not required to allocate the amount of injury caused by each individual exporter. A decision of the Court of Appeals for the Federal Circuit strongly upholds cumulative causation in U.S. anti-dumping injury determinations.[2]

The GATT and the Tokyo Round Antidumping Code are ambiguous on the propriety of cumulation. While GATT Article VI seems to contemplate a country-by-country approach by referring repeatedly to the singular term "country,"[3] the Antidumping Code uses the term "dumped imports," which implicitly permits an aggregate approach.[4] The use of cumulation doctrines in determining material injury in dumping cases has never been criticized by the Committee on Antidumping practices, which is further evidence that the practice of cumulation has been accepted by the signatories to the Tokyo Round GATT Antidumping Code.[5] The Uruguay Round Code expressly permits cumulation.

The Tariff Act requires that the ITC cumulatively assess the volume and effect of reasonably coincident dumped imports from two or more countries of like products subject to investigation if the imports compete with each other and with like United States products.[6] There is, however, an exception for imports from beneficiary countries of the Caribbean Basin Initiative.[7] The ITC has held cumulation to be proper if the factors and conditions of trade in the particular case show its relevance to the determination of injury, and has given a nonexhaustive list of such factors.[8] The list includes the volume of imports, the trend of import volume, the fungibility of imports, competition in the markets for the same end users, common channels of distribution, pricing similarity, simultaneous impact, and any coordinated action by importers.

§ 12.20

1. Horlick, The United States Antidumping System, in Antidumping Law and Practice: A Comparative Study 102 (1989).

2. See Hosiden Corp. v. Advanced Display Mfrs. of America, 85 F.3d 1561 (Fed. Cir.1996).

3. GATT Art. 6(1), 6(6).

4. Antidumping Code, Arts. 3(1), 3(2), 3(4), 3(5) and 3(7).

5. Vermulst, supra Note 2, § 6.3, at 401.

6. 19 U.S.C.A. § 1677(7)(C)(iv). This statutory provision settled a pre–1984 conflict within the Commission concerning whether to cumulate or not.

7. 19 U.S.C.A. § 1677(7)(C)(iv)(II).

8. Certain Steel Products from Belgium, Brazil, France, Italy, Luxembourg, the Netherlands, Romania, the United Kingdom, and West Germany, ITC Pub. 1221, Inv. No. 701–TA–86–144 (February 1986).

From these factors, the ITC determines whether the imports compete with each other and like domestic products. Surprisingly, the ITC found that French and Italian wines do not compete with each other.[9] But an ITC ruling that steel imports from Spain, Brazil and Korea competed with each other was overturned by the Court of International Trade,[10] which also refused to require the ITC to cumulate steel plate imports from Brazil, Korea and Argentina.[11] The ITC has also ruled that, when cumulating, it is not necessary to find for each country a separate causal link between its imports and U.S. material injury.[12] Such multiple country cumulation should be distinguished from the "cross cumulation" allowed by the Tariff Act. Cross cumulation involves consideration by the ITC of both dumped and subsidized imports into the United States.[13] The net effect of U.S. rules on cumulation of import injury is to encourage petitioners to name as many countries as possible as the source of their problems.

§ 12.21   Antidumping   Procedures—Petition   and   Response

In an antidumping proceeding, the ITA determines whether the imports are being sold at less than fair value (LTFV), and the ITC makes a separate determination concerning injury to the domestic industry making like or similar products.

United States antidumping proceedings may be initiated by either the Commerce Department, a union or an aggrieved business—or by a group association of aggrieved workers or businesses.[1] However, the petition must be filed "on behalf of" the entire domestic industry.[2] Unless a majority of the industry actively opposes the petition,[3] such representation is presumed.[4] However, the Commerce Department may commence an antidumping proceeding even if a majority of the industry opposes it.[5]

It has become increasingly difficult to ascertain which firms are part of the domestic industry and thus entitled to file a dumping petition. The Court of International Trade reversed an ITA ruling that a U.S. subsidiary of a Japanese company assembling Brother typewriters in Tennessee was not a member of the domestic industry.[6] The Japanese

---

9. See American Grape Growers Alliance v. United States, 615 F.Supp. 603 (C.I.T.1985).

10. Republic Steel Corp. v. United States, 591 F.Supp. 640 (C.I.T.1984).

11. USX Corp. v. United States, 698 F.Supp. 234 (C.I.T. 1988).

12. Fundicao Tupy S.A. v. United States, 678 F.Supp. 898 (C.I.T.1988), affirmed 859 F.2d 915 (Fed.Cir.1988).

13. See especially Bingham & Taylor Div., Virginia Industries, Inc. v. United States, 815 F.2d 1482 (Fed.Cir.1987).

§ 12.21

1. 19 U.S.C.A. § 1673a.

2. 19 U.S.C.A. § 1673a(b).

3. See Gilmore Steel Corp. v. United States, 585 F.Supp. 670 (C.I.T.1984).

4. NTN Bearing Corp. v. United States, 757 F.Supp. 1425 (C.I.T.1991); Suramericana de Aleaciones Laminadas, C.A. v. United States, 746 F.Supp. 139 (C.I.T.1990), reversed 966 F.2d 660 (Fed.Cir.1992).

5. Id.

6. Brother Industries (USA), Inc. v. United States, 801 F.Supp. 751 (C.I.T. 1992).

subsidiary was thus permitted to file its petition alleging the dumping of typewriters made in Singapore by Smith–Corona, a U.S. firm. And, at least preliminarily, Brother prevailed before the ITA which found a Smith–Corona dumping margin of 16.02 percent.[7] In another proceeding, however, Smith–Corona was also treated as a member of the U.S. domestic industry. Smith–Corona requested an anticircumvention order against Brother under an antidumping order outstanding against the Japanese parent.[8] It does not appear, from these cases, that a significant amount of value must be added in the U.S.A. for a company to be treated as domestic and thus capable of seeking antidumping relief.

The information that must be provided in an antidumping petition is set forth in 19 C.F.R. § 353.12, which is reproduced in Section 6.30 of this chapter. Contact in advance with the ITA and the ITC can often resolve any petitioning issues. The ITA determines whether the petition "alleges the elements necessary for the imposition of a duty," based on the "best information available at the time." [9] Such information cannot include any information furnished by respondents or a respondent's government.[10] In other words, the ITA accepts or rejects the petition almost entirely on the basis of the information supplied by the petitioner.

Once the petition is accepted, the proceeding becomes genuinely adversarial if (as is commonly the case) the parties alleged to be dumping respond to the questionnaires on sales volumes and prices that the ITA creates and later verifies through on-the-spot investigations. It is rare for the "defense" to have more than one month to respond. Any failure to respond or permit verification risks an ITA dumping decision on the "best information available," i.e. most likely the petitioner's or other respondent's submissions.[11] Since this is obviously an undesirable result, the best information available rule functions like a subpoena. Most respondents answer the ITA's questionnaires. Protective orders preserve the confidentiality of the often strategically valuable information submitted to the ITA and ITC in dumping proceedings.[12] Such orders ordinarily preclude release to corporate counsel engaged in competitive decision-making, but permit release to outside counsel and outside experts.[13]

§ 12.22 Administrative Determinations

Antidumping proceedings under U.S. law involve four stages. The ITC first makes a "preliminary determination" that there is reason to believe injury is occurring, again based on the best information available

---

7. 58 Fed.Reg. 7537 (1993).

8. 56 Fed.Reg. 46594 (1991).

9. 19 U.S.C.A. § 1673a(c).

10. United States v. Roses Inc., 706 F.2d 1563 (Fed.Cir.1983).

11. See 19 U.S.C.A. § 1677e(b).

12. 19 U.S.C.A. § 1677f.

13. See Sacilor, Acieries et Laminoirs De Lorraine v. United States, 542 F.Supp. 1020 (C.I.T.1982); Matsushita Electrical Industrial Co., Ltd. v. United States, 929 F.2d 1577 (Fed.Cir.1991).

at that time.[1] If the ITC makes such a finding, the ITA then makes a preliminary determination whether there is a reasonable basis to believe that goods are being sold at LTFV.[2] If the ITA makes such a preliminary determination, it proceeds to make a "final determination" concerning sales at LTFV.[3] If sales at LTFV are found by the ITA, the ITC then must make a final determination concerning injury.[4] Thus the chain of decision-making in antidumping proceedings runs as follows:

ITC Preliminary Injury Determination

ITA Preliminary Dumping Determination

ITA Final Dumping Determination

ITC Final Injury Determination

Congress has repeatedly amended U.S. antidumping law so as to accelerate the rate at which these determinations are made. The chart presented in Section 6.32 details U.S. antidumping investigation procedures. At this point, it is common for the proceeding to be completed within one year. U.S. antidumping duties are then and in the future assessed retrospectively for each importation such that the amount payable varies for each importer and transaction.

Any goods imported after an ITA preliminary determination of sales at LTFV (Stage Two) will be subject to any antidumping duties imposed later, after final determinations are made.[5] In customs law parlance, liquidation of the goods is suspended. In "critical circumstances," the antidumping duties will also be imposed on goods entered 90 days *before* suspension of liquidation.[6] Critical circumstances exist when there is a prior history of dumping or the importer knew or should have known that the sales were below fair value, and there have been massive imports over a relatively short period of time.[7] Since the ITA has demonstrated a willingness to order retroactive antidumping duties and need not find injury as a result of the massive imports,[8] the importer's risks may be substantial.

§ 12.23   The Importance of the ITA Preliminary Dumping Determination

Clearly, the ITA's preliminary determination of sales at LTFV tends to discourage imports. Importers do not know what their liabilities for duties will be and must post an expensive bond in the meantime to gain entry. Foreign exporters frequently raise their "United States prices" to the level of home market prices soon after such a preliminary determination. They may also reduce their home market prices to USP levels. If they do, the antidumping law will have accomplished its

§ 12.22

1. 19 U.S.C.A. § 1673b(a).

2. 19 U.S.C.A. § 1673b(b).

3. 19 U.S.C.A. § 1673d(a).

4. 19 U.S.C.A. § 1673d(b).

5. 19 U.S.C.A. § 1673b(d).

6. 19 U.S.C.A. 1673b(e).

7. Id.

8. See ICC Industries, Inc. v. United States, 812 F.2d 694 (Fed.Cir.1987).

purpose in eliminating dumping. However, unlike European law and the Tokyo Round GATT Antidumping Code, the U.S. antidumping statute disfavors termination of the proceeding on the basis of voluntary undertakings of compliance.[1]

United States antidumping proceedings may be settled by the ITA if the respondents formally agree to cease exporting to the United States within six months or agree to revise their prices so as to eliminate the margin of the dump.[2] Since price revision agreements are hard to monitor, they are disfavored by the ITA. But an agreement to cease exports also cancels any outstanding suspension of liquidation. The total time secured in this manner may allow foreigners a window of opportunity to establish market presence prior to shifting production to the U.S. If requested, final ITA and ITC determinations are reached after settlement is agreed with normal trading resumed if respondents prevail. If petitioners prevail, the settlement agreement remains in effect. All settlement agreements are monitored by the ITA and civil penalties (in addition to antidumping duties) may be assessed if they are breached.[3] The only other settlement alternative involves withdrawal of the petition, something the petitioners may do if the President secures an international trade agreement in their favor.[4]

§ 12.24 AD Duties and Anticircumvention

The ITA final determination of sales at LTFV establishes the amount of any antidumping duties. Since duties are not imposed to support any specific domestic price, they are set at the "margin of dumping" (the amount the foreign market value exceeds the United States price).[1] In the ordinary case, antidumping duties are retroactive to the date of the suspension of liquidation that occurred when the ITA preliminarily found dumping. However, if the ITC final determination is one of threatened (not actual) domestic injury, the duties usually apply as from the ITC's final decision and not retroactively to the suspension date. The antidumping duty remains in force only as long as the dumping occurs. Upon request, annual ITA reviews are conducted. The ITA may review and revoke or modify any antidumping order if changed circumstances warrant such a revocation, but the burden of proof is on the party seeking revocation.[2]

Problems in assessing and collecting antidumping duties may occur because the antidumping duty order applies to goods that do not exactly correspond to normal United States HTS tariff classifications.[3] While the ITA is given some leeway to modify an antidumping order to accommodate such problems, it may not use them as an excuse to

§ 12.23

1. See 19 U.S.C.A. § 1673c.

2. 19 U.S.C.A. § 1673c(b)(1).

3. 19 U.S.C.A. § 1673c(i)(2).

4. See text at Note 12, § 6.5, supra.

§ 12.24

1. 19 U.S.C.A. § 1673e.

2. 19 U.S.C.A. § 1675(b), (c); See Electric Golf Cars—Poland, 1 I.T.R.D. 5511 (1980).

3. See Chapter 5.

exclude merchandise falling within the scope of the order.[4] Where, on the other hand, merchandise was deliberately excluded from the original antidumping order, the ITA may not subsequently include that merchandise in an anticircumvention order.[4.1]

Important amendments to U.S. dumping law undertaken in 1988 focused on the circumvention of antidumping duties. "Anticircumvention" law was at that time being debated within the GATT Uruguay Round. Meanwhile, both the EU and the U.S. incorporated such rules into their dumping statutes. The U.S. anticircumvention provisions are part of the Tariff Act of 1930. They allow, for example, the ITA to ignore fictitious markets in the source nation when calculating foreign market value.[5] Components may be included in the scope of an antidumping duty order when subsequently imported into the U.S. for assembly if there is only a "small" difference between their value and that of the dumped product.[6] This rule is explored in an ITA investigation involving Brother typewriters reaching the conclusion that the value added in the U.S. was not small.[7]

Similarly, when the exporter ships the components to a third country for assembly and subsequent exportation to the U.S., such circumvention efforts can be defeated by imposing the antidumping duties on these goods.[8] Product alterations that are minor and product innovations that result in essentially similar merchandise will not escape a U.S. antidumping order.[9] Even under pre–1988 law, the extension of antidumping duties to imported electric typewriters with new features was upheld.[10] Anticircumvention rules are not precluded by the Uruguay Round WTO Antidumping Code. No substantive WTO anticircumvention rules were agreed upon.

In 2000, the United States adopted the so-called "Byrd amendment." Under this provision of H.R. 4461, antidumping and countervailing tariff duties collected by the U.S. government may be passed on to injured U.S. companies. The Byrd amendment was lobbied heavily by the U.S. steel industry, which has been a major complainant in AD and CVD proceedings. The European Union, Japan and South Korea assert that this provision violates WTO rules and are preparing to challenge it.

§ 12.25　Appeals

The United States—Canada FTA and the NAFTA provide for resolution of antidumping and countervailing duty disputes through binational or trinational panels. Such panels apply the domestic law of the importing country, and provide a substitute for judicial review of the

---

4. Alsthom Atlantique and Cogenel, Inc. v. United States, 787 F.2d 565 (Fed.Cir. 1986).

4.1 Wheatland Tube Co. v. United States, 161 F.3d 1365, 1998 U.S. App.Lexis 29823 (Fed.Cir.1998).

5. 19 U.S.C.A. § 1677b(a)(5).

6. 19 U.S.C.A. § 1677j.

7. Brother Industries (USA), Inc., 56 Fed.Reg. 46594 (1991).

8. 19 U.S.C.A. § 1677j.

9. Id.

10. Smith Corona Corp. v. United States, 698 F.Supp. 240 (C.I.T.1988).

decisions of administrative agencies of the importing country. They are discussed in Chapter 21. Apart from panel review of this kind, final (not preliminary) U.S. dumping determinations of the ITA and injury determinations of the ITC are challenged "on the record" first before the Court of International Trade (CIT).[1] The CIT has demonstrated a willingness to reverse the findings of the ITA and ITC for lack of support by substantial evidence or arbitrariness.[2] Appeals may subsequently be lodged with the Federal Circuit Court of Appeals and ultimately the U.S. Supreme Court.

D. EUROPEAN ANTIDUMPING LAW

§ 12.26 GATT/WTO Code Adherence

Like the United States, the European Union (EU) has become an active enforcer of antidumping law under the Tokyo Round GATT Code. It also adheres to the Uruguay Round WTO Antidumping Code (1994).[1] The increase in European antidumping proceedings has been so remarkable that many outsiders perceive its invocation as protectionist in purpose and effect.

The principal rules on dumping are embodied in Council Regulation 384/96. Some antidumping proceedings involve goods from nonmarket economy states (NMEs). Apart from NMEs, Japanese and United States exports have most frequently been involved in antidumping proceedings. Many of these proceedings are settled by promises of the exporters to raise prices and refrain from dumping. The standing of most exporters and complainants to challenge dumping decisions has been affirmed by the European Court.[2] Such persons would otherwise lack any possible judicial remedy. Importers, on the other hand, have remedies in the national courts of the member states and are therefore generally unable to challenge dumping decisions directly before the European Court.[3] However, importers who are end-users of the product in question and seriously affected by the antidumping duties may challenge anti-dumping determinations.[4]

§ 12.27 Administrative Determinations

"Normal value" under European dumping law is first defined as the comparable price actually paid or payable in the ordinary course of trade for the like product intended for consumption in the exporting country or country of origin. The Commission usually considers all sales made

§ 12.25

1. See Chapter 9.

2. See 19 U.S.C.A. § 1516a and cases discussed in this chapter.

§ 12.26

1. See Chapter 9.

2. Allied Corp. v. Commission (1984) Eur.Comm.Rep. 1005 (named exporters may challenge imposition of dumping duties); Timex Corp. v. Council and Commission (1985) Eur.Comm.Rep. 849 (complainant may challenge antidumping decisions).

3. Alusuisse Italia v. Council and Commission (1982) Eur.Comm.Rep. 3463.

4. Extramet v. Council (1991) Eur. Comm.Rep. 2501 (Case C–358/89).

in the period under investigation (typically 12 months). However, only sales made in the ordinary course of business enter into the calculation. Transactions between related or compensated parties may not be considered in the ordinary course of trade unless the Commission believes they are comparable to arms-length dealings. Sales below cost, for example, are regularly excluded from the Commission's determination of normal value and may trigger "constructed value" determinations. If there are no sales of the like product in the ordinary course of trade on the domestic market of the exporting country or such sales are inadequate to permit a proper comparison, the Commission turns to (1) the "comparable price" of the product as exported to another surrogate country or (2) its constructed value. The constructed value methodology is often used. It involves calculation of production costs plus a reasonable profit. The costs of production include materials, components and manufacturing costs, as well as sales, administrative and other general expenses. The Commission need not follow the exporter's accountings in making these calculations. A profit margin of 10 percent or more has been utilized.

If the goods are from nonmarket economies, the Commission has three options for determining normal value. These are utilization of a price derived from the sale of a like product in a market country, a constructed value price based on the costs of a producer in a market country or (if needed) the price actually paid in the Union adjusted to include a reasonable profit margin.

Once a "normal value" for the goods is established by the Commission, the "export price" is determined. This is defined as the price actually paid or payable for the product sold for export. Relatively speaking, this calculation is less controversial except when the producer sells through its own subsidiary. In addition, certain adjustments must be made to the normal value and export prices so calculated. These adjustments reflect differences in physical attributes, import charges, indirect taxes and selling expenses. The object of making these adjustments is to arrive at comparable "ex-factory" price calculations. The dumping margin is the difference between the adjusted normal value and the adjusted export price. This margin ultimately determines the maximum extra duty the importer must pay provided there also is material injury to an industry and the Commission decides that imposing the duty would be in the region's interest. This "public interest" determination typically pits consumer interests against region's interests. The manufacturers usually win out, but occasionally the consumers' interest in lower-priced imports prevails.[1]

The precise amount of the antidumping duty is supposed to represent only that which is necessary to remove the injury. European antidumping duties are imposed prospectively, applying in most cases to

1. See Commission Dec. May 22, 1990, O.J. L138/48 (May 31, 1990) (photo albums).

all future imports during the next five years. Prospective application of antidumping duties means that the tariff remains unchanged at least until it is up for annual review. While it is possible to obtain refunds of antidumping duties based upon the argument that the actual dumping margins were less than the prospectively assessed duty, this is a rare event. To insure against circumvention of its prospective duties through price reductions intended by the exporter to offset these amounts, Europe has adopted so-called "anti-absorption duties" as a countermeasure.[2]

§ 12.28 Settlements

One United States law professor has noted the utility and frequency of European dumping settlements:

> One consequence of the use of prospective duties is that companies are often interested in settling a dumping proceeding by agreeing to raise their prices. If this is done, the company keeps the higher profits generated by the higher prices. Otherwise, the company's prices in the EC will increase as a result of the duties being applied, but the company will not benefit from those higher prices, as the duties collected go to the EC.
>
> Not surprisingly, the settlement of antidumping cases by acceptance of undertakings is the typical resolution of an antidumping case in the EC. Usually undertakings are accepted only after the Commission's investigation has been completed. The terms of an undertaking are the subject of negotiation and vary from case to case. Typically, the Commission requires at a minimum that the person making the undertaking commit itself to sell above a certain price (which price may be subject to future revision or even indexation), take steps necessary to ensure that the undertaking is not evaded by sales through other parties or other countries, supply the Commission with information concerning its export sales prices on a regular basis (for example, every six months) and agree to give the Commission notice of any termination of the undertaking. If the undertaking is terminated, or if the Commission has reason to believe that it has been violated, the Commission may impose provisional duties on the basis of the facts established before the undertaking was accepted. Prior to doing so, the Commission must consult with the Advisory Committee and give the exporter concerned a chance to comment.[1]

§ 12.29 Anticircumvention and Other Controversies

Although much of the European law on antidumping duties is consistent with the GATT/WTO code, and therefore generally conforms

2. O.J. L170/1 (June 25, 1992).

§ 12.28

1. Davey, "Antidumping Proceedings," in Folsom, Lake and Nanda (eds.), European Community Law After 1992: A Practical Guide for Lawyers Outside the Common Market (Kluwer, 1992).

to United States law on the subject[1] some interesting twists have been applied. One of the most controversial is the so-called "screwdriver plant regulation" aimed mostly at Japanese exporters.[2] These exporters, when faced with antidumping duties on top of the common customs tariff, began to assemble consumer electronics and other products inside Europe using Japanese made components plus a screwdriver. The net effect of this regulatory response was to reimpose dumping duties on these products unless at least 50 percent of the components originate outside the source country (Japan). Similar results have been achieved in certain cases when the Japanese export goods assembled in the U.S. to Europe.[3] In the photocopiers case, the goods had actually qualified as American for purposes of U.S. procurement rules. This origin was rejected by the European Commission. The Japanese successfully challenged the screwdriver regulation within the GATT.

Some have asserted that Europe employs a double standard when calculating export prices and normal values for dumping law purposes. They claim that it has cloaked itself in the technical obscurity of the law so as to systematically inflate normal values and deflate export prices, thereby causing more dumping to be found. Use of asymmetrical methods to reach these determinations has been upheld by the European Court.[4] Additional criticism has been levied against the Commission's refusal to disclose the information upon which it relies in making critical dumping law decisions.[5] Much of this information is admittedly confidential, but could be released under a protective order. Consumer groups will not ordinarily be granted access to non-confidential files accumulated by the Commission in antidumping proceedings.[6]

Selected Bibliography

Alford, When is China Paraguay? An examination of the application of the antidumping and countervailing duty laws of the United States to China and other nonmarket economy nations, 61 So.Cal.L.Rev. 79 (Nov. 1987).

Akakwam, The Standard of Review in the 1994 Antidumping Code, 5 Minn. J. Global Trade 277 (1996).

Barcelo, The Antidumping Law: Repeal It or Revise It, 1 Mich.Yb.Int'l Legal Studies 53 (1979).

§ 12.29

1. 19 U.S.C.A. § 1673.

2. See Council Regulation 1761/87 and Article 13(10) of Regulation 4057/86.

3. See Council Regulation 3205/88 (photocopiers) (assembly does not involve a substantial operation or process so as to alter origin of goods). Accord, Brother International GmbH v. Hauptzollamt Gieben (1989) Eur.Comm.Rep. 4253 (Case 26/88) (suggesting typewriters assembled in Taiwan originate from Japan unless assembly causes the use to which components are put to become definite and the goods to be given their specific qualities).

4. Miniature Bearings, Nippon Seiko v. Council (1987) Eur.Comm.Rep. 1923.

5. See Al–Jubail Fertilizer Co. v. Council (1991) Eur.Comm.Rep. 3187 (Case C–49/88).

6. BEUC v. Commission (1992) Eur. Comm.Rep. II–285 (Case C–170/89).

Bhala, Rethinking Antidumping Law, 29 Geo. Wash. J. Int'l L. & Econ. 1 (1995).

Davey, Antidumping Proceedings, in Folsom Lake and Nanda (eds), European Community Law After 1992: A Practical Guide for Lawyers Outside the Common Market (Kluwer, 1992).

Ehrenhaft, What the Antidumping and Countervailing Duty Provisions (Can) (Will) (Should) Mean for U.S. Trade Policy, 11 Law & Pol'y Int'l Bus. 1361 (1979).

Fisher, The Antidumping Law of the United States: A Legal and Economic Analysis, 5 Law & Policy Int'l Bus. 85 (1973).

Fraedrich, The Japanese Minivan Antidumping Case, 2 Geo. Mason Univ. L.R. 107 (1994).

Horlick & DeBusk, Dispute Resolution Panels of the U.S.–Canada Free Trade Agreement: The First Two and One–Half Years, 37 McGill L.J. 574 (1992).

Horlick & Schuman, Nonmarket Economy Trade and U.S. Antidumping/Countervailing Duty Laws, 18 Int'l Lawyer 807 (1984).

J. Jackson & E. Vermulst (eds), Antidumping Law and Practice: A Comparative Study (1989).

Josephs, The Multinational Corporation, Integrated International Production and U.S. Antidumping Laws, 5 Tul. J. Int'l & Comp. L. 57 (1997).

Lantz, The Search for Consistency: Treatment of Nonmarket Economics in Transition Under U.S. Antidumping and Countervailing Duty Laws, 10 Am. Univ. J. Int'l L. & Pol. 993 (1995).

Long, United States Law and the International Anti–Dumping Code, 3 Int'l Lawyer 464 (1969).

Lorentzen, Overview of Major Changes Contained in the Uruguay Round Antidumping and Subsidies Agreements (P.L.I. 1994).

Macrory and Reade, Fair Value Investigations Under the Antidumping Statute, Federal Bar Ass'n Manual for Practice of U.S. Import Law, Chapter III (Ince and Glick, eds. 1990).

Mock, Cumulation of Import Statistics in Injury Investigations before the International Trade Commission, 7 Northwest.J.Int'l Law & Bus. 433 (1986).

J.E. Pattison, Antidumping and Countervailing Duty Law (1990).

Vermulst, Injury Determinations in Antidumping Investigations in the United States and European Community, 7 N.Y.L.Sch.J.Int'l & Comp.L. 301 (1986).

J. Viner, Dumping: A Problem of International Trade (1923).

W. Wares, The Theory of Dumping and American Commercial Policy (1977).

Chapter 13

SUBSIDIES AND COUNTERVAILING DUTIES

Table of Sections

A. INTRODUCTION

A. INTRODUCTION

§ 13.1 Subsidies and International Trade

The duty payable on an item may be increased above that normally required by the posted tariff schedule because "countervailing duties" (CVD) have been imposed by the country of importation. Countervailing duties are a trade response to unfair "subsidies", typically given by another country to position its exports more competitively in the international marketplace. Thus, a "countervailing duty" is levied as an offset by the country of importation upon goods the production or export of which have been helped by an unfair "subsidy" in the country of origin. Subsidies come in many forms (e.g. tax rebates, investment tax credits, other tax holidays, subsidized financing). Rapidly developing countries often offer to give some form of subsidy for initial foreign investments intended to generate exports. In the United States, the Eximbank offers low cost loans to overseas buyers of products exported from the United States; other countries have similar programs. Many U.S. export incentives could attract the CVD of nations importing U.S. goods.

In theory, the countervailing duty exactly offsets the unfair subsidy. Proponents of countervailing duties argue that they are necessary to keep imports from being unfairly competitive; there must be a level playing field for international trade. Opponents of countervailing duties argue that there is no coherent standard of "fairness" vs. "unfairness" to justify rational application of such duties. They point out that, absent a predatory motive by a foreign government, there is no more reason to justify intervention in favor of a producer disadvantaged by foreign competition than one disadvantaged by domestic competition. The result in each case is that the domestic resources used by the disadvantaged producer are shifted to their next highest value use. Viewing the world market as a unity, production efficiency worldwide is increased. Opponents of countervailing duties also point out that it is often difficult to identify a subsidy.

Countervailing duties (CVD) complement antidumping duties (AD). Unfair international trade practices can arise either through practices of producers or exporters, or through unfair practices of foreign governments. The former are subject to AD law; the latter are subject to CVD law. Either can be equally harmful to domestic industries.

B. GATT/WTO SUBSIDIES AND CVD LAW

§ 13.2 Tokyo Round Subsidies Code (1979)

International concern with unfair subsidies and countervailing duties is reflected in the General Agreement on Tariffs and Trade

(GATT),[1] and countervailing duties are permitted by Articles VI, XVI, and XXIII of the GATT. The criteria for CVDs was set forth in the "Agreement on Subsidies and Countervailing Measures" (the Subsidies Code) adopted at the Tokyo Round MTN in 1979.[2]

The Tokyo Round Subsidies Code provided for extensive consultation and cooperation by countries before countervailing duties are imposed.[3] It recognized that subsidies, other than export subsidies, are used widely as important instruments for promoting economic and social policies, especially in the development programs of third world countries. Countries with domestic subsidies are encouraged to structure them to avoid causing injury overseas.[4] With respect to export subsidies, the Code provided, in part, that "signatories shall not grant export subsidies on products other than certain primary products."[5] Even as to primary products (commodities), signatories agreed not to grant export subsidies in such a manner as to take "more than an equitable share of world trade" in that product, which generally refers to historical shares of that trade.[6]

Under the Tokyo Round GATT Subsidies Code, countervailing duties could be imposed on products of another Contracting State only if two requirements were met. First, there were unfair (countervailable) subsidies.[7] Second, "material injury" to a domestic industry must actually occur or be threatened, or the establishment of such an industry must be "materially retarded."[8] The authorities of the importing country had the power to impose a countervailing duty (CVD) in the amount of the subsidy for as long as the subsidy continues.[9] The CVD could only be imposed after an investigation (ordinarily begun at the request of the affected industry) has "demonstrated" the existence of (1) a countervailable subsidy; (2) material injury or a threat thereof or material retardation of a domestic industry; and (3) a causal link between the subsidy and the alleged injury. It should be noted that countervailing duties, even though available to domestic producers as a trade law remedy, do not have any relation to restrictions on exports into foreign markets. Countervailing duties deal only with unfair selling prices of imported goods.

GATT Article VI allows the Contracting Parties to impose countervailing duties to offset the subsidization of imported merchandise, but only if it can be shown that the subsidies cause or threaten to cause

§ 13.2

1. General Agreement on Tariffs and Trade (hereafter GATT), 55 U.N.T.S. 194 (1947, as amended). The GATT provisions on countervailing duties are set forth in GATT Articles VI, XVI and XXIII. The GATT provisions on antidumping duties are set forth in GATT article VI.

2. Agreement on Implementation of Articles VI, XVI and XXIII of the General Agreement on Tariffs and Trade (Tokyo Round GATT Subsidies Code) (Geneva,

1979) GATT, 26th Supp. B15D 56 (1980). Reprinted at 18 Int'l Legal Mat. 579.

3. GATT Subsidies Code, Arts. 3, 12, 13.

4. GATT Subsidies Code, Art. 11.

5. GATT Subsidies Code, Art. 9(1).

6. GATT Subsidies Code, Art. 10.

7. GATT Subsidies Code, Arts. 4, 5.

8. GATT Subsidies Code, Arts. 5, 6.

9. GATT Subsidies Code, Art. 4.

"material injury" to competing domestic industries. The material injury requirement is intended to prevent trading countries from overly enforcing their CVD laws, and using them as weapons to protect domestic industries.[10] It also provides a degree of uniformity in the general nature of national CVD measures. Under the GATT, countervailing duties may be imposed only if both material injury and a causal link between the subsidized goods and the injury can be shown. These requirements derive from the concern that member countries might otherwise impose CVD even though the allegedly subsidized imports cause only marginal injuries. However, the causal link element was not intended to require that the imports be the principal cause of the domestic injuries.

The Tokyo Round GATT Subsidies Code was an attempt to ensure greater uniformity of its member countries' CVD laws and provides a detailed framework of CVD regulation. One of the characteristics of the injury determination proceeding is its complex factual nature. It is essentially a fact-finding investigation; the allegations, evidence, and nature of the dispute are extremely complex. The types of injury may be very different from one industry to another. Thus, seemingly similar circumstances may lead to opposite or at least differing conclusions. Because of this unique fact-specificity of injury determination, it is unavoidable that CVD laws would be different from one country to another without some form of unifying guidance.

The 1979 Tokyo Round GATT Subsidies Code directed that material injury determinations should involve (1) an objective examination of the volume of the allegedly subsidized imports, (2) the effect of those imports on prices in the domestic market for like products, and (3) the consequent impact of those imports on domestic producers of like products.[11] Then it cautioned that no one or several of these factors can necessarily give decisive guidance.[12] The Subsidies Code also provided that the investigating authorities shall consider: whether there has been a significant increase in the volume of subsidized imports, either in absolute terms or relative to production or consumption in the importing country; whether there has been a significant price undercutting by the imports as compared with the price of a like product of the importing country; or whether the effect of such imports is otherwise to depress prices to a significant degree or to prevent price increases which otherwise would have occurred to a significant degree. Virtually the same criteria apply to injury determinations governed by the Antidumping Code.[13]

The Tokyo Round Subsidies Code envisioned that in examining the impact of subsidized imports on the domestic industry, the investigating authorities would evaluate all relevant economic factors and indices bearing on the state of the industry. The Code provided a nonexhaustive

10. Vermulst, Injury Determinations in Antidumping Investigations in the United States and the European Community, 7 N.Y.L.Sch.J. Int'l & Comp.L. 301, 313 (1986).

11. Tokyo Round GATT Subsidies Code, Art. 6(1).

12. Tokyo Round GATT Subsidies Code, Art. 6(2).

13. See Chapter 12.

list of such factors including: actual and potential decline in output, sales, market share, profits, productivity, return on investments, or utilization of capacity; factors affecting domestic prices; and actual and potential negative effects on cash flow, inventories, employment, wages, growth, ability to raise capital or investments.[14]

As part of an effort to bring its CVD law more in line with the GATT standard, the United States enacted Section 1671 of the Tariff Act under the Trade Agreements Act of 1979.[15] Section 1671 provided a GATT compatible CVD law applicable to "countries under the Agreement." Among other things, this section introduced the concept of material injury into the United States CVD law.

§ 13.3 Uruguay Round WTO Subsidies Code (1994)

Late in 1993, the Uruguay Round of multilateral trade negotiations were concluded. One of the many agreements reached at that time concerns subsidies and countervailing duties. The Uruguay Round Subsidies Code was approved and implemented by Congress in December of 1994 under the Uruguay Round Agreements Act (URAA).[1] The 1994 Code involves a substantial overhaul of prior law.

Subsidies are defined as financial contributions that confer benefits. The Uruguay Round Code distinguishes and provides international trade rules for three categories of subsidies ... prohibited ("red light"), actionable ("yellow light") and nonactionable ("green light"). Export subsidies, including so-called de facto export subsidies, are prohibited. Domestic subsidies that have adverse effects on industries in other countries are actionable when specific in character. Domestic subsidies that are non-specific are not actionable. Specific or non-specific subsidies granted to economically disadvantaged regions, to meet environmental requirements, and for research and precompetitive development are also not actionable.

The Uruguay Round Subsidies Code also creates rules for CVD procedures. The commencement of CVD proceedings, the conduct of CVD investigations, the calculation of the amount of subsidy, and the right of all interested parties to present information are covered. Dispute settlement in the subsidies area will focus upon whether another country's trade interests have been seriously prejudiced. A presumption of such prejudice will exist whenever the total *ad valorem* subsidization of a product exceeds 5 percent, and when the subsidy is by way of debt forgiveness or to cover operating losses.

---

14. Tokyo Round GATT Subsidies Code, Art. 6(3). See also Chapter 12 on antidumping injury determinations.

15. Pub.L. No. 96–39, § 101 et seq., 93 Stat. 162 (1979) (current version at 19 U.S.C.A. § 1671).

§ 13.3

1. Pub. L. No. 103–465, 108 Stat. 4809.

C. U.S. SUBSIDIES AND CVD LAW

§ 13.4 Historical Introduction

The United States considers the use by a foreign nation of a subsidy granted to exporters from that nation to be an unfair trade practice. Unfair subsidy practices have been subject to United States countervailing duty (CVD) laws since 1897, long before the creation of the GATT. The origin of U.S. laws against export "bounties" or "grants" can be traced to Section 5 of the Tariff Act of 1897.[1] For many years, this law vested almost complete discretion in the Treasury Department to levy CVD as it saw fit. Several early CVD tariffs were targeted at tax subsidies on sugar exports.[2] And the U.S. Supreme Court essentially gave the Treasury Department *carte blanche* to impose CVD whenever foreign government regulations favored exports reaching the United States.[3] Prior to the Trade Act of 1974, U.S. law on CVD was largely administered as a branch of U.S. foreign policy, not as a private international trade remedy.[4] It was not until 1974, for example, that negative bounty or grant determinations by the Treasury Department became subject to judicial review. In 1974, also, private parties obtained a number of statutory procedural rights, notably time limits for Treasury decisions on their petitions for CVD relief and mandatory publication of Treasury rulings. It is from this point, therefore, that a systematic body of case law interpreting and applying U.S. bounty, grant and CVD provisions commences.

The next major development in the United States statutes governing this field arrived in the Trade Agreements Act of 1979. This Act, *inter alia,* codified the rules on use of CVDs to counteract unfair "export subsidies" as agreed in the Tokyo Round GATT Subsidies Code. In addition, the 1979 Act authorized limited use of CVDs against foreign *domestic* subsidies, an authorization for which there was no distinct provision in the GATT Subsidies Code. Furthermore, the 1979 Act adopted the GATT requirement of proof of domestic industry injury or the threat or retardation thereof. This requirement had been, and remains for some imports, totally absent from U.S. law on countervailing duties.

The Uruguay Round Agreements Act of 1994 adapted the WTO Subsidies Code to U.S. law. Most importantly, Section 1677(5) of the Tariff Act of 1930 was amended to reflect the "red light," "yellow light" and "green light" categories of subsidies defined in the WTO Code. The

§ 13.4

1. 30 Stat. 205.

2. United States v. Hills Bros., 107 Fed. 107 (2d Cir.1901) (Holland); Downs v. United States, 187 U.S. 496, 23 S.Ct. 222, 47 L.Ed. 275 (1903) (Russia).

3. G.S. Nicholas & Co. v. United States, 249 U.S. 34, 39 S.Ct. 218, 63 L.Ed. 461 (1919).

4. See Energetic Worsted Corp. v. United States, 53 C.C.P.A. 36 (1966) (Uruguay wool); United States v. Hammond Lead Products, 440 F.2d 1024 (C.C.P.A.1971), cert. denied 404 U.S. 1005, 92 S.Ct. 565, 30 L.Ed.2d 558 (1971) (Mexican lead).

Tokyo Round amendments relating to material injury were substantially retained.

§ 13.5 Two Statutory Regimes

The U.S. currently has two statutes on countervailing duties: Section 1671 of the Tariff Act of 1930 for products imported from countries that participate in the WTO Subsidies Code or its equivalent,[1] and Section 1303 for products imported from other nations.[2] Most importantly, duties may be imposed under the latter *without* any finding of injury to a domestic industry (unless the product enters duty free); but may not be imposed under the former without a determination that a U.S. industry is "materially" injured, or threatened with such injury, or its development is materially retarded. As implemented by the United States, the GATT/WTO-derived Section 1671 imposes two conditions on the creation of countervailing duties. First, the International Trade Administration (ITA) in the Department of Commerce must determine that a nation is providing a subsidy to its exporters. Second, the International Trade Commission (ITC) must determine that imports benefiting from the subsidy injure, threaten to injure, or retard the establishment of a domestic industry.[3] This second condition embraces proof of causation, a difficult CVD issue. If these conditions are met, a duty equal to the net subsidy "shall be imposed" upon the imports.

Like antidumping duties, countervailing duties are a statutory remedy, one which the President cannot veto or affect except in Section 1671 (but not Section 1303) proceedings by negotiation of an international trade agreement. If the complaining U.S. industry is not satisfied with such an agreement, it may generally pursue CVD proceedings to their conclusion in spite of the President by refusing to withdraw its complaint. This refusal power typically gives U.S. industries seeking CVD relief substantial leverage over Commerce Department subsidy complaint negotiations. The steel industry, for example, has repeatedly exercised such leverage to its advantage when various Presidents have negotiated voluntary export restraint (VER) agreements with foreign governments.[4] In accepting VERs, the Commerce Department must find them to be in the public interest and consider whether the costs to U.S. consumers will exceed the benefits of protection to U.S. industries.

CVD proceedings under Section 1671 can also be suspended if the foreign government or exporters accounting for substantially all of the exports agree to cease exporting to the U.S. or to eliminate the subsidy within six months.[5] The subsidy may be eliminated by imposition of an export tax or price increases amounting to the net subsidy. In complex "extraordinary circumstances" benefiting the domestic industry, a settlement agreement reducing the subsidy by at least 85 percent and

§ 13.5
1. 19 U.S.C.A. § 1671 et seq.
2. 19 U.S.C.A. § 1303.
3. 19 U.S.C.A. § 1671(a).

4. See especially Note, International Trade: Countervailing Duties and European Steel Imports, 23 Harv.Int'l L.J. 443 (1983).
5. 19 U.S.C.A. § 1671(c)(b).

preventing price cutting in the U.S. can be negotiated.[6] These approaches, which are increasingly common, may effectively give exporters a brief window of opportunity to enter the U.S. market at subsidized price levels prior to shifting production to the United States.

Although the subsidy may arise from either public or private sources, all U.S. determinations to date have involved foreign governmental subsidies. Thus, these cases are usually determined on a country-wide basis (automobiles from Germany), and CVD orders usually apply to all imported goods of a particular tariff classification from a particular country—including indirect imports shipped via other countries. Note that this is one of the few instances in which the GATT/WTO allows an importing nation to engage in discriminatory conduct. In a CVD proceeding involving imports from "a Subsidies Agreement Country" (generally the WTO Subsidies Code), there are at least three separate issues for analysis under U.S. law: the extent of the concept "subsidy," the amount of injury suffered by the domestic industry, and the procedure to be followed by one who wishes to induce the application of countervailing duties.

§ 13.6 U.S. Implementation of the WTO Subsidies Code— Countervailable Subsidies

International concern with unfair subsidies and countervailing duties is reflected in Articles VI, XVI, and XXIII of the GATT 1947 and in the "Agreement on Subsidies and Countervailing Measures" (the SCM Agreement), which is part of the Covered Agreements under WTO. The United States legislation implementing the SCM Agreement changed many concepts under U.S. law. Under the SCM Agreement, the authorities of the importing signatory have the power to impose a countervailing duty (CVD) in the amount of the subsidy for as long as the subsidy continues. The CVD may only be imposed after an investigation, begun on the request of the affected industry, has "demonstrated" the existence of (1) a subsidy; (2) adverse trade effects, such as injury to a domestic industry, and (3) a causal link between the subsidy and the alleged injury.

Under the SCM Agreement there is an attempt to shift the focus of subsidy rules from a national forum, as it was exclusively under GATT, to the multinational forum provided by the Subsidies Committee under WTO and the SCM Agreement. Subsidies complaints can now be brought either in the national forum or the WTO. There are now three classes of subsidies: (1) prohibited ("red light"); (2) permissible, but actionable if they cause adverse trade effects ("yellow light"); and (3) non-actionable and non-countervailable ("green light"). There are special rules which require LDCs to phase out their export subsidies and local content rules, but over 8 and 5 years respectively. Transitional economies are also required to phase out both export subsidies and local content rules, but over a 7 year period.

6.   19 U.S.C.A. § 1671(c)(4).

The U.S. statutory provisions on countervailing duties on products imported from WTO Members is set forth in 19 U.S.C.A. § 1671, et seq. Duties may be imposed if it is found that the product is subsidized and that a U.S. industry is materially injured or threatened with such injury or its development is materially retarded.

A "subsidy" is defined as a "financial contribution" by a government entity which confers a benefit to the manufacturer of the subsidized product.[1] It includes governmental grants, loans, equity infusions and loan guarantees, as well as tax credits and the failure to collect taxes. It can also include the governmental purchase or providing of goods or services on advantageous terms. Further, direct governmental action is not required; a subsidy can also be created if any of the above are provided through a private body. In addition to a "financial contribution" and a "benefit," a subsidy must be specific to a particular industry or enterprise.[2] Red light subsidies are "deemed" to be specific in WTO proceedings, and this concept is incorporated into the provisions on U.S. domestic proceedings for countervailing duties.[3] However, specificity must be proven for other types of actionable subsidies.

"Red light" (prohibited) subsidies include financial contributions which are conditioned upon the export performance of the beneficiary, even where that condition is only one of several criteria (export subsidies). It includes both subsidies legally conditioned on expert performance and also those which are in fact tied to actual or anticipated exportation or export earnings. It does not include, however, all financial contributions to all enterprises which happen to export. "Red light" subsidies also include financial contributions which are conditioned on the use of local goods (import substitutions subsidies).

"Yellow light" (permissible, but actionable) subsidies are permissible under the SCM Agreement, but only so long as they do not cause "adverse trade effects." These subsidies include "financial contributions" which benefit specific enterprises or industries, but are not contingent upon export performance and are not insulated under "green light" criteria. Under U.S. law, such subsidies are subject to countervailing duties if they cause or threaten material injury to an industry in the United States, or materially retard the establishment of an industry in the United States. The definition of "material injury," or a threat thereof, or material retardation of establishment, is the same as in antidumping proceedings.[4] However, there are references in that U.S. definition to two provisions in the SCM Agreement—those dealing with "red light" and "dark amber" subsidies—with instructions that the ITC consider the nature of the subsidy in determining whether the subsidy imposes a material threat to an industry.[5]

§ 13.6

1. 19 U.S.C.A. § 1677(5).

2. 19 U.S.C.A. § 1677(5)(A).

3. 19 U.S.C.A. § 1677(5)(A)(A).

4. 19 U.S.C.A. § 1677(7).

5. 19 U.S.C.A. § 1677(7)(E)(1).

"Dark amber" subsidies are ones which exceed 5% of the cost basis of the product, or provide debt forgiveness, or cover the operating losses of a specific industry or of an enterprise more than once. This "dark amber" type of subsidy (halfway between "red" and "yellow") is a five year experiment under the SCM Agreement to provide "permissible, but actionable" subsidies in which there is a presumption of "adverse trade effects," and the subsidizing Member must rebut that presumption. At the end of the five year period, the Subsidies Committee must decide whether to continue, terminate or modify the "dark amber" provisions.

§ 13.7   National or WTO Proceedings

If a subsidy is either prohibited ("red light") or actionable ("yellow light"), it may be subject to either national or multinational actions. It will be subject to action within the U.S. legal system to impose a countervailing duty on imports of the subsidized product. It will also be subject to multilateral process within the WTO to obtain the withdrawal of the subsidy by the subsidizing Member.

The procedure for deciding whether to impose countervailing duties under domestic U.S. law is the same as that for antidumping duties, described previously, and involving both the ITA and ITC making both preliminary and final determinations. An ITA preliminary determination that a countervailable subsidy exists subjects any goods imported after that date to any countervailing duties imposed later, and therefore usually has the effect of reducing imports of such goods.

The multilateral procedure under WTO first provides for consultations between the complaining Member and the Subsidizing Member. If these do not resolve the dispute within 30 days for a "red light" subsidy, or 60 days for a "yellow light" subsidy, either party is entitled to request that the DSB establish a panel to investigate the dispute and make a written report on it. The DSB panel will have 90 days (red light), or 120 days (yellow light), to investigate and prepare its report. The panel report is appealable on issues of law to the Appellate Body. The Appellate Body has 30 days (red light), or 60 days (yellow light), to decide the appeal. Panel and Appellate Body decisions are adopted without modification by the DSB unless rejected by an "inverted consensus."

If a prohibited or actionable subsidy is found to exist, the subsidizing Member is obligated under WTO to withdraw the subsidy. If the subsidy is not withdrawn within a six month period, the complaining Member can be authorized to take countermeasures. Such countermeasures may not be countervailing duties, but may instead comprise increased tariffs by the complaining Member on exports from the subsidizing Member to the complaining Member.

§ 13.8   Non–Countervailable Subsidies

A new concept found in WTO, and incorporated in U.S. law, is the "green light" (non-actionable) subsidy.[1] Such subsidies are not subject to countervailing duties if they meet the rigorous criteria established in the SCM Agreement. Such subsidies are available for industrial research and development, regional development and adaptation of existing plant to new environmental standards. Green light subsidies are a five year experiment under the SCM Agreement to insulate certain governmental grants from countermeasures by other Members. At the end of the five year period the WTO Subsidies Committee must decide whether to continue, terminate or modify the green light provisions.

Research subsidies must be limited to no more than 75% of the cost of industrial research, or no more than 50% of the cost of pre-competitive development activity. Further, the subsidy must also be limited to specific types of costs.[2]

Regional subsidies must be part of a general framework of regional development, and must be available to persons and enterprises in that region so as not to benefit specific enterprises or industries within the region. The region must be a clearly designated and contiguous geographic area, with an economic and administrative identity. The region must be designated as disadvantaged through neutral and objective criteria, which must be based in part on per capita income or unemployment rate statistics.

Environmental subsidies can be used only to adapt existing facilities to new environmental requirements. It must be available to all enterprises and industries on a non-specific basis. Such subsidies may subsidize only a maximum of 20% of the cost of the adaptation, and the cost calculations must reflect any manufacturing cost savings achieved by the new equipment. The subsidy must be a one-shot, non-recurring measure, and it cannot cover the subsequent cost of replacing any subsidized equipment.

A member which undertakes to provide any of these three types of "green light" subsidies has the option to "notify" the WTO of the subsidy program and seek an evaluation of its features. The notification asks the WTO Secretariat to review the subsidy's provisions and determine whether they satisfy the criteria for the "green light" subsidies. After the review, the Secretariat reports its findings to the Subsidies Committee, which reviews its findings. A Member which disagrees with the Subsidies Committee process may request binding arbitration to determine the matter.

If a "notified" subsidy is determined to satisfy the "green light" criteria, the subsidy cannot later be challenged, except through the Subsidies Committee. It cannot be challenged through the DSB procedure described above in relation to "red light" and "yellow light" subsidies. It also cannot be challenged under U.S. domestic countervailing duty proceedings before the ITA and the ITC, also described above. If

§ 13.8
1.   19 U.S.C.A. § 1677(5B).

2.   19 U.S.C.A. § 1677(5B)(B)(i).

a subsidy has been "notified" under the SCM Agreement, it is expressly exempted from investigation or review under U.S. CVD law.[3] .

However, if a Member believes that a "notified" subsidy is causing "serious adverse effects" to its domestic industry, it may request a review of that "green light" subsidy before the Subsidies Committee. Such a review is similar to the DSB reviews described above, except that it is heard by the Subsidies Committee (which earlier determined it to have "green light," or non-actionable, status), rather than by a DSB panel. If the Subsidies Committee finds that serious adverse effects exist, it "may" recommend that the subsidizing Member modify the subsidy to eliminate the adverse effects. If such a recommendation is made, the subsidizing Member must follow the recommendations within six months or be subject to appropriate countermeasures.

§ 13.9 Export Subsidies

The clearest examples of export subsidies are export incentives, including export credit and loan guarantees at less than commercial rates and differential governmentally set freight tariffs.[1] Governmental infusion of equity into the British Steel Co. after its nationalization was also held to be a subsidy.[2] Where benefits, such as loans with below market interest rates and uncompensated deferrals of payments of the principal, are used to induce the building of a plant with a capacity too large for the local market, such benefits may also be subject to CVDs.[3] Outright cash payments to exporters,[4] export tax credits,[5] and accelerated depreciation benefits for exporters[6] provide additional examples of clearly countervailable export subsidies.

More difficulties are presented in analyzing whether tax rebates confer benefits which should be subject to CVDs. Remission or deferral of, or exemption from, a direct tax on exports is a countervailable subsidy. But the remission of an indirect tax (sales tax, value added tax, etc.) is not subject to a CVD, as long as it is not excessive (the amount remitted is no greater than the amount actually paid).[7] However, the foreign government which makes payments to exporters must show a clear link between the amount, eligibility and purpose of the payments and actual payment of indirect taxes, and then document the links. This

3. 19 U.S.C.A. § 1677(5B)(E)

§ 13.9

1. ASG Industries, Inc. v. United States, 610 F.2d 770 (C.C.P.A.1979), on remand 519 F.Supp. 909 (C.I.T.1981), order vacated 657 F.2d 1226 (C.C.P.A.1981).

2. British Steel Corp. v. United States, 605 F.Supp. 286 (C.I.T.1985), appeal after remand 632 F.Supp. 59 (1986). For important decisions upholding the current Commerce Department method of valuing the amount of past nonrecurring subsidies repaid in privatizations, see British Steel PLC v. United States, 127 F.3d 1471 (Fed.Cir.

1997); Inland Steel Bar Co. v. United States, 155 F.3d 1370 (Fed.Cir.1998).

3. Michelin Tire Corp. v. United States, 3 ITRD 1177 (C.I.T.1981), decision vacated 9 C.I.T. 38 (1985).

4. See Cotton Shop Towels from Pakistan, 49 Fed.Reg. 1408 (1984).

5. See Carbon Steel Products from Brazil, 49 Fed.Reg. 1788 (1984).

6. See Oil Country Tubular Goods from Korea, 49 Fed.Reg. 46776 (1984).

7. Zenith Radio Corp. v. United States, 437 U.S. 443, 98 S.Ct. 2441, 57 L.Ed.2d 337 (1978) (commodity tax).

is less difficult if the indirect taxes have been paid by the exporter, but is much more difficult if they have been paid by several prior producers of the goods and their components. In the latter case ("prior stage cumulative indirect taxes"), the burden of documentation is formidable.[8] The Court of International Trade has held that such a remission of domestic taxes on exported goods can still be subject to countervailing duties, *unless* the exporter can prove that the domestic tax is actually passed on to domestic purchasers of the product—which most authorities believe will be a difficult burden of proof to sustain.[9]

At one time, the amount of a U.S. CVD would be reduced by the "nonexcessive" amount of the remission of an indirect tax. However, the statute now provides a definition of "net subsidy" which includes an exclusive list of permissible offsets,[10] and the prior practice is terminated. The only offsets now permitted under the statutory definition are: 1) application fees to qualify for the subsidy, 2) any reduction in the value of the subsidy due to a governmentally mandated deferral in payment, and 3) export taxes intended to offset the subsidy.

The benefit of tax credits and allowances is usually considered to accrue at the time the exporter receives the benefit on a cash accounting basis. However, when a grant is used to acquire a long-life capital asset, the benefit will be allocated over the useful life of the asset, using data from the company if available.[11]

§ 13.10 Upstream Subsidies

A foreign government may subsidize the product actually exported. Alternatively, it may subsidize component parts or raw materials which are incorporated into the final product or services used in prior production stages. The latter are called "upstream subsidies" and are subject to CVD if they both bestow a competitive benefit on the product exported to the U.S. and have a significant effect on its cost of production.[1] A competitive benefit is bestowed if the price of the subsidized "input" (component or material) to the producer of the final product is less than it would have been "in an arms length transaction."[2] Countervailing duties may be applied to upstream subsidies only if the inputs are granted certain specified domestic subsidies.[3] As in other countervailable domestic subsidies, the benefit cannot be generally available; but the

8. Industrial Fasteners Group v. United States, 525 F.Supp. 885 (C.I.T.1981), 542 F.Supp. 1019 (C.I.T.1982), appeal after remand 542 F.Supp. 1019 (1982), rehearing denied 3 C.I.T. 104 (1982).

9. Zenith Electronics Corp. v. United States, 633 F.Supp. 1382 (C.I.T.1986).

10. 19 U.S.C.A. § 1677(6).

11. Ipsco, Inc. v. United States, 710 F.Supp. 1581 (C.I.T.1989), affirmed 899 F.2d 1192 (Fed.Cir.1990) (remanded on other grounds).

§ 13.10

1. 19 U.S.C.A. § 1677–1(a).

2. 19 U.S.C.A. § 1677–1(b).

3. 19 U.S.C.A. § 1677–1(a), citing the domestic subsidies specified in 19 U.S.C.A. § 1677(5)(B)(i)–(iii).

availability of the subsidized input need not be restricted to any special group.[4]

The amount of the benefit is determined by calculating the subsidy rate on the input and then determining what percentage of the cost of the final product is represented by the subsidized input. The ITA has stated that, if the subsidy so calculated represents more than 5 percent of the total cost, it will presume that there is a "significant effect;" and if it is less than 1 percent, it will presume no significant effect.[5] However, both presumptions are rebuttable, and the ITA will also analyze the importance of price in the competitiveness of the final product.[6]

There are more special rules for processed agricultural products. A subsidy provided to producers of a "raw agricultural product" is deemed to be provided to the producer of the processed agricultural product if (1) the demand for the "raw" product is substantially dependent upon the demand for the processed product, and (2) the processing adds only limited value to the raw product.[7]

§ 13.11 De Minimis Subsidies

De minimis subsidies, defined in U.S. law as subsidies of "less than 0.5 percent *ad valorem*," are disregarded and no CVD is imposed.[1] However, when the ITA calculates country-wide CVD rates, it uses a fair average of aggregate subsidy benefits to exports of all firms from that country. In making such calculations, the ITA must include not only sales by exporters who receive substantial subsidy benefits, but also sales by exporters who receive zero or *de minimis* subsidies, when calculating the weighted average benefit conferred.[2] Thus, in such circumstances, the CVD imposed may not exceed the weighted average benefit received by all exporters of the goods subject to the CVD proceeding.

§ 13.12 Nonmarket Economies Excluded

The Federal Circuit Court of Appeals has ruled that economic incentives given to encourage exportation by the government of a non-market economy (NME) cannot create a countervailable "subsidy."[1] The court's rationale was that, even though an NME government provides export-oriented benefits, the NME can direct sales to be set at any price, so the benefits themselves do not distort competition. The court also suggested that imports from NMEs with unreasonably low prices should be analyzed under antidumping duty provisions. It is believed that this reasoning was implicitly approved by Congress when it enacted the 1988

4. Steel Wheels from Brazil, 54 Fed.Reg. 15,523 (1989).

5. Agricultural Tillage Tools from Brazil, 50 Fed.Reg. 34,525 (1985).

6. *Id.*

7. 19 U.S.C.A. § 1677–2. This section codified prior ITA practice. See Live Swine and Fresh, Chilled and Frozen Pork Products from Canada, 50 Fed.Reg. 13,264 and 25,097 (1985).

§ 13.11

1. 19 C.F.R. § 355.7.

2. Ipsco, Inc. v. United States, 899 F.2d 1192 (Fed.Cir.1990).

§ 13.12

1. Georgetown Steel Corp. v. U.S., 801 F.2d 1308 (Fed.Cir.1986).

amendments to the Tariff Act of 1930, without adding provisions for CVDs on exports from NMEs, and adding several amendments to the antidumping provisions concerning exports from NMEs.[2] Thus, it is expected that unfair trade practices by NMEs will be subjected to AD but not generally to CVD analysis.[3]

The criteria used to determine whether a country has a nonmarket economy in antidumping proceedings[4] are also used by the ITA in deciding NME status for purposes of exclusion under the *Georgetown Steel* precedent from coverage by U.S. countervailing duty law. These criteria focus principally upon government involvement in setting prices or production, private versus collective ownership and market pricing of inputs.[5] Note that such an approach suggests that particular industries and products from countries deemed NMEs may be countervailable if "market-oriented."[6]

§ 13.13　The Injury Determination

CVD proceedings in the United States for Subsidies Agreement countries and only such countries, are conducted in two stages. In the second stage, the International Trade Commission (ITC) must determine whether the subsidization of the imported merchandise has caused or threatens material injury to concerned domestic industries.[1] The ITC's review constitutes the material injury determination under United States law, including injury factors and causation.

The Tariff Act provides that an affirmative injury determination should be made when an industry in the United States is "materially" injured or is threatened with material injury by reason of subsidized imports, or the establishment of an industry in the United States is materially retarded.[2] The "material injury" standard is applied to established industries, and is defined in the statute.[3] The "threat of material injury" standard is separately stated, but has a substantial overlap with the material injury criteria.[4] The standard for "material retardation" of the establishment of an industry is applied to new industries which have made a substantial commitment to begin production, or have recently begun production.[5]

§ 13.14　Like Domestic Products

In a CVD proceeding, it is important to define the relevant industry for injury investigation purposes. In both AD and CVD proceedings, the

2. See, e.g. 19 U.S.C.A. §§ 1677b(c) and 1677(18).

3. See Chapter 12.

4. See Chapter 12.

5. See, e.g., Final Negative CVD Determination: Oscillating and Ceiling Fans from China, 57 Fed.Reg. 24018 (1992).

6. Id.

§ 13.13

1. See 19 U.S.C.A. § 1671(2)

2. 19 U.S.C.A. § 1671(2).

3. 19 U.S.C.A. § 1677(7).

4. 19 U.S.C.A. § 1677(7)(F).

5. BMT Commodity Corp. v. United States, 667 F.Supp. 880 (C.I.T.1987), affirmed 852 F.2d 1285 (Fed.Cir.1988), cert. denied 489 U.S. 1012, 109 S.Ct. 1120, 103 L.Ed.2d 183 (1989).

"industry" means domestic producers of "a like product."[1] However, in AD proceedings, such like products will have been identified in determining a foreign market value for the imported merchandise and in AD injury determinations.[2] In CVD proceedings, the like product identification is used primarily in determining injury. Since the concept of "like product" is used for a different purpose, its definition need not necessarily be the same as that used by the ITA in determining whether dumping has occurred.[3]

The ITC considers a number of factors in determining what are "like products," and what is therefore the relevant domestic injury. These factors include (1) physical appearance, (2) interchangeability, (3) channels of distribution, (4) customer perception, (5) common manufacturing facilities and production employees, and (6) price.[4] Domestic producers who import the foreign products in question or who are related to exporters or importers can be excluded from the industry as defined by the ITC.[5] The ITC is to analyze U.S. production of the domestic like product in terms of production process and profits if useable data is present. If such data is not available, the ITC is to analyze data from "the narrowest range of products which includes the like product" and for which data can be provided.[6]

In addition, the ITC may create regional geographic product markets if the local producers sell most of their production in the regional market, and the demand in the regional market is not supplied by other U.S. producers outside that region.[7] If the relevant domestic injury in such a region is harmed, then there is material injury to a domestic industry. Such analysis of material injury to regional producers or industries is permitted under the Tokyo Round GATT Subsidies Code.[8]

§ 13.15　Material Injury

The Tariff Act defines material injury as "harm which is not inconsequential, immaterial, or unimportant."[1] This is the same standard that applies in AD proceedings and much of the law in the area may therefore be treated as interchangeable. Although the material injury definition seems to require a higher standard than a mere injury

---

§ 13.14

1. 19 U.S.C.A. § 1677(4).

2. See Chapter 12.

3. Mitsubishi Elec. Corp. v. United States, 898 F.2d 1577 (Fed.Cir.1990).

4. Asociacion Colombiana de Exportadores de Flores v. United States, 693 F.Supp. 1165, 1169–70 (C.I.T.1988), appeal after remand 704 F.Supp. 1068 (1988); Torrington Co. v. United States, 747 F.Supp. 744, 749 (C.I.T.1990), judgment affirmed 938 F.2d 1278 (Fed.Cir.1991).

On the other hand, the ITA relies upon factors which include (1) general and physical characteristics of the merchandise, (2)

the expectations of the ultimate purchasers, (3) the channels of trade in which the merchandise moves, (4) the ultimate use of the merchandise, and (5) cost. Diversified Prods. Corp. v. United States, 572 F.Supp. 883, 889 (C.I.T.1983).

5. 19 U.S.C.A. § 1677(4)(B).

6. 19 U.S.C.A. § 1677(4)(D).

7. 19 U.S.C.A. § 1677(4)(C).

8. Tokyo Round GATT Subsidies Code, Art. 6(7).

§ 13.15

1. 19 U.S.C.A. § 1677(7)(A).

requirement, the Senate Finance Committee report did not consider them inconsistent. It stated that the material injury standard was nothing more than a codification of the de minimis standard as it had been construed by the ITC.[2] The ITC's subsequent interpretations suggest that it understood the material injury requirement to codify the de minimis rule.[3]

After the development of the Tokyo Round GATT Subsidies Code, however, the United States amended its statutes to incorporate the Code's principles. The Tariff Act requires the ITC to consider three basic economic aspects in applying the injury standard:

>   (1) The volume of imports of the merchandise subject to investigation;

>   (2) The effect of these imports on prices in the United States for like products; and

>   (3) The impact of these imports on domestic producers of like products, but only in the context of domestic United States production operations.[4]

The Commission is required to explain its analysis of each factor considered and explain its relevance to the agency's determination. The Tariff Act, however, also provides that the "presence or absence" of any of these three factors should "not necessarily give decisive guidance" to the ITC in its material injury determination, and the Commission is not required to give any particular weight to any one factor.[5] The factors are examined through extensive statistical analyses. The analysis is performed for the domestic industry as a whole, and not on a company-by-company basis, and the analysis is industry specific.[6] The ITC may select whatever time period best represents the business cycle and competitive conditions in the industry, and most reasonably allows it to determine whether an injury exists.

Volume of Imports

In compliance with Tokyo Round GATT Subsidies Code Article 6(2), the Tariff Act requires the ITC to consider the absolute volume of imports or any increases in volume in evaluating the volume of imports subject to investigation. This assessment may be made in relation to production or consumption in the United States. The standard in this evaluation is whether the volume of imports, viewed in any of the above ways, is significant.[7]

Data relating to the volume of imports are an important factor in the ITC's injury determinations. In particular, the ITC is more con-

2. Senate Comm. on Finance, Trade Agreements Act of 1979, S.Rep. No. 249, 96th Cong., 1st Sess. 87.

3. Vermulst, supra Note 10, § 7.2, at 364–76.

4. 19 U.S.C.A. § 1677(7)(B).

5. 19 U.S.C.A. § 1677(7)(E)(ii). Compare Tokyo Round GATT Subsidies Code Art. 6(2).

6. Alberta Pork Producers' Marketing Board v. United States, 669 F.Supp. 445 (C.I.T.1987), appeal after remand 683 F.Supp. 1398 (1988).

7. 19 U.S.C.A. § 1677(7)(C)(i).

cerned with the dynamics of market share, such as a significant rise in market penetration, than it is with the size of market share.[8] It is also primarily concerned with the effects that market share changes might have on profits and lost sales. Significant injury has been found when an importer has less than a 2 percent market share, but the imports market share has increased eightfold,[9] while market shares of greater than 2 percent for the subsidized imports have been found to be insignificant.[10] A large market share for the importer may still indicate no injury when coupled with increases in production, domestic shipments, exports, employment and profits of the domestic industry.

Price Effects

Under the Tariff Act, the ITC when making an injury determination may consider the effect of the subsidized imports upon prices for like products in the domestic market. This is done to the extent that such a consideration assists in evaluating whether (1) there is significant price underselling by the imported merchandise as compared with the price of like products of the United States,[11] and (2) whether the effect of the imported merchandise is otherwise to depress domestic prices to a significant degree or prevent price increases, which otherwise would have occurred to a significant degree.[12]

Price underselling is not a *per se* basis for a finding of injury. For example, if the demand for the product is not price sensitive, price underselling will not be a central consideration in any injury finding. There may be no injury from price underselling, even though the domestic producers lost sales in the United States, if the domestic producers' inability to sell goods was not caused by subsidized imports. For example, the industry's decline may have been caused by its failure to develop, produce and market competitive merchandise. A more extensive analysis of causation issues appears in the next section.

Substantial underselling, on the other hand, will lead to an affirmative injury finding, where the market is price sensitive.[13] When the ITC finds that demand for a specific product is price sensitive and importers are engaging in price underselling, it further examines whether domestic producers are being forced into price suppression[14] or actual price cut-

---

8. J. E. Pattison, Antidumping and Countervailing Duty Laws 4–2 (1992).

9. Alberta Pork Producers' Marketing Board v. United States, 669 F.Supp. 445 (C.I.T.1987), appeal after remand 683 F.Supp. 1398 (1988).

10. Cast–Iron Pipe Fittings from Brazil, 7 ITRD 1823 (ITC Final, 1985).

11. 19 U.S.C.A. § 1677(7)(C)(ii)(I).

12. 19 U.S.C.A. § 1677(7)(C)(ii)(II).

13. The ITC views a product as price sensitive when its price is the most important factor in purchasing the product. In Tubeless Tire Valves from the Federal Re-

public of Germany, 46 Fed.Reg. 29,794 (1981), the ITC relied upon the testimony of buyers who had switched their sourcing from domestic producers to the imports that price was the most important factor in purchasing decisions, with availability a secondary but often critical factor. Id. at 29,795.

14. Price suppression arises when the domestic industry can affect smaller price increases on those articles directly competitive with subsidized imports than it can on those articles that directly compete with non-subsidized imports. Tapered Roller bearings from Japan, 40 Fed.Reg. 26,312, 26,314–26,315 (1975).

ting[15] due to this price underselling. Since either price suppression or price cutting can be a severe burden to domestic producers, the ITC will find an injury if it determines that because of the subsidization of the imports, domestic producers have lowered or have been unable to raise their prices to accommodate rising costs.[16]

Domestic Industry Impact

The impact on a domestic industry of an allegedly subsidized product is probably the most important factor in any injury analysis. The Tariff Act employs the same criteria as are set out in the Tokyo Round GATT Subsidies Code.[17] It then provides supplemental factors for ITC consideration, adding the actual and potential negative effects on the existing development and production efforts of the domestic industry, including efforts to develop a derivative or more advanced version of the like product.[18] The ITC relies primarily on two of these factors in making this determination. First, the industry must be in a distressed or a stagnant condition. Second, the ITC analyzes whether low domestic price levels are a factor in the industry's difficulties (e.g., high unemployment or low capacity utilization rate), and whether the low prices are causing low profits.[19]

The ITC will often base an affirmative action determination of material injury on severe downward trends in profitability among domestic producers. For example, loss of profitability in the face of increasing imports can indicate material injury.[20] Thus, it is not necessary that an industry suffer an actual loss as a prerequisite to a finding of material injury.

When a negative determination has been made despite the industry's declining profitability, the ITC has generally indicated that the industry was still in a healthy state, increasing production, shipments, capacity and market share despite losses in profitability.[21] Thus, the ITC

15. Price cutting arises when the domestic industry is compelled to lower its prices to meet the prices of subsidized imports in an attempt to protect its market share.

16. See, e.g., Unrefined Montan Wax from East Germany, 46 Fed.Reg. 45,223, 45,224 (1981).

17. 19 U.S.C.A. § 1677(C)(iii) provides:

In examining the impact required to be considered under subparagraph (B)(iii), the Commission shall evaluate all relevant economic factors which have a bearing on the state of the industry in the United States, including, but not limited to—

(I) actual and potential decline in output, sales, market share, profits, productivity, return on investments, and utilization of capacity,

(II) factors affecting domestic prices,

(III) actual and potential negative effects on cash flow, inventories, employment, wages, growth, ability to raise capital, and investment, and

(IV) actual and potential negative effects on the existing development and production efforts of the domestic industry, including efforts to develop a derivative or more advanced version of the like product.

18. 19 U.S.C.A. § 1677(7)(C)(iii)(IV).

19. Vermulst, supra Note 10, § 7.2, at 369.

20. Cotton Shop Towels from Pakistan, 6 ITRD 1494 (ITC Final, 1984).

21. See, e.g., American Spring Wire Corp. v. United States, 590 F.Supp. 1273 (C.I.T.1984), affirmed sub nom. Armco, Inc. et al. v. United States, 760 F.2d 249 (Fed. Cir.1985).

can make a negative determination concerning material injury, even though the industry has suffered profitability losses.

The effect of subsidized imports on employment in the relevant domestic industry is also considered. Employment data are not dispositive due to the broad spectrum of economic factors related to such data, and many of those factors may not be attributable to foreign subsidization. However, changes in domestic employment during the period under investigation are one factor to be considered. A drop in employment during the period of investigation may be an indication of injury, and an increase in employment and man-hours worked in the domestic industry may be cited by the ITC as one factor in a determination that there has been no material injury. But increasing employment usually is a factor in determinations of no injury only when other factors also indicate that no material injury is present.

The utilization of plant capacity has been considered a factor in many determinations, but such capacity utilization data is treated ambiguously because it is dependent upon diverse factors. Falling capacity utilization may indicate material injury if there is no other explanation, but the ITC can make negative injury determinations despite falling capacity utilization, if the decline is caused by other factors, such as frequent equipment breakdowns and quality control disruptions.

§ 13.16 Causation

Causation of material injury by subsidization is a required element which must be found independently of the finding of material injury, threat of material injury or the material retardation of the establishment of a domestic industry. However, there is a tendency to enter an affirmative injury determination when subsidization and material injury to a concerned industry are found, without a lengthy analysis of the causal link between them. In a negative injury determination, on the other hand, the ITC may engage in a rather detailed analysis of causation.

The Tariff Act requires a simple causation element, stating that material injury must be caused "by reason of" the subsidization of the imports.[1] The same standard applies in AD proceedings and once again the law in this area is largely interchangeable. The causation requirement is not a high one. Imports need only cause material injury, and need not be the most substantial or primary cause of injury being suffered by domestic industry. This causation element of an affirmative

---

§ 13.16

1. 19 U.S.C.A. § 1671(a):

If—

. . .

  (2) the Commission determines that—

  (A) an industry in the United States—

  (i) is materially injured, or

  (ii) is threatened with material injury, or

  (B) the establishment of an industry in the United States is materially retarded,

by reason of imports of that merchandise . . ., then there shall be imposed upon such merchandise a countervailing duty. . . .

injury determination can be satisfied if the subsidized imports contribute, even minimally, to the conditions of the domestic injury.[2] Under this "contributing cause" standard, causation of injuries may be found despite the absence of correlation between subsidized imports and the alleged injuries, if there is substantial evidence that the volume of subsidized imports was a contributing factor to the price depression experienced by the domestic injury.[3]

In examining the causal link between the subsidized imports and the material injury, the ITC is willing to recognize that there can be causal factors other than subsidies which can be responsible for the alleged injury in a particular proceeding.[4] An industry which prospers during times of greater import penetration will find it difficult to persuade the ITC that subsidized imports cause material injury to it. The existence of extraneous injury factors will not, however, necessarily preclude an affirmative finding of material injury for purposes of the Tariff Act,[5] as long as the subsidies are a contributing cause to the material injury of the domestic industry. The ITC is not required to weigh the effects from the subsidized imports against the effects associated with other factors, if the subsidization is a contributing cause of the injury. For example, in evaluating causation, the ITC may uncover other major causes for the problems of the domestic industry. These may include huge unnecessary expenses, chronic excess capacity, inefficiency, poor quality, price sensitivity or increased domestic competition. Nevertheless, the presence of such major alternative causes of injury does not foreclose the possibility that imports have been *a* contributing cause of the industry's problems.[6]

§ 13.17 Cumulative Causation

Can a "material injury" be caused by imports from several exporters in more than one country through the cumulative effect of many small

---

2. British Steel Corp. v. United States, 593 F.Supp. 405, 413 (C.I.T.1984).

3. Id.

4. Such extraneous factors include:

(1) Volume and prices of non-subsidized imports;

(2) Contraction in demand or changes in patterns of consumption;

(3) Trade restrictive practices of and competition between foreign and domestic producers;

(4) Developments in technology; and

(5) The export performance and productivity of the domestic industry.

S.Rep. No. 249 96th Cong., 1st Sess. 57 (1979).

5. At least one Commissioner has argued that although this traditional analysis may be useful in determining material injury, it is not a proper tool to resolve the issue of causation because it does not do well in separating the effects of subsidized imports from the effects of other factors operating in the marketplace. Instead she advocates what is termed the elasticity analysis. This new approach analyzes the elasticity of domestic demand for the product under investigation to determine the effect on the domestic injury of unfair imports, as separated from many other factors that affect the concerned industry. See H. Blinn, The Injury–Test under United States Antidumping and Countervailing Duty Laws as Interpreted by the International Trade Commission and the Department of Commerce: A Comparison Study of the Conventional "Trend–Analysis" and the "Elasticity-test" 23–30 (1991).

6. Iwatsu Electric Co., Ltd. v. United States, 758 F.Supp. 1506 (C.I.T.1991) (small telephone systems); United Engineering & Forging v. United States, 779 F.Supp. 1375 (C.I.T.1991), opinion after remand 14 ITRD 1748 (1992) (crankshafts).

injuries? There are arguments against cumulating each source of subsidized imports to determine whether it is a cause of injury. Such cumulation could penalize small suppliers who would not have caused injury if their subsidization had been examined in isolation.[1] Nevertheless, the injury to a domestic industry is measured by the cumulated results of all subsidies on the ground that injury caused by "many nibbles" is just as harmful as that caused through "one large bite." Cumulation provides administrative ease, since the countervailing duty agency is not required to allocate the amount of injury caused by each individual exporter.

The GATT and the Tokyo Round GATT Subsidies Code were ambiguous on the propriety of cumulation. While GATT Article VI seems to contemplate a country-by-country approach by referring repeatedly to the singular term "country,"[2] the Tokyo Round Subsidies Code used the term "subsidized imports," which implicitly permits an aggregate approach.[3] The Uruguay round expressly permits cumulation.

The Tariff Act requires that the ITC cumulatively assess the volume and effect of reasonably coincident subsidized imports from two or more countries of like products subject to investigation if the imports compete with each other and with like United States products.[4] There is, however, an exception for imports from beneficiary countries of the Caribbean Basin Initiative.[5] The ITC has held multicountry cumulation to be proper if the factors and conditions of trade in the particular case show its relevance to the determination of injury, and has given a nonexhaustive list of such factors.[6] The list includes the volume of imports, the trend of import volume, the fungibility of imports, competition in the markets for the same end users, common channels of distribution, pricing similarity, simultaneous impact, and any coordinated action by importers. From these factors, the ITC determines whether the imports compete with each other and like domestic products. Surprisingly, the ITC found that French and Italian wines do not compete with each other.[7] But an ITC ruling that steel imports from Spain, Brazil and Korea competed with each other was overturned by the Court of International Trade,[8] which also refused to require the ITC to cumulate steel plate imports from Brazil, Korea and Argentina.[9]

The ITC has also ruled that, when cumulating, it is not necessary to find for each country a separate causal link between its imports and U.S.

§ 13.17

1. For a comparable argument, see Horlick, The United States Antidumping System, in Antidumping Law and Practice: A Comparative Study 102 (1989).

2. GATT Art. VI(1), VI(6).

3. Tokyo Round GATT Subsidies Code, Arts. 6(1), 6(2), 6(4), 6(6) and 6(7).

4. 19 U.S.C.A. § 1677(7)(C)(iv). This statutory provision settled a pre–1984 conflict within the Commission concerning whether to cumulate or not.

5. 19 U.S.C.A. § 1677(7)(C)(iv)(II).

6. Certain Steel Products Belgium, Brazil, etc., ITC Pub. No. 1221, U.S.I.T.C. Inv. No. 701–TA–86–144 (February 1986).

7. See American Grape Growers Alliance v. United States, 615 F.Supp. 603 (C.I.T.1985).

8. Republic Steel Corp. v. United States, 591 F.Supp. 640 (C.I.T.1984).

9. USX Corp. v. United States, 698 F.Supp. 234 (C.I.T.1988).

material injury.[10] Such multiple country cumulation should be distinguished form the "cross cumulation" allowed by the Tariff Act. Cross cumulation involves consideration by the ITC of both dumped and subsidized imports into the United States.[11] The net effect of U.S. rules on cumulation of import injury is to encourage petitioners to name as many countries as possible as the source of their problems.

§ 13.18 Countervailing Duty Procedures

For a "Subsidies Agreement Country," the procedures governing the applicability of countervailing duties to its goods will be determined under 19 U.S.C.A. § 1671, not 19 U.S.C.A. § 1303. Section 1671 proceedings can be settled by international agreement; Section 1303 proceedings cannot.[1] Section 1303 CVD can be applied retroactively without limitation whereas Section 1671 CVD can be applied retroactively only in "critical circumstances." The major difference between the two sections is that only a determination that a subsidy exists is necessary under Section 1303, while Section 1671 requires both a determination of a subsidy and an injury determination. Thus the administrative procedure for deciding whether to impose countervailing duties under Section 1671 is the same as that for antidumping duties[2] and involves the ITA and ITC making both preliminary and final determinations. Under either Section 1671 or 1303, an ITA preliminary determination that a countervailable subsidy exists subjects all goods imported after that date to any countervailing duties imposed later. This usually has the effect of immediately reducing imports of such goods.

§ 13.19 Administrative Determinations

Two different governmental agencies are involved in regulating, through countervailing duties, imports into the United States. The International Trade Administration (ITA) is part of the Commerce Department, which in turn is part of the Executive Branch of the government. The International Trade Commission (ITC) is an independent agency. The structure, organization and context of both of these organizations is discussed further in the introductory chapter on U.S. customs and trade regulation.[1]

The chain of decision-making in CVD proceedings depends upon which statutory section controls. If Section 1303 governs, which petitioners (the domestic industry) will ordinarily favor, the proceeding is totally before the ITA with the ITC excluded. This will be a two-stage proceeding:

ITA Preliminary Countervailable Subsidy Determination

10. Fundicao Tupy S.A. v. United States, 678 F.Supp. 898 (C.I.T.1988), decision affirmed 859 F.2d 915 (Fed.Cir.1988).

11. See especially Bingham & Taylor Div., Virginia Industries, Inc. v. United States, 815 F.2d 1482 (Fed.Cir.1987).

§ 13.18

1. See Section 13.5.

2. See Chapter 12.

§ 13.19

1. See Chapter 9.

ITA Final Countervailable Subsidy Determination

If, however, a "country under the Agreement" is the source of the goods, then Section 1671 controls. Respondents (the importers) will generally prefer this because a four-stage proceeding allowing argument over the alleged domestic industry injury will follow:

ITC Preliminary Injury Determination

ITA Preliminary Countervailable Subsidy Determination

ITA Final Countervailable Subsidy Determination

ITC Final Injury Determination

The CVD process may be initiated by either the Department of Commerce, a union or business, or by a group or association of aggrieved workers or businesses—an aggrieved "industry."[2] The required contents of the petition are stipulated at 19 C.F.R. § 355.12 (reproduced in the Selected Documents section of this chapter). Pre-filing contact with the ITA and (if needed) the ITC can often resolve any problems regarding the contents of the petition. Petitioners may also access the ITA's library of information on foreign subsidy practices. The ITA determines whether the petition alleges the elements necessary for the imposition of a duty, based on the best information available at the time.[3] In other words, the ITA accepts or rejects the petition.

Once the petition is accepted, the ITC makes a preliminary determination as to a real or threatened material injury within 45 days of the date the petition was filed based on the best information available to it at that time.[4] If the ITC makes such a finding, the ITA must then make a preliminary determination whether there is "a reasonable basis to believe" based on the best information available that there is a countervailable subsidy with respect to the exported merchandise.[5] The time for making this decision may be extended if the petitioner so requests, or the ITA determines both that the parties are cooperating and that it is an extraordinarily complicated case.[6] The time period may also be extended for "upstream subsidy" investigations.[7]

If the ITA makes a preliminary determination that a countervailable subsidy exists, within 75 days it must make a "final determination" concerning the existence of a countervailable subsidy and calculate the amount of the proposed CVD.[8] If subsidization is found by the ITA, the ITC then must make a final determination concerning material injury within 120 days after the ITA has made an affirmative preliminary determination,[9] or within 75 days after an affirmative final determination by the ITA if its preliminary determination was negative.[10] The chart presented in Section 6.32 details U.S. countervailing duty investi-

---

2. 19 U.S.C.A. § 1671a(a) and (b).

3. 19 U.S.C.A. § 1671a(b).

4. 19 U.S.C.A. § 1671b(a).

5. 19 U.S.C.A. § 1671b(b).

6. 19 U.S.C.A. § 1671b(c).

7. 19 U.S.C.A. § 1671b(h).

8. 19 U.S.C.A. § 1671d(a).

9. 19 U.S.C.A. § 1671d(b)(2).

10. 19 U.S.C.A. § 1671d(b)(3).

gation procedures. As with antidumping, most CVD proceedings are done within a year.

In reaching their determinations, both the ITA and the ITC frequently circulate questionnaires to interested parties, including foreign governments and exporters. Since any failure to respond risks a determination on the "best information available," this results in the flow of significant and often strategically valuable business information to the government. Amendments adopted in 1988 now require release under protective order of all confidential business information to counsel for interested parties.[11] This protection is particularly important because not all domestic producers may support the CVD petition, but they are generally able to access the submissions of others who do. Confidentiality is defined in the regulations at 19 C.F.R. § 355.4 and 19 C.F.R. § 207.6.

§ 13.20 The Importance of the ITA Preliminary Subsidy Determination

An ITA preliminary determination that a countervailable subsidy exists places great pressure on the importers of the foreign goods. Liquidation (entry at a determined rate of tariff) of all such merchandise is suspended by order of customs. Goods imported after an ITA preliminary determination of a countervailable subsidy will be subject to any CVD imposed later, after final determinations are made.[1] Such a preliminary determination, although subject to final determinations by the ITA and the ITC and appealable to the CIT, will effectively cut off further importation of the disputed goods unless an expensive bond is posted until the process has been completed. In this process the respondent importer often wants a speedy resolution as its total costs for the imports are unknown. The statute is replete with time provisions established to protect the importer by requiring action to be completed and decisions to be made within specified time limits. Many CVD proceedings are concluded within a year.

At one level, then, a useful intermediate goal in representing a petitioner is to obtain an ITA preliminary determination concerning a "subsidy" or "bounty" which meets the statutory requirements. The respondent's "defense" to such efforts must be organized quickly, usually within 30 days of the filing of a CVD petition. The importer's ability to present a defense is handicapped by the nature of CVD proceedings . . . the complaint is really lodged against the subsidy practices of foreign governments. Unlike most foreign exporters whose pricing decisions are the focus in AD proceedings, many foreign governments are loath to provide information necessary to an adequate response to a CVD complaint. Since the ITA and ITC are authorized to make decisions on the basis of the best information available, any failure to adequately respond to a CVD complaint can contribute to adverse rulings. Moreover, responses by foreign governments and exporters to ITA questionnaires

11. See 19 U.S.C.A. § 1677f(c)(1).

§ 13.20
1.   19 U.S.C.A. § 1671b(d).

that cannot be verified by on the spot investigations are ignored and thus removed from the best information available for decision-making. This may leave only the petitioner's or other respondent's submissions for review, a one-sided proceeding almost sure to result in affirmative determinations.

The respondent importer's uncertainties over the amount of duty owed after a preliminary ITA determination that a countervailable subsidy exists can increase in Section 1671 (GATT-derived) proceedings if the ITA decides that "critical circumstances" are present. In such cases, the suspension of liquidation of the goods applies not only prospectively from the date of such determination, but also retrospectively for 90 days.[2] Moreover, in traditional Section 1303 proceedings against bounties or grants, there is *no* time limit to the ability to retroactively apply CVD against any unliquidated entries and there need not be any determination that critical circumstances are present.

§ 13.21   CVD Duties and Anticircumvention

The ITA final determination of the existence of a subsidy establishes the amount of any CVD. Since duties are not imposed to support any specific domestic price, they are set only to equal the amount of the net subsidy.[1] The CVD remains in force as long as the subsidization occurs. The ITA may modify or revoke a CVD order if changed circumstances warrant, but the burden of proof is on the party seeking alteration of the CVD order.[2] Circumvention of an existing CVD order, on the other hand, can trigger anticircumvention orders. The statutes authorize such relief when goods subject to a CVD are "downstreamed" (incorporated as a component in another product)[3] or shipped as components for assembly in the United States or a third country.[4]

Another circumvention issue of growing importance is whether subsidies received by a firm that is subsequently sold or privatized pass through to benefit the new owner's exports. The Commerce Department generally has denied the existence of a countervailable subsidy after private sector arm's length acquisitions, but recently sought to impose CVD after steel industry privatization sales by the British and German governments. This effort was strongly rebuked by the Court of International Trade.[5] The CIT declared that the Commerce Department's approach in these cases was in "direct contravention" of the guiding principles of U.S. countervailing duty law, namely to ensure a level playing field. Purchasers in arm's length transactions, whether private or public, do not receive any countervailable benefits since what they have paid includes the value of past subsidies received. The past subsidies either remain with the seller, the shareholders of the selling

2. 19 U.S.C.A. § 1781(b)(e)(1)(B).

§ 13.21
1. 19 U.S.C.A. § 1671e.
2. 19 U.S.C.A. § 1675.
3. 19 U.S.C.A. § 1677i.

4. 19 U.S.C.A. § 1677j.

5. [See Saarstahl, AG v. United States, Inland Steel Bar Co., 858 F.Supp. 187, 11 BNA ATRR 961 (1994).]

corporation upon dissolution, or revert to the state if a privatization sale is involved. If subsidies passed through on arm's length transactions, buyers would have great trouble evaluating the potential CVD liabilities of the firm they purchase. Critics see in this decision the possibility of considerable circumvention through acquisitions of U.S. countervailing duty law.

In 2000, the United States adopted the so-called "Byrd amendment." Under this provision of H.R. 4461, antidumping and countervailing tariff duties collected by the U.S. government may be passed on to injured U.S. companies. The Byrd amendment was lobbied heavily by the U.S. steel industry, which has been a major complainant in AD and CVD proceedings. The European Union, Japan and South Korea assert that this provision violates WTO rules and are preparing to challenge it.

Many petitioners in countervailing duty cases also seek antidumping duties[6] and other relief through escape clause or market disruption proceedings.[7] Thus, domestic producers seeking relief from import competition will often use a "shotgun" approach to obtain protective relief.

§ 13.22 Appeals

Judicial review "on the record" of final (not preliminary) decisions by the ITA and the ITC in both CVD and AD proceedings may be sought before the Court of International Trade (CIT). This is discussed at greater length in the introductory chapter on U.S. customs and trade regulation.[1] However, for proceedings arising out of exports from Canada and Mexico, the United States—Canada FTA and the NAFTA provide for resolution of antidumping and countervailing duty disputes through binational panels.[2] Such panels apply the domestic law of the importing country, and provide a substitute for judicial review of the decisions of administrative agencies of the importing country.[3]

D. EUROPEAN SUBSIDIES AND CVD LAW

§ 13.23 GATT/WTO Code Adherence

The European Union (EU) adhered to the Tokyo Round Subsidies Code. This Code was implemented as part of the Common (External) Commercial Policy. The EU also follows the Uruguay Round Subsidies Code of 1994.[1] The principal rules on countervailing duties are found in Council Regulation 3284/94. In general, European CVD law has developed along lines similar to that of the United States.

The European Court of Justice has said that the concept of a countervailable subsidy presupposes "the grant of an economic advan-

6. See Chapter 12.

7. See Chapter 15.

§ 13.22

1. See Chapter 9.

2. Canada–United States Free Trade Agreement (1989), Chapter 19; NAFTA (1994), Chapter 19.

3. See Chapter 21.

§ 13.23

1. See Section.13.3.

tage through a charge on the public account."[2] For a domestic subsidy to be countervailable, it must have "sectoral specificity" (seek to grant an advantage only to certain firms). For an export subsidy to be countervailable, it must specifically benefit the imported product.[3] As with dumping proceedings, the Commission makes these judgments provisionally and the Council renders final judgment (issued as a customs regulation). The amount of the extra duty corresponds to the amount of the subsidy.

Selected Bibliography

Alexander, The Specificity Test Under U.S. Countervailing Duty Law, 10 Mich.J.Int'l L. 807 (1989).

Alford, When is China Paraguay? An examination of the application of the antidumping and countervailing duty laws of the United States to China and other nonmarket economy nations, 61 So.Cal.L.Rev. 79 (Nov. 1987).

Barcelo, Subsidies and Countervailing Duties—Analysis and Proposal, 9 Law & Policy Int'l Bus. 779 (1977).

Bishop, Multilateral Trade Negotiations, Subsidies and the Great Plains Wheat Case, 16 Int'l Lawyer 339 (1982).

Boger, The United States–European Community Agricultural Export Subsidies Dispute, 16 Law & Pol'y Int'l Bus. 173 (1984).

Ehrenhaft, What the Antidumping and Countervailing Duty Provisions (Can) (Will) (Should) Mean for U.S. Trade Policy, 11 Law & Pol'y Int'l Bus. 1361 (1979).

Guido & Morrone, The Michelin Decision: A Possible New Direction for U.S. Countervailing Duty Law, 6 Law & Pol'y Int'l Bus. 237 (1974).

Horlick & DeBusk, Dispute Resolution Panels of the U.S.–Canada Free Trade Agreement: The First Two and One–Half Years, 37 McGill, J. 574 (1992).

Lantz, The Search for Consistency: Treatment of Nonmarket Economics in Transition Under U.S.Antidumping and Countervailing Duty Laws, 10 Am.U.J. Int'l L. & Pol. 993 (1995).

Note, International Trade: Countervailing Duties and European Steel Imports, 23 Harv.Int'l L.J. 443 (1983).

Note, Upstream Subsidies and U.S. Countervailing Duty Law: The Mexican Ammonia Decision and the Trade Remedies Reform Act of 1984, Law & Pol'y Int'l Bus. 263 (1985).

Schwartz, Countervailing Duties and International Trade, 1978 Sup.Ct. Rev. 294.

Wilcox, GATT–Based Protectionism and the Definition of A Subsidy, 16 B.U. Int'l L.J. 129 (1998).

2. FEDIOL v. Commission (1988) Eur.   **3.** Id.
Comm.Rep. 4193.

Chapter 14

UNITED STATES IMPORT CONTROLS AND NONTARIFF TRADE BARRIERS

Table of Sections

A. INTRODUCTION

§ 14.1 Import Quotas and Licenses

Goods imported into the United States may have to qualify within numerical quota limitations imposed upon importation of that item or upon that kind of item. Import quotas may be "global" limitations (applying to items originating from anywhere in the world), "bilateral" limitations (applying to items originating from a particular country) and "discretionary" limitations. Bilateral limitations may be found in an applicable Treaty of Friendship, Commerce and Navigation or in a more narrow international agreement, such as the 1978 Poland–United States Importation Agreement on Trade in Textiles and Textile Products.[1] Discretionary limitations, when coupled with a requirement that importation of items must be licensed in advance by local authorities, provide an effective vehicle for gathering statistical data and for raising local revenues. "Tariff-rate quotas" admit a specified quantity of goods at a preferential rate of duty. Once imports reach that quantity, tariffs are normally increased.

If a quota system is created, a fundamental subsidiary issue is: How will the quotas be allocated? The Customs Service generally administers quotas on a first-come, first-served basis. This approach creates a race to enter goods into the United States. One potential allocation method is through the use of licenses, which would be the documentation for administration of such quantitative restrictions. Licensing of imports can work a trade restrictive effect. International concern about delays which result from cumbersome licensing procedures was manifested in the 1979 Tokyo Round MTN Import Licensing Code (which most developing countries refused to sign). The United States adhered to this Code, as did a reasonable number of other nations. The Uruguay Round made an Agreement on Import Licensing Procedures (1994) binding on all World Trade Organization members. The Agreement's objectives include facilitating the simplification and harmonization of import licensing and licensing renewal procedures, ensuring adequate publication of rules governing licensing procedures, and reducing the practice of refusing importation because of minor variations in quantity, value or weight of the import item under license.

The President is authorized to sell import licenses at public auctions.[2] One advantage of an auction system is its revenue raising potential. The U.S. Tariff Act of 1930 also provides that to the extent practicable and consistent with efficient and fair administration, the President is to insure against inequitable sharing of imports by a relatively small number of the larger importers.[3] In fact, allocating quotas among U.S. importers rarely happens. Rather, in the past,

§ 14.1

1. TIAS 9064.

2. 19 U.S.C.A. § 2581.

3. Id.

quotas have been part of a "voluntary restraint" or orderly market agreement between the U.S. and one or more foreign governments, and represent adherence by those governments to U.S. initiatives. The negotiations have typically concentrated on obtaining foreign government agreement to limitations on exportation of their products into the U.S. market, and have not pursued limitations on who might use the resulting allocations. Thus, instead of an auction system, the U.S. has usually used a Presidentially managed system of import allocations, especially in regard to agricultural import quotas.

§ 14.2   GATT/WTO Nontariff Trade Barrier Codes

Multilateral negotiations since the end of World War II have led to a significant decline in world tariff levels, particularly on trade with developed nations. As steadily as tariff barriers have disappeared, nontariff trade barriers (NTBs) have emerged. Health and safety regulations, environmental laws, rules regulating products standards, procurement legislation and customs procedures are often said to present NTB problems. Negotiations over nontariff trade barriers dominated the Tokyo Round of the GATT negotiations during the late 1970s. A number of NTB "codes" (sometimes called "side agreements") emerged from the Tokyo Round. These concerned subsidies, dumping, government procurement, technical barriers (products standards), customs valuation and import licensing. In addition, specific agreements regarding trade in bovine meats, dairy products and civil aircraft were also reached. The United States accepted all of these NTB codes and agreements except the one on dairy products. Most of the necessary implementation of these agreements was accomplished in the Trade Agreements Act of 1979.[1]

Additional codes were agreed upon under the Uruguay Round ending in late 1993. They revisit all of the NTB areas covered by the Tokyo Round Codes and create new codes for trade-related investment measures (TRIMs), preshipment inspection, rules of origin, escape clause safeguards and trade-related intellectual property rights (TRIPs). The United States Congress approved and implemented these WTO codes in December of 1994 under the Uruguay Round Agreements Act.

One problem with nontariff trade barriers is that they are so numerous. Intergovernmental negotiation intended to reduce their trade restricting impact is both tedious and difficult. There are continuing attempts through the World Trade Organization to come to grips with additional specific NTB problems. Furthermore, various bilateral agreements of the United States have been undertaken in this field. For example, the Canadian–United States Free Trade Area Agreement and the NAFTA build upon the GATT/WTO agreements to further reduce NTB problems between the United States, Canada and Mexico.[2]

§ 14.2

1. 19 U.S.C.A. § 2501 et seq.

2. See Chapter 21.

§ 14.3 U.S. Import Restraints

In addition to NTBs, the United States has employed import quotas for many years. Tariff-rate quotas have been applied to dairy products, olives, tuna fish, anchovies, brooms, and sugar, syrups and molasses. Quite a few absolute quotas originate under Section 22 of the Agricultural Adjustment Act.[1] These quotas are undertaken when necessary to United States farm price supports or similar agricultural programs. They have used on animals feeds, dairy products, chocolate, cotton, peanuts, and selected syrups and sugars. Some U.S. agricultural quotas are being "tariffied" under the WTO Agreement on Agriculture. Some quotas imposed by the U.S. are sanctions for unfair trade practices, as against tungsten from China. Other quotas originate in international commodity agreements, and important restraints on textile imports are achieved as a result of the international Multi–Fiber Arrangement (phased out under the WTO Textiles Agreement).

The Agricultural Act of 1949 requires the President to impose global import quotas on Upland Cotton whenever the Secretary of Agriculture determines that its average price exceeds certain statutory limits.[2] Whenever this is the case, unlike the ordinary restrictive import quota, the importation of Upland Cotton is duty free. Like the Meat Import Act, this provision tends to be countercyclical to market forces for cotton in the United States.

Lastly, the United States sometimes imposes import restraints for national security or foreign policy reasons. Many of these restraints originate from Section 232 of the Trade Expansion Act of 1962. This provision authorizes the President to "adjust imports" whenever necessary to the national security of the country. Trade embargoes are sometimes imposed on all the goods from politically incorrect nations (e.g., Cuba). Product-specific import bans also exist for selected goods, e.g., narcotic drugs and books urging insurrection against the United States.[3] The importation of "immoral" goods is generally prohibited[4], even for private use, and the obscenity of such items is decided by reviewing the community standards at the port of entry.[5] Generally, as well, goods produced with forced, convict, indentured or bonded child labor are excluded from the United States.[6] This ban has been applied

§ 14.3

1. 7 U.S.C.A. § 624.

2. 7 U.S.C.A. § 1444.

3. 21 U.S.C.A. § 171 and 19 U.S.C.A. § 1305.

4. 19 U.S.C.A. § 1305.

5. United States v. Various Articles of Obscene Merchandise, 536 F.Supp. 50 (S.D.N.Y.1981).

6. 19 U.S.C.A. § 1307. The 1997 Bonded Child Labor Elimination Act amended 19 U.S.C. § 1307 to prohibit the U.S. importation of goods produced by "bonded child labor." Such labor is defined as work or service exacted by confinement against his or her will from persons under age 15 in payment for debts of parents, relatives or guardians, or drawn under false pretexts. Section 307 bans products of convict, forced and indentured labor. See China Diesel Imports, Inc. v. United States, 870 F.Supp. 347 (C.I.T. 1994) (Chinese government documents referring to factory as "Reform through Labor Facility" probative of convict labor origin of goods; exclusion order affirmed; U.S. consumption demand exception applies only to forced and indentured labor). On standing to sue to block importation of prohibited labor goods, see McKin-

to certain goods from the People's Republic of China.[7]

The materials that follow selectively present United States law governing import controls and nontariff trade barriers. A parallel discussion of "voluntary" export restraints (VERs) and orderly marketing agreements (OMAs) limiting exports into the U.S. market can be found in Chapter 9. VERs and OMAs have been applied to textiles, autos, steel, machine tools and semiconductors. Their use is now severely limited by the WTO Agreement on Safeguards.[8]

§ 14.4 U.S. Participation in International Commodity Agreements

The United States has participated in a variety of international commodity agreements, typically negotiated through United Nations organizations. Both supplying and purchasing countries often participate in these agreements. There are a variety of techniques employed to stabilize the price of commodities by agreement. These techniques include buffer stocks, import and export controls, the fixing of prices, and the signing of long term supply contracts. Typically, there is a central organization administering an international commodity agreement. These agreements are generally thought to be desirable in order to avoid wide price fluctuations in certain commodities. The United States has participated in several such agreements including those covering coffee, sugar, wheat, jute, natural rubber and tropical timber. These agreements have not always been effective. For example, the Fifth International Tin Agreement to which the United States was a party expired in June of 1982. The International Sugar Agreement reached in 1977 expired in December of 1984.

The International Coffee Agreement reached in 1983 is presently inoperative. This agreement basically involves export limitations by the source countries. However, the President may request the International Coffee organization to increase coffee supplies if there has been a "unwarranted" increase in coffee prices as a result of market manipulations by at least two parties.[1] When the International Coffee Agreement is operating and its export quotas are in effect, the President is authorized to limit entry into the United States of non-international coffee agreement members. This has led to a Customs Service requirement that exporters provide certificates of origin documenting their source as within the International Coffee Agreement supplying nations.

The United States participates in the International Natural Rubber Agreement of 1979. Various extensions to this Agreement have been undertaken. This particular agreement establishes a buffer stock in-

ney v. U.S. Department of Treasury, 799 F.2d 1544 (Fed.Cir.1986) (causal link between imports and clear economic injury must be shown).

7. See, e.g., 57 Fed.Reg. 9469 (March 18, 1992).

8. See Chapter 15.

§ 14.4

1. See Public Law No. 96–599.

tended to defend natural rubber prices. Its impact is especially important to the United States, which is the largest purchaser in the world of natural rubber. The United States has contributed to the buffer stock fund.[2] There are no provisions for import controls as part of the Natural Rubber Agreement. One of its goals is to expand supplies if the costs of petroleum rise.

§ 14.5 U.S. Participation in the Multi–Fiber Arrangement

There is an international agreement referred to as the Multi–Fiber Arrangement negotiated within the GATT so as to regulate trade in textiles within the world community. The United States participates in the Multi–Fiber Arrangement (MFA) under the authority of Section 204 of the Agricultural Act of 1956.[1] The MFA became effective in 1974 and has been repeatedly extended. Under the Uruguay Round, however, agreement was reached to phase out the MFA over ten years ending in the year 2005. Unlike international commodity agreements, the MFA merely creates a broad framework with guiding principles for the negotiation of bilateral trade agreements between supplying and purchasing countries. In the absence of such an agreement, unilateral trade restraints are authorized. Such restraints can only follow from the fact of market disruption through textile import competition. The importing nation is under a duty to request consultations with the source country and attempt to negotiate a bilateral agreement limiting trade in textiles.

For MFA purposes, market disruption exists whenever domestic producers are suffering "serious damage" or the threat of such damage. In reaching such determinations, the President is to consider the market share, profits, export performance, employment, volume of imports, capacity utilization, productivity, investments, and sales turnover of the United States textile industry. Sharp and substantial increases in textile imports must be found at prices substantially below those prevailing in the importing nation before unilateral trade restraints may be imposed. These criteria originate in the MFA Agreement but are similar to those used in connection with escape clause and market disruption proceedings under the Trade Act of 1974.[2] Unilateral trade restraints cannot exceed certain levels. The actual level of imports during the first 12 of the last 14 months establishes this limitation.

The United States, operating as a signatory in the context of the Multi–Fiber Agreement, has reached a large number of bilateral trade agreements with other nations concerning textiles. These agreements are subject to judicial review.[3] The effect of these agreements is to set aggregate limits on the total imports from those nations that can enter the United States. Within that aggregate, there are quota levels for

---

2. See International Natural Rubber Agreement Implementing Act of 1980.

§ 14.5

1. 7 U.S.C.A. § 1854.

2. See Chapter 15.

3. Associated Dry Goods Corp. v. United States, 521 F.Supp. 473 (C.I.T.1981), mooted 682 F.2d 212 (C.C.P.A.1982).

groups of products such as apparel and wool products. Within each grouping, specific import levels may be set for particular items. On especially sensitive textile imports, a specific level of importation may be designated. The MFA calls for an annual six percent growth in the import restraints established under a bilateral textile agreement. There are now approximately 50 such agreements in place. Special access quotas for Caribbean Basin countries have been established in connection with the United States Caribbean Basin Initiative. These quotas are in addition to those which normally would apply. The effect of these quotas is to liberalize the duty free entry into the United States of textile products from the Caribbean under Section 9802.00.80 of the Harmonized Tariff Schedule.[4]

The Customs Service has issued regulations concerning the rules of origin for textile and apparel products shipped into the United States pursuant to the Multi–Fiber Arrangement.[5] At present, the Multi–Fiber Arrangement governs approximately 75 percent of all United States imports of textiles and apparel goods. Typically, the bilateral agreements undertaken by the United States permit a certain degree of carryover for quotas from one year to the next, as well as swings between portions of quotas in one category to another category. Whenever the United States thinks that there is market disruption as a result of trade in textiles, it will typically initiate consultations with the source country. If after such consultations, a new agreement on trade restraints has not been reached, the United States may impose unilateral quotas. The authority for such action is found in Articles 3 and 4 of the Multi–Fiber Arrangement.

B.   AGRICULTURAL QUOTAS

§ 14.6   Section 22 of the Agricultural Adjustment Act

Like many nations, the United States has long protected its agricultural base with a variety of trade restraints. The primary purpose of these restraints is to insure that imports do not undermine the agricultural price support programs of the nation. Section 22 of the Agricultural Adjustment Act authorizes the President to restrict the importation of agricultural commodities by imposing quotas or fees.[1] Section 22 provides that no trade agreement of the United States (e.g., the GATT) is to be applied in a manner that is inconsistent with its requirements. Section 22 authorizes the President to impose quotas or special fees whenever imports (or the practical certainty of imports) are rendering or tending to render ineffective or materially interfering with any United States farm program. Such restraints may also be imposed when imports substantially reduce the amount processed of any product subject to such a farm program. Import quotas under Section 22 have been

---

4. See Chapter 10.

5. See 50 Fed.Reg. 8710 (March 5, 1985).

§ 14.6

1. 7 U.S.C.A. § 624.

imposed on cotton, peanuts, dairy products, oats, rye, chocolate and other commodities. Under the Uruguay Round accords, however, the United States is committed to a phased withdrawal of import quotas on sugar, dairy products and peanuts. These quotas will be replaced by tariffs.

Agricultural import quotas are undertaken by the President at the advice of the Secretary of Agriculture and its Foreign Agricultural Service (FAS). Before the President may impose a quota or other import restraint, he or she must obtain an advisory report from the International Trade Commission. For example, the ITC found that syrup and molasses imports were materially interfering with the U.S. domestic sugar price supports.[2] This interference was evidenced by the probability that the Commodity Credit Corporation would have to purchase large quantities of domestic sugar. In a later decision, the ITC did not find material interference when tobacco imports were said to be undermining U.S. price supports.[3] The President may impose or reject import restraints regardless of the ITC's determinations on material interference.

The fact that the International Trade Commission believes that imports are materially interfering with U.S. agricultural programs does not require presidential action. The President retains the broadest discretionary authority to determine if, when and how to impose import relief.[4] The President need not await the advice of the International Trade Commission if emergency conditions exist. The President may act pending the report of the International Trade Commission and subsequent final decision by the President under Section 22.[5]

The General Counsel to the International Trade Commission released a memorandum in 1981 which outlines the Commission's approach to determining whether imports "materially interfere" with domestic agricultural programs. In this memorandum, the General Counsel indicates that material interference occurs when there is "more than slight interference but less than major interference."[6] Material interference will always be evaluated in terms of the goals behind United States agricultural support programs. These traditionally have been seen to be the stabilization of commodity prices, satisfactory supply and distribution of those commodities, as well as reasonable prices to producers and consumers. If these objectives are in any way threatened, it would appear likely that such threats may constitute material interference. Other evidence that the International Trade Commission will

---

2. USITC Report No. 22–41 (1978).

3. USITC Report No. 22–47 (Feb. 15, 1985).

4. Farr Man and Company v. United States, 544 F.Supp. 908 (C.I.T.1982). See Zedalis, Agricultural Trade and Section 22, 31 Drake L.R. at 587 (1981). The review of the legislative history to Section 22 found in this article suggests that the President is granted great latitude to accept or reject International Trade Commission recommendations concerning material interference with domestic agricultural support programs.

5. 7 U.S.C.A. § 624(b).

6. General Counsel Memorandum to the International Trade Commission (July 31, 1981) at page 107–10.

consider relates more directly to the import threat, including the level of imports, the level of domestic production, inventories held by the government or elsewhere under the domestic program, and the costs involved in the program. World market prices and supplies will also affect the determination of material interference. The quality attributes of the imports as compared with domestic production are not generally taken into account.[7]

The International Trade Commission has indicated that it believes the "processing clause" which accompanies Section 22 is an integral part of the agricultural protection program, rather than a separate and alternative basis for restricting imports.[8] The language of Section 22 does not seem to support such a connection. On its face, Section 22 would appear to allow processors who suffer reductions as a result of import competition to seek to obtain Section 22 relief. Very few, if any, Section 22 cases focus exclusively on the processing alternative to Section 22 proceedings.

Section 22 quotas cannot be imposed at less than 50 percent of the quantities that have been imported previously during a representative period. Section 22 fees may not exceed 50 percent ad valorem. The President has the power to define which commodities will be subject to an import quota or fee, but may not order the imposition of both an import fee and an import quota with respect to the same product.[9] The President may, however, impose import fees under Section 22 and import quotas under another statutory authorization (e.g., Section 201 of the Trade Act of 1974)[10].

The question whether import restraints imposed under Section 22 are lawful under the General Agreement on Tariffs and Trade was settled in 1955 when a waiver was granted by the GATT to the United States for Section 22 purposes. The extent to which Section 22 restraints can be imposed despite bilateral trade agreements was explored in a case involving sugar from Argentina and other nations. In this decision, the Court of International Trade suggests that only bilateral treaties undertaken prior to 1951 will be subservient to Section 22.[11] This appears to contradict the express language of Section 22(f), which indicates that its terms take precedence over all international agreements "heretofore or hereafter entered into by the United States."[12]

§ 14.7 Meat Imports

The Meat Import Act of 1979[1] requires the President to impose countercyclical quotas on the importation of meat into the United States.

7. Id. at page A–109.

8. U.S. Tariff Commission Report No. 22–25 (September 6, 1962).

9. United States v. Best Foods, Inc., 47 C.C.P.A. 163 (1960).

10. U.S. Cane Sugar Refiners Ass'n v. Block, 544 F.Supp. 883 (C.I.T.1982), affirmed 683 F.2d 399 (C.C.P.A.1982).

11. See Farr Man & Company v. United States, 544 F.Supp. 908 (C.I.T.1982).

12. 7 U.S.C.A. § 624(f).

§ 14.7

1. Public Law No. 96–177.

The only countries exempt from this requirement are Canada and Mexico, and this results from the free trade agreement with those nations. Beef, mutton (but not lamb) and goat meat, as well as processed beef or veal, are generally subject to a meat import quota. The quota is countercyclical in the sense that the greater the domestic production of meat, the more restrictive the quota. If domestic production declines, the quota is expanded. The net result is stabilization of prices for meat in the United States. The Meat Import Act authorizes the President to suspend the quota whenever natural disasters, disease or major national disruptions to the market occur. Typically, presidents have proclaimed quotas as required by the Act, but later suspended those quotas because of the nation's economic interests. Various statutory trigger levels are established for the imposition of meat quotas. One of these is known as the "minimum access floor", a statutory minimum for certain action. This floor does not guarantee a minimum market access to foreign exporters of meat into the United States market.[2]

To avoid meat import quotas, the President has usually negotiated a large number of bilateral agreements with the major meat supplying countries. These agreements are negotiated under the authority of Section 204 of the Agricultural Act of 1956.[3] Such agreements involve "voluntary restraints" by the exporting countries to the effect that they will restrict their shipment of meat into the United States. As a practical matter, the agreements keep the overall meat imports into the United States below the limits permitted by the Meat Import Act. Australia, for example, has entered into successive bilateral agreements with the United States to restrict its export of meat products.

§ 14.8 Sugar Imports

The United States has periodically imposed import quotas on sugar and sugar products under Section 22 of the Agricultural Adjustment Act. In addition, since 1982, heavily restrictive quotas were imposed on the importation of sugars, syrups and molasses under the authority of Note 3 to Chapter 17 of the Harmonized Tariff System of the United States. This caused the importation of sugar to drop from 4.5 million tons in 1981 to 1.25 million tons in 1989. In 1989, a GATT panel ruled that the U.S. sugar import quotas established through the Harmonized Tariff System were illegal under Article XI of the GATT. Generally speaking, the U.S. benefits from an extremely broad waiver of Article XI as applied to Section 22 import quotas.[1]

2. See Australian Meat and Live–Stock Corp. v. Block, 590 F.Supp. 1230 (C.I.T. 1984).

3. 7 U.S.C.A. § 1854.

§ 14.8

1. Waiver granted to the United States in connection with import restrictions imposed under Section 22 of the United States Agricultural Adjustment Act as amended, decision of March 5, 1955 (GATT, 3d Supp. BISD 32–June, 1955).

The United States acceded to the 1989 GATT ruling and in 1990 the President announced the conversion of these quotas into tariff-rate quotas.[2] Under this approach, foreign exporters receive a base quota which permits their sugar to enter at either a rate of approximately 6 cents per pound or duty free if eligible under the GSP or CBI programs. Any exports in excess of a nation's base quota are tariffed at approximately 16 cents a pound. The United States Secretary of Agriculture issues certificates to the various supplying countries for their base quotas. In issuing these certificates, the Secretary is to consider traditional shipping patterns, harvesting periods, United States import requirements, and other relevant factors. How the certificate quota is allocated among exporters within foreign nations is left to them to decide.

Sugar prices are also supported by quotas on U.S. imports of sugar-containing products. Such quotas apply to blended syrups, edibles with over 65 percent sugar (not in containers), sweetened cocoa, flour mixes and doughs with at least 10 percent sugar (except in containers), and edibles with 10 percent sugar (in containers). All of these import restraints are designed to reinforce the nonrecourse loan/price support program that the U.S. administers for the benefit of its sugar-cane and sugar-beet growers and processors.[3]

§ 14.9 Agricultural Marketing Orders

The Agricultural Marketing Agreement Act of 1937 authorizes the issuance of marketing orders by the Secretary of Agriculture. These orders typically restrict the grade, size, quality or maturity of fruits and vegetables sold in the United States market. By mandating restrictions of this type, the price for those fruits and vegetables reaching the market is enhanced and the incomes of growers similarly raised. In order for this agricultural support program to work, import restraints must be imposed. The Act automatically prohibits the importation of commodities whenever a marketing order is in effect unless those commodities meet the same requirements that have been established for U.S.-grown produce.[1]

The United States has issued a significant number of marketing orders since 1937. These often involve raisins, prunes, avocadoes, limes, lemons, tomatoes, grapefruit, oranges, walnuts, peanuts, plums, peaches, grapes, cranberries, lettuce, almonds, and a variety of other fruits and vegetables. The most current regulations governing imports that are subject to U.S. agricultural marketing orders can be found in 7 C.F.R. Parts 944, 980 and 999. The issuance of these regulations is subject to public notice and comment.[2] Size regulations on tomatoes, even if

2. Presidential Proclamation 6179, 55 Fed.Reg. 38293 (1990).

3. See the Food, Agriculture, Conservation and Trade Act of 1990.

§ 14.9

1. 7 U.S.C.A. § 608(e–1).

2. See Walter Holm & Co. v. Hardin, 449 F.2d 1009 (D.C.Cir.1971).

intended to reduce imports, were a valid import restraint.[3] Inspections of grapes upon arrival in the United States were valid even if more likely to bar importation than inspections at the source as with domestic grapes.[4]

§ 14.10   The WTO Agreement on Agriculture

Agricultural issues played a central role in the Uruguay Round negotiations. More than any other issue, they delayed completion of the Round from 1990 to 1993. The agreement reached in December of 1993 is a trade liberalizing, market-oriented effort. Each country has made a number of commitments on market access, reduced domestic agricultural support levels and export subsidies. These are not expected to take effect prior to July, 1995. A supplement to this treatise will analyze the impact upon U.S. law of the Uruguay Round GATT agreement on agriculture if, as expected, it becomes binding.

Broadly speaking nontariff barriers (NTBs) to international agricultural trade are replaced by tariffs that provide substantially the same level of protection. This is known as "tariffication." It applies to virtually all NTBs, including variable levies, import bans, voluntary export restraints and import quotas. Tariffication applies specifically to U.S. agricultural quotas adopted under Section 22 of the Agricultural Adjustment Act. All agricultural tariffs, including those converted from NTBs, are to be reduced by 36 and 24 percent by developed and developing countries, respectively, over 6 and 10 year periods. Certain minimum access tariff quotas apply when imports amount to less than 3 to 5 percent of domestic consumption. An escape clause exists for tariffed imports at low prices or upon a surge of importation depending upon the existing degree of import penetration.

Regarding domestic support for agriculture, some programs with minimal impact on trade are exempt from change. These programs are known as "green box policies." They include governmental support for agricultural research, disease control, infrastructure and food security. Green box policies are also exempt from WTO challenge or countervailing duties for 9 years. Direct payments to producers that are not linked to production are also generally exempt. This will include income support, adjustment assistance, environmental and regional assistance payments. Furthermore, direct payments to support crop reductions and *de minimis* payments are exempted in most cases.

After removing all of the exempted domestic agricultural support programs, the agreement on agriculture arrives at a calculation known as the Total Aggregate Measurement of Support (Total AMS). This measure is the basis for agricultural support reductions under the agreement. Developed nations must reduce their Total AMS by 20 percent over 6 years, developing nations by 13.3 percent over 10 years.

---

3. Id.

4. Cal–Fruit Suma Intern. v. U.S. Dept. of Agriculture, 698 F.Supp. 80 (E.D.Pa. 1988), affirmed 875 F.2d 309 (3d Cir.1989).

United States reductions undertaken in 1985 and 1990 suggest that little or no U.S. action will be required to meet this duty.

Agricultural export subsidies of developed nations must be reduced by 36 percent below 1986–1990 levels over 6 years and the quantity of subsidized agricultural exports by 21 percent. Developing nations must meet corresponding 24 and 14 percent reductions over 10 years.

All conforming tariffications, reductions in domestic support for agriculture and export subsidy alterations are essentially exempt from challenge for 9 years within the WTO on grounds such as serious prejudice in export markets or nullification and impairment of benefits. However, countervailing duties may be levied against all unlawfully subsidized exports of agricultural goods [1] except for subsidies derived from so-called national "green box policies" (discussed above).

C.   NONTARIFF TRADE BARRIERS

§ 14.11   Introduction

There are numerous nontariff trade barriers applicable to United States imports. Many of these barriers arise out of federal or state safety and health regulations. Others concern the environment, consumer protection, product standards and government procurement. Many of the relevant rules were created for legitimate consumer and public protection reasons. They were often created without extensive consideration of their international impact as potential nontariff trade barriers. Nevertheless, the practical impact of legislation of this type is to ban the importation of nonconforming products from the United States market. Thus, unlike tariffs which can always be paid and unlike quotas which permit a certain amount of goods to enter the United States market, nontariff trade barriers have the potential to totally exclude foreign exports.

The diversity of regulatory approaches to products and the environment makes it extremely difficult to generalize about nontariff trade barriers. The material below concerns health restrictions relating to food, safety restrictions relating to consumer products, environmental auto emissions standards and selected other NTBs. These areas have been chosen merely as examples of the types of NTB barriers to the United States market, and are by no means exhaustive. Special NTB rules apply in the context of the Canada–U.S. Free Trade Agreement and the NAFTA.[1] Sanitary and phytosanitary (SPS) measures dealing with food safety and animal and plant health regulations are the subject of a Uruguay Round WTO accord.

The European Union and the United States, and (separately) Canada and the U.S., have agreed to Mutual Recognition Agreements on certain product standards. Each side will test their exports according to

1.   See Chapter 13.   1.   See Chapter 21.

the other's standards. A second test in the country of importation will no longer be necessary. The Agreements should reduce the trade restraining potential of regulations applicable to telecommunications equipment, medical devices, pharmaceuticals, recreational craft, electrical safety and electromagnetic compatibility.

§ 14.12 Food Products

All foods imported into the United States are subject to inspection for their wholesomeness, freedom from contamination, and compliance with labeling requirements (including the 1993 nutritional labeling rules). This examination is conducted by the Food and Drug Administration using samples submitted to it by the United States Customs Service. If these tests result in a finding that the food products cannot be imported into the United States, they must be exported or destroyed.[1] Milk and cream imports are the subject of special permit requirements administered by the Department of Health and Human Services. Basically, the Department certifies that foreign producers operate under sanitary conditions.

There is a broad web of federal rules governing food products, including food imports. These involve, for example, the Federal Insecticide, Fungicide and Rodenticide Act,[2] the Perishable Agricultural Commodities Act,[3] and the Food, Drug and Cosmetic Act.[4] Food which is admitted into the United States under surety bond pending FDA inspection and later found inadmissible must be exported or destroyed. If this does not occur, an action by the Customs Service against the importer and the surety for liquidated damages will typically follow.[5] A strict six-year statute of limitations applies to government complaints seeking liquidated damages running from the importer's breach of the bond.[6]

§ 14.13 Seeds, Plants and Animals

The Customs Service and the Agricultural Marketing Service of the USDA regulate the importation of seeds under the Federal Seed Act of 1939.[1] Seeds that fail to meet the statute's requirements are destroyed unless reexported within one year of their denial of admission into the United States. Another branch of the USDA called APHIS (Animal and Plant Health Inspection Service) regulates plants, domestic animals, and plant and animal products coming into the U.S. This authority is created in the Plant Quarantine Act,[2] Section 306 of the Tariff Act of

§ 14.12

1. See 21 C.F.R. §§ 1.83–1.99.

2. 7 U.S.C.A. § 136 et seq.

3. 7 U.S.C.A. §§ 499a–499t.

4. 21 U.S.C.A. §§ 391–393.

5. See Epstein, The Land of Liquidated Damages: Recent Judicial Decisions and Unresolved Issues, 14 Fordham Int'l L.J. 7 (1990–91).

6. United States v. Cocoa Berkau, Inc., 990 F.2d 610 (Fed.Cir.1993).

§ 14.13

1. 7 U.S.C.A. § 1581 et seq. See 19 C.F.R. § 12.16, 7 C.F.R. § 210.208 et seq.

2. 7 U.S.C.A. § 150aa et seq. See 7 C.F.R. § 352.

1930,[3] the Federal Plant Pest Act,[4] and other statutes.[5] Basically, an import permit system has been established. Applications to import goods of these types must be made to APHIS.

§ 14.14   Consumer Products

The Consumer Products Safety Act bars the importation of consumer products which do not comply with the standards of the Consumer Products Safety Commission.[1] Exporters of consumer products must certify that their goods conform to applicable United States safety and labeling standards. Any product that has a defect which is determined to constitute a "substantial product hazard" or is imminently hazardous may be banned from the United States market. The Customs Service may seize any such nonconforming goods. These goods may be modified in order to conform them to U.S. Consumer Products Safety Commission requirements. Otherwise, such goods must be exported or destroyed.

Another example in this area concerns the Flammable Fabrics Act. This Act prohibits the importation of wearing apparel or interior furnishings that fail to meet its flammability standards.[2] The National Energy Conservation Act requires that any imported consumer appliances be labeled to show their energy efficiency as are domestically made products.[3]

§ 14.15   Motor Vehicles

All automobiles imported into the United States must comply with the safety standards of the Department of Transportation.[1] The exporters of vehicles to the United States must certify compliance to the standards. In addition, most autos and automobile engines must meet federal air pollution control standards as set by the Environmental Protection Agency before they will be allowed into the United States.[2] Both the owner or importer may suffer severe penalties if a nonconforming vehicle is brought into the United States and not subsequently brought into conformity. A common scenario involves the posting of a surety bond by the importer of the auto promising payment of liquidated damages if this does not occur.[3]

Trade barrier conflicts also surround U.S. Corporate Average Fuel Economy (CAFE) standards. Whereas United States manufacturers have been able to average fuel efficient cars and gas guzzlers, European firms largely building premium cars in the U.S. have not been able to do

---

3. 19 U.S.C.A. § 1306. See 9 C.F.R. §§ 92, 94.

4. 7 U.S.C.A. § 150bb et seq. See 7 C.F.R. § 330.

5. See 21 U.S.C.A. § 111.

§ 14.14

1. 15 U.S.C.A. § 2066.

2. 15 U.S.C.A. § 1191 et seq.

3. 31 U.S.C.A. § 316.

§ 14.15

1. 19 C.F.R. §§ 12.73, 12.80. See 49 C.F.R. Part 571.

2. 19 C.F.R. § 12.73.

3. See Epstein, The Land of Liquidated Damages: Recent Judicial Decisions and Unresolved Issues, 14 Fordham Int'l L.J. 7 (1990–91).

so. In 1991, the European Community claimed that 88 percent of the U.S. revenues from CAFE taxes and penalties were disproportionately levied on European carmakers who only have 4 percent of the total U.S. market. The EC is therefore pursuing a GATT complaint against the U.S. on these grounds. The GATT panel report on this complaint was delivered in 1994 and largely upheld CAFE.[4]

§ 14.16 Environmental Regulation

A host of federal and state laws regulating the environment have an impact on international trade. Europeans, for example, have long argued that U.S. auto emissions' requirements amount to a substantial nontariff trade barrier causing them to incur significant costs in producing cars for the United States market. Other environmental controls are more specifically connected to international trade. The Marine Mammal Protection Act [1] prohibits the importation of fish (tuna) caught with methods that incidentally kill marine mammals (dolphins). Under this law, the U.S. undertakes a review of each exporting country's harvesting procedures to see if they are comparable to United States standards. If not, an import ban on fish from that nation and intermediary nations follows. Environmental activists succeeded in 1990 in obtaining a preliminary injunction against tuna imports from Mexico, Panama, Venezuela, Ecuador and Vanuatu under the Act.[2] In 1991, a GATT dispute settlement panel declared the embargo of Mexican tuna an illegal restraint of trade. However, the U.S. and Mexico subsequently "settled" the dispute (over much protest in the world community) with Mexico agreeing to improve its harvesting procedures. In 1994, acting on a complaint filed by the European Union, a second GATT panel ruled against United States tuna embargoes.[3]

Tuna exporting nations that join the Panama Declaration, a multilateral set of principles to protect dolphins from tuna fishermen, may avoid the U.S. Marine Mammal Protection Act. The Panama Declaration was agreed in October 1995 by the United States and eleven Nations (Belize, Colombia, Costa Rica, Ecuador, France, Honduras, Mexico, Panama, Spain, Vanuatu and Venezuela). The U.S. Congress authorized the lifting of the tuna import ban for Panama Declaration adherents in 1997. This is exactly the kind of multilateral accord that opponents of U.S. unilateralism and extraterritorial jurisdiction support.

Other United States environmental or conservation laws notably affecting international trade include:

4. GATT DOC DS 31/R 5.52–5.55 (Sept. 29, 1994).

§ 14.16

1. 16 U.S.C.A. § 1367.

2. Earth Island Institute v. Mosbacher, 929 F.2d 1449 (9th Cir.1991).

3. The GATT Tuna I and Tuna II Panel Decisions are reported in the GATT Basic Instruments and Selected Documents (BISD) 39th Supp. 155 (1993) and GATT Doc. DS 29/R (June 16, 1994).

- The Endangered Species Act of 1973 prohibiting import/export of endangered species.[4]

- The "Pelley Amendment" authorizing import restraints against fish products of nations undermining international fisheries or wildlife conservation agreements.[5]

- The High Seas Driftnet Fisheries Enforcement Act of 1992 banning imports of fish, fish products and sport fishing gear from countries violating the United Nations driftnet moratorium.[6]

- The Sea Turtle Conservation Act prohibiting shrimp imports harvested with adverse effects on sea turtles[7] first used in 1993 against shrimp from several Caribbean nations and now applicable globally to Thailand, India, China and Bangladesh among others.[8]

- The Wild Bird Conservation Act banning imports of tropical wild birds.[9]

- The Antarctic Marine Living Resources Convention Act prohibiting import/export of living resources.[10]

- The African Elephant Conservation Act restricting ivory imports.[11]

§ 14.17 Public Procurement

Where public procurement is involved, and the taxpayer's money is at issue, virtually every nation has some form of legislation or tradition that favors buying from domestic suppliers. In federal nations like the United States, these rules can extend to state and local purchasing requirements. The principal United States statute affecting imports in connection with government procurement is the Buy American Act of 1933.[1] This Act requires the government to buy American unless the acquisition is for use outside the U.S.,[2] there are insufficient quantities of satisfactory quality available in the U.S., or domestic purchases would be inconsistent with the public interest or result in unreasonable costs.

As currently applied, the United States Buy American Act requires federal agencies to treat a domestic bid as unreasonable or inconsistent with the public interest only if it exceeds a foreign bid by more than six percent (customs duties included) or ten percent (customs duties and specific costs excluded). Exceptions to this general approach exist for reasons of national interest, certain designated small business purchases,

4. 16 U.S.C. §§ 1531 et seq.

5. 22 U.S.C. § 1978(1).

6. 16 U.S.C. § 1826a(b).

7. 16 U.S.C. § 1537.

8. See Earth Island Institute v. Christopher, 17 ITRD 2534 (1996), Earth Island Institute v. Albright, 147 F.3d 1352 (Fed. Cir.1998), and the 1998 WTO panel report No. WT/DS58/R condemning the Act as breach of GATT trading rules.

9. 16 U.S.C. § 4901.

10. 16 U.S.C. § 2435.

11. 16 U.S.C. § 4221.

§ 14.17

1. 41 U.S.C.A. §§ 10a–10d.

2. See the U.S. Balance of Payments Program, 48 C.F.R. § 225.302 et seq., creating procurement preferences for materials used outside the U.S. but suspended if the Code on Procurement applies.

domestic suppliers operating in areas of substantial unemployment and demonstrated national security needs. Bids by small businesses and companies located in labor surplus areas are generally protected by a 12 percent margin of preference. Bids from U.S. companies are considered foreign rather than domestic when the materials used in the products concerned are below 50 percent American in origin. These rules apply to civil purchasing by the United States government,[3] but are suspended for purchasing subject to the GATT/WTO Procurement Codes as implemented by the Trade Agreements Act of 1979 and the Uruguay Round Agreements Act of 1994.

The Department of Defense has its own Buy American rules. Generally speaking, a 50 percent price preference (customs duties excluded) or a 6 or 12 percent preference (customs duties included) whichever is more protective to domestic suppliers is applied. However, intergovernmental "Memoranda of Understanding" (MOU) on defense procurement provide important exceptions to the standard Department of Defense procurement rules.[4] Additional procurement preferences are established by the Small Business Act of 1953.[5] Under this Act, federal agencies may set-aside certain procurement exclusively for small U.S. businesses. In practice, the federal government normally sets aside about 30 percent of its procurement needs in this fashion. Special set-aside rules apply to benefit socially and economically disadvantaged minority-owned businesses. These preferences are excepted from U.S. adherence to the GATT/WTO Procurement Codes under a U.S. reservation.

A number of federal statutes also contain specific Buy American requirements. These include various GSA, NASA and TVA appropriations' bills, the AMTRAK Improvement Act of 1978,[6] the Public Works Employment Act of 1977,[7] various highway and transport acts,[8] the Clean Water Act of 1977,[9] and the Rural Electrification Acts of 1936 and 1938.[10] Many of these statutes involve federal funding of state and local procurement. Most are generally excepted from the GATT/WTO Procurement Codes as applied by the United States.

The Buy American Act generally conformed to the GATT Code on Government Procurement negotiated during the Tokyo Round. However, Congress expressed its displeasure with the degree to which that Code opened up sales opportunities for United States firms abroad. It therefore amended the Buy American Act in 1988 to deny the benefits of the Procurement Code when foreign governments are not in good standing under it. United States government procurement contracts are

---

3. See Executive Order No. 10582 (Dec. 17, 1954), 19 Fed.Reg. 8723 as amended by Exec. Order No. 11051 (Sept. 27, 1962), 27 Fed.Reg. 9683 and Exec. Order No. 12148, July 20, 1979, 44 Fed.Reg. 43239.

4. See Self–Powered Lighting, Ltd. v. United States, 492 F.Supp. 1267 (S.D.N.Y. 1980).

5. 15 U.S.C.A. §§ 631–648. See 48 C.F.R. §§ 19.000–.902.

6. Pub.L. 95–421.

7. 42 U.S.C.A. § 6705.

8. See, e.g., Highway Improvement Act of 1982, Pub.L. 97–424.

9. 33 U.S.C.A. § 1295.

10. 7 U.S.C.A. § 903.

also denied to suppliers from countries whose governments "maintain . . . a significant and persistent pattern of practice or discrimination against U.S. products or services which results in identifiable harm to U.S. businesses." [11] Presidential waivers of these statutory denials may occur in the public interest, to avoid single supply situations or to assure sufficient bidders to provide supplies of requisite quality and competitive prices.

The European Union was one of the first to be identified as a persistent procurement discriminator by the USTR. This identification concerns longstanding heavy electrical and telecommunications disputes that were partly settled by negotiation in 1993. The remaining disputes led to U.S. trade sanctions and European retaliation. This did not occur with Greece, Spain and Portugal (where the EU procurement rules do not apply), and with Germany which broke ranks and negotiated a pathbreaking bilateral settlement with the U.S. In 1993, also, Japan was identified as a persistent procurement discriminator in the construction, architectural and engineering areas.

The Tokyo Round GATT Procurement Code was not particularly successful at opening up government purchasing. Only Austria, Canada, the twelve European Union states, Finland, Hong Kong, Israel, Japan, Norway, Singapore, Sweden, Switzerland and the United States adhered to the Procurement Code. This was also partly the result of the 1979 Code's many exceptions. For example, the Code did not apply to contracts below its threshold amount of $150,000 SDR (about $171,000 since 1988), service contracts, and procurement by entities on each country's reserve list (including most national defense items). Because procurement in the European Union and Japan is often decentralized, many contracts fall below the SDR threshold and were therefore exempt. By dividing up procurement into smaller contracts national preferences were retained. U.S. government procurement tends to be more centralized and thus more likely covered by the Code. This pattern helps explain why Congress restrictively amended the Buy American Act in 1988.

In addition to the Buy American Act, state and local purchasing requirements may inhibit import competition in the procurement field. For example, California once had a law which made it mandatory to purchase American products. This law was declared unconstitutional as an encroachment upon the federal power to conduct foreign affairs.[12] A Massachusetts ban on contracts with companies invested in Burma was preempted by federal sanctions adopted in 1997 against Burma.[12.1] State statutes which have copied the federal Buy American Act, on the other hand, and incorporated public interest and unreasonable cost exceptions to procurement preferences, have generally withstood constitutional

11. 41 U.S.C.A. § 10d.

12. Bethlehem Steel Corp. v. Board of Commissioners of the Department of Water and Power of the City of Los Angeles, 276 Cal.App.2d 221, 80 Cal.Rptr. 800 (1969).

12.1 Crosby v. National Foreign Trade Council, 530 U.S. 363, 120 S.Ct. 2288, 147 L.Ed.2d 352 (2000).

challenge.[13] A Pennsylvania statute requiring state and local agencies to ensure that contractors do not provide products containing foreign steel was upheld by the Third Circuit Court of Appeals.[14] This case illustrates the inapplicability of the Tokyo Round Procurement Code to state and local purchasing requirements.[15]

A practice known as "unbalanced bidding" has arisen in connection with the Buy American Act. Unbalanced bidding involves the use of United States labor and parts by foreigners in sufficient degree so as to overcome the bidding preferences established by law for U.S. suppliers. This occurs because the United States value added is *not* included in the calculations of the margin of preference for the U.S. firms. Thus foreign bids minus the value of work done in the U.S. are multiplied by the 6, 12 or 50 percent Buy American Act preference. If the U.S. bids are above the foreign bids but within the margin of preference, the U.S. company gets the contract. If the U.S. bids are higher than the foreign bids plus the margin of preference, the foreigners get the contract.[16]

Chapter 13 of the 1989 Canada–United States Free Trade Area Agreement opens government procurement to U.S. and Canadian suppliers on contracts as small as $25,000. However, the goods supplied must have at least 50 percent U.S. and Canadian content. The NAFTA also establishes distinct procurement regulations. The thresholds are $50,000 for goods and services provided to federal agencies and $250,000 for government-owned enterprises (notably PEMEX and CFE). These regulations are particularly important because Mexico, unlike Canada, has not traditionally joined in GATT/WTO procurement codes.[17]

The Uruguay Round Procurement Code replaced the Tokyo Round agreement. It is one of very few WTO agreements that is optional. The Uruguay Round Code expands the coverage of the current Code to include procurement of services, construction, government-owned utilities, and some state and local (subcentral) contracts. Various improvements to the procedural rules surrounding procurement practices and dispute settlement under the Uruguay Round Code attempt to reduce tensions in this difficult area. For example, an elaborate system for bid protests is established. Bidders who believe the Code's procedural rules have been abused will be able to lodge, litigate and appeal their protests. The United States has agreed, with few exceptions, to bring all procurement by executive agencies subject to the Federal Acquisition Regulations under the Code's coverage (i.e., to suspend application of the normal Buy American preferences to such procurement).

---

13. See K.S.B. Technical Sales Corp. v. North Jersey District Water Supply Commission of the State of New Jersey, 75 N.J. 272, 381 A.2d 774 (1977), appeal dismissed 435 U.S. 982, 98 S.Ct. 1635, 56 L.Ed.2d 76 (1978).

14. Trojan Technologies, Inc. v. Pennsylvania, 916 F.2d 903 (3d Cir.1990), cert. denied 501 U.S. 1212, 111 S.Ct. 2814, 115 L.Ed.2d 986 (1991).

15. See Southwick, Binding the States: A Survey of State Law Conformance with Standards of the GATT Procurement Code, 13 U.Pa.J.Int'l Bus.L. 57 (1992).

16. See Allis–Chalmers Corp. v. Friedkin, 635 F.2d 248 (3d Cir.1980).

17. See generally Chapter 15 on free trade agreements of the United States.

§ 14.18   Product Standards

Widespread use of "standards" requirements as NTB import restraints resulted in 1979 in the GATT Agreement on Technical Barriers to Trade (called the "Standards Code").[1] This Code was made operative in the United States by the Trade Agreements Act of 1979,[2] and was followed by a reasonable number of other nations. Its successor is the Uruguay Round Agreement on Technical Barriers to Trade (1994). This agreement is binding on all WTO members. In general, this Code deals with the problem of countries' manipulation of product standards, product testing procedures, and product certifications in order to slow or stop imported goods. The Code provides, in part and subject to some exceptions, that imported products shall be accorded treatment (including testing treatment and certification) no less favorable than that accorded to like products of national origin or those originating in any other country. It also requires that participating nations establish a central office for standards inquiries, publish advance and reasonable notice of requirements that are applicable to imported goods, and provide an opportunity for commentary by those who may be affected adversely. The Code establishes an international committee to deal with alleged instances of noncompliance.

Under United States law,[3] state and federal agencies may create standards which specify the characteristics of a product, such as levels of quality, safety, performance or dimensions, or its packaging and labelling. However, these "standards-related activities" must not create "unnecessary obstacles to U.S. foreign trade," and must be demonstrably related to "a legitimate domestic objective" such as protection of health and safety, security, environmental or consumer interests. Sometimes there is a conflict between federal and state standards. For example, federal law licensing endangered species' articles preempted California's absolute ban on trade in such goods.[4] The Office of the USTR is charged with responsibility for implementation of the Standards Code within the United States.[5]

The Secretary of Commerce maintains a "standards information center" (National Bureau of Standards, National Center for Standards and Certification Information), in part to "serve as the central national collection facility for information relating to standards, certification systems, and standards-related activities, whether such standards, systems or activities are public or private, domestic or foreign, or international, regional, national, or local [and to] make available to the public at … reasonable fee … copies of information required to be collected."[6]

United States standards have been attacked in international tribunals as violating international obligations. Sometimes the standards have

§ 14.18

1. See 18 Int'l Legal Mat. 1079.

2. 19 U.S.C.A. § 1531 et seq.

3. 19 U.S.C.A. § 2531.

4. Man Hing Ivory and Imports, Inc. v. Deukmejian, 702 F.2d 760 (9th Cir.1983).

5. 19 U.S.C.A. §§ 2541, 2552.

6. 19 U.S.C.A. § 2544.

been upheld, sometimes not. For example, a binational arbitration panel established under Chapter 18 of the Canada–U.S. FTA issued a decision upholding a United States law setting a minimum size on lobsters sold in interstate commerce. The panel found that, since the law applied to both domestic and foreign lobsters, it was not a disguised trade restriction. On the other hand, in 1991, a GATT panel found that United States import restrictions designed to protect dolphin from tuna fishers did violate the GATT. The panel ruled that GATT did not permit any import restrictions based on environmental concerns, whether they were considered disguised trade restrictions or not. This decision suggested repeal of a number of United States laws which concern health, safety and environmental conditions in exporting nations. A 1994 decision by a second GATT panel recognized the legitimacy of extraterritorial environmental regulations, but ruled against the tuna boycott of the U.S. because of its focus on production methods. In 1998, the WTO Appellate Body ruled against a U.S. ban on shrimp imports from nations that fail to use turtle exclusion devises comparable to those required under U.S. law. The Appellate Body found the U.S. ban "arbitrary" and "unjustifiable".

The standards of other nations have also been challenged as violations of GATT obligations. For example, the United States has criticized European Union bans of imports of meat from the United States, first for containing certain hormones, later for unsanitary conditions in U.S. meatpacking facilities. In 1997, the WTO Appellate Body ruled against the EU hormone-treated beef ban, citing lack of an adequate scientific basis as required under the WTO SPS Code. Future disputes with the EU are sure to arise regarding genetically modified food organisms (GMOs).

§ 14.19 Product Markings (Origin, Labels)

The United States requires clear markings of countries of origin on imports. This can be perceived, especially by those abroad, as a non-tariff trade barrier intended to promote domestic purchases. Section 304 of the Tariff act of 1930 establishes the basic rules for origin markings.[1] Every imported article of foreign origin (or its container) must be marked conspicuously, legibly, indelibly and as permanently as practical in English so as to indicate to ultimate purchasers its country of origin.[2]

The principle sanction for failure to properly mark imports is the imposition of statutory tariffs of 10 percent ad valorem, which are imposed in addition to regular duties and even if the goods would ordinarily enter the U.S. duty free. Importers ordinarily receive notice from the Customs Service and an opportunity to comply with marking requirements. Any untimely failure to comply can result in liquidated damages proceedings by Customs against the importer. The amount of damages assessed will vary with the frequency and circumstances of the

§ 14.19
1. 19 U.S.C.A. § 1304.

2. See Precision Specialty Metals, Inc. v. U.S., 116 F.Supp.2d 1350 (C.I.T.2000).

offense, and will be assessed as a percentage of the appraised value of the merchandise. In severe cases, Customs may seek civil penalties under Section 592 of the Tariff Act of 1930.[3] This provision generally sanctions imports under false documents. Furthermore, criminal sanctions are also possible, either for use of false documents[4] or altering a required marking with concealment intended.[5] The latter penalties can rise to $250,000 or one year imprisonment or both. The severity of these sanctions must be measured against the temptation of traders to alter country of origin markings so as to obtain duty free or quota free entry of goods into the United States.

Various exceptions apply to the U.S. country of origin marking requirements.[6] These include goods that are incapable of being marked, goods economically prohibitive to mark (unless the failure to do so was a deliberate attempt at avoiding the law), or goods that will be injured if marked. If the containers will reasonably indicate origin to the ultimate consumer, or the import circumstances or character of the goods necessarily convey knowledge of their source, no marking is required. Nor is it mandatory to mark goods not intended for resale, goods which when processed will obliterate the mark, goods over twenty years old and goods intended for export without entering U.S. commerce. Certain United States fishery products, products of U.S. possessions and products that originally came from the U.S. and are being imported are likewise exempt. Lastly, there is a "J-list" of specific goods that have been individually ruled exempt by the Secretary of the Treasury.[7] These include items like cordage, buttons, nails, etc., all of which must be marked by container.

Special regulations govern the marking requirements for imported textiles. These are created by the Textile Fiber Products Identification Act.[8] This Act is enforced by the U.S. Federal Trade Commission. It mandates disclosure of country of origin, generic fiber contents and the name or identification number of the manufacturer or marketer. Violation of the Textile Fiber Products Identification Act amounts to a violation of Section 5 of the Federal Trade Commission Act.[9] This means that F.T.C. cease and desist order proceedings, injunction actions, civil penalties and consumer redress relief can follow. Similar but not identical labelling requirements are established by the Wool Products Labelling Act[10] (country of origin required) and the Fur Products Labelling Act[11] (country of origin not required). These laws are also enforced by the Federal Trade Commission.

Significant litigation has ensued under the Tariff Act country of origin requirements regarding when a U.S. manufacturer is to be deemed the "ultimate purchaser" which may render the goods exempt

3. 19 U.S.C.A. § 1592.
4. 18 U.S.C.A. § 1001.
5. 19 U.S.C.A. § 1304.
6. See 19 C.F.R. § 134.32.
7. See 19 C.F.R. § 134.33.

8. 15 U.S.C.A. § 70–70K.
9. 15 U.S.C.A. § 45.
10. 15 U.S.C.A. § 68–68j.
11. 15 U.S.C.A. § 69–69j.

from marking. In a major decision by the Court of Customs and Patent Appeals, wooden brush handles from Japan were processed in the U.S. by inserting bristles which obliterated the marking. The CCPA, adopting a common rationale in U.S. customs law, held that the handles had undergone a "substantial transformation" into a new product in the United States and were thus subject only to container marking obligations.[12] In contrast, when leather uppers for shoes were imported from Indonesia, the Court of International Trade required individual markings despite the attachment of soles in the U.S. and argument that a "substantial transformation" had taken place.[13] Gifts of products to ordinary consumers (umbrellas to racetrack patrons) may still require origin markings even if the donor would be exempt.[14]

Other litigation has focused on the duty to mark origin "conspicuously." The Court of International Trade initially reversed a "plainly erroneous" Customs Service position that frozen food markings at the rear of the package (Made in Mexico) were conspicuous.[15] The Court took the position that such markings did not give U.S. consumers realistic choices when shopping and noted the health risks associated with such goods. Subsequently, the Court of International Trade vacated this opinion.

§ 14.20   Maritime Transport

Generally speaking, the United States maintains an open market for competitive trade in services. One major exception is maritime transport. In this area, the U.S. protects its domestic industry from import competition under the Merchant Marine Act of 1920 ("Jones Act") and other statutes. For example, the shipment of Alaskan oil is reserved for U.S.-flag vessels[1] as is the supply of offshore drill rigs.[2] The Jones Act most notably prohibits foreign vessels from transporting goods or passengers between U.S. ports and on U.S. rivers, lakes and canals.[3] The reservation of goods for U.S.-flag ships (such trade is known as cabotage) is very significant economically, amounting to some $6.4 billion annually with a heavy concentration in petroleum products.

D.   NATIONAL SECURITY IMPORT RESTRAINTS

§ 14.21   Section 232 of the Trade Expansion Act

The United States periodically imposes import restraints in order to protect its national security. Apart from the Exon–Florio mergers and

12. United States v. Gibson–Thomsen Co., 27 C.C.P.A. 267 (1940), superseded by regulation as stated in Cumins Engine Co. v. U.S., 83 F.Supp.2d 1366 (C.I.T.1999).

13. Uniroyal, Inc. v. United States, 542 F.Supp. 1026 (C.I.T.1982), affirmed 702 F.2d 1022 (Fed.Cir.1983).

14. Pabrini, Inc. v. United States, 630 F.Supp. 360 (C.I.T.1986).

15. Norcal/Crosetti Foods, Inc. v. United States, 758 F.Supp. 729 (C.I.T.1991), opinion vac'd 790 F.Supp. 302 (C.I.T.1992).

§ 14.20

1. 50 U.S.C.A.App. 2406(d).

2. 43 U.S.C.A. §§ 1333, 1336.

3. 46 U.S.C.A. § 883.

acquisitions' controls,[1] the chief legislative authority for such restraints is Section 232 of the Trade Expansion Act of 1962.[2] This provision authorizes the President to take such action, and for such time, as is deemed necessary to "adjust the imports" of any article that is being imported into the United States in such quantities or under such circumstances as threaten to impair the national security. The concept of national security embodied in Section 232 is broad. The statute makes clear that the economic welfare of the nation is part of the national security of the United States.

Before the President may impose import restraints in the name of national security, he must obtain the advice of the Secretary of Commerce that there is a threatened import impairment of national security. The broad authority given to the President to adjust import competition in the name of national security has been interpreted to include the power to increase tariffs, impose import quotas, and mandate import licensing systems coupled with substantial license fees.[3]

In determining whether imports impair the national security, Section 232 indicates that the President and the Commerce Department are to take into account particular items including the following:

    (1) domestic production for national defense requirements;

    (2) the capacity of domestic industries to meet such requirements;

    (3) existing and anticipated availability of human resources, products, raw materials and other supplies and services essential to the national defense;

    (4) the requirements of growth in such industries; and

    (5) the importation of goods as they affect such industries and the capacity of the United States to meet its national security requirements.

Any interested person may request that the Department of Commerce undertake a national security investigation in connection with import competition. Such investigations can also be initiated at the request of any head of any federal department or agency, or upon the motion of the Department of Commerce itself. The nature of the investigation is left largely to the discretion of the Department of Commerce. However, it must be completed within nine months and a report of its decision must be published in the Federal Register. A public hearing with opportunity to comment will only occur if the Department decides that this is appropriate. Once the report is forwarded to the President, he has 90 days in which to decide whether to take any action, and if so, what kind of action.

§ 14.21

1. See Chapter 31.

2. 19 U.S.C.A. § 1862. See also Section 122 of Trade Act of 1974 authorizing import restraints to assist balance of payments problems.

3. See Federal Energy Administration v. Algonquin SNG, Inc., 426 U.S. 548, 96 S.Ct. 2295, 49 L.Ed.2d 49 (1976).

Although there have been a number of petitions for national security investigations under Section 232, very few remedial actions have been undertaken. Embargoes of oil imports from Iran (1979) and Libya (1982) were based upon Section 232. In 1959, the President established a mandatory oil import program which caused import quotas to remain in effect between 1959 and 1973. In 1973, this quota system was replaced by a license fee system. This system was challenged in the courts and upheld ultimately by the U.S. Supreme Court.[4] A variation on this fee, known as the "gasoline conservation fee," was later successfully challenged in court.[5] Legislative disapproval of the import fee ultimately led to its recission.

Section 232 can occasionally lead to presidential negotiation of voluntary restraint agreements with foreign exporters. In 1986, for example, President Reagan entertained a complaint from United States manufacturers of machine tools. Without formally undertaking a Section 232 sanction, the President negotiated export restraints with Japan, Taiwan, Switzerland and West Germany.

§ 14.22 Trade Embargoes

The President's powers in connection with Section 232 should be contrasted with the various embargoes of goods from some nations (e.g., Libya and Iraq) undertaken through the International Emergency Economic Powers Act.[1] Complete economic embargoes can also be imposed under the Trading with the Enemy Act, chiefly administered by the Foreign Assets Control Office of the Treasury Department.[2] Such import controls may be issued during war or any period of national emergency. President Nixon imposed a 10 percent emergency economic surcharge in 1971 on all U.S. imports, not just those of "the enemy." This surcharge was ultimately upheld in the courts.[3] The Trading with the Enemy Act is the source of U.S. embargoes of North Korean, Libyan, Cuban and (prior to 1994) Vietnamese products.[4] These embargoes include goods that are processed ("tainted") in those nations. The Treasury Department has the power to determine whether goods are so tainted. Felony criminal sanctions attend any violation of the Trading with the Enemy Act, but the Act does not ordinarily extend to sales made by subsidiaries of U.S. firms located abroad.[5] However, the Cuban Democracy Act of 1992 prohibits trade by such subsidiaries with Cuba. The Act also bars ships using Cuban ports from loading or unloading freight in the U.S. for six months after leaving Cuba.

4. Federal Energy Administration v. Algonquin SNG, Inc., 426 U.S. 548, 96 S.Ct. 2295, 49 L.Ed.2d 49 (1976).

5. Independent Gasoline Marketers Council, Inc. v. Duncan and Marathon Oil Corp., Inc. v. Carter, 492 F.Supp. 614 (D.D.C.1980).

§ 14.22

1. 50 U.S.C.A. § 1701 et seq.

2. 50 U.S.C.A.App. § 5(b).

3. See United States v. Yoshida International, Inc., 526 F.2d 560 (C.C.P.A.1975).

4. See Foreign Assets Control Regulations at 31 C.F.R. Part 500.

5. 31 C.F.R. § 515.559.

Any country found to be providing assistance to Cuba as prohibited by the 1992 Act loses its eligibility for U.S. economic aid, debt reduction or debt forgiveness. This is widely seen as an attempt at forcing third world countries to comply with the U.S. embargo of Cuba. The Cuban Democracy Act is to remain in effect until Cuba moves toward democratization and greater respect for human rights, but can be eased if the President determines that "positive developments" occur in Cuba. Reaction abroad to the Act has been almost uniformly negative. The United Nations General Assembly has adopted a nonbinding resolution urging the U.S. to repeal the Act. The British issued a "blocking order" barring all U.K. companies, including U.S. subsidiaries, from complying with the Cuban Democracy Act.

Proponents of the Cuban Democracy Act were also urging adoption of a much harsher act, which would allow litigation by current United States citizens who were Cuban nationals at the time of the Castro expropriations, seeking compensation from persons currently using expropriated properties. This became the Cuban Liberty and Democratic Solidarity (Libertad) Act (more commonly known as Helms–Burton), enacted in March, 1996,[6] because of the emotions aroused due to the shooting down of two aircraft by Cuba near Cuban territory. The Act included two very controversial sections. The first, Title III, created a right of action in United States courts for a U.S. national with a claim that Cuba expropriated property after January 1, 1959 against any person who is "trafficking" in such property. Trafficking is quite broadly defined including not only such actions as selling, buying, leasing or transferring, but also engaging in a "commercial activity using or otherwise benefiting from confiscated property."[7] The Act authorizes the President to suspend the effectiveness of these Title III actions for successive periods of six months. President Clinton issued such suspensions every six months after August, 1996. These suspensions have been the only reason the European Union has kept on hold its request for a panel under the WTO to challenge the extraterritorial effects of the Libertad Act. The U.S. has stated that it would use the national security defense under WTO, and also in response to any similar challenge brought by Canada or Mexico under NAFTA.

The second important part of the Act, Title IV, requires that the Secretary of State deny visas for entry to the United States to corporate officers, principals, shareholders and even the spouse, minor children or agents of such persons, if they are trafficking in or have confiscated property.[8] This authority has been used against officials of Canadian, Israeli and Mexican companies.

Other nations and organizations have responded in very strong terms against the Libertad Act by adopting blocking laws, enacting resolutions, etc.[9] Cuba enacted its own response to the Libertad, which,

6. Pub. L. No. 104–114, 110 Stat. 785 (Mar. 12, 1996).

7. Libertad Act § 4(13).

8. Id at § 401.

9. See, e.g., Mexico: Act to Protect Trade and Investment from Foreign Stat-

inter alia, denies any possible compensation in a future settlement with the government of Cuba to anyone attempting to take advantage of the Libertad Act by using the U.S. courts under Title III.[10]

The Cuban sanctions discussed immediately above represent the most severe sanctions yet adopted. They were partly used as a model for the 1996 Iran and Libya Sanctions Act, often referred to as the D'Amato Act.[11] This Act, following the Libertad Act, requires the President to impose sanctions against foreign companies that invest more than $20 million a year in the development of petroleum resource production in Iran, or more than $40 million in Libya. The $2 billion investment in Iran by the French Total company generated a conflict between France and the U.S. over possible sanctions, which the U.S. President has not imposed, but has been under pressure to do so. If sanctions are imposed, this matter will quickly be taken to the WTO by France. Other petroleum investments have been made in Iran by European companies.

Selected Bibliography

Bhala, National Security and International Trade Law: What the GATT Says, and What the United States Does, 19 Univ. Pa. J. Int'l Econ. L. 263 (1998).

Dick, The EC Hormone Ban Dispute and the Application of the Dispute Settlement Provisions of the Standards Code, 10 Mich.J.Int'l L. 872 (1989).

Donner, The Cuban Democracy Act of 1992, 7 Emory Int'l L.Rev. 259 (Spring 1993).

Echols, Section 301: Access to Foreign Markets from an Agricultural Perspective, 6 Int'l Trade L.J. 4 (1980–81).

Epstein, The Land of Liquidated Damages: Recent Judicial Decisions and Unresolved Issues, 14 Fordham Int'l L.J. 7 (1990–91).

Hudec, Circumventing Democracy: The Political Morality of Trade Negotiations, 25 Int'l Law and Politics 311 (1993).

Janik, A U.S. Perspective on the GATT Agreement on Government Procurement, 20 George Wash.J.Int'l Law & Econ. 501 (1987).

McDorman, The GATT Consistency of U.S. Fish Import Embargoes to Stop Driftnet Fishing and Save Whales, Dolphins and Turtles, 24 Geo.Wash.J.Int'l Law & Econ. 77 (1991).

Note, Buy–American Statutes—An Assessment of Validity under Present Law and A Recommendation for Preemption, 23 Rutgers L.J. 137 (1991).

utes which Contravene International Law, with Introductory note by J. Vargas, 36 Int'l Legal Mat. 133 (1997).

10. Le de Reafirmacion de la Dignidad y Soberania Cubana (Ley No. 80), (Dec. 24, 1996).

11. Pub. L. No. 104–172, 110 Stat. 1541 (1996).

Note, United States Country of Origin Marking Requirements: The Application of a Nontariff Trade Barrier, 6 Law & Pol'y Int'l Bus. 485 (1974).

Note, Waiting for the Big One: Principle, Policy and the Restriction of Imports Under Section 232, 22 Law & Pol'y Int'l Bus. 357 (1991).

O'Connell, Using Trade To Enforce International Environmental Law: Implications for the United States Law, 1 Global L.S.J. 273 (1994).

Southwick, Binding the States: A Survey of State Law Conformance with Standards of the GATT Procurement Code, 13 U.Pa.J.Int'l Bus.L. 57 (1992).

Vaughn, The Buy American Act of 1988: Legislation in Conflict with U.S. International Obligations, 20 Law & Policy Int'l Bus. 603 (1989).

Yechout, In the Wake of Tuna II, 5 Minn.J.Global Trade 247 (1996).

Zedalis, Agricultural Trade and Section 22, 31 Drake L.R. 587 (1981).

Chapter 15

ESCAPE CLAUSE AND MARKET DISRUPTION PROCEEDINGS; TRADE ADJUSTMENT ASSISTANCE

Table of Sections

A. INTRODUCTION

B. ESCAPE CLAUSE PROCEEDINGS

C. MARKET DISRUPTION PROCEEDINGS

D. TRADE ADJUSTMENT ASSISTANCE

A. INTRODUCTION

§ 15.1   Prospects for Relief

One way that United States businesses may seek protection from import competition is by initiating what are known as escape clause or

636

market disruption proceedings under the Trade Act of 1974. In contrast to most other statutory trade law remedies, these proceedings are not targeted at unfair practices. Rather, the goods are assumed to be fairly traded but in such volume that domestic industry relief is temporarily appropriate while adjustments are undertaken. Escape clause proceedings can involve imports from anywhere in the world and are authorized by Section 201 of the Trade Act.[1] Escape clause proceedings are also typically found in the bilateral trade agreements of the United States.

Market disruption proceedings concern imports from communist nations and are authorized by Section 406 of the 1974 Trade Act.[2] These proceedings are similar but not identical. Either may result in the imposition of U.S. import restraints or presidential negotiation of export restraints from the source country. Escape clause and market disruption proceedings are anticipated by Article XIX of the General Agreement on Tariffs and Trade. There has been an ongoing dialogue within the GATT about reforming the law of Article XIX. A "Safeguards Agreement" emerged from the Uruguay Round of negotiations and is outlined below.

Import injury relief available under the Trade Act of 1974 is basically of two kinds: (1) Presidential relief designed to temporarily protect domestic producers of like or directly competitive products; and/or (2) governmental assistance to workers and firms economically displaced by import competition. This assistance is intended to enhance job opportunities and competitiveness. Protective relief tends to be awarded when the President believes that U.S. industry needs sometime to adjust, while governmental assistance is seen as a means to accommodate the injury caused by import competition. Adjustment to import competition is the longer term goal, resulting in competitive U.S. industries and markets.

One reason why protective escape clause relief is difficult to obtain is the fact that most trading partners of the United States are entitled to take compensatory action if the President decides to provide such relief. They are authorized to do this by the General Agreement on Tariffs and Trade. This is the case because escape clause proceedings do not concern any unfair trade practice. Rather, they are simply a reaction to the fact of increased import competition. This perspective helps explain why the President frequently decides that it is not in the national economic interest of the United States to impose escape clause relief. The same factors are much less relevant to market disruption relief because so few communist countries are WTO members.

§ 15.2 Special Rules for Canada and Mexico[1]

Canada and the United States agreed to limit escape clause relief in bilateral cases through 1998 to tariff increases up to most-favored-nation

§ 15.1

1. 19 U.S.C.A. § 2251.
2. 19 U.S.C.A. § 2436.

§ 15.2

1. See R. Folsom and W.D. Folsom, *Understanding NAFTA and Its International*

(MFN) levels or the suspension of further tariff reductions under their Free Trade Agreement. After 1998, no escape clause relief may be applied bilaterally to Canadian–U.S. trade without the consent of the other party. Furthermore, in global escape clause proceedings, Canada and the U.S. can only include each other's trade if it is substantial and contributes importantly to serious domestic injury. Any escape clause relief triggers a duty of compensation. All escape clause disputes as between Canada and the U.S., if not resolved by consultation, are subject to final and binding arbitration.[2] These bilateral provisions remain in place under the NAFTA.

Escape clause rules and procedures are generally applicable to United States–Mexico trade under Chapter 8 of the NAFTA. Chapter 8 permits temporary trade relief against import surges that cause or threaten domestic injury, subject to a right of compensation in the exporting nation. During the 10–year transition period, bilateral escape clause relief may be undertaken as a result of NAFTA tariff reductions only once per product for a maximum in most cases of 3 years. The relief is the "snap-back" to pre-NAFTA tariffs. After 2003, Mexico and the United States can apply bilateral escape clause remedies only by mutual consent.

If a global escape clause proceeding is pursued by one NAFTA partner, the others must be excluded unless their exports account for a substantial share of the imports in question (top five suppliers) and contribute importantly to the serious injury or threat thereof (rate of growth of NAFTA imports must not be appreciably lower than total imports). In global actions, unlike bilateral escape clause proceedings, remedial and corresponding compensatory action may take any form (not just tariff alterations).

The Corn Broom Case

In its first application of Section 302 of the NAFTA Implementation Act, the U.S. International Trade Commission found in 1996 that the elimination of tariffs on Mexican corn brooms resulted in a surge of imports that were the substantial cause of serious injury or its threat to the U.S. broom industry.[3] The ITC subsequently recommended tariff increases starting at 12 percent above the MFN level declining to 3 percent above that level in the fourth year of relief. This recommendation concerned brooms from Mexico and other nations excepting only Canada and Israel.[4]

President Clinton decided against tariff increases, but instructed the USTR to attempt to negotiate solutions with Mexico and other countries while the Labor, Commerce and Agriculture Departments developed an adjustment plan for the U.S. corn broom industry. Mexico, meanwhile, requested consultations under NAFTA Chapter 20 dispute resolution.

Business Implications (1995), Chapter 4 and 5.

2. See Chapter 11, Canada–U.S. Free Trade Agreement (1989).

3. No. NAFTA–302–1.

4. No. TA–201–65, ITC Pub. 3984. Aug. 1996.

Late in 1996, President Clinton deemed the negotiations a failure and imposed substantial tariffs and tariff-rate-quotas (TRQs) on broom imports from Mexico and other countries for 3 years. Mexico, in turn, raised tariffs on U.S. wine, brandy, bourbon, whiskey, wood office and bedroom furniture, flat glass, telephone agendas and chemically-pure sugar, fructose and syrup products. This retaliation was deemed by Mexico "substantially equivalent" to the U.S. broom tariff surcharges valued at roughly $1 million.

Early in 1998, the NAFTA Chapter 20 arbitration panel ruled in Mexico's favor.[5] Specifically, the panel ruled that the ITC had failed to explain why plastic brooms were not directly competitive with corn brooms, and therefore part of the U.S. domestic industry. U.S. officials indicated they would comply, but then took nine months to terminate the safeguards in a decision that does not cite the NAFTA arbitration as a reason for termination. Mexico subsequently removed its retaliatory tariffs.

Special NAFTA Escape Clauses

Textile and apparel goods, some agricultural goods, frozen concentrated orange juice and major household appliances benefit from special escapes from import competition under NAFTA. Many of these provisions were created to secure passage of NAFTA through the United States Congress. For example, textile and apparel goods are subject to a unique import protection scheme found in Annex 300–B. Standard bilateral escape clause relief on originating goods is possible under less demanding conditions until 2003. For non-originating goods, until 2003, quotas may be used as remedies by the United States or Mexico. The most important alteration probably concerns decision-making: the U.S. International Trade Commission does not participate. Instead, the Interagency Committee for the Implementation of Textile Agreements (CITA), thought to be more pro-industry, is the body that determines escape clause relief for textiles and apparel under NAFTA.

A special provision located in Article 703 benefits U.S.-grown chili peppers, eggplants, watermelons, tomatoes, onions and other agricultural goods. These may be protected using tariff-rate-quotas. The United States NAFTA Implementation Act, in Section 309, protects against imports of frozen concentrated orange juice from Mexico until 2007. Additional tariffs apply if the futures price for OJ falls below historic levels for five consecutive days. Once this happens, tariffs on Mexican OJ imports are "snapbacked" to the lower of the present or July 1, 1991 most-favored-nation GATT rates. These tariffs are eliminated when the average historic price level is exceeded for five days. This statistically driven protective mechanism, a monument to Florida politicians, has frequently been triggered.

The President's Statement of Administrative Action (SAA) accompanying the NAFTA Implementation Act contains yet another special

---

5. USA–97–2008–01.

escape from import competition. This time the beneficiaries are United States producers of major household appliances. It is thought that this statement, and its arcane rules of operation under Chapter 8 escape clause relief, secured critical votes in the House of Representatives for the passage of NAFTA.

§ 15.3 The Impact of Limited Judicial Review

Judicial review of escape clause and market disruption proceedings and remedies is limited to procedural irregularities or clear misconstruction of a statute.[1] This flows from the President's broad constitutional powers over foreign affairs. Derivatively, the actions of the International Trade Commission (ITC) in these proceedings are likewise sheltered from extensive judicial review.[2] This means that the decisions of the ITC are critical to obtaining escape clause relief. For example, between 1984 and 1990 the Commission reviewed 14 escape clause petitions. In ten of these petitions, the ITC decided that the statutory criteria for import injury relief were not present. In four of these petitions, the Commission recommended import relief. However, the President refused relief in three of these four cases. Only in a decision concerning wood shakes and shingles imported from Canada did the petitioner actually obtain protective escape clause relief.[3]

GATT compensation duties, U.S. free trade agreements, Presidential prerogatives and the 1988 amendments to Section 201 have significantly reduced the potential for success under these proceedings. During the 1990s, there have been very few Section 201 or Section 406 proceedings. The main focus of U.S. escape clause relief has become trade adjustment assistance, which is discussed below.

§ 15.4 The WTO Safeguards Agreement

A "Safeguards Agreement" on escape clause and related "gray area" protective measures was agreed upon during the Uruguay Round. One of its more important prohibitions is against seeking, undertaking or maintaining voluntary export or import restraint agreements with the exception of one such agreement which could last through 1999.[1] Substantive and procedural escape clause rules are also established, notably on proof of "serious domestic injury," opportunities to present evidence and a maximum 4–year period of protection (extendable to 8 years). The right to retaliate when another country invokes escape clause relief is suspended for the first 3 years of such invocation. Special rules limit the use of escape clause measures to exports from developing nations and extend the potential for their use on imports by such nations.

§ 15.3

1. Sneaker Circus, Inc. v. Carter, 566 F.2d 396 (2d Cir.1977), on remand 457 F.Supp. 771 (E.D.N.Y.1978).

2. Maple Leaf Fish Co. v. United States, 762 F.2d 86 (Fed.Cir.1985).

3. See U.S. International Trade Commission Publication 1826 (March 1986) and 51 Fed.Reg. 19157 (May 28, 1986).

§ 15.5

1. See Section 15.12.

§ 15.5 U.S. Implementation of the WTO Safeguards Agreement

Congress ratified and implemented the Uruguay Round accords in December of 1994 under the Uruguay round Agreements Act.[1] The ITC has summarized the URAA changes to United States escape clause proceedings as follows:

> The legislation amends section 202 of the Trade Act to require the ITC to disclose confidential business information under administrative protective order to authorized representatives of interested parties who are parties to an investigation. As directed in both the legislation and in the accompanying Statement of Administrative Action, the ITC has issued interim regulations that provide for such disclosure in a manner similar to that provided for in the case of investigations under Title VII of the Tariff Act of 1930 and the regulations issued thereunder.

> The legislation also amends section 202 to provide for a new and faster critical circumstances investigation procedure. If a petitioner alleges critical circumstances in a petition, the ITC must, within 60 days of receipt of the petition, make a determination concerning the existence of such circumstances and report to the President its determination and any recommendation concerning provisional relief. Under prior law, the Commission did not make a determination concerning critical circumstances until the end of the 120–day injury phase of an investigation. After receiving an affirmative Commission report, the President has 30 days in which to decide what, if any, action to take, with any such action generally to remain in effect until completion of the ITC investigation and consideration by the President of the ITC recommendation for longer term relief, but in no event longer than 200 days.

> The legislation amends section 202 of the Trade Act to clarify the meaning of the term "domestic industry" and to define the terms "serious injury" and "threat of serious injury," tracking definitions in the Safeguards Agreement. Because the definitions reflect prior law and ITC practice, the Statement of Administrative Action indicated that the incorporation of these definitions into U.S. law "should not affect the outcome of ITC decisions."

> The legislation makes several technical changes in the relief provisions in section 203 of the Trade Act. Under the new law, relief may be provided for an initial period of up to four years, and may be extended one *or more* times, with the overall duration of relief not to exceed eight years. Under prior law, the overall limitation on relief actions were also eight years; however, only one extension of a relief action was permitted, and there was no limitation (short of the full

§ 15.5　　　　　　　　　4809.

1. Public Law No. 103–465, 108 Stat.

eight years) on the duration of the initial period of relief. Under the new law, relief actions that exceed one year must be "phased down at regular intervals" during the relief period. The law does not specify the degree of phase-down period or interval. Under prior law, phase down was required "to the extent feasible" after three years. The term "orderly marketing agreement" has been changed simply to "agreement" to avoid confusion with "orderly marketing arrangements," which are prohibited by the Safeguards Agreement.

The legislation amends Section 204 of the Trade Act to provide for ITC investigations at the request of the President or on petition by industry concerning whether relief action continues to be necessary to prevent or remedy serious injury and whether there is evidence that the industry is making a positive adjustment to import competition. The ITC must transmit its report to the President no later than 60 days before the relief action terminates.[2]

B. ESCAPE CLAUSE PROCEEDINGS

§ 15.6 Petitions

Escape clause proceedings may be initiated by the President, the United States Trade Representative, Congress, and any interested trade association, union or company. It is reasonably common for both labor and management to petition for escape clause relief. Such petitions are filed with the International Trade Commission. Their requirements are detailed in the Selected Documents section of this chapter. Ordinarily the Commission will not commence a second escape clause investigation of the same subject matter unless at least one year has passed since the previous investigation. However, the Commission can waive this rule for good cause.[1] Since 1988, if escape clause relief is imposed, no new investigation regarding the same imports will be initiated until after that relief has expired plus an additional period of time representing the length of the relief originally granted.[2]

The petition must include a statement describing the specific purposes for which relief is being sought. Petitions under Section 201 must show that a substantial number of the companies or workers in the industry support the petition. In this sense, the petitioner is like a class action representative. While it is not necessary for all companies or workers in the industry to support the petition, a substantial proportion must do so since Section 201 is focused upon industry-wide relief.[3]

The statute suggests that the facilitation of the orderly transfer of resources to more productive pursuits, enhancing competitiveness, or other means of adjustment to new conditions of competition are legiti-

2. ITC annual Report, (1995).

§ **15.6**

1. See 19 U.S.C.A. § 2251(e).

2. 19 U.S.C.A. § 2252(h).

3. 19 C.F.R. § 206.9.

mate purposes for seeking Section 201 relief.[4] The petition may request provisional relief pending the outcome of an escape clause proceeding. The petitioner has the option of submitting a plan "to facilitate positive adjustment to import competition." This is often done because the Commission is required in conducting its escape clause investigation to seek information on actions being taken or planned by the firms and workers in the industry to make a positive adjustment to import competition. Moreover, the Commission is authorized to accept "commitments" regarding such action if it affirmatively determines that the statutory criteria of Section 201 are met.[5]

§ 15.7 ITC Investigations

If the industry is unable to adequately document its case for escape clause relief, it may be possible to essentially have the Commission do this under what is known as a Section 332 investigation.[1] If successful, a Section 332 investigation will shift the burden and the cost of preparing for a Section 201 proceeding from the industry or its representatives to the Commission.

As the Commission's investigation proceeds, it will develop an extensive questionnaire to send to domestic producers. This questionnaire focuses on the kinds of information the Commission needs to obtain in order to rule under the statutory criteria for escape clause proceedings. Although industry members typically support escape clause relief, they may not wish to reveal all the information requested in the questionnaire. In this case, the International Trade Commission can obtain subpoena enforcement from the District Court for the District of Columbia.[2] The hearings held by the ITC in connection with escape clause proceedings involve testimony under oath with the right of cross examination by opposing parties. Thus, for example, importers who do not wish to see restrictive measures undertaken, may oppose the domestic industry and its witnesses seeking such relief. The various procedures governing escape clause investigations and proceedings before the International Trade Commission are provided in 19 C.F.R. Parts 201 and 206. The entire ITC investigation normally takes about six months.

§ 15.8 Statutory Criteria

Section 201 of the Trade Act of 1974 requires proof of an increase in imports which substantially cause or threaten to cause serious injury to domestic industries producing like or directly competitive articles before protective trade relief will be considered. It should be noted that the increase in imports can be actual or relative to domestic production. Relative increases occur when domestic production declines when measured against imports. Imports could thus decline but be relatively

---

4. 19 U.S.C.A. § 2252(a)(2).

5. 19 U.S.C.A. § 2252(a)(4)–(7).

§ 15.7

1. See 19 U.S.C.A. § 1332.

2. 19 U.S.C.A. § 1333.

increasing if domestic production declined at an even faster rate.[1] Prior to 1974, escape clause law required the increase in imports to be caused by tariff concessions under trade agreements. This linkage was removed by the 1974 Act.

In conducting its escape clause investigation, Section 201 guides and controls the International Trade Commission's decision making. It defines, for example, the term "substantial cause" to mean a cause which is important and not less than any other cause.[2] In making its determinations with reference to serious injury or the threat of serious injury to a domestic industry producing like or directly competitive articles, the Commission must take into account all economic factors which it considers relevant including (but not limited to):

(1) the significant idling of productive facilities;

(2) the inability of a significant number of firms to carry out domestic production at a reasonable level of profit;

(3) significant unemployment or underemployment within the domestic industry;

(4) declines in sales or market share and higher and growing inventories as well as downward trends in production, profits, wages or employment in the domestic industry;

(5) the extent to which the industry is unable to generate adequate capital to finance modernization or maintain existing levels of research and development; and

(6) the extent to which the United States market is the focal point for the diversion of exports of the article in question by reason of trade restraints in other countries.

In making its determinations in connection with escape clause proceedings, the International Trade Commission must also consider the condition of the domestic industry over the course of its relevant business cycle. However, the Commission may not aggregate the cause of declining demand associated with a recession or economic downturn into a single cause of serious injury or threat of injury.[3] The Commission must also examine factors other than imports which may be a cause of serious injury or the threat of serious injury to the domestic industry. Specifically with reference to the question of "substantial cause," the statutes provide that an increase in imports (either actual or relative to domestic production) and a decline in the proportion of the domestic market supplied by domestic producers must be considered.[4] The term "significant idling of productive facility" includes the closing of plants or underutilization of production capacity.[5]

§ 15.8

1. See 19 U.S.C.A. § 2252(c).

2. 19 U.S.C.A. § 2252(b).

3. 19 U.S.C.A. § 2252(c)(2). Compare Certain Motor Vehicles and Certain Chassis

and Bodies Thereof, USITC Inv. No. TA–201–44, 2 ITRD 5241 (1980).

4. 19 U.S.C.A. § 2252(c)(1)–(2).

5. 19 U.S.C.A. § 2252(c)(6).

In order to determine the existence of a domestic industry producing an article like or directly competitive with the import competition, the ITC must consider only domestic production, may limit its consideration to specific articles of particular producers, and may limit the industry geographically where the imports are focused into a particular part of the United States.[6] For these purposes, a domestic industry includes producers located in the United States as well as its insular possessions.

Escape clause petitions can involved disputes as to the nature of the imported article. Typically, domestic producers will want to define the imported article broadly so as to enhance the possibility of proving domestic injury as well as obtaining broader relief. Importers of the product in question will want to define the imported article narrowly or in terms of separate categories so as to minimize the potential for escape clause remedies. For example, in the non-rubber footwear case,[7] the domestic producers succeeded in persuading the International Trade Commission that the imported competition constituted all non-rubber footwear. They did so over the objection of the importers of this footwear who wished to have the Commission distinguish between athletic and non-athletic footwear.

§ 15.9 Substantial Causation

Despite the elaborate nature of the statutory requirements for ITC determinations of import injury under Section 201, substantial latitude in reaching these decisions still remains. A number of cases turn upon the issue of substantial causation. Restrictive interpretations of escape clause causation under the Trade Expansion Act of 1962 were widely criticized and a major reason for the amended causation criteria of the Trade Act of 1974. The 1962 Act focused on whether the imports were "the major factor" in causing domestic injury, whereas the 1974 Act considers substantial causation (important and not less than any other cause) sufficient. One of the better known decisions in this area under the 1974 Act involves the importation of automobiles from Japan.[1] In this decision, the ITC held that there was an increase in imports of Japanese automobiles which was directly competitive with U.S. production but that other factors were more important to the explanation of the serious injury being suffered by the U.S. auto industry. In particular, the general economic recession of the times was held by the majority to be a more substantial cause of this injury.

In most escape clause proceedings there are often arguably other causes for injury to the domestic industry. Management may be inept, labor underproductive, general economic trends predominantly negative,

6. 19 U.S.C.A. § 2252(c)(4).

7. U.S. International Trade Commission Publication 1545 (July, 1984).

§ 15.9

1. Certain Motor Vehicles and Certain Chassis and Bodies Thereof, U.S. International Trade Commission Investigation No. TA–201–44, 2 ITRD 5241 (1980).

technological innovations affecting competition adversely and so forth. Whether one cause is more substantial than the other is often very difficult to pinpoint with any kind of administrative expertise. The issue of causation may be affected by political currents at the ITC. For example, in a later decision involving the importation of motorcycles, the ITC specifically refused to treat recessionary elements in the United States economy as a more substantial cause for industry injury.[2] It is difficult to reconcile this decision with that concerning auto imports. Congress has since made a recession or an economic downturn incapable of being an aggregate cause of domestic injury for escape clause proceedings.[3]

In evaluating substantial causation under Section 201 of the Trade Act of 1974, the International Trade Commission has considered the following alternative causes of injury to domestic industries:

    (1) Consumer cycles that affect product purchases;

    (2) fundamental changes in consumption;

    (3) governmental regulation;

    (4) industry competition;

    (5) management decision making;

    (6) trends in imports, domestic consumption and production;

    (7) price changes in the product market;

    (8) business cycle changes;

    (9) labor contract negotiations; and

    (10) world price and competitive conditions.[4]

In evaluating declines in domestic consumption, there may be a variety of factors at work. These could include, for example, technological innovation, product substitution or interest rate shifts. It is not clear whether the International Trade Commission will consider these as possible separate and independent causation factors.[5]

§ 15.10 Serious Injury

A less developed but potentially controversial area of ITC determinations under Section 201 involves the question of what constitutes serious injury to the domestic industry. The statutory criteria indicate that loss of production should be the relevant inquiry, whereas loss of market share is relevant primarily to causation. Whether there is serious injury will of course depend upon the definition of the domestic industry. This

2. Heavy Weight Motorcycles, & Engines & Power Train Subassemblies Therefor, U.S. International Trade Commission Investigation No. TA–201–47, 4 ITRD 2469 (1983).

3. See 19 U.S.C.A. § 2252(c).

4. For a review of these alternative causation factors, see especially Carbon & Certain Alloy Steel Products, U.S. International Trade Commission Publication 1553, 6 ITRD 2236 (July 1984).

5. See Stainless Steel and Alloy Tool Steel, U.S. International Trade Commission Publication 1377, 5 ITRD 1411 (May 1983).

is a bit like deciding what is the relevant market in United States antitrust litigation. Sub-markets, including sub-product markets and sub-geographic markets can clearly be domestic industries for purposes of Section 201. In the auto industry case referenced above, the ITC used tariff classifications of the United States in order to determine the domestic industry. Using such classifications has the practical feature of allowing identifiable tariff relief if that is ultimately granted. It is important to remember that the mere threat of serious injury is sufficient to satisfy the statute. There must be a reasonable degree of imminence to the projected import injury.[1]

The International Trade Commission has interpreted the term "serious injury" to mean damage or hurt of a grave or important proportion.[2] In a decision denying relief to U.S. cigar producers, the Commission determined that a marked decline in U.S. consumption of large cigars was a more important cause of injury than import competition.[3] A decline in housing construction was determined to be more important to the injury suffered by door manufacturers than import competition.[4] In most of its decisions concerning causation and serious injury, the Commission ordinarily reviews the economic trends over the past five years so as to screen out temporary problems.

In one decision, the Commission excluded domestic production of certain pigments because they were inorganic in contrast to iron blue pigments which are organic and against which import relief was sought. The different pigments had contrasting commercial uses and were markedly apart in terms of cost. Under these conditions, organic and inorganic pigments were held not to be like or directly competitive products.[5] In determining whether products are competitive with each other, the Commission may consider earlier or later stages of processing.[6] Imports of raw sugar were considered directly competitive with U.S. sugarcane and sugar beets even though these products were not yet processed into sugar. Moreover, U.S. produced refined or processed sugar, even though at a later stage than the imports in questions, could be considered directly competitive with the raw sugar.[7]

In defining the nature of the domestic industry for escape clause purposes, the parties typically engage in argument which seeks to promote either a broader or narrower definition. Importers may contest the definition initially offered by the domestic industry so as to decrease

§ 15.10

1. See Heavy Weight Motorcycles, U.S. International Trade Investigation No. TA–201–47, 4 ITRD 2469, Publication No. 1342 (Feb.1983).

2. Bolts, Nuts & Screws of Iron or Steel, U.S. International Trade Commission Publication 747, 1 ITRD 5142 (November 1975).

3. Wrapper Tobacco, U.S. International Trade Commission Publication 746, 1 ITRD 5137 (November 1975).

4. Birch Plywood Door Skins, U.S. International Trade Commission Publication 743, 1 ITRD 5121 (October 1975).

5. Ferrocyanide and Ferrocyanide Pigments, U.S. International Trade Commission Publication 767 (April 1976).

6. 19 U.S.C.A. § 2481(5).

7. Sugar Imports, U.S. International Trade Commission Publication 807 (March 1977).

the perception that like or directly competitive products are at risk or reduce the measurement of increase in imports. The definition of the industry will also impact on the question of causation. All of these issues were raised in the *Heavy Weight Motorcycles* case. In this decision, the Commission ruled that imported sub-assemblies were not directly competitive with domestic sub-assemblies because the imports were captively consumed.[8] Similar issues were raised in the automobile investigation. The domestic industry argued that passenger cars should be defined as a single industry producing automobiles and light trucks. Importers who opposed the escape clause proceeding sought to subdivide the industry into large automobiles and small automobiles. The Commission's ultimate determination found three different industries, passenger automobiles, light trucks and medium-heavy weight trucks.[9]

Having defined the industry, the Commission then must decide which particular companies belong to it. This is not always easy. In the automobile case, for example, the Commission had to decide whether dealers and independent parts suppliers were part of the domestic industry. It decided that neither were part of the domestic industry because the dealers did not produce any article, and the independent suppliers of parts did not produce products that were like or directly competitive with the final product. If a domestic company is also an importer, the Commission can only consider that part of its business that relates to domestic production to be part of the domestic industry.[10] This legislative provision effectively reverses earlier decisions, such as in *Heavy Weight Motorcycles,* where the Commission found that domestic subsidiaries of Japanese companies were also domestic producers even when the parts they imported comprised more than 50 percent of the final product.

One definition of serious injury is that the industry is "in danger of disappearing or suffering major shrinkage." [11] Section 202 now requires the Commission to specifically consider the significant idling of productive facilities, the inability of a significant number of firms to carry out production at reasonable levels of profit and significant unemployment or underemployment within the industry when determining serious injury.[12] When evaluating the threat of serious injury as opposed to actual injury, the Commission must consider declines in sales or market share, growing inventories, downward trends in production, profits, wages or employment, the inadequacy of capital to finance modernization or maintain existing expenditures for research and development, and the extent to which the United States is the focal point for a

8. See Heavy Weight Motorcycles, U.S. International Trade Investigation No. TA–201–47, 4 ITRD 2469, Publication No. 1342 (Feb. 1983).

9. See Certain Motor Vehicles and Certain Chassis and Bodies Thereof, Investigation No. TA–201–44, 2 ITRD 5241 Publication No. 1110 (December 1980).

10. 19 U.S.C.A. § 2252(c).

11. See Certain Canned Tuna Fish, U.S. International Trade Commission Publication No. 1558, 6 ITRD 2464 (August 1984).

12. 19 U.S.C.A. § 2252(c).

diversion of exports into other markets.[13]   In actual practice, there may be little difference between evaluating potential and actual injury in escape clause proceedings.

One issue concerning the definition of the domestic industry is whether it can involve various stages of processing.   In other words, the issue is whether the imports must be at the same level of processing as the domestic industry.   The International Trade Commission has indicated that when several stages are involved in the production of goods, the domestic industry includes the facilities involved in all of the various stages.[14]   For example, the Commission held that the copper refining industry in the United States includes four stages.   For purposes of determining injury to that industry, it was appropriate to consider all four stages of copper production when gauging the impact of import competition.[15]   The Trade Act of 1974 specifically indicates that various stages of processing can be considered in defining the imported product. This has the practical effect of allowing the imported article to be at a different level of process from that which causes injury to the domestic industry.[16]

§ 15.11   Relief Recommendations of the Commission

If the International Trade Commission affirmatively decides that the statutory criteria of Section 301 are met, it must make recommendations to address the serious injury or threat thereof to the domestic industry as well as consider the most effective means to allow that industry to make a positive adjustment to import competition.[1]   The Commission is authorized to choose from a menu of relief options.   It may recommend an increase in or the imposition of a tariff or a tariff rate quota, modification or imposition of an import quota, various trade adjustment measures including trade adjustment assistance, or any combination of these possibilities.[2]   No recommended relief may exceed an eight-year time limit.   In addition, the Commission may also recommend that the President initiate international negotiations to address the underlying cause of the increase in imports.   Interestingly, only those members of the ITC who voted affirmatively to find a breach of Section 201 are eligible to vote on recommendations to the President.   Dissenting members appear to have no input on relief recommendations.

The Commission's report to the President will also include any adjustment plans submitted by the domestic industry in its petition and any commitments made by firms and workers in that industry in order to facilitate positive adjustment to import competition.   The Commission's report must also analyze the long and short term economic effects of the relief it recommends.

---

13. Id.

14. U.S. International Trade Commission Publication 1558 (August, 1984).

15. U.S. International Trade Commission Publication 1549 (July, 1984).

16. See 19 U.S.C.A. § 2481(5).

§ 15.11

1. 19 U.S.C.A. § 2252(e).

2. Id.

The Commission's Report to the President is advisory, but if the President decides not to follow any recommended import relief, Congress may pass a joint resolution by majority vote of both houses disapproving of the President's action. This joint resolution may be vetoed by the President, and the veto may in turn be overridden by Congress. If this were to occur, then the Commission's original relief recommendations would be implemented.[3]

§ 15.12 Presidential Relief Decisions

After receiving the recommendations and report of the International Trade Commission, the President is required to take all appropriate and feasible action that he or she determines will facilitate efforts by the domestic industry to make a positive adjustment to import competition and which provide greater economic and social benefits than costs. The latter requirement, essentially a cost-benefit analysis, was added to the statute by 1988 amendments.[1] The President need not take any action at all. If the President decides to provide escape clause relief, this may be in the form of a tariff, a tariff rate quota, an import quota, adjustment assistance, orderly marketing agreements with foreign countries, an allocation among importers by auction of import licenses, international negotiations, legislative proposals, or any combination thereof.[2] Duty free treatment under the Generalized System of Tariff Preferences of the United States is automatically suspended if the President decides to impose an escape clause proceeding tariff. No increase in tariff resulting from escape clause proceedings can exceed 50 percent ad valorem of the rate existing at the time of the escape clause proceeding.[3]

Since all escape clause relief is intended to be temporary, no relief ordered by the President may exceed eight years.[4] President Carter denied relief against stainless steel flatware in part because a tariff rate quota had been in effect for more than 13 of the previous 20 years. The President determined that escape clause relief would be inconsistent with the basic concept that this kind of relief is supposed to be temporary in nature.[5]

Petitioners in escape clause proceedings should consider in advance which form of relief they hope to receive. Tariffs may not provide effective relief because of floating currency values. For example, if the dollar declines in value, imports get cheaper and the negative impact of tariffs might be offset. On the other hand, if dollar values are rising, this will cause tariffs to be an effective form of protection because imports become notably more expensive. The point to be made is that the result in connection with tariff relief is uncertain. In either case, tariffs can always be just simply paid if the economics of the transaction

3. See 19 U.S.C.A. § 2253(c).

§ 15.12

1. See 19 U.S.C.A. § 2253(a).

2. 19 U.S.C.A. § 2253(a)(3).

3. 19 U.S.C.A. § 2254(e).

4. 19 U.S.C.A. § 2253(e).

5. Certain Stainless Steel Table Flatware, 43 Fed.Reg. 29259 (July 7, 1978).

support payment. In the *Heavy Weight Motorcycles* case, for example, the relief ultimately determined by the President was a tariff increase with an automatic termination date five years later. In fact, the industry requested an earlier termination and many believe that this is one of the few examples of successful adjustment to import competition under escape clause relief.

The President has provided escape clause relief in less than 20 instances.[6] Congress can (but never has) override any presidential denial of escape clause or market disruption relief recommended by the International Trade Commission, and it may override any decision of the President that differs from the type of relief recommended by the Commission. Congress can do so by adopting a joint resolution of disapproval. Once this is enacted, the President is required to adopt the import relief previously recommended by the Commission. However, the President may veto this joint resolution, in which case an override of the President's veto is required to obtain relief.[7]

If the President decides to impose protective escape clause relief, subsequent proceedings concerning extension, reduction or termination of that relief may be held. The level of the relief granted however cannot be increased. In the subsequent proceedings, the Commission's role is advisory, and it will report upon its monitoring of the existing relief relative to continuing injury and the progress of the domestic industry to adjust to import competition.[8] The President may alter existing escape clause relief if he or she finds that the domestic industry has failed to make adequate efforts to adjust to import competition, the circumstances have sufficiently changed to warrant a reduction or termination in relief, or upon the request of the domestic industry.[9]

In deciding whether to undertake escape clause relief, the President is directed to take into account the report of the Commission, the extent to which the workers and firms in the industry are benefiting from adjustment assistance, the efforts being made by the industry to make a positive adjustment to import competition, the likelihood of effectiveness of relief in facilitating such adjustment, and the short and long term economic and social costs of the relief relative to their short and long term economic and social benefits. The President must also consider

---

6. See Pres.Proc. 4445, June 11, 1976 (orderly marketing agreement for specialty steel); Pres.Proc. 4510, June 22, 1977, (orderly marketing agreement for nonrubber footwear); Pres.Proc. 4511, June 24, 1977, (orderly marketing agreement for color television receivers); Pres.Proc. 4561, April 7, 1978, (duty on CB radios); Pres.Proc. 4608, November 15, 1978, (duty on high-carbon ferrochromium); Pres.Proc. 4632, January 4, 1979, (duty on bolts, nuts and large screws); Pres.Proc. 4640, February 23, 1979, (import quota on wooden clothespins); Pres.Proc. 4713, January 16, 1980, (duty on certain nonelectric steel cookware); Pres.Proc. 4801, October 29, 1980,

(duty on canned and other prepared mushrooms); Pres.Proc. 5050, April 15, 1983, (tariff-rate quota on certain heavyweight motorcycles); Pres.Proc. 5074, July 19, 1983, (duty and import quota on certain specialty steel); Pres.Proc. 5498, June 6, 1986, (duty on wood shingles and shakes of western red cedar).

7. See 19 U.S.C.A. § 2253(b).

8. See Color Television Receivers and Subassemblies Thereof, U.S. International Trade Commission Publication 1068, 2 ITRD 5046 (May 1980).

9. 19 U.S.C.A. § 2253(a).

other factors related to the national economic interest of the United States including but not limited to the economic and social costs if relief is not granted, the impact on consumers and on competition in domestic markets, and the impact on United States industries if other nations take compensatory action. Consumer interests have sometimes been critical to the President's decision to deny escape clause relief. Various presidents have noted that such relief can as a practical matter increase prices to consumers and that this would be adverse to the national economic interests of the United States.[10] The argument that escape clause relief may cause inflation in the United States is a variation on this theme.[11] The fact that the imposition of escape clause relief may provoke retaliation has also been used to justify denial of such relief by several Presidents.[12]

The President is further directed to consider the extent to which there is a diversion of foreign exports to the U.S. markets by reason of foreign restraints, the potential for circumvention of any relief taken, the national security interests of the United States, and those factors that the Commission is required to consider in reaching its recommendations.[13] These considerations have frequently in the past caused presidents to deny escape clause relief. This is consistent with the President's primary role in the foreign affairs of the nation. Thus, for example, the President decided not to grant escape clause relief regarding imports of honey because it might have an adverse effect on the bargaining position of the United States in international trade negotiations.[14] Similar results were achieved in connection with imports of copper when there were ongoing GATT negotiations as well as UNCTAD negotiations about commodities trade.[15] Later rejections of other efforts to obtain import relief in connection with copper were based upon considerations of the need for the exporters of copper to obtain adequate export earnings.[16]

Amendments to the Trade Act of 1974 adopted in 1988 promote the goal of adjustment to import competition instead of trade restrictive relief. This has been sought by strongly encouraging the submission of adjustment plans and commitments by petitioners for Section 201 relief, and by expanding the range of remedies the Commission can recommend to the President in escape clause proceedings to *any* action that will facilitate adjustment. Furthermore, the standards for presidential relief mandate a determination that such relief will facilitate efforts by the domestic industry to make a positive adjustment to import competition. Finally there is increased monitoring of Section 201 relief plans and limitations on the right to petition for further relief. Thus, Section 201

10. See Certain Stainless Steel Flatware, supra.

11. See Nonrubber Footwear, U.S. International Trade Commission Publication No. 1717, 7 ITRD 2125 (July 1985).

12. See High Carbon Verochrominium, 43 Fed.Reg. 4245 (November 6, 1978).

13. 19 U.S.C.A. § 2253(a).

14. Honey, 41 Fed.Reg. 3787 (Sept. 1, 1976).

15. Domestic Copper Industry, 43 Fed. Reg. 49523 (October 24, 1978).

16. Copper Import Relief Determination, 49 Fed.Reg. 35609 (1984).

of the Trade Act is now considerably less protectionist and more adjustment oriented than previously.

§ 15.13 Orderly Marketing and Voluntary Restraint Agreements

A common form of protective relief that Presidents have selected under Section 201 is the negotiation of orderly marketing agreements (OMAs). Such agreements result in the restriction at the source of the offending imports. Orderly marketing agreements, for example, have periodically been used in connection with the import of footwear from Asia to the United States. They should be distinguished from voluntary restraint agreements (VRAs) which are negotiated outside of the context of escape clause proceedings. In the auto imports case, since the International Trade Commission refused to determine injury to the United States automobile industry, the President was unable to negotiate an orderly marketing agreement with Japan. However, the near equivalent of such an arrangement was achieved by the President through negotiations resulting in a voluntary restraint agreement limiting the export of Japanese automobiles to the United States market. The President's authority under the foreign affairs power to enter into VRA negotiations was challenged in court but upheld as long as legally enforceable obligations are not established through these negotiations.[1]

Many have criticized the economic effects of orderly marketing agreements and voluntary restraint agreements. When effective, these agreements often permit exporters based abroad to raise prices and profit margins on the artificially limited supply of their products in the United States market.[2] However, since most OMAs and VRAs are targeted at particular countries and production can be shifted to other nations not subject to such agreements, they may not provide effective protection against import competition. The GATT Uruguay Round Escape Clause Code prohibits signatories from seeking, maintaining or undertaking export or import restraint agreements with the exception of one such agreement which may last through 1999.

United States importation of steel products has frequently been limited by voluntary restraint agreements with foreign exporting countries. The authority for such agreements is found in the Steel Import Stabilization Act of 1984, adopted as Title VIII of the Trade and Tariff Act of 1984.[3] Excessive imports can be remedied by Customs Service action, and foreign steel producers do not have standing to challenge such determinations.[4] This authority was renewed in the Steel Trade

§ 15.13

1. See Consumers Union of the United States, Inc. v. Kissinger, 506 F.2d 136 (D.C.Cir.1974), cert. denied 421 U.S. 1004, 95 S.Ct. 2406, 44 L.Ed.2d 673 (1975).

2. See FTC Staff Report, Bureau of Economics, "Effects of Restrictions on United States Imports: Five Case Studies & Theories" (June 1980).

3. Public Law 98–573.

4. Sacilor, Acieries Et Laminoirs de Lorraine v. United States, 815 F.2d 1488 (Fed. Cir.1987), cert. denied 484 U.S. 924, 108 S.Ct. 285, 98 L.Ed.2d 245 (1987).

Liberalization Program Implementation Act of 1989.[5] In general, the 1989 Act endorses the liberalization program of President Bush. This program calls for the eventual restoration of market forces and the removal of voluntary restraint agreements. After this time, U.S. steel producers will rely on Section 201, Section 301 and other domestic trade law protective devices. Such a program will replace the approximately 30 bilateral voluntary restraint agreements that have traditionally governed steel exports to the United States markets. These agreements have usually accounted for approximately 20 percent of United States steel imports. The major agreements have been with the European Union and Brasil. The steel VRAs expired March 31, 1992. In the absence of a multilateral agreement, the U.S. steel industry filed massive antidumping petitions.

C. MARKET DISRUPTION PROCEEDINGS

§ 15.14 Statutory Criteria

Section 406 of the Trade Act of 1974 authorizes what are known as "market disruption proceedings." These proceedings in many ways parallel the law concerning escape clause proceedings discussed above. However, the focus of market disruption proceedings are imports from communist countries.[1] It is noteworthy that Section 406 applies to communist countries, regardless of whether their economies can be characterized as market oriented or nonmarket in orientation. Thus, Congress denoted Section 406 in terms of political systems rather than market structures. This contrasts with a number of other United States trade laws which focus more on nonmarket economy nations rather than communist countries. The legislative history to the provisions concerning market disruption makes it clear that Congress was concerned about the overdependence on communist nations for vital raw materials and that such countries might use their control over domestic production to flood the United States with low priced goods. Moreover, Congress believed that traditional remedies such as antidumping, countervailing duty and escape clause proceedings were ineffective or inappropriate against imports from communist countries.[2] These perceptions fostered easier statutory criteria than exist under Section 201.

The petitioning and investigation procedures outlined above in connection with escape clause proceedings apply equally to market disruption proceedings. One difference is that the President may take action in connection with market disruption only with reference to the specific countries involved. In contrast, escape clause proceedings can result in relief which is global. Another difference is that market disruption investigations by the ITC last only three months not six.

---

5. Public Law 101–221.

§ 15.14

1. 19 U.S.C.A. § 2436.

2. See 1974 U.S.Code Congressional and Administrative News 7186 (Senate Report No. 1298, 93rd Congress, 2nd Session 210 (1974)).

Section 406 indicates that market disruption exists within a domestic industry whenever imports of like or directly competitive articles are increasing *rapidly* (either absolutely or relatively) so as to be a *significant* cause of *material* injury or the threat thereof. Note the difference between Section 406 and Section 201 language. The causation test under Section 406 uses the term significant not substantial, and the injury test is one of materiality not seriousness. However, Section 406 requires imports to be increasing rapidly, whereas Section 201 merely requires an increase. In one decision, the International Trade Commission found that imports were increasing rapidly when ammonia from the Soviet Union had constituted merely two percent of U.S. production in 1978, four percent in 1979 and was expected to reach 12 percent by 1981.[3] In determining whether imports are rapidly increasing for purposes of Section 406, the Commission has suggested that the increase in imports must be abnormal relative to previous trends from that country.[4] These imports must have increased in a recent period, generally taken to be within the past three years.[5] As under escape clause law, it does not matter whether the increase is absolute or relative.[6]

The material injury standard of Section 206 is the same as used in dumping and subsidy law.[7] But neither dumping nor subsidy law require proof of substantial or significant causation, issues only found in Section 201 and Section 406 proceedings. Section 406(e) indicates that "significant" refers to a cause that contributes significantly to the material injury of the domestic industry but need not be equal to or greater than any other cause.

The question of what constitutes significant cause under Section 406 has yet to be fully resolved. This standard is less than the substantial causation requirement of Section 201 yet apparently more than the important causation requirement associated with adjustment assistance. One feature of an analysis of causation under Section 406 that distinguishes it from Section 201 concerns the consideration of other imports. It is possible in Section 406 proceedings that other imports are more significant than the imports that are being contested. In one decision contesting glove imports from the People's Republic of China, the Commission found no significant cause of injury in part because the Chinese gloves accounted for only 20 percent of all imports to the United States while Hong Kong was the source of 40 percent of those imports during the same period.[8] In another decision the Commission noted that Brazilian and Canadian imports of ferrosilicon amounted to more than

3. Anhydrous Ammonia from the U.S.S.R., U.S. International Trade Commission Publication 1051, 1 ITRD 5355 (April 1980).

4. See Clothespins from the PRC, Poland and Romania, United States International Trade Commission Publication No. 902, 1 ITRD 5435 (August 1978).

5. See Canned Mushrooms from the People's Republic of China, U.S. International Trade Commission Publication No. 1293, 4 ITRD 2061 (October 1982).

6. 19 U.S.C.A. § 2436(e).

7. See Chapters 6 and 7.

8. See Certain Gloves from the People's Republic of China, U.S. International Trade Commission Publication No. 867, 1 ITRD 5371 (March 1978).

twice those coming from the Soviet Union for which relief was sought under Section 406.[9] This perspective tends to undermine the argument of petitioners for Section 406 relief that communist country exports are a significant cause of domestic injury. In an extreme case, the Commission noted that imports of kitchenware from Japan, Korea and Taiwan "dwarfed" the importance of such imports from the People's Republic of China.[10]

§ 15.15   Relief Measures

Despite a number of ITC investigations and a few recommendations of relief, few market disruption proceedings have produced concrete import injury relief. One reason for this is that Section 406 exists as an alternative to Section 201 which also can be made to apply to imports from communist countries. Global relief will almost always be preferred by petitioners over country-specific relief. Another reason is the highly political nature of any trade relief proceeding targeted at a communist country. In one instance, for example, the President declined to follow an ITC recommendation for relief against ammonia from the Soviet Union. A few days later, the Soviets invaded Afghanistan and the President imposed emergency import restraints on ammonia on the basis of changed circumstances. This emergency provision permitting the President to impose temporary relief without a hearing or other administrative process is not found in connection with Section 201 escape clause proceedings. In order to impose emergency relief under Section 406, the President need only find that there is reasonable grounds to believe that market disruption exists.[1] The ITC ultimately refused to go along with this decision, issuing a negative 406 determination which had the effect of terminating the President's emergency quota.[2] Another ITC recommendation for relief, this one regarding tungsten products from China, did result in an orderly marketing agreement for 4 years.[3]

D.   TRADE ADJUSTMENT ASSISTANCE

§ 15.16   Individual and Company Assistance Criteria

The idea of trade adjustment assistance has its origins in programs intended to assist people who were dislocated when the European Community (now Union) was established. Its adoption in the United States has had a checkered history, particularly as regards Congressional willingness to fund trade adjustment assistance. The first authority for

9. Ferrosilicon from the U.S.S.R., U.S. International Trade Commission Publication No. 1484, 6 ITRD 1319 (February 1984).

10. Certain Ceramic Kitchenware and Tableware from the People's Republic of China, U.S. International Trade Commission Publication No. 1279, 4 ITRD 1470 (August 1982).

§ 15.15

1. 19 U.S.C.A. § 2436(c).

2. See U.S. International Trade Commission Publications 1006 (Oct. 1979) and 1051 (April 1980) and Presidential Proclamation 4714 (Jan. 18, 1980).

3. See Pres. Proclamation 5718 (Oct. 2, 1987).

such assistance was provided in the Trade Expansion Act of 1962. However, no assistance was actually provided until 1969. The Trade Act of 1974 made trade adjustment assistance a greater possibility. But dramatic increases in payments to workers under the program during the early 1980s caused the Reagan Administration to actively seek to repeal the Trade Adjustment Assistance Program. During the 1980s, tighter eligibility requirements and shrinking budgetary allocations reduced the scope of the program. It was not until the Omnibus Trade and Competitiveness Act of 1988 that significant funds were committed to trade adjustment assistance and the program was reauthorized through 1993. Even so, actual payment of adjustment assistance to workers has occurred slowly, and assistance to companies has been extremely difficult to obtain.

There is a growing trend in escape clause law to provide adjustment assistance to workers and companies impacted by import competition rather than protective relief through presidential action. The Trade Act of 1974 facilitates the provision of such assistance either as an alternative to or in addition to protective presidential relief under Sections 201 or 406 of the Trade Act of 1974. Workers, for example, may petition the Secretary of Labor for trade adjustment assistance.[1] In order for such relief to be granted, the Secretary must certify that (1) a significant number or proportion of the workers have become totally or partially separated or threatened to become so separated, (2) that sales or production or both of the firm in question have decreased absolutely, and (3) that increased imports of articles like or directly competitive with those made by the workers or the firm for which the workers provide essential goods or services "contributed importantly" to such separation and decline.[2]

All three criteria must be met.[3] These criteria are related but not identical to those considered by the International Trade Commission in connection with escape clause proceedings. For example, the term "contributed importantly" means a cause which is important but not necessarily more important than any other cause. This is a lesser standard than substantial causation in connection with Section 201 proceedings. Whether imports are "like or directly competitive" with domestic products is a question of interchangeability or substitutability.[4] The fact that imports are actually decreasing does not per se eliminate the possibility of trade adjustment assistance. The critical issue is whether those imports have contributed importantly to unemployment.[5]

Adjustment assistance for workers, when granted, often resembles supplemental cash unemployment compensation. Such benefits are now

§ 15.16

1. 19 U.S.C.A. § 2271.

2. 19 U.S.C.A. § 2272.

3. Former Employees of Asarco's Amarillo Copper Refinery v. United States, 675 F.Supp. 647 (C.I.T.1987).

4. International Union, UAW v. Donovan, 592 F.Supp. 673 (C.I.T.1984).

5. United Rubber, Cork, Linoleum and Plastic Workers of America, Local 798 v. Donovan, 652 F.2d 702 (7th Cir.1981).

conditioned upon participation in job training and job search programs. Adjustment assistance for companies has sometimes involved income maintenance through loans like the Chrysler bail-out. At this point, assistance to companies is primarily limited to technical aid.[6] Companies may receive adjustment assistance only if the Secretary of Commerce finds that a significant number of their workers have been separated or threatened with separation, that sales or production have decreased absolutely, and increased importation of like or directly competitive articles contributed importantly to these results.[7] Agricultural firms may apply for adjustment assistance. Although once authorized by statute, Congress has not been willing to fund trade adjustment assistance for communities impacted by import competition.

It should be emphasized that it is not necessary for the ITC to determine that import injury has occurred under the criteria of Section 201 or Section 406 in order for adjustment assistance to be rendered. Such assistance flows from the separate determinations by the Secretaries of Labor and Commerce under the Trade Act of 1974. One important difference is the fact that in adjustment assistance proceedings the effect of imports on the industry as a whole is not at issue. The focus is on specific workers and specific companies. Whenever the International Trade Commission commences an investigation for purposes of Section 201 escape clause proceedings, the Secretary of Labor is required to begin a parallel investigation as to the likelihood and number of workers who may be certified as eligible for trade adjustment assistance. The Secretary of Labor then compiles a report which is forwarded to the President along with the report of the International Trade Commission concerning the escape clause petition.

§ 15.17 Secretary of Labor Determinations

The Circuit Court of Appeals for the District of Columbia has indicated that when the Secretary of Labor determines worker eligibility for trade adjustment assistance, it is appropriate to ask whether the buyers of the imports alleged to have caused injury have decreased their purchases from the employer in question. Such decreases, combined with evidence of increases in purchases of imported glass, supported the conclusion that imports contributed importantly to unemployment at a glass plant.[1] When deciding whether imports have increased for purposes of making these determinations, the Secretary of Labor can limit consideration to the immediate preceding year as a base period in the absence of any valid reason to consider a different year.[2] The Secretary of Labor cannot deviate from past practices focusing on the immediate

---

6. See 19 U.S.C.A. § 2431.

7. 19 U.S.C.A. § 2341(c).

§ 15.17

1. United Glass and Ceramic Workers of North America, AFL–CIO v. Marshall, 584 F.2d 398 (D.C.Cir.1978).

2. Paden v. U.S. Department of Labor, 562 F.2d 470 (7th Cir.1977).

preceding year. To do so may result in reversible error.[3] In deciding
what constitutes "an appropriate subdivision" for purposes of worker
eligibility, the Secretary of Labor must demonstrate clear reasons for
such decisions. In a case where the Secretary took the position that a
subdivision could never be larger than a plant, this decision upon review
was remanded for clarification of the underlying reasons.[4] On the other
hand, the Secretary's determination that the appropriate subdivision
could only be that which produces articles which are like or directly
competitive with imports was not erroneous and withstood challenge on
appeal.[5]

In making determinations as to worker eligibility, the Secretary of
Labor is given a subpoena power.[6] It is no defense to such subpoenas
that the information requested is confidential.[7] No prior judicial determination of the nature of the materials and their possible exemption
from disclosure under the Freedom of Information Act is permissible.[8]
Judicial review of worker eligibility determinations by the Secretary of
Labor are now filed in the Court of International Trade. On review, the
question is whether the findings of fact by the Secretary are supported
by substantial evidence.[9] It has been said the Secretary's determinations will be reversed only if arbitrary or not based on substantial
evidence.[10]

The Secretary of Labor may conduct investigations by mail rather
than in the field when determining worker eligibility. This is not an
abuse of discretion.[11] The Secretary of Labor is absolutely required to
publish notice of the fact that he or she has received petitions for
certification for eligibility for trade adjustment assistance benefits, and
must publish a summary of the determinations on that petition in the
Federal Register.[12] Any failure to do so will amount to substantial
prejudice to the petitioners and a court order requiring further action by
the Secretary.[13] However, a petition filed by only one worker where the
record does not indicate that that person was an official or certified
representative of a union or other worker representative does not impose
upon the Secretary of Labor the duty to commence an investigation.[14]
Once an investigation is commenced, the nature and the extent of the

3. Katunich v. Donovan, 594 F.Supp.
744 (C.I.T.1984), appeal after remand 599
F.Supp. 985 (1984).

4. International Union, United Auto.,
Aerospace and Agricultural Implement
Workers of America, UAW v. Marshall, 584
F.2d 390 (D.C.Cir.1978), appeal after re-
mand 627 F.2d 559 (D.C.Cir.1980).

5. Paden v. U.S. Department of Labor,
562 F.2d 470.

6. 19 U.S.C.A. § 2321.

7. Usery v. Whitin Machine Works, Inc.,
554 F.2d 498 (1st Cir.1977).

8. Id.

9. Id.

10. United Glass and Ceramic Workers
of North America, AFL–CIO v. Marshall,
584 F.2d 398 (D.C.Cir.1978).

11. Abbott v. Donovan, 570 F.Supp. 41
(C.I.T.1983), appeal after remand 588
F.Supp. 1438 (1984).

12. Woodrum v. Donovan, 544 F.Supp.
202 (C.I.T.1982), rehearing denied 4 C.I.T.
(1982).

13. Id.

14. Former Employees of USX Corp. v.
United States, 660 F.Supp. 961 (C.I.T.
1987).

investigations are discretionary matters for the Secretary.[15] This means, for example, that petitioners do not have a right to a trial-type hearing with cross examination of the witnesses of the Department of Labor as part of the process of determining eligibility for trade adjustment assistance.[16]

The importation of fully manufactured televisions sets was held not directly competitive with a manufacturer of printed circuit boards and other parts used in televisions. The workers at a plant which produced those parts were therefore not entitled to trade adjustment assistance.[17] Shipyard workers who customized various parts failed to show an increase in imports of such articles causing a decrease in their business and therefore were ineligible for trade adjustment assistance.[18] The question of whether imports contribute importantly to worker unemployment is a critical one in trade adjustment proceedings. A large number of the cases taken up on judicial review suggest that the Secretary's determinations on these questions will be ordinarily upheld.[19] Coal miners, for example, were ineligible to receive trade adjustment assistance as a result of increased importation of steel into the United States. Coal could not be regarded as a substitute or directly competitive with steel.[20] Likewise, handknitting yarn was held not like or directly competitive with cotton and synthetic sewing thread. This caused the workers in question to be ineligible for trade adjustment assistance.[21]

Services do not appear to be covered by worker adjustment assistance programs. Thus it was held that airline services are not "articles" within the meaning of the statute.[22] Likewise, former employees of an independently owned automobile dealership were not entitled to assistance since they were engaged in service activities that did not produce an import-impacted article.[23] Workers at a shipyard who were mainly involved in repair and maintenance and thus did not produce or create articles as required for trade adjustment assistance were similarly ineligible.[24]

15. Cherlin v. Donovan, 585 F.Supp. 644 (C.I.T.1984).

16. United Electric, Radio and Machine Workers of America v. Brock, 731 F.Supp. 1082 (C.I.T.1990), appeal after remand 14 C.I.T. 818 (1990).

17. Morristown Magnavox Former Employees v. Marshall, 671 F.2d 194 (6th Cir. 1982), cert. denied 459 U.S. 1041, 103 S.Ct. 458, 74 L.Ed.2d 610 (1982).

18. Pemberton v. Marshall, 639 F.2d 798 (D.C.Cir.1981).

19. See Local 167, International Molders and Allied Workers' Union, AFL–CIO v. Marshall, 643 F.2d 26 (1st Cir.1981); International Union, United Auto., Aerospace and Agricultural Implement Workers of America v. Marshall, 627 F.2d 559 (D.C.Cir. 1980); Former Employees of CSX Oil and Gas Corp. v. United States, 720 F.Supp. 1002 (C.I.T.1989); Former Employees of Asarco's Amarillo Copper Refinery v. United States, 675 F.Supp. 647 (C.I.T.1987).

20. United Mine Workers of America v. Brock, 664 F.Supp. 543 (C.I.T.1987).

21. Kelley v. Secretary, 626 F.Supp. 398 (C.I.T.1985).

22. Fortin v. Marshall, 608 F.2d 525 (1st Cir.1979).

23. Miller v. Donovan, 568 F.Supp. 760 (C.I.T.1983). Accord Woodrum v. United States, 737 F.2d 1575 (Fed.Cir.1984).

24. Pemberton v. Marshall, 639 F.2d 798 (D.C.Cir.1981).

§ 15.18 NAFTA Trade Adjustment

Worker training and trade adjustment assistance for persons displaced by NAFTA was adopted unilaterally as part of U.S. law. These provisions can be found in the NAFTA Implementation Act, Title V, entitled the "NAFTA Worker Safety Act."[1]

Under this Act, workers can petition the Secretary of Labor for assistance if a significant number of employees have been or are threatened with job losses. NAFTA imports must have "contributed importantly" to this result. Assistance is also available if production of like or directly competitive articles has been shifted to Mexico or Canada. Income support (extended beyond regular state unemployment benefits) and job search and relocation reimbursements are possible, but only if job training is undertaken.

In the first three years of operation, the Secretary of Labor certified nearly 100,000 U.S. workers as being "at risk" because of NAFTA imports or job shifts. Not all of these workers actually lost their jobs. Mexico was the source country in 60 percent of these certifications, Canada in 23 percent and 17 percent involved no single source. Of these 100,000 workers, only slightly more than 12,000 applied for NAFTA trade adjustment benefits. Another 20,000 certified workers opted for regular (non-NAFTA) trade adjustment benefits where job training requirements can be waived.

Selected Bibliography

Berg, Petitioning and Responding Under the Escape Clause: One Practitioner's View of How To Do It, 6 N.C.J.Int'l Law & Comm.Reg. 407 (1981).

Calabrese, Market Disruption Caused By Imports from Communist Countries: Analysis of Section 406 of the Trade Act of 1974, 14 Cornell Int'l L.J. 117 (1981).

Derrick, The Evolution of the Escape Clause: The United States' Quest for Effective Relief from Fairly Traded Imports, 13 N.Carolina J.Int'l L. & Comm.Policy 348 (1988).

Lowenfeld, Fair or Unfair Trade: Does It Matter?, 13 Cornell Int'l L.J. 205 (1980).

Mashigan, Orderly Marketing Agreements: Analysis of U.S. Automobile Industry Efforts to Obtain Relief, 6 Hastings Int'l & Comp.L.Rev. 161 (1982).

Note, Car Wars. Auto Imports and the Escape Clause, 13 Law & Policy Int'l Bus. 591 (1981).

Note, The Harley–Davidson Case: Escaping the Escape Clause, 16 Law & Policy Int'l Bus. 325 (1984).

§ 15.18   1. 17 Stat. § 501 (et seq.)

Note, Letting Obsolete Firms Die: Trade Adjustment Assistance in the U.S. and Japan, 22 Harv.Int'l L.J. 595 (1981).

Note, Trade Adjustment Assistance: An Analysis, 6 Conn.J.Int'l L. 251 (Fall 1990).

Rosenthal and Gilbert, The 1988 Amendments to Section 201: It Isn't Just for Import Relief Anymore, 20 Law & Policy Int'l Bus. 403 (1988).

Smith, Trade Adjustment Assistance: An Underdeveloped Alternative To Import Restrictions, 56 Albany L.Rev. 943 (1993).

Sykes, Protectionism as a "Safeguard": A Positive Analysis of the GATT "Escape Clause" with Normative Speculations, 58 U.Chi.L.Rev. 255 (Winter 1991).

Chapter 16

UNITED STATES EXPORT CONTROLS

Table of Sections

A. INTRODUCTION

B. DETERMINING WHEN A LICENSE IS NEEDED—THE 29 STEPS

C. SCOPE OF THE EXPORT ADMINISTRATIVE REGULATIONS

D. GENERAL PROHIBITIONS

E. COMMERCE CONTROL LIST OVERVIEW AND THE COUNTRY CHART

F. SPECIAL CONTROLS

A. INTRODUCTION

§ 16.1   Governance of Imports

The regulatory format for exports is quite different than for imports. Imports are governed by a series of trade acts beginning with the Tariff Act of 1930, and continuing to the most recent trade act legislation. Each successive trade act normally both amends portions of one or more of the earlier principal trade acts, and creates some new trade controls. Thus, it is necessary to check several trade acts for a complete coverage of import regulation. A considerable part of the U.S. trade law governing imports consists of the implementation of WTO rules. The reason for this complexity is clear. Nations often create barriers to imports in order to protect their own industries. Tariffs help establish trade barriers and also raise revenue. The WTO helps reduce tariff and nontariff barriers. The end result is a lengthy, detailed and disorganized group of national laws. Imports even have their own courts. The U.S. Court of International Trade (CIT) is an Article III court parallel to a federal district court (and formerly known as the U.S. Customs Court). The CIT principally deals with issues relating to imports, such as customs valuation and classification, subsidies, dumping, escape clause, etc. Appeals are to the Court of Appeals for the Federal Circuit (CAFC), a court parallel to a federal circuit court of appeals (and formerly known as the Court of Customs and Patent Appeals).

§ 16.2   Governance of Exports

Unlike the control of imports, the law regulating exports is briefer and relies on the issuance of extensive regulations. For example, the statutes prohibiting U.S. persons from assisting boycotts against friendly nations fill only a few pages. But the regulations and examples of prohibited and permissible conduct fill many pages in the Code of Federal Regulations. The control of exports, meaning their limitation, quite expectantly creates some conflict by way of the diminished economic benefit to the nation that may be gained from export trade. Indeed, the EAA in its statement of policy indicates that it is only after consideration of the impact of restrictions on the economy that export restrictions are adopted, and only to the extent necessary.[1]

Exports are controlled for three reasons stated in the governing rules—(1) to protect against the drain of scarce materials and reduce inflation from foreign demand, (2) to further U.S. foreign policy and (3) to assure national security.[2] These goals are expressed in the principal export enactment, the Export Administration Act (EAA), and are implemented by means of licensing requirements.[3] But the EAA does not contain many substantive provisions regulating exports. They are con-

§ 16.2

1. 50 U.S.C.A.App. § 2402.

2. 15 C.F.R. § 730.6 Foreign policy has caused the United States to limit exports at great cost both to U.S. companies and to foreign relations. The United States imposed severe export restrictions after the USSR invaded Poland in 1982. The controls limited the sales of U.S. companies' subsidiaries in Europe, and gained the wrath of several European nations. The use of export controls for political ends is discussed briefly in Ralph H. Folsom, Michael Wallace Gordon & John A. Spanogle, International Business Transactions: A Problem–Oriented Coursebook (4th ed. 1999).

3. The EAA of 1979 has been amended several times. It expired in 1994 but has been kept in force ever since by the President declaring a state of emergency under the International Emergency Economic Powers Act (IEEPA). 50 U.S.C.A. §§ 1701–1706. The President is required to report to Congress every six months on the national emergency. The report is more an outline of changes in export rules and actions taken than a disclosure of any conditions which any "reasonable man" might conclude constitute a national emergency.

The Congress and the President have allowed the EAA to expire because of the continuing conflict regarding control over export trade between the Congress and the President. Unhappy with what Congress presents as a new framework, that often grants little discretion to the President, the President may veto the new act and allow the provisions of the old act to remain in force under the International Emergency Economic Powers Act, while waiting for a "better" new law from Congress which does not so severely limit discretionary power of the President to curtail exports to countries for U.S. foreign policy reasons. At the time of writing prospects for a new EAA by early–2001 appeared dim. Legislators annually predict that it will be passed "this year". In addition to the usual debate between Congress and the administration, the business community has been very vocal in assuring that its interests are met. While that mostly means limited controls, it means to some industries protection of scarce local supplies, such as some hardwoods. The debate over encryption has been the most contentious, with numerous new regulations, and more likely to come.

tained in the Export Administration Regulations (EAR).[4] These Regulations, in 15 C.F.R., constitute an extensive set of provisions detailing the governance of exports.

Governing exports does not include taxing them. The Constitution prohibits taxes on exports.[5] In 1995 the CIT held harbor maintenance taxes (for dredging) on exports by sea (0.125% of value) in violation of the Constitution.[6] The tax brings in over $600 million annually (expected to reach $2 billion in 2000) and the court both allowed continued collection and deferred refunds pending a certain appeal.

One of the most significant changes in 1996 was the decision of the President to transfer administration of certain encryption products from the Department of State to the Department of Commerce. The President issued an Executive Order governing the administration of export controls on encryption devices.[7]

The governance of exports in the European Union has yet to be harmonized. It has been extensively discussed—the intention is to establish EU guidelines for the issuance of export licenses. A 1992 Commission proposal would require all member states to jointly approve a list of controlled technologies and destinations that would apply in all EU nations. Obstacles remain, especially the transition period to adapt national rules to the new requirements. EU member states continue to impose separate national restrictions on exports not only to nations outside the EU, but also to other EU nations.

§ 16.3   The Meaning of a "License"

Prior to the 1996 changes, exporters sent items abroad under either a "general" license or a "validated" license. The general license was used for most exports and it did not require prior Department of Commerce approval. When most goods were shipped and a "Shipper's Export Declaration (SED)" was filled out, the SED constituted a general license. Validated licenses were issued upon application to the Department of Commerce.

The new regulations eliminate the terms "general license" and "validated license". "License" now refers to an authorization to export granted by the Department of Commerce. The change is to some degree

4. Changes to the structure of licensing were adopted in 1996, effective March 1997. The new regulations are in 15 C.F.R. 730, et seq. The regulations include a useful part-by-part analysis, at the end of which is a list of subjects. This is followed by the detailed section-by-section provisions.

The new regulations are supposed to be easier to use. They essentially do not require any export license unless a license is required in the regulations. This contrasts with the previous regulations, which deny exports of all listed items unless an export license is obtained. Whether they are truly easier to use will be decided by the users—

U.S. exporters. The regulations consume more than 200 pages of the Federal Register, without including the lengthy Part 774, the Commerce Control List of ECCN numbers. Even before the regulations became effective, an additional 15 pages were issued to amend the License Exception provisions.

5. Art. I, § 9, cl. 5.

6. U.S. Shoe Corp. v. United States, 907 F.Supp. 408, (CIT 1995), affirmed 114 F.3d 1564 (1997), affirmed 523 U.S. 360, 118 S.Ct. 1790, 140 L.Ed.2d 453 (1998).

7. Executive Order, Nov. 15, 1996.

a matter of semantics. General licenses, which were in a sense "self-granted", are abolished in favor of referring to such exports as exports permitted without any license. The new "license" replaces the old "validated license." But much more was accomplished in this complete rearrangement of the regulations. The myriad of "special" licenses has been redone. The EAR is arranged more user-friendly. There are now ten general prohibitions making up Part 736, rather than the previous scattering of the prohibitions throughout the regulations. These prohibitions indicate the circumstances where a license must be obtained. The Country Group listings remain, but better reflect the end of the Cold War, and current foreign policy. The Commerce Control List (CCL) also remains (now Part 774), but is redesigned to better state the reasons for control within each Export Control Classification Number (ECCN). The CCL may be used with the Country Chart to assist in determining whether a license is required for an ECCN to any country.

§ 16.4 Export Administration Regulations

The Export Administration Regulations[1] govern most export activity, including the issuance of licenses. The Regulations include helpful provisions for the exporter, that attempt to explain the regulations in simple terms.

The Regulations introduce the exporter to considerable new terminology.[2] The export of some commodities and technical data is absolutely prohibited, while other commodities are permitted to be exported under a range of lenient to severe restrictions. Special provisions of the EAA apply to further control the proliferation of missiles, and chemical and biological weapons.[3] The EAR has integrated the role of the former Coordinating Committee for Multilateral Export Controls (COCOM), a group of nations which sought to keep sensitive material from communist dominated nations. COCOM was abolished soon after the Soviet Union was dismantled.[4] The United States has enacted the Enhanced Proliferation Control Initiative (EPCI), motivated by the Iraq conflict. This enactment seeks to establish greater control where commodities or technical data are destined for a prohibited nuclear, chemical or biological weapons or missile development use or end user. Considerable emphasis is placed on making the exporter aware of the nature of the buyer and where the items are going.

There is considerable discretion given to the Department of Commerce to allow exports where they are subject to licensing. In addition, certain *items* may be subject to mandatory controls, just as certain *destinations* may be subject to mandatory controls (e.g., a boycott that

---

§ 16.4

1. 15 C.F.R. §§ 730–774. The Department of Commerce publishes a separate edition of the EAR, avoiding the need to have the full C.F.R.

2. Terms are defined in 50 U.S.C.A.App. § 2415, and in 15 C.F.R. § 772.

3. 50 U.S.C.A.App. §§ 2410b and c.

4. COCOM expired in 1994. It has been replaced by the Wassenaar Arrangement, discussed below in § 16.34.

disallows most or all exports). Actually these mandatory controls allow some deviation, usually by the President rather than an agency exercising discretion. Some examples of mandatory controls include the Nuclear Non–Proliferation Act regulations governing exports that have nuclear explosive capability, unprocessed timber under the Forest Resources Conservation and Shortage Relief Act (FRCSRA 1990), oil for purposes of conservation or to establish reserves, and oil from certain locations such as the North Slope of Alaska. Exports are thus subject to a mix of regulations *by* different persons or agencies, *of* different products, *for* different purposes, and *to* different places.

B. DETERMINING WHEN A LICENSE IS NEEDED—THE 29 STEPS

§ 16.5 General Information

Part 730 provides a general introduction to the EAR. It is a most useful place to start for the first time user. This part outlines the scope of the regulations, statutory authority, defines "dual use" exports (generally civil versus military), other agencies which participate in the regulation of exports, extraterritorial application of regulations, purposes of control, and limited situations requiring licenses. But the most useful portion of this part is titled "How to proceed and where to get help".[1] It briefly notes how an exporter proceeds to determine the need for a license, whether items are subject to the EAR, EAR requirements when licenses are required, filing process, clearing shipments with Customs, and the location of such special rules as restrictive trade practices, boycotts, and record keeping. This part also outlines the organization of the Bureau of Export Administration (BXA).[2]

§ 16.6 Steps for Using the Export Administration Regulations

Part 732 includes the 29 steps for using the EAR. They are in sections which include an overview, steps regarding the scope of the EAR, the ten general prohibitions, License Exceptions, Shipper's Export Declaration and other documents and records, and other requirements.

The overview of the steps notes some important questions which the exporter must give thought to, such as—What is the item?, Where is it going?, Who will actually receive and use it?, and What will it be used for?[1] This will help the exporter determine whether the EAR are applicable. The ten General Prohibitions are outlined, which offer a good indication of what is **not** allowed without a license.

If none of the ten General Prohibitions apply, the exporter moves on to steps which discuss the Shipper's Export Declaration filed with

Customs, Destination Control Statements, and record keeping requirements. But if a license is required, the next step is to determine whether an exception is available. Licenses may be available when General Prohibitions One through Three apply, but not when Four through Ten apply.[2]

§ 16.7   Steps One Through Six—Scope of the EAR

The first six steps regarding the scope of the EAR cover (1) items subject to the exclusive jurisdiction of another federal agency; (2) publicly available technology and software; (3) reexport of U.S. origin items; (4) foreign made items incorporating less than a de minimis level of U.S. parts, components and materials; (5) foreign made items incorporating more than a de minimis level of U.S. parts, components and materials, and (6) foreign made items produced with certain U.S. technology for export to specified destinations.[1] This presents a rough outline of whether or not the EAR are applicable.

§ 16.8   Steps Seven Through Nineteen—The General Prohibitions

The next steps are Steps 7 through 19 and stipulate the ten general prohibitions.[1] They must be considered if the first steps suggest the EAR are applicable. General prohibitions One through Three are product controls that require use of the CCL and Country Chart. General Prohibitions Four through Ten include prohibitions on certain activities that are not allowed without BXA authorization.

Step 7 is classification, that requires the exporter to determine the proper CCL entry. It may not be easy, but it is critical and the exporter is held liable for errors in classification. The exporter may ask the BXA to provide assistance and the BXA must do so.[2]

Step 8 is the determination of the country of ultimate destination, usually not a difficult determination.

Step 9 uses the Country Chart and "License Requirements" section of the ECCN to determine whether a license is required under General Prohibitions One, Two or Three to a particular destination. The ECCN will note the reasons for control, such as national security or antiterrorism. Using the Country Chart column identifiers in the ECCN, will show whether an "x" is marked in the cell (box) next to the destination. An "x" indicates a license is required for General Prohibitions One through Three. Where there is an "x" in one or more applicable cells, the exporter may qualify for a License Exception.[3] There may be additional

---

2. There are, however, some exceptions for embargoed destinations (Part 746) and goods subject to short supply controls (Part 754).

§ 16.7

1. 15 C.F.R. § 732.2

§ 16.8

1. 15 C.F.R. § 732.3.

2. If the item is not listed on the CCL, it receives a classification of EAR99. This same "basket" number appears at the end of each category on the CCL.

3. License Exceptions are contained in 15 C.F.R. Part 740. This Part was amended

controls described in Steps 12 through 18. If the export is from the United States, the exporter goes directly to Step 12.

The Country Chart is not used to determine whether a license is required in two instances. First is for items controlled for short supply reasons.[4] Second is where an ECCN contained on the CCL does not identify a Country Chart column identifier. In such instance the ECCN itself notes whether a license is required and for which destinations.

Step 10 includes instructions for foreign made items incorporating U.S. origin items and the de minimis rule. A 10 percent de minimis rule applies for embargoed and terrorist-supporting countries, while a 25 percent rule applies for all other countries. Even though the de minimis rule might allow shipments from the foreign destination, they may not be made if in violation of General Prohibition Seven, governing the proliferation of weapons of mass destruction and missiles.

Step 11 applies to foreign produced direct products, and outlines some considerations when items are produced abroad that would require a license for national security reasons. Important are the country of destination, scope of technology or software used to create the products, and scope of products subject to the prohibition.

Step 12 denies export privileges to certain persons, under General Prohibition Four. This includes a transferee, ultimate end-user, any intermediate consignee, or any other part to a transaction. The exporter should check the Denied Persons List before exporting. No License Exceptions are available, and special BXA permission is rarely given when denied persons are involved.

Step 13, General Prohibition Five, directs the exporter to review the end-uses and end-users prohibited under General Prohibition Five.[5]

Step 14, General Prohibition Six, governs export to embargoed countries and special destinations. If the destination is Bosnia–Herzegovina, Croatia, Cuba, Iran, Iraq, Libya, North Korea, Rwanda or Serbia and Montenegro, Part 746 controls apply. A license is needed (under a License Exception in Part 746) unless the export is technology or software publicly available, or items outside the scope of the EAR.

Step 15 is to consider General Prohibition Seven, the proliferation activity of U.S. persons unrelated to exports and reexports. This is a broad prohibition, extending to items subject to General Prohibitions One through Three, and also to services and dealing in wholly foreign origin items.

Step 16, General Prohibition Eight, applies to shippers and operators of vessels and aircraft to determine the countries where items may not be unladen or shipped in-transit.

in December, 1996. See 61 Fed. Reg. 64272 (Dec. 4, 1996).

4. See 15 C.F.R. Part 754.

5. 15 C.F.R. Part 744.

Step 17 involves General Prohibition Ten, that prohibits the violation of any orders, terms and conditions imposed under the EAR. Terms and conditions are usually contained in a license.

Step 18 is application of the final General Prohibition Ten, which prohibits anyone from proceeding with a transaction when there is knowledge that a violation of the EAR has or is about to occur. It applies to related shipping, financial and other services. The step suggests a review of the license requirements including classification, end-use, end-user, ultimate destination and conduct of U.S. persons, all as noted above in earlier steps. Review policy of the BXA is outlined in Part 742.

Step 19 is the review completion, and awareness of any of the General Prohibitions that may apply to the transaction. If none apply, no license is needed. In such case, the exporter may skip Steps 20 through 26, that apply to license exceptions, and go to the final Steps 27 and 28, governing Shipper's Export Declaration and other documents and record keeping, and other requirements.

If the export is subject to the EAR and to General Prohibitions One through Three, there may be exceptions.[6] Steps 20 through 26 are used when there may be an exception.

§ 16.9 Steps Twenty Through Twenty–Six—Exceptions

Step 20 directs the exporter to determine whether any of the General Prohibitions in § 736.2(b) apply. If none apply, the export may be made without review of the Part 740 License Exceptions.

Step 21, followed if Step 20 does not allow the export with further inquiry, refers the exporter to § 740.2 of the License Exceptions. If any of the restrictions apply, no License Exceptions apply and a license must be obtained.

Step 22, followed if none of the restrictions from the above step apply, directs the exporter to the License Exceptions. Eligibility is based on the item, country of ultimate destination, end-use, end-user, and any special conditions a specific License Exception imposes. More than one License Exception may be available, and the one most favorable may be used.

Step 23 notes that some License Exceptions are limited by country or type of item, referring the exporter to Supplement No. 1 to Part 740. Emphasized is the fact that License Exceptions do not apply to any embargoed destinations.

Step 24 assumes a License Exception has been found, and directs the exporter to proceed with meeting all the terms and conditions of the applicable License Exception.

6. Exceptions may be allowed to General Prohibition Five (end-use, end-user) and are contained in Part 744, or to General Prohibition Six (embargoed countries) and are contained in Part 746.

Step 25 reemphasizes the fact that if there is no applicable License Exception, a license must be obtained before exporting.

Step 26 suggests reviewing the requirements of Part 748 in proceeding with a license application.

§ 16.10 Steps Twenty–Seven Through Twenty–Nine— Shipping Documentation and Records

Steps 27 through 29 apply to an exporter who is preparing the shipping documentation and records of the transaction.

Step 27 outlines the Shipper's Export Declaration,[1] and the use of "NLR" (no license required) for exports not requiring a license. It is used for items not on the CCL (classified EAR99) and for some items listed on the CCL but not requiring a license to all destinations under General Prohibitions One through Three. If exporting under a License Exception, the proper symbol (e.g., LVS, GBS, etc.) must be listed. If exporting under a license the license number is to be listed.

Step 27 is the requirement to list an appropriate Destination Control Statement (DCS) as governed by § 758.6.

Lastly, Step 29 affirms that records must be kept of the transaction as required by Part 762.

Following these steps is Supplement No 1., the BXA's "Know Your Customer" Guidance and Red Flags. This guide lists 12 red flags that are warnings that an unlawful diversion might be planned by the exporter's customer.

C. SCOPE OF THE EXPORT ADMINISTRATIVE REGULATIONS

§ 16.11 Function of the Scope Regulations[1]

This part helps to determine whether items are subject to the EAR.[2] That does not necessarily mean that a license is required, but that the BXA may have some authority, such as in requiring the maintenance of records. There are also definitions of "export" and "reexport", although a comprehensive listing of definitions is in Part 772. This part further includes the de minimis rules, which stipulate percentages where U.S. content is considered too low to bring the item within the EAR.[3]

Where information is published it is generally not within the scope of the EAR,[4] which may extend to information resulting from fundamental research.[5] Other educational information may similarly be exempt.[6]

§ 16.10
1. See § 16.36 infra.

§ 16.11
1. 15 C.F.R. Part 734.
2. 15 C.F.R. §§ 734.2 & 734.3.

3. 15 C.F.R. § 734.4.
4. 15 C.F.R. § 734.7.
5. 15 C.F.R. § 734.8.
6. 15 C.F.R. § 734.9.

This part includes two useful supplements. Supplement No. 1 includes questions and answers regarding technology and software subject to the EAR, and Supplement No. 2 includes instructions on the calculation of values for de minimis rules.

D. GENERAL PROHIBITIONS[1]

§ 16.12 Introduction

The ten General Prohibitions have been discussed above, as they constitute Steps 7 through 19. If an export is subject to the EAR, these general prohibitions, as well as the License Exceptions, must be reviewed to determine if a license is necessary. This part informs the exporter of both the facts that make the proposed transaction subject to the general prohibitions, and the nature of the general prohibitions.

§ 16.13 Determination of the Applicability of the General Prohibitions

Five factors help determine the obligations of the exporter under the ten general prohibitions.[1] They are:

    1. Classification of the item using the CCL.

    2. Destination of the item using the CCL and Country Chart.

    3. End-user referring to a list of persons the exporter may not deal with.[2]

    4. End-use.[3]

    5. Conduct such as contracting, financing and freight forwarding in support of a proliferation project.[4]

The ten general prohibitions follow, with commentary under the following headings:

    1. General Prohibition One—Export and reexport of controlled items to listed countries (Exports and Reexports).

    2. General Prohibition Two—Reexport and export from abroad of foreign-made items incorporating more than a de minimis amount of controlled U.S. content (Parts and Components Reexports).

    3. General Prohibition Three—Reexport and export from abroad of the foreign-produced direct product of U.S. technology and software (Foreign–Produced Direct Product Reexports).

    4. General Prohibition Four—Engaging in actions prohibited by a denial order (Denial Orders).

---

1. 15 C.F.R. Part 736.

§ **16.13**

1. 15 C.F.R. § 736.2.

2. 15 C.F.R. Parts 744 and 764, and § 736.2(b)(4).

3. 15 C.F.R. Part 744 and § 736.2(b)(5).

4. 15 C.F.R. Part 744.

5. General Prohibition Five—Export or reexport to prohibited end-uses or end-users (End–Use End–User).

6. General Prohibition Six—Export or reexport to embargoed destinations (Embargo).

7. General Prohibition Seven—Support of Proliferation Activities (U.S. Person Proliferation Activity).

8. General Prohibition Eight—In transit shipments and items to be unladen from vessels or aircraft (Intransit).

9. General Prohibition Nine—Violation of any order, terms, and conditions (Orders, Terms, and Conditions).

10. General Prohibition Ten—Proceeding with transactions with knowledge that a violation has occurred or is about to occur (Knowledge Violation to Occur).

In preparing these prohibitions, the Commerce Department rejected a number of suggestions to liberalize existing reexport controls, such as to create a separate part for reexports. Reexports create a problem with the nation from which the item may be reexported, which nation may object to any extraterritorial application of the U.S. rules. Some comments noted that the new regulations were intended to be easier to use and less complex than the old, but that the new regulations created a system just as complex.

E. COMMERCE CONTROL LIST OVERVIEW AND THE COUNTRY CHART

§ 16.14 Introduction

The Commerce Control List (CCL—Part 774) is maintained by the BXA. The CCL includes all items (i.e., commodities, software, and technology) subject to BXA controls. The CCL does not include items exclusively governed by other agencies. But where there is shared governance, the CCL will note other agency participation. Knowing the Harmonized Code (customs classification for tariff purposes) Schedule B number does not help to determine whether or not an export license is required. That number is used by the Census Bureau for trade statistics. It is only the ECCN that will indicate whether or not an export license is required.

§ 16.15 The Commerce Control List (CCL)

The CCL is contained in Supplement No. 1 to Part 774. Supplement No. 2 to Part 774 contains the General Technology and Software Notes relevant to entries in the CCL. The CCL basic structure includes the following ten general categories:

0. Nuclear Materials, Facilities and Equipment and Miscellaneous

1. Materials, Chemicals, "Microorganisms," and Toxins

   2. Materials Processing

   3. Electronics

   4. Computers

   5. Telecommunications and Information Security

   6. Lasers and Sensors

   7. Navigation and Avionics

   8. Marine

   9. Propulsion Systems, Space Vehicles and Related Equipment

Within each of the above ten categories are five different groups of items, identified by the letters A through E, as follows:

   A. Equipment, Assemblies and Components

   B. Test, Inspection and Production Equipment

   C. Materials

   D. Software

   E. Technology

To classify an item the exporter determines the general characteristics that will usually be expressed by one of the categories. Having the appropriate category, the next step is to match the characteristics and functions with one of the groups. For example, a common television would be in category 3 and group A. The first digit and letter of the ECCN would thus be 3A.

This is followed by another digit that differentiates individual entries by the types of controls associated with the second digit. The Reasons for Control are as follows:

0. National Security reasons (including Dual Use and International Munitions List) and Items on the NSG Dual Use Annex and Trigger List

1. Missile Technology reasons

2. Nuclear Nonproliferation reasons

3. Chemical & Biological Weapons reasons

9. Anti-terrorism, Crime Control, Regional Stability, Short Supply, UN Sanctions, etc.

There may be more than one reason for control of a particular item. If so the first digit in the above list would appear as the second digit in the ECCN. The third digit in the ECCN reflects the possible unilateral and multilateral controls.

§ 16.16 License Requirements, License Exceptions and List of Items Controlled Sections

Next to each ECCN is a brief description, followed by "License Requirements", "License Exceptions", and "List of Items Controlled" sections.

"License Requirements" identifies all possible Reasons for Control in order of precedence. Items within a particular ECCN number may be controlled for more than one reason. All the possible Reasons for Control are as follows:[1]

AT Anti–Terrorism

CB Chemical & Biological Weapons

CC Crime Control

EI Encryption Items

MT Missile Technology

NS National Security

NP Nuclear Nonproliferation

RS Regional Stability

SS Short Supply

XP Computers

SI Significant Items

The applicable reasons appear in one of two columns in the License Requirements, entitled "Control(s)". The second column, entitled "Country Chart", identifies a column name and number for each applicable Reason for Control (e.g., CB Column 1). Once the exporter has determined that the item is controlled by a specific ECCN, information contained in the "License Requirements" section of the ECCN in combination with the Country Chart will allow a decision regarding the need for a license.

"License Exceptions" is used after it is determined that a license is required. It provides a brief eligibility statement for each ECCN-driven License Exception that may be applicable to the transaction. This is intended to help the exporter decide which ECCN-driven License Exception should be considered before submitting an application.[2] License Exceptions, the subject of Part 740, includes numerous categories. In the interim regulations, several exceptions were "bundled" under the grouping symbol LST (limited value shipments (LVS), shipments to group B countries (GBS), civil end-users (CIV), technology and software under restriction (TSR) and computers (CTP)). But objections by exporters with automated processes, who complained that an additional step was created, resulted in December 1996 changes which dropped the LST, "debundled" the process, putting each exception into its own section. This makes them similar to other separated exceptions (i.e., temporary imports and exports(TMP), servicing and parts replacement(RPL), governments and international organizations(GOV), gift parcels and humanitarian donations(GFT),[3] some technology and soft-

§ 16.16
1. 15 C.F.R. § 738.2(d)(2)(i).
2. 15 C.F.R. § 738.2(d)(2)(ii).

3. Supplement No. 2 to Part 740 lists items which may be donated to meet basic needs under this exception.

ware(TSU), baggage(BAG), aircraft and vessels(AVS) and additional permissive reexports(APR)). Part 740 is an extensive and important part of the EAR. It is followed by Supplement No. 1 to Part 740, which is the Country Group listing countries under A,B,D, or E, allowing the above exceptions to be limited to certain country groups.

"List of Items Controlled" defines the unit of measure applicable to the entry, may add definitions, notes related controls by other agencies or departments, and lists all items controlled by an entry.

§ 16.17 The Commerce Country Chart

The Country Chart is essential in determining the need for a license It is useful in all cases except where short-supply reasons apply, or where there are unique entries.[1] The Country Chart is Supplement No. 1 to Part 738, and over several pages lists countries alphabetically. Territories, possessions and departments are not listed, but are subject to the same rules as the governing country. On the right of the listed countries are the numerous columns identifying the various Reasons for Control. There may be one, two or three columns under a particular Reason for Control. They correlate to references in the License Requirements section of the applicable ECCN. There may be an "x" in one or more of the cells. Where it appears in more than one cell, there will be multiple reviews.

§ 16.18 Determining the Need for a License[1]

Having determined that the item to be exported is controlled by a specific ECCN number, the exporter uses information in the "License Requirements" section of the ECCN entry in combination with the Country Chart. The need for a license is thus determined. Using the CCL "Controls" the exporter learns the reasons for control. Turning to the Country Chart and finding the appropriate country and the heading(s) for the reason(s), and with the column identifiers from the ECCN, the exporter looks for an "x". If found in the cell on the Country Chart, the exporter knows a license is required. A license application must be submitted unless a License Exception applies. Turning to the License Exceptions in the ECCN entry list, if a "yes" appears a further search of Part 740 will disclose whether an exception is available. Where there is no "x" in the cell on the Country Chart, a license is not required for control and destination, but one or more of General Prohibitions Four through Ten may prohibit the export. One can thus go to Parts 758 and 762 for information on export clearance procedures and record keeping.

§ 16.17   § 16.18

1. 15 C.F.R. § 738.3   1. 15 C.F.R. § 738.4.

F. SPECIAL CONTROLS

§ 16.19 Country Control List Based Controls[1]

This part provides the reasons for the controls reflected in the Country Chart in Supplement No. 1 to Part 738. Furthermore, it includes licensing requirements and policies for such items as are not in the Country Chart as specially designed implements of torture, high performance computers and communications intercepting devices.

This part includes regulations governing proliferation of chemical and biological weapons, nuclear nonproliferation, national security, missile technology, regional stability, crime control and anti-terrorism. There are numerous special provisions dealing with countries considered unstable and especially troublesome to U.S. interests. Formerly known as Country Z nations, they are now called Country Group E nations.[2] The special provisions are often quite restrictive and include specific policy considerations to be used when reviewing license applications.

§ 16.20 End–User and End–Use Based Controls[1]

This part includes prohibitions against exports to certain end-users and end-uses. It includes restrictions on certain nuclear, missile, chemical and biological and maritime nuclear propulsion end-uses, and on certain activities of U.S. persons, exports to and for the use of certain vessels or aircraft, and certain exports to all countries for Libyan aircraft. For the most part, there are no license exceptions for the covered exports.

§ 16.21 Embargoes and Other Special Controls[1]

This part implements broad based controls, including comprehensive controls applying to Cuba, Libya, North Korea, Iran and Iraq, and special controls applying to Rwanda. The comprehensive controls include all BXA licensing requirements, licensing policies and license exceptions for those countries subject to general embargoes. The second category, currently applicable only to Rwanda, are controls set forth in the Country Chart in part 738.

A third coverage of this part is to provide descriptions of controls maintained by the Office of Foreign Assets Control in the Treasury Department and the Office of Defense Trade Controls in the Department of State.[2] It sets forth the allocation of licensing responsibilities between the BXA and these other agencies.

§ 16.19

1. 15 C.F.R. Part 742.

2. 15 C.F.R. Supplement No. 1 to Part 740. In early 1999 they included Angola, Bosnia & Herzegovina, Cuba, Iraq, North Korea, Libya and Rwanda.

§ 16.20

1. 15 C.F.R. Part 744.

§ 16.21

1. 15 C.F.R. Part 746.

2. This includes U.N. arms embargoes administered by the Department of State.

§ 16.22 Short Supply Controls[1]

Occasionally items are in short supply in the United States and special controls apply. They are not based on the more common foreign policy, national security or nonproliferation grounds. Part 754 implements rules governing some specific short supply items, such as crude oil, other petroleum products, unprocessed western red cedar, and horses. The regulations also allow for the registration of agricultural commodities for exemption from short supply controls.

G. SPECIAL COMPREHENSIVE LICENSE[1]

§ 16.23 Consolidation of Previous Separate Licenses

Under the previous regulations, a number of special licenses were available. The new Special Comprehensive License (SCL) combines the earlier Project, Distribution, Service Supply, Service Facilities, Aircraft and Vessel Repair Station Procedure, and Special Chemical Licenses.

§ 16.24 Eligible Activities, Items and Countries

Under the SCL, the BXA may authorize various activities, such as service activities or distribution activities.[1] A limited number of items may be eligible for the SCL,[2] and all except a few countries are classified as eligible.[3]

§ 16.25 Procedures for Obtaining a SCL

The regulations outline three steps for obtaining the SCL, and note the appropriate BXA forms for different variations of the license, such as a multipurpose application, or end user appendix.[1] Five Supplements are included providing instructions on filling out the forms.

H. APPLICATION FOR A LICENSE AND ADVISORY OPINIONS

§ 16.26 The Application Procedure

Application for a license is made on Form BXA–748P.[1] It may be made in writing or electronically. Because the applicant may not know the correct Export Control Classification Number (ECCN), BXA may be asked to provide the correct number in a "Classification Request." BXA will advise whether a license is required, and if required whether it is likely to be granted.

§ 16.22
1. 15 C.F.R. Part 754.
1. 15 C.F.R. Part 752.

§ 16.24
1. 15 C.F.R. § 752.2.
2. 15 C.F.R. § 752.3.

3. 15 C.F.R. § 752.4.

§ 16.25
1. 15 C.F.R. § 752.5.

§ 16.26
1. 15 C.F.R. § 748.1.

§ 16.27 Advisory Opinions

A party who wishes to know whether a license is required may obtain an Advisory Opinion from the BXA. The regulations outline what should be included in the request.[1] Receipt of an opinion does not mean the subsequent application will be granted by the BXA, opinions are not binding. But the BXA is likely to help the applicant in the preparation of an application which will meet the Advisory Opinion's requirements.

An applicant may wish to avoid asking for an Advisory Opinion for fear that the opinion will be unfavorable. But if an export is made without an opinion and is in violation of the law, the sanctions may be severe.[2] Certainly, obtaining an unfavorable opinion and then exporting without a license creates a rather clear case of intent to disregard the law. But the Advisory Opinion is a good route to follow. If an unfavorable opinion is received, the BXA may explain what is required to obtain permission, unless the case is a clear one where no exports are permitted.

"Unique" license application requirements apply for certain items or types of transactions, ranging from medicines to ship stores.[3] In such cases additional requirements may apply.

Support documents may be required along with an application.[4] Numerous countries are exempt from the need of support documents, mostly (1) any exports or reexports in the Western Hemisphere, (2) sales to government purchasers, and licenses submitted under special procedures, such as by A.I.D., or under the Special Comprehensive License procedure. When support documentation is required, the required data is to gain information about the disposition of the items, and to answer questions about national security controls and certain destinations. The transaction may require an End–User Certificate, or a Statement of Ultimate Consignee and Purchaser.[5]

I.   REVIEW OF APPLICATIONS

§ 16.28 Issuance and/or Denial of Applications[1]

Part 750 describes the BXA's process for reviewing a license application, including processing times, denials, revocations, issuance, duplicates, transfers, and shipping tolerances on approved licenses. The part also includes information on processing Advisory Opinion requests.

§ 16.27

1. 15 C.F.R. § 748.3.

2. Persons convicted of a violation of any statute specified in § 11(h) of the EAA may not apply for any export license for ten years. 15 C.F.R. § 748.4(c).

3. 15 C.F.R. § 748.8.

4. 15 C.F.R. § 748.9.

5. See also 15 C.F.R. § 748.10–13, and Supplements.

§ 16.28

1. 15 C.F.R. Part 750.

§ 16.29   Review by BXA and Other Departments or Agencies

The BXA undertakes a complete review of the application, including an analysis of the license and support documentation, plus a consideration of the reliability of each party to the transaction, including any intelligence information. The Departments of Defense, Energy, State and the Arms Control and Disarmament Agency may also have review authority. Furthermore, the BXA may request review by other departments or agencies, which may agree to review, or waive review.

If there are disputes between or among agencies within the U.S. government,[1] they are dealt with by various internal groups initially. Appeals are made to the Export Administration Review Board, chaired by the Secretary of Commerce. The Secretary may discuss the most difficult cases with the Secretaries of Defense, State or Energy. Final Review goes to the President.

There has been a continuing dispute between Commerce and State over control of technology that seems to fall within the jurisdiction of each department. While the Arms Export Control Act gives State exclusive authority to issue jurisdiction determinations, Commerce has attempted to obtain concurrent authority to issue commodity jurisdiction determinations. Hearings were held in 1995 by the Senate Armed Services Committee after complaints that Commerce had issued export licenses for stealth technology that was under the jurisdiction of State. State intervened to stop the shipments, determined that they had jurisdiction, and denied the license. This kind of dispute has made it difficult to reach agreement on a new Export Administration Act. With proposals to abolish Commerce and transfer much of its export jurisdiction to State, the issue could become moot. There is little likelihood that State will agree to the transfer of any authority to Commerce.

Delay has been used by the government, especially by the Department of Defense, as a means of discouraging exports which might be permissible, but to which the Department objects. The *Daedalus Enterprises, Inc. v. Baldrige* case is an example.[2] Twenty-nine months after the filing of an application, the Department of Commerce had not reached a decision. The company had to seek a court order that the Secretary comply with the statutory timetable. There is little a company can do. It may not export the goods when the time period has expired if no response has been made by the government. It must go to court at each stage when the government fails to comply with the statute. Fortunately, the *Daedalus* case is an exception, and this kind of delay has been much diminished. The filing process is considerably improved.

§ 16.29

1. Where there is initial disagreement, some 85% are settled by informal discussion.

2. 563 F.Supp. 1345 (D.D.C.1983).

While there may be turf conflicts, the President in 1996 made a major transfer of authority over encryption devices from the Department of State to the Department of Commerce.

§ 16.30   Timetable for Application Review

The BXA is required to resolve all applications, or refer them to the President, within 90 calendar days from the date of registration by the BXA. That is the date the BXA enters the application into the electronic license processing system.[1] Where there are deficiencies, the BXA tries to contact the applicant to obtain needed information. If no contact is made, the license is returned with notations of the deficiencies. This may cause a suspension in the processing time. If another department or agency is involved, or if government-to-government assurances or consultations are involved, there are additional time requirements for making requests and analyzing their results. When certain countries are involved, such as Congressional designated terrorist supporting nations, Congress may have to be notified, delaying the application for another 60 days. The status of an application may be learned by contacting the BXA.[2]

§ 16.31   Issuance of a License[1]

A license is issued for a transaction, or series of transactions. The application may be approved in whole or in part. A license number is issued and a validation date. The license number must be used when preparing a Shipper's Export Declaration (SED), and in discussing the license with the Department of Commerce. Nonmaterial changes may be made without obtaining a "Replacement" license.

§ 16.32   Revocation or Suspension of a License[1]

All licenses may be revised, suspended, or revoked. This may occur without notice when the BXA learns that the EAR have been violated or are about to be violated. The exporter may have to stop a shipment about to be made, or if possible one that is already en route. When revocation or suspension occurs, the exporter is required to return the license to the BXA.

§ 16.33   Appeals[1]

Appeals from actions taken under the EAA or the EAR by the BXA are allowed for most actions.[2] There is an internal appeal process prior to appealing to the federal courts.

§ 16.30

1. 15 C.F.R. § 750.4.

2. See 15 C.F.R. § 750.5(a) for current telephone numbers.

§ 16.31

1. 15 C.F.R. § 750.7.

§ 16.32

1. 15 C.F.R. § 750.8.

§ 16.33

1. 15 C.F.R. Part 756.

2. 15 C.F.R. § 756.1.

§ 16.34   Review of Export Applications by International Agencies

In December, 1995, 28 nations,[1] including the United States, agreed to establish a new export control regime which would assume some of the functions of the expired COCOM. The Wassenaar Arrangement on Export Controls for Conventional Arms and Dual–Use Goods and Technologies (the organizational meeting was in Wassenaar, the Netherlands) fell short of U.S. expectations, not containing a requirement of prior notification of sales by one country to other countries in the group. A second concern is the lack of agreement on prohibiting dual-use goods and conventional weapons to civilian as well as military end-users in such nations as Iran, Iraq, Libya and North Korea. An additional concern is the lack of transparency in exchanging information on exports of dual use goods and conventional arms. The Wassenaar Arrangement established its secretariat in Vienna.

The Arrangement includes reporting requirements. The United States has sought compliance by amending several EAR processes to conform to the Wassenaar Arrangement, Annex 1 (Sensitive List) and Annex 2 (Very Sensitive List) requirements.

J.   EXPORT CLEARANCE REQUIREMENTS

§ 16.35   Responsibilities

The exporter is responsible for following the regulations that govern carrying out the export. This is so whether a license is issued or the exporter relies on a License Exception. The most important responsibility is the proper preparation of the Shipper's Export Declaration (SED).[1]

§ 16.36   Shipper's Export Declaration (SED)

The SED is a statement to the U.S. government.[1] It is used for gathering information to prepare trade statistics. Most exports require an SED, but most to Canada do not. Limited value (not over $500) mail shipments do not require an SED.

As many as one-half the SEDs contain errors of omission or commission, according to the Bureau of Census and U.S. Customs Service. The two organizations have compared SEDs with outboard vessel manifests and discovered numerous inaccuracies in the vessel manifests as well as the SEDs. Cargo is often manifested not on the vessel actually carrying the goods, but on the manifest of a later departing vessel. The reason is

§ 16.34

1. Australia, Austria, Belgium, Canada, the Czech Republic, Denmark, Finland, France, Germany, Greece, Hungary, Iceland, Italy, Japan, Luxembourg, the Netherlands, New Zealand, Norway, Poland, Portugal, the Russian Federation, the Slovak Republic, Spain, Sweden, Switzerland, Turkey, the United Kingdom, and the United States. Several other nations have since joined.

§ 16.35

1. 15 C.F.R. § 758.3.

§ 16.36

1. 15 C.F.R. § 758.3.

the failure of exporters (and forwarders) to supply SEDs with complete and accurate information when the goods are shipped. This causes difficulties for Customs in detecting export law violations, and creates inaccurate trade statistics. The usual fine is up to $1,000, but sometimes shipments are detained. Unless voluntary compliance improves, Customs may delay or detain an increasing number of shipments unless SEDs are presented with complete and accurate information.

The Commerce Department conducts audits of SEDs to disclose violations of the export laws. The Customs Service screens SEDs and compares commodities and values. An internal compliance program is a common procedure within companies selling abroad to assure SEDs are proper. A single program is often useful to assure compliance with general export laws, antiboycott laws, specific country prohibitions (Cuba, Libya, etc.) and the Foreign Corrupt Practices Act.

K. ENFORCEMENT

§ 16.37 Fines, Suspensions and Revocation of Export Authority

Some means of enforcement is necessary to assure compliance with rules. The export laws and regulations are no exception. Violation of laws and regulations governing exports brings into play both the basic law and the regulations. The Export Administrative Act contains provisions governing violations of the EAA and EAR.[1] The Export Administrative Regulations contain supplementary provisions.[2]

The general sanction for violations of the export laws, where the conduct was entered into *knowingly,* is a fine of the higher of $50,000 or five times the value of the exports.[3] This can obviously be *very* substantial.[4]

Willful violations, with knowledge that the commodities or technology will be used to benefit, or are destined for, a controlled country, may result in a fine for business entities of the higher of $1 million or five times the value of the exports.[5] For individuals who engage in such willful violations the fine is $250,000 and/or 10 years imprisonment. This provision covers misuse of licenses. Cases involving violations of the licensing requirements tend to be quite complex.[6]

If the party exported to a controlled country commodities or technology under a license with knowledge that the commodities or technology were being used for military or intelligence gathering purposes, and willfully fails to report this use, the business entity fine is the same as

§ 16.37

1. 50 U.S.C.A.App. § 2410.

2. 15 C.F.R. Part 764.

3. 50 U.S.C.A. App. § 2410(a).

4. See United States v. Ortiz de Zevallos, 748 F.Supp. 1569, 1573 (S.D.Fla.1990),

judgment reversed 994 F.2d 1526 (11th Cir. 1993).

5. 50 U.S.C.A. App. § 2410(b)(1).

6. United States v. Pervez, 871 F.2d 310 (3d Cir.1989); *cert. denied* 492 U.S. 925, 109 S.Ct. 3258, 106 L.Ed.2d 603 (1989).

above, the higher of $1 million or five times the value of the exports, but for the individual the imprisonment drops to five years, with the fine remaining the same, $250,000.[7]

Even possession of goods or technology either with the intent to export in violation of the law, or knowing that the goods might be so exported, can result in a fine.

Perhaps the most severe statutory penalty in the EAA is in the civil penalty section. The Department of Commerce may impose a fine of $10,000 for violations (in certain cases up to $100,000), and they may *suspend or revoke the authority to export.*[8] This is a most severe sanction, used only in extreme cases. It was used in the Toshiba dispute, where Toshiba (Japan) and Köngsberg (Norway) enterprises sold the Soviet Union technology allegedly useful for developing submarine propellers which would be sufficiently silent to avoid detection.[9] The result was enactment of the Multilateral Export Control Enhancements Act in 1988,[10] amending the EAA and providing trade prohibition sanctions for two to five years.[11] These sanctions are applied whether or not the other nations take action against their companies.

The EAR repeat and expand upon these statutory sanctions. They further add provisions dealing with "causing, aiding, or abetting" a violation,[12] and "solicitation and attempt", and "conspiracy."[13] Further details are provided addressing misrepresentation and concealment of facts, or evasion,[14] failing to comply with reporting and record keeping requirements',[15] alterations of documents,[16] and acting contrary to the terms of a denial order.[17]

The political nature of export controls is emphasized by judicial refusal to agree to a settlement negotiated between a company accused of violations of the export laws and the Justice Department. In one instance a bargained for $1 million fine was rejected by the court, which imposed a $3 million fine.[18]

§ 16.38 Administrative Proceedings

Administrative procedures which supplement the Administrative

7. 50 U.S.C.A. App. § 2410(b)(2).

8. 50 U.S.C.A. § 2410(c).

9. The case is discussed briefly in Ralph H. Folsom, Michael Wallace Gordon & John A. Spanogle, Jr., International Business Transactions: A Problem–Oriented Course-book 632 (4th ed. 1999). See also Robert van den Hoven van Genderen, Cooperation on Export Control Between the United States and Europe: A Cradle of Conflict in Technology Transfer? 14 N.C.J.Int'l L. & Com.Reg. 391 (1989).

10. It was part of the 1988 Omnibus Trade and Competitiveness Act. See 50 U.S.C.A.App. § 2410a.

11. 50 U.S.C.A.App. § 2410a.

12. 15 C.F.R. § 764(2)(b).

13. 15 C.F.R. § 764(2)(c) & (d).

14. 15 C.F.R. § 764.2(g) & (h).

15. 15 C.F.R. § 764.2(i).

16. 15 C.F.R. § 764.2(j).

17. 15 C.F.R. § 764.2(k).

18. United States v. Datasaab Contracting A.B., (D.D.C.Criminal No. § 84–00130, 4–27–84).

Procedures Act, are the subject of a separate Part of the EAA and EAR.[1] They provide the framework for proceedings dealing largely with denial of export privileges and civil penalties. Appeals are the subject of several parts of the regulations.[2]

§ 16.39 Denial Orders

The denial of export rights occurs principally either as an administrative sanction for violation of the EAR;[1] or as a temporary measure when there is evidence of an imminent violation of the EAR.[2]

A denial order prohibits the party from any exports, unless there are exceptions in the order. The denial order states the extent to which exports are restricted. Because all denial orders are not the same, it is important to read carefully any specific denial order to determine the extent of the denial.

The denial order also affects persons dealing with the denied party.[3] The denied party may not be part of a transaction nor receive any benefit from a transaction. What are subject to regulation are essentially items of U.S. origin, or foreign items which require reexport permission. A person who deals with a denied party is not innocent if there is no knowledge of the denial status; everyone is responsible for knowing that any person with whom they engage in transactions is *not* on the denial list.

Licensed items to be shipped to a denied party may place the exporter at risk. The denial order must be checked to determine the extent of the loss of export privileges *if* the sale to the denied party is a product to be reexported, or it releases controlled technical data to a denied foreign national. A person may buy products from a denied party in the United States, however, unless the intention is to subsequently export the product, which would give a "benefit" to the denied party. A transaction within a foreign country may be prohibited, as the foreign recipient of U.S. origin items may not sell them to a denied party even if the sale occurs within the foreign nation.[4] This purportedly applies whether the foreign firm is a U.S. subsidiary or not.

§ 16.38

1. 50 U.S.C.A.App. § 2412; 15 C.F.R. Parts 756, 764, and 766. One court has held that attorneys' fees of a prevailing defendant are not allowable under § 2412, because Congress did not make the equal Access to Justice Act part of the EAA. See Dart v. United States, 961 F.2d 284 (D.C.Cir.1992).

2. 15 C.F.R. Part 766.21. See Iran Air v. Kugelman, 996 F.2d 1253 (D.C.Cir.1993).

§ 16.39

1. 15 C.F.R. § 764.3(a)(2).

2. 15 C.F.R. § 766.23.

3. It could even limit employment of a denied party, to the extent that the party could not engage in transactions subject to the EAR.

4. This is not likely to be acceptable to the foreign country, which is likely to consider the prohibition an unreasonable extension of United States laws into its territory. A foreign court might order the transaction to take place.

Selected Bibliography

Linda Andros, Chemical Weapons Proliferation: Extraterritorial Jurisdiction and United States Export Controls: When Too Much Is Not Enough, 13 N.Y.L.Sch.J.Int'l & Comp.L. 257 (1992).

Joseph I. Burkemper, Export Verboten: Export Controls in the United States and Germany, 67 So.Cal.L.R. 149 (1993).

Carlson, Corporate Counsel's Guide to Records Retention Under the Export Control Laws, 5 Int'l Q. 162 (1993).

Carlson, Compliance with U.S. Export Control Laws, 9 Corp. Counsel's Q. 26 (1993).

Department of Commerce BXA website—www.bxa.doc.gov. (listing new cases of violations of export laws)

Export Administration Act, 74 Proc.Am.Soc'y Int'l L. 82 (1980).

Export Management System Guidelines, U.S. Department of Commerce, Bureau of Export Administration (Sept. 1992).

Tom Harris, The Extraterritorial Application of U.S. Export Controls: A British Perspective, 19 N.Y.U.J.Int'l L. & Pol. 959 (1987).

Homer E. Moyer, et al., Law and Policy of Export Controls (ABA 1994).

The OEL Insider, monthly newsletter from the Bureau of Export Administration of the Department of Commerce.

Practicing Law Institute, Coping with U.S. Export Controls (1998).

Peter Swan, A Road Map to Understanding Export Controls: National Security in a Changing Global Environment, 30 Am.Bus.L.J. 607 (1993).

Chapter 17

THE FOREIGN CORRUPT PRACTICES ACT AND ILLEGAL PAYMENTS ABROAD

Table of Sections

A. INTRODUCTION

B. SCOPE OF THE FCPA

C. ACCOUNTING STANDARDS

D. PERSONS SUBJECT TO THE FCPA

E. THE ACT OF OFFERING, PROMISING OR GIVING CORRUPTLY

F. PROHIBITED PERSONS (RECIPIENTS) AND PURPOSES

A. INTRODUCTION

§ 17.1 Foreign Policy–Based Laws—The Antiboycott Laws and the FCPA

Two special sets of laws which mainly affect exports (and foreign investments) have been enacted to address specific foreign policy issues. First, the antiboycott laws and regulations that are discussed in the following chapter were enacted to reduce United States participation in the Arab nations' boycott of Israel. Second, the Foreign Corrupt Practices Act of 1977 (FCPA) was enacted to reduce United States participation in making certain payments or giving of items of value to foreign government officials, or to agents who would pass them on to foreign government officials, when done in an attempt to influence government decisions.

These are two examples of laws enacted to achieve political, as opposed to international trade, goals. The antiboycott laws arose from the increasingly intrusive boycott of Israel by the Arab nations. These laws address the political relationships with Israel and the Arab nations, and the intention of the U.S. government to prevent other nations (i.e., Arab) from using U.S. persons to carry out foreign political goals (i.e., the demise of Israel).[1] The Foreign Corrupt Practices Act also sought to achieve political goals by preventing U.S. persons from making payments to officials abroad which might destabilize foreign policy relationships between the foreign nation and the United States. Payments which caused friendly governments to fall were not deemed to be in the best interests of the United States. Had it not been for the Watergate investigations, which disclosed payments made abroad, there might never have been a FCPA.

§ 17.2 History of the FCPA

The FCPA resulted from disclosures made to the Special Investigator of the Watergate investigations that many U.S. corporations had made payments to foreign officials to influence official government decisions affecting the companies. The FCPA is a response to real and perceived harm to U.S. foreign relations with important, developed friendly nations, and the interest of the United States to prevent U.S. persons from making payments which embarrass the United States in conducting foreign policy.[1]

§ 17.1

1. The law nowhere mentions the words "Arab" or "Israel", but applies generally to boycotts against nations friendly to the United States.

§ 17.2

1. There was also a more general distrust of business during the Carter Administration. All was not attributable to the President; Senator Frank Church and others in Congress appeared to view multinational corporations as inherently evil, and the FCPA as a law necessary to govern their immoral behavior.

The Securities and Exchange Commission's investigations in the mid–1970s commenced after the first disclosures by the Watergate Special Investigator. The investigations disclosed a large number of payments by U.S. corporations to foreign officials. The response by Congress to these disclosures was far more rapid than it had been when the Arab boycott had become known. There were in Congress a number of members outspokenly opposed to a litany of alleged abuses perpetrated by multinational corporations in developing nations.[2] The vigor with which some entities, such as the Senate Subcommittee on Multinational Corporations, pursued the issue of payments abroad, itself threatened foreign relations. Names of alleged recipients were disclosed, causing considerable embarrassment (Prince Bernard of the Netherlands), and even withdrawal or removal from office (Prime Minister Tanaka of Japan[3]), of national leaders. Ultimately, many consent agreements were concluded between the U.S. government and U.S. companies charged with making questionable payments. The agreements usually provided that names of foreign officials who received payments would be held confidential if the companies would disclose the payments. Considerable debate ensued in the press, generally attacking the U.S. companies and including little about the way business was conducted in many other nations, where bribes were not only commonplace but a precondition to doing business. There were legitimate concerns that several large U.S. corporations' payments had been extremely harmful to U.S. foreign relations. Some new legislation was inevitable. Morality was at stake. Many foreign observers, especially from other major exporting nations, did not object to the proposed legislation. Preventing U.S. persons from making such payments would give foreign businesses a competitive advantage. Some foreign observers wondered why Americans needed to make such public disclosure of their moments of transgression. The inevitable legislation occurred in 1977 with the enactment of the FCPA.[4] It has had two principal amendments: in 1988 and 1998.

§ 17.3   Amendments in 1988

The FCPA was first amended in 1988.[1] The amendments removed some of the strictness of the initial act. The level of conduct required to violate the Act was altered in favor of U.S. business by substantial elimination of the "reason to know" standard when payments made to agents might be passed on to foreign officials. The amendment requires that payments to agents must have been knowingly made, and includes a definition of such knowledge. One leading proponent of the original

---

2. It was not payments made to officials in small developing nations, such as Honduras, which were as much concern as those to officials in major trading nations, such as Japan, Italy and the Netherlands.

3. Lockheed was alleged to have paid $1.4 million to Prime Minister Tanaka, which led to his removal and imprisonment. See 134 Cong. Rec. S9617–18 (July 14,

1988)(quoting statement of Senator Proxmire).

4. Pub.L. 95–213, 91 Stat. 1494, Dec. 19, 1977 (amending the Securities Exchange Act of 1934, 15 U.S.C.A. §§ 78q(b), 78dd, 78ff(a)).

§ 17.3

1. 15 U.S.C.A. §§ 78q(b), 78dd, 78ff(a).

provision in the Senate was so incensed at the change that he suggested that the new loophole established by the amendment was "big enough to fly a Lockheed through."[2]

§ 17.4 Amendments in 1998

The FCPA was again amended in 1998, in order to comply with U.S. obligations arising from the signing of the OECD Convention on Combating Bribery of Foreign Officials in International Business Transactions. The Convention was concluded in Paris in late 1997. The U.S. Congress adopted amendments to the FCPA to bring the FCPA into line with the new Convention.[1] The Convention included language, added to the FCPA, making it unlawful to make payments to gain "any improper advantage" in order to obtain or renew business. The FCPA was further amended to expand its scope to cover prohibited acts by "any person." The FCPA had only covered issuers with securities registered with the SEC and "domestic concerns." Only certain U.S. persons were covered. There must also have been some use of the mails or any means or instrumentality of interstate commerce. The 1998 amendments make very significant additions as to whom is covered and add an alternate jurisdiction provision. Domestic concerns other than issuers and "other" persons are now included, the latter making the FCPA cover all *foreign* natural and legal persons who commit acts while in the United States.[2] They do not have to meet the "use of the mails or any means or instrumentality of interstate commerce" jurisdictional mandate.[3] The amendments also reach payments by U.S. businesses and persons taking place wholly outside the United States, and payments to officials of international agencies. Finally, penalties for non-U.S. citizen employees and agents of U.S. employers and principals, previously limited to civil sanctions, now include the same criminal sanctions as for U.S. citizen employees and agents.

§ 17.5 Responses From Other Nations

There was an outcry in the 1970s by the press within the United States and abroad about the disclosed payments made by U.S. corporations. But there was almost no legislative response from other nations individually,[1] and only a very modest response internationally.[2] The United States thus stood nearly alone in responding to the general condemnation of payments to foreign officials by enacting the FCPA.

2. Lockheed Aircraft Corp. was one of the corporations involved in the investigations in the mid–1970s. It was alleged to have made payments to Prime Minister Tanaka in Japan and to a member of the royal family in the Netherlands.

§ 17.4

1. Pub.L. 105–366, Nov 10, 1998 (International Anti-bribery & Fair Competition Act).

2. 15 U.S.C.A. §§ 78dd–2, 78dd–3.

3. 15 U.S.C.A. § 78dd–1(g).

§ 17.5

1. Swedish law provides for criminal sanctions. See Michael Bogdan, International Trade and the New Swedish Provision on Corruption, 27 Am.J.Comp.L. 665 (1979).

2. The very modest response of the United Nations is discussed below.

Many U.S. businesses objected to the United States adopting a law prohibiting foreign payments. These businesses had to compete abroad for contracts with enterprises from nations which had no such laws, and which in some cases, even allowed foreign bribes to be considered ordinary and necessary business expenses which received tax deductions. The FCPA was criticized severely by many in the U.S. business community. When the FCPA was first enacted the U.S. government denied that U.S. businesses would suffer. But that view changed as other nations were urged but failed to adopt similar laws.[3] One argument in favor of the law was that foreign officials would become aware that they should not talk about payments to U.S. business persons, since such payments were prohibited. But that presumes a more perfect world than what exists. Most observers believe that payments to foreign officials have continued, but are made with much greater care and with less of a paper trail than before.

Bribery in some nations has reached epidemic proportions. A UK organization, Control Risks, suggests three classes of corruption. First is the payment of bribes to officials and businesses for favorable treatment. Second is nepotism carried to a level of domination of business by family and clan interests. Third is the evolution of corruption into organized crime, with the participation of officials at the highest levels of government. This last class seems the case with Russia, creating a potentially serious risk of extortion and kidnaping to all persons transacting business in the country.[4] Recent disclosures of corruption in China appear to involve government officials, but perhaps without the participation of organized crime. The Chinese People's Procuratorate reported that in the first half of 1996, 34,070 cases of economic crimes (bribes, embezzlement, graft, etc.) were reported involving more than 7,000 officials, including 3,017 managers of state owned industries and 2,141 involved with banking and negotiable securities.

Following the conclusion of the OECD Convention in 1997, several nations have adopted domestic antibribery laws. But as of February 2000, the number is disappointing to the Convention's advocates. In the first year of the Convention, only 12 of 34 signatories enacted domestic laws to implement the Convention. Thirteen signatories had not yet ratified the Convention, including France and six other EU members. The European Union's foot-dragging may be related to the EU Commission's internal corruption disclosures in March 1999. Japan, contrastingly, has taken the bribery issue seriously. Japan's Ministry of International Trade and Industry (MITI) began in 1997 to adopt measures consistent with the OECD guidelines. Canada enacted an antibribery law in February 1999, which adopted the OECD recommendation to

3. The U.S. Undersecretary of State for Economic, Business and Agricultural Affairs stated in early 2000 that he estimated that U.S. businesses lost tens of billions of dollars in international contracts because of bribery.

4. An Assessment of Prospects for U.S. Assistance to Support the Rule of Law in Russia, Global Studies Research Program, University of Wisconsin–Madison 57 (Jan. 3, 1994).

prohibit tax deductions for bribes.[5] The Canadian law provides for significant fines and jail sentences.

B. SCOPE OF THE FCPA

§ 17.6 Definitional Challenges

One difficulty with the FCPA is defining what constitutes a wrongful payment. Because the payment is made to a foreign official, cultural standards of that official's nation may affect the payment. Conflicts of interest by government officials are governed by very different notions in each countries. While apparently no foreign country has written laws permitting foreign officials to accept bribes to influence their conduct, the "operational code" or unwritten law of many countries makes that very conduct commonplace. The FCPA imposes a U.S. ethic on conduct in the United States and abroad by U.S. persons, and to conduct within the United States by foreign persons. But the FCPA does not prohibit bribes qua bribes: it prohibits only actions which violate the express language of the Act.

§ 17.7 Exempting Minor Payments

In defining what conduct would violate the FCPA it was acknowledged in considering the legislation that certain minor payments to minor foreign officials for minor activities should not be condemned. But how to write such law? The original act adopted language defining "foreign official" so as to exclude foreign employees "whose duties are essentially ministerial or clerical."[1] But the 1988 amendments altered this to specifically exclude acts which were "routine government action."[2] Because there have been only a few court decisions interpreting the language of the FCPA, there is little judicial assistance available to guide one's understanding of the meaning of this language. The definitions in the amended law are nevertheless useful, in spite of their limited meaning.

§ 17.8 Who Is Covered?

In addition to limiting prohibited payments to certain kinds of payments, the drafters of the Act also had to consider the scope of coverage regarding who would fall within the prohibitions of the Act. That meant both which persons would be subject to an action for making prohibited payments, and which persons abroad were to be the recipients of the payments in order to be unlawful. The former would depend on the permissible reach of federal law; the latter would depend on who might cause embarrassment to the United States were such payments revealed.

5. A guide to the act is at http:/canada.justice.gc.ca.

2. 15 U.S.C.A. § 78dd–1(b).

§ 17.7

1. 15 U.S.C.A. § 78dd–1(b) (1977).

The amendments in 1998 implementing the Convention expanded the scope of coverage of payors. The amendments extend coverage to "any person", natural or legal, United States or foreign, acting within United States territory. Omitted are foreign persons acting outside the United States. But as to payees the Convention mandates are quite narrow, and required no amendments to the FCPA. The Convention, for example, does not cover payments to political parties, party officials, or candidates (except in some one-party states). Such payments are covered under the FCPA.

§ 17.9　Prohibited Payments

The 1977 FCPA amended the Securities Exchange Act of 1934 (SEA). The FCPA made it unlawful for an issuer of registered securities under § 12 of the SEA, or an issuer required to file reports under § 15(d) of the SEA, to make certain payments to foreign officials or other persons. The FCPA also requires those issuers to maintain accurate financial records which would disclose such payments.[1] The Act additionally extends the scope of prohibited payments to any issuer *or domestic concern* making use of the mails or any means or instrumentality of interstate commerce,[2] thus effectively extending the liability to all corporations, in a manner not unlike the insider trading provisions of § 10 of the SEA. Some persons involved in the SEC investigation have suggested that there were no moral judgments being made during the development of these rules. They allegedly were based on a shareholder's right to know if its corporation books were inaccurate, if management used corporate money to violate U.S. or foreign laws, if bribes were paid with corporate funds, or if payments were made to consultants with no accountability as to the disbursements by the consultants.[3]

The FCPA of 1977 was a concise act, including only three substantive sections. The 1988 amendments retained much of the 1977 act's structure, but made very important changes and additions. There were important changes to the accounting standards. But the most significant and controversial change was removing the "reason to know" language from the provision regulating payments to third persons which might be passed on to government officials.[4] This language was replaced with a "knowing" standard for liability, and a complex definition of "knowing" violations.[5] The amendments in 1998 expanded the scope of prohibited payments by including payments made to secure "any improper advantage." This may not actually expand the meaning of the 1988 FCPA language before the amendments, but the new words seem to confirm an expansive intent.

§ 17.9

1.　15 U.S.C.A. § 78m(b).

2.　15 U.S.C.A. §§ 78dd–1(a), 78dd–2(a). The latter part also defines both "domestic concern" and "interstate commerce." See § 78dd–2(h)(1) and (5).

3.　Wallace Timmeny, An Overview of the FCPA, 9 Syracuse J. Int'l L. & Com. 235 (1982).

4.　15 U.S.C.A. §§ 78dd–1(a)(3), 78dd–2(a)(3) (1977).

5.　15 U.S.C.A. § 78dd–1(f)2.

The current, twice-amended FCPA remains relatively concise. After establishing accounting standards,[6] it prohibits payments to certain foreign officials directly, or by way of third persons, when such payments are for the purpose of influencing any act or decision of the foreign official,[7] inducing the foreign official to act or refrain from acting in violation of the official's duty,[8] inducing the foreign official to use influence with a foreign government or instrumentality to influence that government's or instrumentality's act or decision,[9] or to secure any improper advantage.[10] There is next an important exception for routine government action,[11] which is further defined in a separate section.[12] The Act then establishes as an affirmative defense, cases where the payment was lawful under the *written* laws of the foreign country, or was a "reasonable and bona fide expenditure."[13]

The Attorney General is required by the 1988 amendments to make a report on the extent to which compliance with the law "would be enhanced and the business community would be assisted by further clarification" of the provisions. The Attorney General may issue guidelines to illustrate conformance, and adopt general precautionary procedures to conform conduct to Department of Justice enforcement policy.[14] The Attorney General must also provide a procedure for responding to specific inquiries by issuers regarding conformance with the enforcement policy.[15]

The Act next provides definitions of "foreign official", "public international organization", "knowing" and "routine governmental action."[16]

Added in 1998 is a provision for alternative jurisdiction.[17] This provision extends jurisdiction to issuers and U.S. persons who are officers, directors, employees or agents (and shareholders acting on behalf) of issuers acting corruptly *outside* the United States, regardless of whether the act involved the use of the mails or any means or instrumentality of interstate commerce. "U.S. person" is defined.

Concluding provisions of the Act consist of a penalty section with some exceptionally severe sanctions, including fines up to $1 million and ten years' imprisonment for individuals, and fines to $2.5 million for enterprises.[18]

---

6. 15 U.S.C.A. § 78m(b).

7. 15 U.S.C.A. § 78dd–1(a)(1)(A)(i).

8. 15 U.S.C.A. § 78dd–1(a)(1)(A)(ii).

9. 15 U.S.C.A. § 78dd–1(a)(1)(B).

10. 15 U.S.C.A.§§ 78dd–1(a)(1)(A)(iii), 78dd–1(a)(2)(A)(iii), 78dd–1(a)(3)(A)(iii). The content of these provisions is essentially repeated in sections 78dd–2 and 78dd–3.

11. 15 U.S.C.A. § 78dd–1(b).

12. 15 U.S.C.A. § 78dd–1(f)(2).

13. 15 U.S.C.A. § 78dd–1(c).

14. 15 U.S.C.A. §§ 78dd–1(d), 78dd–2(e).

15. 15 U.S.C.A. §§ 78dd–1(e), 78dd–2(f).

16. 15 U.S.C.A. §§ 78dd–1(f), 78dd–2(h). Section 78dd–2(h) also defines "domestic concern" and "interstate commerce."

17. 15 U.S.C.A. § 78dd–1(g).

18. 15 U.S.C.A. § 78ff.

C. ACCOUNTING STANDARDS

§ 17.10 Approach of Accounting Standards

One approach used in the FCPA to discourage illegal payments is to require issuers subject to the SEA to maintain certain accounting records that will assist in disclosing payments that might violate the other substantive sections of the FCPA. The original law generated considerable criticism about standards that threatened harsh penalties for even slight, incorrect accounting entries. The standards further required considerable documentation of foreign transactions.[1] The 1988 amendments address what was a concern for "reasonable detail" and "reasonable assurances" in internal accounting controls, and indicate that the Act does not cover technical or insignificant errors in record keeping.[2] Liability is to be imposed on persons who "knowingly circumvent or knowingly fail to implement a system of internal controls or knowingly falsify any book, record or account."[3] The OECD Convention does not call for the adoption of any specific accounting standards. But it does require signatories to enact rules to prevent false records or separate books. The United States was disappointed that the Convention failed to prohibit signatories from considering foreign payments as tax deductible as business expenses.

§ 17.11 ABA/SEC Disagreement

The American Bar Association and the SEC disagree on the scope of the accounting provisions of the FCPA. The ABA believes that if the conduct in question does not cause an impact upon the financial statements, then that conduct does not come within the accounting provisions. The SEC has repeatedly argued that Congress intended a broader application of the accounting provisions in order to make corporations accountable for questionable payments.[1]

§ 17.12 First Standard: Books, Records and Accounts

The regulated issuers must meet two standards. First is to maintain books, records and accounts which in reasonable detail possess such accuracy as to fairly reflect any transaction and disposition of assets of the issuer.[1] This means maintaining records of any payment made by the issuer to a person, such as one the Act defines as a foreign official, or

§ 17.10

1. This exposed persons to criminal sanctions for what might be technical errors or incomplete internal accounting controls.

2. See H.R.Conf.Rep. No. 576, 100th Cong. 916 (1988).

3. 15 U.S.C.A. § 78m(b)5.

§ 17.11

1. American Bar Ass'n, Commission on Corp. Law and Accounting, A Guide to the New Section 13(b)(2) Accounting Requirements of the Securities Exchange Act of 1934, 34 Bus. Lawyer 307 (1978). Section 13(b)(2) was not changed by the 1988 amendments.

§ 17.12

1. 15 U.S.C.A. § 78m(b)(2)(A). For a decision where a defendant pleaded guilty in federal court in New York to aiding and abetting acts of false record keeping under the FCPA, and was denied a request to withdraw the guilty plea after alleged co-conspirators were acquitted in a federal court in California, see United States v. O'Hara, 960 F.2d 11 (2d Cir.1992).

some other person (agent). Failure to maintain such record is an offense separate to the actual prohibited payment.

§ 17.13 Second Standard: Internal Accounting Control

The second required accounting standard is to establish and maintain a system of internal accounting controls in order to give reasonable assurance that:

(1) management's authorizations are properly executed,

(2) transactions are recorded so as to allow the preparation of financial statements which conform to generally accepted accounting principles or other applicable criteria, and to allow continued accountability for assets,

(3) management's authorizations regarding access to assets is maintained, and

(4) there is periodic accountability of assets and appropriate action when differences are discovered.[1]

These statutory principles should be part of any internal management policy established to avoid violations of the FCPA. They actually are accounting standards which serve many other legitimate business purposes, such as carrying out management decisions. One purpose for their structural form is to place responsibility on management for having allowed funds to end up in the hands of foreign officials, however they might have gotten there.[2]

§ 17.14 Sole Exemption: National Security

There is one exemption from compliance with the accounting requirement. It is unlikely to be available to many firms in many instances. It is where compliance would threaten national security.[1]

D. PERSONS SUBJECT TO THE FCPA

§ 17.15 Issuers, Domestic Concerns and Other Persons

The true heart of the FCPA consists of the provisions which prohibit certain forms payments by persons under the jurisdiction of the Act. The initial use of the securities laws to govern the prohibited conduct mandated that persons subject to the FCPA provisions have met the jurisdictional requirements of the SEA. But the 1998 amendments expanded the scope of jurisdiction. The Act has three very similarly worded sections, 78dd–1, 78dd–2, and 78dd–3, each of which contains the "prohibited foreign trade practices" language. Federal jurisdiction is

§ 17.13
1. 15 U.S.C.A. § 78m(b)(2)(B).
2. The accounting standards are supplemented by SEC regulations. See 17 C.F.R. §§ 240.13b2–1, 240.13b2–2.

§ 17.14
1. 15 U.S.C.A. § 78m(b)(3)(A).

based on the use of the mails or means or instrumentality of interstate commerce. But an alternative jurisdiction, which does not require the use of the mails or means or instrumentality of interstate commerce, is provided for in the amendments.[1] The pattern of the Act is to commence the provisions of each of the three prohibited classes (i.e., issuers in 78dd–1, domestic concerns in 78dd–2, and persons other than issuers or domestic concerns in 78dd–3) with a jurisdictional basis. A person in any class may not make use of the mails or any means or instrumentality of interstate commerce to commit acts in violation of the law. Added in 1998 was both the third class, persons other than issuers or domestic concerns, and a separate section supplementing the first two classes providing for alternative jurisdiction (78dd–1(g), 78dd–2(i)). The alternative jurisdiction is for acts outside the United States and does not require any use of the mails or any means or instrumentality of interstate commerce. This alternative jurisdiction does not apply to the third class, persons other than issuers or domestic concerns.

§ 17.16　Issuers of Securities

The first section, 78dd–1, has three classes of persons to which the prohibitory language applies:

    1.　issuers of securities registered under § 78*l* of the SEA, or required to file reports under § 78o(d) of the SEA;

    2.　officers, directors, employees or agents of such issuers; and

    3.　shareholders acting on behalf of such issuers.[1]

§ 17.17　Domestic Concerns Other Than Issuers

The second section, 78dd–2, extends the scope of the prohibitory language much further, to domestic concerns other than issuers subject to the first section 78dd–1. "Domestic concerns" includes:

    1.　individuals who are citizens, nationals or residents of the United States;

    2.　any form of business with a principal place of business in the United States; and

    3.　any form of business organized in one of the United States, a territory, possession or commonwealth of the United States.[1]

This language encompasses nearly anyone who might be involved in the transactions which are prohibited by the language that follows the jurisdictional reach. It is essential to realize that the statute does not provide for personal jurisdiction. The usual constitutional due process requirements to obtain jurisdiction over the person charged with making payments must be met. But that should not be difficult in most cases since the law addresses payments by U.S. persons or foreign persons

§ 17.15
1.　15 U.S.C.A. § 77dd–1(g).

§ 17.16
1.　15 U.S.C.A. § 77dd–1(a).

§ 17.17
1.　15 U.S.C.A. § 78dd–2(h)(1).

while in the United States, not any payments by foreign persons made outside the United States, or the receipt of payments by foreign persons.

§ 17.18 Foreign Natural and Legal Persons Who Commit Acts While in the United States

The third section, 77dd–3, was added in the 1998 amendments, to extend the reach of the FCPA beyond persons covered by the two above-noted sections. The linkage with the use of the mails or means or instrumentality of interstate commerce for jurisdiction remains, because the acts must occur in the United States.

The FCPA of 1977 was intended to govern the conduct only of *U.S.* persons as defined in the Act. It did not allow actions to be brought against foreign officials for violations of the Act.[1] Any such attempt was thought to be certain to generate criticism from abroad, and lead to little cooperation from foreign governments. Unless the foreign official chanced to be in the United States, there would be additional problems of personal jurisdiction. Actions in absentia would receive negative reaction from abroad and foreign relations could be adversely affected. The original Act did not allow suits against foreign *individual* agents.

The participation of foreign officials in payments prohibited by the FCPA could create difficulties in suits brought in the United States against U.S. persons. If the suit required consideration of whether foreign officials violated their domestic law in their territory, the U.S. court might refuse to go forward under the act of state doctrine.[2] But the U.S. Supreme Court, in *W.S. Kirkpatrick & Co., Inc. v. Environmental Tectonics Corp., Int'l*,[3] a case involving the FCPA and Nigeria, ruled in 1990 that the act of state doctrine does not apply when the court is not called upon to decide the effect of official action of a foreign sovereign, but only to examine the motives of the foreign official involved.

The 1998 FCPA amendments reflect the OECD Convention language which extends the scope of covered persons to include foreign persons. The amendments add the third class, persons other than issuers and domestic concerns, but this means only those who act *in* the United States. While the application of the Act to such foreign persons would have the blessing of the OECD Convention, it may nevertheless cause some foreign policy conflicts when important foreign persons are implicated.

§ 17.19 Foreign Subsidiaries of U.S. Companies

The extraterritorial application of any U.S. law is likely to create uneasiness abroad. The United States has a reputation for adopting and

---

§ 17.18

1. See United States v. Castle, 925 F.2d 831 (5th Cir.1991); United States v. Blondek, 741 F.Supp. 116 (N.D.Tex.1990). But see United States v. Young & Rubicam, 741 F.Supp. 334 (D.Conn.1990)(holding infringement of the FCPA could be a basis for violation of the Travel Act which could then serve as a basis for RICO charges).

2. Act of state with regard to expropriation is discussed in chapter 33, infra.

3. 493 U.S. 400, 110 S.Ct. 701, 107 L.Ed.2d 816 (1990).

pursuing an enforcement approach which interferes with the sovereignty of foreign nations. There is little question that many U.S. laws purport to apply extraterritorially. The FCPA is on the list. A parent corporation may be liable for payments made by a foreign subsidiary, if the parent knew or should have known of its subsidiary's actions.[1] Congress' intent seems to have been to make the parent liable only when it participated directly or indirectly in the foreign payment, not when the payment was initiated by the foreign subsidiary. A subsidiary more than 50 percent owned by a U.S. parent which is subject to the FCPA must additionally comply with the accounting requirements. The parent should make a considerable effort to have any subsidiary adopt policies which comply with the accounting rules.

E. THE ACT OF OFFERING, PROMISING OR GIVING CORRUPTLY

§ 17.20 What Is Given?

The persons described above who are subject to the Act may not "make use of the mails or any means or instrumentality of interstate commerce *corruptly*" where the act is "in furtherance of" any one of several actions, including an:

1. offer,
2. payment,
3. promise to pay, or
4. authorization of the payment

"of any money", or an:

1. offer,
2. gift,
3. promise to give, or
4. authorization of the giving

"of anything of value."[1]

Thus, the Act divides numerous "giving" actions between giving either money or anything of value. The fact that an item offered, promised or given has a very small value does not remove it from the Act. There is no *de minimis* exemption. The exemptions exist in *to whom* the item is offered, promised or given, or *for what purpose* the item is offered, promised or given.

§ 17.21 Acting "Corruptly"

The act of offering, promising or giving must be done *corruptly.* "Corruptly" is not defined in the Act. Its insertion in the Act raises the

§ 17.19
1. 123 Cong.Rec. 38600 (Dec. 6, 1977).

§ 17.20
1. 15 U.S.C.A. §§ 78dd–1(a), 78dd–2(a).

question whether, if all of the provisions are met, i.e., a payment is made to a defined foreign official and there is no statutory affirmative defense, the government nevertheless has to prove that the act was done corruptly. Or does the giving to a foreign official where there is no statutory defense constitute a corrupt act? The word "corruptly" seems unnecessary; the FCPA prohibits certain conduct, about which persons might debate endlessly regarding whether it is corrupt conduct. One decision suggests that the word "corruptly" means the that the court or jury concludes that the conduct violates the provisions of the Act, rather than meeting some external definition of "corrupt".[1] The party charged must be the one who acts corruptly; carrying out an employer's instructions might not be acting corruptly.[2] Thus, an employee of a U.S. aircraft-maintenance contractor who made a "gesture" to the chief of maintenance for Nigerian Air Force cargo planes, in the form of purchasing airline tickets for the official's honeymoon, after the contract was awarded to the U.S. company, was entitled to a new trial to determine whether the employee met the "corrupt" standard.[3]

An unusual comment in the Senate Committee Report on the 1977 Act stated:

> That the payment may have been first proposed by the recipient rather than the U.S. company does not alter the corrupt purpose on the part of the person paying the bribe. On the other hand true extortion situations would not be covered by this provision since a payment to an official to keep an oil rig from being dynamited should not be held to be made with the requisite corrupt purpose.[4]

This would be a useful defense where there is clearly an attempt to extort money from the company or individual. But it may be very difficult to prove, and may require the kind of dramatic case noted in the Senate Report.

F. PROHIBITED PERSONS (RECIPIENTS) AND PURPOSES

§ 17.22 Foreign Official

The offer, promise or gift may not be made to any person in one of three classes. One class is a payment to any *foreign official* if the offer, promise or gift is either (1) to influence an official act or decision, induce an act or omission in violation of lawful duty, or secure any advantage, or (2) to induce the use of the official's influence with a foreign government or instrumentality in order to "affect or influence" any act thereof, and where the ultimate purpose is assisting the issuer in either obtaining or retaining business, or directing business to any person.[1]

§ 17.21

1. See United States v. Liebo, 923 F.2d 1308 (8th Cir.1991).

2. Id.

3. Id.

4. Senate Report No. 114, 95th Cong.10 (1977).

§ 17.22

1. 15 U.S.C.A. §§ 78dd–1(a)(1), 78dd–2(a)(1).

The "obtaining or retaining" business language has been discussed in *United States v. Liebo,* where the court held the standard had been met.[2]

In addition to defining "knowing", the Act offers some help in defining the term "foreign official."[3] A foreign official is any "officer or employee" of any foreign government, or department, agency or instrumentality thereof. "Official" is thus very broadly defined to include the lowest-level employee.[4] Also included are persons acting in an *official capacity* for or on behalf of a government or international organization. Added in 1998 were officers or employees of international organizations.

The addition of international organizations substantially expands the scope of the FCPA. Where payments to only foreign *government* officials were covered, it was necessary to define "government." That is not always easy. Some entities, such as the Vatican, the PLO, or a territory over which there is some government control, may or may not be considered governments. The Foreign Sovereign Immunities Act has generated many helpful discussions about the definition of a "state", which may assist in defining a foreign government. With the inclusion of payments to foreign officials of international organizations, the definition difficulty is shifted to "international organizations" rather than "governments".

§ 17.23 Foreign Political Party, Official or Candidate

An offer, promise or gift may not be made to any *foreign political party* or *official of that party* or *candidate for political office,* if it is (1) to influence such party in an official act or decision, induce an act or omission in violation of lawful duty, or secure any improper advantage, or (2) to induce the use of that party's influence with a foreign government or instrumentality to "affect or influence" any act thereof. The ultimate purpose must be to assist the issuer in either obtaining or retaining business, or directing business to any person.[1] "Candidate" may be difficult to define, since it may not be clear that a person is a candidate at the time of making a payment. The act does not specifically cover a person intending to become a candidate.

§ 17.24 Any Person "While Knowing"

An offer, promise or gift may not be made to *any person,* while *knowing* it will be offered, promised or given to (1) a foreign official, (2) a foreign political party, (3) an official of a foreign political party, or (4) a candidate for foreign political office, where the purpose is the same as in

---

2. 923 F.2d 1308 (8th Cir.1991).

3. 15 U.S.C.A. §§ 78dd–1(f)(1), 78dd–2(h)(2).

4. But the exceptions for routine government actions are most likely to apply to payments to relatively low-level employees.

§ 17.23

1. 15 U.S.C.A. §§ 78dd–1(a)(3), 78dd–2(a)(3).

the first two sections above.[1] This third category of persons to whom payments are prohibited governs payments to persons hired as agents or consultants, but adds the very important requirement that a payment to such third party be made "while knowing" that the money or item of value will be passed on to a prohibited person. The alteration to the knowing language was the most important provision in the 1988 amendments to the Act. In the original Act, the language was "knowing or having reason to know."[2] The "having reason to know" was the subject of continual criticism by business persons and their counsel, who believed it created an unfair and ambiguous standard which placed the burden on the business to prove that its conduct was proper. Although proponents of the original language lost the fight to retain it in the amendments, added to the Act was a broad definition of "knowing". The definition seems to be so broad to possibly include within the definition of the word "knowing" some actual "reason to know" criteria. The definition of "knowing" states that knowing conduct is where either (1) the person is *aware* of the conduct, that "such circumstance" exists, or the result is "substantially certain" to occur, or (2) the person has a "firm belief" that such circumstance exists or the result is substantially certain to occur.[3] The provision then adds that the knowing standard is met if the person is "aware of a high probability" of the existence of such circumstance, *unless* the person "actually believes" that such circumstance does not exist.[4] Does the "high probability" language carry the knowing standard into the territory of a reason to know standard? The definition certainly modifies what might normally be considered a knowing standard, and will be the subject of considerable debate when it comes to an argument before the courts.

G. ROUTINE GOVERNMENTAL ACTION EXEMPTION

§ 17.25   De Minimis or "Grease" Payments

Without more than what has been discussed above, the FCPA might leave one with the sense that the Act extended far beyond what Congress initially wished to label as corrupt, into the area of the myriad of minor "grease" payments made to government officials (usually too nominal in amount to have a third party involved) to do what they are supposed to do, but to do it in a shorter period of time.

Probably very few persons who have crossed a border into Mexico or further South driving a car filled with personal belongings (but no illegal items) have not paid the customs officials a few dollars to avoid having to unload every item, and to speed the car on its way without a lengthy

---

§ 17.24

1. 15 U.S.C.A. §§ 78dd–1(a)(3), 78dd–2(a)(3).

2. 15 U.S.C.A. §§ 78dd–1(a)(3), 78dd–2(a)(3) (1977).

3. 15 U.S.C.A. §§ 78dd–1(f)(2)(A), 78dd–2(h)(3)(A).

4. 15 U.S.C.A. §§ 78dd–1(f)(2)(B), 78dd–2(h)(3)(B).

inspection. Probably many business persons have paid a small amount to a customs official to expedite the processing of goods needed for an impatient customer. The FCPA needed some exception for "minor" payments, without compromising its premise that "corrupt" payments ought not be allowed. The result is that corruption has a *de minimis* element, but it is not defined by dollar amount. Payments made to obtain or retain business are not minor payments. Furthermore, even *de minimis* payments may be subject to the accounting requirements.

§ 17.26 "Facilitating or Expediting Routine Governmental Action"

The original Act exempted payments to minor government officials for acts that were ministerial, using language to exempt payments to foreign government employees "whose duties are essentially ministerial or clerical."[1] The 1988 amendments changed that to create an exception for "facilitating or expediting" payments when the purpose is to "expedite or to secure the performance of a routine governmental action."[2]

A "routine governmental action" is defined in the Act,[3] in four specific sections and one general subsection. Specifically allowed are payments made when:

1. obtaining permits, licenses or other official documents which are part of the process of qualifying to do business in the country,

2. processing such papers as visas and work orders,

3. providing police protection, mail pick-up and delivery, or scheduling inspections which are associated with the performance of a contract or related to transit of goods across country, and

4. providing telephone service, power and water supply, loading and unloading cargo, or protecting perishables from deterioration.

A final, fifth class encompasses "actions of a similar nature."

Specifically exempted from being considered a "routine governmental action" is any decision by a foreign official about the terms of a new contract, the awarding of such contract, continuing business, or any action by any official involved in the process of new or renewal business.[4]

There is a very large gap between what is specifically allowed and what is specifically disallowed. One of the least clear areas involves the extent to which foreign officials may be entertained. Entertaining is not always motivated solely by courtesy. Foreign officials are usually entertained as part of the process of receiving the award of a contract, or establishing or continuing a business. The line of legitimacy must fall

§ 17.26

1. 15 U.S.C.A. § 77dd–1(b) (1977).

2. 15 U.S.C.A. §§ 78dd–1(b), 78dd–2(b).

3. 15 U.S.C.A. §§ 78dd–1(f)(3), 78dd–2(h)(4).

4. 15 U.S.C.A. §§ 78dd–1(f)(3)(B), 78dd–2(h)(4)(B).

somewhere between reasonable expenses associated with normal business, and unreasonable expenses associated with unreasonable influence. Finding that line is helped by the special provisions providing affirmative defenses.[5]

H.   AFFIRMATIVE DEFENSES

§ 17.27   Lawful Under "Written" Laws

The FCPA establishes two basic classes of affirmative defenses. The first is when the payment, gift, offer or promise is lawful under the *written* laws and regulations of the foreign country.[1] Since nations are not known for enacting laws to give legitimacy to what may be common but unlawful practices of its officials, this section is likely to be of little use. Were it to allow payments where the *unwritten* laws, i.e., the expected and common practice, mandate payments, the loophole would be considerably wider than merely enough to fly a Lockheed through. To be safe, counsel should obtain an opinion in writing from foreign local counsel that identifies the written law or regulation which allows a payment. It is of course possible that payments may be allowed to political campaigns under local written law, but not personally to serving officials to influence their official decisions.

§ 17.28   "Reasonable and Bona Fide Expenditures"

The second specific affirmative defense is when the payment, gift, offer or promise is a "reasonable and bona fide expenditure, such as travel and lodging expenses" that a foreign official incurs, and which is related to either (1) the promotion, demonstration or explanation of products or services, or (2) the execution or performance of a contract.[1] While the first part of this section broadens the permissible payments, the second part narrows it. Noticeably excluded are such payments when the contract is being considered, either initially or for renewal. But a carefully crafted corporate policy might provide that even in the advance of obtaining a contract or having it renewed, payments to foreign officials are exclusively based on promotions, demonstrations and/or explanations relating to the performance of the contract if granted or renewed.

I.   ENFORCEMENT AND PENALTIES

§ 17.29   Enforcement Authority

The severity of penalties for violations of the FCPA mandates close consideration of its provisions by all persons doing business abroad. Violations of the FCPA are dealt with principally by the SEC (which

---

5.   15 U.S.C.A. §§ 78dd–1(c), 78dd–2(c).

§ 17.27

1.   15 U.S.C.A. § 77dd–1(c)(1).

§ 17.28

1.   15 U.S.C.A. § 77dd–1(c)(2).

monitors the record keeping) and the Department of Justice (which enforces the antibribery provisions).

Comparatively few actions for FCPA violations have been brought by the Department of Justice and reached the appellate courts.[1] One example, involving the International Harvester Company, alleged participation in a series of charges relating to dealings with officials of Petroleos Mexicanos (PEMEX), the national oil company.[2] But it is not only the largest U.S. corporations which have been the subject of actions. Another action involved an individual who owned a postage stamp concession for a Caribbean island and who paid for flights for citizens to return to the island to vote for the reelection of the president, allegedly to influence the government to renew the concession.[3]

Investigations are often reported in the news, suggesting that U.S. persons and companies have not ceased making payments to foreign officials.[4] Some of the most controversial allegations in the past few years involved IBM and Mexico in 1993, during the sensitive negotiations for the North American Free Trade Agreement.[5] An Iranian-born British businessman was retained by IBM to be its agent in a tender bid for a new air-control system in Mexico City.[6] The agent alleged that soon after a meeting with several Mexican officials at which they tried to obtain a $1 million bribe, IBM's bid was rejected and the contract given to the French Thomson Company. The agents' subsequent public disclosure and numerous newspaper articles led nowhere, but caused a sensation in Mexico early in 1993. The Minister of Communications was ousted in a cabinet reorganization. The agent alleged that the Mexican government later tried to buy him off. IBM did not support the agent in his claims, and settled with the agent out of court. The whole episode illustrates many problems. The U.S. government showed no inclination to become involved or investigate the matter. There were foreign policy problems, NAFTA priorities, perhaps a sense that the whole story was not implausible, but a realization that this is how things work. Aliases or no names, secret meetings, finger pointing, and leaks to the press are all part of the game. No one seems to have asked how the French Thomson Company got the bid so quickly after IBM was rejected.

§ 17.29

1. The Department of Justice shares information from investigations with the SEC, which does not have criminal jurisdiction.

2. The company pleaded guilty to conspiracy to violate the FCPA. See McLean v. International Harvester Co., 902 F.2d 372 (5th Cir.1990); McLean v. International Harvester Co., 817 F.2d 1214 (5th Cir. 1987); Executive Legal Summary No. 5, Business Laws, Inc. 100.03 (Hancock ed., Oct. 1988).

3. Executive Legal Summary No. 5, Business Laws, Inc., 100.03, 100.04 (Hancock ed., Oct. 1988).

4. See, e.g., Some Weapons Makers Are Said To Continue Illicit Foreign Outlays, Wall St.J., Nov. 5, 1993, at 1, discussing GE, Teledyne Inc., Litton Industries, Inc., Loral Corp., and United Technologies Corp. problems.

5. See The Independent, August 29, 1993, Sunday Review at 2; The Financial Post, Oct. 27, 1993, at 13.

6. His contract with IBM included, allegedly at his demand, provisions that he would not be asked to perform, nor would he undertake, any act in violation of the FCPA.

IBM was later again in the news regarding an investigation of bribes in Argentina to obtain a $250 million contract to modernize the computer system for the Banco de la Nación.[7] IBM allegedly paid bribes to CCR, a computer systems company, in connection with obtaining a contract with Nación, money which soon found its way into Swiss accounts.[8]

§ 17.30   Consent Decrees

Few of the cases investigated ever come to court.[1] Most cases are resolved by consent decrees. Corporations prefer to accept a negotiated fine rather than litigate in the federal courts.[2] Furthermore, corporations usually prefer to avoid the publicity accompanying charges of making foreign payments corruptly. There is also the problem that the payment usually occurs in a foreign country and proof of the payment is difficult to establish. The foreign country is not likely to assist in allowing discovery or taking depositions.

§ 17.31   Charges of Accounting and Illegal Payment Violations

More actions have been brought charging violations of the accounting provisions as opposed to making illegal payments. The proof of accounting violations is mostly available in the United States, since the charge relates to the books the corporation maintains in the United States. But the books often disclose little to auditors, since payments may be made to persons who appear to be legitimate foreign consultants, and thus are listed only as payments made to consultants, not to foreign officials. There can be complications where the payments are made through subsidiaries abroad, especially when the nations where the subsidiaries are located have blocking laws limiting access to documents.

§ 17.32   Additional Charges

Persons charged by the government with violations of either the accounting requirements or the payments provisions may face other charges. Competitors may brings claims under RICO, antitrust or direct FCPA theories. Employees who are dismissed for refusing to comply with orders to make foreign payments may bring unlawful discharge suits, usually in the form of a breach of contract action, or become whistle-blowers and tell all to the government.[1] Shareholders may initiate

---

7. National Law Journal, Mar. 3, 1997, at B16.

8. Financial Times, Oct. 19, 1995, at 5.

§ 17.30

1. See United States v. McLean, 738 F.2d 655 (5th Cir.1984), *cert. denied* 470 U.S. 1050, 105 S.Ct. 1748, 84 L.Ed.2d 813 (1985).

2. The FCPA Reporter includes information regarding consent decrees and guilty pleas. The names of corporations charged are well known, including such companies as Ashland Oil, General Electric, Goodyear International, International Harvester, and Lockheed Martin.

§ 17.32

1. A whistle-blower's experience at GE is described in Some Weapons Makers Are Said To Continue Illicit Foreign Outlays, Wall St.J., Nov. 5, 1993, at 1.

derivative suits. Finally, a foreign government whose officials are offered bribes may take action.

§ 17.33   Penalties: Record Keeping and Accounting Violations

Section 78m(b) violations, the record-keeping and internal accounting-control standards section, may lead to penalties of $100 per day during the period in which the company fails to comply with the requirements. These are civil rather than criminal penalties. But where there is (1) a willful violation of the provisions, or (2) a willful and knowing making of a false or misleading statement in filed applications, statements or reports, a criminal penalty may be imposed of not more than $1,000,000, or not more than ten years imprisonment, or both.[1]

§ 17.34   Penalties: Illegal Payment Violations

Section 78dd–1 and § 78dd–2 violations for making illegal payments are governed in these two different provisions, for issuers and domestic concerns, respectively, and their officers, directors, agents and shareholders acting on behalf of the entity. Each section leads to the same levels of penalties.[1] The entities are subject to fines of not more than $2 million, and civil penalties of not more than $10,000. The officers, directors, employees, agents, and shareholders acting on behalf of the concerns are subject to fines up to $100,000, or five years' imprisonment, or both, if the violation was willful.[2] They are also subject to civil penalties up to $10,000, without the willful requirement. Any fine imposed on a person under the above provisions, criminal or civil, may not be paid by the company, directly or indirectly. These latter penalties illustrate that the government is serious about violations of the FCPA.[3]

J.   DEPARTMENT OF JUSTICE REVIEW PROCEDURE

§ 17.35   Review Process

The FCPA requires the Department of Justice to establish a procedure allowing persons to request an opinion about proposed activity that might create some FPCA concern.[1] The first step is for the person or

§ 17.33

1. 15 U.S.C.A. § 78ff(a). An exchange may be fined up to $2,500,000. Proof of no knowledge of the rule or regulation will avoid imprisonment. Id.

§ 17.34

1. 15 U.S.C.A. §§ 78ff(c) and 78dd–2(g).

2. Only willful violations are subject to criminal penalties. See Trane Co. v. O'Connor Securities, 718 F.2d 26 (2d Cir.1983).

3. Two units of Litton Industries pleaded guilty in 1999 to fraud and conspiracy in making payments to obtain defense business in Greece and Taiwan. Litton agreed to pay $18.5 million to settle the matter (including an amount to reimburse the Department of Justice for the costs of the investigation).

§ 17.35

1. 15 U.S.C.A. §§ 78dd–1(e), 78dd–2(f). The review procedure is contained in 28 C.F.R. § 50.18.

company to present to the Department of Justice details of the proposed transaction. The Department has 30 days within which to respond. The person or company may only rely upon a review letter signed by the Assistant Attorney General (or delegate) in charge of the criminal division. The procedure, begun in 1980 under the original law, has not been used very often, possibly because of concern about identifying foreign officials and the consequences if the review request information is not held confidential.[2] The 1988 amendments provide more definitional information of what may be allowed, and may lead to even less use of the review procedure.

§ 17.36   When to Use Review Process?

The review process should be used when a company is clearly uncertain about the lawfulness of the proposed payments, and believes that the information it will provide to the Department will not be disclosed, or will not cause injury if disclosed, and that the protection afforded by the request outweighs the potential harm to the company if it does not disclose and is later challenged.

K.   RIGHTS OF ACTION

§ 17.37   Actions by the Government

The FCPA was drafted with the intent that the Department of Justice and the SEC would enforce the law. The former would challenge illegal payments and the latter record keeping and accounting procedures. That is the way the Act has functioned. But, as in the case of many federal laws, questions have been raised regarding the extent to which the FCPA creates private rights of action and other suits.

§ 17.38   Private Right of Action

There have not been many suits charging violations of the FCPA initiated by private individuals or companies against other private parties. One federal circuit court has held that there is no private right of action under the FCPA.[1] The case involved donations Philip Morris allegedly promised a Venezuelan Children's Foundation (the wife of the President of Venezuela was the president of the Foundation) for benefits to Philip Morris in obtaining Venezuelan tobacco. Two U.S. tobacco producers sued Philip Morris for harm caused by the alleged violation of

---

2. Furthermore, information provided in a review request might be used against the person in a criminal prosecution. See John W. Bagby, Enforcement of the Accounting Standards in the Foreign Corrupt Practices Act, 21 Am.Bus.L.J. 213 (1983).

§ 17.38

1. Lamb v. Phillip Morris, Inc., 915 F.2d 1024 (6th Cir.1990), *cert. denied* 498 U.S. 1086, 111 S.Ct. 961, 112 L.Ed.2d 1048 (1991). See also Citicorp Int'l Trading Co.,

Inc. v. Western Oil & Refining Co., 771 F.Supp. 600 (S.D.N.Y.1991) (applying the well established four-part Cort v. Ash test to determine that there is no private cause of action); Shields on Behalf of Sundstrand Corp. v. Erickson, 710 F.Supp. 686 (N.D.Ill. 1989) (violations of financial and accounting controls do not give rise to private right); Lewis v. Sporck, 612 F.Supp. 1316 (N.D.Cal.1985) (same conclusion).

the FCPA (and antitrust law). The *Lamb* decision is influential and law in the Sixth Circuit, but may not be the last word on the issue.

§ 17.39 Employee Suits

If a company intends to make payments to foreign officials that appear likely to be in violation of the FCPA, the payments will obviously require acts by company employees. Very large payments are likely to be authorized and possibly made directly by senior officers. Other payments may be authorized by senior officials but made by lower level employees who are in more frequent contact with the foreign officials. In some cases, the lower-level employees, such as sales or purchasing agents, will decided upon and make the payments on their own. The payments may be made by any of the above directly or to a third-party agent who makes the final disbursements to the government officials. If executives who have made the decision to make payments delegate making those payments to another employee, the decision makers are in jeopardy of the employee refusing and, if dismissed for the refusal, bringing a lawsuit. The FCPA itself does not provide any basis for a corporate employee to bring a claim against the corporation where the corporation appears to have made the employee the scapegoat for allegedly unlawful payments.[1]

The original 1977 Act included what was known as the Eckhardt provision, which did not allow actions to be brought against employees without first going against the employer. The amendments in 1988 reverse this and allow such actions. An employer may now urge the government to bring suit directly against the employee who made the payment, even if the payment was authorized by other higher-level officers. The possibility of a scapegoat is back. But the scapegoat employee may not be without a remedy. That employee is likely to be or soon become a *former* employee, and may have an action against the company.

Ashland Oil Inc., learned that firing an employee for refusing to make an illegal payment abroad is costly.[2] William McKay, an Ashland Oil vice-president, was instructed to make but refused to participate in an illegal payment to an official in Oman. McKay later cooperated with SEC and IRS investigations of the payment. Another executive, Harry Williams, was sympathetic to McKay's attempt to change the corporate policy at Ashland. Both were soon no longer employed. They sued Ashland for wrongful discharge and received a verdict of nearly $70 million, later settled for $25 million. A key to the settlement was a provision in McKay's employment contract that he would not be compelled to make unlawful payments. It is an appropriate employment contract provision for an officer, because many states do not allow suits for termination in the absence of a contractual provision. Any suit

§ 17.39

1. McLean v. International Harvester Co., 817 F.2d 1214 (5th Cir.1987), *appeal after remand* 902 F.2d 372 (5th Cir.1990).

2. See Marshall Sella, More Big Bucks in Jury Verdicts, 75 A.B.A. Journal 69 (July 1989). See also Williams v. Hall, 683 F.Supp. 639 (E.D.Ky.1988).

commenced under such a contract provision would be based on the contract and not the FCPA. It would therefore not face the uncertain issue noted above of bringing private suits under the Act. Because it is a suit based on breach of the employment contract, it requires inquiry only regarding the company's act of demanding a payment that, if made, would be a violation.[3]

Teledyne Systems faced another possible use of the FCPA: whistle-blower suits. A significant military contractor, Teledyne became involved in several whistle-blower suits in the early 1990s. One filed by a former program manager for Teledyne in the Middle East alleged a payment to an Egyptian general to help obtain Air Force contracts.[4]

§ 17.40 Suits Charging Competitor With Violation of FCPA

A person or company believing that a competitor violated the FCPA and obtained business at the company's expense has several choices. First, a direct suit charging a violation of the FCPA may fail as in the case of the Philip Morris experience discussed above, because it is an attempt to bring a private cause of action.[1] Second, the suit might be based on violations of antitrust laws. A third choice is a violation of the Racketeer Influenced and Corrupt Organizations Act (RICO).[2] In each of the latter two actions, the corrupt payment would be *evidence* of the wrong alleged, but not used as the basis of the suit, and thus the suit would not fail as a disallowed private right of action.[3] A fourth possible cause of action would be for tortious interference with a current or prospective business relationship.[4]

A RICO action was brought in *W.S. Kirkpatrick & Co., Inc. v. Environmental Tectonics Corp., Int'l,*[5] a case important to the development of the act of state doctrine. Environmental Tectonics was an unsuccessful bidder for a contract with the Nigerian Air Force. The company complained that Kirkpatrick had paid unlawful bribes to Nigerian officials. The company sued under the federal RICO statute. The court ruled that the act of state doctrine did not apply because the

---

3. See also Pratt v. Caterpillar Tractor Co., 149 Ill.App.3d 588, 102 Ill.Dec. 900, 500 N.E.2d 1001 (1986), *appeal denied* 114 Ill.2d 556, 107 Ill.Dec. 68, 506 N.E.2d 959 (1987), holding that the FCPA did not create a basis for a state claim of retaliatory discharge.

4. See At Teledyne, A Chorus of Whistle-Blowers, Business Week, Dec. 14, 1992, at 40.

§ 17.40

1. Lamb v. Phillip Morris, Inc., 915 F.2d 1024 (6th Cir.1990), *cert. denied* 498 U.S. 1086, 111 S.Ct. 961, 112 L.Ed.2d 1048 (1991).

2. 18 U.S.C.A. §§ 1961–1968. Treble damages are allowed under § 1964(c).

There is some question about whether RICO damage must be caused directly by acts of racketeering defined by statute, such as bribery. See Dooley v. United Technologies Corp., 803 F.Supp. 428 (D.D.C.1992) (RICO claim upheld, part of claim based on FCPA violations).

3. For a RICO action allowed where an employee was discharged, see Williams v. Hall, 683 F.Supp. 639 (E.D.Ky.1988).

4. See discussion in Citicorp Int'l Trading Co., Inc. v. Western Oil & Refining Co., Inc., 771 F.Supp. 600 (S.D.N.Y.1991).

5. 493 U.S. 400, 110 S.Ct. 701, 107 L.Ed.2d 816 (1990).

lawfulness of acts of a foreign government in its own territory were not at issue, but only the motives of foreign officials in accepting payments. The case was remanded. RICO thus may be an effective method for private suits involving violations of the FCPA, unless RICO is amended to diminish its scope.

As the incidents of such cases as the above, involving Ashland and Environmental Tectonics, become more common, companies may be more inclined to develop serious internal policies which are intended both to prevent company officials from making such payments abroad and to assure that they are in fact not made. Facing litigation by dismissed employees who refused to make illegal payments, and by competitors injured by such payments, companies may find it better to stop such payments rather than to attempt to hide them.

L.   COMPANY RESPONSES

§ 17.41   Responses to Foreign Officials' Requests for Payments

When a foreign official requests a payment that would likely violate the FCPA, the U.S. person or company has essentially two choices. The first is to make the payment, hoping it will not be disclosed, but if it is disclosed, assuming the consequences as a cost of doing business. The end result is most likely to be a negotiated settlement with the Department of Justice, and payment of a fine which, if added to the payments made abroad, may nevertheless total far less than the profits from having the contract. If a company can obtain business worth millions in profit for illegal payments of a few hundred thousand, it may be hard to comply with the Act. That becomes even more difficult when the history of enforcement is understood. But the company nevertheless *must* take all necessary measures not to violate the FCPA. The penalties for noncompliance are appropriately severe.

The second choice for the person or company is refusing any requested payment, and, quite possibly, losing the contract. But that is not necessarily the result. The foreign government may need the products, technology, or investment from the particular U.S. source. A company with such leverage is foolish to submit to any payment demand, from either a legal or business viewpoint. Colgate–Palmolive reportedly rejected demands from Chinese officials for jobs for relatives and foreign trips, but was able to go forward with a joint venture.[1]

Even if a company does not have leverage or a willingness to test the foreign officials who are demanding payments, it may be possible to obtain the assistance of the U.S. government to avoid making requested payments, yet not lose the business. When an officer of the Campbell Soup Company was asked by an Argentine government official for an illegal payment, Campbell went to the U.S. government. The govern-

§ 17.41
1.   Business China (BNA), Aug. 23, 1993.

ment worked directly with President Menem in Argentina, who both increased anti-corruption efforts, and gave Campbell the sought after tax exemption to which it was entitled under Argentine law.[2]

One problem with making a requested payment is the fact that the company is unlikely to be left alone in the future. It is marked as a company willing to make payments to obtain favorable decisions, and the number of open palms and size of future requests may increase. But the hard, cold fact to many businesses is the thought that if payments are not made, especially when they are commonly made by other nations' companies whose national laws do not prohibit such payments, business will be lost. Viewed as a legitimate cost of doing business by many business persons in the United States, payments will continue to be made in the future.

A company receiving a request for a payment is not required to report that request to any government agency, as in the case of requests related to supporting or assisting a boycott against a nation friendly to the United States, under the antiboycott laws of the United States. But when a request for a payment which would violate the FCPA is received by a U.S. person or company, it may be appropriate policy to contact officials in the Department of State and Department of Commerce. For a company rejecting such request and losing the business, it is helpful to the U.S. government to know how the foreign nation's officials are acting. It may lead to an investigation of the practices of the company which did obtain the business, if the company is a U.S. person and was thought to have been able to obtain the business only if it agreed to payments. Any U.S. government inquiry may help the United States reporting company prepare evidence for a suit against the company making the payment, such as in the *Kirkpatrick* decision discussed above. Or the United States may place pressure on higher foreign officials to investigate the matter, such as the Campbell Soup case in Argentina.

§ 17.42 Company Policy to Prohibit Payments in Violation of the FCPA

Every company involved in foreign business transactions should have a written policy which prohibits payments which violate the FCPA. Some internal control is *required* to comply with the accounting provisions in the Act. Several suggestions were made above in the comments on accounting standards. But a policy should do more. It should prohibit unlawful payments and explain to company employees what kinds of payments are unlawful. A policy will not assure that illegal payments are not made. But even if foreign payments are later found to have been made, a written policy, acknowledged by employees' signatures, will to establish the company's good intentions and should help in minimizing penalties.

2. Legal Times, June 24, 1991, at 2;
Wall St.J., Jan. 21, 1991, at A7.

The possible policies are numerous. One alternative is to merely state in a company policy manual that any payment in violation of the FCPA is prohibited under any circumstances. But a detailed policy is more appropriate. There should be some attempt to educate all company employees in positions where they might be asked to make unlawful payments. The policy should outline the content of the FCPA, and how the company views payments which are on the margin, and might be exempt. Officials should be required to sign a statement that they understand the company policy and agree to comply. The policy should also state that it is company practice that any request made by one person in the company to another, to carry out an illegal foreign payment, is considered grounds for the dismissal of the former, and may be grounds for a suit against the company by the latter. But it is unlikely that many companies will offer to include in an employment contract the language that was in the officer's contract in the Ashland Oil case, at least without some urging by the officer being hired. Any person in a position to negotiate an employment contract, rather than simply take what is offered, should insist on the inclusion of a statement similar to the one in the Ashland case.

Dealing with unknown agents creates special problems. The agent should be asked for details about the existence of any relatives or business associates of the agent, who are in the government. The company should contact various persons in the U.S. government to check on the reputation of an agent. Such offices as the respective country desk officer at State or Commerce are useful. The commercial affairs officer at the country's embassy in Washington, the U.S. commercial and/or economic affairs officer at the United States embassy in the respective country, and any U.S. associated chamber of commerce in that country, all might help the company avoid using an agent with a poor reputation. Local counsel may help in the inquiry. Such contacts may help to later establish that the company did not act "while knowing", the standard in the FCPA. Finally, the agreement with the agent should contain a clause that none of the funds paid to the agent will be used in any manner which might violate the FCPA.

M. FOREIGN NATION AND MULTINATIONAL ORGANIZATION CONTROLS ON CORRUPT FOREIGN PAYMENTS

§ 17.43 Specific Nations' Laws and U.S. Agency Procedures

The United States' effort to govern corporate behavior abroad with regard to paying bribes to foreign officials extends far beyond governing U.S. and some foreign persons. It has pursued the adoption of similar laws on a multinational level.[1] Until the conclusion of the 1997 OECD

---

§ 17.43

1. The FCPA required the President to report on progress in obtaining an interna-

tional agreement on corrupt business practices.

Convention, only Sweden had adopted a law with sanctions similar to the United States'.[2] Most nations rejected the idea of enacting domestic laws to govern foreign payments, and France as part of its export-insurance program (COFACE[3]) usually covered "commissions" to foreign persons as part of the export risk. The European attitude appeared to be that the regulation of bribery is the responsibility of the host government. But no host government *permits* bribes in the written law. The likelihood that many capital-importing nations will enact and enforce tough domestic antibribery laws is so commonly thought to be so slim that it makes the European policy unrealistic.

The U.S. interagency Trade Promotion Coordinating Committee *National Export Strategy* report in 1996 suggested that there was evidence that U.S. firms lost at least 36 contracts worth some $11 billion because of corrupt payments. United States firms suggested the figures to be closer to 139 contracts worth about $64 billion. Repeated and quite similar annual disclosures led the United States to increase pressure on other nations and international organizations to adopt laws similar to the FCPA. Furthermore, Commerce will require firms in the United States with foreign parents or other foreign affiliates, when seeking Commerce advocacy for a specific contract, to stipulate that no corrupt practices are present. The U.S. Export–Import Bank will demand certification to reduce the possibility of corrupt payments involved with its loans, guarantees and insurance. The Overseas Private Investment Corporation (OPIC) will add to political risk insurance applications provisions intended to reduce such payments. International business persons may thus expect to discover several levels of inquiries, mandates, certifications and other methods of addressing this issue, when dealing with various government agencies.

§ 17.44 Organization for Economic Cooperation and Development (OECD)

The OECD in 1976, at the urging of the United States, adopted a set of decisions and guidelines (a voluntary code) for its member nations. They *suggested* that corporations should not offer bribes or questionable payments, nor should they expect to receive offers of bribes or questionable payments. All of the OECD nations endorsed the guidelines by signature. A few of the nations circulated information to corporations incorporated under its law about the guidelines, and urged the corporations to adopt policies consistent with the guidelines. But for the most part the guidelines disappeared.

The OECD next began to develop firmer rules to reduce bribery of foreign officials. But agreement was slow, allegedly because the United

---

2. See Michael Bogdan, International Trade and the New Swedish Provision on Corruption, 27 Am.J.Comp.L. 665 (1979).

3. Compagnie Francaise d'Assurance pour le Commerce Exterieur.

States wanted a tougher stance taken than was agreeable to other member nations. Finally, in 1997 the OECD Convention on Combating Bribery of Foreign Public Officials in International Business Transactions was completed.[1] Many OECD nations signed the Convention, and some non-OECD nations also signed, including Argentina, Brazil, China and the Czech Republic. The United States signed and in 1998 amended the FCPA to bring it in line with the Convention. The major disappointment for the United States in the Convention was the failure to ban tax deductibility of bribes, a common practice in many nations.[2] France, the most notable of these nations, separately agreed to eliminate the practice. The principal focus of the Convention is to require participants to make the payment of bribes to foreign officials a crime and to impose severe sanctions. While the motivation may appear in print, what has been absent is any serious compliance mechanism. There is little that one nation can do if another ignores its obligations. But however limited the Convention appears, it is an important step and perhaps the first time many of the participants acknowledged that there was even a problem requiring attention. The use of a Convention, rather than the OECD's more common practice of drafting guidelines, emphasized the concern about the issue.

§ 17.45   General Agreement on Tariffs and Trade (GATT/WTO)

The United States presented to the GATT the issue of questionable foreign payments by way of a Senate Resolution in 1975. There was no interest in considering the issue and the GATT thus took no action. The Uruguay Round did not result in the adoption of any such provisions. But the United States subsequently indicated that it would attempt to have the WTO (successor to the GATT) adopt rules prohibiting foreign corrupt practices. No such rules were included in the WTO.

§ 17.46   United Nations

The United Nations Economic and Social Council (ECOSOC) adopted a resolution to draft a treaty to govern foreign payments.[1] A draft was prepared using the FCPA as a model. The efforts of the drafting group of ECOSOC were later combined with the ongoing work in the UN on a code of conduct for transnational corporations. The last text proposed in 1988 included provision 21, comprising two brief paragraphs which stated that transnational corporations should not make

---

§ 17.44

1. The OECD Convention and a useful Commentaries on the Convention are in www.usdoj.gov./criminal/fraud/oecd-com.htm.

2. The OECD issued a Recommendation in May 1997, that requested member states to prohibit tax deductibility of bribes, as well as to adopt standardized accounting procedures to help disclose illegal payments, to impose sanctions for violations, and to disqualify firms violating the laws from public procurement.

§ 17.46

1. Resolution to Convene a Conference to Draft a Treaty on Corrupt Practices, U.N.DOC.No. E/Res/1978/71 (1978).

bribes and should maintain accounting records of payments to officials.[2] Typical of the efforts of the UN at the time, no suggestion was included that foreign officials should not request or accept bribes. These provisions are now part of the history of unsuccessful efforts within the UN to control real and perceived evils of multinationals operating in third-world and nonmarket economies. Most of these nations are now focused on encouraging multinational corporations to offer their benefits for development. But within the institutional structure of the UN lurk a few remnants of the restrictionism of the 1970s.

§ 17.47 Other Organizations

The Organization of American States (OAS) has completed the Inter–American Convention Against Corruption.[1] It is quite extensive in its list of acts which constitute corruption. The Convention is intended to require nations to adopt laws which establish as a criminal offense the acts of corruption. It further considers violations to be extraditable offenses. The OAS Convention thus reaches beyond the regulatory process of the FCPA. One such extension is including as an offense the "illicit enrichment" of a public official. Appropriately, it develops some means for international cooperation in investigating and enforcing the rules. This hemispheric action is extremely important, but must be tempered with the history of a very great gap between what nations are willing to place on the books, and what they are willing to enforce.

The International Chamber of Commerce (ICC) has urged companies to adopt rules of conduct intended to address issues of extortion and bribery in international trade.[2] In rules announced March 1996, the ICC urged nations to implement the 1994 recommendations of the OECD on curtailing bribery.

Transparency International was formed in 1993 as a non-governmental organization (NGO) to attempt to curtail corruption.[3] Its goal is to build "broad coalitions" against corruption, create national chapters to join the fight, and encourage corporations to take first steps by refusing to participate in corrupt acts. TI publishes an annual list ranking nations on the basis of its Corruption Perception Index. The CPI is not welcomed by the nations which each year tend to remain at or near the most corrupt end of the index.

---

2. Proposed text of the Draft Code of Conduct on Transnational Corporations, Para. 21. E/1988/39 Add. 1, E/1983/17/Rev. 1–E/C.10/1983/S/5 Rev/1. annex II.

§ 17.47

1. Inter–American Convention Against Corruption, adopted by the OAS Specialized Conference on the draft-Inter–American Convention Against Corruption, Caracas, Venezuela, March 29, 1996. The United States signed the Convention, but it has not been ratified by the Congress. The United States executive believes that the FCPA satisfies the Convention and no further legislation is needed.

2. International Chamber of Commerce Press release 6641889 E (10/21/96). The new ICC rules are stricter than the ICC rules published in 1977.

3. See Transparency International (ti@transparency.org).

The IBRD and IDA of the World Bank have adopted guidelines which apply to procurement, and establish the absence of corruption as a condition of lending. If there is evidence of corruption in projects requesting financing it will be denied, and for projects underway it will be withdrawn.[4] The action of the World Bank is likely to generate similar conditions for lending in regional financial institutions.

N. CONCLUSIONS

§ 17.48 Repeal Unlikely

Much of the activity addressing payments abroad occurred in the mid to late 1970s, including the various actions, or inactions, of multinational organizations such as the OECD, the GATT and the UN. The adoption of the FCPA was followed by a surge of U.S. efforts to have similar rules adopted either by international organizations or by individual nations. Repeatedly criticized, the law has been amended twice, but there have been few serious urgings for additional amendments to either further weaken the law, or return it to its stricter, original version, with the "reason to know" language. But as the enforcement section above suggests, the law continues to be the subject of actions, investigations, and accusations. Any full repeal of the FCPA is very unlikely. The FCPA breathes morality. Who in the Congress wants to attach his or her name to the bill which abolishes prohibiting *corrupt* payments? If it ever is abolished, it is likely to be by burying its demise in an omnibus trade bill with little discussion of its repeal.

§ 17.49 Warning Signs of Violations of the FCPA

Any company doing business abroad should be aware of signs that violations of the FCPA may be occurring in the company. Some such signs include:

1. Previous company history of FCPA violations.

2. Previous history of FCPA violations by officers and directors.

3. Previous industry history of FCPA violations.

4. Doing business in a nation with a reputation for corruption, and for FCPA violations.

5. Transactions where local distributor or agent is related to, or has business links with, or is recommended by, government officials.

6. Transactions where local distributor or agent wishes commissions to be paid to third-nation account, especially a numbered account in a nation known as a safe haven.

4. In 1997 the World Bank refused to grant Kenya new credits because of corrup-   tion.

7. Transactions with local distributor or agent who suggests irregular procedures, such as incorrect dates on invoices, double invoicing for customs, checks for more than the invoice amount, different check dates, cash or bearer instrument payments, excessive credit line, advance payments, etc.

8. Transactions with local distributor or agent which call for excessive commissions.

9. Transactions with local distributor or agent with poor reputation.

10. Transactions with local distributor or agent without any experience in the field of business.

11. Transactions with local distributor or agent who insists on anonymity.

12. Transactions with local distributor or agent who refuses to sign company policy that the FCPA not be violated.

13. Transactions with local distributor or agent who appears not to have adequate facilities and staff to undertake task by effort versus by bribes.

O. SELECTED DOCUMENTS

§ 17.50 Company Policy Regarding the FCPA

The Corporation adopts as a policy the nonparticipation of any of its directors, officers, employees or agents in any activity which would be in violation of the Foreign Corrupt Practices Act (FCPA). Any action by any such person shall be grounds for dismissal or termination of any agency relationship with possible forfeiture of compensation.

[Further recommended are provisions which define what kind of payments are likely to be in violation, relating such payments to the type of business in which the company is engaged.]

§ 17.51 Officer Contract Provision Regarding Making Unlawful Payments

The corporation agrees that no director, officer, agent or employee is authorized to request or demand that _____ make any payment which in the opinion of _____ might violate any United States law, or the law of any foreign nation in which the corporation is doing business, including but not limited to payments in violation of the Foreign Corrupt Practices Act of the United States. Any such request or demand may be refused by _____, and any dismissal following such refusal, whether or not such dismissal states it is for reasons of such refusal, shall be considered a breach of this contract of employment.

Selected Bibliography

Katherine M. Albright & Grace Won, Foreign Corrupt Practices Act, 30 Am.Crim.L.R. 773 (1993).

Arthur Aronoff, Antibribery Provisions of the Foreign Corrupt Practices Act, The Commerce Department Speaks 1992: Developments in Import Administration, Export and Investment Abroad 799, Practicing Law Institute Corporate Law and Practice Course Handbook Series No. B–789 (1992).

John W. Bagby, Enforcement of the Accounting Standards in the Foreign Corrupt Practices Act, 21 Amer. Bus. L.J. 213 (1983).

Jeffrey P. Bialos & Gregory Husisian, Foreign Corrupt Practices Act: Coping with Corruption in Russia and Other Transitional Economies, Practicing Law Institute Commercial and Practice Course Handbook Series (Oct. 1995).

Stephen F. Black, Complying with the Foreign Corrupt Practices Act (1997).

Bartley A. Brennan, The Foreign Corrupt Practices Act Amendments of 1988: "Death" of a Law, 15 North Car.J.Int'l L. & Comm.Reg. 229 (1990).

H. Lowell Brown, Parent Subsidiary Liability Under the Foreign Corrupt Practices Act, 50 Baylor L. Rev. 1 (1998).

Christopher F. Corr and Judd Lawler, Damned if You Do, Damned if You Don't? The OECD Convention and the Globalization of Anti-bribery Measures. 32 Vand. J. Transnat'l L. 1249 (1999)

Donald R. Crover, Complying with the Foreign Corrupt Practices Act: A Guide for U.S. Firms Doing Business in the International Marketplace (1999).

Raymond J. Dowd, Civil RICO Misread: The Judicial Repeal of the 1988 Amendments to the Foreign Corrupt Practices Act, 14 Fordham Int'l L.J. 946 (1991).

Executive Legal Summary No. 5, Business Laws, Inc. 100.01 et seq. (Hancock ed., Oct. 1988).

Foreign Corrupt Practices Act Antibribery Provisions, Corporate Law and Practice Course Handbook Series, Practicing Law Institute Order No. B4–7145 (1996).

Foreign Corrupt Practices Act Reporter.

John E. Impert, A Program for Compliance with the Foreign Corrupt Practices Act and Foreign Law Restrictions on the Use of Sales Agents, 24 Int'l Lawyer 1009 (1990).

Pamela J. Jadwin & Monica Shilling, Foreign Corrupt Practices Act, 31 Am. Crim. L. Rev. 677 (1994).

G. Jones, et al., The Foreign Corrupt Practices Act, Doing Business in Kuwait and Saudi Arabia 84–99 (Smith, Currie & Hancock 1991).

Robert E. Klitgaard, Controlling Corruption (1991).

Laura E. Longobardi, Reviewing the Situation: What is to be Done with the Foreign Corrupt Practices Act? 20 Vand.J. of Transnat'l L. 431 (1987).

Middle East Executive Reports.

Lawrence W. Newman & Michael Burrows, Private Claims Under the Foreign Corrupt Practices Act, 207 N.Y. L.J. 3 (1992).

Philip M. Nichols, Regulating Transnational Bribery in Times of Globalization and Fragmentation, 24 Yale J. Int'l L. 257 (1999).

W. Michael Reisman, Folded Lies (1979).

SEC Report on Questionable and Illegal Corporate Payments and Practices, 94th Cong. (1976).

Steven R. Salbu, Extraterritorial Restriction of Bribery: A Premature Evocation of the Normative Global Village, 24 Yale J. Int'l L. 223 (1999).

Bill Shaw, Foreign Corrupt Practices Act: Amendments of 1988, 14 Md.J. Int'l L. & Trade 161 (1990).

Symposium: A Hemispheric Approach to Combating Corruption, 15 Am. U. Int'l L.R. 759 (2000).

Symposium: The Foreign Corrupt Practices Act: Domestic and International Implications, 9 Syracuse J.Int'l L. & Com. (1982).

Jay Vogelson, Corrupt Practices in the Conduct of International Business: ABA Section on Int'l Law Recommendations and Reports, 30 Int'l Law. 193 (1996)

H. Weisberg & E. Reichenberg, Research Report: The Price of Ambiguity More than Three Years Under the Foreign Corrupt Practices Act, Chamber of Commerce of the United States (1981).

Bruce Zagaris, Avoiding Criminal Liability in the Conduct of International Business, 21 Wm. Mitchell L. Rev. 749 (1996).

Don Zarin, Doing Business Under the Foreign Corrupt Practices Act (1995).

Note, No More "This for That"? The Effect of the OECD Convention on Combating Bribery of Foreign Public Officials in International Business Transactions, 8 Cardozo J. Int'l & Comp. L. 139 (2000).

Note, Amending the Foreign Corrupt Practices Act to Include a Private Right of Action, 82 Cal. L.R. 185 (1994).

Note, The Foreign Corrupt Practices Act of 1988: Clarification or Visceration?, 20 L. & Pol'y Int'l Bus. 441 (1989).

Chapter 18

UNITED STATES BOYCOTT AND ANTI-BOYCOTT LAW

Table of Sections

A. INTRODUCTION

A. INTRODUCTION

§ 18.1 Boycott and Antiboycott Laws

The United States engages in both boycott and antiboycott practices. In the past few decades the United States has boycotted or embargoed goods from or to such countries as Cuba, Iran, Iraq, Libya, Nicaragua, North Korea, South Africa, Rhodesia and Vietnam. The effectiveness of these boycotts in achieving political goals has been widely debated.[1]

The U.S. boycotts have not all been unilateral. It has engaged in collective sanctions when many others have joined, such as the U.N. trade boycott against Iraq after the invasion of Kuwait,[2] or against Serbia and Montenegro after the Serbian-promoted invasion of Bosnia.[3] Less "collective" were the trade sanctions imposed on Argentina by the United States and the European Economic Community after the Argentine invasion of the Falklands/Malvinas Islands.[4]

The United States has engaged in boycotts when many have participated, such as the U.N. collective sanctions noted above. It has also stood nearly alone among major nations in implementing other boycotts, such as that directed to Cuba. Additionally, the United States has engaged in long term boycotts, notably against Cuba, and very brief boycotts, such as limits on exports to Europe which might be used in the construction of a gas pipeline from the USSR after the Soviet invasion of Poland. There is little doubt that in the future unilateral or collective boycotts will continue to be part of U.S. foreign policy.

§ 18.1

1. See Gary C. Hufbauer, Jeffrey J. Schott & Kimberly Ann Elliot, Economic Sanctions Reconsidered (1990).

2. See United Nations Security Council Resolution 661 (1990).

3. See United Nations Security Council Resolution 757 (1992).

4. See Domingo E. Acevedo, The U.S. Measures Against Argentina Resulting from the Malvinas Conflict, 78 Am.J.Int'l L. 323 (1984).

The United States has only one significant experience with the use of antiboycott law. That is the Arab boycott of Israel, which forms the major part of this chapter. The law was adopted exclusively because of the Arab boycott of Israel. But nowhere does the law specifically mention either Arabs or Israel. Furthermore, the law is likely to remain on the books long after the Arab boycott ends. The law is directed to prohibiting U.S. persons from participating in or supporting boycotts by foreign nations against other foreign nations friendly to the United States.

§ 18.2 Boycott Laws and International Law

International law scholars have long debated whether boycotts violate international law.[1] But boycotts have been used frequently as an instrument of international law to achieve political goals,[2] such as actions by the United Nations. A primary boycott, which involves a curtailment of trade with another nation, generally is regarded as not constituting a violation of international law. But that view may differ when the boycotted nation is little more than an economic dependent of the boycotting nation. Even when the boycott assumes secondary or tertiary characteristics, international law may not be violated. It is when the boycotting nation carries the boycott to a stage of economic warfare, such as a blockade, that it more readily conflicts with international law, especially when human rights issues arise. Further obscuring the issue is whether there must be some act by the nation boycotted which justifies the boycotting action of the other.[3]

A *blockade* of another nation may constitute a violation of international law, as will such more aggressive activities as mining the harbors of the foreign nation. The blockade may be viewed as an acceptable alternative to war, causing some reluctance in labeling the blockade a violation of international law. Few disagree as to the less harmful alternative, but that does not reject the idea that both may be violations of acceptable international conduct.

However elevated the argument over the norms of international law may soar to academic heights, nations will continue to use boycotts as an instrument of foreign policy. The use of boycotts by the United States illustrates that it is quite an extensive, although perhaps not always effective, instrument of that policy.

§ 18.2

1. See, e.g., Margaret P. Doxey, Economic Sanctions and International Enforcement (1980); Christopher C. Joyner, The Transnational Boycott as Economic Coercion in International Law: Policy, Place and Practice, 17 Vand.J.Transnat'l L. 205 (1984).

2. They may be referred to as "self-help" or unilateral measures. The Restatement (Third) of Foreign Relations Law addresses unilateral measures in § 905, as does the International Law Commission's Draft Articles on State Responsibility (Part Two), in Articles 12–14. Both assume similar approaches. Neither constitute law; they reflect the perceptions (and sometimes goals) of their drafters.

3. A critical point is whether the boycotted state must have committed an illegal act. The majority view seems to be that the act need not be illegal, it may simply be "unfriendly.".

B. UNITED STATES BOYCOTTS

§ 18.3 The Structure of United States Boycott Law

With whom the United States does not trade tends to be the decision of the President, although the Congress may act in special situations to deny trade benefits. Trade embargoes are often imposed quickly following some act which the U.S. President finds politically unacceptable; he responds with trade sanctions. The Department of Commerce participates in the process of enforcing trade sanctions by controls on exports to various nations.[1] Although the Congress governs foreign commerce and specifically *exports* by means of the Export Administration Act, Congress tends to leave to presidential discretion the imposition of sanctions against specific countries. This is not always the case, however. Congress may enact specific laws targeting particular nations. An example is the Cuban Democracy Act of 1992, which placed severe limitations on trade with Cuba, including trade by U.S. controlled subsidiaries abroad.[2] When Congress does act, it usually provides that its law will be carried out with additional regulations. The Export Administration Act has substantial regulations which are enforced largely by the Department of Commerce.

When the United States wishes to go further than to simply deny most favored nation status to a foreign nation, it may totally prohibit trade. Congressional action is likely to target a specific nation. When Congress prohibits trade, or delegates such authority to the President, there is a shift of much of the enforcement (and enactment of regulations) responsibility from the Department of Commerce to the Department of the Treasury. Part of the reason is that Treasury has an extensive framework of regulations governing the control of foreign assets.[3]

The Office of Foreign Assets Control of Treasury has jurisdiction over a broad range of controls on transactions between U.S. persons and persons in foreign countries.[4] When those latter persons are in certain foreign countries, the controls may prohibit nearly any form of "transaction" or "transfer". A transaction or transfer may involve money or goods or services. Certain transactions or transfers may be absolutely prohibited, others may be subject to special licensing.[5]

The general regulations governing foreign assets control,[6] are fol-

§ 18.3

1. Export controls are the subject of chapter 16.

2. Pub.L. No. 102–484, §§ 1706–12, 106 Stat. 2315, 2578–81 (1992).

3. 31 C.F.R. Parts 500–585.

4. For a clash of OFAC and the Constitution see Looper v. Morgan, 1995 WL 499816 (S.D.Tex.1995)(regarding the search of an attorney's briefcase upon entry to the United States in search of documents supporting violations of the Libyan sanctions).

5. Licensing is in 31 C.F.R. Part 500, subpart E.

6. 31 C.F.R. Parts 500 and 505.

lowed by a series of mostly country-specific regulations.[7] These regulations vary in intensity of restrictiveness, but follow a general format including (1) the relation of the regulations to other laws and regulations, (2) what transactions are prohibited, (3) definitions, (4) interpretations, (5) licensing process, (6) reports, (7) penalties and (8) procedures. Some of the provisions are brief, others extensive.[8] To give an idea of how these restrictions function, the experience of Cuba is outlined in the following section.

The Office of Foreign Assets Control has two forms of sanctions. One is financial sanctions and asset freezes. The second is trade and commercial embargoes. They may be used selectively or quite comprehensively.[9] Selective sanctions may include blocking assets held in the United States, limitations on engaging in contracts, in travel, in transportation or even in exporting any goods or services. Selective sanctions have been used against various countries, including former "communist bloc" nations, South Africa, Iran and Angola. Comprehensive sanctions usually involve all the available options, and have been used against Cuba, Iran, Iraq, Libya, North Korea and parts of the former Yugoslavia.

The Cuban sanctions discussed immediately below represent the most severe sanctions yet adopted. They were partly used as a model for the 1996 Iran and Libya Sanctions Act, often referred to as the D'Amato Act.[10] This Act, following the Libertad Act, requires the President to impose sanctions against *foreign* companies that invest more than $20 million a year in the development of petroleum resource production in Iran, or more than $40 million in Libya. The proposed $2 billion investment in Iran by the French Total company in the late 1990s generated a conflict between France and the United States over possible sanctions,[11] which the U.S. President did not impose, although he was under pressure to do so.[12] If sanctions had been imposed, this matter quickly would have been taken to the WTO by the European Union on behalf of[13] France.

Although the focus of this chapter is on federal law, in the past few years a number of state and local governments have adopted boycott provisions. The provisions for the most part limit government procure-

---

7. The consolidation of regulations as of July 10, 2000, included specific regulations for Angola, Burma, Cuba, Iran (two parts), Iraq, Libya, Sudan and Yugoslavia (two parts: Bosnian Serb-controlled areas of Republic [part 585] and Kosovo [part 586]).

8. The restrictions on trade with Libya list many companies which are considered to be part of the government.

9. The President's Export Council June 1997 report on Unilateral Economic Sanctions listed 49 such measures against 18 countries by state and local governments.

10. Pub.L. No. 104–172, 110 Stat. 1541 (1996).

11. See Roger Cohen, France Scoffs at U.S. Protest Over Iran Deal, N.Y. Times, Sep. 30, 1997, at A1.

12. President Clinton waived sanctions in return for an agreement by the three companies to eliminate the sale of nuclear technology to Iran. See Jane Perley & Steve LeVine, U.S. Oilmen Chafing at Curbs on Iran, N.Y. Times, Aug. 9, 1998, § 1, at 8; see also Douglas Jehl, Tehran Smiles After U.S. Waives Sanctions Against 3 Companies, N.Y. Times, May 20, 1998, at A13.

13. See Youssef M. Ibrahim, French Oil Official Asks if U.S. Law Reaches Iran, N.Y. Times, Oct. 3, 1997, at A6.

ment for reasons of perceived violations of human rights (a principal target is Burma (Myanmar)), religious freedom (many countries), and the failure to deal with the return of Holocaust assets (Switzerland). These laws have created a separate (from federal sanctions) opposition among some foreign nations. The EU initiated a challenge under the WTO government procurement rules against a 1996 Massachusetts law addressed to Burma. Federal sanctions were authorized against Burma in 1997,[14] but the law did not discuss preemption. In a case against the Massachusetts law brought by the National Foreign Trade Council, the federal district court, the federal circuit court and the U.S. Supreme Court all held for the NFTC.[15] The federal ruling caused the EU to withdraw its action under the WTO dispute resolution procedures.

§ 18.4   Trade Restrictions: The Case of Cuba

The trade boycott of Cuba illustrates how the United States carries out a unilateral boycott. The Cuban boycott has endured longer than the other current sanctions. Furthermore, it has received attention by Congress and the U.S. President of varying levels of forcefulness over the past three decades, often in direct relation to political campaigns.

The boycott of Cuba began as a response to the Cuban nationalization of all U.S. citizens' properties in 1959 and 1960,[1] and to the trade agreement concluded by Cuba with the USSR in February, 1960. The U.S. Congress amended the Sugar Act of 1948 giving the President authority to alter the Cuban sugar quota. The President used this authority during the height of the July, 1960, bitterness to nearly totally remove the extensive quotas, leaving Cuba with no access to the U.S. sugar market. In October, 1960, the President imposed an extensive embargo on shipments of goods to Cuba, except for nonsubsidized food, medicines and medical supplies. With the cessation of diplomatic relations, the United States has continued the boycott without a break, but the intensity of the boycott has varied.

The boycott provisions were amended in 1975 to allow foreign subsidiaries of U.S. companies to trade with Cuba. These amendments followed U.S. threats to tighten controls on foreign subsidiaries which caused several foreign governments to angrily denounce the policy, and even threaten nationalization of the companies.[2] After 1975, U.S. subsid-

14. Omnibus Consolidated Appropriations Act, Pub.L. No. 104–208, § 570, 110 Stat. 3009, 3009–166–167, on September 30, 1996.

15. National Foreign Trade Council v. Baker, 26 F.Supp.2d 287 (D.Mass.1998), *aff'd,* National Foreign Trade Council v. Natsios, 181 F.3d 38 (1st Cir.1999), *aff'd sub nom.,* Crosby v. National Foreign Trade Council, 530 U.S. 363, 120 S.Ct. 2288, 147 L.Ed.2d 352 (2000)(holding Massachusetts' Burma law invalid under the Supremacy Clause because it threatens to frustrate federal statutory objectives).

§ 18.4

1. The expropriations effectively commenced under the Agrarian Reform Law on June 1, 1959, but did not reach their zenith until the resolutions issued under the authority of the major nationalization law of July, 1960. See Michael Wallace Gordon, The Cuban Nationalizations: The Demise of Foreign Private Property (1976).

2. The threats were fewer in number than those which followed the enactment of the Cuban Democracy Act, but were more

iaries abroad developed significant trade with Cuba. This trade angered anti-Castro groups in the United States, and led to the enactment of the Cuban Democracy Act in 1992. The Cuban Assets Control Regulations were amended to reflect the Act's strict provisions.

Proponents of the Cuban Democracy Act were also urging adoption of a much harsher act, which would allow litigation by current U.S. citizens who were Cuban nationals at the time of the Castro expropriations, seeking compensation from persons currently using expropriated properties. This became the Cuban Liberty and Democratic Solidarity (Libertad) Act (more commonly known as Helms–Burton), enacted in March, 1996,[3] only because of the emotions aroused due to the shooting down of two U.S. civilian aircraft by Cuba near Cuban territory. The Act included two very controversial sections. The first, Title III, created a right of action in U.S. courts for a U.S. national with a claim that Cuba expropriated property after January 1, 1959, against any person who is "trafficking" in such property. Trafficking is quite broadly defined, including not only such actions as selling, buying, leasing or transferring, but also engaging in a "commercial activity using or otherwise benefitting from confiscated property."[4] The Act authorizes the President to suspend the effectiveness of Title III actions for successive periods of six months. President Clinton issued such suspension every six months since August, 1996, throughout his term. These suspensions were the only reason the European Union kept on hold its request for a panel under the WTO to challenge the extraterritorial effects of the Libertad Act. The United States has stated that it would use the national-security defense under the WTO, and also in response to any similar challenge brought by Canada or Mexico under the NAFTA.[5]

The second important part of the Act, Title IV, requires that the Secretary of State deny visas for entry into the United States to corporate officers, principals, shareholders and even the spouse, minor children or agents of such persons, if they are trafficking in or have confiscated property.[6] This authority has been used against officials of Canadian, Israeli and Mexican companies.

Other nations and organizations have responded in very strong terms against the Libertad Act by adopting blocking laws, enacting resolutions, etc.[7] Cuba enacted its own response to the Libertad, which,

successful in causing the United States to change its policy.

3. Pub.L. No. 104–114, 110 Stat. 785 (Mar. 12, 1996).

4. Libertad Act § 4(13).

5. The use of the national security defense was strongly criticized in such a case, where there was no foreseeable security threat.

6. Id. at § 401.

7. See, e.g., Peter Glossop, Canada's Foreign Extraterritorial Measures Act and U.S. Restrictions on Trade with Cuba, 32 Int'l Lawyer 93 (1998); Mexico: Act to Protect Trade and Investment from Foreign Statutes which Contravene International Law, with Introductory note by Jorge Vargas, 36 Int'l Legal Materials 133 (1997); Douglas H. Forsythe, Introductory Note, Canada: Foreign Extraterritorial Measures Act Incorporating the Amendments Countering the U.S. Helms–Burton Act, 36 Int'l Legal Materials 111 (1997); Protecting Against the Effects of the Extraterritorial Application of Legislation Adopted by the Third Country, E.U. Council Regulation

inter alia, denies any possible compensation in a future settlement with the government of Cuba to anyone attempting to take advantage of the Libertad Act by using the U.S. courts under Title III.[8]

The Cuban Assets Control Regulations, approximately four dozen pages and nearly 150 separate provisions, are the principal regulations which govern trade with Cuba. The application of the Regulations is limited by the Cuban Democracy Act, which removed administrative discretion in allowing some trade with Cuba from foreign subsidiaries. Furthermore, the Regulations may not conflict with the Trading with the Enemy Act,[9] or the Foreign Assistance Act of 1961, both as amended.[10] The administration of the Regulations is delegated to the Office of Foreign Assets Control (OFAC) of the Department of the Treasury.[11]

The Regulations prohibit certain transactions and transfers, where Cuba or a Cuban national is involved. The scope is very wide, including various transfers involving (1) currency, securities, and gold or silver coin or bullion; (2) property or indebtedness; and (3) any form where the transfer is one which attempts to evade or avoid the first two prohibitions.[12] But the Secretary of the Treasury is given authority to authorize such transfers.[13] Imports are prohibited if (1) Cuban in origin,[14] (2) the goods have been in Cuba (including transported through), or (3) made from any Cuban parts.[15] There are few exceptions to the trade restrictions. One is a limited exception allowing trade in informational materials, such as some books.[16] The prohibitions conclude with a restriction that disallows (1) any vessel which has entered a Cuban port for trade purposes from entering a U.S. port for 180 days after the departure from Cuba, or (2) any vessel carrying goods or passengers to or from Cuba (or goods in which a Cuban has any interest) from entering any U.S. port with such goods or passengers on board.[17]

The prohibitions are followed by quite extensive definitions.[18] While nearly all of the definitions create little problem, one is of considerable importance to U.S. businesses with subsidiaries. A "person subject to the

---

2271/96, 1996 O.J. (L 309), reprinted in 36 Int'l Legal Materials 127 (1997).

8. Ley de Reafirmacion de la Dignidad y Soberania Cubana (Ley No. 80), Dec. 24, 1996.

9. The original powers of the President were in the Trading With the Enemy Act (TWEA) of 1917. The President delegated authority to Treasury in accordance with the TWEA. The International Emergency Economic Powers Act (IEEPA) was enacted in 1988 and substantially replaced the TWEA. The authority of the President continues under the IEEPA.

10. 31 C.F.R. § 515.101.

11. The Cuban Democracy Act mandates that the Office establish a branch in Miami to "strengthen the enforcement" of the Act.

12. 31 C.F.R. § 515.201.

13. Id.

14. See, e.g., United States v. Plummer, 221 F.3d 1298 (11th Cir.2000).

15. 31 C.F.R. § 515.204. Exports would require a validated license which is not available for goods destined to Cuba. Export controls are discussed in chapter 16.

16. 31 C.F.R. § 515.206. This Regulation is followed by several examples of prohibited and permitted informational transfers.

17. 31 C.F.R. § 515.207. These vessel restrictions were added to comply with § 1706(b) of the Cuban Democracy Act.

18. 31 C.F.R. Subpart C.

jurisdiction of the United States," upon whom the Regulations impose trade restrictions, includes, "any corporation, partnership, or association, wherever organized or doing business, that is owned or controlled by persons" citizen or resident of the United States or where an entity is organized under the laws of the United States.[19] The meaning of "owned" or "controlled" is not included in the Regulations. The focus of the Cuban Democracy Act is to limit trade with Cuba from foreign subsidiaries of U.S. corporations. It has brought negative responses from the European Union (and separately from member states of the EU), Canada, Argentina, Mexico and the U.N. General Assembly. It is one more example of the extraterritorial application of U.S. laws, and one more example of foreign rejection of such application.

Following the definitions in the Regulations are several "interpretations."[20] They both allow some flexibility in the application of the restrictions, (i.e., allowing some professional travel to Cuba[21]) and provide some strict interpretations of the restrictions (i.e., limiting access to safe-deposit boxes wherein may lie property owned by a Cuban).

Until this point, the Regulations are mostly prohibitory. But the next section contains important provisions covering "licenses, authorizations, and statements of licensing policy."[22] These provisions authorize the Secretary of the Treasury to issue licenses in a wide variety of circumstances, including (1) for certain judicial proceedings to take place, (2) to determine persons to be unblocked nationals, (3) and to allow transfers by operations of law. The provisions of most importance for U.S. business interests allow some limited trade with Cuba by U.S. owned or controlled firms.[23] But it was this provision which was the principal focus of the Cuban Democracy Act, which reversed a decade old policy allowing Treasury to license foreign subsidiaries to trade with Cuba.[24] The current law prohibits the issuance of any such licenses to contracts entered into after the enactment of the Cuban Democracy Act. The governments of the foreign nations in which many U.S. subsidiaries are located, however, have enacted laws which mandate that the subsidiaries disregard the U.S. restrictions. It must be assumed that some trade continues, without any attempt of obtaining a license.

The subsequent subpart governs reports, and requires reports by any person engaging in any transaction subject to the Regulations.[25] Thus, a U.S. company trading through a subsidiary may twice violate the law, first by trading and second by failing to report the trade. Penalties are contained in the next provisions,[26] and are severe. Fines may reach

19. 31 C.F.R. § 515.329(d).

20. 31 C.F.R. Subpart D.

21. These provisions are the basis for much of the permitted travel to Cuba. They are quite detailed, even prohibiting travel by bird-watching groups. In late 2000 the U.S. Congress enacted legislation prohibiting the President from altering the travel regulations without Congressional approval. It was part of a bill principally intended to allow some sales of food and medicine to Cuba.

22. 31 C.F.R. Subpart E.

23. 31 C.F.R. § 515.559.

24. Cuban Democracy Act § 1706(a).

25. 31 C.F.R. § 515.601.

26. 31 C.F.R. Subpart F.

$1 million for willful violations, with a maximum of $500,000 as civil penalties. If experience with the antiboycott Regulations discussed below offers any parallel, consent decrees are likely to be the method used to respond to investigated violations. Just as the antiboycott provisions have not stopped violations, these boycott provisions are unlikely to stop violations. That becomes even more clear when it is realized that with antiboycott violations there is no violation of foreign law when the violation of the U.S. law occurs. But in the case of these boycott Regulations, a U.S. firm in violation of some of the provisions may have a mitigating argument not present in the antiboycott situation—to comply with the U.S. law means violation of the law of the nation in which the U.S. subsidiary is incorporated and operating.

Three final areas complete the structure of the Cuban Assets Control Regulations, covering procedures and miscellaneous provisions. As noted in the section above, the structure of the Cuban Assets Control Regulations follows a kind of generic pattern for dealing with other boycotted nations. How forceful the regulations are in practice depends on foreign policy rather than economic considerations.[27]

C. ENACTING THE ANTIBOYCOTT LAWS

§ 18.5 United States Reaction to the Arab Boycott of Israel: The Antiboycott Laws

Two important historic events surrounding the conflict between businesses' freedom to export and the government's political goals led to special rules governing exports.[1] The first was the Arab nations' extensive international primary, secondary and tertiary boycott of Israel.[2] The boycott is inconsistently applied by the Arab nations. Where the product or project is of high priority, the Arab nations either ignore their own boycott[3] or grant a waiver.[4]

The Arab boycott of Israel led to the adoption of U.S. laws and regulations essentially prohibiting U.S. persons from complying with or supporting any boycott by a foreign nation against a nation friendly to

27. See, e.g., Michael Krinsky & David Golove (eds.), United States Economic Measures Against Cuba (1993).

§ 18.5

1. These rules also govern foreign investment, but more often affect exports. It is clear that loss of a business opportunity is not a justification for violating the antiboycott laws.

2. A primary boycott is where one nation, for example, Oman, refuses to deal with another, for example, Israel. The boycott is secondary when the boycotting nation (Oman) refuses to deal with any third party nation, such as the United States, if

that nation deals with the boycotted nation, Israel. The tertiary boycott arises when the boycotting nation (Oman) refuses to deal with the third party nation (the United States), if any of the elements of its products are from a fourth party nation company (e.g., The Netherlands) which trades with the boycotted nation (e.g., Israel).

3. See Guzzardi, That Curious Barrier on the Arab Frontiers, Fortune, July 1975, at 82.

4. See Abrams v. Baylor College of Medicine, 581 F.Supp. 1570, 1576 n. 3, (S.D.Tex.1984) for an example of a waiver of the boycott regarding medical equipment from a blacklisted company.

the United States.[5] Nowhere in the law is there any direct reference to either Israel or any specific Arab nation, but these provisions owe their existence to a long and bitter struggle within Congress, and between Congress and the administration, over the creation of rules which would prohibit U.S. companies from assisting the Arab nations in their attempts to harm Israel.[6] Prior to the enactment of federal export laws dealing with the Arab boycott of Israel, several states enacted similar laws, and the federal tax and antitrust laws were used to deter U.S. companies from compliance with boycott requests.[7] Although the boycott of Israel by the Arab nations is the reason the federal law exists, there has been some question raised about the applicability of the law to foreign boycotts against South Africa. The Department of Commerce interpreted the law as not applicable to the (since terminated) boycotts against South Africa.[8] The law does affect many commercial relationships between U.S. persons and Middle Eastern governments, private individuals and banks.

The second event leading to special rules governing exports evolved from the discovery during the Watergate investigations that many U.S. companies had made payments to foreign officials to encourage those officials to purchase the goods of the company making the payments or extend other favors, such as allowing a foreign investment. Congressional reaction was much swifter than in the case of the Arab boycott. Congress adopted amendments to the securities laws to prohibit certain payments and regulate reporting of payments, in legislation called the Foreign Corrupt Practices Act.[9] Congress instead might have further

5. Export Administration Act of 1979, 50 App.U.S.C.A. § 2407; Export Administrative Regulations, 15 C.F.R. Part 769.

6. The history of the boycott provisions is contained in Trane v. Baldrige, 552 F.Supp. 1378 (W.D.Wis.1983). There are numerous references to Arab nations in the Supplements to 15 C.F.R. Part 769, which include interpretations of the regulations. For example, Supplement No. 3 notes that as a result of the Israel–Egypt Peace Treaty of 1980, the boycott of Israel by Egypt was officially ended and requests for information directed to U.S. persons involved with business in Egypt that were previously assumed to be boycott related would have to be considered differently. There was considerable pressure on the Arab nations to formally terminate the boycott, but as of early 2001 no such action had been taken by the Arab nations. However, six more nations lifted the secondary and tertiary boycotts of Israel. See Elaine Sciolino, Saudis and 5 Other Gulf Nations Will Ease Their Boycott of Israel, N.Y. Times, Oct. 1, 1994, § 1, at 1. But in 1997 some of the boycott appeared to be reactivated. See Arabs Vow Boycott of Israel, N.Y. Times, Apr. 1, 1997, § A, at 2.

7. Since 1976 the Internal Revenue Code has contained provisions which, first,

require companies to report operations in or related to a boycotting country, and second, cause such companies to forfeit certain tax benefits such as part of a foreign tax credit, deferral on undistributed earnings, and deferral of tax on export earnings. See IRC §§ 952(a)(3), 999(c)(1)–(2). See also Richard L. Kaplan, A Critical Examination of the Treasury Department's Report on the Arab Boycott, 1983 U.Ill.L.Rev. 23. The antitrust challenge came principally on the theory of refusals to deal constituting a violation of U.S. antitrust law. See Note: The Arab Boycott: The Antitrust Challenge of the United States v. Bechtel in Light of the Export Administration Amendments of 1977, 92 Harv.L.Rev. 1440 (1979). The enactment of the EAA and regulations shifted the focus of attack from this periphery of tax and antitrust laws to the more direct antiboycott laws. But they did not end the possible use of tax and antitrust laws to address the boycott issue.

8. See Supplement No. 14 to Part 769.

9. Foreign Corrupt Practices Act of 1977 (as amended in 1988 and 1998), 15 U.S.C.A. §§ 78q(b), 78dd, 78ff(a). The FCPA is the subject of the previous chapter.

amended the Export Administration Act to prohibit such payments, but the securities laws already addressed reporting and accounting requirements and that was one method used to regulate payments abroad. The FCPA added new reporting and accounting requirements which would help identify payments abroad. Prohibiting certain payments abroad, the second part of the FCPA, could be monitored by a company's records of payments. Use of the securities laws additionally meant that the Department of Justice would be the agency to pursue violations. The antiboycott provisions were under the jurisdiction of the Department of Commerce, thought to be somewhat more lenient than Justice.[10]

§ 18.6 Addressing Boycotts Contrary to United States Interests by Other Laws

While the antiboycott provisions of the Export Administration Act are the principal means of challenging boycotts against friendly nations which draw into their net U.S. persons, other laws also may be applicable. Some were used prior to the adoption of the antiboycott provisions.

Antitrust law. Because cooperating with the Arab nations' boycott may involve refusing to deal with Israel, the refusal to deal alone may constitute a violation of the Sherman Act. The Department of Justice initiated an action against the U.S. Bechtel Corporation with such view, alleging that Bechtel's refusal to deal with blacklisted companies constituted a combination and conspiracy with those blacklisted companies that violated the antitrust laws. The case never went to trial.[1] But the consent decree illustrated in detail those acts of compliance with Arab nation requests which were permissible, and which also have been exempted from the antiboycott laws.[2] The Justice Department subsequently stated that it was allowed to modify any terms in the consent decree which were more restrictive than what might be enacted in the proposed antiboycott legislation. Bechtel and Justice had later disagreements regarding the continued effectiveness of the consent decree and the issue of the applicability of the antitrust laws and boycotts remains unanswered.

Securities regulation. As in the case of foreign payments, the securities laws may challenge any failure to disclose activities which might constitute participation in a boycott and which might involve mandated reporting under the securities laws. There was never a *Bechtel*-kind of action commenced with regard to the securities laws. The applicability of the securities laws thus remains quite uncertain.[3]

---

10. There have been attempts by businesses to shift the jurisdiction of the FCPA from Justice to Commerce.

§ 18.6

1. See Note, The Arab Boycott: The Antitrust Challenge of United States v. Bechtel in Light of the Export Administrative Amendments of 1977, 92 Harv.L.Rev. 1440 (1979).

2. These deal mainly with the right of the Arab party to designate suppliers. The final judgment is in United States v. Bechtel Corp., 1979 WL 1582 (N.D.Cal.1979).

3. See Roth, The Arab Boycott and the Federal Securities Laws, 5 Sec.Reg.L.J. 318 (1978).

State laws. New York, with a substantial Jewish population and groups monitoring any anti-Semitic activity, enacted legislation which prohibited assistance to the Arab boycott. Other states enacted similar laws.[4] These state laws have had relatively little impact, because they were followed by the federal enactment of the antiboycott laws. The latter tend not to preempt the state laws, however, since the state laws are usually directed at antidiscriminatory practices.[5]

Internal Revenue Code. The IRC and the Regulations provide for sanctions against a taxpayer who participates in or cooperates with a boycott not acknowledged by the United States. There is not an exact convergence between what is a violation of the antiboycott laws and what will cause a loss of tax benefits. To be denied tax benefits, there must be an agreement to comply with a boycott.[6] Where a violation occurs, tax credits, tax deferrals and benefits under the Foreign Sales Corporations provisions may be lost. A second part of the tax laws requires reports on boycotts. If a U.S. States taxpayer is engaged in operations in countries named on a list maintained by the Secretary of the Treasury, reporting may be required. It is difficult for a company to determine the reporting requirements under the EAA and the IRC when there is any indication of participation in a boycott that is not sanctioned by the United States.

D.   THE ANTIBOYCOTT LAW

§ 18.7 Export Administration Act

The Export Administration Act (EAA) governs the export of goods from the United States. It additionally includes the antiboycott provisions. These antiboycott provisions, and the subsequently issued regulations, prohibit U.S. persons from participating in boycotts by a foreign nation against third nations that are friendly towards the United States. The statutory language is very broad, not unlike the concept of the U.S. antitrust laws. The EAA structure requires the President to issue regulations that prohibit any U.S. person from engaging principally in two different areas of activity, *refusals to deal* and *furnishing information*, if such actions further or support a boycott by one foreign nation against another foreign nation that is friendly to the United States.[1] There is a further provision that applies particularly to banks, that prohibits certain actions with regard to letters of credit which also may further or support a boycott.[2] These prohibitions are included in six

---

4. See Maurice Portley, State Legislative Responses to the Arab Boycott of Israel, Mich. J.L. Reform (1977).

5. There are also federal anti-discriminatory laws, principally the Civil Rights Act of 1964, which prohibit most employment discrimination based on religion. See Howard M. Friedman, Confronting the Arab Boycott: A Lawyer's Baedeker, 19 Harv. Int'l L.J. 443 (1978). See, supra, § 18.3.

6. The EAA rules go much further, to the prohibition of furnishing certain information in furtherance of a boycott.

§ 18.7

1. 50 App.U.S.C.A. § 2407(a)(1).

2. 50 App.U.S.C.A. § 2407(a)(1)(F).

sections of the law.[3] The law subsequently states that the regulations should provide exceptions governing some six classes of activity.[4] Further mandated is the reporting to the Secretary of Commerce of any request to furnish information.[5] Violations of these provisions are subject to the same statutes that govern other violations of the export laws, that were discussed in chapter 16.[6]

§ 18.8   Export Administration Regulations

Supplementing the EAA are Export Administration Regulations (EAR).[1] They include very extensive examples of conduct which provide guidance in determining whether specific conduct may constitute a violation of the EAA and EAR. Many of the examples are of common occurrences where companies are in jeopardy of refusing to deal or furnishing prohibited information.[2] Use of these examples is essential to determining both the sense of the administration in interpreting the law, and the likelihood that the conduct in question may be challenged. The examples in the Regulations follow the pattern of the principal statute. Thus, the Regulations begin (after a section with definitions[3]) with examples of the six classes of prohibited conduct,[4] and are followed by examples of the six classes of exceptions.[5] Following the Regulations are a series of 16 Supplements that include Department of Commerce interpretations of various provisions, with some suggested contractual provisions that may avoid challenges by the Department.

E.   ANTIBOYCOTT LAW—PROHIBITED CONDUCT

§ 18.9   Prohibited Actions Must Be Done Intentionally

The purpose of the antiboycott provisions is to prohibit any U.S. person "from taking or knowingly agreeing to take [certain actions] with intent to comply with, further, or support any boycott" against a country friendly to the United States.[1] It specifically exempts boycotts pursuant to U.S. law.[2]

The requirement of intent is essential, but what constitutes intent

3.   50 App.U.S.C.A. § 2407(a)(1)(A)–(F).

4.   50 App.U.S.C.A. § 2407(a)(2)(A)–(F).

5.   50 App.U.S.C.A. § 2407(b)(2).

6.   50 App.U.S.C.A. §§ 2410, 2411 and 2412.

§ 18.8

1.   15 C.F.R. Part 769.

2.   Also important to check are the supplements to Part 769. Supplement No. 5 contains some specific classes of information which may be furnished without having to qualify under one of the exceptions in the EAA. See also Supplement No. 15(c) to Part 769, and Supplement No. 16.

3.   15 C.F.R. § 769.1. These definitions may be supplemented by the formal "supplements" which appear at the end of the Regulations. For example, Supplement No. 4 to Part 769 further defines § 769.1(d)(12) with respect to foreign made goods with United States made spare parts. Supplement No. 8 to Part 769 further defines interstate or foreign commerce of the United States.

4.   15 C.F.R. § 769.2.

5.   15 C.F.R. § 769.3.

§ 18.9

1.   50 App.U.S.C.A. § 2407(a)(1).

2.   Id.

may seem marginal. In *United States v. Meyer*,[3] the defendant Meyer was held to have knowledge that a form required by Saudi Arabia to have a trademark registered in that country was not used to obtain information needed for the registration, but to further the boycott of Israel. Meyer claimed that his actions were inadvertent and not intentional, but Meyer's knowledge and intention were rather clearly illustrated by his receipt of information from the U.S. Department of State that it could not notarize the form because of the boycott, and his subsequent acquisition of a notarization through the U.S.–Arab Chamber of Commerce.[4] The *Meyer* decision involves a rather clear attempt to find a way past the law. It is thus not very helpful for a case where the intent is based on less apparent criteria. But it does emphasize that *inadvertent* compliance is not a violation.

§ 18.10 Refusals to Deal

The first prohibition in the EAA is against directly refusing to do business with or in the boycotted country, or with a national or resident of that country. Also prohibited is any refusal to do business with the boycotted country by agreement with or response to requests from any other person.[1] This means a U.S. company may not refuse to do business with Israel at the request of the central boycott office of the Arab nations in Damascus. Intent to refuse to do business is not established by the absence of any business relationship with the boycotted country.[2]

The Export Administration Regulations, which include ten subsections further defining the meaning of refusing to do business, expand upon this prohibition.[3] The Regulations make it clear that a refusal to do business may be established by a course of conduct as well as a specific refusal, or by a use of any "blacklist" or "whitelist". They emphasize, nevertheless, that intent to comply with or support a boycott is required. The Regulations also suggest what does *not* constitute a refusal to do business, such as an agreement to comply generally with the laws of the boycotting country.[4] There does not have to be an agreement not to do business. Compliance with a request, or a unilateral decision, if for boycott reasons, will suffice. These Regulations raise one especially difficult issue—the use of a list of suppliers. The Regulations give a specific example, although specific examples are usually left for the "examples" section.[5] A U.S. person under contract to provide management services for a construction contract may provide a list of qualified

3. 864 F.2d 214 (1st Cir.1988).

4. A strong dissent inappropriately relied on an inapplicable case to argue that the required level of intent was not met.

§ 18.10

1. 50 App.U.S.C.A. § 2407(a)(1)(A).

2. Id.

3. 15 C.F.R. § 769.2(a). See also Supplements No. 6(a), 7, and 15(a) to Part 769.

4. Supplement No. 1 to Part 769 includes an interpretation of contractual clauses regarding import laws of boycotting countries.

5. 15 C.F.R. § 769.2(a)(6).

bidders for the client if the service is customary, and if qualified persons are not excluded because they are blacklisted.[6]

The Regulations and especially the examples in the Regulations disclose the nearly unlimited possible configurations of fact situations that may give rise to problems. Consider only a few possible variations, from which numerous additional variations may be easily considered:

1.   A U.S. company is doing business in Israel, but wants to do business in Arab nations while retaining the Israel business. This creates a problem if the Arab nations have alternative sources for the goods, especially from companies in nations which do not have antiboycott laws, meaning essentially all other nations in the world.

2.   Same as above but the company would like to terminate the business in Israel because:

    a.   it believes in or doesn't really care about the boycott. The company is in danger of challenge by the Department of Commerce. But is a business likely to state that it believes in or doesn't care about the boycott?

    b.   the Israel business is not as large as the potential Arab nations business and the company does not have the capacity to do business in both. As long as the decision is not boycott based, it is proper to drop the Israel business. But it may have to prove that its motives were business and not boycott based.

    c.   the company had planned to close the Israel business because it has been losing money. It had best be able to prove that loss.

3.   The company trades with Arab nations and would also like to do business with Israel. It knows if it does do business with Israel it may lose the business with the Arab nations.

4.   The same but the company is willing to drop the business with the Arab nations. It may do so without violating the boycott rules because Israel is not boycotting the Arab nations.

5.   The company is doing business in both Israel and Arab nations. The Arabs do not know this. The company wants to drop the Israel business because it fears that the Arabs will learn of that business and terminate very profitable Arab business.

Prior to 1985–86, the focus of the Department of Commerce was on reporting violations. But in 1986 the Department, concerned with its limited resources, began to concentrate on the blacklist, religious discrimination and refusals to deal. These are viewed by the Department as the most serious violations.

The Regulations attempt to cover many variations, but obviously cannot offer an example for each possible situation. Refusals to deal arise for reasons both directly related and totally unrelated to the boycott.

---

6. Id.

When normally justified business reasons for refusing to deal begin to show a pattern of not dealing for reasons consistent with a boycott, however, the party is in some danger of a challenge from Commerce. But the law does include language of intent, which is most difficult to show from a pattern of conduct that indicates good business reasons for refusing to deal.

§ 18.11 Discriminatory Actions

The second statutorily prohibited conduct is refusing to employ or otherwise discriminating against any U.S. person on the basis of race, religion, sex or national origin, where such conduct is intentional and in furtherance of an unlawful boycott.[1] This section addresses the Arab nations' attempt to injure Jewish people wherever they may live, rather than to harm Israel as a nation. Thus, a company may not refuse to employ Jewish persons so that it may gain favor with Arab clients. In one of the few court decisions involving the antiboycott provisions, Baylor College of Medicine was found to have persistently appointed non-Jewish persons for a project with Saudi Arabia.[2]

The antidiscrimination section of the EAA includes both refusals to employ and *other discrimination*. For example, a requirement that a U.S. company not use a six-pointed star on its packaging of products to be sent to the Arab nation would be a violation because it is part of the enforcement effort of the boycott. But it is not a violation if the demand is that no symbol of Israel be included on the packaging. The former is a religious symbol generally, the latter an acceptable request which does not include reference to any person's religion.[3] This illustrates a general attempt to acknowledge that the boycotting nations are entitled to have *some* control over what comes into their nation. They are entitled to say no imports may be stamped "Products of Israel", but they may not attack the Jewish religion more broadly by requiring certification that no religious symbols appear on any packages. The United States is attempting to say that the Arab nations may have a right to engage in a primary boycott against Israel, but they may not draw U.S. persons into supporting that boycott.

The Regulations governing discriminatory actions make it clear that such actions must involve "intent to comply with, further or support an unsanctioned foreign boycott."[4] The Regulations further state that the boycott provisions do not supersede or limit U.S. civil rights laws.[5]

§ 18.11

1. 50 App.U.S.C.A. § 2407(a)(B). Even if employment discrimination is not boycott based, and thus not a violation of the EAA, it may violate other laws, such as civil rights legislation.

2. Abrams v. Baylor College of Medicine, 581 F.Supp. 1570 (S.D.Tex.1984), *aff'd*, 805 F.2d 528 (5th Cir.1986). The case also deals with the issue of the right to bring a private action. Using the Cort v. Ash factors test it held that there is an implied right under the EAA. But see the discussion infra § 18.27.

3. These are examples included in 15 C.F.R. § 769.2(b), examples (viii) and (ix). See Supplement No. 6(b) & (c) to Part 769.

4. 15 C.F.R. § 769.2(b)(2).

5. 15 C.F.R. § 769.2(b)(3).

§ 18.12 Furnishing Information Regarding Race, Religion, Sex or National Origin

The third specific prohibition is related to the prohibition of the refusal to hire for reasons of race, etc., discussed immediately above. This provision prohibits furnishing information with respect to race, religion, sex or national origin.[1] This brief provision is supplemented in the Regulations that state that it shall apply whether the information is specifically requested or offered voluntarily and whether stated in the affirmative or negative.[2] Furthermore, prohibited information includes place of birth or nationality of the parents, and information in code words or symbols that would identify a person's race, religion, sex or national origin.[3] The Regulations also reaffirm the element of intent.[4]

The examples in the Regulations illustrate the difficulty of clearly defining "prohibited information". If the boycotting nation requests a U.S. company to give all employees who will work in the boycotting nation visa forms, and these visa forms request otherwise prohibited information, the company is not in violation for giving the forms to its employees or for sending the forms back to the boycotting country party. This is considered a ministerial function and not support of the boycott. But the company may not itself provide the information on race, religion, sex or nationality of its employees, if it meets the intent requirement. The company might certify that none of its employees to be sent to the boycotting nation are women, where the laws of the boycotting country prohibit women from working. The reason for the submission has nothing to do with the boycott.

§ 18.13 Furnishing Information Regarding Business Relationships—The Use of "Blacklists"

The fourth prohibition is one which is often at issue, because it involves the use of blacklists. The Arab nations maintain a blacklist of persons and companies with whom they will not do business. Arab nations often ask a prospective commercial agreement party to certify that none of the goods will include components obtained from any companies on the blacklist.

Persons are prohibited from furnishing information about an extensive list of business activities ("including a relationship by way of sale, purchase, legal or commercial representation, shipping or other transport, insurance, investment, or supply"[1]), with an equally extensive list of business relationships ("with or in the boycotted country, with any business concern organized under the laws of the boycotted country, with any national or resident of the boycotted country, or with any other person which is known or believed to be restricted from having any

§ 18.12
1. 50 App.U.S.C.A. § 2407(a)(C).
2. 15 C.F.R. § 769.2(c)(2).
3. 15 C.F.R. § 769.2(c)(3).

4. 15 C.F.R. § 769.2(c)(4).

§ 18.13
1. 50 App.U.S.C.A. § 2407(a)(D).

business relationship with or in the boycotting country"[2]). At the end is a statement that the section does not prohibit furnishing "normal business information in a commercial context as defined by the Secretary."[3] Thus, clients are very extensively governed with regard to the flow of information between the company and the boycotting country.

The Regulations expand upon this already expansive section.[4] The prohibited information may not be given whether directly or indirectly requested or furnished on the initiative of the U.S. person.[5] The Secretary's definition of normal business in a commercial context is that related "to factors such as financial fitness, technical competence, or professional experience" as might be normally found in documents available to the public, such as "annual reports, disclosure statements concerning securities, catalogues, promotional brochures, and trade and business handbooks."[6] Such public information may not be supplied if in response to a boycott request.[7] But it may be supplied if it could be used by the boycotting country to further the boycott—knowledge and intent on the part of the U.S. person is the key to making the furnishing of the information unlawful. There are numerous examples of this prohibition, many referring to use of blacklists. For example, a person may not certify that its suppliers are not on a furnished blacklist.[8] If a company is on the blacklist, or if it wishes to know whether it is on the blacklist, it may request such information.[9] That is not furnishing information. But if it furnishes information in order to be removed, it may be in violation. If a company believes it is on the blacklist but no longer would be listed were the Arab nations to know the facts, supplying those facts may constitute a violation.[10] The same may occur when a company believes it is mistakenly listed, and wishes to make this known to the Arab nations. Companies have removed their names, but it must be done with great care.[11]

Supplement No. 1 to Part 769 of the Regulations includes Department of Commerce interpretation of shipping and insurance certification and certificates of origin.[12] Examples of positive shipping and insurance certifications, and a certification of origin, are provided. Their use avoids problems with negative certificates, especially use of blacklists. Supplement No. 2 to Part 769 adds a later interpretation regarding shipping and insurance certifications with Saudi Arabia.

2. Id.
3. Id.
4. 15 C.F.R. § 769.2(d).
5. 15 C.F.R. § 769.2(d)(2)(ii).
6. 15 C.F.R. § 769.2(d)(3).
7. 15 C.F.R. § 769.2(d)(4).
8. 15 C.F.R. § 769.2(d) example (x).
9. 15 C.F.R. § 769.2(d) example (xv).
10. A U.S. subsidiary of the French cosmetics company L'Oreal provided the parent information to assist in removal from the blacklist. Providing this information and failing to report to the Commerce department led to L'Oreal agreeing to pay $1.4 million in civil penalties. See, e.g, Los Angeles Times, August 30, 1995, at Part D.

11. See Nancy Turck, The Arab Boycott of Israel, 55 For. Affairs 472 (April 1977).

12. See also Supplement No. 13 to Part 769.

The most publicized blacklist case involved Baxter International Inc., a large U.S. medical supply company.[13] As a result of an informant's disclosure, Baxter was investigated and charged with violating the EAA because of the way in which it attempted to have its name removed from the Arab blacklist.[14] Commerce was prepared to charge Baxter and a senior officer with providing over 300 items of prohibited information to Syrian authorities and a Saudi Arabian firm. The company and the officer admitted civil and criminal violations and were assessed total civil penalties of $6,060,600—the highest at the time.[15] The case would not have succeeded without the informant providing substantial documentation of the violations.

§ 18.14 Furnishing Information Regarding Charitable or Fraternal Organizations

The fifth section, and third dealing with furnishing information, prohibits furnishing information about contributions to or associations or activities with charitable or fraternal organizations which support the boycotted country.[1] The law is intended to deny access to Arab nations to information identifying U.S. persons who provide assistance to Israel. The Regulations further elaborate on this section, indicating that the prohibition applies to a charitable or fraternal organization which has as a stated purpose support of the boycotted country through financial contributions or other means, or undertakes as a major activity such support.[2] The information may be that information furnished directly or indirectly or furnished voluntarily by the U.S. person. The type of information may concern membership, financial contributions, or other association or involvement.[3] Information about normal business in a commercial context is permissible. The Regulation refers back to the previous section for the definition of that normal business information. Three examples are provided in the Regulations, emphasizing the intent requirement and the need that the furnished information was boycott related.

§ 18.15 Use of Letters of Credit

The sixth and final prohibition is directed to banks.[1] It prohibits several acts, including paying, honoring, confirming or otherwise implementing any letter of credit, if that letter of credit has a condition or requirement that would mandate compliance with some activity which is in violation of the antiboycott laws.[2] A U.S. person is not obligated to

13. See, e.g., The Case Against Baxter International, Business Week, Oct. 7, 1991, pg. 106.

14. See 5 OEL Insider 7 (Dec. 1993).

15. The admission of criminal violations was a first.

§ 18.14

1. 50 App.U.S.C.A. § 2407(a)(E).

2. 15 C.F.R. § 769.2(e)(2).

3. Id.

§ 18.15

1. 50 App.U.S.C.A. § 2407(a)(F).

2. In addition to the Regulations, Supplement No. 15(b) to Part 769 applies to letters of credit.

pay, honor or implement any such letter of credit. This prohibition covers a wide expanse of banking letter of credit activity, and the Regulations are quite extensive. They are divided into several categories.[3] The initial Regulations expand upon the statutory language. "Implementing" a letter of credit is defined to include issuing or opening, honoring by acceptance, paying a draft or demand under a letter of credit, confirming, negotiating by voluntarily purchasing a draft and presenting the draft for reimbursement, or taking any action implementing a letter of credit.[4] A bank is not prohibited from advising a beneficiary of the existence of a letter of credit, or taking ministerial actions to dispose of a letter of credit which it is prohibited from implementing.[5]

When a bank complies with this provision, it has an absolute defense in any action demanding implementation or for damages for failure to implement.[6] This offers a defense in addition to those in the Uniform Commercial Code, Uniform Customs and Practices for Documentary Credits, or other applicable law or rules.

Following these provisions the Regulations create several new subheadings with further regulations. The first applies to "letters of credit to which this section applies," and reaffirms that the section applies only where the actions are undertaken with intent to comply with, further or support an unsanctioned boycott, and only when the transaction to which the letter of credit applies is in U.S. commerce and the beneficiary is a U.S. person.[7]

The second subheading is "implementation of letters of credit in the United States," and states that such implementation will be assumed to apply to a transaction in U.S. commerce and to be in favor of a U.S. beneficiary if the beneficiary's address is in the United States.[8] Where the beneficiary's address is not in the United States the above presumption is not established.[9]

The third subheading is "implementation of letters of credit outside the United States," which if implemented by a U.S. person has the same presumption as above, *if* the address of the beneficiary is in the United States, and if the letter calls for documents indicating shipment from the United States or that the goods are of U.S. origin.[10] If the address of the beneficiary is not in the United States, the beneficiary is presumed to be other than a U.S. person. Also, if the required documents do not show shipment from the United States or goods of U.S. origin, the transaction is presumed to be outside of U.S. commerce.[11]

The final subheading is "grace period", and states that if Part 769 of the EAR allows a grace period for the underlying transaction,[12] the

3. 15 C.F.R. § 769.2(f); see also Supplement No. 10 to Part 769.

4. 15 C.F.R. § 769.2(f)(2).

5. 15 C.F.R. § 769.2(f)(4).

6. 15 C.F.R. § 769.2(f)(5).

7. 15 C.F.R. § 769.2(f)(6).

8. 15 C.F.R. § 769.2(f)(7). These are rebuttable presumptions.

9. 15 C.F.R. § 769.2(f)(8).

10. 15 C.F.R. § 769.2(f)(9).

11. 15 C.F.R. § 769.2(f)(10).

12. The grace period mechanism is included in § 769.7.

implementation of the letter of credit shall be entitled to that same grace period.[13] Furthermore, the letter of credit may be implemented after the grace period applicable to the underlying transaction provided all the prohibited boycott certifications were given (or boycott-related acts undertaken) prior to the expiration of the grace period.

The Regulations are followed by numerous examples intended to assist in interpreting the complexities of the combination of letter of credit law and the antiboycott provisions.

F.   ANTIBOYCOTT LAW—EXCEPTIONS

§ 18.16   Function of the Exceptions

The EAA follows the six specific prohibitions with six specific areas where regulations must provide for exceptions. Each refers to some "compliance" activity, usually compliance with laws in the boycotting country which are deemed to require respect, even though one might argue that such compliance may further the boycott. The function of these exceptions is to acknowledge some rights of boycotting nations to limit contact with the boycotted nation. The purpose of the antiboycott law is not to deny the boycotting nations any right to engage in a boycott. The United States has numerous boycotts in effect. The purpose of the law is to prevent U.S. persons from complying with or furthering a boycott against a friendly nation. It is an attempt to balance the U.S. friendship with both the Arab nations and Israel, and not to assist the Arab nations in their boycott of Israel. The balance does not always seem in balance, and the exceptions do not always seem consistent with the purpose of the laws. As in the case of the prohibitions, the exceptions are not only expanded upon in the regulations, but followed by examples which are intended to show the dimensions of the antiboycott structure.

§ 18.17   Import Requirements of the Boycotting Country

The law requires that regulations provide for exceptions where the U.S. person is complying with requirements of the boycotting country which either (i) prohibit the import of goods or services from any business organized under the laws of the boycotted country or from nationals or residents thereof,[1] or (ii) prohibit the shipment of goods to the boycotting country on a carrier of the boycotted country, or by means of a shipping route other than prescribed by the boycotting country.[2] This allows an Arab nation to prohibit entry of any Israeli product, and to prohibit an Israeli ship from entering its ports. It also allows an Arab nation to stipulate that a ship coming from the United States not stop at an Israeli port on the way to the Arab nation.

---

13.   15 C.F.R. § 769.2(f)(11).

§ 18.17

1.   See Supplement No. 6(a) to Part 769 for a reference to the practice of Kuwait.

2.   50 App.U.S.C.A. § 2407(a)(2)(A).

The Regulations, divided into two groups affecting first goods and services and second shipping, restate the law in more outline form, and additionally state that a U.S. person may comply with such requirements even without a specific request. Thus, a U.S. shipper may purchase only non-Israeli made components for goods ordered by Arab nations without being reminded by the Arab nations that their laws prohibit the import of Israeli made goods.[3] But the U.S. person must be careful not to violate the provisions regulating furnishing information and the import and shipping document requirements.[4]

An example of this exception would allow a U.S. building contractor, awarded a contract in Oman, to reject the bid (the lowest) of an Israeli company for some of the goods, because Omani law does not allow Israeli goods to enter Oman.[5] But the U.S. company could not reject another bid from the Israeli company for work on a project in Bolivia under this same provision, although there would have to be proof of intent to comply with, support or further the Arab boycott in rejecting the bid for work in Bolivia.[6]

The shipping compliance exception, which applies to both carriers of boycotted nations and routes of shipment for any carriers, also allows the U.S. party to make its own judgment regarding the boycotting nation's law, but there must be reason to know that such law exists. The exception applies whether the boycotting nation or purchaser states explicitly that the ship should not pass through a boycotted country's port, or describes a route that does not include a boycotted country's port.[7] The carrier of a boycotted nation includes one flying the flag of the boycotted nation, or which is owned, chartered, leased or operated by a boycotted country or its nationals or residents.[8]

Under these Regulations it is clear that Israeli ships are not to be used in shipping goods to Arab nations. But even U.S. carriers may have their route prescribed so that they do not stop at an Israeli port on the way *to* the Arab nation. The exception applies only to the route *to* the Arab nation, not to the carrier's route after the shipment is completed.

§ 18.18 Import and Shipping Document Requirements

The exceptions allow a U.S. party to comply with import and shipping document requirements in some five areas:

1. country of origin,
2. name of carrier,
3. route of shipment,
4. name of supplier of shipment, and

---

3. 15 C.F.R. § 769.3(a–1)(2).

4. 15 C.F.R. § 769.3(a–1)(3), referring to §§ 769.2(d) and 769.3(b) respectively.

5. 15 C.F.R. § 769.3(a–1) example (iii).

6. 15 C.F.R. § 769.3(a–1) example (iv).

7. 15 C.F.R. § 769.3(a–2)(2).

8. 15 C.F.R. § 769.3(a–2)(3).

5.   name of provider of services.[1]

However, the above information may not be provided knowingly in "negative, blacklisting, or similar exclusionary terms," except with respect to carriers or routes of shipments as permitted by regulations to comply with "precautionary requirements protecting against war risks and confiscation."[2] This is a complex rule, first constituting an exception to a prohibition, then having an exception to the exception, and ending with a further exception. Its effectiveness was delayed to allow persons to adjust their practices and use positive rather than negative terms in import and shipping documentation.

The Regulations are followed by numerous examples of compliance with import and shipping document requirements. They illustrate the shift from negative to positive terms. For example, certifying that goods being shipped did not originate in a blacklisted country is no longer acceptable, the certification would have to state the name of the country of origin.

§ 18.19   Compliance With Unilateral Selection

The law mandates an exception where, in the normal course of business, the U.S. person complies with the unilateral and specific selection by the boycotting country of the use of certain carriers, insurers, suppliers of services to be performed in the boycotting country, or specific goods identifiable by source when imported into the boycotting country.[1] Unilateral selection allows a boycotting country to carry out the boycott by providing "whitelists", which do not include any firms with any connection to Israel or even with any Jewish employees. While the EAA provision is brief, the Regulations are very extensive, including some 18 sections followed by many examples.

The Regulations clarify that the section applies to what response is allowed a U.S. person who receives a unilateral or specific selection for services or goods supplied by a third person.[2] The act of making the selection is governed by another section.[3] Also separately governed is provision by a U.S. person of its own services or goods.

The "character" of the unilateral and specific selection is governed by four provisions.[4] They first emphasize that the selection must be unilateral and specific. "Specific" is a selection stated affirmatively and specifying a particular supplier of goods or services. "Unilateral" is where the discretion of selection is exercised solely by the boycotting country buyer. The selection is not unilateral when the U.S. person has provided the buyer with any boycott-based assistance. Use of "pre-

§ 18.18

1.   50 App.U.S.C.A. § 2407(a)(2)(B).

2.   Id.

§ 18.19

1.   50 App.U.S.C.A. § 2407(a)(2)(C).

2.   15 C.F.R. § 769.3(c)(2).

3.   15 C.F.R. § 769.3(c). See Supplement No. 13 to Part 769.

4.   15 C.F.R. §§ 769.3(c)(3)–(6). Supplement No. 1 of Part 769 includes an interpretation of contractual clauses regarding unilateral and specific selections. A suggested contractual clause is included.

selection" or "pre-award" services (i.e., providing lists of qualified suppliers, subcontractors or bidders) does not of itself negate the unilateral aspect of the selection, as long as they are not boycott based. They also must be of services that are customarily provided in similar transactions by the firm as measured by practices in non-boycotting countries as well as boycotting countries. If they are not services customarily provided *or* if they are provided in a way to exclude blacklisted persons from participating, then the unilateral character is destroyed. It is often clear that the real reason that boycotting nations provide lists is to further the boycott. But lists are customarily used in business. A violation is likely to require such a pattern of denial to boycotted country suppliers that the reason becomes fairly obvious. This is not an easy section to apply or with which to comply.

The next four sections of the Regulations apply to selections made by a boycotting country resident.[5] The resident may be a U.S. person who is a bona fide temporary or permanent resident of the boycotting country. Factors to determine bona fide residency are (i) physical presence, (ii) necessity of residence for legitimate business purposes, (iii) continuity of residency, (iv) residency intent, (v) prior residency, (vi) size and nature of presence, (vii) whether person is registered to do business or incorporated, (viii) valid work visa, and (ix) presence of residency in both boycotting and non-boycotting countries in connection with similar business activities. These factors are all used to determine the legitimacy of the person's presence in the boycotting country, as opposed to presence in that country exclusively for the purpose of allowing the U.S. person to carry out, further or support the boycott. The boycotting country resident must be the party making the selection. A selection made by a non-resident agent, parent, subsidiary, affiliate, or home or branch office of the boycotting country resident is not a selection under this section. But another person may transmit the selection for the bona fide boycotting country resident to the U.S. person.

The duty of inquiry is the subject of two provisions that require a U.S. recipient of a unilateral selection that the U.S. person believes was made for boycotting reasons to inquire about the selection and determine its true source.[6] Any course of conduct that suggests a selection is boycott based raises this duty of inquiry. There is a "know or reason to know" provision which is consistent with the statute.

Selection of services is addressed in separate regulations.[7] These provisions apply only to services to be performed in the boycotting country, and are only the type of services customarily performed within the country of the recipient of the services, and when they are necessary and constitute a not insignificant part of the total services performed. "Customary and necessary" depends on the usual practices of the supplier as measured by practices in non-boycotting countries as well as boycotting countries.

5.   15 C.F.R. §§ 769.3(c)(7)(10).

6.   15 C.F.R. §§ 769.3(c)(11)–(12).

7.   15 C.F.R. §§ 769.3(c)(13)–(15).

Selection of goods has similar provisions, in that they must be goods that in the normal course of business are identifiable as to their source or origin when entering the boycotting country. "Specifically identifiable goods" are identifiable as to source or origin by (a) uniqueness of design or appearance, or (b) trademark, trade name or other identification normally on the items or packaging.[8]

A final "general" provision in the Regulations states that when the above conditions are met, a U.S. person may comply even if he knows or has reason to know that the selection was boycott based. But compliance is not permitted if the person knows or has reason to know that the purpose of the selection is to effect discrimination against any U.S. person on the basis of race, religion, sex or national origin.[9]

Several pages of examples follow the above regulations, under headings of "Specific and Unilateral Selection," "Examples of Boycotting Country Buyer," "Examples of Suppliers of Services," "Examples of Specifically Identifiable Goods," and "Examples of Discrimination on Basis of Race, Religion, Sex, or National Origin."

§ 18.20 Compliance With Shipment and Transshipment Requirements

The EAA allows compliance with export requirements of the boycotting country which relate to shipments or transshipment.[1] The Regulations are brief, essentially repeating the statute and further defining what shipments are covered.[2] The restrictions may be on direct exports to the boycotted country from the boycotting country; on indirect exports which pass through third parties; on exports to residents, nationals or business concerns of the boycotted country, including where located in third countries. The exception also applies to restrictions on routes if related to preventing the exports from contact with or under the jurisdiction of the boycotted country. This latter exception applies whether a boycotting country or vendor of the shipment (i) specifically restricts the route, or (ii) affirmatively describes a route that omits the boycotted country. This compliance exception does not allow a U.S. person to refuse on an across-the-board basis to do business with a boycotted country or national or resident of a boycotted country. The examples provide several illustrations of permitted and disallowed conduct involving compliance with shipping requirements.

§ 18.21 Compliance With Immigration, Passport, Visa or Employment Requirements

The statute allows compliance with immigration, passport or visa requirements of the boycotting nation, with respect to individuals or

---

8. 15 C.F.R. §§ 769.3(c)(16)–(17). This definition is the same as used for § 769.3(f) on "Compliance with Local Law."

9. 15 C.F.R. § 769.3(c)(18).

§ 18.20

1. 50 App.U.S.C.A. § 2407(a)(2)(D).

2. 15 C.F.R. §§ 769.3(d)(1)–(4).

family members. It further allows compliance with requests for information regarding employment requirements of the individual.[1]

The Regulations state that compliance with the above requirements may be made in order to allow the boycotting country to determine whether the individual meets requirements for employment within the boycotting country, *but* information may be given only about the individual or a member of his family and not about any other U.S. individual, such as an employee, employer or co-worker.[2] A U.S. individual is a person resident or national of the United States. "Family" includes such immediate family members as parents, siblings, spouse, children and other dependents living in the individual's home.[3] A U.S. person is not permitted to furnish information about its employees or executives, but it may allow any individual to respond individually regarding information for immigration, passport, visa or employment requirements.[4] The U.S. person may perform ministerial acts to assist processing by individuals, such as (i) informing employees of boycotting country visa requirements, (ii) typing, (iii) translations, (iv) messenger and similar services, and (v) assisting or arranging for expeditious processing.[5] The boycotting country's denial of admission of some employees does not require the company to stop a project in a boycotting country, but employees may not be selected for the project in a manner intended to comply with the boycott.[6]

§ 18.22   Compliance With Local Law

This statutory provision deals with both activities exclusively in a foreign country and compliance with local import law. The statute allows compliance by a person resident in a boycotting country or by means of an agreement with such country, with the laws of that nation with respect to activities within the boycotting nation. The Regulations are allowed to provide exceptions which govern imports of trademarked, trade-named or similarly specifically identifiable goods or components for the person's own use, including performing contractual services.[1]

The Regulations have three parts: (f) Compliance with local law, (f–1) Activities exclusively within a foreign country, and (f–2) Compliance with local import law.[2]

Compliance with local law has two parts: first with local law applicable to a U.S. person's activities exclusively within a foreign country, and second, with regard to local import laws. Local laws include statutes, regulations, decrees and other official sources with the effect of law. This

---

§ 18.21

1. 50 App.U.S.C.A. § 2407(a)(2)(E).
2. 15 C.F.R. § 769.3(e)(1).
3. 15 C.F.R. § 769.3(e)(2).
4. 15 C.F.R. § 769.3(e)(3).
5. Id.
6. 15 C.F.R. § 769.3(e)(4).

§ 18.22

1. 50 App.U.S.C.A. § 2407(a)(2)(F).
2. 15 C.F.R. §§ 769.3(f)–(f–2). In addition, Supplement No. 5 includes in part B an interpretation of the availability of the exception permitting compliance with local law for establishing a foreign branch.

section does not include "presumed policies or understandings of policies" unless reflected in sources having the effect of law. Both parts of this section apply exclusively to U.S. persons who are bona fide residents in a foreign country, which does include temporary residence.[3] The factors are the same as those in the Regulations discussed above governing compliance with unilateral and specific selection.[4] Numerous examples of bona fide residency follow the Regulations.

The first part of this exception, activities undertaken exclusively within a foreign country, defines such activities as (i) contracts providing that local law applies, (ii) employing residents of the host country, (iii) retaining local contractors, (iv) purchasing or selling goods from or to host country residents, and (v) furnishing information within the host country.[5] Activities which are exclusively undertaken within the country do not include importing goods or services. They are the subject of the next subpart.

The second part of this exception applies to a foreign nation's import laws. Compliance with import laws is allowed, provided that (i) the items are for the U.S. person's own use[6] (title is not the determining factor[7]) or use in performing contractual services in the host country, and (ii) the items, in the normal course of business, are identifiable as to their source or origin at the time of entry either by (a) uniqueness of design or appearance or (b) trademark, trade name or other normal identification.[8] The factors used for such identification are as outlined in the initial paragraph (f). A person who is a bona fide resident may act through an agent outside the country, but the agent must not have discretion to act but be solely under the control of the resident. This allows the resident to direct an agent in the United States, but disallows any discretion in the United States by the agent.[9] This second part of the local law exception does not apply to the import of *services*.[10]

The Regulations for this exception state specifically that use of this exception will be monitored and continually reviewed for consistency with the national interest.[11] This exception is followed by numerous examples. The Regulation should be checked for changes, which may appear when political and economic relations with the boycotting nations change.

3. 15 C.F.R. § 769.3(f)(2).

4. 15 C.F.R. § 769.3(f)(3); see 15 C.F.R. § 769.3(c)(8).

5. 15 C.F.R. § 769.3(f–1)(1); see also Supplement No. 9 to Part 769 for an interpretation of activities exclusively within a boycotting country. This interpretation even includes several illustrative examples.

6. Goods are for the person's own use if they are (i) to be consumed by that person, (ii) to remain in that person's possession and to be used by that person, (iii) to be used in the performance of contractual services for another, (iv) to be further pro-

cessed, or (v) to be put into a project to be constructed for another. 15 C.F.R. § 769.3(f–2)(6). Goods acquired to fill an order for another do not qualify as for a person's own use. 15 C.F.R. § 769.3(f–2)(7).

7. 15 C.F.R. § 769.3(f–2)(5).

8. 15 C.F.R. § 769.3(f–2)(1). The "specifically identifiable" test is that used in 15 C.F.R. § 769.3(c).

9. 15 C.F.R. § 769.3(f–2)(3).

10. 15 C.F.R. § 769.3(f–2)(8).

11. 15 C.F.R. § 769.3(f–2)(9).

G. ANTIBOYCOTT LAW—MISCELLANEOUS

§ 18.23   Prohibition of Intentional Evasion

The EAA and the Regulations both include a section which states that no U.S. person may take any action with intent to evade the law.[1] Permitted activities are not to be considered an evasion of the law. An example of an evasion is placing a person at a commercial disadvantage or imposing on that person special burdens because that person is blacklisted or otherwise restricted from business relations for boycott reasons.[2] Another evasion may be use of risk-of-loss provisions that expressly impose a financial risk on another because of the import laws of a boycotting country, unless customarily used.[3] Two final suggested evasions are the use of dummy corporations or other devices to mask prohibited activities, or diverting boycotting country orders to a foreign subsidiary.[4] A number of further examples follow this Regulation, in the form of examples similar to those appearing throughout the prohibitions and exceptions discussed above.

§ 18.24   Reporting Requirements

Under the title "Foreign policy controls," the EAA includes very important provisions which require the reporting of the receipt of any request for the "furnishing of information, the entering into or implementing of agreements, or the taking of any other action" outlined in the policy section[1] of the EAA.[2] The receipt of any such request must be reported to the Secretary of Commerce. Failure to report boycott-associated requests is perhaps the most frequent violation of the EAA. The report must include any information the Secretary deems appropriate and must state whether the person intends to comply or has complied with the request. These reports are made public records, except to the extent that certain confidential information is included which would cause a competitive disadvantage to the reporting person.

The Regulations include quite extensive provisions, covering (a) the scope of reporting requirements, (b) the manner of reporting, and (c) the disclosure of information.

Scope of reporting requirements. Whenever a person receives a written or oral request to take any action in furtherance or support of a boycott against a friendly foreign country it must be reported. The request may be to enter into or implement an agreement. It may involve a solicitation, directive, legend or instruction asking for information or action (or inaction). The request must be reported whether or not the action

§ 18.23

1. 50 App. U.S.C.A. § 2407(a)(5); 15 C.F.R. § 769.4; see also Supplement No. 12 to Part 769 for an interpretation dealing with use of an agent.

2. 15 C.F.R. § 769.4(c).

3. 15 C.F.R. § 769.4(d).

4. 15 C.F.R. § 769.4(e).

§ 18.24

1. 50 App. U.S.C.A. § 2402(5).

2. 50 App. U.S.C.A. § 2407(b).

requested is prohibited, except as the regulations provide.[3] That essentially means reporting is required if the person knows or has reason to know that the purpose of the request is to enforce, implement or otherwise support, further or secure compliance with the boycott.[4]

When a request is received by a U.S. person located outside the United States (subsidiary, branch, partnership, affiliate, office or other controlled permanent foreign establishment), it is reportable if received in connection with a transaction in interstate or foreign commerce.[5] A general boycott questionnaire, unrelated to any specific transaction, must be reported when that person has or anticipates a business relationship with or in the boycotting country, also in interstate or foreign commerce.

The reporting requirements apply whether the U.S. person is an exporter, bank or other financial institution, insurer, freight forwarder, manufacturer, or other person.[6] If the information about a country's boycotting requirements is learned by means of the receipt or review of books, pamphlets, legal texts, exporter's guidebooks and other similar publications, it is not considered a reportable request. The same is true of receipt of an unsolicited bid where there is no intention to respond.[7]

The Regulations including ten specific requests which are not reportable. They were added because of the customary use of certain terms for boycott and non-boycott purposes, Congressional mandates for clear guidelines in uncertain areas, and the Department of Commerce's desire to reduce paperwork and costs. They are as follows:[8]

(i) request to refrain from shipping goods on a carrier flying the flag of a particular country, or that is owned, chartered, leased or operated by a particular country or its nationals or residents; or a request for certification to such effect;

(ii) request to ship goods, or refrain from shipping goods, on a prescribed route, or a certification request of either;

(iii) request for an affirmative statement or certification regarding the country of origin of goods;

(iv) request for an affirmative statement or certification of supplier's or manufacturer's or service provider's name;

(v) request to comply with laws of another country except where it requires compliance with that country's boycott laws;

(vi) request to individual for personal information about himself or family for immigration, passport, visa or employment requirements;

3. 15 C.F.R. § 769.6(a)(1).

4. 15 C.F.R. § 769.6(a)(2).

5. Id., citing 15 C.F.R. §§ 769.1(c) and (d). The definition of "interstate or foreign commerce" is the subject of a Department of Commerce interpretation in Supplement No. 8 to Part 769.

6. 15 C.F.R. § 769.6(a)(3).

7. 15 C.F.R. § 769.6(a)(4). A definition of "unsolicited invitation to bid" is included in Supplement No. 11 to Part 769.

8. 15 C.F.R. § 769.6(a)(5); see also Supplement No. 10(b) to Part 769.

(vii) request for an affirmative statement or certification stating destination of exports or confirming or indicating the cargo will be unloaded at a particular destination;

(viii) request for certification from owner, master, charterer, or any employee thereof, that a vessel, aircraft, truck or other transport is eligible, permitted, nor restricted from or allowed to enter, a particular port, country or group of countries under the laws, rules, or regulations of that port, country or countries;

(ix) request for certification from insurance company stating the issuing company has an agent or representative (plus name and address) in a boycotting country; or

(x) request to comply with term or condition that vendor bears the risk of loss and indemnify the purchaser if goods are denied entry for any reason if this clause was in use by the purchaser prior to January 18, 1978.

The Department of Commerce periodically is to survey domestic concerns to determine the worldwide scope of boycott requests received by U.S. subsidiaries and controlled affiliates regarding activities outside U.S. commerce.[9] This is to cover requests that would be required to be reported but for the fact that they involve commerce outside the United States. Information collected from U.S. persons will include the number and nature of non-reportable requests received, action requested, action taken, and countries making such requests.

Manner of reporting requests. Every request must be reported; however, only the first need be reported when the same request is received in several forms.[10] But each different request regarding the same transaction must be reported. Each U.S. person receiving a request must report the request, but one person may designate another to make the report, such as a parent reporting on behalf of a subsidiary.[11] The person who designates another to make the report remains responsible for the report.

Reports are to be submitted in duplicate to the Department of Commerce.[12] Where the person receiving the request is in the United States the report must be made at the end of the month received, where received outside the United States an additional month is allowed. The forms must be completely filled in, and where it is not certain what action will be taken, that must be reported within 10 business days of deciding.

Disclosure of information. The third part of the regulations applying to reporting states that the reports shall become public records, except for "certain proprietary information."[13] The reporting party may certify that the disclosure of information relating to the (1) quantity, (2) description, or (3) value of any articles, materials or supplies (including technical

---

9. 15 C.F.R. § 769.6(a)(7).

10. 15 C.F.R. § 769.6(b)(1).

11. 15 C.F.R. § 769.6(b)(2).

12. 15 C.F.R. § 769.6(b)(5).

13. 15 C.F.R. § 769.6(c)(1).

data and other information), may place the company at a competitive disadvantage. In such case the information will not be made public. But the reporting party must edit the public inspection copy of the accompanying documents as noted below, and the Secretary may reject the request for confidentiality for reasons either of disagreement regarding the competitive disadvantage, or of national interest in not withholding the information.[14] If such decision is made, the party must be given an opportunity to comment.

Because the report is made public, one copy must be submitted intact and the other may be edited in accordance with the above limitations. Any additional material considered confidential may also be deleted, as may be any material not required to be reported.[15] The copy is to be marked "Public Inspection Copy."

The Regulations are followed by many examples of situations raising questions of reporting.

§ 18.25   Supplements to the Regulations

Following the Regulations are supplements which contain Department of Commerce views on various parts of the antiboycott provisions. These supplements apply to different provisions discussed above and are referred to in the discussion of each respective area. They provide considerable assistance in understanding how the Department interprets some of the more complex provisions.

§ 18.26   Violations and Enforcement

Violations and enforcement of the antiboycott laws are subject to the same provisions as violations and enforcement of the export laws.[1] The enforcement of the antiboycott laws has generated few court decisions.[2] Most have involved issues of constitutionality, creation of private rights of action, or the statute of limitations.[3] Through 1986, 275 persons were charged with violations.[4] Several persons had licenses suspended and fines exceeding $5 million had been levied. Most of these cases involved the receipt of requests for information from Arab countries. In instances where the companies had complied with the request, the Department of Commerce and the company usually agreed on a fine as part of a consent

---

14. Id.

15. 15 C.F.R. § 769.6(c)(2).

§ 18.26

1. 50 App.U.S.C.A. §§ 2410, 2411 and 2412. See supra, chapter 17.

2. See Michael Wallace Gordon, United States Anti-bribery and Anti-boycott Legislation of 1977, 44 Bulletin Int'l Bureau Fiscal Documentation 150 (Mar. 1990).

3. United States v. Core Laboratories, Inc., No. 3–54–09 51–C (N.D.Tex. July 24, 1984), aff'd 759 F.2d 480 (5th Cir.1985)

(EAA and the statute of limitations); Abrams v. Baylor College of Medicine, 581 F.Supp. 1570 (S.D.Tex.1984), aff'd 805 F.2d 528 (5th Cir.1986) (EAA and affirming private right of action); Bulk Oil (ZUG) A.G. v. Sun Co., Inc., 583 F.Supp. 1134 (S.D.N.Y. 1983), aff'd 742 F.2d 1431 (2d Cir.1984), cert. denied 469 U.S. 835, 105 S.Ct. 129, 83 L.Ed.2d 70 (1984) (EAA and rejecting private right).

4. Howard Fenton, United States Antiboycott Laws: An Assessment of Their Impact Ten Years After Adoption, 10 Hastings Int'l and Comp.L.R. 211 (1987).

decree. The procedures were dealt with administratively,[5] and the decisions are found only in some private reporters.[6] One of the largest civil penalties was imposed in a settlement with Baxter International Inc., in 1993. Baxter, a Swiss subsidiary, and an officer paid a penalty of $6,060,600.

The Department of Commerce began in 1986 to emphasize what it considered the most serious violations, involving the blacklist, religious discrimination and refusals to deal. The number of reported court decisions remains very small. Although in the early 1990s the number of reported Arab requests for information had diminished, cases such as Baxter illustrate that violations continue to occur.

U.S. subsidiaries which carry out boycott activities of foreign parents are within the reach of the provisions. The French L'Oreal, S.A. cosmetics company requested information from two U.S. subsidiaries, Parbel of Florida, Inc. (formerly Helena Rubenstein, Inc.) and Cosmair, Inc., about their business relationships in or with Israel. More than 100 items of information were provided, and no report of the request was made to Commerce. The two subsidiaries (and individual corporate counsel for Cosmair) agreed to fines exceeding $1.4 million in 1995.

§ 18.27　Private Right of Action

As is the case with so many laws, there is no clear indication whether the EAA includes a private right of action. A federal district court in Texas, in *Abrams v. Baylor College of Medicine*,[1] addressing a claim by two Jewish medical students that Baylor University denied them opportunities when it excluded Jews from medical teams it sent to Saudi Arabia, found an implied right of action by applying the factors in the *Cort v. Ash* decision of the U.S. Supreme Court.[2] The Fifth Circuit upheld the decision. But in *Bulk Oil (ZUG) A.G. v. Sun Co.*, the Second Circuit rejected the existence of a private right of action, affirming a New York federal district court decision involving an accusation of violation of the antiboycott provisions by failing to deliver oil to Israel.[3]

H.　COMPANY POLICY

§ 18.28　Responses to Requests From Arab Nations

As discussed above, the law requires a company to report any requests for furnishing information to the Department of Commerce. Additionally, there may be reporting requirements to the Internal Revenue Service. With regard to the former, experience suggests that the

---

5. The administrative procedures are found in 50 App.U.S.C.A. § 2412.

6. See Int'l Boycotts (Business Law Inc.); Boycott L. Bull.

§ 18.27

1. 581 F.Supp. 1570 (S.D.Tex.1984), aff'd 805 F.2d 528 (5th Cir.1986).

2. 422 U.S. 66, 95 S.Ct. 2080, 45 L.Ed.2d 26 (1975).

3. 583 F.Supp. 1134 (S.D.N.Y.1983), aff'd 742 F.2d 1431 (2d Cir.1984), *cert. denied* 469 U.S. 835, 105 S.Ct. 129, 83 L.Ed.2d 70 (1984).

Central Office for the Boycott of Israel in Damascus has made many requests to companies for information. Furthermore, individual Arab governments make such requests. The Department of Commerce has forms to use to report such requests. Every company should be prepared to respond according to the law if any request for information is received. But a company should do more. It should be prepared to deal with the boycott by adopting a company policy which complies with the law. All too often company personnel act without any awareness of the boycott rules.

§ 18.29   Company Policy to Comply With Law

The company policy must accommodate all laws which affect the company's actions related to the boycott. This will include the EAA and IRC rules, and may also require attention to civil rights law and state antiboycott rules. Penalties for violations are severe. The *Baxter* case, discussed above, illustrates not only how severe penalties may be, but that companies which intentionally violate the law cannot avoid the possibility that some employee may accumulate documentation of violations and submit the documentation to the Department of Commerce.

The first function of a company policy should be educating company employees as to the *existence* of antiboycott rules and their possible impact on the company's operations. Every part of the company which might be involved in boycott-related activities must be included, and the policy should extend to subsidiaries. The more difficult issue is the extent to which the policy should include foreign subsidiaries. Where U.S. law extends extraterritorially, if it conflicts with the law of the nation in which the subsidiary is incorporated and located, the policy should not violate local law. The most difficult decision is where the U.S. law and foreign host-nation law are in clear conflict. There is no simple solution, whatever action is taken is likely to result in the violation of the law of one nation.

Once an awareness of the existence of the law is established in the company policy, the policy should have guidelines regarding how to deal with the law. These guidelines should cover every part of the company involved, including persons who deal with letters of credit. Employees should be able to identify a request for information which might violate the law and forward that request to the proper persons, most likely the legal department. The policy should clearly outline how the company's compliance program functions and who is in charge of the program.

Finally, there should be a periodic review of the company's policy, and continuing education of employees as to changes in the boycott rules or the company's policy, and education for new employees. A sincere, comprehensive policy should help any company which comes in conflict with the laws. The policy may be important in how the Department of Commerce, or another applicable federal or state agency, reacts to information that the company may be in violation of the law.

I.   SELECTED DOCUMENTS

§ 18.30   Ashland   Chemical   Antiboycott   Compliance Guide and Policy Statement *

I.   Introduction

The antiboycott laws and regulations are intended to prevent United States companies and foreign concerns controlled by or affiliated with United States companies from taking action in support of a boycott imposed by a foreign country upon a country which is friendly to the United States.

There are two federal statutes which govern international boycott activity. The Export Administration Act is enforced by the Department of Commerce, and the Tax Reform Act of 1976 is enforced by the Treasury Department (Internal Revenue Service). Each of these entities has adopted comprehensive regulations and guidelines that supplement these laws.

Although these two sets of laws have their differences, generally taken together they prohibit a U.S. person and its foreign subsidiaries and affiliates, including branches, from refusing or agreeing to refuse to do business (1) with or in a boycotted country, or (2) with any business concern organized under the laws of a boycotted country, or (3) with any national or resident of a boycotted country, or (4) with any person who has dealt with a boycotted person or country, when such refusal is pursuant to an unsanctioned foreign boycott. Also prohibited is the furnishing of information for boycott-related purposes, including not only past, present, or future business relationships with or in a boycotted country or with a company in the boycotted country, but any information, public or not, whether connected with boycott-related matters or provided for boycott-related purposes. The furnishing of information with respect to race, religion, sex, or for other discriminatory purposes is also prohibited. In addition, there are prohibitions on implementing letters of credit containing boycott-related conditions. The laws and regulations also require that boycott-related requests be promptly reported. Although the current laws were passed primarily to respond to the boycott of Israel by several Middle Eastern nations, there are other boycotts such as the Pakistani boycott of India that are covered.

References to the boycott and the receipt of boycott-related requests are frequently associated with transactions that involve sales to buyers

* *Thanks to Mr. Charles Saunders, Jr., Associate General Counsel, Ashland Chemi-* *cal, Inc., Columbus, Ohio, for permission to reprint this material.*

in boycotting countries. However, the laws and regulations are equally applicable to purchases made from such countries. Therefore, the principles contained in this Guide must be considered whenever a transaction with a buyer or a seller from a boycotting country is being considered. Further, boycott-related requests may appear from third countries that are rendered pursuant to transactions connected with boycotting countries and these requests also must be reported.

This Guide and Policy Statement is not designed to be all encompassing or to make you an expert in the area of international boycotts. It is intended to clearly state the Company's Policy which prohibits any activity in support of unsanctioned boycotts and to give a basic understanding of the law so that boycott requests will be properly identified and the appropriate action taken. For purposes of this Guide, no distinction has been made between the provisions or requirements of the two Acts, even though some differences exist. If you have any questions about the information contained in the Guide or if you have any questions about a particular business transaction, you should contact your General Counsel of your operating unit, the Corporate Law Department or the Corporate Tax Department in Ashland, Kentucky.

II. Policy Statement

It is the Policy of Ashland Oil, Inc., its subsidiaries, and affiliates to comply with the antiboycott laws and regulations of the United States.

Compliance with this Policy is mandatory. No employee has the authority to act contrary to the provisions of this Policy or to authorize, direct or condone violations of it by any other employee or by any agent.

No employee shall refuse to do business with any country, company, or person for boycott-related purposes. Further, no employee shall provide information, statements, certificates or any other communication, whether written or oral, which would be in violation of U.S. antiboycott laws and regulations. More specifically, no employee shall provide any information with regard to the Company's relationship with a boycotted country or any national of a boycotted country, whether in positive or negative terms, or provide any other information if requested or provided for boycott-related purposes.

Any employee who has knowledge of facts or incidents which he or she believes may be a violation of this Policy has an obligation, promptly after learning of such fact or incident, to review the matter with the General Counsel of his operating unit, the Corporate Law Department, or the Corporate Tax Department in Ashland, Kentucky.

Any employee who violates this Policy or who orders another to violate this Policy or who knowingly permits a subordinate to violate this Policy will be subject to appropriate disciplinary action.

III. Summary of the Law

This summary is not designed to answer all questions that may arise relating to the antiboycott laws and regulations. Rather, it is intended to provide a basic understanding of them and thereby enable you to recognize and avoid potential violations. When you encounter a request that you believe may be boycott-related, you are to immediately contact your General Counsel.

Since the law applies to a boycott imposed by any foreign country against a country friendly to the United States, it is impossible to identify with precision the countries that may be described as "boycotting countries." Boycott requests will most frequently originate from countries that are members of the Arab League. At the present time, the following are members of the Arab League and, thus, business transactions with these countries must be closely reviewed:

Algeria	Lebanon	Saudi Arabia	Tunisia
Bahrain	Libya	Yemen Arab	United Arab
Egypt	Mauritania	Republic	Emirates
Iraq	Morocco	Somalia	Peoples Demo-
Jordan	Oman	Sudan	cratic Repub-
Kuwait	Qatar	Syria	lic of Yemen

The Arab Emirates is a federation of seven Emirates:

Abu Dhabi	Ras Al–Khaimah	Fujairah	Umm Al–
Ajman	Sharjah	Dubai	Quaiwain

Egypt has terminated its boycott of Israel and, though Iran may not have formally adopted a policy of boycotting Israel, boycott requests may be associated with Iranian transactions.

A boycott-related request may be oral or written and may or may not require you to take any specific action. For example, an invitation to bid may contain a statement that "the bidder agrees to comply with all local boycott laws." No specific action is required in response to such a statement, but it is a boycott-related request and it must be reported even if a bid is not going to be submitted.

A. [Prohibited Activities]

The following activities are prohibited under the antiboycott laws and regulations:

(1) agreeing, refusing, or requiring any other person to refuse to do business with any person or entity pursuant to an agreement with, a requirement of, or a request from or on behalf of a boycotting country;

(2) agreeing, refusing, or requiring any other person to refuse to employ or otherwise discriminate against a United States person on the basis of the race, religion, sex or national origin of such person;

(3) furnishing or agreeing to furnish information with respect to the race, religion, sex, or national origin of any United States person or personnel of the entity involved in the proposed transaction;

(4) furnishing or agreeing to furnish information concerning any person's (including those of Ashland and any of its divisions and

subsidiaries) business relationships in a boycotted country or with companies, residents, or nationals of the boycotted country or with regard to any person believed to be restricted from doing business in boycotting countries;

(5) furnishing or agreeing to furnish information about whether any person is a member of, has made contributions to, or is otherwise associated with charitable organizations which support a boycotted country;

(6) paying, honoring, or confirming letters of credit which contain any conditions or requirements which are prohibited by the antiboycott laws or regulations.

B.   Forms of Transactions and Requests

It is essential that the Company avoid taking any action or agreeing to take any action with respect to a boycott other than those actions that are clearly permitted under these procedures.   An "agreement" to take any prohibited action in response to a boycott request would constitute a violation of U.S. antiboycott laws even if the Company does not intend to abide by the agreement.   It is not necessary that there be a formal written "contract" specifically detailing the duties of the parties in order for an agreement to exist.   An agreement may be oral or an agreement may result merely by the acceptance of an order detailed in a purchase order which contains a boycott request.   Further, compliance with the conditions of a letter of credit is an agreement in that the letter of credit is considered a part of the overall contract.

1.   *Purchase Orders.*   Purchase orders and other similar documents received from customers in boycotting countries must be examined with great care to determine if they contain boycott requests or statements. Acceptance of an order placed pursuant to a purchase order or other similar document containing a boycott-related request may constitute an act in support of a boycott even though the Company does not expressly do or undertake to do any specific act in response to the request.   In the event a purchase order or similar document is received that contains a boycott request, the order must be rejected completely unless an agreement is reached with the customer to withdraw the request.   The agreement to withdraw must be reached prior to the acceptance of the order.

For example, a purchase order may state that the goods cannot be shipped on a blacklisted vessel (or on vessels "not eligible" or "not allowed" to enter Arab ports).   Acceptance of the order would amount to an agreement not to use a blacklisted vessel and result in a violation of the law, even though it is the Company's practice to ship all of its goods on the vessels of a particular company, which company just happens not to be blacklisted.   The purchaser must be informed immediately that the purchase order cannot be accepted unless the restrictive language is deleted.   While this request should be handled diplomatically, it must not be accompanied by any informal assurance that the Company will act in accordance with the deleted request. If efforts to delete the offensive language are unsuccessful, the order must be rejected.

2. *Letters of Credit.* Letters of credit frequently contain restrictive provisions or shipping conditions that are boycott-related. If they originate from customers located in the Middle East, they should be thoroughly reviewed for boycott-related requests before processing. Paying, honoring, confirming, or otherwise implementing a letter of credit that contains an objectionable provision is considered to be an agreement to comply with a boycott request and therefore a violation of the antiboycott laws.

3. *Contracts and Invitations to Bid.* No contract may be executed that contains a boycott-related request. Likewise, no bid shall be submitted that responds to an invitation to bid that contains a boycott-related request. Contractual provisions that require the Company to "comply with," "follow," or otherwise abide by the law of the country of the customer are highly suspect and should be immediately referred to your General Counsel. The foregoing holds true even if merely requested to comply with, abide by, or go along with laws generally of a country known to be a boycotting country. This is because any such agreement by necessity would have to include the boycott laws of that country. Clauses that specifically state that the contract is "subject to" the laws of a boycotting country or that such laws will "apply to" the contract are permissible. No statement of any kind that specifically refers to the boycott laws of the country is permitted. Since the language distinctions are often not obvious, all such clauses referring to local laws should be referred to the General Counsel.

As discussed in the section dealing with purchase orders, prohibited language must be deleted from the contract or the invitation to bid before an agreement can be reached or a bid submitted.

4. *Oral Agreements.* The antiboycott laws and regulations cover oral statements and agreements as well as written requests and agreements contained in documents and contracts. Discussions concerning boycott requests or compliance with boycott requirements generally should be avoided. It is particularly important to avoid an oral understanding that the parties will honor a boycott request even though it is being deleted from a document.

5. *Requests for Information.* Boycott questionnaires and general requests for information are occasionally received that solicit information about the Company's activities in a boycotted country, its business relationships with other U.S. companies or companies from a boycotted country or about its officers, directors, employees, or shareholders. It is prohibited to provide any such information, even if publicly available, if requested or provided for boycott-related purposes.

The antiboycott laws and regulations prohibit the furnishing of information about a person's race, religion, sex, or national origin and from furnishing information about the Company's relationship with companies or nationals of a boycotted country or with companies that may engage in business activities with a boycotted country. However, an individual is able to provide such information about himself or his family when, for example, he is applying for a visa.

C. Examples of Boycott–Related Requests

The following are some examples of boycott-related requests that you may encounter. The list is obviously not complete and should be viewed only as instructive as to the form and wording that such requests may take. Be aware that particular requests may vary markedly from these examples.

1. A request for a statement or a certificate that the goods or services involved are not manufactured in Israel or do not contain any Israeli materials or were not produced with any Israeli capital or labor. Requests for statements of this type may also be styled as a request for the "Israeli declaration" or a request for a "non-Israeli clause."

   a. This type of request is known as a negative certificate of origin and is prohibited. The transaction cannot be agreed to until the request has been withdrawn.

   b. The alternative to such a request is to provide a positive statement of origin, that is, one that states in positive terms the country from which the goods or their components originated. For example, "the goods are of U.S. origin and contain only U.S. materials."

   c. Even if an agreement with the purchaser is reached to withdraw the request for the negative statement of origin (or any other prohibited boycott-related statement) and substitute a positive statement, the request still must be reported. *See* Section IV, Reporting Requirements.

2. A request for a statement or certificate that the goods or materials involved were not manufactured by a blacklisted company.

   a. Compliance with this request is prohibited. The transaction cannot be agreed to until the request has been withdrawn.

3. A request for a statement or certificate that the goods were not shipped on a blacklisted vessel.

   a. Compliance with this request is prohibited. The transaction cannot be agreed to until the request has been withdrawn.

   b. A related type of request is that the carrier with whom the goods are shipped certify that it is "not blacklisted," that its vessels are "not blacklisted," or that its vessels are "eligible" or "allowed" to enter a particular port, or that they are "not prohibited" from entering a particular port or ports. These related requests are considered to be equivalent to a "not blacklisted" statement and are prohibited.

   c. An exception to this prohibition is a statement that the vessel is "eligible" to enter the ports of Saudi Arabia. This exception was granted because Saudi Arabia presented proof that it requires such statements for valid commercial reasons and, therefore, the statements are not considered to be boycott related.

d. The prohibition against compliance with this type of request should be distinguished from the shipping certification found in the next example, which is permitted.

4. A request for a statement or certificate that the goods will not be shipped on an Israeli-owned or Israeli-flagged vessel and that the vessel will not call at an Israeli port en route to the purchaser.

a. This request may be complied with and it need not be reported.

b. This is the only negative statement that is specifically allowed by the antiboycott law. It is critical that the words "en route to the purchaser" or words of similar meaning be used. The exception is permitted to prevent possible confiscation of the goods prior to their delivery. Once the goods are delivered, there is no longer a justification to support a statement that it will not call at Arab ports. Language indicating that a carrier will not stop at an Israeli port or airport during its entire journey is similar to a statement that the vessel is not blacklisted and is, therefore, prohibited.

5. A request for a statement or certificate that the goods are not insured by a blacklisted company or by a company from a boycotted country.

a. Compliance with this request is prohibited. The transaction cannot be agreed to until the request has been withdrawn.

6. A request for a statement or certificate that the insurer is qualified to do business in the country of destination or that the insurer "has a duly qualified and appointed agent or representative" in the country of destination.

a. Compliance with this request is prohibited. The transaction cannot be agreed to until the request has been withdrawn.

b. A related type of request or requirement is that the identity of the shipper's agent or representative in the boycotting country be provided. Compliance with this request is also prohibited.

c. There is an exception for this specific request with respect to Saudi Arabia, under the same rationale as contained in 3(c), which has explained that these requirements are for commercial reasons and, therefore, are not boycott related.

7. A request for a statement that neither the exporting company nor any of its affiliates is blacklisted. A similar request is for a statement that the manufacturer is not a subsidiary of, or a parent company of, a firm on the Israeli Boycott Blacklist.

a. Compliance with this request is prohibited. The transaction cannot be agreed to until the request has been withdrawn.

8. Request for a statement or certificate that the exporting company does not maintain an office or have a branch in a boycotted country.

    a. Compliance with this request is prohibited. The transaction cannot be agreed to until the request has been withdrawn.

9. A request for a statement or certificate that the exporting company will comply with the laws and regulations of the country of the purchaser, or that it will comply with the boycott laws of that country.

    a. If the request asks for compliance with the boycott laws it is clearly boycott related and compliance with it is prohibited. The transaction cannot be agreed to until the request has been withdrawn.

    b. If the request is for a statement of general compliance with the laws and regulations of the purchaser's country even though there is no mention of boycott laws you must presume the request is boycott related. Compliance with this request is prohibited unless advice to the contrary is received from the General Counsel of your operating unit, the Corporate Law Department, or the Corporate Tax Department.

    c. An agreement may contain a clause that provides specifically that the laws of the boycotting country "will apply" to the performance of the contract or that its performance is "subject to" the laws of such country.

10. A request for information concerning the race, religion, sex, or national origin of the officers, directors, employees, or shareholders of the Company.

    a. Compliance with this request is prohibited. The transaction cannot be agreed to until the request has been withdrawn.

    b. The prohibition against providing information is directed toward employers. An individual may provide information of this type about himself and members of his immediate family for employment purposes or for purposes of securing a visa.

11. As noted, the above list is not all inclusive and boycott requests may appear in other forms. In particular, any request, direction or contract provision that contains the words "boycott" or "blacklist" or any reference to Israel, Israeli goods or Israeli nationals should be considered to be boycott related. If documents containing any of these terms are received, you should, as with any other boycott-related request, immediately contact the General Counsel of your operating unit.

IV. Reporting Requirements

The regulations of the Commerce Department and the Treasury Department require that the mere receipt of a boycott request be reported in a timely manner. The report must also describe the action that the Company has taken in response to the request. Therefore, even if an agreement with the purchaser is reached to withdraw the request, a report must still be filed.

A. The Commerce Department Regulations require that boycott-related requests must be reported by the last day of the month after the end of the calendar quarter in which they were received if the recipient is a company located in the United States. If the recipient of the request is a foreign division, subsidiary or affiliate of a U.S. company the request must be reported by the last day of the second month after the end of the calendar quarter in which it was received.

Failure to report requests in a timely manner is a violation of the law, even if no action to comply with the request is taken. To be sure that reports are properly filed, all boycott-related requests are to be promptly sent to the General Counsel of your respective operation. The General Counsel will advise as to the proper course of action to take and he will file the necessary report. Since the reports require information about the goods or services being purchased, the price involved and the date the request was received, a copy of the document in which the request is contained as well as the purchase order, contract, letter of credit and related documents should also be submitted.

B. The Treasury Department Regulations require that boycott-related requests be reported annually. The Law Department will provide copies of all boycott-related requests received to the Tax Department to assist it in filing.

V. Compliance Procedures

Compliance with the antiboycott laws and regulations demands the attention of each employee who may be involved in business transactions with Middle East customers. To facilitate compliance, the following procedures will be implemented.

A. An Antiboycott Compliance Officer shall be appointed at each of the Company's locations that engages in business transactions or that may engage in business transactions with Middle East customers. An alternate Compliance Officer will be appointed to function as the compliance officer in the absence of the Antiboycott Compliance Officer (referred to herein collectively as the Compliance Officer).

1. The person responsible for the operation of the location, or his designee, will appoint the Compliance Officer and the alternate.

2. The identity of the individuals appointed will be provided, in writing, to the General Counsel responsible for the particular location.

B. The Compliance Officer will be responsible for reviewing all documents and requests for information that relate to transactions with Middle East customers. The Compliance Officer may appoint others to process the documents as long as all such individuals are familiar with the material contained in this Compliance Guide and instructed to suspend the processing of any transaction that appears to relate to a boycott request and immediately report the receipt of the material to the Compliance Officer.

1.   The Compliance Officer will promptly review the related document and make a preliminary determination as to whether the request is covered by the laws or regulations.

2.   Unless the Compliance Officer is sure that the request is not objectionable, he must immediately contact the General Counsel responsible for his operation and seek guidance.   The transaction is to remain suspended until advice from the General Counsel is received.

C.   The Compliance Officer is responsible for distributing copies of the Antiboycott Compliance Guide and Policy Statement and any supplemental material that may be provided to all affected employees and for periodically securing a Compliance Statement from each such employee. The Compliance Statement will provide that the employee has received a copy of the Antiboycott Compliance Guide and Policy Statement, that he is familiar with it and the related procedures, that he is familiar with the Corporate Policy that prohibits activity in violation of the antiboycott laws and regulations and that he agrees to abide by it.

D.   The General Counsel of the operating unit is responsible for providing advice when boycott-related questions arise and for maintaining copies of the designations of the Compliance Officer and the alternates and the Antiboycott Compliance Statements.   In the event of his unavailability, the Corporate Law Department should be contacted.

1.   The General Counsel of each operating unit shall conduct Antiboycott Compliance Seminars for all employees who are involved in transactions with Middle East customers.   These Seminars, the form and frequency of which may be structured to address the needs of the particular entity involved, should discuss the substance of the antiboycott laws and regulations and provide those in attendance with an opportunity to ask questions.

2.   The General Counsel of each operating unit must periodically conduct Antiboycott Compliance Audits to assure that compliance with the antiboycott laws and regulations is being followed.

3.   The General Counsel of each operating unit must periodically provide to the General Counsel of Ashland Oil, Inc. a report that details compliance efforts undertaken and the effectiveness of such efforts.

E.   The General Counsel of Ashland Oil, Inc., or his designee, is to provide advice and guidance to the operating entities, receive and review the reports from the various entities and take whatever additional steps he deems necessary to assure that compliance with the antiboycott laws and regulations is being achieved.

VI. Penalties

The antiboycott laws of the Commerce Department and the antiboycott laws of the Treasury Department each contain penalty provisions, and any activity could be found to be in violation of both of these statutes.

    A. A violation of the Export Administration Act, the statute administered by the Commerce Department, provides for criminal and civil penalties.

    1. *Criminal.* Anyone who knowingly violates the Export Administration Act or any order, regulation, or license issued thereunder, may be fined $25,000 and imprisoned for one year. Subsequent violations are subject to a fine of $50,000 and five years' imprisonment.

    2. *Civil.* The applicable penalties to the Company are a civil fine of not more than $10,000 for each violation and/or denial to the Company of export privileges. Although a fine could be substantial, the denial of export privileges could have a far more devastating effect on the Company's business.

    B. A violation of the Tax Reform Act of 1976 may be punished by a reduction of available foreign tax credit, the denial of certain benefits otherwise allowable as shareholder of a foreign controlled corporation, and the denial of deferral of tax. Once the Internal Revenue Service finds a violation in one transaction with a customer, it will presume that all transactions involving customers in boycotting countries are violations. The burden shifts to the Company to show that it has not violated the law with respect to each transaction. The cost of such proof could be considerable.

Selected Bibliography

Boycott Law Bulletin.

C. Lloyd Brown–John, Multilateral Sanctions in International Law—A Comparative Analysis (1975).

Pavel K. Chudzicki, The European Union's Response to the LIBERTAD Act and the Iran-Libya Act: Extraterritoriality Without Boundaries?, 28 Loy. U. Chi. L.J. 505 (1997).

Brice M. Clagett, AGORA: The Cuban Liberty and Democratic Solidarity (LIBERTAD) Act, Continued: A Reply to Professor Lowenfeld, 90 Am. J. Int'l L. 641 (1996).

Brice M. Clagett, Title III of the Helms–Burton Act is Consistent with International Law, 90 Am. J. Int'l L. 434 (1996).

William Lawrence Craig, Application of the Trading with the Enemy Act to Foreign Corporations Owned by Americans: Reflections on *Freuhauf v. Massardy*, 83 Harv. L. Rev. 579 (1970).

Arthur T. Downey, Extraterritorial Sanctions in the Canada/U.S. Context—A U.S. Perspective, 24 Can.-U.S. L.J. 215 (1998).

Ellicott, Corporate Directive and Procedure for Compliance with United States Antiboycott Legislation, 5 Int'l Q. 98 (1993).

Export Control News.

Howard Fenton, Antiboycott Report: FY 1992 Activities, 15 Middle East Executive Rep. 9 (1992).

Howard Fenton, United States Antiboycott Laws: An Assessment of Their Impact Ten Years After Adoption, 10 Hastings Int'l & Comp. L.R. 211 (1987).

Peter L. Fitzgerald, "If Property Rights Were Treated Like Human Rights, They Could Never Get Away with This": Blacklisting and Due Process in U.S. Economic Sanctions Programs, 51 Hastings L.J. 73 (1999).

Peter L. Fitzgerald, Pierre Goes Online: Blacklisting and Secondary Boycotts in U.S. Trade Policy, 31 Vand. J. Transnat'l L. 1 (1998).

Douglas H. Forsythe, Introductory Note, Canada: Foreign Extraterritorial Measures Act Incorporating Amendments Countering the U.S. Helms–Burton Act, 36 Int'l Legal Materials 111 (1997).

Digna B. French, Economic Sanctions Imposed by the United States Against Cuba: The Thirty-nine Year Embargo Culminating with the Cuban Liberty and Democratic Solidarity (LIBERTAD) Act of 1996, 7 Int'l & Comp. L. Rev. 1 (1998).

Howard M. Friedman, Confronting the Arab Boycott: A Lawyer's Baedeker, 19 Harv.Int'l L.J. 443 (1978).

Craig R. Giesze, Helms–Burton in Light of the Common Law and Civil Law Legal Traditions: Is Legal Analysis Alone Sufficient to Settle Controversies Arising Under International Law on the Eve of the Second Summit of the Americas?, 32 Int'l Lawyer 51 (1991).

Peter Glossop, Canada's Foreign Extraterritorial Measures Act and U.S. Restrictions on Trade with Cuba, 32 Int'l Lawyer 93 (1998).

Gary C. Hufbauer et al., Economic Sanctions Reconsidered: History and Current Policy (2d ed. 1990).

Inter–American Juridical Committee Opinion Examining the U.S. Helms–Burton Act, O.A.S. Doc. No. OEA/Ser. G, CP/doc. 2803/96, Aug. 27, 1996, reprinted in 35 Int'l Legal Materials 1322 (1996).

International Boycotts (Bus.Law Inc.).

Christopher C. Joyner, The Transnational Boycott as Economic Coercion in International Law: Policy, Place, and Practice, 17 Vand. J. Transnat'l L. 205 (1984).

Richard L. Kaplan, A Critical Examination of the Treasury Department's Report on the Arab Boycott, 1983 Ill.L.R. 23 (1983).

Sheldon H. Klein, United States Antiboycott Legislation: Consequences for Intellectual Property Owners and Their Counsel, 80 Trademark Rep. 354 (1990).

Michael Krinsky and David Golove (eds.), United States Economic Measures Against Cuba (1993).

Monroe Leigh, Export Administrative Act—Antiboycott Amendments—Private Right of Action Not Implied, 78 Am.J.Int'l L. 910 (1984).

Monroe Leigh, Export Administration Act—Extraterritorial Jurisdiction Over Foreign Incorporated Subsidiaries of U.S. Parent Companies Upheld in United States Court, 77 Am. J. Int'l L. 626 (1983).

Andreas F. Lowenfeld, AGORA: The Cuban Liberty and Democratic Solidarity (LIBERTAD) Act, 90 Am. J. Int'l L. 419 (1996),

Andreas F. Lowenfeld, "... Sauce for the Gander": The Arab Boycott and United States Political Trade Controls, 12 Texas Int'l L.J. 25 (1977).

Andreas F. Lowenfeld, Trade Controls for Political Ends, International Economic Law (2d ed. 1983).

Eugene A. Ludwig & John T. Smith II, The Business Effects of the Antiboycott Provisions of the Export Administration Amendments of 1977—Morality Plus Pragmatism Equals Complexity, 8 Ga. J. Int'l & Comp. L. 581 (1979).

Michael P. Malloy, Economic Sanctions and U.S. Trade (1990).

Karl M. Meessen, Extraterritorial Jurisdiction in Theory and Practice (1961).

Memorandum of Understanding Concerning the U.S. Helms–Burton Act and the U.S. Iran and Libya Sanctions Act, Apr. 11, 1997, Dept. Comm. Bull., reprinted at 36 Int'l Legal Materials 529 (1997).

National Association of Manufacturers, A Catalog of New U.S. Unilateral Economic Sanctions for Foreign Policy Purposes 1993–1996 (1997).

Richard W. Parker, The Problem with Scorecards: How (and How Not) to Measure the Cost–Effectiveness of Economic Sanctions, 21 Michigan J. Int'l L. 235 (2000).

Practicing Law Institute, Coping with U.S. Export Controls (1998).

President's Export Council, Unilateral Economic Sanctions (June 1997).

Martin P. Sherman, Outline and Checklist of Arab Boycott and U.S. Antiboycott Laws, 17 Int'l Lawyer 711 (1983).

Henry J. Steiner, Pressures and Principles—The Politics of the Antiboycott Legislation, 8 Ga. J. Int'l & Comp. L. 529 (1978).

Symposium: State's Rights vs. International Trade: The Massachusetts Burma Law, 19 N.Y.L. Sch. J. Int'l & Comp. L. 348 (2000).

Symposium: The Arab Boycott and the International Response, 8 Ga.J. Int'l & Comp.L. 527 (1978).

U.K. Statement and Order Concerning the American Export Embargo with Regard to the Soviet Gas Pipeline, 21 Int'l Legal Materials 851 (1982).

Bureau of Export Administration (BXA), U.S. Department of Commerce, Annual Reports.

Michael Peter Waxman, Threats of Foreign Group Boycotts of American Industry in Response to U.S. Government Trade Policy: Illegal Anticompetitive Activity or Protected Lobbying Under the *Noerr-Pennington* Doctrine?, 29 Geo. Wash. J. Int'l L. & Econ. 659 (1996).

†

0–314–26254–7 (Vol. 1)

90000

9 780314 262547

0–314–10181–0 SET

90000

9 780314 101815